ASIA
MAPS 26 – 45

AFRICA
MAPS 46 – 57

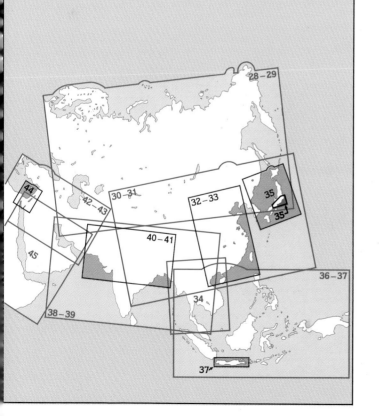

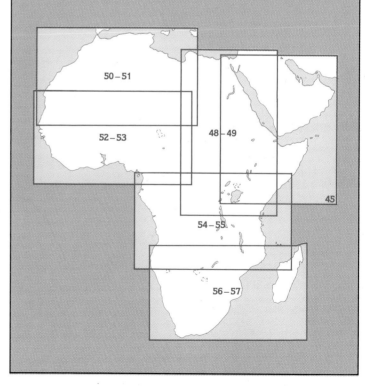

Continued on Back Endpaper

COLLINS
CONCISE
ATLAS
OF THE WORLD

COLLINS
CONCISE
ATLAS
OF THE WORLD

COLLINS

LONDON · GLASGOW · SYDNEY · AUCKLAND · TORONTO · JOHANNESBURG

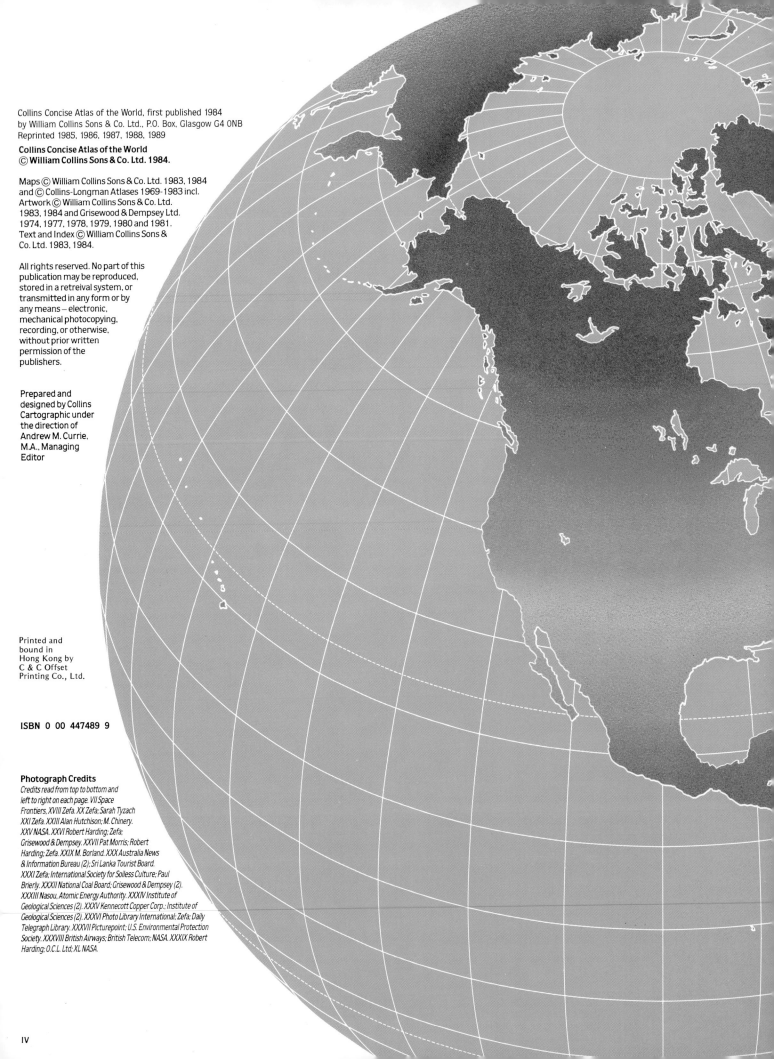

Collins Concise Atlas of the World, first published 1984
by William Collins Sons & Co. Ltd., P.O. Box, Glasgow G4 0NB
Reprinted 1985, 1986, 1987, 1988, 1989

Collins Concise Atlas of the World
© William Collins Sons & Co. Ltd. 1984.

Maps © William Collins Sons & Co. Ltd. 1983, 1984
and © Collins-Longman Atlases 1969-1983 incl.
Artwork © William Collins Sons & Co. Ltd.
1983, 1984 and Grisewood & Dempsey Ltd.
1974, 1977, 1978, 1979, 1980 and 1981.
Text and Index © William Collins Sons &
Co. Ltd. 1983, 1984.

Prepared and
designed by Collins
Cartographic under
the direction of
Andrew M. Currie,
M.A., Managing
Editor

Printed and
bound in
Hong Kong by
C & C Offset
Printing Co., Ltd.

ISBN 0 00 447489 9

Photograph Credits
*Credits read from top to bottom and
left to right on each page. VII Space
Frontiers, XVIII Zefa. XX Zefa; Sarah Tyzach
XXI Zefa. XXIII Alan Hutchison; M. Chinery.
XXV NASA. XXVI Robert Harding; Zefa;
Grisewood & Dempsey. XXVII Pat Morris; Robert
Harding; Zefa. XXIX M. Borland. XXX Australia News
& Information Bureau (2); Sri Lanka Tourist Board.
XXXI Zefa; International Society for Soiless Culture; Paul
Brierly. XXXII National Coal Board; Grisewood & Dempsey (2).
XXXIII Nasou, Atomic Energy Authority. XXXIV Institute of
Geological Sciences (2). XXXV Kennecott Copper Corp.; Institute of
Geological Sciences (2). XXXVI Photo Library International; Zefa; Daily
Telegraph Library. XXXVII Picturepoint; U.S. Environmental Protection
Society. XXXVIII British Airways; British Telecom; NASA. XXXIX Robert
Harding; O.C.L. Ltd; XL NASA.*

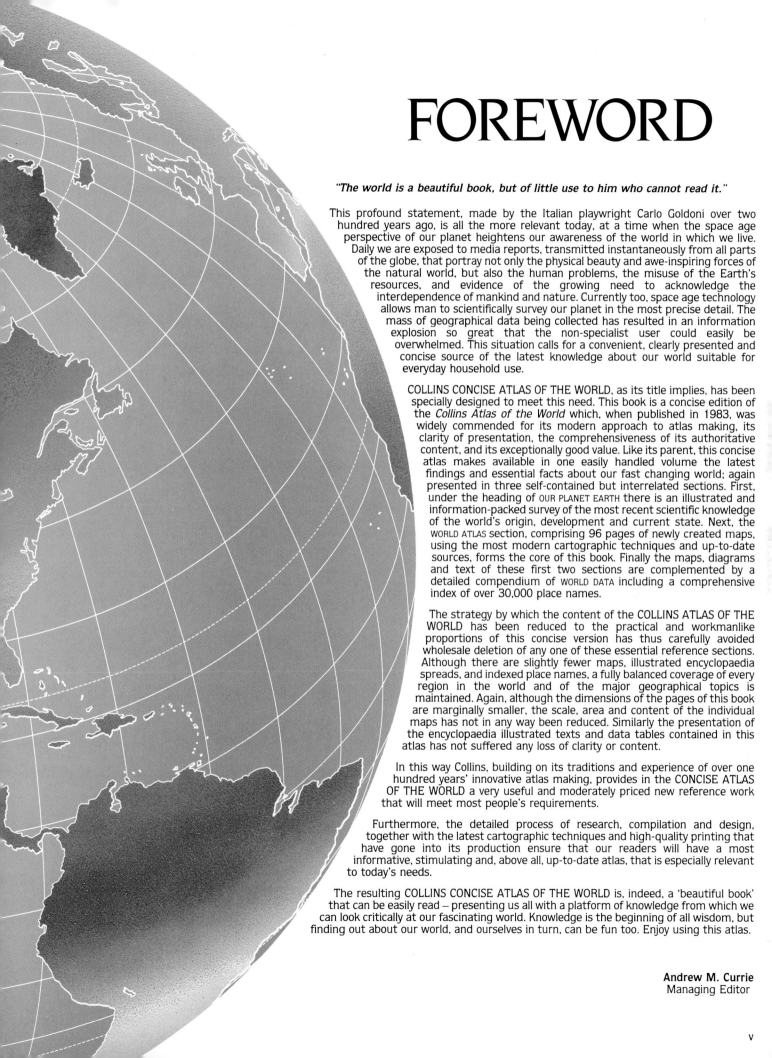

FOREWORD

"The world is a beautiful book, but of little use to him who cannot read it."

This profound statement, made by the Italian playwright Carlo Goldoni over two hundred years ago, is all the more relevant today, at a time when the space age perspective of our planet heightens our awareness of the world in which we live. Daily we are exposed to media reports, transmitted instantaneously from all parts of the globe, that portray not only the physical beauty and awe-inspiring forces of the natural world, but also the human problems, the misuse of the Earth's resources, and evidence of the growing need to acknowledge the interdependence of mankind and nature. Currently too, space age technology allows man to scientifically survey our planet in the most precise detail. The mass of geographical data being collected has resulted in an information explosion so great that the non-specialist user could easily be overwhelmed. This situation calls for a convenient, clearly presented and concise source of the latest knowledge about our world suitable for everyday household use.

COLLINS CONCISE ATLAS OF THE WORLD, as its title implies, has been specially designed to meet this need. This book is a concise edition of the *Collins Atlas of the World* which, when published in 1983, was widely commended for its modern approach to atlas making, its clarity of presentation, the comprehensiveness of its authoritative content, and its exceptionally good value. Like its parent, this concise atlas makes available in one easily handled volume the latest findings and essential facts about our fast changing world; again presented in three self-contained but interrelated sections. First, under the heading of OUR PLANET EARTH there is an illustrated and information-packed survey of the most recent scientific knowledge of the world's origin, development and current state. Next, the WORLD ATLAS section, comprising 96 pages of newly created maps, using the most modern cartographic techniques and up-to-date sources, forms the core of this book. Finally the maps, diagrams and text of these first two sections are complemented by a detailed compendium of WORLD DATA including a comprehensive index of over 30,000 place names.

The strategy by which the content of the COLLINS ATLAS OF THE WORLD has been reduced to the practical and workmanlike proportions of this concise version has thus carefully avoided wholesale deletion of any one of these essential reference sections. Although there are slightly fewer maps, illustrated encyclopaedia spreads, and indexed place names, a fully balanced coverage of every region in the world and of the major geographical topics is maintained. Again, although the dimensions of the pages of this book are marginally smaller, the scale, area and content of the individual maps has not in any way been reduced. Similarly the presentation of the encyclopaedia illustrated texts and data tables contained in this atlas has not suffered any loss of clarity or content.

In this way Collins, building on its traditions and experience of over one hundred years' innovative atlas making, provides in the CONCISE ATLAS OF THE WORLD a very useful and moderately priced new reference work that will meet most people's requirements.

Furthermore, the detailed process of research, compilation and design, together with the latest cartographic techniques and high-quality printing that have gone into its production ensure that our readers will have a most informative, stimulating and, above all, up-to-date atlas, that is especially relevant to today's needs.

The resulting COLLINS CONCISE ATLAS OF THE WORLD is, indeed, a 'beautiful book' that can be easily read – presenting us all with a platform of knowledge from which we can look critically at our fascinating world. Knowledge is the beginning of all wisdom, but finding out about our world, and ourselves in turn, can be fun too. Enjoy using this atlas.

Andrew M. Currie
Managing Editor

CONTENTS AND

COLLINS CONCISE ATLAS OF THE WORLD consists of three self-contained but interrelated sections, as is clearly indicated in the list of contents below.

OUR PLANET EARTH

WORLD ATLAS

THE WORLD

EUROPE

ASIA

This concise encyclopaedia section, by use of stimulating illustration and informative text, brings together many of the latest scientific discoveries and conclusions about our world; our place in the universe, the origin, structure and dynamics of our planet, the distribution of peoples and resources, and the increasingly significant effects of man on his environment. Each double-page opening has been carefully designed to highlight an important facet of our world as we know it today. As a special feature, every subject presentation includes a *Factfinder* panel, to which quick and easy reference can be made in order to find out particularly notable facts. All statistics quoted in this section are presented in metric terms in accordance with the System International d'Unites (S. I. units).

The main section of 96 pages of maps has been carefully planned and designed to meet the contemporary needs of the atlas user. Full recognition has been given to the many different purposes that currently call for map reference.

Map Coverage extends to every part of the world in a balanced scheme that avoids any individual country or regional bias. Map areas are chosen to reflect the social, economic, cultural or historical importance of a particular region. Each double spread or single page map has been planned deliberately to cover an entire physical or political unit. Generous map overlaps are included to maintain continuity. Following two world maps, giving separate coverage of the main political and physical features, each of the continents is treated systematically in a subsection of its own. Apart from being listed in the contents, full coverage of all regional maps of each continent is also clearly depicted in the *Key to Maps* to be found on the front and back endpapers. Also at the beginning of each continental subsection, alongside a special *Global View* political map, all map coverage, country by country, is identified in an additional handy page index. Finally as a further aid to the reader in locating the required area, a postage stamp key map is incorporated into the title margin of each map page.

Map projections have been chosen to reflect the different requirements of particular areas. No map can be absolutely true on account of the impossibility of representing a spheroid accurately on a flat surface without some distortion in either area, distance, direction or shape. In a general world atlas it is the equal area property that is most important to retain for comparative map studies and feature size evaluation and this principle has been followed wherever possible in this map section. As a special feature of this atlas, the *Global View* projections

used for each continental political map have been specially devised to allow for a realistic area comparison between the land areas of each continent and also between land and sea.

Map scales, as expressions of the relationship which the distance between any two points of the map bears to the corresponding distance on the ground, are in the context of this atlas grouped into three distinct categories.

Large scales, of between 1 : 1 000 000 (1 centimetre to 10 kilometres or 1 inch to 16 miles) and 1 : 2 500 000 (1 centimetre to 25 kilometres or 1 inch to 40 miles), are used to cover particularly dense populated areas of Western Europe, United States, Canada and Japan.

Medium scales, of between 1 : 2 500 000 and 1 : 7 500 000 are used for maps of important parts of Europe, North America, Australasia, India, China, etc.

Small scales, of less than 1 : 7 500 000 (e.g. 1 : 10 000 000, 1 : 15 000 000, 1 : 25 000 000 etc.) are selected for maps of the complete world, continents, oceans, polar regions and many of the larger countries.

The actual scale at which a particular area is mapped therefore reflects its shape, size and density of detail, and as a basic principle the more detail required to be shown of an area, the greater its scale. However, throughout this atlas, map scales have been limited in number, as far as possible, in order to facilitate comparison between maps.

Map Measurements give preference to the metric system which is now used in nearly every country throughout the world. All spot heights and ocean depths are shown in metres and the relief and submarine layer delineation is based on metric contour levels. However, all linear scalebar and height reference column figures are given in

GUIDE TO THE ATLAS

metric and Imperial equivalents to facilitate conversion of measurements for the non-metric reader.

Map symbols used are fully explained in the legend to be found on the first page of the World Atlas section. Careful study and frequent reference to this legend will aid in the reader's ability to extract maximum information.

Topography is shown by the combined means of precise spot heights, contouring, layer tinting and three-dimensional hill shading. Similar techniques are also used to depict the sea bed on the World Physical map and those of the oceans and polar regions.

Hydrographic features such as coastlines, rivers, lakes, swamps and canals are clearly differentiated.

Communications are particularly well represented with the contemporary importance of airports and road networks duly emphasized.

International boundaries and national capitals are fully documented and internal administrative divisions are shown with the maximum detail that the scale will allow. Boundary delineation reflects the 'de facto' rather than the 'de jure' political interpretation and where relevant an undefined or disputed boundary is distinguished. However there is no intended implication that the publishers necessarily endorse or accept the status of any political entity recorded on the maps.

Settlements are shown by a series of graded town stamps, each representing a population size category, based on the latest census figures.

Other features, such as notable ancient monuments, oases, national parks, oil and gas fields, are selectively included on particular maps that merit their identification.

Lettering styles used in the maps have been chosen with great care to ensure maximum legibility and clear distinction of named feature

categories. The size and weight of the various typefaces reflect the relative importance of the features. Town names are graded to correspond with the appropriate town stamp.

Map place names have been selected in accordance with maintaining legibility at a given scale and at the same time striking an appropriate balance between natural and man-made features worthy of note. Name forms have been standardized according to the widely accepted principle, now well established in international reference atlases, of including place names and geographical terms in the local language of the country in question. In the case on non-Roman scripts (e.g. Arabic), transliteration and transcription have either been based on the rules recommended by the Permanent Committee on Geographical Names and the United States Board of Geographical Names, or as in the case of the adopted Pinyin transcription of Chinese names, a system officially proposed by the country concerned. The diacritical signs used in each language or transliteration have been retained on all maps and throughout the index. However the English language reader's requirements have also been recognised in that the names of all countries, oceans, major seas and land features as well as familiar alternative name versions of important towns are presented in English.

Map Sources used in the compilation of this atlas were many and varied, but always of the latest available information. At each stage of their preparation the maps were submitted to a thorough process of research and continual revision to ensure that on publication all data would be as accurate as practicable. A well-documented data bank was created to ensure consistency and validity of all information represented on the maps.

This detailed data section forms an appropriate complement to the preceding maps and illustrated texts. There are two parts, each providing a different type of essential geographical information.

World Facts and Figures Drawn from the latest available official sources, these tables present an easy reference profile of significant world physical, political and demographic as well as national data.

World Index This concluding part of the atlas lists in alphabetical order all individual place names to be found on the maps, which total over 30,000. Each entry in the index is referenced to the appropriate map page number, the country or region in which the name is located and the position of the name on the map, given by its co-ordinates of latitude and longitude. A full explanation of how to use the index is to be found on page 103.

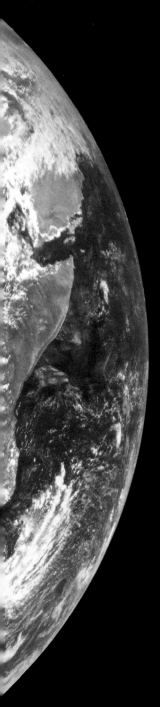

OUR PLANET EARTH

The Space Age, which began in 1957 with the triumphant launch of the Russian satellite Sputnik I, has already greatly enriched our understanding of the Solar System.

It has also afforded us a new perspective on our own planet, not least through photographs taken by astronauts that remind us that the Earth is a mere speck in space.

These photographs have dispelled the dangerous notion that our world is boundless in extent, with limitless resources. To view our planet from space is to recognize its finite nature and that we misuse it at our peril.

The Earth is a dynamic planet, with an ever-changing face. Movements in the restless atmosphere and hydrosphere are plain to see, while cataclysmic volcanic eruptions and earthquakes testify to the massive forces that operate beneath the Earth's crust.

Continental drift is slowly but inexorably changing the world map, creating new ocean basins and lofty mountain ranges.

Change ensures that the Earth's resources are constantly renewed. But nature works slowly, while our exploitation of those resources increases year by year — a consequence of a massive population explosion, which is most marked in the poorer nations, where malnutrition and short average life expectancies are features of everyday life. For example, an expanding population must be fed. But in many areas, over-intensive farming and over-grazing can rapidly transform once lush farmland into bleak desert.

Many question marks hang over the future of mankind, divided as it is by race, religion, language and political philosophies. And the plunder of our planet home is threatening many other life forms with extinction. One contribution we can all make to the survival of our world is to study and comprehend the delicate and infinetly varied environments that make Earth such a fascinating planet on which to live. Perhaps then our world can be preserved as, in the words of astronaut Neil Armstrong, 'a beautiful jewel in space.'

THE WHIRLING EARTH

The Earth moves in three ways: it spins on its axis; it orbits the Sun; and it moves around the Milky Way galaxy with the rest of the Solar System. As it spins on its axis, the Sun appears to move around the sky once every 24 hours. This, the mean solar day, is slightly longer than the sidereal day of 23 hours, 56 minutes and 4 seconds. The difference between the two is explained by the fact that the Earth is orbiting the Sun while it spins on its axis, with the effect that it must rotate 1/365th of a revolution more than a sidereal day in order that the same meridian exactly faces the Sun again.

As the Earth spins on its axis, the time at any point on the surface is calculated from the position of the Sun in the sky. This is called the local or apparent time. Because the Earth rotates 360° in 24 hours, local time changes by one hour for every 15° of longitude or 4 minutes for every 1° of longitude. For practical purposes, however, we use standard or zone time, so that the times are fixed over extensive north-south zones that also take account of national boundaries. By an international agreement in 1884, time zones are measured east and west of the prime meridian (0° longitude) which passes through Greenwich, London. Because clocks are advanced by 12 hours 180° east of Greenwich, but put back by 12 hours 180° west of Greenwich, there is a time difference of 24 hours at the International Date Line. This is approximately 180°W or E, although internationally agreed deviations prevent confusion of dates in island groups and land areas.

People crossing the International Date Line from west to east gain a day. Those going from east to west lose a day.

The Seasons

Because the Earth's axis is tilted by 23½°, the Sun appears to travel in a higher or lower path across the sky at various times of the year, giving differing lengths of daylight. The diagram at the top of the page shows that, at the spring equinox in the northern hemisphere (March 21), the Sun is overhead at the Equator. After March 21, the overhead Sun moves northwards as the northern hemisphere tilts towards the Sun. On June 21, the summer solstice in the northern hemisphere, the Sun is overhead at the Tropic of Cancer (latitude 23½° North). By September 23, the Sun is again overhead at the Equator. By about December 21, the Sun is overhead at the Tropic of Capricorn (23½° S). This is the winter solstice in the northern hemisphere. The seasons are reversed in the southern hemisphere.

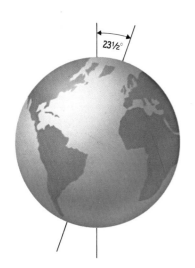

Above: The Earth's axis (joining the North and South poles via the centre of the Earth) is tilted by 23½°. The Earth rotates on its axis once every 23 hours, 56 minutes and 4 seconds. The tilt of the axis remains constant as the Earth orbits the Sun.

Right: The path of the Sun across the sky is highest on Midsummer Day, the longest day, and lowest at midwinter (December 21), the shortest day. The total variation in altitude is 47°, which is twice the angle by which the Earth's axis is tilted.

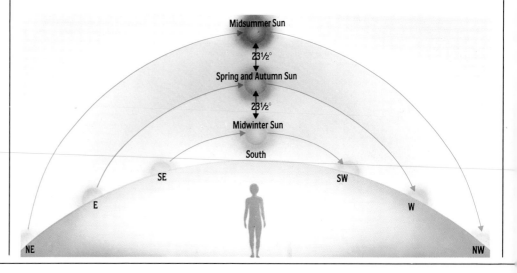

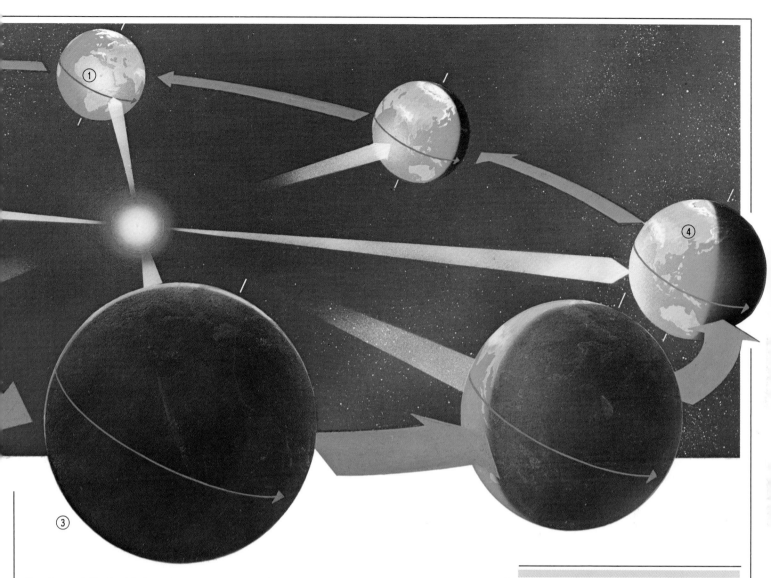

Above: Because the Earth's axis is tilted during its annual orbit of the Sun, there are variations in solar radiation that cause seasons. On March 21, the spring or vernal equinox in the northern hemisphere, the Sun is overhead at the Equator (1). On June 21, it is overhead at the Tropic of Cancer, the summer solstice (2). On September 23, it is overhead at the Equator, the autumn equinox (3). On December 21, it is overhead at the Tropic of Capricorn, the winter solstice (4).

Below: The world is divided into time zones. The standard time at Greenwich (0° longitude) on the map is 12.00 Greenwich Mean Time (not British Summer Time). East of Greenwich, standard times are ahead of GMT, while west of Greenwich, they are behind it. Ideally, time zones should be longitudinal bands of 15° or 7½° (representing time differences of 1 hour or 30 minutes). But time zones are irregular in shape to prevent small countries having two standard times.

FACTFINDER

Length of day: Mean solar day, 24 hours. Sidereal day (measured against fixed stars) 23·93 hours.

Speed of the Earth's rotation on its axis: At the Equator, it is rotating at 1660 km/h. It is less away from the Equator: at 30°N and S, it is 1438 km/h; at 60° N and S, it is 990 km/h.

Equinoxes: The vernal equinox is on March 21, and the autumn equinox on September 23 in the northern hemisphere. The equinoxes are reversed in the southern hemisphere.

Solstices: In the northern hemisphere, the summer solstice is on June 21 and the winter solstice on December 21. The reverse applies in the southern hemisphere.

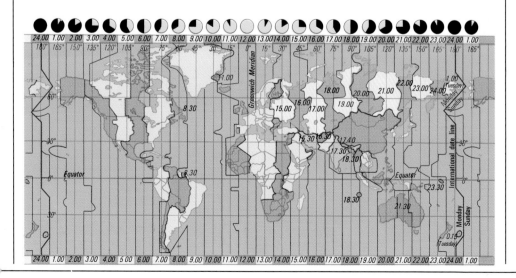

THE EARTH'S STRUCTURE

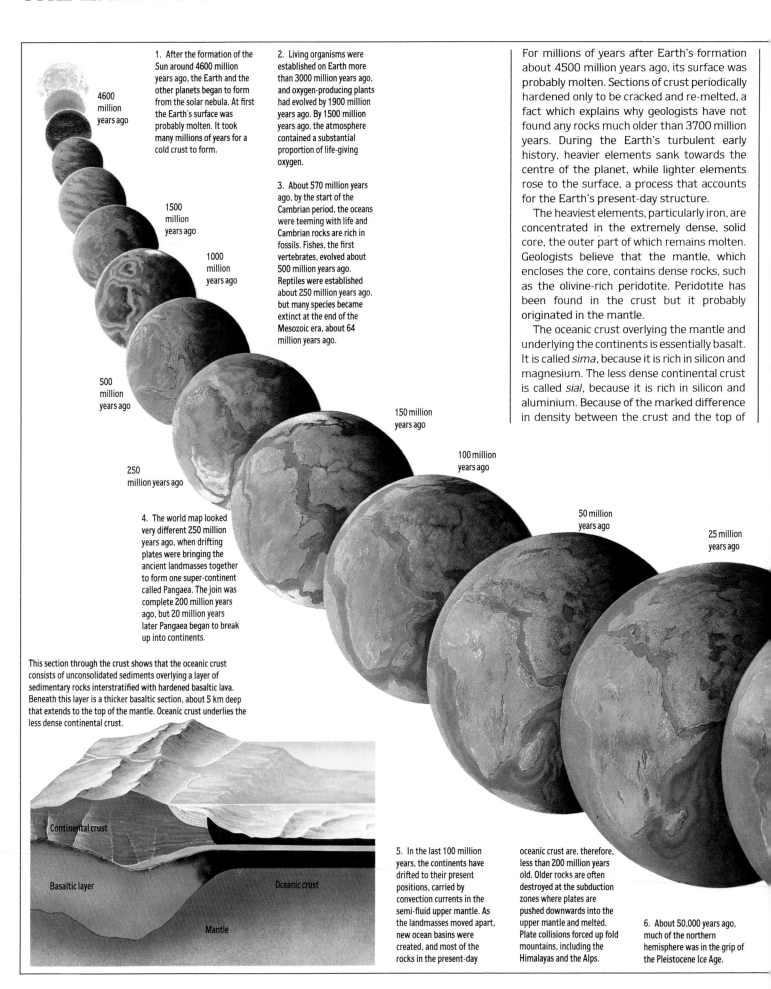

1. After the formation of the Sun around 4600 million years ago, the Earth and the other planets began to form from the solar nebula. At first the Earth's surface was probably molten. It took many millions of years for a cold crust to form.

2. Living organisms were established on Earth more than 3000 million years ago, and oxygen-producing plants had evolved by 1900 million years ago. By 1500 million years ago, the atmosphere contained a substantial proportion of life-giving oxygen.

3. About 570 million years ago, by the start of the Cambrian period, the oceans were teeming with life and Cambrian rocks are rich in fossils. Fishes, the first vertebrates, evolved about 500 million years ago. Reptiles were established about 250 million years ago, but many species became extinct at the end of the Mesozoic era, about 64 million years ago.

4600 million years ago

1500 million years ago

1000 million years ago

500 million years ago

250 million years ago

150 million years ago

100 million years ago

50 million years ago

25 million years ago

For millions of years after Earth's formation about 4500 million years ago, its surface was probably molten. Sections of crust periodically hardened only to be cracked and re-melted, a fact which explains why geologists have not found any rocks much older than 3700 million years. During the Earth's turbulent early history, heavier elements sank towards the centre of the planet, while lighter elements rose to the surface, a process that accounts for the Earth's present-day structure.

The heaviest elements, particularly iron, are concentrated in the extremely dense, solid core, the outer part of which remains molten. Geologists believe that the mantle, which encloses the core, contains dense rocks, such as the olivine-rich peridotite. Peridotite has been found in the crust but it probably originated in the mantle.

The oceanic crust overlying the mantle and underlying the continents is essentially basalt. It is called *sima*, because it is rich in silicon and magnesium. The less dense continental crust is called *sial*, because it is rich in silicon and aluminium. Because of the marked difference in density between the crust and the top of

4. The world map looked very different 250 million years ago, when drifting plates were bringing the ancient landmasses together to form one super-continent called Pangaea. The join was complete 200 million years ago, but 20 million years later Pangaea began to break up into continents.

This section through the crust shows that the oceanic crust consists of unconsolidated sediments overlying a layer of sedimentary rocks interstratified with hardened basaltic lava. Beneath this layer is a thicker basaltic section, about 5 km deep that extends to the top of the mantle. Oceanic crust underlies the less dense continental crust.

Continental crust

Basaltic layer

Oceanic crust

Mantle

5. In the last 100 million years, the continents have drifted to their present positions, carried by convection currents in the semi-fluid upper mantle. As the landmasses moved apart, new ocean basins were created, and most of the rocks in the present-day

oceanic crust are, therefore, less than 200 million years old. Older rocks are often destroyed at the subduction zones where plates are pushed downwards into the upper mantle and melted. Plate collisions forced up fold mountains, including the Himalayas and the Alps.

6. About 50,000 years ago, much of the northern hemisphere was in the grip of the Pleistocene Ice Age.

FACTFINDER

The Earth's crust: The oceanic crust averages 6 km thick; density, 3·0 g/cm³. The continental crust averages 35–40 km, reaching 60–70 km under high mountains; density 2·7 g/cm³.

Mantle: About 2900 km thick; density, 3·4–4·5 g/cm³.

Core: Diameter 6740 km. Outer core 2000 km thick, molten iron and nickel. Inner core, a solid metal ball, 1370 km thick. Density of core, 10–13 g/cm³. Temperature at 2700°C, under pressure of 3800 tonnes per sq cm.

Surface area of the Earth: 510,066,000 km². About 148,326,000 km², or just over 29 per cent of the Earth's surface, is land.

Mass: 5976 million million million tonnes.

Shape and size: Oblate spheroid, slightly flattened at the poles and bulging at the Equator. So, at sea level, the diameter of the Earth between the poles is 12,713 km, as compared with a diameter of 12,756 km, across the plane of the Equator. Similarly, the equatorial circumference of 40,075 km is greater than the polar circumference of 40,007 km.

Below are eight rocks found in the Earth's crust. There are three main kinds of rocks: igneous, sedimentary and metamorphic. Igneous rocks, including obsidian and granite, are forms of hardened magma. Many sedimentary rocks, such as sandstone and conglomorate, are composed of worn fragments of other rocks, while coal is compressed plant remains. Metamorphic rocks, such as marble and slate, are formed when great heat and pressure alter igneous or sedimentary rocks.

the mantle, the crust cannot sink. It is split into large, rigid plates that 'float' on the denser mantle. Plate movements cause earthquakes, mountain building and volcanic activity – occurrences that remind us of the restless nature of our world.

About 85 per cent of the top 16 km of the crust are either igneous rocks (rocks formed from molten magma) or metamorphic rocks (igneous or sedimentary rocks that have been changed by heat, pressure or, sometimes, chemical action). However, sedimentary rocks cover 75 per cent of the surface of landmasses. Many sedimentary rocks are clastic (formed from eroded rock fragments), some, such as coal, are organic, and some are formed by chemical action, such as rock salt precipitated from water.

Obsidian is a glassy, extrusive igneous rock, formed on the surface.

Granite is a coarse-grained, intrusive igneous rock, which forms in huge underground masses.

Marble is formed by the action of great heat and pressure on limestone.

Slate is usually formed by the metamorphism of shale.

Coal is a fossil fuel formed in ancient swamps.

Limestones are sedimentary rocks composed mainly of calcium carbonate.

Sandstone contains grains of quartz and other minerals bound together by tough mineral cements.

Conglomerates contain pebbles cemented in a fine silt or sand matrix.

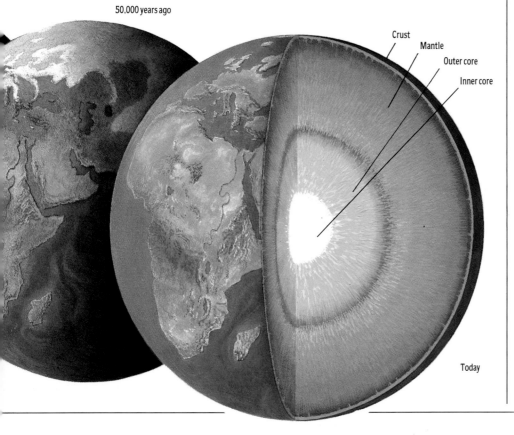

50,000 years ago

Crust
Mantle
Outer core
Inner core

Today

THE VIOLENT EARTH

Ever since the Earth formed, volcanic activity has continued ceaselessly. It was responsible for releasing pockets of gas from the rocks to form an atmosphere and water vapour to fill the oceans. It was molten magma that formed the Earth's first, fragile, potentially life-supporting crust and, even today, newly formed volcanic soils are among the world's most fertile.

Most volcanoes lie near plate edges. Some, including Surtsey – a volcanic island that appeared off Iceland in 1963 – are on the ocean ridges where new crustal rock is being created as magma wells up from the interior (see pages XVI–XVII). Other volcanoes are near subduction zones where descending plates are melted to produce pockets of magma. A few volcanoes are far from plate edges. They are apparently situated above radioactive heat sources in the mantle.

Magma, molten rock at temperatures around 1100°C to 1200°C, reaches the surface as lava. Gases in thick, pasty lava cannot easily escape; they expand, shatter and eject the lava in fragments, called *pyroclasts*, ranging in size from loaf-shaped volcanic bombs to fine dust and ash. Quiet volcanoes, however, emit thin, runny lava, usually basalt, from which gases escape easily. Quiet eruptions build up flattish, shield mountains, contrasting with the ash cones of explosive eruptions. Most volcanoes are intermediate, sometimes erupting explosively, sometimes quietly.

Magma may also emerge from long fissures and build up huge plateaux, such as the Deccan Plateau in India. Other magma solidifies underground in huge batholiths and laccoliths, or in thin dykes and sills. In some areas, where volcanic activity has almost ceased, fumaroles (holes from which steam and gases emerge under pressure), hot springs, geysers and boiling mud pools still testify to past activity.

Most volcanoes in populated areas are now carefully observed for signs of activity, including changes in pressure and temperature, earth tremors, tilts of slopes caused by magma swelling below, and changes in the composition of gases from fumaroles. But prediction of eruptions remains inexact.

FACTFINDER

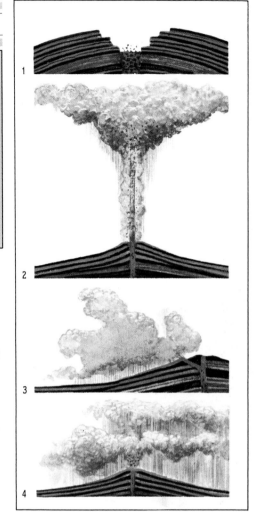

Below: The section through a volcanic landscape shows a large pocket of magma (1) in the crust. Periodically, magma rises under pressure through a vent (2) and spills out as lava (3). This volcanic cone is made up of alternating layers of hardened lava and compacted ash. Magma is also injected into rock layers to form dykes (4) that cut across existing rock layers and sills (5), which are sheets of hardened magma that are parallel to the rock strata. Large, dome-shaped intrusions of magma, like those that underlie mountain ranges, are called batholiths. They extend over hundreds of square kilometres and appear to replace rather than displace the invaded rocks. They are revealed when the overlying rocks have been worn away. Small batholiths, or laccoliths (6), arch up overlying strata. Magma sometimes flows on to the surface through long fissures and spreads over huge areas (8). In volcanic regions, where activity is declining, high temperatures still produce hot springs and geysers (7). Extinct volcanoes may contain large lakes in their craters (9). These lakes are known as *calderas*, from the Spanish word for kettle.

Right: Types of Volcanic Eruptions
1. Quiet volcanoes, as in Hawaii, discharge little gas so there are no explosive eruptions. They emit fluid lava streams that flow a long way before they harden. Hence, in cross-section, they are gently sloping.
2. Explosive volcanoes are characterized by sudden, violent eruptions in which the magma is shattered into hot dust, ash and volcanic bombs. These pyroclasts are hurled high into the air. Explosive volcanoes are often said to be Plinian in type, after the Roman writer Pliny who witnessed the explosive eruption of Mount Vesuvius in southern Italy in AD 79.
3. Peléan volcanoes, named after Mount Pelée in Martinique in the West Indies, which erupted in 1902, produce *nuées ardentes*, or 'glowing clouds' of hot gas and ash that roll downhill, burning all in their path.
4. Vesuvian volcanoes are intermediate in type. Although intermediate volcanoes may erupt explosively, lava streams accompany most eruptions.

THE DRIFTING CONTINENTS

In the early 20th century, the German meteorologist Alfred Wegener and the American scientist F. B. Taylor both advanced the theory of continental drift. The idea sprang from the similarities between the shapes of the continents on either side of the Atlantic Ocean and studies showed that there were many similar rock structures and fossils found in landmasses that are now separated by thousands of kilometres.

The study of the ocean floor after World War II produced much evidence to support the theory. Mapping of the oceans revealed that there were enormous mountain ranges, called oceanic ridges, running through the oceans. These ridges were zones of seismic activity and temperature studies showed a concentration of heat along the rift valleys that run through the centre of the ridges. Further, the youngest rocks always came from the centre of the ridges and rocks

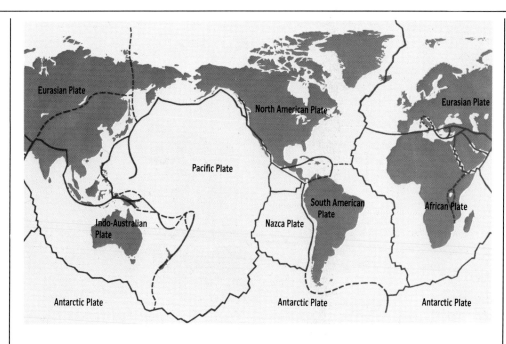

increased in age in both directions away from the ridges.

This and other evidence suggested that molten rock is welling up beneath the ridges from the semi-molten asthenosphere. This molten rock is spreading out under the crust, flowing considerable distances before cooling and sinking again. These convection currents are pulling the two sides of the ocean apart, while magma wells up to form new crustal rock along the ridges to fill the gap.

The oceanic ridges, therefore, contain breaks in the crust between rigid blocks on either side. The blocks are known as plates.

The oceans are being widened by between one and 10 cm per year, but the Earth is not growing any larger, and so there must be places where crustal rock is destroyed. These places are at the bottom of deep oceanic trenches, where the advancing edge of one plate is thrust under another in a subduction zone. As it descends into the asthenosphere, the plate is melted and magma rises through volcanoes in the overlying plate. Some plate edges are collision zones, which are former subduction zones where the plates continue

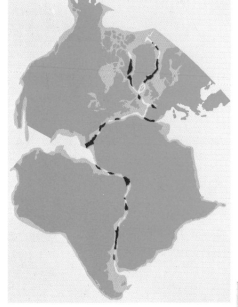

Top right: The map shows the chief plates into which the Earth's crust is divided. Plate edges are zones of intense seismic and volcanic activity.
Above: The similarity between the shapes of the landmasses on either side of the Atlantic Ocean suggests that they were once joined together. The map, which takes as the continental edge an underwater line, 1000 metres below sea level, reveals an even better fit than coastlines, which are not the true edges of the continents.

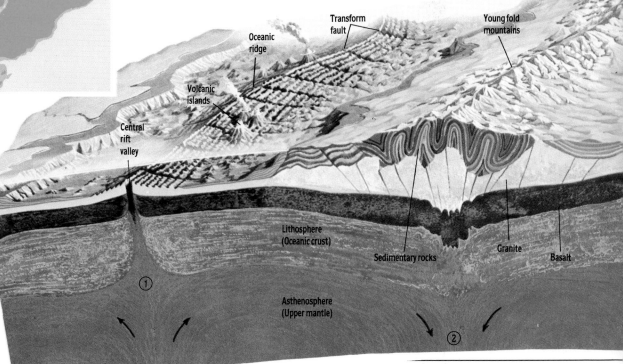

FACTFINDER

to push against each other. Plates sliding alongside each other are transform faults.

The study of plate tectonics has greatly increased our understanding of many phenomena, including vulcanicity, seismology and orogenesis. It has also thrown light on the changing face of the Earth, particularly since the start of the Jurassic period, 200 million years ago. (In Earth history, periods are subdivisions of longer eras, epochs are subdivisions of periods, and ages are subdivisions of epochs.)

Below: Convection currents in the semi-molten asthenosphere (the upper mantle) pull plates apart along the oceanic ridges. Magma wells up (1) to fill the gap along the central rift valley in the ridge. This process is called ocean spreading. Lateral movements of plates cause plate collisions. The force of two plates pushing against each other can force up sedimentary rocks on intervening sea beds into new fold mountains until, finally, the plates become locked together in a collision zone. (2). In subduction zones (3), the edge of one plate is thrust beneath another along an oceanic trench. Pressure, friction and heat melt the descending plate edge, and magma rises to the surface (4). Oceanic ridges, collision zones and subduction zones are types of plate edges. The fourth is the transform fault (5), like the San Andreas Fault in California. Here plates move alongside each other.

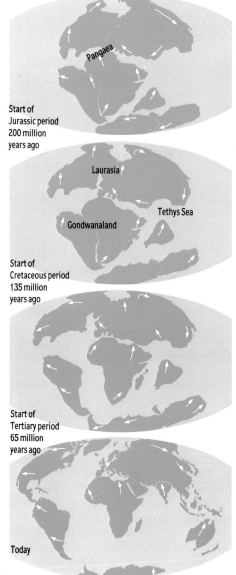

Start of Jurassic period 200 million years ago

Start of Cretaceous period 135 million years ago

Start of Tertiary period 65 million years ago

Today

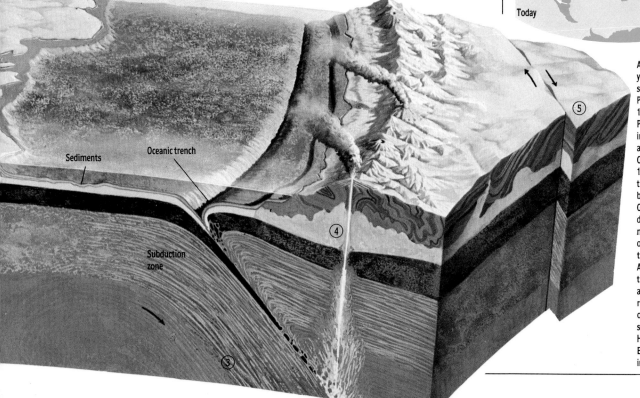

Sediments

Oceanic trench

Subduction zone

Above: About 200 million years ago, there was one super-continent, called Pangaea, or 'all Earth'. About 180 million years ago, Pangaea began to break up into the northern Laurasia and the southern Gondwanaland. The map of 135 million years ago shows that a plate bearing India had broken away from Gondwanaland and was drifting northwards. This movement continued as other landmasses drifted to their present positions. Around 53 million years ago, the Indian Plate was pushing against Asia. Sedimentary rocks on the intervening bed of the Tethys Sea were squeezed up to form the lofty Himalayas. The Indian and Eurasian Plates are now interlocked.

THE RESTLESS EARTH

Plate movements keep the Earth's crust on the move. But the movements are not smooth, because the rough plate edges become jammed. The tension mounts until the rocks snap and the plates lurch forward in sudden, violent jerks, causing earthquakes. An earthquake's point of origin is the focus, while the spot on the Earth's surface directly above it is the epicentre. Vibrations spreading outwards from the focus, are sometimes so intense that buildings collapse, fires start and destructive waves (tsunami) are generated in the sea. The intensity of the vibrations decreases away from the focus, but faint seismic waves can be detected by seismographs on the other side of the world.

The most violent earthquakes occur near plate edges, but they can occur anywhere where rocks move along faults, or where the ground is shaken by avalanches, explosions or landslides. Ways of predicting earthquakes are being sought and some successes have been claimed, but much research remains to be done.

Plate collisions are responsible for crustal deformation, when horizontal sedimentary rock layers are folded, squeezed and fractured. Intensely folded ranges include the Himalayas, which have been compressed by as much as 650 km, and the Alps. The Alps were raised up in the last 26 million years as the African plate pushed a small plate bearing Italy against the Eurasian Plate. Fracturing produces major fault lines along which horizontal and vertical movements occur. Vertical movements raise up horsts, such as the Vosges and Harz mountains, and even larger block mountains, such as the Ruwenzori range in East Africa. The Ruwenzoris overlook the world's largest rift valley, a trough formed between plate systems of roughly parallel faults. The East African Rift Valley runs from Syria in the Middle East to Mozambique in the south.

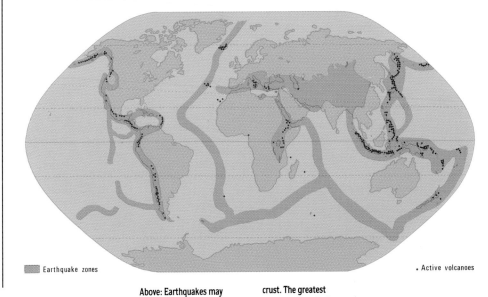

Left: An earthquake in Alaska in 1964 caused great devastation. The focus of the earthquake was offshore in the Prince William Sound.

San Andreas Fault

Sierra Nevada

Great Valley

■ Earthquake zones

. Active volcanoes

Above: Earthquakes may occur anywhere, but the main earthquake zones are near plate edges, the geologically active parts of the Earth's crust. The greatest concentration of volcanoes is in Indonesia, which has more than 160 active volcanoes and frequent earthquakes.

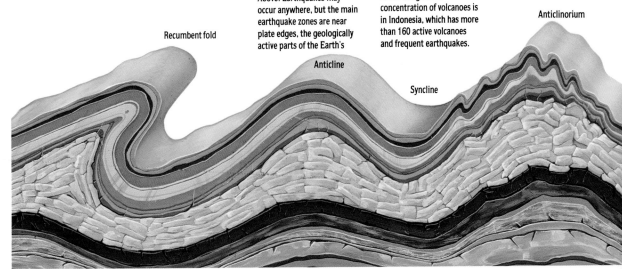

Recumbent fold

Anticline

Syncline

Anticlinorium

Enormous lateral pressure caused by plate collisions can squeeze horizontal layers of rocks into folds. A simple upfold is an anticline and a simple downfold is a syncline. If a large anticline contains a number of small folds, it is called an anticlinorium. Overfolds in which the axial plane is sharply inclined are called recumbent folds. Recumbent folds are sometimes sheared away and forced long distances. These folds are called nappes.

Left: California is split by faults into a series of blocks. Vertical movements have created block mountains and downfaulted depressions. Along the San Andreas Fault, two plates are sliding past each other at an average annual rate of 6 cm a year.

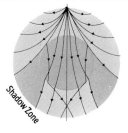

Above: Seismic waves are deflected by zones of differing density in the Earth. The core reflects shock waves such that shadow zones occur where no waves are recorded.

Garlock Fault

Mojave Desert

San Bernardino Mountains

Los Angeles

Salton Sea

FACTFINDER

SOME DEVASTATING EARTHQUAKES

Concepción, Chile: An earthquake south of Concepción in 1960 was the most massive ever recorded, ranking 9·5 on the revised Richter scale (in use since 1977). Death toll: 2000.

Lisbon, Portugal: The earthquake of 1775 was one of the world's greatest. Caused by sudden fault movements and fissuring on the seabed to the west and south, there were three major shocks. Fires and tsunami destroyed the city. Lakes in Norway swayed. Death toll: about 60,000.

Prince William Sound, Alaska: The 1964 earthquake (9·2 on the revised Richter scale) generated a 67-metre tsunami that battered Alaska's southern coasts. Death toll: 114. (The highest recorded tsunami appeared off Ishigaki Island in the Ryukyu chain in 1971. It was 85 metres high).

Sagami Bay, Japan: An earthquake in Sagami Bay in 1923 was the world's most destructive. On the Kwanto Plain, in nearby Tokyo and Yokohama, about 570,000 houses were destroyed. The cost of the damage was estimated at £1000 million (it would now be more than four times that figure). Death toll: 143,000.

Shaanxi (formerly Shensi) province, China: An earthquake in 1556 was the world's greatest killer. In widespread landslides and floods, more than 800,000 people perished.

Tangshan, China: An earthquake in 1976 was the greatest killer of recent times. Death toll: about 750,000.

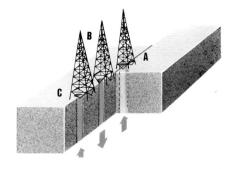

Above: The diagram shows a transform fault which is a plate edge, like California's San Andreas Fault. Movements along the fault are jerky. Sudden jerks cause earthquakes.

Below: Plate movements create tension in the crust some way from the plate edges. Such tension can fracture rocks and produce long fault lines. Tugging movements cause some

blocks of land to slip down between roughly parallel faults to create graben, or rift valleys. Other blocks are squeezed up to form steep-walled horsts, or block mountains.

Above: Earthquake prevention is an important area of scientific research. American scientists have found that water lubricates faults and causes rock slippages. This principle might be applied along the San Andreas Fault. To relieve the mounting tension before a violent earthquake occurs, scientists propose that a series of wells be drilled along the fault. By pumping water *out* of wells A and C, the fault would become locked at these points. Water could then be pumped *into* the intervening well B, lubricating the fault and causing a small earthquake. Such small movements made along the entire fault might prevent a disaster.

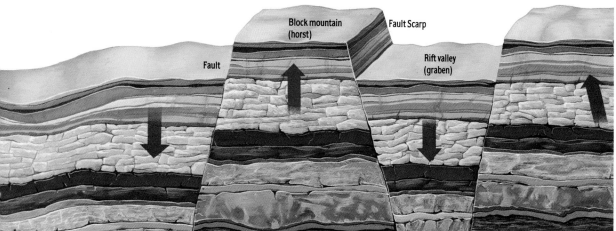

Fault

Block mountain (horst)

Fault Scarp

Rift valley (graben)

THE SCULPTURED EARTH

Natural erosion is a slow process and landscapes do not appear to change much in a person's lifetime. But even as mountains rise, natural forces, including weathering, wear them down. Weathering can be mechanical or chemical. In cool, moist areas, mechanical weathering includes action by frost. As water freezes it expands. Frost forming in cracks in the rocks exerts pressure which eventually splits the rocks apart. In hot, dry regions, the Sun's heat expands the outer layer of rocks which peel away, a process called exfoliation.

Chemical weathering includes the dissolving of minerals by water, and hydrolysis, when minerals react with water to produce new compounds, such as kaolin from potash feldspars in granite. Carbonation occurs because rainwater is a weak carbonic acid, which reacts with calcium carbonate, the chief constituent of limestone, wearing the limestone away to create karst scenery and limestone caves.

Major sculptors of the landscape are ice, the wind and running water. Although ice sheets and valley glaciers are now confined to polar and mountain regions, large parts of the northern hemisphere were sculpted by ice during the Pleistocene Ice Age. Glaciers, which form from compacted snow, contain rocks frozen into the bottom and sides. These jagged rocks give the moving ice a powerful cutting-edge, enabling it to deepen the basins and valleys that it occupies. Glaciated features include knife-edged arêtes, basins called cirques, pointed horns, and U-shaped valleys. The moraine carried by the ice ranges from boulders to fine clay. Some moraine is dumped in ridges of terminal moraine. Some is washed out by melt water and spread out as glaciofluvial deposits.

The chief agent of erosion in hot deserts is the wind. Wind-blown sand can undercut cliffs, carve rocks into the shape of mushrooms, and scour out deep hollows. Sand covers about one-fifth of the world's hot deserts; migrating dunes are a constant threat to human settlements at oases.

Valley glaciers flow from snowfields where glacier ice is formed from compressed snow. The rate of flow is determined by the rate of ice formation at the source.

Above left: Seas of sand cover about one-fifth of the world's hot deserts.
Left: A barchan is a crescent-shaped sand dune formed in regions with winds that blow constantly from the same direction.

Below: Sand dunes usually accumulate around some irregularity or obstacle. Once formed, they advance in the direction of the prevailing wind as sand is blown up the windward side and down the leeward side.

Left: Glaciated uplands contain several typical features, including pointed peaks, or horns (1), which are formed when three or more cirques (steep-sided basins, 2) form back to back. Cirques are separated by knife-edged ridges called arêtes (3). Overdeepening of the main valleys by glaciers creates truncated spurs (4) and typical U-shaped valleys (5). Tributary valleys (6) are left hanging above the overdeepened main valleys.

Above: Glaciated lowlands contain features formed both by glacial erosion and deposition. Many lakes occupy ice-worn hollows (1) or basins dammed by moraine. Ice-scoured rocks are striated (scratched) in the direction of the ice flow. Roches moutonneés (2) are rocks that have been smoothed by the ice on the upstream side, but are jagged on the downstream side. Moraine forms winding ridges called eskers (3) and hummocks called drumlins (4). Long ridges of terminal moraine (5) mark the snouts of ancient glaciers. Beyond, melt water has spread eroded material over a glacial outwash plain (6).

Direction of wind

The Karst district of Yugoslavia has given its name to limestone landscapes in general. Typical features are gorges formed when the roofs of caves collapse.

FACTFINDER

Largest cave system: Mammoth Cave National Park, Kentucky, Unites States; 345 km of mapped passageways.

Largest cavern: Sarawak Chamber in Gunung National Park, Sarawak; 700 m long; 300 m wide; lowest height: 70m.

Ice sheets and glaciers: Ice covers 10·4 per cent of the world's land surfaces. It constitutes 2·15 per cent of the world's

water. The largest ice sheet of Antarctica contains more than seven times as much ice as the Greenland sheet.

Longest glacier: Lambert Glacier, 400 km long. With the Fish Glacier limb, it forms a continuous ice passage of over 510 km.

Largest desert: The Sahara in north Africa covers 5½ per cent of the earth's surface or 8½ million sq km.

Limestone is eroded by carbonation, caused by the reaction of the rock with rainwater containing carbon dioxide. Vertical cracks (1) are enlarged into grikes, which enclose blocks called clints (2). Streams plunge into sink or swallow holes (3). Pot-holers may enter limestone caves through dry swallow holes (4). They find dry galleries (5) and underground streams (6), which surface at resurgences (7). Limestone caves often contain features formed from calcite deposited from dripping water, including stalactites (8), stalagmites (9), plate stalagmites (10), balcony stalagmites (11) and fir cone stalagmites (12). Pillars (13) form when stalactites and stalagmites meet. Balconies (14) are deposited from water dripping over a ledge.

WATER SHAPES THE LAND

On fine summer days, mountain streams and sea waves may seem harmless enough. But when the streams are in flood and the waves are whipped up by strong winds, both become powerful sculptors of the landscape.

River Action and Valley Development

Rivers are the leading agent of erosion, transportation and deposition in moist, temperate regions. Their power depends on their speed, a function of the gradient, and their volume. Rivers have three distinct sections. The youthful stage includes the steepest gradients and is often marked by waterfalls and rapids which form where the river crosses resistant rocks. A youthful river in flood becomes a torrent, capable of further deepening its V-shaped valley. In the mature stage, the volume of water is increased, although the gradients are gentler. The river remains vigorous and sweeping meanders constantly broaden the valleys. In the old age stage, the river flows over the flattest part of its course. Little erosion occurs, but the water carries huge loads of sediment, worn by attrition into fine particles. The Mississippi sweeps an estimated 700 million tonnes of sediment past New Orleans every year. Some is dumped in the advancing delta. The rest spreads over the floor of the Gulf of Mexico. River profiles are slowly flattened, but if the land is uplifted, steeper gradients rejuvenate the river. For example, the Colorado River in the United States has been rejuvenated by the uplift of the Colorado Plateau, which was formerly a nearly flat coastal plain. With its steadily increasing gradient, the Colorado River eroded the magnificent Grand Canyon.

Power of the Sea

Sea waves constantly batter coasts by lifting up shingle and hurling it at the shore. Wave erosion is most marked during storms. The sea also dissolves some rocks and shatters others by compressing air in cracks. Wave erosion carves out bays in softer rocks, but it also slowly wears away headlands of resistant rock. The sea also has a constructive side. Eroded material is carried along the shore by waves and currents. At points where the land changes direction, the water often drops the material to form low shingle ridges called spits. Spits are often curved because waves deflect their growth towards the shore. Sometimes, spits extend from one headland to another, sealing off a bay or lagoon. Such spits are called baymouth bars. Some bars are built up offshore and are not attached to land. Tombolos are spits linking the mainland to offshore islands, such as the Tombolo di Feniglio and the Tombolo di Gianetta in Italy. Chesil Beach in southern England links the former Isle of Portland to the mainland.

Opposite: Glaciers (1) are one of the sources of rivers. Here melt water feeds a lake (2), which is drained by a river. The youthful stage of a river is marked by deep, V-shaped valleys (3) eroded by the river in flood. Waterfalls (4) and rapids occur where the river passes over particularly hard rock outcrops. Gorges (5) are other features usually associated with youthful rivers, especially in semi-arid regions where there is little weathering of the valley sides. The mature stage of a river is characterized by vigorous meanders (6). The river's power here is concentrated on lateral erosion so that the valley is widened rather than deepened. Lateral erosion sometimes undercuts the banks along the necks of meanders until the river straightens its course. The abandoned meander then becomes a stagnant oxbow lake (7). In the old age stage, the sluggish river lacks erosive power as it winds over a nearly flat flood plain (8). But large amounts of sediment are suspended in the water. This sediment may accumulate in deltas (9), or currents may sweep it out to sea where it settles on the seabed to form new sedimentary rocks (10).

FACTFINDER

Power of rivers: At speeds of 0·5 km/h, rivers move fine sand; at 10 km/h, small stones are transported; at 30 km/h, rivers shift large boulders.

Greatest flow of any river: Amazon River discharges an average of 120,000 m³/sec. In full flood, nearly 1·66 times as much water is emptied into the Atlantic Ocean.

Largest river canyon: Grand Canyon, Arizona, United States; length: 349 km; width: 6–20 km; depth: up to 2133 metres.

Longest river: River Nile, northeast Africa. Length: 6695 km.

Highest waterfall: Angel Falls, Venezuela has a drop of 979m It is on a branch of the River Carrao and was discovered by an American pilot, Jimmy Angel, in 1935.

Largest delta: Ganges-Brahmaputra delta, area: 75,000 km².

Highest sea cliffs: Molokai Island, Hawaii, 1005 metres.

(1)

(2)

(3)

Above: Sea waves undercut headlands, forming caves which may be linked to the surface by blowholes (1). Caves on either side of a headland may unite to form a natural arch (2). When the arch collapses, only a stack (3) remains.

Above: A bar of sand and shingle encloses a lagoon on the coast of Tanzania.

Below: Sand and shingle are moved along the shore in a series of zig-zags.

Below: Spits and bars are features of the Baltic coast of northern Germany.

Above: This stack is being undercut along its bedding planes (lines of weakness).

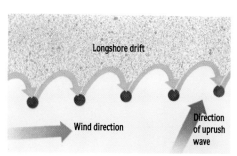

Longshore drift

Wind direction

Direction of uprush wave

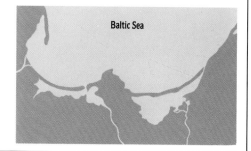

Baltic Sea

THE ATMOSPHERE AND CLOUDS

The atmosphere is a thin skin of gases, chiefly nitrogen and life-giving oxygen, that encircles and protects the Earth. It moderates temperatures, preventing enormous diurnal changes in heating that would destroy life on Earth. And, in the stratosphere, one of the five main layers of the atmosphere, is a belt of ozone that absorbs most of the Sun's dangerous ultraviolet radiation. The depth of the atmosphere cannot be defined precisely, because it becomes increasingly rarefied with height. But more than 99 per cent of its mass is within 40 km of the surface.

Air Pressure
Air has weight and the total weight of the atmosphere is about 5000 million million tonnes. However, we do not feel the constant pressure of about one tonne of air on our shoulders, because there is an equal air pressure inside our bodies. Air pressure varies, a major factor in weather. Generally, pressures are lower in warm, expanding air which tends to rise, as at the doldrums. It is higher in cold, dense air which sinks downwards, as at the high pressure horse latitudes.

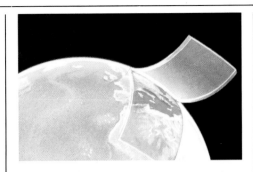

The Earth is surrounded by a thin layer of gases, known as the atmosphere.

This section through the atmosphere shows its five main layers.

EXOSPHERE, which begins at about 500 km above the surface, is extremely rarefied and composed mainly of hydrogen and helium. The exosphere merges into space.

IONOSPHERE, between 80 and 500 km, contains gas molecules that are ionized, or electrically charged, by cosmic or solar rays. Disturbances in the ionosphere cause glowing lights, called aurorae. Temperatures rise steadily with height from about −80°C at 80 km to 2200°C at 400 km.

MESOSPHERE, between 50 and 80 km, is marked by a fall in temperature from 10°C at 50 km to −80°C.

STRATOSPHERE, stretches above the tropopause (the name for the upper boundary of the troposphere) to 50 km height. It has a layer of ozone (oxygen with three rather than two atoms) that filters out most of the Sun's ultraviolet rays. Temperatures rise from −55°C to 10°C at 50 km. The noctilucent clouds are probably composed of meteoric dust.

TROPOSPHERE is the lowest 18km of the atmosphere over the Equator, the lowest 10 to 11 km in the middle latitudes, and the lowest 8 km over the poles. It contains most of the atmosphere's mass. Temperatures fall with height, but stabilize at the tropopause.

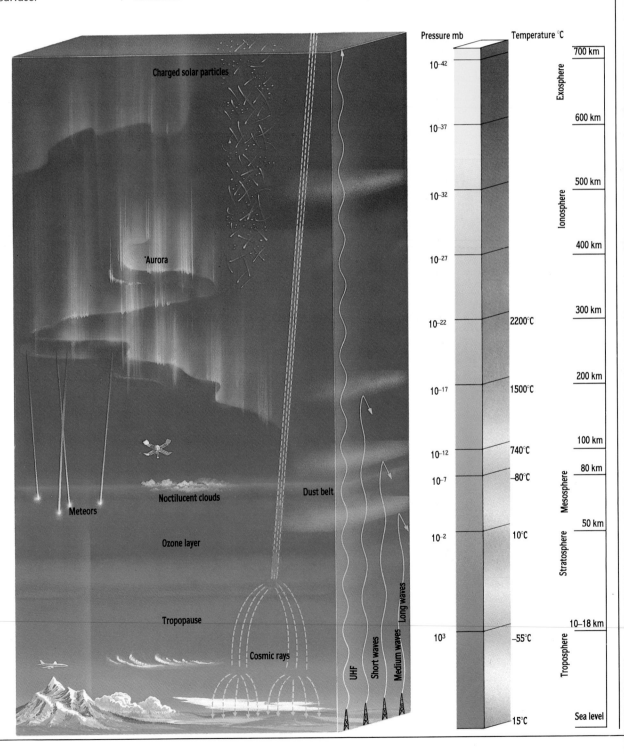

Charged solar particles

Aurora

Meteors

Noctilucent clouds

Dust belt

Ozone layer

Tropopause

Cosmic rays

UHF

Short waves

Medium waves

Long waves

Pressure mb	Temperature °C	
10^{-42}		700 km
		Exosphere
10^{-37}		600 km
		500 km
10^{-32}		Ionosphere
		400 km
10^{-27}		
	2200°C	300 km
10^{-22}		
		200 km
10^{-17}	1500°C	
		100 km
10^{-12}	740°C	
10^{-7}	−80°C	80 km Mesosphere
		50 km
10^{-2}	10°C	Stratosphere
		10–18 km
10^3	−55°C	Troposphere
	15°C	Sea level

The clouds on this photograph reveal a hurricane, a rotating low pressure air system.

FACTFINDER

Composition of the air: Nitrogen (78·09 per cent); oxygen (20·95 per cent); argon (0·93 per cent).
Other gases include carbon dioxide, helium, hydrogen, krypton, methane, neon, ozone, and xenon.

Average surface pressure: 1013 mb.

Atmospheric level reached by radio waves (frequency in kilohertz)

Long waves (below 500 kHz)	: 50 km
Medium waves (500 – 1500 kHz)	: 95 km
Short (1500 – 30,000 kHz by day)	: 200 km
waves (1500 – 30,000 kHz by night)	: 280 km

Very short wavelengths (UHF) penetrate all layers.

Cloud Formation

All air contains water vapour, but warm air holds much more than cold air. When air is cooled it can hold less water vapour. At dew point, it is saturated, containing all the water vapour it can at that temperature. Further cooling causes water vapour to condense around specks of dust or salt in the air to form tiny, visible water droplets or ice crystals, masses of which form clouds.

Circulation of Air

Air is invisible but, powered by energy from the Sun, it is always moving. Generally, winds blow from areas of high air pressure, such as the horse latitudes, towards areas of low pressure, such as the doldrums. Winds are deflected by the Coriolis effect, which is caused by the Earth's rotation. Local factors, such as mountains, also affect winds. Monsoons are seasonal reversals of winds. For example, over northern India in winter, cold, dense air masses develop, from which winds blow outwards. But heating in summer creates low air pressure and moist winds are sucked on to the land.

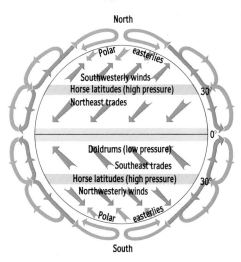

Above: The diagram shows the main movements of air in the atmosphere and across the surface in the prevailing wind systems. Winds generally blow towards low pressure regions, such as the doldrums, and outwards from high pressure systems at the horse latitudes and the poles.

Cloud Types

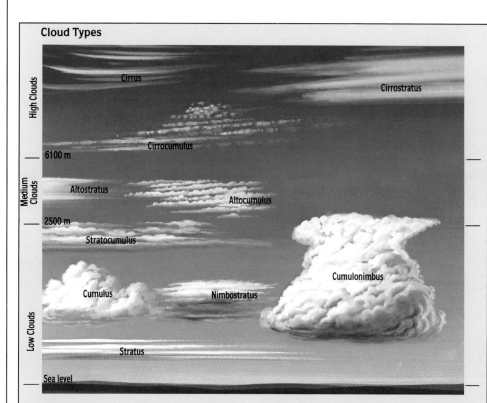

High Clouds
High clouds form above 6100 metres above ground level, as follows:
CIRRUS is a delicate feathery cloud, sometimes called mares' tails or ice banners. It is often the first sign of an approaching depression.
CIRROSTRATUS is a thin layer cloud, with ripples and rounded masses. It veils but does not block out the Sun.
CIRROCUMULUS is a patchy cloud composed of small white balls. Formed from ice crystals, it is often called mackerel sky.

Medium Clouds
Medium clouds occur between about 2500 and 6100 metres, as follows:
ALTOSTRATUS is a greyish or bluish layer cloud that may become so thick that it blocks out the Sun. It is a sign of an advancing depression.
ALTOCUMULUS resembles a mass of tiny clouds. It indicates unsettled weather.

Low Clouds
Low clouds form below 2500 metres above ground level as follows:
STRATOCUMULUS is a greyish-white cloud, consisting of rounded masses.
NIMBOSTRATUS is a dark cloud, associated with rain and snow, which often occurs along the warm fronts of depressions.
CUMULUS is a white, heap cloud, usually with a flat base and a dome-shaped top. In summer, fluffy cumulus is a feature of fine weather. Heavy cumulus can develop into cumulonimbus cloud.
STRATUS is a grey layer cloud that often forms ahead of warm fronts in depressions where warm air is rising fairly slowly over cold air. Such clouds bring drizzle, rain and snow.
CUMULONIMBUS is a dark, heavy cloud. It may rise 4500 metres or more from its ragged base to its often anvil-shaped top. It is associated with thunder, lightning, rain and snow.

Cloud Classification. There are three main types of cloud shapes: feathery cirrus; heap or cumuliform clouds; and layer or stratiform clouds.

THE WATER OF LIFE

In some countries, people take their regular supply of fresh water for granted, while elsewhere, in desert lands, it is a prized commodity. Water reaches us, in one way or another, through the hydrological, or water, cycle, whereby land areas are supplied with precipitation that originates in the saline oceans, where more than 97 per cent of the world's water is found.

Another vital resource, also taken for granted in many places, is the soil, the character of which is largely determined by the climate. The delicate balance between climate, water, and plant life is something that we disturb at our peril.

Soil is the thin layer of loose material derived from and overlying the bedrock. Soils vary in thickness. Mineral grains, the product of weathering, make up more than 90 per cent of most dry soils. Soil also contains humus, including the remains of dead plants and animals. About 40 per cent of moist soils is made up of spaces, occupied by air or water. Soils vary according to the climate, for example, soils in tropical rainy regions are leached by heavy rain. By contrast, some soils in arid regions contain mineral salts deposited by water rising *upwards* towards the surface.

Plant life shows remarkable adaptations to a vast variety of environments. The main vegetation zones are largely determined by climate. But, like climatic regions, vegetation zones have no marked boundaries; they merge imperceptibly with one another.

Vegetation zones usually refer to the original plant cover, or optimum growth, before it was altered by human activity. Human interference with nature can be disastrous. For example, semi-arid grasslands have been ploughed up. Prolonged droughts have reduced the exposed soil to a powdery dust which is removed by the wind, creating dust bowls and encouraging the spread of deserts. The destruction of tropical forests, such as in Brazil, is a matter of concern today. Plants that have never been identified are being destroyed for ever, when they might be sources of new drugs. A massive forest clearance might change world climates.

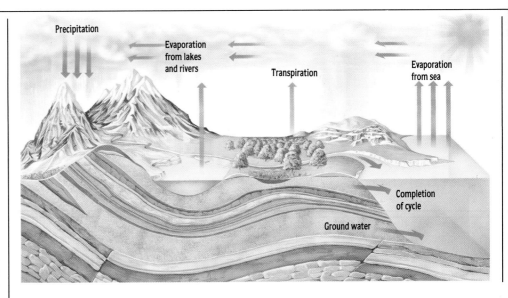

Precipitation
Evaporation from lakes and rivers
Transpiration
Evaporation from sea
Completion of cycle
Ground water

Above: The water cycle provides landmasses with fresh water. The water comes mainly from moisture evaporated from the oceans, to which the water eventually returns.

Right: The map shows the world's chief vegetation zones.

Below: The photographs show major vegetation regions:
1. Tundra is the name for treeless regions near the poles and near the tops of high mountains that are snow-covered for most of the year. But mosses, lichens and some flowering plants flourish in the short summer.
2. Coniferous forests, or taiga, cover a broad belt south of the tundra in the northern hemisphere. The shapes of conifers prevent their being overloaded by snow. The needle-like leaves reduce transpiration, while the thick bark and pitch-like sap reduce evaporation.
3. Broadleaf, or deciduous, forests grow in warm temperate regions. By shedding their leaves, deciduous trees are better able to survive the winter.
4. Scrub and semi-arid grasslands cover large areas of the world. They are highly susceptible to soil erosion if the vegetation cover is removed. Scrub, called maquis, fynbos, chaparral and mallee scrub, are typical of Mediterranean lands where the original forest cover has been destroyed.
5. Tropical grassland includes the llanos of Venezuela. The palm trees in the photograph are growing in a swamp. Tropical grassland is also called campos or savanna.
6. Evergreen tropical rain forest flourishes in regions which are hot and have ample rain throughout the year.

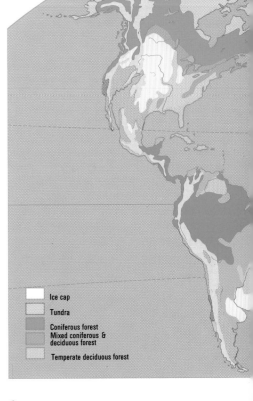

Ice cap
Tundra
Coniferous forest
Mixed coniferous & deciduous forest
Temperate deciduous forest

1

2

3

FACTFINDER

Water distribution: 97·2% is in the oceans (about 1360 million km³); 2·15% is frozen in bodies of ice; 0·625% is ground water; 0·171% is in rivers and lakes; 0·001 is water vapour in the atmosphere.

Average daily water consumption: In the United States: about 200 litres (flushing toilet, washing and bathing, 78%; kitchen use, 6%; drinking, 5%; other, 11%). In many hot countries, the daily per capita water consumption is less than 4 litres.

Common soils: Laterites (leached soils in tropical rainy regions); grey marginal soils (deserts); chestnut-brown soils (arid grasslands); brown forest earths (Mediteranean lands); podsols (cold temperate regions).

Vegetation: Ice covers about 10% of the world's land surfaces and hot deserts 20%. The largest forest is the coniferous forest of the northern USSR, which covers 1100 million hectares – 27% of the world's total forests.

Below: Well-developed soils have three layers, called the A, B and C horizons, overlying the parent rock.

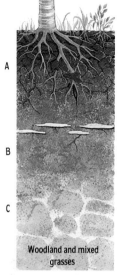

Right: Prairie soils occur in regions that are wet enough in places to support woodland. The A horizon contains much humus, but it is also much leached by seeping water.

A
B
C

Woodland and mixed grasses

A
B
C

Tall bunch grass

Chernozem soils, sometimes called black earths, contain much humus (mainly decomposed grass). They occur in steppelands which have less rainfall than prairies.

A
B

Short grass and xerophytic shrubs

Chestnut-brown soils are typical of particularly arid grasslands. They occur south of the Russian steppes and in the drier parts of Argentina, South Africa and the United States.

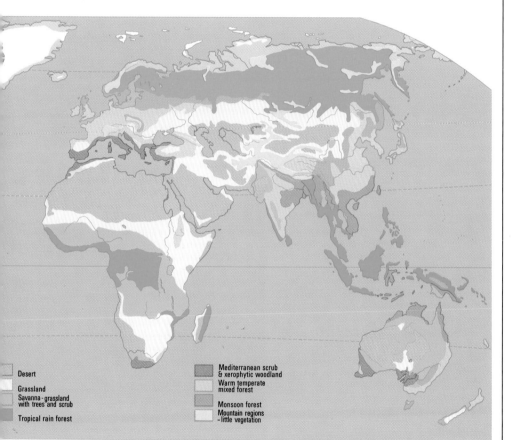

Desert

Grassland

Savanna - grassland with trees and scrub

Tropical rain forest

Mediterranean scrub & xerophytic woodland

Warm temperate mixed forest

Monsoon forest

Mountain regions – little vegetation

4

5

6

THE POPULATION EXPLOSION

One of the world's most serious problems is the population explosion and the difficulties that can be foreseen in feeding the people of the world in the future. On an average estimated rate of population increase of 1·8 per cent a year between 1970 and 1975, the world's population will double in the next 39 years, although recent data suggests that the rate in the 1970s is less than that in the 1960s. The problems arising from the population explosion are most marked in the developing world and least in the industrial nations where people see advantages in population control.

Population explosions occur when average birth rates far exceed death rates. In recent years, death rates have everywhere declined mainly because of improved medical care. In industrial countries, birth rates have also fallen so that a growing proportion of people is in the senior age groups. But while such countries must finance retirement pensions, developing nations have the highest expenditures on health and other children's services, because 40 per cent or more of their population is under 15. This contrast between developing and developed nations is also illustrated by the average life expectancies of 52 years in India and 74 years in the United States.

The distribution of people throughout the world is uneven, because few people live in the vast hot and cold deserts, mountain regions and rain forests. In the world's most densely populated areas, the proportions of urban dwellers is increasing quickly. Urban growth is also a problem in developing nations where unqualified youngsters flock to the cities only to become unemployed occupants of unhealthy shanty towns.

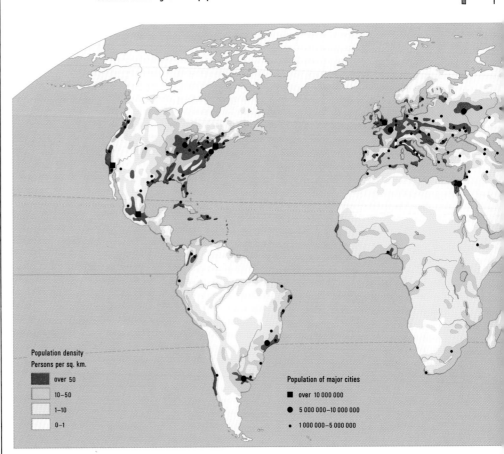

Countries according to size of population

☐ = 10 m people

Population density
Persons per sq. km.
- over 50
- 10–50
- 1–10
- 0–1

Population of major cities
- ■ over 10 000 000
- ● 5 000 000–10 000 000
- • 1 000 000–5 000 000

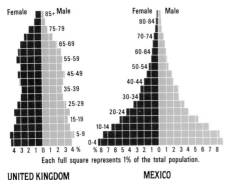

UNITED KINGDOM

MEXICO

Each full square represents 1% of the total population.

Left: The graphs depict the population structures of two nations according to sex and age. Developed nations, such as the United Kingdom (left), have a high proportion of older people, while developing nations such as Mexico (right) have a young population, with as many as 40 per cent of the people being under 15 years of age.

Above: The map shows the uneven distribution of the world's population, a feature that is emphasized by the cartogram, top, which represents the size of nations by their populations rather than by their areas.

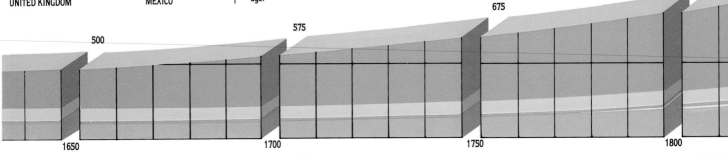

FACTFINDER

Population distribution: The mainly developed continents of North America, Europe and Oceania and the USSR contain 23% of the world's people. The rest live in the mainly developing continents of Africa, Latin America and Asia.

Urbanization: Ranges from 2% in Burundi to 90% in the United Kingdom (1980).

Population density: Gibraltar had 5333 people per sq km in 1979, as compared with 2 per sq km in Australia.

Largest country: USSR (by area); China (by population).

Largest metropolitan area: New York 16,479,000.

The world's population was around 300 million in AD 1000. It passed the 1000 million mark around 1850, but the Industrial Revolution led to an acceleration of population growth. The 2000 million mark was passed in the 1920s and the 4000 million mark in the 1970s. By the year 2000, if the present growth rates of 1·8% per year continue, there will be more than 6000 million people on Earth. (for the purposes of this graph, the Americas have been divided into Anglo-Saxon – and Spanish-speaking America).

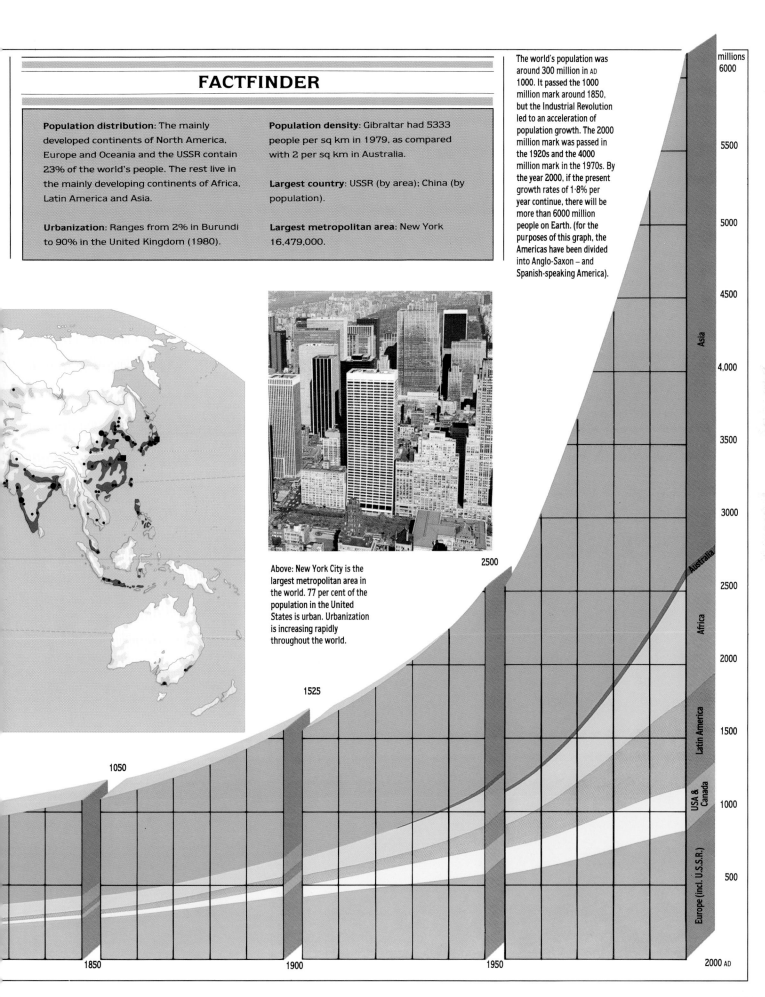

Above: New York City is the largest metropolitan area in the world. 77 per cent of the population in the United States is urban. Urbanization is increasing rapidly throughout the world.

FEEDING THE WORLD

The basic human activity is agriculture. There are two main kinds of agriculture: arable and pastoral. Arable land covers nearly 10 per cent of the world's land area, and meadows and pastures another 20 per cent. In terms of producing food, arable farming is more efficient than pastoral farming. For instance, a given area of cereals will produce six times as many food calories as the milk obtained from dairy cattle grazing on an equal area of grass. Hence, pastoral farming is generally practised on land that is unsuitable for arable farming.

Cereals, the chief food crops, now grow on two-thirds of the world's cultivated land. The main cereals in temperate regions are barley, oats, rye and wheat, and in warmer areas maize, millet, rice (the staple food of more people than any other) and sorghum.

Another important food crop, sugar, is made from sugarcane in tropical regions and from sugar beet in temperate regions. Fruit and vegetables also vary according to the climate. An important group of plants, including groundnuts, oil palms and olives, are grown to make cooking oils, while other crops are grown to make beverages or to produce fibres. Pastoral farming may be extensive, as in the vast cattle or sheep ranches of Argentina, Australia, the United States and the USSR, or intensive as in the factory farming of chickens. Methods of farming vary greatly as do crop yields. For instance, average yields of arable farms in North America are more than three times as high as those of Africa.

Because of the population explosion, agriculture has to provide food for an increasing number of people every year. This involves improving methods of farming and increasing yields. Better farming methods include the use of fertilizers, land conservation and land reclamation. To raise yields, selective breeding of animals and plants will continue. In the last thirty years, many new plant varieties have been developed to raise yields in developing nations.

Another important source of food for the future may come from fish farming in inland and coastal waters. Despite all the modern fishing vessels, fishing is still primitive compared with agriculture. However, yields could probably be increased greatly by breeding young fish in fish farms and then releasing them into nutrient-rich and penned-off parts of the continental shelves.

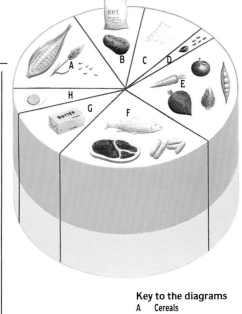

Key to the diagrams
A   Cereals
B   Starchy foods, such as potatoes
C   Sugar
D   Nuts and pulses
E   Vegetables
F   Meat and fish
G   Fats
H   Eggs

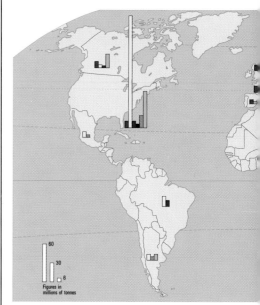

60
30
6
Figures in millions of tonnes

Above: The map shows the chief producers of cereals. North America stands out as the leading source of maize while South and East Asia grow mainly rice.

Below: Cattle ranching is extensive in semi-arid regions. Wheat (2) is the chief food in many temperate areas. Tea (3) is grown in tropical countries.

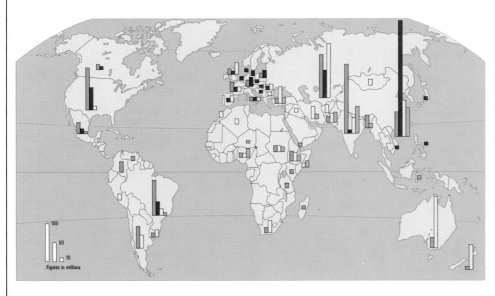

100
50
10
Figures in millions

Major Animal Food Resources
Cattle   Pigs
Sheep   Goats

Above: The map shows the chief producers of live-stock. The leading exporters are in the southern hemisphere, with importers in the northern hemisphere.

1

2

3

The diagrams compare the diets of people in developed nations, left, with those in the developing world, below. They show that people in the developed nations enjoy far more balanced diets with plenty of proteins and vitamins. In developing nations, protein-deficiency diseases, such as kwashiorkor in children, are common.

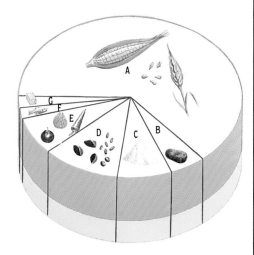

Major net exporters of food and livestock: United States, Australia, Netherlands, Brazil, Denmark.

Major net importers of food and livestock: Japan, West Germany, United Kingdom, Italy, USSR.

Yields of cereals (1981): World 2248 kilogrammes/hectare; North America 3860 kg/ha; Western Europe 3659 kg/ha; Asia 2152 kg/ha; Latin America 1991 kg/ha; Eastern Europe and the USSR 1801 kg/ha; Africa 1045 kg/ha.

Leading cereal producers (1980): **Barley**: USSR (27 per cent of the total); France (7 per cent); Canada (7 per cent); United Kingdom (6 per cent). **Maize**: United States (43 per cent); China (15 per cent); Brazil (5 per cent); Romania (3 per cent). **Rice**: China (36 per cent); India (21 per cent);

Indonesia (7 per cent); Bangladesh (5 per cent). **Rye**: USSR (37 per cent); Poland (24 per cent); West Germany (8 per cent); China (7 per cent). **Wheat**: USSR (22 per cent); United States (14 per cent); China (12 per cent); India (7 per cent).

Livestock producers (1980): **Cattle**: India (15 per cent); USSR (9 per cent); United States (9 per cent); Brazil (8 per cent). **Sheep**: USSR (13 per cent); Australia (12 per cent); China (9 per cent); New Zealand (6 per cent).

Beverage crops (1980): **Cocoa**: Ivory Coast (21 per cent); Brazil (19 per cent); Ghana (16 per cent); Nigeria (11 per cent). **Coffee**: Brazil (22 per cent); Colombia (16 per cent); Ivory Coast (5 per cent); Indonesia (5 per cent). **Tea**: India (31 per cent); China (17 per cent); Sri Lanka (10 per cent); USSR (7 per cent).

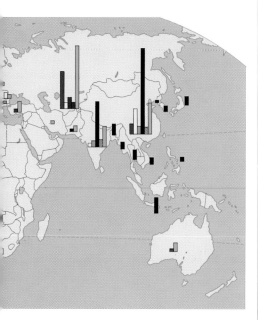

Major Cereal Food Resources

■ Barley	■ Millet	■ Rice	▨ Sorghum	
□ Maize	■ Oats	■ Rye	■ Wheat	

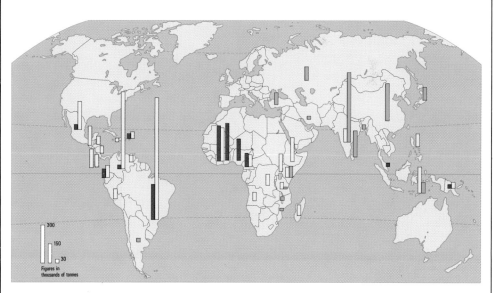

300
150
30
Figures in
thousands of tonnes

Below: New food-producing methods include oyster farming (4), hydroponics (growing plants in water, 5) and making protein-rich meat substitutes from soya beans (6).

Above: The map shows the chief producers of the world's leading beverages which are grown in the tropics or subtropics mainly as cash export crops.

Major Beverage Cash Crops

■ Cocoa	▨ Tea
□ Coffee	

4
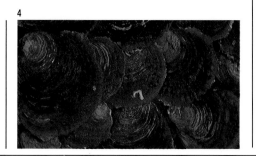

5

6

ALTERNATIVE ENERGY

All forms of energy come directly or indirectly from the Sun. Prehistoric people had only their own labour, but as life styles changed and technology developed, draught animals, the burning of wood, windmills, waterwheels and sails to propel ships were all employed. With the onset of the Industrial Revolution, another abundant source of energy, the fossil fuel coal, was used to power 'the age of steam'. And recently, oil and natural gas have become the main fossil fuels, chiefly because they are fairly cheap to extract, easy to transport, and weight for weight they are more heat-efficient than coal. In consequence, world coal production has remained roughly stable over the last thirty years, although in some industrial nations, such as France, West Germany and the United Kingdom, it has declined. And yet coal may again become important if the existing reserves of oil start to run out, as predicted on current levels of consumption, in the early 21st century.

Despite the recent pre-eminence of oil and natural gas, alternative forms of energy that could replace fossil fuels have been successfully developed, notably hydro-electricity and, in the last thirty years, nuclear power. Hydro-electricity is now the chief form of electrical energy in such countries as Norway, where it supplies 100 per cent of the nation's electrical supply, Brazil (93 per cent), Switzerland (79 per cent) and Canada (70 per cent). But hydro-electricity is clearly unsuited to flat nations, such as the Netherlands.

Nuclear power, using the heat of nuclear fission, can be generated anywhere and, in several Western nations, including the United States and the United Kingdom, it already supplies more than one tenth of the total electrical supply. Uranium, the raw material used in nuclear fission, is generally abundant, and is produced in the West by the United States, South Africa and Canada.

But nuclear power is surrounded by controversy, particularly concerning the disposal of radioactive nuclear wastes. This factor, together with the finite nature of fossil fuel reserves, have led conservationists to explore many other possible forms of energy, employing the latest modern technology. The diagram, right, summarizes the main possibilities that are currently under investigation, including the harnessing of solar radiation, the power of winds and moving water, and the exploitation of the heat that exists not far beneath the Earth's surface.

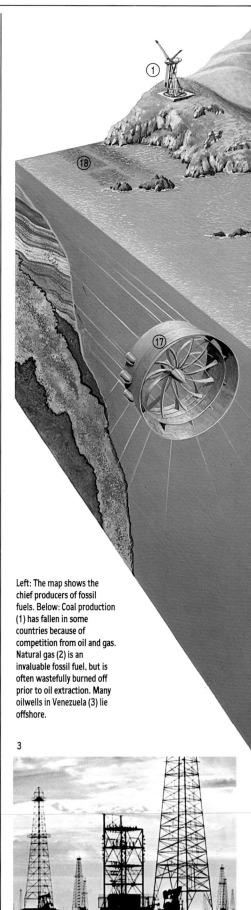

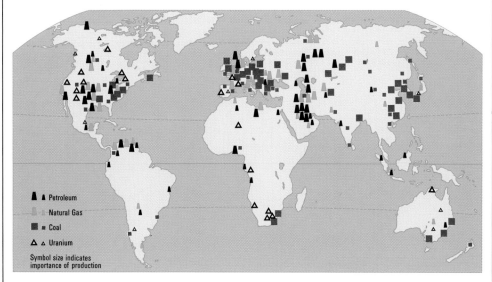

- ▲ ▲ Petroleum
- ▲ ▲ Natural Gas
- ■ ■ Coal
- △ △ Uranium

Symbol size indicates importance of production

Left: The map shows the chief producers of fossil fuels. Below: Coal production (1) has fallen in some countries because of competition from oil and gas. Natural gas (2) is an invaluable fossil fuel, but is often wastefully burned off prior to oil extraction. Many oilwells in Venezuela (3) lie offshore.

1

2

3

Energy consumption (per capita, in equivalents of kg of coal, 1980): Africa 370; Far East 544; Middle East 1123; Oceania 3247; Western Europe 4204; North America 10,394.

Largest oil producers (1981): USSR (21 per cent of world production); Saudi Arabia (17 per cent); United States (17 per cent); Rest of Middle East (9 per cent); Mexico (4 per cent); Venezuela (4 per cent); United Kingdom (3 per cent).

Oil reserves (1978): Saudia Arabia (20 per cent); Kuwait (13 per cent); USSR (10 per cent); Iran (8 per cent); Iraq (6 per cent); United Arab Emirates (6 per cent); Mexico, United States and Malaysia (5 per cent each).

Nuclear power: Belgium (25 per cent of its electrical energy production in 1978); Sweden (22 per cent); Bulgaria (20 per cent); Switzerland (17 per cent); United Kingdom (14 per cent).

Left: Alternative energy sources include improved windmills (1) and pump storage reservoirs (2), into which water is pumped when energy is abundant and then used to drive turbine generators. Hydro-electric stations (3) are important in many countries, while solar power stations, powered by concentrated sunlight, could get microwave energy beamed from a satellite (4) or from banks of angled mirrors or heliostats (5). Decaying waste (6) is a source of heat, as are geysers (7) in volcanic areas. Mud (8) can be used to store heat, while greenhouses (9) are familiar ways of utilizing solar energy. Shallow solar ponds (10) produce heated water to drive generators, and solar houses (11) are self-supporting. Geothermal energy (12) comes from heat inside the Earth. Tidal power stations (13) have much potential, and wave power (14) could be harnessed by moving floats ('bobbing ducks'). Ordinary powered ships might use aluminium sails (15) as an extra form of energy. Floating thermal stations (16) could tap heat under the sea, while huge underwater turbines (17) could be driven by ocean currents. Even kelp (18), a seaweed, could be cultivated as a plant fuel. Solar furnaces (19) can produce temperatures of 4000°C by concentrating the Sun's rays with a paraboloid mirror.

Below: Hydro-electricity is a major alternative to fossil fuels in upland areas with abundant rivers that can be dammed (4). Nuclear power stations (5), a recent development, now supply a substantial proportion of the total electrical energy in several developed nations.

4

5

MINERAL WEALTH

In the Stone Age, people used flint and obsidian tools and, around 10,000 years ago, copper implements were first made. The invention of bronze, an alloy of copper and tin about 5000 years ago, was a major breakthrough. But modern history began with the start of the Iron Age, around 3300 years ago. Since then, metal technology has expanded greatly. For example, since the early 19th century, aluminium, which is obtained from bauxite, has become important, because it is light, strong and corrosion-resistant. And today new alloys are invented to meet all modern needs.

Scientists have identified nearly 3000 minerals, but only about 100 are of economic importance. Iron ore, from which a wide range of ferro-alloys is made, incorporating such metals as chromium, cobalt, manganese, molybdenum, nickel, tungsten and vanadium, remains the leading metallic ore. Various light and base metals, including aluminium, copper, lead, tin and zinc, are also important. The Earth's crust also yields gold, silver and platinum, such precious stones as diamond, emerald, ruby and sapphire, and non-metallic resources, such as phosphate rock which is used as a fertilizer.

Economic minerals – those that can be mined at a profit – are unevenly distributed. Nations with a wide range of minerals and fuels, such as the United States and the USSR have become rich and powerful, while those with few minerals have largely subsistence economies. Some developing countries have rich reserves of one or more minerals, such as copper-rich Zambia and bauxite-rich Guinea in Africa. But many such countries lack the other resources, capital and the skilled manpower to develop industries based on their mineral riches. Instead, they export most of their production to industrial nations. Minerals with strategic value influence political decisions. For example, the United States import manganese. But the chief producers of manganese are the Soviet Union and South Africa. Hence, calls to the United States to boycott South African exports of manganese are likely to be disregarded.

The demand for economic minerals has increased greatly as a result of the population explosion. Today, as the diagram below indicates, the economic reserves of some ores are close to exhaustion. New reserves must be prospected and new methods devised to mine in places where it is now uneconomic to do so. For example, many minerals, such as gold, are dissolved in seawater, but the extraction of these minerals, apart from bromine, magnesium and salt, is currently too expensive. On parts of the seabed are enormous numbers of manganese nodules, potato-like lumps also containing cobalt, copper, iron, nickel and other metals, but again the problem is how to extract them economically. One important source of metals, before we start thinking about mining on the Moon, is the waste products of our society. The recycling of old cars and other junk could be a major factor in overcoming the inevitable shortages in the future.

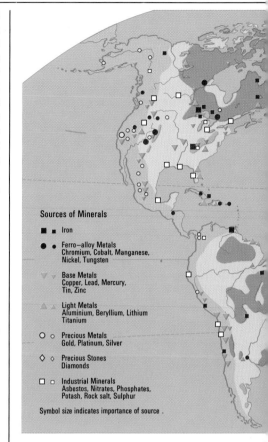

Sources of Minerals

- ■ ▪ Iron
- ● ● Ferro–alloy Metals
  Chromium, Cobalt, Manganese, Nickel, Tungsten
- ▼ ▽ Base Metals
  Copper, Lead, Mercury, Tin, Zinc
- ▲ △ Light Metals
  Aluminium, Beryllium, Lithium Titanium
- ○ ○ Precious Metals
  Gold, Platinum, Silver
- ◇ ◇ Precious Stones
  Diamonds
- □ ▫ Industrial Minerals
  Asbestos, Nitrates, Phosphates, Potash, Rock salt, Sulphur

Symbol size indicates importance of source.

Below: Several methods have been proposed for mining the manganese nodules that litter parts of the seabed. The ship on the left is using the suction pump shown below and the ships in the middle are moving a series of dredge buckets. Remote-controlled collectors, right and bottom, shuttle between a surface platform and the seabed.

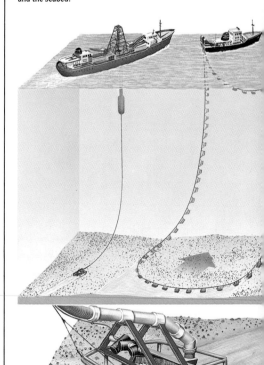

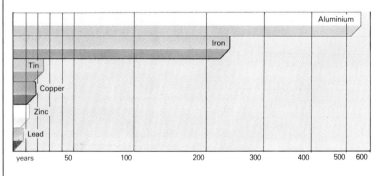

Left: The two leading metals used in construction, aluminium and iron, are abundant and the diagram shows that known reserves of other important metals, including tin, copper, zinc and lead, could run out in twenty to thirty years.

Malachite and azurite are major ores of copper.

Galena is the chief ore from which lead is extracted.

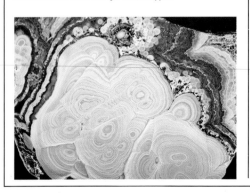

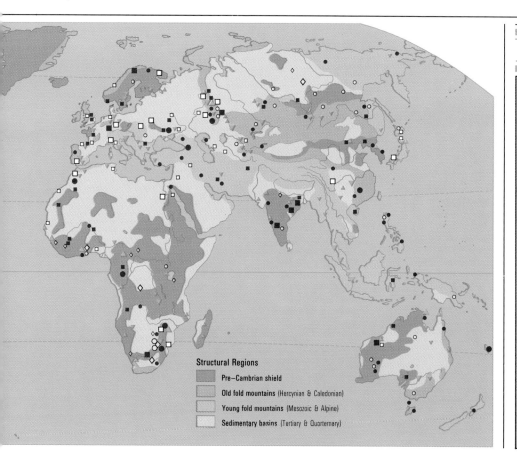

Structural Regions

- ▰ Pre–Cambrian shield
- ▱ Old fold mountains (Hercynian & Caledonian)
- ▱ Young fold mountains (Mesozoic & Alpine)
- ▱ Sedimentary basins (Tertiary & Quaternary)

Major mineral exporters (excluding fuels): United States, Canada, Australia, USSR.

Major mineral importers (excluding fuels): Japan, Italy, United Kingdom, France.

Leading metal producers (1980): **Copper**: United States (15 per cent of the total); USSR (15 per cent); Chile (14 per cent). **Iron Ore**: USSR (28 per cent); Australia (11 per cent). **Tin**: Malaysia (26 per cent); Thailand (14 per cent); Bolivia (14 per cent). **Zinc**: Canada (17 per cent); USSR (16 per cent); Peru (8 per cent).

Deepest mine: Western Deep Levels Mine, South Africa; 3582 metres deep.

Largest excavation: Bingham Canyon Copper Mine. Utah, United States. Area: over 7 km²; depth: over 775 metres.

Above: The map shows the locations of the producers of the most important metal ores, precious stones and other minerals needed by the industrialized world.

Right: The world's largest excavation is the open-cast Bingham Canyon Copper Mine, south of Salt Lake City, in Utah in the western United States.

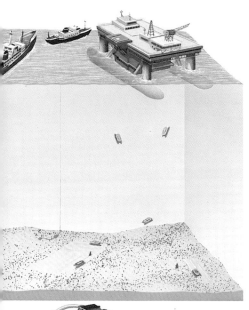

The mineral calcite is used in smelting metallic ores.

Quartz, a common mineral, is used in watchmaking.

ENVIRONMENT IN DANGER

Because of the population explosion and the industrial and technological developments of the last 200 years, great damage has been done to the environment in many areas by the disruption of the balance of nature.

Pollution has become a major problem particularly in modern industrial societies. For example, air pollution in the form of smog has made cities unpleasant and unhealthy. It causes bronchitis and various other respiratory diseases – the London smog of 1952 killed an estimated 4000 people.

Water pollution by sewage and industrial wastes has fouled rivers, lakes and even seas, notably parts of the almost tideless Mediterranean. The flora and fauna have been destroyed and people's health has been directly affected as at Minamata in Japan in the 1950s. Here perhaps as many as 10,000 people suffered death, deformity or acute illness after eating fish poisoned by acetaldehyde waste pumped into the sea by a chemical company.

The land, too, has been polluted in many ways. For example, the pesticide DDT was once regarded as a means of raising food production. But it has also wiped out large populations of birds and, because of its persistence, it has damaged the fragile ecology of soils by weakening the micro-organisms in it.

Steps have been taken in many places to control the dangers of smog, Minamata disease and DDT. But many other, perhaps even more serious, problems lie ahead if the balance of nature is disturbed. For example, if jet airliners and rocket discharges damage the ozone layer in the stratosphere, it could expose the Earth to the Sun's broiling ultraviolet rays. And no one is sure of the consequences of the rising content in the air of carbon dioxide, which increased by seven per cent between 1958 and 1980. One estimate is that it could double by the year 2030. The atmosphere would then increasingly block long-wave radiation from the Earth, like the glass roof of a greenhouse, and temperatures would rise by an average of 3°C. Climatic zones would change and ice sheets would melt, submerging coastal plains and cities.

Radioactive fallout from nuclear weapons' tests (1) pollutes the air, as do kerosene combustion products, soot and unburned fuel expelled by aircraft (2). The build-up of carbon dioxide in the air (3), caused mainly by the burning of fossil fuels and the cutting down of forests may have a greenhouse effect, causing the atmosphere to overheat.

Aerial crop spraying (4) can introduce poisons into the soil that can disturb its ecology for years, while nuclear power stations (5) may discharge radioactive coolants, and thermal power stations (6) and city air conditioning systems may cause thermal and chemical pollution.

Below: Rubbish dumps for cars (1), open-cast mines (2) and oil spillages (3) that foul beaches are all examples of pollution.

1

2

3

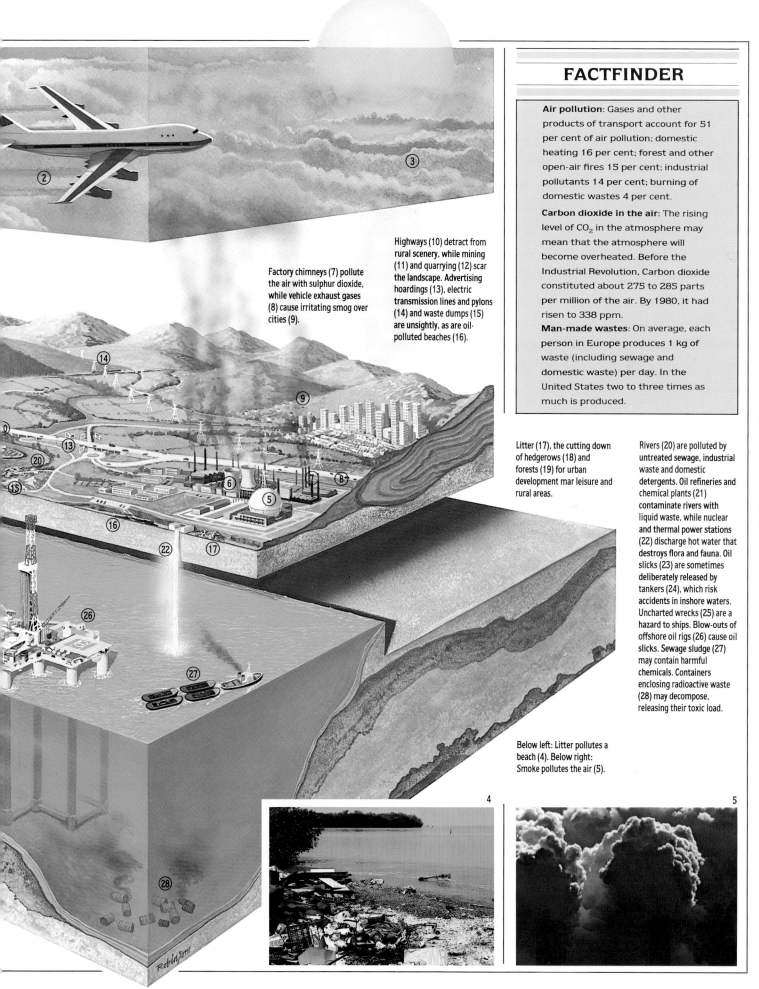

Air pollution: Gases and other products of transport account for 51 per cent of air pollution; domestic heating 16 per cent; forest and other open-air fires 15 per cent; industrial pollutants 14 per cent; burning of domestic wastes 4 per cent.

Carbon dioxide in the air: The rising level of CO_2 in the atmosphere may mean that the atmosphere will become overheated. Before the Industrial Revolution, Carbon dioxide constituted about 275 to 285 parts per million of the air. By 1980, it had risen to 338 ppm.

Man-made wastes: On average, each person in Europe produces 1 kg of waste (including sewage and domestic waste) per day. In the United States two to three times as much is produced.

Highways (10) detract from rural scenery, while mining (11) and quarrying (12) scar the landscape. Advertising hoardings (13), electric transmission lines and pylons (14) and waste dumps (15) are unsightly, as are oil-polluted beaches (16).

Factory chimneys (7) pollute the air with sulphur dioxide, while vehicle exhaust gases (8) cause irritating smog over cities (9).

Litter (17), the cutting down of hedgerows (18) and forests (19) for urban development mar leisure and rural areas.

Rivers (20) are polluted by untreated sewage, industrial waste and domestic detergents. Oil refineries and chemical plants (21) contaminate rivers with liquid waste, while nuclear and thermal power stations (22) discharge hot water that destroys flora and fauna. Oil slicks (23) are sometimes deliberately released by tankers (24), which risk accidents in inshore waters. Uncharted wrecks (25) are a hazard to ships. Blow-outs of offshore oil rigs (26) cause oil slicks. Sewage sludge (27) may contain harmful chemicals. Containers enclosing radioactive waste (28) may decompose, releasing their toxic load.

Below left: Litter pollutes a beach (4). Below right: Smoke pollutes the air (5).

4

5

THE SHRINKING WORLD

Photographs taken from the Moon emphasize that the Earth and its resources are finite. They remind us that, if we squander those resources or make the planet uninhabitable through ecological blunders or nuclear war, we have as yet nowhere else to go.

The Space Age has enabled scientists to achieve major advances in communications, which, with the revolution in transport which began in the late 17th century, has made the world shrink. Only 500 years ago, before Columbus made his epic journey across the Atlantic Ocean, the world seemed boundless, with new continents awaiting discovery. Columbus took five weeks to sail from the Canary Islands to the Bahamas, but today a trans-Atlantic crossing in a supersonic airliner takes 3½ hours.

The increasing speed of all forms of transport has given us much greater mobility. However, problems lie ahead. For example, unless alternative fuels are invented, shortages of petroleum-based fuels in the early 21st century will probably restrict the use of private transport. Instead, public systems, operated by alternative engines, will be the main forms of transport, carrying enormous numbers of passengers at speeds of thousands of kilometres per hour. In cities, computer-controlled passenger cars will pick up people and drop them at their destinations. A world shortage of petroleum will probably render the diesel locomotive obsolete. Instead, trains will be electric and will probably employ the already known principles of air-cushion vehicles. They will be capable of speeds of 800 km/h.

Telecommunications have also undergone a revolution. As late as 1860, the Pony Express was carrying messages between Missouri and California in the United States, but we can now communicate, via wire and microwave radio links or communications satellites, with people on the other side of the world. Powered by sunlight, communications satellites are located in geo-synchronous orbit over the Equator, such that they move at the same speed as the rotation of the Earth. Although they have a limited lifespan, their lofty positions enable them to transmit signals to any place on Earth without interference from the Earth's curvature. More powerful communications satellites will allow simultaneous intercontinental television broadcasts directly to home aerials, without the need for ground stations.

Below: Air transport has come within the range of many people in the rich developed nations in the last thirty years.

Opposite: Modern highways, like this road on a dyke across the IJsselmeer in the Netherlands, have speeded up private travel.

Opposite: The use of prepacked containers makes the loading and unloading of cargo ships much faster and more efficient.

Right: The space age has given us a new perspective on our planet Earth. Teams of astronauts in Skylab (1), an American space station launched into orbit at 435 km above the Earth in 1973, were able to observe our planet's surface. The development of the American shuttle *Columbia* makes the establishment of similar stations economically feasible. Various weather satellites, including *Nimbus* (2), have advanced our knowledge of the atmosphere and provided much data for weather forecasters. Communications satellites (3), in stationary orbit over the Equator at about 35,900 km, can transmit telecommunications and television signals to any part of the world. Landsat earth science satellites (4) orbit the Earth from pole to pole at heights of about 920 km. They obtain detailed survey pictures. They also monitor crop growth and pollution, and obtain information used in mineral prospecting.

Below: Viewphones using satellite communications may become commonplace in the next twenty years, although they may look different from this model.

FACTFINDER

Transport speeds: Before the Industrial Revolution, stage wagons travelled at about 5 km/h, while horse transport and sailing boats reached 16 km/h. The 'age of steam' which began in the 18th century, led to speeds of 100 km/h by steam locomotives and 50 km/h by steamboats. Piston-engined aircraft flew at 500–600 km/h after World War II. Jet airliners now fly at more than 1000 km/h, while supersonic airliners reach 2250 km/h. On land, high-speed trains reach 210 km/h.

Air travel: The British Handley Page (1932) carried 38 passengers at 170 km/h; the British Bristol Britannia (1955) carried 110 passengers at 650 km/h; the Boeing 747 now carries up to 500 passengers at 950 km/h or more.

Shipping: Until 1800, it took a month or more to cross the Atlantic. In 1827 the first crossing by a power vessel took 22 days from Rotterdam to the West Indies. In 1952 the *United States* made the fastest crossing of 3 days, 10 hours and 40 minutes from New York City to Le Havre.

Car ownership: In 1912, there were 600,000 motor vehicles in the United States. By 1940, there were 32 million. In 1979, there were 159·4 million vehicles that covered 2,454,000 million km (or 330 km per week per driver).

Highest traffic density: Hong Kong (1977) had 191,146 vehicles on 1091 km of roads – a density of 5·7 metres per vehicle (as compared with the United Kingdom, 19·4 metres per vehicle in 1979).

Telecommunications: First successful launch of international communications satellite (Comsat or Syncom), 1963.

The problems that face mankind are truly monumental. According to the United Nations Environment Programme (UNEP), a recently established agency, soil erosion and soil degradation were still widespread in the early 1980s, and one third of the world's arable land was at risk of becoming desert because of human misuse. Tropical forests were disappearing at an estimated rate of 50 hectares a minute — a rate that, if it continues, will eliminate all tropical forests in forty years. One plant or animal species was also being lost per day — a rate that was accelerating. And in human terms, UNEP estimated that every day some 40,000 infants and young children were dying from hunger or from pollution-related disease.

Disease and malnutrition are features of everyday life in the developing world and, despite all the aid that goes to developing nations, the economic gap between them and the developed world is enormous and increasing. In 1980, the per capita gross national products of the United Kingdom, United States and Switzerland were, respectively, US $7920, $11,360 and $16,440. By contrast, the per capita GNPs of Chad, Burma and India were $120, $170 and $240. A world split into two sectors — one rich and one poor — is a world fraught with danger. And the population explosion, which is most marked in the poorest countries, could cause global chaos.

The world's problems must be tackled with a real understanding of all the factors involved. People once talked of 'taming' Nature, as if Nature were hostile towards and separate from them. However, in recent years, we have begun to realize that the key to our future lies not in 'taming' but in comprehending Nature, particularly the highly complex ecological relationships that exist between us, the Earth and the millions of animals and plant species that the Earth supports. A view from space has made us realize that damage has been and is still being done. But hopefully it is not too late for us to heal the wounds we have inflicted.

WORLD ATLAS

SYMBOLS

Relief

		Feet	Relief	Metres
〰	Land contour	16404		5000
▲ 8848	Spot height (metres)	9843		3000
⋈	Pass	6562		2000
		3281		1000
▭	Permanent ice cap	1640		500
		656		200
		0		Sea Level
	Land Dep.	656		200
		13123		4000
		22966		7000

Hydrography

〰	Submarine contour
▼11034	Ocean depth (metres)
(217)	Lake level (metres)
⌒⌒⌒	Reef
〜	River
⋯〜	Intermittent river
⌒⌒	Falls
⌒⊤⌒	Dam
⋎	Gorge
⊥⊥⊥	Canal
⬭	Lake/Reservoir
⬭	Intermittent lake
⁕⁕⁕	Marsh/Swamp

Communications

Tunnel ⊶	Main railway
⊕	Main airport
- - - -	Track

Road representation varies with the scale category.

══════	Principal road	} 1:1M-1:2½M
────────	Other main road	
────────	Principal road	} 1:2½M-1:7½M
────────	Other main road	
────────	Principal road	1:7½M or smaller

Administration

──────	International boundary
- - -	Undefined/Disputed international boundary
-·-·-	Internal division : First order
········	Internal division : Second order
◪ ⊙ ◎ / ◉ ⊡ ⊡	National capitals

Settlement

Each settlement is given a town stamp according to its population size and scale category.

	1:1M-1:2½M	1:2½M-1:7½M	1:7½M or smaller
◪	over 1 000 000	over 1 000 000	over 1 000 000
◉	500 000-1 000 000	500 000-1 000 000	500 000-1 000 000
◎	100 000-500 000	100 000-500 000	100 000-500 000
⊙	25 000-100 000	25 000-100 000	under 100 000
○	10 000-25 000	under 25 000	—
•	under 10 000	—	—
▰	Major urban area (1:1M-1:2½M only)		

The size of type used for each settlement is graded to correspond with the appropriate town stamp.

Other features

∴	Ancient monument
∪	Oasis
⬭	National Park
▲	Oil field
△	Gas field
⊶⊶⊶	Oil/Gas pipeline

Lettering

Various styles of lettering are used - each one representing a different type of feature.

ALPS	Physical feature	KENYA	Country name
Red Sea	Hydrographic feature	IOWA	Internal division
Paris	Settlement name	(Fr.)	Territorial administration

THE WORLD : Political

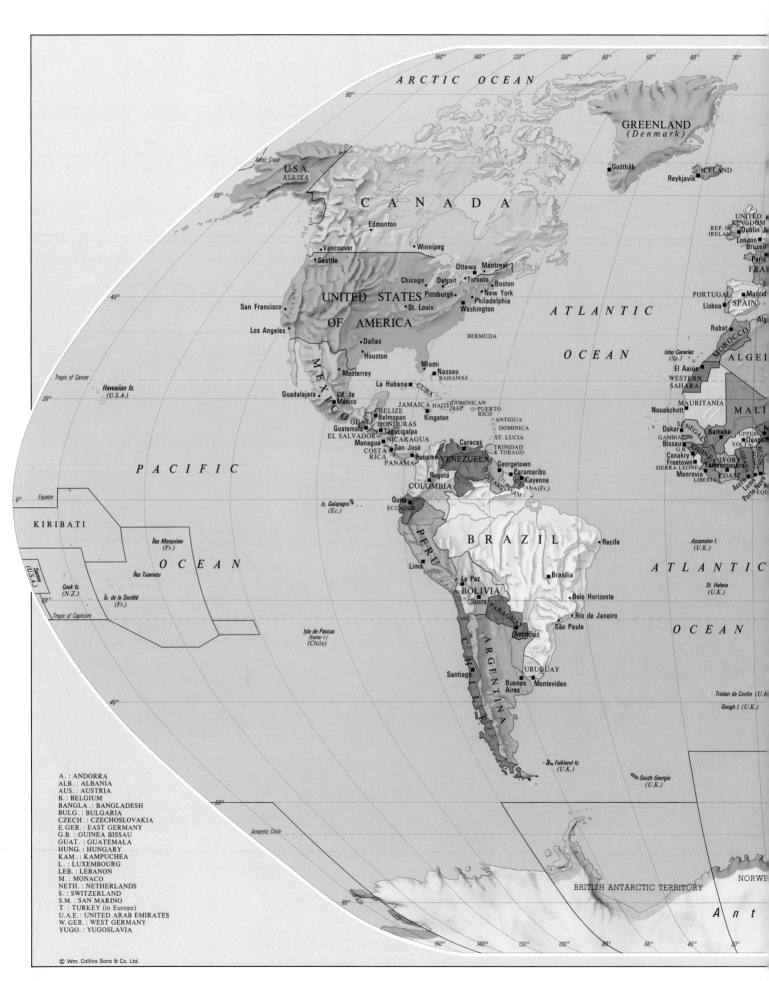

ARCTIC OCEAN

GREENLAND
(Denmark)

Godthåb

ICELAND

Reykjavík

Arctic Circle

U.S.A.
ALASKA

C A N A D A

Edmonton

Vancouver • Winnipeg

Seattle

Ottawa • Montreal

UNITED KINGDOM
REP. OF IRELAND
Dublin
London
Bruxel
Paris
FRA

Chicago • Detroit • Toronto

Pittsburgh • Boston
New York

UNITED STATES
OF AMERICA

St. Louis • Philadelphia
Washington

ATLANTIC

San Francisco

PORTUGAL • Madrid
Lisboa SPAIN
Alg

Los Angeles

OCEAN

Rabat

MOROCCO

Dallas

BERMUDA

Islas Canarias
(Sp.)
El Aaiún
WESTERN
SAHARA

ALGE

Tropic of Cancer

Houston

Hawaiian Is.
(U.S.A.)

Monterrey

Miami
Nassau
BAHAMAS

MAURITANIA

Nouakchott

MALI

Guadalajara

La Habana CUBA
Cd. de
México
JAMAICA HAITI DOMINICAN
REP.
PUERTO
RICO
ANTIGUA
DOMINICA
ST. LUCIA

Dakar SENEGAL
GAMBIA
Bissau G.B.
Conakry GUINEA
SIERRA LEONE Freetown
Monrovia
LIBERIA

Bamako
UPPER
VOLTA Ouaga
GHANA IVORY
Yamoussoukro COAST
Accra
Lomé
Porto-Novo Equ

BELIZE
Belmopan
GUAT. HONDURAS
Guatemala Tegucigalpa
EL SALVADOR NICARAGUA
Managua
COSTA San José
RICA Panamá
PANAMA

Kingston

TRINIDAD
& TOBAGO
Caracas
VENEZUELA
Georgetown
Paramaribo
Bogotá Cayenne
GUIANA (Fr.)
COLOMBIA
SURINAM

PACIFIC

KIRIBATI

Is. Galapagos
(Ec.)
Quito
ECUADOR

Equator

Ascension I.
(U.K.)

ATLANTIC

Îles Marquises
(Fr.)

OCEAN

PERU

B R A Z I L

• Recife

Lima

Îles Tuamotu

Cook Is.
(N.Z.)

Samoa
(U.S.A.)

La Paz

Brasília

BOLIVIA

Belo Horizonte

St. Helena
(U.K.)

Îs. de la Société
(Fr.)

Sucre

PARAGUAY

Rio de Janeiro
São Paulo

OCEAN

Tropic of Capricorn

Isla de Pascua
(Easter I.)
(Chile)

Asunción

Santiago

CHILE

ARGENTINA

URUGUAY

Buenos Montevideo
Aires

Tristan da Cunha (U.K

Gough I. (U.K.)

Falkland Is.
(U.K.)

South Georgia
(U.K.)

Antarctic Circle

BRITISH ANTARCTIC TERRITORY

NORWE

Ant

A. : ANDORRA
ALB. : ALBANIA
AUS. : AUSTRIA
B. : BELGIUM
BANGLA. : BANGLADESH
BULG. : BULGARIA
CZECH. : CZECHOSLOVAKIA
E. GER. : EAST GERMANY
G.B. : GUINEA BISSAU
GUAT. : GUATEMALA
HUNG. : HUNGARY
KAM. : KAMPUCHEA
L. : LUXEMBOURG
LEB. : LEBANON
M. : MONACO
NETH. : NETHERLANDS
S. : SWITZERLAND
S.M. : SAN MARINO
T. : TURKEY (in Europe)
U.A.E. : UNITED ARAB EMIRATES
W. GER. : WEST GERMANY
YUGO. : YUGOSLAVIA

© Wm. Collins Sons & Co. Ltd.

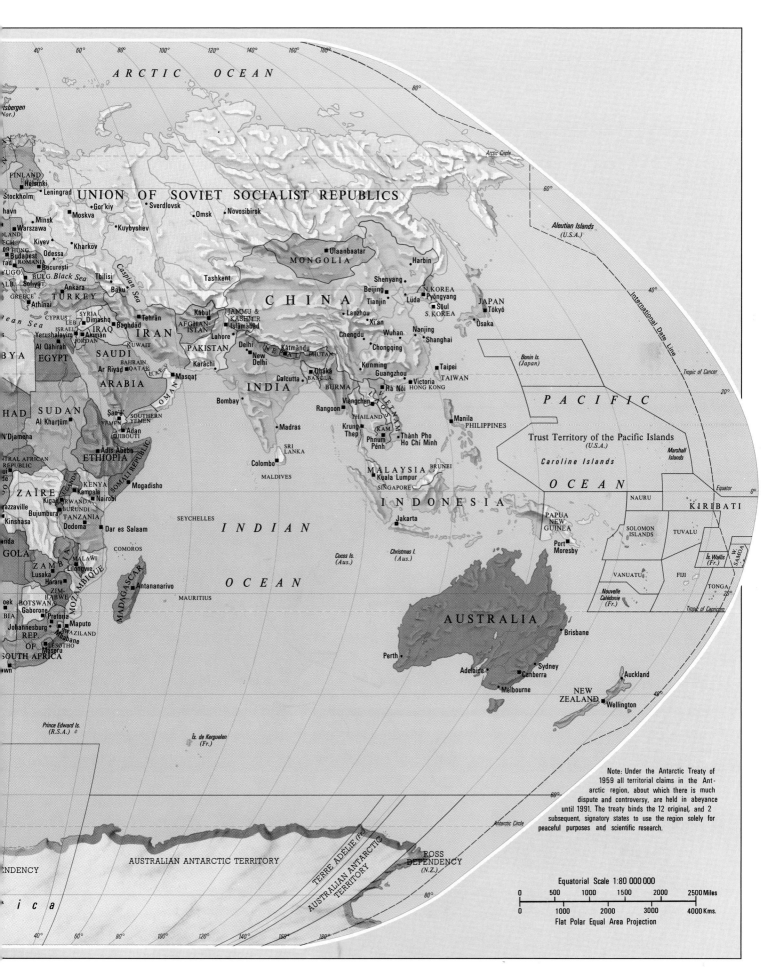

ARCTIC OCEAN

rtsbergen
(Nor.)

FINLAND
Helsinki
Stockholm •Leningrad
havn
•Gor'kiy   •Sverdlovsk   •Omsk   •Novosibirsk
•Minsk   •Moskva
•Kuybyshev
Warszawa
Kiyev   Kharkov
Odessa
Budapest
ROMANIA
Bucureşti
BULG. Black Sea
Sofiya
Ankara   Tbilisi   Baku
GREECE
Athínai   TURKEY
CYPRUS LEB. Dimashq   •Kābul
an Sea   SYRIA   Baghdād   AFGHAN-
ISRAEL   IRAQ   ISTAN
Yerushalayim   Ammān   IRAN
JORDAN
BYA   KUWAIT
EGYPT   SAUDI   BAHRAIN
Ar Riyāḍ QATAR
ARABIA   U.A.E.   Masqaṭ
OMAN

UNION OF SOVIET SOCIALIST REPUBLICS

•Ulaanbaatar
MONGOLIA

Tashkent

CHINA

•Harbin

Shenyang
Beijing   Lüda   N.KOREA
Tianjin   Pyŏngyang
Lanzhou   •Xi'an   S.KOREA   Sŏul
Chengdu   Wuhan   Nanjing
Chongqing   Shanghai
Kunming   Guangzhou
Victoria
HONG KONG
Hà Nôi

JAPAN
Tōkyō
Ōsaka

Arctic Circle

Aleutian Islands
(U.S.A.)

International Date Line

Bonin Is.
(Japan)

Tropic of Cancer

PACIFIC

Kābul   JAMMU &
KASHMIR   Islāmābād
Lahore
Delhi
PAKISTAN   New
Delhi
Karāchi
NEPAL   Kātmāndu
BHUTAN
Dhākā
BANGLA.
Calcutta
Bombay   INDIA   BURMA
Madras
Rangoon
VIETNAM
THAILAND
Krung   (KAM.)
Thep   Phnum
Pénh
Colombo   SRI LANKA
MALDIVES

Taipei
TAIWAN

Thành Pho
Ho Chí Minh

Manila
PHILIPPINES

Trust Territory of the Pacific Islands
(U.S.A.)
Caroline Islands

Marshall
Islands

OCEAN

HAD   SUDAN
Al Khartūm   SOUTHERN
YEMEN
Şan'ā
•Adan
DJIBOUTI
N'Djamena
NTRAL AFRICAN
REPUBLIC   ÁDIS ÁBEBA
nda   ETHIOPIA
ZAÏRE   UGANDA   KENYA
Kigali   RWANDA   Nairobi
Bujumbura   BURUNDI
Kinshasa   TANZANIA
Dodoma
anda   Dar es Salaam
GOLA   COMOROS
ZAMBIA   MALAWI
Lusaka   Lilongwe
Harare
ZIM-
BABWE
MOZAMBIQUE
oek   BOTSWANA   Antananarivo
BIA   Gaborone
Johannesburg   Pretoria
REP.   SWAZILAND
OF   Mbabane
SOUTH AFRICA   LESOTHO
wn   Maseru

MALAYSIA
Kuala Lumpur
SINGAPORE

BRUNEI

INDONESIA

Jakarta

SEYCHELLES

INDIAN

OCEAN

Cocos Is.
(Aus.)

Christmas I.
(Aus.)

MAURITIUS

MADAGASCAR

NAURU

KIRIBATI

PAPUA
NEW
GUINEA
Port
Moresby

SOLOMON
ISLANDS

TUVALU

VANUATU

Nouvelle
Calédonie
(Fr.)

Îs. Wallis
(Fr.)

FIJI

W.
SAMOA

TONGA

Equator   0°

20°

AUSTRALIA

Brisbane

Perth
Adelaide
Melbourne

Sydney
Canberra

Auckland

NEW
ZEALAND
Wellington

Tropic of Capricorn

40°

Prince Edward Is.
(R.S.A.)

Îs. de Kerguelen
(Fr.)

Note: Under the Antarctic Treaty of
1959 all territorial claims in the Antarctic region, about which there is much
dispute and controversy, are held in abeyance
until 1991. The treaty binds the 12 original, and 2
subsequent, signatory states to use the region solely for
peaceful purposes and scientific research.

60°

Antarctic Circle

ENDENCY

AUSTRALIAN ANTARCTIC TERRITORY

TERRE ADÉLIE (Fr.)

ROSS
DEPENDENCY
(N.Z.)

AUSTRALIAN ANTARCTIC
TERRITORY

ica

80°

Equatorial Scale 1:80 000 000

0   500   1000   1500   2000   2500 Miles
0   1000   2000   3000   4000 Kms.
Flat Polar Equal Area Projection

40°   60°   80°   100°   120°   140°   160°   180°

3

THE WORLD : Physical

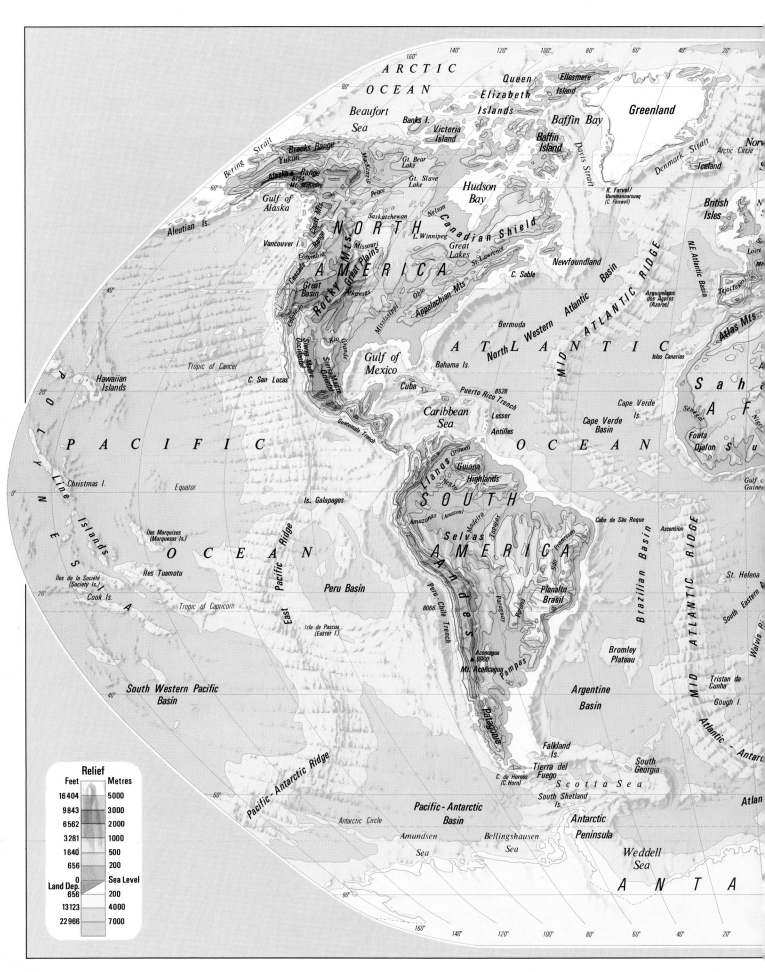

ARCTIC OCEAN

Queen Elizabeth Islands

Ellesmere Island

Greenland

Beaufort Sea

Banks I.

Victoria Island

Baffin Bay

Baffin Island

Denmark Strait

Iceland

Arctic Circle

Nor

Brooks Range

Yukon

Alaska Range
6194
Mt. McKinley

Gulf of Alaska

Aleutian Is.

Bering Strait

MacKenzie

Gt. Bear Lake

Gt. Slave Lake

Peace

Hudson Bay

Davis Strait

K. Farvel/ Uummannarsuaq (C. Farewell)

British Isles

N

Vancouver I.

Columbia

Cascade Range

Coast Mts.

Great Basin

Rocky Mts.

NORTH AMERICA

Saskatchewan

Nelson

L. Winnipeg

Missouri

Great Plains

Canadian Shield

Great Lakes

St. Lawrence

C. Sable

Newfoundland

Western Atlantic Basin

MID ATLANTIC RIDGE

N.E. Atlantic Basin

Loire

Te

Colorado

Arkansas

Ohio

Mississippi

Appalachian Mts.

Bermuda

North Atlantic

Arquipelagos dos Açores (Azores)

Atlas Mts.

Tropic of Cancer

Sierra Madre Occidental

Rio Grande

C. San Lucas

Gulf of Mexico

Bahama Is.

Cuba

A T L A N T I C   O C E A N

Islas Canarias

Sah

A F

Hawaiian Islands

Sierra Madre Oriental

Guatemala Trench

Puerto Rico Trench   8528

Caribbean Sea

Lesser Antilles

Cape Verde Is.

Cape Verde Basin

Senegal

Fouta Djalon

S

u

P A C I F I C

Christmas I.

Equator

Is. Galapagos

Llanos

Orinoco

Neg ro

Guiana Highlands

SOUTH AMERICA

Amazonas (Amazon)

Madeira

Tapajos

Cabo de São Roque

Ascension

Gulf of Guinea

L I N E   I S L A N D S

Îles Marquises (Marquesas Is.)

Pacific Ridge

Selvas

A N D E S

São Francisco

Pará

Brazilian Basin

MID   ATLANTIC   RIDGE

St. Helena

Îles de la Société (Society Is.)

Îles Tuamotu

O C E A N

Peru Basin

Peru Chile Trench

Paraguay

Planalto Brasil

South Eastern

Cook Is.

Tropic of Capricorn

Isla de Pascua (Easter I.)

East Pacific

8066

Bromley Plateau

Walvis R

Aconcagua 6960
Mt. Aconcagua

Pampas

Argentine Basin

Tristan da Cunha

Gough I.

South Western Pacific Basin

Patagonia

Falkland Is.

Atlantic - Antar

Pacific - Antarctic Ridge

C. de Hornos (C. Horn)

Tierra del Fuego

South Georgia

Scotia Sea

South Shetland Is.

Atlan

Pacific - Antarctic Basin

Antarctic Circle

Antarctic Peninsula

Amundsen Sea

Bellingshausen Sea

Weddell Sea

A N T A

Relief

Feet		Metres
16404		5000
9843		3000
6562		2000
3281		1000
1640		500
656		200
0		Sea Level
Land Dep.		
656		200
13123		4000
22966		7000

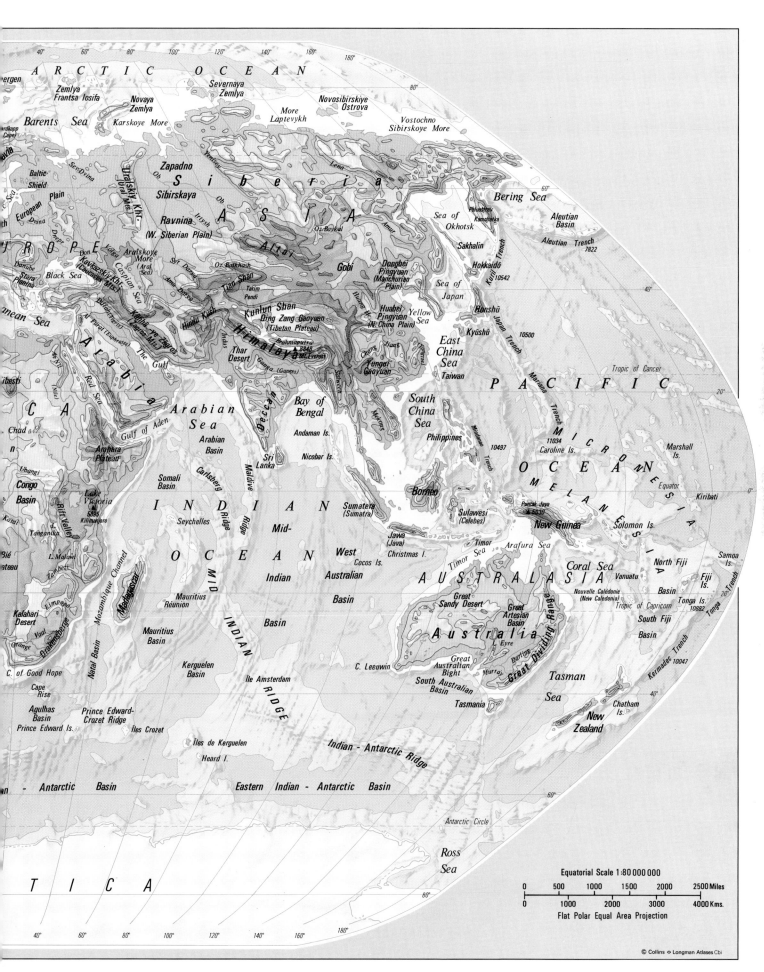

ARCTIC OCEAN

Spergen
Nordkapp
(North Cape)

Zemlya
Frantsa Iosifa
Novaya
Zemlya
Severnaya
Zemlya
More
Laptevykh
Novosibirskiye
Ostrova
Vostochno
Sibirskoye More

Barents Sea
Karskoye More

80°

Baltic
Shield
Sev. Dvina
Ob
Yenisey
Zapadno
Sibirskaya
Lena
 Amur
Bering Sea
Kamchatka
Poluostrov
Aleutian
Basin

EUROPE

Ural'skiy Khr.
(Ural Mts.)

S I B E R I A
Ravnina
(W. Siberian Plain)

A S I A
60°
Aleutian Trench
7822

European
Plain
Dnepr
Drina
Volga
Irtysh
Ob
Oz Baykal
Altai

Sea of
Okhotsk
Sakhalin
Hokkaidō

C. Sea

Don
Stara
Planina
Black Sea
Kavkazskiy Khr.
(Caucasus Mts.)
Caspian Sea
Aral'skoye
More
(Aral
Sea)
Syr Dar'ya
Oz Balkhash
Amu Dar'ya
Tarim
Pendi
Gobi
Dongbei
Pingyuan
(Manchurian
Plain)
Amur
Sea of
Japan
Honshū
Kuril Trench
10542
40°

Danube
Kizil-Ye Zagros
(Zagros Mts.)
Hindu Kush
Tian Shan
Kunlun Shan
Huabei
Pingyuan
(N. China Plain)
Yellow
Sea
Kyūshū
Japan Trench
10500

A r a b i a
Al Furat (Euphrates)
The Gulf
Indus
Qing Zang Gaoyuan
(Tibetan Plateau)
Huang He
Chang Jiang
East
China
Sea
Mariana Trench

Tigris
Ganga (Ganges)
Thar
Desert
Brahmaputra
8848 Mt Everest
Himalaya
Chang
Jiang
Yunguı
Gaoyuan
Taiwan
P A C I F I C
Tropic of Cancer
20°

nean Sea

AFRICA
Tibesti
Nile
Red Sea
Gulf of Aden
Arabian
Sea
Arabian
Basin
Ganges
Bay of
Bengal
Andaman Is.
South
China
Sea
Philippines
Mindanao Trench
10497
11034
Caroline Is.
M I C R O N E S I A
Marshall
Is.

Chad
Amhara
Plateau
Somali
Basin
Carlsberg
Maldive
Sri
Lanka
Nicobar Is.
O C E A N
Equator
0°

Congo
Basin
Ubangi
Kasai
Rift Valley
Lake
Victoria
5895
Kilimanjaro
Seychelles
Ridge
Ridge
Mid-
Sumatera
(Sumatra)
Borneo
Sulawesi
(Celebes)
Puncak Jaya
5030
New Guinea
M E L A N E S I A
Solomon Is.
Kiribati

Bié
Plateau
Tanganika
L. Malawi
Zambezi
I N D I A N
Indian
West
Australian
Cocos Is.
Jawa
(Java)
Christmas I.
Timor
Sea
Timor
Arafura Sea
A U S T R A L A S I A
Coral Sea
Vanuatu
Nouvelle Calédonie
(New Caledonia)
North Fiji
Basin
Samoa
Is.
Fiji
Is.

Kalahari
Desert
Limpopo
Orange
Vaal
Mozambique Channel
Madagascar
O C E A N
Mauritius
Réunion
Basin
Basin
Great
Sandy Desert
Great
Artesian
Basin
A u s t r a l i a
L. Eyre
Great Dividing Range
Tropic of Capricorn
20°
South Fiji
Basin
Tonga Is.
10882
Tonga Trench

Drakensberge
C. of Good Hope
Cape
Rise
Natal Basin
Mauritius
Basin
Kerguelen
Basin
Île Amsterdam
C. Leeuwin
Great
Australian
Bight
South Australian
Basin
Darling
Murray
Tasman
Sea
Kermadec Trench
10047

Agulhas
Basin
Prince Edward-
Crozet Ridge
Prince Edward Is.
Îles Crozet
I N D I A N
Îles de Kerguelen
Heard I.
South Australian
Basin
Tasmania
40°
Chatham
Is.
New
Zealand

R I D G E
Indian - Antarctic Ridge

- Antarctic Basin
Eastern Indian - Antarctic Basin
60°

Antarctic Circle

Ross
Sea

T I C A
80°

40°   60°   80°   100°   120°   140°   160°   180°

Equatorial Scale 1:80 000 000

0   500   1000   1500   2000   2500 Miles
0   1000   2000   3000   4000 Kms.

Flat Polar Equal Area Projection

© Collins ◇ Longman Atlases Cbi

5

North America

ARCTIC OCEAN

Spitsbergen
(Nor.)

Barents
Sea

Novaya
Zemlya
(U.S.S.R.)

Denmark Strait   70°

Arctic Circle

ICELAND

Reykjavik

60°

NORWAY

SWEDEN

FINLAND

Bergen   Oslo

Helsinki

Leningrad

U.S.S.R.

Gor'kiy

North
Sea

Göteborg

Stockholm

Moskva

ATLANTIC

OCEAN

50°

REP.
OF
IRE.

Dublin

UNITED
KINGDOM

Birmingham

London

Århus
DENMARK

Kobenhavn

Minsk

(in Europe)

Kubyshev

Hamburg

NETH.

Berlin
EAST
GERMANY

POLAND
Warszawa

Łódź

Kiyev

Kharkov

Amsterdam
B.
Bruxelles
LUX.

Leipzig

Bonn

Praha

Brno
CZECH.

40°

Bay
of
Biscay

Paris

WEST
GERMANY

Wien

AUSTRIA

Budapest

HUNGARY

Odessa

FRANCE

Bern
SW.

Zürich

L.

Zagreb

ROMANIA

Beograd

Bucureşti

Caspian Sea

Lyon

M.

Milano

S.M.

YUGOSLAVIA

Sofiya

BULGARIA

Black Sea

Oporto

AN.

ITALY

Tirane

Istanbul

Lisboa

PORTUGAL

Madrid

SPAIN

Corse
(Fr.)

Roma

ALB.

T.

Barcelona

Thessaloniki

Is.
Baleares
(Sp.)

Sardegna
(It.)

GREECE

30°

Madeira
(Port.)

Islas Canarias
(Sp.)

Sicilia

Athínai

MALTA

Kríti

Mediterranean Sea

Tropic of Cancer

20°

Africa

10°

20° Equator

10°

0°

ATLANTIC

OCEAN

10°

South America

OCEAN

20°

40°

30°

Tropic of Capricorn

30°

50°

ALB. : ALBANIA
AN. : ANDORRA
B. : BELGIUM
CZECH. : CZECHOSLOVAKIA
L. : LIECHTENSTEIN
LUX. : LUXEMBOURG
M. : MONACO
NETH. : NETHERLANDS
REP. OF IRE. : REPUBLIC OF IRELAND
S.M. : SAN MARINO
SW. : SWITZERLAND
T. : TURKEY (in Europe)

© Wm. Collins Sons & Co. Ltd.

EUROPE

BRITISH ISLES

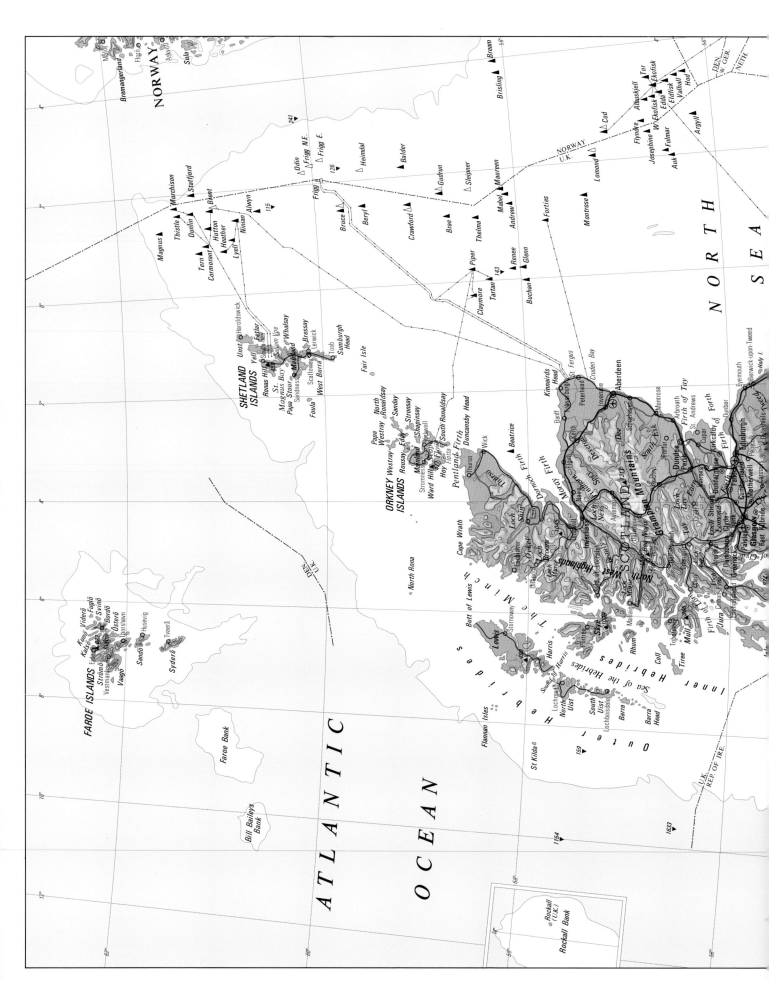

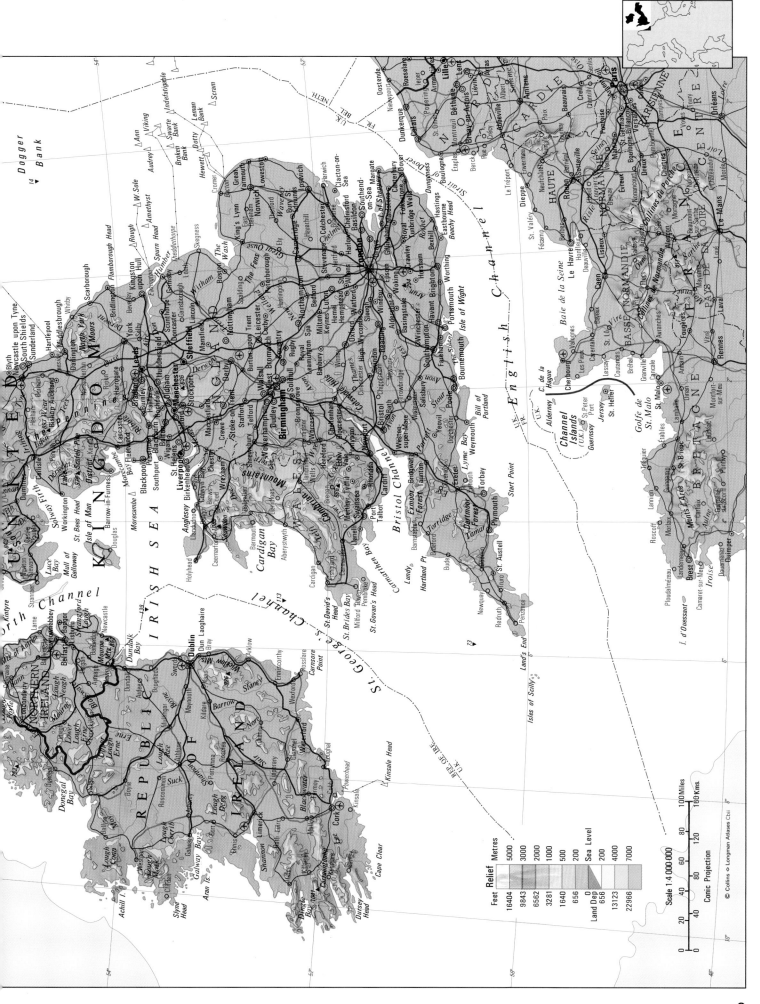

ENGLAND AND WALES

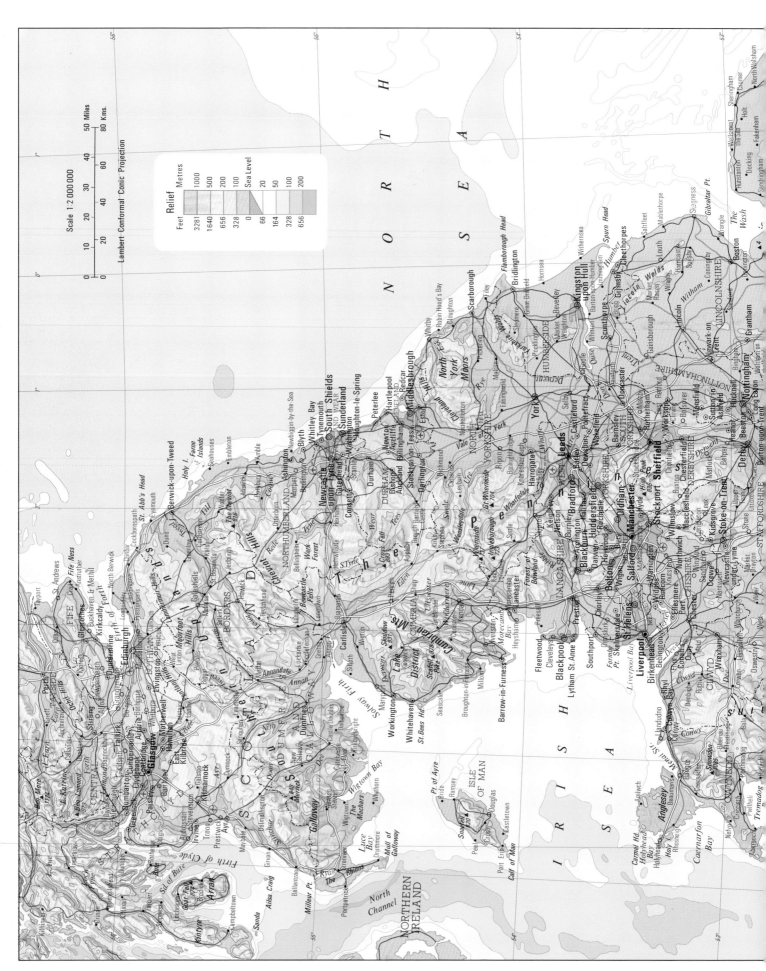

Scale 1:2 000 000

Lambert Conformal Conic Projection

50 Miles
80 Kms.

Relief			Sea Level		
Metres					
1000	500	200	100	20	50	100	200
Feet					
3281	1640	656	328	0	66	164	328	656

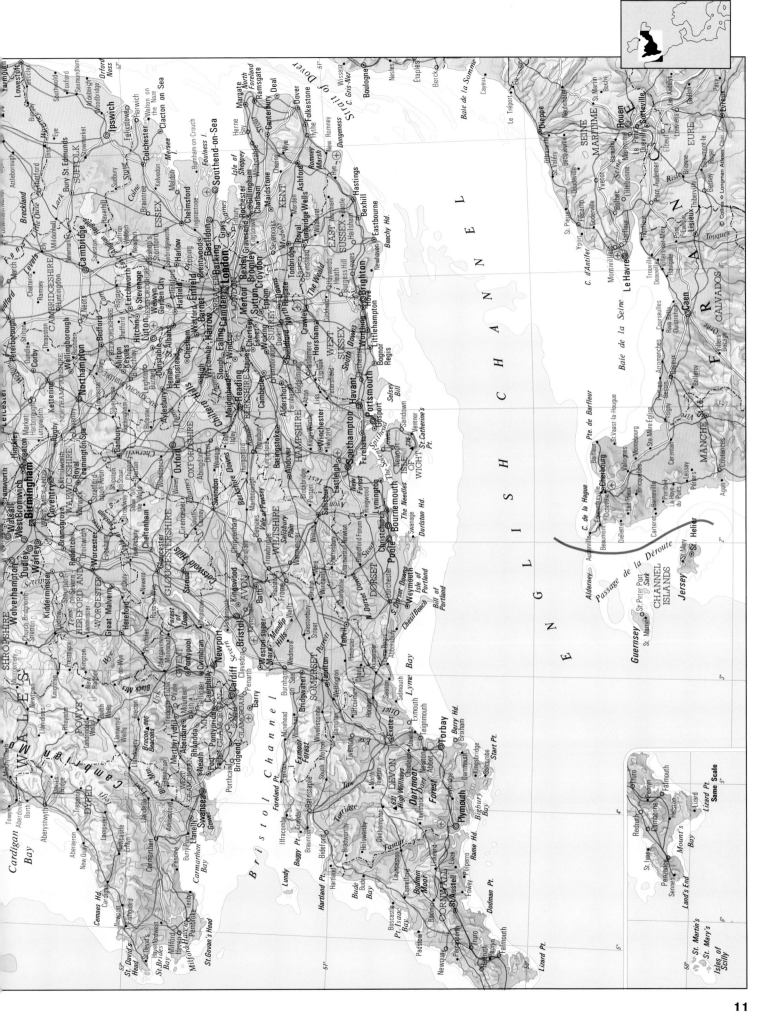

SCOTLAND

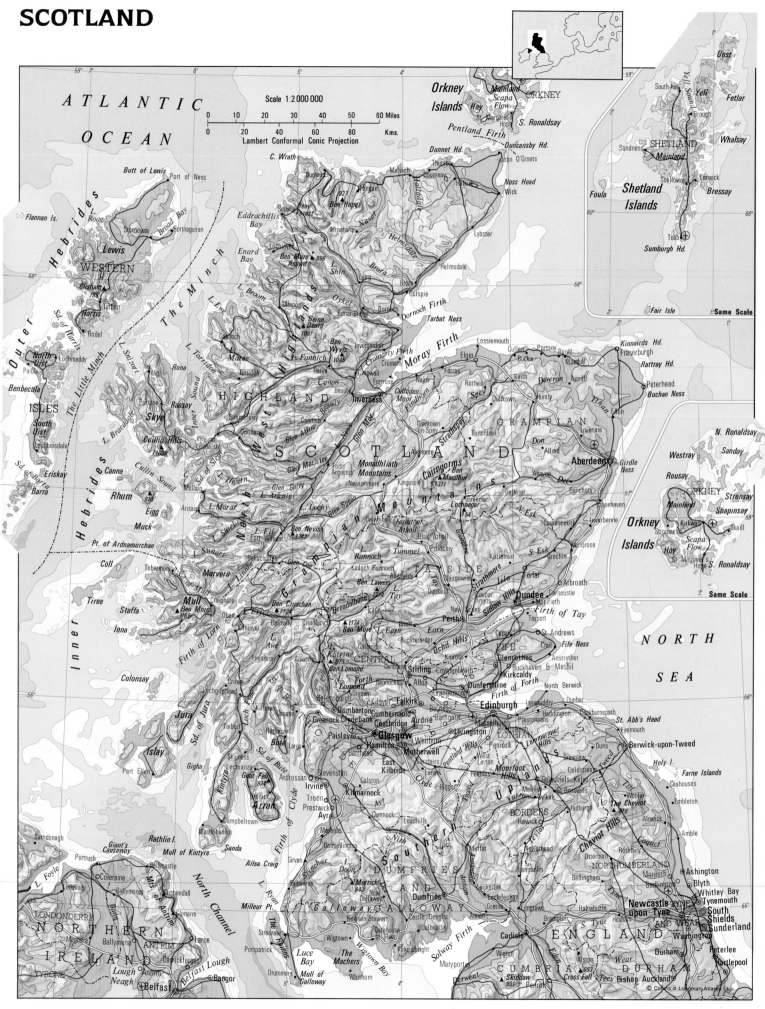

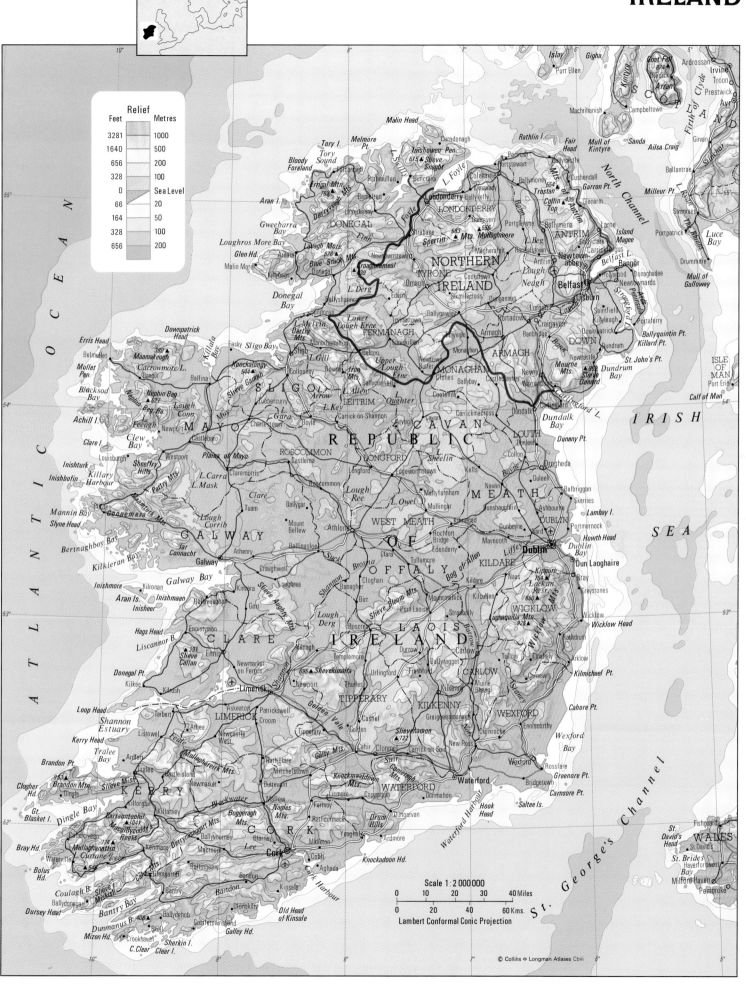

IRELAND

THE LOW COUNTRIES

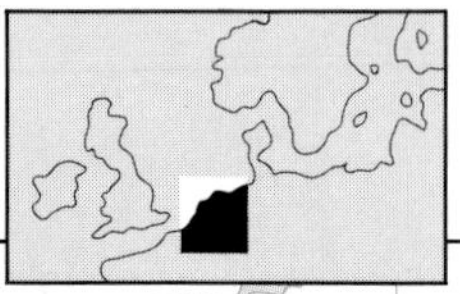

Scale 1:2 000 000

Conic Projection

Relief

Feet	Metres
16 404	5000
9843	3000
6562	2000
3281	1000
1640	500
656	200
0	Sea Level
Land Dep. 656	200
13 123	4000
22 966	7000

NORTH SEA

NETHERLANDS

BELGIUM

GERMANY

LUXEMBOURG

FRANCE

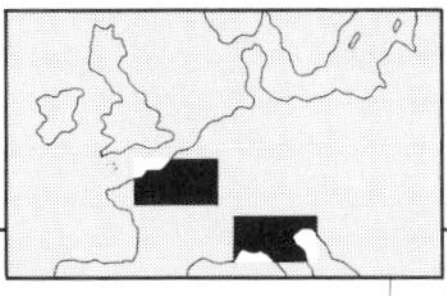

Scale 1:2 500 000

0 10 20 30 40 Miles
0 20 40 60 Kms

Conic Equidistant Projection

Baie de la Seine

BASSE-NORMANDIE
HAUTE-NORMANDIE
NORMANDIE
CALVADOS
MANCHE
ORNE
EURE
SEINE-MARITIME
OISE
PICARDIE
AISNE
ARDENNES
CHAMPAGNE-ARDENNE
MARNE
AUBE
VAL D'OISE
PARISIENNE
Paris
YVELINES
ESSONNE
SEINE-ET-MARNE
EURE-ET-LOIRE
MAYENNE
SARTHE
ILLE-ET-VILAINE
PAYS DE LA LOIRE
MAINE-ET-LOIRE
LOIRE-ATLANTIQUE
LOIR-ET-CHER
LOIRET
INDRE-ET-LOIRE
YONNE
COTE-D'OR
BEAUCE

Rennes · Laval · Le Mans · Angers · Tours · Orléans · Chartres · Caen · Rouen · Le Havre · Cherbourg · Beauvais · Amiens · St. Quentin · Laon · Reims · Épernay · Troyes · Sens · Auxerre · Nantes · Saumur · Blois · Vendôme

© Wm. Collins Sons & Co. Ltd.

Scale 1:2 500 000

0 10 20 30 40 Miles
0 20 40 60 Kms

Conic Equidistant Projection

PIEMONTE
LOMBARDIA
VALLE D'AOSTA
SAVOIE
EMILIA-ROMAGNA
FRIULI-VENEZIA GIULIA
VENETO
ADIGE
DOLOMITI
Alpi Lepontine
Alpi Pennines
Alpes Pennines
Monte Rosa
Matterhorn
Mont Blanc
Gran Paradiso
ALPES MARITIMES
Appennino Ligure
Appennino Tosco-Emiliano
Riviera di Levante
Riviera di Ponente
Golfo di Genova (G. of Genoa)

Torino (Turin) · Milano (Milan) · Genova (Genoa) · Aosta · Novara · Vercelli · Pavia · Bergamo · Brescia · Verona · Vicenza · Padova (Padua) · Venezia (Venice) · Treviso · Udine · Pordenone · Belluno · Bolzano (Bozen) · Trento · Rovereto · Mantova · Cremona · Piacenza · Parma · Reggio · Modena · Bologna · Ferrara · Ravenna · Forlì · Cesena · Rimini · Pesaro · SAN MARINO · Alessandria · Asti · Cuneo · Savona · La Spezia · Massa · Carrara

Gulf of Venice

ADRIATIC SEA

© Wm. Collins Sons & Co. Ltd.

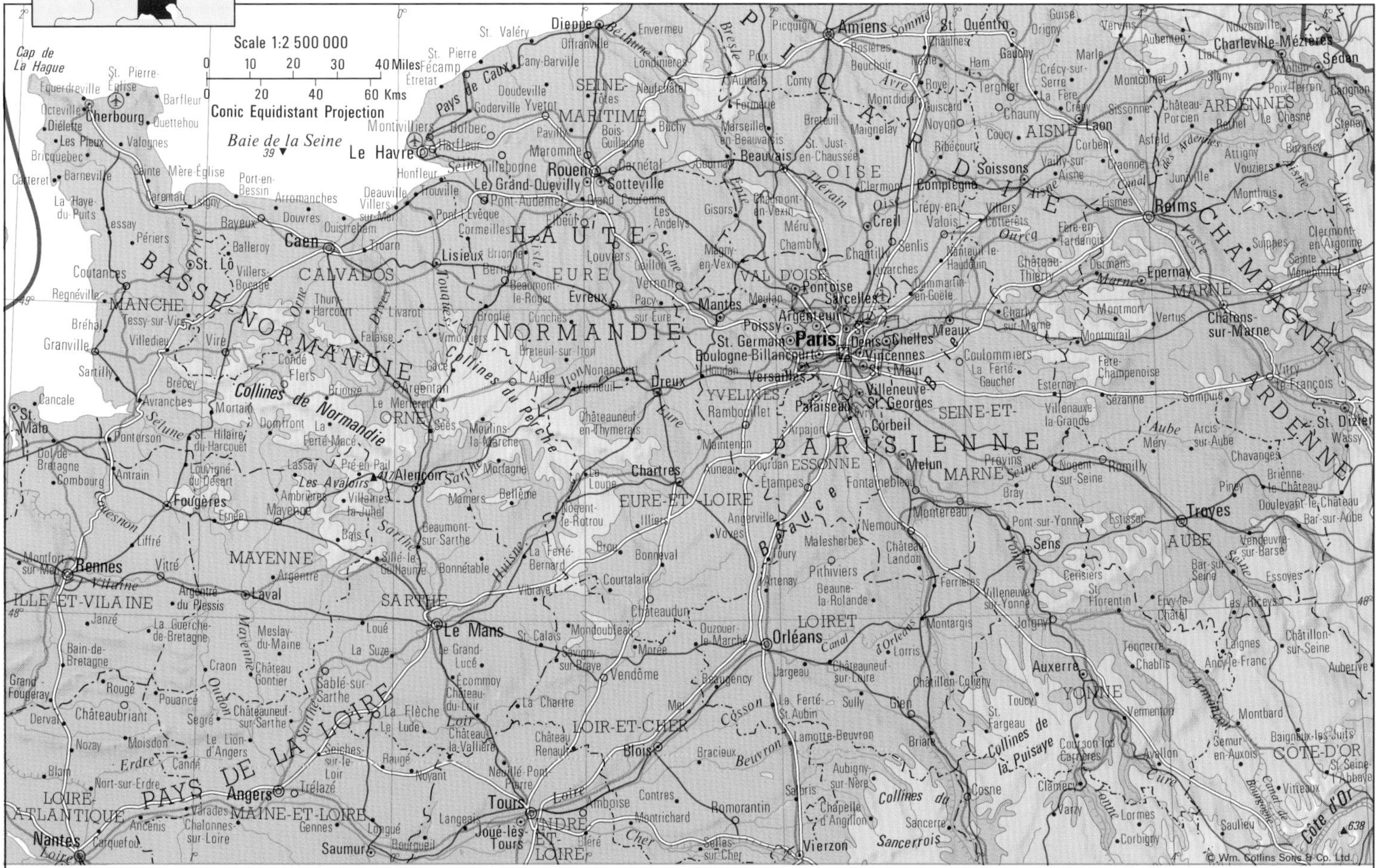

SPAIN AND PORTUGAL

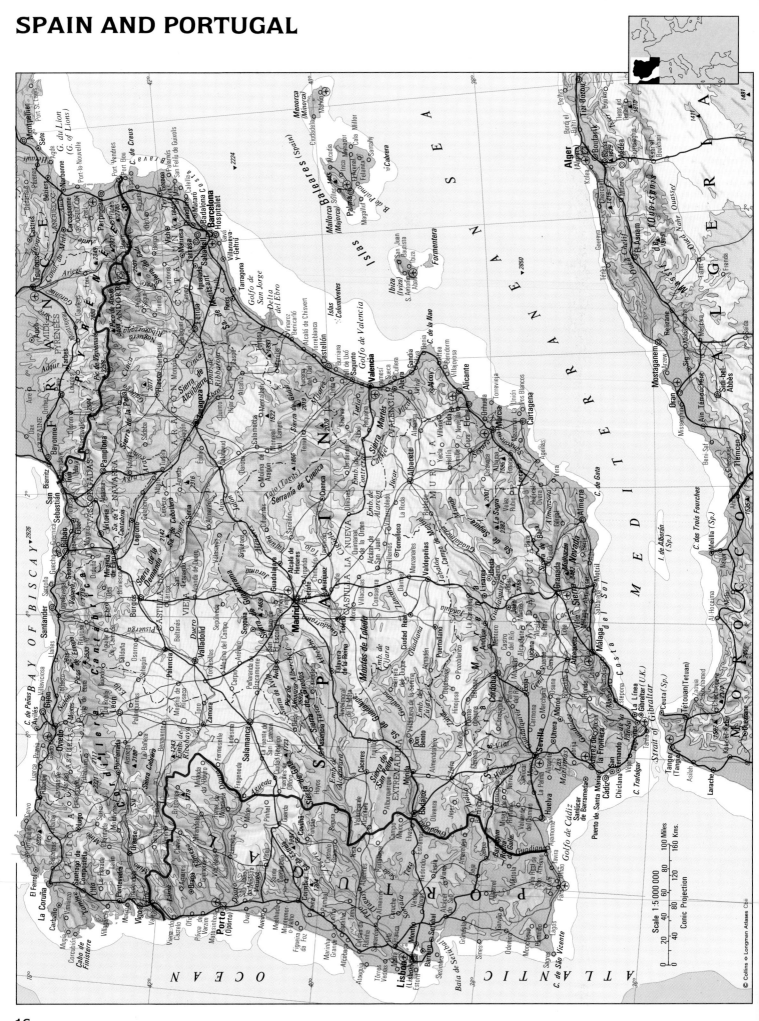

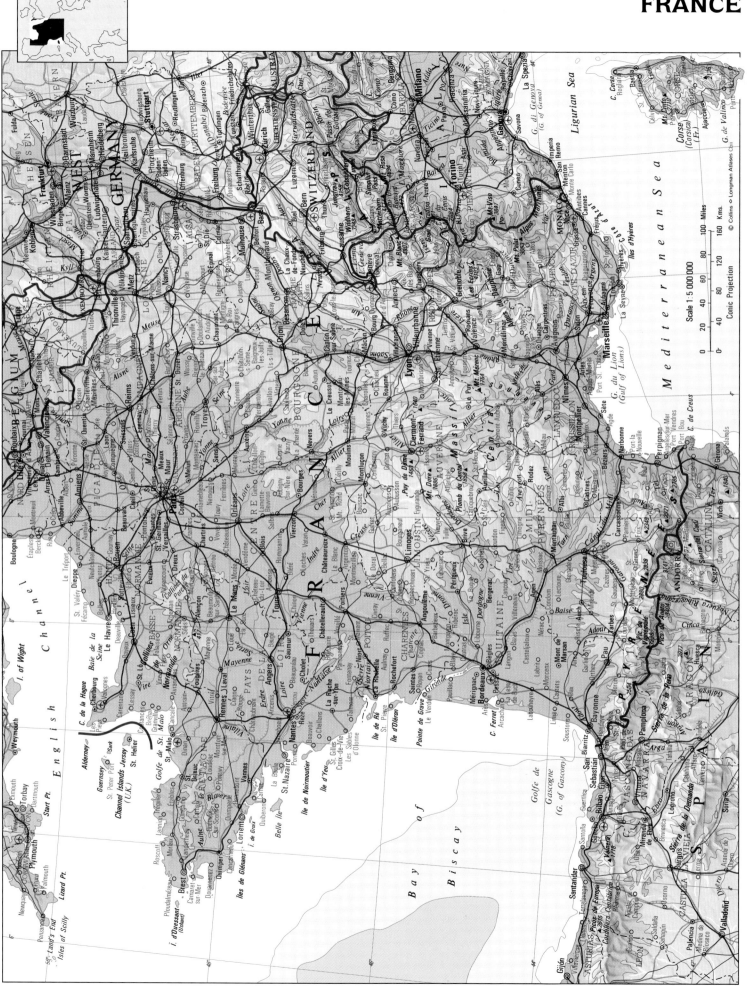

FRANCE

Scale 1:5 000 000
Conic Projection

© Longman Atlases Collins

ITALY AND THE BALKANS

19

CENTRAL EUROPE

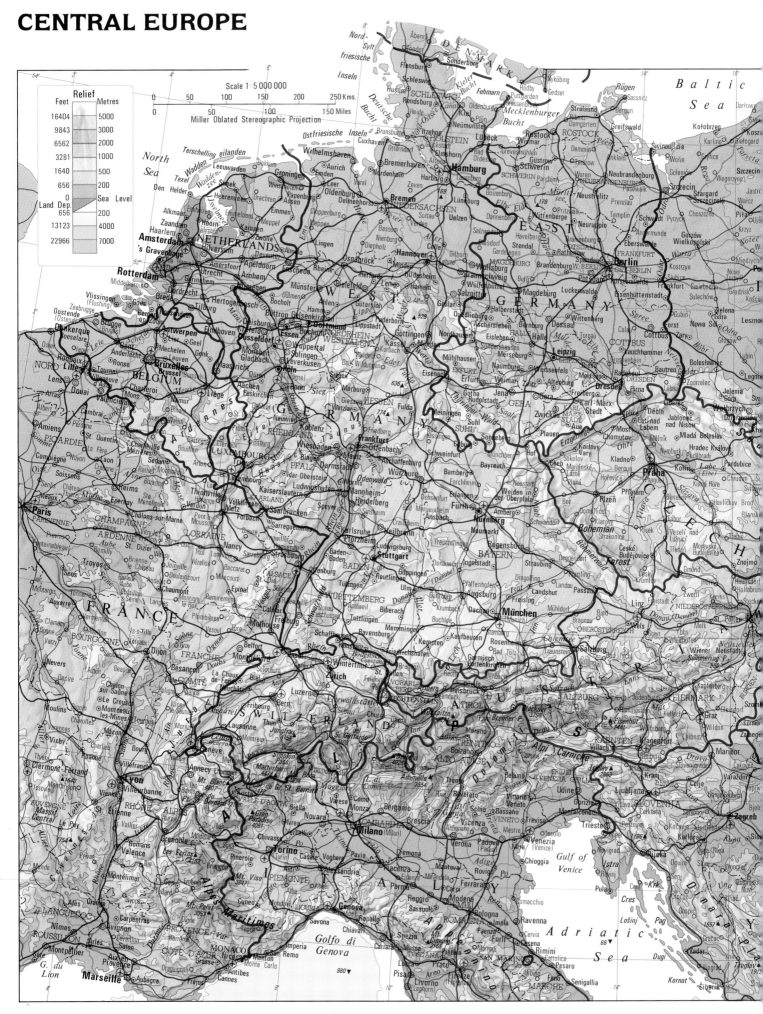

Gulf of Danzig

POLAND

LITOVSKAYA S.S.R.

R.S.F.S.R.

BELORUSSKAYA S.S.R.

Polesye

Nizmennost

Minsk

Bobruysk

Gomel

Kiyev

U.S.S.R.

UKRAINSKAYA S.S.R.

Warszawa (Warsaw)

Brest

Lublin

Lvov

Chernovtsy

Carpathians

SLOVAKIA

Budapest

HUNGARY

MOLDAVSKAYA S.S.R.

Kishinev

Odessa

Tiraspol

ROMANIA

Cluj

Bucureşti

Wallachia

Beograd

SRBIJA (SERBIA)

YUGOSLAVIA

HERCEGOVINA

Sarajevo

BULGARIA

Delta Dunării (Mouths of the Danube)

Gura Portiţei

Black Sea

Nos. Kaliakra

Varna

© Wm. Collins, Sons & Co. Ltd.

21

SCANDINAVIA AND BALTIC LANDS

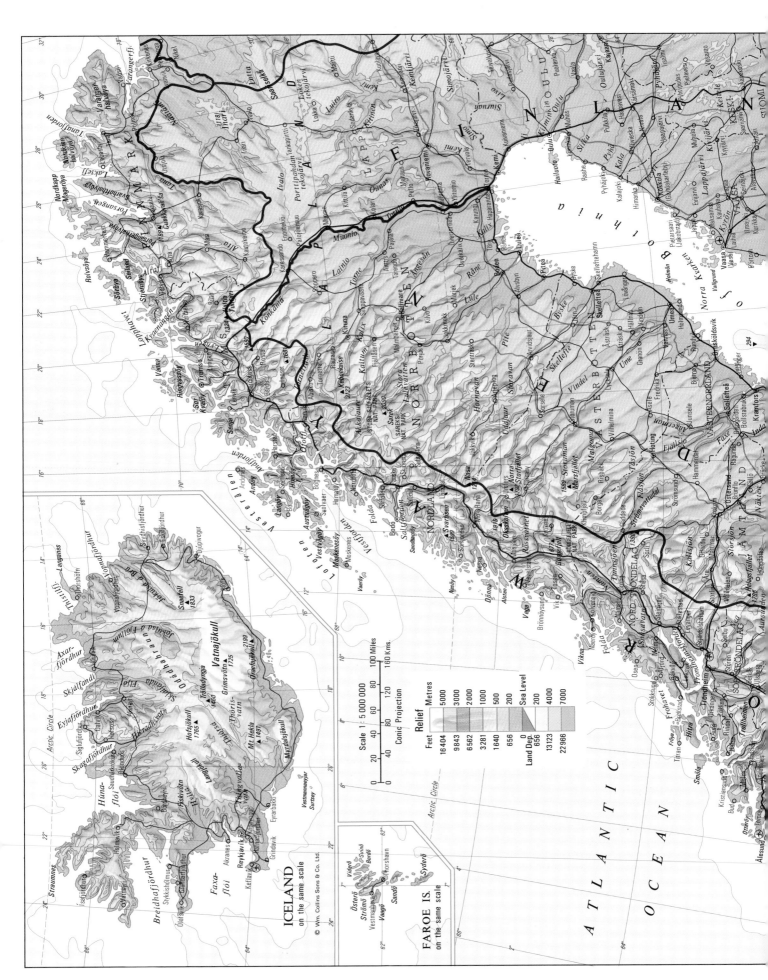

ICELAND
on the same scale

© Wm. Collins Sons & Co. Ltd.

FAROE IS.
on the same scale

Scale 1 : 5 000 000

Conic Projection

Relief

Feet	Metres
16404	5000
9843	3000
6562	2000
3281	1000
1640	500
656	200
0	Sea Level
	Land Dep.
656	200
13123	4000
22966	7000

ATLANTIC OCEAN

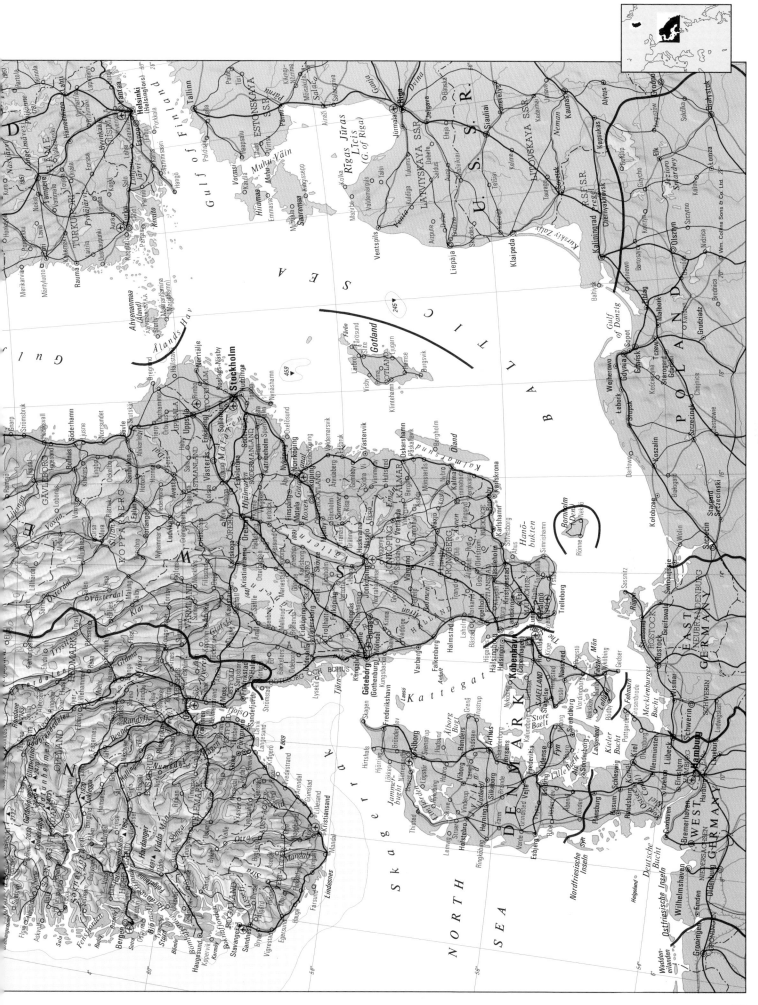

U.S.S.R. IN EUROPE

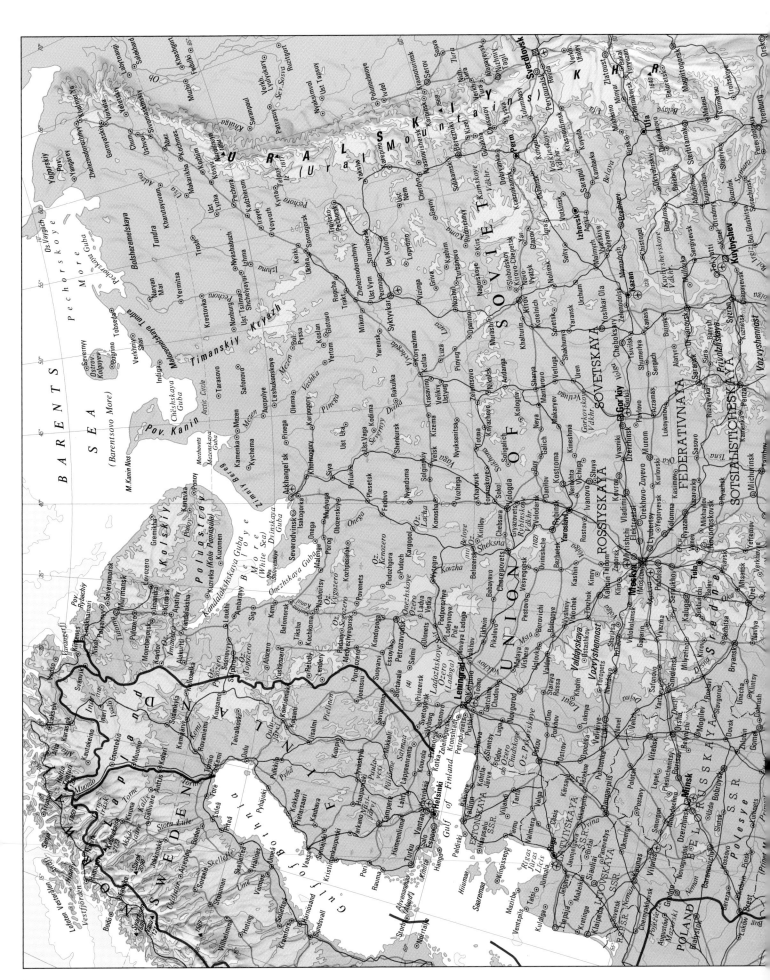

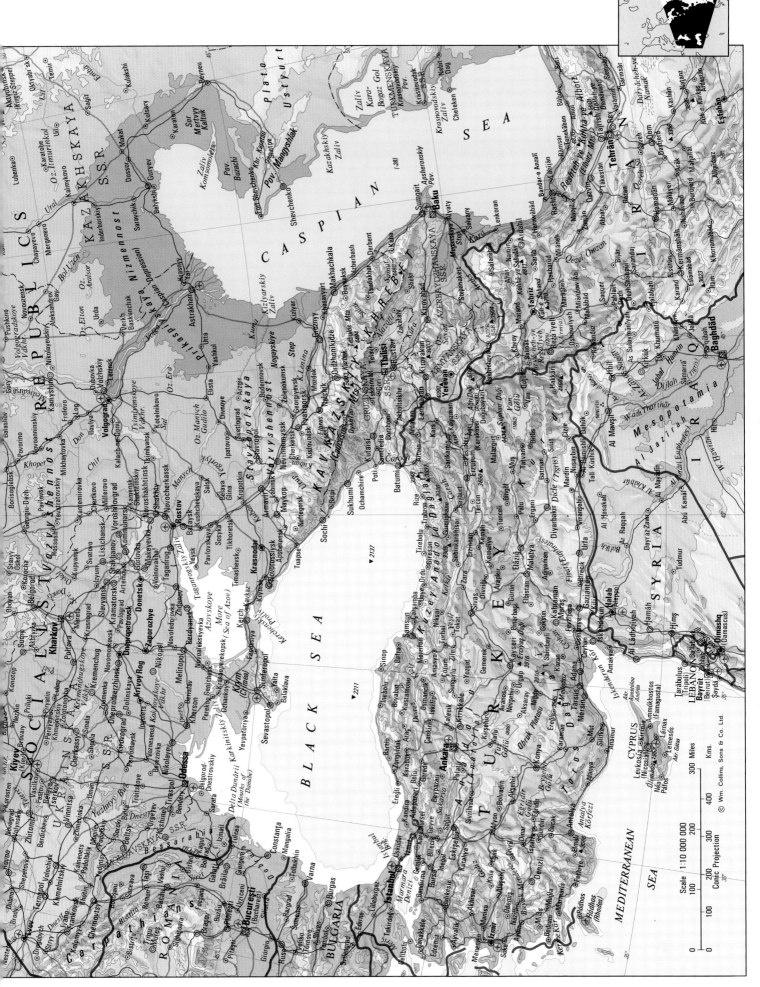

25

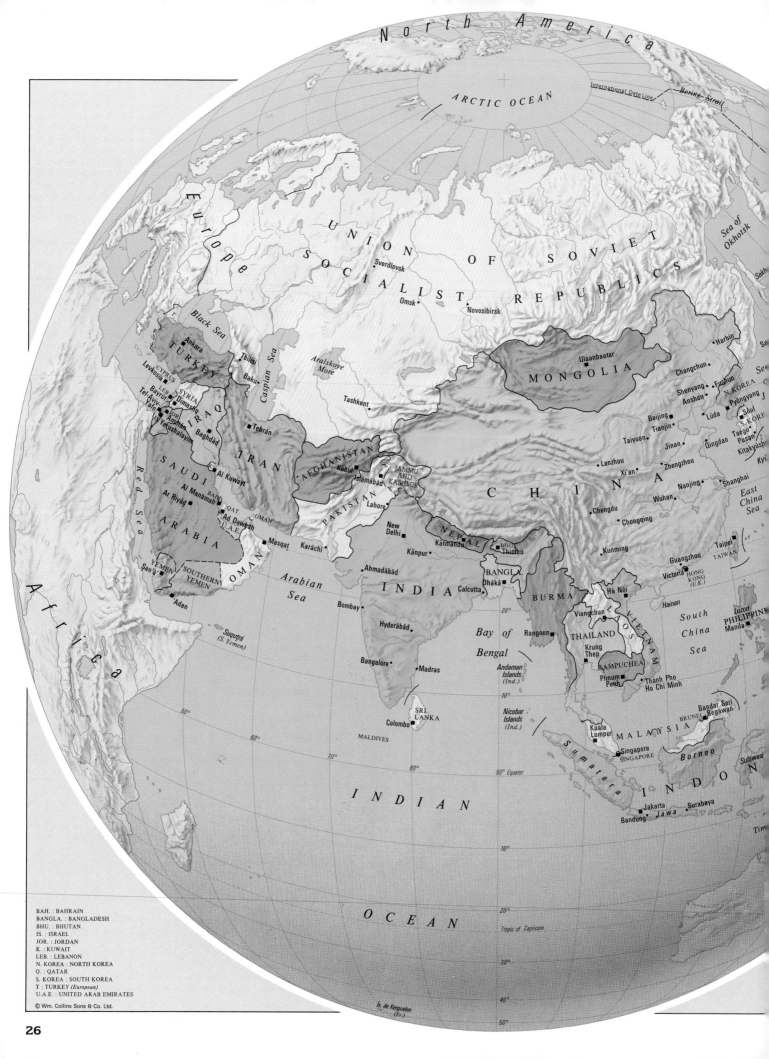

North America

ARCTIC OCEAN

International Date Line

Bering Strait

Europe

UNION   OF   SOVIET

SOCIALIST   REPUBLICS

Sea of Okhotsk

Sverdlovsk

Omsk

Novosibirsk

Sakh

Black Sea

Ankara

TURKEY

Levkosía
CYPRUS
LEB.
Bayrūt
Tel Aviv-
Yafo
Yerushalayim
SYRIA
Dimashq
JOR.
Ammān
IRAQ
Baghdād

Tbilisi

Baku

Caspian Sea

Aralskoye More

Tashkent

Tehrān

MONGOLIA

Ulaanbaatar

Harbin

Changchun

Fushun

Shenyang

N. KOREA

Pyŏngyang

Anshan

Lüda

S. KOREA

Sŏul

Taegu

Pusan

Kitakyūshū

SAUDI

Al Kuwayt

Al Manamah
BAH.
Ar Riyād
QAT.
Ad Dawhah
U.A.E.

OMAN

Masqat

Red Sea

ARABIA

YEMEN
San'a
SOUTHERN
YEMEN

Adan

AFGHANISTAN

Kābul

Islāmābād

JAMMU
AND
KASHMIR

PAKISTAN

Lahore

IRAN

Beijing

Tianjin

Taiyuan

Jinan

Qingdao

CHINA

Lanzhou

Xi'an

Zhengzhou

Nanjing

Shanghai

Wuhan

Chengdu

Chongqing

East
China
Sea

NEPAL

Kātmāndu

BHU.
Thimbu

Kunming

Guangzhou

Taipei

TAIWAN

New
Delhi

Kānpur

BANGLA.

Dhākā

Karāchi

Ahmadābād

INDIA

Calcutta

BURMA

Hà Nôi

Hainan

Victoria

HONG
KONG
(U.K.)

Suqutrā
(S. Yemen)

Arabian
Sea

Bombay

Hyderābād

Bay   of

Bengal

Rangoon

Viangchan
LAOS
THAILAND

VIETNAM

South
China
Sea

Luzon

PHILIPPINES

Manila

Africa

Bangalore

Madras

Andaman
Islands
(Ind.)

20°

Krung
Thep

KAMPUCHEA

Phnum
Penh

Thành Pho
Ho Chí Minh

Bandar Seri
Begawan

50°

60°

70°

80°

SRI
LANKA

Colombo

MALDIVES

Nicobar
Islands
(Ind.)

10°

90° Equator

Kuala
Lumpur

Singapore
SINGAPORE

Sumatera

MALAYSIA

BRUNEI

Borneo

Sulawesi

INDON

INDIAN

Jakarta

Surabaya

Bandung
Jawa

Tim

10°

20°

OCEAN

Tropic of Capricorn

30°

Is. de Kerguelen
(Fr.)

40°

50°

BAH. : BAHRAIN
BANGLA. : BANGLADESH
BHU. : BHUTAN
IS. : ISRAEL
JOR. : JORDAN
K. : KUWAIT
LEB. : LEBANON
N. KOREA : NORTH KOREA
Q. : QATAR
S. KOREA : SOUTH KOREA
T : TURKEY (European)
U.A.E. : UNITED ARAB EMIRATES

© Wm. Collins Sons & Co. Ltd.

ASIA

U.S.S.R.

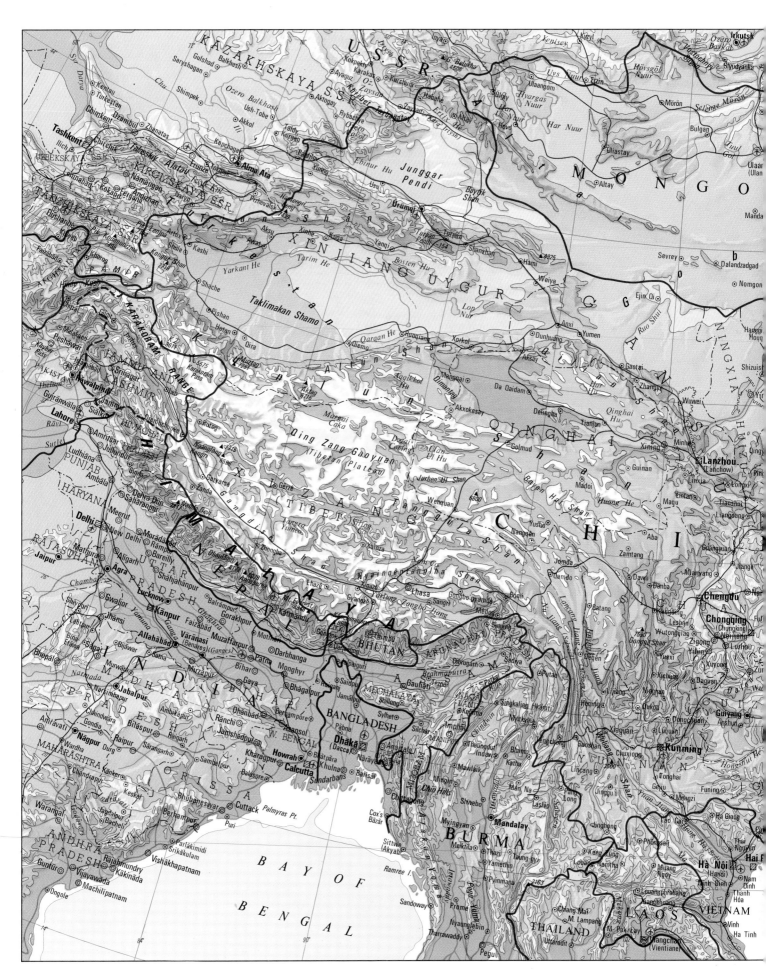

EAST CHINA

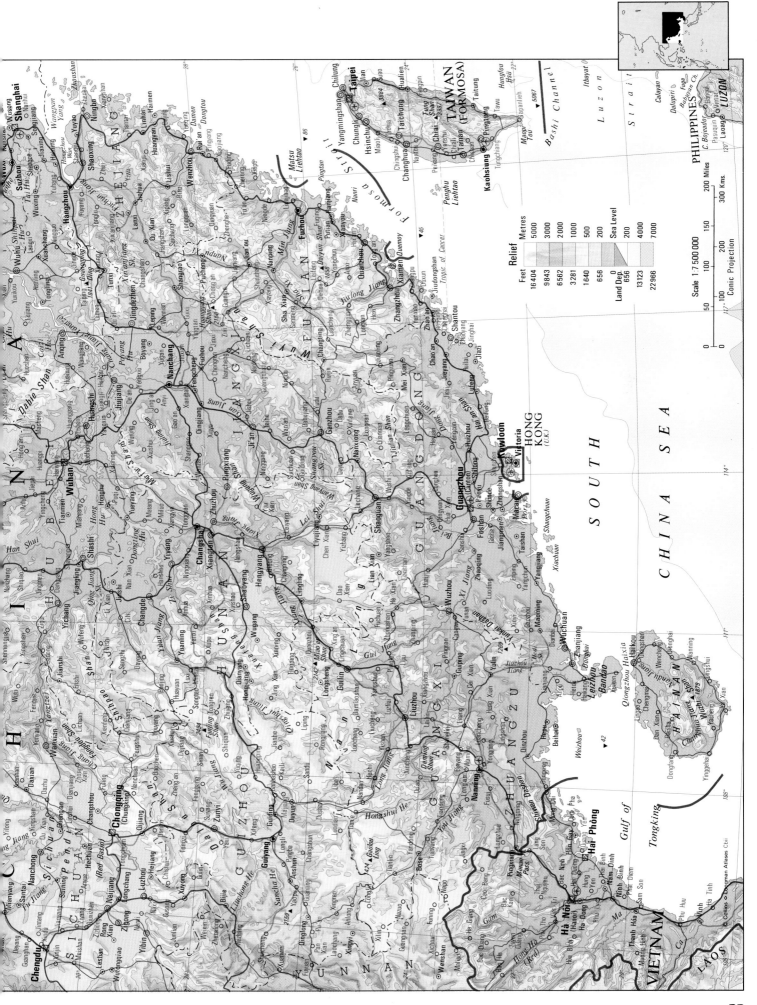

INDO-CHINA

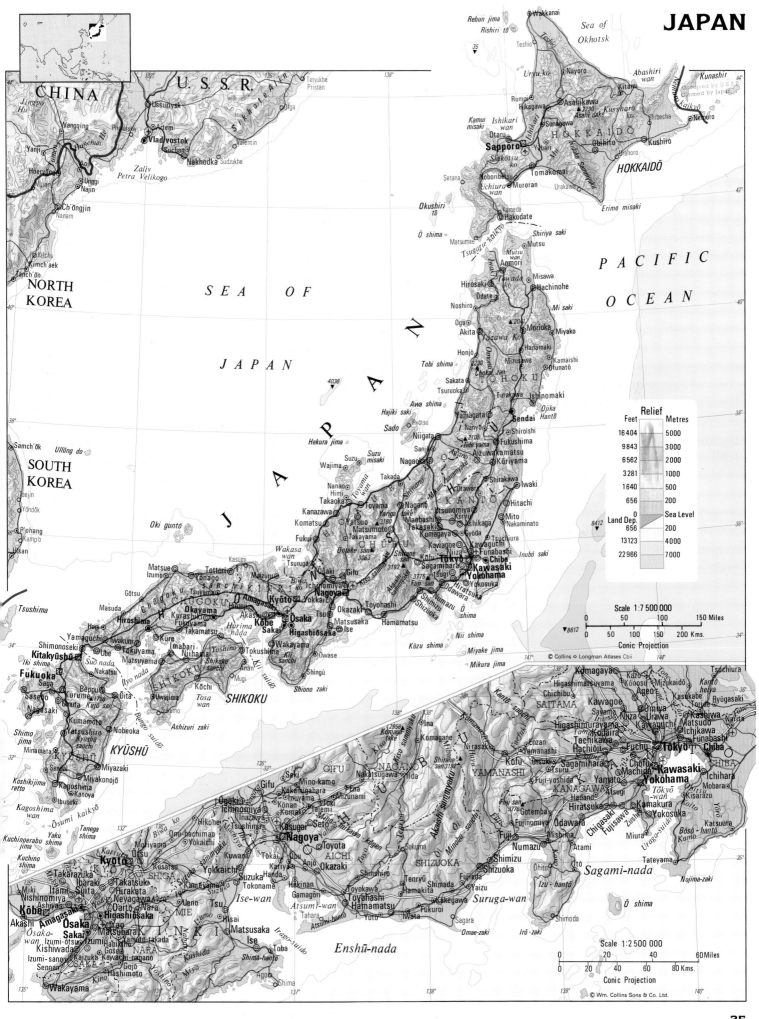

JAPAN

SOUTHEAST ASIA

SOUTH ASIA

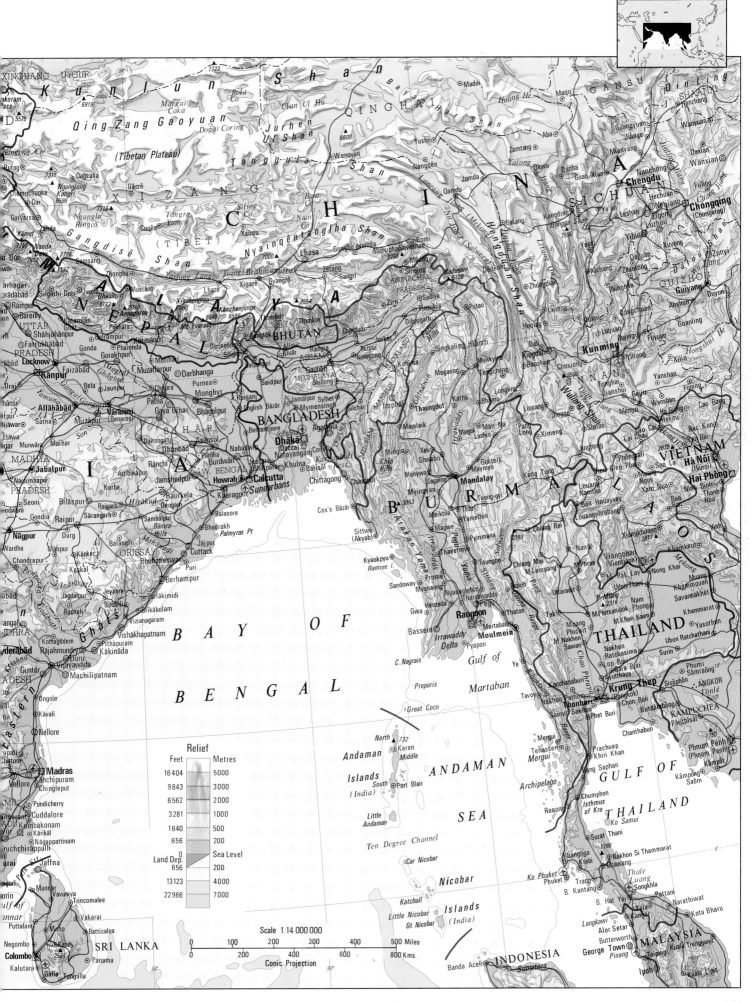

XINJIANG UYGUR
akoram
Pass
D 5575
Bangong Co
Butog
rabad
Rampur
n
Bareilly
UTTAR
Lucknow
PRADESH
Kanpur
rais
hānsi
MADHYA
PRADESH
Jabalpur
Nāgpur
Wardha
Chandrapur
andra
angal
DHRA
ADESH
yderabad

Kunlun Shan
Margai
Caka
Qing Zang Gaoyuan
(Tibetan Plateau)
Oagreka
Ngangl òng
Kangri
Gèrzê
Gar
Garyarsa
Xainza
Kemet
Namc
Nanda
MALAYA
Gangdisê Shan
Zhongba
Xigazê
Gyangzê
Samsang
Mustāng
Lhaze
Siling
Co
Nam Co
Nyainqentanglha Shan
Lhasa
(TIBET)
Kailas Zangbo Jiang/Brahmaputra

Rola
Co
Ulan Ul Hu
QINGHAI
Jurhen Ul Shan
6800
Wenquan
Tanggula Shan
Gongho oyamda

7723
Madoi
Huang He
Maqu
GANSU
Qinling
SHAN
Hanzho
Zamtang
Nangqên
Yushu
Yalong
Danba
Dawu
Jomda
Qamdo
Batang
Kangding
Litang
Xichang
Zhongdian
Heqing
Dali
Chuxiong
Kunming
Yuxi

CHINA
Aba
Mianyang
Guangyuan
Wanxian
Daxian
Nanchong
Chengdu
SICHUAN
Ya'an
Leshan
Yibin
Luzhou
Neijiang
Zigong
Chongqing
Luzhou
GUIZHOU
Guiyang
Duyun
Anshun
Guanling
Huishui
Hongshui He

NEPAL
Dhaulagiri
Annapurna
8172
Pokhara
Kathmandu
Mt Everest
8840
8586
HIMALAYA
Darjeeling
BHUTAN
Thimphu
Phunkar
Siliguri
Duar
Rangia
Gauhati
ASSAM
Shillong
MEGHALAYA
Sylhet
Mymensingh
BANGLADESH
Dhaka (Dacca)
Narayanganj Comilla
Khulna
Barisal
Sunderbans
Chittagong
Cox's Bāzār

ARUNACHAL PRADESH
Tezpur
Nowgong
Kohima
Imphal
MANIPUR
Silchar
MIZORAM
Chin
Hills
Agartala
Barak

BAY OF
BENGAL

BURMA
Myitkyina
Bhamo
Katha
Mogaung
Shwebo
Mandalay
Monywa
Sagaing
Meiktila
Magwe
Pyinmana
Prome
Henzada
Bassein
Irrawaddy
Delta
Rangoon
C. Negrais
Moulmein
Martaban
Sittwe
(Akyab)
Arakan Yoma
Pegu Yoma
Toungoo
Pegu
Thaton
Sandoway
Myanaung
Gwa

YUNNAN
Baoshan
Longling
Lincang
Simao
Jinghong
Ximeng

LAOS
Muang Sing
Louang
Namtha
Ban Houayxay
Louangphrabang
Viangchan
(Vientiane)
Pak Lay
Muang Khammouan
Savannakhét

VIETNAM
Hà Nôi
Hai Phòng
Thanh Hoa

THAILAND
Chiang Rai
Chiang Mai
M.Lampang
M.Phrae
Uttaradit
M.Phitsanulok
Tak
M.Nakhon
Sawan
Nakhon
Ratchasima
Surin
Ubon Ratchathani
Krung Thep
(Bangkok)
Thonburi
Phet Buri
Chanthaburi
Prachuap
Khiri Khan
Bang Saphan
Chumphon
Isthmus
of Kra
Ranong
Surat Thani
Ko Phuket
Phuket
Trang
Songkhla
Pattani
B. Hat Yai
Yala
Narathiwat

KAMPUCHEA
Phnum Pénh
(Phnom Penh)
ANGKOR
Tônlé
Sap
Kâmpôt
Saôm

GULF OF
THAILAND

GULF OF
MARTABAN
Gulf of
Martaban

ANDAMAN
SEA
Preparis
Great Coco
North
Karen
Middle
Andaman
Islands
South
Port Blair
(India)
Little
Andaman
Ten Degree Channel
Car Nicobar
Nicobar
Katchall
Little Nicobar
Gt Nicobar
Islands
(India)

Madras
Kānchipuram
Chingleput
Pondicherry
Cuddalore
Kumbakonam
Kārikāl
Nāgappattinam
ruchchirāppalli
urai
Jaffna
Vavuniya
Trincomalee
Vakarai
Batticaloa
orin
Puttalam
Negombo
Colombo
Kalutara
SRI LANKA
Kandy
Panama
Galle
Tangalla

Relief
Feet	Metres
16 404	5000
9843	3000
6562	2000
3281	1000
1640	500
656	200
0	Sea Level
Land Dep.	
656	200
13 123	4000
22 966	7000

Scale 1:14 000 000
0   100   200   300   400   500 Miles
0   200   400   600   800 Kms.
Conic Projection

INDONESIA
Banda Aceh
Sumatera

MALAYSIA
George Town
Pinang
Butterworth
Taiping
Ipoh
Kuala Trengganu
Kota Bharu
Alor Setar
Langkawi

NORTHERN INDIA, PAKISTAN AND BANGLADESH

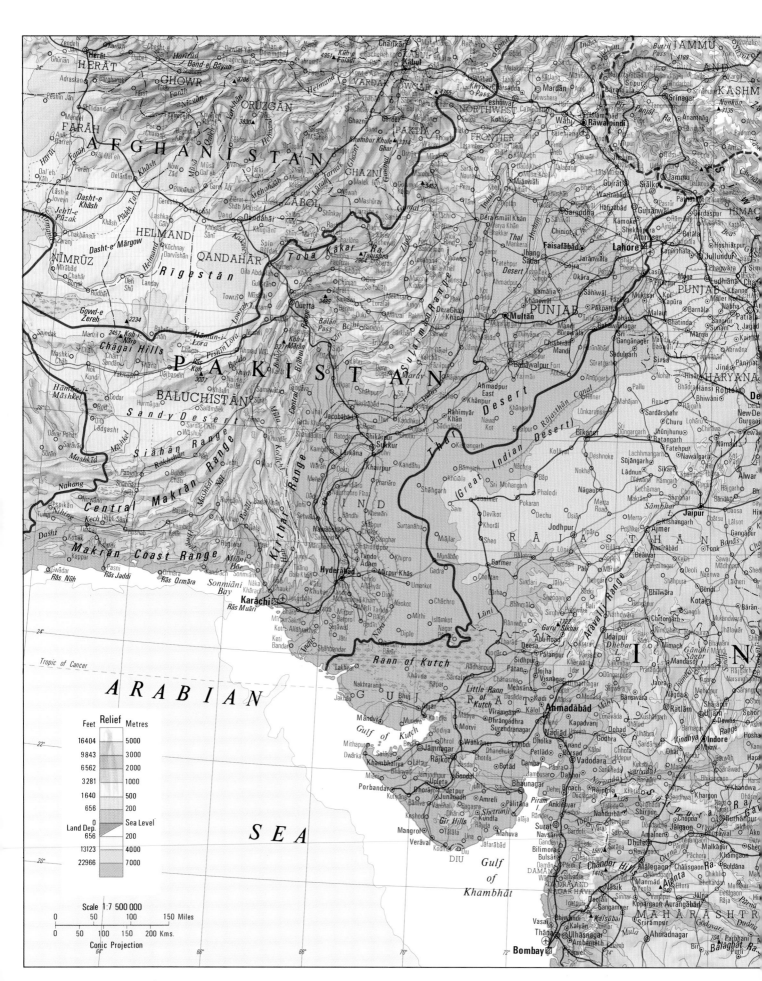

41

SOUTHWEST ASIA

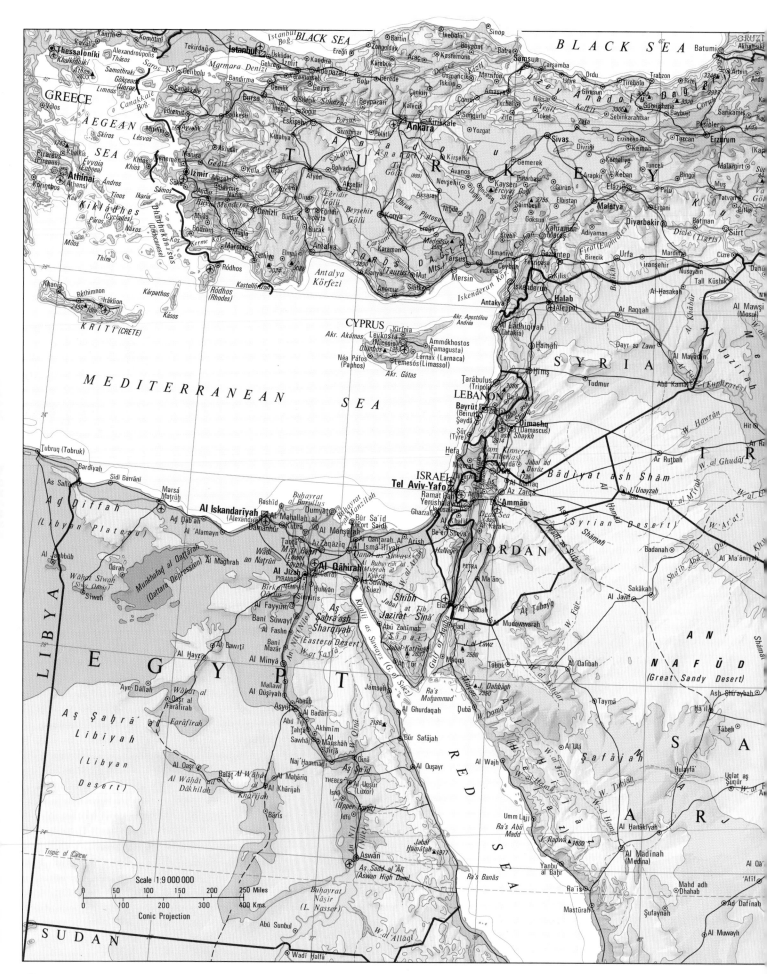

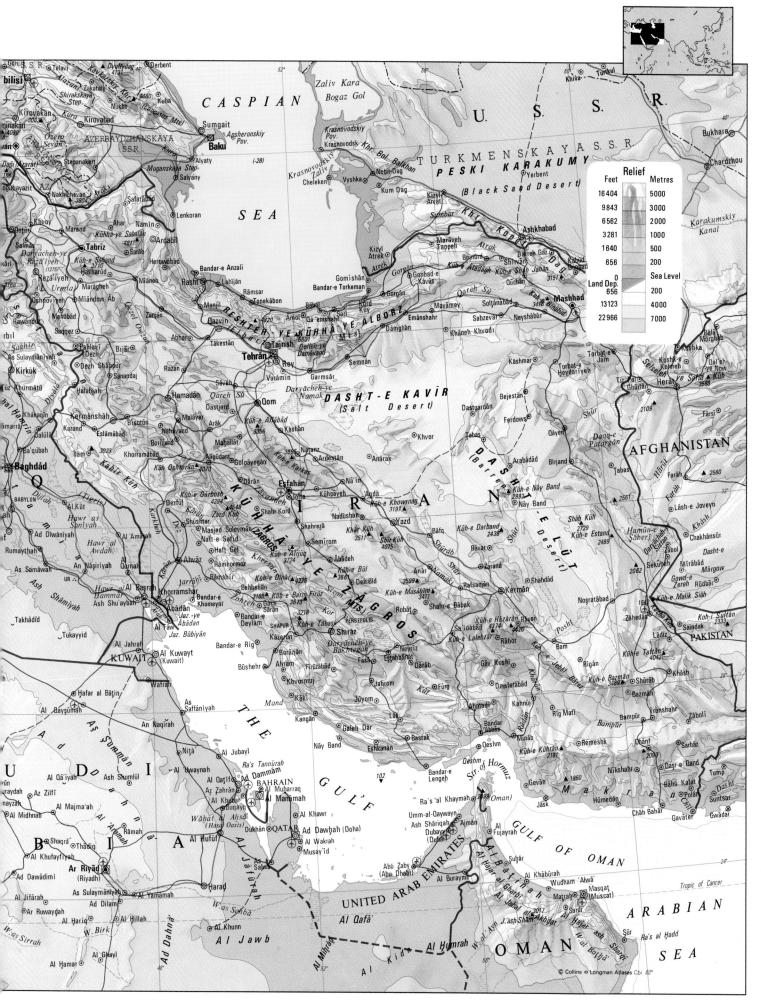

THE LEVANT

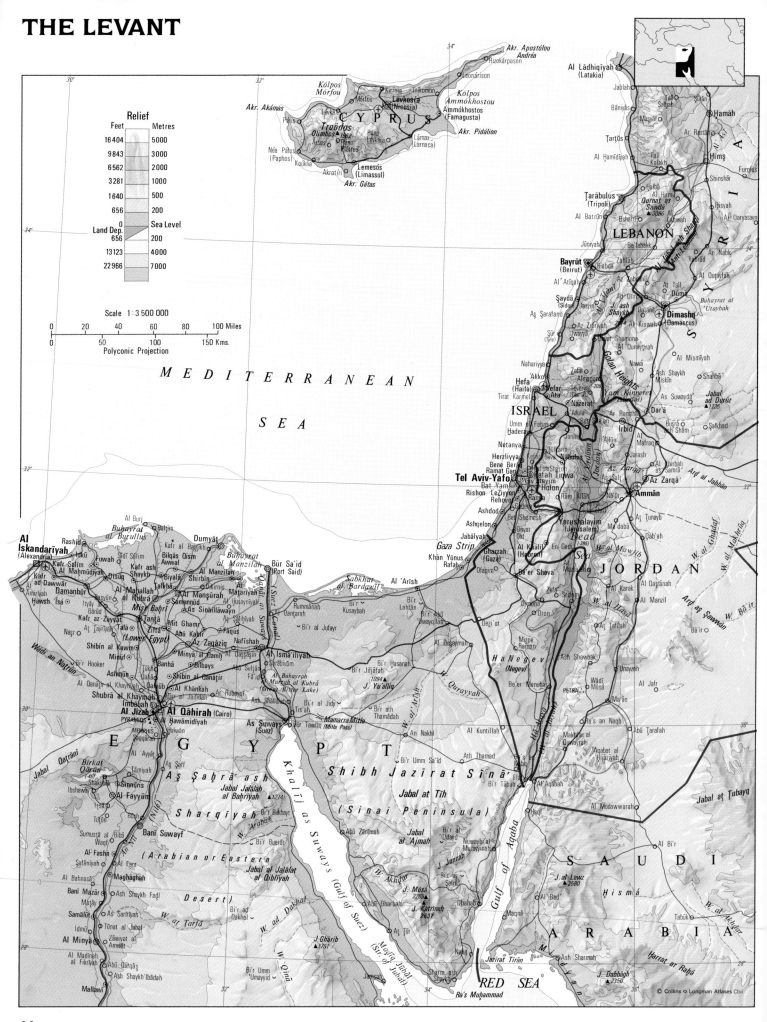

Relief

Feet	Metres
16 404	5000
9843	3000
6562	2000
3281	1000
1640	500
656	200
0	Sea Level
Land Dep.	
656	200
13123	4000
22966	7000

Scale 1:3 500 000

0 20 40 60 80 100 Miles
0 50 100 150 Kms.
Polyconic Projection

MEDITERRANEAN SEA

CYPRUS

LEBANON

SYRIA

ISRAEL

JORDAN

EGYPT

(Lower Egypt)

(Arabian or Eastern Desert)

Shibh Jazīrat Sīnā' (Sinai Peninsula)

SAUDI ARABIA

RED SEA

Khalīj as Suways (Gulf of Suez)

Gulf of Aqaba

© Collins · Longman Atlases Cbii

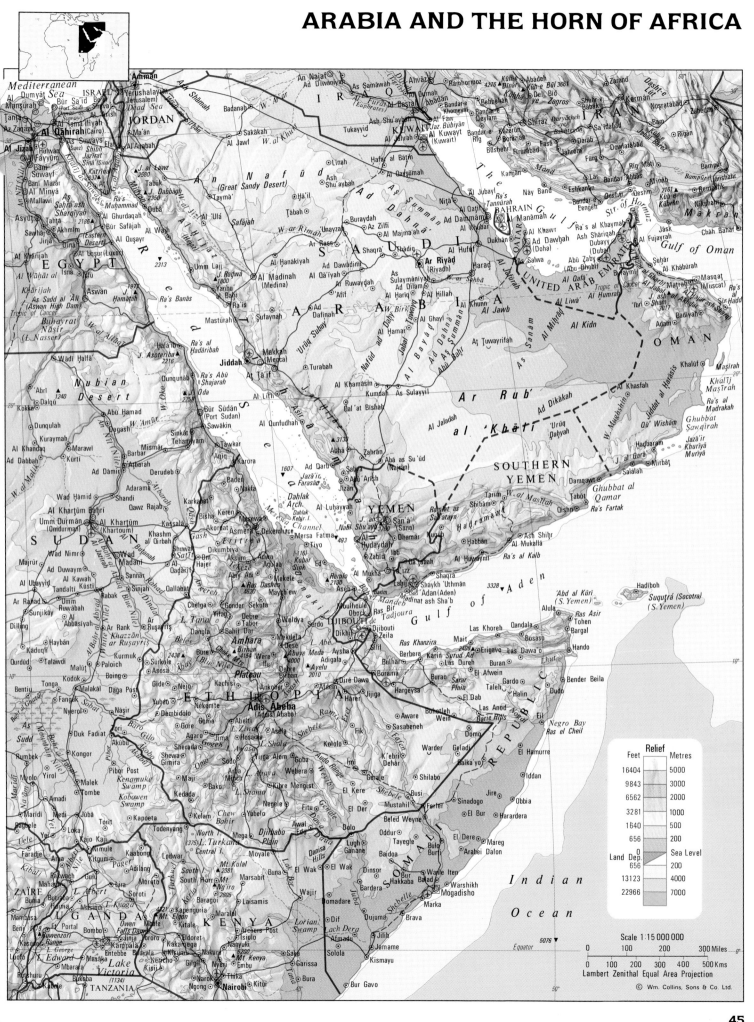

ARABIA AND THE HORN OF AFRICA

North America

Arctic Circle

Europe

60°

50°

ATLANTIC

40°

Mediterranean Sea

Alger
Tunis
TUNISIA
Ṭarābulus
Al Iskandarīyah
Al Jīzah
Al Qāhirah

30°

Rabat
Casablanca
Madeira
(Port.)

MOROCCO

OCEAN

Islas
Canarias
(Sp.)
El Aaiún

ALGERIA

LIBYA

EGYPT

Red Sea

Tropic of Cancer

WESTERN SAHARA

20°

MAURITANIA

NIGER

CHAD

Al Khartūm

SUDAN

Nouakchott

M A L I

CAPE
VERDE

Dakar
SENEGAL
Bamako
GAMBIA
Banjul
Bissau

Niamey
UPPER
VOLTA
Ouagadougou

DJIBOUTI
Djibouti Gulf of Aden

Ādis Ābeba

ETHIOPIA

GUINEA
N'Djamena

10°

Conakry
Freetown S.L.

IVORY
COAST
Yamoussoukro

GHANA
TOGO
BENIN

NIGERIA
Ibadan
Abuja
Lagos

CENTRAL
AFRICAN REPUBLIC

SOMALI REPUBLIC

Monrovia

LIBERIA

Accra
Lomé Porto-
Novo

Bangui

Abidjan
Malabo
CAMEROON
Yaoundé

Mogadisho

Gulf of Guinea
EQUATORIAL
GUINEA

UGANDA
Kampala

KENYA

SÃO TOMÉ
AND
PRÍNCIPE

Principe

Libreville

CONGO

ZAÏRE

Kigali R.W.
BUR.
Bujumbura

Nairobi

São
Tomé

GABON

0° Equator

SEYCH

20° 10° 0°

10°

20° Equator

30°

40°

ATLANTIC

Brazzaville

Kinshasa

TANZANIA
Dodoma

Dar es Salaam

ANGOLA
Kananga

10°

Luanda

OCEAN

COMOROS

ANGOLA
ZAMBIA MAL.
Lusaka Lilongwe

South
America

20°

ANGOLA

NAMIBIA

BOTSWANA

Harare
(Salisbury)
ZIMBABWE

MOZAMBIQUE

Mozambique Channel

MADAGASCAR
Antananarivo

MAUR

Tropic of Capricorn

R.S.A.
Windhoek

Gaborone
Johannesburg
Soweto
REPUBLIC
OF
SOUTH AFRICA

Pretoria
Maputo
Mbabene
SW.
Maseru
LES. Durban

30°

Cape Town

40°

50°

60°

Antarctic Circle

70°

Antarctica

BUR. : BURUNDI
G.B. : GUINEA BISSAU
LES. : LESOTHO
MAL. : MALAWI
R.S.A. : REPUBLIC OF SOUTH AFRICA
R.W. : RWANDA
S.L. : SIERRA LEONE
SW. : SWAZILAND

© Wm. Collins Sons & Co. Ltd.

46

AFRICA

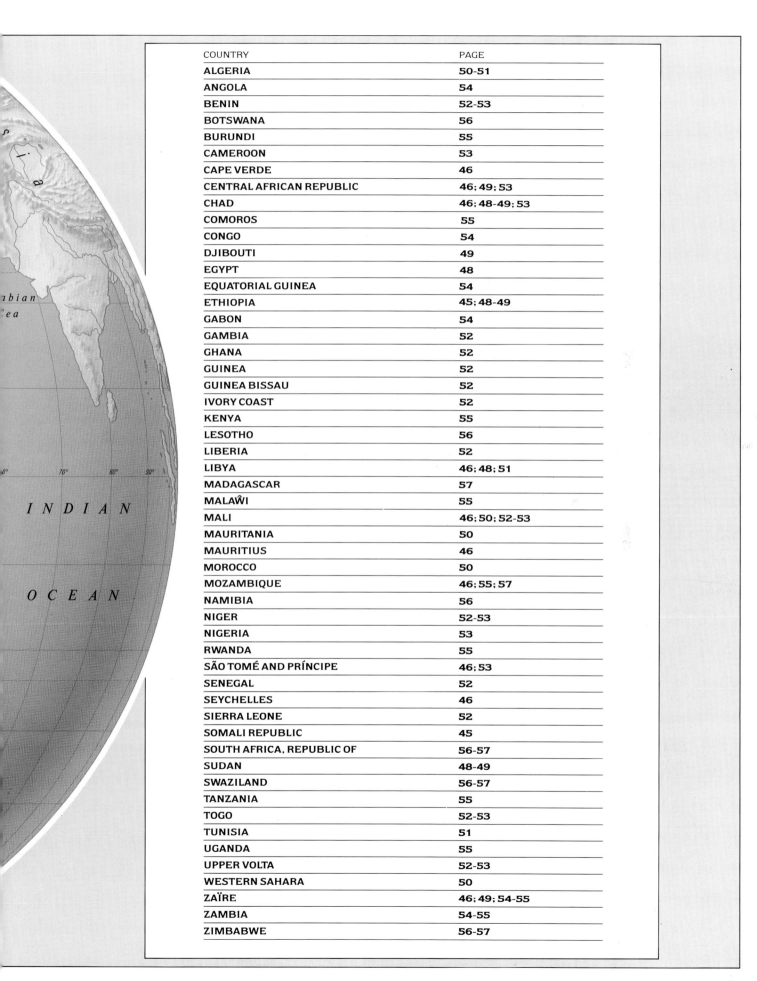

NILE VALLEY

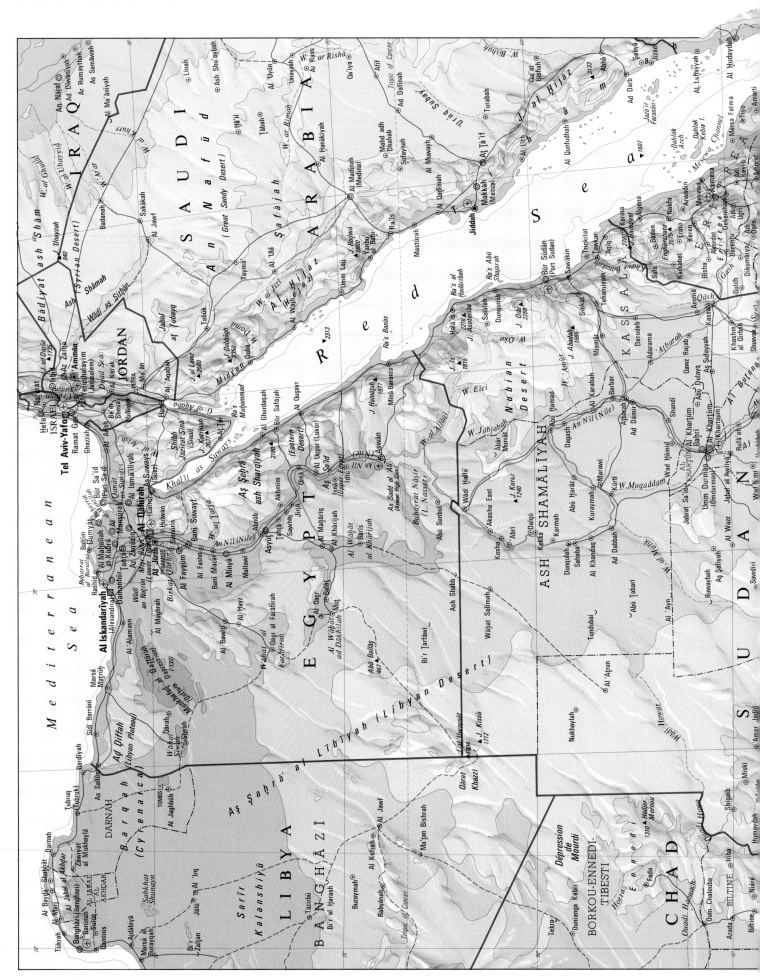

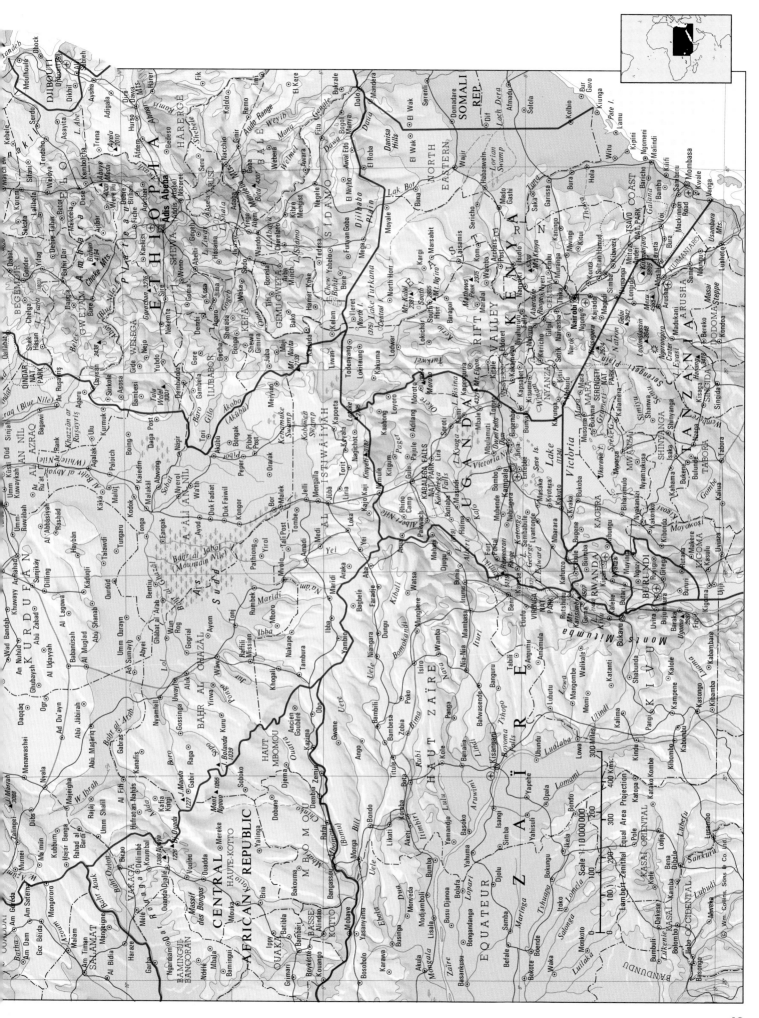

49

NORTHWEST AFRICA

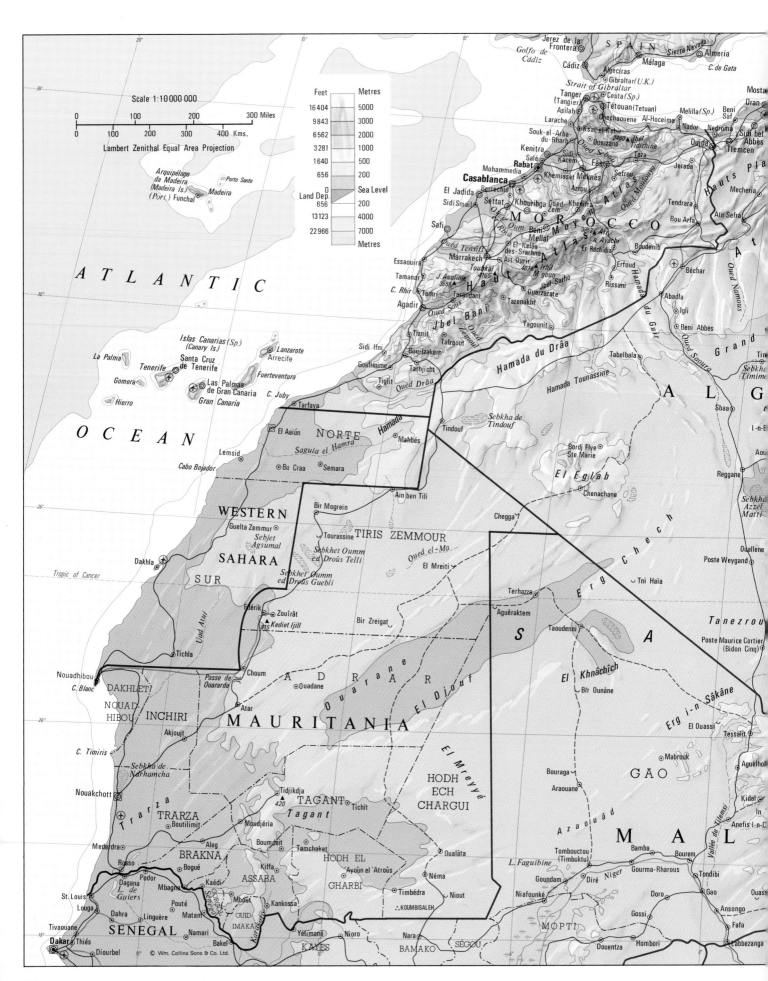

Alger (Algiers) Tizi-Ouzou Jijel Skikda Annaba Menzel Bizert (Bizerte) C. Bon Catania Siracusa GREECE
Boufarik Bejaïa Tabarka Bourguiba Tunis Sicilia (Sicily) Ragusa Akr. Akrítas
Blida Bordj Bou El Eulma Guelma Béja La Goulette C. Passero Akr. Taínaron
El Asnam Médéa Arreridj Constantine Souk Ahras El Kef Hammam Lif Nabeul
Ksar el Sétif Aïn Beida Ouenza Enfida Msaken Sousse MALTA Valletta
Boukhari Batna Tébessa El Kairouan Monastir
Tiaret Bou Saâda Barika Khenchela 1278 Djebel Mrhila El Mahdia Lampedusa (Italy)
Aflou Djelfa Biskra El Kasserine Ra's Kaboudia
Laghouat Chott Melrhir El Metlaoui Gafsa Sfax Íles Kerkenna
Hassi er Oued Ittel Tozeur G. de Gabès
Rmel Nefta Gabès Île de Djerba
Ghardaïa El Oued Chott Kebíli Médenine
Touggourt Djerid TUNISIA Tarábulus (Tripoli) Al Bayḍā' Shaḥḥāt
Ouargla Ksar Zuwārah Tripolitanía Al Mari Tūkrah Al Jabal al Akhḍar
Hassi Messaoud Rhilane AZ ZĀWIYAH TARĀBULUS Banghāzī (Benghazi) Baninah
Fort Lallemand Dehibat Gharyān Al Qaṣabāt Miṣrātāh Qamīnis Sulūq AL JABAL AL AKHDAR
Al Jawsh Bani Walid Khalīj Surt (Gulf of Sidra)
Fort Saint Nālūt W. Sawfajjīn Daryat al Bu'ayrāt As Sulṭān Surt Ra's al Unūf Ajdābiyā
Ghadāmis Dirj GHARYĀN Jādū Mizdah Sinawin Qaddāhīyah Hasūn An Nawfalīyah Al 'Uqaylah Marsā al Sabkhat Shunayn
Tarābulus Abyār ash Shuwayrif Buraygah
Hassi bel Guebbour (Tripolitania) Waddān Marādah Bi'r Al 'Irq
Ohanet AL KHUMS Zaltan Jālū
Bordj Omar Jabal as Sawdá' Zillah Sarīr Kalanshiyū
Driss SĀBHĀ
Miliana Amguid Birāk Al Harūj al Aswad Tāzirbū
I-n-Salah W. Irauen Sabhā Samnū LIBYA Bi'r al Harash BANGHĀZĪ
Illizi Awbārī Ghaddūwah Tmassah
Tadjmout Tassili-n-Ajjer Al 'Uwaynāt Hamādat Marzūq Zawīlah Şahrā' Rabyānah Rabyānah
Arak W. Barjūj Marzūq Wāw al Kabīr (Rebiana Sand Sea) Buzaymah
Garet el Djenoun Azao Zaouatallaz AWBĀRĪ Al Qaṭrūn Tropic of Cancer
2327 2158 Ghāt Şahrā' Marzūq Sarīr Tibastī
I-n-Eker Idèles Djanet Tajarhī
I-n-Amguel Ahaggar Djebel I-n-Ezzane Bette 2286
Tit 2918 2132 2306 Serkout Toummo Aozou Tarso Ouri Quri
Abalessa Tahat Plateau Bardai 3150
Tamanrasset du Djado Wour 3265 Tibesti
Silet Amsel 3325 Tarso Ahōn
Ténéré du Djado Plateau du Tchigai 3415 Emi Koussi
1994 Mt. Grébaun Tafassasset Zouar
Admer Séguédine Tekro
Anou Ti-n- AGADEZ Gouro
Elhaoua Aney Ounianga Kébir
1795 BORKOU-ENNEDI-TIBESTI
Iferouâne Aïr Bilma Grand Erg de Bilma Largeau Horta
Sidaouet (Azbine) Aïn Galakka Fada
In Abbangarit Bodélé CHAD
Teguidda I-n-Tessoum Ouadi Haouach
Agadez Koro Toro Oum Chalouba
I-n-Gall NIGER DIFFA Bahr el Ghazal Arada
TAHOUA Tegouma KANEM BATHA BILTINE
508 ZINDER Tanout Nokou Zigey Biltine

WEST AFRICA

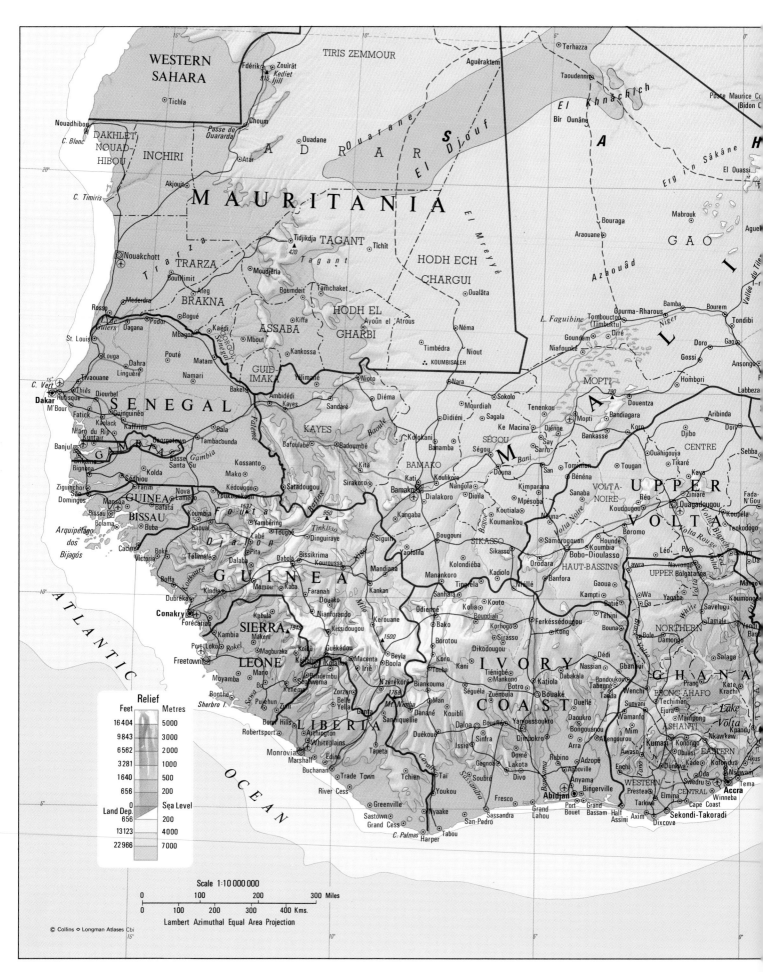

WESTERN SAHARA

TIRIS ZEMMOUR

• Terhazza

Fdérik • Zouirât
Kediet
Ijill

Aguêraktem

Poste Maurice Co
(Bidon C

• Tichla

Nouadhibou

Taoudenni

El khnáchích

C. Blanc
DAKHLET
NOUAD-
HIBOU

INCHIRI

Passe de
Ouararda

• Choum

• Ouadane

R Ouârâne

A D R A R

El Djouf

A

Bir Ounâne

Erg in Sâkâne

Aguel

El Ouassi

• Atar

• Akjoujt

M A U R I T A N I A

Bouraga •

GAO

Mabrouk •

• El Ouassi

Nouakchott

Trarza
TRARZA

BoutIimit •

Aleg
BRAKNA

• Bogué

Tidjikdja

TAGANT

420

Tichît •

HODH ECH
CHARGUI

El Mreyyé

Araouane •

Azbouâd

I

Rosso •
Mederdra •

• Podor
Dagana

Louga •
Dahra •
• Tivaouane
Linguère •

St. Louis •

Mbagne
Kaédi

Moudjéria •
Boumdeit •

Tamchaket •

HODH EL
GHARBI

Ayoûn el 'Atroûs •

• Ouâlâta

L. Faguibine
Tombouctou
(Timbuktu)

Goundam •

Gourma-Rharous •
Diré •

Bamba •
Bourem •

Niger

Vallée du Tileï

Tondibi •

C. Vert
DIourbel
Thiès •
Rufisque •
Dakar
M'Bour •
Fatick •

Pouté •
Matam •
Namari •

GUID-
IMAKA

Vélimané •

Nioto •

• Diéma

Nara •

Sokolo •

Tenenkou •

MOPTI

790

Douentza •

Niafounké •

Gao •

Gossi •

Doro •

Ansongo •

Hombori •

Labbeza •

S E N E G A L

Guinguinéo •
Kaolack •
N'Ioro du Rip •
Kuntaïr •

Bala •
Georgetown •
Tambacounda •

Ambidédi •
Kayes •

Sandaré •

Mourdiah •

• Didiéni
Sagala •

Ke Macina •
Djénné •

Bandiagara •

Koro •

Aribinda •

Djibo •

Dori •

Banjul
GAMBIA
Brikama •
Bignona •
Ziguinchor •
São Domingos •

Kaffrine •
Basse
Santa Su •

KAYES

Bafoulabé •
Badoumbé •

Banamba •
Kolokani •

SÉGOU
Séou •

Say •

Sarro •

Douna •
San •

CENTRE

Ouahigouya •

Tikaré •

Sebba •

Kita •
BAMAKO

Kati •
Koulikoro •

Nángola •

Dioïla •

Mpésoba •

Sanaba •
Réo •

Koudougou •

Tougan •

Bénéna •

UPPER

Fada-
N'Gou

Koupela •

CENTRE

Mansôa •
GUINEA
BISSAU
Bissau •
Bolama •
Buba •

Balatá •
Nova
Lamego •

Kossanto •
Mako •
Satadougou •

Kédougou •
Youkoukoun •

Sirakoro •
Bamako
Dialakoro •

Kangaba •

Bougouni •

Koutiala •

Kimparana •

SIKASSO

VOLTA-
NOIRE

Bobo-Dioulasso •

Léo •
Po •

Boromo •

Koupela •
Tenkodogo •

Arquipélago
dos
Bijagós

Cacheu •
Victoria •

Boffa •
Kindia •

Télimélé •

Koumbia •

Youla •
Diaoun

1537

Labé •
Pita •

Dalaba •

Gaoual •

Yambéring •
Tougé •

Dinguiraye •

Tinkisso

Dabola •
Bissikrima •

Mamou •
Kaba •

Mandiana •

Odienné •
Sikasso •
Kadiolo •
N'Tellé •

Orodara •
Banfora •

Kampti •

Gaoua •

HAUT-BASSINS

Wa •
Batié •

Yagaba •

Lawra •

UPPER

Bolgatanga •

Koumongou

Mango •

Yendi •
Bas

Conakry
Forécariah •

SIERRA
Kambia •

Port Loko •

Dubréka •
Kouroussa •

G U I N E A

Faranah •
Douako •

Nianforando •

Kankan •

Kérouane •

Sanhala •
Tingrela •

Kolondiéba •

Kong •

Kadiolo •

Tehini •

Boundiali •

NORTHERN

Salaga •

Kete
Krachi

Freetown

Makeni •
Magburaka •

Kailahun •

1948

Kissidougou •

Bako •

Korhogo •

Ferkéssédougou •

Bouna •

Damongo •

Tamale •

Moyamba •
Séguéla •

Koidu •
Kolahun •

Macenta •
Irié •

Beyla •
Boola •

Koro •

Kani •

Séguéla •

Katiola •

Bole •

GHANA

BRONG-AHAFO

Prang •

Kete
Krachi

Bonthe •
Sherbro I.

Pujehun •
Zimi •

Belle
Yella •

N'zérékoré •
Zorzor •

Biankouma •

Man •

1768

Danané •
Sanniquellie •

Kouibli •

TIÉNIGBÉ •

Dabakala •
Bondoukou •

Wenchi •
Techiman •

Sunyani •

Ejura •

ASHANTI
Kumasi •

Mampong •

Lake
Volta

Kpandu •
Nkawkaw •

Sewa

LIBERIA

Robertsport •
Arthington •
Whiteplains •

Monrovia
Marshall •
Edina •

Mt. Nimba
Ganta •
Tapeta •

Duékoué •

Daloa •
Sinfra •

C O A S T

Bouaké •

Daoukro •
Bongouanou •

Ouellé •

Yamoussoukro •

Dimbokro •

Agboville •

Oumé •
Gagnoa •
Lakota •

Divo •

Adzopé •

Abengourou •
Mim •

Sunyani •

Awaso •
Dunkwa •
Obuasi •

EASTERN
Koforidua •

Buchanan •

Trade Town •
Tchien •

Tai •

Youkou •

River Cess •

Nyaake •

Sastown •
Grand Cess •
C. Palmas •
Harper

Greenville

San-Pedro •

Sassandra •

Fresco •

Gagnoa •

Issia •

Arra •
Rubino •

Anyama •

Bingerville •
Abidjan

Tabou •

Sekondi-Takoradi

WESTERN
Enchi •

Presteá •
Tarkwa •
Dixcove •

CENTRAL

Elmina •
Cape Coast •

Accra

Winneba •
Tema

Grand
Lahou •
Grand
Bassam •
Half
Assini •

Port
Bouët •
Axim •

ATLANTIC

OCEAN

Relief

Feet		Metres
16 404		5000
9843		3000
6562		2000
3281		1000
1640		500
656		200
0		Sea Level
Land Dep.		
656		200
13 123		4000
22 966		7000

Scale 1:10 000 000

| 0 | 100 | 200 | 300 Miles |

| 0 | 100 | 200 | 300 | 400 Kms. |

Lambert Azimuthal Equal Area Projection

© Collins ◊ Longman Atlases Cbi

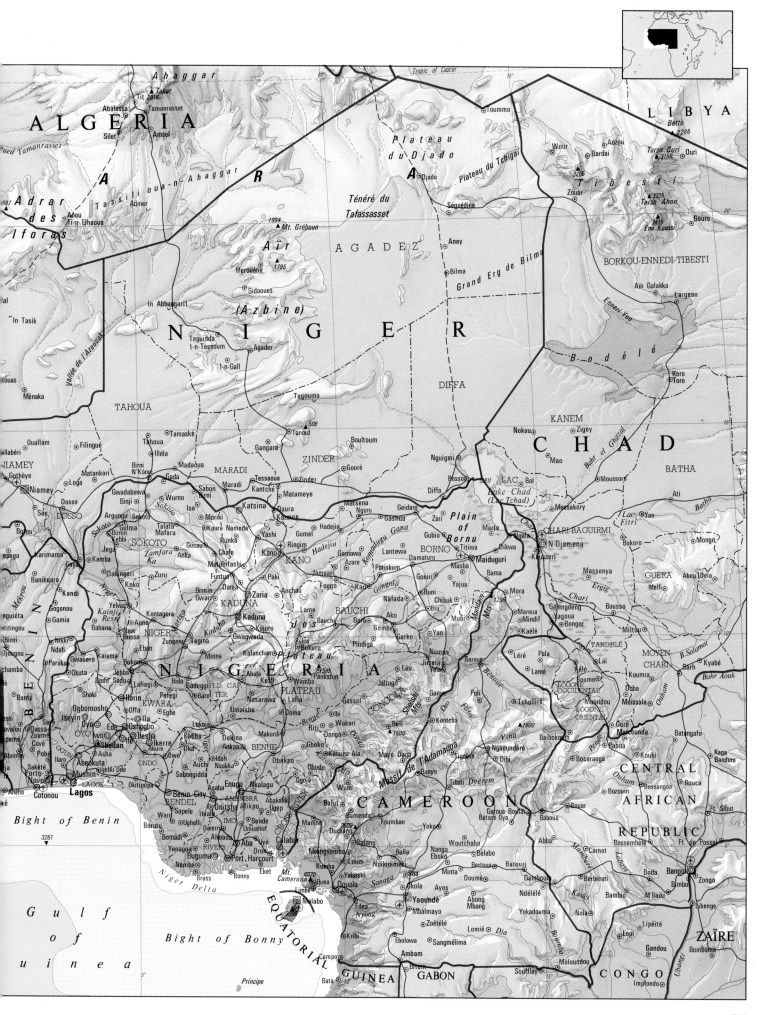

ALGERIA

Ahaggar

LIBYA

Tahat 2918
Abalessa
Tamanrasset
Amsel
Silet
Tit

A H A G G A R

*Plateau
du Djado*

Toummo
Wour
Aozou
Bardai
Bette 2286
Tarso Ouri
Ouri

*Adrar
des
Iforas*

Anou
Aïn Elhaoua

Tassili oua-n-Ahaggar
Admer

Djado
Séguédine

Plateau du Tchigaï
Zouar
Tibesti
3265
Tarso Ahon

In Tasik

Mt. Gréboun 1994

*Ténéré du
Tafassasset*

Aney

Emi Koussi
Gouro

BORKOU-ENNEDI-TIBESTI

In Abbangarit

*Air
(Azbine)*

1795
Iferouâne
Sidaouet

A G A D E Z

Bilma

Grand Erg de Bilma

Aïn Galakka
Largeau

Ennedi Yoo

N I G E R

B o d é l é

Koro
Toro

Teguidda
I-n-Tessoum
Agadez
I-n-Gall

DIFFA

KANEM

Tegouma

Nokou
Mao
Zigey

C H A D

BATHA

TAHOUA

Tamaské
Tanout

508

Boultoum
Gangara

Nguigmi
Bosso
Bol
LAC
Lake Chad
(Lac Tchad)

Massakory
Lac Fitri
Yao
Ati

Batha

Ouallam
Filingué
Tahoua
Illéla
Madaoua

Gada
Birni
N'Konni

ZINDER

Gouré
Diffa

Nokou

Mongo
CHARI-BAGUIRMI
N'Djamena

NIAMEY
Gothèye
Niamey
Loga
Dosso
Say

Matankari
Gwadabawa
Binji
Argungu
Sokoto

Wurno
Isa
Sokoto
Sabon Birni

MARADI
Maradi
Kantché
Tessaoua
Zinder

Matsena
Nguru
Gashua

Zari

Gubio
Plain of Bornu
Marte

Ngala
Kousseri
Zigey

Massenya
Ergig
GUERA
Abou Deïa
Melfi

DOSSO
Karimama

Gwarzo
Talata Mafara
Gusau

Kaura Namoda
Yashi

Gamiawa
Lantewa

BORNO
Titiwa
Dikwa
Maiduguri

Gombe
Yagoua
Bongor
Bousso

Gélengdeng
Mindif
Kaélé

Chari

Banikoara
Goya
Kamba
Jega
SOKOTO
Zamfara
Ka
Anka

Runka
Chafe
Maru
Funtua
Katsina
Daura
Kazaure

Hadejia
Gumel
Ringim
Gamawa
Azare
Jamaari

Kano
KANO
Gana
Potiskum
Damaturu
Masba
Bama

Goniri
Yajua

Biu
Mubi

Maroua
TANDJILÉ
Léré
Pala
Lai
Kélo

MOYEN
CHARI
Sarh
Kyabé
Bahr Aouk

BENIN
Gogonou
Gamia

Yelwa
Kainji Res.

Zuru
Birnin
Gwari

Danja
Zaria
KADUNA
Kaduna
Kajuru

Anchau
Lame
Bauchi
BAUCHI
Bara

Foggo
Kapo
Nafada
Buni
Chibuk

Ako
Gombe
Garko
Yan
Mora

Mbang
Léré

Nikki
Ndali
Gwaseró
Kaiama
Bokani
Eban

New Bussa
NIGER
Zungeru
Tegina
Minna

Gwagwada
Kafanchan
Bukuru
Jos
*Jos
plateau*

Pindiga
Numan
Jimeta
Barou
Benoue

1296
Kaélé
Moundou

Gore
Doba
Moïssala

CENTRAL

Okuta
Shaki
Ilorin
KWARA
Offa

Bida
Badeggi
Barol
FED. CAP.
TER.
Keffi
Abuja

Wamba
PLATEAU
Lafia
Nasarawa
Doma

Wukari
GONGOLA
Lau
Jalingo

Poli
Kontcha
Tcholliré

1500

Ngaoundéré
Baïbokoum

Bocaranga
Kouki
Pabua

AFRICAN

Iseyin
Oyo
OYO
Ede
Oshogbo
Ilesha
Ikerre

Egbe
Lokoja
Makurdi

Riti
Donga
Beli
Mayo Daga

Dibi

Bétaré Oya
Baboua

Garoua Boulaï

Bocaranga

Batangafo

REPUBLIC

Ibadan
Ife
Akure
Owo
Oka
Kabba
Dekina
Ankpa
BENUE
Gboko
Katsina-Ala

Wum
Bafut
Bamenda

Banyo

Tibati Dyérem
Tignère

Ngaoundéré

Garoua Boulaï

Bouar

Bossangoa
Bouca
Ft. Sibut

Abeokuta
OGUN
Mushin
Ilaro
Ijebu Ode
Okitipupa
ONDO
Auchi
Idah
Nsukka
Oturkpo
Obudu
Ogoja

Mamfe
Foumban
Dschang
Yoko

Woutchaba
Nanga Eboko
Bélabo
Bertoua

Batouri

Carnot
Berbérati
Boda
Bangui
Bimbo

CAMEROON

Cotonou
Porto Novo
Lagos
Benin City
BENDEL
Sapele
Warri
Ughelli
IMO
Onitsha
ANAMBRA
Afikpo
Abakaliki
Ugep
Bende
Umuahia

Bafang
Bafia
Loum
Ndikinimeki
Saa
Minta
Doumé

M'Baiki
Nola
Lipéïté

Gandou

ZAÏRE

Bight of Benin

3261

Bomadi
Yenagoa
RIVERS
Nembe
Aba
Uyo
Oron
Calabar

Buguma
Port Harcourt
Eket
Bonny
Brass

CROSS RIVER

Nkongsamba
Kumba
Yabassi
Mt. Cameroun 4070
Buea
Limbe
Douala

Loum
Saa
Okola
Ayos
Ndélélé

Abong Mbang

Yokadouma

Lomié
Dja

Bania
Bambio

Libenge

Niger Delta

Bonny

Malabo

EQUATORIAL

Edea
Nyong

Yaoundé
Mbalmayo
Zoétélé

Ebolowa
Sangmélima
Ambam

Moloundou
Souflay

CONGO
Impfondo

*Gulf
of
Guinea*

Bight of Bonny

Principe

Bata

GUINEA
GABON

Kribi
Campo
Bitam

ZAÏRE

53

CENTRAL AND EAST AFRICA

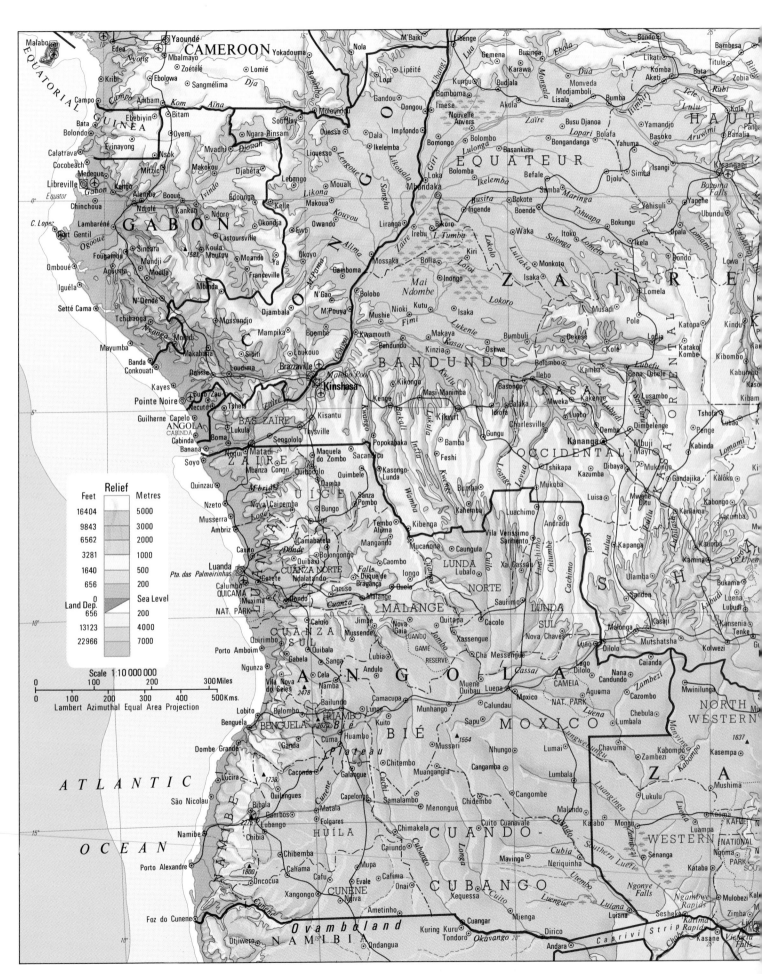

SOUTHERN AFRICA AND MADAGASCAR

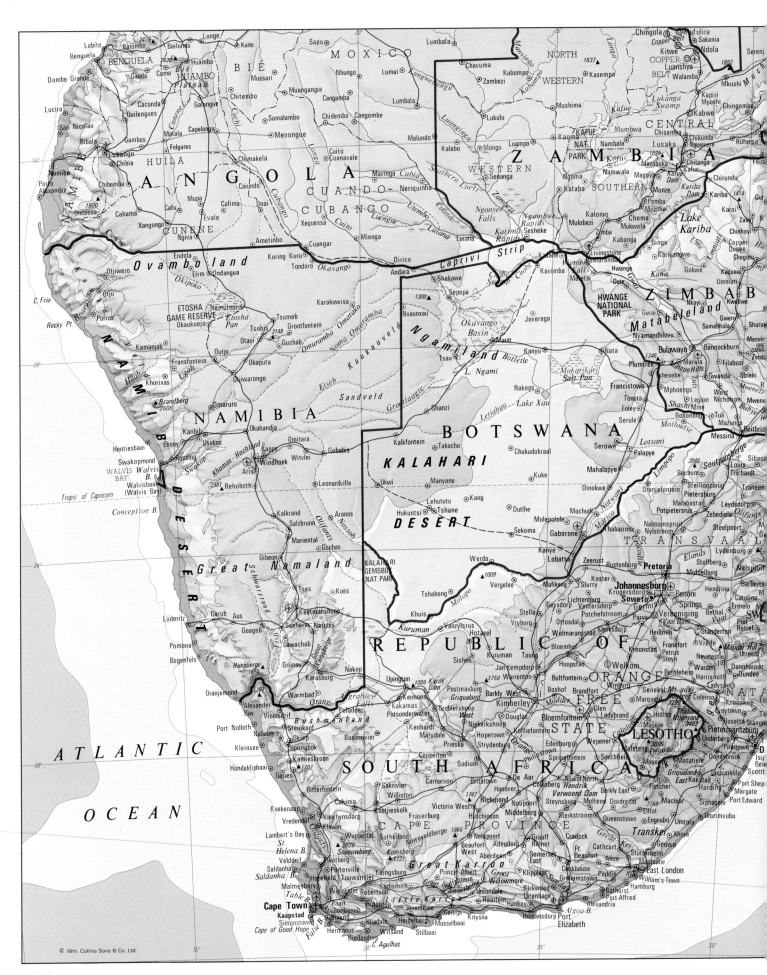

I N D I A N

O C E A N

Mozambique Channel

Relief

Feet		Metres
16 404		5000
9 843		3000
6 562		2000
3 281		1000
1 640		500
656		200
0		Sea Level
Land Dep.		
656		200
13 123		4000
22 966		7000

Scale 1:10 000 000

0   100   200   300 Miles

0   100   200   300   400   500 Kms.

Lambert Azimuthal Equal Area Projection

57

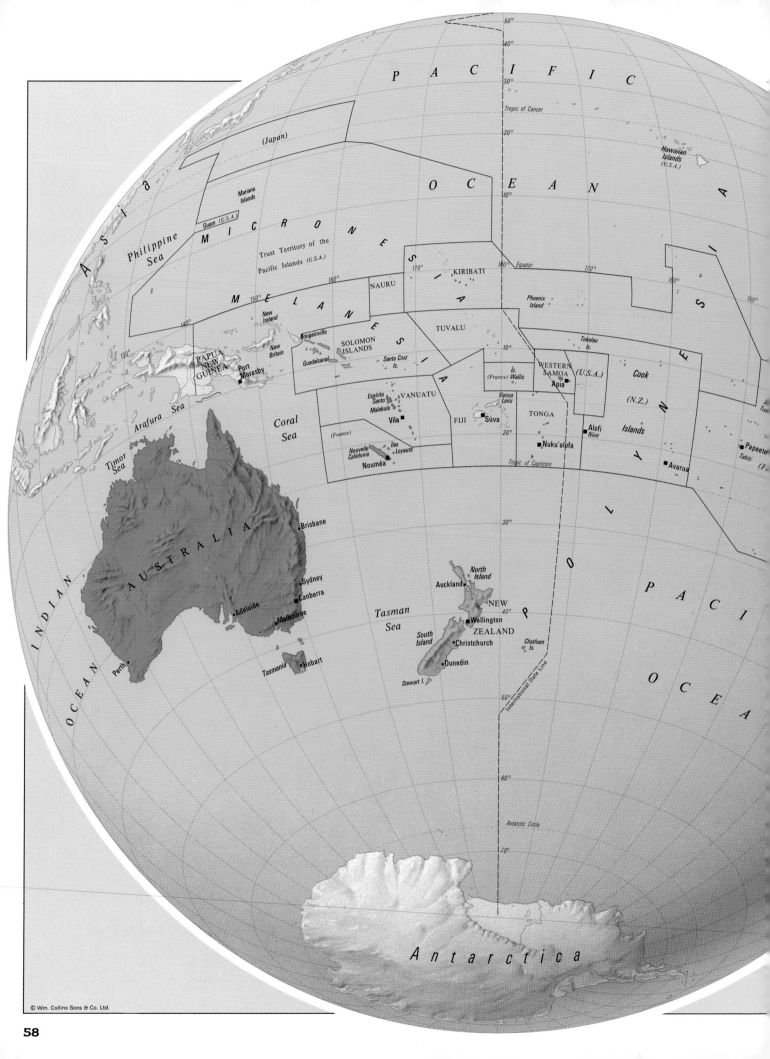

P A C I F I C

Tropic of Cancer

O C E A N

Hawaiian
Islands
(U.S.A.)

A s i a

(Japan)

Philippine
Sea

Mariana
Islands

Guam (U.S.A.)

M I C R O N E S I A

Trust Territory of the
Pacific Islands (U.S.A.)

160°

150°

140°

130°

M E L A N E S I A

NAURU

KIRIBATI

Equator

170°

170°

160°

150°

Phoenix
Island

New
Ireland

Bougainville

New
Britain

SOLOMON
ISLANDS

Guadalcanal

TUVALU

Tokelau
Is.

PAPUA
NEW
GUINEA

Port
Moresby

Santa Cruz
Is.

Is.
(France) Wallis

WESTERN
SAMOA

Apia

(U.S.A.)

Cook

Arafura Sea

Coral
Sea

Espiritu
Santo
Malekula

VANUATU

Vila

Vanua
Levu

FIJI   Suva

TONGA

Alofi
Niue

(N.Z.)

Islands

Papeete
Tahiti (Fr

Timor
Sea

(France)

Nouvelle
Calédonie

Iles
Loyauté

Nouméa

Tropic of Capricorn

Nuku'alofa

Avarua

P O L Y N E S I A

P A C I

Brisbane

30°

A U S T R A L I A

Sydney

Adelaide

Canberra

Melbourne

North
Island

Auckland

NEW

Tasman
Sea

ZEALAND

Wellington

40°

P A C I

Perth

Tasmania   Hobart

South
Island

Christchurch

Chatham
Is.

I N D I A N

O C E A N

Dunedin

Stewart I.

O C E A

International Date Line

50°

60°

Antarctic Circle

70°

A n t a r c t i c a

OCEANIA

Oceania as a continental name is used for the area extending from Australia in the west, to the most easterly island of Polynesia and from New Zealand in the south, to the Hawaiian Islands in the north. Australasia is that portion of Oceania which lies between the equator and 47°S but in general the term is not often used because of confusion with Australia the country name.

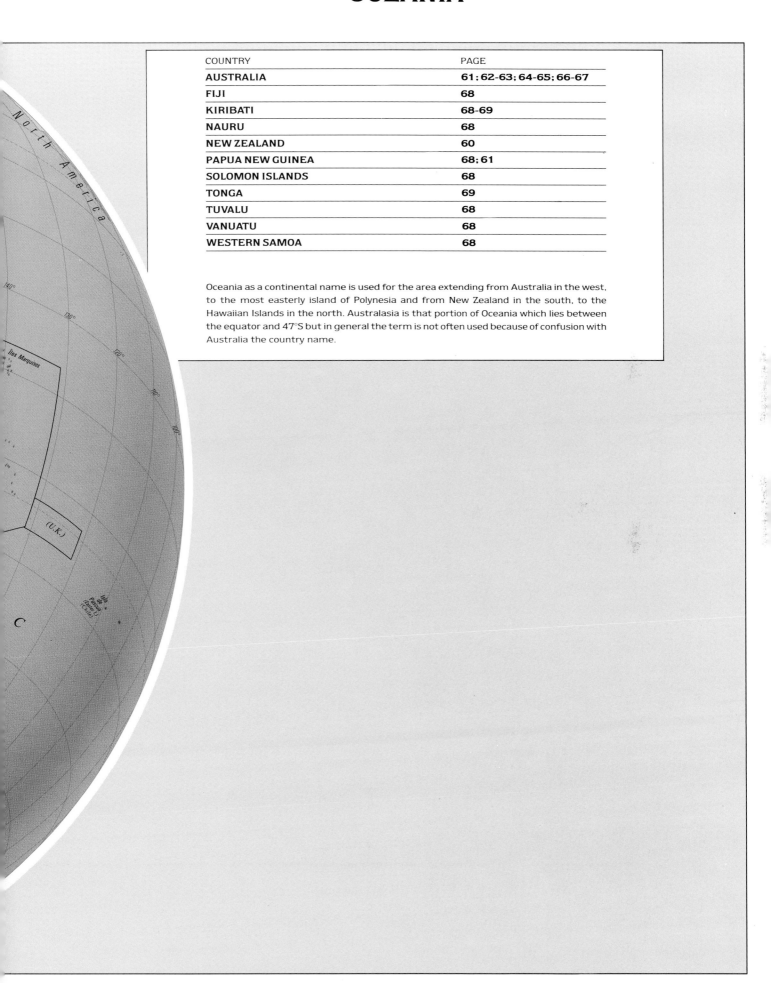

NEW ZEALAND

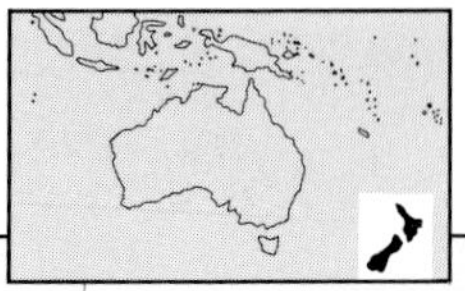

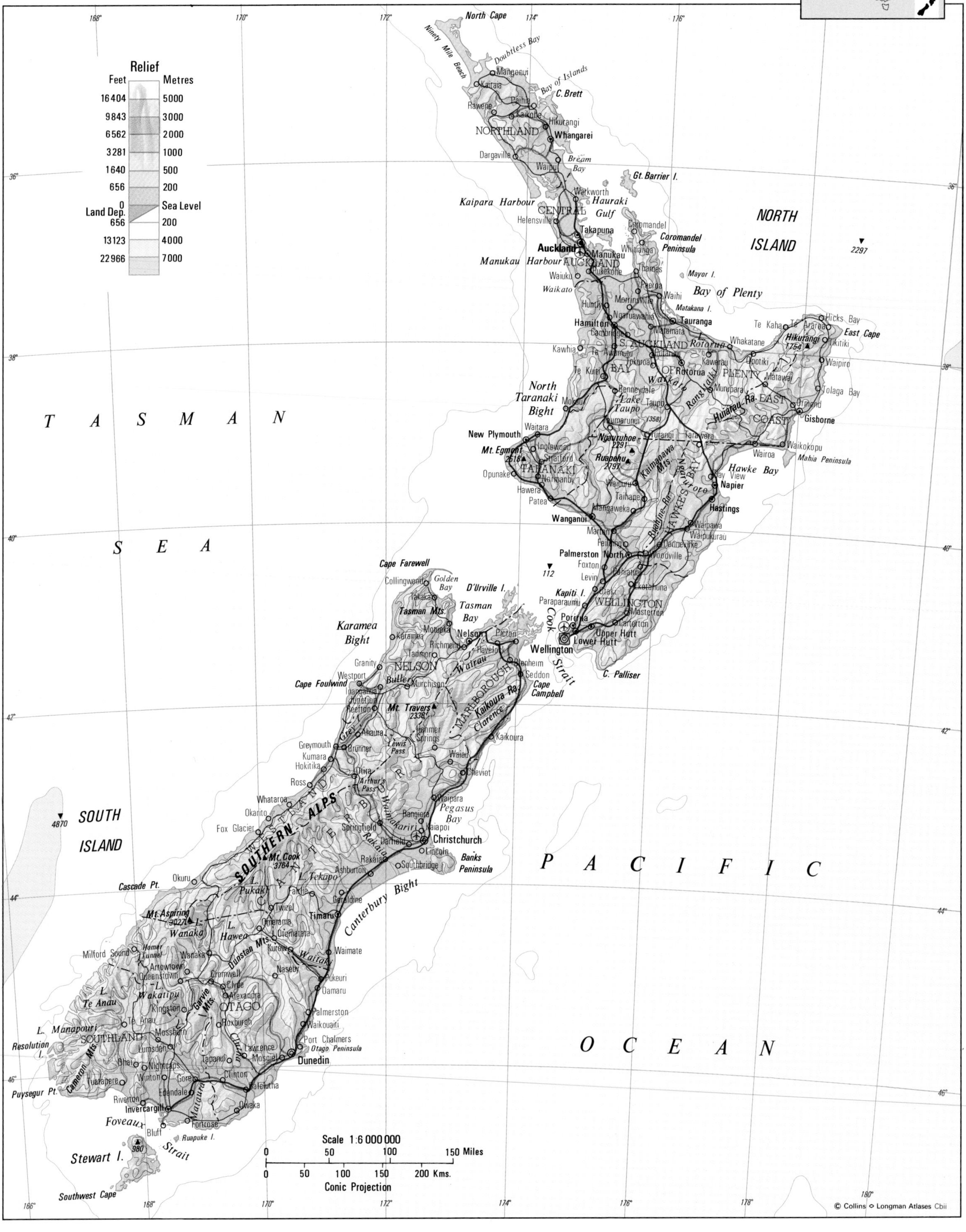

Relief

Feet		Metres
16 404		5000
9 843		3000
6 562		2000
3 281		1000
1 640		500
656		200
0		Sea Level

Land Dep.

656		200
13 123		4000
22 966		7000

North Cape

Ninety Mile Beach

Doubtless Bay

Mangonui
Karaia
Rawene
Pahia
Bay of Islands
C. Brett
Kaikohe
Hikurangi
NORTHLAND
Whangarei

Dargaville
Waipu
Bream Bay

Gt. Barrier I.

Warkworth
Kaipara Harbour
CENTRAL
Hauraki Gulf
Helensville
Coromandel
Coromandel Peninsula
Takapuna
Whitianga
Auckland
Manukau
AUCKLAND
Manukau Harbour
Waiuku
Pukekohe
Thames
Mayor I.
Waikato
Morrinsville
Paeroa
Waihi
Tauranga
Bay of Plenty
Huntly
Matakana I.
Te Kaha
Hicks Bay
Te Araroa
Hamilton
Cambridge
Matamata
Whakatane
East Cape
Kawhia
S. AUCKLAND
Te Awamutu
Rotorua
Te Kuiti
Tokoroa
Kawerau
Ruatoki
Te Karoa
BAY OF ROTORUA
WAIKATO
PLENTY
Opotiki
Raukumara Ra.
EAST
Hikurangi
1754
Waipiro
Tolaga Bay
Murupara
Matawai

North Taranaki Bight
Mokau
Lake Taupo
Waitara
New Plymouth
Inglewood
Ngauruhoe
2291
Rangitaiki
Hikurangi
Huiarau Ra.
EAST COAST
Gisborne
Mt. Egmont
2518
Stratford
Taumarunui
(358)
Ruapehu
2797
Kaimanawa
TARANAKI MTS.
Eltham
Opunake
Normanby
Waiouru
Tutira
Hay View
Hawke Bay
Hawera
Waipawa
Napier
Patea
Taihape
Mangaweka
Hastings
Waipukurau
Wanganui
HAWKES BAY
Ruahine Ra.
Marton
Feilding
Dannevirke
Palmerston North
Woodville
Foxton
Pahiatua
Levin
112
Kapiti I.
Paraparaumu
WELLINGTON
Masterton
Otaki
Porirua
Carterton
Upper Hutt
Lower Hutt
Wellington
Cook Strait
C. Palliser

NORTH ISLAND
2297

TASMAN SEA

Cape Farewell
Collingwood
Golden Bay
D'Urville I.
Takaka
Tasman Mts.
Tasman Bay
Karamea Bight
Karamea
Motueka
Nelson
Picton
Richmond
Granity
Tadmor
Havelock
Blenheim
Westport
Cape Foulwind
Inangahua
NELSON
Murchison
Wairau
MARLBOROUGH
Seddon
Cape Campbell
Buller
Reefton
Mt. Travers
2338
Hanmer Springs
Kaikoura Ra.
Greymouth
Ahaura
Clarence
Kumara
Brunner
Lewis Pass
Waiau
Kaikoura
Hokitika
Grey
Otira
Arthur's Pass
Ross
THE BULLER
Hanmer Springs
Waipara
Cheviot
Whataroa
Rakaia
Waimakariri
Rangiora
Okarito
SOUTHERN ALPS
Springfield
Kaiapoi
Pegasus Bay
Fox Glacier
Darfield
Christchurch
Okuru
Mt. Cook
3764
Rakaia
Lincoln
4870
Tekapo
Ashburton
Southbridge
Banks Peninsula
Pukaki
THE
Cascade Pt.
Mt. Aspiring
3027
L. Wanaka
Fairlie
Geraldine
Canterbury Bight
Twizel
SOUTH ISLAND
Hamer Tunnel
Wanaka
L. Hawea
Omarama
Timaru
Milford Sound
Arrowtown
Dunstan Mts.
Kurow
Waimate
L. Te Anau
Queenstown
Clyde
Waitaki
L. Wakatipu
Cromwell
Naseby
Pokeuri
Kingston
Alexandra
Oamaru
Te Anau
Garvie Mts.
OTAGO
Roxburgh
Palmerston
L. Manapouri
Mossburn
Waikouaiti
Resolution I.
SOUTHLAND
Lumsden
Lawrence
Port Chalmers
Otago Peninsula
Ohai
Nightcaps
Clutha
Mosgiel
Dunedin
Puysegur Pt.
Cameron Mts.
Tuatapere
Winton
Gore
Clinton
Mataura
Balclutha
Riverton
Edendale
Invercargill
Owaka
Foveaux Strait
Fortrose
Bluff
Ruapuke I.
Stewart I.
980
Southwest Cape

PACIFIC OCEAN

Scale 1:6 000 000

0	50	100	150 Miles

| 0 | 50 | 100 | 150 | 200 Kms. |

Conic Projection

© Collins ◇ Longman Atlases Cbii

AUSTRALIA

WESTERN AUSTRALIA

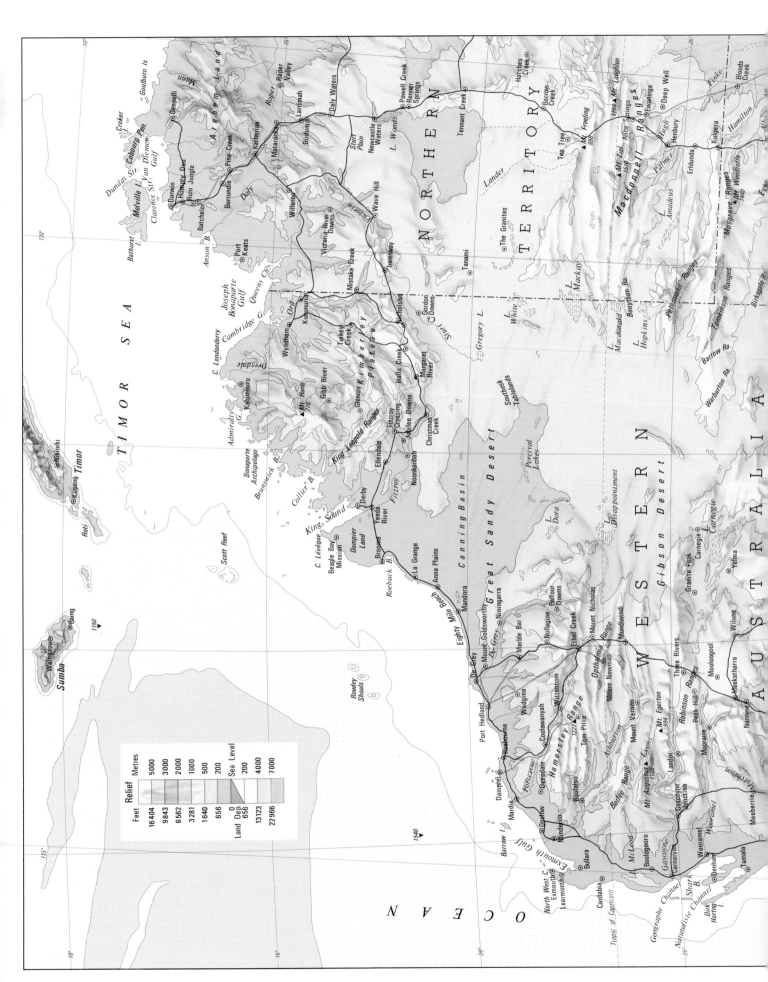

TIMOR SEA

Goulburn Is
Croker
Croker
Dundas Str.
Coburg Pen.
Van Diemen Gulf
Bathurst I.
Melville I.
Clarence Str.
Anson B.
Darwin
Batchelor
Humpty Doo
Rum Jungle
Burrundie
Pine Creek
Port Keats
Joseph Bonaparte Gulf
Queens Ch.
Cambridge G.
C. Londonderry
C. Londonderry
Drysdale
Admiralty G.
Kalumburu
Bonaparte Archipelago
Brunswick B.
Collier B.
King Sound
C. Lévêque
Beagle Bay Mission
Dampier Land
Broome
Roebuck B.
La Grange
Anna Plains
Eighty Mile Beach
Mandora
Roti
Kupang Timor
Timor
Sumba
Waingapu
Baing
Nikiniki
Rowley Shoals
Scott Reef
Dampier
Onslow

Arnhem Land
Mann
Oenpelli
Roper
Roper Valley
Katherine
Mataranka
Daly Waters
Larrimah
Birdum
Willeroo
Daly
Wave Hill
Victoria River Downs
Inverway
Victoria
Mistake Creek
Kununurra
Nicholson
Ord
Wyndham
Turkey Creek
Halls Creek
Margaret River
Gordon Downs
Gibb River
Mt. Ham
King Leopold Ranges
Glenoy
Fitzroy Crossing
Jubilee Downs
Christmas Creek
Ellendale
Noonkanbah
Derby
Yeeda River
Fitzroy

NORTHERN TERRITORY
Powell Creek
Renner Springs
Newcastle Waters
L. Woods
Barrow Creek
Tennant Creek
Sturt Plain
Tea Tree
Mt. Freeling 998
Mt. Zeil 1510
Alice Springs
Ewaninga
Deep Well
Hugh
Henbury
Erldunda
Kulgera
Hamilton
Finke
Bloods Creek
Mt. Laughlen
MacDonnell Ranges
Palmer
Musgrave Ranges
Mt. Woodroffe 1440
Birksgate Ra.
L. Amadeus
Petermann Ranges
Tomkinson Ranges
Warburton Ra.
Barrow Ra.
Lander
Tanami
The Granites
Stirt
Gregory L.
L. Mackay
L. White
L. Macdonald
Southesk Tablelands
L. Hopkins
L. Disappointment
L. Dora

WESTERN AUSTRALIA
Great Sandy Desert
Canning Basin
Gibson Desert
Percival Lakes
Granite Peak
Carnegie
Carnegie
Yelma
Wiluna
Mount Goldsworthy
Marble Bar
Niningarra
Nullagine
Balfour Downs
Mount Nicholas
Mundiwindi
Three Rivers
Mooloogool
De Grey
Da Grey
Wodgina
Ethel Creek
Mount Newman
Mount Egerton 904
Nannine
Meekatharra
Ophthalmia Range
Port Hedland
Roebourne
Coolawanyah
Wittenoom
Hamersley Range 1227
Tom Price
Mount Vernon
Peak Hill
Robinson Ranges
Ashburton
Mt. Augustus 1105
Landor
Moorarie
Barlee Range
Lyons
Dampier
Nanutarra
Pannawonica
Wandagee
Fortescue
Boolatoo
Deepdale
Mardie
Minderoo
Gascoyne Junction
Gascoyne
Boologooro
Wooramel
Wooramel
Woorameł
Meeberrie
Barrow I.
North West C.
Exmouth
Learmonth
Cardabia
Bullara
Exmouth Gulf
McLeod
Carnarvon
Geographe Channel
Shark B.
Denham
Dirk Hartog I.
Naturaliste Channel
Tamala
Hutt

INDIAN OCEAN

Tropic of Capricorn

Relief

Feet	Metres
16404	5000
9843	3000
6562	2000
3281	1000
1640	500
656	200
0	Sea Level
Land Dep. 656	200
13123	4000
22966	7000

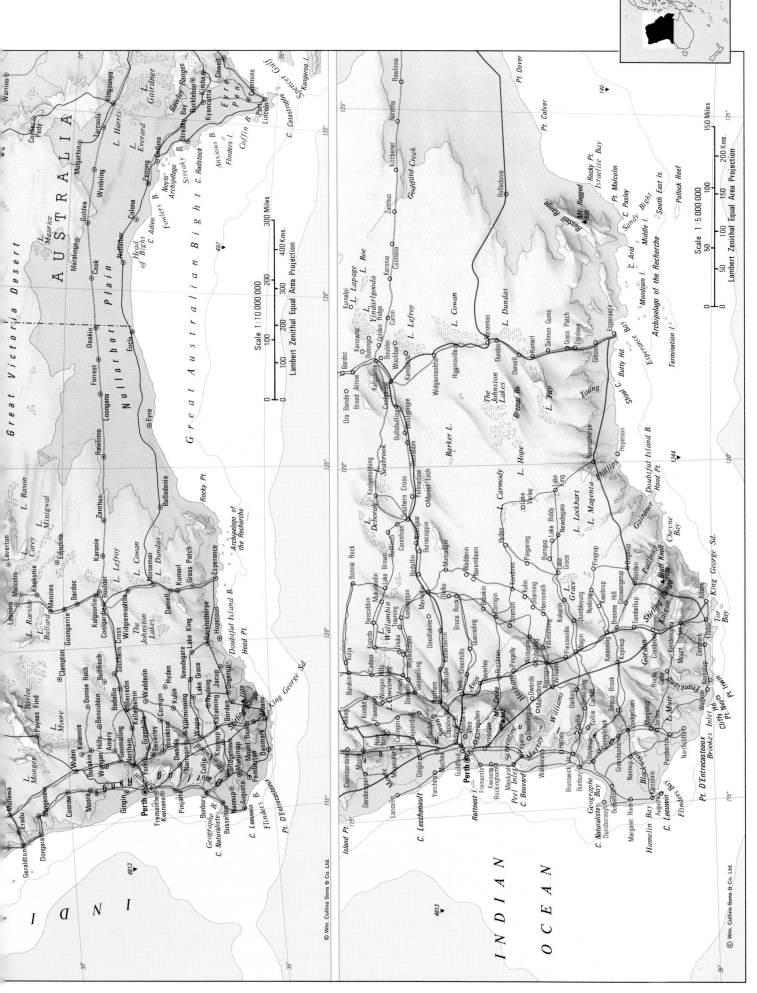

INDIAN OCEAN

AUSTRALIA

Great Victoria Desert

Nullarbor Plain

Great Australian Bight

Spencer Gulf

Eyre Pen.

Scale 1:10 000 000
Lambert Zenithal Equal Area Projection

Scale 1:5 000 000
Lambert Zenithal Equal Area Projection

Perth

Russell Range

Archipelago of the Recherche

Stirling Range

King George Sd.

© Wm. Collins Sons & Co. Ltd.

© Wm. Collins Sons & Co. Ltd.

63

EASTERN AUSTRALIA

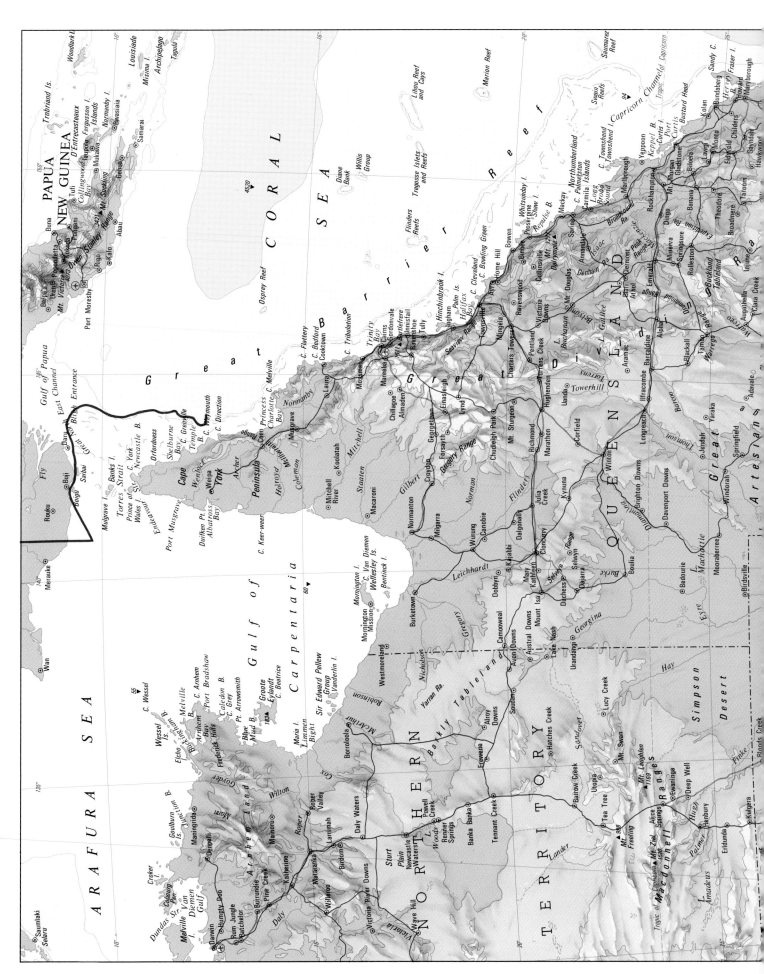

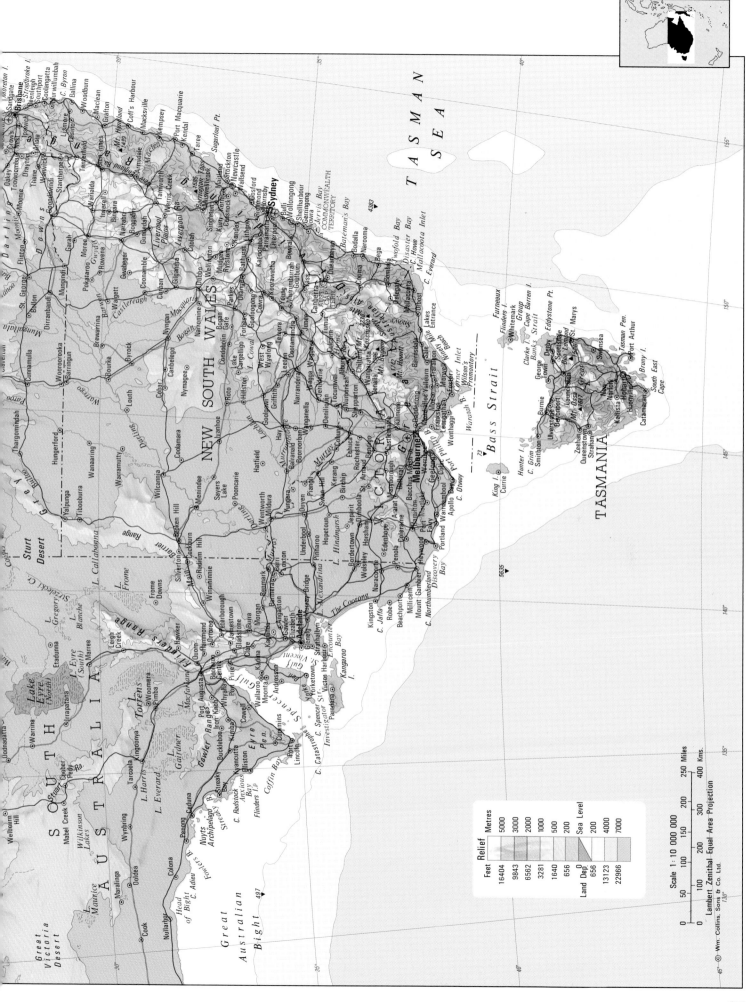

SOUTHEAST AUSTRALIA

PACIFIC OCEAN

HAWAIIAN ISLANDS
(U.S.A.)

Scale 1:10 000 000

KIRITIMATI (CHRISTMAS I.)
(Kiribati)

Scale 1:2 500 000

TONGA

Scale 1:7 500 000

MARQUESAS ISLANDS
(France)

Scale 1:10 000 000

EASTER ISLAND
(Chile)

Scale 1:1 000 000

SOCIETY ISLANDS
(France)

TAHITI
(France)

Scale 1:2 500 000

Îles de la Société
(Society Islands)

Scale 1:7 500 000

Scale 1:60 000 000

0 200 400 600 800 1000 Miles
0 400 800 1200 1600 Kms.

Modified Zenithal Equidistant Projection

69

Asia

Europ

ARCTIC OCEAN

Ellesmere I.

GREENLAND
(Den.)

Denmark
Strait

Arctic Circle

Parry Islands

Baffin
Bay

Bering Strait

ALASKA
U.S.A.

Anchorage

Baffin Island

Godthåb/
Nuuk

Victoria
Island

Hudson
Bay

International Date Line

C A N A D A

Newfoundland

Edmonton

50°

Seattle   Vancouver

Winnipeg

Quebec

Montreal
Ottawa

Portland

U N I T E D   S T A T E S

Toronto

Hamilton   Buffalo
Detroit   Paterson
Newark   Boston

40°

Milwaukee
Chicago   Cleveland   New York
Pittsburgh   Philadelphia
Indianapolis   Baltimore
Cincinnati   Washington

San Francisco
San Jose

O F

Denver

Kansas City   St. Louis

PACIFIC

A M E R I C A

Honolulu

Hawaiian
Islands
(U.S.A.)

Los Angeles   San Bernadino
San Diego
Tijuana

30°

Atlanta

Dallas

BERMUDA

Ciudad
Juárez

I. de
Guadalupe
(Mex.)

Houston   New Orleans

Miami

BAHAMAS

Tropic of Cancer

Gulf of

M E X I C O

Monterray

Mexico   Havana   CUBA   Santiago
de Cuba

20°

PUERTO
RICO

HAITI   DOM.
REP.

León

Is. de
Revilla Gigedo
(Mex.)

Guadalajara

Ciudad
de México

JAMAICA   Port-   Santo
Kingston   au-   Domingo   ST
Prince

Caribbean   Sea

10°

Belmopan
BELIZE

(Neth.)

GUA

Guatemala   Honduras   Tegucigalpa
San Salvador   EL   NICARAGUA
SAL.

180°   150°   Equator

O C E A N

Managua

Panama

COSTA RICA

San José

PANAMA

A

150°   140°   130°   120°   110°   100°   90°   Equator

10°

20°

Tropic of Capricorn

30°

DOM. REP.: DOMINICAN REPUBLIC
EL SAL.: EL SALVADOR
GUA.: GUATEMALA
ST.V. AND G.: ST.VINCENT AND THE GRENADINES

© Wm. Collins Sons & Co. Ltd.

70

NORTH AMERICA

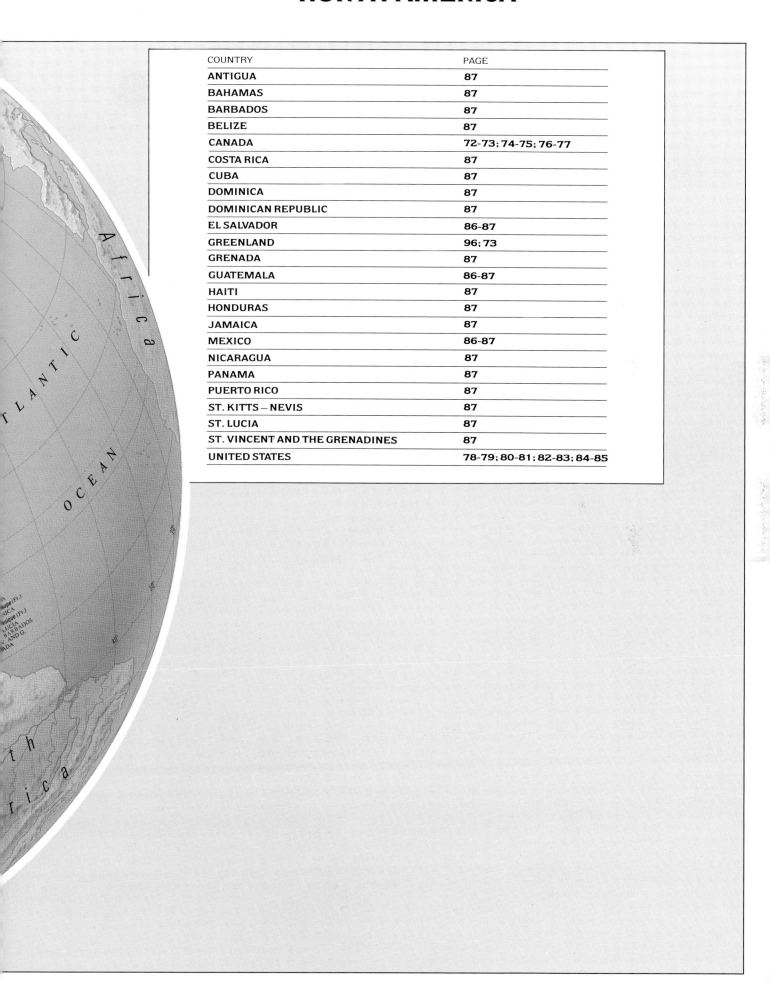

CANADA AND ALASKA

Relief

Feet		Metres
16 404		5000
9843		3000
6562		2000
3281		1000
1640		500
656		200
0		Sea Level
Land Dep.		
656		200
13 123		4000
22 966		7000

Scale 1 : 17 000 000

0 100 200 300 400 500 Miles

0 100 200 300 400 500 600 700 800 Kms.

Bonne Projection

WESTERN CANADA

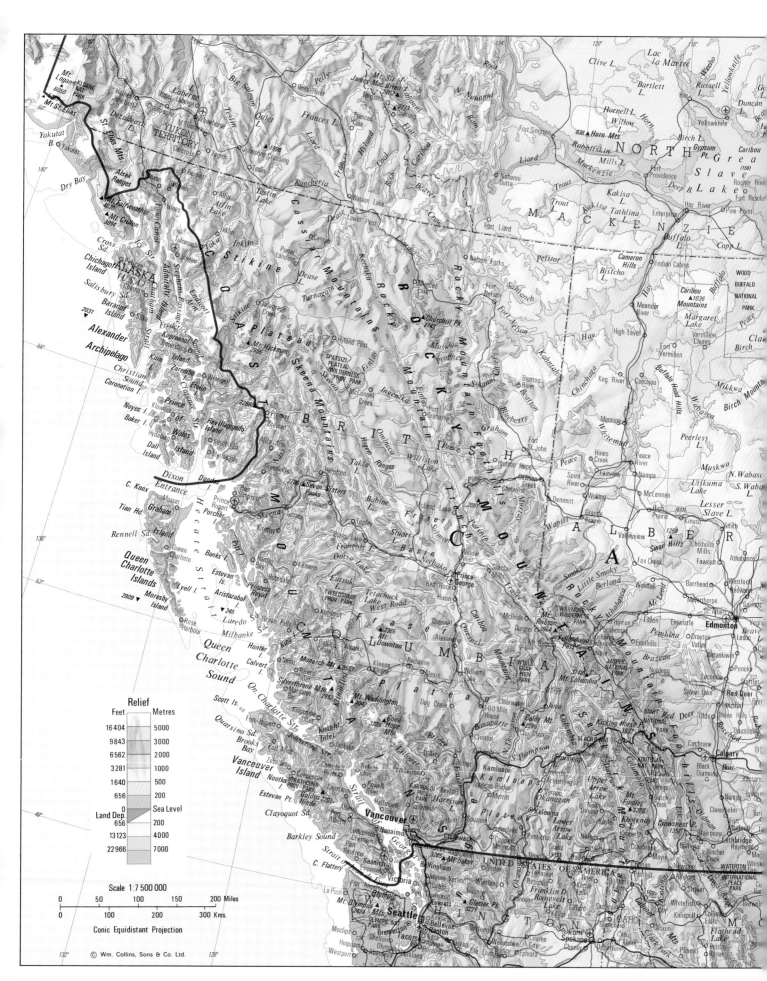

Relief

Feet		Metres
16 404		5000
9843		3000
6562		2000
3281		1000
1640		500
656		200
0		Sea Level
Land Dep.		
656		200
13 123		4000
22 966		7000

Scale 1:7 500 000

0   50   100   150   200 Miles
0   100   200   300 Kms.

Conic Equidistant Projection

© Wm. Collins, Sons & Co. Ltd.

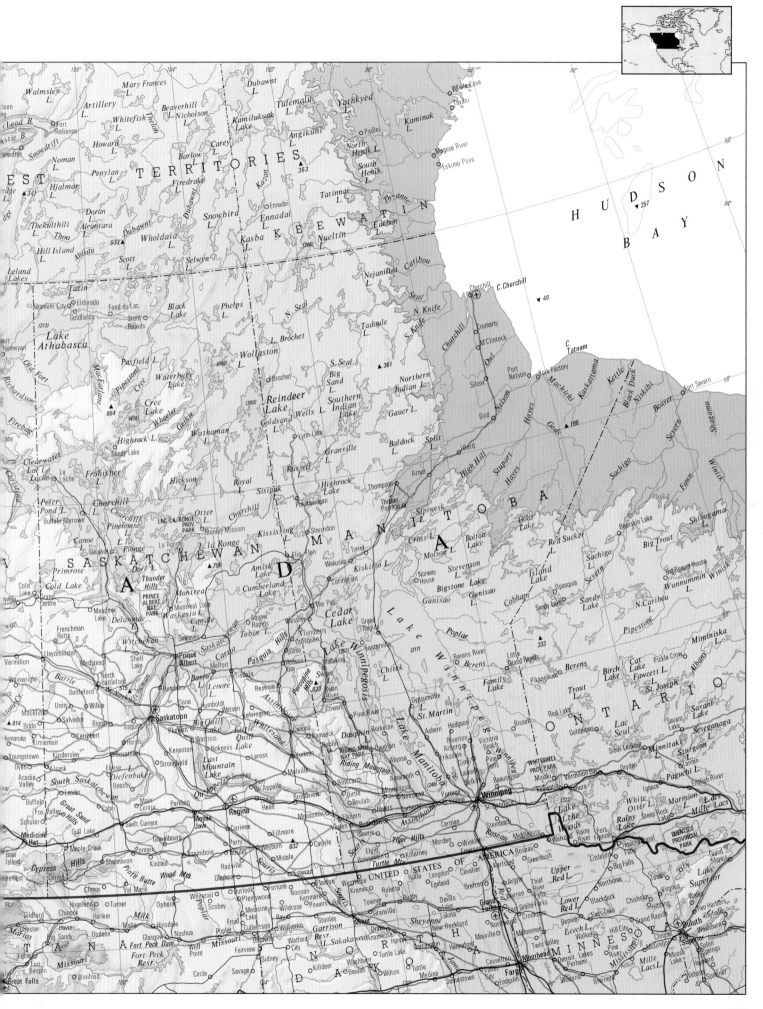

EASTERN CANADA

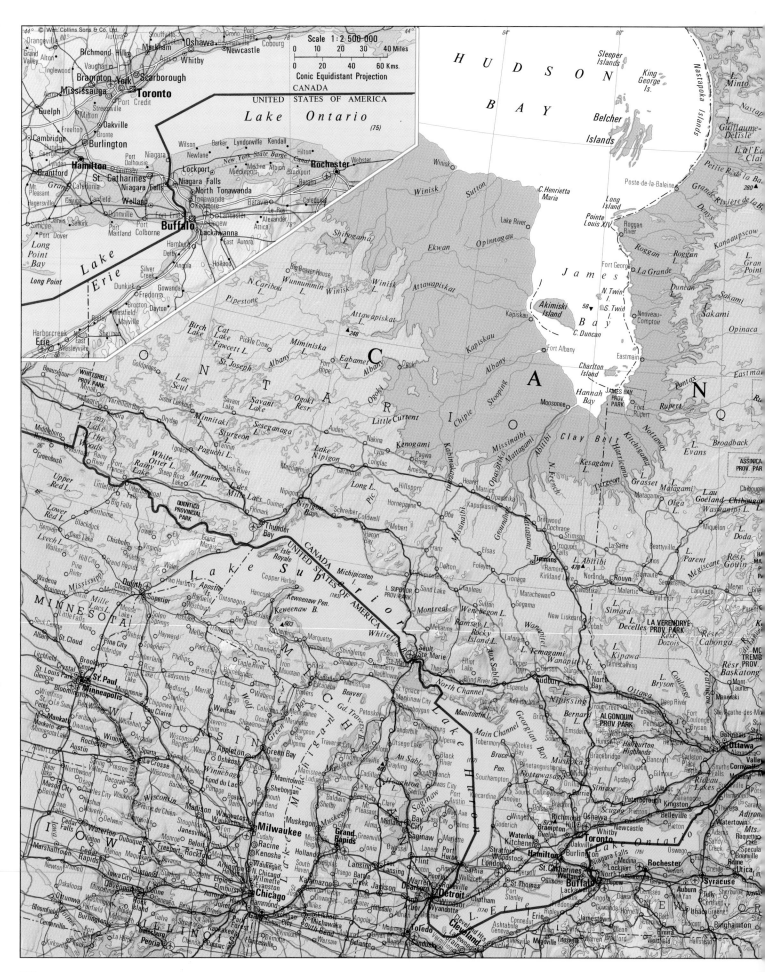

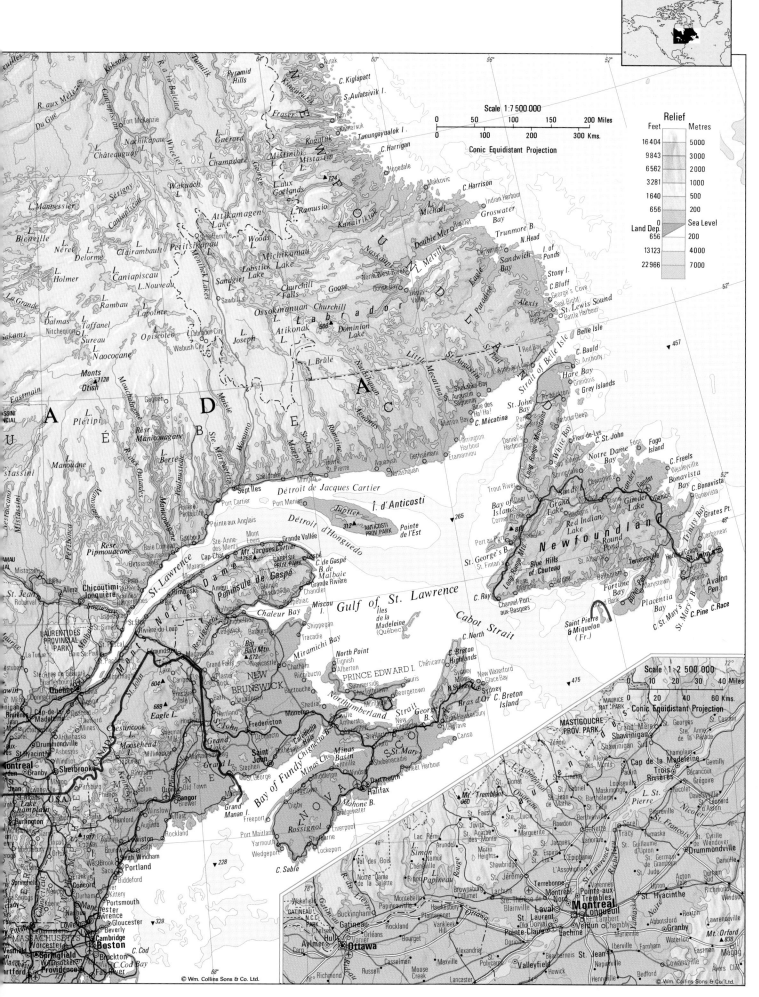

Scale 1:7 500 000

0	50	100	150	200 Miles

0	100	200	300 Kms.

Conic Equidistant Projection

Relief

Feet	Metres
16 404	5000
9843	3000
6562	2000
3281	1000
1640	500
656	200
0	Sea Level
Land Dep.	
656	200
13 123	4000
22 966	7000

© Wm. Collins Sons & Co. Ltd.

Scale 1:2 500 000

0	10	20	30	40 Miles

0	20	40	60 Kms.

Conic Equidistant Projection

© Wm. Collins Sons & Co. Ltd.

77

UNITED STATES

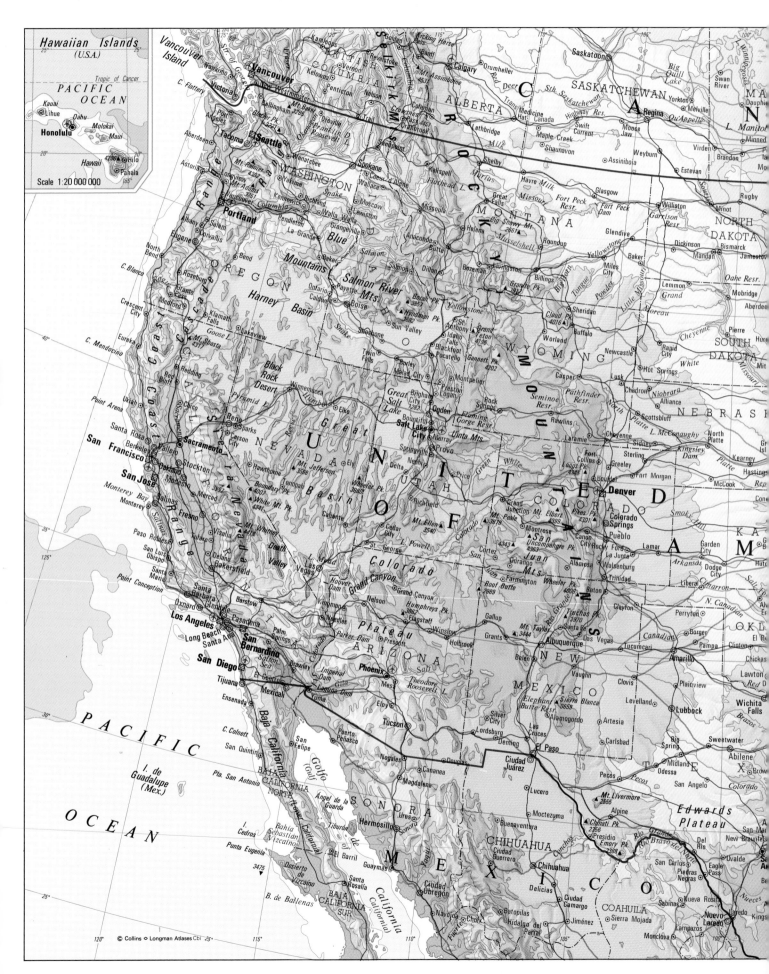

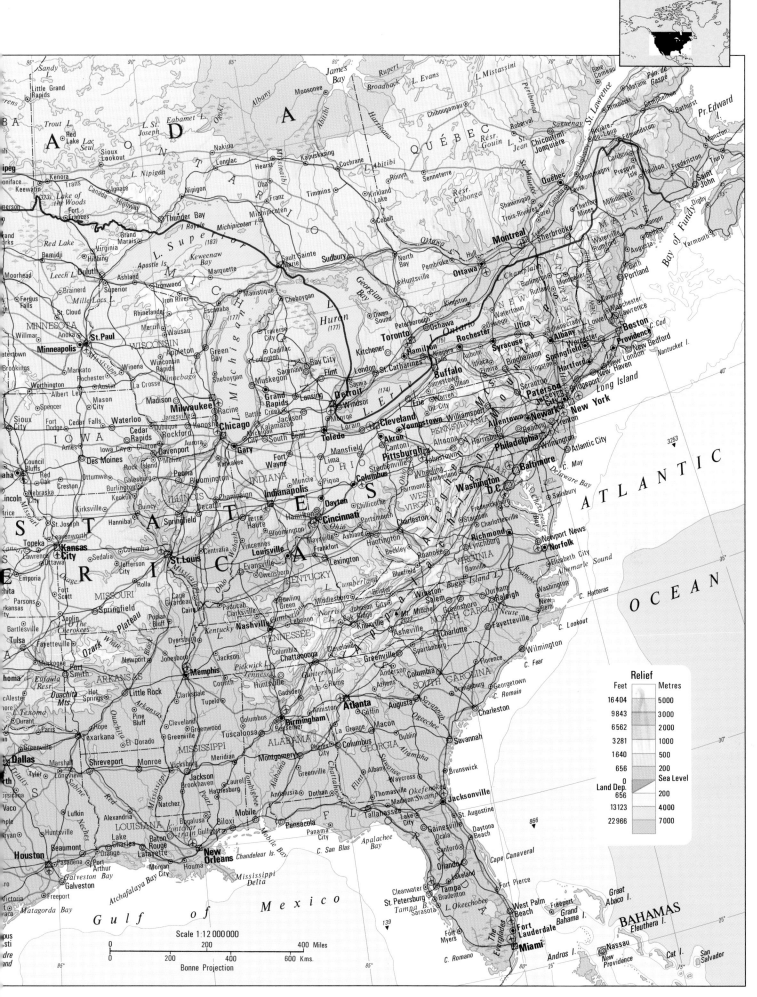

WESTERN UNITED STATES

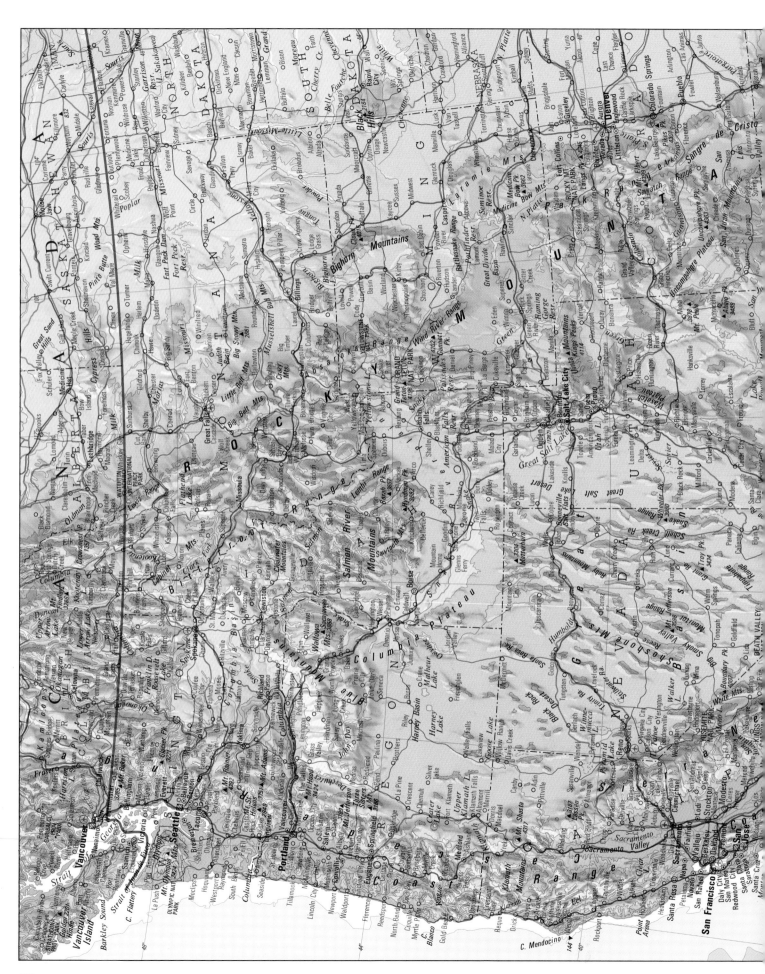

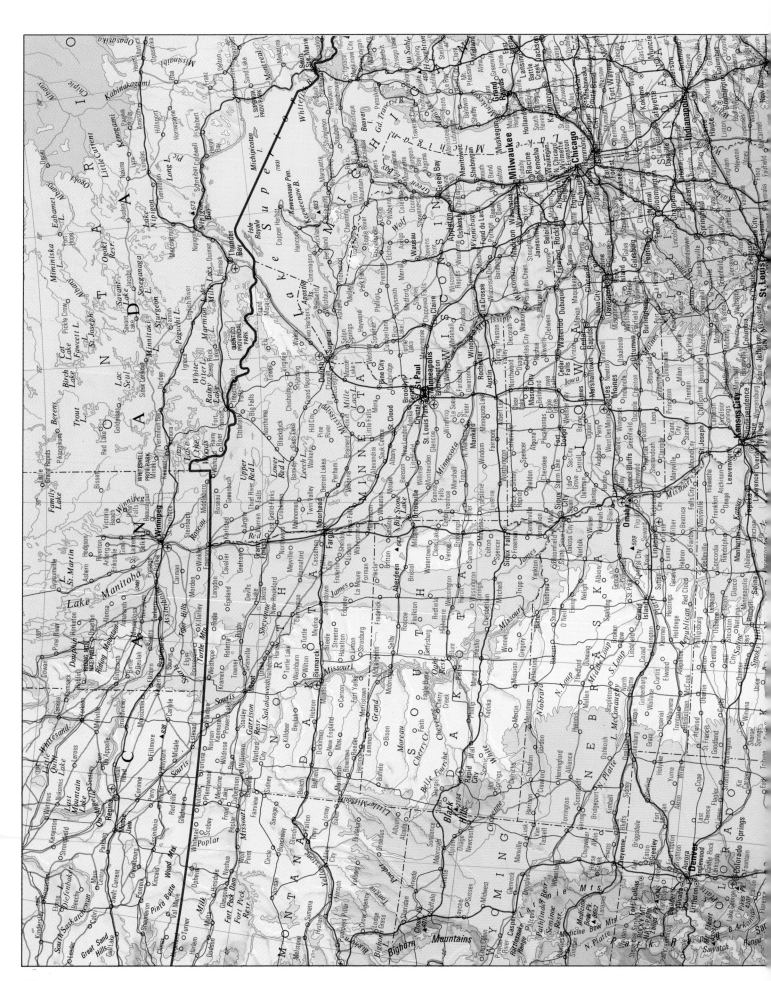

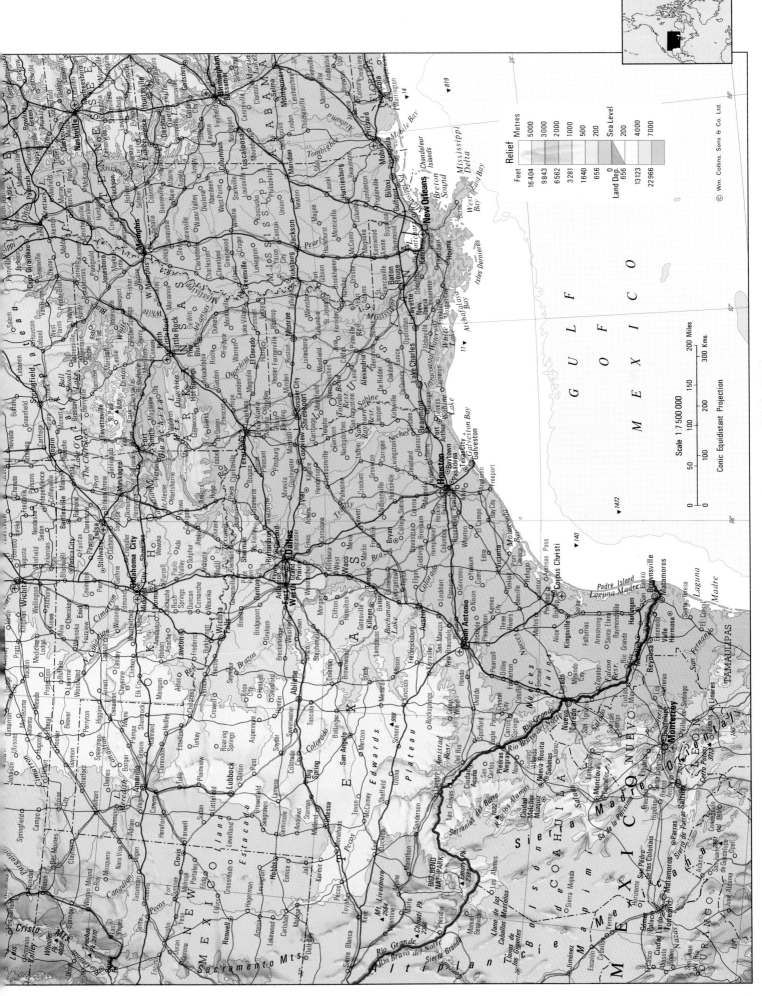

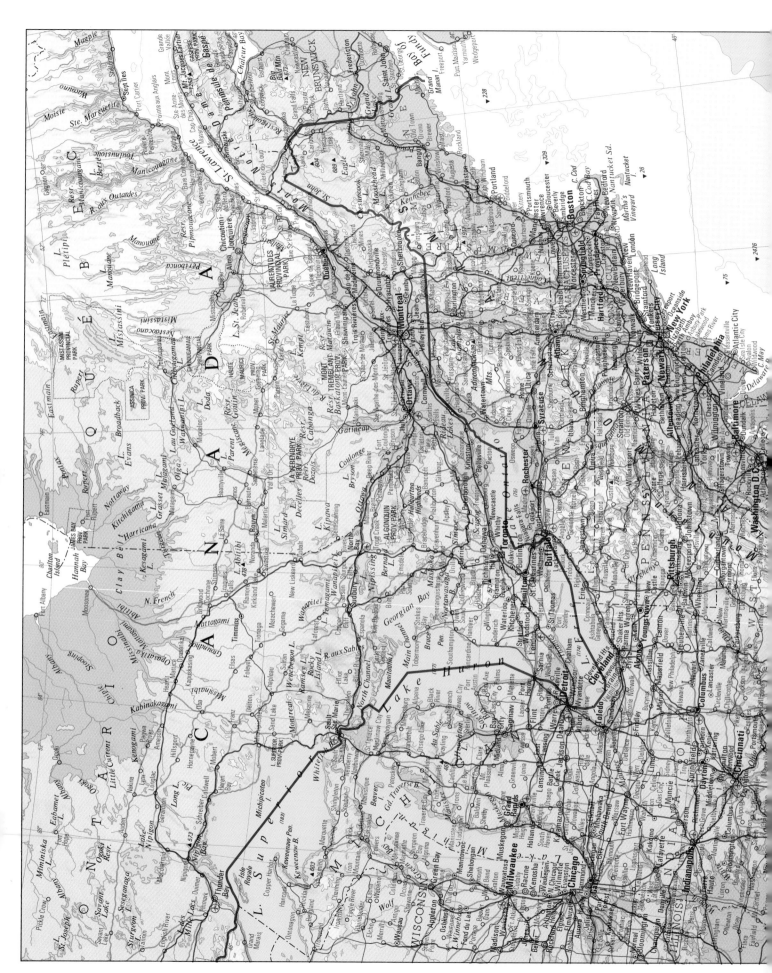

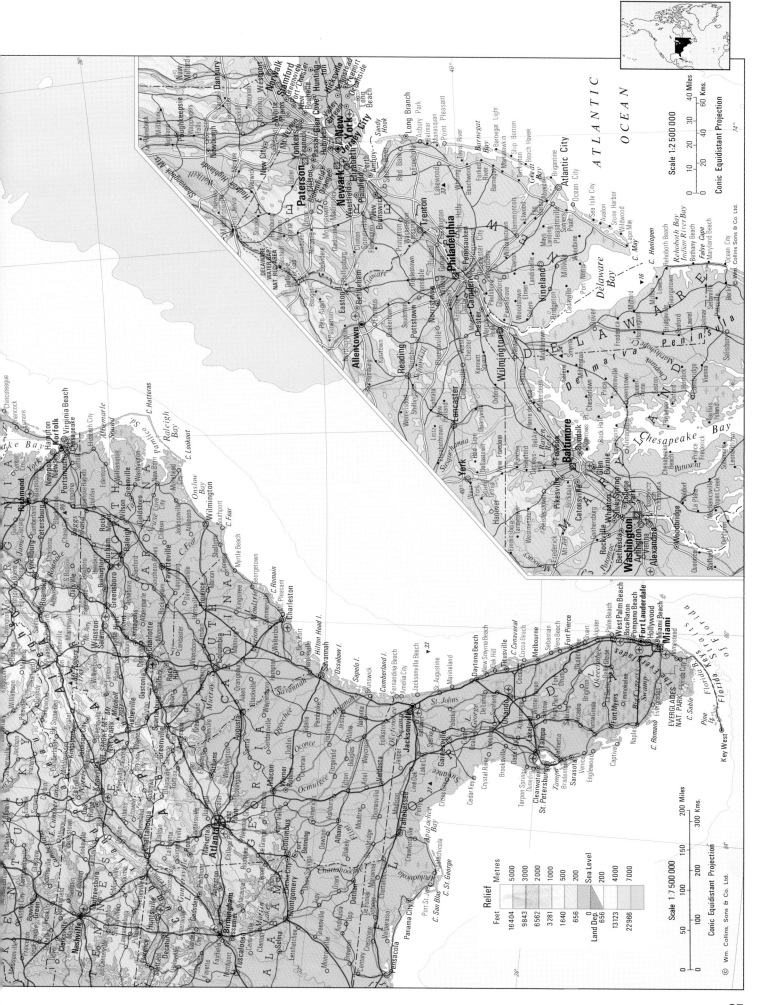

ATLANTIC OCEAN

Scale 1:2 500 000

Conic Equidistant Projection

| 0 | 10 | 20 | 30 | 40 Miles |
| 0 | 20 | 40 | 60 Kms. |

© Wm. Collins Sons & Co. Ltd.

Relief

Feet	Metres
16404	5000
9843	3000
6562	2000
3281	1000
1640	500
656	200
	Sea Level
0	Land Dep.
656	200
13123	4000
22966	7000

Scale 1:7 500 000

Conic Equidistant Projection

| 0 | 50 | 100 | 150 | 200 Miles |
| 0 | 100 | 200 | 300 Kms. |

© Wm. Collins, Sons & Co. Ltd.

CENTRAL AMERICA AND THE CARIBBEAN

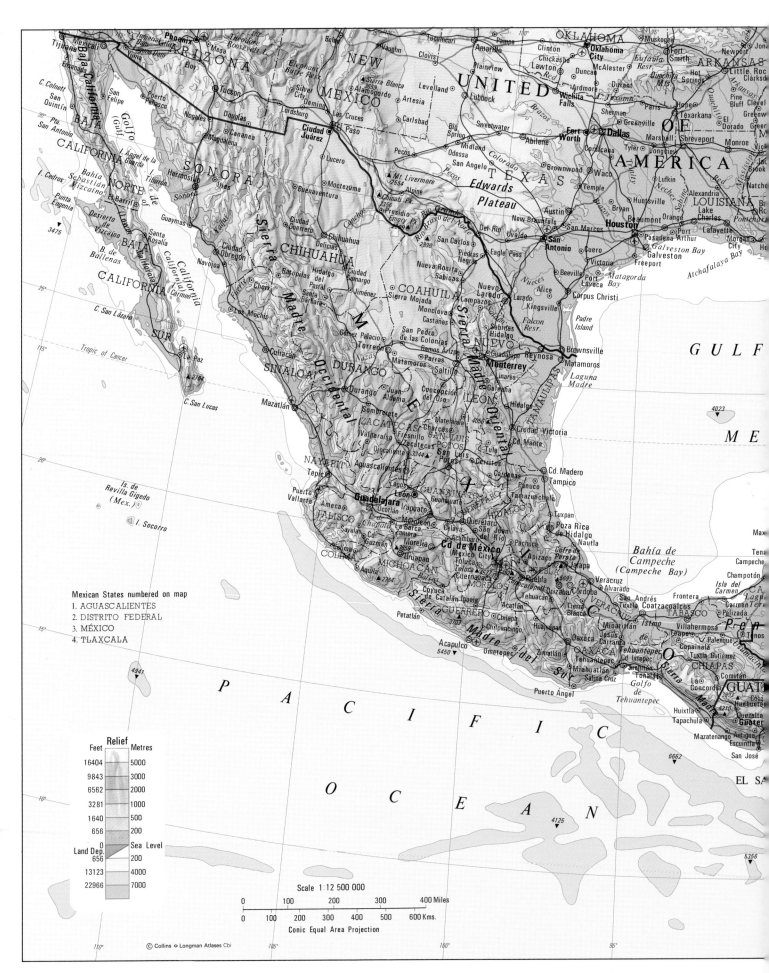

Mexican States numbered on map
1. AGUASCALIENTES
2. DISTRITO FEDERAL
3. MÉXICO
4. TLAXCALA

Relief
Feet		Metres
16404		5000
9843		3000
6562		2000
3281		1000
1640		500
656		200
0		Sea Level
Land Dep.		
656		200
13123		4000
22966		7000

Scale 1:12 500 000

0   100   200   300   400 Miles

0   100 200 300 400 500 600 Kms.

Conic Equal Area Projection

© Collins ◇ Longman Atlases Cbi

86

TENNESSEE
Columbia
Asheville
NORTH
Charlotte
Fayetteville
New Bern
C. Lookout
Chattanooga
Cleveland
Spartanburg
CAROLINA
Huntsville
Greenville
Greenville
SOUTH
Wilmington
Corinth
Tenn.
Anderson
Columbia
Florence
C. Fear
Gadsden
Rome
CAROLINA
TATES
Birmingham
Atlanta
Augusta
Orangeburg
C. Romain
Bessemer
Anniston
Athens
Georgetown
ALABAMA
GEORGIA
Columbus
Macon
Dublin
Savannah
Charleston
Montgomery
Phenix
City
Greenville
Albany
Waycross
ATLANTIC
Andalusia
Dothan
Thomasville
Brunswick
Mobile
Pensacola
Madison
OCEAN
Biloxi
Panama
City
Tallahassee
Jacksonville
Gulfport
Lake City
St. Augustine
Chandeleur
Is
Apalachee
Gainesville
Ocala
Daytona Beach
866
Mississippi
Bay
C. San Blas
Sanford
Delta
Orlando
Cape Canaveral
Clearwater
Lakeland
1137
St. Petersburg
Tampa
Fort Pierce
Sarasota
Bradenton
West
Palm
Great
OF
Fort Myers
Lake
Beach
Freeport
Abaco
Okeechobee
Grand
Bahama I.
C. Romano
Fort
Lauderdale
Eleuthera I.
CO
C. Sable
Miami
Nicolls
Rock Sound
Cat I.
Town
Nassau
San
Key West
Florida Keys
New
Providence
Salvador
Andros
Florida
Andros
Town
The Bight
Straits
Rolleville
Rum Cay
Samana Cay
La Habana
Cárdenas
Archo. de Sabana
Gt.
Exuma
Long I.
(Havana)
Matanzas
Archo. de Camagüey
Plana Cays
Mayaguana I.
Marianao
Sagua
la Grande
Crooked I.
Acklin's I.
Turks and Caicos Is.
Pinar del Río
Güines
Santa Clara
Caibarién
(U.K.)
Guane
Golfo de
Cienfuegos
Sancti
Morón
Ciego de Ávila
Caicos Is.
Turks Is.
Batabanó
Spíritus
Nuevitas
Great
Matthew
Nueva
Archo. de los
Holguín
Inagua I
Town
Gerona
Canarreos
CUBA
Camagüey
Banes
Isla de Pinos
Jardines de la
Victoria
Baracoa
Cap-Haïtien
de las Tunas
Bayamo
S. Luis
Manzanillo
Reina
Sa. Maestra
Guantánamo
Little
Turquino 1971
C. Cruz
Santiago
Cayman
de Cuba
Cayman Brac
Grand Cayman
Cayman Is.
Georgetown
(U.K.)
Montego Bay
St. Ann's Bay
Port
Antonio
Black River
JAMAICA
May Pen
Kingston

87

North America

ATLANTIC

Caribbean Sea

OCEAN

Tropic of Cancer

Barranquilla
Maracaibo • Caracas
TRINIDAD
AND TOBAGO
VENEZUELA
Georgetown
Medellín
Paramaribo
Bogotá
GUYANA
SURINAM
Cayenne
Cali
GUIANA
(Fr.)
COLOMBIA
Belém
Quito
ECUADOR
Islas
Galápagos
(Ec.)
Guayaquil
Fortaleza
B R A Z I L
Equator
P E R U
Recife
Lima
Salvador
La Paz
B O L I V I A
Brasília
PACIFIC
Sucre
Belo
Horizonte
PARAGUAY
Rio de
Janeiro
San Félix (Chile)
San Ambrosio
São Paulo
Santo André
Asunción
Curitiba
Tropic of Capricorn
Islas
Juan
Fernández
(Chile)
Córdoba
Pôrto
Alegre
URUGUAY
Valparaíso
Rosario
OCEAN
Santiago
Buenos
Aires
Montevideo
La Plata
OC
ARGENTINA
CHILE

International Date Line

Falkland
Is. (U.K.)

South
Georgia
(U.K.)

Tierra del
Fuego

Antarctic Circle

Antarctica

© Wm. Collins Sons & Co. Ltd.

88

SOUTH AMERICA

South America as a continental name is used for the land area extending south from the Isthmus of Panama to Cape Horn and lying between 34°W and 82°W. Latin America is a term widely used to cover those parts of the Americas where Spanish, or Portuguese as in Brazil, are the adopted national languages, and thus refers to an area that includes all of South America, Central America, Mexico and the Caribbean, except for the few English, French and Dutch speaking countries and dependencies.

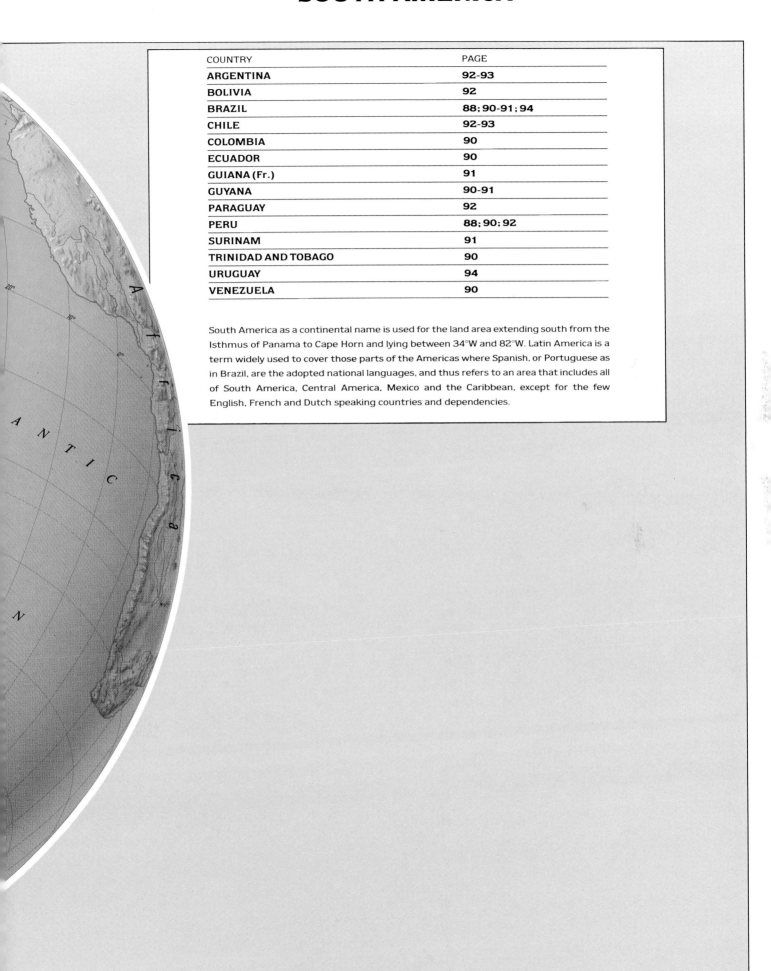

90

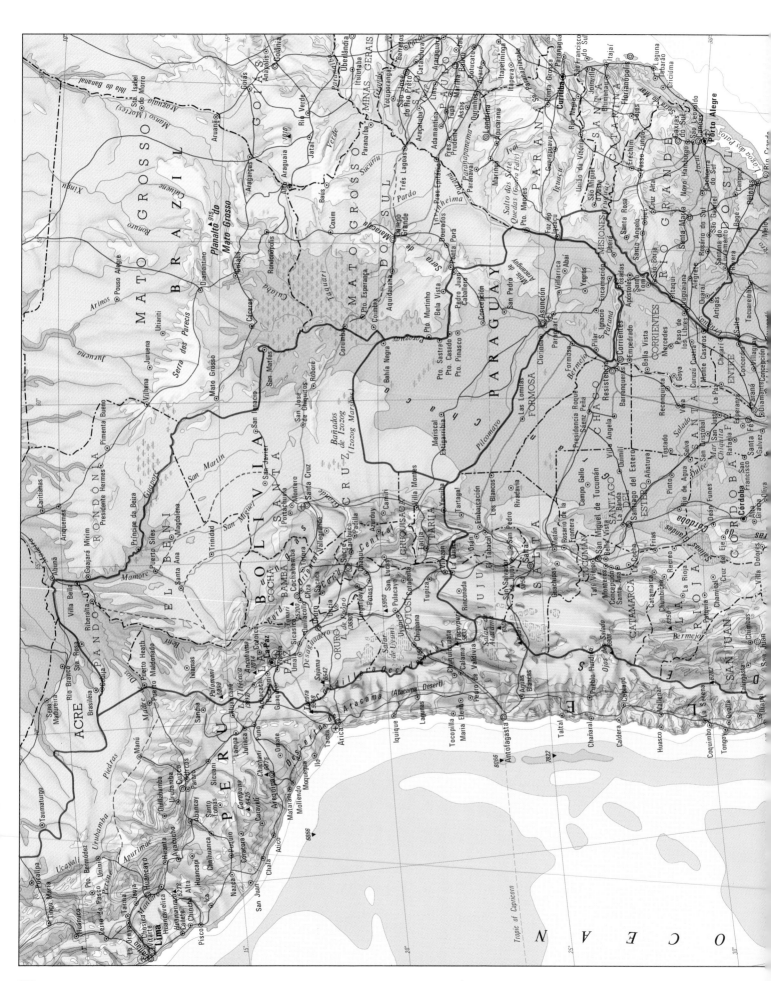

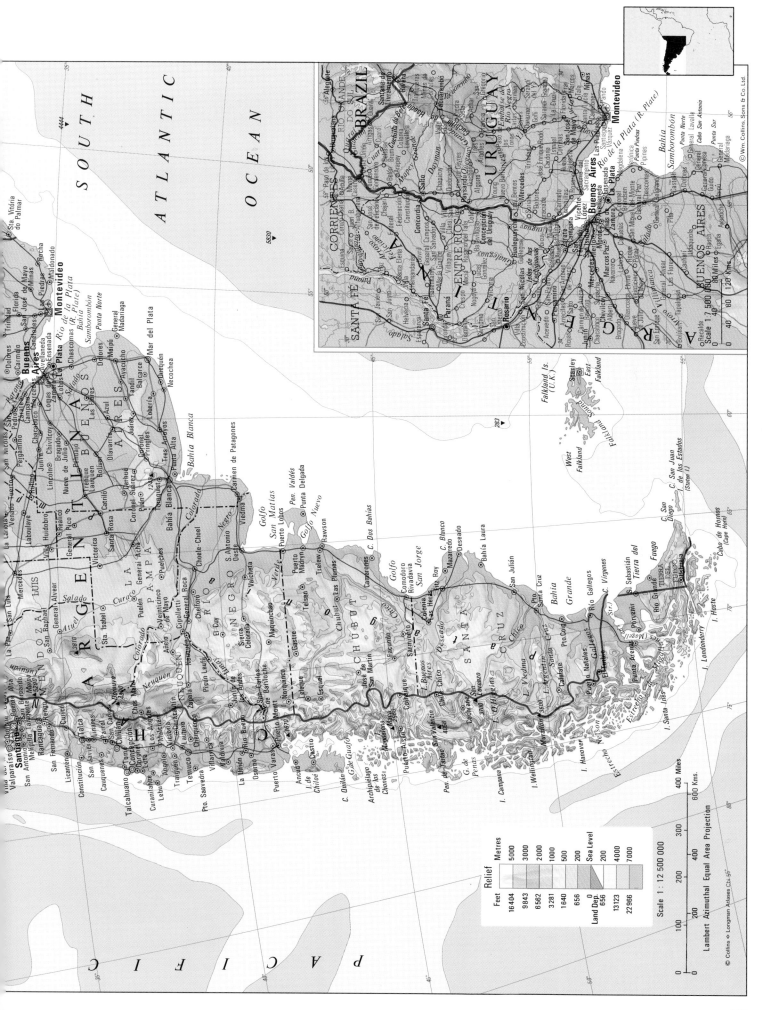

SOUTH

ATLANTIC

OCEAN

•444

•5830

•283

S O U T H

A T L A N T I C

O C E A N

Falkland Is.
(U.K.)

Stanley
East
Falkland

West
Falkland

Falkland Sound

P A C I F I C

P A C I F I C

BRAZIL

URUGUAY

Montevideo

Río de la Plata (R. Plate)

Buenos
Aires

La Plata

Rosario

CORRIENTES

SANTA FÉ

ENTRE RIOS

BUENOS AIRES

A R G E N T I N A

Paraná

Paraná

Uruguay

Río de la Plata
(R. Plate)

Bahía
Samborombón

Scale 1:7 500 000
0   40   80   Miles
0 40 80 120 Kms.

© Wm. Collins, Sons & Co. Ltd.

Montevideo

Buenos
Aires
La Plata

Avellaneda
Ensenada

Bahía
Samborombón

Mar del Plata

A R G E N T I N A

B U E N O S   A I R E S

Bahía Blanca

Carmen de Patagones

Golfo
San Matías

Pen. Valdés

Punta Delgada

Puerto Lobos

Golfo Nuevo

Puerto Madryn

Rawson

Trelew

C. Dos Bahías

Comodoro
Rivadavia

Golfo
San Jorge

C. Blanca

Deseado

Bahía Laura

San Julián

Santa Cruz

Río Gallegos

Bahía
Grande

C. San
Diego

C. de los Estados
(Staten I.)

Cabo de Hornos
(Cape Horn)

TIERRA
DEL
FUEGO

Ushuaia

Río Grande

Punta Arenas

R I O   N E G R O

N E U Q U É N

C H U B U T

S A N T A   C R U Z

L A   P A M P A

M E N D O Z A

S A N   L U I S

C H I L E

Santiago

Valparaíso

Concepción

Temuco

Valdivia

Puerto Montt

I. de Chiloé

Archipiélago
de los
Chonos

G. de Penas

Pen. de Taitao

I. Wellington

I. Campana

I. Hanover

Estrecho de Magallanes

P A C I F I C

Relief

Metres				Feet
5000				16404
3000				9843
2000				6562
1000				3281
500				1640
200				656
Sea Level				0
Land Dep.				
200				656
4000				13123
7000				22966

Scale 1 : 12 500 000

0   100   200   300   400 Miles
0   200   400   600 Kms.

Lambert Azimuthal Equal Area Projection

© Collins · Longman Atlases CLs-95

93

Guaporé
Vilhena
Juruena
Planalto do Mato Grosso
Utiarita
Ronuro
Culuene
Parana
Ibotirama
Planalto
Diamantino
▲916
Manso (Mortes)
Araguaia
Tocantins
Campos Belos
Barreiras
Patagonaçu
BAHIA Brasil
Serra dos Pareeis
MATO GROSSO
Cuiabá
Aruanã
Niquelândia
1006▲
Serra Geral
Jequié
Brumado
Ipiaú
San Martin
Mato Grosso
Cáceres
(Brazilian Highlands)
1500
Vitória da Conquista
Itabuna
Ibirarei
San Javier
San Ignacio
San Matías
Rondonópolis
Goiás
DISTRITO FEDERAL
Formosa
Januária
Monte Azul
Tapetinga
Porto da Divisa
SANTA CRUZ
Anápolis
Brasília
Luziânia
Montes Claros
Teófilo Otoni
BOLIVIA
Banados de Izozog (Izozog Marshes)
Roboré
Coxim
Baús
Jataí
Rio Verde
GOIÁS
Goiânia
Corumbá
Paracatú
Patacató
Pirapora
Serra do Espinhaço
2033▲
Diamantina
Governador Valadares
Santa Cruz
Montero
San José de Chiquitos
Bahía Negra
Aquidauana
Patos de Minas
Represa Três Marías
Curvelo
Itabira
Caratinga
ESPÍRITO
Villa Montes
MATO GROSSO DO SUL
Campo Grande
Paranaíba
Uberlândia
MINAS GERAIS
Sete Lagoas
Bom Despacho
Belo Horizonte
Nova Lima
SANTO
Vila Velha
Vitória
Mariscal Estigarribia
Pto. Esperança
Corumbá
Bahía Negra
Três Lagoas
São José do Rio Prêto
Votuporanga
Uberaba
Araxá
Divinópolis
Formiga
Passos
Barbacena
João del Rei
Lavras
Cachoeiro de Itapemirim
Pto. Murtinho
Bela Vista
SÃO PAULO
Catanduva
Ribeirão Prêto
Poços de Caldas
Varginha
Itajubá
Campos
Pedro Juan Caballero
Dourados
Ponta Porã
Pres. Epitácio
Adamantina
Lins
São Carlos
Rio Claro
Limeira
Volta Redonda
Barra do Pirai
RIO
Niterói
Rio de Janeiro
PARAGUAY
Concepción
Pres. Prudente
Tupã
Bauru
Jaú
Piracicaba
Campinas
Jundiaí
Taubaté
Petrópolis
Nova Iguaçu
Formosa
San Pedro
Iya
Paranavaí
Avaré
Botucatu
São Paulo
Sto. André
São José dos Campos
C. Frio
Rivadavia
Las Lomitas
Salto das Sete Quedas (Guaíra) Falls
Maringá
Apucarana
Itapetininga
São Vicente
Santos
I. de São Sebastião
Clorinda
Asunción
Villarrica
Abaí
Yegros
Pto. Mendes
Londrina
PARANÁ
Itapeva
Ponta Grossa
SANTIAGO DEL ESTERO
Presidencia Roque Sáenz Peña
Formosa
Pilar
S. Ignacio
Encarnación
União da Vitória
Foz do Iguaçu
Guarapuava
Curitiba
Paranaguá
Campo Gallo
CHACO
Resistencia
Villa Angela
Barranqueras
Corrientes
Posadas
MISIONES
Santa Rosa
União da Vitória
São Miguel d'Oeste
Uruguai
Rio Negro
Joinville
São Francisco do Sul
Quimilí
Empedrado
Bella Vista
Apóstoles
Santo Tomé
Santo Angelo
Ijuí
Erechim
SANTA CATARINA
Blumenau
Itajaí
Añatuya
CORRIENTES
Goya
Mercedes
Itaqui
Cruz Alta
Passo Fundo
Lajes
Florianópolis
ARGENTINA
Reconquista
Vera
Paso de Los Libres Uruguaiana
Alegrete
Santa Maria
Novo Hamburgo
São Leopoldo
Caxias do Sul
Tubarão
Criciúma
Pinto
Tostado
Selva
San Cristóbal
Curuzú Cuatiá
Monte Caseros
Quaraí
Rosário do Sul
Cachoeira do Sul
São Gabriel do Sul
Jacuí
Canoas
Porto Alegre
Ojo de Agua
SANTA FE
San Justo
Rafaela
San Francisco
Santa Fé
Paraná
ENTRE RIOS
Villaguay
Concordia
Salto
Artigas
Santana do Livramento
Rivera
Bagé
Canguçu
Pelotas
Rio Grande
Lagoa dos Patos
CORDOBA
Oliva
Villa María
Cañada de Gómez
Bell Ville
Galvez
Diamante
Nogoyá
Victoria
Gualeguay
Paysandú
Durazno
Tacuarembó
Melo
L. Mirim
L. Mangueira
Jaguarão
Rosario
Casilda
Villa Constitución
San Nicolás
Concepción del Uruguay
Gualeguaychú
Fray Bentos
Mercedes
Trinidad
Florida
URUGUAY
Treinta y Tres
Sta. Vitória do Palmar
Venado Tuerto
Pergamino
Zarate
Campana
Dolores
Carmelo
San José de Mayo
Minas
Rocha
General Pico
Rufino
Chacabuco
Lincoln
Chivilcoy
Mercedes
Lobos
Buenos Aires
Avellaneda
Ensenada
La Plata
Montevideo
Río de la Plata (R. Plate)
Bragado
Nueve de Julio
Zárate
Lomas de Zamora
Piedras
Chascomús
Bahía Samborombón
Punta Norte
LA PAMPA
Catriló
Lanquen
Bolívar
Las Flores
Dolores
BUENOS AIRES
Azul
Maipú
General Madariaga
Santa Rosa
Coronel Suárez
Plum
Juárez
Tandil
Balcarce
Ayacucho
Olavarría
Carhué
Coronel Pringles
Loberia
Quequén
1243▲
Tornquist
Bahía Blanca
Punta Alta
Necochea
Mar del Plata
Colorado
Bahía Blanca

Relief

Feet		Metres
16 404		5000
9843		3000
6562		2000
3281		1000
1640		500
656		200
0	Sea Level	
Land Dep.		
656		200
13 123		4000

Scale 1:12 500 000

0   100   200   300   400 Miles
0   100   200   300   400   500   600 Kms.

Lambert Azimuthal Equal Area Projection

Scale 1:7 500 000
0   40   80 Miles
0   40   80   120 Kms.

Belo Horizonte
Divinópolis
MINAS GERAIS
São João del Rei
Juiz de Fora
Barbacena
Ouro Preto
Conselheiro Lafaiete
Volta Redonda
Barra do Pirai
Teresópolis
Petrópolis
RIO DE JANEIRO
Duque de Caxias
Niterói
Rio de Janeiro
Cabo Frio
Tropic of Capricorn
Ribeirão Prêto
SÃO PAULO
Bauru
Piracicaba
Campinas
São José dos Campos
Taubaté
Santos
São Vicente
São Paulo
Santo André
São Caetano do Sul

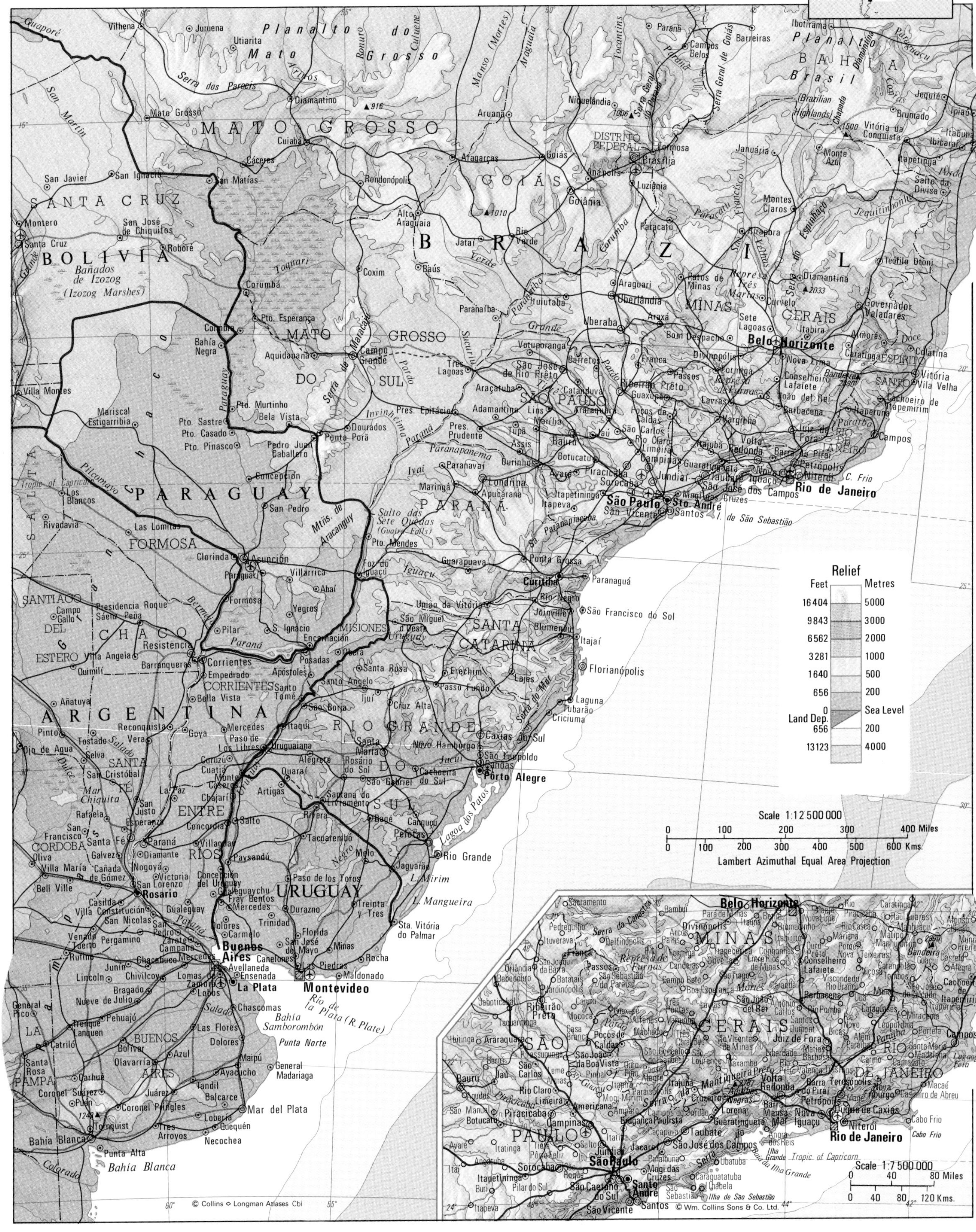

BERMUDA
Scale 1:1 000 000

St. George's I.
St. David's I.
St. George
Ireland I.
Castle Harbour
Somerset I.
Flatts Village
Great Sound
Hamilton

CANARY ISLANDS (Spain)
Scale 1:10 000 000

Lanzarote
Arrecife
Fuerteventura
Los Llanos de Aridane
La Palma
Tenerife
Santa Cruz de Tenerife
La Orotava
Arucas
Tuineje
Gomera
3718
Las Palmas de Gran Canaria
Hierro
Maspalomas
Gran Canaria
Islas Canarias (Canary Isles)
WESTERN SAHARA

MADEIRA ISLANDS
Scale 1:4 000 000 (Portugal)

Porto Santo
Porto Moniz
Santana
Madeira
Paúl do Mar
1862
Funchal
Sta. Cruz
Arquipélago da Madeira (Madeira Is.)
Deserta Grande

CANADA
Fort Chimo
Nain
Hudson B.
Hudson Str.
Davis Strait
Denmark Str.
GREENLAND
ICELAND
Reykjavík
Arctic Circle
Faroe Is. (Den.)
SWEDEN
Bergen
NORWAY
North Sea
UNITED KINGDOM
Glasgow
Birmingham
NETH.
BEL.
London
Bruxelles
Brussel
Paris
FRANCE
SWITZ.
K. Farvel/ Uummannarsuaq (C. Farewell)
3008
Rockall Bank
REP. OF IRELAND
Dublin
Nantes
Bordeaux
B. of Biscay
Lyon
Marseille
Barcelona
Madrid
Valencia
Alger
Algiers
Mediterranean Sea

Québec
Sept Îles
G. of St. Lawrence
Newfoundland
Labrador Basin
2920
Ottawa
Montreal
Pittsburgh
Cincinnati
Boston
New York
Philadelphia
Washington
UNITED STATES OF AMERICA
Memphis
Dallas
Birmingham
Mobile
Houston
New Orleans
Gulf of Mexico
Jacksonville
C. Hatteras
Bermuda Rise
6532
Halifax
C. Race
North Eastern Atlantic Basin
5819
NORTH
Arquipélago dos Açores (Azores) (Port.)
265
C. Finisterre
PORTUGAL
Lisboa
SPAIN
Sevilla
Tangier
Rabat
Oran
Casablanca
Marrakech
MOROCCO
Atlas Mts.
ALGERIA
LIBYA
In-Salah
Ahaggar
2918
Tibesti
3415
SUDAN

La Habana (Havana)
Miami
5462
Nassau
BAHAMAS
Sargasso Sea
Western Atlantic Basin
North America Basin
6995
West Indies
Cape Verde Basin
Islas Canarias (Canary Is.) (Sp.)
El Aaiún
WESTERN SAHARA
Sahara
Air
NIGER
Agadez
CHAD
L. Chad
N'Djamena
Botele

Yucatan
MEXICO
Gulf of Honduras
Cayman
7680
CUBA
Greater
HAITI
DOM. REP.
9218 Puerto Rico Trench
PUERTO RICO
DOMINICA
Guadeloupe (Fr.)
Martinique (Fr.)
BARBADOS
GRENADA
TRINIDAD AND TOBAGO
5420
1429
CAPE VERDE
Nouadhibou
MAURITANIA
Nouakchott
MALI
Tombouctou
Gao
Niamey
UPPER VOLTA
Ouagadougou
Kano
Jos
NIGERIA
Abuja
CENTRAL AFRICAN REPUBLIC
Bangui

HONDURAS
NICARAGUA
COSTA RICA
Bracos Reef
JAMAICA
Caribbean Sea
Colombian Basin
Venezuelan Basin
Lesser Antilles
Cape Verde Basin
Dakar
SENEGAL
GAMBIA
Banjul
Bamako
BENIN
CAMEROON
ZAIRE

PANAMA
Barranquilla
Maracaibo
Caracas
Georgetown
Paramaribo
Cayenne
GUINEA BISSAU
Conakry
Freetown
SIERRA LEONE
Monrovia
LIBERIA
Yamoussoukro
IVORY COAST
GHANA
Accra
Porto Novo
Lagos
Ibadan
Port Harcourt
Douala
Yaoundé
GABON
Libreville
CONGO
Brazzaville

Medellín
Bogota
Cali
COLOMBIA
Ciudad Bolívar
VENEZUELA
Orinoco
GUIANA HIGHLANDS
GUYANA
SURINAM
FRENCH GUIANA
5140
Abidjan
Gulf of Guinea
Guinea Basin
São Tomé
Annobón
Congo Basin
Kananga
Kinshasa
Cabinda
Luanda

ECUADOR
Quito
Guayaquil
6369
Trujillo
PERU
Manaus
Amazonas
Amazonas (Amazon)
Madeira
Juruá
Negro
Branco
Tapajós
Belém
São Luís
Fortaleza
St. Paul Rocks
6040
Rocas
Fernando de Noronha
C. de São Roque
Recife
6537
Ascension (U.K.)
84
MID-ATLANTIC RIDGE
South Eastern Atlantic Basin
6013
St. Helena (U.K.)
Lobito
Huambo
ANGOLA

Lima
Cuzco
Arequipa
BOLIVIA
La Paz
Titicaca
Sucre
Arica
Santa Cruz
5633
BRAZIL
Planalto do Mata Grosso
Cuiabá
Goiânia
Brasília
Planalto
Brasil
São Francisco
Salvador
Belo Horizonte
Ribeirão Preto
Niterói
Rio de Janeiro
São Paulo
Curitiba
Brazilian Basin
6022
Martin Vaz (Brazil)
Ascension (U.K.)
SOUTH
MID-ATLANTIC RIDGE
Walvis Ridge
892
Walvis Bay
NAMIBIA
Windhoek
Kalahari Desert
BOTSWANA
Kimberley
REP. OF SOUTH AFRICA

Antofagasta
8066
S. Ambrosio (Chile)
ANDES
PARAGUAY
Asunción
San Miguel de Tucumán
Córdoba
Santa Fe
Rosario
PARANA
URUGUAY
Florianópolis
Porto Alegre
Pelotas
Santiago
Islas Juan Fernández (Chile)
Buenos Aires
Montevideo
Río de la Plata
ARGENTINA
Concepción
Mar del Plata
Bahía Blanca
Argentine Basin
5585
Martin Vaz
514
Tristan da Cunha (U.K.)
Gough I. (U.K.)
5457
411
ATLANTIC
Cape Basin
Cape Town
Kaapstad
C. of Good Hope
Port Elizabeth
Agulhas Basin

ST. HELENA (U.K.)
Scale 1:1 000 000

Georgetown
Portland Pt.
S.E. Head
The Peak
859
ASCENSION (U.K.)
Scale 1:1 000 000

Jamestown
Flagstaff
Longwood
Gill Pt.
Diana's Peak
823
Sandy B.
S.W. Pt.

Peurto Montt
Comodoro Rivadavia
6212
Punta Arenas
Tierra del Fuego
Cabo de Hornos (Cape Horn)
Falkland Is. (U.K.)
Stanley
Scotia Sea
Drake Passage
S. Georgia (U.K.)
S. Sandwich Is. (U.K.)
8428
5552
Scotia Ridge
S. Orkney Is. (U.K.)
S. Sandwich Trench
Bouvetøya (Norway)
Atlantic-Antarctic Ridge
Settlement of Edinburgh
2160
Tristan da Cunha

Scale 1:60 000 000
0 500 1000 1500 Miles
0 500 1000 1500 2000 2500 Kms.
Zenithal Equal-Area Projection
Atlantic-Indian-Antarctic Basin
Pacific Antarctic Basin
Antarctic Peninsula
Antarctic Circle
Inaccessible I.
Nightingale I.
TRISTAN DA CUNHA (U.K.)
Scale 1:1 000 000

© Wm. Collins Sons & Co. Ltd.

POLAR REGIONS

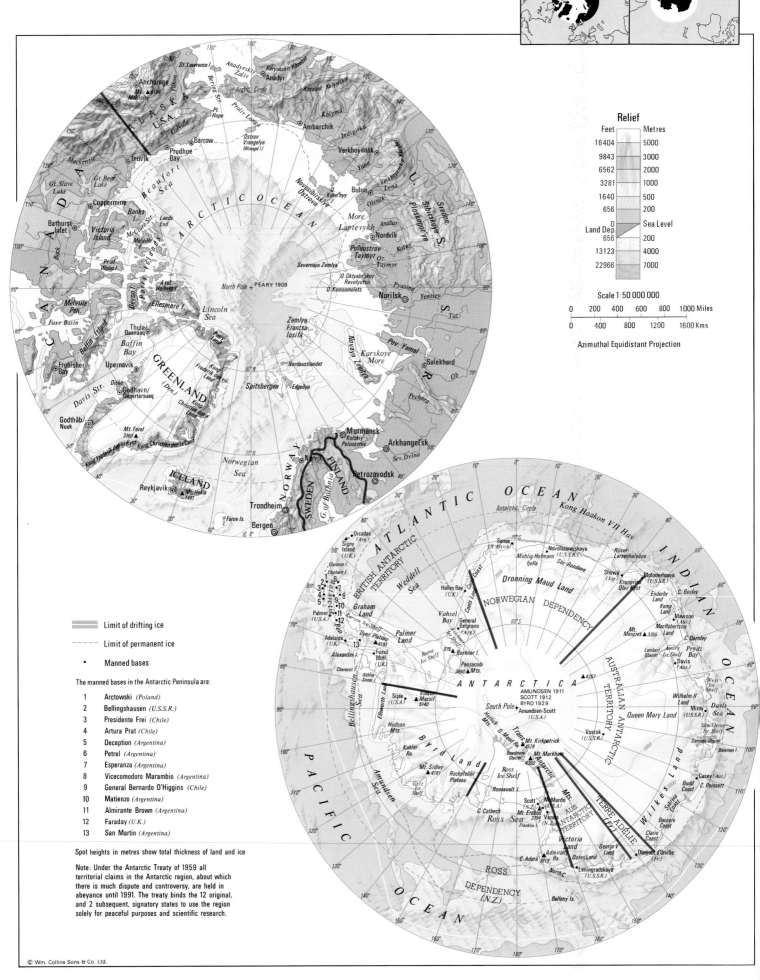

Relief

Feet		Metres
16404		5000
9843		3000
6562		2000
3281		1000
1640		500
656		200
0	Sea Level	
Land Dep.		
656		200
13123		4000
22966		7000

Scale 1:50 000 000

0   200   400   600   800   1000 Miles

0   400   800   1200   1600 Kms.

Azimuthal Equidistant Projection

━━━ Limit of drifting ice

- - - Limit of permanent ice

•   Manned bases

The manned bases in the Antarctic Peninsula are:

1   Arctowski   *(Poland)*
2   Bellingshausen   *(U.S.S.R.)*
3   Presidente Frei   *(Chile)*
4   Artura Prat   *(Chile)*
5   Deception   *(Argentina)*
6   Petrel   *(Argentina)*
7   Esperanza   *(Argentina)*
8   Vicecomodoro Marambio   *(Argentina)*
9   General Bernardo O'Higgins   *(Chile)*
10   Matienzo   *(Argentina)*
11   Almirante Brown   *(Argentina)*
12   Faraday   *(U.K.)*
13   San Martin   *(Argentina)*

Spot heights in metres show total thickness of land and ice

Note: Under the Antarctic Treaty of 1959 all
territorial claims in the Antarctic region, about which
there is much dispute and controversy, are held in
abeyance until 1991. The treaty binds the 12 original,
and 2 subsequent, signatory states to use the region
solely for peaceful purposes and scientific research.

WORLD DATA

WORLD PHYSICAL DATA

Earth's Dimensions

Superficial area	510 066 000 km²
Land surface	148 326 000 km²
Water surface	361 740 000 km²
Equatorial circumference	40 075 km
Meridional circumference	40 007 km
Volume	1 083 230x10⁶ km³
Mass	5.976x10²¹ tonnes

Oceans and Sea Areas

Pacific Ocean	165 384 000 km²
Atlantic Ocean	82 217 000 km²
Indian Ocean	73 481 000 km²
Arctic Ocean	14 056 000 km²
Mediterranean Sea	2 505 000 km²
South China Sea	2 318 000 km²
Bering Sea	2 269 000 km²
Caribbean Sea	1 943 000 km²
Gulf of Mexico	1 544 000 km²
Okhotskoye More (Sea of Okhotsk)	1 528 000 km²
East China Sea	1 248 000 km²
Hudson Bay	1 233 000 km²
Sea of Japan	1 008 000 km²
North Sea	575 000 km²
Black Sea	461 000 km²

River Lengths

An Nīl (Nile); Africa	6695 km
Amazonas (Amazon); South America	6570 km
Mississippi - Missouri; North America	6020 km
Chang Jiang (Yangtze); Asia	5471 km
Ob-Irtysh; Asia	5410 km
Huang He (Hwang Ho); Asia	4840 km
Zaïre; Africa	4630 km
Amur; Asia	4416 km
Lena; Asia	4269 km
Mackenzie; North America	4240 km
Niger; Africa	4183 km
Mekong; Asia	4180 km
Yenisey; Asia	4090 km
Murray - Darling; Oceania	3717 km
Volga; Europe	3688 km

Lake and Inland Sea Areas

Some areas are subject to seasonal variations.

Caspian Sea; U.S.S.R./Iran	371 795 km²
Lake Superior; U.S.A./Canada	82 413 km²
Lake Victoria; East Africa	69 485 km²
Aralskoye More (Aral Sea); U.S.S.R.	66 457 km²
Lake Huron; U.S.A./Canada	59 596 km²
Lake Michigan; U.S.A.	58 016 km²
Lake Tanganyika; East Africa	32 893 km²
Great Bear Lake; Canada	31 792 km²
Ozero Baykal (Lake Baikal); U.S.S.R.	30 510 km²
Great Slave Lake; Canada	28 930 km²
Lake Malaŵi; Malaŵi/Mozambique	28 490 km²
Lake Erie; U.S.A./Canada	25 667 km²
Lake Winnipeg; Canada	24 514 km²
Lake Ontario; U.S.A./Canada	19 529 km²
Ladozhskoye Ozero (Lake Ladoga); U.S.S.R.	18 390 km²

The Continents

Asia	44 391 162 km²
Africa	30 244 049 km²
North America	24 247 038 km²
South America	17 821 028 km²
Antarctica	13 338 500 km²
Europe	10 354 636 km²
Oceania	8 547 000 km²

Island Areas

Greenland; Arctic/Atlantic Ocean	2 175 597 km²
New Guinea; Indonesia/Papua New Guinea	828 057 km²
Borneo; Malaysia/Indonesia/Brunei	751 929 km²
Madagascar; Indian Ocean	587 042 km²
Baffin Island; Canada	476 068 km²
Sumatera (Sumatra); Indonesia	422 170 km²
Honshū; Japan	230 455 km²
Great Britain; United Kingdom	229 867 km²
Ellesmere Island; Canada	212 688 km²
Victoria Island; Canada	212 199 km²
Sulawesi (Celebes); Indonesia	179 370 km²
South Island; New Zealand	150 461 km²
Jawa (Java); Indonesia	126 500 km²
North Island; New Zealand	114 688 km²
Cuba; Caribbean Sea	114 525 km²

Mountain Heights (Selected)

Everest; Nepal/China	8848 m
K2; Jammu & Kashmir/China	8611 m
Kānchenjunga; Nepal/India	8586 m
Dhaulāgiri; Nepal	8172 m
Annapurna; Nepal	8078 m
Aconcagua; Argentina	6960 m
Ojos del Salado; Argentina/Chile	6908 m
McKinley; Alaska U.S.A.	6194 m
Logan; Canada	6050 m
Kilimanjaro; Tanzania	5895 m
Elbrus; U.S.S.R.	5633 m
Kenya; Kenya	5200 m
Vinson Massif; Antarctica	5139 m
Puncak Jaya; Indonesia	5030 m
Blanc; France/Italy	4807 m

Volcanoes (Selected)

	Last Eruption	Height
Cameroun; Cameroon	1922	4070 m
Cotopaxi; Ecuador	1975	5897 m
Elbrus; U.S.S.R.	extinct	5633 m
Erebus; Antarctica	1979	3794 m
Etna; Sicilia, Italy	1983	3340 m
Fuji san (Fujiyama); Japan	extinct	3776 m
Hekla; Iceland	1981	1491 m
Kilimanjaro; Tanzania	extinct	5895 m
Mauna Loa; Hawaii	1978	4171 m
Ngauruhoe; New Zealand	1975	2291 m
Popocatépetl; Mexico	1920	5452 m
St. Helens; U.S.A.	1981	2949 m
Stromboli; Italy	1975	926 m
Tristan da Cunha; Atlantic Ocean	1962	2160 m
Vesuvio (Vesuvius); Italy	1944	1277 m

WORLD POLITICAL DATA

National Areas

Union of Soviet Socialist Republics; Asia/Europe	22 402 000 km²
Canada; North America	9 976 000 km²
China; Asia	9 596 961 km²
United States; North America	9 363 123 km²
Brazil; South America	8 511 965 km²
Australia; Oceania	7 686 848 km²
India; Asia	3 287 590 km²
Argentina; South America	2 766 889 km²
Sudan; Africa	2 505 813 km²
Algeria; Africa	2 381 741 km²
Zaïre; Africa	2 345 409 km²
Greenland; North America	2 175 600 km²
Saudi Arabia; Asia	2 149 690 km²
Mexico; North America	1 972 547 km²
Indonesia; Asia	1 904 345 km²
Libya; Africa	1 759 540 km²
Iran; Asia	1 648 000 km²
Mongolia; Asia	1 565 000 km²
Peru; South America	1 285 216 km²
Chad; Africa	1 284 000 km²

National Populations

China; Asia	982 550 000
India; Asia	683 810 000
Union of Soviet Socialist Republics; Asia/Europe	265 542 000
United States; North America	227 640 000
Indonesia; Asia	147 383 000
Brazil; South America	123 032 000
Japan; Asia	117 057 000
Bangladesh; Asia	86 656 000
Pakistan; Asia	82 441 000
Nigeria; Africa	77 082 000
Mexico; North America	71 911 000
West Germany; Europe	61 658 000
Italy; Europe	57 140 000
United Kingdom; Europe	55 945 000
France; Europe	53 788 000
Vietnam; Asia	52 742 000
Philippines; Asia	48 400 000
Thailand; Asia	46 455 000
Turkey; Asia/Europe	45 218 000
Egypt; Africa	41 995 000

World Cities

New York; United States	16 479 000
Ciudad de México (Mexico City); Mexico	13 994 000
Tōkyō; Japan	11 695 000
Shanghai; China	10 820 000
Los Angeles; United States	10 607 000
Paris; France	9 863 000
Buenos Aires; Argentina	8 436 000
Moskva (Moscow); U.S.S.R.	8 011 000
Chicago; United States	7 664 000
Beijing (Peking); China	7 570 000
São Paulo; Brazil	7 199 000
Calcutta; India	7 031 000
Sŏul (Seoul); South Korea	6 879 000
London; United Kingdom	6 696 000
Bombay; India	5 971 000

Major International Organisations

United Nations - On December 1981 the United Nations had 157 members. Independent states not represented include Liechtenstein, Monaco, Nauru, North Korea, San Marino, South Korea, Switzerland, Taiwan, Tonga.

Commonwealth

Australia	Bahamas	Bangladesh	Barbados
Belize	Botswana	Brunei	Canada
Cyprus	Dominica	Fiji	Gambia
Ghana	Grenada	Guyana	Hong Kong
India	Jamaica	Kenya	Kiribati
Lesotho	Malaŵi	Malaysia	Maldives
Malta	Mauritius	Nauru	New Zealand
Nigeria	Papua New Guinea	St. Kitts-Nevis	St. Lucia
St. Vincent	Seychelles	Sierra Leone	Singapore
Solomon Islands	Sri Lanka	Swaziland	Tanzania
Tonga	Trinidad & Tobago	Tuvalu	Uganda
United Kindom	Vanuatu	Western Samoa	Zambia
Zimbabwe			

OAU - Organisation of African Unity

Algeria	Angola	Benin	Botswana
Burundi	Cameroon	Cape Verde	Central African Rep.
Chad	Comoros	Congo	Djibouti
Egypt	Equatorial Guinea	Ethiopia	Gabon
Gambia	Ghana	Guinea	Guinea Bissau
Ivory Coast	Kenya	Lesotho	Liberia
Libya	Madagascar	Malaŵi	Mali
Mauritania	Mauritius	Morocco	Mozambique
Niger	Nigeria	Rwanda	São Tomé & Príncipe
Senegal	Seychelles	Sierra Leone	Somali Rep.
Sudan	Swaziland	Tanzania	Togo
Tunisia	Uganda	Upper Volta	Western Sahara
Zaïre	Zambia	Zimbabwe	

OAS - Organisation of American States

Argentina	Barbados	Bolivia	Brazil
Chile	Colombia	Costa Rica	Dominica
Dominican Rep.	Ecuador	El Salvador	Grenada
Guatemala	Haiti	Honduras	Jamaica
Mexico	Nicaragua	Panama	Paraguay
Peru	St. Lucia	Surinam	Trinidad & Tobago
United States	Uruguay	Venezuela	

EEC - European Economic Community

Belgium	Denmark	France	Greece
Ireland	Italy	Luxembourg	Netherlands
United Kingdom	West Germany		

EFTA - European Free Trade Association

Austria	Finland (assoc.)	Iceland	Norway
Portugal	Sweden	Switzerland	

COMECON - Council for Mutual Economic Assistance

Bulgaria	Cuba	Czechoslovakia	East Germany
Hungary	Mongolia	Poland	Romania
U.S.S.R.	Vietnam	Yugoslavia (assoc.)	

ASEAN - Association of Southeast Asian Nations

Brunei	Indonesia	Malaysia	Philippines
Singapore	Thailand		

ECOWAS - Economic Community of West African States

Benin	Cape Verde	Gambia	Ghana
Guinea	Guinea Bissau	Ivory Coast	Liberia
Mali	Mauritania	Niger	Nigeria
Senegal	Sierra Leone	Togo	Upper Volta

CARICOM - Caribbean Community and Common Market

Antigua	Barbados	Belize	Dominica
Grenada	Guyana	Jamaica	Monserrat
St. Kitts - Nevis	St. Lucia	St. Vincent	Trinidad & Tobago

NATIONS OF THE WORLD

COUNTRY	AREA sq. km.	POPULATION total	per sq. km.	FORM OF GOVERNMENT	CAPITAL CITY	MAIN LANGUAGES	CURRENCY
AFGHANISTAN	647 497	15 540 000	24	democratic republic	Kābul	Pushtu, Dari (Persian)	afghani
ALBANIA	28 748	2 734 000	95	socialist people's republic	Tiranë	Albanian	lek
ALGERIA	2 381 741	18 594 000	8	republic	Alger (Algiers)	Arabic	dinar
ANDORRA	453	34 000	75	principality	Andorra	Catalan	French franc, Spanish peseta
ANGOLA	1 246 700	7 078 000	5.6	people's republic	Luanda	Portuguese	kwanza
ANTIGUA AND BARBUDA	442	74 000	167	independent political entity	St John's	English	East Caribbean dollar
ARGENTINA	2 766 889	27 863 000	10	federal republic	Buenos Aires	Spanish	peso
AUSTRALIA	7 686 848	14 727 000	1.9	monarchy (federal)	Canberra	English	dollar
AUSTRIA	83 849	7 507 000	89	federal republic	Wien (Vienna)	German	schilling
BAHAMAS	13 935	223 000	16	constitutional monarchy	Nassau	English	dollar
BAHRAIN	622	364 000	585	emirate	Al Manāmah	Arabic	dinar
BANGLADESH	143 998	86 656 000	601	people's republic	Dhākā	Bengali	taka
BARBADOS	431	250 000	580	independent political entity	Bridgetown	English	dollar
BELGIUM	30 513	9 859 000	323	constitutional monarchy	Bruxelles/Brussel (Brussels)	French, Dutch, German	franc
BELIZE	22 965	145 000	6.3	constitutional monarchy	Belmopan	English	dollar
BENIN	112 622	3 567 000	31	people's republic	Porto-Novo	French	CFA franc
BHUTAN	47 000	1 298 000	27	monarchy (Indian protection)	Thimbu	Dzongkha	Indian rupee, ngultrum
BOLIVIA	1 098 581	5 600 000	5	republic	La Paz/Sucre	Spanish	peso
BOTSWANA	600 372	819 000	1.3	republic	Gaborone	English, Tswana	pula
BRAZIL	8 511 965	123 032 000	14	federal republic	Brasília	Portuguese	cruzeiro
BRUNEI	5 765	213 000	37	sultanate	Bandar Seri Begawan	Malay	dollar
BULGARIA	110 912	8 862 000	79	people's republic	Sofiya (Sofia)	Bulgarian	lev
BURMA	676 552	35 289 000	52	federal republic	Rangoon	Burmese	kyat
BURUNDI	27 834	4 512 000	162	republic	Bujumbura	French, Kirundi	franc
CAMEROON	475 442	8 503 000	17	republic	Yaoundé	French, English	CFA franc
CANADA	9 976 139	23 941 000	2.4	monarchy (federal)	Ottawa	English, French	dollar
CAPE VERDE	4 033	314 000	78	republic	Praia	Portuguese, Creole	escudo
CENTRAL AFRICAN REPUBLIC	622 984	2 370 000	3.8	republic	Bangui	French, Sango	CFA franc
CHAD	1 284 000	4 524 000	3.5	republic	N'Djamena	French	CFA franc
CHILE	756 945	11 104 000	15	republic	Santiago	Spanish	peso
CHINA	9 596 961	982 550 000	102	people's republic	Beijing (Peking)	Mandarin	yuan
COLOMBIA	1 138 914	27 520 000	24	republic	Bogotá	Spanish	peso
COMOROS	2 171	320 000	147	federal republic	Moroni	Comoran, Arabic, French	CFA Franc
CONGO	342 000	1 537 000	4.4	republic	Brazzaville	French	CFA franc
COSTA RICA	50 700	2 245 000	44	republic	San José	Spanish	colon
CUBA	114 524	9 833 000	86	people's republic	La Habana (Havana)	Spanish	peso
CYPRUS	9 251	629 000	68	republic	Levkosía (Nicosia)	Greek	pound
CZECHOSLOVAKIA	127 869	15 312 000	119	federal socialist republic	Praha (Prague)	Czech, Slovak	koruna
DENMARK	43 069	5 124 000	119	constitutional monarchy	København (Copenhagen)	Danish	krone
DJIBOUTI	22 000	119 000	5.4	republic	Djibouti	French, Somali, Afar	franc
DOMINICA	751	81 000	108	republic	Roseau	English, French	East Caribbean dollar
DOMINICAN REPUBLIC	48 734	5 431 000	111	republic	Santo Domingo	Spanish	peso
EAST GERMANY	108 178	16 737 000	155	people's republic	Berlin	German	mark
ECUADOR	283 561	8 354 000	29	republic	Quito	Spanish	sucre
EGYPT	1 001 449	41 995 000	41	republic	Al Qāhirah (Cairo)	Arabic	pound
EL SALVADOR	21 041	4 813 000	228	republic	San Salvador	Spanish	colón
EQUATORIAL GUINEA	28 051	363 000	13	republic	Malabo	Spanish	ekuele
ETHIOPIA	1 221 900	31 065 000	25	provisional military government	Ādīs Ābeba (Addis Ababa)	Amharic	birr
FIJI	18 272	631 000	34	monarchy (federal)	Suva	English, Fijian, Hindustani	dollar
FINLAND	337 009	4 788 000	14	republic	Helsinki	Finnish, Swedish	mark
FRANCE	547 026	53 788 000	98	republic	Paris	French	franc
GABON	267 667	551 000	2.1	republic	Libreville	French	CFA franc
GAMBIA	11 295	601 000	53	republic	Banjul	English	dalasi
GHANA	238 537	11 450 000	48	republic	Accra	English	cedi
GREECE	131 944	9 599 000	72	republic	Athínai (Athens)	Greek	drachma
GREENLAND	2 175 600	50 000	0.1	overseas territory (Denmark)	Godthåb/Nuuk	Danish, Greenlandic	kroner
GRENADA	344	97 000	281	independent political entity	St George's	English	East Caribbean dollar
GUATEMALA	108 889	7 262 000	66	republic	Guatemala	Spanish	quetzal
GUIANA	91 000	64 000	0.6	overseas department (France)	Cayenne	French	franc

COUNTRY	AREA sq. km.	POPULATION total	per sq. km.	FORM OF GOVERNMENT	CAPITAL CITY	MAIN LANGUAGES	CURRENCY
GUINEA	245 857	5 014 000	20	republic	Conakry	French	syli
GUINEA BISSAU	36 125	777 000	22	republic	Bissau	Portuguese	peso
GUYANA	214 969	884 000	4.1	republic	Georgetown	English	dollar
HAITI	27 750	5 009 000	180	republic	Port-au-Prince	French, Créole	gourde
HONDURAS	112 088	3 691 000	32	republic	Tegucigalpa	Spanish	lempira
HONG KONG	1 045	5 068 000	4 850	colony (U.K.)		English, Chinese	dollar
HUNGARY	93 030	10 711 000	115	republic	Budapest	Magyar	forint
ICELAND	103 000	228 000	2.2	republic	Reykjavík	Icelandic	króna
INDIA	3 287 590	683 810 000	208	republic	New Delhi	Hindi	rupee
INDONESIA	1 904 345	147 383 000	77	republic	Jakarta	Bahasa Indonesia	rupiah
IRAN	1 648 000	37 447 000	22	islamic republic	Tehrān	Persian	rial
IRAQ	434 924	13 084 000	30	republic	Baghdād	Arabic	dinar
IRELAND, REPUBLIC OF	70 023	3 365 000	48	republic	Dublin	English, Irish	punt
ISRAEL	20 770	3 871 000	186	republic	Yerushalayim (Jerusalem)	Hebrew	shekel
ITALY	301 225	57 140 000	189	republic	Roma (Rome)	Italian	lira
IVORY COAST	322 462	7 973 000	25	republic	Yamoussoukro	French	CFA franc
JAMAICA	10 991	2 192 000	199	constitutional monarchy	Kingston	English	dollar
JAPAN	372 313	117 057 000	314	monarchy	Tōkyō	Japanese	yen
JORDAN	97 740	2 779 000	28	monarchy	'Ammān	Arabic	dinar
KAMPUCHEA	181 035	8 872 000	49	people's republic	Phnum Pénh (Phnom Penh)	Cambodian, Khmer	riel
KENYA	582 646	16 402 000	28	republic	Nairobi	Swahili, English	shilling
KIRIBATI	886	63 000	71	republic	Bairiki	English, Gilbertese (I-Kiribati)	Australian dollar
KUWAIT	17 818	1 356 000	76	sheikdom	Al Kuwayt (Kuwait)	Arabic	dinar
LAOS	236 800	3 721 000	15	people's republic	Viangchan (Vientiane)	Lao	kip
LEBANON	10 400	3 161 000	304	republic	Bayrūt (Beirut)	Arabic	pound
LESOTHO	30 355	1 339 000	44	monarchy	Maseru	English, Sesotho	loti
LIBERIA	111 369	1 873 000	16	republic	Monrovia	English	dollar
LIBYA	1 759 540	2 977 000	1.6	republic	Ṭarābulus (Tripoli)	Arabic	dinar
LIECHTENSTEIN	157	26 000	166	constitutional monarchy	Vaduz	German	Swiss franc
LUXEMBOURG	2 586	364 000	140	constitutional monarchy	Luxembourg	Letzeburgish, French, German	franc
MADAGASCAR	587 041	8 742 000	14	republic	Antananarivo	Malagasy	Malagasy franc
MALAWI	118 484	5 968 000	50	republic	Lilongwe	English, Chichewa	kwacha
MALAYSIA	329 749	13 436 000	40	constitutional monarchy	Kuala Lumpur	Malay	ringgit
MALDIVES	298	143 046	480	republic	Malé	Divehi	rupee
MALI	1 240 000	6 906 000	5.5	republic	Bamako	French, Bambara	franc
MALTA	316	369 000	1 167	republic	Valletta	Maltese, English	pound
MAURITANIA	1 030 700	1 634 000	1.5	republic	Nouakchott	French, Arabic	ouguiya
MAURITIUS	2 045	924 000	452	independent political entity	Port Louis	English, Creole	rupee
MEXICO	1 972 547	71 911 000	35	federal republic	Ciudad de México (Mexico City)	Spanish	peso
MONACO	1.5	26 000	17 333	constitutional monarchy	Monaco	French	French franc
MONGOLIA	1 565 000	1 595 000	1.1	people's republic	Ulaanbaatar (Ulan Bator)	Mongol	tugrik
MOROCCO	446 550	20 242 000	44	monarchy	Rabat	Arabic	dirham
MOZAMBIQUE	783 000	12 130 000	13	people's republic	Maputo	Portuguese	escudo
NAMIBIA	824 292	852 000	1.1	South African mandate	Windhoek	Afrikaans, English	R.S.A. rand
NAURU	21	8 000	381	republic	Nauru	Nauruan, English	Australian dollar
NEPAL	140 797	14 010 000	99	monarchy	Kātmāndu	Nepali	rupee
NETHERLANDS	40 844	14 220 000	348	constitutional monarchy	Amsterdam	Dutch	guilder
NEW ZEALAND	268 676	3 164 000	12	monarchy	Wellington	English	dollar
NICARAGUA	130 000	2 703 000	20	republic	Managua	Spanish	córdoba
NIGER	1 267 000	5 305 000	4.1	republic	Niamey	French	CFA franc
NIGERIA	923 768	77 082 000	83	federal republic	Abuja	English	naira
NORTH KOREA	120 538	17 914 000	148	people's republic	Pyŏngyang	Korean	won
NORWAY	324 219	4 092 000	13	constitutional monarchy	Oslo	Norwegian	krone
OMAN	212 457	891 000	4.1	sultanate	Masqaṭ (Muscat)	Arabic	rial
PAKISTAN	803 943	82 441 000	103	federal republic	Islāmābād	Urdu, Punjabi, English	rupee
PANAMA	75 650	1 837 000	24	republic	Panamá	Spanish	balboa
PAPUA NEW GUINEA	461 691	3 082 000	6.7	republic	Port Moresby	English	kina
PARAGUAY	406 752	3 067 000	7.5	republic	Asunción	Spanish, Guaraní	guaraní

NATIONS OF THE WORLD

COUNTRY	AREA sq. km.	POPULATION total	per sq. km.	FORM OF GOVERNMENT	CAPITAL CITY	MAIN LANGUAGES	CURRENCY
PERU	1 285 216	17 780 000	14	republic	Lima	Spanish	sol
PHILIPPINES	300 000	48 400 000	161	republic	Manila	Pilipino	peso
POLAND	312 677	35 815 000	115	people's republic	Warszawa (Warsaw)	Polish	zloty
PORTUGAL	92 082	9 933 000	107	republic	Lisboa (Lisbon)	Portuguese	escudo
PUERTO RICO	8 897	3 188 000	358	commonwealth (U.S.A.)	San Juan	Spanish, English	dollar
QATAR	11 000	220 000	20	emirate	Ad Dawḩah (Doha)	Arabic	riyal
ROMANIA	237 500	22 201 000	93	socialist republic	Bucureşti (Bucharest)	Romanian	leu
RWANDA	26 338	5 046 000	191	republic	Kigali	Kinyarwanda, French	franc
ST KITTS - NEVIS	266	62 000	233	independent political entity	Basseterre	English	East Caribbean dollar
ST LUCIA	616	113 000	183	independent political entity	Castries	English, French	East Caribbean dollar
ST VINCENT AND THE GRENADINES	389	96 000	247	independent political entity	Kingstown	English	East Caribbean dollar
SAN MARINO	61	21 000	344	republic	San Marino	Italian	Italian lira
SÃO TOMÉ AND PRÍNCIPE	964	82 750	86	republic	São Tomé	Portuguese, Creole	dobra
SAUDI ARABIA	2 149 690	8 367 000	3.8	monarchy	Ar Riyāḑ (Riyadh)	Arabic	riyal
SENEGAL	,196 192	5 661 000	28	republic	Dakar	French	CFA franc
SEYCHELLES	280	61 900	221	republic	Victoria	English, French	rupee
SIERRA LEONE	71 740	3 474 000	48	republic	Freetown	English	leone
SINGAPORE	602	2 391 000	3 972	republic	Singapore	Malay, English, Chinese, Tamil	dollar
SOLOMON ISLANDS	28 446	221 000	7.8	constitutional monarchy	Honiara	English	dollar
SOMALI REPUBLIC	637 657	3 645 000	5.7	republic	Mogadisho	Arabic, Italian, English, Somali	shilling
SOUTH AFRICA, REPUBLIC OF	1 221 037	29 285 000	23	federal republic	Cape Town (Kaapstad) / Pretoria	Afrikaans, English	rand
SOUTH KOREA	98 484	37 605 000	382	republic	Sŏul (Seoul)	Korean	won
SOUTHERN YEMEN	332 968	1 969 000	5.9	people's republic	'Adan (Aden)	Arabic	dinar
SPAIN	504 782	37 430 000	74	constitutional monarchy	Madrid	Spanish	peseta
SRI LANKA	65 610	14 738 000	225	republic	Colombo	Sinhala, Tamil	rupee
SUDAN	2 505 813	18 681 000	7.4	republic	Al Kharṭūm (Khartoum)	Arabic	pound
SURINAM	163 265	352 000	2.1	republic	Paramaribo	Dutch, English	guilder
SWAZILAND	17 363	547 000	31	monarchy	Mbabane	English, Siswati	R.S.A. rand, lilangeni
SWEDEN	449 964	8 320 000	18	constitutional monarchy	Stockholm	Swedish	krona
SWITZERLAND	41 288	6 329 000	153	federal republic	Bern (Berne)	German, French, Italian, Romansh	franc
SYRIA	185 180	8 979 000	48	republic	Dimashq (Damascus)	Arabic	pound
TAIWAN	35 961	17 479 000	486	republic	Taipei	Mandarin	dollar
TANZANIA	945 087	17 982 000	19	republic	Dar es Salaam / Dodoma	Swahili	shilling
THAILAND	514 000	46 455 000	90	monarchy	Krung Thep (Bangkok)	Thai	baht
TOGO	56 000	2 699 000	48	republic	Lomé	French	CFA franc
TONGA	699	97 000	139	monarchy	Nuku'alofa	Tongan, English	dollar
TRINIDAD AND TOBAGO	5 128	1 156 000	225	republic	Port of Spain	English	dollar
TUNISIA	163 610	6 363 000	39	republic	Tunis	Arabic	dinar
TURKEY	780 576	45 218 000	57	republic	Ankara	Turkish	lira
TUVALU	24	7 000	292	constitutional monarchy	Funafuti	Tuvalu, English	dollar
U.S.S.R.	22 402 200	265 542 000	12	federal socialist republic	Moskva (Moscow)	Russian	rouble
UGANDA	236 036	13 225 000	56	republic	Kampala	English	shilling
UNITED ARAB EMIRATES	83 600	1 040 000	12	self-governing union		Arabic	dirham
UNITED KINGDOM	244 046	55 945 000	229	constitutional monarchy	London	English	pound
UNITED STATES OF AMERICA	9 363 123	227 640 000	24	federal republic	Washington	English	dollar
UPPER VOLTA	274 200	6 908 000	25	republic	Ouagadougou	French	CFA franc
URUGUAY	177 508	2 899 000	16	republic	Montevideo	Spanish	peso
VANUATU	14 763	112 000	7.6	republic	Vila	English, French	vatu
VENEZUELA	912 050	13 913 000	15	federal republic	Caracas	Spanish	bolívar
VIETNAM	333 000	52 742 000	158	people's republic	Hà Nôi (Hanoi)	Vietnamese	dong
WEST GERMANY	248 577	61 658 000	248	federal republic	Bonn	German	mark
WESTERN SAHARA	266 000	135 000	0.5		El Aaiún	Arabic	peseta
WESTERN SAMOA	2 842	156 000	55	constitutional monarchy	Apia	Samoan, English	tala
YEMEN	195 000	5 926 000	30	republic	Şan'ā	Arabic	riyal
YUGOSLAVIA	255 804	22 471 000	87	socialist federal republic	Beograd (Belgrade)	Serbo-Croat, Macedonian, Slovene	dinar
ZAÏRE	2 345 409	28 291 000	12	republic	Kinshasa	French, Lingala	zaïre
ZAMBIA	752 614	5 680 000	7.5	republic	Lusaka	English	kwacha
ZIMBABWE	390 580	7 360 000	18	republic	Harare	English	dollar

Introduction to World Index

The Index includes an alphabetical list of all names appearing on the maps in the World Atlas section. Each entry indicates the country or region of the world in which the name is located. This is followed by a page reference and finally the name's location on the map, given by latitude and longitude co-ordinates. Most features are indexed to the largest scale map on which they appear, however when the name applies to countries or other extensive features it is generally indexed to the map on which it appears in its entirety. Areal features are generally indexed using co-ordinates which indicate the centre of the feature. The latitude and longitude indicated for a point feature gives the location of the point on the map. In the case of rivers the mouth or confluence is always taken as the point of reference.

Names in the Index are generally in the local language and where a conventional English version exists, this is cross referenced to the entry in the local language. Names of features which extend across the boundaries of more than one country are usually named in English if no single official name exists. Names in languages not written in the Roman alphabet have been transliterated using the official system of the country if one exists, e.g. Pinyin system for China, otherwise the systems recognised by the United States Board on Geographical Names have been used.

Names abbreviated on the maps are given in full in the Index. Abbreviations are used for both geographical terms and administrative names in the Index. All abbreviations used in the Index are listed below.

Abbreviations of Geographical Terms

b., B.	bay, Bay	f.	physical feature e.g. valley, plain, geographic district or region	mts., Mts.	mountains, Mountains
c., C.	cape, Cape			pen., Pen.	peninsula, Peninsula
d.	internal division e.g. county, region, state.	g., G.	gulf, Gulf	Pt.	Point
		i., I., is., Is.	island, Island, islands, Islands	r.	river
des.	desert	l., L.	lake, Lake	resr., Resr.	reservoir, Reservoir
est.	estuary	mtn., Mtn.	mountain, Mountain	Sd.	Sound
				str., Str.	strait, Strait

Abbreviations of Country / Administrative Names

Afghan.	Afghanistan	Mass.	Massachusetts	R.S.F.S.R.	Rossiyskaya Sovetskaya Federativnaya Sotsialisticheskaya Respublika
Ala.	Alabama	Md.	Maryland		
Alas.	Alaska	Mich.	Michigan		
Alta.	Alberta	Minn.	Minnesota	S.A.	South Australia
Ariz.	Arizona	Miss.	Mississippi	Sask.	Saskatchewan
Ark.	Arkansas	Mo.	Missouri	S.C.	South Carolina
Bangla.	Bangladesh	Mont.	Montana	Sch.-Hol.	Schleswig-Holstein
B.C.	British Columbia	M.S.S.R.	Moldavskaya Sovetskaya Sotsialisticheskaya Respublika	S. Dak.	South Dakota
B.S.S.R.	Belorusskaya Sovetskaya Sotsialisticheskaya Respublika			Shrops.	Shropshire
		N.B.	New Brunswick	S. Korea	South Korea
Calif.	California	N.C.	North Carolina	Sogn og Fj.	Sogn og Fjordane
C.A.R.	Central African Republic	N. Dak.	North Dakota	Somali Rep.	Somali Republic
Char. Mar.	Charente Maritime	Nebr.	Nebraska	Strath.	Strathclyde
Colo.	Colorado	Neth.	Netherlands	Switz.	Switzerland
Conn.	Connecticut	Nev.	Nevada	S. Yemen	Southern Yemen
C.P.	Cape Province	Nfld.	Newfoundland	Tas.	Tasmania
Czech.	Czechoslovakia	N.H.	New Hampshire	Tenn.	Tennessee
D. and G.	Dumfries and Galloway	N.J.	New Jersey	Tex.	Texas
D.C.	District of Colombia	N. Korea	North Korea	Tk. S.S.R.	Turkmenskaya Sovetskaya Sotsialisticheskaya Respublika
Del.	Delaware	N. Mex.	New Mexico		
Derbys.	Derbyshire	Northum.	Northumberland	Trans.	Transvaal
Dom. Rep.	Dominican Republic	N.S.	Nova Scotia	U.A.E.	United Arab Emirates
E. Germany	East Germany	Nschn.	Niedersachen	U.K.	United Kingdom
Equat. Guinea	Equatorial Guinea	N.S.W.	New South Wales	Ukr. S.S.R.	Ukrainskaya Sovetskaya Sotsialisticheskaya Respublika
Fla.	Florida	N.-Westfalen	Nordrhein-Westfalen		
Ga.	Georgia	N.W.T.	Northwest Territories	U.S.A.	United States of America
Glos.	Gloucestershire	N.Y.	New York State	U.S.S.R.	Union of Soviet Socialist Republics
G.M.	Greater Manchester	N. Yorks.	North Yorkshire		
Guang. Zhuang.	Guangxi Zhuangzu	O.F.S.	Orange Free State	Uttar P.	Uttar Pradesh
Himachal P.	Himachal Pradesh	Okla.	Oklahoma	U. Volta	Upper Volta
H. Zaïre	Haut Zaïre	Ont.	Ontario	Va.	Virginia
Ill.	Illinois	Oreg.	Oregon	Vic.	Victoria
Ind.	Indiana	P.E.I.	Prince Edward Island	Vt.	Vermont
I.o.M.	Isle of Man	Penn.	Pennsylvania	W.A.	Western Australia
Kans.	Kansas	Phil.	Philippines	Wash.	Washington
K. Oriental	Kasai Oriental	P.N.G.	Papua New Guinea	W. Bengal	West Bengal
Ky.	Kentucky	Pyr. Or.	Pyrénées Orientales	W. Germany	West Germany
La.	Lousiana	Qld.	Queensland	Wisc.	Wisconsin
Liech.	Liechtenstein	Que.	Québec	W. Isles	Western Isles
Lit. S.S.R.	Litovskaya Sovetskaya Sotsialisticheskaya Respublika	Raj.	Rājasthān	W. Sahara	Western Sahara
		Rep. of Ire.	Republic of Ireland	W. Va.	West Virginia
Lux.	Luxembourg	Rhein.-Pfalz	Rheinland-Pfalz	Wyo.	Wyoming
Madhya P.	Madhya Pradesh	R.I.	Rhode Island	Xin Uygur	Xinjiang Uygur
Man.	Manitoba	R.S.A.	Republic of South Africa	Yugo.	Yugoslavia

Aachen to **Além Paraíba**

A

Aachen W. Germany 14 50.46N 6.06E
A 'âli an Nîl d. Sudan 49 9.00N 32.00E
Aalsmeer Neth. 14 52.17N 4.46E
Aalst Belgium 14 50.57N 4.03E
Äänekoski Finland 22 62.36N 25.44E
Aarau Switz. 20 47.24N 8.04E
Aardenburg Neth. 14 51.16N 3.26E
Aare r. Switz. 20 47.37N 8.13E
Aarschot Belgium 14 50.59N 4.50E
Aba China 39 32.55N101.42E
Aba Nigeria 53 5.06N 7.21E
Aba Zaïre 49 3.52N 30.14E
Abā as Su'ūd Saudi Arabia 45 17.28N 44.06E
Abadab, Jabal mtn. Sudan 48 18.53N 35.59E
Ābādān Iran 43 30.21N 48.15E
Abadan, Jazīreh-ye i. Iran 43 30.10N 48.30E
Ābādeh Iran 43 31.10N 52.40E
Abadla Algeria 50 31.01N 2.44W
Abaetetuba Brazil 91 1.45S 48.54W
Abagnar Qi China 32 43.58N116.02E
Abag Qi China 32 43.53N114.33E
Abaí Paraguay 92 26.01S 55.57W
Abajo Peak mtn. U.S.A. 80 37.51N109.28W
Abakaliki Nigeria 53 6.17N 8.04E
Abakan U.S.S.R. 29 53.43N 91.25E
Abalessa Algeria 51 22.54N 4.50E
Abancay Peru 92 13.35S 72.55W
Abariringa i. Kiribati 68 2.50S171.40W
Ābār Murrāt wells Sudan 48 21.03N 32.55E
Abasolo Mexico 83 25.18N104.40W
Abau P.N.G. 64 10.10S148.40E
Ābay r. Ethiopia see Azraq, Al Baḥr al r. Sudan 48
Abay U.S.S.R. 28 49.40N 72.47E
Abaya, L. Ethiopia 49 6.20N 37.55E
Abba C.A.R. 53 5.20N 15.11E
Abbeville France 17 50.06N 1.51E
Abbeville La. U.S.A. 83 29.58N 92.08W
Abbeville S.C. U.S.A. 85 34.10N 82.23W
Abbiategrasso Italy 15 45.24N 8.54E
Abbotsbury U.K. 11 50.40N 2.36W
Abbotsford Canada 77 45.27N 72.55W
Abbottābād Pakistan 40 34.09N 73.13E
'Abd al Kūrī i. S. Yemen 45 12.12N 52.13E
Abdulino U.S.S.R. 24 53.42N 53.40E
Abe, L. Ethiopia 49 11.06N 41.50E
Abéché Chad 48 13.49N 20.49E
Abelti Ethiopia 49 8.10N 37.37E
Abengourou Ivory Coast 52 6.42N 3.27W
Åbenrå Denmark 23 55.02N 9.26E
Abeokuta Nigeria 53 7.10N 3.26E
Aberayron U.K. 11 52.15N 4.16W
Abercrombie r. Australia 67 33.50S149.10E
Aberdare U.K. 11 51.43N 3.27W
Aberdare Range mts. Kenya 55 0.20S 36.40E
Aberdeen R.S.A. 56 32.28S 24.03E
Aberdeen U.K. 12 57.08N 2.07W
Aberdeen Md. U.S.A. 85 39.30N 76.10W
Aberdeen Miss. U.S.A. 83 33.49N 88.33W
Aberdeen Ohio U.S.A. 84 38.39N 83.46W
Aberdeen S. Dak. U.S.A. 82 45.28N 98.29W
Aberdeen Wash. U.S.A. 80 46.59N123.50W
Aberdovey U.K. 11 52.33N 4.03W
Aberfeldy U.K. 12 56.37N 3.54W
Abergavenny U.K. 11 51.49N 3.01W
Abersoch U.K. 10 52.50N 4.31W
Aberystwyth U.K. 11 52.25N 4.06W
Abetone Italy 15 44.08N 10.40E
Abez U.S.S.R. 24 66.33N 61.51E
Abhā Saudi Arabia 48 18.13N 42.30E
Abhar Iran 43 36.09N 49.13E
Abidjan Ivory Coast 52 5.19N 4.01W
Abilene Kans. U.S.A. 82 38.55N 97.13W
Abilene Tex. U.S.A. 83 32.27N 99.44W
Abingdon U.K. 11 51.40N 1.17W
Abisko Sweden 22 68.20N 18.51E
Abitau r. Canada 75 59.53N109.03W
Abitibi r. Canada 76 51.03N 80.55W
Abitibi, L. Canada 76 48.42N 79.45W
Abiy Adi Ethiopia 49 13.36N 39.00E
Abnūb Egypt 42 27.16N 31.09E
Åbo see Turku Finland 23
Abohar India 40 30.08N 74.12E
Abomey Benin 53 7.14N 2.00E
Abong Mbang Cameroon 53 3.59N 13.12E
Abou Deïa Chad 53 11.20N 19.20E
Aboyne U.K. 12 57.05N 2.48W
Abrantes Portugal 16 39.28N 8.12W
'Abrī Sudan 48 20.48N 30.20E
Abring Jammu & Kashmir 40 33.42N 76.35E
Abrud Romania 21 46.17N 23.04E
Abruzzi d. Italy 18 42.05N 13.45E
Absaroka Range mts. U.S.A. 80 44.45N109.50W
Absecon U.S.A. 85 39.26N 74.30W
Abū 'Arīsh Saudi Arabia 45 16.58N 42.50E
Abū Baḥr f. Saudi Arabia 45 21.30N 48.15E
Abū Ballāṣ hill Egypt 48 24.26N 27.39E
Abu Dhabi see Abū Ẓaby U.A.E. 43
Abū Dharbah Egypt 44 28.29N 33.20E
Abū Dulayq Sudan 48 15.54N 33.49E
Abū Ḥamad Sudan 48 19.32N 33.19E
Abū Ḥarāz Sudan 48 19.04N 32.07E
Abuja Nigeria 53 9.12N 7.11E
Abū Jābirah Sudan 49 11.04N 26.51E
Abū Kabīr Egypt 44 30.44N 31.40E
Abū Kamāl Syria 42 34.27N 40.55E
Abū Madd, Ra's c. Saudi Arabia 42 24.50N 37.07E
Abū Maṭāriq Sudan 49 10.58N 26.17E
Abunã Brazil 90 9.41S 65.20W
Abū Qurqāṣ Egypt 44 27.56N 30.50E
Abu Road town India 40 24.29N 72.47E
Abū Shajarah, Ra's c. Sudan 48 21.04N 37.14E
Abū Shanab Sudan 49 10.47N 29.32E
Abū Sulṭān Egypt 44 30.25N 32.19E
Abū Sunbul Egypt 42 22.18N 31.40E
Abū Ṭabarī well Sudan 48 17.35N 28.31E
Abū Ṭarafah Jordan 44 30.00N 35.56E
Abū Tīj Egypt 42 27.06N 31.17E
Abuya Mexico 81 24.16N107.01W
Abuye Meda mtn. Ethiopia 49 10.28N 39.44E
Abū Zabad Sudan 49 12.21N 29.15E
Abū Ẓaby U.A.E. 43 24.27N 54.23E
Abū Zanīmah Egypt 44 29.03N 33.06E
Abwong Sudan 49 9.07N 32.12E
Åby Sweden 23 58.40N 16.11E
Abyaḍ Sudan 48 13.46N 26.28E
Abyaḍ, Al Baḥr al r. Sudan 48 15.38N 32.31E
Abyār ash Shuwayrif wells Libya 51 29.59N 14.16E
Abyei Sudan 49 9.36N 28.26E
Acacio Mexico 83 24.50N102.44W
Acadia Valley town Canada 75 51.08N110.13W
Acámbaro Mexico 86 20.01N101.42W
Acapulco Mexico 86 16.51N 99.56W
Acará Brazil 91 1.57S 48.11W
Acarigua Venezuela 90 9.35N 69.12W
Acatlán Mexico 86 18.12N 98.02W
Accra Ghana 52 5.33N 0.15W
Accrington U.K. 10 53.46N 2.22W
Aceh d. Indonesia 36 4.00N 97.30E
Acevedo Argentina 93 33.46S 60.27W
Achacachi Bolivia 92 16.03S 68.43W
Achalpur India 41 21.16N 77.31E
Achar Uruguay 93 32.25S 56.10W
Acheng China 31 45.32N126.59E
Achill I. Rep. of Ire. 13 53.57N 10.00W
Āchīn Afghan. 40 34.08N 70.42E
Achinsk U.S.S.R. 28 56.10N 90.10E
Acklin's I. Bahamas 87 22.30N 74.10W
Aconcagua mtn. Argentina 92 32.39S 70.00W
Açores, Arquipélago dos is. Atlantic Oc. 95 38.30N 28.00W
Acqui Italy 15 44.41N 8.28E
Acraman, L. Australia 66 32.02S135.26E
Acre d. Brazil 90 8.50S 71.30W
Acton Canada 76 43.37N 80.02W
Acton Vale Canada 77 45.39N 72.34W
Açu Brazil 91 5.35S 36.57W
Acuña Argentina 93 29.54S 57.57W
Ada U.S.A. 83 34.46N 96.41W
Adaba Ethiopia 49 7.07N 39.20E
Adair, Bahía de b. Mexico 81 31.30N113.50W
Adair, C. Canada 73 71.24N 71.13W
Adam Oman 45 22.23N 57.32E
Adamantina Brazil 94 21.42S 51.04W
Adamaoua, Massif de l' mts. Cameroon/Nigeria 53 7.05N 12.00E
Adamello mtn. Italy 15 46.10N 10.35E
Adaminaby Australia 67 36.04S148.42E
Adamintina Brazil 92 21.42S 51.04W
Adams N.Y. U.S.A. 84 43.49N 76.01W
Adams, Mt. U.S.A. 80 46.12N121.28W
'Adan S. Yemen 45 12.50N 45.00E
Adana Turkey 42 37.00N 35.19E
Adapazari Turkey 42 40.45N 30.23E
Adarama Sudan 48 17.05N 34.54E
Adare, C. Antarctica 96 71.30S171.00E
Adavale Australia 64 25.55S144.36E
Adda r. Italy 15 45.08N 9.55E
Aḍ Ḍab'ah Egypt 42 31.02N 28.26E
Ad Dabbah Sudan 48 18.03N 30.57E
Ad Dafīnah Saudi Arabia 42 23.18N 41.58E
Ad Dahnā' des. Saudi Arabia 43 26.00N 47.00E
Ad Dāmir Sudan 48 17.35N 33.58E
Ad Dammām Saudi Arabia 43 26.23N 50.08E
Ad Darb Saudi Arabia 48 17.44N 42.15E
Ad Dawādimī Saudi Arabia 43 24.29N 44.23E
Ad Dawḥah Qatar 43 25.15N 51.34E
Aḍ Ḍiffah f. Africa 42 30.45N 26.00E
Ad Dikākah f. Saudi Arabia 45 19.25N 51.30E
Ad Dilam Saudi Arabia 43 23.59N 47.10E
Ad Dīmās Syria 44 33.35N 36.05E
Addis Ababa see Ādīs Ābeba Ethiopia 49
Ad Dīwānīyah Iraq 43 31.59N 44.57E
Ad Du'ayn Sudan 49 11.26N 26.09E
Ad Duwaym Sudan 48 14.00N 32.19E
Adel U.S.A. 85 31.07N 83.27W
Adelaide Australia 66 34.56S138.36E
Adelaide Pen. Canada 73 68.09N 97.45W
Adelong Australia 67 35.21S148.04E
Aden see 'Adan S. Yemen 45
Aden, G. of Indian Oc. 45 13.00N 50.00E
Adendorp R.S.A. 56 32.18S 24.31E
Adi i. Indonesia 37 4.10S133.10E
Adi Daro Ethiopia 48 14.27N 38.16E
Adieu, C. Australia 63 31.59S132.09E
Adigala Ethiopia 49 10.25N 42.17E
Adige r. Italy 15 45.10N 12.20E
Adigrat Ethiopia 48 14.18N 39.31E
Adi Keyih Ethiopia 48 14.49N 39.23E
Ādilābād India 41 19.40N 78.32E
Adilang Uganda 55 2.44N 33.28E
Adin U.S.A. 80 41.12N120.57W
Adirondack Mts. U.S.A. 84 44.00N 74.00W
Ādīs Ābeba Ethiopia 49 9.03N 38.42E
Adi Ugri Ethiopia 48 14.55N 38.53E
Adiyaman Turkey 42 37.46N 38.15E
Adjud Romania 21 46.04N 27.11E
Admer well Algeria 51 20.23N 5.27E
Admiralty G. Australia 62 14.20S125.50E
Admiralty I. U.S.A. 74 57.50N134.30W
Admiralty Is. P.N.G. 37 2.30S147.20E
Admiralty Range mts. Antarctica 96 72.00S164.00E
Adour r. France 17 43.28N 1.35W
Adra Spain 16 36.43N 3.03W
Adrano Italy 18 37.39N 14.49E
Adrar d. Mauritania 50 21.00N 10.00W
Adrar des Iforas mts. Mali/Algeria 51 20.00N 2.30E
Adraskan Afghan. 40 33.39N 62.16E
Adria Italy 15 45.03N 12.03E
Adrian Mich. U.S.A. 84 41.55N 84.01W
Adrian Mo. U.S.A. 82 38.24N 94.21W
Adrian Tex. U.S.A. 83 35.16N102.40W
Adriatic Sea Med. Sea 18 42.30N 16.00E
Ādwa Ethiopia 48 14.12N 38.56E
Adzopé Ivory Coast 52 6.07N 3.49W
Adzwa r. U.S.S.R. 24 66.30N 59.30E
Aegean Sea Med. Sea 19 39.00N 25.00E
Āfdem Ethiopia 49 9.26N 41.02E
Afghanistan Asia 40 32.45N 65.00E
'Afīf Saudi Arabia 42 23.53N 42.59E
Afikpo Nigeria 53 5.53N 7.55E
Afjord Norway 22 63.57N 10.12E
Aflou Algeria 51 34.07N 2.06E
Afmadu Somali Rep. 55 0.27N 42.05E
Afobaka Surinam 91 5.00N 55.05W
Afognak I. U.S.A. 72 58.15N152.30W
Afonso Cláudio Brazil 94 20.05S 41.06W
Afsluitdijk f. Neth. 14 53.04N 5.11E
'Afula Israel 44 32.36N 35.17E
Afyon Turkey 42 38.46N 30.32E
Agadez Niger 53 17.00N 7.56E
Agadez d. Niger 53 19.25N 11.00E
Agadir Morocco 50 30.26N 9.36W
Agalak Sudan 49 11.01N 32.42E
Agana Guam 37 13.28N144.45E
Agapa U.S.S.R. 29 71.29N 86.16E
Agar India 40 23.42N 76.01E
Agaro Ethiopia 49 7.50N 36.40E
Agartala India 41 23.49N 91.16E
Agaru Sudan 49 10.59N 34.44E
Agboville Ivory Coast 52 5.55N 4.15W
Agde France 17 43.19N 3.28E
Agen France 17 44.12N 0.38E
Ageo Japan 35 35.58N139.36E
Agger r. W. Germany 14 50.45N 7.06E
Aghada Rep. of Ire. 13 51.50N 8.13W
Agia India 41 26.05N 90.32E
Aginskoye U.S.S.R. 29 51.10N114.32E
Agnew Australia 63 28.01S120.30E
Ago Japan 35 34.17N136.48E
Agordo Italy 15 46.17N 12.02E
Agouma Gabon 54 1.33S 10.08E
Āgra India 41 27.11N 78.01E
Agra r. Spain 16 42.12N 1.43W
Agraciada Uruguay 93 33.48S 58.15W
Agreda Spain 16 41.51N 1.55W
Agri r. Italy 19 40.13N 16.45E
Agri Turkey 42 39.44N 43.04E
Agri Daği mtn. Turkey 43 39.45N 44.15E
Agrigento Italy 18 37.19N 13.36E
Agrihan i. Mariana Is. 37 18.44N145.39E
Agropoli Italy 18 40.21N 15.00E
Agryz U.S.S.R. 24 56.30N 53.00E
Agsumal, Sebjet f. W. Sahara 50 24.21N 12.52W
Agua Caliente, Cerro mtn. Mexico 81 26.27N106.12W
Aguanish Canada 77 50.16N 62.10W
Aguanus r. Canada 77 50.12N 62.10W
Agua Prieta Mexico 81 31.18N109.34W
Aguas Blancas Chile 92 24.13S 69.50W
Aguascalientes Mexico 86 21.51N102.18W
Aguascalientes d. Mexico 86 22.00N102.00W
Agudos Brazil 94 22.27S 49.03W
Águeda r. Spain 16 41.00N 6.56W
Aguelhok Mali 50 19.28N 0.52E
Aguema Angola 54 12.03S 21.52E
Aguêraktem well Mali 50 23.07N 6.12W
Aguilar de Campóo Spain 16 42.47N 4.15W
Aguilas Spain 16 37.25N 1.35W
Aguit China 32 41.42N113.20E
Agulaa Ethiopia 48 13.42N 39.35E
Agulhas, C. R.S.A. 56 34.50S 20.00E
Agulhas Basin f. Indian Oc. 95 43.00S 25.00E
Agulhas Negras mtn. Brazil 94 22.20S 44.43W
Agung, Gunung mtn. Indonesia 37 8.20S115.28E
Ahaggar f. Algeria 51 23.36N 5.50E
Ahar Iran 43 38.25N 47.07E
Ahaura New Zealand 60 42.21S171.33E
Ahaus W. Germany 14 52.04N 7.01E
Ahklun Mts. U.S.A. 72 59.15N161.00W
Ahlen W. Germany 14 51.47N 7.52E
Ahmadābād India 40 23.02N 72.37E
Aḥmadī Iran 43 27.56N 56.42E
Ahmadnagar India 40 19.05N 74.44E
Ahmadpur East Pakistan 40 29.09N 71.16E
Ahmadpur Siāl Pakistan 40 30.41N 71.46E
Ahmad Wāl Pakistan 40 29.25N 65.56E
Ahmar Mts. Ethiopia 49 9.15N 41.00E
Ahoada Nigeria 53 5.06N 6.39E
Ahr r. W. Germany 14 50.34N 7.16E
Ahram Iran 43 28.52N 51.16E
Ahraura India 41 25.01N 83.01E
Aḥsā', Wāḥat al oasis Saudi Arabia 43 25.37N 49.40E
Ähtäri Finland 22 62.34N 24.06E
Åhus Sweden 23 55.55N 14.17E
Ahvāz Iran 43 31.17N 48.44E
Ahvenanmaa d. Finland 23 60.15N 20.00E
Ahvenanmaa is. Finland 23 60.15N 20.00E
Aichi d. Japan 35 35.02N137.15E
Aigle Switz. 15 46.19N 6.58E
Aigues-Mortes France 17 43.34N 4.11E
Aiken U.S.A. 85 33.34N 81.44W
Ailette r. France 14 49.35N 3.09E
Ailsa Craig i. U.K. 12 55.15N 5.07W
Aim U.S.S.R. 29 58.50N134.15E
Aimorés Brazil 94 19.30S 41.04W
Ain r. France 17 45.47N 5.12E
Aïna r. Gabon 54 0.38N 12.47E
Ainaži U.S.S.R. 23 57.52N 24.21E
Aïn Beïda Algeria 51 35.50N 7.27E
Aïn ben Tili Mauritania 50 26.00N 9.32W
Aïn Galakka Chad 51 18.04N 18.24E
Aïn Sefra Algeria 50 32.45N 0.35W
Aïr mts. Niger 53 18.30N 8.30E
Airdrie U.K. 12 55.52N 3.59W
Aire France 17 43.39N 0.15W
Aire r. France 15 49.19N 4.49E
Aire r. U.K. 10 53.42N 0.54W
Aisne d. France 15 49.30N 3.30E
Aisne r. France 15 49.27N 2.51E
Aitape P.N.G. 37 3.10S142.17E
Aitkin U.S.A. 82 46.32N 93.43W
Aït Ourir Morocco 50 31.38N 7.42W
Aitutaki Atoll Cook Is. 69 18.52S159.46W
Aiud Romania 21 46.19N 23.44E
Aix-en-Provence France 17 43.31N 5.27E
Aix-les-Bains France 17 45.42N 5.55E
Aíyina i. Greece 19 37.43N 23.30E
Aíyion Greece 19 38.15N 22.05E
Aizpute U.S.S.R. 23 56.43N 21.38E
Ajaccio France 17 41.55N 8.43E
Ajanta Range mts. India 40 20.15N 75.30E
Ajax Canada 76 43.51N 79.02W
Ajdābiyā Libya 48 30.46N 20.14E
Ajibar Ethiopia 49 10.41N 38.37E
'Ajlūn Jordan 44 32.20N 35.45E
'Ajmah, Jabal al f. Egypt 44 29.12N 33.58E
'Ajmān U.A.E. 43 25.23N 55.26E
Ajmer India 40 26.27N 74.38E
Ajnāla India 40 31.51N 74.47E
Ajo U.S.A. 81 32.22N112.52W
Akaishi sammyaku mts. Japan 35 35.20N138.10E
Akámas, Akrotírion c. Cyprus 44 35.06N 32.17E
'Akasha East Sudan 48 21.05N 30.43E
Akashi Japan 35 34.38N134.59E
Akbarpur India 41 26.25N 82.33E
Akbulak U.S.S.R. 25 51.00N 55.40E
Akelamo Indonesia 37 1.35N129.40E
Akershus d. Norway 23 60.00N 11.10E
Aketi Zaïre 54 2.46N 23.51E
Akhaltsikhe U.S.S.R. 42 41.37N 42.59E
Akhḍar, Al Jabal al mts. Libya 48 32.30N 21.30E
Akhḍar, Al Jabal al mts. Oman 43 23.10N 57.25E
Akhḍar, Wādī r. Egypt 44 28.42N 33.41E
Akhḍar, Wādī al r. Saudi Arabia 44 28.30N 36.48E
Akhelóös Greece 19 38.20N 21.04E
Akhisar Turkey 19 38.54N 27.49E
Akhmīm Egypt 42 26.34N 31.44E
Akhtyrka U.S.S.R. 25 50.19N 34.54E
Akimiski I. Canada 76 53.00N 81.20W
Akita Japan 31 39.44N140.05E
Akjoujt Mauritania 50 19.44N 14.26W
Akkajaure l. Sweden 22 67.40N 17.30E
'Akko Israel 44 32.55N 35.04E
Akkol U.S.S.R. 30 45.04N 75.39E
Aklavik Canada 72 68.12N135.00W
Ako Nigeria 53 10.19N 10.48E
Ākobo r. Ethiopia 49 8.30N 33.15E
Akola India 40 20.44N 77.00E
Akordat Ethiopia 48 15.35N 37.55E
Akot India 40 21.11N 77.04E
Akpatok I. Canada 73 60.30N 68.30W
Akranes Iceland 22 64.19N 22.05W
Akron Colo. U.S.A. 82 40.10N103.13W
Akron Ohio U.S.A. 84 41.04N 81.31W
Akrotíri Cyprus 44 34.36N 32.57E
Aksaray Turkey 42 38.22N 34.02E
Aksarka U.S.S.R. 28 66.31N 67.50E
Aksay China 30 39.28N 94.15E
Aksay U.S.S.R. 25 51.24N 52.11E
Akşehir Turkey 42 38.22N 31.24E
Aksu China 30 42.10N 80.00E
Āksum Ethiopia 48 14.08N 38.48E
Aktag mtn. China 30 36.45N 84.40E
Aktogay U.S.S.R. 30 46.59N 79.42E
Aktyubinsk U.S.S.R. 25 50.16N 57.13E
Akūbū Sudan 49 7.47N 33.01E
Akūbū r. Sudan see Ākobo r. Sudan 49
Akula Zaïre 54 2.22N 20.11E
Akure Nigeria 53 7.14N 5.08E
Akureyri Iceland 22 65.41N 18.04W
Akuse Ghana 52 6.04N 0.12E
Akxokesay China 30 36.48N 91.06E
Akyab see Sittwe Burma 34
Ål Norway 23 60.38N 8.34E
Alabama d. U.S.A. 85 32.50N 87.00W
Alabama r. U.S.A. 83 31.08N 87.57W
Al 'Abbāsīyah Sudan 49 14.27N 33.31E
Ālādāgh, Kūh-e mts. Iran 43 37.15N 57.30E
Alagoas d. Brazil 91 9.30S 37.00W
Alagoinhas Brazil 91 12.09S 38.21W
Alagón Spain 16 41.46N 1.12W
Alakol, Ozero l. U.S.S.R. 30 46.00N 81.40E
Alakurtti U.S.S.R. 24 67.00N 30.23E
Al 'Alamayn Egypt 42 30.49N 28.57E
Alamagan i. Mariana Is. 37 17.35N145.50E
Al 'Amārah Iraq 43 31.52N 47.50E
Al Āmirīyah Egypt 44 31.01N 29.48E
Alamogordo U.S.A. 81 32.54N105.57W
Alamos, Rio de los r. Mexico 83 27.53N101.12W
Alamosa U.S.A. 80 37.28N105.52W
Åland is. see Ahvenanmaa is. Finland 23
Ålands Hav sea Finland 23 60.00N 19.30E
Alanreed U.S.A. 83 35.14N100.45W
Alanya Turkey 42 36.32N 32.02E
Alaotra, Lac l. Madagascar 57 17.30S 48.30E
Alapayevsk U.S.S.R. 24 57.55N 61.42E
Al 'Aqabah Jordan 44 29.32N 35.00E
Al 'Aramah f. Saudi Arabia 43 25.30N 46.30E
Alarcón, Embalse de resr. Spain 16 39.36N 2.10W
Al 'Arīsh Egypt 44 31.08N 33.48E
Alaşehir Turkey 19 38.22N 28.29E
Alaska d. U.S.A. 72 65.00N153.00W
Alaska, G. of U.S.A. 72 58.45N145.00W
Alaska Pen. U.S.A. 72 56.00N160.00W
Alaska Range mts. U.S.A. 72 62.10N152.00W
Alassio Italy 15 44.00N 8.10E
Al 'Aṭīqah Lebanon 44 33.42N 35.27E
Al 'Aṭrūn Sudan 48 18.11N 26.36E
Alatyr U.S.S.R. 24 54.51N 46.35E
Alausí Ecuador 90 2.00S 78.50W
Alavus Finland 22 62.35N 23.37E
Alawoona Australia 66 34.44S140.33E
Al 'Ayn wells Sudan 48 16.36N 29.19E
Al 'Ayyāṭ Egypt 44 29.37N 31.15E
Alazani r. U.S.S.R. 43 41.06N 46.40E
Alba Italy 15 44.42N 8.02E
Albacete Spain 16 39.00N 1.52W
Al Bad' Saudi Arabia 44 28.29N 35.02E
Al Badārī Egypt 42 26.59N 31.25E
Al Bahnasā Egypt 44 28.32N 30.39E
Alba-Iulia Romania 21 46.04N 23.33E
Albania Europe 19 41.00N 20.00E
Albany Australia 63 34.57S117.54E
Albany r. Canada 76 52.10N 82.00W
Albany Ga. U.S.A. 85 31.37N 84.10W
Albany Ky. U.S.A. 85 36.42N 85.08W
Albany Minn. U.S.A. 82 45.38N 94.34W
Albany N.Y. U.S.A. 84 42.39N 73.45W
Albany Oreg. U.S.A. 80 44.38N123.06W
Al Baṣrah Iraq 43 30.33N 47.50E
Al Bāṭinah f. Oman 43 24.25N 56.50E
Albatross B. Australia 64 12.45S141.43E
Al Batrūn Lebanon 44 34.16N 35.40E
Al Bawīṭī Egypt 42 28.21N 25.52E
Al Bayāḍ f. Saudi Arabia 45 22.00N 47.00E
Al Bayḍā' Libya 51 32.46N 21.43E
Albemarle Sd. U.S.A. 79 36.10N 76.00W
Albenga Italy 15 44.03N 8.13E
Alberche r. Spain 16 40.00N 4.45W
Alberga Australia 65 27.12S135.28E
Alberga r. Australia 65 27.12S135.28E
Albermarle U.S.A. 85 35.21N 80.12W
Albermarle Sd. U.S.A. 85 36.03N 76.12W
Alberni Canada 74 49.20N124.50W
Albert Australia 67 32.21S147.33E
Albert France 14 50.00N 2.38E
Albert, L. Australia 66 35.38S139.17E
Albert, L. Uganda/Zaïre 55 1.45N 31.00E
Alberta d. Canada 74 54.00N115.00W
Alberti Argentina 93 35.01S 60.16W
Albertirsa Hungary 21 47.15N 19.38E
Albert Kanaal canal Belgium 14 51.00N 5.15E
Albert Lea U.S.A. 82 43.39N 93.22W
Albert Nile r. Uganda 55 3.30N 32.00E
Alberton Canada 77 46.49N 64.04W
Albi France 17 43.56N 2.08E
Al Bidia Chad 49 10.33N 20.13E
Albin U.S.A. 80 41.26N104.08W
Albina Surinam 91 5.30N 54.03W
Albino Italy 15 45.46N 9.47E
Albion Mich. U.S.A. 84 42.14N 84.45W
Albion Mont. U.S.A. 80 45.11N104.15W
Albion Nebr. U.S.A. 82 41.42N 98.00W
Albion N.Y. U.S.A. 76 43.15N 78.12W
Albion Penn. U.S.A. 84 41.53N 80.22W
Al Bi'r Saudi Arabia 44 28.52N 36.15E
Alborán, Isla de i. Spain 16 35.55N 3.10W
Ålborg Denmark 23 57.03N 9.56E
Ålborg Bugt b. Denmark 23 56.45N 10.30E
Alborz, Reshteh-ye Kūhhā-ye mts. Iran 43 36.00N 52.30E
Albuquerque U.S.A. 81 35.05N106.40W
Al Buraymī U.A.E. 43 24.15N 55.45E
Al Burj Egypt 44 31.35N 30.59E
Alburquerque Spain 16 39.13N 6.59W
Albury Australia 67 36.03S146.53E
Al Buṭanah f. Sudan 48 14.50N 34.30E
Alby Sweden 22 62.30N 15.25E
Alcácer do Sal Portugal 16 38.22N 8.30W
Alcalá de Chisvert Spain 16 40.19N 0.13E
Alcalá de Henares Spain 16 40.28N 3.22W
Alcalá la Real Spain 16 37.28N 3.55W
Alcamo Italy 18 37.59N 12.58E
Alcañiz Spain 16 41.03N 0.09W
Alcántara, Embalse de resr. Spain 16 39.45N 6.25W
Alcantara L. Canada 75 60.57N108.09W
Alcaudete Spain 16 37.35N 4.05W
Alcázar de San Juan Spain 16 39.24N 3.12W
Alcira Spain 16 39.10N 0.27W
Alcobaça Portugal 16 39.33N 8.59W
Alcova U.S.A. 80 42.35N106.34W
Alcoy Spain 16 38.42N 0.29W
Alcubierre, Sierra de mts. Spain 16 41.40N 0.20W
Alcudia Spain 16 39.51N 3.09E
Aldan U.S.S.R. 29 58.44N125.22E
Aldan r. U.S.S.R. 29 63.30N130.00E
Aldeburgh U.K. 11 52.09N 1.35E
Alderney i. U.K. 11 49.42N 2.11W
Aldershot U.K. 11 51.15N 0.47W
Alderson Canada 75 50.20N111.25W
Aldridge U.K. 11 52.36N 1.55W
Aledo U.S.A. 82 41.12N 90.45W
Aleg Mauritania 50 17.03N 13.55W
Alegre Brazil 94 20.44S 41.30W
Alegrete Brazil 93 29.46S 55.46W
Aleksandrov Gay U.S.S.R. 25 50.08N 48.34E
Aleksandrovsk Sakhalinskiy U.S.S.R. 29 50.55N142.12E
Alembe Gabon 54 0.03N 10.57E
Além Paraíba Brazil 94 21.49S 42.36W

Alençon to Aney

Alençon France 15 48.25N 0.05E
Alenuihaha Channel Hawaiian Is. 69 20.26N156.00W
Aleppo see Ḩalab Syria 42
Aléria France 17 42.05N 9.30E
Alès France 17 44.08N 4.05E
Alessandria Italy 15 44.54N 8.37E
Ålesund Norway 22 62.28N 6.11E
Aleutian Basin Bering Sea 68 57.00N179.00E
Aleutian Is U.S.A. 68 52.00N176.00W
Aleutian Range mts. U.S.A. 72 58.00N156.00W
Aleutian Trench Pacific Oc. 68 50.00N176.00W
Alexander U.S.A. 76 42.54N 78.16W
Alexander Archipelago is. U.S.A. 74 56.30N134.30W
Alexander Bay town R.S.A. 56 28.36S 16.26E
Alexander I. Antarctica 96 72.00S 70.00W
Alexandra Australia 67 37.12S145.14E
Alexandra New Zealand 60 45.14S169.26E
Alexandria B.C. Canada 74 52.35N122.27W
Alexandria Ont. Canada 77 45.18N 74.39W
Alexandria see Al Iskandarīyah Egypt 44
Alexandria Romania 21 43.58N 25.20E
Alexandria R.S.A. 56 33.39S 26.24E
Alexandria La. U.S.A. 83 31.18N 92.27W
Alexandria Minn. U.S.A. 82 45.53N 95.22W
Alexandria Va. U.S.A. 85 38.48N 77.03W
Alexandrina, L. Australia 66 35.26S139.10E
Alexandroúpolis Greece 19 40.50N 25.53E
Alexis r. Canada 77 52.32N 56.08W
Alexis Creek town Canada 74 52.05N123.20W
Aleysk U.S.S.R. 28 52.32N 82.45E
Al Fant Egypt 44 28.46N 30.53E
Alfaro Spain 16 42.11N 1.45W
Al Fāshir Sudan 49 13.38N 25.21E
Al Fashn Egypt 44 28.49N 30.54E
Al Fāw Iraq 43 29.57N 48.30E
Al Fayyūm Egypt 44 29.19N 30.50E
Alfeld W. Germany 20 51.59N 9.50E
Alfenas Brazil 94 21.28S 45.48W
Al Fifi Sudan 49 10.03N 25.01E
Alfiós r. Greece 19 37.37N 21.27E
Alfonsine Italy 15 44.30N 12.03E
Alford U.K. 12 57.14N 2.42W
Al Fujayrah U.A.E. 43 25.10N 56.20E
Al Furāt r. Asia 43 31.00N 47.27E
Alga U.S.S.R. 28 49.49N 57.16E
Ålgård Norway 23 58.46N 5.51E
Al Gebir Sudan 49 13.43N 29.49E
Algeciras Spain 16 36.08N 5.27W
Algemesí Spain 16 39.11N 0.27W
Algena Ethiopia 48 16.20N 38.34E
Alger Algeria 51 36.50N 3.00E
Algeria Africa 50 28.00N 2.00E
Al Ghayl Saudi Arabia 43 22.36N 46.19E
Alghero Italy 18 40.33N 8.20E
Al Ghurdaqah Egypt 42 27.14N 33.50E
Algiers see Alger Algeria 51
Algoa B. R.S.A. 56 33.50S 26.00E
Algoma U.S.A. 82 44.36N 87.27W
Algona U.S.A. 82 43.04N 94.14W
Algonquin Prov. Park Canada 76 45.27N 78.26W
Algorta Uruguay 93 32.25S 57.23W
Al Ḩajar al Gharbī mts. Oman 43 24.00N 56.30E
Al Ḩajar ash Sharqī mts. Oman 43 22.45N 58.45E
Alhama Spain 16 37.51N 1.25W
Al Ḩamād des. Saudi Arabia 42 31.45N 39.00E
Al Ḩamar Saudi Arabia 43 22.26N 46.12E
Alhambra U.S.A. 81 34.06N118.08W
Al Ḩamīdīyah Syria 44 34.43N 35.56E
Al Ḩanākīyah Saudi Arabia 42 24.53N 40.30E
Al Ḩarīq Saudi Arabia 43 23.37N 46.31E
Al Harūj al Aswad hills Libya 51 27.00N 17.10E
Al Ḩasakah Syria 42 36.29N 40.45E
Al Ḩawāmidīyah Egypt 44 29.54N 31.15E
Al Ḩayz Egypt 42 28.02N 28.39E
Al Ḩijāz f. Saudi Arabia 42 26.00N 37.30E
Al Ḩillah Iraq 43 32.28N 44.29E
Al Ḩillah Saudi Arabia 43 23.30N 46.51E
Al Hirmil Lebanon 44 34.25N 36.23E
Al-Hoceima Morocco 50 35.15N 3.55W
Al Ḩudaydah Yemen 48 14.50N 42.58E
Al Hufūf Saudi Arabia 43 25.20N 49.34E
Al Ḩumrah des. U.A.E. 43 22.45N 55.10E
Al Ḩusaynīyah Egypt 44 30.52N 31.55E
Al Ḩuwaymī S. Yemen 45 14.05N 47.44E
Alīābād, Kūh-e mtn. Iran 43 34.09N 50.48E
Aliákmon r. Greece 19 40.30N 22.38E
Alicante Spain 16 38.21N 0.29W
Alice R.S.A. 56 32.47S 26.49E
Alice U.S.A. 83 27.45N 98.04W
Alice Arm Canada 74 55.29N129.31W
Alice Springs town Australia 64 23.42S133.52E
Alīgarh India 41 27.53N 78.05E
Alīgūdarz Iran 43 33.25N 49.38E
'Alījūq, Kūh-e mtn. Iran 43 31.27N 51.43E
Alima r. Congo 54 1.36S 16.35E
Alindao C.A.R. 49 5.02N 21.13E
Alingsås Sweden 23 57.56N 12.31E
Alīpur Pakistan 40 29.23N 70.55E
Alīpur Duār India 41 26.29N 89.44E
Alīpur Janūbī Pakistan 40 30.13N 71.18E
Aliquippa U.S.A. 84 40.38N 80.16W
Al 'Irq Libya 51 29.05N 15.48E
Ali Sabieh Djibouti 49 11.09N 42.42E
Al Iskandarīyah Egypt 44 31.13N 29.55E
Al Ismā'īlīyah Egypt 44 30.36N 32.15E
Al Istiwā'īyah d. Sudan 49 5.00N 32.30E
Aliwal North R.S.A. 56 30.41S 26.41E
Al Jabal al Akhḑar d. Libya 51 32.00N 21.30E
Al Jafr Jordan 44 30.16N 36.11E
Al Jāfūrah des. Saudi Arabia 43 24.40N 50.20E
Al Jaghbūb Libya 48 29.45N 24.31E
Al Jahrah Kuwait 43 29.20N 47.41E
Al Jaladah f. Saudi Arabia 45 18.30N 46.25E
Al Jawārah Oman 38 18.55N 57.17E
Al Jawb f. Saudi Arabia 43 23.00N 50.00E
Al Jawf Libya 48 24.12N 23.18E
Al Jawf Saudi Arabia 42 29.49N 39.52E
Al Jawsh Libya 51 32.00N 11.40E
Al Jazīrah f. Iraq 42 35.00N 41.00E
Al Jazīrah f. Sudan 48 14.25N 33.00E
Al Jifārah Saudi Arabia 43 23.59N 45.11E
Al Jīzah Egypt 44 30.01N 31.12E
Al Jubayl Saudi Arabia 43 27.59N 49.40E
Al Junaynah Sudan 49 13.27N 22.27E
Aljustrel Portugal 16 37.55N 8.10W
Al Karabah Sudan 48 18.33N 33.42E
Al Karak Jordan 44 31.11N 35.42E
Al Kawah Sudan 49 13.44N 32.30E
Al Khābūr r. Syria 42 35.07N 40.30E
Al Khābūrah Oman 43 23.58N 57.10E
Al Khalīl Jordan 44 31.32N 35.06E
Al Khamāsīn Saudi Arabia 45 20.29N 44.49E
Al Khandaq Sudan 48 18.36N 30.34E
Al Khānkah Egypt 44 30.12N 31.21E
Al Khārijah Egypt 42 25.26N 30.33E
Al Kharṭūm Sudan 48 15.33N 32.35E
Al Kharṭūm d. Sudan 48 15.45N 32.30E
Al Kharṭūm Baḩrī Sudan 48 15.39N 32.34E
Al Khasfah well Oman 45 19.45N 54.19E
Al Khawr Qatar 43 25.39N 51.32E
Al Khirbah as Samrā' Jordan 44 32.11N 36.10E
Al Khubar Saudi Arabia 43 26.18N 50.06E
Al Khufayfīyah Saudi Arabia 43 24.55N 44.42E
Al Khums Libya 51 32.39N 14.16E
Al Khums d. Libya 51 31.20N 14.10E
Al Khunn Saudi Arabia 43 23.18N 49.15E
Al Kidn des. Saudi Arabia 43 22.20N 54.20E
Al Kiswah Syria 44 33.21N 36.14E
Alkmaar Neth. 14 52.37N 4.44E
Al Kufrah Libya 48 24.14N 23.15E
Al Kuntillah Egypt 44 30.00N 34.41E
Al Kūt Iraq 43 32.30N 45.51E
Al Kuwayt Kuwait 43 29.20N 48.00E
Al Labwah Lebanon 44 34.11N 36.21E
Al Lādhiqīyah Syria 44 35.31N 35.47E
Al Lagowa Sudan 49 11.24N 29.08E
Allāhābād India 41 25.27N 81.51E
Allakaket U.S.A. 72 66.30N152.45W
Allanche France 17 45.14N 2.56E
'Allāqī, Wādī al r. Egypt 42 22.55N 33.02E
Allegheny r. U.S.A. 84 40.27N 80.00W
Allegheny Mts. U.S.A. 84 38.30N 80.00W
Allen, Lough Rep. of Ire. 13 54.07N 8.04W
Allentown U.S.A. 85 40.37N 75.30W
Alleppey India 38 9.30N 76.22E
Aller r. W. Germany 20 52.57N 9.11E
Alliance Nebr. U.S.A. 82 42.06N102.52W
Allier r. France 17 46.58N 3.04E
Al Līṭānī r. Lebanon 44 33.22N 35.14E
Al Līth Saudi Arabia 48 20.09N 40.16E
Al Līwā' f. U.A.E. 45 23.00N 54.00E
Alloa U.K. 12 56.07N 3.49W
Allora Australia 65 28.02S151.59E
Allos France 17 44.14N 6.38E
Al Luḩayyah Yemen 48 15.43N 42.42E
Alluitsup-Paa see Sydpröven Greenland 73
Alma Canada 77 48.32N 71.40W
Alma Ga. U.S.A. 85 31.33N 82.29W
Alma Mich. U.S.A. 84 43.23N 84.40W
Al Ma'ānīyah well Iraq 42 30.44N 43.00E
Alma-Ata U.S.S.R. 30 43.19N 76.55E
Almaden Australia 64 17.20S144.41E
Almadén Spain 16 38.47N 4.50W
Al Madīnah Saudi Arabia 42 24.30N 39.35E
Al Madīnah al Fikrīyah Egypt 44 27.56N 30.49E
Al Mafraq Jordan 44 32.20N 36.12E
Al Maghrah well Egypt 42 30.14N 28.56E
Almagor Israel 44 32.55N 35.36E
Al Maḩallah al Kubrá Egypt 44 30.59N 31.12E
Al Maḩārīq Egypt 42 25.37N 30.39E
Al Maḩmūdīyah Egypt 44 31.10N 30.30E
Al Majma'ah Saudi Arabia 43 25.52N 45.25E
Al Manāmah Bahrain 43 26.12N 50.36E
Almanor U.S.A. 80 40.15N121.08W
Almansa Spain 16 38.52N 1.06W
Al Manshāh Egypt 42 26.28N 31.48E
Al Manṣūrah Egypt 44 31.03N 31.23E
Al Manzil Jordan 44 31.03N 36.01E
Al Manzilah Egypt 44 31.10N 31.56E
Almanzor, Pico de mtn. Spain 16 40.20N 5.22W
Almanzora r. Spain 16 37.16N 1.49W
Al Marj Libya 48 32.30N 20.50E
Al Maṭarīyah Egypt 44 31.12N 32.02E
Al Matnah Sudan 48 13.47N 35.03E
Al Mawṣil Iraq 42 36.21N 43.08E
Al Mayādīn Syria 42 35.01N 40.28E
Almazán Spain 16 41.29N 2.31W
Al Mazra'ah Jordan 44 31.16N 35.31E
Almeirim Portugal 16 39.12N 8.37W
Almelo Neth. 14 52.21N 6.40E
Almendralejo Spain 16 38.41N 6.26W
Almería Spain 16 36.50N 2.26W
Älmhult Sweden 23 56.33N 14.08E
Al Midhnab Saudi Arabia 43 25.52N 44.15E
Al Miḩrāḑ des. Saudi Arabia 43 20.00N 52.30E
Al Minyā Egypt 44 28.06N 30.45E
Al Mismīyah Syria 44 33.08N 36.24E
Almonte Spain 16 37.16N 6.31W
Almora India 41 29.37N 79.40E
Al Mudawwarah Jordan 44 29.20N 36.00E
Al Muglad Sudan 49 11.02N 27.44E
Al Muḩarraq Bahrain 43 26.16N 50.38E
Al Mukallā S. Yemen 45 14.34N 49.09E
Al Mukhā Yemen 49 13.19N 43.15E
Almuñécar Spain 16 36.44N 3.41W
Al Muwayh Saudi Arabia 42 22.41N 41.37E
Alnwick U.K. 10 55.25N 1.41W
Alofi Niue 68 19.03S169.55W
Alofi B. Niue 68 19.02S169.55W
Alónnisos i. Greece 19 39.08N 23.50E
Alonsa Canada 75 50.50N 99.00W
Alor i. Indonesia 37 8.20S124.30E
Alor Setar Malaysia 36 6.06N100.23E
Alozero U.S.S.R. 24 65.02N 31.10E
Alpena U.S.A. 84 45.04N 83.27W
Alpes Maritimes mts. France 17 44.07N 7.08E
Alpha Australia 64 23.39S146.38E
Alphen Neth. 14 52.08N 4.40E
Alpine U.S.A. 83 30.22N103.40W
Alps mts. Europe 17 46.00N 7.30E
Al Qaḑārif Sudan 48 14.02N 35.24E
Al Qaḑīmah Saudi Arabia 48 22.21N 39.09E
Al Qafā' des. U.A.E. 38 23.25N 53.50E
Al Qafā' des. U.A.E. 43 23.30N 53.30E
Al Qāhirah Egypt 44 30.03N 31.15E
Al Qā'īyah Saudi Arabia 42 24.18N 43.30E
Al Qā'īyah well Saudi Arabia 43 26.27N 45.35E
Al Qalībah Saudi Arabia 42 28.24N 37.42E
Al Qanāṭir al Khayrīyah Egypt 44 30.12N 31.08E
Al Qanṭarah Egypt 44 30.52N 32.20E
Al Qaryatayn Syria 44 34.13N 37.13E
Al Qaşabāt Libya 51 32.35N 14.03E
Al Qaşr Egypt 42 25.43N 28.54E
Al Qaşşāşīn Egypt 44 30.34N 31.56E
Al Qaṭīf Saudi Arabia 43 26.31N 50.00E
Al Qaṭrānah Jordan 44 31.15N 36.03E
Al Qaṭrūn Libya 51 24.56N 14.38E
Al Qayşūmah Saudi Arabia 43 28.20N 46.07E
Al Qunayṭirah Syria 44 33.08N 35.49E
Al Qunfudhah Saudi Arabia 48 19.08N 41.05E
Al Qurnah Iraq 43 31.00N 47.26E
Al Quşaymah Egypt 44 30.40N 34.22E
Al Quşayr Egypt 42 26.06N 34.17E
Al Qūşīyah Egypt 42 27.26N 30.49E
Al Quṭayfah Syria 44 33.44N 36.36E
Alroy Downs town Australia 64 19.18S136.04E
Als i. Denmark 23 54.59N 9.55E
Alsace d. France 17 48.25N 7.40E
Alsask Canada 75 51.23N109.59W
Alsasua Spain 16 42.54N 2.10W
Älsborg d. Sweden 23 58.00N 12.20E
Alsek Ranges mts. Canada 74 59.21N137.05W
Alsfeld W. Germany 20 50.45N 9.16E
Alsten i. Norway 22 65.55N 12.35E
Alston U.K. 12 54.48N 2.26W
Alta Norway 22 70.00N 23.15E
Alta r. Norway 22 69.50N 23.30E
Altafjorden est. Norway 22 70.10N 23.00E
Alta Gracia Argentina 92 31.40S 64.26W
Altagracia de Orituco Venezuela 90 9.54N 66.24W
Altai mts. Mongolia 30 46.30N 93.30E
Altamaha r. U.S.A. 85 31.19N 81.17W
Altamira Brazil 91 3.12S 52.12W
Altamont Oreg. U.S.A. 80 42.12N121.44W
Altamura Italy 19 40.50N 16.32E
Altar, Desierto de des. Mexico 81 31.50N114.15W
Altavista U.S.A. 85 37.07N 79.18W
Altay China 30 47.48N 88.07E
Altay Mongolia 30 46.20N 97.00E
Altea Spain 16 38.37N 0.03W
Altenburg E. Germany 20 50.59N 12.27E
Altenkirchen W. Germany 14 50.41N 7.40E
Altiboullin, L. Australia 66 29.50S142.50E
Altiplanicie Mexicana mts. Mexico 83 29.00N105.00W
Altnaharra U.K. 12 58.16N 4.26W
Alto Araguaia Brazil 91 17.19S 53.10W
Alto Molocue Mozambique 55 15.38S 37.42E
Alton Canada 76 43.52N 80.04W
Alton U.K. 11 51.08N 0.59W
Alton U.S.A. 82 38.55N 90.10W
Altona Australia 62 27.34S120.00E
Altona W. Germany 20 53.32N 9.56E
Altoona U.S.A. 84 40.30N 78.24W
Altun Shan mts. China 30 38.10N 87.50E
Altus U.S.A. 83 34.38N 99.20W
Al Ubayyiḑ Sudan 49 13.11N 30.13E
Al Uḑayyah Sudan 49 12.03N 28.17E
Aluk Sudan 49 8.26N 27.32E
Al 'Ulá Saudi Arabia 42 26.39N 37.58E
'Alula Somali Rep. 45 11.58N 50.48E
Al 'Uqaylah Libya 51 30.16N 19.12E
Al Uqşur Egypt 42 25.41N 32.24E
Al Urduun r. Asia 44 31.47N 35.31E
Al 'Uwaynah well Saudi Arabia 43 26.46N 48.13E
Al 'Uwaynāt Libya 51 25.48N 10.33E
Al 'Uyūn Saudi Arabia 43 26.32N 43.41E
Alva U.S.A. 83 36.48N 98.40W
Alvarado Mexico 86 18.49N 95.46W
Älvdalen Sweden 23 61.14N 14.02E
Alvesta Sweden 23 56.54N 14.33E
Älvho Sweden 23 61.30N 14.46E
Alvin U.S.A. 83 29.25N 95.15W
Älvkarleby Sweden 23 60.34N 17.27E
Älvsbyn Sweden 22 65.39N 20.59E
Al Wajh Saudi Arabia 42 26.16N 36.28E
Al Wakrah Qatar 43 25.09N 51.36E
Alwar India 40 27.34N 76.36E
Al Wazz Sudan 48 15.01N 30.10E
Al Yamāmah Saudi Arabia 43 24.11N 47.21E
Alyaty U.S.S.R. 43 39.59N 49.20E
Alytus U.S.S.R. 21 54.24N 24.03E
Alzada U.S.A. 80 45.01N104.26W
Alzette r. Lux. 14 49.52N 6.07E
Amadeus, L. Australia 62 24.50S130.45E
Amadi Sudan 49 5.31N 30.20E
Amadjuak Canada 73 64.00N 72.50W
Amadjuak L. Canada 73 65.00N 71.00W
Amagasaki Japan 35 34.43N135.25E
Åmål Sweden 23 59.03N 12.42E
Amaliás Greece 19 37.48N 21.21E
Amalner India 40 21.03N 75.04E
Amami ō shima i. Japan 31 28.20N129.30E
Amamula Zaïre 55 0.17S 27.49E
Amanã, L. Brazil 90 2.35S 64.40W
Amānganj India 41 24.26N 80.02E
Amangeldy U.S.S.R. 28 50.12N 65.11E
Amapá Brazil 91 2.00N 50.50W
Amapá d. Brazil 91 2.00N 52.00W
Amarante Brazil 91 6.14S 42.51W
Amaranth Canada 75 50.36N 98.43W
Amareleja Portugal 16 38.12N 7.13W
Amares Portugal 16 41.38N 8.21W
Amarillo U.S.A. 83 35.13N101.49W
Amar Jadīd Sudan 48 14.28N 25.14E
Amarkantak India 41 22.40N 81.45E
Amaro, Monte mtn. Italy 18 42.06N 14.04E
Amarti Ethiopia 48 14.16N 41.10E
Amasya Turkey 42 40.37N 35.50E
Amazon r. see Amazonas r. Brazil 91
Amazonas d. Brazil 90 4.50S 64.00W
Amazonas r. Brazil 91 2.00S 52.00W
Amazonas, Estuario do Rio f. Brazil 91 0.00 50.30W
Amazon Delta see Amazonas, Estuario do Rio f. Brazil 91
Amb Pakistan 40 34.19N 72.51E
Ambāla India 40 30.23N 76.46E
Ambalavao Madagascar 57 21.50S 46.56E
Ambam Cameroon 53 2.25N 11.16E
Ambarawa Indonesia 37 7.12S110.30E
Ambarchik U.S.S.R. 29 69.39N162.27E
Ambarnāth India 40 19.11N 73.10E
Ambarnyy U.S.S.R. 24 65.59N 33.53E
Ambato Ecuador 90 1.18S 78.36W
Ambato-Boeni Madagascar 57 16.28S 46.43E
Ambatofinandrahana Madagascar 57 20.33S 46.48E
Ambatolampy Madagascar 57 19.23S 47.25E
Ambatondrazaka Madagascar 57 17.50S 48.25E
Amberg W. Germany 20 49.27N 11.52E
Ambergris Cay i. Belize 87 18.00N 87.58W
Ambidédi Mali 52 14.35N 11.47W
Ambikāpur India 41 23.07N 83.12E
Ambilobe Madagascar 57 13.12S 49.04E
Amble U.K. 10 55.20N 1.34W
Ambleside U.K. 10 54.26N 2.58W
Ambodifototra Madagascar 57 16.59S 49.52E
Ambohidratrimo Madagascar 57 18.50S 47.26E
Ambohimahasoa Madagascar 57 21.07S 47.13E
Ambohimanga du Sud Madagascar 57 20.52S 47.36E
Amboise France 15 47.25N 1.00E
Ambon Indonesia 37 4.50S128.10E
Ambositra Madagascar 57 20.31S 47.15E
Ambovombe Madagascar 57 25.11S 46.05E
Amboy U.S.A. 81 34.33N115.44W
Ambre, Cap d' c. Madagascar 57 11.57S 49.17E
Ambrières France 15 48.24N 0.38W
Ambrim i. Vanuatu 68 16.15S168.10E
Ambriz Angola 54 7.54S 13.12E
Ambunten Indonesia 37 6.55S113.45E
Am Dam Chad 49 12.46N 20.29E
Amderma U.S.S.R. 28 69.44N 61.35E
Amdo China 41 32.22N 91.07E
Ameca Mexico 86 20.33N104.02W
Ameland i. Neth. 14 53.28N 5.48E
Amelia City U.S.A. 85 30.37N 81.27W
Americana Brazil 94 22.44S 47.19W
American Falls Resr. U.S.A. 80 43.00N113.00W
American Fork U.S.A. 80 40.23N111.48W
Americus U.S.A. 85 32.04N 84.14W
Amersfoort Neth. 14 52.10N 5.23E
Amery Australia 63 31.09S117.05E
Ames U.S.A. 82 42.02N 93.37W
Ameson Canada 76 49.50N 84.35W
Ametinho Angola 54 17.20S 17.20E
Amga U.S.S.R. 29 60.51N131.59E
Amga r. U.S.S.R. 29 62.40N135.20E
Am Géréda Chad 49 12.52N 21.10E
Amgu U.S.S.R. 31 45.48N137.36E
Amguid Algeria 51 26.26N 5.22E
Amgun r. U.S.S.R. 29 53.10N139.47E
Amhara Plateau f. Ethiopia 49 11.00N 38.00E
Amherst Canada 77 45.49N 64.14W
Amiata mtn. Italy 18 42.53N 11.37E
Amiens Australia 67 28.35S151.46E
Amiens France 15 49.54N 2.18E
Amīr Chāh well Pakistan 40 29.13N 62.28E
Amisk L. Canada 75 54.35N102.13W
Amistad Resr. U.S.A. 83 29.34N101.15W
Amite U.S.A. 83 30.44N 90.33W
Amla India 41 21.56N 78.07E
Amlekhganj Nepal 41 27.17N 85.00E
Åmli Norway 23 58.47N 8.30E
Amlwch U.K. 10 53.24N 4.21W
'Ammān Jordan 44 31.57N 35.56E
Ammanford U.K. 11 51.48N 4.00W
Ammassalik Greenland 73 65.40N 38.00W
Ammókhostos Cyprus 44 35.07N 33.57E
Ammókhostou, Kólpos b. Cyprus 44 35.12N 34.05E
Amo r. India 41 25.58N 89.36E
Āmol Iran 43 36.26N 52.24E
Amorgós i. Greece 19 36.50N 25.55E
Amory U.S.A. 83 33.59N 88.29W
Amos Canada 76 48.35N 78.05W
Ampala Honduras 87 13.16N 87.39W
Ampanihy Madagascar 57 24.42S 44.45E
Amparo Brazil 94 22.44S 46.44W
Ampezzo Italy 15 46.25N 12.48E
Amphitheatre Australia 66 37.12S143.25E
Amqui Canada 77 48.28N 67.26W
Amrāvati India 41 20.56N 77.45E
Amreli India 40 21.37N 71.14E
Amritsar India 40 31.38N 74.53E
Amroha India 41 28.55N 78.28E
Am Saterna Chad 49 12.26N 21.25E
Amsel Algeria 51 22.37N 5.26E
Amstelveen Neth. 14 52.18N 4.51E
Amsterdam Neth. 14 52.22N 4.54E
Amsterdam N.Y. U.S.A. 84 42.57N 74.11W
Am Timan Chad 49 11.02N 20.17E
Amu Darya r. U.S.S.R. 28 43.50N 59.00E
Amulet Canada 75 49.40N104.45W
Amundsen G. Canada 72 70.30N122.00W
Amundsen Sea Antarctica 96 72.00S120.00W
Amuntai Indonesia 36 2.24S115.14E
Amur r. U.S.S.R. 29 53.17N140.00E
'Amūr, Wādī r. Sudan 48 18.56N 33.34E
Amurzet U.S.S.R. 31 47.50N131.05E
Anabar r. U.S.S.R. 29 72.40N113.30E
Ana Branch r. Australia 66 34.08S141.46E
Anaco Venezuela 90 9.27N 64.28W
Anaconda U.S.A. 80 46.08N112.57W
Anadarko U.S.A. 83 35.04N 98.15W
Anadolu f. Turkey 42 38.00N 35.00E
Anadyr U.S.S.R. 29 64.40N177.32E
Anadyr r. U.S.S.R. 29 65.00N176.00E
Anadyrskiy Zaliv g. U.S.S.R. 29 64.30N177.50W
Anáfi i. Greece 19 36.21N 25.50E
Anaheim U.S.A. 81 33.51N117.57W
Analalava Madagascar 57 14.38S 47.45E
Anambas, Kepulauan is. Indonesia 36 3.00N106.10E
Anambra d. Nigeria 53 6.20N 7.25E
Anamoose U.S.A. 82 47.53N100.15W
Anamur Turkey 42 36.06N 32.49E
Ānand India 40 22.34N 72.56E
Anandpur India 41 21.16N 86.13E
Anantapur India 38 14.41N 77.36E
Anantnāg Jammu & Kashmir 40 33.44N 75.09E
Anápolis Brazil 91 16.19S 48.58W
Anapú r. Brazil 91 1.53S 50.53W
Anār Iran 43 30.54N 55.18E
Anārak Iran 43 33.20N 53.42E
Anār Darreh Afghan. 40 32.46N 61.39E
Anatahan i. Mariana Is. 37 16.22N145.38E
Anatolia f. see Anadolu f. Turkey 42
Anatone U.S.A. 80 46.08N117.08W
Añatuya Argentina 92 28.26S 62.48W
Ancenis France 15 47.21N 1.10W
Anchau Nigeria 53 11.00N 8.23E
Anchorage U.S.A. 72 61.10N150.00W
Ancien Goubéré C.A.R. 49 5.51N 26.46E
Ancohuma mtn. Bolivia 92 16.05S 68.36W
Ancón Peru 90 11.50S 77.10W
Ancona Italy 18 43.37N 13.33E
Ancuabe Mozambique 55 13.00S 39.50E
Ancud Chile 93 41.05S 73.50W
Ancy-le-Franc France 15 47.46N 4.10E
Anda China 31 46.25N125.20E
Åndalsnes Norway 22 62.33N 7.43E
Andalucía d. Spain 16 37.36N 4.30W
Andalusia U.S.A. 85 31.20N 86.30W
Andaman Is. India 34 12.00N 92.45E
Andaman Sea Indian Oc. 34 10.00N 95.00E
Andamooka Australia 66 30.27S137.12E
Andanga U.S.S.R. 24 59.11N 45.44E
Andara Namibia 56 18.04S 21.26E
Andelot France 17 48.15N 5.18E
Andenes Norway 22 69.18N 16.10E
Andenne Belgium 14 50.29N 5.04E
Anderlecht Belgium 14 50.51N 4.18E
Andernach W. Germany 14 50.25N 7.24E
Anderson r. Canada 72 69.45N129.00W
Anderson Ind. U.S.A. 84 40.05N 85.41W
Anderson S.C. U.S.A. 85 34.30N 82.39W
Andes mts. S. America 93 32.40S 70.00W
Andevoranto Madagascar 57 18.57S 49.06E
Andfjorden est. Norway 22 69.55N 16.00E
Andhra Pradesh d. India 39 17.00N 79.00E
Andikíthira i. Greece 19 35.52N 23.18E
Andizhan U.S.S.R. 30 40.48N 72.23E
Andorra town Andorra 17 42.30N 1.31E
Andorra Europe 17 42.30N 1.32E
Andover U.K. 11 51.13N 1.29W
Andover N.J. U.S.A. 85 40.59N 74.45W
Andöy i. Norway 22 69.05N 15.40E
Andrada Angola 54 7.41S 21.22E
Andrews N.C. U.S.A. 85 35.13N 83.49W
Andrews Tex. U.S.A. 83 32.19N102.33W
Andreyevo-Ivanovka U.S.S.R. 21 47.28N 30.29E
Andria Italy 18 41.13N 16.18E
Andriba Madagascar 57 17.36S 46.55E
Androka Madagascar 57 25.02S 44.05E
Ándros Greece 19 37.50N 24.57E
Ándros i. Greece 19 37.50N 24.50E
Andros I. Bahamas 87 24.25N 78.00W
Andros Town Bahamas 87 24.43N 77.47W
Andrushevka U.S.S.R. 21 50.00N 28.59E
Andújar Spain 16 38.02N 4.03W
Andulo Angola 54 11.28S 16.43E
Anefis I-n-Darane Mali 52 17.57N 0.35E
Anegada i. B.V.Is. 87 18.46N 64.24W
Anécho Togo 53 6.17N 1.40E
Aneityum i. Vanuatu 68 20.12S169.45E
Añelo Argentina 93 38.20S 68.45W
Aneto, Pico de mtn. Spain 16 42.40N 0.19E
Aney Niger 53 19.24N 12.56E

Angara to Åsnen

Angara r. U.S.S.R. 29 58.00N 93.00E
Angarsk U.S.S.R. 29 52.31N103.55E
Angaston Australia 66 34.30S139.03E
Angatuba Brazil 94 23.27S 48.25W
Ånge Sweden 22 62.31N 15.40E
Ángel de la Guarda, Isla i. Mexico 81 29.20N113.25W
Angel Falls f. Venezuela 90 5.55N 62.30W
Ängelholm Sweden 23 56.15N 12.50E
Angels Camp U.S.A. 80 38.04N120.32W
Angereb r. Ethiopia 49 13.45N 36.40E
Ångerman r. Sweden 22 63.00N 17.43E
Angermünde E. Germany 20 53.01N 14.00E
Angers France 15 47.29N 0.32W
Angerville France 15 48.19N 2.00E
Ångesån r. Sweden 22 66.22N 22.58E
Angikuni L. Canada 75 62.00N100.00W
Angkor ruins Kampuchea 34 13.30N103.50E
Angledool Australia 67 29.06S147.57E
Anglesey i. U.K. 10 53.16N 4.25W
Angleton U.S.A. 83 29.10N 95.26W
Ango Zaïre 49 4.02N 25.52E
Angoche Mozambique 57 16.10S 39.57E
Angol Chile 93 37.48S 72.43W
Angola Africa 54 11.00S 18.00E
Angola Ind. U.S.A. 84 41.38N 85.01W
Angola N.Y. U.S.A. 84 42.39N 79.02W
Angoram P.N.G. 37 4.04S144.04E
Angoulême France 17 45.40N 0.10E
Angra dos Reis Brazil 94 22.59S 44.17W
Ang Thong Thailand 34 14.35N100.25E
Anguilla i. Leeward Is. 87 18.14N 63.05W
Angul India 41 20.51N 85.06E
Angumu Zaïre 55 0.10S 27.38E
Anholt i. Denmark 23 56.42N 11.34E
Anholt W. Germany 14 51.51N 6.26E
Anh Son Vietnam 34 18.54N105.18E
Anhua China 33 28.24N111.13E
Anhui d. China 33 32.00N117.00E
Aniak U.S.A. 72 61.32N159.40W
Animas U.S.A. 81 31.57N108.48W
Anin Burma 34 15.40N 97.46E
Anina Romania 21 45.05N 21.51E
Anivorano Madagascar 57 18.44S 48.58E
Anjad India 40 22.02N 75.03E
Anjangaon India 40 21.10N 77.18E
Anjār India 40 23.08N 70.01E
Anjō Japan 35 34.57N137.05E
Anjouan i. Comoros 55 12.12S 44.28E
Anjozorobe Madagascar 57 18.24S 47.52E
Anju N. Korea 31 39.36N125.42E
Anka Nigeria 53 12.06N 5.56E
Ankang China 32 32.38N109.12E
Ankara Turkey 42 39.55N 32.50E
Ankaramena Madagascar 57 21.57S 46.39E
Ankazoabo Madagascar 57 22.18S 44.31E
Ankazobe Madagascar 57 18.21S 47.07E
Anklam E. Germany 20 53.51N 13.41E
Anklesvar India 40 21.38N 72.59E
Ånkober Ethiopia 49 9.30N 39.44E
Ankpa Nigeria 53 7.26N 7.38E
Anlong China 33 25.06N105.31E
Anlu China 33 31.15N113.40E
Anna U.S.A. 83 37.28N 89.15W
Annaba Algeria 51 36.55N 7.47E
An Nabk Syria 44 34.02N 36.43E
Anna Creek town Australia 66 28.50S136.07E
An Nafūd des. Saudi Arabia 42 28.40N 41.30E
An Najaf Iraq 43 31.59N 44.19E
An Nakhl Egypt 44 29.55N 33.45E
Annam Highlands see Annamitique, Chaîne mts. Laos / Vietnam 34
Annamitique, Chaîne mts. Laos / Vietnam 34 17.00N106.00E
Annan U.K. 12 54.59N 3.16W
Annan r. U.K. 12 54.58N 3.16W
Annandale Australia 64 21.57S148.18E
Annandale f. U.K. 12 55.12N 3.25W
Anna Plains Australia 62 19.18S121.34E
Annapolis U.S.A. 85 38.59N 76.30W
Annapurna mtn. Nepal 41 28.34N 83.50E
An Naqīrah well Saudi Arabia 43 27.53N 48.15E
Ann Arbor U.S.A. 84 42.18N 83.43W
An Nāşirīyah Iraq 43 31.04N 46.16E
An Nawfalīyah Libya 51 30.47N 17.50E
Annecy France 17 45.54N 6.07E
An Nil al Azraq d. Sudan 49 13.00N 33.00E
Anniston U.S.A. 85 33.38N 85.50W
Annobón i. Equat. Guinea 95 1.25S 5.36E
Annonay France 17 45.15N 4.40E
Annuello Australia 66 34.52S142.54E
An Nuhūd Sudan 49 12.42N 28.26E
Anoka U.S.A. 82 45.11N 93.20W
Anorotsangana Madagascar 57 13.56S 47.55E
Anou Ti-n Elhaoua well Algeria 51 20.02N 2.55E
Anpu China 33 21.27N110.01E
Anqing China 33 30.40N117.03E
Ansbach W. Germany 20 49.18N 10.36E
Anshan China 32 41.06N122.58E
Anshun China 33 26.11N105.50E
Anson B. Australia 62 13.10S130.00E
Ansongo Mali 52 15.40N 0.30E
Anstruther U.K. 12 56.14N 2.42W
Ansudu Indonesia 37 2.11S139.22E
Antakya Turkey 42 36.12N 36.10E
Antalaha Madagascar 57 14.53S 50.16E
Antalya Turkey 42 36.53N 30.42E
Antalya Körfezi g. Turkey 42 36.38N 31.00E
Antananarivo Madagascar 57 18.55S 47.31E
Antarctica 96
Antarctic Pen. f. Antarctica 95 65.00S 64.00W
Antas Brazil 91 10.20S 38.20W
Antequera Spain 16 37.01N 4.34W
Anthony U.S.A. 83 37.09N 89.02W
Antibes France 17 43.35N 7.07E
Anticosti, Île d' i. Canada 77 49.20N 63.00W
Anticosti Prov. Park Canada 77 49.20N 63.00W
Antifer, Cap d' c. France 15 49.41N 0.10E
Antigo U.S.A. 82 45.09N 89.09W
Antigua Guatemala 86 14.33N 90.42W
Antigua i. Leeward Is. 87 17.09N 61.49W
Anti-Lebanon mts. see Sharqī, Al Jabal ash mts. Lebanon 44
Antipodes Is. Pacific Oc. 68 49.42S178.50E
Antlers U.S.A. 83 34.14N 95.47W
Antofagasta Chile 92 23.39S 70.24W
Antônio Bezerra Brazil 91 3.44S 38.35W
Antônio Carlos Brazil 94 21.18S 43.48W
Antonito U.S.A. 80 37.05N106.00W
Antrain France 15 48.28N 1.30W
Antrim U.K. 13 54.43N 6.14W
Antrim d. U.K. 13 54.58N 6.20W
Antrim, Mts. of U.K. 13 55.00N 6.10W
Antsalova Madagascar 57 18.40S 44.37E
Antsirabé Madagascar 57 19.51S 47.02E
Antsiranana Madagascar 57 12.16S 49.17E
Antsohihy Madagascar 57 14.52S 47.59E
Anttis Sweden 22 67.16N 22.52E
Antwerpen Belgium 14 51.13N 4.25E
Antwerpen d. Belgium 14 51.16N 4.45E
Anūpgarh India 40 29.11N 73.12E
Anvik U.S.A. 72 62.38N160.20W
Anxi Fujian China 33 25.03N118.13E
Anxi Gansu China 30 40.32N 95.57E
Anxious B. Australia 66 33.25S134.35E
Anyama Ivory Coast 52 5.30N 4.03W
Anyang China 32 36.05N114.20E
Anyer Lor Indonesia 37 6.02S105.57E
Anyi China 33 28.50N115.32E
Anyuan China 33 25.09N115.21E
Anyue China 33 30.09N105.18E
Anzhero-Sudzhensk U.S.S.R. 28 56.10N 86.10E
Anzio Italy 18 41.27N 12.37E
Ao Ban Don b. Thailand 34 9.00N 99.20E
Aohan Qi China 32 42.23N119.59E
Aomori Japan 31 40.50N140.43E
Aopo W. Samoa 68 13.29S172.30W
Aosta Italy 15 45.43N 7.19E
Aoulef Algeria 50 26.58N 1.05E
Aoulime, Jbel mtn. Morocco 50 30.48N 8.50W
Aozou Chad 53 21.49N 17.25E
Apache U.S.A. 83 34.54N 98.22W
Apalachee B. U.S.A. 85 30.00N 84.13W
Apalachicola U.S.A. 85 29.43N 85.01W
Apalachicola r. U.S.A. 85 29.44N 84.59W
Apaporis r. Colombia 90 1.40S 69.20W
Aparri Phil. 37 18.22N121.40E
Apatin Yugo. 19 45.40N 18.59E
Apatity U.S.S.R. 24 67.32N 33.21E
Apeldoorn Neth. 14 52.13N 5.57E
Api mtn. Nepal 41 30.01N 80.56E
Apia W. Samoa 68 13.48S171.45W
Apizaco Mexico 86 19.25N 98.09W
Apoka Uganda 49 3.42N 33.38E
Apollo Bay town Australia 66 38.45S143.40E
Apostle Is. U.S.A. 82 46.50N 90.30W
Apóstoles Argentina 92 27.55S 55.45W
Apostólou Andréa, Akrotírion c. Cyprus 44 35.40N 34.35E
Apoteri Guyana 90 4.02N 58.32W
Appalachian Mts. U.S.A. 84 41.00N 77.00W
Appennino mts. Italy 18 42.00N 13.30E
Appennino Ligure mts. Italy 15 44.30N 9.00E
Appennino Tosco-Emiliano mts. Italy 15 44.05N 11.00E
Appiano Italy 15 46.28N 11.15E
Appingedam Neth. 14 53.18N 6.52E
Appleby U.K. 10 54.35N 2.29W
Appleton U.S.A. 82 44.16N 88.25W
Apsheronsk U.S.S.R. 25 44.26N 39.45E
Apsheronskiy Poluostrov pen. U.S.S.R. 43 40.28N 50.00E
Apsley Australia 66 36.58S141.08E
Apsley Canada 76 44.45N 78.06W
Apucarana Brazil 94 23.34S 51.28W
Apure r. Venezuela 90 7.40N 66.30W
Apurimac r. Peru 90 10.43S 73.55W
Aqaba, G. of Asia 44 28.45N 34.45E
Aqabat al Ḩijāzīyah Jordan 44 29.40N 35.55E
'Aqdā Iran 43 32.25N 33.38E
'Aqīq Sudan 48 18.14N 38.12E
Aqqikkol Hu l. China 30 35.44N 81.34E
Aquidauana Brazil 92 20.27S 55.45W
Aquila Mexico 86 18.30N103.50W
Aquitaine d. France 17 44.40N 0.00
'Arab, Baḩr al r. Sudan 49 9.12N 29.28E
Arabābād Iran 43 33.02N 57.41E
'Arabah, Wādī r. Egypt 44 29.07N 32.40E
Arabei Dalon Somali Rep. 45 3.34N 46.30E
Arabian Sea Asia 38 16.00N 65.00E
Araç Turkey 42 41.14N 33.20E
Aracaju Brazil 91 10.54S 37.07W
Aracanguy, Montañas de mts. Paraguay 92 24.00S 55.50W
Aracati Brazil 91 4.32S 37.45W
Araçatuba Brazil 94 21.12S 50.24W
Arad Romania 21 46.12N 21.19E
Arada Chad 51 15.01N 20.40E
Arafura Sea Austa. 64 9.00S133.00E
Aragarças Brazil 91 15.55S 52.12W
Aragats mtn. U.S.S.R. 43 40.32N 44.11E
Aragón d. Spain 16 41.25N 1.00W
Aragón r. Spain 16 42.20N 1.45W
Araguacema Brazil 91 8.50S 49.34W
Araguaia r. Brazil 91 5.20S 48.30W
Araguari Brazil 94 18.38S 48.13W
Araguari r. Brazil 91 1.15N 50.05W
Arak Algeria 51 25.18N 3.45E
Arāk Iran 43 34.06N 49.44E
Araka Sudan 49 4.16N 30.21E
Arakan d. Burma 34 19.00N 94.15E
Arakan Yoma mts. Burma 34 19.30N 94.30E
Araks r. U.S.S.R. 43 40.00N 48.28E
Aral Sea see Aralskoye More sea U.S.S.R. 28
Aralsk U.S.S.R. 28 46.56N 61.43E
Aralskoye More sea U.S.S.R. 28 45.00N 60.00E
Aralsor, Ozero l. U.S.S.R. 25 49.00N 48.40E
Aramac Australia 64 22.59S145.14E
Arāmbāgh India 41 22.53N 87.47E
Aramia r. P.N.G. 37 8.00S143.20E
Aranda de Duero Spain 16 41.40N 3.41W
Aran I. Rep. of Ire. 13 53.07N 9.38W
Aran Is. Rep. of Ire. 13 53.07N 9.38W
Aranjuez Spain 16 40.02N 3.37W
Aranos Namibia 56 24.09S 19.09E
Aransas Pass town U.S.A. 83 27.54N 97.09W
Araouane Mali 52 18.53N 3.31W
Arapahoe U.S.A. 82 40.18N 99.54W
Arapey Uruguay 93 30.58S 57.30W
Arapey Grande r. Uruguay 93 30.55S 57.49W
Arapiraca Brazil 91 9.45S 36.40W
Arapkir Turkey 42 39.03N 38.29E
'Ar'ar, Wādī r. Iraq 42 32.00N 42.30E
Araraquara Brazil 94 21.46S 48.08W
Araras Brazil 94 22.20S 47.23W
Ararat Australia 66 37.20S143.00E
Ararat mtn. see Ağri Daği mtn. Turkey 43
Aras r. Turkey see Araks r. U.S.S.R. 42
Arauca Colombia 90 7.04N 70.41W
Arauca r. Venezuela 90 7.05N 70.45W
Araure Venezuela 90 9.36N 69.15W
Arāvalli Range mts. India 40 25.00N 73.45E
Araxá Brazil 94 19.37S 46.50W
Araxes r. Iran see Araks r. U.S.S.R. 43
Arba Minch Ethiopia 49 6.02N 37.40E
Arbatax Italy 18 39.56N 9.41E
Arboga Sweden 23 59.24N 15.50E
Arborg Canada 75 50.55N 97.15W
Arbroath U.K. 12 56.34N 2.35W
Arcachon France 17 44.40N 1.11W
Arcadia Fla. U.S.A. 85 27.12N 81.52W
Arcadia Wisc. U.S.A. 82 44.15N 91.30W
Arcata U.S.A. 80 40.52N124.05W
Archer r. Australia 64 13.28S141.41E
Archers Post Kenya 55 0.42N 37.40E
Arcis-sur-Aube France 15 48.32N 4.08E
Arckaringa r. Australia 66 27.56S134.45E
Arco Italy 15 45.55N 10.53E
Arco U.S.A. 80 43.38N113.18W
Arcoona Australia 66 31.06S137.19E
Arcoordaby Australia 66 31.10S135.00E
Arcos Brazil 94 20.12S 45.30W
Arcos Spain 16 36.45N 5.45W
Arcoverde Brazil 91 8.23S 37.00W
Arctic Bay town Canada 73 73.05N 85.20W
Arctic Ocean 96
Arctic Red r. Canada 72 67.26N133.48W
Arctic Red River town Canada 72 67.27N133.46W
Arda r. Greece 19 41.39N 26.30E
Ardabīl Iran 43 38.15N 48.18E
Ardahan Turkey 42 41.08N 42.41E
Årdalstangen Norway 23 61.14N 7.43E
Ardara Rep. of Ire. 13 54.46N 8.25W
Arḑ aş Şawwān f. Jordan 44 30.45N 37.15E
Ardèche r. France 17 44.31N 4.40E
Ardee Rep. of Ire. 9 53.51N 6.33W
Ardennes mts. Belgium 14 50.10N 5.30E
Ardennes d. France 15 49.40N 4.40E
Ardennes, Canal des France 15 49.26N 4.02E
Ardestān Iran 43 33.22N 52.25E
Ardfert Rep. of Ire. 13 52.20N 9.48W
Ardila r. Portugal 16 38.10N 7.30W
Ardlethan Australia 67 34.20S146.53E
Ardmore Rep. of Ire. 13 51.58N 7.43W
Ardmore Okla. U.S.A. 83 34.10N 97.08W
Ardmore Penn. U.S.A. 85 40.01N 75.18W
Ardnamurchan, Pt. of U.K. 12 56.44N 6.14W
Ardrossan Australia 66 34.25S137.55E
Ardrossan U.K. 12 55.38N 4.49W
Ards Pen. U.K. 13 54.30N 5.30W
Åre Sweden 22 63.25N 13.05E
Arecibo Puerto Rico 87 18.29N 66.44W
Areia Branca Brazil 91 4.56S 37.07W
Arena, Pt. U.S.A. 78 38.58N123.44W
Arena, Punta c. Mexico 81 23.32N109.30W
Arendal Norway 23 58.27N 8.48E
Arequipa Peru 90 16.25S 71.32W
Arès France 17 44.47N 1.08W
Arévalo Spain 16 41.03N 4.43W
Arezzo Italy 18 43.27N 11.52E
Arfak mtn. Indonesia 37 1.30S133.50E
Arganda Spain 16 40.19N 3.26W
Argelès-sur-Mer France 17 42.33N 3.01E
Argens r. France 17 43.10N 6.45E
Argenta Italy 15 44.37N 11.50E
Argentan France 15 48.45N 0.01W
Argenton France 15 48.45N 0.01W
Argentera Italy 15 44.24N 6.57E
Argentera mtn. Italy 15 44.10N 7.18E
Argenteuil France 15 48.57N 2.15E
Argentia Canada 77 47.18N 53.59W
Argentina S. America 93 36.00S 63.00W
Argentine Basin f. Atlantic Oc. 95 40.00S 40.00W
Argentino, L. Argentina 93 50.15S 72.25W
Argenton France 17 46.36N 1.30E
Argentré France 15 48.05N 0.39W
Argentré du Plessis France 15 48.03N 1.08W
Argeş r. Romania 19 44.13N 26.22E
Arghandāb r. Afghan. 40 31.27N 64.23E
Árgos Greece 19 37.37N 22.45E
Argostólion Greece 19 38.10N 20.30E
Arguello, Pt. U.S.A. 81 34.35N120.39W
Argun r. U.S.S.R. 31 53.30N121.48E
Argungu Nigeria 53 12.45N 4.35E
Argyle U.S.A. 82 48.20N 96.49W
Ar Horqin Qi China 32 43.45N120.00E
Århus Denmark 23 56.09N 10.13E
Ariah Park town Australia 67 34.20S147.10E
Ariano Italy 18 41.04N 15.00E
Ariano nel Polesine Italy 15 44.56N 12.07E
Aribinda Mali 52 14.17N 0.52W
Arica Chile 92 18.29S 70.20W
Arica Colombia 90 2.07S 71.46W
Arid, C. Australia 63 33.58S123.05E
Arieş r. Romania 21 46.26N 23.59E
Ārifwāla Pakistan 40 30.17N 73.04E
Arīḩā Al Quds Jordan 44 31.51N 35.27E
Arima Trinidad 90 10.38N 61.17W
Arinos r. Brazil 91 10.20S 57.35W
Aripuanã Brazil 90 9.10S 60.38W
Aripuanã r. Brazil 90 5.05S 60.30W
Ariquemes Brazil 90 9.56S 63.04W
Aris Namibia 56 22.48S 17.10E
Arisaig U.K. 12 56.55N 5.51W
'Arīsh, Wādī al r. Egypt 44 31.09N 33.49E
Aristazabal I. Canada 74 52.40N129.10W
Arivonimamo Madagascar 57 19.01S 47.15E
Ariza Spain 16 41.19N 2.03W
Arizona d. U.S.A. 78 34.00N112.00W
Årjäng Sweden 23 59.23N 12.08E
Arjeplog Sweden 22 66.00N 17.58E
Arjona Colombia 90 10.14N 75.22W
Arkadelphia U.S.A. 83 34.07N 93.04W
Arkaig, Loch U.K. 12 56.58N 5.08W
Arkansas d. U.S.A. 83 34.20N 92.00W
Arkansas r. U.S.A. 83 33.48N 91.04W
Arkansas City U.S.A. 83 37.04N 97.02W
Arkhangel'sk U.S.S.R. 24 64.32N 41.10E
Árki i. Greece 19 37.22N 26.45E
Arklow Rep. of Ire. 13 52.47N 6.10W
Arkville U.S.A. 84 42.09N 74.37W
Arlberg Pass Austria 20 47.00N 10.05E
Arles France 17 43.41N 4.38E
Arlington Colo. U.S.A. 80 38.20N103.19W
Arlington Oreg. U.S.A. 80 45.16N120.13W
Arlington Tex. U.S.A. 83 32.44N 97.07W
Arlington Va. U.S.A. 85 38.52N 77.05W
Arlington Heights town U.S.A. 82 42.06N 88.00W
Arlon Belgium 14 49.41N 5.49E
Armadale Australia 63 32.10S115.57E
Armagh U.K. 13 54.21N 6.41W
Armagh d. U.K. 13 54.16N 6.35W
Armançon r. France 15 47.57N 3.30E
Armavir U.S.S.R. 25 44.59N 41.10E
Armenia Colombia 90 4.32N 75.40W
Armeniş Romania 21 45.12N 22.19E
Armentières France 14 50.41N 2.53E
Armidale Australia 67 30.32S151.40E
Armori India 41 20.28N 79.59E
Armstrong Canada 74 50.25N119.10W
Armstrong U.S.A. 83 26.55N 97.47W
Armūr India 41 18.48N 78.17E
Armyanskaya S.S.R. d. U.S.S.R. 43 40.00N 45.00E
Arnaud r. Canada 73 60.00N 69.45W
Årnes Norway 23 60.09N 11.28E
Arnett U.S.A. 83 36.08N 99.46W
Arnhem Neth. 14 52.00N 5.55E
Arnhem, C. Australia 64 12.10S137.00E
Arnhem B. Australia 64 12.20S136.12E
Arnhem Land f. Australia 64 13.10S134.30E
Arno r. Italy 18 43.43N 10.17E
Arno Bay town Australia 66 33.54S136.34E
Arnot Canada 75 55.46N 96.41W
Arnprior Canada 76 45.26N 76.21W
Arnsberg W. Germany 14 51.24N 8.03E
Aroma Sudan 48 15.49N 36.08E
Arona Italy 15 45.46N 8.34E
Arorangi Rarotonga Cook Is. 68 21.13S159.49W
Arpajon France 15 48.35N 2.15E
Arra Ivory Coast 52 6.42N 3.57W
Arrah India 41 25.34N 84.40E
Ar Rahad Sudan 49 12.43N 30.39E
Ar Ramādī Iraq 42 33.27N 43.19E
Ar Ramthā Jordan 44 32.34N 36.00E
Arran i. U.K. 12 55.35N 5.14W
Ar Rank Sudan 49 11.45N 32.48E
Ar Raqqah Syria 42 35.57N 39.03E
Arras France 14 50.17N 2.46E
Ar Rass Saudi Arabia 42 25.54N 43.30E
Ar Rastān Syria 44 34.55N 36.44E
Arrecife Canary Is. 50 28.57N 13.32W
Arrecifes Argentina 93 34.05S 60.05W
Arrey U.S.A. 81 32.51N107.19W
Ar Riyāḑ Saudi Arabia 43 24.39N 46.44E
Arrochar U.K. 12 56.12N 4.44W
Arromanches France 15 49.20N 0.38W
Arrow, Lough Rep.of Ire. 13 54.03N 8.20W
Arrowsmith, Pt. Australia 64 13.18S136.24E
Arrowtown New Zealand 60 44.56S168.50E
Arroyo Feliciano r. Argentina 93 31.06S 59.53W
Arroyo Villimanca r. Argentina 93 35.36S 59.05W
Ar Ru'at Sudan 49 12.21N 32.17E
Ar Rub' al Khālī des. Saudi Arabia 38 20.20N 52.30E
Ar Rubayqī Egypt 44 30.10N 31.46E
Ar Rumaythah Iraq 43 31.32N 45.12E
Ar Ruşayriş Sudan 49 11.51N 34.23E
Ar Ruţbah Iraq 42 33.03N 40.18E
Ar Ruwayḑah Saudi Arabia 43 23.46N 44.46E
Ársos Cyprus 44 34.50N 32.46E
Árta Greece 19 39.10N 20.57E
Artemovsk U.S.S.R. 25 48.35N 38.00E
Artenay France 15 48.05N 1.50E
Artesia U.S.A. 81 32.51N104.24W
Arthabaska Canada 77 46.02N 71.55W
Arthal Jammu & Kashmir 40 33.16N 76.11E
Arthington Liberia 52 6.35N 10.45W
Arthur's Pass New Zealand 60 42.50S171.45E
Artigas Uruguay 93 30.24S 56.28W
Artillery L. Canada 75 63.09N107.52W
Artois f. France 14 50.16N 2.50E
Artux China 30 39.40N 75.49E
Artvin Turkey 42 41.12N 41.48E
Aru, Kepulauan is. Indonesia 37 6.00S134.30E
Arua Uganda 55 3.02N 30.56E
Aruanã Brazil 91 14.54S 51.05W
Aruba i. Neth. Ant. 87 12.30N 70.00W
Arucas Canary Is. 95 28.08N 15.32W
Arun r. U.K. 9 50.48N 0.32W
Arunachal Pradesh d. India 39 28.40N 94.60E
Arundel Canada 77 45.58N 74.37W
Arusha Tanzania 55 3.21S 36.40E
Arusha d. Tanzania 55 4.00S 37.00E
Ārusī d. Ethiopia 49 7.50N 39.50E
Aruwimi r. Zaïre 54 1.20N 23.36E
Arvada Colo. U.S.A. 80 39.50N105.05W
Arvada Wyo. U.S.A. 80 44.39N105.05W
Arvagh Rep. of Ire. 13 53.56N 7.35W
Arvi India 41 20.59N 78.14E
Arvidsjaur Sweden 22 65.35N 19.07E
Arvika Sweden 23 59.39N 12.36E
Arwadin Ethiopia 48 16.16N 38.46E
Arzamas U.S.S.R. 24 55.24N 43.48E
Arzgir U.S.S.R. 25 45.24N 44.04E
Arzignano Italy 15 45.31N 11.20E
Asaba Nigeria 53 6.12N 6.44E
Asadābād Afghan. 40 34.52N 71.09E
Asahi dake mtn. Japan 31 43.42N142.54E
Asahikawa Japan 31 43.50N142.20E
Asansol India 41 23.41N 86.59E
Åsarna Sweden 22 62.40N 14.20E
Asayita Ethiopia 49 11.33N 41.30E
Asbestos Canada 77 45.46N 71.57W
Asbury Park U.S.A. 85 40.14N 74.00W
Ascension i. Atlantic Oc. 95 7.57S 14.22W
Aschaffenburg W. Germany 20 49.58N 9.10E
Aschendorf W. Germany 14 53.03N 7.20E
Aschersleben E. Germany 20 51.46N 11.28E
Ascoli Piceno Italy 18 42.52N 13.36E
Ascona Switz. 15 46.09N 8.46E
Aseb Ethiopia 49 13.01N 42.47E
Åseda Sweden 23 57.10N 15.20E
Asedjrad Algeria 51 24.42N 1.40E
Asela Ethiopia 49 7.59N 39.08E
Åsele Sweden 22 64.10N 17.20E
Åsenbruk Sweden 23 58.54N 12.40E
Asenovgrad Bulgaria 19 42.00N 24.53E
Åseral Norway 23 58.37N 7.25E
Asfeld France 15 49.27N 4.05E
Asha Nigeria 53 7.07N 3.43E
Ashanti d. Ghana 52 6.30N 1.30W
Ashbourne Rep. of Ire. 13 53.31N 6.25W
Ashburn U.S.A. 85 31.42N 83.41W
Ashburton r. Australia 62 21.15S115.00E
Ashburton New Zealand 60 43.54S171.46E
Ashby de la Zouch U.K. 11 52.45N 1.29W
Ashcroft Canada 74 50.40N121.20W
Ashdod Israel 44 31.48N 34.38E
Asheboro U.S.A. 85 35.42N 79.50W
Ashern Canada 75 51.11N 98.21W
Asheville U.S.A. 85 35.35N 82.35W
Ashewat Pakistan 40 31.22N 68.32E
Ash Flat town U.S.A. 83 36.12N 91.38W
Ashford Kent U.K. 11 51.08N 0.53E
Ash Fork U.S.A. 81 35.13N112.29W
Ashington U.K. 10 55.11N 1.34W
Ashiya Japan 35 34.43N135.17E
Ashkhabad U.S.S.R. 43 37.58N 58.24E
Ashland Ky. U.S.A. 84 38.28N 82.40W
Ashland Oreg. U.S.A. 80 42.12N122.42W
Ashland Wisc. U.S.A. 82 46.35N 90.53W
Ashley Australia 67 29.19S149.52E
Ashley U.S.A. 82 38.20N 89.10W
Ashley Snow I. Antarctica 96 72.30S 77.00W
Ashmūn Egypt 44 30.18N 30.59E
Ashoknagar India 41 24.34N 77.43E
Ashqelon Israel 44 31.40N 34.35E
Ash Shabb well Egypt 48 22.19N 29.46E
Ash Shallūfah Egypt 44 30.07N 32.34E
Ash Shāmah des. Saudi Arabia 42 31.20N 38.00E
Ash Shamālīyah d. Sudan 48 19.30N 31.30E
Ash Shāmīyah des. Iraq 43 30.30N 45.30E
Ash Shāriqah U.A.E. 43 25.20N 55.26E
Ash Sharmah Saudi Arabia 44 28.01N 35.14E
Ash Shawbak Jordan 44 30.33N 35.35E
Ash Shaykh Faḑl Egypt 44 28.29N 30.50E
Ash Shaykh 'Ibādah Egypt 44 27.48N 30.52E
Ash Shaykh Miskīn Syria 44 32.49N 36.09E
Ash Shiḩr S. Yemen 45 14.45N 49.36E
Ash Shu'aybah Iraq 43 30.30N 47.40E
Ash Shu'aybah Saudi Arabia 42 27.53N 42.43E
Ash Shumlūl Saudi Arabia 43 26.29N 47.20E
Ashta India 40 23.01N 76.43E
Ashtabula U.S.A. 84 41.53N 80.47W
Ashton R.S.A. 56 33.49S 20.04E
Ashton U.S.A. 80 44.04N111.27W
'Āsī r. Lebanon 44 34.37N 36.30E
Asiago Italy 15 45.52N 11.30E
Asilah Morocco 50 35.32N 6.00W
Asinara i. Italy 18 41.04N 8.18E
Asinara, Golfo dell' g. Italy 18 41.00N 8.32E
'Asīr f. Saudi Arabia 45 19.00N 42.00E
Asir, Ras c. Somali Rep. 45 11.48N 51.22E
Aska India 41 19.36N 84.39E
Askeaton Rep. of Ire. 13 52.36N 9.00W
Askersund Sweden 23 58.53N 14.54E
Askim Norway 23 59.35N 11.10E
Askvoll Norway 23 61.21N 5.04E
Åsmera Ethiopia 48 15.20N 38.58E
Åsnen l. Sweden 23 56.38N 14.42E

Asola to **Baleares, Islas**

Asola Italy 15 45.13N 10.24E
Asosa Ethiopia 49 10.03N 34.32E
Asoteriba, Jabal *mtn.* Sudan 48 21.51N 36.30E
Aspen U.S.A. 80 39.11N106.49W
Aspermont U.S.A. 83 33.08N100.14W
Aspiring, Mt. New Zealand 60 44.20S168.45E
Asquith Canada 75 52.08N107.13W
Assaba *d.* Mauritania 50 16.40N 11.40W
As Sadd al 'Ālī *dam* Egypt 48 23.59N 32.54E
Aş Şaff Egypt 44 29.34N 31.17E
As Saffānīyah Saudi Arabia 43 28.00N 48.48E
Aş Şāfiyah Sudan 48 15.31N 30.07E
Aş Şa'īd *f.* Egypt 42 25.30N 32.00E
Aş Şāliḩīyah Egypt 44 30.47N 31.59E
As Sallūm Egypt 42 31.31N 25.09E
As Salṭ Jordan 44 32.03N 35.44E
As Salwa Saudi Arabia 43 24.44N 50.50E
Assam *d.* India 39 26.30N 93.00E
As Samāwah Iraq 43 31.18N 45.18E
As Sanām *f.* Saudi Arabia 45 22.00N 51.10E
Aş Şarafand Lebanon 44 33.27N 35.18E
As Sarīrīyah Egypt 44 28.20N 30.45E
Assebroek Belgium 14 51.11N 3.16E
Assen Neth. 14 53.00N 6.34E
As Sinbillāwayn Egypt 44 30.53N 31.27E
Assiniboia Canada 75 49.38N105.59W
Assiniboine *r.* Canada 75 49.53N 97.08W
Assinica Prov. Park Canada 76 50.24N 75.00W
Assis Brazil 94 22.37S 50.25W
As Sudd Sudan 49 7.50N 30.00E
Aş Şufayyah Sudan 48 15.30N 34.42E
As Sulaymānīyah Iraq 43 35.32N 45.27E
As Sulaymānīyah Saudi Arabia 43 24.10N 47.20E
As Sulayyil Saudi Arabia 45 20.27N 45.34E
As Sulṭān Libya 51 31.07N 17.09E
As Sumayḩ Sudan 49 9.49N 27.39E
Aş Şummān *f.* Saudi Arabia 43 27.00N 47.00E
As Suwaydā' Syria 44 32.43N 36.33E
As Suways Egypt 44 29.59N 32.33E
Asti Italy 15 44.54N 8.13E
Astipálaia *i.* Greece 19 36.35N 26.25E
Astorga Spain 16 42.30N 6.02W
Astoria U.S.A. 80 46.11N123.50W
Astorp Sweden 23 56.08N 12.57E
Astrakhan U.S.S.R. 25 46.22N 48.00E
Asträsk Sweden 22 64.38N 20.00E
Asturias *d.* Spain 16 43.20N 6.00W
Asuncion *i.* Mariana Is. 37 19.34N145.24E
Asunción Paraguay 94 25.15S 57.40W
Aswân Egypt 42 24.05N 32.56E
Aswan High Dam *see* As Sadd al 'Ālī Egypt 42
Asyût Egypt 42 27.14N 31.07E
Atacama, Desierto *des.* S. America 92 20.00S 69.00W
Atacama, Salar de *f.* Chile 92 23.30S 68.46W
Atacama Desert *see* Atacama, Desierto *des.* S. America 92
Atafu Pacific Oc. 68 8.40S172.40W
Atakpamé Togo 53 7.34N 1.14E
Atami Japan 35 35.05N139.04E
Atapupu Indonesia 37 9.00S124.51E
Atar Mauritania 50 20.32N 13.08W
Atara U.S.S.R. 29 63.10N129.10E
Atasu U.S.S.R. 28 48.42N 71.38E
'Aṭbarah Sudan 48 17.42N 33.59E
'Aṭbarah *r.* Sudan 48 17.40N 33.58E
Atchafalaya B. U.S.A. 83 29.25N 91.20W
Atchison U.S.A. 82 39.34N 95.07W
Ath Belgium 14 50.38N 3.45E
Athabasca Canada 74 54.45N113.20W
Athabasca *r.* Canada 74 58.40N110.50W
Athabasca, L. Canada 75 59.07N110.00W
Athea Rep. of Ire. 13 52.28N 9.19W
Athenry Rep. of Ire. 13 53.18N 8.45W
Athens *see* Athínai Greece 19
Athens Ga. U.S.A. 85 33.57N 83.24W
Athens Tenn. U.S.A. 85 35.27N 84.38W
Athens Tex. U.S.A. 83 32.12N 95.51W
Athínai Greece 19 37.59N 23.42E
Athlone Rep. of Ire. 13 53.26N 7.57W
Atholl, Forest of U.K. 12 56.50N 3.55W
Áthos *mtn.* Greece 19 40.09N 24.19E
Ath Thamad Egypt 44 29.40N 34.18E
Ati Chad 53 13.11N 18.20E
Atico Peru 90 16.12S 73.37W
Atikonak L. Canada 77 52.40N 64.30W
Atimaono Tahiti 69 17.46S149.28W
Atkarsk U.S.S.R. 25 51.55N 45.00E
Atkinson U.S.A. 85 34.33N 78.12W
Atlanta Ga. U.S.A. 85 33.45N 84.23W
Atlanta Tex. U.S.A. 83 33.07N 94.10W
Atlantic Iowa U.S.A. 82 41.24N 95.01W
Atlantic-Antarctic Ridge *f.* Atlantic Oc. 95 53.00S 0.00
Atlantic City U.S.A. 85 39.22N 74.26W
Atlantic-Indian-Antarctic Basin *f.* Atl.Oc./Ind.Oc. 95 61.00S 0.00
Atlas Saharien *mts.* Algeria 51 34.00N 2.00E
Atlin Canada 74 59.31N133.41W
Atlin L. Canada 74 59.26N133.45W
Atmore U.S.A. 83 31.02N 87.29W
Atnarko Canada 74 52.25N126.00W
Atnosen Norway 23 61.44N 10.49E
Atoka U.S.A. 83 34.23N 96.08W
Atouat *mtn.* Laos 34 16.03N107.17E
Atouguia Portugal 16 39.20N 9.20W
Atrak *r.* Iran *see* Atrek *r.* Asia 43
Ätran *r.* Sweden 23 56.53N 12.30E
Atrato *r.* Colombia 90 8.15N 76.58W
Atrauli India 41 28.02N 78.17E
Atrek *r.* Asia 43 37.23N 54.00E
Atsugi Japan 35 35.27N139.22E
Atsumi-hantō *pen.* Japan 35 34.40N137.20E
Atsumi-wan *b.* Japan 35 34.45N137.10E
Aṭ Ṭafīlah Jordan 44 30.52N 35.36E
Aṭ Ṭā'if Saudi Arabia 48 21.15N 40.21E
At Tall Syria 44 33.36N 36.18E
Attapu Laos 36 14.51N106.56E
Attar, Oued el *wadi* Algeria 51 33.23N 5.12E
Attawapiskat *r.* Canada 76 53.00N 82.30W
Attawapiskat L. Canada 76 52.20N 88.00W
Aṭ Ṭayrīyah Egypt 44 30.39N 30.46E
Attendorn W. Germany 14 51.07N 7.54E
Attica N.Y. U.S.A. 76 42.52N 78.17W
Attigny France 15 49.29N 4.35E
Attikamagen L. Canada 77 55.00N 66.38W
Attleborough U.K. 11 52.31N 1.01E
Aṭ Ṭubayq *mts.* Saudi Arabia 42 29.30N 37.15E
Aṭ Ṭunayb Jordan 44 31.48N 35.56E
Aṭ Ṭūr Egypt 44 28.14N 33.36E
At Tuwayrifah *well* Saudi Arabia 45 21.30N 49.35E
Atucha Argentina 93 33.58S 59.17W
Atuel *r.* Argentina 93 36.15S 66.55W
Atui, Uad *wadi* Mauritania 50 20.03N 15.35W
Atui I. Cook Is. 69 20.00S158.07W
Atuona Is. Marquises 69 9.48S139.02W
Åtvidaberg Sweden 23 58.12N 16.00E
Atwater U.S.A. 80 37.21N120.36W
Atwood U.S.A. 82 39.48N101.03W
Aubagne France 17 43.17N 5.35E
Aube *d.* France 15 48.15N 4.05E
Aube *r.* France 15 48.30N 3.37E
Aubenton France 15 49.50N 4.12E
Auberive France 15 47.47N 5.03E
Aubigny-sur-Nère France 15 47.29N 2.26E
Aubin France 17 44.32N 2.14E
Auburn Ala. U.S.A. 85 32.38N 85.38W
Auburn Calif. U.S.A. 80 38.54N121.04W
Auburn Ind. U.S.A. 84 41.22N 85.02W
Auburn Maine U.S.A. 84 44.06N 70.14W
Auburn N.Y. U.S.A. 84 42.57N 76.34W
Auburn Wash. U.S.A. 80 47.18N122.13W
Aubusson France 17 45.57N 2.11E
Auce U.S.S.R. 23 56.28N 22.53E
Auch France 17 43.40N 0.36E
Auchi Nigeria 53 7.05N 6.16E
Auchterarder U.K. 12 56.18N 3.43W
Auckland New Zealand 60 36.55S174.45E
Auckland Is. Pacific Oc. 68 50.35S166.00E
Aude *r.* France 17 43.13N 2.20E
Auden Canada 76 50.17N 87.54W
Audo Range *mts.* Ethiopia 49 6.30N 41.30E
Audubon U.S.A. 82 41.43N 94.55W
Aue E. Germany 20 50.35N 12.42E
Augathella Australia 64 25.48S146.35E
Augrabies Falls *f.* R.S.A. 56 28.33S 20.27E
Augsburg W. Germany 20 48.21N 10.54E
Augusta Australia 63 34.19S115.09E
Augusta Italy 18 37.13N 15.13E
Augusta Ga. U.S.A. 85 33.29N 82.00W
Augusta Ill. U.S.A. 82 40.14N 90.56W
Augusta Kans. U.S.A. 83 37.41N 96.58W
Augusta Maine U.S.A. 84 44.19N 69.47W
Augustín Codazzi Colombia 90 10.01N 73.10W
Augustów Poland 21 53.51N 22.59E
Augustus, Mt. Australia 62 24.20S116.49E
Aulla Italy 15 44.12N 9.58E
Aulnay France 17 46.02N 0.22W
Aulne *r.* France 17 48.30N 4.11W
Aulnoye-Aymeries France 14 50.13N 3.50E
Ault U.S.A. 80 40.35N104.44W
Aumale France 15 49.46N 1.45E
Aumont-Aubrac France 17 44.43N 3.17E
Auna Nigeria 53 10.11N 4.46E
Auneau France 15 48.27N 1.46E
Auraiya India 41 26.28N 79.31E
Aurangābād Bihār India 41 24.45N 84.22E
Aurangābād Mahār India 40 19.53N 75.20E
Aurdal Norway 23 60.56N 9.24E
Aure Norway 22 63.16N 8.34E
Aurich W. Germany 14 53.28N 7.29E
Aurillac France 17 44.56N 2.26E
Aurora Canada 76 44.00N 79.28W
Aurora Colo. U.S.A. 80 39.44N104.52W
Aurora Ill. U.S.A. 82 41.45N 88.20W
Aurora Mo. U.S.A. 83 36.58N 93.43W
Aursunden *l.* Norway 22 62.37N 11.40E
Aus Namibia 56 26.41S 16.14E
Au Sable *r.* U.S.A. 84 44.27N 83.21W
Aust-Agder *d.* Norway 23 58.50N 8.20E
Austin Minn. U.S.A. 82 43.40N 92.59W
Austin Nev. U.S.A. 80 39.30N117.04W
Austin Penn. U.S.A. 84 41.38N 78.05W
Austin Tex. U.S.A. 83 30.16N 97.45W
Austin, L. Australia 62 27.40S118.00E
Austral Downs *town* Australia 64 20.28S137.55E
Australia Austa. 61
Australian Alps *mts.* Australia 67 36.30S148.30E
Australian Antarctic Territory Antarctica 96 73.00S 90.00E
Australian Capital Territory *d.* Australia 67 35.30S149.00E
Austral Ridge Pacific Oc. 69 24.00S148.00W
Austria Europe 20 47.30N 14.00E
Austvågöy *i.* Norway 22 68.20N 14.40E
Autun France 17 46.58N 4.18E
Auvergne *d.* France 17 45.20N 3.00E
Auxerre France 15 47.48N 3.35E
Aux Sables *r.* Canada 76 46.13N 82.04W
Auzances France 17 46.02N 2.29E
Ava Burma 34 21.49N 95.57E
Avallon France 15 47.30N 3.54E
Avaloirs, Les *hills* France 15 48.28N 0.07W
Avalon U.S.A. 85 39.06N 74.43W
Avalon Pen. Canada 77 47.00N 53.15W
Avanos Turkey 42 38.44N 34.51E
Avaré Brazil 94 23.06S 48.57W
Avarua Rarotonga Cook Is. 68 21.12S159.46W
Avatele Niue 68 19.06S169.55W
Avatele B. Niue 68 19.05S169.56W
Avatiu Rarotonga Cook Is. 68 21.12S159.47W
Aveiro Portugal 16 40.40N 8.35W
Avellaneda Argentina 93 34.40S 58.20W
Avellino Italy 18 40.55N 14.46E
Aversa Italy 18 40.58N 14.12E
Avery U.S.A. 80 47.15N115.49W
Avesnes France 14 50.08N 3.57E
Avesta Sweden 23 60.09N 16.12E
Aveyron *r.* France 17 44.09N 1.10E
Avezzano Italy 18 42.03N 13.26E
Aviemore U.K. 12 57.12N 3.50W
Avignon France 17 43.56N 4.48E
Ávila Spain 16 40.39N 4.42W
Ávila, Sierra de *mts.* Spain 16 40.35N 5.08W
Avilés Spain 16 43.35N 5.57W
Avoca *r.* Australia 66 35.56S143.44E
Avola Canada 74 51.45N119.19W
Avon *r.* Australia 63 31.40S116.07E
Avon *d.* U.K. 11 51.35N 2.40W
Avon *r.* Avon U.K. 9 51.30N 2.43W
Avon *r.* Dorset U.K. 11 50.43N 1.45W
Avon *r.* Glos. U.K. 11 52.00N 2.10W
Avon Downs *town* Australia 64 20.05S137.30E
Avonmouth U.K. 11 51.30N 2.42W
Avon Park *town* U.S.A. 85 27.36N 81.30W
Avranches France 15 48.42N 1.21W
Avre *r.* France 15 49.53N 2.20E
Awal Edo Ethiopia 49 4.14N 40.39E
Awara Ethiopia 49 5.30N 40.00E
Aware Ethiopia 45 8.15N 44.10E
Awasa, L. Ethiopia 49 7.05N 38.25E
Āwash *r.* Ethiopia 49 11.45N 41.05E
Awaso Ghana 52 6.20N 2.22W
Awat China 30 40.38N 80.22E
Awbārī Libya 51 26.35N 12.46E
Awbārī *d.* Libya 51 25.10N 12.45E
Awbārī, Şaḩrā' *des.* Libya 51 27.30N 11.30E
Awdah, Hawr al *l.* Iraq 43 31.36N 46.53E
Awe, Loch U.K. 12 56.18N 5.24W
Axarfjördhur *est.* Iceland 22 66.10N 16.30W
Axat France 17 42.48N 2.14E
Axel Heiberg I. Canada 73 79.30N 90.00W
Axim Ghana 52 4.53N 2.14W
Axiós *r.* Greece 19 40.31N 22.43E
Axminster U.K. 11 50.47N 3.01W
Ayabaca Peru 90 4.40S 79.53W
Ayachi, Ari n' *mtn.* Morocco 50 32.29N 4.57W
Ayacucho Argentina 93 37.10S 58.30W
Ayacucho Peru 90 13.10S 74.15W
Ayaguz U.S.S.R. 30 47.59N 80.27E
Ayamonte Spain 16 37.12N 7.24W
Ayan U.S.S.R. 29 56.29N138.00E
Aydin Turkey 42 37.52N 27.50E
Ayelu *mtn.* Ethiopia 49 10.04N 40.46E
Ayers Cliff *town* Canada 77 45.10N 72.03W
Áyios Evstrátios *i.* Greece 19 39.30N 25.00E
Aylesbury U.K. 11 51.48N 0.49W
Aylmer Que. Canada 77 45.23N 75.51W
Aylmer L. Canada 72 64.05N108.30W
Aylsham U.K. 10 52.48N 1.16E
'Ayn, Wādī al *r.* Oman 43 22.18N 55.35E
'Ayn Dāllah *well* Egypt 42 27.19N 27.20E
Ayod Sudan 49 8.07N 31.26E
Ayom Sudan 49 7.52N 28.23E
Ayon, Ostrov *i.* U.S.S.R. 29 70.00N169.00E
Ayos Cameroon 53 3.55N 12.30E
'Ayoûn el' Atroûs Mauritania 50 16.40N 9.37W
Ayr Australia 64 19.35S147.24E
Ayr U.K. 12 55.28N 4.37W
Ayr *r.* U.K. 12 55.28N 4.38W
Ayre, Pt. of U.K. 10 54.25N 4.22W
Aysha Ethiopia 49 10.46N 42.37E
Ayutthaya Thailand 34 14.20N100.40E
Ayvalik Turkey 19 39.19N 26.42E
Azamgarh India 41 26.04N 83.11E
Azao *mtn.* Algeria 51 25.12N 8.08E
Azaouâd *des.* Mali 52 18.00N 3.00W
Azaouak, Vallée de l' *f.* Mali 53 16.00N 3.40E
Azare Nigeria 53 11.40N 10.08E
Azbine *mts. see* Aïr *mts.* Niger 53
Azerbaydzhanskaya S.S.R. *d.* U.S.S.R. 43 40.10N 47.50E
Azogues Ecuador 90 2.35S 78.00W
Azopolye U.S.S.R. 24 65.15N 45.18E
Azores *is. see* Açores, Arquipélago dos *is.* Atlantic Oc. 95
Azoum *r.* Chad 49 10.53N 20.15E
Azov, Sea of *see* Azovskoye More U.S.S.R. 25
Azovskoye More *sea* U.S.S.R. 25 46.00N 36.30E
Azraq, Al Baḩr al *r.* Sudan 48 15.38N 32.31E
Azrou Morocco 50 33.27N 5.14W
Aztec U.S.A. 81 32.48N113.26W
Azua Dom. Rep. 87 18.29N 70.44W
Azuaga Spain 16 38.16N 5.40W
Azuero, Península de *pen.* Panama 87 7.30N 80.30W
Azul Argentina 93 36.46S 59.50W
'Azūm, Wādī *r.* Sudan *see* Azoum *r.* Chad 49
Azurduy Bolivia 92 19.59S 64.29W
Az Zāb al Kabīr *r.* Iraq 43 35.37N 43.20E
Az Zāb aş Şaghīr *r.* Iraq 43 35.15N 43.27E
Az Zabdānī Syria 44 33.43N 36.05E
Aẓ Ẓahrān Saudi Arabia 43 26.18N 50.08E
Az Zaqāziq Egypt 44 30.36N 31.30E
Az Zarqā' Jordan 44 32.04N 36.05E
Az Zarqā' *r.* Jordan 44 32.08N 35.32E
Az Zāwiyah *d.* Libya 51 32.40N 12.10E
Azzel Matti, Sebkha *f.* Algeria 50 26.00N 0.55E
Az Zilfī Saudi Arabia 43 26.15N 44.50E
Az Zrārīyah Lebanon 44 33.21N 35.20E

B

Baan Baa Australia 67 30.28S149.58E
Baarle-Hertog Neth. 14 51.26N 4.56E
Babadag Romania 21 44.54N 28.43E
Babahoyo Ecuador 90 1.53S 79.31W
Babai Gaxun China 32 40.30N104.43E
Babakin Australia 63 32.11S117.58E
Babana Nigeria 53 10.26N 3.51E
Babanka U.S.S.R. 21 48.41N 30.30E
Babanūsah Sudan 49 11.20N 27.48E
Babar, Kepulauan *is.* Indonesia 37 8.00S129.30E
Babayevo U.S.S.R. 24 59.24N 35.50E
B'abdā Lebanon 44 33.50N 35.31E
Babia Gora *mtn.* Czech./Poland 21 49.38N 19.38E
Babīna India 41 25.15N 78.28E
Babine L. Canada 74 54.48N126.00W
Babo Indonesia 37 2.33S133.25E
Bābol Iran 43 36.32N 52.42E
Baboua C.A.R. 53 5.49N 14.51E
Babuyan Channel Phil. 33 18.40N121.30E
Babuyan Is. Phil. 37 19.20N121.30E
Babylon *ruins* Iraq 43 32.33N 44.25E
Bacabal Maranhão Brazil 91 4.15S 44.45W
Bacabal Para Brazil 91 5.20S 56.45W
Bacău Romania 21 46.32N 26.59E
Baccarat France 17 48.27N 6.45E
Bacchus Marsh *town* Australia 66 37.41S144.27E
Bacharach W. Germany 14 50.03N 7.48E
Bacheli India 39 18.40N 81.16E
Bachelina U.S.S.R. 28 57.45N 67.20E
Back *r.* Canada 73 66.37N 96.00W
Bac Kan Vietnam 33 22.06N105.57E
Bäckefors Sweden 23 58.48N 12.10E
Backstairs Passage *str.* Australia 66 35.42S138.05E
Bac Lieu Vietnam 34 9.16N105.45E
Bac Ninh Vietnam 34 21.10N106.04E
Bacolod Phil. 37 10.38N122.58E
Bac Phan *f.* Vietnam 34 22.00N105.00E
Bac Quang Vietnam 33 22.30N104.52E
Badagara India 38 11.36N 75.35E
Badajós, Lago *l.* Brazil 90 3.15S 62.47W
Badajoz Spain 16 38.53N 6.58W
Badal Khān Goth Pakistan 40 26.31N 67.06E
Badalona Spain 16 41.27N 2.15E
Badanah Saudi Arabia 42 30.59N 41.02E
Bad Axe U.S.A. 84 43.49N 82.59W
Baddo *r.* Pakistan 40 28.15N 65.00E
Badeggi Nigeria 53 9.04N 6.09E
Bad Ems W. Germany 14 50.21N 7.42E
Baden Austria 20 48.01N 16.14E
Baden Ethiopia 48 17.00N 38.00E
Baden-Baden W. Germany 20 48.45N 8.15E
Baden-Württemberg *d.* W. Germany 20 48.30N 9.00E
Badgastein Austria 20 47.07N 13.09E
Bad Godesberg W. Germany 14 50.41N 7.09E
Bad Honnef W. Germany 14 50.39N 7.13E
Badīn Pakistan 40 24.39N 68.50E
Bad Ischl Austria 20 47.43N 13.38E
Badīyah Oman 45 22.27N 58.48E
Bādiyat ash Shām *des.* Asia 42 32.00N 39.00E
Bad Kissingen W. Germany 20 50.12N 10.04E
Bad Kreuznach W. Germany 14 49.51N 7.52E
Bad Mergentheim W. Germany 20 49.30N 9.46E
Bad Münstereifel W. Germany 14 50.34N 6.47E
Badnera India 41 20.52N 77.44E
Bad Neuenahr-Ahrweiler W. Germany 14 50.33N 7.07E
Bad Oldesloe W. Germany 20 53.48N 10.22E
Badong China 33 31.02N110.20E
Badou Togo 52 7.37N 0.37E
Badoumbé Mali 52 13.42N 10.09W
Badrīnāth India 41 30.44N 79.29E
Bad Tölz W. Germany 20 47.46N 11.34E
Bad Wildungen W. Germany 20 51.07N 9.07E
Baerami Australia 67 32.23S150.30E
Baeza Spain 16 37.57N 3.25W
Bafang Cameroon 53 5.11N 10.12E
Bafatá Guinea Bissau 52 12.09N 14.38W
Baffin B. Canada 73 74.00N 70.00W
Baffin I. Canada 73 68.50N 70.00W
Bafia Cameroon 53 4.39N 11.14E
Bafing *r.* Mali 52 14.48N 12.10W
Bafoulabé Mali 52 13.49N 10.50W
Bāfq Iran 43 31.35N 55.21E
Bafra Turkey 42 41.34N 35.56E
Bafut Cameroon 53 6.06N 10.02E
Bafwasende Zaïre 55 1.09N 27.12E
Bagaha India 41 27.06N 84.05E
Bagamoyo Tanzania 55 6.26S 38.55E
Bagasra India 40 21.29N 70.57E
Bagawi Sudan 49 12.19N 34.21E
Bagbele Zaïre 49 4.21N 29.17E
Bagdarin U.S.S.R. 29 54.28N113.38E
Bagé Brazil 94 31.22S 54.06W
Baggy Pt. U.K. 11 51.08N 4.15W
Baghdād Iraq 43 33.20N 44.26E
Bāgherhāt Bangla. 41 22.40N 89.48E
Bagheria Italy 18 38.05N 13.30E
Baghlān Afghan. 38 36.11N 68.44E
Baghrān Khowleh Afghan. 40 33.01N 64.58E
Bagni di Lucca Italy 15 44.01N 10.35E
Bagnois-sur-Cèze France 17 44.10N 4.37E
Bagodar India 41 24.05N 85.52E
Bagoé *r.* Mali 52 12.34N 6.30W
Bagolino Italy 15 45.49N 10.28E
Bagrationovsk U.S.S.R. 21 54.26N 20.38E
Baguio Phil. 37 16.25N120.37E
Bāh India 41 26.53N 78.36E
Bahamas C. America 87 24.15N 76.00W
Bahāwalnagar Pakistan 40 29.59N 73.16E
Bahāwalpur Pakistan 40 29.24N 71.41E
Baheri India 41 28.47N 79.30E
Bahi Tanzania 55 5.59S 35.15E
Bahia *d.* Brazil 91 12.30S 42.30W
Bahía, Islas de la *is.* Honduras 87 16.10N 86.30W
Bahía Blanca Argentina 94 38.45S 62.15W
Bahía de Caráquez Ecuador 90 0.40S 80.25W
Bahía Kino Mexico 81 28.50N111.55W
Bahía Laura Argentina 93 48.18S 66.30W
Bahía Negra Paraguay 94 20.15S 58.12W
Bahir Dar Ethiopia 49 11.35N 37.28E
Bahraich India 41 27.35N 81.36E
Bahrain Asia 43 26.00N 50.35E
Baḩr al Ghazāl *d.* Sudan 49 8.00N 27.30E
Bahrāmābād Iran 38 30.24N 56.00E
Bahrām Chāh Afghan. 40 29.26N 64.03E
Bahr Aouk *r.* C.A.R. 53 8.50N 18.50E
Bahr el Ghazal *r.* Chad 53 12.26N 15.25E
Bahr Salamat *r.* Chad 53 9.30N 18.10E
Bāhū Kalāt Iran 43 25.42N 61.28E
Baia-Mare Romania 21 47.40N 23.35E
Baião Brazil 91 2.41S 49.41W
Baia Sprie Romania 21 47.40N 23.42E
Baïbokoum Chad 53 7.46N 15.43E
Baicheng China 32 45.40N122.52E
Baidoa Somali Rep. 55 3.08N 43.34E
Baie Comeau Canada 77 49.13N 68.10W
Baie des Ha! Ha! *town* Canada 77 50.56N 58.58W
Baie St. Paul *town* Canada 77 47.27N 70.30W
Baigneux-les-Juifs France 15 47.31N 4.39E
Baihar India 41 22.06N 80.33E
Baijnāth India 41 29.55N 79.37E
Baikunthapur India 41 23.15N 82.33E
Băileşti Romania 21 44.02N 23.21E
Bailleul France 14 50.44N 2.44E
Bailundo Angola 54 12.13S 15.46E
Baimuru P.N.G. 37 7.30S144.49E
Bainang China 41 29.10N 89.15E
Bainbridge U.S.A. 85 30.54N 84.33W
Bain-de-Bretagne France 15 47.50N 1.41W
Baing Indonesia 62 10.15S120.34E
Baingoin China 41 31.45N 89.50E
Bāir Jordan 44 30.46N 36.41E
Bā'ir, Wādī *r.* Jordan 44 31.10N 36.55E
Baird Mts. U.S.A. 72 67.35N161.30W
Bairin Zuoqi China 32 43.59N119.11E
Bairnsdale Australia 67 37.51S147.38E
Bais France 15 48.15N 0.22W
Baise *r.* France 17 44.15N 0.20E
Baisha China 33 19.13N109.26E
Baiyang Dian *l.* China 32 38.55N116.00E
Baiyin China 32 36.40N104.15E
Baja Hungary 21 46.12N 18.58E
Baja California *pen.* Mexico 81 28.40N114.40W
Baja California Norte *d.* Mexico 81 29.45N115.30W
Baja California Sur *d.* Mexico 81 26.00N113.00W
Bakal U.S.S.R. 24 54.58N 58.45E
Bakali *r.* Zaïre 54 3.58S 17.10E
Bakel Senegal 52 14.54N 12.26W
Baker Calif. U.S.A. 81 35.16N116.04W
Baker Mont. U.S.A. 80 46.22N104.17W
Baker Oreg. U.S.A. 80 44.47N117.50W
Baker, Mt. U.S.A. 80 48.47N121.49W
Baker I. U.S.A. 74 55.20N133.36W
Baker Lake *town* Canada 73 64.20N 96.10W
Bakersfield U.S.A. 81 35.23N119.01W
Bâ Kêv Kampuchea 34 13.42N107.12E
Bako Ethiopia 49 5.50N 36.40E
Bako Ivory Coast 52 9.08N 7.40W
Bakouma C.A.R. 49 5.42N 22.47E
Baku U.S.S.R. 43 40.22N 49.53E
Bala Senegal 52 14.01N 13.08W
Bala U.K. 10 52.54N 3.36W
Balabac *i.* Phil. 36 7.57N117.01E
Balabac Str. Malaysia/Phil. 36 7.30N117.00E
Ba'labakk Lebanon 44 34.00N 36.12E
Balaclava Australia 66 32.09S141.25E
Balad Somali Rep. 45 2.22N 45.25E
Bālāghāt India 41 21.48N 80.11E
Bālāghāt Range *mts.* India 40 19.00N 76.30E
Balaguer Spain 16 41.50N 0.50E
Balaka Malaŵi 55 15.00S 34.56E
Balaka Zaïre 54 4.51S 19.57E
Balaklava Australia 66 34.08S138.24E
Balaklava U.S.S.R. 25 44.31N 33.35E
Balakovo U.S.S.R. 24 52.04N 47.46E
Balama Mozambique 55 13.19S 38.35E
Bālā Morghāb Afghan. 43 35.34N 63.20E
Balāngīr India 41 20.43N 83.29E
Balarāmpur India 41 23.07N 86.13E
Balashov U.S.S.R. 25 51.30N 43.10E
Balasore India 41 21.30N 86.56E
Balassagyarmat Hungary 21 48.05N 19.18E
Balāṭ Egypt 42 25.33N 29.16E
Balaton *l.* Hungary 21 46.55N 17.50E
Balboa Panama 87 8.37N 79.33W
Balbriggan Rep. of Ire. 13 53.36N 6.12W
Balcarce Argentina 93 37.52S 58.15W
Balchik Bulgaria 21 43.24N 28.10E
Balclutha New Zealand 60 46.16S169.46E
Baldock L. Canada 75 56.33N 97.57W
Baldwin Fla. U.S.A. 85 30.18N 81.59W
Baldwin Mich. U.S.A. 84 43.54N 85.50W
Baldwin Penn. U.S.A. 84 40.23N 79.58W
Baldy Mt. Canada 74 51.28N120.02W
Balē Ethiopia 49 6.30N 40.45E
Baleanoona Australia 66 30.33S139.22E
Baleares, Islas *is.* Spain 16 39.30N 2.30E

Baleine, Grande rivière de la to Beattyville

Baleine, Grande rivière de la *r.* Canada **76** 55.20N 77.40W
Baleine, Petite rivière de la *r.* Canada **76** 56.00N 76.45W
Balfate Honduras **87** 15.48N 86.25W
Balfour Downs *town* Australia **62** 22.57S120.46E
Bali India **40** 25.50N 74.05E
Bali *d.* Indonesia **37** 8.45S114.56E
Bali *i.* Indonesia **37** 8.20S115.07E
Bali, Laut *sea* Indonesia **37** 7.30S115.15E
Bali, Selat *str.* Indonesia **37** 8.21S114.30E
Balikesir Turkey **19** 39.38N 27.51E
Balīkh *r.* Syria **42** 35.58N 39.05E
Balikpapan Indonesia **36** 1.15S116.50E
Bali Sea *see* Bali, Laut Indonesia **37**
Balkan Mts. *see* Stara Planina *mts.* Bulgaria **19**
Balkhash U.S.S.R. **30** 46.51N 75.00E
Balkhash, Ozero *l.* U.S.S.R. **30** 46.40N 75.00E
Ballachulish U.K. **12** 56.40N 5.08W
Balladonia Australia **63** 32.27S123.51E
Ballālpur India **41** 19.50N 79.22E
Ballandean Australia **67** 28.39S151.50E
Ballantrae U.K. **12** 55.06N 5.01W
Ballarat Australia **66** 37.36S143.58E
Ballard, L. Australia **63** 29.27S120.55E
Ballater U.K. **12** 57.03N 3.03W
Ballenas, Bahía de *b.* Mexico **81** 26.45N113.25W
Ballenas, Canal de *str.* Mexico **81** 29.10N113.30W
Balleny Is. Antarctica **96** 66.30S163.00E
Balleroy France **15** 49.11N 0.50W
Ballia India **41** 25.45N 84.10E
Ballina Australia **67** 28.50S153.37E
Ballina Rep. of Ire. **13** 54.08N 9.10W
Ballinasloe Rep. of Ire. **13** 53.20N 8.15W
Ballingeary Rep. of Ire. **13** 51.50N 9.15W
Ballinger U.S.A. **83** 31.44N 99.57W
Ball's Pyramid *i.* Pacific Oc. **68** 31.45S159.15E
Ballybay Rep. of Ire. **13** 54.08N 6.56W
Ballycastle U.K. **13** 55.12N 6.15W
Ballyclare U.K. **13** 54.45N 6.00W
Ballyconnell Rep. of Ire. **13** 54.06N 7.37W
Ballydehob Rep. of Ire. **13** 51.34N 9.28W
Ballydonegan Rep. of Ire. **13** 51.38N 10.04W
Ballygar Rep. of Ire. **13** 53.32N 8.20W
Ballygawley U.K. **13** 54.28N 7.03W
Ballykelly U.K. **13** 55.03N 7.00W
Ballymena U.K. **13** 54.52N 6.17W
Ballymoney U.K. **13** 55.04N 6.31W
Ballyquintin Pt. U.K. **13** 54.40N 5.30W
Ballyragget Rep. of Ire. **13** 52.47N 7.21W
Ballyshannon Rep. of Ire. **13** 54.30N 8.11W
Ballyvaughan Rep.of Ire. **13** 53.06N 9.09W
Ballyvourney Rep. of Ire. **13** 51.57N 9.10W
Balmoral Australia **66** 37.17S141.50E
Balombo Angola **54** 12.20S 14.45E
Balonne *r.* Australia **67** 28.30S148.20E
Bālotra India **40** 25.50N 72.14E
Balpunga Australia **66** 33.44S141.50E
Balrāmpur India **41** 27.26N 82.11E
Balranald Australia **66** 34.37S143.37E
Balş Romania **21** 44.21N 24.06E
Balsas *r.* Brazil **91** 9.00S 48.10W
Balsas *r.* Mexico **86** 18.10N102.05W
Balta U.S.S.R. **21** 47.58N 29.39E
Baltanás Spain **16** 41.56N 4.15W
Baltasar Brum Uruguay **93** 30.44S 57.19W
Baltic Sea Europe **23** 57.00N 20.00E
Balṭīm Egypt **44** 31.34N 31.05E
Baltimore Md. U.S.A. **85** 39.17N 76.37W
Baltiysk U.S.S.R. **23** 54.39N 19.55E
Baluchistān *d.* Pakistan **40** 28.30N 65.00E
Baluchistan *f.* Pakistan **38** 28.00N 66.00E
Bālurghāt India **41** 25.13N 88.46E
Balygychan U.S.S.R. **29** 63.55N154.12E
Balykshi U.S.S.R. **25** 47.04N 51.55E
Bām Iran **43** 29.07N 58.20E
Bama Nigeria **53** 11.35N 13.40E
Bamako Mali **52** 12.40N 7.59W
Bamako *d.* Mali **52** 12.40N 7.55W
Bamba Kenya **55** 3.33S 39.32E
Bamba Mali **52** 17.05N 1.23W
Bamba Zaïre **54** 5.45S 18.23E
Bambari C.A.R. **49** 5.45N 20.40E
Bamberg W. Germany **20** 49.54N 10.53E
Bambesa Zaïre **54** 3.27N 25.43E
Bambesi Ethiopia **49** 9.45N 34.40E
Bambili Zaïre **54** 3.34N 26.07E
Bambio C.A.R. **53** 3.55N 16.57E
Bambuí Brazil **94** 20.01S 45.59W
Bam Co *l.* China **41** 31.30N 91.10E
Bamenda Cameroon **53** 5.55N 10.09E
Bāmīān Afghan. **40** 34.50N 67.50E
Bamingui C.A.R. **49** 7.34N 20.11E
Bamingui Bangoran *d.* C.A.R. **49** 8.30N 20.30E
Bampton Devon U.K. **11** 51.00N 3.29W
Bampūr Iran **43** 27.13N 60.29E
Bampūr *r.* Iran **43** 27.18N 59.02E
Bāmra Hills India **41** 21.20N 84.30E
Banaba *i.* Kiribati **68** 0.52S169.35E
Banagher Rep. of Ire. **13** 53.12N 8.00W
Banalia Zaïre **54** 1.33N 25.23E
Banamba Mali **52** 13.29N 7.22W
Banana Australia **64** 24.30S150.08E
Banana Zaïre **54** 5.55S 12.27E
Bananal, Ilha do *f.* Brazil **91** 11.30S 50.15W
Ban Aranyaprathet Thailand **34** 13.43N102.31E
Banās *r.* India **40** 25.54N 76.45E
Banās, Ra's *c.* Egypt **42** 23.54N 35.48E
Ban Ban Laos **34** 19.38N103.34E
Banbridge U.K. **13** 54.21N 6.17W
Ban Bua Chum Thailand **34** 15.15N101.15E
Banbury U.K. **11** 52.04N 1.21W
Banchory U.K. **12** 57.03N 2.30W
Bancroft Canada **76** 45.03N 77.51W
Band Afghan. **40** 33.17N 68.39E
Banda Gabon **54** 3.47S 11.04E
Banda Madhya P. India **41** 24.03N 78.57E
Bānda Uttar P. India **41** 25.29N 80.20E
Banda *i.* Indonesia **37** 4.30S129.55E
Banda, Laut *sea* Indonesia **37** 5.00S128.00E
Banda Aceh Indonesia **36** 5.35N 95.20E
Bānda Dāūd Shāh Pakistan **40** 33.16N 71.11E
Bandama *r.* Ivory Coast **52** 5.10N 4.59W
Bandar 'Abbās Iran **43** 27.10N 56.15E
Bandar-e Anzalī Iran **43** 37.26N 49.29E
Bandar-e Deylam Iran **43** 30.05N 50.11E
Bandar-e Khomeynī Iran **43** 30.26N 49.03E
Bandar-e Lengeh Iran **43** 26.34N 54.53E
Bandar-e Rīg Iran **43** 29.30N 50.40E
Bandar-e Torkeman Iran **43** 36.55N 54.05E
Bandar Seri Begawan Brunei **36** 4.56N114.58E
Banda Sea *see* Banda, Laut *sea* Indonesia **37**
Bandawe Malaŵi **55** 11.57S 34.11E
Bandeira *mtn.* Brazil **94** 20.25S 41.45W
Bāndhi Pakistan **40** 26.36N 68.18E
Bandiagara Mali **52** 14.12N 3.29W
Bāndikūi India **40** 27.03N 76.34E
Bandīpur Nepal **41** 27.56N 84.25E
Bandipura Jammu & Kashmir **40** 34.25N 74.39E
Bandirma Turkey **19** 40.22N 28.00E
Bandon Rep. of Ire. **13** 51.45N 8.45W
Bandon *r.* Rep. of Ire. **13** 51.43N 8.38W
Bandundu Zaïre **54** 3.20S 17.24E
Bandundu *d.* Zaïre **54** 4.00S 18.30E
Bandung Indonesia **37** 6.57S107.34E
Banes Cuba **87** 20.59N 75.24W
Banff Canada **74** 51.10N115.34W
Banff U.K. **12** 57.40N 2.31W
Banff Nat. Park Canada **74** 51.30N116.15W
Banfora U. Volta **52** 10.36N 4.45W
Bangalore India **38** 12.58N 77.35E
Bangassou C.A.R. **49** 4.50N 23.07E
Banggai, Kepulauan *is.* Indonesia **37** 1.30S123.10E
Banggi *i.* Malaysia **36** 7.17N117.12E
Banghāzī Libya **51** 32.07N 20.05E
Banghāzī *d.* Libya **51** 25.40N 21.00E
Bangil Indonesia **37** 7.34S112.47E
Bangka *i.* Indonesia **36** 2.20S106.10E
Bangkalan Indonesia **37** 7.05S112.44E
Bangkog Co *l.* China **41** 31.45N 89.30E
Bangkok *see* Krung Thep Thailand **34**
Bangladesh Asia **41** 24.30N 90.00E
Bangong Co *l.* China **39** 33.45N 79.15E
Bangor Rep. of Ire. **13** 54.09N 9.44W
Bangor U.K. **13** 54.40N 5.41W
Bangor U.K. **10** 53.13N 4.09W
Bangor Maine U.S.A. **84** 44.49N 68.47W
Bangor Penn. U.S.A. **85** 40.52N 75.13W
Bang Saphan Thailand **34** 11.14N 99.31E
Bangui C.A.R. **53** 4.23N 18.37E
Bangui Phil. **33** 18.33N120.45E
Banguru Zaïre **55** 0.30N 27.10E
Bangweulu, L. Zambia **55** 11.15S 29.45E
Banhā Egypt **44** 30.28N 31.11E
Ban Hat Yai Thailand **34** 7.10N100.28E
Ban Houayxay Laos **34** 20.21N100.32E
Bani *r.* Mali **52** 14.30N 4.15W
Bani, Jbel *mtn.* Morocco **50** 30.00N 8.00W
Banikoara Benin **53** 11.21N 2.25E
Banī Mazār Egypt **44** 28.29N 30.48E
Banīnah Libya **51** 32.05N 20.16E
Banī Suwayf Egypt **44** 29.05N 31.05E
Banī Walīd Libya **51** 31.46N 13.59E
Bāniyās Syria **44** 35.09N 35.58E
Banja Luka Yugo. **19** 44.47N 17.10E
Banjarmasin Indonesia **36** 3.22S114.36E
Banjul Gambia **52** 13.28N 16.39W
Bānka India **41** 24.53N 86.55E
Banka Banka Australia **64** 18.48S134.01E
Ban Kan Vietnam **34** 22.08N105.49E
Ban Kantang Thailand **34** 7.25N 99.35E
Bankasse Mali **52** 14.01N 3.29W
Banks Group *is.* Australia **66** 34.35S136.12E
Banks I. Australia **64** 10.12S142.16E
Banks I. B.C. Canada **74** 53.25N130.10W
Banks I. N.W.T. Canada **72** 73.00N122.00W
Banks Is. Vanuatu **68** 13.50S167.30E
Banks Pen. New Zealand **60** 43.45S173.10E
Banks Str. Australia **65** 40.37S148.07E
Bānkura India **41** 23.15N 87.04E
Ban-m'drack Vietnam **34** 12.45N108.50E
Bann *r.* U.K. **13** 55.10N 6.46W
Ban Na San Thailand **34** 8.53N 99.17E
Bannockburn U.K. **12** 56.06N 3.55W
Bannockburn Zimbabwe **56** 20.16S 29.51E
Bannu Pakistan **40** 32.59N 70.36E
Ban Pak Phraek Thailand **34** 8.13N100.13E
Bānsda India **40** 20.45N 73.22E
Banská Bystrica Czech. **21** 48.44N 19.07E
Bānswāra India **40** 23.33N 74.27E
Banté Benin **53** 8.26N 1.54E
Bantry Rep. of Ire. **13** 51.41N 9.27W
Bantry B. Rep. of Ire. **13** 51.40N 9.40W
Bāntva India **40** 21.29N 70.05E
Banyak, Kepulauan *is.* Indonesia **36** 2.15N 97.10E
Banyo Cameroon **53** 6.47N 11.50E
Banyuwangi Indonesia **37** 8.12S114.22E
Banzare Coast *f.* Antarctica **96** 66.30S125.00E
Baode China **32** 39.00N111.05E
Baoding China **32** 38.50N115.26E
Bao Ha Vietnam **33** 22.10N104.22E
Baoji China **32** 34.20N107.17E
Baojing China **33** 28.43N109.37E
Bao-Loc Vietnam **34** 11.30N107.54E
Baoshan China **39** 25.07N 99.08E
Baotou China **32** 40.35N109.59E
Baoulé *r.* Mali **52** 13.47N 10.45W
Bāp India **40** 27.23N 72.21E
Bapaume France **14** 50.07N 2.51E
Baqên China **41** 31.56N 94.00E
Ba'qūbah Iraq **43** 33.45N 44.38E
Bar Albania **19** 42.05N 19.06E
Bar U.S.S.R. **21** 49.05N 27.40E
Bara Nigeria **53** 10.24N 10.43E
Barabinsk U.S.S.R. **28** 55.20N 78.18E
Baraboo U.S.A. **82** 43.28N 89.50W
Baracoa Cuba **87** 20.23N 74.31W
Baradero Argentina **93** 33.50S 59.30W
Baradine Australia **67** 30.56S149.05E
Baradine *r.* Australia **67** 30.17S148.27E
Baragoi Kenya **49** 1.47N 36.47E
Bārah Sudan **49** 13.42N 30.22E
Barahona Dom. Rep. **87** 18.13N 71.07W
Baraka Zaïre **55** 4.09S 29.05E
Barakī Barak Afghan. **40** 33.56N 68.55E
Bārākot India **41** 21.33N 85.01E
Bāramūla Jammu & Kashmir **40** 34.12N 74.21E
Bārān India **40** 25.06N 76.31E
Baranagar India **41** 22.38N 88.22E
Baranoa Colombia **90** 10.50N 74.55W
Baranof I. U.S.A. **74** 57.00N135.00W
Baranovichi U.S.S.R. **24** 53.09N 26.00E
Baratta Australia **66** 32.01S139.10E
Barbacena Brazil **94** 21.13S 43.47W
Barbados Lesser Antilles **87** 13.20N 59.40W
Barbar Sudan **48** 18.01N 33.59E
Barbastro Spain **16** 42.02N 0.07E
Barberton R.S.A. **56** 25.46S 31.02E
Barbezieux France **17** 45.28N 0.09W
Barbil India **41** 22.06N 85.20E
Barbuda *i.* Leeward Is. **87** 17.41N 61.48W
Barcaldine Australia **64** 23.31S145.15E
Barcellona Italy **18** 38.10N 15.13E
Barcelona Spain **16** 41.25N 2.10E
Barcelona Venezuela **90** 10.08N 64.43W
Barcelos Brazil **90** 0.59S 62.58W
Barcoo *r.* Australia **64** 25.30S142.50E
Barcs Hungary **21** 45.58N 17.28E
Barcs Yugo. **19** 45.58N 17.28E
Bardai Chad **53** 21.21N 16.56E
Bardejov Czech. **21** 49.18N 21.16E
Bardera Somali Rep. **55** 2.18N 42.18E
Bardi Italy **15** 44.38N 9.44E
Bardia Nepal **41** 28.18N 81.23E
Bardīyah Libya **48** 31.46N 25.06E
Bardnovichi U.S.S.R. **21** 53.09N 26.00E
Bardoc Australia **63** 30.20S121.17E
Bardoli India **40** 21.07N 73.07E
Bardsey *i.* U.K. **10** 52.45N 4.48W
Bardu Norway **22** 68.54N 18.20E
Bardufoss Norway **22** 69.00N 18.30E
Bareilly India **41** 28.21N 79.25E
Barellan Australia **67** 34.17S146.34E
Barengapāra India **41** 25.14N 90.14E
Barentsovo More *see* Barents Sea Arctic Oc. **24**
Barents Sea Arctic Oc. **24** 73.00N 40.00E
Barentu Ethiopia **48** 15.04N 37.37E
Barfleur France **15** 49.40N 1.15W
Barga China **41** 30.51N 81.20E
Bargal Somali Rep. **45** 11.18N 51.07E
Bargarh India **41** 21.20N 83.37E
Barge Italy **15** 44.43N 7.20E
Barghanak Afghan. **40** 33.56N 62.26E
Barguzin U.S.S.R. **29** 53.40N109.35E
Barharwa India **41** 24.52N 87.47E
Barhi India **41** 24.18N 85.25E
Bāri Madhya P. India **41** 23.03N 78.05E
Bāri Rāj. India **41** 26.39N 77.36E
Bari Italy **19** 41.08N 16.52E
Baricho Kenya **55** 3.07S 39.47E
Barika Algeria **51** 35.25N 5.19E
Barīm *i.* S. Yemen **45** 12.40N 43.24E
Barinas Venezuela **90** 8.36N 70.15W
Baripāda India **41** 21.56N 86.43E
Bariri Brazil **94** 22.04S 48.41W
Bārīs Egypt **42** 24.40N 30.36E
Bari Sādri India **40** 24.25N 74.28E
Barisāl Bangla. **41** 22.42N 90.22E
Barisan, Pegunungan *mts.* Indonesia **36** 3.30S102.30E
Barito *r.* Indonesia **36** 3.35S114.35E
Barjūj, Wādī Libya **51** 26.03N 12.50E
Barker U.S.A. **76** 43.20N 78.33W
Barker L. Australia **63** 31.45S120.05E
Bārkhān Pakistan **40** 29.54N 69.31E
Barking U.K. **11** 51.32N 0.05E
Barkley Sd. Canada **74** 48.53N125.20W
Barkly East R.S.A. **56** 30,58S 27.33E
Barkly Tableland *f.* Australia **64** 19.00S136.40E
Barkly West R.S.A. **56** 28.32S 24.29E
Bar-le-Duc France **17** 48.46N 5.10E
Barlee, L. Australia **63** 29.30S119.30E
Barlee Range *mts.* Australia **62** 23.40S116.00E
Barletta Italy **18** 41.20N 16.15E
Barlow L. Canada **75** 62.00N103.00W
Barmedman Australia **67** 34.08S147.25E
Barmer India **40** 25.45N 71.23E
Barmera Australia **66** 34.15S140.31E
Barm Fīrūz, Kūh-e *mtn.* Iran **43** 30.21N 52.00E
Barmouth U.K. **10** 52.44N 4.03W
Barnagar India **40** 23.03N 75.22E
Barnāla India **40** 30.22N 75.33E
Barnard Castle *town* U.K. **10** 54.33N 1.55W
Barnato Australia **67** 31.38S144.59E
Barnaul U.S.S.R. **28** 53.21N 83.15E
Barnegat U.S.A. **85** 39.45N 74.13W
Barnegat B. U.S.A. **85** 39.52N 74.07W
Barnegat Light U.S.A. **85** 39.46N 74.06W
Barnet U.K. **11** 51.39N 0.11W
Barneveld Neth. **14** 52.10N 5.39E
Barneville France **15** 49.23N 1.45W
Barneys L. Australia **66** 33.16S144.13E
Barnsley U.K. **10** 53.33N 1.29W
Barnstaple U.K. **11** 51.05N 4.03W
Baro *r.* Ethiopia **49** 8.26N 33.13E
Baro Nigeria **53** 8.37N 6.19E
Barpeta India **41** 26.19N 91.00E
Barqah *f.* Libya **48** 31.00N 23.00E
Barquisimeto Venezuela **90** 10.03N 69.18W
Barra Brazil **91** 11.06S 43.15W
Barra *i.* U.K. **12** 56.59N 7.28W
Barra, Sd. of U.K. **12** 57.04N 7.20W
Barraba Australia **67** 30.24S152.36E
Barra do Corda Brazil **91** 5.30S 45.15W
Barra do Piraí Brazil **94** 22.28S 43.49W
Barra Head U.K. **8** 56.47N 7.36W
Barra Mansa Brazil **94** 22.35S 44.12W
Barranca Peru **90** 4.50S 76.40W
Barrancabermeja Colombia **90** 7.06N 73.54W
Barrancas Venezuela **90** 8.45N 62.13W
Barrancos Portugal **16** 38.10N 7.01W
Barranqueras Argentina **94** 27.30S 58.55W
Barranquilla Colombia **90** 11.10N 74.50W
Barraute Canada **76** 48.26N 77.39W
Barre U.S.A. **84** 44.12N 72.30W
Barreiras Brazil **91** 12.09S 44.58W
Barreiro Portugal **16** 38.40N 9.05W
Barreiros Brazil **91** 8.49S 35.12W
Barrême France **20** 43.57N 6.22E
Barretos Brazil **94** 20.37S 48.38W
Barrhead Canada **74** 54.10N114.24W
Barrhead U.K. **12** 55.47N 4.24W
Barrie Canada **76** 44.22N 79.42W
Barrington Tops *mts.* Australia **67** 32.30S151.28E
Barringun Australia **67** 29.01S145.43E
Barron U.S.A. **80** 48.44N120.43W
Barrow *r.* Rep. of Ire. **13** 52.17N 7.00W
Barrow U.S.A. **72** 71.16N156.50W
Barrow Creek *town* Australia **64** 21.32S133.53E
Barrow I. Australia **62** 21.40S115.27E
Barrow-in-Furness U.K. **10** 54.08N 3.15W
Barrow Range *mts.* Australia **62** 26.04S127.28E
Barry U.K. **11** 51.23N 3.19W
Barstow U.S.A. **81** 34.54N117.01W
Bar-sur-Aube France **15** 48.14N 4.43E
Bar-sur-Seine France **15** 48.07N 4.22E
Bartica Guyana **90** 6.24N 58.38W
Bartin Turkey **42** 41.37N 32.20E
Bartlefrere *mt.* Australia **64** 17.23S145.49E
Bartlesville U.S.A. **83** 36.45N 95.59W
Bartlett L. Canada **74** 63.05N118.20W
Bartolomeu Dias Mozambique **57** 21.10S 35.09E
Barton-upon-Humber U.K. **10** 53.41N 0.27W
Bartoszyce Poland **21** 54.16N 20.49E
Bartow U.S.A. **85** 27.54N 81.51W
Bāruni India **41** 25.29N 85.59E
Barwāh India **40** 22.16N 76.03E
Barwāni India **40** 22.02N 74.54E
Barwa Sāgar India **41** 25.23N 78.44E
Barwon *r.* Australia **67** 30.00S148.05E
Barysh U.S.S.R. **24** 53.40N 47.09E
Basāl Pakistan **40** 33.33N 72.15E
Basankusu Zaïre **54** 1.12N 19.50E
Basavilbaso Argentina **93** 32.20S 58.52W
Basel Switz. **20** 47.33N 7.36E
Bashi Channel Taiwan/Phil. **33** 21.30N121.00E
Basilan Phil. **37** 6.40N121.59E
Basilan *i.* Phil. **37** 6.40N122.10E
Basildon U.K. **11** 51.34N 0.25E
Basilicata *d.* Italy **18** 40.30N 16.20E
Basin U.S.A. **80** 44.23N108.02W
Basingstoke U.K. **11** 51.15N 1.05W
Basin L. Canada **75** 52.38N105.18W
Baskatong, Résr. Canada **76** 46.48N 75.50W
Basmat India **40** 19.19N 77.10E
Bāsoda India **41** 23.51N 77.56E
Basoko Zaïre **49** 1.20N 23.30E
Basongo Zaïre **49** 4.23S 20.28E
Bassano Canada **74** 50.48N112.20W
Bassano Italy **15** 45.46N 11.44E
Bassari Togo **52** 9.12N 0.18E
Bassein Burma **34** 16.46N 94.45E
Basse-Kotto *d.* C.A.R. **49** 5.00N 21.30E
Basse Normandie *d.* France **15** 49.00N 0.00
Basse Santa Su Gambia **52** 13.23N 14.15W
Basse-Terre Guadeloupe **87** 16.00N 61.43W
Bassett U.S.A. **82** 42.35N 99.32W
Bass Str. Australia **65** 39.45S146.00E
Bassum W. Germany **20** 52.51N 8.43E
Båstad Sweden **23** 56.26N 12.51E
Bastak Iran **43** 27.15N 54.26E
Bastelica France **17** 42.00N 9.03E
Basti India **41** 26.48N 82.43E
Bastia France **17** 42.41N 9.26E
Bastogne Belgium **14** 50.00N 5.43E
Bastrop U.S.A. **83** 32.47N 91.55W
Basyūn Egypt **44** 30.57N 30.49E
Bas Zaïre *d.* Zaïre **54** 5.15S 14.00E
Bata Equat. Guinea **54** 1.51N 9.49E
Batabanó, Golfo de *g.* Cuba **87** 23.15N 82.30W
Batāla India **40** 31.48N 75.13E
Batalha Portugal **16** 39.39N 8.50W
Batang China **39** 30.02N 99.01E
Batangafo C.A.R. **53** 7.27N 18.11E
Batangas Phil. **37** 13.46N121.01E
Batan Is. Phil. **37** 20.50N121.55E
Bátaszék Hungary **21** 46.12N 18.44E
Batatais Brazil **94** 20.54S 47.37W
Batavia U.S.A. **76** 43.00N 78.11W
Bataysk U.S.S.R. **25** 47.09N 39.46E
Batchelor Australia **64** 13.04S131.01E
Bătdâmbâng Kampuchea **34** 13.06N103.12E
Bateman's B. Australia **65** 35.55S150.09E
Batemans Bay *town* Australia **67** 35.55S150.09E
Batesville Ark. U.S.A. **83** 35.46N 91.39W
Batesville Miss. U.S.A. **83** 34.18N 90.00W
Bath Canada **77** 46.31N 67.37W
Bath U.K. **11** 51.22N 2.22W
Bath Maine U.S.A. **84** 43.55N 69.49W
Bath N.Y. U.S.A. **84** 42.20N 77.19W
Batha *d.* Chad **53** 14.30N 18.30E
Batha *r.* Chad **53** 12.47N 17.34E
Baṭḥā, Wādī al *r.* Oman **43** 20.01N 59.39E
Bathgate U.K. **12** 55.44N 3.38W
Bathurst Australia **67** 33.27S149.35E
Bathurst Canada **77** 47.36N 65.39W
Bathurst R.S.A. **56** 33.30S 26.48E
Bathurst, C. Canada **72** 70.30N128.00W
Bathurst I. Australia **62** 11.45S130.15E
Bathurst I. Canada **73** 76.00N100.00W
Bathurst Inlet *town* Canada **72** 66.48N108.00W
Batibla C.A.R. **49** 5.56N 21.09E
Batié U. Volta **52** 9.42N 2.53W
Batina Yugo. **21** 45.51N 18.51E
Batley U.K. **10** 53.43N 1.38W
Batlow Australia **67** 35.32S148.10E
Batman Turkey **42** 37.52N 41.07E
Batna Algeria **51** 35.35N 6.11E
Baton Rouge U.S.A. **83** 30.23N 91.11W
Batopilas Mexico **81** 27.00N107.45W
Batouri Cameroon **53** 4.26N 14.27E
Batson U.S.A. **83** 30.15N 94.37W
Batticaloa Sri Lanka **39** 7.43N 81.42E
Battle *r.* Canada **75** 52.43N108.15W
Battle U.K. **11** 50.55N 0.30E
Battle Creek *town* U.S.A. **84** 42.20N 85.11W
Battleford Canada **75** 52.45N108.15W
Battle Harbour Canada **77** 52.17N 55.35W
Batu *mtn.* Ethiopia **49** 6.55N 39.46E
Batu, Kepulauan *is.* Indonesia **36** 0.30S 98.20E
Batumi U.S.S.R. **42** 41.37N 41.36E
Batu Pahat Malaysia **36** 1.50N102.48E
Baturaja Indonesia **36** 4.10S104.10E
Baturité Brazil **91** 4.20S 38.53W
Bat Yam Israel **44** 32.01N 34.45E
Baubau Indonesia **37** 5.30S122.37E
Bauchi Nigeria **53** 10.16N 9.50E
Bauchi *d.* Nigeria **53** 10.40N 10.00E
Baudh India **41** 20.50N 84.19E
Baugé France **15** 47.33N 0.06W
Bauld, C. Canada **77** 51.38N 55.25W
Bauru Brazil **94** 22.19S 49.07W
Baús Brazil **94** 18.19S 53.10W
Bauska U.S.S.R. **23** 56.24N 24.14E
Bautzen E. Germany **20** 51.11N 14.29E
Bavay France **14** 50.18N 3.48E
Bawean *i.* Indonesia **37** 5.50S112.39E
Bawku Ghana **52** 11.05N 0.13W
Bayamo Cuba **87** 20.23N 76.39W
Bayamón Puerto Rico **87** 18.24N 66.10W
Bāyan, Band-e *mts.* Afghan. **40** 34.20N 65.00E
Bayāna India **40** 26.54N 77.17E
Bayan Har Shan *mts.* China **30** 34.00N 97.20E
Bayan Nur China **32** 38.14N103.56E
Bayburt Turkey **42** 40.15N 40.16E
Bay City Mich. U.S.A. **84** 43.35N 83.52W
Bay City Tex. U.S.A. **83** 28.59N 95.58W
Baydaratskaya Guba *b.* U.S.S.R. **28** 70.00N 66.00E
Bayern *d.* W. Germany **20** 48.30N 11.30E
Bayeux France **15** 49.16N 0.42W
Bayfield U.S.A. **82** 46.49N 90.49W
Baykal, Ozero *l.* U.S.S.R. **30** 53.30N100.00E
Baykit U.S.S.R. **29** 61.45N 96.22E
Bayombong Phil. **37** 16.27N121.10E
Bayonne France **17** 43.30N 1.28W
Bayovar Peru **90** 5.50S 81.03W
Bayreuth W. Germany **20** 49.56N 11.35E
Bayrūt Lebanon **44** 33.52N 35.30E
Baytik Shan *mts.* China **30** 45.15N 90.50E
Baytown U.S.A. **83** 29.44N 94.58W
Bay View New Zealand **60** 39.26S176.52E
Baza Spain **16** 37.30N 2.45W
Baza, Sierra de *mts.* Spain **16** 37.15N 2.45W
Bazaliya U.S.S.R. **21** 49.42N 26.29E
Bazaruto, Ilha do *i.* Mozambique **57** 21.40S 35.28E
Bazas France **17** 44.26N 0.13W
Bazdār Pakistan **40** 26.21N 65.03E
Bazhong China **33** 31.51N106.42E
Bazmān Iran **43** 27.48N 60.12E
Bazmān, Kūh-e *mtn.* Iran **43** 28.06N 60.00E
Beach U.S.A. **82** 46.55N103.52W
Beach Haven U.S.A. **85** 39.34N 74.14W
Beachport Australia **66** 37.29S140.01E
Beachwood U.S.A. **85** 39.56N 74.12W
Beachy Head U.K. **11** 50.43N 0.15E
Beacon U.S.A. **85** 41.30N 73.58W
Beagle Bay Mission Australia **62** 16.58S122.40E
Bealanana Madagascar **57** 14.33S 48.44E
Beardstown U.S.A. **82** 40.01N 90.26W
Bear L. U.S.A. **80** 42.00N111.20W
Bearskin Lake *town* Canada **75** 53.58N 91.02W
Beas *r.* India **40** 31.10N 75.00E
Beatrice U.S.A. **82** 40.16N 96.44W
Beatrice, C. Australia **64** 14.15S136.59E
Beatton *r.* Canada **74** 56.15N120.45W
Beatton River *town* Canada **74** 57.26N121.20W
Beatty U.S.A. **80** 36.54N116.46W
Beattyville Canada **76** 48.53N 77.10W

Beauce to Bilimora

Beauce f. France 15 48.22N 1.50E
Beaufort Australia 66 37.28S143.28E
Beaufort U.S.A. 85 32.26N 80.40W
Beaufort Sea N. America 72 72.00N141.00W
Beaufort West R.S.A. 56 32.20S 22.34E
Beaugency France 15 47.47N 1.38E
Beauharnois Canada 77 45.19N 73.52W
Beaulieu r. Canada 74 62.03N113.11W
Beauly U.K. 12 57.29N 4.29W
Beauly r. U.K. 12 57.29N 4.25W
Beaumaris U.K. 10 53.16N 4.07W
Beaumetz-lès-Loges France 14 50.15N 2.36E
Beaumont Belgium 14 50.14N 4.16E
Beaumont Miss. U.S.A. 83 31.11N 88.55W
Beaumont Tex. U.S.A. 83 30.05N 94.06W
Beaumont-le-Roger France 15 49.05N 0.47E
Beaumont-sur-Sarthe France 15 48.13N 0.07E
Beaune France 17 47.02N 4.50E
Beaune-la-Rolande France 15 48.04N 2.26E
Beaupréau France 17 47.12N 0.59W
Beauséjour Canada 75 50.04N 96.33W
Beauvais France 15 49.26N 2.05E
Beauval Canada 75 55.09N107.35W
Beauvoir France 17 46.55N 2.01W
Beaver r. N.W.T. Canada 74 59.43N124.16W
Beaver r. Ont. Canada 75 55.55N 87.50W
Beaver Alaska U.S.A. 72 66.22N147.24W
Beaver Okla. U.S.A. 83 36.49N100.31W
Beaver Dam town U.S.A. 82 43.28N 88.50W
Beaverhill L. Alta. Canada 74 53.27N112.32W
Beaverhill L. N.W.T. Canada 75 63.02N104.22W
Beaver I. U.S.A. 84 45.42N 85.28W
Beāwar India 40 26.06N 74.19E
Bebedouro Brazil 94 20.54S 48.31W
Bebington U.K. 10 53.23N 3.01W
Bécancour Canada 77 46.20N 72.26W
Beccles U.K. 11 52.27N 1.33E
Bečej Yugo. 21 45.37N 20.03E
Béchar Algeria 50 31.37N 2.13W
Beckley U.S.A. 85 37.46N 81.12W
Beckum W. Germany 14 51.45N 8.02E
Beclean Romania 21 47.11N 24.10E
Bédarieux France 17 43.35N 3.10E
Bedeso Ethiopia 49 8.50N 40.45E
Bedford U.K. 11 52.08N 0.29W
Bedford Canada 77 45.07N 72.59W
Bedford U.S.A. 84 38.51N 86.30W
Bedford, C. Australia 64 15.14S145.21E
Bedford Levels f. U.K. 11 52.35N 0.08W
Bedfordshire d. U.K. 11 52.04N 0.28W
Bedi India 40 22.30N 70.02E
Bedlington U.K. 10 55.08N 1.34W
Bedourie Australia 64 24.21S139.28E
Beech Grove U.S.A. 84 39.42N 86.06W
Beechworth Australia 67 36.23S146.42E
Beenleigh Australia 67 27.43S153.09E
Be'er Menuha Israel 44 30.19N 35.08E
Be'er Sheva' Israel 44 31.15N 34.47E
Beerta Neth. 14 53.12N 7.07E
Beeston U.K. 10 52.55N 1.11W
Beeville U.S.A. 83 28.24N 97.45W
Befale Zaïre 54 0.27N 21.01E
Befandriana Madagascar 57 15.16S 48.32E
Befandriana Madagascar 57 22.06S 43.54E
Beg, Lough U.K. 13 54.47N 6.29W
Bega Australia 67 36.41S149.50E
Begamganj India 41 23.36N 78.20E
Begēmdir d. Ethiopia 49 12.30N 37.30E
Bègles France 17 44.48N 0.32W
Begna r. Norway 23 60.32N 10.00E
Begusarai India 41 25.25N 86.08E
Behara Madagascar 57 25.00S 46.25E
Behbehān Iran 43 30.35N 50.17E
Bei'an China 31 48.17N126.33E
Beihai China 33 21.29N109.09E
Bei Jiang r. China 33 23.19N112.51E
Beijing China 32 39.55N116.25E
Beijing d. China 32 40.00N116.30E
Beijing Shi d. China 31 40.15N116.30E
Beilen Neth. 14 52.51N 6.31E
Beinn Dearg mtn. U.K. 12 57.47N 4.55W
Beipa'a P.N.G. 64 8.30S146.35E
Beipiao China 32 41.47N120.40E
Beira see Sofala Mozambique 57
Beirut see Bayrūt Lebanon 44
Beitang China 32 39.06N117.43E
Beitbridge Zimbabwe 56 22.10S 30.01E
Beiuş Romania 21 46.40N 22.21E
Beja Portugal 16 38.01N 7.52W
Béja Tunisia 51 36.44N 9.11E
Bejaïa Algeria 51 36.45N 5.05E
Béjar Spain 16 40.24N 5.45W
Bejestān Iran 43 34.32N 58.08E
Bejhi r. Pakistan 40 29.47N 67.58E
Bejoording Australia 63 31.22S116.30E
Békés Hungary 21 46.46N 21.08E
Békéscsaba Hungary 21 46.41N 21.06E
Bekily Madagascar 57 24.13S 45.19E
Bela India 41 25.56N 81.59E
Bela Pakistan 40 26.14N 66.19E
Bélabo Cameroon 53 5.00N 13.20E
Bela Crkva Yugo. 21 44.54N 21.26E
Bel Air U.S.A. 85 39.32N 76.21W
Belalcázar Spain 16 38.35N 5.10W
Belampalli India 41 19.02N 79.30E
Belang Indonesia 37 0.58N124.56E
Belau Pacific Oc. 37 7.00N134.25E
Bela Vista Brazil 92 22.05S 56.22W
Bela Vista Mozambique 57 26.20S 32.41E
Belaya r. U.S.S.R. 28 55.40N 52.30E
Belaya Glina U.S.S.R. 25 46.04N 40.54E
Belaya Tserkov U.S.S.R. 21 49.49N 30.10E
Belcher Is. Canada 76 56.00N 79.00W
Belcoo U.K. 13 54.18N 7.53W
Belda India 41 22.05N 87.21E
Belebey U.S.S.R. 24 54.05N 54.07E
Beled Weyne Somali Rep. 45 4.47N 45.12E
Belém Brazil 91 1.27S 48.29W
Belem Mozambique 57 14.11S 35.59E
Belén Uruguay 93 30.47S 57.47W
Belen U.S.A. 81 34.40N106.46W
Belén, Cuchilla de mts. Uruguay 93 30.49S 56.28W
Beles r. Ethiopia 45 11.10N 35.10E
Belev U.S.S.R. 24 53.50N 36.08E
Belfast U.K. 13 54.36N 5.57W
Belfast Maine U.S.A. 84 44.27N 69.01W
Belfast Lough U.K. 13 54.42N 5.45W
Belfield U.S.A. 82 46.53N103.12W
Belfort France 17 47.38N 6.52E
Belfry U.S.A. 80 45.09N109.01W
Belgaum India 38 15.54N 74.36E
Belgium Europe 14 51.00N 4.30E
Belgorod U.S.S.R. 25 50.38N 36.36E
Belgorod-Dnestrovskiy U.S.S.R. 21 46.10N 30.19E
Belgrade see Beograd Yugo. 21
Beli Nigeria 53 7.53N 10.59E
Belitung i. Indonesia 36 3.00S108.00E
Belize Belize 87 17.29N 88.20W
Belize C. America 87 17.00N 88.30W
Belka Australia 63 31.45S118.09E
Bellac France 17 46.07N 1.04E
Bella Coola Canada 74 52.25N126.40W
Bellagio Italy 15 45.59N 9.15E
Bellaire Tex. U.S.A. 83 29.44N 95.03W
Bellaria Italy 15 44.09N 12.28E
Bellary India 38 15.11N 76.54E
Bellata Australia 67 29.55S149.50E
Bella Unión Uruguay 93 30.15S 57.35W
Bella Vista Corrientes Argentina 92 28.30S 59.00W
Bella Vista Tucuman Argentina 92 27.02S 65.19W
Bellbrook Australia 67 30.48S152.30E
Bellefontaine U.S.A. 84 40.22N 83.45W
Belle Fourche r. U.S.A. 82 44.26N102.19W
Belle Glade U.S.A. 85 26.41N 80.41W
Belle Île France 17 47.20N 3.10W
Belle Isle Canada 77 51.55N 55.20W
Belle Isle, Str. of Canada 77 51.35N 56.30W
Bellême France 15 48.22N 0.34E
Belleoram Canada 77 47.32N 55.28W
Belleville Canada 76 44.10N 77.22W
Belleville Kans. U.S.A. 82 39.49N 97.38W
Bellevue Canada 74 49.35N114.22W
Bellevue Idaho U.S.A. 80 43.28N114.16W
Bellevue Penn. U.S.A. 84 40.32N 80.08W
Bellevue Wash. U.S.A. 80 47.37N122.12W
Belle Yella Liberia 52 7.24N 10.09W
Bellin Canada 73 60.01N 70.01W
Bellingen Australia 67 30.28S152.43E
Bellingham U.K. 10 55.09N 2.15W
Bellingham U.S.A. 80 48.46N122.29W
Bellingshausen Sea Antarctica 96 70.00S 88.00W
Bellinzona Switz. 15 46.11N 9.02E
Bello Colombia 90 6.20N 75.41W
Bellpat Pakistan 40 28.59N 68.00E
Belluno Italy 15 46.09N 12.13E
Bell Ville Argentina 93 32.35S 62.41W
Belmar U.S.A. 85 40.11N 74.01W
Bélmez Spain 16 38.17N 5.17W
Belmond U.S.A. 82 42.51N 93.37W
Belmopan Belize 87 17.25N 88.46W
Belmullet Rep. of Ire. 13 54.14N 10.00W
Belogradchik Bulgaria 21 43.38N 22.41E
Belo Horizonte Brazil 94 19.45S 43.54W
Beloit Kans. U.S.A. 82 39.28N 98.06W
Beloit Wisc. U.S.A. 82 42.31N 89.02W
Belo Jardim Brazil 91 8.22S 36.22W
Belokorovichi U.S.S.R. 21 51.04N 28.00E
Belomorsk U.S.S.R. 24 64.34N 34.45E
Belonia India 41 23.15N 91.27E
Beloretsk U.S.S.R. 24 53.59N 58.20E
Belorusskaya S.S.R. d. U.S.S.R. 21 53.30N 28.00E
Beloye More sea U.S.S.R. 24 65.30N 38.00E
Beloye Ozero l. U.S.S.R. 24 60.12N 37.45E
Belozersk U.S.S.R. 24 60.00N 37.49E
Belper U.K. 10 53.02N 1.29W
Beltana Australia 66 30.40S138.27E
Belterra Brazil 91 2.38S 54.57W
Belton Australia 66 32.12S138.45E
Belton U.S.A. 83 31.04N 97.28W
Beltsy U.S.S.R. 21 47.45N 27.59E
Belukha, Gora mtn. U.S.S.R. 30 49.48N 86.40E
Belvidere U.S.A. 85 40.49N 75.05W
Belyando r. Australia 64 21.38S146.50E
Belyayevka U.S.S.R. 21 46.30N 30.12E
Belynichi U.S.S.R. 21 54.00N 29.42E
Belyy, Ostrov U.S.S.R. 28 73.10N 70.45E
Belyy Yar U.S.S.R. 28 58.28N 85.03E
Bełżec Poland 21 50.24N 23.26E
Bemaraha, Plateau du mts. Madagascar 57 20.00S 45.15E
Bemarivo r. Madagascar 57 15.27S 47.40E
Bemidji U.S.A. 82 47.29N 94.53W
Bena Dibele Zaïre 54 4.07S 22.50E
Benagerie Australia 66 31.30S140.21E
Benalla Australia 67 36.35S145.58E
Benanee Australia 66 34.32S142.56E
Benares see Vārānasi India 41
Benavente Spain 16 42.00N 5.40W
Benbecula i. U.K. 12 57.26N 7.18W
Bencha China 32 32.31N120.53E
Ben Cruachan mtn. U.K. 12 56.26N 5.18W
Bencubbin Australia 63 30.48S117.52E
Bend U.S.A. 80 44.03N121.19W
Bende Nigeria 53 5.34N 7.37E
Bendel d. Nigeria 53 6.10N 6.00E
Bender Beila Somali Rep. 45 9.30N 50.30E
Bendery U.S.S.R. 21 46.50N 29.29E
Bendigo Australia 66 36.48S144.21E
Bendoc Australia 67 37.10S148.55E
Bendorf W. Germany 14 50.26N 7.34E
Bénéna Mali 52 13.09N 4.17W
Benenitra Madagascar 57 23.27S 45.05E
Benešov Czech. 20 50.45N 14.22E
Benevento Italy 18 41.07N 14.46E
Bengal, B. of Indian Oc. 41 20.00N 90.00E
Bengbu China 32 32.53N117.26E
Benghazi see Banghāzī Libya 51
Bengkulu Indonesia 36 3.46S102.16E
Benguela Angola 54 12.34S 13.24E
Benguela d. Angola 54 12.45S 14.00E
Ben Hope mtn. U.K. 12 58.24N 4.36W
Beni r. Bolivia 92 10.23S 65.24W
Beni Zaïre 55 0.29N 29.27E
Beni Abbes Algeria 50 30.08N 2.10W
Benicarló Spain 16 40.25N 0.25E
Benidorm Spain 16 38.33N 0.09W
Beni-Mellal Morocco 50 32.22N 6.29W
Benin Africa 53 9.00N 2.30E
Benin, Bight of Africa 53 5.30N 3.00E
Benin City Nigeria 53 6.19N 5.41E
Beni Saf Algeria 50 35.19N 1.23W
Benjamin Constant Brazil 90 4.22S 70.02W
Benkelman U.S.A. 82 40.03N101.32W
Ben Lawers mtn. U.K. 12 56.33N 4.14W
Ben Lomond mtn. N.S.W. Australia 67 30.04S151.43E
Ben Lomond mtn. Tas. Australia 65 41.33S147.40E
Ben Lomond mtn. U.K. 12 56.12N 4.38W
Ben Macdhui mtn. U.K. 12 57.04N 3.40W
Ben More mtn. Central U.K. 12 56.23N 4.31W
Ben More mtn. Strath. U.K. 12 56.26N 6.02W
Ben More Assynt mtn. U.K. 12 58.07N 4.52W
Bennett Canada 74 59.49N135.01W
Bennettsville U.S.A. 85 34.36N 79.40W
Ben Nevis mtn. U.K. 12 56.48N 5.00W
Benneydale New Zealand 60 38.31S175.21E
Benoni R.S.A. 56 26.12S 28.18E
Bénoué r. Cameroon see Benue r. Nigeria 53
Benson Ariz. U.S.A. 81 31.58N110.18W
Benson Minn. U.S.A. 82 45.19N 95.36W
Bentinck I. Australia 64 17.04S139.30E
Bentiu Sudan 49 9.14N 29.50E
Benton U.S.A. 82 38.01N 88.54W
Benton Harbor U.S.A. 84 42.07N 86.27W
Benue d. Nigeria 53 7.20N 8.00E
Benue r. Nigeria 53 7.52N 6.45E
Ben Wyvis mtn. U.K. 12 57.40N 4.35W
Benxi China 32 41.21N123.47E
Beograd Yugo. 21 44.49N 20.28E
Beohāri India 41 24.03N 81.23E
Beowawe U.S.A. 80 40.35N116.29W
Berat Albania 19 40.42N 19.59E
Berau, Teluk b. Indonesia 37 2.20S133.00E
Berbera Somali Rep. 45 10.28N 45.02E
Berbérati C.A.R. 53 4.19N 15.51E
Berceto Italy 15 44.31N 9.59E
Berchem Belgium 14 50.48N 3.32E
Berck France 17 50.25N 1.36E
Bercu France 14 50.32N 3.15E
Berdichev U.S.S.R. 21 49.54N 28.39E
Berdsk U.S.S.R. 28 54.51N 82.51E
Berdyansk U.S.S.R. 25 46.45N 36.47E
Beregovo U.S.S.R. 21 48.13N 22.39E
Bereko Tanzania 55 4.27S 35.43E
Berens r. Canada 75 52.21N 97.02W
Berens River town Canada 75 52.22N 97.02W
Beresford Australia 66 29.14S136.40E
Berettyóújfalu Hungary 21 47.14N 21.32E
Berevo Madagascar 57 19.44S 44.58E
Bereza U.S.S.R. 21 52.32N 25.00E
Berezhany U.S.S.R. 21 49.27N 24.56E
Berezina r. U.S.S.R. 21 54.10N 28.10E
Berezna U.S.S.R. 21 51.34N 31.46E
Berezniki U.S.S.R. 24 59.26N 56.49E
Berezno U.S.S.R. 21 51.00N 26.41E
Berezovka U.S.S.R. 21 47.12N 30.56E
Berezovo U.S.S.R. 28 63.58N 65.00E
Berga Spain 16 42.06N 1.48E
Berga Sweden 23 57.14N 16.03E
Bergama Turkey 19 39.08N 27.10E
Bergamo Italy 15 45.42N 9.40E
Bergen E. Germany 20 54.25N 13.26E
Bergen Neth. 14 52.40N 4.41E
Bergen Norway 23 60.23N 5.20E
Bergen U.S.A. 76 43.05N 77.57W
Bergen op Zoom Neth. 14 51.30N 4.17E
Bergerac France 17 44.50N 0.29E
Bergheim W. Germany 14 50.58N 6.39E
Berghem Neth. 14 51.46N 5.32E
Bergisch Gladbach W. Germany 14 50.59N 7.10E
Bergkamen W. Germany 14 51.35N 7.39E
Bergkvara Sweden 23 56.23N 16.05E
Bergland U.S.A. 84 46.36N 89.33W
Bergues France 14 50.58N 2.21E
Bergum Neth. 14 53.14N 5.59E
Berhampore India 41 24.06N 88.15E
Berhampur India 41 19.19N 84.47E
Bering Sea N. America/Asia 72 65.00N170.00W
Bering Str. U.S.S.R./U.S.A. 72 65.00N170.00W
Berislav U.S.S.R. 25 46.51N 33.26E
Berja Spain 16 36.50N 2.56W
Berkåk Norway 22 62.48N 10.03E
Berkel r. Neth. 14 52.10N 6.12E
Berkeley U.S.A. 80 37.57N122.18W
Berkner I. Antarctica 96 79.30S 50.00W
Berkshire d. U.K. 11 51.25N 1.03W
Berkshire Downs hills U.K. 11 51.32N 1.36W
Berland r. Canada 74 54.00N116.50W
Berlin E. Germany 20 52.32N 13.25E
Berlin Md. U.S.A. 85 38.20N 75.13W
Berlin N.H. U.S.A. 84 44.29N 71.10W
Bermagui Australia 67 36.28S150.03E
Bermejo r. San Juan Argentina 92 31.40S 67.15W
Bermejo r. Tucumán Argentina 92 26.47S 58.30W
Bermo India 41 23.47N 85.57E
Bermuda Atlantic Oc. 95 32.18N 64.45W
Bermuda Rise f. Atlantic Oc. 95 34.00N 60.00W
Bern Switz. 20 46.57N 7.26E
Bernard L. Canada 76 45.44N 79.24W
Bernay France 15 48.06N 0.36E
Bernburg E. Germany 20 51.48N 11.44E
Berne see Bern Switz. 17
Bernina mtn. Italy/Switz. 15 46.22N 9.57E
Bernkastel W. Germany 14 49.55N 7.05E
Beroroha Madagascar 57 21.41S 45.10E
Beroun Czech. 20 49.58N 14.04E
Berrechid Morocco 50 33.17N 7.35W
Berri Australia 66 34.17S140.36E
Berrigan Australia 67 35.41S145.48E
Berry Head U.K. 11 50.24N 3.28W
Berryville Ark. U.S.A. 83 36.22N 93.34W
Bersenbrück W. Germany 14 52.36N 7.58E
Bershad U.S.S.R. 21 48.20N 29.30E
Berté, Lac l. Canada 77 50.47N 68.30W
Berthierville Canada 77 46.05N 73.10W
Bertinoro Italy 15 44.09N 12.08E
Bertoua Cameroon 53 4.34N 13.42E
Bertraghboy B. Rep. of Ire. 13 53.23N 9.52W
Berwick-upon-Tweed U.K. 10 55.46N 2.00W
Besalampy Madagascar 57 16.45S 44.30E
Besançon France 17 47.14N 6.02E
Bessarabia f. U.S.S.R. 21 46.30N 28.40E
Bessemer U.S.A. 85 33.22N 87.00W
Betafo Madagascar 57 19.50S 46.51E
Betanzos Spain 16 43.17N 8.13W
Bétaré Oya Cameroon 53 5.34N 14.09E
Bethal R.S.A. 56 26.26S 29.27E
Bethany Beach town U.S.A. 85 38.31N 75.04W
Bethel Alas. U.S.A. 72 60.48N161.46W
Bethesda U.S.A. 85 38.59N 77.06W
Bethlehem R.S.A. 56 28.13S 28.18E
Bethlehem U.S.A. 85 40.36N 75.22W
Béthune France 14 50.32N 2.38E
Béthune r. France 15 49.53N 1.09E
Betim Brazil 94 19.55S 44.07W
Betioky Madagascar 57 23.42S 44.22E
Betor Ethiopia 49 11.40N 39.00E
Betroka Madagascar 57 23.16S 46.06E
Bet She'an Israel 44 32.30N 35.30E
Bet Shemesh Israel 44 31.45N 35.00E
Betsiamites Canada 77 48.56N 68.38W
Betsiboka r. Madagascar 57 16.03S 46.36E
Bette mtn. Libya 51 22.00N 19.12E
Bettiah India 41 26.48N 84.30E
Bettles U.S.A. 72 66.53N151.51W
Betūl India 41 21.55N 77.54E
Betwa r. India 41 25.55N 80.12E
Betws-y-Coed U.K. 9 53.05N 3.48W
Betzdorf W. Germany 14 50.48N 7.54E
Beulah Australia 66 35.59S142.26E
Beulah Canada 75 50.16N101.02W
Beulah U.S.A. 82 47.16N101.47W
Beuvron r. France 15 47.29N 3.31E
Beverley Australia 63 32.06S116.56E
Beverley U.K. 10 53.52N 0.26W
Beverley Hills town U.S.A. 81 34.04N118.26W
Beverly Mass. U.S.A. 84 42.33N 70.53W
Beverwijk Neth. 14 52.29N 4.40E
Bewcastle Fells hills U.K. 10 55.05N 2.50W
Bexhill U.K. 11 50.51N 0.29E
Bexley U.K. 11 51.26N 0.10E
Beyla Guinea 52 8.42N 8.39W
Beyneu U.S.S.R. 25 45.16N 55.04E
Beypazari Turkey 42 40.10N 31.56E
Beyşehir Gölü l. Turkey 42 37.47N 31.30E
Bezhanovo Bulgaria 19 43.13N 24.26E
Bezhetsk U.S.S.R. 24 57.49N 36.40E
Bezhitsa U.S.S.R. 24 53.19N 34.17E
Béziers France 17 43.21N 3.13E
Bhadohi India 41 25.25N 82.34E
Bhādra India 40 29.07N 75.10E
Bhadrakh India 41 21.04N 86.30E
Bhāg Pakistan 40 29.02N 67.49E
Bhāgalpur India 41 25.15N 87.00E
Bhāi Pheru Pakistan 40 31.12N 73.57E
Bhaironghāti India 41 31.01N 78.53E
Bhaisa India 41 19.06N 77.58E
Bhakkar Pakistan 40 31.38N 71.04E
Bhaktapur Nepal 41 27.42N 85.27E
Bhalwāl Pakistan 40 32.16N 72.54E
Bhamo Burma 34 24.10N 97.30E
Bhandāra India 41 21.10N 79.39E
Bhānvad India 40 21.56N 69.47E
Bharatpur India 41 27.13N 77.29E
Bharthana India 41 26.45N 79.14E
Bhātāpāra India 41 21.44N 81.56E
Bhatewar India 40 24.40N 74.05E
Bhātiāpāra Ghāt Bangla. 41 23.12N 89.42E
Bhatinda India 40 30.13N 74.56E
Bhatkal India 38 13.58N 74.34E
Bhātpāra India 41 22.52N 88.24E
Bhaunagar India 40 21.46N 72.09E
Bhawāni Mandi India 40 24.25N 75.50E
Bhawānipatna India 41 19.54N 83.10E
Bhera Pakistan 40 32.29N 72.55E
Bhikangaon India 40 21.52N 75.57E
Bhilai India 41 21.13N 81.26E
Bhilwāra India 40 25.21N 74.38E
Bhima r. India 38 16.30N 77.10E
Bhind India 41 26.34N 78.48E
Bhīnmāl India 40 25.00N 72.15E
Bhiwandi India 40 19.18N 73.04E
Bhiwāni India 40 28.47N 76.08E
Bhognīpur India 41 26.12N 79.48E
Bhojpur Nepal 41 27.11N 87.02E
Bhokardan India 40 20.16N 75.46E
Bhopāl India 41 23.16N 77.24E
Bhor India 38 18.12N 73.53E
Bhuban India 41 20.53N 85.50E
Bhubaneswar India 41 20.15N 85.50E
Bhuj India 40 23.16N 69.40E
Bhusāwal India 40 21.03N 75.46E
Bhutan Asia 41 27.15N 91.00E
Bia, Phou mtn. Laos 34 18.59N103.11E
Bīābānak Afghan. 40 32.11N 64.11E
Biak Indonesia 37 1.10S136.05E
Biak i. Indonesia 37 0.55S136.00E
Biała Podlaska Poland 21 52.02N 23.06E
Białogard Poland 20 54.00N 16.00E
Białystok Poland 21 53.09N 23.10E
Biankouma Ivory Coast 52 7.51N 7.34W
Biaora India 40 23.55N 76.54E
Biarritz France 17 43.29N 1.33W
Biasca Switz. 15 46.22N 8.58E
Bibā Egypt 44 28.56N 30.59E
Bibala Angola 54 14.46S 13.21E
Bibbenluke Australia 67 36.42S149.20E
Biberach W. Germany 20 48.20N 8.02E
Bic Canada 77 48.22N 68.42W
Bicas Brazil 94 21.44S 43.04W
Bicester U.K. 11 51.53N 1.09W
Bida Nigeria 53 9.06N 5.59E
Bīdar India 38 17.54N 77.33E
Biddeford U.S.A. 84 43.30N 70.26W
Bideford U.K. 11 51.01N 4.13W
Bidon Cinq see Poste Maurice Cortier Algeria 50
Bi Doup mtn. Vietnam 34 12.05N108.40E
Bié d. Angola 54 12.30S 17.30E
Biel Switz. 17 47.09N 7.16E
Bielefeld W. Germany 20 52.02N 8.32E
Biella Italy 15 45.34N 8.03E
Bielsko-Biała Poland 21 49.49N 19.02E
Bielsk Podlaski Poland 21 52.47N 23.12E
Bien Hoa Vietnam 34 10.58N106.50E
Bienville, Lac l. Canada 77 55.05N 72.40W
Bié Plateau f. Angola 54 13.00S 16.00E
Big Bald Mtn. Canada 77 47.12N 66.25W
Big Bear Lake town U.S.A. 81 34.15N116.53W
Big Beaver House town Canada 76 52.59N 89.50W
Big Belt Mts. U.S.A. 80 46.40N111.25W
Big Bend Nat. Park U.S.A. 83 29.12N103.12W
Bigbury B. U.K. 11 50.15N 3.56W
Big Cypress Swamp f. U.S.A. 85 26.10N 81.38W
Big Falls town U.S.A. 82 48.12N 93.48W
Biggar Canada 75 52.04N107.59W
Biggar U.K. 12 55.38N 3.31W
Bighorn r. U.S.A. 80 46.09N107.28W
Bighorn L. U.S.A. 80 45.06N108.08W
Bighorn Mts. U.S.A. 80 44.00N107.30W
Bight, Head of b. Australia 65 31.29S131.16E
Bignasco Switz. 15 46.20N 8.36E
Bignona Senegal 52 12.48N 16.18W
Big Pine U.S.A. 80 37.10N118.17W
Big Piney U.S.A. 80 42.32N110.07W
Big Quill L. Canada 75 51.55N104.22W
Big Salmon Canada 72 61.53N134.55W
Big Salmon r. Canada 74 61.52N134.56W
Big Sand L. Canada 75 57.45N 99.42W
Big Sandy U.S.A. 80 48.11N110.07W
Big Smoky Valley f. U.S.A. 80 38.30N117.15W
Big Snowy Mtn. U.S.A. 80 46.50N109.30W
Big Spring town U.S.A. 83 32.15N101.28W
Big Stone Gap town U.S.A. 85 36.52N 82.46W
Bigstone L. Canada 75 53.42N 95.44W
Big Stone L. U.S.A. 82 45.25N 96.40W
Big Sur U.S.A. 81 36.15N121.48W
Big Timber U.S.A. 80 45.50N109.57W
Big Trout L. Canada 75 53.40N 90.00W
Bihać Yugo. 18 44.49N 15.53E
Bihar India 41 25.11N 85.31E
Bihar d. India 41 24.30N 86.00E
Biharamulo Tanzania 55 2.34S 31.20E
Bihor mtn. Romania 21 46.26N 22.43E
Bihu China 33 28.21N119.47E
Bijagós, Arquipélago dos is. Guinea Bissau 52 11.30N 16.00W
Bijainagar India 40 25.56N 74.38E
Bijaipura India 41 24.46N 77.48E
Bijāpur India 41 18.48N 80.49E
Bijāpur India 38 16.52N 75.47E
Bījār Iran 43 35.52N 47.39E
Bijāwar India 41 24.38N 79.30E
Bijbān Chāh Pakistan 40 26.54N 64.42E
Bijeljina Yugo. 19 44.45N 19.13E
Bijeypur India 40 26.03N 77.22E
Bijie China 33 27.28N105.20E
Bijnor India 41 29.22N 78.08E
Bikaner India 40 28.42N 73.25E
Bikin U.S.S.R. 31 46.52N134.15E
Bikini i. Pacific Oc. 68 11.35N165.23E
Bikoro Zaïre 54 0.45S 18.09E
Bilāra India 40 26.10N 73.42E
Bilāspur India 39 22.03N 82.12E
Bilāspur Himachal P. India 40 31.19N 76.45E
Bilāspur Madhya P. India 41 22.05N 82.09E
Bilauktaung Range mts. Thailand 34 13.00N 99.15E
Bilbao Spain 16 43.15N 2.56W
Bilbays Egypt 44 30.25N 31.34E
Bilecik Turkey 42 40.10N 29.59E
Bilgrām India 41 27.11N 80.02E
Bili r. Zaïre 49 4.09N 22.29E
Bilibino U.S.S.R. 29 68.02N166.15E
Bilimora India 40 20.45N 72.57E

Billabong to Bory Tucholskie

Billabong *r.* Australia **66** 35.04S144.06E
Bill Baileys Bank *f.* Atlantic Oc. **8** 60.45N 10.30W
Billeroo Australia **66** 31.13S139.58E
Billingham U.K. **10** 54.36N 1.18W
Billings U.S.A. **80** 45.47N108.27W
Bill of Portland *c.* U.K. **11** 50.32N 2.28W
Bilma Niger **51** 18.41N 12.56E
Biloela Australia **64** 24.24S150.30E
Biloxi U.S.A. **83** 30.24N 88.53W
Bilqās Qism Awwal Egypt **44** 31.14N 31.22E
Biltine Chad **51** 14.32N 20.55E
Biltine *d.* Chad **51** 15.00N 21.00E
Bilto Norway **22** 69.26N 21.35E
Bima *r.* Zaïre **54** 3.24N 25.10E
Bimberi, Mt. Australia **67** 35.40S148.47E
Bimbo C.A.R. **53** 4.15N 18.33E
Bīna-Etāwa India **41** 24.11N 78.11E
Binaija *mtn.* Indonesia **37** 3.10S129.30E
Bīnālūd, Kūh-e *mts.* Iran **43** 36.15N 59.00E
Binbee Australia **64** 20.20S147.55E
Binche Belgium **14** 50.25N 4.10E
Bindki India **41** 26.02N 80.36E
Bindura Zimbabwe **57** 17.18S 31.20E
Binga Zimbabwe **56** 17.38S 27.19E
Binga, Mt. Zimbabwe **57** 19.47S 33.03E
Bingara Australia **67** 29.51S150.38E
Bingen W. Germany **14** 49.58N 7.55E
Bingerville Ivory Coast **52** 5.20N 3.53W
Bingham U.K. **10** 52.57N 0.57W
Bingham U.S.A. **84** 45.03N 69.53W
Binghamton U.S.A. **84** 42.08N 75.54W
Bingkor Malaysia **36** 5.26N116.15E
Bingöl Turkey **25** 38.54N 40.29E
Bingol Dağlari *mtn.* Turkey **42** 39.21N 41.22E
Binhai China **32** 34.00N119.55E
Binh Dinh Vietnam **34** 13.53N109.07E
Binjai Indonesia **36** 3.37N 98.25E
Binji Nigeria **53** 13.12N 4.55E
Binnaway Australia **67** 31.33S148.50E
Binscarth Canada **75** 50.37N101.16W
Bintan *i.* Indonesia **36** 1.10N104.30E
Bintulu Malaysia **36** 3.12N113.01E
Bin Xian China **32** 35.02N108.04E
Binya Australia **67** 34.14S146.22E
Binyang China **33** 23.12N108.48E
Binzert Tunisia **51** 37.17N 9.51E
Biograd Yugo. **18** 43.56N 15.27E
Bīr India **40** 18.59N 75.46E
Bir, Ras *c.* Djibouti **45** 11.59N 43.25E
Bi'r Abū 'Uwayqīlah *well* Egypt **44** 30.50N 34.07E
Bi'r ad Dakhal *well* Egypt **44** 28.40N 32.24E
Birāk Libya **51** 27.32N 14.17E
Bi'r al Ḩarash *well* Libya **51** 25.30N 22.06E
Bi'r al Jidy *well* Egypt **44** 30.13N 33.03E
Bi'r al Jufayr *well* Egypt **44** 30.49N 32.40E
Bi'r al 'Udayd *well* Egypt **44** 28.59N 34.05E
Birao C.A.R. **49** 10.17N 22.47E
Bi'r aş Şafrā' *well* Egypt **44** 28.46N 34.20E
Bi'r ath Thamadah *well* Egypt **44** 30.10N 33.28E
Birātnagar Nepal **41** 26.18N 87.17E
Bi'r Buerāt *well* Egypt **44** 28.59N 32.10E
Bi'r Bukhayt *well* Egypt **44** 29.13N 32.17E
Birch *r.* Canada **74** 58.30N112.15W
Birchip Australia **66** 35.59S142.59E
Birch L. N.W.T. Canada **74** 62.04N116.33W
Birch L. Ont. Canada **76** 51.24N 92.20W
Birch Mts. Canada **74** 57.30N112.30W
Bird Canada **75** 56.30N 94.13W
Birdsboro U.S.A. **85** 40.16N 75.48W
Birdsville Australia **64** 25.54S139.22E
Birdum Australia **62** 15.38S133.12E
Birecik Turkey **42** 37.03N 37.59E
Birganj Nepal **41** 27.01N 84.54E
Birhan *mtn.* Ethiopia **49** 11.00N 37.50E
Bi'r Ḩasanah *well* Egypt **44** 30.29N 33.47E
Bi'r Hooker *well* Egypt **44** 30.23N 30.20E
Birjand Iran **43** 32.54N 59.10E
Bi'r Jifjafah *well* Egypt **44** 30.28N 33.11E
Birk, Wādī *r.* Saudi Arabia **43** 24.08N 47.35E
Birkenfeld Rhein.-Pfalz W. Germany **14** 49.39N 7.10E
Birkenhead U.K. **10** 53.24N 3.01W
Birksgate Range *mts.* Australia **62** 27.10S129.45E
Bi'r Kusaybah *well* Egypt **44** 22.41N 29.55E
Bîrlad Romania **21** 46.14N 27.40E
Bi'r Lahfān *well* Egypt **44** 31.01N 33.52E
Birmingham U.K. **11** 52.30N 1.55W
Birmingham Ala. U.S.A. **85** 33.30N 86.55W
Birmitrapur India **41** 22.24N 84.46E
Bir Mogreïn Mauritania **50** 25.14N 11.35W
Birni Benin **53** 9.59N 1.34E
Birnin Gwari Nigeria **53** 11.02N 6.47E
Birnin Kebbi Nigeria **53** 12.30N 4.11E
Birni N'Konni Niger **53** 13.49N 5.19E
Birobidzhan U.S.S.R. **31** 48.49N132.54E
Bîr Ounâne *well* Mali **50** 21.02N 3.18W
Birr Rep. of Ire. **13** 53.06N 7.56W
Birrie *r.* Australia **67** 29.43S146.37E
Birsilpur India **40** 28.11N 72.15E
Birsk U.S.S.R. **24** 55.28N 55.31E
Bi'r Tābah *well* Egypt **44** 29.30N 34.53E
Bi'r Ţarfāwī *well* Egypt **48** 22.55N 28.53E
Birtle Canada **75** 50.32N101.02W
Bi'r Umm Sa'īd *well* Egypt **44** 29.40N 33.34E
Bi'r Umm 'Umayyid *well* Egypt **44** 27.53N 32.30E
Biržai U.S.S.R. **24** 56.10N 24.48E
Bi'r Zalţan *well* Libya **51** 28.27N 19.46E
Bir Zreigat Mauritania **50** 22.27N 8.53W
Bisalpur India **41** 28.18N 79.48E
Bisbee U.S.A. **81** 31.27N109.55W
Biscay, B. of France **17** 45.30N 4.00W
Bisceglie Italy **19** 41.14N 16.31E
Bisha Ethiopia **48** 15.28N 37.34E
Bishnupur India **41** 23.05N 87.19E
Bishop Calif. U.S.A. **80** 37.22N118.24W
Bishop Tex. U.S.A. **83** 27.35N 97.48W
Bishop Auckland U.K. **10** 54.40N 1.40W
Bishop's Stortford U.K. **11** 51.53N 0.09E
Bisina, L. Uganda **55** 1.35N 34.08E
Biskra Algeria **51** 34.48N 5.40E
Bismarck U.S.A. **82** 46.48N100.47W
Bismarck Range *mts.* P.N.G. **37** 6.00S145.00E
Bismarck Sea Pacific Oc. **37** 4.00S146.30E
Bison U.S.A. **82** 45.31N102.28W
Bīsotūn Iran **43** 34.22N 47.29E
Bispgården Sweden **22** 63.02N 16.40E
Bissau Guinea Bissau **52** 11.52N 15.39W
Bissett Canada **75** 51.02N 95.40W
Bissikrima Guinea **52** 10.50N 10.58W
Bistcho L. Canada **74** 59.45N118.50W
Bistrița Romania **21** 47.08N 24.30E
Bistrița *r.* Romania **21** 46.30N 26.54E
Biswān India **41** 27.30N 81.00E
Bitam Gabon **54** 2.05N 11.30E
Bitburg W. Germany **14** 49.58N 6.31E
Bitéa, Ouadi *wadi* Chad **49** 13.11N 20.10E
Bitlis Turkey **42** 38.23N 42.04E
Bitola Yugo. **19** 41.02N 21.21E
Bitter Creek *town* U.S.A. **80** 41.31N109.27W
Bitterfontein R.S.A. **56** 31.02S 18.14E
Bitterroot Range *mts.* U.S.A. **80** 47.06N115.10W
Biu Nigeria **53** 10.36N 12.11E
Biumba Rwanda **55** 1.38S 30.02E
Biwa ko *l.* Japan **35** 35.10N136.00E
Biyalā Egypt **44** 31.11N 31.13E
Biysk U.S.S.R. **28** 52.35N 85.16E
Bizerte *see* Binzert Tunisia **51**
Bjelovar Yugo. **19** 45.54N 16.51E
Bjorli Norway **23** 62.16N 8.13E
Björna Sweden **22** 63.32N 18.36E
Björnafjorden *est.* Norway **23** 60.06N 5.22E
Black *r.* Ark. U.S.A. **83** 35.38N 91.19W
Black *r. see* Đà *r.* Vietnam **34**
Blackall Australia **64** 24.25S145.28E
Blackburn U.K. **10** 53.44N 2.30W
Black Diamond Canada **74** 50.45N114.14W
Blackduck U.S.A. **82** 47.44N 94.33W
Black Duck *r.* U.S.A. **75** 56.51N 89.02W
Blackfoot U.S.A. **80** 43.11N112.20W
Black Hills U.S.A. **82** 44.00N104.00W
Black L. Canada **75** 59.10N105.20W
Black Mtn. U.K. **11** 51.52N 3.50W
Black Mts. U.K. **11** 51.52N 3.09W
Blackpool U.K. **10** 53.48N 3.03W
Black River *town* Jamaica **87** 18.02N 77.52W
Black River *town* Mich. U.S.A. **84** 44.51N 83.21W
Black Rock *town* U.S.A. **80** 38.41N112.59W
Black Rock Desert U.S.A. **80** 41.10N119.00W
Black Sand Desert U.S.S.R. **43** 37.45N 60.00E
Black Sea Europe **21** 44.00N 30.00E
Blacksod B. Rep. of Ire. **13** 54.04N 10.00W
Blackstone U.S.A. **85** 37.05N 78.02W
Black Sugarloaf Mt. Australia **67** 31.24S151.34E
Blackville Australia **67** 31.34S150.10E
Blackville U.S.A. **85** 33.22N 81.17W
Black Volta *r.* Ghana **52** 8.14N 2.11W
Blackwater *r.* Waterford Rep. of Ire. **13** 51.58N 7.52W
Blackwater *r.* U.K. **9** 54.31N 6.36W
Blackwell U.S.A. **83** 36.48N 97.17W
Blackwood *r.* Australia **63** 34.15S115.10E
Blaenau Ffestiniog U.K. **10** 53.00N 3.57W
Blagoevgrad Bulgaria **19** 42.02N 23.04E
Blagoveshchensk U.S.S.R. **31** 50.19N127.30E
Blain France **15** 47.29N 1.46W
Blair U.S.A. **82** 41.33N 96.08W
Blair Athol Australia **64** 22.42S147.33E
Blair Atholl U.K. **12** 56.46N 3.51W
Blairgowrie U.K. **12** 56.36N 3.21W
Blairmore Canada **74** 49.40N114.25W
Blairsville Ga. U.S.A. **85** 34.52N 83.52W
Blakely U.S.A. **85** 31.22N 84.58W
Blanc, Cap *c.* Mauritania **52** 20.44N 17.05W
Blanc, Mont *mtn.* Europe **17** 45.50N 6.52E
Blanca, Bahía *b.* Argentina **93** 39.20S 62.00W
Blanca, Sierra *mtn.* U.S.A. **81** 33.23N105.48W
Blanchard U.S.A. **80** 48.01N116.59W
Blanche, L. Australia **66** 29.15S139.40E
Blanchetown Australia **66** 34.21S139.38E
Blanchewater Australia **66** 29.32S139.28E
Blanco, C. Argentina **93** 47.12S 65.20W
Blanco, C. Costa Rica **87** 9.36N 85.06W
Blanco, C. U.S.A. **80** 42.50N124.34W
Bland *r.* Australia **67** 33.42S147.30E
Blandford Forum U.K. **11** 50.52N 2.10W
Blankenberge Belgium **14** 51.18N 3.08E
Blansko Czech. **20** 49.22N 16.39E
Blantyre Malaŵi **55** 15.46S 35.00E
Blarney Rep. of Ire. **13** 51.56N 8.34W
Blatnica Bulgaria **21** 43.42N 28.31E
Blavet *r.* France **17** 47.43N 3.18W
Blaye France **17** 45.08N 0.40W
Blayney Australia **67** 33.32S149.19E
Blednaya, Gora *mtn.* U.S.S.R. **28** 76.23N 65.08E
Bleiburg Austria **20** 46.35N 14.48E
Blekinge *d.* Sweden **23** 56.20N 15.00E
Blenheim New Zealand **60** 41.32S173.58E
Bléré France **15** 47.20N 0.59E
Blerick Neth. **14** 51.22N 6.08E
Bletchley U.K. **11** 51.59N 0.45W
Blida Algeria **51** 36.30N 2.50E
Bligh Entrance Australia **64** 9.18S144.10E
Blind River *town* Canada **76** 46.15N 83.00W
Blinman Australia **66** 31.05S138.11E
Blitar Indonesia **37** 8.06S112.12E
Blitta Togo **53** 8.23N 1.06E
Bloemfontein R.S.A. **56** 29.07S 26.14E
Bloemhof R.S.A. **56** 27.37S 25.34E
Blois France **15** 47.36N 1.20E
Blönduós Iceland **22** 65.39N 20.18W
Bloods Creek *town* Australia **64** 26.28S135.17E
Bloody Foreland *c.* Rep. of Ire. **13** 55.09N 8.17W
Bloomfield Iowa U.S.A. **82** 40.45N 92.25W
Bloomfield Nebr. U.S.A. **82** 42.36N 97.39W
Bloomfield N.J. U.S.A. **85** 40.48N 74.12W
Bloomington Ill. U.S.A. **82** 40.29N 89.00W
Bloomington Ind. U.S.A. **84** 39.10N 86.31W
Bloomington Minn. U.S.A. **82** 44.50N 93.17W
Bloomsburg U.S.A. **84** 41.00N 76.27W
Blora Indonesia **37** 6.55S111.29E
Blueberry *r.* Canada **74** 56.45N120.49W
Bluefield U.S.A. **85** 37.14N 81.17W
Bluefields Nicaragua **87** 12.00N 83.49W
Blue Hills of Couteau Canada **77** 47.59N 57.43W
Blue Mts. Australia **67** 33.30S150.15E
Blue Mts. U.S.A. **80** 45.30N118.15W
Blue Mud B. Australia **64** 13.26S135.56E
Blue Nile *r. see* Azraq, Al Baḩr al *r.* Sudan **48**
Bluenose L. Canada **72** 68.30N119.35W
Blue River *town* Canada **74** 52.05N119.09W
Blue Stack Mts. Rep. of Ire. **13** 54.44N 8.09W
Bluff New Zealand **60** 46.38S168.21E
Bluff U.S.A. **80** 37.17N109.33W
Bluff, C. Canada **77** 52.48N 55.53W
Bluff Knoll *mtn.* Australia **63** 34.25S118.15E
Blumenau Brazil **94** 26.55S 49.07W
Blunt U.S.A. **82** 44.31N 99.59W
Blyth Northum. U.K. **10** 55.07N 1.29W
Blythe U.S.A. **81** 33.37N114.36W
Bö Nordland Norway **22** 68.38N 14.35E
Bö Telemark Norway **23** 59.25N 9.04E
Bo Sierra Leone **52** 7.58N 11.45W
Boa Esperança Brazil **94** 21.03S 45.37W
Bo'ai Henan China **32** 35.10N113.04E
Boane Mozambique **57** 26.02S 32.19E
Boa Vista Brazil **90** 2.51N 60.43W
Bobadah Australia **67** 32.18S146.42E
Bobadilla Spain **16** 37.02N 4.44W
Bobbili India **39** 18.34N 83.22E
Bobbio Italy **15** 44.46N 9.23E
Bobo-Dioulasso U. Volta **52** 11.11N 4.18W
Bobonong Botswana **56** 21.59S 28.29E
Bóbr *r.* Poland **20** 52.04N 15.04E
Bobr U.S.S.R. **21** 54.19N 29.18E
Bobruysk U.S.S.R. **21** 53.08N 29.10E
Bôca do Acre Brazil **90** 8.45S 67.23W
Bocaranga C.A.R. **53** 7.01N 15.35E
Boca Raton U.S.A. **85** 26.22N 80.05W
Bochnia Poland **21** 49.58N 20.26E
Bocholt W. Germany **14** 51.49N 6.37E
Bochum R.S.A. **56** 23.12S 29.12E
Bochum W. Germany **14** 51.28N 7.11E
Bockum-Hövel W. Germany **14** 51.42N 7.41E
Boconó Venezuela **90** 9.17N 70.17W
Boda C.A.R. **53** 4.19N 17.26E
Bodalla Australia **67** 36.05S150.03E
Bodallin Australia **63** 31.22S118.52E
Bodélé Chad **51** 16.30N 16.30E
Bodélé *f.* Chad **53** 16.50N 17.10E
Boden Sweden **22** 65.50N 21.42E
Bodensee *l.* Europe **20** 47.40N 9.30E
Bode Sadu Nigeria **53** 8.57N 4.49E
Bodfish U.S.A. **81** 35.36N118.30W
Bodmin U.K. **11** 50.28N 4.44W
Bodmin Moor U.K. **11** 50.53N 4.35W
Bodo Canada **75** 52.11N110.04W
Bodö Norway **22** 67.18N 14.26E
Bodrum Turkey **42** 37.03N 27.28E
Boembé Congo **54** 2.59S 15.34E
Boende Zaïre **54** 0.15S 20.49E
Boffa Guinea **52** 10.12N 14.02W
Bogale Burma **34** 16.17N 95.24E
Bogalusa U.S.A. **83** 30.47N 89.52W
Bogan *r.* Australia **67** 30.00S146.20E
Bogan Gate *town* Australia **67** 33.08S147.50E
Bogata U.S.A. **83** 33.28N 95.13W
Bogcang Zangbo *r.* China **41** 31.50N 87.25E
Bogenfels Namibia **56** 27.26S 15.22E
Boggabilla Australia **67** 28.36S150.21E
Boggabri Australia **67** 30.42S150.02E
Boggeragh Mts. Rep. of Ire. **13** 52.03N 8.53W
Bogia P.N.G. **37** 4.16S145.00E
Bognes Norway **22** 68.15N 16.00E
Bognor Regis U.K. **11** 50.47N 0.40W
Bog of Allen *f.* Rep. of Ire. **13** 53.17N 7.00W
Bogol Manya Ethiopia **49** 4.32N 41.32E
Bogong, Mt. Australia **67** 36.45S147.21E
Bogor Indonesia **36** 6.34S106.45E
Bogor *mtn.* Indonesia **37** 6.34S106.45E
Bogotá Colombia **90** 4.38N 74.05W
Bogra Bangla. **41** 24.51N 89.22E
Bogué Mauritania **50** 16.35N 14.16W
Boguslav U.S.S.R. **21** 49.32N 30.52E
Bo Hai *b.* China **32** 38.30N119.30E
Bohain France **14** 49.59N 3.28E
Bohai Wan *b.* China **32** 38.30N117.55E
Bohemian Forest *see* Böhmerwald *mts.* W. Germany / Czech. **20**
Böhmerwald *mts.* W. Germany / Czech. **20** 49.20N 13.10E
Bohol *i.* Phil. **37** 9.45N124.10E
Bohotleh Wein Somali Rep. **45** 8.16N 46.24E
Boiaçu Brazil **90** 0.27S 61.46W
Boigu *i.* Australia **64** 9.16S142.12E
Boing Sudan **49** 9.58N 33.44E
Bois, Lac des *l.* Canada **72** 66.40N125.15W
Boise U.S.A. **80** 43.37N116.13W
Boise City U.S.A. **83** 36.44N102.31W
Bois-Guillaume France **15** 49.28N 1.08E
Boissevain Canada **75** 49.15N100.00W
Boizenburg E. Germany **20** 53.22N 10.43E
Bojador, Cabo *c.* W. Sahara **50** 26.08N 14.30W
Bojeador, C. Phil. **33** 18.30N120.36E
Bojnūrd Iran **43** 37.28N 57.20E
Bojonegoro Indonesia **37** 7.06S111.50E
Bokani Nigeria **53** 9.27N 5.13E
Boké Guinea **52** 10.57N 14.13W
Bokhara *r.* Australia **67** 29.55S146.42E
Boknafjorden *est.* Norway **23** 59.10N 5.35E
Bokoro Chad **53** 12.17N 17.04E
Bokote Zaïre **54** 0.05S 20.08E
Bokpyin Burma **34** 11.16N 98.46E
Bokungu Zaïre **54** 0.44S 22.28E
Bol Chad **53** 13.27N 14.40E
Bolac, L. Australia **66** 37.45S142.55E
Bolafa Zaïre **54** 1.23N 22.06E
Bolama Guinea Bissau **52** 11.35N 15.30W
Bolān *r.* Pakistan **40** 29.05N 67.45E
Bolanda, Jabal *mtn.* Sudan **49** 7.44N 25.28E
Bolān Pass Pakistan **40** 29.45N 67.35E
Bolbec France **15** 49.34N 0.28E
Bole Ghana **52** 9.03N 2.23W
Bolesławiec Poland **20** 51.16N 15.34E
Bolgatanga Ghana **52** 10.42N 0.52W
Bolgrad U.S.S.R. **21** 45.42N 28.40E
Bolia Zaïre **54** 1.36S 18.23E
Bolívar Argentina **93** 36.14S 61.07W
Bolivar Tenn. U.S.A. **83** 35.16N 88.59W
Bolivia S. America **92** 17.00S 65.00W
Bollnäs Sweden **23** 61.21N 16.25E
Bollon Australia **65** 28.02S147.28E
Bollstabruk Sweden **22** 62.59N 17.42E
Bolmen *l.* Sweden **23** 56.55N 13.40E
Bolobo Zaïre **54** 2.10S 16.17E
Bologna Italy **15** 44.30N 11.20E
Bologoye U.S.S.R. **24** 57.58N 34.00E
Bolomba Zaïre **54** 0.30N 19.13E
Bolombo Zaïre **54** 3.59S 21.22E
Bolondo Equat. Guinea **54** 1.40N 9.38E
Bolongongo Angola **54** 8.28S 15.16E
Bolovens, Plateau des *f.* Laos **34** 15.10N106.30E
Bolsena, Lago di *l.* Italy **18** 42.36N 11.55E
Bolshaya Glushitsa U.S.S.R. **24** 52.28N 50.30E
Bolshaya Pyssa U.S.S.R. **24** 64.11N 48.44E
Bolsherechye U.S.S.R. **28** 56.07N 74.40E
Bol'shevik, Ostrov *i.* U.S.S.R. **29** 78.30N102.00E
Bolshezemelskaya Tundra *f.* U.S.S.R. **24** 67.00N 56.10E
Bolshoy Atlym U.S.S.R. **28** 62.17N 66.30E
Bol'shoy Balkhan, Khrebet *mts.* U.S.S.R. **43** 39.38N 54.30E
Bol'shoy Irgiz *r.* U.S.S.R. **24** 52.00N 47.20E
Bol'shoy Lyakhovskiy, Ostrov *i.* U.S.S.R. **29** 73.30N142.00E
Bol'shoy Onguren U.S.S.R. **29** 53.40N107.40E
Bolshoy Uzen *r.* U.S.S.R. **25** 49.00N 49.40E
Bolsover U.K. **10** 53.14N 1.18W
Bolton U.K. **10** 53.35N 2.26W
Bolton L. Canada **75** 54.16N 95.47W
Bolu Turkey **42** 40.45N 31.38E
Bolus Head Rep. of Ire. **13** 51.47N 10.20W
Bolvadin Turkey **42** 38.43N 31.02E
Bolzano Italy **15** 46.30N 11.20E
Boma Zaïre **54** 5.50S 13.03E
Bomaderry Australia **67** 34.21S150.34E
Bomadi Nigeria **53** 5.13N 6.01E
Bombala Australia **67** 36.55S149.16E
Bombay India **40** 18.58N 72.50E
Bombo Uganda **45** 0.35N 32.32E
Bomboma Zaïre **54** 2.25N 18.54E
Bom Despacho Brazil **94** 19.46S 45.15W
Bomi China **30** 29.50N 95.45E
Bomi Hills Liberia **52** 7.01N 10.38W
Bömlafjorden *est.* Norway **23** 59.39N 5.20E
Bömlo *i.* Norway **23** 59.46N 5.13E
Bomokandi *r.* Zaïre **55** 3.37N 26.09E
Bomongo Zaïre **54** 1.30N 18.21E
Bomu *r.* Zaïre *see* Mbomou *r.* C.A.R. **49**
Bon, Cap *c.* Tunisia **51** 37.05N 11.03E
Bonaigarh India **41** 21.50N 84.57E
Bonaire *i.* Neth. Antilles **90** 12.15N 68.27W
Bonanza U.S.A. **80** 40.01N109.11W
Bonaparte *r.* Canada **74** 50.46N121.17W
Bonaparte Archipelago *is.* Australia **62** 14.17S125.18E
Bonar-Bridge *town* U.K. **12** 57.53N 4.21W
Bonavista Canada **77** 48.39N 53.07W
Bonavista, C. Canada **77** 48.42N 53.05W
Bonavista B. Canada **77** 48.45N 53.20W
Bon Bon Australia **66** 30.26S135.28E
Bondeno Italy **15** 44.53N 11.25E
Bondo Zaïre **54** 1.22S 23.53E
Bondo Zaïre **54** 3.47N 23.45E
Bondoukou Ivory Coast **52** 8.03N 2.15W
Bondowoso Indonesia **37** 7.54S113.50E
Bone, Teluk *b.* Indonesia **37** 4.00S120.50E
Bo'ness U.K. **12** 56.01N 3.36W
Bonga Ethiopia **49** 7.17N 36.15E
Bongaigaon India **41** 26.28N 90.34E
Bongak Sudan **49** 7.27N 33.14E
Bongandanga Zaïre **54** 1.28N 21.03E
Bongor Chad **53** 10.18N 15.20E
Bongos, Massif des *mts.* C.A.R. **49** 8.20N 21.35E
Bongouanou Ivory Coast **52** 6.44N 4.10W
Bonham U.S.A. **83** 33.35N 96.11W
Bonifacio, Str. of Med. Sea **18** 41.18N 9.10E
Bonin Is. Japan **68** 27.00N142.10E
Bonn W. Germany **14** 50.44N 7.06E
Bonners Ferry U.S.A. **80** 48.41N116.18W
Bonnétable France **15** 48.11N 0.26E
Bonneval France **15** 48.11N 1.24E
Bonneville Salt Flats *f.* U.S.A. **80** 40.45N113.52W
Bonney, L. Australia **66** 37.47S140.23E
Bonnie Rock *town* Australia **63** 30.32S118.21E
Bonny Nigeria **53** 4.25N 7.10E
Bonny, Bight of Africa **53** 2.58N 7.00E
Bonnyville Canada **75** 54.16N110.44W
Bonshaw Australia **67** 29.08S150.53E
Bontang Indonesia **36** 0.05N117.31E
Bonthain Indonesia **36** 5.32S119.58E
Bonthe Sierra Leone **52** 7.32N 12.30W
Bonython Range *mts.* Australia **62** 23.51S129.00E
Boogah Australia **67** 28.24S147.25E
Bookaloo Australia **66** 31.56S137.21E
Boola Guinea **52** 8.22N 8.41W
Boolaboolka, L. Australia **66** 32.40S143.13E
Boolaloo Australia **62** 22.30S115.51E
Booleroo Centre Australia **66** 32.53S138.21E
Booligal Australia **67** 33.54S144.54E
Boologooro Australia **62** 24.21S114.02E
Boom Belgium **14** 51.07N 4.21E
Boomrivier R.S.A. **56** 29.34S 20.26E
Boonah Australia **67** 28.00S152.36E
Boone U.S.A. **82** 42.04N 93.53W
Booneville U.S.A. **83** 34.39N 88.34W
Boonville Mo. U.S.A. **82** 38.58N 92.44W
Boonville N.Y. U.S.A. **84** 43.29N 75.20W
Boorabbin Australia **63** 31.14S120.21E
Boorindal Australia **67** 30.23S146.11E
Booroorban Australia **67** 34.56S144.46E
Boorowa Australia **67** 34.26S148.48E
Boort Australia **66** 36.08S143.46E
Boorthanna Australia **66** 28.32S135.52E
Boothia, G. of Canada **73** 70.00N 90.00W
Boothia Pen. Canada **73** 70.30N 95.00W
Bootra Australia **66** 30.00S143.00E
Booué Gabon **54** 0.00 11.58E
Bopeechee Australia **66** 29.36S137.23E
Boppard W. Germany **14** 50.13N 7.35E
Boquilla, Presa de la *l.* Mexico **81** 27.30N105.30W
Bor Czech. **20** 49.43N 12.47E
Bor Sudan **49** 6.12N 31.33E
Bor Yugo. **19** 44.05N 22.07E
Bora Bora *i.* Îs. de la Société **69** 16.30S151.45W
Borah Peak *mtn.* U.S.A. **80** 44.08N113.38W
Borama Somali Rep. **45** 9.58N 43.07E
Borås Sweden **23** 57.43N 12.55E
Borāzjān Iran **43** 29.14N 51.12E
Borba Brazil **90** 4.24S 59.35W
Borda, C. Australia **66** 35.45S136.34E
Bordeaux France **17** 44.50N 0.34W
Borden Australia **63** 34.05S118.16E
Borden I. Canada **72** 78.30N111.00W
Borden Pen. Canada **73** 73.00N 83.00W
Borders *d.* U.K. **12** 55.30N 2.53W
Bordertown Australia **66** 36.18S140.49E
Bordheyri Iceland **22** 65.12N 21.06W
Bordighera Italy **15** 43.46N 7.39E
Bordj Bou Arreridj Algeria **51** 36.04N 4.46E
Bordj Flye Sainte Marie Algeria **50** 27.17N 2.59W
Bordj Omar Driss Algeria **51** 28.09N 6.49E
Bordö *i.* Faroe Is. **22** 62.10N 7.13W
Bore Ethiopia **49** 4.40N 37.40E
Boreda Ethiopia **49** 6.32N 37.48E
Borgå Finland **23** 60.24N 25.40E
Borga Sweden **22** 64.49N 15.05E
Börgefjell *mtn.* Norway **22** 65.20N 13.45E
Börgefjell Nat. Park Norway **22** 65.00N 13.58E
Borger Neth. **14** 52.57N 6.46E
Borger U.S.A. **83** 35.39N101.24W
Borgholm Sweden **23** 56.53N 16.39E
Borghorst W. Germany **14** 52.08N 7.27E
Borgo Italy **15** 46.03N 11.27E
Borgomanero Italy **15** 45.42N 8.28E
Borgo San Dalmazzo Italy **15** 44.20N 7.30E
Borgo San Lorenzo Italy **15** 43.57N 11.23E
Borgosesia Italy **15** 45.43N 8.16E
Borgo Val di Taro Italy **15** 44.29N 9.46E
Borgund Norway **23** 61.03N 7.49E
Borislav U.S.S.R. **21** 49.18N 23.28E
Borisoglebsk U.S.S.R. **25** 51.23N 42.02E
Borisov U.S.S.R. **21** 54.09N 28.30E
Borispol U.S.S.R. **21** 50.21N 30.59E
Borja Peru **90** 4.20S 77.40W
Borken W. Germany **14** 51.50N 6.52E
Borkou-Ennedi-Tibesti *d.* Chad **51** 18.15N 20.00E
Borkum W. Germany **14** 53.34N 6.41E
Borkum *i.* W. Germany **14** 53.35N 6.45E
Borlänge Sweden **23** 60.29N 15.25E
Borley, C. Antarctica **96** 66.15S 55.00E
Bormio Italy **15** 46.28N 10.22E
Borndiep *g.* Neth. **14** 53.28N 5.35E
Borneo *i.* Asia **36** 1.00N114.00E
Bornheim W. Germany **14** 50.45N 7.00E
Bornholm *i.* Denmark **23** 55.10N 15.00E
Borno *d.* Nigeria **53** 12.20N 12.40E
Bornu, Plain of *f.* Nigeria **53** 12.30N 13.00E
Boro *r.* Sudan **49** 8.52N 26.11E
Borodyanka U.S.S.R. **21** 50.38N 29.59E
Boromo U. Volta **52** 11.43N 2.53W
Borotou Ivory Coast **52** 8.46N 7.30W
Boroughbridge U.K. **10** 54.06N 1.23W
Borovichi U.S.S.R. **24** 58.22N 34.00E
Borrika Australia **66** 35.00S140.05E
Borroloola Australia **64** 16.04S136.17E
Borşa Romania **21** 47.39N 24.40E
Borşa Romania **21** 46.56N 23.40E
Borsad India **40** 22.25N 72.54E
Borth U.K. **11** 52.29N 4.03W
Borūjerd Iran **43** 33.54N 48.47E
Bory Tucholskie *f.* Poland **21** 53.45N 17.30E

Borzhomi to **Bunia**

Borzhomi U.S.S.R. **25** 41.49N 43.23E
Borzna U.S.S.R. **25** 51.15N 32.25E
Borzya U.S.S.R. **29** 50.24N 116.35E
Bosa Italy **18** 40.18N 8.29E
Bosanska Gradiška Yugo. **19** 45.09N 17.15E
Bosanski Novi Yugo. **20** 45.03N 16.23E
Bosaso Somali Rep. **45** 11.13N 49.08E
Boscastle U.K. **11** 50.42N 4.42W
Bose China **33** 23.58N 106.32E
Boshan China **32** 36.29N 117.50E
Boshof R.S.A. **56** 28.32S 25.12E
Bosna *r.* Yugo. **19** 45.04N 18.27E
Bosna i Hercegovina *d.* Yugo. **19** 44.00N 18.10E
Bosnik Indonesia **37** 1.09S 136.14E
Bosobolo Zaïre **49** 4.11N 19.54E
Bōsō-hantō *pen.* Japan **35** 35.08N 140.00E
Bosporus *str.* see Istanbul Boğazi *str.* Turkey **19**
Bossangoa C.A.R. **53** 6.27N 17.21E
Bossembélé C.A.R. **53** 5.10N 17.44E
Bossier City U.S.A. **83** 32.31N 93.43W
Bosso Niger **53** 13.43N 13.19E
Bostān Pakistan **40** 30.26N 67.02E
Bosten Hu *l.* China **30** 42.00N 87.00E
Boston U.K. **10** 52.59N 0.02W
Boston U.S.A. **84** 42.21N 71.04W
Boston B. Australia **66** 34.35S 136.02E
Botād India **40** 22.10N 71.40E
Botany B. Australia **67** 34.04S 151.08E
Botev *mtn.* Bulgaria **19** 42.43N 24.55E
Botevgrad Bulgaria **19** 42.55N 23.57E
Bothnia, G. of Europe **22** 63.30N 20.30E
Botletle *r.* Botswana **56** 21.06S 24.47E
Botoşani Romania **21** 47.44N 26.41E
Botou U. Volta **53** 12.47N 2.02E
Botrange *mtn.* Belgium **14** 50.30N 6.04E
Botro Ivory Coast **52** 7.51N 5.19W
Botswana Africa **56** 22.00S 24.15E
Bottrop W. Germany **14** 51.31N 6.55E
Botucatu Brazil **94** 22.52S 48.30W
Bouaflé Ivory Coast **52** 7.01N 5.47W
Bouaké Ivory Coast **52** 7.42N 5.00W
Bouar C.A.R. **53** 5.58N 15.35E
Bou Arfa Morocco **50** 32.30N 1.59W
Bouca C.A.R. **53** 6.30N 18.21E
Bouchoir France **15** 49.45N 2.41E
Boudenib Morocco **50** 31.57N 4.38W
Boufarik Algeria **51** 36.36N 2.54E
Bougainville *i.* Pacific Oc. **68** 6.00S 155.00E
Bougouni Mali **52** 11.25N 7.28W
Bouillon Belgium **14** 49.48N 5.03E
Bouïra Algeria **51** 36.23N 3.54E
Bou-Izakarn Morocco **50** 29.09N 9.44W
Boulder Australia **63** 30.55S 121.32E
Boulder U.S.A. **82** 40.01N 105.17W
Boulder City U.S.A. **81** 35.59N 114.50W
Boulia Australia **64** 22.54S 139.54E
Boulogne France **17** 50.43N 1.37E
Boulogne-Billancourt France **15** 48.50N 2.15E
Boultoum Niger **53** 14.45N 10.25E
Boumba *r.* Cameroon **53** 2.00N 15.10E
Boumdeit Mauritania **50** 17.26N 9.50W
Boumo Chad **53** 9.01N 16.24E
Bouna Ivory Coast **52** 9.19N 2.53W
Boundary Peak *mtn.* U.S.A. **80** 37.51N 118.21W
Boundiali Ivory Coast **52** 9.30N 6.31W
Bountiful U.S.A. **80** 40.53N 111.53W
Bounty Is. Pacific Oc. **68** 48.00S 178.30E
Bouraga *well* Mali **52** 19.00N 3.36W
Bourail N. Cal. **68** 21.34S 165.30E
Bourem Mali **52** 16.59N 0.20W
Bourg France **17** 46.12N 5.13E
Bourganeuf France **17** 45.57N 1.44E
Bourges France **17** 47.05N 2.23E
Bourget Canada **77** 45.26N 75.09W
Bourg Madame France **17** 42.26N 1.55E
Bourgogne *d.* France **17** 47.10N 4.20E
Bourgogne, Canal de France **15** 47.58N 3.30E
Bourgoin France **17** 45.35N 5.17E
Bourgueil France **15** 47.17N 0.10E
Bourke Australia **67** 30.09S 145.59E
Bournemouth U.K. **11** 50.43N 1.53W
Bou Saâda Algeria **51** 35.12N 4.11E
Boussac France **17** 46.22N 2.13E
Bousso Chad **53** 10.32N 16.45E
Boutilimit Mauritania **50** 17.33N 14.42W
Bouvard, C. Australia **63** 32.40S 115.34E
Bouvetöya *i.* Atlantic Oc. **95** 54.26S 3.24E
Bovill U.S.A. **80** 46.51N 116.24W
Bovril Argentina **93** 31.22S 59.25W
Bow *r.* Canada **74** 51.10N 115.00W
Bowelling Australia **63** 33.25S 116.27E
Bowen Australia **64** 20.00S 148.15E
Bowen, Mt. Australia **67** 37.11S 148.34E
Bowie Ariz. U.S.A. **81** 32.19N 109.29W
Bowie Tex. U.S.A. **83** 33.34N 97.51W
Bow Island *town* Canada **75** 49.52N 111.22W
Bowling Green U.S.A. **85** 37.00N 86.29W
Bowling Green, C. Australia **64** 19.19S 146.25E
Bowman U.S.A. **82** 46.11N 103.24W
Bowman I. Antarctica **96** 65.00S 104.00E
Bowmanville Canada **76** 43.55N 78.41W
Bowral Australia **67** 34.30S 150.24E
Bowser Australia **67** 36.19S 146.23E
Boxholm Sweden **23** 58.12N 15.03E
Bo Xian China **32** 33.50N 115.46E
Boxing China **32** 37.08N 118.05E
Box Tank Australia **66** 32.13S 142.17E
Boxtel Neth. **14** 51.36N 5.20E
Boyabat Turkey **42** 41.27N 34.45E
Boyang China **33** 28.59N 116.42E
Boyanup Australia **63** 33.29S 115.40E
Boyarka U.S.S.R. **21** 50.20N 30.26E
Boyd *r.* Australia **67** 29.51S 152.25E
Boykétté C.A.R. **49** 5.28N 20.50E
Boyle Rep. of Ire. **13** 53.58N 8.19W
Boyne *r.* Rep. of Ire. **13** 53.43N 6.17W
Boyoma Falls *f.* Zaïre **54** 0.18N 25.32E
Boyup Brook Australia **63** 33.50S 116.22E
Bozca Ada *i.* Turkey **19** 39.49N 26.03E
Bozeman U.S.A. **80** 45.41N 111.02W
Bozen see Bolzano Italy **15**
Bozoum C.A.R. **53** 6.16N 16.22E
Bra Italy **15** 44.42N 7.51E
Brabant *d.* Belgium **14** 50.47N 4.30E
Brač *i.* Yugo. **19** 43.20N 16.38E
Bracadale, Loch U.K. **12** 57.22N 6.30W
Bracebridge Canada **76** 45.02N 79.19W
Bracieux France **15** 47.33N 1.33E
Bräcke Sweden **22** 62.44N 15.30E
Brad Romania **19** 46.06N 22.48E
Bradano *r.* Italy **19** 40.23N 16.52E
Bradenton U.S.A. **85** 27.29N 82.33W
Bradford Canada **76** 44.07N 79.34W
Bradford U.K. **10** 53.47N 1.45W
Bradford Penn. U.S.A. **84** 41.58N 78.39W
Bradley U.S.A. **83** 33.06N 93.39W
Bradworthy U.K. **11** 50.54N 4.22W
Brady U.S.A. **83** 31.08N 99.20W
Braemar U.K. **12** 57.01N 3.24W
Braga Portugal **16** 41.32N 8.26W
Bragado Argentina **93** 35.10S 60.30W
Bragança Brazil **91** 1.03S 46.46W
Bragança Portugal **16** 41.47N 6.46W
Bragança Paulista Brazil **94** 22.59S 46.32W
Bragin U.S.S.R. **21** 51.49N 30.16E
Brāhmanbāria Bangla. **41** 23.59N 91.07E
Brāhmani *r.* India **41** 20.39N 86.46E
Brahmaputra *r.* Asia **41** 23.50N 89.45E
Braidwood Australia **67** 35.27S 149.50E
Brăila Romania **21** 45.18N 27.58E
Brainerd U.S.A. **79** 46.20N 94.10W
Braintree U.K. **11** 51.53N 0.32E
Brakna *d.* Mauritania **50** 17.00N 13.20W
Brålanda Sweden **23** 58.34N 12.22E
Brampton Canada **76** 43.41N 79.46W
Brampton U.K. **10** 54.56N 2.43W
Bramsche W. Germany **14** 52.26N 7.59E
Branco *r.* Brazil **90** 1.00S 62.00W
Brandberg *mtn.* Namibia **56** 21.08S 14.35E
Brandbu Norway **23** 60.28N 10.30E
Brande Denmark **23** 55.57N 9.07E
Brandenburg E. Germany **20** 52.25N 12.34E
Brandfort R.S.A. **56** 28.41S 26.27E
Brandon Canada **75** 49.50N 99.57W
Brandon Mtn. Rep. of Ire. **13** 52.14N 10.15W
Brandon Pt. Rep. of Ire. **13** 52.17N 10.11W
Braniewo Poland **21** 54.24N 19.50E
Bransby Australia **66** 28.40S 142.00E
Branson U.S.A. **83** 36.39N 93.13W
Brantas *r.* Indonesia **37** 7.13S 112.45E
Brantford Canada **76** 43.08N 80.16W
Branxholme Australia **66** 37.51S 141.49E
Bras d'Or L. Canada **77** 45.52N 60.50W
Brasil, Planalto *mts.* Brazil **91** 17.02S 50.00W
Brasiléia Brazil **90** 11.00S 68.44W
Brasília Brazil **91** 15.45S 47.57W
Braşov Romania **21** 45.40N 25.35E
Brass Nigeria **53** 4.20N 6.15E
Brasschaat Belgium **14** 51.18N 4.28E
Bratislava Czech. **21** 48.10N 17.10E
Bratsk U.S.S.R. **29** 56.20N 101.15E
Bratsk Vodokhranilishche *resr.* U.S.S.R. **29** 54.40N 103.00E
Bratslav U.S.S.R. **21** 48.49N 28.51E
Braunau Austria **20** 48.15N 13.02E
Braunschweig W. Germany **20** 52.15N 10.30E
Braunton U.K. **11** 51.06N 4.09W
Brava Somali Rep. **55** 1.02N 44.02E
Bravo del Norte, Rio *r.* Mexico see Rio Grande *r.* Mexico/U.S.A. **83**
Brawley U.S.A. **81** 32.59N 115.31W
Bray France **15** 48.25N 3.14E
Bray Rep. of Ire. **13** 53.12N 6.07W
Bray Head Kerry Rep. of Ire. **13** 51.53N 10.26W
Brazeau *r.* Canada **74** 52.55N 115.15W
Brazilian Basin *f.* Atlantic Oc. **95** 15.00S 25.00W
Brazilian Highlands see Brasil, Planalto *mts.* Brazil **91**
Brazos *r.* U.S.A. **83** 28.53N 95.23W
Brazzaville Congo **54** 4.14S 15.10E
Brčko Yugo. **21** 44.53N 18.48E
Brda *r.* Poland **21** 53.07N 18.08E
Breadalbane *f.* U.K. **12** 56.30N 4.20W
Bream B. New Zealand **60** 36.00S 174.30E
Brebes Indonesia **37** 6.54S 109.00E
Brécey France **15** 48.44N 1.10W
Brechin U.K. **12** 56.44N 2.40W
Breckenridge U.S.A. **83** 32.45N 98.54W
Breckland *f.* U.K. **11** 52.28N 0.40E
Břeclav Czech. **20** 48.46N 16.53E
Brecon U.K. **11** 51.57N 3.23W
Brecon Beacons *mts.* U.K. **11** 51.53N 3.27W
Breda Neth. **14** 51.35N 4.46E
Bredasdorp R.S.A. **56** 34.31S 20.03E
Bredbo Australia **67** 35.57S 149.10E
Bregenz Austria **20** 47.31N 9.46E
Bregovo Bulgaria **19** 44.08N 22.39E
Bréhal France **15** 48.53N 1.30W
Breidhafjördhur *est.* Iceland **22** 65.15N 23.00W
Breim Norway **23** 61.44N 6.25E
Brekstad Norway **22** 63.42N 9.40E
Bremangerland *i.* Norway **23** 61.51N 5.02E
Bremen W. Germany **20** 53.05N 8.48E
Bremerhaven W. Germany **20** 53.33N 8.35E
Bremer Range *mts.* Australia **63** 32.40S 120.55E
Bremerton U.S.A. **80** 47.34N 122.38W
Brenda Australia **67** 29.00S 147.12E
Brenham U.S.A. **83** 30.10N 96.24W
Brenner Pass Italy/Austria **20** 47.00N 11.30E
Breno Italy **15** 45.57N 10.18E
Brent Canada **76** 46.00N 78.24W
Brenta *r.* Italy **15** 45.25N 12.15E
Brentwood U.K. **11** 51.38N 0.18E
Brescia Italy **15** 45.33N 10.12E
Breskens Neth. **14** 51.24N 3.34E
Bressay *i.* U.K. **12** 60.08N 1.05W
Bressuire France **17** 46.50N 0.28W
Brest France **17** 48.23N 4.30W
Brest U.S.S.R. **21** 52.08N 23.40E
Bretagne *d.* France **17** 48.15N 2.30W
Breteuil France **15** 49.38N 2.18E
Breteuil-sur-Iton France **15** 48.50N 0.55E
Breton Sd. U.S.A. **83** 29.30N 89.30W
Brett, C. New Zealand **60** 35.15S 174.20E
Breuil-Cervinia Italy **15** 45.56N 7.38E
Brevik Norway **23** 59.04N 9.42E
Brewarrina Australia **67** 29.57S 147.54E
Brewer U.S.A. **84** 44.48N 68.46W
Brewster N.Y. U.S.A. **85** 41.24N 73.37W
Brewton U.S.A. **85** 31.07N 87.04W
Brezhnev U.S.S.R. **24** 55.42N 52.20E
Brezovo Bulgaria **19** 42.20N 25.06E
Bria C.A.R. **49** 6.32N 21.59E
Briançon France **17** 44.53N 6.39E
Briare France **15** 47.38N 2.44E
Bribbaree Australia **67** 34.07S 147.51E
Bribie I. Australia **65** 27.00S 153.07E
Brichany U.S.S.R. **21** 48.20N 27.01E
Bricquebec France **15** 49.28N 1.38W
Bride U.K. **10** 54.23N 4.24W
Bridge *r.* Canada **74** 50.50N 122.40W
Bridgend U.K. **11** 51.30N 3.35W
Bridgeport Calif. U.S.A. **80** 38.10N 119.13W
Bridgeport Conn. U.S.A. **84** 41.12N 73.12W
Bridgeport Nebr. U.S.A. **82** 41.40N 103.06W
Bridgeport Tex. U.S.A. **83** 33.13N 97.45W
Bridger U.S.A. **80** 45.18N 108.55W
Bridgeton U.S.A. **85** 39.26N 75.14W
Bridgetown Australia **63** 33.57S 116.08E
Bridgetown Barbados **87** 13.06N 59.37W
Bridgetown Canada **77** 44.51N 65.18W
Bridgetown Rep. of Ire. **13** 52.14N 6.33W
Bridgeville U.S.A. **85** 38.45N 75.36W
Bridgewater Canada **77** 44.23N 64.31W
Bridgewater, C. Australia **66** 38.25S 141.28E
Bridgnorth U.K. **11** 52.33N 2.25W
Bridgwater U.K. **11** 51.08N 3.00W
Bridlington U.K. **10** 54.06N 0.11W
Brie *f.* France **15** 48.40N 3.20E
Brienne-le-Château France **15** 48.24N 4.32E
Brig Switz. **15** 46.19N 8.00E
Brig Switz. **20** 46.19N 8.00E
Brigantine U.S.A. **85** 39.24N 74.22W
Brigg U.K. **10** 53.33N 0.30W
Briggsdale U.S.A. **82** 40.38N 104.20W
Brigham City U.S.A. **80** 41.31N 112.01W
Bright Australia **67** 36.42S 146.58E
Brighton U.K. **11** 50.50N 0.09W
Brighton Colo. U.S.A. **80** 39.59N 104.49W
Brighton Fla. U.S.A. **85** 27.13N 81.06W
Brighton Downs *town* Australia **64** 23.20S 141.34E
Brikama Gambia **52** 13.15N 16.39W
Brindisi Italy **19** 40.38N 17.57E
Brinkley U.S.A. **83** 34.53N 91.12W
Brinkworth Australia **66** 33.42S 138.24E
Brionne France **15** 49.12N 0.43E
Briouze France **15** 48.42N 0.22W
Brisbane Australia **67** 27.30S 153.00E
Brisighella Italy **15** 44.13N 11.46E
Bristol U.K. **11** 51.26N 2.35W
Bristol Penn. U.S.A. **85** 40.06N 74.52W
Bristol S.Dak. U.S.A. **82** 45.21N 97.45W
Bristol Tenn. U.S.A. **85** 36.33N 82.11W
Bristol B. U.S.A. **72** 58.00N 158.50W
Bristol Channel U.K. **11** 51.17N 3.20W
British Antarctic Territory Antarctica **96** 70.00S 50.00W
British Columbia *d.* Canada **74** 55.00N 125.00W
British Mts. Canada **72** 69.00N 140.20W
British Virgin Is. C. America **87** 18.30N 64.30W
Britstown R.S.A. **56** 30.34S 23.30E
Britt Canada **76** 45.46N 80.35W
Britton U.S.A. **82** 45.48N 97.45W
Brive France **17** 45.09N 1.32E
Briviesca Spain **16** 42.33N 3.19W
Brixham U.K. **11** 50.24N 3.31W
Brno Czech. **20** 49.11N 16.39E
Broach India **40** 21.42N 72.58E
Broad Arrow Australia **63** 30.32S 121.20E
Broad B. U.K. **12** 58.15N 6.15W
Broadback *r.* Canada **76** 51.20N 78.50W
Broadford Australia **67** 37.16S 145.03E
Broadmere Australia **64** 25.30S 149.30E
Broadsound Range *mts.* Australia **64** 22.30S 149.30E
Broadus U.S.A. **80** 45.27N 105.25W
Broadview Canada **75** 50.20N 102.30W
Broadwater Australia **67** 28.59S 13.16E
Broadway U.K. **11** 52.02N 1.51W
Brochet Canada **75** 57.53N 101.40W
Brochet, L. Canada **75** 58.36N 101.35W
Brockport U.S.A. **76** 43.13N 77.56W
Brockton U.S.A. **84** 42.05N 71.01W
Brockville Canada **84** 44.35N 75.41W
Brockway Mont. U.S.A. **80** 47.15N 105.45W
Brocton U.S.A. **76** 42.23N 79.27W
Brod Hrvatska Yugo. **21** 45.09N 18.02E
Brodeur Pen. Canada **73** 73.00N 88.00W
Brodick U.K. **12** 55.34N 5.09W
Brodnica Poland **21** 53.16N 19.23E
Brodribb River *town* Australia **67** 37.42S 148.37E
Brody U.S.S.R. **21** 50.05N 25.08E
Broglie France **15** 49.01N 0.32E
Broken Arrow U.S.A. **83** 36.03N 95.48W
Broken B. Australia **67** 33.34S 151.18E
Broken Bow U.S.A. **82** 41.24N 99.38W
Broken Hill *town* Australia **66** 31.57S 141.30E
Bromley U.K. **11** 51.24N 0.02E
Bromley Plateau *f.* Atlantic Oc. **95** 30.00S 34.00W
Bromsgrove U.K. **9** 52.20N 2.03W
Brönderslev Denmark **23** 57.16N 9.58E
Brong-Ahafo *d.* Ghana **52** 7.45N 1.30W
Brönnöysund Norway **22** 65.30N 12.10E
Bronte Canada **76** 43.23N 79.43W
Brookes Inlet Australia **63** 33.55S 116.25E
Brooke's Point *town* Phil. **36** 8.50N 117.52E
Brookfield U.S.A. **82** 39.47N 93.04W
Brookhaven U.S.A. **83** 31.35N 90.26W
Brookings Oreg. U.S.A. **80** 42.03N 124.17W
Brookings S.Dak. U.S.A. **82** 44.19N 96.48W
Brooklin Canada **76** 43.57N 78.57W
Brooklyn Center U.S.A. **82** 45.05N 93.20W
Brooks Canada **72** 50.35N 111.53W
Brooks B. Canada **74** 50.15N 127.55W
Brooks Range *mts.* U.S.A. **72** 68.50N 152.00W
Brooksville U.S.A. **85** 28.34N 82.24W
Brookton Australia **63** 32.22S 117.01E
Broom, Loch U.K. **12** 57.52N 5.07W
Broome Australia **62** 17.58S 122.15E
Broome Hill *town* Australia **63** 33.50S 117.35E
Brora U.K. **12** 58.01N 3.52W
Brora *r.* U.K. **12** 58.00N 3.51W
Brosna *r.* Rep.of Ire. **13** 53.13N 7.58W
Brothers U.S.A. **80** 43.49N 120.36W
Brou France **15** 48.13N 1.11E
Brough England U.K. **10** 54.32N 2.19W
Brough Scotland U.K. **12** 60.29N 1.12W
Broughton *r.* Australia **66** 33.21S 137.46E
Broughton in Furness U.K. **10** 54.17N 3.12W
Brouwershaven Neth. **14** 51.44N 3.53E
Brovary U.S.S.R. **21** 50.30N 30.45E
Brovst Denmark **23** 57.06N 9.32E
Brown, Mt. Australia **66** 32.33S 138.02E
Brownfield U.S.A. **83** 33.11N 102.16W
Browning U.S.A. **80** 48.34N 113.01W
Brownsburg Canada **77** 45.41N 74.25W
Brownsville Tenn. U.S.A. **83** 35.36N 89.15W
Brownsville Tex. U.S.A. **83** 25.54N 97.30W
Brownwood U.S.A. **83** 31.43N 98.59W
Bruay-en-Artois France **14** 50.29N 2.36E
Bruce Pen. Canada **76** 44.50N 81.20W
Bruce Rock *town* Australia **63** 31.52S 118.09E
Bruges see Brugge Belgium **14**
Brugge Belgium **14** 51.13N 3.14E
Brühl W. Germany **14** 50.50N 6.55E
Brûlé, Lac *l.* Canada **77** 52.17N 63.52W
Brumadinho Brazil **94** 20.09S 44.11W
Brumado Brazil **91** 14.13S 41.40W
Brunei Asia **36** 4.56N 114.58E
Brünen W. Germany **14** 51.45N 6.41E
Brunflo Sweden **22** 63.04N 14.50E
Brunner New Zealand **60** 42.28S 171.12E
Brunsbüttel W. Germany **20** 53.44N 9.05E
Brunssum Neth. **14** 50.57N 5.59E
Brunswick Ga. U.S.A. **85** 31.09N 81.30W
Brunswick Maine U.S.A. **84** 43.55N 69.58W
Brunswick B. Australia **62** 15.05S 125.00E
Brunswick Junction Australia **63** 33.15S 115.45E
Bruny I. Australia **65** 43.15S 147.16E
Brusilovka U.S.S.R. **25** 50.39N 54.59E
Brussel see Bruxelles Belgium **14**
Brussels see Bruxelles Belgium **14**
Bruthen Australia **67** 37.44S 147.49E
Bruton U.K. **11** 51.06N 2.28W
Bruxelles Belgium **14** 50.50N 4.23E
Bryan Ohio U.S.A. **84** 41.30N 84.34W
Bryan Tex. U.S.A. **83** 30.40N 96.22W
Bryan, Mt. Australia **66** 33.26S 138.27E
Bryansk U.S.S.R. **24** 53.15N 34.09E
Bryne Norway **23** 58.44N 5.39E
Bryson Canada **76** 45.41N 76.37W
Bryson, Lac *l.* Canada **76** 46.19N 77.27W
Bryson City U.S.A. **85** 35.26N 83.27W
Brzeg Poland **21** 50.52N 17.27E
Bsharrī Lebanon **44** 34.15N 36.00E
Bua *r.* Malaŵi **55** 12.42S 34.15E
Bua Yai Thailand **34** 15.34N 102.24E
Bu'ayrāt al Ḥasūn Libya **51** 31.24N 15.44E
Buba Guinea Bissau **52** 11.36N 14.55W
Būbīyān, Jazīrat *i.* Kuwait **45** 29.45N 48.15E
Bubye *r.* Zimbabwe **56** 22.18S 31.00E
Bucak Turkey **42** 37.28N 30.36E
Bucaramanga Colombia **90** 7.08N 73.10W
Buchach U.S.S.R. **21** 49.09N 25.20E
Buchan Australia **67** 37.30S 148.09E
Buchanan Liberia **52** 5.57N 10.02W
Buchanan, L. Australia **64** 21.28S 145.52E
Buchanan L. U.S.A. **83** 30.48N 98.25W
Buchan Ness *c.* U.K. **12** 57.28N 1.47W
Buchans Canada **77** 48.49N 56.52W
Bucharest see Bucureşti Romania **21**
Buchloe W. Germany **20** 48.02N 10.44E
Buchy France **15** 49.35N 1.22E
Buckambool Mt. Australia **67** 31.55S 145.40E
Buckhaven and Methil U.K. **10** 56.11N 3.03W
Buckie U.K. **12** 57.40N 2.58W
Buckingham U.K. **11** 52.00N 0.59W
Buckingham Canada **77** 45.35N 75.25W
Buckingham B. Australia **64** 12.10S 135.46E
Buckinghamshire *d.* U.K. **11** 51.50N 0.48W
Buckland Tableland *f.* Australia **64** 25.00S 148.00E
Buckleboo Australia **66** 32.55S 136.12E
Buckley U.S.A. **82** 40.35N 88.04W
Bucklin U.S.A. **83** 37.33N 99.38W
Buco Zau Angola **54** 4.46S 12.34E
Bucquoy France **14** 50.09N 2.43E
Bu Craa W. Sahara **50** 26.21N 12.57W
Buctouche Canada **77** 46.28N 64.43W
Bucureşti Romania **21** 44.25N 26.06E
Bucyrus U.S.A. **84** 40.47N 82.57W
Bud Norway **22** 62.54N 6.56E
Budapest Hungary **21** 47.30N 19.03E
Budaun India **41** 28.03N 79.07E
Budda Australia **66** 31.12S 144.16E
Budd Coast *f.* Antarctica **96** 67.00S 112.00E
Buddh Gaya India **41** 24.42N 84.59E
Bude U.K. **11** 50.49N 4.33W
Bude B. U.K. **11** 50.50N 4.40W
Budennovsk U.S.S.R. **25** 44.50N 44.10E
Budjala Zaïre **54** 2.38N 19.48E
Buea Cameroon **53** 4.09N 9.13E
Buenaventura Colombia **90** 3.54N 77.02W
Buenaventura Mexico **81** 29.51N 107.29W
Buena Vista U.S.A. **85** 37.44N 79.22W
Buenos Aires Argentina **93** 34.40S 58.25W
Buenos Aires *d.* Argentina **93** 36.30S 59.00W
Buenos Aires, L. Argentina/Chile **93** 46.35S 72.00W
Buffalo Canada **75** 50.49N 110.42W
Buffalo *r.* Canada **74** 60.55N 115.00W
Buffalo Mo. U.S.A. **83** 37.39N 93.06W
Buffalo N.Y. U.S.A. **84** 42.52N 78.55W
Buffalo Okla. U.S.A. **83** 36.50N 99.38W
Buffalo S.Dak. U.S.A. **82** 45.35N 103.33W
Buffalo Wyo. U.S.A. **80** 44.21N 106.42W
Buffalo Head Hills Canada **74** 57.25N 115.55W
Buffalo L. Canada **74** 60.10N 115.30W
Buffalo Narrows *town* Canada **75** 55.51N 108.30W
Bug *r.* Poland **21** 52.29N 21.11E
Buga Colombia **90** 3.53N 76.17W
Bugaldie Australia **67** 31.02S 149.08E
Bugembe Uganda **55** 0.26N 33.16E
Bugene Tanzania **55** 1.34S 31.07E
Buggs Island L. U.S.A. **85** 36.35N 78.28W
Bugrino U.S.S.R. **24** 68.45N 49.15E
Bugt China **31** 48.45N 121.58E
Bugulma U.S.S.R. **24** 54.32N 52.46E
Buguma Nigeria **53** 4.43N 6.53E
Buguruslan U.S.S.R. **24** 53.36N 52.30E
Buhera Zimbabwe **57** 19.21S 31.25E
Buhuşi Romania **21** 46.43N 26.41E
Builth Wells U.K. **11** 52.09N 3.24W
Buinsk U.S.S.R. **24** 54.58N 48.15E
Buitenpost Neth. **14** 53.15N 6.09E
Buji P.N.G. **64** 9.07S 142.26E
Bujumbura Burundi **55** 3.22S 29.21E
Bukama Zaïre **54** 9.16S 25.52E
Bukavu Zaïre **55** 2.30S 28.49E
Bukene Tanzania **55** 4.13S 32.52E
Bukhara U.S.S.R. **43** 39.47N 64.26E
Buki U.S.S.R. **21** 49.02N 30.29E
Bukima Tanzania **55** 1.48S 33.25E
Bukittinggi Indonesia **36** 0.18S 100.20E
Bukoba Tanzania **55** 1.20S 31.49E
Bukrale Ethiopia **49** 4.30N 42.03E
Bukuru Nigeria **53** 9.48N 8.52E
Būl, Kūh-e *mtn.* Iran **43** 30.48N 52.45E
Bula Indonesia **37** 3.07S 130.27E
Bulan Phil. **37** 12.40N 123.53E
Bulandshahr India **41** 28.24N 77.51E
Bulawayo Zimbabwe **56** 20.10S 28.43E
Buldāna India **40** 20.32N 76.11E
Buldern W. Germany **14** 51.52N 7.21E
Bulgan Mongolia **30** 48.34N 103.12E
Bulgaria Europe **19** 42.30N 25.00E
Bulhar Somali Rep. **45** 10.23N 44.27E
Bullabulling Australia **63** 31.05S 120.52E
Bullara Australia **62** 22.40S 114.03E
Buller *r.* New Zealand **60** 41.45S 171.35E
Buller, Mt. Australia **67** 37.11S 146.26E
Bullfinch Australia **63** 30.59S 119.06E
Bulli Australia **67** 34.20S 150.55E
Bull Mts. U.S.A. **80** 46.05N 109.00W
Bulloo *r.* Australia **66** 28.43S 142.27E
Bulloo Downs *town* Australia **66** 28.30S 142.45E
Bull Shoals L. U.S.A. **83** 36.30N 92.50W
Bulo Burti Somali Rep. **45** 3.52N 45.40E
Bulolo P.N.G. **37** 7.13S 146.35E
Bulong Australia **63** 30.44S 121.48E
Bulsār India **40** 20.38N 72.56E
Bultfontein R.S.A. **56** 28.17S 26.09E
Bulu Indonesia **37** 4.34N 126.45E
Bulu, Gunung *mtn.* Indonesia **36** 3.00N 116.00E
Bulun U.S.S.R. **29** 70.50N 127.20E
Bulunde Tanzania **55** 4.19S 32.57E
Bumba Bandundu Zaïre **54** 6.55S 19.16E
Bumba Equateur Zaïre **54** 2.15N 22.32E
Bumbuli Zaïre **54** 3.25S 20.30E
Buna Kenya **55** 2.49N 39.27E
Buna P.N.G. **64** 8.40S 148.25E
Bunbury Australia **63** 33.20S 115.34E
Buncrana Rep. of Ire. **13** 55.08N 7.27W
Bundaberg Australia **64** 24.50S 152.21E
Bundaleer Australia **67** 28.39S 146.31E
Bundarra Australia **67** 30.11S 151.04E
Bunde W. Germany **14** 53.12N 7.16E
Bundella Australia **67** 31.35S 149.59E
Būndi India **40** 25.27N 75.39E
Bundoran Rep. of Ire. **13** 54.28N 8.17W
Būndu India **41** 23.11N 85.35E
Bungay U.K. **11** 52.27N 1.26E
Bungo Angola **54** 7.26S 15.23E
Bungu Tanzania **55** 7.37S 39.07E
Bunguran *i.* Indonesia **36** 4.00N 108.20E
Bunguran Selatan *i.* Indonesia **36** 3.00N 108.50E
Buni Nigeria **53** 11.20N 11.59E
Bunia Zaïre **55** 1.30N 30.10E

Buninyong to Carlos Reyles

Buninyong Australia 66 37.41S143.58E
Bunkie U.S.A. 83 30.57N 92.11W
Bunyala Kenya 45 0.07N 34.00E
Bunyan Australia 67 36.11S149.09E
Buol Indonesia 37 1.12N121.28E
Buqayq Saudi Arabia 43 25.55N 49.40E
Bura Coast Kenya 55 3.30S 38.19E
Bura Coast Kenya 55 1.09S 39.55E
Burakin Australia 63 30.30S117.08E
Buran Somali Rep. 45 10.10N 48.48E
Burang China 41 30.16N 81.11E
Burao Somali Rep. 45 9.30N 45.30E
Buras U.S.A. 83 29.21N 89.32W
Buraydah Saudi Arabia 43 26.18N 43.58E
Burcher Australia 67 33.32S147.18E
Burdur Turkey 25 37.44N 30.17E
Burdwān India 41 23.15N 87.51E
Bure Ethiopia 49 10.40N 37.04E
Burg E. Germany 20 52.17N 11.51E
Burgas Bulgaria 19 42.30N 27.29E
Bur Gavo Somali Rep. 49 1.10S 41.50E
Burgenland *d.* Austria 20 47.30N 16.20E
Burgeo Canada 77 47.36N 57.34W
Burgess Hill U.K. 11 50.57N 0.07W
Burgos Spain 16 42.21N 3.41W
Burgsteinfurt W. Germany 14 52.09N 7.21E
Burgsvik Sweden 23 57.03N 18.16E
Bur Hakkaba Somali Rep. 55 2.43N 44.10E
Burhānpur India 40 21.18N 76.14E
Buri Brazil 94 23.46S 48.39W
Burias *i.* Phil. 37 12.50N123.10E
Burica, Punta *c.* Panama 87 8.05N 82.50W
Burin Pen. Canada 77 47.00N 55.40W
Buriram Thailand 34 14.59N103.08E
Burkburnett U.S.A. 83 34.06N 98.34W
Burke *r.* Australia 64 23.12S139.33E
Burketown Australia 64 17.44S139.22E
Burley U.S.A. 80 42.32N113.48W
Burlington Canada 76 43.19N 79.48W
Burlington Iowa U.S.A. 82 40.49N 91.14W
Burlington Kans. U.S.A. 82 38.12N 95.45W
Burlington N.C. U.S.A. 85 36.05N 79.27W
Burlington N.J. U.S.A. 85 40.04N 74.49W
Burlington Vt. U.S.A. 84 44.29N 73.13W
Burlington Wisc. U.S.A. 82 42.41N 88.17W
Burma Asia 34 21.45N 97.00E
Burngup Australia 63 33.00S118.39E
Burnham-on-Crouch U.K. 11 51.37N 0.50E
Burnham-on-Sea U.K. 11 51.15N 3.00W
Burnie Australia 65 41.03S145.55E
Burnley U.K. 10 53.47N 2.15W
Burns Australia 66 32.10S141.03E
Burns Oreg. U.S.A. 80 43.35N119.03W
Burns Wyo. U.S.A. 80 41.11N104.21W
Burnside *r.* Canada 72 66.51N108.04W
Burns Lake *town* Canada 74 54.20N125.45W
Burra Australia 66 33.40S138.57E
Burracoppin Australia 63 31.22S118.30E
Burren Junction Australia 67 30.08S148.59E
Burrewarra Pt. Australia 67 35.56S150.12E
Burriana Spain 16 39.54N 0.05W
Burrinjuck Australia 67 35.01S148.33E
Burrinjuck Resr. Australia 67 35.00S148.40E
Burro, Serranías del *mts.* Mexico 83 29.20N102.00W
Burrundie Australia 62 13.32S131.40E
Burry Port U.K. 11 51.41N 4.17W
Bursa Turkey 19 40.11N 29.04E
Būr Safājah Egypt 42 26.44N 33.56E
Būr Sa'īd Egypt 44 31.17N 32.18E
Būr Sūdān Sudan 48 19.39N 37.01E
Burta Australia 66 32.30S141.05E
Būr Tawfīq Egypt 44 29.57N 32.34E
Burton upon Trent U.K. 10 52.58N 1.39W
Burtundy Australia 66 33.45S142.22E
Buru *i.* Indonesia 37 3.30S126.30E
Burullus, Buḥayrat al *l.* Egypt 44 31.30N 30.45E
Burundi Africa 55 3.00S 30.00E
Bururi Burundi 55 3.58S 29.35E
Burutu Nigeria 53 5.20N 5.31E
Bury G.M. U.K. 10 53.36N 2.19W
Bury St. Edmunds U.K. 11 52.15N 0.42E
Burzil Jammu & Kashmir 40 34.52N 75.07E
Burzil Pass Jammu & Kashmir 40 34.54N 75.06E
Busalla Italy 15 44.34N 8.57E
Busca Italy 15 44.31N 7.29E
Būsh Egypt 44 29.09N 31.07E
Būshehr Iran 43 28.57N 50.52E
Bushkill U.S.A. 85 41.06N 75.00W
Bushmanland *f.* R.S.A. 56 29.25S 19.40E
Busi Ethiopia 45 5.30N 44.30E
Busigny France 14 50.03N 3.29E
Businga Zaïre 54 3.16N 20.55E
Busira *r.* Zaïre 54 0.05N 18.18E
Buskerud Norway 23 60.20N 9.00E
Buṣrá ash Shām Syria 44 32.30N 36.29E
Busselton Australia 63 33.43S115.15E
Bussum Neth. 14 52.17N 5.10E
Bustard Head *c.* Australia 64 24.02S151.48E
Busto Arsizio Italy 15 45.37N 8.51E
Busu Djanoa Zaïre 54 1.42N 21.23E
Buta Zaïre 54 2.50N 24.50E
Butari Rwanda 55 2.38S 29.43E
Butaritari *i.* Kiribati 68 3.07N172.48E
Bute Australia 66 33.24S138.01E
Bute *i.* U.K. 12 55.51N 5.07W
Bute, Sd. of U.K. 12 55.44N 5.10W
Butedale Canada 74 53.12N128.45W
Butiaba Uganda 55 1.48N 31.15E
Butler Mo. U.S.A. 83 38.16N 94.20W
Butler N.J. U.S.A. 85 41.00N 74.21W
Butte Mont. U.S.A. 80 46.00N112.32W
Butte Nebr. U.S.A. 82 42.58N 98.51W
Butterworth Malaysia 36 5.24N100.22E
Buttevant Rep. of Ire. 13 52.14N 8.41W
Butt of Lewis *c.* U.K. 12 58.31N 6.15W
Butty Head Australia 63 33.52S121.35E
Butuan Phil. 37 8.56N125.31E
Butung *i.* Indonesia 37 5.00S122.50E
Butwal Nepal 41 27.42N 83.28E
Buxton U.K. 10 53.16N 1.54W
Buy U.S.S.R. 24 58.23N 41.27E
Buyaga U.S.S.R. 29 59.42N126.59E
Buynaksk U.S.S.R. 25 42.48N 47.07E
Büyük Menderes *r.* Turkey 19 37.30N 27.05E
Buzachi, Poluostrov *pen.* U.S.S.R. 25 45.00N 51.55E
Buzancy France 15 49.30N 4.59E
Buzău Romania 21 45.10N 26.49E
Buzău *r.* Romania 21 45.24N 27.48E
Buzaymah Libya 51 24.55N 22.02E
Buzi *r.* Mozambique 57 19.52S 34.00E
Buzuluk U.S.S.R. 24 52.49N 52.19E
Bwasiaia P.N.G. 64 10.06S150.48E
Byala Bulgaria 19 42.53N 27.55E
Byam Martin I. Canada 72 75.15N104.00W
Bydgoszcz Poland 21 53.16N 17.33E
Byemoor Canada 74 52.00N112.17W
Bygland Norway 23 58.48N 7.50E
Byhalia U.S.A. 83 34.52N 89.41W
Bykhov U.S.S.R. 21 53.30N 30.15E
Bykle Norway 23 59.21N 7.20E
Bylot I. Canada 73 73.00N 78.30W
Byrd Land *f.* Antarctica 96 79.30S125.00W
Byrock Australia 67 30.40S146.25E
Byron, C. Australia 67 28.37S153.40E
Byron Bay *town* Australia 67 28.43S153.34E
Byrranga, Gory *mts.* U.S.S.R. 29 74.50N101.00E
Byske Sweden 22 64.57N 21.12E
Byske *r.* Sweden 22 64.57N 21.13E
Byten U.S.S.R. 21 52.50N 25.28E
Bytom Poland 21 50.22N 18.54E
Bzipi U.S.S.R. 25 43.15N 40.24E

C

Ca *r.* Vietnam 33 18.47N105.40E
Caballos Mesteños, Llano de los *f.* Mexico 83 28.15N104.00W
Cabanatuan Phil. 37 15.30N120.58E
Cabimas Venezuela 90 10.26N 71.27W
Cabinda Angola 54 5.34S 12.12E
Cabinet Mts. U.S.A. 80 48.08N115.46W
Cabo Delgado *d.* Mozambique 55 12.30S 39.00E
Cabo Frio *town* Brazil 94 22.51S 42.03W
Cabonga, Résr. Canada 76 47.35N 76.40W
Cabool U.S.A. 83 37.07N 92.06W
Caboolture Australia 65 27.05S152.57E
Cabo Pantoja Peru 90 1.00S 75.10W
Cabora Bassa Dam Mozambique 55 15.36S 32.41E
Cabot Str. Canada 77 47.20N 59.30W
Cabras Italy 18 39.56N 8.32E
Cabrera *i.* Spain 16 39.08N 2.56E
Cabrera, Sierra *mts.* Spain 16 42.10N 6.30W
Cabri Canada 75 50.37N108.28W
Cabriel *r.* Spain 16 39.13N 1.07W
Cabruta Venezuela 90 7.40N 66.16W
Čačak Yugo. 21 43.53N 20.21E
Caçapava Brazil 94 23.05S 45.40W
Cáceres Brazil 91 16.05S 57.40W
Cáceres Spain 16 39.29N 6.23W
Cacharí Argentina 93 36.23S 59.29W
Cachimo *r.* Zaïre 54 7.02S 21.13E
Cachoeira Brazil 91 12.35S 38.59W
Cachoeira do Sul Brazil 94 30.03S 52.52W
Cachoeiro de Itapemirim Brazil 94 20.51S 41.07W
Cacín *r.* Spain 16 37.10N 4.01W
Cacine Guinea 52 11.08N 14.57W
Cacolo Angola 54 10.09S 19.15E
Caconda Angola 54 13.46S 15.06E
Cacuso Angola 54 9.26S 15.43E
Čadca Czech. 21 49.26N 18.48E
Cader Idris *mtn.* U.K. 11 52.40N 3.55W
Cadí, Sierra del *mts.* Spain 16 42.12N 1.35E
Cadibarrawirracanna, L. Australia 66 28.52S135.27E
Cadillac U.S.A. 84 44.15N 85.23W
Cadiz Phil. 37 10.57N123.18E
Cádiz Spain 16 36.32N 6.18W
Cádiz, Golfo de *g.* Spain 16 37.00N 7.10W
Cadomin Canada 74 53.02N117.20W
Cadoux Australia 63 30.47S117.05E
Caen France 15 49.11N 0.22W
Caernarfon U.K. 10 53.08N 4.17W
Caernarfon B. U.K. 10 53.05N 4.25W
Caerphilly U.K. 11 51.34N 3.13W
Caeté Brazil 94 19.54S 43.37W
Cafima Angola 54 16.34S 16.30E
Cafu Angola 54 16.30S 15.14E
Cagayan de Oro Phil. 37 8.29N124.40E
Cagliari Italy 18 39.14N 9.07E
Cagliari, Golfo di *g.* Italy 18 39.07N 9.15E
Cagnes France 15 43.40N 7.09E
Caguán *r.* Colombia 90 0.08S 74.18W
Caguas Puerto Rico 87 18.08N 66.00W
Cahama Angola 54 16.16S 14.23E
Caha Mts. Rep. of Ire. 13 51.44N 9.45W
Caherciveen Rep. of Ire. 13 51.51N 10.14W
Cahir Rep. of Ire. 13 52.23N 7.56W
Cahore Pt. Rep. of Ire. 13 52.34N 6.12W
Cahors France 17 44.28N 0.26E
Cahuapanas Peru 90 5.15S 77.00W
Caianda Angola 54 11.02S 23.29E
Caibarién Cuba 87 22.31N 79.28W
Caicó Brazil 91 6.25S 37.04W
Caicos Is. Turks & Caicos Is. 87 21.30N 72.00W
Caird Coast *f.* Antarctica 96 75.00S 20.00W
Cairngorms *mts.* U.K. 12 57.04N 3.30W
Cairns Australia 64 16.51S145.43E
Cairo *see* Al Qāhirah Egypt 44
Cairo Ill. U.S.A. 83 37.01N 89.09W
Cairo Montenotte Italy 15 44.24N 8.16E
Caiundo Angola 54 15.43S 17.30E
Caiwarro Australia 67 28.38S144.45E
Caizhai China 32 37.20N118.10E
Caizi Hu *l.* China 33 30.50N117.06E
Cajamarca Peru 90 7.09S 78.32W
Cajàzeiras Brazil 91 6.52S 38.31W
Cajuru Brazil 94 21.15S 47.18W
Čakovec Yugo. 20 46.23N 16.26E
Calabar Nigeria 53 4.56N 8.22E
Calabozo Venezuela 90 8.58N 67.28W
Calabria *d.* Italy 19 39.00N 16.30E
Calafat Romania 21 43.59N 22.57E
Calafate Argentina 93 50.20S 72.16W
Calahorra Spain 16 42.18N 1.58W
Calama Brazil 90 8.03S 62.53W
Calama Chile 92 22.30S 68.55W
Calamar Colombia 90 10.15N 74.55W
Calamian Group *is.* Phil. 37 12.00N120.05E
Cala Millor Spain 16 39.35N 3.22E
Calamocha Spain 16 40.54N 1.18W
Calapan Phil. 37 13.23N121.10E
Călăraşi Romania 21 44.11N 27.21E
Calatayud Spain 16 41.21N 1.39W
Calatrava Equat. Guinea 54 1.09N 9.24E
Calau E. Germany 20 51.45N 13.56E
Calayan *i.* Phil. 33 19.20N121.25E
Calbayog Phil. 37 12.04N124.58E
Calcutta India 41 22.32N 88.22E
Caldaro Italy 15 46.25N 11.14E
Caldas Colombia 90 6.05N 75.36W
Caldas da Rainha Portugal 16 39.24N 9.08W
Caldera Chile 92 27.04S 70.50W
Caldwell Idaho U.S.A. 80 43.40N116.41W
Caldwell Ohio U.S.A. 84 39.44N 81.32W
Caledon *r.* R.S.A. 56 30.27S 26.12E
Caledon B. Australia 64 12.58S136.52E
Caledonia Canada 76 43.04N 79.56W
Caledonia Hills Canada 77 45.40N 65.00W
Calella Spain 16 41.37N 2.40E
Calexico Mexico 81 32.40N115.30W
Calf of Man *i.* U.K. 10 54.03N 4.49W
Calgary Canada 74 51.00N114.10W
Cali Colombia 90 3.24N 76.30W
Calicut India 38 11.15N 75.45E
Caliente U.S.A. 80 37.37N114.31W
California *d.* U.S.A. 80 37.29N119.58W
California, G. of *see* California, Golfo de *g.* Mexico 86
California, Golfo de *g.* Mexico 81 28.00N112.00W
Calingasta Argentina 92 31.15S 69.30W
Calingiri Australia 63 31.07S116.27E
Callabonna *r.* Australia 66 29.37S140.08E
Callabonna, L. Australia 66 29.47S140.07E
Callander U.K. 12 56.15N 4.13W
Callao Peru 92 12.05S 77.08W
Caloocan Phil. 37 14.38N120.58E
Caltagirone Italy 18 37.14N 14.30E
Caltanissetta Italy 18 37.30N 14.05E
Calulo Angola 54 10.05S 14.56E
Calumbo Angola 54 9.08S 13.24E
Calumet Canada 77 45.39N 74.41W
Calundau Angola 54 12.05S 19.10E
Calvados *d.* France 15 49.10N 0.30W
Calvert I. Canada 74 51.30N128.00W
Calvi France 17 42.34N 8.44E
Calvinia R.S.A. 56 31.29S 19.44E
Cam *r.* U.K. 11 52.34N 0.21E
Camabatela Angola 54 8.20S 15.29E
Camacupa Angola 54 12.01S 17.22E
Camagüey Cuba 87 21.25N 77.55W
Camagüey, Archipiélago de Cuba 87 22.30N 78.00W
Camaiore Italy 15 43.56N 10.18E
Camarès France 17 43.49N 2.53E
Camaret-sur-Mer France 17 48.16N 4.37W
Camarón, C. Honduras 87 15.59N 85.00W
Camaronero, Laguna *l.* Mexico 81 23.00N106.07W
Camarones Argentina 93 44.45S 65.40W
Camas U.S.A. 80 45.35N122.24W
Cambay India 40 22.18N 72.37E
Camberley U.K. 11 51.21N 0.45W
Camborne U.K. 11 50.12N 5.19W
Cambrai France 17 50.10N 3.14E
Cambria U.S.A. 81 35.34N121.05W
Cambrian Mts. U.K. 11 52.33N 3.33W
Cambridge Canada 76 43.22N 80.19W
Cambridge New Zealand 60 37.53S175.29E
Cambridge U.K. 11 52.13N 0.08E
Cambridge Idaho U.S.A. 80 44.34N116.41W
Cambridge Mass. U.S.A. 84 42.22N 71.06W
Cambridge Md. U.S.A. 85 38.34N 76.04W
Cambridge Minn. U.S.A. 82 45.31N 93.14W
Cambridge Bay *town* Canada 72 69.09N105.00W
Cambridge G. Australia 62 15.00S128.05E
Cambridgeshire *d.* U.K. 11 52.15N 0.05E
Camden U.K. 11 51.33N 0.10W
Camden Ark. U.S.A. 83 33.35N 92.50W
Camden N.J. U.S.A. 85 39.57N 75.07W
Camden S.C. U.S.A. 85 34.16N 80.36W
Camden Haven *b.* Australia 67 31.40S152.49E
Cameia Nat. Park Angola 54 12.00S 21.30E
Camelford U.K. 11 50.37N 4.41W
Cameron Ariz. U.S.A. 81 35.51N111.25W
Cameron La. U.S.A. 83 29.48N 93.19W
Cameron Mo. U.S.A. 82 39.44N 94.14W
Cameron Tex. U.S.A. 83 30.51N 96.59W
Cameron Hills Canada 74 59.48N118.00W
Cameron Mts. New Zealand 60 45.50S167.00E
Cameroon Africa 53 6.00N 12.30E
Cameroun, Mont *mtn.* Cameroon 53 4.20N 9.05E
Cametá Brazil 91 2.12S 49.30W
Camiri Bolivia 92 20.03S 63.31W
Camocim Brazil 91 2.55S 40.50W
Camooweal Australia 64 19.55S138.07E
Camopi Guiana 91 3.12N 52.15W
Campana Argentina 93 34.10S 58.57W
Campana, Isla *i.* Chile 93 48.25S 75.20W
Campania *d.* Italy 18 41.00N 14.30E
Campbell, C. New Zealand 60 41.45S174.15E
Campbell I. Pacific Oc. 68 52.30S169.02E
Campbellpore Pakistan 40 33.46N 72.22E
Campbell River *town* Canada 74 50.05N125.20W
Campbellsville U.S.A. 85 37.20N 85.21W
Campbellton Canada 77 48.00N 66.40W
Campbelltown Australia 67 34.04S150.49E
Campbeltown U.K. 12 55.25N 5.36W
Campeche Mexico 86 19.50N 90.30W
Campeche *d.* Mexico 86 19.00N 90.00W
Campeche, Bahía de *b.* Mexico 86 19.30N 94.00W
Campeche B. *see* Campeche, Bahía de *b.* Mexico 86
Camperdown Australia 66 38.15S143.14E
Cam Pha Vietnam 34 21.07N107.19E
Campina Grande Brazil 91 7.15S 35.50W
Campinas Brazil 94 22.54S 47.06W
Campo Cameroon 53 2.22N 9.50E
Campo *r.* Cameroon 54 2.21N 9.51E
Campo U.S.A. 83 37.06N102.35W
Campobasso Italy 18 41.34N 14.39E
Campo Belo Brazil 94 20.52S 45.16W
Campo Gallo Argentina 92 26.35S 62.50W
Campo Grande Brazil 92 20.24S 54.35W
Campo Maior Brazil 91 4.50S 42.12W
Campo Maior Portugal 16 39.01N 7.04W
Campos Brazil 94 21.45S 41.18W
Campos Belos Brazil 91 13.09S 47.03W
Campos do Jordão Brazil 94 23.28S 46.10W
Camp Wood U.S.A. 83 29.40N100.01W
Cam Ranh Vietnam 34 11.54N109.14E
Camrose Canada 74 53.00N112.50W
Canada N. America 72 60.00N105.00W
Cañada de Gómez Argentina 92 32.49S 61.25W
Canadian U.S.A. 83 35.55N100.23W
Canadian *r.* U.S.A. 83 35.27N 95.03W
Çanakkale Turkey 19 40.09N 26.26E
Çanakkale Boğazi *str.* Turkey 19 40.15N 26.30E
Canal du Midi France 17 43.18N 2.00E
Cananea Mexico 81 30.57N110.18W
Canarias, Islas *is.* Atlantic Oc. 50 28.00N 15.00W
Canary Is. *see* Canarias, Islas *is.* Atlantic Oc. 50
Canastra, Serra da *mts.* Brazil 94 20.05S 46.30W
Canaveral, C. U.S.A. 85 28.27N 80.32W
Canavieiras Brazil 91 15.44S 38.58W
Canbelego Australia 67 31.33S146.19E
Canberra Australia 67 35.18S149.08E
Canby Calif. U.S.A. 80 41.27N120.52W
Canby Minn. U.S.A. 82 44.43N 96.16W
Cancale France 15 48.40N 1.50W
Cancon France 17 44.32N 0.38E
Candé France 15 47.34N 1.02W
Candeias Brazil 94 20.44S 45.18W
Candeleda Spain 16 40.10N 5.14W
Candle L. Canada 75 53.50N105.18W
Canelli Italy 15 44.43N 8.17E
Canelones Uruguay 93 34.32S 56.17W
Cañete Peru 90 13.00S 76.30W
Canfield Canada 76 42.59N 79.43W
Cangamba Angola 54 13.40S 19.50E
Cangas de Narcea Spain 16 43.11N 6.33W
Cangkuang, Tanjung *c.* Indonesia 37 6.45S105.15E
Cangombe Angola 54 14.27S 20.00E
Canguçu Brazil 92 31.24S 52.41W
Cangwu China 33 23.27N111.17E
Cangzhou China 32 38.15N116.58E
Caniapiscau *r.* Canada 77 57.40N 69.30W
Caniapiscau, Lac *l.* Canada 77 54.10N 69.55W
Çankiri Turkey 42 40.35N 33.37E
Canna *i.* U.K. 12 57.03N 6.30W
Cannes France 17 43.33N 7.00E
Cannich U.K. 12 57.20N 4.45W
Canning Basin *f.* Australia 62 19.50S123.35E
Cannock U.K. 11 52.42N 2.02W
Cann River *town* Australia 67 37.35S149.06E
Canōas Brazil 94 29.55S 51.10W
Canobie Australia 64 19.28S140.38E
Canoe L. Canada 75 55.11N108.15W
Canonba Australia 67 31.33S147.22E
Canon City U.S.A. 80 38.27N105.14W
Canopus Australia 66 33.30S140.57E
Canora Canada 75 51.37N102.26W
Canossa *site* Italy 15 44.35N 10.27E
Canowindra Australia 67 33.34S148.30E
Canso Canada 77 45.20N 61.00W
Cantabria, Sierra de *mts.* Spain 16 42.40N 2.30W
Cantábrica, Cordillera *mts.* Spain 16 42.55N 5.10W
Cantagalo Brazil 94 21.59S 42.22W
Cantaura Venezuela 90 9.22N 64.24W
Canterbury *d.* New Zealand 60 43.30S172.00E
Canterbury U.K. 11 51.17N 1.05E
Canterbury Bight New Zealand 60 44.15S172.00E
Can Tho Vietnam 34 10.03N105.40E
Canton *see* Guangzhou China 33
Canton Miss. U.S.A. 83 32.37N 90.02W
Canton N.C. U.S.A. 85 35.33N 82.51W
Canton Ohio U.S.A. 84 40.48N 81.23W
Canton Okla. U.S.A. 83 36.03N 98.35W
Cantù Italy 15 45.44N 9.08E
Cantua Creek *town* U.S.A. 81 36.30N120.19W
Cantung Canada 74 62.00N128.09W
Cañuelas Argentina 93 35.03S 58.44W
Canumã *r.* Brazil 90 3.55S 59.10W
Canutama Brazil 90 6.32S 64.20W
Canutillo Mexico 81 26.21N105.25W
Cany-Barville France 15 49.47N 0.38E
Canyon Tex. U.S.A. 83 34.59N101.55W
Canyon Wyo. U.S.A. 80 44.43N110.32W
Cao Bang Vietnam 33 22.37N106.18E
Caombo Angola 54 8.45S 16.50E
Caorle Italy 15 45.36N 12.53E
Capanema Brazil 91 1.08S 47.07W
Cap-Chat Canada 77 48.56N 66.53W
Cap-de-la-Madeleine *town* Canada 77 46.22N 72.32W
Cape Barren I. Australia 65 40.25S148.15E
Cape Basin *f.* Atlantic Oc. 95 38.00S 10.00E
Cape Breton Highlands Canada 77 46.45N 60.45W
Cape Breton I. Canada 77 46.00N 60.30W
Cape Coast *town* Ghana 52 5.10N 1.13W
Cape Cod B. U.S.A. 84 41.50N 70.17W
Cape Dyer *town* Canada 73 66.30N 61.20W
Cape Girardeau *town* U.S.A. 83 37.19N 89.32W
Cape Johnson Depth Pacific Oc. 37 10.20N127.20E
Capellen Lux. 14 49.39N 5.59E
Capelongo Angola 54 14.28S 16.25E
Cape May *town* U.S.A. 85 38.56N 74.55W
Cape Province *d.* R.S.A. 56 31.30S 23.30E
Cape Town R.S.A. 56 33.55S 18.27E
Cape Verde Atlantic Oc. 95 16.00N 24.00W
Cape Verde Basin *f.* Atlantic Oc. 95 15.00N 35.00W
Cape York Pen. Australia 64 12.40S142.20E
Cap-Haïtien *town* Haiti 87 19.47N 72.17W
Capim *r.* Brazil 91 1.40S 47.47W
Capoompeta, Mt. Australia 67 29.22S151.59E
Cappoquin Rep. of Ire. 13 52.09N 7.52W
Capraia *i.* Italy 18 43.03N 9.50E
Caprera *i.* Italy 18 41.48N 9.27E
Capri *i.* Italy 18 40.33N 14.13E
Capricorn Channel Australia 64 23.00S152.14E
Caprivi Strip *f.* Namibia 56 17.50S 23.10E
Captiva U.S.A. 85 26.31N 82.12W
Caqueta *r.* Colombia 90 1.20S 70.50W
Caracal Romania 21 44.08N 24.18E
Caracas Venezuela 90 10.35N 66.56W
Caraghnan Mt. Australia 67 31.20S149.03E
Caraguatatuba Brazil 94 23.39S 45.26W
Carandaí Brazil 94 20.55S 43.46W
Carangola Brazil 94 20.44S 42.03W
Caransebeş Romania 21 45.25N 22.13E
Caratasca, Laguna de *b.* Honduras 87 15.10N 84.00W
Caratinga Brazil 94 19.50S 42.06W
Caravaca Spain 16 38.06N 1.51W
Caravaggio Italy 15 45.30N 9.38E
Caravelí Peru 90 15.45S 73.25W
Carballo Spain 16 43.13N 8.41W
Carberry Canada 75 49.52N 99.20W
Carbonara, Capo *c.* Italy 18 39.06N 9.32E
Carbondale Ill. U.S.A. 83 37.44N 89.13W
Carbondale Penn. U.S.A. 84 41.35N 75.30W
Carbonear Canada 77 47.45N 53.14W
Carbonia Italy 18 39.11N 8.32E
Carcajou Canada 74 57.47N117.06W
Carcassonne France 17 43.13N 2.21E
Carcross Canada 74 60.13N134.45W
Cardabia Australia 62 23.06S113.48E
Cárdenas Cuba 87 23.02N 81.12W
Cárdenas Mexico 86 22.00N 99.40W
Cardenete Spain 16 39.46N 1.42W
Cardiff U.K. 11 51.28N 3.11W
Cardigan U.K. 11 52.06N 4.41W
Cardigan B. U.K. 11 52.30N 4.30W
Cardona Spain 16 41.56N 1.40E
Cardona Uruguay 93 33.53S 57.23W
Carei Romania 21 47.42N 22.28E
Carentan France 15 49.18N 1.14W
Carey U.S.A. 80 43.18N113.56W
Carey, L. Australia 63 29.05S122.15E
Carey L. Canada 75 62.12N102.55W
Carhaix France 17 48.16N 3.35W
Carhué Argentina 93 37.11S 62.45W
Caribbean Sea C. America 87 15.00N 75.00W
Cariboo Mts. Canada 74 53.00N121.00W
Caribou *r.* Man. Canada 75 59.20N 94.44W
Caribou *r.* N.W.T. Canada 74 61.27N125.45W
Caribou U.S.A. 84 46.52N 68.01W
Caribou Is. Canada 74 61.55N113.15W
Caribou Mts. Canada 74 59.12N115.40W
Carignan France 15 49.38N 5.10E
Carinda Australia 67 30.29S147.45E
Carinhanha Brazil 91 14.18S 43.47W
Carini Italy 18 38.08N 13.11E
Caritianas Brazil 90 9.25S 63.06W
Carleton Place Canada 76 45.08N 76.09W
Carlingford Rep. of Ire. 13 54.03N 6.12W
Carlingford Lough Rep. of Ire. 13 54.03N 6.09W
Carlinville U.S.A. 82 39.17N 89.52W
Carlisle U.K. 10 54.54N 2.55W
Carlos Reyles Uruguay 93 33.03S 56.29W

Carlow to Chelva

Carlow Rep. of Ire. 13 52.50N 6.46W
Carlow d. Rep. of Ire. 13 52.43N 6.50W
Carlsbad Calif. U.S.A. 81 33.10N117.21W
Carlsbad N.Mex. U.S.A. 81 32.25N104.14W
Carlyle Canada 75 49.38N102.16W
Carmacks Canada 72 62.04N136.21W
Carmagnola Italy 15 44.51N 7.43E
Carman Canada 75 49.32N 98.00W
Carmarthen U.K. 11 51.52N 4.20W
Carmarthen B. U.K. 11 52.30N 4.30W
Carmaux France 17 44.03N 2.09E
Carmel U.S.A. 85 41.26N 73.41W
Carmel Head U.K. 10 53.24N 4.35W
Carmelo Uruguay 93 34.00S 58.17W
Carmen Colombia 90 9.46N 75.06W
Carmen Mexico 86 18.38N 91.50W
Carmen Uruguay 93 33.15S 56.01W
Carmen, Isla i. Mexico 81 25.55N111.10W
Carmen, Isla del i. Mexico 86 18.35N 91.40W
Carmen de Areco Argentina 93 34.20S 59.50W
Carmen de Patagones Argentina 93 40.48S 63.00W
Carmi U.S.A. 82 38.05N 88.11W
Carmichael U.S.A. 80 38.38N121.19W
Carmila Australia 64 21.55S149.25E
Carmo Brazil 94 21.56S 42.37W
Carmody, L. Australia 63 32.27S119.20E
Carmona Spain 16 37.28N 5.38W
Carnac France 17 47.35N 3.05W
Carnarvon Australia 62 24.53S113.40E
Carnarvon R.S.A. 56 30.58S 22.07E
Carndonagh Rep. of Ire. 13 55.15N 7.15W
Carnegie Australia 62 25.43S122.59E
Carnegie, L. Australia 62 26.15S123.00E
Carnew Rep. of Ire. 13 52.43N 6.31W
Carniche, Alpi mts. Austria/Italy 18 46.40N 12.48E
Car Nicobar i. India 34 9.11N 92.45E
Carnot C.A.R. 53 4.59N 15.56E
Carnot, C. Australia 66 34.57S135.38E
Carnoustie U.K. 12 56.30N 2.44W
Carnsore Pt. Rep. of Ire. 13 52.10N 6.21W
Carolina Brazil 91 7.20S 47.25W
Carolina Puerto Rico 87 18.23N 65.57W
Carolina R.S.A. 56 26.04S 30.07E
Caroline I. Kiribati 69 10.00S150.30W
Caroline Is. Pacific Oc. 37 7.50N145.00E
Caroline-Solomon Ridge Pacific Oc. 68 8.00N150.00E
Caroní r. Venezuela 90 8.20N 62.42W
Carora Venezuela 90 10.12N 70.07W
Carp Canada 77 45.21N 76.02W
Carpathians mts. Europe 21 48.45N 23.45E
Carpaţii Meridionali mts. Romania 21 45.35N 24.40E
Carpentaria, G. of Australia 64 14.00S139.00E
Carpentras France 17 44.03N 5.03E
Carpi Italy 15 44.47N 10.53E
Carpio Spain 16 41.13N 5.07W
Carpolac Australia 66 36.45S141.20E
Carquefou France 15 47.18N 1.30W
Carra, Lough Rep. of Ire. 13 53.41N 9.15W
Carrara Italy 15 44.04N 10.06E
Carrathool Australia 67 34.25S145.24E
Carrauntoohil mtn. Rep. of Ire. 13 52.00N 9.45W
Carrickfergus U.K. 13 54.43N 5.49W
Carrickmacross Rep. of Ire. 13 53.58N 6.43W
Carrick-on-Shannon Rep. of Ire. 13 53.57N 8.06W
Carrick-on-Suir Rep. of Ire. 13 52.21N 7.26W
Carrieton Australia 66 32.28S138.34E
Carrington U.S.A. 82 47.27N 99.08W
Carrizo Springs town U.S.A. 83 28.31N 99.52W
Carrizozo U.S.A. 81 33.38N105.53W
Carroll U.S.A. 82 42.04N 94.52W
Carrollton Mo. U.S.A. 82 39.22N 93.30W
Carrot r. Canada 75 53.50N101.17W
Carrowmore Lough Rep. of Ire. 13 54.11N 9.47W
Çarşamba Turkey 42 41.13N 36.43E
Çarşamba r. Turkey 42 37.52N 31.48E
Carson U.S.A. 82 46.25N101.34W
Carson City U.S.A. 80 39.10N119.46W
Carstairs U.K. 12 55.42N 3.41W
Cartagena Colombia 90 10.24N 75.33W
Cartagena Spain 16 37.36N 0.59W
Cartago Colombia 90 4.45N 75.55W
Cartago Costa Rica 87 9.50N 83.52W
Carter U.S.A. 80 41.27N110.25W
Carteret France 15 49.22N 1.48W
Cartersville U.S.A. 85 34.09N 84.49W
Carterton New Zealand 60 41.01S175.31E
Carthage Mo. U.S.A. 83 37.11N 94.19W
Carthage S.Dak. U.S.A. 82 44.10N 97.43W
Carthage Tex. U.S.A. 83 32.09N 94.20W
Cartwright Canada 77 53.50N 56.45W
Caruarú Brazil 91 8.15S 35.55W
Carúpano Venezuela 90 10.39N 63.14W
Caruthersville U.S.A. 83 36.11N 89.39W
Carvin France 14 50.30N 2.58E
Carvoeiro Brazil 90 1.24S 61.59W
Caryapundy Swamp Australia 66 29.00S142.36E
Casablanca Morocco 50 33.39N 7.35W
Casa Branca Brazil 94 21.45S 47.06W
Casa Grande U.S.A. 81 32.53N111.45W
Casale Italy 15 45.08N 8.27E
Casa Nova Brazil 91 9.25S 41.08W
Casarano Italy 19 40.00N 18.10E
Cascade Idaho U.S.A. 80 44.31N116.02W
Cascade Mont. U.S.A. 80 47.16N111.42W
Cascade Pt. New Zealand 60 44.01S168.22E
Cascade Range mts. U.S.A. 80 46.15N121.00W
Caserta Italy 18 41.06N 14.21E
Cashel Tipperary Rep. of Ire. 13 52.31N 7.54W
Casilda Argentina 93 33.03S 61.10W
Casimiro de Abreu Brazil 94 22.28S 42.12W
Casino Australia 67 28.50S153.02E
Casma Peru 90 9.30S 78.20W
Caspe Spain 16 41.14N 0.03W
Casper U.S.A. 80 42.51N106.19W
Caspian Depression see Prikaspiyskaya Nizmennost ost U.S.S.R. 25
Caspian Sea U.S.S.R. 25 42.00N 51.00E
Cassai r. Angola 54 10.38S 22.15E
Cassano allo Ionio Italy 19 39.47N 16.20E
Cass City U.S.A. 84 43.37N 83.11W
Casselman Canada 77 45.19N 75.05W
Casselton U.S.A. 82 46.54N 97.13W
Cassiar Canada 74 59.16N129.40W
Cassiar Mts. Canada 74 59.00N129.00W
Cassilis Australia 67 32.01S149.59E
Cass Lake town U.S.A. 82 47.22N 94.35W
Castaños Mexico 83 26.48N101.26W
Castelfranco Veneto Italy 15 45.40N 11.55E
Casteljaloux France 17 44.19N 0.06W
Castell' Arquato Italy 15 44.51N 9.52E
Castelli Argentina 93 36.07S 57.50W
Castellón Spain 16 39.59N 0.03W
Castelmassa Italy 15 45.01N 11.18E
Castelnovo ne'Monti Italy 15 44.26N 10.24E
Castelnuovo di Garfagnana Italy 15 44.06N 10.24E
Castelo Brazil 94 20.33S 41.14W
Castelo Branco Portugal 16 39.50N 7.30W
Castel San Giovanni Italy 15 45.04N 9.26E
Castelvetrano Italy 18 37.41N 12.47E
Casterton Australia 66 37.35S141.25E
Castets France 17 43.53N 1.09W
Castilla Peru 90 5.16S 80.36W
Castilla la Nueva d. Spain 16 40.00N 3.45W
Castilla la Vieja d. Spain 16 41.30N 4.00W
Castilletes Colombia 90 11.55N 71.20W
Castlebar Rep. of Ire. 13 53.52N 9.19W
Castleblayney Rep. of Ire. 13 54.08N 6.46W
Castle Douglas U.K. 12 54.56N 3.56W
Castleford U.K. 10 53.43N 1.21W
Castlegar Canada 74 49.20N117.40W
Castlegate U.S.A. 80 39.44N110.52W
Castle Harbour b. Bermuda 95 32.20N 64.40W
Castleisland Rep. of Ire. 13 52.13N 9.28W
Castlemaine Australia 66 37.05S144.19E
Castlerea Rep. of Ire. 13 53.45N 8.30W
Castlereagh r. Australia 67 30.12S147.32E
Castle Rock town Colo. U.S.A. 80 39.22N104.51W
Castle Rock town Wash. U.S.A. 80 46.17N122.54W
Castletown U.K. 10 54.04N 4.38W
Castletownshend Rep. of Ire. 13 51.32N 9.12W
Castres France 17 43.36N 2.14E
Castries St. Lucia 87 14.01N 60.59W
Castro Chile 93 42.30S 73.46W
Castro del Río Spain 16 37.41N 4.29W
Casula Mozambique 55 15.26S 33.32E
Cataguases Brazil 94 21.23S 42.39W
Çatalca Turkey 19 41.09N 28.29E
Catalina Pt. Guam 68 13.31N144.55E
Cataluña d. Spain 16 42.00N 2.00E
Catamaran Australia 65 43.33S146.49E
Catamarca Argentina 92 28.30S 65.45W
Catamarca d. Argentina 92 27.45S 67.00W
Catanduanes i. Phil. 37 13.45N124.20E
Catanduva Brazil 94 21.03S 49.00W
Catania Italy 18 37.31N 15.05E
Catanzaro Italy 19 38.55N 16.35E
Catarman Phil. 37 12.28N124.50E
Catastrophe, C. Australia 66 34.59S136.00E
Catbalogan Phil. 37 11.46N124.55E
Catete Angola 54 9.09S 13.40E
Cathcart Australia 67 36.49S149.25E
Cathcart R.S.A. 56 32.17S 27.08E
Cat I. Bahamas 87 24.33N 75.36W
Cat L. Canada 76 51.40N 91.50W
Catoche, C. Mexico 87 21.38N 87.08W
Catonsville U.S.A. 85 39.16N 76.44W
Catriló Argentina 93 36.23S 63.24W
Catterick U.K. 10 54.23N 1.38W
Cattolica Italy 15 43.58N 12.44E
Catuane Mozambique 57 26.49S 32.17E
Cauca r. Colombia 90 8.57N 74.30W
Caucasus Mts. see Kavkazskiy Khrebet mts. U.S.S.R. 25
Caudry France 17 50.07N 3.22E
Caungula Angola 54 8.26S 18.35E
Cauquenes Chile 93 35.58S 72.21W
Caura r. Venezuela 90 7.38N 64.53W
Cavaillon France 17 43.50N 5.02E
Cavalese Italy 15 46.17N 11.26E
Cavalier U.S.A. 82 48.48N 97.37W
Cavally r. Ivory Coast 52 4.25N 7.39W
Cavan Rep. of Ire. 13 54.00N 7.22W
Cavan d. Rep. of Ire. 13 53.58N 7.10W
Cavarzere Italy 15 45.08N 12.05E
Caviana, Ilha i. Brazil 91 0.02N 50.00W
Cavite Phil. 37 14.30N120.54E
Cawndilla L. Australia 66 32.30S142.18E
Caxambu Brazil 94 21.59S 44.54W
Caxias Brazil 91 4.53S 43.20W
Caxias do Sul Brazil 94 29.14S 51.10W
Caxito Angola 54 8.32S 13.38E
Cayambe Ecuador 90 0.03N 78.08W
Cayenne Guiana 91 4.55N 52.18W
Cayman Brac i. Cayman Is. 87 19.44N 79.48W
Cayman Is. C. America 87 19.00N 81.00W
Cayman Trough Carib. Sea 95 18.00N 8.00W
Cayuga Canada 76 42.56N 79.51W
Cazères France 17 43.13N 1.05E
Cazombo Angola 54 11.54S 22.56E
Ceara d. Brazil 91 4.50S 39.00W
Ceba Canada 75 53.07N102.14W
Ceballos Mexico 83 26.32N104.09W
Cebollera, Sierra de mts. Spain 16 41.58N 2.30W
Cebu Phil. 37 10.17N123.56E
Cebu i. Phil. 37 10.15N123.45E
Cecina Italy 18 43.18N 10.30E
Cedar City U.S.A. 80 37.41N113.04W
Cedar City U.S.A. 78 37.40N113.04W
Cedar Falls town U.S.A. 82 42.32N 92.27W
Cedar Key U.S.A. 85 29.08N 83.03W
Cedar L. Canada 75 53.20N100.00W
Cedar Rapids town U.S.A. 82 41.59N 91.40W
Cedarville U.S.A. 85 39.20N 75.12W
Cedros, Isla i. Mexico 81 28.10N115.15W
Ceduna Australia 66 32.07S133.42E
Ceepeecee Canada 74 49.52N126.42W
Cefalù Italy 18 38.01N 14.03E
Cegléd Hungary 21 47.10N 19.48E
Cela Angola 54 11.26S 15.05E
Celaya Mexico 86 20.32N100.48W
Celebes i. see Sulawesi i. Indonesia 37
Celebes Sea Indonesia 37 3.00N122.00E
Celina U.S.A. 84 40.34N 84.35W
Celje Yugo. 18 46.15N 15.16E
Celle W. Germany 20 52.37N 10.05E
Cemaes Head U.K. 11 52.08N 4.42W
Ceno r. Italy 15 44.41N 10.05E
Center Cross U.S.A. 85 37.48N 76.48W
Centerville Iowa U.S.A. 82 40.43N 92.52W
Centerville S.Dak. U.S.A. 82 43.07N 96.58W
Centerville Tenn. U.S.A. 85 35.45N 87.29W
Cento Italy 15 44.43N 11.17E
Central d. Ghana 52 5.30N 1.10W
Central d. Kenya 55 0.30S 37.00E
Central d. U.K. 12 56.10N 4.20W
Central d. Zambia 56 14.30S 29.30E
Central, Cordillera mts. Bolivia 92 18.30S 65.00W
Central, Cordillera mts. Colombia 90 5.00N 75.20W
Central Auckland d. New Zealand 60 36.45S174.45E
Central Brāhui Range mts. Pakistan 40 29.15N 67.15E
Central City Ky. U.S.A. 85 37.17N 87.08W
Central City Nebr. U.S.A. 82 41.07N 98.00W
Central I. Kenya 55 3.30N 36.02E
Centralia Ill. U.S.A. 82 38.32N 89.08W
Centralia Wash. U.S.A. 80 46.43N122.58W
Central Makrān Range mts. Pakistan 40 26.30N 65.00E
Central Siberian Plateau see Sredne Sibirskoye Ploskogor'ye f. U.S.S.R. 29
Centre d. France 17 47.40N 1.45E
Centre d. U. Volta 52 13.30N 1.00W
Centreville Ala. U.S.A. 85 32.57N 87.08W
Centreville Md. U.S.A. 85 39.03N 76.04W
Century Fla. U.S.A. 85 30.59N 87.18W
Cepu Indonesia 37 7.07S111.35E
Ceram i. see Seram i. Indonesia 37
Ceram Sea see Seram, Laut sea Pacific Oc. 37
Ceres U.S.A. 80 37.35N120.57W
Ceresole Reale Italy 15 45.26N 7.15E
Cereté Colombia 90 8.54N 75.51W
Cerignola Italy 18 41.17N 15.53E
Cérilly France 17 46.37N 2.50E
Cerisiers France 15 48.08N 3.29E
Cerknica Yugo. 18 45.48N 14.22E
Cernavodă Romania 21 44.20N 28.02E
Cerralvo, Isla i. Mexico 81 24.17N109.52W
Cerritos Mexico 86 22.26N100.17W
Cerro de Pasco Peru 90 10.43S 76.15W
Cervera Lérida Spain 16 41.40N 1.16E
Cervia Italy 15 44.15N 12.22E
Cervignano del Friuli Italy 15 45.49N 13.20E
Cervo Spain 16 43.40N 7.24W
Cesena Italy 15 44.08N 12.15E
Cesenatico Italy 15 44.12N 12.24E
Cēsis U.S.S.R. 24 57.18N 25.18E
České Budějovice Czech. 20 49.00N 14.30E
Český Krumlov Czech. 20 48.49N 14.19E
Cessnock Australia 67 32.51S151.21E
Cetinje Yugo. 19 42.24N 18.55E
Ceuta Spain 16 35.53N 5.19W
Ceva Italy 15 44.23N 8.01E
Cévennes mts. France 17 44.25N 4.05E
Ceyhan Turkey 42 37.02N 35.48E
Ceyhan r. Turkey 42 36.54N 34.58E
Chablis France 15 47.47N 3.48E
Chacabuco Argentina 93 34.38S 60.29W
Chachani mtn. Peru 90 16.12S 71.32W
Chachapoyas Peru 90 6.13S 77.54W
Chāchro Pakistan 40 25.07N 70.15E
Chaco d. Argentina 92 26.30S 60.00W
Chad, L. Africa 53 13.30N 14.00E
Chadron U.S.A. 82 42.50N103.02W
Chafe Nigeria 53 11.56N 6.55E
Chāgai Pakistan 40 29.18N 64.42E
Chāgai Hills Pakistan 40 29.10N 63.35E
Chagda U.S.S.R. 29 58.44N130.38E
'Chaghcharān Afghan. 40 34.32N 65.15E
Cha'gyüngoinba China 41 31.10N 90.42E
Chahār Borjak Afghan. 40 30.17N 62.03E
Chāh Bahār Iran 43 25.17N 60.41E
Chāh Sandan well Pakistan 40 28.59N 63.27E
Chaibāsā India 41 22.34N 85.49E
Chainat Thailand 34 15.10N100.10E
Chaiyaphum Thailand 34 15.46N101.57E
Chajarí Argentina 93 30.45S 57.59W
Chākāi India 41 24.34N 86.24E
Chakdaha India 41 23.05N 88.31E
Chake Chake Tanzania 55 5.13S 39.46E
Chakhānsūr Afghan. 40 31.10N 62.04E
Chakradharpur India 41 22.42N 85.38E
Chakwāl Pakistan 40 32.56N 72.52E
Chala Peru 90 15.48S 74.20W
Chaleur B. Canada 77 48.00N 65.45W
Chalhuanca Peru 90 14.20S 73.10W
Chālisgaon India 40 20.28N 75.01E
Challans France 17 46.51N 1.52W
Challenger Depth Pacific Oc. 37 11.19N142.15E
Challis U.S.A. 80 44.30N114.14W
Chalonnes-sur-Loire France 15 47.21N 0.46W
Châlons-sur-Marne France 15 48.58N 4.22E
Chalon-sur-Saône France 17 46.47N 4.51E
Cham W. Germany 20 49.13N 12.41E
Chama U.S.A. 80 36.54N106.35W
Chama Zambia 55 11.09S 33.10E
Chaman Pakistan 40 30.55N 66.27E
Chamba India 40 32.34N 76.08E
Chambal r. India 41 26.29N 79.15E
Chamberlain U.S.A. 82 43.49N 99.20W
Chambersburg U.S.A. 84 39.56N 77.39W
Chambéry France 17 45.34N 5.55E
Chambeshi Zambia 55 10.57S 31.04E
Chambeshi r. Zambia 55 11.15S 30.37E
Chambly France 15 49.10N 2.15E
Chambly Canada 77 45.27N 73.17W
Chamburi Kalāt Pakistan 40 26.09N 64.43E
Cha Messengue Angola 54 11.04S 18.56E
Chamical Argentina 92 30.22S 66.19W
Chamoli India 41 30.24N 79.21E
Chamonix France 17 45.55N 6.52E
Chāmpa India 41 22.03N 82.39E
Champagne Canada 74 60.47N136.29W
Champagne-Ardenne d. France 14 49.42N 4.30E
Champaign U.S.A. 82 40.07N 88.14W
Champdoré, Lac l. Canada 77 55.55N 65.50W
Champéry Switz. 15 46.10N 6.52E
Champlain Canada 77 46.27N 72.21W
Champlain, L. U.S.A. 84 44.45N 73.15W
Champotón Mexico 86 19.21N 90.43W
Chāmpua India 41 22.05N 85.40E
Chañaral Chile 92 26.21S 70.37W
Chānasma India 40 23.43N 72.07E
Chandausi India 41 28.27N 78.46E
Chāndbāli India 41 20.46N 86.49E
Chandeleur Is. U.S.A. 83 29.48N 88.51W
Chandigarh India 40 30.44N 76.47E
Chandigarh d. India 40 30.45N 76.45E
Chāndil India 41 22.58N 86.03E
Chandler Canada 77 48.21N 64.41W
Chandler U.S.A. 83 35.42N 96.53W
Chāndor Hills India 40 20.30N 74.00E
Chāndpur Bangla. 41 23.13N 90.39E
Chāndpur Bangla. 39 22.08N 91.55E
Chāndpur India 41 29.09N 78.16E
Chandrapur India 41 19.57N 79.18E
Chāndvad India 40 20.20N 74.15E
Chānf Iran 43 26.40N 60.31E
Chang, Ko i. Thailand 34 12.04N102.23E
Changchun China 32 43.51N125.15E
Changde China 33 29.00N111.35E
Changfeng China 32 32.27N117.09E
Changhua Jiang r. China 33 19.20N108.38E
Chang Jiang r. China 33 31.40N121.15E
Changjin N. Korea 31 40.21N127.20E
Changle China 32 36.42N118.49E
Changli China 32 39.43N119.08E
Changling China 32 44.16N123.58E
Changning China 33 26.24N112.24E
Changping China 32 40.12N116.12E
Changsha China 33 28.09N112.59E
Changshan China 33 28.57N118.31E
Changshan Qundao is. China 32 39.20N123.00E
Changshou China 33 29.50N107.02E
Changshu China 33 31.48N120.52E
Changshun China 33 25.59N106.25E
Changting China 33 25.42N116.20E
Changyi China 32 36.51N119.23E
Changzhi China 32 36.10N113.00E
Changzhou China 33 31.46N119.58E
Channel Is. U.K. 11 49.28N 2.13W
Channel Is. U.S.A. 81 34.00N120.00W
Channel-Port-aux-Basques town Canada 77 47.35N 59.11W
Channing Mich. U.S.A. 84 46.08N 88.06W
Channing Tex. U.S.A. 83 35.41N102.20W
Chantada Spain 16 42.36N 7.46W
Chanthaburi Thailand 34 12.35N102.05E
Chantilly France 15 49.12N 2.28E
Chanute U.S.A. 83 37.41N 95.27W
Chao'an China 33 23.40N116.32E
Chao Hu l. China 33 31.32N117.30E
Chaonde Mozambique 57 13.43S 40.31E
Chao Phraya r. Thailand 34 13.34N100.35E
Chao Xian China 33 31.36N117.52E
Chaoyang Guangdong China 33 23.25N116.31E
Chaoyang Liaoning China 32 41.35N120.20E
Chapada das Mangabeiras mts. Brazil 91 10.00S 46.30W
Chapada Diamantina Brazil 94 13.30S 42.30W
Chapala, Lago de l. Mexico 86 20.00N103.00W
Chapayevo U.S.S.R 25 50.12N 51.09E
Chapayevsk U.S.S.R. 24 52.58N 49.44E
Chapelle-d'Angillon France 15 47.22N 2.26E
Chapicuy Uruguay 93 31.39S 57.54W
Chapleau Canada 76 47.50N 83.24W
Chāpra India 41 25.46N 84.45E
Chaqui Bolivia 92 19.36S 65.32W
Charcot I. Antarctica 96 70.00S 75.00W
Charay Mexico 81 26.01N108.50W
Charcas Mexico 86 23.08N101.07W
Chard U.K. 11 50.52N 2.59W
Charduār India 41 26.52N 92.46E
Chardzhou U.S.S.R. 43 39.09N 63.34E
Charente r. France 17 45.57N 1.00W
Chari r. Chad 53 13.00N 14.30E
Chari-Baguirmi d. Chad 53 12.20N 15.30E
Chārīkār Afghan. 40 35.01N 69.11E
Charing U.K. 11 51.12N 0.49E
Chariton U.S.A. 82 41.01N 93.19W
Charleroi Belgium 14 50.25N 4.27E
Charlesbourg Canada 77 46.52N 71.16W
Charles City U.S.A. 82 43.04N 92.40W
Charleston Miss. U.S.A. 83 34.00N 90.04W
Charleston S.C. U.S.A. 85 32.48N 79.58W
Charleston W.Va. U.S.A. 84 38.23N 81.40W
Charlestown Rep. of Ire. 13 53.57N 8.48W
Charlestown Ind. U.S.A. 84 38.28N 85.40W
Charlesville Zaïre 54 5.27S 20.58E
Charleville Australia 64 26.25S146.13E
Charleville-Mézières France 15 49.46N 4.43E
Charlieu France 17 46.10N 4.10E
Charlotte N.C. U.S.A. 85 35.03N 80.50W
Charlotte Va. U.S.A. 85 37.03N 78.44W
Charlottesville U.S.A. 85 38.02N 78.29W
Charlottetown Canada 77 46.14N 63.08W
Charlton Australia 66 36.18S143.27E
Charlton I. Canada 76 52.00N 79.30W
Charly-sur-Marne France 15 48.58N 3.17E
Charolles France 17 46.26N 4.17E
Chārsadda Pakistan 40 34.09N 71.44E
Charters Towers Australia 64 20.05S146.16E
Chartres France 15 48.27N 1.30E
Chascomas Argentina 93 35.35S 58.00W
Chase City U.S.A. 85 36.59N 78.30W
Châteaubriant France 15 47.43N 1.22W
Château-du-Loir France 15 47.42N 0.25E
Châteaudun France 15 48.04N 1.20E
Château Gontier France 15 47.50N 0.42W
Châteauguay, Lac l. Canada 77 56.27N 70.05W
Château Landon France 15 48.09N 2.42E
Château-la-Vallière France 15 47.33N 0.19E
Châteauneuf-en-Thymerais France 15 48.35N 1.15E
Châteauneuf-sur-Loire France 15 47.52N 2.14E
Chateauneuf-sur-Sarthe France 15 47.41N 0.30W
Château-Porcien France 15 49.32N 4.15E
Château Renault France 15 47.35N 0.55E
Châteauroux France 17 46.49N 1.41E
Château-Thierry France 15 49.03N 3.24E
Châtelet Belgium 14 50.24N 4.32E
Châtellerault France 17 46.49N 0.33E
Chatham N.B. Canada 77 47.02N 65.28W
Chatham Ont. Canada 76 42.24N 82.11W
Chatham U.K. 11 51.23N 0.32E
Chatham Alas. U.S.A. 74 57.30N135.00W
Chatham Is. Pacific Oc. 68 44.00S176.35W
Chatham Rise Pacific Oc. 68 43.30S178.00W
Chatham Str. U.S.A. 74 57.30N134.45W
Châtillon Italy 15 45.45N 7.37E
Châtillon-Coligny France 15 47.50N 2.51E
Châtillon-sur-Seine France 15 47.52N 4.35E
Chatra India 41 24.13N 84.52E
Chatrapur India 41 19.21N 84.59E
Chātsu India 40 26.36N 75.57E
Chattahoochee U.S.A. 85 30.42N 84.51W
Chattahoochee r. U.S.A. 85 30.52N 84.57W
Chattanooga U.S.A. 85 35.02N 85.18W
Chatteris U.K. 11 52.27N 0.03E
Chauk Burma 34 20.52N 94.50E
Chaulnes France 15 49.49N 2.48E
Chaumont France 17 48.07N 5.08E
Chaumont-en-Vexin France 15 49.16N 1.53E
Chaungwabyin Burma 34 13.41N 98.22E
Chauny France 15 49.37N 3.13E
Chaupāran India 41 24.23N 85.15E
Chau Phu Vietnam 34 10.42N105.03E
Chausy U.S.S.R. 21 53.49N 30.57E
Chavanges France 15 48.31N 4.34E
Chaves Brazil 91 0.10S 49.55W
Chaves Portugal 16 41.44N 7.28W
Chavuma Zambia 54 13.04S 22.43E
Chawang Thailand 34 8.25N 99.32E
Cheb Czech. 20 50.04N 12.20E
Cheboksary U.S.S.R. 24 56.08N 47.12E
Cheboygan U.S.A. 84 45.40N 84.28W
Chebsara U.S.S.R. 24 59.14N 38.59E
Chebula Angola 54 12.27S 23.49E
Chech, Erg des. Mali/Algeria 50 24.30N 2.30W
Chechaouene Morocco 50 35.10N 5.16W
Chechersk U.S.S.R. 21 52.54N 30.54E
Checiny Poland 21 50.48N 20.28E
Cheduba I. Burma 34 18.50N 93.35E
Chegdomyn U.S.S.R. 29 51.09N133.01E
Chegga well Mauritania 50 25.30N 5.46W
Chegutu Zimbabwe 56 18.09S 30.07E
Chehalis U.S.A. 80 46.40N122.58W
Cheil, Ras el c. Somali Rep. 45 7.45N 49.48E
Cheiron, Cime du mtn. France 15 43.49N 6.58E
Cheju S. Korea 31 33.31N126.29E
Cheju do i. S. Korea 31 33.20N126.30E
Cheleken U.S.S.R. 43 39.26N 53.11E
Chelforó Argentina 93 39.04S 66.33W
Chelga Ethiopia 49 12.30N 37.04E
Chelif, Oued r. Algeria 51 36.15N 2.05E
Chelkar U.S.S.R. 28 47.48N 59.39E
Chelles France 15 48.53N 2.36E
Chełm Poland 21 51.10N 23.28E
Chelmer r. U.K. 9 51.43N 0.40E
Chelmsford U.K. 11 51.44N 0.28E
Chełmża Poland 21 53.12N 18.37E
Chelsea Canada 77 45.29N 75.48W
Cheltenham U.K. 11 51.53N 2.07W
Chelva Spain 16 39.45N 1.00W

Chelyabinsk to **Cobourg**

Chelyabinsk U.S.S.R. 28 55.10N 61.25E
Chelyuskin, Mys c. U.S.S.R. 29 77.20N106.00E
Chemainus Canada 74 48.55N123.48W
Chemba Mozambique 55 17.11S 34.53E
Chemult U.S.A. 80 43.13N121.47W
Chĕn, Gora mtn. U.S.S.R. 29 65.30N141.20E
Chenāb r. Pakistan 40 29.23N 71.02E
Chenachane Algeria 50 26.00N 4.15W
Chénéville Canada 77 45.53N 75.03W
Cheney U.S.A. 80 47.29N117.34W
Chengchow see Zhengzhou China 32
Chengde China 32 41.00N117.52E
Chengdu China 33 30.41N104.05E
Chenggu China 32 33.10N107.22E
Chenghai China 33 23.31N116.43E
Chengkou China 33 31.58N108.48E
Chengmai China 33 19.44N109.59E
Cheng Xian China 32 33.42N105.36E
Chenoa U.S.A. 82 40.44N 88.43W
Chen Xian China 33 25.45N113.00E
Chepen Peru 90 7.15S 79.20W
Chepstow U.K. 11 51.38N 2.40W
Cher r. France 15 47.12N 2.04E
Cherbourg France 15 49.38N 1.37W
Cherdyn U.S.S.R. 24 60.25N 55.22E
Cherelato Ethiopia 49 6.00N 38.10E
Cheremkhovo U.S.S.R. 29 53.08N103.01E
Cherepovets U.S.S.R. 24 59.05N 37.55E
Chergui, Chott ech f. Algeria 51 34.21N 0.30E
Cherikov U.S.S.R. 21 53.35N 31.23E
Cherkassy U.S.S.R. 25 49.27N 32.04E
Cherkessk U.S.S.R. 25 44.14N 42.05E
Cherkovitsa Bulgaria 19 43.41N 24.49E
Cherlak U.S.S.R. 28 54.10N 74.52E
Chernigov U.S.S.R. 21 51.30N 31.18E
Chernikovsk U.S.S.R. 24 54.51N 56.06E
Chernobyl U.S.S.R. 21 51.17N 30.15E
Chernovtsy U.S.S.R. 21 48.19N 25.52E
Chernyakhov U.S.S.R. 21 50.30N 28.38E
Chernyakhovsk U.S.S.R. 23 54.38N 21.49E
Cherokee Iowa U.S.A. 82 42.45N 95.33W
Cherokee Okla. U.S.A. 83 36.45N 98.21W
Cherquenco Chile 93 38.41S 72.00W
Cherrapunji India 41 25.18N 91.42E
Cherry Creek r. U.S.A. 82 44.36N101.30W
Cherry Creek town Nev. U.S.A. 80 39.54N113.53W
Cherry Creek town S.Dak. U.S.A. 82 44.36N101.26W
Cherskogo, Khrebet mts. U.S.S.R. 29 65.50N143.00E
Chertkovo U.S.S.R. 25 49.22N 40.12E
Chertsey U.K. 11 51.23N 0.27W
Chervonograd U.S.S.R. 21 50.25N 24.10E
Cherwell r. U.K. 11 51.44N 1.15W
Chesapeake Va. U.S.A. 85 36.43N 76.15W
Chesapeake B. U.S.A. 84 38.40N 76.25W
Chesapeake Beach town U.S.A. 85 38.41N 76.32W
Chesham U.K. 11 51.43N 0.38W
Cheshire d. U.K. 10 53.14N 2.30W
Chëshskaya Guba g. U.S.S.R. 24 67.20N 46.30E
Chesht-e Sharīf Afghan. 40 34.21N 63.44E
Chesil Beach f. U.K. 11 50.37N 2.33W
Chester U.K. 10 53.12N 2.53W
Chester Mont. U.S.A. 80 48.31N110.58W
Chester Penn. U.S.A. 85 39.51N 75.21W
Chesterfield U.K. 10 53.14N 1.26W
Chesterfield, Îles is. N. Cal. 68 20.00S159.00E
Chesterfield Inlet town Canada 73 63.00N 91.00W
Chestertown Md. U.S.A. 85 39.13N 76.04W
Chesuncook L. U.S.A. 84 46.00N 69.20W
Chéticamp Canada 77 46.38N 61.01W
Chetumal Mexico 87 18.30N 88.17W
Chetumal B. Mexico 87 18.30N 88.00W
Chetwynd Canada 74 55.45N121.45W
Cheviot New Zealand 60 42.49S173.16E
Cheviot U.S.A. 84 39.10N 84.32W
Chew Bahir l. Ethiopia 49 4.40N 36.50E
Cheyenne r. U.S.A. 82 44.40N101.15W
Cheyenne Okla. U.S.A. 83 35.37N 99.40W
Cheyenne Wyo. U.S.A. 80 41.08N104.49W
Cheyne B. Australia 63 34.35S118.50E
Chhabra India 40 24.40N 76.50E
Chhātak Bangla. 41 25.02N 91.40E
Chhatarpur Bihār India 41 24.23N 84.11E
Chhatarpur Madhya P. India 41 24.54N 79.36E
Chhattīsgarh f. India 41 21.00N 82.00E
Chhindwāra India 41 22.04N 78.56E
Chhota-Chhindwāra India 41 23.03N 79.29E
Chhota Udepur India 40 22.19N 74.01E
Chiali Taiwan 33 23.10N120.11E
Chiang Mai Thailand 34 18.48N 98.59E
Chiapas d. Mexico 86 16.30N 93.00W
Chiari Italy 15 45.32N 9.56E
Chiavari Italy 15 44.19N 9.19E
Chiavenna Italy 15 46.19N 9.24E
Chiba Japan 35 35.36N140.07E
Chiba d. Japan 35 35.10N140.00E
Chibemba Angola 56 15.43S 14.07E
Chibia Angola 54 15.10S 13.32E
Chibougamau Canada 76 49.56N 74.24W
Chibougamau Lac l. Canada 76 49.50N 74.20W
Chibougamau Prov. Park Canada 77 49.25N 73.50W
Chibuk Nigeria 53 10.52N 12.50E
Chibuto Mozambique 57 24.41S 33.32E
Chicago U.S.A. 82 41.50N 87.45W
Chichagof I. U.S.A. 74 57.55N135.45W
Chichagof I. U.S.A. 72 57.55N135.45W
Chicheng China 32 40.52N115.50E
Chichester U.K. 11 50.50N 0.47W
Chichibu Japan 35 35.59N139.05E
Chickasha U.S.A. 83 35.02N 97.58W
Chiclana Spain 16 36.26N 6.09W
Chiclayo Peru 90 6.47S 79.47W
Chico r. Chubut Argentina 93 43.45S 66.10W
Chico r. Santa Cruz Argentina 93 50.03W 68.35W
Chico U.S.A. 80 39.44N121.50W
Chicomo Mozambique 57 24.33S 34.11E
Chicoutimi-Jonquière Canada 77 48.26N 71.06W
Chicualacuala Mozambique 57 22.06S 31.42E
Chidambarum India 39 11.24N 79.42E
Chidembo Angola 54 14.34S 19.17E
Chidenguele Mozambique 57 24.54S 34.13E
Chidley, C. Canada 73 60.30N 65.00W
Chiemsee l. W. Germany 20 47.55N 12.30E
Chiengi Zambia 55 8.42S 29.07E
Chieri Italy 15 45.01N 7.49E
Chieti Italy 18 42.22N 14.12E
Chifeng China 32 42.13N118.56E
Chigasaki Japan 35 35.19N139.24E
Chignecto B. Canada 77 45.35N 64.45W
Chiguana Bolivia 92 21.05S 67.58W
Chigubo Mozambique 57 22.38S 33.18E
Chigu Co l. China 41 28.40N 91.50E
Chihuahua Mexico 81 28.38N106.05W
Chihuahua d. Mexico 81 28.40N106.00W
Chiili U.S.S.R. 28 44.10N 66.37E
Chikhli India 40 20.21N 76.15E
Chikumbi Zambia 55 15.14S 28.21E
Chikwawa Malaŵi 55 16.00S 34.54E
Chīl r. Iran 43 25.12N 61.30E
Chilanga Zambia 56 15.33S 28.17E
Chilapa Mexico 86 17.38N 99.11W
Chilcoot U.S.A. 80 39.49N120.08W
Childers Australia 64 25.14S152.17E
Childress U.S.A. 83 34.25N100.13W
Chile S. America 92 32.30S 71.00W
Chile Basin Pacific Oc. 69 34.20S 80.00W
Chile Chico Chile 93 46.33S 71.44W
Chilka L. India 41 19.46N 85.20E
Chilko L. Canada 72 51.20N124.05W
Chillagoe Australia 64 17.09S144.32E
Chillán Chile 93 36.36S 72.07W
Chillicothe Mo. U.S.A. 82 39.48N 93.33W
Chillicothe Ohio U.S.A. 84 39.20N 82.59W
Chillingollah Australia 66 35.17S143.07E
Chilliwack Canada 74 49.10N122.00W
Chiloé, Isla de i. Chile 93 43.00S 73.00W
Chilonga Zambia 55 12.02S 31.17E
Chilpancingo Mexico 86 17.33N 99.30W
Chiltern Australia 67 36.11S146.36E
Chiltern Hills U.K. 11 51.40N 0.53W
Chilton U.S.A. 82 44.04N 88.10W
Chilumba Malaŵi 55 10.25S 34.18E
Chilwa, L. Malaŵi 55 15.15S 35.45E
Chimakela Angola 54 15.12S 16.58E
Chimanimani Zimbabwe 57 19.48S 32.52E
Chimay Belgium 14 50.03N 4.20E
Chimbas Argentina 92 31.28S 68.30W
Chimborazo mtn. Ecuador 90 1.29S 78.52W
Chimbote Peru 90 9.04S 78.34W
Chimishliya U.S.S.R. 21 46.30N 28.50E
Chimkent U.S.S.R. 30 42.16N 69.05E
Chimoio Mozambique 57 19.04S 33.29E
Chin d. Burma 34 22.00N 93.30E
China Asia 30 33.00N103.00E
China Lake town U.S.A. 81 35.46N117.39W
Chinandega Nicaragua 87 12.35N 87.10W
Chinati Peak U.S.A. 81 29.57N104.29W
Chincha Alta Peru 90 13.25S 76.07W
Chinchaga r. Canada 74 58.50N118.20W
Chinchón Spain 16 40.09N 3.26W
Chinchoua Gabon 54 0.00 9.48E
Chincoteague U.S.A. 85 37.55N 75.23W
Chinde Mozambique 57 18.37S 36.24E
Chindio Mozambique 55 17.46S 35.23E
Chindwin r. Burma 34 21.30N 95.12E
Chinga Mozambique 55 15.14S 38.40E
Chingleput India 39 12.42N 79.59E
Chingola Zambia 55 12.29S 27.53E
Chingombe Zambia 55 14.25S 29.56E
Chingshui Taiwan 33 24.15N120.35E
Chin Hills Burma 34 22.30N 93.30E
Chinhoyi Zimbabwe 56 17.22S 30.10E
Chini India 41 31.32N 78.15E
Chiniot Pakistan 40 31.43N 72.59E
Chinjan Pakistan 40 30.34N 67.58E
Chinko r. C.A.R. 49 4.50N 23.53E
Chinle U.S.A. 81 36.09N109.33W
Chinon France 17 47.10N 0.15E
Chinook U.S.A. 80 48.35N109.14W
Chino Valley town U.S.A. 81 34.45N112.27W
Chinsali Zambia 55 10.33S 32.05E
Chintheche Malaŵi 55 11.50S 34.13E
Chiny Belgium 14 49.45N 5.20E
Chiôco Mozambique 55 16.27S 32.49E
Chioggia Italy 15 45.13N 12.17E
Chipata Zambia 55 13.37S 32.40E
Chipera Mozambique 55 15.20S 32.35E
Chipie r. Canada 76 51.25N 83.20W
Chipinge Zimbabwe 57 20.12S 32.38E
Chippenham U.K. 11 51.27N 2.07W
Chippewa Falls town U.S.A. 82 44.56N 91.24W
Chipping Norton U.K. 11 51.56N 1.32W
Chiquian Peru 90 10.10S 77.00W
Chiquinquirá Colombia 90 5.37N 73.50W
Chir r. U.S.S.R. 25 48.34N 42.53E
Chirāwa India 40 28.15N 75.38E
Chirchik U.S.S.R. 30 41.28N 69.31E
Chiredzi Zimbabwe 57 21.03S 31.39E
Chiredzi r. Zimbabwe 57 21.10S 31.50E
Chiricahua Peak mtn. U.S.A. 81 31.52N109.20W
Chiriquí mtn. Panama 87 8.49N 82.38W
Chiriquí, Laguna de b. Panama 87 9.00N 82.00W
Chiromo Malaŵi 55 16.28S 35.10E
Chirripó mtn. Costa Rica 87 9.31N 83.30W
Chirundu Zimbabwe 56 16.04S 28.51E
Chisamba Zambia 56 14.58S 28.23E
Chishan Taiwan 33 22.53N120.29E
Chisholm U.S.A. 82 47.29N 92.53W
Chisholm Mills Canada 74 54.55N114.09W
Chishtiān Mandi Pakistan 40 29.48N 72.52E
Chishui China 33 28.29N105.38E
Chisone r. Italy 15 44.49N 7.25E
Chistopol U.S.S.R. 24 55.25N 50.38E
Chita U.S.S.R. 31 52.03N113.35E
Chitek L. Canada 75 52.25N 99.20W
Chitembo Angola 54 13.33S 16.47E
Chitipa Malaŵi 55 9.41S 33.19E
Chitorgarh India 40 24.53N 74.38E
Chitrakūt Dham India 41 25.11N 80.52E
Chitrāl Pakistan 38 35.52N 71.58E
Chittagong Bangla. 41 22.20N 91.50E
Chittoor India 39 13.13N 79.06E
Chiumbe r. Zaïre 54 6.37S 21.04E
Chiuta, L. Malaŵi/Mozambique 55 14.45S 35.50E
Chivasso Italy 15 45.11N 7.53E
Chivhu Zimbabwe 56 19.01S 30.53E
Chivilcoy Argentina 93 34.52S 60.02W
Chiwanda Tanzania 55 11.21S 34.55E
Chobe r. Namibia/Botswana 56 17.48S 25.12E
Chobe Swamp f. Namibia 56 18.20S 23.40E
Chocolate Mts. U.S.A. 81 33.20N115.15W
Chocope Peru 90 7.47S 79.12W
Choele-Choel Argentina 93 39.15S 65.30W
Chōfu Japan 35 35.39N139.33E
Chohtan India 40 25.29N 71.04E
Choix Mexico 81 26.43N108.17W
Chojnice Poland 21 53.42N 17.32E
Choke Mts. Ethiopia 49 11.00N 37.30E
Cholet France 17 47.04N 0.53W
Cholon Vietnam 34 10.40N106.30E
Choluteca Honduras 87 13.16N 87.11W
Choma Zambia 55 16.51S 27.04E
Chomu India 40 27.10N 75.44E
Chomutov Czech. 20 50.28N 13.25E
Chon Buri Thailand 34 13.20N101.02E
Chone Ecuador 90 0.44S 80.04W
Chong'an China 33 27.46N118.01E
Ch'ŏngjin N. Korea 31 41.55N129.50E
Ch'ŏngju S. Korea 31 36.39N127.31E
Chŏng Kal Kampuchea 34 13.57N103.35E
Chongming i. China 33 31.36N121.33E
Chongqing China 33 29.31N106.35E
Chongren China 33 27.44N116.02E
Chŏnju S. Korea 31 35.50N127.05E
Chonos, Archipelago de los is. Chile 93 45.00S 74.00W
Cho Oyu mtn. China/Nepal 41 28.06N 86.40E
Chopda India 40 21.15N 75.18E
Choptank r. U.S.A. 85 38.38N 76.13W
Chorley U.K. 10 53.39N 2.39W
Chortkov U.S.S.R. 21 49.01N 25.42E
Chorzów Poland 21 50.19N 18.56E
Chosica Peru 90 11.55S 76.38W
Chos Malal Argentina 93 37.20S 70.15W
Choszczno Poland 20 53.10N 15.26E
Choteau U.S.A. 80 47.49N112.11W
Chotila India 40 22.25N 71.11E
Choum Mauritania 50 21.10N 13.00W
Chowchilla U.S.A. 80 37.07N120.16W
Christchurch New Zealand 60 43.33S172.40E
Christchurch U.K. 11 50.44N 1.47W
Christian Sd. U.S.A. 74 55.56N134.40W
Christianshåb Greenland 73 68.50N 51.00W
Christie B. Canada 75 62.32N111.10W
Christina r. Canada 75 56.40N111.03W
Christmas Creek town Australia 62 18.55S125.56E
Christmas I. Indian Oc. 36 10.30S105.40E
Christmas I. see Kiritimati i. Kiribati 69
Chrudim Czech. 20 49.57N 15.48E
Chu r. U.S.S.R. 30 42.30N 76.10E
Chuādānga Bangla. 41 23.38N 88.51E
Chubbuck U.S.A. 81 34.22N115.20W
Chūbu d. Japan 35 35.25N137.40E
Chubut d. Argentina 93 44.00S 68.00W
Chubut r. Argentina 93 43.18S 65.06W
Chu Chua Canada 74 51.22N120.10W
Chudleigh U.K. 11 50.35N 3.36W
Chudleigh Park town Australia 64 19.41S144.06E
Chudnov U.S.S.R. 21 50.05N 28.01E
Chudovo U.S.S.R. 24 59.10N 31.41E
Chudskoye, Ozero l. U.S.S.R. 24 58.30N 27.30E
Chugwater U.S.A. 80 41.46N104.49W
Chuiquimula Guatemala 87 15.52N 89.50W
Chukai Malaysia 36 4.16N103.24E
Chukotskiy Poluostrov pen. U.S.S.R. 29 66.00N174.30W
Chukudukraal Botswana 56 22.30S 23.22E
Chula Vista U.S.A. 81 32.39N117.05W
Chulman U.S.S.R. 29 56.54N124.55E
Chulucanas Peru 90 5.08S 80.00W
Chulym U.S.S.R. 28 55.09N 80.59E
Chum U.S.S.R. 24 67.05N 63.15E
Chumbicha Argentina 92 28.50S 66.18W
Chumikan U.S.S.R. 29 54.40N135.15E
Chumphon Thailand 34 10.34N 99.15E
Chuna r. U.S.S.R. 29 58.00N 94.00E
Ch'unch'ŏn S. Korea 31 37.53N127.45E
Chungking see Chongqing China 33
Chunya Tanzania 55 8.31S 33.28E
Chuquicamata Chile 92 22.20S 68.56W
Chuquisaca d. Bolivia 92 21.00S 64.00W
Chur Switz. 17 46.52N 9.32E
Churchill Canada 75 58.46N 94.10W
Churchill r. Man. Canada 75 58.47N 94.12W
Churchill r. Nfld. Canada 77 53.20N 60.11W
Churchill, C. Canada 75 58.46N 93.12W
Churchill Falls f. Canada 77 53.35N 64.27W
Churchill L. Canada 75 55.55N108.20W
Churchill Peak mtn. Canada 74 58.10N125.10W
Church Stretton U.K. 11 52.32N 2.49W
Churia Range mts. Nepal 41 28.40N 81.30E
Churu India 40 28.18N 74.57E
Chusovoy U.S.S.R. 24 58.18N 57.50E
Chu Xian China 32 32.25N118.15E
Chuxiong China 39 25.03N101.33E
Chu Yang Sin mtn. Vietnam 34 12.25N108.25E
Ciamis Indonesia 37 7.20S108.21E
Cianjur Indonesia 37 6.50S107.09E
Cibatu Indonesia 37 7.10S107.59E
Ciechanów Poland 21 52.53N 20.38E
Ciego de Avila Cuba 87 21.51N 78.47W
Ciénaga Colombia 90 11.11N 74.15W
Cienfuegos Cuba 87 22.10N 80.27W
Cieszyn Poland 21 49.45N 18.38E
Cieza Spain 16 38.14N 1.25W
Cifuentes Spain 16 40.47N 2.37W
Cigüela r. Spain 16 39.47N 3.00W
Cijara, Embalse de resr. Spain 16 39.20N 4.50W
Cijulang Indonesia 37 7.44S108.30E
Cikampek Indonesia 37 6.21S107.25E
Cilacap Indonesia 37 7.44S109.00E
Ciledug Indonesia 37 6.56S108.43E
Cili China 33 29.24N111.04E
Cimanuk r. Indonesia 37 6.20S108.12E
Cimarron U.S.A. 83 37.48N100.21W
Cimarron r. U.S.A. 83 36.10N 96.17W
Cimone, Monte mtn. Italy 15 44.12N 10.42E
Cîmpina Romania 19 45.08N 25.44E
Cîmpulung Romania 19 45.16N 25.03E
Cinca r. Spain 16 41.22N 0.20E
Cincinnati U.S.A. 84 39.10N 84.30W
Ciney Belgium 14 50.17N 5.06E
Cinto, Monte mtn. France 17 42.23N 8.57E
Cipolletti Argentina 93 38.56S 67.59W
Circle U.S.A. 80 47.25N105.35W
Circleville Ohio U.S.A. 84 39.36N 82.57W
Circleville Utah U.S.A. 80 38.10N112.16W
Cirebon Indonesia 37 6.46S108.33E
Cirencester U.K. 11 51.43N 1.59W
Ciriè Italy 15 45.14N 7.36E
Cirò Marina Italy 19 39.22N 17.08E
Cisco U.S.A. 83 32.23N 98.59W
Citra U.S.A. 85 29.24N 82.06W
Cittadella Italy 15 45.39N 11.47E
Cittanova Italy 18 38.21N 16.05E
Ciudad Acuña Mexico 83 29.18N100.55W
Ciudad Allende Mexico 83 28.20N100.51W
Ciudad Bolívar Venezuela 90 8.06N 63.36W
Ciudad Camargo Mexico 81 27.40N105.10W
Ciudad de México Mexico 86 19.25N 99.10W
Ciudadela Spain 16 40.00N 3.50E
Ciudad Guayana Venezuela 90 8.22N 62.40W
Ciudad Guerrero Mexico 86 28.33N107.28W
Ciudad Guzmán Mexico 86 19.41N103.29W
Ciudad Ixtepec Mexico 86 16.32N 95.10W
Ciudad Jiménez Mexico 81 27.08N104.55W
Ciudad Juárez Mexico 81 31.44N106.29W
Ciudad Lerdo Mexico 83 25.32N103.32W
Ciudad Madero Mexico 86 22.19N 97.50W
Ciudad Mante Mexico 86 22.44N 98.57W
Ciudad Melchor Múzquiz Mexico 83 27.53N101.31W
Ciudad Mier Mexico 83 26.26N 99.09W
Ciudad Obregón Mexico 81 27.29N109.56W
Ciudad Ojeda Venezuela 90 10.05N 71.17W
Ciudad Piar Venezuela 90 7.27N 63.19W
Ciudad Real Spain 16 38.59N 3.55W
Ciudad Rodrigo Spain 16 40.36N 6.33W
Ciudad Victoria Mexico 86 23.43N 99.10W
Civitanova Italy 18 43.19N 13.40E
Civitavecchia Italy 18 42.06N 11.48E
Civray France 17 46.09N 0.18E
Çivril Turkey 42 38.18N 29.43E
Ci Xian China 32 36.22N114.23E
Cizre Turkey 42 37.21N 42.11E
Clackline Australia 63 31.43S116.31E
Clacton on Sea U.K. 11 51.47N 1.10E
Clairambault, Lac l. Canada 77 54.45N 69.22W
Claire, L. Canada 74 58.30N112.00W
Clamecy France 15 47.27N 3.31E
Clampton Australia 63 29.56S119.06E
Clanton U.S.A. 85 32.50N 86.38W
Clara Rep. of Ire. 13 53.21N 7.37W
Clara Creek town Australia 64 26.00S146.50E
Clare N.S.W. Australia 66 33.27S143.55E
Clare S.A. Australia 66 33.50S138.38E
Clare d. Rep. of Ire. 13 52.52N 8.55W
Clare r. Rep. of Ire. 13 53.17N 9.04W
Clare U.S.A. 84 43.49N 84.47W
Clare I. Rep. of Ire. 13 53.48N 10.00W
Claremore U.S.A. 83 36.19N 95.36W
Claremorris Rep. of Ire. 13 53.44N 9.00W
Clarence r. Australia 67 29.25S153.02E
Clarence r. New Zealand 60 42.10S173.55E
Clarence I. Antarctica 96 61.30S 53.50W
Clarence Str. Australia 62 12.00S131.00E
Clarence Str. U.S.A. 74 55.40N132.10W
Clarendon U.S.A. 83 34.56N100.53W
Claresholm Canada 74 50.00N113.30W
Clarie Coast f. Antarctica 96 67.00S133.00E
Clarinda U.S.A. 82 40.44N 95.02W
Clark, L. U.S.A. 72 60.15N154.15W
Clarke I. Australia 65 40.30S148.10E
Clark Fork r. U.S.A. 80 48.09N116.15W
Clarksburg U.S.A. 84 39.16N 80.22W
Clarksdale U.S.A. 83 34.12N 90.34W
Clarkston U.S.A. 80 46.26N117.02W
Clarksville Ark. U.S.A. 83 35.28N 93.28W
Clarksville Tenn. U.S.A. 85 36.31N 87.21W
Clarksville Tex. U.S.A. 83 33.37N 95.03W
Clary France 14 50.05N 3.21E
Claverton Australia 65 27.24S145.55E
Clayoquot Sd. Canada 74 49.11N126.08W
Clayton r. Australia 66 29.06S137.59E
Clayton Idaho U.S.A. 80 44.16N114.25W
Clayton N.J. U.S.A. 85 39.39N 75.06W
Clayton N.Mex. U.S.A. 83 36.27N103.11W
Clear, C. Rep. of Ire. 9 51.25N 9.32W
Clearfield Utah U.S.A. 80 41.07N112.01W
Clear I. Rep. of Ire. 13 51.26N 9.30W
Clear L. U.S.A. 80 39.02N122.50W
Clear Lake town Iowa U.S.A. 82 43.08N 92.23W
Clear Lake town S.Dak. U.S.A. 82 44.45N 96.41W
Clearwater Canada 74 51.38N120.02W
Clearwater r. Canada 75 56.40N109.30W
Clearwater U.S.A. 85 27.57N 82.48W
Clearwater Mts. U.S.A. 80 46.00N115.30W
Cle Elum U.S.A. 80 47.12N120.56W
Cleethorpes U.K. 10 53.33N 0.02W
Clermont Australia 64 22.49S147.39E
Clermont France 15 49.23N 2.24E
Clermont-en-Argonne France 15 49.05N 5.05E
Clermont-Ferrand France 17 45.47N 3.05E
Clervaux Lux. 14 50.04N 6.01E
Cles Italy 15 46.22N 11.02E
Cleve Australia 66 33.37S136.32E
Clevedon U.K. 11 51.26N 2.52W
Cleveland d. U.K. 10 54.37N 1.08W
Cleveland Miss. U.S.A. 83 33.45N 90.50W
Cleveland Ohio U.S.A. 84 41.30N 81.41W
Cleveland Tenn. U.S.A. 85 35.10N 84.51W
Cleveland Tex. U.S.A. 83 30.21N 95.05W
Cleveland, C. Australia 64 19.11S147.01E
Cleveland Heights town U.S.A. 84 41.30N 81.34W
Cleveland Hills U.K. 10 54.25N 1.10W
Cleveleys U.K. 10 53.52N 3.01W
Clew B. Rep. of Ire. 13 53.50N 9.47W
Clifden Rep. of Ire. 13 53.29N 10.02W
Cliffy Head Australia 63 34.58S116.24E
Clifton Ariz. U.S.A. 81 33.03N109.18W
Clifton N.J. U.S.A. 85 40.53N 74.08W
Clifton Tex. U.S.A. 83 31.47N 97.35W
Clifton Forge U.S.A. 85 37.49N 79.49W
Climax Canada 75 49.13N108.23W
Clint U.S.A. 81 31.35N106.14W
Clinton B.C. Canada 74 51.05N121.35W
Clinton New Zealand 60 46.13S169.23E
Clinton Ark. U.S.A. 83 35.36N 92.38W
Clinton Ill. U.S.A. 82 40.10N 88.59W
Clinton Iowa U.S.A. 82 41.51N 90.12W
Clinton Mo. U.S.A. 82 38.22N 93.46W
Clinton N.C. U.S.A. 85 35.00N 78.20W
Clinton N.J. U.S.A. 85 40.38N 74.55W
Clinton Okla. U.S.A. 83 35.31N 98.59W
Clintwood U.S.A. 85 37.09N 82.30W
Clipperton i. Pacific Oc. 69 10.17N109.13W
Clisham mtn. U.K. 12 57.58N 6.50W
Clive L. Canada 74 63.13N118.54W
Cliza Bolivia 92 17.36S 65.56W
Cloghan Offaly Rep. of Ire. 13 53.13N 7.54W
Clogher Head Kerry Rep. of Ire. 13 52.09N 10.28W
Clonakilty Rep. of Ire. 13 51.37N 8.54W
Cloncurry Australia 64 20.42S140.30E
Clones Rep. of Ire. 13 54.11N 7.16W
Clonmel Rep. of Ire. 13 52.21N 7.44W
Clonroche Rep. of Ire. 13 52.27N 6.45W
Cloppenburg W. Germany 14 52.52N 8.02E
Cloquet U.S.A. 82 46.43N 92.28W
Clorinda Argentina 92 25.20S 57.40W
Cloud Peak mtn. U.S.A. 80 44.25N107.10W
Cloughton U.K. 10 54.20N 0.27W
Cloverdale U.S.A. 80 38.48N123.01W
Clovis Calif. U.S.A. 80 36.49N119.42W
Clovis N.Mex. U.S.A. 83 34.24N103.12W
Clowne U.K. 10 53.18N 1.16W
Cluj Romania 21 46.47N 23.37E
Cluny France 17 46.26N 4.39E
Clusone Italy 15 45.53N 9.57E
Clutha r. New Zealand 60 46.18S169.05E
Clwyd d. U.K. 10 53.07N 3.20W
Clwyd r. U.K. 10 53.19N 3.30W
Clyde Canada 73 70.30N 68.30W
Clyde New Zealand 60 45.11S169.19E
Clyde r. U.K. 12 55.58N 4.53W
Clydebank U.K. 12 55.53N 4.23W
Coachella U.S.A. 81 33.41N116.10W
Coahuila d. Mexico 83 27.40N102.00W
Coal r. Canada 74 59.39N126.57W
Coalgate U.S.A. 83 34.32N 96.13W
Coalinga U.S.A. 81 36.09N120.21W
Coalville U.K. 11 52.43N 1.21W
Coast d. Kenya 55 3.00S 39.30E
Coast Mts. Canada 74 55.00N129.00W
Coast Range mts. U.S.A. 80 42.40N123.30W
Coatbridge U.K. 12 55.52N 4.02W
Coatesville U.S.A. 85 39.59N 75.49W
Coats I. Canada 73 62.30N 83.00W
Coats Land f. Antarctica 96 77.00S 25.00W
Coatzacoalcos Mexico 86 18.10N 94.25W
Cobalt Canada 76 47.25N 79.42W
Cobán Guatemala 86 15.28N 90.20W
Cobar Australia 67 31.32S145.51E
Cobargo Australia 67 36.24S149.52E
Cobden Australia 66 38.21S143.07E
Cobden Canada 76 45.38N 76.53W
Cobh Rep. of Ire. 13 51.50N 8.18W
Cobham L. Australia 66 30.09S142.05E
Cobija Bolivia 92 11.02S 68.44W
Cobourg Canada 76 43.58N 78.10W

Cobourg Pen. to Crucero

Cobourg Pen. Australia 64 11.20S132.15E
Cobram Australia 67 35.56S145.40E
Cobre U.S.A. 80 41.07N114.25W
Cobue Mozambique 55 12.10S 34.50E
Coburg W. Germany 20 50.15N 10.58E
Coburg I. Canada 73 76.00N 79.25W
Cochabamba Bolivia 92 17.24S 66.09W
Cochabamba d. Bolivia 92 17.30S 65.40W
Cochem W. Germany 14 50.08N 7.10E
Cochin India 38 9.56N 76.15E
Cochise U.S.A. 81 32.06N109.56W
Cochran U.S.A. 85 32.22N 83.21W
Cochrane Alta. Canada 74 51.11N114.30W
Cochrane Ont. Canada 76 49.00N 81.00W
Cochrane Chile 93 47.20S 72.30W
Cockburn Australia 66 32.05S141.00E
Cockburnspath U.K. 12 55.56N 2.22W
Cockeysville U.S.A. 85 39.29N 76.39W
Coco r. Honduras 87 14.58N 83.15W
Coco, Isla del i. Pacific Oc. 69 5.32N 87.04W
Cocoa U.S.A. 85 28.21N 80.46W
Cocoa Beach town U.S.A. 85 28.19N 80.36W
Cocobeach Gabon 54 0.59N 9.36E
Cocoparra Range mts. Australia 67 34.00S146.00E
Cod, C. U.S.A. 84 41.42N 70.15W
Codăeşti Romania 21 46.52N 27.46E
Codajás Brazil 90 3.55S 62.00W
Codigoro Italy 15 44.49N 12.08E
Codó Brazil 91 4.28S 43.51W
Codogno Italy 15 45.09N 9.42E
Codroipo Italy 15 45.58N 12.59E
Cody U.S.A. 80 44.32N109.03W
Coen Australia 64 13.56S143.12E
Coesfeld W. Germany 14 51.55N 7.13E
Coeur d'Alene U.S.A. 78 47.40N116.46W
Coevorden Neth. 14 52.39N 6.45E
Coffeyville U.S.A. 83 37.02N 93.37W
Coffin B. Australia 66 34.27S135.19E
Coff's Harbour Australia 67 30.19S153.05E
Cofre de Perote mtn. Mexico 86 19.30N 97.10W
Coghinas r. Italy 18 40.57N 8.50E
Cognac France 17 45.42N 0.19W
Cohoes U.S.A. 84 42.46N 73.42W
Cohuna Australia 66 35.47S144.15E
Coiba, Isla de i. Panama 87 7.23N 81.45W
Coihaique Chile 93 45.35S 72.08W
Coimbatore India 38 11.00N 76.57E
Coimbra Brazil 94 19.55S 57.47W
Coimbra Portugal 16 40.12N 8.25W
Coín Spain 16 36.40N 4.45W
Cojimies Ecuador 90 0.20N 80.00W
Cokeville U.S.A. 80 42.05N110.57W
Coko Range mts. Australia 66 30.35S141.46E
Colac Australia 66 38.22S143.38E
Colatina Brazil 94 19.35S 40.37W
Colbeck, C. Antarctica 96 77.20S159.00W
Colby U.S.A. 82 39.24N101.03W
Colchester U.K. 11 51.54N 0.55E
Cold L. Canada 75 54.33N110.05W
Cold Lake town Canada 75 54.27N110.10W
Coldstream U.K. 12 55.39N 2.15W
Coldwater U.S.A. 84 41.57N 85.01W
Coldwell Canada 76 48.45N 86.30W
Coleman r. Australia 64 15.06S141.38E
Coleman Tex. U.S.A. 83 31.50N 99.26W
Coleman Wisc. U.S.A. 82 45.04N 88.02W
Colenso R.S.A. 56 28.43S 29.49E
Coleraine Australia 66 37.36S141.42E
Coleraine U.K. 13 55.08N 6.40W
Colesberg R.S.A. 56 30.43S 25.05E
Colfax U.S.A. 83 31.31N 92.42W
Colgong India 41 25.16N 87.13E
Colico Italy 15 46.08N 9.22E
Colima Mexico 86 19.14N103.41W
Colima d. Mexico 86 19.05N104.00W
Colinas Brazil 91 6.02S 44.14W
Coll i. U.K. 12 56.38N 6.34W
College U.S.A. 72 64.54N147.55W
College Park town Ga. U.S.A. 85 33.39N 84.28W
College Park town Md. U.S.A. 85 39.00N 76.55W
College Station town U.S.A. 83 30.37N 96.21W
Collerina Australia 67 29.22S146.32E
Collie N.S.W. Australia 67 31.41S148.22E
Collie W.A. Australia 63 33.21S116.09E
Collie Cardiff Australia 63 33.27S116.09E
Collier B. Australia 62 16.10S124.15E
Collingswood U.S.A. 85 39.55N 75.04W
Collingwood Canada 76 44.29N 80.13W
Collingwood New Zealand 60 40.41S172.41E
Collingwood B. P.N.G. 64 9.20S149.30E
Collinsville Australia 64 20.34S147.51E
Collin Top mtn. U.K. 13 54.58N 6.08W
Collon Rep. of Ire. 13 53.47N 6.30W
Collooney Rep. of Ire. 13 54.11N 8.29W
Colmar France 17 48.05N 7.21E
Colmenar Viejo Spain 16 40.39N 3.46W
Colne r. Essex U.K. 11 51.50N 0.59E
Colnett, C. Mexico 86 31.00N116.20W
Colnett, Cabo c. Mexico 81 31.00N116.20W
Colo r. Australia 67 33.26S150.53E
Cologne see Köln W. Germany 14
Colombia S. America 90 4.00N 72.30W
Colombian Basin f. Carib. Sea 95 14.00N 76.00W
Colombo Sri Lanka 39 6.55N 79.52E
Colón Argentina 93 32.15S 58.10W
Colón Panama 90 9.21N 79.54W
Colona Australia 65 31.38S132.05E
Colonelganj India 41 27.08N 81.42E
Colonia del Sacramento Uruguay 93 34.28S 57.51W
Colonia Las Heras Argentina 93 46.33S 68.57W
Colonia Lavelleja Uruguay 93 31.06S 57.01W
Colonsay i. U.K. 12 56.04N 6.13W
Colorado r. Argentina 93 39.50S 62.02W
Colorado d. U.S.A. 80 39.07N105.27W
Colorado r. Ariz. U.S.A. 81 31.45N114.40W
Colorado r. Tex. U.S.A. 83 28.36N 95.58W
Colorado City U.S.A. 83 32.24N100.52W
Colorado Plateau f. U.S.A. 81 36.30N108.00W
Colorado Springs town U.S.A. 80 38.50N104.49W
Colton S.Dak. U.S.A. 82 43.47N 96.56W
Columbia r. U.S.A. 80 46.15N124.05W
Columbia La. U.S.A. 83 32.06N 92.05W
Columbia Miss. U.S.A. 83 31.15N 89.56W
Columbia Mo. U.S.A. 82 38.57N 92.20W
Columbia S.C. U.S.A. 85 34.00N 81.00W
Columbia Tenn. U.S.A. 85 35.37N 87.02W
Columbia, Mt. Canada 74 52.08N117.20W
Columbia, Sierra mts. Mexico 81 29.30N114.50W
Columbia Basin f. U.S.A. 80 46.55N117.36W
Columbia Falls town U.S.A. 80 48.23N114.11W
Columbia Plateau f. U.S.A. 80 44.00N117.30W
Columbretes, Islas is. Spain 16 39.50N 0.40E
Columbus Ga. U.S.A. 85 32.28N 84.59W
Columbus Ind. U.S.A. 84 39.12N 85.57W
Columbus Miss. U.S.A. 83 33.30N 88.25W
Columbus Mont. U.S.A. 80 45.38N109.15W
Columbus Nebr. U.S.A. 82 41.25N 97.22W
Columbus N.Mex. U.S.A. 81 31.50N107.38W
Columbus Ohio U.S.A. 84 39.59N 83.03W
Columbus Tex. U.S.A. 83 29.42N 96.33W
Colville r. U.S.A. 72 70.06N151.30W
Colwyn Bay town U.K. 10 53.18N 3.43W
Comacchio Italy 15 44.42N 12.11E
Comacchio, Valli di b. Italy 15 44.38N 12.06E
Comai China 41 28.28N 91.33E
Comanche U.S.A. 83 34.22N 97.58W
Comayagua Honduras 87 14.30N 87.39W
Comblain-au-Pont Belgium 14 50.29N 5.32E
Combles France 14 50.01N 2.52E
Combourg France 15 48.25N 1.45W
Comboyne Australia 67 31.35S152.27E
Comeragh Mts. Rep. of Ire. 13 52.17N 7.34W
Comilla Bangla. 41 23.28N 91.10E
Comitán Mexico 86 16.15N 92.08W
Commentry France 17 46.17N 2.44E
Commerce U.S.A. 83 33.15N 95.54W
Commonwealth Territory d. Australia 67 35.00S151.00E
Como Italy 15 45.48N 9.04E
Como, Lago di l. Italy 15 46.05N 9.17E
Comodoro Rivadavia Argentina 93 45.50S 67.30W
Comorin, C. India 38 8.04N 77.35E
Comoros Africa 55 12.15S 44.00E
Compiègne France 15 49.24N 2.50E
Cona China 41 27.59N 91.59E
Co Nag l. China 41 32.00N 91.15E
Conakry Guinea 52 9.30N 13.43W
Concarneau France 17 47.53N 3.55W
Conceição Mozambique 57 18.45S 36.10E
Conceição do Araguaia Brazil 91 8.15S 49.17W
Concepción Argentina 92 27.20S 65.36W
Concepción Chile 93 36.50S 73.03W
Concepción r. Mexico 81 30.32N112.59W
Concepción Paraguay 92 23.22S 57.26W
Concepción del Oro Mexico 83 24.38N101.25W
Concepción del Uruguay Argentina 93 32.30S 58.14W
Conception, Pt. U.S.A. 81 34.27N120.27W
Conception B. Namibia 56 23.53S 14.28E
Conches France 15 48.58N 0.58E
Conchillas Uruguay 93 34.15S 58.04W
Conchos r. Mexico 81 29.32N104.25W
Concord N.C. U.S.A. 85 35.25N 80.34W
Concord N.H. U.S.A. 84 43.12N 71.32W
Concordia Argentina 93 31.24S 58.02W
Concórdia Brazil 90 4.35S 66.35W
Concordia Mexico 81 23.17N106.04W
Concordia U.S.A. 82 39.34N 97.39W
Condé France 15 48.51N 0.33W
Condé-sur-l'Escaut France 14 50.28N 3.35E
Condobolin Australia 67 33.03S147.11E
Condom France 17 43.58N 0.22E
Conegliano Italy 15 45.53N 12.18E
Confolens France 17 46.01N 0.40E
Conghua China 33 23.33N113.34E
Congleton U.K. 10 53.10N 2.12W
Congo Africa 54 1.00S 16.00E
Congo r. see Zaïre r. Zaïre 54
Congonhas Brazil 94 20.30S 43.53W
Coningsby U.K. 10 53.07N 0.09W
Coniston U.K. 10 54.22N 3.06W
Conkouati Congo 54 4.00S 11.16E
Conn, Lough Rep. of Ire. 13 54.01N 9.15W
Connah's Quay town U.K. 10 53.13N 3.03W
Conneaut U.S.A. 84 41.58N 80.34W
Connecticut d. U.S.A. 84 41.45N 72.45W
Connecticut r. U.S.A. 84 41.17N 72.21W
Connellsville U.S.A. 84 40.01N 79.35W
Connemara f. Rep. of Ire. 13 53.32N 9.56W
Conon r. U.K. 12 57.33N 4.33W
Conrad U.S.A. 80 48.10N111.57W
Conroe U.S.A. 83 30.19N 95.27W
Conselheiro Lafaiete Brazil 94 20.40S 43.48W
Consett U.K. 10 54.52N 1.50W
Con Son is. Vietnam 34 8.45N106.38E
Constance, L. see Bodensee Europe 20
Constanța Romania 19 44.10N 28.31E
Constantina Spain 16 37.54N 5.36W
Constantine Algeria 51 36.22N 6.38E
Constitución Chile 93 35.20S 72.25W
Constitución Uruguay 93 31.05S 57.50W
Consuegra Spain 16 39.28N 3.43W
Consul Canada 75 49.21N109.30W
Contact U.S.A. 80 41.48N114.46W
Contai India 41 21.47N 87.45E
Contamana Peru 90 7.19S 75.00W
Contas r. Brazil 91 14.15S 39.00W
Contreras, Embalse de resr. Spain 16 39.32N 1.30W
Contres France 15 47.25N 1.26E
Contwoyto L. Canada 72 65.42N110.50W
Conty France 15 49.44N 2.09E
Conway Ark. U.S.A. 83 35.05N 92.26W
Conway N.H. U.S.A. 84 43.59N 71.07W
Conway S.C. U.S.A. 85 33.51N 79.04W
Conway, L. Australia 66 28.17S135.35E
Conwy r. U.K. 9 53.17N 3.49W
Coober Pedy Australia 66 29.01S134.43E
Cooch Behār India 41 26.19N 89.26E
Cook Australia 65 30.37S130.25E
Cook, C. Canada 72 50.08N127.55W
Cook, Mt. New Zealand 60 43.45S170.12E
Cooke, Mt. Australia 63 32.26S116.18E
Cookeville U.S.A. 85 36.10N 85.30W
Cookhouse R.S.A. 56 32.44S 25.47E
Cook Inlet U.S.A. 72 60.30N152.00W
Cook Is. Pacific Oc. 68 15.00S160.00W
Cookstown U.K. 13 54.39N 6.46W
Cook Str. New Zealand 60 41.15S174.30E
Cooktown Australia 64 15.29S145.15E
Coolabah Australia 67 31.02S146.45E
Coolah Australia 67 31.48S149.45E
Coolamara Australia 66 31.59S143.42E
Coolangatta Australia 67 28.10S153.26E
Coolawanyah Australia 62 21.47S117.48E
Coolgardie Australia 63 31.01S121.12E
Coolidge U.S.A. 81 32.59N111.31W
Cooma Australia 67 36.15S149.07E
Coombah Australia 66 32.58S141.39E
Coomberdale Australia 63 30.29S116.03E
Coonalpyn Australia 66 35.41S139.52E
Coonamble Australia 67 30.55S148.26E
Coonana Australia 63 31.01S123.05E
Coonawarra Australia 66 37.16S140.50E
Coondambo Australia 66 31.07S135.20E
Cooper Creek r. Australia 66 28.33S137.46E
Coopernook Australia 67 31.49S152.38E
Coorow Australia 63 29.53S116.01E
Cooroy Australia 64 26.29S152.50E
Coos Bay town U.S.A. 80 43.22N124.13W
Cootamundra Australia 67 34.41S148.03E
Cootehill Rep. of Ire. 13 54.05N 7.05W
Copainalá Mexico 86 17.05N 93.12W
Copán ruins Honduras 87 14.52N 89.10W
Cope U.S.A. 80 39.40N102.51W
Copenhagen see København Denmark 23
Copiapó Chile 92 27.22S 70.20W
Copparo Italy 15 44.54N 11.49E
Copperbelt d. Zambia 56 13.00S 28.00E
Copper Belt f. Zambia 55 12.40S 28.00E
Copper Center U.S.A. 72 61.58N145.19W
Copper Cliff town Canada 76 46.28N 81.04W
Copper Harbor U.S.A. 84 47.28N 87.54W
Coppermine r. Canada 72 67.54N115.10W
Coppermine town Canada 72 67.49N115.12W
Copper Mountain town Canada 74 49.20N120.30W
Copper Queen Zimbabwe 56 17.31S 29.20E
Copperton R.S.A. 56 30.00S 22.15E
Copp L. Canada 74 60.14N114.40W
Coqên China 41 31.13N 85.12E
Coquet r. U.K. 10 55.21N 1.35W
Coquille U.S.A. 80 43.11N124.11W
Coquimbo Chile 92 29.58S 71.21W
Corabia Romania 19 43.45N 24.29E
Coracora Peru 90 15.02S 73.48W
Coral Harbour town Canada 73 64.10N 83.15W
Coral Sea Pacific Oc. 64 14.30S149.30E
Coral Sea Basin Pacific Oc. 68 14.00S152.00E
Corangamite, L. Australia 66 38.10S143.25E
Corbeil France 15 48.37N 2.29E
Corbeny France 15 49.28N 3.49E
Corbigny France 15 47.15N 3.40E
Corbin U.S.A. 85 36.58N 84.06W
Corby U.K. 11 52.29N 0.41W
Corcubión Spain 16 42.56N 9.12W
Córdoba Argentina 92 31.25S 64.10W
Córdoba d. Argentina 92 30.30S 64.30W
Córdoba Mexico 86 18.55N 96.55W
Córdoba Spain 16 37.53N 4.46W
Córdoba, Sierras de mts. Argentina 92 30.30S 64.40W
Cordova U.S.A. 72 60.33N139.44W
Corentyne r. Guyana 91 5.10N 57.20W
Corfield Australia 64 21.43S143.22E
Corfu i. see Kérkira i. Greece 19
Coricudgy, Mt. Australia 67 32.51S150.25E
Corigliano Italy 19 39.36N 16.31E
Corindi Australia 67 30.00S153.21E
Corinne Canada 75 50.04N104.40W
Corinth Miss. U.S.A. 83 34.56N 88.31W
Corinthian Australia 63 31.05S119.13E
Corinto Nicaragua 87 12.29N 87.14W
Cork Rep. of Ire. 13 51.54N 8.28W
Cork d. Rep. of Ire. 13 52.00N 8.40W
Cork Harbour est. Rep. of Ire. 13 51.50N 8.17W
Cormeilles France 15 49.15N 0.23E
Cormorant Canada 75 54.14N100.35W
Corner Brook town Canada 77 48.57N 57.57W
Corner Inlet b. Australia 67 38.43S146.20E
Corning Ark. U.S.A. 83 36.24N 90.35W
Corning N.Y. U.S.A. 84 42.09N 77.04W
Corno, Monte mtn. Italy 18 42.29N 13.33E
Cornwall Canada 76 45.02N 74.45W
Cornwall d. U.K. 11 50.26N 4.40W
Cornwallis I. Canada 73 75.00N 95.00W
Coro Venezuela 90 11.27N 69.41W
Coroatá Brazil 91 4.08S 44.08W
Čoroch r. U.S.S.R. 25 41.36N 41.35E
Coroico Bolivia 92 16.10S 67.44W
Coromandel New Zealand 60 36.46S175.30E
Coromandel Pen. New Zealand 60 36.45S175.30E
Corona U.S.A. 81 34.15N105.36W
Coronation G. Canada 72 68.00N112.00W
Coronation I. U.S.A. 74 55.52N134.20W
Coronda Argentina 93 31.55S 60.55W
Coronel Chile 93 37.01S 73.08W
Coronel Brandsen Argentina 93 35.10S 58.15W
Coronel Pringles Argentina 93 37.56S 61.25W
Coronel Suárez Argentina 93 37.30S 61.52W
Coropuna mtn. Peru 90 15.31S 72.45W
Corowa Australia 67 36.00S146.20E
Corozal Belize 87 18.23N 88.23W
Corpus Christi U.S.A. 83 27.48N 97.24W
Correggio Italy 15 44.46N 10.47E
Correntes, Cabo das c. Mozambique 57 24.11S 35.35E
Corrib, Lough Rep. of Ire. 13 53.26N 9.14W
Corrientes Argentina 92 27.30S 58.48W
Corrientes d. Argentina 92 28.00S 57.00W
Corrientes, Cabo c. Colombia 90 5.30N 77.34W
Corrigan U.S.A. 83 31.00N 94.50W
Corrigin Australia 63 32.21S117.52E
Corrimal Australia 67 34.21S150.54E
Corry U.S.A. 84 41.56N 79.39W
Corryong Australia 67 36.11S147.58E
Corse d. France 17 42.00N 9.10E
Corse i. France 17 42.00N 9.10E
Corse, Cap c. France 17 43.00N 9.21E
Corsham U.K. 11 51.25N 2.11W
Corsica i. see Corse i. France 17
Corsicana U.S.A. 83 32.06N 96.28W
Corte France 17 42.18N 9.08E
Cortegana Spain 16 37.55N 6.49W
Cortez Colo. U.S.A. 80 37.21N108.35W
Cortez Nev. U.S.A. 80 40.09N116.38W
Cortina Italy 18 46.32N 12.08E
Cortland N.Y. U.S.A. 84 42.36N 76.11W
Cortona Italy 18 43.16N 11.59E
Coruche Portugal 16 38.58N 8.31W
Çoruh r. Turkey see Čoroch r. U.S.S.R. 42
Çorum Turkey 42 40.31N 34.57E
Corumbá Brazil 92 19.00S 57.27W
Corumbá r. Brazil 94 18.15S 48.55W
Corunna Australia 66 32.47S137.08E
Corvallis U.S.A. 80 44.34N123.16W
Corwen U.K. 10 52.59N 3.23W
Cosenza Italy 18 39.17N 16.14E
Cosne France 15 47.25N 2.55E
Coso Junction U.S.A. 81 36.03N117.58W
Cosson r. France 15 47.30N 1.15E
Costa Brava f. Spain 16 41.30N 3.00E
Costa del Sol f. Spain 16 36.30N 4.00W
Costa Mesa U.S.A. 81 33.39N117.55W
Costa Rica C. America 87 10.00N 84.00W
Costeşti Romania 19 44.40N 24.53E
Cotabato Phil. 37 7.14N124.15E
Cotagaita Bolivia 92 20.50S 65.41W
Côte d'Azur f. France 17 43.20N 6.45E
Côte-d'Or d. France 15 47.30N 4.50E
Côte d'Or f. France 15 47.10N 4.50E
Cotonou Benin 53 6.24N 2.31E
Cotopaxi mtn. Ecuador 90 0.40S 78.28W
Cotswold Hills U.K. 11 51.50N 2.00W
Cottage Grove U.S.A. 80 43.48N123.03W
Cottbus E. Germany 20 51.43N 14.21E
Cottbus d. E. Germany 20 51.45N 14.00E
Cottonwood U.S.A. 81 34.45N112.01W
Cotulla U.S.A. 83 28.26N 99.14W
Coucy France 15 49.31N 3.19E
Couer d'Alene U.S.A. 80 47.41N117.00W
Couesnon r. France 15 48.37N 1.31W
Coulagh B. Rep. of Ire. 13 51.42N 10.00W
Coulee City U.S.A. 80 47.37N119.17W
Coulommiers France 15 48.49N 3.05E
Coulonge r. Canada 76 45.51N 76.46W
Council U.S.A. 72 64.55N163.44W
Council Bluffs U.S.A. 82 41.16N 95.52W
Coupar Angus U.K. 12 56.33N 3.17W
Courson-les-Carrières France 15 47.36N 3.30E
Courtalain France 15 48.05N 1.09E
Courtenay Canada 74 49.41N125.00W
Coutances France 15 49.03N 1.29W
Coutras France 17 45.02N 0.07W
Couvin Belgium 14 50.03N 4.30E
Cové Benin 53 7.16N 2.20E
Cove City U.S.A. 85 35.11N 77.20W
Coventry U.K. 11 52.25N 1.31W
Covilhã Portugal 16 40.17N 7.30W
Covington Ga. U.S.A. 85 33.35N 83.52W
Covington Ky. U.S.A. 84 39.04N 84.30W
Covington Okla. U.S.A. 83 36.18N 97.35W
Covington Tenn. U.S.A. 83 35.34N 89.38W
Covington Va. U.S.A. 85 37.48N 80.01W
Cowal, L. Australia 67 33.36S147.22E
Cowan Canada 75 52.05N100.45W
Cowan, L. Australia 63 32.00S122.00E
Cowangie Australia 66 35.14S141.28E
Cowansville Canada 77 45.12N 72.45W
Cowcowing, L. Australia 63 31.01S117.18E
Cowdenbeath U.K. 12 56.07N 3.21W
Cowell Australia 66 33.41S136.55E
Cowes U.K. 11 50.45N 1.18W
Cowra Australia 67 33.50S148.45E
Cox r. Australia 64 15.19S135.25E
Coxim Brazil 92 18.28S 54.37W
Cox's Bāzār Bangla. 41 21.26N 91.59E
Coyuca de Catalán Mexico 86 18.20N100.39W
Cozad U.S.A. 82 40.52N 99.59W
Cozes France 17 45.35N 0.50W
Cozumel, Isla de i. Mexico 87 20.30N 87.00W
Craboon Australia 67 32.02S149.29E
Cradock R.S.A. 56 32.10S 25.35E
Craig Alas. U.S.A. 74 55.29N133.09W
Craig Colo. U.S.A. 80 40.31N107.33W
Craigavon U.K. 13 54.28N 6.25W
Craignure U.K. 12 56.28N 5.42W
Craigsville U.S.A. 85 38.04N 79.23W
Crail U.K. 12 56.16N 2.38W
Crailsheim W. Germany 20 49.09N 10.06E
Craiova Romania 19 44.18N 23.46E
Cranbrook Australia 63 34.15S117.32E
Cranbrook Canada 74 49.30N115.46W
Crane U.S.A. 80 43.25N118.34W
Cranston U.S.A. 84 41.47N 71.26W
Craon France 15 47.50N 0.58W
Craonne France 15 49.27N 3.46E
Crater L. U.S.A. 80 42.56N122.06W
Crateús Brazil 91 5.10S 40.39W
Crati r. Italy 19 39.43N 16.29E
Crato Amazonas Brazil 90 7.25S 63.00W
Crato Ceará Brazil 91 7.10S 39.25W
Craughwell Rep. of Ire. 13 53.14N 8.44W
Crawford U.S.A. 82 42.41N103.25W
Crawfordsville U.S.A. 84 40.03N 86.54W
Crawfordville U.S.A. 85 30.12N 84.21W
Crawley U.K. 11 51.07N 0.10W
Crazy Mts. U.S.A. 80 46.08N110.20W
Crécy France 17 50.15N 1.53E
Crécy-sur-Serre France 15 49.42N 3.37E
Cree r. Canada 75 59.00N105.47W
Creede U.S.A. 80 37.51N106.56W
Cree L. Canada 75 57.30N106.30W
Creil France 15 49.16N 2.29E
Crema Italy 15 45.22N 9.41E
Cremona Italy 15 45.08N 10.03E
Crépy France 15 49.36N 3.31E
Crépy-en-Valois France 15 49.14N 2.54E
Cres i. Yugo. 18 44.50N 14.20E
Cres town Yugo. 18 44.58N 14.25E
Crescent U.S.A. 80 43.29N121.41W
Crescent City U.S.A. 80 41.45N124.12W
Crespo Argentina 93 32.02S 60.20W
Cressy Australia 66 38.02S143.38E
Crest France 17 44.44N 5.02E
Creston Canada 74 49.10N116.31W
Creston Iowa U.S.A. 82 41.04N 94.22W
Creston Oriental de la Sierra Madre mts. Mexico 81 28.40N107.50W
Crestview U.S.A. 85 30.44N 86.34W
Crete i. see Kríti i. Greece 19
Crete U.S.A. 82 40.38N 96.58W
Crete, Sea of see Kritikón Pélagos sea Greece 19
Creus, Cabo de c. Spain 16 42.20N 3.19E
Creuse r. France 17 47.00N 0.35E
Crewe U.K. 10 53.06N 2.28W
Crianlarich U.K. 12 56.23N 4.37W
Criccieth U.K. 10 52.55N 4.15W
Criciúma Brazil 94 28.40S 49.23W
Crieff U.K. 12 56.23N 3.52W
Crillon, Mt. U.S.A. 74 58.39N137.14W
Crimea pen. see Krym pen. U.S.S.R. 25
Crinan U.K. 12 56.06N 5.34W
Cristóbal Colón mtn. Colombia 90 10.53N 73.48W
Crişu Alb r. Romania 21 46.42N 21.17E
Crna r. Yugo. 19 41.33N 21.58E
Crna Gora d. Yugo. 19 43.00N 19.30E
Croaghnameal mtn. Rep. of Ire. 13 54.40N 7.57W
Croatia d. see Hrvatska d. Yugo. 19
Crockett U.S.A. 83 31.19N 95.28W
Crocodile r. Trans. R.S.A. 56 24.11S 26.48E
Croker I. Australia 64 11.12S132.32E
Cromarty Canada 75 58.03N 94.09W
Cromarty U.K. 12 57.40N 4.02W
Cromarty Firth est. U.K. 12 57.41N 4.10W
Cromer U.K. 10 52.56N 1.18E
Cromwell New Zealand 60 45.03S169.14E
Crooked I. Bahamas 87 22.45N 74.00W
Crookhaven Rep. of Ire. 13 51.29N 9.45W
Crookston U.S.A. 82 47.47N 96.37W
Crookwell Australia 67 34.27S149.28E
Croom Rep. of Ire. 13 52.31N 8.43W
Croppa Creek town Australia 67 29.08S150.20E
Crosby U.K. 10 54.11N 4.34W
Crosby U.S.A. 83 31.17N 91.04W
Cross City U.S.A. 85 29.39N 83.09W
Crossett U.S.A. 83 33.08N 91.58W
Cross Fell mtn. U.K. 10 54.43N 2.28W
Cross L. Canada 75 54.45N 97.30W
Cross River d. Nigeria 53 5.45N 8.25E
Crossroads U.S.A. 83 33.30N103.21W
Cross Sd. U.S.A. 74 58.10N136.30W
Crossville U.S.A. 85 35.57N 85.02W
Crotone Italy 19 39.05N 17.06E
Crow r. Canada 74 59.41N124.20W
Crow Agency U.S.A. 80 45.36N107.27W
Crowell U.S.A. 83 33.59N 99.43W
Crowes Australia 66 38.38S143.12E
Crowl r. Australia 67 31.58S144.53E
Crow's Nest Australia 65 27.16S152.03E
Crowsnest Pass Canada 74 49.40N114.40W
Croydе U.K. 11 51.07N 4.13W
Croydon Australia 61 18.12S142.14E
Croydon Australia 64 18.12S142.14E
Croydon U.K. 11 51.23N 0.06W
Crucero U.S.A. 81 35.03N116.10W

Cruger to **Demmin**

Cruger U.S.A. 83 33.14N 90.14W
Cruz, Cabo *c.* Cuba 87 19.52N 77.44W
Cruz Alta Brazil 94 28.38S 53.38W
Cruz del Eje Argentina 92 30.44S 64.49W
Cruzeiro Brazil 94 22.33S 44.59W
Cruzeiro do Sul Brazil 90 7.40S 72.39W
Crystal U.S.A. 82 45.00N 93.25W
Crystal Bridge *town* Australia 66 33.21S138.13E
Crystal City U.S.A. 83 28.41N 99.50W
Crystal River *town* U.S.A. 85 28.54N 82.36W
Csorna Hungary 21 47.37N 17.16E
Csurgó Hungary 21 46.16N 17.06E
Cuamba Mozambique 55 14.48S 36.32E
Cuando *r.* Angola 56 18.30S 23.32E
Cuando-Cubango *d.* Angola 56 16.00S 20.00E
Cuangar Angola 54 17.34S 18.39E
Cuango *r. see* Kwango *r.* Zaïre 54
Cuanza *r.* Angola 54 9.20S 13.09E
Cuanza Norte *d.* Angola 54 8.45S 15.00E
Cuanza Sul *d.* Angola 54 11.00S 15.00E
Cua Rao Vietnam 34 19.16N104.27E
Cuaró Uruguay 93 30.37S 56.54W
Cuaró *r.* Uruguay 93 30.15S 57.01W
Cuauhtémoc Mexico 81 28.25N106.52W
Cuba C. America 87 22.00N 79.00W
Cuba U.S.A. 81 36.01N107.04W
Cuballing Australia 63 32.50S117.07E
Cubango *r. see* Okavango *r.* Angola 54
Cubia *r.* Angola 54 16.00S 21.46E
Cubo Mozambique 57 23.48S 33.55E
Cuchi *r.* Angola 56 15.23S 17.12E
Cuckfield U.K. 11 51.00N 0.08W
Cucuí Brazil 90 1.12N 66.50W
Cúcuta Colombia 90 7.55N 72.31W
Cudahy U.S.A. 82 42.57N 87.52W
Cuddalore India 39 11.43N 79.46E
Cue Australia 62 27.25S117.54E
Cuenca Ecuador 90 2.54S 79.00W
Cuenca Spain 16 40.04N 2.07W
Cuenca, Serranía de *mts.* Spain 16 40.25N 2.00W
Cuernavaca Mexico 86 18.57N 99.15W
Cuero U.S.A. 83 29.06N 97.18W
Cuervo U.S.A. 81 35.02N104.24W
Cuiabá Brazil 91 15.32S 56.05W
Cuiabá *r.* Brazil 92 18.00S 57.25W
Cuidado, Punta *c.* I. de Pascua 69 27.08S109.19W
Cuillin Hills U.K. 12 57.12N 6.13W
Cuilo *r. see* Kwilu *r.* Zaïre 54
Cuito *r.* Angola 54 18.01S 20.50E
Cuito Cuanavale Angola 56 15.11S 19.11E
Culbertson U.S.A. 80 48.09N104.31W
Culcairn Australia 67 35.40S147.03E
Culemborg Neth. 14 51.57N 5.14E
Culgoa *r.* Australia 67 29.56S146.20E
Culiacán Mexico 81 24.48N107.24W
Culiacán *r.* Mexico 81 24.30N107.31W
Cullarin Range *mts.* Australia 67 34.30S149.32E
Cullen U.K. 12 57.41N 2.50W
Cullera Spain 16 39.10N 0.15W
Cullin Sd. U.K. 12 57.03N 6.13W
Culloden Moor U.K. 12 57.29N 3.55W
Culpeper U.S.A. 84 38.28N 77.53W
Cultowa Australia 66 31.24S144.10E
Culuene *r.* Brazil 91 12.56S 52.51W
Culver, Pt. Australia 63 32.52S124.41E
Cuma Angola 54 12.52S 15.05E
Cumaná Venezuela 90 10.29N 64.12W
Cumberland *r.* U.S.A. 85 37.09N 88.25W
Cumberland Ky. U.S.A. 85 36.58N 82.59W
Cumberland Md. U.S.A. 84 39.39N 78.46W
Cumberland Va. U.S.A. 85 37.31N 78.16W
Cumberland Wisc. U.S.A. 82 45.32N 92.01W
Cumberland, C. Vanuatu 68 14.39S166.37E
Cumberland, L. U.S.A. 85 36.45N 84.51W
Cumberland I. U.S.A. 85 30.51N 81.27W
Cumberland L. Canada 75 54.02N102.17W
Cumberland Pen. Canada 73 66.50N 64.00W
Cumberland Plateau *f.* U.S.A. 85 36.00N 85.00W
Cumberland Sd. Canada 73 65.00N 65.30W
Cumbernauld U.K. 12 55.57N 4.00W
Cumbria *d.* U.K. 10 54.30N 3.00W
Cumbrian Mts. U.K. 10 54.32N 3.05W
Cuminá *r.* Brazil 91 1.30S 56.00W
Cummins Australia 66 34.16S135.44E
Cumnock Australia 67 32.56S148.46E
Cumnock U.K. 12 55.27N 4.15W
Cunderdin Australia 63 31.39S117.15E
Cunene *d.* Angola 54 16.00S 16.00E
Cunene *r.* Angola 54 17.15S 11.50E
Cuneo Italy 15 44.22N 7.32E
Cungena Australia 66 32.33S134.40E
Cunnamulla Australia 67 28.04S145.40E
Cuokkaraš'ša *mtn.* Norway 22 69.57N 24.32E
Cuorgnè Italy 15 45.23N 7.39E
Cupar U.K. 12 56.19N 3.01W
Cupica, Golfo de *g.* Colombia 90 6.35N 77.25W
Curaçao *i.* Neth. Antilles 90 12.15N 69.00W
Curacautín Chile 93 38.26S 71.53W
Curaco *r.* Argentina 93 38.49S 65.01W
Curanilahue Chile 93 37.28S 73.21W
Curaray *r.* Peru 90 2.20S 74.05W
Curban Australia 67 31.33S148.36E
Curdlawidny L. Australia 66 30.16S136.20E
Cure *r.* France 15 47.40N 3.41E
Curiapo Venezuela 90 8.33N 61.05W
Curicó Chile 93 34.59S 71.14W
Curitiba Brazil 94 25.24S 49.16W
Curlewis Australia 67 31.08S150.16E
Curnamona Australia 66 31.40S139.35E
Currane, Lough Rep. of Ire. 13 51.50N 10.07W
Currant U.S.A. 80 38.44N115.30W
Curranyalpa Australia 67 30.57S144.33E
Currie Australia 65 39.56S143.52E
Currie U.S.A. 80 40.17N114.44W
Curtin Australia 63 30.50S122.05E
Curtis U.S.A. 82 40.38N100.31W
Curtis I. Australia 64 23.38S151.09E
Curuá *r.* Brazil 91 5.23S 54.22W
Cururupu Brazil 91 1.50S 44.52W
Curuzú Cuatiá Argentina 93 29.50S 58.05W
Curvelo Brazil 94 18.45S 44.27W
Cushendall U.K. 13 55.06N 6.05W
Cushing U.S.A. 83 35.59N 96.46W
Cusna, Monte *mtn.* Italy 15 44.17N 10.23E
Cutana Australia 66 32.14S140.25E
Cut Bank U.S.A. 80 48.38N112.20W
Cuttaburra *r.* Australia 67 29.18S145.00E
Cuttack India 41 20.30N 85.50E
Cuxhaven W. Germany 20 53.52N 8.42E
Cuyuni *r.* Guyana 90 6.24N 58.38W
Cuzco Peru 90 13.32S 71.57W
Cwmbran U.K. 11 51.39N 3.01W
Cyclades *is. see* Kikládhes *is.* Greece 19
Cynthiana U.S.A. 84 38.22N 84.18W
Cypress Hills Canada 75 49.40N109.30W
Cyprus Asia 44 35.00N 33.00E
Cyrenaica *f. see* Barqah *f.* Libya 48
Czechoslovakia Europe 20 49.30N 15.00E
Czeremcha Poland 21 52.32N 23.15E
Czersk Poland 21 53.48N 18.00E
Częstochowa Poland 21 50.49N 19.07E

D

Dà *r.* Vietnam 34 21.20N105.24E
Da'an China 32 45.30N124.18E
Ḍab'ah Jordan 44 31.36N 36.04E
Dabakala Ivory Coast 52 8.19N 4.24W
Daba Shan *mts.* China 33 32.00N109.00E
Dabat Ethiopia 49 12.58N 37.48E
Dabbāgh, Jabal *mtn.* Saudi Arabia 44 27.51N 35.43E
Dabhoi India 40 22.11N 73.26E
Dabie Shan *mts.* China 33 31.15N115.20E
Dabola Guinea 52 10.48N 11.02W
Dabra India 41 25.54N 78.20E
Dabu Jiangxi China 33 26.47N116.04E
Dacca *see* Dhākā Bangla. 41
Dachau W. Germany 20 48.15N 11.26E
Dadanawa Guyana 90 2.30N 59.30W
Dade City U.S.A. 85 28.23N 82.11W
Dādhar Pakistan 40 29.28N 67.39E
Dādra & Nagar Haveli *d.* India 40 20.05N 73.00E
Dādu Pakistan 40 26.44N 67.47E
Dadu He *r.* China 39 28.47N104.40E
Daet Phil. 37 14.07N122.58E
Dagali Norway 23 60.25N 8.27E
Dagana Senegal 52 16.28N 15.35W
Daga Post Sudan 49 9.12N 33.58E
Dagash Sudan 48 19.22N 33.24E
Dagu China 32 38.58N117.40E
Dagua P.N.G. 37 3.25S143.20E
Daguan China 30 27.44N103.53E
Dagupan Phil. 37 16.02N120.21E
Dagzê China 41 29.45N105.45E
Dagzê Co *l.* China 41 31.45N 87.50E
Dahan-e Qowmghī Afghan. 40 34.28N 66.31E
Da Hinggan Ling *mts.* China 31 50.00N122.10E
Dahlak Archipelago *is.* Ethiopia 48 15.45N 40.30E
Dahlak Kebir I. Ethiopia 48 15.38N 40.11E
Dahlem W. Germany 20 50.23N 6.33E
Dahlgren U.S.A. 85 38.20N 77.03W
Dahra Senegal 52 15.21N 15.29W
Dahujiang China 33 26.06N114.58E
Dahūk Iraq 42 36.52N 43.00E
Daḩy, Nafūd ad *f.* Saudi Arabia 45 22.00N 45.25E
Ḍaḩyah, 'Urūq *f.* S. Yemen 45 18.45N 51.15E
Dai Hai *l.* China 32 40.31N112.43E
Dailekh Nepal 41 28.50N 81.43E
Daimiel Spain 16 39.05N 3.35W
Daitō Japan 35 34.42N135.38E
Daiyun Shan *mtn.* China 33 25.41N118.11E
Dājal Pakistan 40 29.33N 70.23E
Dajarra Australia 64 21.42S139.31E
Dajing China 33 28.25N121.10E
Dakar Senegal 52 14.38N 17.27W
Dakhal, Wādī ad *r.* Egypt 44 28.49N 32.45E
Dākhilah, Al Wāḩāt ad *oasis* Egypt 42 25.30N 28.10E
Dakhla W. Sahara 50 23.43N 15.57W
Dakhlet Nouadhibou *d.* Mauritania 50 20.30N 16.00W
Dakingari Nigeria 53 11.40N 4.06E
Dakota City U.S.A. 82 42.25N 96.25W
Dakovica Yugo. 19 42.23N 20.25E
Dal *r.* Sweden 23 60.38N 17.27E
Dala Congo 54 1.40N 16.39E
Dalaba Guinea 52 10.47N 12.12W
Dalai Nur *l.* China 32 43.27N116.25E
Dalandzadgad Mongolia 32 43.30N104.18E
Da Lat Vietnam 34 11.56N108.25E
Dālbandin Pakistan 40 28.53N 64.25E
Dalbeattie U.K. 12 54.55N 3.49W
Dalby Australia 65 27.11S151.12E
Dalby Sweden 23 55.40N 13.20E
Dale Hordaland Norway 23 60.35N 5.49E
Dale Sogn og Fj. Norway 23 61.22N 5.24E
Dalen Norway 23 59.27N 8.00E
Dalgety Australia 67 36.30S148.50E
Dalgonally Australia 64 20.09S141.16E
Dalhart U.S.A. 83 36.04N102.31W
Dalhousie Canada 77 48.04N 66.23W
Dalhousie Jammu & Kashmir 40 32.32N 75.59E
Dali China 30 25.42N100.11E
Dalkeith U.K. 12 55.54N 3.04W
Dallas Oreg. U.S.A. 80 44.55N123.19W
Dallas Tex. U.S.A. 83 32.47N 96.48W
Dallastown U.S.A. 85 39.54N 76.39W
Dall I. U.S.A. 74 55.00N133.00W
Dalli Rajhāra India 41 20.35N 81.04E
Dalmally U.K. 12 56.25N 4.58W
Dalmas, Lac *l.* Canada 77 53.27N 71.50W
Dalmellington U.K. 12 55.19N 4.24W
Dalnerechensk U.S.S.R. 31 45.55N133.45E
Daloa Ivory Coast 52 6.56N 6.28W
Dalou Shan *mts.* China 33 28.25N107.15E
Dalqū Sudan 48 20.07N 30.35E
Dalrymple, Mt. Australia 64 21.02S148.38E
Dalsingh Sarai India 41 25.40N 85.50E
Dalton Canada 76 48.10N 84.00W
Dalton U.S.A. 85 34.46N 84.59W
Daltonganj India 41 24.02N 84.04E
Dalupiri *i.* Phil. 33 19.05N121.13E
Dalveen Australia 67 28.26S151.55E
Dalvik Iceland 22 65.58N 18.28W
Dalwhinnie U.K. 12 56.56N 4.15W
Daly *r.* Australia 62 13.20S130.19E
Daly City U.S.A. 80 37.42N122.29W
Daly Waters *town* Australia 64 16.15S133.22E
Damā, Wādī *r.* Saudi Arabia 42 27.04N 35.48E
Damān India 40 20.25N 72.51E
Damān *d.* India 40 20.10N 73.00E
Damanhūr Egypt 44 31.03N 30.28E
Damar *i.* Indonesia 37 7.10S128.30E
Damascus *see* Dimashq Syria 44
Damaturu Nigeria 53 11.49N 11.50E
Damāvand, Qolleh-ye *mtn.* Iran 43 35.47N 52.04E
Damba Angola 54 6.44S 15.17E
Damen *i.* China 33 27.58N121.05E
Dāmghān Iran 43 36.09N 54.22E
Damiaoshan China 33 24.43N109.15E
Daming Shan *mts.* China 33 23.23N108.30E
Dammartin-en-Goële France 15 49.03N 2.41E
Dāmodar *r.* India 41 22.17N 88.05E
Damoh India 41 23.50N 79.27E
Damongo Ghana 52 9.06N 1.48W
Dampier Australia 62 20.45S116.50E
Dampier, Selat *str.* Pacific Oc. 37 0.30S130.50E
Dampier Land Australia 62 17.20S123.00E
Damqawt S. Yemen 45 16.34N 52.50E
Damxung China 41 30.32N 91.06E
Dana Canada 75 52.18N105.42W
Danakil *f.* Ethiopia 49 13.00N 41.00E
Danané Ivory Coast 52 7.21N 8.10W
Da Nang Vietnam 34 16.04N108.13E
Dānāpur India 41 25.38N 85.03E
Danba China 30 30.57N101.55E
Danbury Conn. U.S.A. 85 41.24N 73.26W
Dand Afghan. 40 31.37N 65.41E
Dandaragan Australia 63 30.40S115.42E
Dande *r.* Angola 54 8.30S 13.23E
Dandeldhura Nepal 41 29.17N 80.36E
Dandenong Australia 67 37.59S145.14E
Dandong China 32 40.10N124.25E
Danger Is. Cook Is. 68 10.53S165.49W
Dangla Ethiopia 49 11.18N 36.54E
Dangqên China 41 31.41N 91.51E
Dangriga Belize 87 16.58N 88.13W
Dangshan China 32 34.25N116.24E
Dangyang China 33 30.52N111.40E
Daniel U.S.A. 80 42.52N110.04W
Daniell Australia 63 32.37S121.30E
Daniel's Harbour Canada 77 50.14N 57.35W
Danilov U.S.S.R. 24 58.10N 40.12E
Daning China 32 36.32N110.47E
Danisa Hills Kenya 55 3.10N 39.37E
Danja Nigeria 53 11.29N 7.30E
Danlí Honduras 87 14.02N 86.30W
Dannenberg W. Germany 20 53.06N 11.05E
Dannevirke New Zealand 60 40.12S176.08E
Dannhauser R.S.A. 56 28.00S 30.03E
Dansville U.S.A. 84 42.34N 77.41W
Dantewāra India 41 18.54N 81.21E
Danube *r.* Europe 21 45.26N 29.38E
Danube, Mouths of the *see* Dunării, Delta *f.* Romania 21
Danville Canada 77 45.47N 72.01W
Danville Ill. U.S.A. 82 40.09N 87.37W
Danville Ky. U.S.A. 85 37.40N 84.49W
Danville Va. U.S.A. 85 36.34N 79.25W
Dan Xian China 33 19.30N109.35E
Danzig, G. of Poland 21 54.45N 19.15E
Daordeng China 32 40.47N119.05E
Daosa India 40 26.53N 76.20E
Daoukro Ivory Coast 52 7.10N 3.58W
Dao Xian China 33 25.32N111.35E
Daozhen China 33 28.46N107.45E
Dapango Togo 52 10.51N 0.15E
Dapingfang China 32 41.25N120.07E
Da Qaidam China 30 37.44N 95.08E
Daqinggou China 32 41.22N114.13E
Daqing Shan *mts.* China 32 41.00N111.00E
Daqqāq Sudan 49 12.56N 26.58E
Daqq-e Patargān *f.* Iran 43 33.30N 60.40E
Dar'ā Syria 44 32.37N 36.06E
Dārāb Iran 43 28.45N 54.34E
Darāban Pakistan 40 31.44N 70.20E
Darabani Romania 21 48.11N 26.35E
Darakht-e Yahyá Afghan. 40 31.50N 68.08E
Dārān Iran 43 33.00N 50.27E
Darband, Kūh-e *mtn.* Iran 43 31.33N 57.08E
Darbhanga India 41 26.10N 85.54E
Darby Mont. U.S.A. 80 46.01N114.11W
Darby Penn. U.S.A. 85 39.54N 75.15W
D'Arcy Canada 74 50.33N122.32W
Dardanelles *see* Çanakkale Boğazi *str.* Turkey 19
Dareel Australia 67 28.50S148.49E
Dar es Salaam Tanzania 55 6.51S 39.18E
Dar es Salaam *d.* Tanzania 55 6.45S 39.10E
Darfield New Zealand 60 43.29S172.07E
Dārfūr *d.* Sudan 49 13.20N 25.00E
Dargan Ata U.S.S.R. 28 40.30N 62.10E
Dargaville New Zealand 60 35.57S173.53E
Dargo Australia 67 37.30S147.16E
Darhan Mongolia 30 49.34N106.23E
Darie Hills Somali Rep. 45 8.15N 47.25E
Darién, Golfo del *g.* Colombia 90 9.20N 77.30W
Darjeeling India 41 27.02N 88.16E
Darkan Australia 63 33.19S116.42E
Darke Peak *mtn.* Australia 66 33.28S136.12E
Darling *r.* Australia 66 34.05S141.57E
Darling Downs *f.* Australia 65 28.00S149.45E
Darling Range *mts.* Australia 63 32.00S116.30E
Darlington U.K. 10 54.33N 1.33W
Darlington Point *town* Australia 67 34.36S146.01E
Darłowe Poland 20 54.26N 16.23E
Darmstadt W. Germany 20 49.52N 8.30E
Darnah Libya 48 32.45N 22.39E
Darnah *d.* Libya 48 31.30N 23.30E
Darnétal France 15 49.27N 1.09E
Darnick Australia 66 32.55S143.39E
Darnley, C. Antarctica 96 68.00S 69.00E
Daroca Spain 16 41.09N 1.25W
Darreh Gaz Iran 43 37.22N 59.08E
Dar Rounga *f.* C.A.R. 49 9.25N 21.30E
Dartmoor Australia 66 37.58S141.19E
Dartmoor Forest *hills* U.K. 11 50.33N 3.55W
Dartmouth Canada 77 44.40N 63.34W
Dartmouth U.K. 11 50.21N 3.35W
Dartry Mts. Rep. of Ire. 13 54.23N 8.25W
Daru P.N.G. 64 9.04S143.12E
Darvaza U.S.S.R. 28 40.12N 58.24E
Darvel, Teluk *b.* Malaysia 36 4.40N118.30E
Darwen U.K. 10 53.42N 2.29W
Dārwha India 41 20.19N 77.46E
Darwin Australia 64 12.23S130.44E
Daryācheh-ye Bakhtegān *l.* Iran 43 29.20N 54.05E
Daryācheh-ye Namak *l.* Iran 43 34.45N 51.36E
Daryācheh-ye Rezā'īyeh *l.* Iran 43 37.40N 45.28E
Daryācheh-ye Sīstān *f.* Iran 43 31.00N 61.15E
Darya Khān Pakistan 40 31.48N 71.06E
Daryāpur India 40 20.56N 77.20E
Dasāda India 40 23.19N 71.50E
Dasht *r.* Pakistan 40 25.10N 61.40E
Dashte-e Māṛgow *des.* Afghan. 43 30.45N 63.00E
Dasht-e Kavīr *des.* Iran 43 34.40N 55.00E
Dasht-e Lūt *des.* Iran 43 31.30N 58.00E
Dashui Nur China 32 42.45N116.47E
Daspalla India 41 20.21N 84.51E
Dassa-Zoumé Benin 53 7.50N 2.13E
Dastgardān Iran 43 34.19N 56.51E
Dastjerd Iran 43 34.33N 50.15E
Datia India 41 25.40N 78.28E
Datong China 32 40.10N113.15E
Datteln W. Germany 14 51.40N 7.20E
Datu, Tanjung *c.* Malaysia 36 2.00N109.30E
Datu Piang Phil. 37 7.02N124.30E
Daua *r.* Kenya *see* Dawa *r.* Ethiopia 49
Dāud Khel Pakistan 40 32.53N 71.34E
Daudnagar India 41 25.02N 84.24E
Daugavpils U.S.S.R. 24 55.52N 26.31E
Daun W. Germany 14 50.11N 6.50E
Dauphin Canada 75 51.09N100.03W
Dauphiné, Alpes du *mts.* France 17 44.35N 5.45E
Dauphin L. Canada 75 51.17N 99.48W
Daura Nigeria 53 13.05N 8.18E
Dāvangere India 38 14.30N 75.52E
Davao Phil. 37 7.05N125.38E
Davao G. Phil. 37 6.30N126.00E
Daveluyville Canada 77 46.12N 72.08W
Davenport U.S.A. 82 41.32N 90.36W
Davenport Downs *town* Australia 64 24.09S141.08E
Daventry U.K. 11 52.16N 1.10W
David Panama 87 8.26N 82.26W
David-Gorodok U.S.S.R. 21 52.04N 27.10E
Davis U.S.A. 80 38.33N121.44W
Davis Creek *town* U.S.A. 80 41.44N120.24W
Davis Sea Antarctica 96 66.00S 90.00E
Davis Str. N. America 73 66.00N 58.00W
Davlekanovo U.S.S.R. 24 54.12N 55.00E
Davos Switz. 20 46.47N 9.50E
Dawa China 32 40.58N122.00E
Dawa *r.* Ethiopia 49 4.11N 42.06E
Dawaxung China 41 31.26N 85.06E
Dawlish U.K. 11 50.34N 3.28W
Dawna Range *mts.* Burma 34 17.00N 98.00E
Dawson Canada 72 64.04N139.24W
Dawson U.S.A. 85 31.47N 84.27W
Dawson Creek *town* Canada 74 55.45N120.15W
Dawson Range *f.* Canada 72 62.40N139.00W
Dawu China 30 31.00N101.09E
Dax France 17 43.43N 1.03W
Daxian China 33 31.10N107.28E
Daxing China 32 39.44N116.20E
Daylesford Australia 66 37.22S144.12E
Dayman *r.* Uruguay 93 31.25S 58.00W
Dayong Hunan China 33 29.06N110.24E
Dayr az Zawr Syria 42 35.20N 40.08E
Dayton N.Y. U.S.A. 76 42.25N 78.58W
Dayton Ohio U.S.A. 84 39.45N 84.10W
Dayton Tenn. U.S.A. 85 35.30N 85.01W
Dayton Wash. U.S.A. 80 46.19N117.59W
Daytona Beach *town* U.S.A. 85 29.11N 81.01W
Dayu China 33 25.24N114.22E
Da Yunhe *canal* China 32 39.10N117.12E
Dazhu China 33 30.50N107.12E
De Aar R.S.A. 56 30.39S 24.01E
Dead Sea Jordan 44 31.25N 35.30E
Deakin Australia 63 30.46S128.58E
Deal U.K. 11 51.13N 1.25E
De'an China 33 29.20N115.46E
Deán Funes Argentina 92 30.25S 64.20W
Dearborn U.S.A. 84 42.18N 83.14W
Dease *r.* Canada 74 59.54N128.30W
Dease Arm *b.* Canada 72 66.52N119.37W
Dease L. Canada 74 58.05N130.04W
Death Valley *f.* U.S.A. 81 36.30N117.00W
Death Valley *town* U.S.A. 81 36.18N116.25W
Death Valley Nat. Monument U.S.A. 80 36.30N117.00W
Deauville France 15 49.21N 0.04E
Debar Yugo. 19 41.31N 20.31E
Debica Poland 21 50.04N 21.24E
Deblin Poland 21 51.35N 21.50E
Deborah, L. Australia 63 30.45S119.07E
Debre Birhan Ethiopia 49 9.40N 39.33E
Debrecen Hungary 21 47.30N 21.37E
Debre Tabor Ethiopia 49 11.50N 38.05E
Decatur Ala. U.S.A. 85 34.36N 87.00W
Decatur Ga. U.S.A. 85 33.45N 84.17W
Decatur Ill. U.S.A. 82 39.51N 89.32W
Decatur Ind. U.S.A. 84 40.50N 84.57W
Deccan *f.* India 38 18.30N 77.30E
Decelles, Lac *l.* Canada 76 47.40N 78.10W
Dechu India 40 26.47N 72.20E
Děčín Czech. 20 50.48N 14.15E
Decize France 20 46.50N 3.27E
De Cocksdorp Neth. 14 53.12N 4.52E
Decorah U.S.A. 82 43.18N 91.48W
Deda Romania 21 46.57N 24.53E
Dédi Ivory Coast 52 8.34N 3.33W
Dediāpada India 40 21.35N 73.40E
Dedza Malaŵi 55 14.20S 34.24E
Dee *r.* D. and G. U.K. 12 54.50N 4.05W
Dee *r.* Grampian U.K. 12 57.07N 2.04W
Dee *r.* Wales U.K. 10 53.13N 3.05W
Deep B. Canada 74 61.15N116.35W
Deepdale Australia 62 21.42S116.11E
Deep River *town* Canada 76 46.04N 77.29W
Deep Well Australia 64 24.25S134.05E
Deer Lake *town* Canada 77 49.07N 57.35W
Deer Lodge U.S.A. 80 46.24N112.44W
Deesa India 40 24.15N 72.10E
Deeth U.S.A. 80 41.04N115.18W
Defiance U.S.A. 84 41.17N 84.21W
De Funiak Springs *town* U.S.A. 85 30.41N 86.08W
Deggendorf W. Germany 20 48.51N 12.59E
De Grey Australia 62 20.10S119.09E
De Grey *r.* Australia 62 20.12S119.11E
Deh Bīd Iran 43 30.38N 53.12E
Dehej India 40 21.42N 72.35E
Dehibat Tunisia 51 32.01N 10.42E
Dehra Dūn India 41 30.19N 78.02E
Dehri India 41 24.52N 84.11E
Deh Shū Afghan. 40 30.28N 63.25E
Dehua China 33 25.30N118.14E
Deinze Belgium 14 50.59N 3.32E
Dej Romania 21 47.08N 23.55E
Deje Sweden 23 59.36N 13.28E
Dejiang China 33 28.19N108.05E
Dekemhare Ethiopia 48 15.05N 39.02E
Dekese Zaïre 54 3.25S 21.24E
Dekina Nigeria 53 7.43N 7.04E
De Land U.S.A. 85 29.02N 81.18W
Delano U.S.A. 81 35.41N119.15W
Delārām Afghan. 40 32.11N 63.25E
Delaronde L. Canada 75 54.05N107.05W
Delaware *d.* U.S.A. 85 39.10N 75.30W
Delaware *r.* U.S.A. 85 39.20N 75.25W
Delaware *town* U.S.A. 84 40.18N 83.06W
Delaware B. U.S.A. 85 39.05N 75.15W
Delaware Water Gap *town* U.S.A. 85 40.59N 75.09W
Delaware Water Gap Nat. Recreation Area U.S.A. 85 41.07N 75.06W
Delegate Australia 67 37.03S148.58E
Delfinópolis Brazil 94 20.21S 46.51W
Delft Neth. 14 52.01N 4.23E
Delfzijl Neth. 14 53.20N 6.56E
Delgado, C. Mozambique 55 10.45S 40.38E
Delhi India 40 28.40N 77.13E
Delhi *d.* India 40 28.37N 77.10E
Delicias Mexico 81 28.13N105.28W
Délimbé C.A.R. 49 9.53N 22.37E
Delingha China 30 37.16N 97.12E
Dell City U.S.A. 81 31.56N105.12W
Delmar U.S.A. 85 38.27N 75.34W
Delmarva Pen. U.S.A. 85 38.48N 75.47W
Delmenhorst W. Germany 20 53.03N 8.37E
De Long Mts. U.S.A. 72 68.20N162.00W
Delorme, Lac *l.* Canada 77 54.40N 69.50W
Delphos U.S.A. 84 40.50N 84.21W
Del Rio U.S.A. 83 29.22N100.54W
Delta Colo. U.S.A. 80 38.44N108.04W
Delta Utah U.S.A. 80 39.21N112.35W
Delungra Australia 67 29.38S150.50E
Demak Indonesia 37 6.53S110.40E
Demba Zaïre 54 5.28S 22.14E
Dembi Ethiopia 49 8.05N 36.27E
Dembia C.A.R. 49 5.07N 24.25E
Dembidolo Ethiopia 49 8.30N 34.48E
Demer *r.* Belgium 14 50.59N 4.42E
Deming U.S.A. 81 32.16N107.45W
Demmin E. Germany 20 53.54N 13.02E

Demmitt to **Drogheda**

Demmitt Canada **74** 55.20N119.50W
Demonte Italy **15** 44.19N 7.17E
Demopolis U.S.A. **83** 32.31N 87.50W
Demotte U.S.A. **84** 41.07N 87.14W
Dêmqog China **41** 32.43N 79.29E
Denain France **14** 50.20N 3.24E
Denbigh U.K. **10** 53.11N 3.25W
Den Burg Neth. **14** 53.03N 4.47E
Dendermonde Belgium **14** 51.01N 4.07E
Dendre *r.* Belgium **14** 51.01N 4.07E
Dengkou China **32** 40.18N106.59E
Deng Xian China **32** 32.44N112.00E
Denham Australia **62** 25.54S113.35E
Denham Range *mts.* Australia **64** 21.55S147.46E
Den Helder Neth. **14** 52.58N 4.46E
Denia Spain **16** 38.51N 0.07E
Deniliquin Australia **67** 35.33S144.58E
Denison Iowa U.S.A. **82** 42.01N 95.21W
Denison Tex. U.S.A. **83** 33.45N 96.33W
Denizli Turkey **42** 37.46N 29.05E
Denmark Australia **63** 34.54S117.25E
Denmark Europe **23** 55.50N 10.00E
Denmark Str. Greenland/Iceland **95** 66.00N 25.00W
Den Oever Neth. **14** 52.56N 5.01E
Denpasar Indonesia **37** 8.40S115.14E
Denton Mont. U.S.A. **80** 47.19N109.57W
Denton Tex. U.S.A. **83** 33.13N 97.08W
D'Entrecasteaux, Pt. Australia **63** 34.50S116.00E
D'Entrecasteaux, Recifs *reef* N. Cal. **68** 18.00S163.10E
D'Entrecasteaux Is. P.N.G. **64** 9.30S150.40E
Denver U.S.A. **80** 39.43N105.01W
Denys *r.* Canada **76** 55.05N 77.22W
Deo *r.* Cameroon **53** 8.33N 12.45E
Deogarh *mtn.* India **41** 23.32N 82.16E
Deogarh Madhya P. India **41** 24.33N 78.15E
Deogarh Orissa India **41** 21.32N 84.44E
Deogarh Rāj. India **40** 25.32N 73.54E
Deogarh Hills India **41** 23.45N 82.30E
Deoghar India **41** 24.29N 86.42E
Deolāli India **40** 19.57N 73.50E
Deoli India **40** 25.45N 75.23E
Deori India **41** 23.08N 78.41E
Deoria India **41** 26.31N 83.47E
Deori Khās India **41** 23.24N 79.01E
Deosil India **41** 23.42N 82.15E
De Peel *f.* Belgium **14** 51.30N 5.50E
Depew U.S.A. **84** 42.54N 78.41W
Dêqên China **30** 28.45N 98.58E
De Queen U.S.A. **83** 34.02N 94.21W
De Quincy U.S.A. **83** 30.27N 93.26W
Dera Bugti Pakistan **40** 29.02N 69.09E
Dera Ghāzi Khān Pakistan **40** 30.03N 70.38E
Dera Ismāil Khān Pakistan **40** 31.50N 70.54E
Derazhnya U.S.S.R. **21** 49.18N 27.28E
Derbent U.S.S.R. **43** 42.03N 48.18E
Derby Tas. Australia **65** 41.08S147.47E
Derby W.A. Australia **62** 17.19S123.38E
Derby U.K. **10** 52.55N 1.28W
Derby N.Y. U.S.A. **76** 42.41N 78.58W
Derbyshire *d.* U.K. **10** 52.55N 1.28W
Derg, Lough Donegal Rep. of Ire. **13** 54.37N 7.55W
Derg, Lough Tipperary Rep. of Ire. **13** 52.57N 8.18W
De Ridder U.S.A. **83** 30.51N 93.17W
Dernieres, Isles *is.* U.S.A. **83** 29.02N 90.47W
Déroute, Passage de la *str.* France/U.K. **11** 49.10N 1.45W
Derrynasaggart Mts. Rep. of Ire. **13** 51.58N 9.15W
Derryveagh Mts. Rep. of Ire. **13** 55.00N 8.07W
Derudeb Sudan **48** 17.32N 36.06E
Derval France **15** 47.40N 1.40W
Derwent *r.* Cumbria U.K. **10** 54.38N 3.34W
Derwent *r.* Derbys. U.K. **9** 52.52N 1.19W
Derwent *r.* N. Yorks. U.K. **10** 53.44N 0.57W
Desaguadero *r.* Bolivia **92** 18.24S 67.05W
Desappointement, Îles du *is.* Pacific Oc. **69** 14.02S141.24W
Descanso Mexico **81** 32.14N116.58W
Deschutes *r.* U.S.A. **80** 45.38N120.54W
Desē Ethiopia **49** 11.05N 39.41E
Deseado Argentina **93** 47.39S 65.20W
Deseado *r.* Argentina **93** 47.45S 65.50W
Desenzano del Garda Italy **15** 45.28N 10.32E
Deserta Grande *is.* Madeira Is. **95** 32.32N 16.30W
Desert Center U.S.A. **81** 33.44N115.25W
Deshnoke India **40** 27.48N 73.21E
Des Moines *r.* U.S.A. **82** 40.22N 91.26W
Des Moines Iowa U.S.A. **82** 41.35N 93.37W
Des Moines N.Mex. U.S.A. **80** 36.46N103.50W
Desna *r.* U.S.S.R. **21** 50.32N 30.37E
De Soto U.S.A. **83** 38.08N 90.33W
Dessau E. Germany **20** 51.51N 12.15E
D'Estrees B. Australia **66** 35.50S137.58E
Dete Zimbabwe **56** 18.39S 26.49E
Detroit U.S.A. **84** 42.23N 83.05W
Detroit Lakes *town* U.S.A. **82** 46.49N 95.51W
Deūlgaon Rāja India **40** 20.01N 76.02E
Deurne Belgium **14** 51.13N 4.26E
Deurne Neth. **14** 51.29N 5.44E
Deutsche Bucht *b.* W. Germany **20** 54.00N 8.15E
Deva Romania **21** 45.54N 22.55E
Deventer Neth. **14** 52.15N 6.10E
Deveron *r.* U.K. **12** 57.40N 2.30W
Devikot India **40** 26.42N 71.12E
Devil's Bridge U.K. **11** 52.23N 3.50W
Devils Lake *town* U.S.A. **82** 48.07N 98.59W
Devin Bulgaria **19** 41.44N 24.24E
Devizes U.K. **11** 51.21N 2.00W
Devon *d.* U.K. **11** 50.50N 3.40W
Devon I. Canada **73** 75.00N 86.00W
Devonport Australia **65** 41.09S146.16E
Devrez *r.* Turkey **42** 41.07N 34.25E
Dewās India **40** 22.58N 76.04E
De Witt U.S.A. **83** 34.18N 91.20W
Dewsbury U.K. **10** 53.42N 1.38W
Dexter Mo. U.S.A. **83** 36.48N 89.57W
Deyang China **33** 31.05N104.18E
Dez *r.* Iran **43** 31.38N 48.54E
Dezadeash L. Canada **74** 60.28N136.58W
Dezfūl Iran **43** 32.24N 48.27E
Dezhou China **32** 37.23N116.16E
Dezh Shāhpūr Iran **43** 35.31N 46.10E
Dhahab Egypt **44** 28.30N 34.31E
Dhākā Bangla. **41** 23.43N 90.25E
Dhamār Yemen **45** 14.33N 44.24E
Dhamtari India **41** 20.41N 81.34E
Dhānbād India **41** 23.48N 86.27E
Dhandhuka India **40** 22.22N 71.59E
Dhangarhi Nepal **41** 28.41N 80.38E
Dhankuta Nepal **41** 26.59N 87.21E
Dhār India **40** 22.36N 75.18E
Dharampur India **40** 20.32N 73.11E
Dharān Bāzār Nepal **41** 26.49N 87.17E
Dharangaon India **40** 21.01N 75.16E
Dhāri India **40** 21.20N 71.01E
Dharmābād India **41** 18.54N 77.51E
Dharmjaygarh India **41** 22.28N 83.13E
Dharmsāla India **40** 32.13N 76.19E
Dhārni India **40** 21.33N 76.53E
Dhaulāgiri *mtn.* Nepal **41** 28.42N 83.31E
Dhebar L. India **40** 24.16N 74.00E
Dhenkānāl India **41** 20.40N 85.36E
Dhodhekánisos *is.* Greece **19** 37.00N 27.00E
Dholka India **40** 22.43N 72.28E
Dholpur India **41** 26.42N 77.54E
Dhorāji India **40** 21.44N 70.27E
Dhrāngadhra India **40** 22.59N 71.28E
Dhrol India **40** 22.34N 70.25E
Dhubri India **41** 26.02N 89.58E
Dhule India **40** 20.54N 74.47E
Dhuliān India **41** 24.41N 87.58E
Dialakoro Mali **52** 12.18N 7.54W
Diamante Argentina **93** 32.05S 60.35W
Diamantina *r.* Australia **64** 26.45S139.10E
Diamantina Brazil **94** 18.17S 43.37W
Diamantina, Chapada *hills* Brazil **91** 13.00S 42.30W
Diamantino Brazil **94** 14.25S 56.29W
Diamond Harbour India **41** 22.12N 88.12E
Diana's Peak *mtn.* St. Helena **95** 15.58S 5.42W
Dianbai China **33** 21.30N111.01E
Diane Bank *is.* Australia **64** 15.50S149.48E
Dianjiang China **33** 30.14N107.27E
Diapaga U. Volta **53** 12.04N 1.48E
Dibai India **41** 28.13N 78.15E
Dibaya Zaïre **54** 6.31S 22.57E
Dibi Cameroon **53** 7.09N 13.43E
Dibrugarh India **39** 27.29N 94.56E
Dibs Sudan **49** 14.18N 24.23E
Dickinson U.S.A. **82** 46.53N102.47W
Dicle *r.* Turkey *see* Dijlah *r.* Asia **42**
Didcot U.K. **11** 51.36N 1.14W
Didiéni Mali **52** 14.05N 7.50W
Didwāna India **40** 27.24N 74.34E
Die France **17** 44.45N 5.23E
Diefenbaker, L. Canada **75** 51.00N106.55W
Diekirch Lux. **14** 49.52N 6.10E
Diélette France **15** 49.33N 1.52W
Diéma Mali **52** 14.32N 9.03W
Diemen Neth. **14** 52.22N 4.58E
Diemuchuoke Jammu & Kashmir **41** 32.42N 79.29E
Dien Bien Phu Vietnam **34** 21.23N103.02E
Diepholz W. Germany **20** 52.35N 8.21E
Dieppe France **15** 49.55N 1.05E
Dierdorf W. Germany **14** 50.33N 7.38E
Dieren Neth. **14** 52.03N 6.06E
Dierks U.S.A. **83** 34.07N 94.01W
Diesdorf E. Germany **20** 52.45N 10.52E
Diest Belgium **14** 50.59N 5.03E
Dieuze France **17** 48.49N 6.43E
Dif Kenya **55** 1.04N 40.57E
Dif Somali Rep. **49** 1.00N 41.00E
Diffa Niger **53** 13.19N 12.35E
Diffa *d.* Niger **53** 16.00N 13.00E
Dig India **40** 27.20N 77.25E
Digby Canada **77** 44.30N 65.47W
Dighton U.S.A. **82** 38.29N100.28W
Digne France **17** 44.05N 6.14E
Digoin France **17** 46.29N 3.59E
Digras India **41** 20.07N 77.43E
Digri Pakistan **40** 25.10N 69.07E
Digul *r.* Indonesia **37** 7.10S139.08E
Dijlah *r.* Asia **43** 31.00N 47.27E
Dijle *r.* Belgium **14** 51.02N 4.25E
Dijon France **17** 47.20N 5.02E
Dikhil Djibouti **49** 11.06N 42.22E
Dikili Turkey **19** 39.05N 26.52E
Dikirnis Egypt **44** 31.05N 31.35E
Dikodougou Ivory Coast **52** 9.00N 5.45W
Diksmuide Belgium **14** 51.01N 2.52E
Dikumbiya Ethiopia **48** 14.42N 37.30E
Dikwa Nigeria **53** 12.01N 13.55E
Dili Indonesia **37** 8.35S125.35E
Dilley U.S.A. **83** 28.40N 99.10W
Dilling Sudan **49** 12.03N 29.39E
Dillingham U.S.A. **72** 59.02N158.29W
Dillon U.S.A. **80** 45.13N112.38W
Dilolo Zaïre **54** 10.39S 22.20E
Dimashq Syria **44** 33.30N 36.19E
Dimbelenge Zaïre **54** 5.32S 23.04E
Dimbokro Ivory Coast **52** 6.43N 4.46W
Dimboola Australia **66** 36.27S142.02E
Dîmbovița *r.* Romania **21** 44.13N 26.22E
Dimitrovgrad Bulgaria **19** 42.01N 25.34E
Dimona Israel **44** 31.04N 35.01E
Dinagat *i.* Phil. **37** 10.15N125.30E
Dinājpur Bangla. **41** 25.38N 88.38E
Dinan France **17** 48.27N 2.02W
Dinant Belgium **14** 50.16N 4.55E
Dinar Turkey **42** 38.05N 30.09E
Dīnār, Kūh-e *mtn.* Iran **43** 30.45N 51.39E
Dinara Planina *mts.* Yugo. **20** 44.00N 16.30E
Dindar *r.* Sudan **48** 14.06N 33.40E
Dindar Nat. Park Sudan **49** 12.00N 35.00E
Dindigul India **38** 10.23N 78.00E
Dindori India **41** 22.57N 81.05E
Dinga Pakistan **40** 25.26N 67.10E
Dingbian China **32** 37.36N107.38E
Dinggyê China **41** 28.18N 88.06E
Dingle Rep. of Ire. **13** 52.09N 10.17W
Dingle B. Rep. of Ire. **13** 52.05N 10.12W
Dingo Australia **64** 23.40S149.21E
Dingolfing W. Germany **20** 48.38N 12.31E
Dinguiraye Guinea **52** 11.19N 10.49W
Dingwall U.K. **12** 57.35N 4.26W
Dingxi China **32** 35.33N104.32E
Ding Xian China **32** 38.30N115.00E
Dingxing China **32** 39.17N115.46E
Dinokwe Botswana **56** 23.24S 26.40E
Dinsor Somali Rep. **45** 2.28N 43.00E
Dinuba U.S.A. **81** 36.32N119.23W
Diö Sweden **23** 56.38N 14.13E
Diodār India **40** 24.06N 71.47E
Dioïla Mali **52** 12.30N 6.49W
Diourbel Senegal **52** 14.30N 16.10W
Diplo Pakistan **40** 24.28N 69.35E
Dipolog Phil. **37** 8.34N123.28E
Dirdal Norway **23** 58.47N 6.14E
Diré Mali **52** 16.16N 3.24W
Direction, C. Australia **64** 12.51S143.32E
Dirē Dawa Ethiopia **49** 9.35N 41.50E
Dirico Angola **54** 17.58S 20.40E
Dirj Libya **51** 30.09N 10.26E
Dirk Hartog I. Australia **62** 25.50S113.00E
Dirranbandi Australia **67** 28.35S148.10E
Disappointment, L. Australia **62** 23.30S122.55E
Disaster B. Australia **67** 37.20S149.58E
Discovery Canada **72** 63.10N113.58W
Discovery B. Australia **66** 38.12S141.07E
Disko *i.* Greenland **73** 69.45N 53.00W
Diss U.K. **11** 52.23N 1.06E
District of Columbia *d.* U.S.A. **85** 38.55N 77.00W
Distrito Federal *d.* Brazil **91** 15.45S 47.50W
Distrito Federal *d.* Mexico **86** 19.20N 99.10W
Disûq Egypt **44** 31.09N 30.39E
Diu India **40** 20.42N 70.59E
Diu *d.* India **40** 20.45N 70.59E
Diver Canada **76** 46.44N 79.30W
Dives *r.* France **15** 49.19N 0.05W
Divinópolis Brazil **94** 20.08S 44.55W
Divnoye U.S.S.R. **25** 45.55N 43.21E
Divo Ivory Coast **52** 5.48N 5.15W
Divrigi Turkey **42** 39.23N 38.06E
Dīwāl Qol Afghan. **40** 34.19N 67.54E
Dixcove Ghana **52** 4.49N 1.57W
Dixie U.S.A. **80** 45.34N115.28W
Dixon Ill. U.S.A. **82** 41.50N 89.29W
Dixon N.Mex. U.S.A. **81** 36.12N105.33W
Dixon Entrance *str.* U.S.A./Canada **74** 54.25N132.30W
Diyālā *r.* Iraq **43** 33.13N 44.33E
Diyarbakir Turkey **42** 37.55N 40.14E
Dja *r.* Cameroon **54** 1.38N 16.03E
Djabéta Gabon **54** 0.45N 14.00E
Djado Niger **53** 21.00N 12.20E
Djado, Plateau du *f.* Niger **53** 22.00N 12.30E
Djambala Congo **54** 2.33S 14.38E
Djanet Algeria **51** 24.34N 9.29E
Djelfa Algeria **51** 34.40N 3.15E
Djema C.A.R. **49** 6.03N 25.19E
Djénné Mali **52** 13.55N 4.31W
Djerba, Île de *i.* Tunisia **51** 33.48N 10.54E
Djerid, Chott *f.* Tunisia **51** 33.42N 8.26E
Djibo U. Volta **52** 14.09N 1.38W
Djibouti Africa **49** 12.00N 42.50E
Djibouti *town* Djibouti **49** 11.35N 43.11E
Djilbabo Plain *f.* Ethiopia **49** 4.00N 39.10E
Djolu Zaïre **54** 0.35N 22.28E
Djouah *r.* Gabon **54** 1.16N 13.12E
Djougou Benin **53** 9.40N 1.47E
Djugu Zaïre **55** 1.55N 30.31E
Djúpivogur Iceland **22** 64.41N 14.16W
Dmitriya Lapteva, Proliv *str.* U.S.S.R. **29** 73.00N142.00E
Dnepr *r.* U.S.S.R. **21** 50.00N 31.00E
Dneprodzerzhinsk U.S.S.R. **25** 48.30N 34.37E
Dnepropetrovsk U.S.S.R. **25** 48.29N 35.00E
Dneprovskaya Nizmennost *f.* U.S.S.R. **21** 52.30N 29.45E
Dneprovsko-Bugskiy Kanal U.S.S.R. **21** 52.03N 25.35E
Dnestr *r.* U.S.S.R. **21** 46.21N 30.20E
Dno U.S.S.R. **24** 57.50N 30.00E
Doba Chad **53** 8.40N 16.50E
Dobane C.A.R. **49** 6.24N 24.42E
Dobbyn Australia **64** 19.48S140.00E
Dobele U.S.S.R. **23** 56.37N 23.16E
Dobo Indonesia **37** 5.46S134.13E
Doboj Yugo. **21** 44.44N 18.02E
Dobrodzień Poland **21** 50.44N 18.27E
Dobruja *f.* Romania **21** 44.30N 28.15E
Dobrush U.S.S.R. **21** 52.24N 31.19E
Dobryanka U.S.S.R. **24** 58.30N 56.26E
Dobzha China **41** 28.28N 88.13E
Doce *r.* Brazil **94** 19.32S 39.57W
Docking U.K. **10** 52.55N 0.39E
Doda Jammu & Kashmir **40** 33.08N 75.34E
Doda, Lac *l.* Canada **76** 49.24N 75.14W
Dodecanese *is. see* Dhodhekánisos *is.* Greece **19**
Dodge City U.S.A. **83** 37.45N100.01W
Dodman Pt. U.K. **11** 50.13N 4.48W
Dodoma Tanzania **55** 6.10S 35.40E
Dodoma *d.* Tanzania **55** 6.00S 36.00E
Dodson U.S.A. **80** 48.24N108.15W
Doetinchem Neth. **14** 51.57N 6.17E
Dogai Coring *l.* China **39** 34.30N 89.00E
Dog Creek *town* Canada **74** 51.35N122.14W
Dogger Bank *f.* North Sea **9** 54.45N 2.00E
Doğubayazit Turkey **43** 39.32N 44.08E
Do'gyaling China **41** 31.58N 88.24E
Doha *see* Ad Dawḥah Qatar **43**
Dohad India **40** 22.50N 74.16E
Dohhi India **41** 24.32N 84.54E
Doilungdêqên China **41** 30.06N 90.32E
Dokkum Neth. **14** 53.20N 6.00E
Dokri Pakistan **40** 27.23N 68.06E
Dolbeau Canada **77** 48.53N 72.14W
Dol-de-Bretagne France **15** 48.33N 1.45W
Dole France **17** 47.05N 5.30E
Dolgellau U.K. **11** 52.44N 3.53W
Dolina U.S.S.R. **21** 49.00N 23.59E
Dolinskaya U.S.S.R. **25** 48.06N 32.46E
Dolisie Congo **54** 4.09S 12.40E
Dollard *b.* W. Germany **14** 53.20N 7.10E
Dolny Kubín Czech. **21** 49.12N 19.17E
Dolo Somali Rep. **45** 4.13N 42.08E
Dolomiti *mts.* Italy **15** 46.25N 11.50E
Dolores Argentina **93** 36.19S 57.40W
Dolores Mexico **81** 28.53N108.27W
Dolores Uruguay **93** 33.33S 58.13W
Dolores U.S.A. **80** 37.28N108.30W
Dolphin and Union Str. Canada **72** 69.20N118.00W
Doma Nigeria **53** 8.23N 8.21E
Domadare Somali Rep. **49** 1.48N 41.13E
Domažlice Czech. **20** 49.27N 12.56E
Dombås Norway **23** 62.05N 9.08E
Dombe Grande Angola **54** 13.00S 13.06E
Dombey, C. Australia **66** 37.12S139.43E
Dombóvár Hungary **21** 46.23N 18.08E
Domburg Neth. **14** 51.35N 3.31E
Domfront France **15** 48.36N 0.39W
Dominica Windward Is. **87** 15.30N 61.30W
Dominican Republic C. America **87** 18.00N 70.00W
Dominion L. Canada **77** 52.40N 61.42W
Dommel *r.* Neth. **14** 51.44N 5.17E
Domo Ethiopia **45** 7.54N 46.52E
Domodossola Italy **15** 46.07N 8.17E
Domuyo *mtn.* Argentina **93** 36.37S 70.28W
Don Mexico **81** 26.26N109.02W
Don *r.* England U.K. **10** 53.41N 0.50W
Don *r.* Scotland U.K. **12** 57.10N 2.05W
Don *r.* U.S.S.R. **25** 47.06N 39.16E
Donaghadee U.K. **13** 54.39N 5.33W
Donald Australia **66** 36.25S143.04E
Donaldsonville U.S.A. **83** 30.06N 90.59W
Donau *r.* W. Germany *see* Danube *r.* Europe **20**
Donaueschingen W. Germany **20** 47.57N 8.29E
Donauwörth W. Germany **20** 48.44N 10.48E
Don Benito Spain **16** 38.57N 5.52W
Doncaster U.K. **10** 53.31N 1.09W
Dondaicha India **40** 21.20N 74.34E
Dondo Angola **54** 9.40S 14.25E
Dondo Mozambique **57** 19.39S 34.39E
Donegal Rep. of Ire. **13** 54.39N 8.06W
Donegal *d.* Rep. of Ire. **13** 54.52N 8.00W
Donegal B. Rep. of Ire. **13** 54.32N 8.18W
Donegal Pt. Rep. of Ire. **13** 52.43N 9.38W
Donetsk U.S.S.R. **25** 48.00N 37.50E
Donga Nigeria **53** 7.45N 10.05E
Donga *r.* Nigeria **53** 8.20N 10.00E
Dongara Australia **63** 29.15S114.56E
Dongargarh India **41** 21.12N 80.44E
Dongbei Pingyuan *f.* China **32** 42.30N123.00E
Dongchuan China **30** 26.10N103.02E
Dongco China **41** 32.07N 84.35E
Dongfang China **33** 19.05N108.39E
Donggala Indonesia **36** 0.48S119.45E
Donggou China **32** 39.52N124.08E
Dongguang China **32** 37.53N116.32E
Donghai China **32** 34.35N118.49E
Donghai *i.* China **33** 21.02N110.25E
Dong Hoi Vietnam **34** 17.32N106.35E
Dong Jiang *r.* China **33** 23.00N113.33E
Dongkalang Indonesia **37** 0.12N120.07E
Dongling China **32** 41.44N123.32E
Dongou Congo **54** 2.05N 18.00E
Dongping Hu *l.* China **32** 35.55N116.15E
Dongqiao China **41** 31.57N 90.30E
Dongsheng China **32** 39.49N109.59E
Dongtai China **32** 32.42N120.26E
Dongting Hu *l.* China **33** 29.10N113.00E
Dongtou *i.* China **33** 27.50N121.08E
Dong Ujimqin Qi China **32** 45.33N116.50E
Dongxi China **33** 28.42N106.40E
Dongxing China **33** 21.33N107.58E
Donington U.K. **10** 52.55N 0.12W
Donja Stubica Yugo. **20** 45.59N 15.58E
Dönna *i.* Norway **22** 66.05N 12.30E
Donnacona Canada **77** 46.40N 71.47W
Donnybrook Australia **63** 33.34S115.47E
Donnybrook R.S.A. **56** 29.55S 29.51E
Doodlakine Australia **63** 31.41S117.23E
Doon, Loch U.K. **12** 55.15N 4.23W
Doondi Australia **67** 28.16S148.25E
Dora, L. Australia **62** 22.05S122.55E
Dora Baltea *r.* Italy **15** 45.11N 8.05E
Doran L. Canada **75** 61.13N108.06W
Dora Riparia *r.* Italy **15** 45.05N 7.44E
Dorchester U.K. **11** 50.52N 2.28W
Dorchester, C. Canada **73** 65.29N 77.30W
Dordogne *r.* France **17** 45.03N 0.34W
Dordrecht Neth. **14** 51.48N 4.40E
Dordrecht R.S.A. **56** 31.22S 27.02E
Dore, Mont *mtn.* France **17** 45.32N 2.49E
Doré L. Canada **75** 54.46N107.17W
Dori U. Volta **52** 14.03N 0.02W
Dorion Canada **77** 45.23N 74.03W
Dorking U.K. **11** 51.14N 0.20W
Dormagen W. Germany **14** 51.05N 6.50E
Dormans France **15** 49.04N 3.38E
Dornie U.K. **12** 57.16N 5.31W
Dornoch U.K. **12** 57.52N 4.02W
Dornoch Firth *est.* U.K. **12** 57.50N 4.04W
Dornogovĭ *d.* Mongolia **32** 44.00N110.00E
Dornum W. Germany **14** 53.39N 7.26E
Doro Mali **52** 16.09N 0.51W
Dorohoi Romania **21** 47.57N 26.24E
Dörpen W. Germany **14** 52.58N 7.20E
Dorrigo Australia **67** 30.20S152.41E
Dorris U.S.A. **80** 41.58N121.55W
Dorset *d.* U.K. **11** 50.48N 2.25W
Dorset, C. Canada **73** 64.10N 76.40W
Dorsten W. Germany **14** 51.38N 6.58E
Dortmund W. Germany **14** 51.32N 7.27E
Dortmund-Ems Kanal W. Germany **14** 52.20N 7.30E
Dorval Canada **77** 45.27N 73.44W
Dos Bahías, C. Argentina **93** 44.55S 65.32W
Dosquet Canada **77** 46.28N 71.32W
Dosso Niger **53** 13.03N 3.10E
Dosso *d.* Niger **53** 13.00N 3.15E
Dossor U.S.S.R. **25** 47.31N 53.01E
Dothan U.S.A. **85** 31.12N 85.25W
Douai France **14** 50.22N 3.05E
Douako Guinea **52** 9.45N 10.08W
Douala Cameroon **53** 4.05N 9.43E
Douarnenez France **17** 48.05N 4.20W
Double Mer *g.* Canada **77** 54.05N 59.00W
Doubs *r.* France **17** 46.57N 5.03E
Doubtful Island B. Australia **63** 34.15S119.30E
Doubtless B. New Zealand **60** 35.10S173.30E
Doudeville France **15** 49.43N 0.48E
Douentza Mali **52** 14.58N 2.48W
Douglas *r.* Australia **66** 28.35S136.50E
Douglas R.S.A. **56** 29.03S 23.45E
Douglas U.K. **10** 54.09N 4.29W
Douglas Ariz. U.S.A. **81** 31.21N109.33W
Douglas Ga. U.S.A. **85** 31.30N 82.54W
Douglas Mich. U.S.A. **84** 42.38N 86.13W
Douglas Wyo. U.S.A. **80** 42.45N105.24W
Doulaincourt France **17** 48.19N 5.12E
Doulevant-le-Château France **15** 48.23N 4.55E
Doumé Cameroon **53** 4.13N 13.30E
Douna Mali **52** 12.40N 6.00W
Dounreay U.K. **12** 58.35N 3.42W
Dourados Brazil **92** 22.09S 54.52W
Dourdan France **15** 48.32N 2.01E
Douro *r.* Portugal **16** 41.10N 8.40W
Douvres France **15** 49.17N 0.23W
Dove *r.* Derbys. U.K. **10** 52.50N 1.35W
Dover U.K. **11** 51.07N 1.19E
Dover Del. U.S.A. **85** 39.10N 75.32W
Dover N.H. U.S.A. **84** 43.12N 70.56W
Dover N.J. U.S.A. **85** 40.53N 74.34W
Dover Ohio U.S.A. **84** 40.32N 81.30W
Dover Tenn. U.S.A. **85** 36.30N 87.50W
Dover, Pt. Australia **63** 32.32S125.30E
Dover, Str. of U.K. **11** 51.00N 1.30E
Dovey *r.* U.K. **11** 52.33N 3.56W
Dovrefjell *mts.* Norway **23** 62.06N 9.25E
Dovsk U.S.S.R. **21** 53.07N 30.29E
Dowa Malaŵi **55** 13.40S 33.55E
Dowagiac U.S.A. **84** 41.58N 86.06W
Dowerin Australia **63** 31.15S117.00E
Dowlatābād Iran **43** 28.19N 56.40E
Dowlat Yār Afghan. **40** 34.33N 65.47E
Down *d.* U.K. **13** 54.20N 6.00W
Downey U.S.A. **80** 42.26N112.07W
Downham Market U.K. **11** 52.36N 0.22E
Downpatrick U.K. **13** 54.21N 5.43W
Downpatrick Head Rep. of Ire. **13** 54.20N 9.22W
Downton, Mt. Canada **74** 52.42N124.51W
Dowra Rep. of Ire. **13** 54.11N 8.02W
Doylestown U.S.A. **85** 40.19N 75.08W
Dozois, Résr. Canada **76** 47.30N 77.00W
Drâa, Hamada du *f.* Algeria **50** 29.00N 6.00W
Drâa, Oued *wadi* Morocco **50** 28.40N 11.06W
Drachten Neth. **14** 53.05N 6.06E
Drăgășani Romania **21** 44.40N 24.16E
Dragoman, Pasul *pass* Bulgaria/Yugo. **19** 42.56N 22.52E
Dragon's Mouth *str.* Trinidad **90** 11.00N 61.35W
Dragovishtitsa Bulgaria **19** 42.22N 22.39E
Draguignan France **17** 43.32N 6.28E
Drake Australia **67** 28.55S152.24E
Drake U.S.A. **82** 47.55N100.23W
Drakensberge *mts.* R.S.A./Lesotho **56** 30.00S 29.05E
Drake Passage *str.* Atlantic Oc. **95** 59.00S 65.00W
Dráma Greece **19** 41.09N 24.11E
Drammen Norway **23** 59.44N 10.15E
Drās Jammu & Kashmir **40** 34.27N 75.46E
Drau *r.* Austria *see* Drava *r.* Yugo. **20**
Drava *r.* Yugo. **21** 45.34N 18.56E
Drayton Australia **65** 27.40S151.50E
Drayton Valley *town* Canada **74** 53.25N114.58W
Drenthe *d.* Neth. **14** 52.52N 6.30E
Dresden E. Germany **20** 51.03N 13.45E
Dresden *d.* E. Germany **20** 51.10N 14.00E
Dreux France **15** 48.44N 1.23E
Driftwood Canada **76** 49.08N 81.23W
Drin *r.* Albania **19** 41.45N 19.34E
Drina *r.* Yugo. **21** 44.53N 19.20E
Dröbak Norway **23** 59.39N 10.39E
Drogheda Rep. of Ire. **13** 53.42N 6.23W

Drogobych to Ely

Drogobych U.S.S.R. 21 49.10N 23.30E
Droitwich U.K. 11 52.16N 2.10W
Drokiya U.S.S.R. 21 48.07N 27.49E
Dromedary, C. Australia 67 36.18S150.15E
Dronero Italy 15 44.28N 7.22E
Dronfield U.K. 10 53.18N 1.29W
Dronne r. France 17 45.02N 0.09W
Dronning Maud Land f. Antarctica 96 74.00S 10.00E
Drumheller Canada 74 51.25N112.40W
Drum Hills Rep. of Ire. 13 52.03N 7.42W
Drummond Range mts. Australia 64 23.30S147.15E
Drummondville Canada 77 45.53N 72.30W
Drummore U.K. 12 54.41N 4.54W
Druskininkai U.S.S.R. 21 53.48N 23.58E
Drut r. U.S.S.R. 21 53.03N 30.42E
Drvar Yugo. 20 44.22N 16.24E
Dry B. U.S.A. 74 59.08N138.25W
Dryden Canada 76 49.47N 92.50W
Drymen U.K. 12 56.04N 4.27W
Drysdale r. Australia 62 13.59S126.51E
Dschang Cameroon 53 5.28N 10.02E
Dua r. Zaïre 54 3.12N 20.55E
Du'an China 33 24.01N108.06E
Ḍubā Saudi Arabia 42 27.21N 35.40E
Dubai see Dubayy U.A.E. 43
Dubawnt r. Canada 73 62.50N102.00W
Dubawnt L. Canada 75 63.04N101.42W
Dubayy U.A.E. 43 25.13N 55.17E
Dubbo Australia 67 32.16S148.41E
Dubica Yugo. 20 45.11N 16.48E
Dublin Rep. of Ire. 13 53.21N 6.18W
Dublin d. Rep. of Ire. 13 53.20N 6.18W
Dublin U.S.A. 85 32.31N 82.54W
Dublin B. Rep. of Ire. 13 53.20N 6.09W
Dubno U.S.S.R. 21 50.28N 25.40E
Dubois Idaho U.S.A. 80 44.10N112.14W
Du Bois Penn. U.S.A. 84 41.07N 78.46W
Dubovka U.S.S.R. 25 49.04N 44.48E
Dubréka Guinea 52 9.50N 13.32W
Dubrovitsa U.S.S.R. 21 51.38N 26.40E
Dubrovnik Yugo. 19 42.40N 18.07E
Dubuque U.S.A. 82 42.30N 90.41W
Duchesne U.S.A. 80 40.10N110.24W
Duchess Australia 64 21.22S139.52E
Duchess Australia 61 21.22S139.52E
Ducie I. Pacific Oc. 69 24.40S124.48W
Du Couëdic, C. Australia 66 36.00S136.10E
Dudhnai India 41 25.59N 90.44E
Dudinka U.S.S.R. 29 69.27N 86.13E
Dudley U.K. 11 52.30N 2.05W
Dudna r. India 40 19.07N 76.54E
Dudo Somali Rep. 45 9.20N 50.14E
Duékoué Ivory Coast 52 6.50N 7.22W
Duero r. Spain see Douro r. Portugal 16
Duff Creek town Australia 66 28.28S135.51E
Dufftown U.K. 12 57.27N 3.09W
Duga Resa Yugo. 20 45.27N 15.30E
Dugi i. Yugo. 20 44.04N 15.00E
Du Gué r. Canada 77 57.20N 70.48W
Duifken Pt. Australia 64 12.33S141.38E
Duisburg W. Germany 14 51.26N 6.45E
Duitama Colombia 90 5.50N 73.01W
Duiveland i. Neth. 14 51.39N 4.00E
Dujuma Somali Rep. 55 1.14N 42.37E
Duk Fadiat Sudan 49 7.45N 31.25E
Duk Faiwil Sudan 49 7.30N 31.29E
Dukhān Qatar 43 25.24N 50.47E
Duki Pakistan 40 30.09N 68.34E
Dukou China 30 26.33N101.44E
Dukye Dzong Bhutan 41 27.20N 89.30E
Dulce r. Argentina 92 30.40S 62.00W
Duleek Rep. of Ire. 13 53.39N 6.24W
Dülmen W. Germany 14 51.49N 7.17E
Dulovo Bulgaria 21 43.49N 27.09E
Duluth U.S.A. 82 46.47N 92.06W
Dūmā Syria 44 33.33N 36.24E
Dumaguete Phil. 37 9.20N123.18E
Dumai Indonesia 36 1.41N101.27E
Dumaran i. Phil. 36 10.33N119.50E
Dumaresq r. Australia 67 28.40S150.28E
Dumaring Indonesia 36 1.36N118.12E
Dumas Ark. U.S.A. 83 33.53N 91.29W
Dumas Tex. U.S.A. 83 35.52N101.58W
Dumbarton U.K. 12 55.57N 4.35W
Dumbleyung Australia 63 33.18S117.42E
Dumbrăveni Romania 21 46.14N 24.35E
Dum-Dum India 41 22.35N 88.24E
Dumfries U.K. 12 55.04N 3.37W
Dumfries and Galloway d. U.K. 12 55.05N 3.40W
Dumka India 41 24.16N 87.15E
Dumraon India 41 25.33N 84.09E
Dumyāṭ Egypt 44 31.26N 31.48E
Duna r. Hungary see Danube r. Europe 21
Dunaföldvár Hungary 21 46.48N 18.55E
Dunajec r. Poland 21 50.15N 20.44E
Dunajská Streda Czech. 21 48.01N 17.35E
Dunany Pt. Rep. of Ire. 13 53.51N 6.15W
Dunărea r. Romania see Danube r. Europe 21
Dunării, Delta f. Romania 21 45.05N 29.45E
Dunav r. Bulgaria see Danube r. Europe 21
Dunav r. Yugo. see Danube r. Europe 21
Dunbar U.K. 12 56.00N 2.31W
Dunblane U.K. 12 56.12N 3.59W
Dunboyne Rep. of Ire. 13 53.26N 6.30W
Duncan Canada 74 48.45N123.40W
Duncan r. Canada 74 50.11N116.57W
Duncan U.S.A. 83 34.30N 97.57W
Duncan, C. Canada 76 52.40N 80.48W
Duncan L. N.W.T. Canada 74 62.51N113.58W
Duncan L. Que. Canada 76 53.35N 77.55W
Duncansby Head U.K. 12 58.39N 3.01W
Dundalk Rep. of Ire. 13 54.01N 6.25W
Dundalk U.S.A. 85 39.15N 76.31W
Dundalk B. Rep. of Ire. 13 53.55N 6.17W
Dundas Australia 63 32.20S121.48E
Dundas Canada 76 43.16N 79.58W
Dundas, L. Australia 63 32.35S121.50E
Dundas I. Canada 74 54.33N130.50W
Dundas Str. Australia 64 11.20S131.35E
Dundee R.S.A. 56 28.09S 30.14E
Dundee U.K. 12 56.28N 3.00W
Dundgovi d. Mongolia 32 45.00N106.00E
Dundrum U.K. 13 54.16N 5.51W
Dundrum B. U.K. 13 54.12N 5.46W
Dunedin New Zealand 60 45.52S170.30E
Dunedin U.S.A. 85 28.02N 82.47W
Dunfermline U.K. 12 56.04N 3.29W
Dungannon U.K. 13 54.31N 6.47W
Dūngarpur India 40 23.50N 73.43E
Dungarvan Rep. of Ire. 13 52.06N 7.39W
Dungeness c. U.K. 11 50.55N 0.58E
Dungiven U.K. 13 54.56N 6.56W
Dungog Australia 67 32.24S151.46E
Dungu Zaïre 55 3.40N 28.40E
Dunhuang China 30 40.00N 94.40E
Dunkeld Qld. Australia 65 26.55S148.00E
Dunkeld Vic. Australia 66 37.40S142.23E
Dunkeld U.K. 12 56.34N 3.36W
Dunkerque France 14 51.02N 2.23E
Dunkirk see Dunkerque France 20
Dunkirk U.S.A. 84 42.29N 79.21W
Dunkwa Central Ghana 52 5.59N 1.45W
Dun Laoghaire Rep. of Ire. 13 53.17N 6.09W
Dunlap U.S.A. 82 41.51N 95.36W
Dunleer Rep. of Ire. 13 53.49N 6.24W
Dunmahon Rep. of Ire. 13 52.09N 7.23W
Dunmore U.S.A. 84 41.25N 75.38W
Dunnet Head U.K. 12 58.40N 3.23W
Dunning U.S.A. 82 41.50N100.06W
Dunnville Canada 76 42.54N 79.36W
Dunoon U.K. 12 55.57N 4.57W
Dunqulah Sudan 48 19.10N 30.29E
Dunqunāb Sudan 48 21.06N 37.05E
Duns U.K. 12 55.47N 2.20W
Dunsborough Australia 63 33.37S115.06E
Dunshaughlin Rep. of Ire. 13 53.30N 6.34W
Dunstable U.K. 11 51.53N 0.32W
Dunstan Mts. New Zealand 60 44.45S169.45E
Dunster Canada 74 53.08N119.50W
Dunyāpur Pakistan 40 29.48N 71.44E
Duolun China 32 42.09N116.21E
Duong Dong Vietnam 34 10.12N103.57E
Dupont U.S.A. 84 38.53N 85.30W
Duque de Bragança Angola 54 9.06S 16.11E
Duque de Caxias Brazil 94 22.47S 43.18W
Du Quoin U.S.A. 83 38.01N 89.14W
Duran U.S.A. 81 34.28N105.24W
Durance r. France 17 43.55N 4.48E
Durango Mexico 86 24.01N104.00W
Durango d. Mexico 83 24.30N104.00W
Durango Spain 16 43.13N 2.40W
Durango U.S.A. 80 37.16N107.53W
Durant U.S.A. 83 34.00N 96.23W
Durazno Uruguay 93 33.22S 56.31W
Durban R.S.A. 56 29.50S 30.59E
Durbe U.S.S.R. 23 56.35N 21.21E
Dureji Pakistan 40 25.53N 67.18E
Düren W. Germany 14 50.48N 6.30E
Durg India 41 21.11N 81.17E
Durgāpur India 41 23.29N 87.20E
Durham U.K. 10 54.47N 1.34W
Durham d. U.K. 10 54.42N 1.45W
Durham N.C. U.S.A. 85 36.00N 78.54W
Durham N.H. U.S.A. 84 43.08N 70.56W
Durham Sud Canada 77 45.39N 72.19W
Durlston Head c. U.K. 11 50.35N 1.58W
Durmitor mtn. Yugo. 19 43.08N 19.03E
Durness U.K. 12 58.33N 4.45W
Durrës Albania 19 41.19N 19.27E
Durrow Rep. of Ire. 13 52.51N 7.25W
Dursey Head Rep. of Ire. 13 51.35N 10.15W
Durūz, Jabal ad mtn. Syria 44 32.42N 36.42E
D'Urville I. New Zealand 60 40.45S173.50E
Dushak U.S.S.R. 28 37.13N 60.01E
Dushan China 33 25.50N107.30E
Dushanbe U.S.S.R. 30 38.38N 68.51E
Duskotna Bulgaria 19 42.52N 27.10E
Düsseldorf W. Germany 14 51.13N 6.47E
Dutch Creek town Canada 74 50.18N115.58W
Dutlhe Botswana 56 23.55S 23.47E
Dutton, L. Australia 66 31.49S137.08E
Duvno Yugo. 21 43.43N 17.14E
Duxun China 33 23.57N117.37E
Duyun China 33 26.12N107.29E
Dvina r. U.S.S.R. 28 57.03N 24.02E
Dvinskaya Guba b. U.S.S.R. 24 64.40N 39.30E
Dwarda Australia 63 32.45S116.23E
Dwārka India 40 22.14N 68.58E
Dwellingup Australia 63 32.42S116.04E
Dyatlovichi U.S.S.R. 21 52.08N 30.49E
Dyatlovo U.S.S.R. 21 53.28N 25.28E
Dyer, C. Canada 73 67.45N 61.45W
Dyérem r. Cameroon 53 6.36N 13.10E
Dyer Plateau Antarctica 96 70.00S 65.00W
Dyersburg U.S.A. 83 36.03N 89.23W
Dyfed d. U.K. 11 52.00N 4.17W
Dykh Tau mtn. U.S.S.R. 25 43.04N 43.10E
Dymer U.S.S.R. 21 50.50N 30.20E
Dyulevo Bulgaria 19 42.22N 27.10E
Dyultydag mtn. U.S.S.R. 43 41.55N 46.52E
Dzamïn Üüd Mongolia 32 43.50N111.53E
Dzerzhinsk B.S.S.R. U.S.S.R. 21 53.40N 27.01E
Dzerzhinsk R.S.F.S.R. U.S.S.R. 24 56.15N 43.30E
Dzhambul U.S.S.R. 30 42.50N 71.25E
Dzhankoy U.S.S.R. 25 45.42N 34.23E
Dzhardzhan U.S.S.R. 29 68.49N124.08E
Dzhelinde U.S.S.R. 29 70.09N114.00E
Dzhetygara U.S.S.R. 28 52.14N 61.10E
Dzhezkazgan U.S.S.R. 28 47.48N 67.24E
Dzhizak U.S.S.R. 28 40.06N 67.45E
Dzhugdzhur, Khrebet mts. U.S.S.R. 29 57.30N138.00E
Dzhurin U.S.S.R. 21 48.40N 28.16E
Działdowo Poland 21 53.15N 20.10E
Dzierzoniów Poland 20 50.44N 16.39E
Dzodze Ghana 52 6.14N 1.00E

E

Eabamet L. Canada 76 51.30N 88.00W
Eads U.S.A. 82 38.29N102.47W
Eagle r. Canada 77 53.35N 57.25W
Eagle U.S.A. 82 39.39N106.50W
Eagle Butte town U.S.A. 82 45.00N101.14W
Eagle Grove U.S.A. 82 42.40N 93.54W
Eagle L. U.S.A. 84 46.17N 69.20W
Eagle Lake town U.S.A. 84 47.02N 68.36W
Eagle Pass town U.S.A. 83 28.43N100.30W
Eagle River town U.S.A. 82 45.55N 89.15W
Ealing U.K. 11 51.31N 0.20W
Earlimart U.S.A. 81 35.53N119.16W
Earn r. U.K. 12 56.21N 3.18W
Earn, Loch U.K. 12 56.23N 4.12W
Easingwold U.K. 10 54.08N 1.11W
Easky Rep. of Ire. 13 54.17N 8.58W
Easley U.S.A. 85 34.50N 82.34W
East Anglian Heights hills U.K. 11 52.03N 0.15E
East Aurora U.S.A. 76 42.46N 78.37W
East B. U.S.A. 83 29.30N 94.35W
Eastbourne U.K. 11 50.46N 0.18E
East C. New Zealand 60 37.45S178.30E
East Caroline Basin Pacific Oc. 68 3.00N147.00E
East China Sea Asia 31 29.00N125.00E
East Coast d. New Zealand 60 38.20S177.45E
East Dereham U.K. 9 52.40N 0.57E
Easter I. see Pascua, Isla de i. Pacific Oc. 69
Eastern d. Ghana 52 6.20N 0.45W
Eastern d. Kenya 55 0.00 38.00E
Eastern Desert see Sharqīyah, Aş Şaḥrā' ash des. Egypt 44
Eastern Ghāts mts. India 39 16.30N 80.30E
Easterville Canada 75 53.06N 99.53W
East Falkland i. Falkland Is. 93 51.45S 58.50W
East Germany Europe 20 52.15N 12.30E
East Grand Forks U.S.A. 82 47.56N 96.55W
East Grinstead U.K. 11 51.08N 0.01W
East Ilsley U.K. 11 51.33N 1.15W
East Kilbride U.K. 12 55.46N 4.09W
East Lansing U.S.A. 84 42.45N 84.30W
Eastleigh U.K. 11 50.58N 1.21W
East London R.S.A. 56 33.00S 27.54E
Eastmain Canada 76 52.15N 78.30W
Eastmain r. Canada 76 52.15N 78.30W
Eastman Canada 77 45.18N 72.19W
Easton Md. U.S.A. 85 38.46N 76.04W
Easton Penn. U.S.A. 85 40.41N 75.13W
Easton Wash. U.S.A. 80 47.14N121.11W
East Orange U.S.A. 85 40.46N 74.14W
East Pacific Ridge Pacific Oc. 69 15.00S112.00W
East Point town U.S.A. 85 33.41N 84.29W
East Retford U.K. 10 53.19N 0.55W
East St. Louis U.S.A. 82 38.34N 90.04W
East Sussex d. U.K. 11 50.56N 0.12E
Eaton U.S.A. 82 40.32N104.42W
Eau Claire U.S.A. 82 44.50N 91.30W
Eau-Claire, Lac à l' l. Canada 76 56.10N 74.30W
Eauripik i. Caroline Is. 37 6.42N143.04E
Eauripik-N. Guinea Rise Pacific Oc. 68 2.00N141.00E
Eban Nigeria 53 9.41N 4.54E
Ebbw Vale U.K. 11 51.47N 3.12W
Ebebiyin Equat. Guinea 54 2.09N 11.20E
Eberswalde E. Germany 20 52.50N 13.50E
Ebinur Hu l. China 30 45.00N 83.00E
Ebola r. Zaïre 49 3.20N 20.57E
Eboli Italy 18 40.37N 15.04E
Ebolowa Cameroon 54 2.56N 11.11E
Ebon i. Pacific Oc. 68 4.38N168.43E
Ebony Namibia 56 22.05S 15.15E
Ebro r. Spain 16 40.43N 0.54E
Ebro, Delta del f. Spain 16 40.43N 0.54E
Ecclefechan U.K. 10 55.03N 3.18W
Echeng China 33 30.26N114.00E
Echternach Lux. 14 49.49N 6.25E
Echuca Australia 67 36.10S144.20E
Écija Spain 16 37.33N 5.04W
Écommoy France 15 47.50N 0.16E
Ecuador S. America 90 1.40S 79.00W
Ed Ethiopia 48 13.52N 41.40E
Ed Sweden 23 58.55N 11.55E
Edam Neth. 14 52.30N 5.02E
Eday i. U.K. 8 59.11N 2.47W
Eddrachillis B. U.K. 12 58.17N 5.15W
Eddystone Pt. Australia 65 40.58S148.12E
Ede Neth. 14 52.03N 5.40E
Ede Nigeria 53 7.45N 4.26E
Edea Cameroon 54 3.47N 10.15E
Edehon L. Canada 75 60.25N 97.15W
Eden Australia 67 37.04S149.54E
Eden r. Cumbria U.K. 10 54.57N 3.02W
Eden U.S.A. 80 42.03N109.26W
Edenburg R.S.A. 56 29.44S 25.55E
Edendale New Zealand 60 46.19S168.47E
Edenderry Rep. of Ire. 13 53.21N 7.05W
Edenhope Australia 66 37.04S141.20E
Edenton U.S.A. 85 36.04N 76.39W
Edeowie Australia 66 31.28S138.29E
Eder r. W. Germany 20 51.13N 9.27E
Ederny U.K. 13 54.32N 7.40W
Edgeley U.S.A. 82 40.07N 98.43W
Edgeöya i. Arctic Oc. 96 77.45N 22.30E
Edgeworthstown Rep. of Ire. 13 53.42N 7.38W
Édhessa Greece 19 40.47N 22.03E
Ediacara Australia 66 30.18S137.50E
Edina Liberia 52 6.01N 10.10W
Edinburgh U.K. 12 55.57N 3.13W
Edirne Turkey 19 41.40N 26.35E
Edithburgh Australia 66 35.06S137.44E
Edjudina Australia 63 29.48S122.23E
Edmond U.S.A. 83 35.39N 97.29W
Edmonton Canada 74 53.30N113.30W
Edmundston Canada 77 47.22N 68.20W
Edna U.S.A. 83 28.59N 96.39W
Edo r. Japan 35 35.37N139.53E
Edolo Italy 15 46.11N 10.20E
Edounga Gabon 54 0.03S 13.43E
Edremit Turkey 19 39.35N 27.02E
Edsbruk Sweden 23 58.02N 16.28E
Edson Canada 74 53.35N116.26W
Edward, L. Uganda / Zaïre 55 0.30S 29.30E
Edward's Creek town Australia 66 28.15S135.49E
Edwards Plateau f. U.S.A. 83 31.20N101.00W
Eeklo Belgium 14 51.11N 3.34E
Eel r. U.S.A. 80 40.40N124.20W
Efate i. Vanuatu 68 17.40S168.25E
Effingham U.S.A. 82 39.07N 88.33W
Egaña Argentina 93 36.57S 59.06W
Egbe Nigeria 53 8.13N 5.31E
Egeland U.S.A. 82 48.38N 99.10W
Eger Hungary 21 47.54N 20.23E
Egersund Norway 23 58.27N 6.00E
Egerton, Mt. Australia 62 24.44S117.40E
Egg Harbor U.S.A. 85 39.32N 74.39W
Egmont, Mt. New Zealand 60 39.20S174.05E
Egridir Turkey 42 37.52N 30.51E
Egridir Gölü l. Turkey 42 38.04N 30.55E
Egypt Africa 48 26.00N 30.00E
Eiao i. Is. Marquises 69 8.00S140.40W
Éibar Spain 16 43.11N 2.28W
Eidsvåg Norway 22 62.47N 8.03E
Eidsvold Australia 64 25.23S151.08E
Eifel f. W. Germany 14 50.10N 6.45E
Eigg i. U.K. 12 56.53N 6.09W
Eighty Mile Beach f. Australia 62 19.00S121.00E
Eil Somali Rep. 45 8.00N 49.51E
Eil, Loch U.K. 12 56.51N 5.12W
Eildon Resr. Australia 67 37.10S146.00E
Einasleigh Australia 64 18.31S144.05E
Eindhoven Neth. 14 51.26N 5.30E
Eirunepé Brazil 90 6.40S 69.52W
Eiseb r. Namibia 56 20.26S 20.05E
Eisenach E. Germany 20 50.59N 10.19E
Eisenerz Austria 20 47.33N 14.53E
Eisenhut mtn. Austria 20 47.00N 13.45E
Eisenhüttenstadt E. Germany 20 52.09N 14.41E
Eišiškes U.S.S.R. 21 54.09N 24.55E
Eisleben E. Germany 20 51.32N 11.33E
Eitorf W. Germany 14 50.46N 7.27E
Ejde Faroe Is. 8 62.03N 7.06W
Ejin Qi China 30 41.50N100.50E
Ejura Ghana 52 7.24N 1.20W
Ekalaka U.S.A. 80 45.53N104.33W
Eket Nigeria 53 4.39N 7.56E
Eketahuna New Zealand 60 40.39S175.44E
Ekibastuz U.S.S.R. 28 51.45N 75.22E
Ekimchan U.S.S.R. 29 53.09N133.00E
Eksjö Sweden 23 57.40N 14.47E
Ekträsk Sweden 22 64.29N 19.50E
Ekuku Zaïre 54 0.42S 21.38E
Ekwan r. Canada 76 53.30N 84.00W
El Aaiún W. Sahara 50 27.09N 13.12W
El Afweín Somali Rep. 45 9.55N 47.14E
Elands r. Trans. R.S.A. 56 24.52S 29.20E
El Arco Mexico 81 28.00N113.25W
El Arenal Spain 16 39.30N 2.45E
El Asnam Algeria 51 36.10N 1.20E
Elat Israel 44 29.33N 34.56E
Elâzig Turkey 42 38.41N 39.14E
Elba i. Italy 18 42.47N 10.17E
El Barril Mexico 81 28.22N113.00W
Elbasan Albania 19 41.07N 20.04E
El Baúl Venezuela 90 8.59N 68.16W
Elbe r. W. Germany 20 53.33N 10.00E
El Beni d. Bolivia 92 14.00S 65.30W
Elbert, Mt. U.S.A. 82 39.07N106.27W
Elberton U.S.A. 85 34.05N 82.54W
Elbeuf France 15 49.17N 1.01E
Elbistan Turkey 42 38.14N 37.11E
Elbląg Poland 21 54.10N 19.25E
Elbrus mtn. U.S.S.R. 25 43.21N 42.29E
El Bur Somali Rep. 45 4.40N 46.40E
Elburg Neth. 14 52.27N 5.50E
Elburz Mts. see Alborz, Reshteh-ye Kūhhā-ye ye Iran 43
El Cajon U.S.A. 81 32.48N116.58W
El Callao Venezuela 90 7.18N 61.48W
El Campo U.S.A. 83 29.12N 96.16W
El Casco Mexico 83 25.34N104.35W
El Centro U.S.A. 81 32.48N115.34W
Elche Spain 16 38.16N 0.41W
Elcho U.S.A. 82 45.26N 89.11W
Elcho I. Australia 64 11.55S135.45E
El Corral Mexico 83 25.09N 97.58W
El Cozón Mexico 81 31.18N112.29W
El Cuy Argentina 93 39.57S 68.20W
Elda Spain 16 38.29N 0.47W
El Dab Somali Rep. 45 8.58N 46.38E
Elde r. E. Germany 20 53.17N 12.40E
El Der Ethiopia 45 5.08N 43.08E
Elder, L. Australia 66 30.39S140.13E
El Dere Somali Rep. 45 3.55N 47.10E
El Desemboque Mexico 81 29.30N112.27W
El Djouf des. Mauritania 50 20.30N 7.30W
Eldon U.S.A. 82 38.21N 93.35W
Eldorado Canada 75 59.35N108.30W
El Dorado Ark. U.S.A. 83 33.13N 92.40W
El Dorado Kans. U.S.A. 83 37.49N 96.52W
El Dorado Venezuela 90 6.45N 61.37W
Eldoret Kenya 55 0.31N 35.17E
Electra U.S.A. 83 34.02N 98.55W
El Eglab f. Algeria 50 26.30N 4.15W
Elei, Wādī Sudan 48 22.04N 34.27E
Eleja U.S.S.R. 23 56.26N 23.42E
Elektrostal U.S.S.R. 24 55.46N 38.30E
Elephant Butte Resr. U.S.A. 81 33.19N107.10W
Elephant I. Antarctica 96 61.00S 55.00W
El Eulma Algeria 51 36.09N 5.41E
Eleuthera I. Bahamas 87 25.15N 76.20W
Elevtheroúpolis Greece 19 40.55N 24.16E
El Ferrol Spain 16 43.29N 8.14W
Elgå Norway 23 62.11N 11.07E
Elgin Canada 75 49.26N100.15W
Elgin U.K. 12 57.39N 3.20W
Elgin Ill. U.S.A. 82 42.03N 88.19W
Elgin Nev. U.S.A. 80 37.21N114.30W
Elgin Oreg. U.S.A. 80 45.34N117.55W
Elgin Tex. U.S.A. 83 30.21N 97.22W
El Golea Algeria 51 30.34N 2.53E
Elgon, Mt. Kenya / Uganda 55 1.07N 34.35E
El Hamurre Somali Rep. 45 7.11N 48.55E
Elida U.S.A. 83 33.57N103.39W
Elim Namibia 56 17.47S 15.30E
Elista U.S.S.R. 25 46.18N 44.14E
Elizabeth Australia 66 34.45S138.39E
Elizabeth N.J. U.S.A. 85 40.40N 74.13W
Elizabeth W.Va. U.S.A. 84 39.04N 81.24W
Elizabeth City U.S.A. 85 36.18N 76.16W
Elizabethtown Ky. U.S.A. 85 37.41N 85.51W
Elizabethtown Penn. U.S.A. 85 40.09N 76.36W
El Jadida Morocco 50 33.16N 8.30W
Elk r. Canada 74 49.10N115.14W
Elk Poland 21 53.50N 22.22E
El Kairouan Tunisia 51 35.41N 10.07E
El Kasserine Tunisia 51 35.11N 8.48E
Elk City U.S.A. 83 35.25N 99.25W
El Kef Tunisia 51 36.11N 8.43E
El-Kelâa-des-Srarhna Morocco 50 32.02N 7.23W
El Kere Ethiopia 49 5.48N 42.10E
Elkhart Ind. U.S.A. 82 41.52N 85.56W
Elkhart Kans. U.S.A. 83 37.00N101.54W
El Khnâchîch f. Mali 52 21.50N 3.45W
Elkhorn Canada 75 49.58N101.14W
Elkhovo Bulgaria 19 42.10N 26.35E
Elkins N.Mex. U.S.A. 81 33.41N104.04W
Elkins W.Va. U.S.A. 84 38.55N 79.51W
Elko U.S.A. 80 40.50N115.46W
Elkton Md. U.S.A. 85 39.36N 75.50W
Elleker Australia 63 34.55S117.40E
Ellen, Mt. U.S.A. 78 38.06N110.50W
Ellendale Australia 62 17.56S124.48E
Ellensburg U.S.A. 80 47.00N120.32W
Ellesmere I. Canada 73 78.00N 82.00W
Ellesmere Port U.K. 10 53.17N 2.55W
Elliot R.S.A. 56 31.19S 27.49E
Elliot Lake town Canada 76 46.35N 82.35W
Ellis U.S.A. 82 38.56N 99.34W
Elliston Australia 66 33.39S134.55E
Ellon U.K. 12 57.22N 2.05W
Ellora India 40 20.01N 75.10E
El Mahdía Tunisia 51 35.30N 11.04E
Elmali Turkey 42 36.43N 29.56E
El Maneadero Mexico 81 31.45N116.35W
Elmer U.S.A. 85 39.36N 75.10W
El Metlaoui Tunisia 51 34.20N 8.24E
Elmhurst U.S.A. 82 41.54N 87.56W
Elmina Ghana 52 5.07N 1.21W
Elmira U.S.A. 84 42.06N 76.49W
Elmore Australia 67 36.30S144.40E
El Mreiti well Mauritania 50 23.29N 7.52W
El Mreyyé f. Mauritania 50 19.30N 7.00W
Elmshorn W. Germany 20 53.46N 9.40E
El Niybo Ethiopia 49 4.32N 39.59E
Elo d. Ethiopia 49 11.30N 40.00E
El Ouassi well Mali 52 20.23N 0.12E
El Oued Algeria 51 33.20N 6.53E
Eloy U.S.A. 81 32.45N111.33W
El Paso U.S.A. 81 31.45N106.29W
El Portal U.S.A. 80 37.41N119.47W
El Quelite Mexico 81 23.32N106.28W
El Real Panama 87 8.06N 77.42W
El Reno U.S.A. 83 35.32N 97.57W
El Roba Kenya 55 3.57N 40.01E
Elrose Canada 75 51.13N108.01W
El Salto Mexico 81 23.47N105.22W
El Salvador C. America 87 13.30N 89.00W
Elsas Canada 76 48.32N 82.55W
Elsdorf W. Germany 14 50.56N 6.35E
Elsinore U.S.A. 80 38.41N112.09W
El Sueco Mexico 81 29.54N106.24W
El Tabacal Argentina 92 23.15S 64.14W
El Tigre Venezuela 90 8.44N 64.18W
Elton, Ozero l. U.S.S.R. 25 49.10N 46.34E
El Turbio Argentina 93 51.41S 72.05W
Elūru India 39 16.45N 81.10E
Elvas Portugal 16 38.53N 7.10W
Elvdal Norway 23 61.38N 11.56E
Elverum Norway 23 60.53N 11.34E
Elvira Argentina 93 35.15S 59.30W
El Wak Kenya 55 2.45N 40.52E
El Wak Somali Rep. 55 2.50N 41.03E
Elwood Nebr. U.S.A. 82 40.36N 99.52W
Elwood N.J. U.S.A. 85 39.35N 74.43W
Ely U.K. 9 52.24N 0.16E

Ely to **Fetlar**

Ely Minn. U.S.A. **82** 47.53N 91.52W
Ely Nev. U.S.A. **80** 39.15N114.53W
Elyria U.S.A. **84** 41.22N 82.06W
Emae *i.* Vanuatu **68** 17.04S168.24E
Emån *r.* Sweden **23** 57.08N 16.30E
Emāmshahr Iran **43** 36.25N 55.00E
Emba U.S.S.R. **28** 48.47N 58.05E
Emba *r.* U.S.S.R. **25** 46.38N 53.00E
Embarcación Argentina **92** 23.15S 64.10W
Embleton U.K. **10** 55.30N 1.37W
Embrun France **17** 44.34N 6.30E
Embu Kenya **55** 0.32S 37.28E
Emden W. Germany **14** 53.23N 7.13E
Emerald Australia **64** 23.32S148.10E
Emerson Canada **75** 49.00N 97.12W
Emi Koussi *mtn.* Chad **53** 19.58N 18.30E
Emilia-Romagna *d.* Italy **15** 44.35N 11.00E
Emlichheim W. Germany **14** 52.37N 6.50E
Emmaboda Sweden **23** 56.38N 15.32E
Emmaste U.S.S.R. **23** 58.42N 22.36E
Emmaus U.S.A. **85** 40.32N 75.30W
Emmaville Australia **67** 29.25S151.39E
Emmeloord Neth. **14** 52.43N 5.46E
Emmen Neth. **14** 52.48N 6.55E
Emmerich W. Germany **14** 51.49N 6.16E
Emmett U.S.A. **80** 43.52N116.30W
Emmitsburg U.S.A. **85** 39.42N 77.20W
Emory Peak *mtn.* U.S.A. **83** 29.13N103.17W
Empalme Mexico **81** 27.58N110.51W
Empangeni R.S.A. **57** 28.45S 31.54E
Empedrado Argentina **92** 27.59S 58.47W
Emporia Kans. U.S.A. **82** 38.24N 96.11W
Emporia Va. U.S.A. **85** 36.42N 77.33W
Ems *r.* W. Germany **14** 53.14N 7.25E
Emsdale Canada **76** 45.28N 79.18W
Emsdetten W. Germany **14** 52.14N 7.32E
Ems-Jade Kanal W. Germany **14** 53.28N 7.40E
Emyvale Rep. of Ire. **13** 54.20N 6.59W
Enard B. U.K. **12** 58.05N 5.20W
Encarnación Paraguay **94** 27.20S 55.50W
Enchi Ghana **52** 5.53N 2.48W
Encinal U.S.A. **83** 28.02N 99.21W
Encino U.S.A. **81** 34.39N105.28W
Encontada, Cerro de la *mtn.* Mexico **81** 27.03N112.31W
Encontrados Venezuela **90** 9.03N 72.14W
Encounter B. Australia **66** 35.35S138.44E
Ende Indonesia **37** 8.51S121.40E
Endeavour Str. Australia **64** 10.50S142.15E
Enderbury I. Kiribati **68** 3.08S171.05W
Enderby Canada **74** 50.35N119.10W
Enderby Land *f.* Antarctica **96** 67.00S 53.00E
Enderlin U.S.A. **82** 46.37N 97.36W
Endicott U.S.A. **84** 42.06N 76.03W
Endicott Arm *f.* U.S.A. **74** 57.38N133.22W
Endicott Mts. U.S.A. **72** 68.00N152.00W
Endola Namibia **56** 17.37S 15.50E
Enfida Tunisia **51** 36.08N 10.22E
Enfield U.K. **11** 51.40N 0.05W
Engaño, C. Phil. **37** 18.30N122.20E
Engcobo R.S.A. **56** 31.39S 28.01E
'En Gedi Israel **44** 31.28N 35.23E
Engels U.S.S.R. **25** 51.30N 46.07E
Enggano *i.* Indonesia **36** 5.20S102.15E
Enghershatu *mtn.* Ethiopia **48** 16.40N 38.20E
Enghien Belgium **14** 50.42N 4.02E
England U.K. **10** 53.00N 2.00W
Englewood Colo. U.S.A. **80** 39.39N104.59W
Englewood Fla. U.S.A. **85** 26.58N 82.21W
English Bāzār India **41** 25.00N 88.09E
English Channel U.K. **11** 50.15N 1.00W
English River *town* Canada **76** 49.20N 91.00W
Enid U.S.A. **83** 36.19N 97.48W
Eniwetok *i.* Pacific Oc. **68** 11.30N162.15E
Enkhuizen Neth. **14** 52.42N 5.17E
Enköping Sweden **23** 59.38N 17.04E
Enna Italy **18** 37.34N 14.15E
Ennadai Canada **75** 61.08N100.53W
Ennadai L. Canada **75** 61.00N101.00W
Ennedi *f.* Chad **48** 17.15N 22.00E
Enneri Yoo *wadi* Chad **53** 19.24N 16.38E
Enngonia Australia **67** 29.20S145.53E
Ennis Rep. of Ire. **13** 52.51N 9.00W
Ennis U.S.A. **83** 32.20N 96.38W
Enniscorthy Rep. of Ire. **13** 52.30N 6.35W
Enniskillen U.K. **13** 54.21N 7.40W
Ennistymon Rep. of Ire. **13** 52.56N 9.18W
Enns *r.* Austria **20** 48.14N 14.22E
Enontekiö Finland **22** 68.23N 23.38E
Enping China **33** 22.11N112.18E
Ensay Australia **67** 37.24S147.52E
Enschede Neth. **14** 52.13N 6.54E
Ensenada Argentina **93** 34.51S 57.55W
Ensenada Baja Calif. Norte Mexico **81** 31.52N116.37W
Ensenada Nuevo León Mexico **83** 25.56N 97.50W
Enshi China **33** 30.18N109.29E
Enshū-nada *sea* Japan **35** 34.30N137.30E
Entebbe Uganda **55** 0.08N 32.29E
Enterprise Canada **74** 60.47N115.45W
Entre Rios *d.* Argentina **93** 32.10S 59.00W
Entre Rios de Minas Brazil **94** 20.39S 44.06W
Entwistle Canada **74** 53.30N115.00W
Enugu Nigeria **53** 6.20N 7.29E
Envermeu France **15** 49.53N 1.15E
Envigado Colombia **90** 6.09N 75.35W
Enza *r.* Italy **15** 44.54N 10.31E
Enzan Japan **35** 35.42N138.44E
Eolie, Isole *is.* Italy **18** 38.35N 14.45E
Epe Neth. **14** 52.21N 5.59E
Epernay France **15** 49.02N 3.58E
Ephraim U.S.A. **80** 39.22N111.35W
Ephrata Penn. U.S.A. **85** 40.11N 76.10W
Ephrata Wash. U.S.A. **80** 47.19N119.33W
Epi *i.* Vanuatu **68** 16.43S168.15E
Épila Spain **16** 41.36N 1.17W
Épinal France **17** 48.10N 6.28E
Epping U.K. **11** 51.42N 0.07E
Epsom U.K. **11** 51.20N 0.16W
Epte *r.* France **15** 49.04N 1.37E
Equateur *d.* Zaïre **54** 0.00 21.00E
Equatorial Guinea Africa **54** 2.00N 10.00E
Equerdreville France **15** 49.40N 1.40W
Era, Ozero *l.* U.S.S.R. **25** 47.38N 45.18E
Eraclea Italy **15** 45.35N 12.40E
Eradu Australia **63** 28.41S115.02E
Erciyaş Daği *mtn.* Turkey **42** 38.33N 35.25E
Erdre *r.* France **15** 47.27N 1.34W
Erebus, Mt. Antarctica **96** 77.40S167.20E
Erechim Brazil **94** 27.35S 52.15W
Eregli Konya Turkey **42** 37.30N 34.02E
Eregli Zonguldak Turkey **42** 41.17N 31.26E
Erenhot China **32** 43.48N112.00E
Erer *r.* Ethiopia **45** 7.35N 42.05E
Erfoud Morocco **50** 31.28N 4.10W
Erft *r.* W. Germany **14** 51.12N 6.45E
Erfurt E. Germany **20** 50.58N 11.02E
Erfurt *d.* E. Germany **20** 51.10N 10.45E
Ergani Turkey **42** 38.17N 39.44E
Ergene *r.* Turkey **19** 41.02N 26.22E
Ergig *r.* Chad **53** 11.30N 15.30E
Erica Neth. **14** 52.44N 6.56E
Erie U.S.A. **84** 42.07N 80.05W
Erie, L. Canada/U.S.A. **76** 42.15N 81.00W
Erigavo Somali Rep. **45** 10.40N 47.20E
Eriksdale Canada **75** 50.52N 98.06W
Eriskay *i.* U.K. **12** 57.04N 7.17W
Eritrea *d.* Ethiopia **48** 15.30N 39.00E
Eritrea *f.* Ethiopia **48** 15.30N 38.00E
Erkelenz W. Germany **14** 51.05N 6.18E
Erlangen W. Germany **20** 49.36N 11.02E
Erldunda Australia **64** 25.14S133.12E
Ermelo Neth. **14** 52.19N 5.38E
Ermelo R.S.A. **56** 26.30S 29.59E
Erne *r.* Rep. of Ire. **9** 54.30N 8.17W
Ernée France **15** 48.18N 0.56W
Erode India **38** 11.21N 77.43E
Eromanga *i.* Vanuatu **68** 18.45S169.05E
Eroto Ethiopia **48** 16.13N 37.57E
Er Rachidia Morocco **50** 31.58N 4.25W
Errego Mozambique **55** 16.02S 37.11E
Errigal Mtn. Rep. of Ire. **13** 55.02N 8.08W
Erris Head Rep. of Ire. **13** 54.19N 10.00W
Ertix He *r.* U.S.S.R. **30** 48.00N 84.20E
Erudina Australia **66** 31.30S139.23E
Ervy-le-Châtel France **15** 48.02N 3.55E
Erzgebirge *mts.* E. Germany/Czech. **20** 50.30N 12.50E
Erzin U.S.S.R. **30** 50.16N 95.14E
Erzincan Turkey **42** 39.44N 39.30E
Erzurum Turkey **42** 39.57N 41.17E
Esbjerg Denmark **23** 55.28N 8.27E
Esbo *see* Espoo Finland **23**
Escalante U.S.A. **80** 37.47N111.36W
Escalón Mexico **83** 26.45N104.20W
Escanaba U.S.A. **84** 45.47N 87.04W
Esch Lux. **14** 49.31N 5.59E
Eschweiler W. Germany **14** 50.49N 6.16E
Escondido *r.* Nicaragua **87** 11.58N 83.45W
Escondido U.S.A. **81** 33.07N117.05W
Escuinapa Mexico **81** 22.51N105.48W
Escuintla Guatemala **86** 14.18N 90.47W
Esens W. Germany **14** 53.40N 7.40E
Eşfahān Iran **43** 32.42N 51.40E
Esher U.K. **11** 51.23N 0.22W
Eshkanān Iran **43** 27.10N 53.38E
Eshowe R.S.A. **56** 28.53S 31.29E
Esk *r.* N. Yorks. U.K. **10** 54.29N 0.37W
Eskifjördhur *town* Iceland **22** 65.05N 14.00W
Eskilstuna Sweden **23** 59.22N 16.30E
Eskimo Point *town* Canada **75** 61.10N 94.03W
Eskişehir Turkey **42** 39.46N 30.30E
Esla *r.* Spain **16** 41.29N 6.03W
Eslāmābād Iran **43** 34.08N 46.35E
Eslöv Sweden **23** 55.50N 13.20E
Esmeraldas Ecuador **90** 0.56N 79.40W
Espanola Canada **76** 46.15N 81.46W
Espe U.S.S.R. **28** 43.50N 74.10E
Esperance Australia **63** 33.49S121.52E
Esperance B. Australia **63** 33.51S121.53E
Esperanza Argentina **93** 31.30S 61.00W
Esperanza Mexico **81** 27.35N109.56W
Espinal Colombia **90** 4.08N 75.00W
Espinhaço, Serra do *mts.* Brazil **94** 17.15S 43.10W
Espírito Santo *d.* Brazil **94** 20.00S 40.30W
Espírtu Santo I. Vanuatu **68** 15.50S166.50E
Espoo Finland **23** 60.13N 24.40E
Espungabera Mozambique **57** 20.28S 32.48E
Esquel Argentina **93** 42.55S 71.20W
Esquimalt Canada **74** 48.30N123.23W
Esquina Argentina **93** 30.00S 59.30W
Essaouira Morocco **50** 31.30N 9.47W
Essen W. Germany **14** 51.27N 6.57E
Essequibo *r.* Guyana **90** 6.30N 58.40W
Essex *d.* U.K. **11** 51.46N 0.30E
Essex U.S.A. **81** 34.45N115.15W
Essonne *d.* France **15** 48.36N 2.20E
Essoyes France **15** 48.04N 4.32E
Essoyla U.S.S.R. **24** 61.47N 33.11E
Es Suki Sudan **49** 13.24N 33.55E
Est *d.* U. Volta **52** 12.45N 0.25E
Est, Pointe de l' *c.* Canada **77** 49.08N 61.41W
Estacado, Llano *f.* U.S.A. **83** 33.30N102.40W
Estados, Isla de los *i.* Argentina **93** 54.45S 64.00W
Eşţahbānāt Iran **43** 29.05N 54.03E
Estância Brazil **91** 11.15S 37.28W
Estand, Kūh-e *mtn.* Iran **43** 31.18N 60.03E
Este Italy **15** 45.14N 11.39E
Estelline U.S.A. **83** 34.33N100.26W
Estepona Spain **16** 36.26N 5.09W
Esternay France **15** 48.44N 3.34E
Estevan Canada **75** 49.07N103.05W
Estevan Is. Canada **74** 53.03N129.38W
Estevan Pt. Canada **74** 49.23N126.33W
Estherville U.S.A. **82** 43.24N 94.50W
Estissac France **15** 48.16N 3.49E
Estivane Mozambique **57** 24.07S 32.38E
Eston U.K. **10** 54.34N 1.07W
Estonskaya S.S.R. *d.* U.S.S.R. **23** 58.35N 24.35E
Estoril Portugal **16** 38.42N 9.23W
Estrela, Serra da *mts.* Portugal **16** 40.20N 7.40W
Estremoz Portugal **16** 38.50N 7.35W
Esztergom Hungary **21** 47.48N 18.45E
Étables France **17** 48.37N 2.50W
Etadunna Australia **66** 28.43S138.38E
Etah India **41** 27.38N 78.40E
Etamamiou Canada **77** 50.16N 59.58W
Étampes France **15** 48.26N 2.10E
Étaples France **17** 50.31N 1.39E
Etāwah India **41** 26.46N 79.02E
Ethel Creek *town* Australia **62** 23.05S120.14E
Ethiopia Africa **49** 9.00N 39.00E
Etive, Loch U.K. **12** 56.27N 5.15W
Etna, Monte *mtn.* Italy **18** 37.43N 14.59E
Etolin I. U.S.A. **74** 56.10N132.30W
Etosha Game Res. Namibia **56** 18.50S 15.40E
Etosha Pan *f.* Namibia **56** 18.50S 16.20E
Etowah U.S.A. **85** 35.20N 84.30W
Étretat France **15** 49.42N 0.12E
Ettelbrück Lux. **14** 49.51N 6.06E
Eua *i.* Tonga **69** 21.23S174.55W
Euabalong Australia **67** 33.07S146.28E
Eubank U.S.A. **85** 37.16N 84.40W
Euboea *see* Évvoia *i.* Greece **19**
Eucla Australia **63** 31.40S128.51E
Euclid U.S.A. **84** 41.34N 81.33W
Eucumbene, L. Australia **67** 36.05S148.45E
Eudora U.S.A. **83** 33.07N 91.16W
Eudunda Australia **66** 34.09S139.04E
Eufaula Resr. U.S.A. **79** 35.15N 95.35W
Eugene U.S.A. **80** 44.02N123.05W
Eugenia, Punta *c.* Mexico **81** 27.50N115.03W
Eumungerie Australia **67** 31.57S148.39E
Eunice La. U.S.A. **83** 30.30N 92.25W
Eunice N.Mex. U.S.A. **83** 32.26N103.09W
Eupen Belgium **14** 50.38N 6.04E
Euphrates *r. see* Al Furāt *r.* Asia **43**
Eurdon U.S.A. **83** 33.55N 93.09W
Eure *d.* France **15** 49.10N 1.00E
Eure *r.* France **15** 48.18N 1.12E
Eure et Loire *d.* France **15** 48.30N 1.30E
Eureka Calif. U.S.A. **80** 40.47N124.09W
Eureka Kans. U.S.A. **83** 37.49N 96.17W
Eureka Nev. U.S.A. **80** 39.31N115.58W
Eureka Utah U.S.A. **80** 39.57N112.07W
Eurinilla *r.* Australia **66** 30.50S140.01E
Euriowie Australia **66** 31.22S141.42E
Euroa Australia **67** 36.46S145.35E
Europa, Picos de *mts.* Spain **16** 43.10N 4.40W
Euskirchen W. Germany **14** 50.40N 6.47E
Euston Australia **66** 34.34S142.49E
Eutsuk L. Canada **74** 53.20N126.45W
Evale Angola **54** 16.24S 15.50E
Evans, Lac *l.* Canada **76** 50.50N 77.00W
Evans Head *c.* Australia **67** 29.06S153.25E
Evanston Ill. U.S.A. **82** 42.02N 87.41W
Evanston Wyo. U.S.A. **80** 41.16N110.58W
Evansville U.S.A. **84** 38.00N 87.33W
Evelyn Creek *r.* Australia **66** 28.20S134.50E
Everard, C. Australia **67** 37.50S149.16E
Everard, L. Australia **66** 31.25S135.05E
Everard Range *mts.* Australia **65** 27.05S132.28E
Everest, Mt. China/Nepal **41** 27.59N 86.56E
Everett Wash. U.S.A. **80** 47.59N122.13W
Everglades U.S.A. **85** 25.52N 81.23W
Everglades Nat. Park U.S.A. **85** 25.27N 80.53W
Evesham U.K. **11** 52.06N 1.57W
Evijärvi Finland **22** 63.22N 23.29E
Evinayong Equat. Guinea **54** 1.27N 10.34E
Evje Norway **23** 58.36N 7.51E
Évora Portugal **16** 38.34N 7.54W
Évreux France **15** 49.03N 1.11E
Évry France **15** 48.38N 2.27E
Évvoia *i.* Greece **19** 38.30N 23.50E
Ewaninga Australia **64** 23.58S133.58E
Ewe, Loch U.K. **12** 57.48N 5.38W
Ewing U.S.A. **82** 42.16N 98.21W
Ewo Congo **54** 0.48S 14.47E
Excelsior Springs *town* U.S.A. **82** 39.20N 94.13W
Exe *r.* U.K. **11** 50.40N 3.28W
Exeter U.K. **11** 50.43N 3.31W
Exeter Nebr. U.S.A. **82** 40.39N 97.27W
Exmoor Forest *hills* U.K. **11** 51.08N 3.45W
Exmore U.S.A. **85** 37.32N 75.49W
Exmouth Australia **62** 21.54S114.10E
Exmouth U.K. **11** 50.37N 3.24W
Exmouth G. Australia **62** 22.00S114.20E
Expedition Range *mts.* Australia **64** 24.30S149.05E
Extremadura *d.* Spain **16** 39.00N 6.00W
Exuma Is. Bahamas **87** 24.00N 76.00W
Eyasi, L. Tanzania **55** 3.40S 35.00E
Eye U.K. **11** 52.19N 1.09E
Eyemouth U.K. **12** 55.52N 2.05W
Eygurande France **17** 45.40N 2.26E
Eyjafjördhur *est.* Iceland **22** 65.54N 18.15W
Eyrarbakki Iceland **22** 63.52N 21.09W
Eyre Australia **63** 32.15S126.18E
Eyre *r.* Australia **64** 26.40S139.00E
Eyre, L. Australia **66** 28.30S137.25E
Eyre Pen. Australia **66** 34.00S135.45E

F

Faaone Tahiti **69** 17.40S149.18W
Fåberg Norway **23** 61.10N 10.22E
Fåborg Denmark **23** 55.06N 10.15E
Fabriano Italy **18** 43.20N 12.54E
Facatativá Colombia **90** 4.48N 74.32W
Facundo Argentina **93** 45.19S 69.59W
Fada Chad **48** 17.14N 21.33E
Fada-N'Gourma U. Volta **52** 12.03N 0.22E
Faenza Italy **15** 44.17N 11.52E
Fafa Mali **52** 15.20N 0.43E
Fafen *r.* Ethiopia **45** 6.07N 44.20E
Fagamalo W. Samoa **68** 13.24S172.22W
Făgăraş Romania **21** 45.51N 24.58E
Fagernes Norway **23** 60.59N 9.17E
Fagersta Sweden **23** 60.00N 15.47E
Faguibine, Lac *l.* Mali **52** 16.45N 3.54W
Fagus Egypt **44** 30.44N 31.47E
Fā'id Egypt **44** 30.19N 32.19E
Fairbanks U.S.A. **72** 64.50N147.50W
Fairborn U.S.A. **84** 39.48N 84.03W
Fairbury U.S.A. **82** 40.08N 97.11W
Fairfax U.S.A. **83** 36.34N 96.42W
Fairfield Ala. U.S.A. **85** 33.29N 86.59W
Fairfield Calif. U.S.A. **80** 38.15N122.03W
Fairfield Ill. U.S.A. **82** 38.22N 88.23W
Fairfield Iowa U.S.A. **82** 40.56N 91.57W
Fair Head U.K. **13** 55.13N 6.09W
Fair Isle U.K. **12** 59.32N 1.38W
Fairlie New Zealand **60** 44.06S170.50E
Fairmont Minn. U.S.A. **82** 43.39N 94.28W
Fairmont W.Va. U.S.A. **84** 39.28N 80.08W
Fairview Canada **74** 56.05N118.25W
Fairview Mont. U.S.A. **80** 47.51N104.03W
Fairview Okla. U.S.A. **83** 36.16N 98.29W
Fairview Utah U.S.A. **80** 39.38N111.26W
Fairweather, Mt. U.S.A. **74** 59.00N137.30W
Faisalābād Pakistan **40** 31.25N 73.05E
Faith U.S.A. **82** 45.02N102.02W
Faizābād India **41** 26.47N 82.08E
Fajr, Wādī *r.* Saudi Arabia **42** 30.00N 38.25E
Fakaofo Pacific Oc. **68** 9.30S171.15W
Fakenham U.K. **10** 52.50N 0.51E
Fakfak Indonesia **37** 2.55S132.17E
Falaise France **15** 48.54N 0.11W
Falam Burma **34** 22.58N 93.45E
Falcarragh Rep. of Ire. **13** 55.08N 8.06W
Falcone, Capo del *c.* Italy **18** 40.57N 8.12E
Falcon Resr. U.S.A. **83** 26.37N 99.11W
Falealupo W. Samoa **68** 13.29S172.47W
Falémé *r.* Senegal **52** 14.55N 12.00W
Faleshty U.S.S.R. **21** 47.30N 27.45E
Falfurrias U.S.A. **83** 27.14N 98.09W
Falkenberg Sweden **23** 56.54N 12.28E
Falkirk U.K. **12** 56.00N 3.48W
Falkland Is. Atlantic Oc. **93** 51.45W 59.00W
Falkland Sd. *str.* Falkland Is. **93** 51.45W 59.25W
Falköping Sweden **23** 58.10N 13.31E
Fallbrook U.S.A. **81** 33.23N117.15W
Fallon U.S.A. **80** 46.50N105.07W
Fall River *town* U.S.A. **84** 41.43N 71.08W
Falls City U.S.A. **82** 40.03N 95.36W
Falmouth U.K. **11** 50.09N 5.05W
False B. R.S.A. **56** 34.10S 18.40E
False C. U.S.A. **85** 38.29N 74.59W
False Pt. India **41** 20.22N 86.52E
Falster *i.* Denmark **23** 54.48N 11.58E
Fălticeni Romania **21** 47.28N 26.18E
Falun Sweden **23** 60.36N 15.38E
Famagusta *see* Ammókhostos Cyprus **44**
Family L. Canada **75** 51.54N 95.30W
Famoso U.S.A. **81** 35.36N119.14W
Fandriana Madagascar **57** 20.14S 47.23E
Fangak Sudan **49** 9.04N 30.53E
Fangcheng China **32** 33.18N112.59E
Fangdou Shan *mts.* China **33** 30.36N108.45E
Fang Xian China **33** 32.04N110.47E
Fanjing Shan *mtn.* China **33** 27.57N108.50E
Fannich, Loch U.K. **12** 57.38N 5.00W
Fanning I. *see* Tabuaeran *i.* Kiribati **69**
Fano Italy **15** 43.50N 13.01E
Fan Xian China **32** 35.59N115.31E
Faradje Zaïre **55** 3.45N 29.43E
Faradofay Madagascar **57** 25.02S 47.00E
Farafangana Madagascar **57** 22.49S 47.50E
Farāfirah, Wāḥāt al *oasis* Egypt **42** 27.15N 28.10E
Farāh Afghan. **40** 32.22N 62.07E
Farāh *d.* Afghan. **40** 33.00N 62.00E
Farāh *r.* Afghan. **40** 31.29N 61.24E
Farallon de Medinilla *i.* Mariana Is. **37** 16.01N146.04E
Farallon de Pajaros *i.* Mariana Is. **37** 20.33N144.59E
Faranah Guinea **52** 10.01N 10.47W
Farasān, Jazā'ir *is.* Saudi Arabia **48** 16.48N 41.54E
Faratsiho Madagascar **57** 19.24S 46.57E
Faraulep *is.* Mariana Is. **37** 8.36N144.33E
Fareara, Pt. Tahiti **69** 17.52S149.39W
Fareham U.K. **11** 50.52N 1.11W
Farewell, C. *see* Farvel, Kap *c.* Greenland **73**
Farewell, C. New Zealand **60** 40.30S172.35E
Fargo U.S.A. **82** 46.52N 96.48W
Faribault U.S.A. **82** 44.18N 93.16W
Farīdpur Bangla. **41** 23.36N 89.50E
Farim Guinea Bissau **52** 12.30N 15.09W
Farina Australia **66** 30.05S138.20E
Farkwa Tanzania **55** 5.26S 35.15E
Farmerville U.S.A. **83** 32.47N 92.24W
Farmington Mo. U.S.A. **83** 37.47N 90.25W
Farmington N.Mex. U.S.A. **80** 36.44N108.12W
Farnborough U.K. **11** 51.17N 0.46W
Farne Is. U.K. **10** 55.38N 1.36W
Farnham U.K. **11** 51.13N 0.49W
Farnham Canada **77** 45.17N 72.59W
Faro Brazil **91** 2.11S 56.44W
Faro Portugal **16** 37.01N 7.56W
Faroe Bank *f.* Atlantic Oc. **8** 61.00N 9.00W
Faroe Is. Europe **8** 62.00N 7.00W
Fårön *i.* Sweden **23** 57.56N 19.08E
Fårösund Sweden **23** 57.52N 19.03E
Farrell U.S.A. **84** 41.13N 80.31W
Farrukhābād India **41** 27.24N 79.34E
Fársala Greece **19** 39.17N 22.22E
Fārsī Afghan. **40** 33.47N 63.15E
Farsund Norway **23** 58.05N 6.48E
Fartak, Ra's *c.* S. Yemen **45** 15.38N 52.15E
Farvel, Kap *c.* Greenland **73** 60.00N 44.20W
Farwell U.S.A. **83** 34.23N103.02W
Fasā Iran **43** 28.55N 53.38E
Fastov U.S.S.R. **21** 50.08N 29.59E
Fatehābād India **40** 29.31N 75.28E
Fatehjang Pakistan **40** 33.34N 72.39E
Fatehpur Rāj. India **40** 27.59N 74.57E
Fatehpur Uttar P. India **41** 25.56N 80.48E
Fatehpur Pakistan **40** 31.10N 71.13E
Fatehpur Sīkri India **41** 27.06N 77.40E
Fatick Senegal **52** 14.19N 16.27W
Fatu Hiva *i.* Îs. Marquises **69** 10.27S138.39W
Fatwā India **41** 25.31N 85.19E
Faulkton U.S.A. **82** 45.02N 99.08W
Făurei Romania **21** 45.04N 27.15E
Fauske Norway **22** 67.17N 15.25E
Favara Italy **18** 37.19N 13.40E
Favignana *i.* Italy **18** 37.57N 12.19E
Fawcett Canada **74** 54.34N114.06W
Fawcett L. Canada **76** 51.20N 91.46W
Fawn *r.* Canada **75** 55.20N 88.20W
Faxaflói *b.* Iceland **22** 64.30N 22.50W
Faxe *r.* Sweden **22** 63.15N 17.15E
Fayette U.S.A. **85** 33.42N 87.50W
Fayetteville Ark. U.S.A. **83** 36.04N 94.10W
Fayetteville N.C. U.S.A. **85** 35.03N 78.53W
Fayetteville Tenn. U.S.A. **85** 35.08N 86.33W
Fāzilka India **40** 30.24N 74.02E
Fāzilpur Pakistan **40** 29.18N 70.27E
Fdérik Mauritania **50** 22.30N 12.30W
Feale *r.* Rep. of Ire. **13** 52.28N 9.37W
Fear, C. U.S.A. **85** 33.50N 77.58W
Fécamp France **15** 49.45N 0.23E
Federación Argentina **93** 31.00S 57.55W
Federal Argentina **93** 30.55S 58.45W
Federal Capital Territory *d.* Nigeria **53** 8.50N 7.00E
Fedovo U.S.S.R. **24** 62.22N 39.21E
Fedulki U.S.S.R. **24** 65.00N 66.10E
Feeagh, Lough Rep. of Ire. **13** 53.56N 9.35W
Fehmarn *i.* W. Germany **20** 54.30N 11.05E
Feia, Lagoa *l.* Brazil **94** 22.00S 41.20W
Feijó Brazil **90** 8.09S 70.21W
Feilding New Zealand **60** 40.10S175.25E
Feira Zambia **55** 15.30S 30.27E
Feira de Santana Brazil **91** 12.17S 38.53W
Felanitx Spain **16** 39.27N 3.08E
Feldkirch Austria **20** 47.15N 9.38E
Felixstowe U.K. **11** 51.58N 1.20E
Feltre Italy **15** 46.01N 11.54E
Femunden *l.* Norway **23** 62.12N 11.52E
Femundsenden Norway **23** 61.55N 11.55E
Fenerwa Ethiopia **49** 13.05N 38.58E
Fengcheng Jiangxi China **33** 28.10N115.45E
Fengcheng Liaoning China **32** 40.29N124.00E
Fengfeng China **32** 36.35N114.28E
Fenggang China **33** 27.58N107.47E
Fengjie China **33** 31.02N109.31E
Fengnan China **32** 39.30N117.58E
Fengpin Taiwan **33** 23.36N121.31E
Fengrun China **32** 39.51N118.08E
Fen He *r.* China **32** 35.30N110.38E
Feni Bangla. **41** 23.01N 91.20E
Fenoarivo Madagascar **57** 18.26S 46.34E
Fenoarivo Atsinanana Madagascar **57** 17.22S 49.25E
Fensfjorden *est.* Norway **23** 60.51N 4.50E
Fenton U.S.A. **84** 42.48N 83.42W
Fenwick U.S.A. **85** 38.14N 80.36W
Fenyang China **32** 37.10N111.40E
Feodosiya U.S.S.R. **25** 45.03N 35.23E
Ferdows Iran **43** 34.00N 58.10E
Fère-Champenoise France **15** 48.45N 3.59E
Fère-en-Tardenois France **15** 48.12N 3.31E
Ferfer Somali Rep. **45** 5.07N 45.07E
Fergana U.S.S.R. **30** 40.23N 71.19E
Fergus Falls *town* U.S.A. **82** 46.17N 96.04W
Ferguson U.S.A. **82** 38.46N 90.19W
Fergusson I. P.N.G. **64** 9.30S150.40E
Ferkéssédougou Ivory Coast **52** 9.30N 5.10W
Fermanagh *d.* U.K. **13** 54.21N 7.40W
Fermo Italy **18** 43.09N 13.43E
Fermoselle Spain **16** 41.19N 6.24W
Fermoy Rep. of Ire. **13** 52.08N 8.17W
Fernandina Beach *town* U.S.A. **85** 30.40N 81.26W
Fernando de Noronha *i* Atlantic Oc. **95** 3.50S 32.25W
Fernlee Australia **67** 28.12S147.05E
Ferrara Italy **15** 44.49N 11.38E
Ferreñafe Peru **90** 6.42S 79.45W
Ferret, Cap *c.* France **17** 44.42N 1.16W
Ferriday U.S.A. **83** 31.38N 91.33W
Ferrières France **15** 48.05N 2.48E
Fès Morocco **50** 34.05N 4.57W
Feshi Zaïre **54** 6.08S 18.12E
Festubert Canada **77** 47.15N 72.40W
Festus U.S.A. **82** 38.13N 90.24W
Feteşti Romania **21** 44.23N 27.50E
Fethiye Turkey **42** 36.37N 29.06E
Fetlar *i.* U.K. **12** 60.37N 0.52W

Feuilles, Rivière aux to Galatina

Feuilles, Rivière aux r. Canada 73 58.47N 70.06W
Fevzipaşa Turkey 42 37.07N 36.38E
Fianarantsoa Madagascar 57 21.26S 47.05E
Fiche Ethiopia 49 9.52N 38.46E
Fidenza Italy 15 44.52N 10.03E
Fier Albania 19 40.43N 19.34E
Fife d. U.K. 12 56.10N 3.10W
Fife Ness c. U.K. 12 56.17N 2.36W
Figeac France 17 44.32N 2.01E
Figueira da Foz Portugal 16 40.09N 8.51W
Figueras Spain 16 42.16N 2.57E
Fihaonana Madagascar 57 18.36S 47.12E
Fiherenana r. Madagascar 57 23.19S 43.37E
Fiji Pacific Oc. 68 18.00S178.00E
Fik Ethiopia 49 8.10N 42.18E
Filabusi Zimbabwe 56 20.34S 29.20E
Filey U.K. 10 54.13N 0.18W
Filiaşi Romania 21 44.33N 23.31E
Filiatrá Greece 19 37.09N 21.35E
Filingué Niger 53 14.21N 3.22E
Filipstad Sweden 23 59.43N 14.10E
Fillmore Canada 75 49.50N103.25W
Fillmore Calif. U.S.A. 81 34.24N118.55W
Fimi r. Zaïre 54 3.00S 17.00E
Finale Emilia Italy 15 44.50N 11.17E
Finale Ligure Italy 15 44.10N 8.20E
Findhorn r. U.K. 12 57.38N 3.37W
Findlay U.S.A. 84 41.02N 83.40W
Findlay, Mt. Canada 74 50.04N116.10W
Finisterre, Cabo de c. Spain 16 42.54N 9.16W
Finke r. Australia 65 27.00S136.10E
Finland Europe 24 64.30N 27.00E
Finland, G. of Finland/U.S.S.R. 23 59.30N 24.00E
Finlay r. Canada 74 57.00N125.05W
Finley Australia 67 35.40S145.34E
Finmark Canada 76 48.36N 89.44W
Finn r. Rep. of Ire. 13 54.50N 7.30W
Finnmark d. Norway 22 70.10N 26.00E
Finschhafen P.N.G. 37 6.35S147.51E
Finse Norway 23 60.36N 7.30E
Finspång Sweden 23 58.43N 15.47E
Fiorenzuola d'Arda Italy 15 44.56N 9.55E
Firat r. Turkey see Al Furāt r. Asia 42
Firebag r. Canada 75 57.45N111.20W
Firedrake L. Canada 75 61.25N104.30W
Firenze Italy 18 43.46N 11.15E
Firenzuola Italy 15 44.07N 11.23E
Fīrozābād India 41 27.09N 78.25E
Fīrozpur India 40 30.55N 74.38E
Fīrozpur Jhirka India 40 27.48N 76.57E
Firth of Clyde est. U.K. 12 55.35N 4.53W
Firth of Forth est. U.K. 12 56.05N 3.00W
Firth of Lorn est. U.K. 12 56.20N 5.40W
Firth of Tay est. U.K. 12 56.24N 3.08W
Fīrūzābād Iran 43 28.50N 52.35E
Firyuza U.S.S.R. 28 37.55N 58.03E
Fish r. Namibia 56 28.07S 17.45E
Fisher U.S.A. 83 35.30N 90.58W
Fisher Str. Canada 73 63.00N 84.00W
Fishguard U.K. 11 51.59N 4.59W
Fiskenaesset Greenland 73 63.05N 50.40W
Fiskivötn f. Iceland 22 64.50N 20.45W
Fismes France 15 49.18N 3.41E
Fitu Ethiopia 49 5.05N 40.42E
Fitzgerald U.S.A. 85 31.43N 83.16W
Fitz Roy Argentina 93 47.00S 67.15W
Fitzroy r. Australia 62 17.31S123.35E
Fitzroy Crossing Australia 62 18.13S125.33E
Fivizzano Italy 15 44.14N 10.08E
Fizi Zaïre 55 4.18S 28.56E
Fjällåsen Sweden 22 67.29N 20.10E
Fjällsjo r. Sweden 22 63.27N 17.06E
Flå Norway 23 60.25N 9.26E
Flagler U.S.A. 80 39.18N103.04W
Flagstaff U.S.A. 81 35.12N111.39W
Flagstaff B. St. Helena 95 15.55S 5.40W
Flåm Norway 23 60.50N 7.07E
Flamborough Head U.K. 10 54.06N 0.05W
Flaming Gorge Resr. U.S.A. 80 41.15N109.30W
Flandre f. Belgium 14 50.52N 3.00E
Flannan Is. U.K. 12 58.16N 7.40W
Flåsjön l. Sweden 22 64.06N 15.51E
Flat r. Canada 74 61.51N126.00W
Flathead L. U.S.A. 80 47.52N114.08W
Flatonia U.S.A. 83 29.47N 97.06W
Flattery, C. Australia 64 14.58S145.21E
Flattery, C. U.S.A. 78 48.23N124.43W
Flatts Village Bermuda 95 32.19N 64.44W
Flaxton U.S.A. 82 48.54N102.24W
Fleetwood U.K. 10 53.55N 3.01W
Flekkefjord town Norway 23 58.17N 6.41E
Flemington U.S.A. 85 40.31N 74.52W
Flen Sweden 23 59.04N 16.35E
Flensburg W. Germany 20 54.47N 9.27E
Flers France 15 48.45N 0.34W
Fleur-de-Lys Canada 77 50.06N 56.08W
Flinders r. Australia 64 17.30S140.45E
Flinders B. Australia 63 34.23S115.19E
Flinders I. S.A. Australia 66 33.44S134.30E
Flinders I. Tas. Australia 65 40.00S148.00E
Flinders Range mts. Australia 66 31.25S138.45E
Flinders Reefs Australia 64 17.37S148.31E
Flin Flon Canada 75 54.46N101.53W
Flint U.K. 10 53.15N 3.07W
Flint U.S.A. 84 43.03N 83.40W
Flint r. Ga. U.S.A. 85 30.52N 84.38W
Flint I. Kiribati 69 11.26S151.48W
Flinton Australia 65 27.54S149.34E
Flisa Norway 23 60.34N 12.06E
Flora U.S.A. 82 38.40N 88.30W
Florac France 17 44.19N 3.36E
Florence see Firenze Italy 18
Florence Ala. U.S.A. 85 34.48N 87.40W
Florence Ariz. U.S.A. 81 33.02N111.23W
Florence Colo. U.S.A. 80 38.23N105.08W
Florence Oreg. U.S.A. 80 43.58N124.07W
Florence S.C. U.S.A. 85 34.12N 79.44W
Florence, L. Australia 66 28.52S138.08E
Florencia Colombia 90 1.37N 75.37W
Florennes Belgium 14 50.14N 4.35E
Florenville Belgium 14 49.42N 5.19E
Flores i. Indonesia 37 8.40S121.20E
Flores, Laut sea Indonesia 37 7.00S121.00E
Floreshty U.S.S.R. 21 47.52N 28.12E
Flores Sea see Flores, Laut sea Indonesia 37
Floriano Brazil 91 6.45S 43.00W
Florianópolis Brazil 94 27.35S 48.34W
Florida Uruguay 93 34.06S 56.13W
Florida d. U.S.A. 85 28.00N 82.00W
Florida, Str. of U.S.A. 85 24.00N 81.00W
Florida B. U.S.A. 85 25.00N 80.45W
Florida City U.S.A. 85 25.27N 80.30W
Florida Keys is. U.S.A. 85 24.45N 81.00W
Florina Australia 66 32.23S139.58E
Flórina Greece 19 40.48N 21.25E
Florö Norway 23 61.36N 5.00E
Fluessen l. Neth. 14 52.58N 5.23E
Flushing see Vlissingen Neth. 14
Fly r. P.N.G. 64 8.22S142.23E
Focşani Romania 21 45.40N 27.12E
Foggia Italy 18 41.28N 15.33E
Foggo Nigeria 53 11.21N 9.57E
Fogo Canada 77 49.43N 54.17W
Fogo I. Canada 77 49.40N 54.13W
Foix France 17 42.57N 1.35E
Folda est. Nordland Norway 22 67.36N 14.50E
Folda est. N. Trönd. Norway 22 64.45N 11.20E
Folégandros i. Greece 19 36.35N 24.55E
Foley Botswana 56 21.34S 27.21E
Foleyet Canada 76 48.05N 82.26W
Folgares Angola 56 14.55S 15.03E
Folgares Angola 54 14.55S 15.03E
Folgefonna glacier Norway 23 60.00N 6.20E
Foligno Italy 18 42.56N 12.43E
Folkestone U.K. 11 51.05N 1.11E
Folkston U.S.A. 85 30.49N 82.02W
Folsom U.S.A. 80 38.41N121.15W
Fominskoye U.S.S.R. 24 59.45N 42.03E
Fond du Lac Canada 75 59.17N106.00W
Fond du Lac U.S.A. 82 43.48N 88.27W
Fonsagrada Spain 16 43.08N 7.04W
Fonseca, Golfo de g. Honduras 87 13.10N 87.30W
Fontainebleau France 15 48.24N 2.42E
Fonte Boa Brazil 90 2.33S 65.59W
Fontenay France 17 46.28N 0.48W
Fonuafo'ou i. Tonga 69 18.47S173.58W
Foothills town Canada 74 53.04N116.47W
Forbach France 17 49.11N 6.54E
Forbes Australia 67 33.24S148.03E
Forbesganj India 41 26.18N 87.15E
Forchheim W. Germany 20 49.43N 11.04E
Förde Norway 23 61.27N 5.52E
Ford's Bridge Australia 67 29.46S145.25E
Fordyce U.S.A. 83 33.49N 92.25W
Forécariah Guinea 52 9.28N 13.06W
Forel, Mt. Greenland 73 67.00N 37.00W
Foreland Pt. U.K. 11 51.15N 3.47W
Foremost Canada 75 49.29N111.25W
Forest of Bowland hills U.K. 10 53.57N 2.30W
Forest of Dean f. U.K. 11 51.48N 2.32W
Forfar U.K. 12 56.38N 2.54W
Forked River town U.S.A. 85 39.51N 74.12W
Forlì Italy 15 44.13N 12.02E
Forman U.S.A. 82 46.07N 97.38W
Formby Pt. U.K. 10 53.34N 3.07W
Formentera i. Spain 16 38.41N 1.30E
Formerie France 15 49.39N 1.44E
Formiga Brazil 94 20.30S 45.27W
Formosa Argentina 92 26.06S 58.14W
Formosa d. Argentina 92 25.00S 60.00W
Formosa see Taiwan Asia 33
Formosa Brazil 91 15.30S 47.22W
Formosa, Serra mts. Brazil 91 12.00S 55.20W
Formosa Str. China/Taiwan 33 24.30N119.30E
Fornovo di Taro Italy 15 44.42N 10.06E
Forres U.K. 12 57.37N 3.38W
Forrest Australia 63 30.49S128.03E
Fors Sweden 23 60.13N 16.18E
Forsayth Australia 64 18.35S143.36E
Forssa Finland 23 60.49N 23.38E
Forst E. Germany 20 51.46N 14.39E
Forsyth U.S.A. 80 46.16N106.41W
Fort Abbās Pakistan 40 29.12N 72.52E
Fort Adams U.S.A. 83 31.05N 91.33W
Fort Albany Canada 76 52.15N 81.35W
Fortaleza Brazil 91 3.45S 38.35W
Fort Atkinson U.S.A. 82 42.56N 88.50W
Fort Augustus U.K. 12 57.09N 4.41W
Fort Beaufort R.S.A. 56 32.46S 26.36E
Fort Benning U.S.A. 85 32.20N 84.58W
Fort Benton U.S.A. 80 47.49N110.40W
Fort Carnot Madagascar 57 21.53S 47.28E
Fort Chimo Canada 73 58.10N 68.15W
Fort Chipewyan Canada 75 58.42N111.08W
Fort Collins U.S.A. 80 40.35N105.05W
Fort Coulonge Canada 76 45.51N 76.44W
Fort-de-France Martinique 87 14.36N 61.05W
Fort de Possel C.A.R. 53 5.03N 19.16E
Fort Dodge U.S.A. 82 42.30N 94.10W
Fort Drum U.S.A. 85 27.31N 80.49W
Forte dei Marmi Italy 15 43.57N 10.10E
Fort Erie Canada 76 42.54N 78.56W
Fortescue r. Australia 62 21.00S116.06E
Fort Frances Canada 76 48.35N 93.25W
Fort Franklin Canada 72 65.11N123.45W
Fort Garland U.S.A. 80 37.26N105.26W
Fort George Canada 76 53.50N 79.00W
Fort Good Hope Canada 72 66.16N128.37W
Fort Grahame Canada 74 56.30N124.35W
Fort Grey Australia 66 29.04S141.13E
Forth r. U.K. 12 56.06N 3.48W
Fort Hancock U.S.A. 81 31.17N105.53W
Fort Hope Canada 76 51.32N 88.00W
Fort Klamath U.S.A. 80 42.42N122.00W
Fort Lallemand Algeria 51 31.18N 6.20E
Fort Lauderdale U.S.A. 85 26.08N 80.08W
Fort Liard Canada 74 60.15N123.28W
Fort Lupton U.S.A. 80 40.05N104.49W
Fort Mackay Canada 75 57.12N111.41W
Fort Macleod Canada 74 49.45N113.30W
Fort MacMahon Algeria 51 29.46N 1.37E
Fort Madison U.S.A. 82 40.38N 91.27W
Fort Maguire Malaŵi 55 13.38S 34.59E
Fort McKenzie Canada 77 56.50N 68.59W
Fort McMurray Canada 75 56.45N111.27W
Fort McPherson Canada 72 67.29N134.50W
Fort Miribel Algeria 51 29.26N 3.00E
Fort Morgan U.S.A. 80 40.15N103.48W
Fort Myers U.S.A. 85 26.39N 81.51W
Fort Nelson Canada 74 58.49N122.39W
Fort Nelson r. Canada 74 59.30N124.00W
Fort Norman Canada 72 64.55N125.29W
Fort Peck Dam U.S.A. 80 47.52N106.38W
Fort Peck Resr. U.S.A. 80 47.45N106.50W
Fort Pierce U.S.A. 85 27.28N 80.20W
Fort Portal Uganda 55 0.40N 30.17E
Fort Providence Canada 74 61.21N117.39W
Fort Qu'Appelle Canada 75 50.45N103.50W
Fort Randall U.S.A. 72 55.10N162.47W
Fort Reliance Canada 75 63.00N109.20W
Fort Resolution Canada 74 61.10N113.40W
Fortrose New Zealand 60 46.34S168.48E
Fortrose U.K. 12 57.34N 4.09W
Fort Rupert B.C. Canada 74 50.39N127.27W
Fort Rupert Que. Canada 76 51.29N 78.45W
Fort Saint Tunisia 51 30.19N 9.30E
Fort St. John Canada 74 56.15N120.51W
Fort Sandeman Pakistan 40 31.20N 69.27E
Fort Saskatchewan Canada 74 53.40N113.15W
Fort Scott U.S.A. 83 37.50N 94.42W
Fort Severn Canada 75 56.00N 87.40W
Fort Shevchenko U.S.S.R. 25 44.31N 50.15E
Fort Sibut C.A.R. 53 5.46N 19.06E
Fort Simpson Canada 74 61.46N121.15E
Fort Smith Canada 75 60.00N111.51W
Fort Smith U.S.A. 83 35.23N 94.25W
Fort Stockton U.S.A. 83 30.53N102.53W
Fort Sumner U.S.A. 81 34.28N104.15W
Fort Thomas U.S.A. 81 33.02N109.58W
Fortuna Calif. U.S.A. 80 40.36N124.09W
Fortuna N.Dak. U.S.A. 82 48.55N103.47W
Fortune B. Canada 77 47.25N 55.25W
Fort Valley U.S.A. 85 32.32N 83.56W
Fort Vermilion Canada 74 58.24N116.00W
Fort Wayne U.S.A. 84 41.05N 85.08W
Fort William U.K. 12 56.49N 5.07W
Fort Worth U.S.A. 83 32.45N 97.20W
Fort Yates U.S.A. 82 46.05N100.38W
Forty Mile town Canada 72 64.24N140.31W
Fort Yukon U.S.A. 72 66.35N145.20W
Foshan China 33 23.08N113.08E
Fossano Italy 15 44.33N 7.43E
Foster Australia 67 38.39S146.12E
Fostoria U.S.A. 84 41.10N 83.25W
Fougamou Gabon 54 1.10S 10.31E
Fougères France 15 48.21N 1.12W
Foula i. U.K. 12 60.08N 2.05W
Foulness I. U.K. 11 51.35N 0.55E
Foulwind, C. New Zealand 60 41.45S171.30E
Foumban Cameroon 53 5.43N 10.50E
Fountain U.S.A. 80 38.41N104.42W
Fourmies France 14 50.01N 4.02E
Foúrnoi i. Greece 19 37.34N 26.30E
Fouta Djalon f. Guinea 52 11.30N 12.30W
Foveaux Str. New Zealand 60 46.40S168.00E
Fowey U.K. 11 50.20N 4.39W
Fowler U.S.A. 80 38.08N104.01W
Fowlers B. Australia 65 31.59S132.27E
Fowlerton U.S.A. 83 28.28N 98.48W
Fox Creek town Canada 74 54.26N116.55W
Foxe Basin b. Canada 73 67.30N 79.00W
Foxe Channel Canada 73 65.00N 80.00W
Foxe Pen. Canada 73 65.00N 76.00W
Fox Glacier town New Zealand 60 43.28S170.01E
Foxton New Zealand 60 40.27S175.18E
Fox Valley town Canada 75 50.29N109.28W
Foyle r. U.K. 13 55.00N 7.20W
Foyle, Lough U.K. 13 55.05N 7.10W
Foz do Cunene Angola 54 17.15S 11.48E
Foz do Iguaçu Brazil 94 25.33S 54.31W
Franca Brazil 94 20.33S 47.27W
Francavilla Fontana Italy 19 40.31N 17.35E
France Europe 17 47.00N 2.00E
Frances Australia 66 36.41S140.59E
Frances r. Canada 74 60.16N129.10W
Frances L. Canada 74 61.23N129.30W
Frances Lake town Canada 74 61.15N129.12W
Francesville U.S.A. 84 40.59N 86.54W
Franceville Gabon 54 1.38S 13.31E
Franche-Comté d. France 17 47.10N 6.00E
Francia Uruguay 93 32.33S 56.37W
Francistown Botswana 56 21.12S 27.29E
François L. Canada 74 54.00N125.40W
Franeker Neth. 14 53.13N 5.31E
Frankfort R.S.A. 56 27.15S 28.30E
Frankfort Kans. U.S.A. 82 39.42N 96.25W
Frankfort Ky. U.S.A. 84 38.11N 84.53W
Frankfurt E. Germany 20 52.20N 14.32E
Frankfurt d. E. Germany 20 52.30N 14.00E
Frankfurt W. Germany 20 50.06N 8.41E
Frankland r. Australia 63 34.58S116.49E
Franklin d. Canada 73 73.00N100.00W
Franklin Ky. U.S.A. 85 36.42N 86.35W
Franklin La. U.S.A. 83 29.48N 91.30W
Franklin N.H. U.S.A. 84 43.27N 71.39W
Franklin Tex. U.S.A. 83 31.02N 96.29W
Franklin W.Va. U.S.A. 84 38.39N 79.20W
Franklin B. Canada 72 70.00N126.30W
Franklin D. Roosevelt L. U.S.A. 80 48.20N118.10W
Franklin Harbour Australia 66 33.42S136.56E
Franklin I. Antarctica 96 76.10S168.30E
Frankston Australia 67 38.08S145.07E
Fransfontein Namibia 56 20.12S 15.01E
Frantsa Iosifa, Zemlya is. U.S.S.R. 28 81.00N 54.00E
Franz Canada 76 48.28N 84.25W
Franz Josef Land is. see Frantsa Iosifa, Zemlya ya U.S.S.R. 28
Fraser r. B.C. Canada 74 49.07N123.11W
Fraser r. Nfld. Canada 77 56.35N 61.55W
Fraser, I. Australia 64 25.15S153.10E
Fraser Basin f. Canada 74 54.29N124.00W
Fraserburg R.S.A. 56 31.55S 21.29E
Fraserburgh U.K. 12 57.42N 2.00W
Fraser Plateau f. Canada 74 52.52N124.00W
Fraustro Mexico 83 25.51N101.04W
Fray Bentos Uruguay 93 33.08S 58.18W
Fray Marcos Uruguay 93 34.11S 55.44W
Frederica U.S.A. 85 39.01N 75.28W
Fredericia Denmark 23 55.35N 9.46E
Frederick Md. U.S.A. 85 39.23N 77.25W
Frederick Okla. U.S.A. 83 34.23N 99.01W
Frederick S.Dak. U.S.A. 82 45.50N 98.30W
Frederick Hills Australia 64 12.41S136.00E
Fredericksburg Tex. U.S.A. 83 30.17N 98.52W
Fredericksburg Va. U.S.A. 79 38.18N 77.30W
Frederick Sd. U.S.A. 74 57.00N133.00W
Fredericton Canada 77 45.58N 66.39W
Frederikshåb Greenland 73 62.05N 49.30W
Frederikshavn Denmark 23 57.26N 10.32E
Fredonia Kans. U.S.A. 83 37.32N 95.49W
Fredonia N.Y. U.S.A. 84 42.27N 79.22W
Fredrika Sweden 22 64.05N 18.24E
Fredrikstad Norway 23 59.13N 10.57E
Freehold U.S.A. 85 40.16N 74.17W
Freeling, Mt. Australia 64 22.35S133.06E
Freeling Heights mts. Australia 66 30.10S139.16E
Freels, C. Canada 77 49.15N 53.28W
Freelton Canada 76 43.22N 80.02W
Freeman U.S.A. 82 43.21N 97.26W
Freeport Bahamas 87 26.30N 78.45W
Freeport N.S. Canada 77 44.17N 66.19W
Freeport Ill. U.S.A. 82 42.17N 89.38W
Freeport N.Y. U.S.A. 85 40.40N 73.35W
Freeport Tex. U.S.A. 83 28.58N 95.22W
Freetown Sierra Leone 52 8.30N 13.17W
Freiberg E. Germany 20 50.54N 13.20E
Freiburg W. Germany 20 48.00N 7.52E
Freilingen W. Germany 14 50.33N 7.50E
Freising W. Germany 20 48.24N 11.45E
Freistadt Austria 20 48.31N 14.31E
Fréjus France 17 43.26N 6.44E
Fremantle Australia 63 32.07S115.44E
Fremont Calif. U.S.A. 80 37.34N122.01W
Fremont Nebr. U.S.A. 82 41.26N 96.30W
Fremont Ohio U.S.A. 84 41.21N 83.08W
Frenchglen U.S.A. 80 42.48N118.56W
French I. Australia 67 38.20S145.20E
Frenchman Butte town Canada 75 53.35N109.38W
Frenda Algeria 51 35.04N 1.03E
Freren W. Germany 14 52.29N 7.32E
Fresco r. Brazil 91 7.10S 52.30W
Fresco Ivory Coast 52 5.03N 5.31W
Freshford Rep. of Ire. 13 52.44N 7.23W
Fresnillo Mexico 86 23.10N102.53W
Fresno U.S.A. 80 36.45N119.45W
Frewena Australia 64 19.25S135.25E
Fria, C. Namibia 56 18.25S 12.01E
Frias Argentina 92 28.40S 65.10W
Fribourg Switz. 20 46.50N 7.10E
Friedberg Hessen W. Germany 20 50.20N 8.45E
Friedrichshafen W. Germany 20 47.39N 9.29E
Friesland d. Neth. 14 53.05N 5.45E
Friesoythe W. Germany 14 53.02N 7.52E
Frio, Cabo c. Brazil 94 22.59S 42.00W
Friuli-Venezia Giulia d. Italy 15 46.15N 12.45E
Frobisher B. Canada 73 63.00N 66.45W
Frobisher Bay town Canada 73 63.45N 68.30W
Frobisher L. Canada 75 56.25N108.20W
Frohavet est. Norway 22 63.55N 9.05E
Froid U.S.A. 80 48.20N104.30W
Frolovo U.S.S.R. 25 49.45N 43.40E
Frome r. Australia 66 29.49S138.40E
Frome U.K. 11 51.16N 2.17W
Frome, L. Australia 66 30.48S139.48E
Frome Downs town Australia 66 31.13S139.46E
Frontera Mexico 86 18.32N 92.38W
Frosinone Italy 18 41.36N 13.21E
Fröya i. Norway 22 63.45N 8.45E
Frunze U.S.S.R. 30 42.53N 74.46E
Frunzovka U.S.S.R. 21 47.19N 29.44E
Frýdek-Místek Czech. 21 49.41N 18.22E
Fu'an China 33 27.04N119.37E
Fuchū Japan 35 35.40N139.29E
Fuchuan China 33 24.50N111.16E
Fuchun Jiang r. China 33 30.05N120.00E
Fuding China 33 27.18N120.12E
Fuefuki r. Japan 35 35.33N138.28E
Fuente-obejuna Spain 16 38.15N 5.25W
Fuentes de Oñoro Spain 16 40.33N 6.52W
Fuerte r. Mexico 81 25.50N109.25W
Fuerteventura i. Canary Is. 50 28.20N 14.10W
Fuga i. Phil. 33 18.53N121.22E
Fuglö i. Faroe Is. 8 62.22N 6.15W
Fugou China 32 34.04N114.23E
Fugu China 32 39.02N111.03E
Fuji Japan 35 35.09N138.39E
Fuji r. Japan 35 35.07N138.38E
Fujian d. China 33 26.00N118.00E
Fu Jiang r. China 33 30.02N106.20E
Fujieda Japan 35 34.52N138.16E
Fujin China 31 47.15N131.59E
Fujinomiya Japan 35 35.12N138.38E
Fuji san mtn. Japan 35 35.22N138.44E
Fujisawa Japan 35 35.21N139.29E
Fuji-yoshida Japan 35 35.38N138.42E
Fukui Japan 31 36.04N136.12E
Fukuoka Japan 31 33.39N130.21E
Fukuroi Japan 35 34.45N137.55E
Fūlādī, Kūh-e mtn. Afghan. 40 34.38N 67.32E
Fulda W. Germany 20 50.35N 9.45E
Fulda r. W. Germany 20 50.33N 9.41E
Fuling China 33 29.40N107.20E
Fulton Mo. U.S.A. 82 38.52N 91.57W
Fulton N.Y. U.S.A. 84 43.20N 76.26W
Fumay France 14 49.59N 4.42E
Funabashi Japan 35 35.42N139.59E
Funafuti Tuvalu 68 8.31S179.13E
Funchal Madeira Is. 95 32.40N 16.55W
Fundão Portugal 16 40.08N 7.30W
Fundy, B. of Canada 77 45.00N 66.00W
Funing China 33 23.37N105.36E
Funiu Shan mts. China 32 33.40N112.20E
Funtua Nigeria 53 11.34N 7.18E
Funyan Goba Ethiopia 49 4.22N 37.58E
Fuping China 32 38.52N114.12E
Fuqing China 33 25.43N119.22E
Furancungo Mozambique 55 14.51S 33.38E
Fūrg Iran 43 28.19N 55.10E
Furnas, Reprêsa de resr. Brazil 94 20.45S 46.00W
Furneaux Group is. Australia 65 40.15S148.15E
Furqlus Syria 44 34.38N 37.08E
Fürstenau W. Germany 14 52.32N 7.41E
Fürstenwalde E. Germany 20 52.22N 14.04E
Fürth W. Germany 20 49.28N 11.00E
Furu-tone r. Japan 35 35.58N139.51E
Fusagasugá Colombia 90 4.22N 74.21W
Fushun China 32 41.50N123.55E
Fusong China 31 42.17N127.19E
Fusui China 33 22.35N107.57E
Fuwah Egypt 44 31.12N 30.33E
Fu Xian Liaoning China 32 39.35N122.07E
Fu Xian Shaanxi China 32 36.00N109.20E
Fuxin China 32 42.08N121.45E
Fuyang Anhui China 32 32.52N115.52E
Fuyang Zhejiang China 33 30.03N119.57E
Fuyang He r. China 32 38.10N116.08E
Fuyu China 31 45.12N124.49E
Fuyuan Heilongjiang China 31 48.20N134.18E
Fuyuan Yunnan China 33 25.40N104.14E
Fuzhou Fujian China 33 26.09N119.21E
Fuzhou Jiangxi China 33 28.01N116.13E
Fyn i. Denmark 23 55.20N 10.30E
Fyne, Loch U.K. 12 55.55N 5.23W

G

Ga Ghana 52 9.48N 2.28W
Gabela Angola 54 10.52S 14.24E
Gabès Tunisia 51 33.53N 10.07E
Gabès, Golfe de g. Tunisia 51 34.00N 10.25E
Gabir Sudan 49 8.35N 24.40E
Gabon Africa 54 0.00 12.00E
Gabon r. Gabon 54 0.15N 10.00E
Gaborone Botswana 56 24.45S 25.55E
Gabras Sudan 49 10.16N 26.14E
Gabrovo Bulgaria 19 42.52N 25.19E
Gacé France 15 48.48N 0.18E
Gach Sārān Iran 43 30.13N 50.49E
Gada Nigeria 53 13.50N 5.40E
Gādarwāra India 41 22.55N 78.47E
Gäddede Sweden 22 64.30N 14.15E
Gadra Pakistan 40 25.40N 70.37E
Gadsden U.S.A. 85 34.00N 86.00W
Gaeta Italy 18 41.13N 13.35E
Gaeta, Golfo di g. Italy 18 41.05N 13.30E
Gaferut i. Caroline Is. 37 9.14N145.23E
Gaffney U.S.A. 85 35.03N 81.40W
Gafsa Tunisia 51 34.25N 8.48E
Gagarin U.S.S.R. 24 55.38N 35.00E
Gagnoa Ivory Coast 52 6.04N 5.55W
Gagnon Canada 77 51.53N 68.10W
Gaibānda Bangla. 41 25.19N 89.33E
Gaillac France 17 43.54N 1.53E
Gaillon France 15 49.10N 1.20E
Gainesville Fla. U.S.A. 85 29.37N 82.21W
Gainesville Ga. U.S.A. 85 34.17N 83.50W
Gainesville Mo. U.S.A. 83 36.36N 92.26W
Gainesville Tex. U.S.A. 83 33.37N 97.08W
Gainsborough U.K. 10 53.23N 0.46W
Gairdner r. Australia 63 34.20S119.30E
Gairdner, L. Australia 66 31.30S136.00E
Gairloch U.K. 12 57.43N 5.40W
Gaithersburg U.S.A. 85 39.09N 77.12W
Gai Xian China 32 40.25N122.15E
Galana r. Kenya 55 3.12S 40.09E
Galangue Angola 54 13.40S 16.00E
Galapagos, Islas is. Pacific Oc. 69 0.30S 90.30W
Galashiels U.K. 12 55.37N 2.49W
Galaţi Romania 21 45.27N 27.59E
Galatina Italy 19 40.10N 18.10E

Galdhöpiggen to Gods L.

Galdhöpiggen *mtn.* Norway 23 61.37N 8.17E
Galeana Mexico 83 24.50N100.04W
Galeh Dār Iran 43 27.36N 52.42E
Galena Australia 63 27.50S114.41E
Galena Alas. U.S.A. 72 64.43N157.00W
Galena Md. U.S.A. 85 39.20N 75.55W
Galesburg U.S.A. 82 40.57N 90.22W
Galich U.S.S.R. 24 58.20N 42.12E
Galicia *d.* Spain 16 43.00N 8.00W
Galilee, L. Australia 64 22.21S145.48E
Galiuro Mts. U.S.A. 81 32.40N110.20W
Galka'yo Somali Rep. 45 6.49N 47.23E
Gallarate Italy 15 45.40N 8.47E
Gallatin U.S.A. 85 36.22N 86.28W
Galle Sri Lanka 39 6.01N 80.13E
Gállego *r.* Spain 16 41.40N 0.55W
Gallegos *r.* Argentina 93 51.35S 69.00W
Galley Head Rep. of Ire. 13 51.32N 8.57W
Galliate Italy 15 45.29N 8.42E
Gallinas, Punta *c.* Colombia 90 12.20N 71.30W
Gallipoli Italy 19 40.02N 18.01E
Gallipolis U.S.A. 84 38.49N 82.14W
Gällivare Sweden 22 67.07N 20.45E
Gällö Sweden 22 62.56N 15.15E
Galloway *f.* U.K. 12 55.00N 4.28W
Gallup U.S.A. 81 35.32N108.44W
Galong Australia 67 34.37S148.34E
Galston U.K. 12 55.36N 4.23W
Galty Mts. Rep. of Ire. 13 52.20N 8.10W
Galva U.S.A. 82 41.10N 90.03W
Galveston U.S.A. 83 29.18N 94.48W
Galveston B. U.S.A. 83 29.36N 94.57W
Galvez Argentina 92 32.03S 61.14W
Galway Rep. of Ire. 13 53.17N 9.04W
Galway *d.* Rep. of Ire. 13 53.25N 9.00W
Galway B. Rep. of Ire. 13 53.12N 9.07W
Gam *r.* Vietnam 33 18.47N105.40E
Gamagōri Japan 35 34.50N137.14E
Gamawa Nigeria 53 12.10N 10.31E
Gamba China 41 28.18N 88.32E
Gambela Ethiopia 49 8.18N 34.37E
Gambia Africa 52 13.10N 16.00W
Gambia *r.* Gambia 52 13.28N 15.55W
Gambier, Îles *is.* Pacific Oc. 69 23.10S135.00W
Gambier I. Australia 66 35.12S136.32E
Gambo Canada 77 48.46N 54.14W
Gamboli Pakistan 40 29.50N 68.26E
Gamboma Congo 54 1.50S 15.58E
Gambos Angola 54 14.49S 14.34E
Gamboula C.A.R. 53 4.05N 15.10E
Gamia Benin 53 10.24N 2.45E
Gamlakarleby *see* Kokkola Finland 22
Gamleby Sweden 23 57.54N 16.24E
Ganado U.S.A. 81 35.43N109.33W
Gananoque Canada 76 44.20N 76.10W
Ganbashao China 33 26.37N107.41E
Ganda Angola 54 12.58S 14.39E
Gandajika Zaïre 54 6.46S 23.58E
Gandak *r.* India 41 25.40N 85.13E
Gāndarbal Jammu & Kashmir 40 34.14N 74.47E
Gandāva Pakistan 40 28.37N 67.29E
Gander Canada 77 48.57N 54.34W
Gander *r.* Canada 77 49.15N 54.30W
Gander L. Canada 77 48.55N 54.40W
Gandevi India 40 20.49N 73.00E
Gāndhi Sāgar *resr.* India 40 24.18N 75.21E
Gandía Spain 16 38.59N 0.11W
Gandou Congo 54 2.25N 17.25E
Ganga *r.* India 41 23.22N 90.32E
Gangāpur Rāj. India 40 26.29N 76.43E
Gangāpur Rāj. India 40 25.13N 74.16E
Gangara Niger 53 14.35N 8.40E
Gangārāmpur India 41 25.24N 88.31E
Gangdhār India 40 23.57N 75.37E
Gangdisê Shan *mts.* China 41 31.15N 82.00E
Ganges *r. see* Ganga *r.* India 41
Gangotri India 41 30.56N 79.02E
Gangtok India 41 27.20N 88.37E
Gangu China 32 34.30N105.30E
Gan Jiang *r.* China 33 29.10N116.00E
Ganmain Australia 67 34.47S147.01E
Gannat France 17 46.06N 3.11E
Gannett Peak *mtn.* U.S.A. 80 43.11N109.39W
Ganquan China 32 36.19N109.19E
Gansu *d.* China 30 36.00N103.00E
Ganta Liberia 52 7.15N 8.59W
Gantheaume, C. Australia 66 36.05S137.27E
Ganye Nigeria 53 8.24N 12.02E
Ganyu China 32 34.50N119.07E
Ganzhou China 33 25.49N114.50E
Gao Mali 52 16.19N 0.09W
Gao *d.* Mali 52 18.30N 1.15W
Gao'an China 33 28.25N115.22E
Gaohe China 33 22.46N112.57E
Gaolan China 32 36.23N103.55E
Gaolou Ling *mtn.* China 33 24.47N106.48E
Gaomi China 32 36.23N119.44E
Gaoping China 32 35.48N112.55E
Gaotai China 30 39.20N 99.58E
Gaoua U. Volta 52 10.20N 3.09W
Gaoual Guinea 52 11.44N 13.14W
Gaoxiong Taiwan 33 22.40N120.18E
Gaoyou China 32 32.40N119.30E
Gaoyou Hu *l.* China 32 32.50N119.25E
Gaozhou China 33 21.58N110.59E
Gap France 17 44.33N 6.05E
Gar China 41 32.11N 79.59E
Gara, Lough Rep. of Ire. 13 53.57N 8.27W
Garah Australia 67 29.04S149.38E
Garanhuns Brazil 91 8.53S 36.28W
Garba C.A.R. 49 9.12N 20.30E
Gārbosh, Kūh-e *mtn.* Iran 43 32.36N 50.02E
Gard *r.* France 17 43.52N 4.40E
Garda Italy 15 45.34N 10.42E
Garda, Lago di *l.* Italy 15 45.40N 10.40E
Gardelegen E. Germany 20 52.31N 11.23E
Garden City Ala. U.S.A. 85 34.01N 86.55W
Garden City Kans. U.S.A. 83 37.58N100.53W
Garden Reach India 41 22.33N 88.17E
Gardēz Afghan. 40 33.37N 69.07E
Gardiner U.S.A. 80 45.02N110.42W
Gardnerville U.S.A. 80 38.56N119.45W
Gardo Somali Rep. 45 9.30N 49.03E
Gardone Val Trompia Italy 15 45.41N 10.11E
Garessio Italy 15 44.12N 8.02E
Garet el Djenoun *mtn.* Algeria 51 25.05N 5.25E
Garhākota India 41 23.46N 79.09E
Garhi Khairo Pakistan 40 28.04N 67.59E
Garibaldi Prov. Park Canada 74 49.50N122.40W
Garies R.S.A. 56 30.34S 18.00E
Garigliano *r.* Italy 18 41.13N 13.45E
Garissa Kenya 55 0.27S 39.49E
Garko Nigeria 53 11.45N 8.53E
Garland Tex. U.S.A. 83 32.54N 96.39W
Garland Utah U.S.A. 80 41.45N112.10W
Garlasco Italy 15 45.12N 8.55E
Garlin France 17 43.34N 0.15W
Garm Āb Afghan. 40 32.14N 65.01E
Garmisch Partenkirchen W. Germany 20 47.30N 11.05E
Garmsār Iran 43 35.15N 52.21E
Garnett U.S.A. 82 38.17N 95.14W
Garo Hills India 41 25.45N 90.30E
Garonne *r.* France 17 45.00N 0.37W
Garoua Cameroon 53 9.17N 13.22E
Garoua Boulaï Cameroon 53 5.54N 14.33E
Garrison U.S.A. 83 31.49N 94.30W
Garrison Resr. U.S.A. 82 48.00N102.30W
Garron Pt. U.K. 13 55.03N 5.57W
Garry L. Canada 73 66.00N100.00W
Garson Canada 76 46.34N 80.52W
Garub Namibia 56 26.33S 16.00E
Garut Indonesia 37 7.15S107.55E
Garvão Portugal 16 37.42N 8.21W
Garve U.K. 12 57.37N 4.41W
Garvie Mts. New Zealand 60 45.15S169.00E
Garwa India 41 24.11N 83.49E
Gary U.S.A. 84 41.34N 87.20W
Garyarsa China 30 31.30N 80.40E
Gar Zangbo *r.* China 41 32.25N 79.40E
Garzón Colombia 90 2.14N 75.37E
Gas City U.S.A. 84 40.28N 85.37W
Gascogne, Golfe de *g.* France 17 44.00N 2.40W
Gascony, G. of *see* Gascogne, Golfe de France 17
Gascoyne *r.* Australia 62 25.00S113.40E
Gascoyne Junction Australia 62 25.02S115.15E
Gash *r.* Ethiopia *see* Qāsh *r.* Sudan 48
Gashua Nigeria 53 12.53N 11.02E
Gaspé Canada 77 48.50N 64.30W
Gaspé, Cap de *c.* Canada 77 48.45N 64.09W
Gaspé, Péninsule de *pen.* Canada 77 48.30N 65.00W
Gaspésie Prov. Park Canada 77 48.50N 65.45W
Gassol Nigeria 53 8.34N 10.25E
Gastonia U.S.A. 85 35.14N 81.12W
Gastre Argentina 93 42.17S 69.15W
Gata, Cabo de *c.* Spain 16 36.45N 2.11W
Gata, Sierra de *mts.* Spain 16 40.20N 6.30W
Gátas, Akrotírion *c.* Cyprus 44 34.33N 33.03E
Gatchina U.S.S.R. 24 59.32N 30.05E
Gatehouse of Fleet U.K. 12 54.53N 4.12W
Gateshead U.K. 10 54.57N 1.35W
Gatesville U.S.A. 83 31.26N 97.45W
Gatineau Canada 77 45.29N 75.38W
Gatineau *r.* Canada 77 45.27N 75.40W
Gatineau N.C.C. Park Canada 77 45.30N 75.52W
Gattinara Italy 15 43.37N 8.22E
Gatun L. Panama 87 9.20N 80.00W
Gauchy France 15 49.49N 3.13E
Gauer L. Canada 75 57.00N 97.50W
Gauhāti India 41 26.11N 91.44E
Gaurela India 41 22.45N 81.54E
Gauri Sankar *mtn.* China / Nepal 41 27.57N 86.21E
Gavá Spain 16 41.18N 2.00E
Gavāter Iran 43 25.10N 61.31E
Gāv Koshī Iran 43 28.39N 57.13E
Gävle Sweden 23 60.40N 17.10E
Gävleborg *d.* Sweden 23 61.30N 16.15E
Gávrion Greece 19 37.52N 24.46E
Gawachab Namibia 56 27.03S 17.50E
Gāwilgarh Hills India 40 21.30N 77.00E
Gawler Australia 66 34.38S138.44E
Gawler Ranges *mts.* Australia 66 32.30S136.00E
Gaya India 41 24.47N 85.00E
Gaya Niger 53 11.53N 3.31E
Gayndah Australia 64 25.37S151.36E
Gayny U.S.S.R. 24 60.17N 54.15E
Gaysin U.S.S.R. 21 48.50N 29.29E
Gayvoron U.S.S.R. 21 48.20N 29.52E
Gaza *see* Ghazzah Egypt 44
Gaza *d.* Mozambique 57 23.20S 32.35E
Gaza Strip *f.* Egypt 44 31.32N 34.23E
Gaziantep Turkey 42 37.04N 37.21E
Gbanhui Ivory Coast 52 8.12N 3.02W
Gboko Nigeria 53 7.22N 8.58E
Gcuwa R.S.A. 56 32.20S 28.09E
Gdańsk Poland 21 54.22N 18.38E
Gdov U.S.S.R. 24 58.48N 27.52E
Gdynia Poland 21 54.31N 18.30E
Gebe *i.* Indonesia 37 0.05S129.20E
Gebze Turkey 42 40.48N 29.26E
Gecha Ethiopia 49 7.31N 35.22E
Gedera Israel 44 31.48N 34.46E
Gediz *r.* Turkey 19 38.37N 26.47E
Gedser Denmark 23 54.35N 11.57E
Geel Belgium 14 51.10N 5.00E
Geelong Australia 66 38.10S144.26E
Gê'gyai China 41 32.25N 84.05E
Gehua P.N.G. 64 10.20S150.25E
Geidam Nigeria 53 12.55N 11.55E
Geikie *r.* Canada 75 57.45N103.52W
Geilenkirchen W. Germany 14 50.58N 6.08E
Geilo Norway 23 60.31N 8.12E
Gejiu China 30 23.25N103.05E
Gela Italy 18 37.03N 14.15E
Geladi Ethiopia 45 6.58N 44.30E
Gelai *mtn.* Tanzania 55 2.37S 36.07E
Gelderland *d.* Neth. 14 52.05N 6.00E
Geldermalsen Neth. 14 51.53N 5.17E
Geldern W. Germany 14 51.31N 6.19E
Geldrop Neth. 14 51.26N 5.31E
Geleen Neth. 14 50.58N 5.51E
Gélengdeng Chad 53 10.56N 15.32E
Gelibolu Turkey 19 40.25N 26.31E
Gelligaer U.K. 11 51.40N 3.18W
Gelsenkirchen W. Germany 14 51.30N 7.05E
Gem Canada 74 50.58N112.11W
Gemas Malaysia 36 2.35N102.35E
Gembloux Belgium 14 50.34N 4.42E
Gemena Zaïre 54 3.14N 19.48E
Gemerek Turkey 42 39.13N 36.05E
Gemlik Turkey 42 40.26N 29.10E
Gemona del Friuli Italy 15 46.16N 13.09E
Gemu Gwefa *d.* Ethiopia 49 6.00N 37.00E
Genale *r.* Ethiopia 49 4.15N 42.10E
Genappe Belgium 14 50.37N 4.25E
Gendringen Neth. 14 51.52N 6.26E
General Acha Argentina 93 37.20S 64.35W
General Alvear Buenos Aires Argentina 93 36.00S 60.00W
General Alvear Mendoza Argentina 93 34.59S 67.42W
General Belgrano Argentina 93 35.45S 58.30W
General Campos Argentina 93 31.30S 58.25W
General Conesa Argentina 93 36.30S 57.19W
General Guido Argentina 93 36.40S 57.45W
General Lavalle Argentina 93 36.22S 56.55W
General Madariaga Argentina 93 37.00S 57.05W
General Paz Argentina 93 35.32S 58.18W
General Pico Argentina 93 35.38S 63.46W
General Roca Argentina 93 39.02S 67.33W
General Santos Phil. 37 6.05N125.15E
Geneseo Ill. U.S.A. 82 41.27N 90.09W
Geneseo N.Y. U.S.A. 84 42.46N 77.49W
Geneva *see* Genève Switz. 20
Geneva Nebr. U.S.A. 82 40.32N 97.36W
Geneva N.Y. U.S.A. 84 42.53N 76.59W
Geneva Ohio U.S.A. 84 41.48N 80.57W
Geneva, L. *see* Léman, Lac *l.* Switz. 20
Genève Switz. 20 46.13N 6.09E
Genichesk U.S.S.R. 25 46.10N 34.49E
Genil *r.* Spain 16 37.42N 5.20W
Genk Belgium 14 50.58N 5.34E
Gennep Neth. 14 51.43N 5.58E
Gennes France 15 47.20N 0.14W
Genoa Australia 67 37.29S149.35E
Genoa *see* Genova Italy 15
Genoa U.S.A. 82 41.27N 97.44W
Genoa, G. of *see* Genova, Golfo di *g.* Italy 15
Genova Italy 15 44.24N 8.54E
Genova, Golfo di *g.* Italy 15 44.12N 8.55E
Gent Belgium 14 51.02N 3.42E
Gentilly Canada 77 46.24N 72.17W
Geographe B. Australia 63 33.35S115.15E
Geographe Channel Australia 62 24.40S113.20E
George *r.* Australia 66 28.24S136.39E
George *r.* Canada 73 58.30N 66.00W
George R.S.A. 56 33.57S 22.27E
George, L. N.S.W. Australia 67 35.07S149.22E
George, L. S.A. Australia 66 37.26S140.00E
George, L. Uganda 55 0.00 30.10E
George, L. Fla. U.S.A. 85 29.17N 81.36W
George B. Canada 77 45.50N 61.45W
George's Cove Canada 77 52.40N 55.50W
Georgetown Ascension 95 7.56S 14.25W
Georgetown Qld. Australia 64 18.18S143.33E
George Town Tas. Australia 65 41.04S146.48E
Georgetown Canada 77 46.11N 62.32W
Georgetown Cayman Is. 87 19.20N 81.23W
Georgetown Gambia 52 13.31N 14.50W
Georgetown Guyana 90 6.46N 58.10W
George Town Malaysia 36 5.30N100.16E
Georgetown Del. U.S.A. 85 38.42N 75.23W
Georgetown S.C. U.S.A. 85 33.23N 79.18W
Georgetown Tex. U.S.A. 83 30.38N 97.41W
George V Land *f.* Antarctica 96 69.00S145.00E
Georgia *d.* U.S.A. 85 32.50N 83.15W
Georgia, Str. of Canada 74 49.25N124.00W
Georgian B. Canada 76 45.15N 80.45W
Georgina *r.* Australia 64 23.12S139.33E
Georgiu-Dezh U.S.S.R. 25 51.00N 39.30E
Georgiyevsk U.S.S.R. 25 44.10N 43.30E
Gera E. Germany 20 50.51N 12.11E
Gera *d.* E. Germany 20 50.45N 11.45E
Geraardsbergen Belgium 14 50.47N 3.53E
Geral de Goiás, Serra *mts.* Brazil 91 13.00S 45.40W
Geraldine New Zealand 60 44.05S171.15E
Geral do Paraná, Serra *mts.* Brazil 91 14.40S 47.30W
Geraldton Australia 63 28.49S114.36E
Geraldton Canada 76 49.44N 86.59W
Gerale Ethiopia 45 6.20N 42.32E
Gerede Turkey 42 40.48N 32.13E
Gereshk Afghan. 40 31.48N 64.34E
Gérgal Spain 16 37.07N 2.31W
Gering U.S.A. 82 41.50N103.40W
Gerlach U.S.A. 80 40.40N119.21W
Gerlachovsky *mtn.* Czech. 21 49.10N 20.05E
Germiston R.S.A. 56 26.14S 28.10E
Gerolstein W. Germany 14 50.14N 6.40E
Gerona Spain 16 41.59N 2.49E
Gerringong Australia 67 34.45S150.50E
Gêrzê China 41 32.16N 84.12E
Gescher W. Germany 14 51.58N 7.00E
Getafe Spain 16 40.18N 3.44W
Gete *r.* Belgium 14 50.58N 5.07E
Gethsémani Canada 77 50.13N 60.40W
Gettysburg S.Dak. U.S.A. 82 45.01N 99.57W
Gevān Iran 43 26.03N 57.17E
Gevelsberg W. Germany 14 51.20N 7.20E
Geysdorp R.S.A. 56 26.31S 25.17E
Geyser U.S.A. 80 47.16N110.30W
Geyve Turkey 42 40.32N 30.18E
Ghābat al 'Arab Sudan 49 9.02N 29.29E
Ghadaf, Wādī al *r.* Jordan 44 31.46N 36.50E
Ghadāmis Libya 51 30.08N 9.30E
Ghaddūwah Libya 51 26.26N 14.18E
Ghāghra *r.* India 41 25.47N 84.37E
Ghana Africa 52 8.00N 1.00W
Ghanzi Botswana 56 21.42S 21.39E
Ghardaïa Algeria 51 32.29N 3.40E
Gharghoda India 41 22.10N 83.21E
Ghārib, Jabal *mtn.* Egypt 44 28.06N 32.54E
Gharo Pakistan 40 24.44N 67.35E
Gharyān Libya 51 32.10N 13.01E
Gharyān *d.* Libya 51 30.35N 12.00E
Ghāt Libya 51 24.58N 10.11E
Ghātsīla India 41 22.36N 86.29E
Ghazāl, Baḩr al *r.* Sudan 49 9.31N 30.25E
Ghāziābād India 41 28.40N 77.26E
Ghāzīpur India 41 25.35N 83.34E
Ghazlūna Pakistan 40 31.24N 67.49E
Ghaznī Afghan. 40 33.33N 68.26E
Ghaznī *d.* Afghan. 40 32.45N 68.30E
Ghaznī *r.* Afghan. 40 32.35N 67.58E
Ghazzah Egypt 44 31.30N 34.28E
Ghedi Italy 15 45.24N 10.16E
Gheorghe-Gheorghiu-Dej Romania 21 46.14N 26.44E
Gheorgheni Romania 21 46.43N 25.36E
Gherla Romania 21 47.02N 23.55E
Ghotki Pakistan 40 28.01N 69.19E
Ghowr *d.* Afghan. 40 34.00N 64.15E
Ghubaysh Sudan 49 12.09N 27.21E
Ghudāf, Wādī al *r.* Iraq 42 32.54N 43.33E
Ghūriān Afghan. 40 34.21N 61.30E
Gia Dinh Vietnam 34 10.54N106.43E
Gibb River *town* Australia 62 15.39S126.38E
Gibeon Namibia 56 25.09S 17.44E
Gibraltar Europe 16 36.07N 5.22W
Gibraltar, Str. of Africa / Europe 16 36.00N 5.25W
Gibraltar Pt. U.K. 10 53.05N 0.20E
Gibson Australia 63 33.39S121.48E
Gibson Desert Australia 62 24.30S123.00E
Giddings U.S.A. 83 30.11N 96.56W
Gide Ethiopia 49 9.40N 35.16E
Gien France 15 47.41N 2.37E
Giessen W. Germany 20 50.35N 8.42E
Gieten Neth. 14 53.01N 6.45E
Gifford *r.* Canada 73 70.21N 83.05W
Gifford U.S.A. 80 48.20N118.08W
Gifhorn W. Germany 20 52.29N 10.33E
Gifu Japan 35 35.25N136.45E
Gifu *d.* Japan 35 35.32N137.15E
Giganta, Sierra de la *mts.* Mexico 81 25.30N111.15W
Gigantes, Llanos de los *f.* Mexico 81 30.00N105.00W
Gigha *i.* U.K. 12 55.41N 5.44W
Giglio *i.* Italy 18 42.21N 10.53E
Gijón Spain 16 43.32N 5.40W
Gila *r.* U.S.A. 81 32.43N114.33W
Gila Bend U.S.A. 81 32.57N112.43W
Gila Bend Mts. U.S.A. 81 33.10N113.10W
Gilbert *r.* Australia 64 16.35S141.15E
Gildford U.S.A. 80 48.34N110.18W
Gilé Mozambique 55 16.10S 38.17E
Gilgandra Australia 67 31.42S148.40E
Gil Gil *r.* Australia 67 29.10S148.50E
Gilgil Kenya 55 0.29S 36.19E
Gilgit Jammu & Kashmir 38 35.54N 74.20E
Gilgunnia Australia 67 32.25S146.04E
Gill, Lough Rep. of Ire. 13 54.15N 8.14W
Gilles, L. Australia 66 32.50S136.45E
Gillette U.S.A. 80 44.18N105.30W
Gillingham Kent U.K. 11 51.24N 0.33E
Gill Pt. *c.* St. Helena 95 15.59S 5.38W
Gilmour Canada 76 44.48N 77.37W
Gilo *r.* Ethiopia 49 8.10N 33.15E
Gimli Canada 75 50.39N 97.00W
Gingin Australia 63 31.21S115.42E
Ginir Ethiopia 49 7.07N 40.46E
Ginzo de Limia Spain 16 42.03N 7.47W
Gióna *mtn.* Greece 19 38.38N 22.14E
Girardot Colombia 90 4.19N 74.47W
Girdle Ness U.K. 12 57.06N 2.02W
Giresun Turkey 42 40.55N 38.25E
Gīr Hills India 40 21.10N 71.00E
Giri *r.* Zaïre 54 0.30N 17.58E
Girīdīh India 41 24.11N 86.18E
Girilambone Australia 67 31.14S146.55E
Girna *r.* India 40 21.08N 75.19E
Gironde *r.* France 17 45.35N 1.00W
Girvan U.K. 12 55.15N 4.51W
Girwa *r.* India 41 27.20N 81.25E
Gisborne New Zealand 60 38.41S178.02E
Gisors France 15 49.17N 1.47E
Gitega Burundi 55 3.25S 29.58E
Giulianova Italy 18 42.45N 13.57E
Giurgiu Romania 21 43.52N 25.58E
Giv'atayim Israel 44 32.04N 34.49E
Givet France 17 50.08N 4.49E
Gīzāb Afghan. 40 33.23N 65.55E
Gizhiga U.S.S.R. 29 62.00N160.34E
Gizhiginskaya Guba *g.* U.S.S.R. 29 61.00N158.00E
Giżycko Poland 21 54.03N 21.47E
Gjerstad Norway 23 58.54N 9.00E
Gjirokastër Albania 19 40.05N 20.10E
Gjoa Haven *town* Canada 73 68.39N 96.08W
Gjövik Norway 23 60.48N 10.42E
Glace Bay *town* Canada 77 46.12N 59.57W
Glacier Nat. Park Canada 74 51.15N117.30W
Glacier Peak *mtn.* U.S.A. 80 48.07N121.06W
Gladewater U.S.A. 83 32.33N 94.56W
Gladmar Canada 75 49.12N104.31W
Gladstone Qld. Australia 64 23.52S151.16E
Gladstone S.A. Australia 66 33.17S138.22E
Gladstone Mich. U.S.A. 84 45.52N 87.02W
Gladstone N.J. U.S.A. 85 40.43N 74.40W
Glafsfjorden *l.* Sweden 23 59.34N 12.37E
Glåma *r.* Norway 23 59.15N 10.55E
Glamoč Yugo. 19 44.03N 16.51E
Glan *r.* W. Germany 14 49.46N 7.43E
Glanaman U.K. 11 51.49N 3.54W
Glandorf W. Germany 14 52.05N 8.00E
Glasco Kans. U.S.A. 82 39.22N 97.50W
Glasgow U.K. 12 55.52N 4.15W
Glasgow Ky. U.S.A. 85 36.59N 85.56W
Glasgow Mont. U.S.A. 80 48.12N106.38W
Glassboro U.S.A. 85 39.42N 75.07W
Glastonbury U.K. 11 51.09N 2.42W
Glazov U.S.S.R. 24 58.09N 52.42E
Gleisdorf Austria 20 47.06N 15.44E
Glen R.S.A. 56 28.57S 26.19E
Glen Affric *f.* U.K. 12 57.15N 5.03W
Glénans, Îles de *is.* France 17 47.43N 3.57W
Glenarm U.K. 13 54.57N 5.58W
Glenburnie Australia 66 37.49S140.56E
Glen Burnie U.S.A. 85 39.10N 76.37W
Glencoe Australia 66 37.41S140.05E
Glen Coe *f.* U.K. 12 56.40N 5.03W
Glencoe U.S.A. 82 44.45N 94.10W
Glen Cove U.S.A. 85 40.52N 73.37W
Glendale Ariz. U.S.A. 81 33.32N112.11W
Glendale Calif. U.S.A. 81 34.10N118.17W
Glendale Oreg. U.S.A. 80 42.44N123.26W
Glen Davis Australia 67 33.07S150.22E
Glendive U.S.A. 80 47.06N104.43W
Glenelg Australia 66 34.59S138.31E
Glenelg *r.* Australia 66 38.03S141.00E
Glengarriff Rep. of Ire. 13 51.45N 9.33W
Glen Garry *f.* Highland U.K. 12 57.03N 5.04W
Glen Head Rep. of Ire. 13 54.44N 8.46W
Glen Ina Australia 66 31.45S143.33E
Glen Innes Australia 67 29.42S151.45E
Glen Lyon Australia 66 31.41S142.06E
Glen Mòr *f.* U.K. 12 57.15N 4.30W
Glenmora U.S.A. 83 30.59N 92.35W
Glen Moriston U.K. 12 57.09N 4.50W
Glenns Ferry U.S.A. 80 42.57N115.18W
Glenrock U.S.A. 80 42.52N105.52W
Glenrothes U.K. 12 56.12N 3.10W
Glenroy Australia 62 17.23S126.01E
Glens Falls *town* U.S.A. 84 43.19N 73.39W
Glenshee *f.* U.K. 12 56.45N 3.25W
Glen Spean *f.* U.K. 12 56.53N 4.40W
Glenwood Ark. U.S.A. 83 34.20N 93.33W
Glenwood Iowa U.S.A. 82 41.03N 95.45W
Glenwood Oreg. U.S.A. 80 45.39N123.16W
Glenwood Springs *town* U.S.A. 80 39.33N107.19W
Glittertind *mtn.* Norway 23 61.39N 8.33E
Gliwice Poland 21 50.17N 18.40E
Globe U.S.A. 81 33.24N110.47W
Głogów Poland 20 51.40N 16.06E
Glotovo U.S.S.R. 24 63.25N 49.28E
Gloucester Australia 67 31.59S151.58E
Gloucester U.K. 11 51.52N 2.15W
Gloucester U.S.A. 84 42.41N 70.39W
Gloucester City U.S.A. 85 39.54N 75.07W
Gloucestershire *d.* U.K. 11 51.45N 2.00W
Głubczyce Poland 21 50.13N 17.49E
Glückstadt W. Germany 20 53.47N 9.25E
Glusha U.S.S.R. 21 53.03N 28.55E
Gmünd Austria 20 48.47N 14.59E
Gnarp Sweden 23 62.03N 17.16E
Gnesta Sweden 23 59.03N 17.18E
Gniewkowo Poland 21 52.24N 18.25E
Gniezno Poland 21 52.32N 17.32E
Gnjilane Yugo. 19 42.28N 21.58E
Gnosjö Sweden 23 57.22N 13.44E
Gnowangerup Australia 63 33.57S117.58E
Gnuka Australia 63 31.08S117.24E
Goa *d.* India 38 15.30N 74.00E
Goageb Namibia 56 26.45S 17.18E
Goālpāra India 41 26.10N 90.37E
Goat Fell *mtn.* U.K. 12 55.37N 5.12W
Goba Ethiopia 49 7.02N 40.00E
Goba Mozambique 57 26.11S 32.08E
Gobabis Namibia 56 22.28S 18.58E
Gobi *des.* Asia 32 45.00N108.00E
Goch W. Germany 14 51.41N 6.09E
Gochas Namibia 56 24.50S 18.48E
Godalming U.K. 11 51.11N 0.37W
Godar Pakistan 40 28.10N 63.14E
Godāvari *r.* India 39 16.40N 82.15E
Godbout Canada 77 49.19N 67.37W
Goddard Creek *r.* Australia 63 31.10S124.30E
Goderich Canada 76 43.45N 81.43W
Goderville France 15 49.39N 0.22E
Godhavn Greenland 73 69.20N 53.30W
Godhra India 40 22.45N 73.38E
Godoy Cruz Argentina 93 32.55S 68.50W
Gods *r.* Canada 75 56.22N 92.51W
Gods L. Canada 75 54.45N 94.00W

Godthåb to Gualeguay

Godthåb Greenland 73 64.10N 51.40W
Goéland, Lac au l. Canada 76 49.47N 76.41W
Goélands, Lac aux l. Canada 77 55.25N 64.20W
Goes Neth. 14 51.30N 3.54E
Gogama Canada 76 47.35N 81.35W
Gogeb r. Ethiopia 49 7.10N 37.27E
Gogeh Ethiopia 49 8.12N 38.27E
Gogonou Benin 53 10.50N 2.50E
Gogra r. see Ghāghra India 41
Gogrial Sudan 49 8.32N 28.07E
Gohad India 41 26.26N 78.27E
Goiana Brazil 91 7.30S 35.00W
Goiânia Brazil 91 16.43S 49.18W
Goiás Brazil 91 15.57S 50.07W
Goiás d. Brazil 91 12.00S 48.00W
Goichran India 41 31.04N 78.07E
Goito Italy 15 45.15N 10.40E
Gojō Japan 35 34.21N135.42E
Gojra Pakistan 40 31.09N 72.41E
Gökçeada i. Turkey 19 40.10N 25.51E
Göksun Turkey 42 38.03N 36.30E
Gokteik Burma 39 22.26N 97.00E
Gokwe Zimbabwe 56 18.14S 28.54E
Gol Norway 23 60.42N 8.57E
Gola Gokaran Nath India 41 28.05N 80.28E
Golan Heights mts. Syria 44 32.55N 35.42E
Golconda U.S.A. 80 40.57N117.30W
Goldap Poland 21 54.19N 22.19E
Gold Beach town U.S.A. 80 42.25N124.25W
Golden Canada 74 51.20N117.00W
Golden Rep. of Ire. 13 52.30N 7.59W
Golden U.S.A. 80 39.46N105.13W
Golden B. New Zealand 60 40.45S172.50E
Goldendale U.S.A. 80 45.49N120.50W
Golden Hinde mtn. Canada 74 49.40N125.44W
Golden Ridge town Australia 63 30.51S121.42E
Golden Vale f. Rep. of Ire. 13 52.30N 8.07W
Goldfield U.S.A. 80 37.42N117.14W
Goldfields Canada 75 59.28N108.31W
Goldpines Canada 76 50.45N 93.05W
Goldsand L. Canada 75 56.58N101.02W
Goldsboro U.S.A. 85 35.23N 78.00W
Goleniów Poland 20 53.36N 14.50E
Golets Skalisty mtn. U.S.S.R. 29 56.00N130.40E
Golfito Costa Rica 87 8.42N 83.10W
Golfo degli Aranci town Italy 18 41.00N 9.38E
Gol Gol Australia 66 34.10S142.17E
Goliad U.S.A. 83 28.40N 97.23W
Golling Austria 20 47.36N 13.10E
Golmud China 30 36.22N 94.55E
Golovanevsk U.S.S.R. 21 48.25N 30.30E
Golpāyegān Iran 43 33.23N 50.18E
Golspie U.K. 12 57.58N 3.58W
Goma Ethiopia 49 8.25N 36.53E
Goma Zaïre 55 1.37S 29.10E
Gomang Co l. China 41 31.10N 89.10E
Gombe Nigeria 53 10.17N 11.20E
Gombe r. Tanzania 55 4.43S 31.30E
Gomel U.S.S.R. 21 52.25N 31.00E
Gomera i. Canary Is. 50 28.08N 17.14W
Gómez Palacio Mexico 83 25.34N103.30W
Gomīshān Iran 43 37.04N 54.06E
Gompa Jammu & Kashmir 40 35.02N 77.20E
Gonaïves Haiti 87 19.29N 72.42W
Gonâve, Golfe de la g. Haiti 87 19.20N 73.00W
Gonâve, Île de la i. Haiti 87 18.50N 73.00W
Gonbad-e Kāvūs Iran 43 37.15N 55.11E
Gonda India 41 27.08N 81.56E
Gondal India 40 21.58N 70.48E
Gonder Ethiopia 49 12.39N 37.29E
Gondia India 41 21.27N 80.12E
Gongbo'gyamda China 41 29.56N 93.23E
Gonggar China 41 29.15N 90.50E
Gongga Shan mtn. China 30 29.30N101.30E
Gongola d. Nigeria 53 8.40N 11.30E
Gongola r. Nigeria 53 9.30N 12.06E
Gongolgon Australia 67 30.22S146.56E
Goñi Uruguay 93 33.31S 56.24W
Goniri Nigeria 53 11.30N 12.15E
Gonzaga Italy 15 44.57N 10.49E
Gonzales U.S.A. 83 29.30N 97.27W
Good Hope, C. of R.S.A. 56 34.21S 18.28E
Good Hope Mtn. Canada 74 51.09N124.10W
Gooding U.S.A. 80 42.56N114.43W
Goodland U.S.A. 82 39.21N101.43W
Goodooga Australia 67 29.08S147.30E
Goodsprings U.S.A. 81 35.50N115.26W
Goole U.K. 10 53.42N 0.52W
Goolgowi Australia 67 33.59S145.42E
Goolma Australia 67 32.21S149.20E
Gooloogong Australia 67 33.37S148.43E
Goolwa Australia 66 35.31S138.45E
Goomalling Australia 63 31.19S116.49E
Goombalie Australia 67 29.59S145.24E
Goondiwindi Australia 67 28.30S150.17E
Goongarrie Australia 63 30.03S121.09E
Goor Neth. 14 52.16N 6.33E
Goose r. Canada 77 53.18N 60.23W
Goose Bay town Canada 77 53.19N 60.24W
Goose L. U.S.A. 80 41.57N120.25W
Gopālganj Bangla. 41 23.01N 89.50E
Gopālganj India 41 26.28N 84.26E
Göppingen W. Germany 20 48.43N 9.39E
Gorakhpur India 41 26.45N 83.22E
Goras India 40 25.32N 76.56E
Gordon Australia 66 32.05S138.08E
Gordon r. Australia 63 34.12S117.00E
Gordon U.S.A. 82 42.48N102.12W
Gordon Downs town Australia 62 18.43S128.33E
Gordon L. Canada 74 63.05N113.11W
Gordonvale Australia 64 17.05S145.47E
Goré Chad 53 7.57N 16.31E
Gore Ethiopia 49 8.08N 35.33E
Gore New Zealand 60 46.06S168.58E
Gorgān Iran 43 36.50N 54.29E
Gorgān r. Iran 43 37.00N 54.00E
Gorgol d. Mauritania 50 15.45N 13.00W
Gori U.S.S.R. 43 41.59N 44.05E
Gorinchem Neth. 14 51.50N 4.59E
Gorizia Italy 18 45.58N 13.37E
Gorki see Gor'kiy U.S.S.R. 24
Gor'kiy U.S.S.R. 24 56.20N 44.00E
Gorkovskoye Vodokhranilishche resr. U.S.S.R. 24 56.49N 43.00E
Görlitz E. Germany 20 51.09N 15.00E
Gorlovka U.S.S.R. 25 48.17N 38.05E
Gorna Oryakhovitsa Bulgaria 19 43.07N 25.40E
Gorno Altaysk U.S.S.R. 28 51.59N 85.56E
Gorno Filinskoye U.S.S.R. 28 60.06N 69.58E
Gornyatskiy U.S.S.R. 24 67.30N 64.03E
Gorochan mtn. Ethiopia 49 9.22N 37.04E
Gorodenka U.S.S.R. 21 48.40N 25.30E
Gorodishche B.S.S.R. U.S.S.R. 21 53.18N 26.00E
Gorodishche B.S.S.R. U.S.S.R. 21 53.45N 29.45E
Gorodnitsa U.S.S.R. 21 50.50N 27.19E
Gorodnya U.S.S.R. 21 51.54N 31.37E
Gorodok U.S.S.R. 21 49.48N 23.39E
Goroka P.N.G. 37 6.02S145.22E
Goroke Australia 66 36.43S141.30E
Gorokhov U.S.S.R. 21 50.30N 24.46E
Gorongosa r. Mozambique 57 20.29S 34.36E
Gorontalo Indonesia 37 0.33N123.05E
Gort Rep. of Ire. 13 53.04N 8.49W
Goryn r. U.S.S.R. 21 52.08N 27.17E
Gorzów Wielkopolski Poland 20 52.42N 15.12E
Gose Japan 35 34.27N135.44E
Gosford Australia 67 33.25S151.18E
Goslar W. Germany 20 51.54N 10.25E
Gospić Yugo. 20 44.34N 15.23E
Gosport U.K. 11 50.48N 1.08W
Gossi Mali 52 15.49N 1.17W
Gossinga Sudan 49 8.39N 25.59E
Gostivar Yugo. 19 41.47N 20.24E
Gostynin Poland 21 52.26N 19.29E
Göta r. Sweden 23 57.42N 11.52E
Göta Kanal Sweden 23 58.50N 13.58E
Göteborg Sweden 23 57.43N 11.58E
Göteborg och Bohus d. Sweden 23 58.30N 11.30E
Gotemba Japan 35 35.18N138.56E
Götene Sweden 23 58.32N 13.29E
Gotha E. Germany 20 50.57N 10.43E
Gothenburg see Göteborg Sweden 23
Gothenburg U.S.A. 82 40.56N100.09W
Gothèye Niger 53 13.51N 1.31E
Gotland d. Sweden 23 57.30N 18.30E
Gotland i. Sweden 23 57.30N 18.33E
Göttingen W. Germany 20 51.32N 9.57E
Gottwaldov Czech. 21 49.13N 17.41E
Gouda Neth. 14 52.01N 4.43E
Gough I. Atlantic Oc. 95 40.20S 10.00W
Gouin, Résr. Canada 76 48.38N 74.54W
Goulburn Australia 67 34.47S149.43E
Goulburn r. Australia 67 36.08S144.30E
Goulburn Is. Australia 64 11.33S133.26E
Goulimime Morocco 50 28.56N 10.04W
Goundam Mali 52 17.27N 3.39W
Gourdon France 17 44.45N 1.22E
Gouré Niger 53 13.59N 10.15E
Gourma-Rharous Mali 52 16.58N 1.50W
Gournay France 15 49.29N 1.44E
Gouro Chad 51 19.33N 19.33E
Gourock Range mts. Australia 67 35.45S149.25E
Governador Valadares Brazil 94 18.51S 42.00W
Govind Balabh Pant Sāgar resr. India 41 24.05N 82.50E
Govind Sāgar resr. India 40 31.20N 76.45E
Gowanda U.S.A. 84 42.28N 78.57W
Gowd-e Zereh des. Afghan. 43 30.00N 62.00E
Gower pen. U.K. 11 51.37N 4.10W
Gowmal r. Afghan. see Gumal r. Pakistan 40
Gowmal Kalay Afghan. 40 32.29N 68.55E
Goya Argentina 92 29.10S 59.20W
Goyder r. Australia 64 12.38S135.11E
Goz Béïda Chad 49 12.13N 21.25E
Gozo i. Malta 18 36.03N 14.16E
Graaff Reinet R.S.A. 56 32.15S 24.31E
Gračac Yugo. 20 44.18N 15.51E
Grace, L. Australia 63 33.18S118.15E
Gracias á Dios, Cabo c. Honduras/Nicaragua 87 15.00N 83.10W
Grado Italy 15 45.40N 13.23E
Grado Spain 16 43.23N 6.04W
Grafton Australia 67 29.40S152.56E
Grafton N.Dak. U.S.A. 82 48.25N 97.25W
Grafton Wisc. U.S.A. 82 43.20N 87.58W
Grafton W.Va. U.S.A. 84 39.21N 80.03W
Graham r. Canada 74 56.31N122.17W
Graham U.S.A. 83 33.06N 98.35W
Graham, Mt. U.S.A. 81 32.42N109.52W
Graham I. Canada 74 53.40N132.30W
Graham Land f. Antarctica 96 67.00S 60.00W
Grahamstown R.S.A. 56 33.18S 26.30E
Graiguenamanagh Rep. of Ire. 13 52.33N 6.57W
Grajaú r. Brazil 91 3.41S 44.48W
Grampian d. U.K. 12 57.22N 2.35W
Grampian Mts. U.K. 12 56.55N 4.00W
Grampians mts. Australia 66 37.12S142.34E
Granada Nicaragua 87 11.58N 85.59W
Granada Spain 16 37.10N 3.35W
Granby Canada 77 45.23N 72.44W
Gran Canaria i. Canary Is. 50 28.00N 15.30W
Gran Chaco f. S. America 92 22.00S 60.00W
Grand r. Canada 76 42.51N 79.34W
Grand r. S.Dak. U.S.A. 82 45.40N100.32W
Grand Bahama I. Bahamas 87 26.40N 78.20W
Grand Bank town Canada 77 47.06N 55.47W
Grand Bassam Ivory Coast 52 5.14N 3.45W
Grand Canal see Da Yunhe canal China 32
Grand Canyon f. U.S.A. 81 36.10N112.45W
Grand Canyon town U.S.A. 81 36.03N112.09W
Grand Canyon Nat. Park U.S.A. 81 36.15N112.58W
Grand Cayman i. Cayman Is. 87 19.20N 81.30W
Grand Centre Canada 75 54.25N110.13W
Grand Cess Liberia 52 4.40N 8.12W
Grand Couronne France 15 49.21N 1.00E
Grande r. Bolivia 92 15.10S 64.55W
Grande r. Bahia Brazil 91 11.05S 43.09W
Grande r. Minas Gerais Brazil 92 20.00S 51.00W
Grande, Bahía b. Argentina 93 51.30S 67.30W
Grande, Ilha i. Brazil 94 23.07S 44.16W
Grande, Sierra mts. Mexico 81 29.35N104.55W
Grande Cascapédia Canada 77 48.19N 65.54W
Grande Comore i. Comoros 55 11.35S 43.20E
Grande do Gurupá, Ilha i. Brazil 91 1.00S 51.30W
Grande-Pointe, Lac l. Canada 76 53.52N 75.32W
Grande Prairie Canada 74 55.15N118.50W
Grand Erg de Bilma des. Niger 53 18.30N 14.00E
Grand Erg Occidental des. Algeria 50 30.10N 0.20E
Grand Erg Oriental des. Algeria 51 30.00N 7.00E
Grande Rivière town Canada 77 48.24N 64.30W
Grandes, Salinas f. Argentina 92 29.37S 64.56W
Grandes Bergeronnes Canada 77 48.15N 69.33W
Grande Vallée Canada 77 49.14N 65.08W
Grand Falls town N.B. Canada 77 46.55N 67.45W
Grand Falls town Nfld. Canada 77 48.56N 55.40W
Grand Forks Canada 74 49.00N118.30W
Grand Forks U.S.A. 82 47.55N 97.03W
Grand Fougeray France 15 47.44N 1.44W
Grand Island town U.S.A. 82 40.55N 98.21W
Grand Junction U.S.A. 80 39.05N108.33W
Grand L. N.B. Canada 77 45.38N 67.38W
Grand L. Nfld. Canada 77 49.00N 57.25W
Grand L. U.S.A. 84 45.15N 67.50W
Grand Lahou Ivory Coast 52 5.09N 5.01W
Grand Manan I. Canada 77 44.40N 66.50W
Grand Marais U.S.A. 82 47.45N 90.20W
Grand' Mère Canada 77 46.37N 72.41W
Grandois Canada 77 51.07N 55.46W
Grândola Portugal 16 38.10N 8.34W
Grand Passage N. Cal. 68 18.45S163.10E
Grand Prairie town U.S.A. 83 32.45N 96.59W
Grand Rapids town Canada 75 53.08N 99.20W
Grand Rapids town Mich. U.S.A. 84 42.57N 85.40W
Grand Rapids town Minn. U.S.A. 82 47.14N 93.31W
Grand Récif de Cook reef N. Cal. 68 19.25S163.50E
Grand St. Bernard, Col du pass Italy/Switz. 15 45.52N 7.11E
Grand Teton mtn. U.S.A. 80 43.44N110.48W
Grand Teton Nat. Park U.S.A. 80 43.30N110.37W
Grand Traverse B. U.S.A. 84 45.02N 85.30W
Grand Valley Canada 76 43.54N 80.19W
Grand Valley town U.S.A. 80 39.27N108.03W
Grandville U.S.A. 84 42.54N 85.48W
Grangemouth U.K. 12 56.01N 3.44W
Granger U.S.A. 80 41.35N109.58W
Grängesberg Sweden 23 60.05N 14.59E
Grangeville U.S.A. 80 45.56N116.07W
Granite City U.S.A. 82 38.43N 90.04W
Granite Falls town U.S.A. 82 44.49N 95.31W
Granite Peak town Australia 62 25.38S121.21E
Granite Peak mtn. U.S.A. 78 45.10N109.50W
Granity New Zealand 60 41.38S171.51E
Granja Brazil 91 3.06S 40.50W
Gränna Sweden 23 58.01N 14.28E
Granollers Spain 16 41.37N 2.18E
Granön Sweden 22 64.15N 19.19E
Gran Paradiso mtn. Italy 15 45.31N 7.15E
Grant Mich. U.S.A. 84 43.20N 85.49W
Grant Nebr. U.S.A. 82 40.50N101.56W
Grant City U.S.A. 82 40.29N 94.25W
Grantham U.K. 10 52.55N 0.39W
Grantown-on-Spey U.K. 12 57.20N 3.38W
Grant Range mts. U.S.A. 80 38.25N115.30W
Grants U.S.A. 81 35.09N107.52W
Grants Pass town U.S.A. 80 42.26N123.19W
Grantsville U.S.A. 84 38.55N 81.07W
Granville France 15 48.50N 1.35W
Granville N.Dak. U.S.A. 82 48.16N100.47W
Granville L. Canada 75 56.18N100.30W
Gras, Lac de l. Canada 72 64.30N110.30W
Graskop R.S.A. 56 24.55S 30.50E
Grasse France 17 43.40N 6.56E
Grasset, L. Canada 76 49.55N 78.00W
Grass Patch Australia 63 33.14S121.43E
Grass Valley town Calif. U.S.A. 80 39.13N121.04W
Grass Valley town Oreg. U.S.A. 80 45.22N120.47W
Grates Pt. Canada 77 48.09N 52.57W
Grave Neth. 14 51.45N 5.45E
Grave, Pointe de c. France 17 45.35N 1.04W
Gravelbourg Canada 75 49.53N106.34W
Gravenhurst Canada 76 44.55N 79.22W
Gravesend Australia 67 29.35S150.20E
Gravesend U.K. 11 51.27N 0.24E
Gray France 17 47.27N 5.35E
Grayling U.S.A. 84 44.40N 84.43W
Grays U.K. 11 51.29N 0.20E
Graz Austria 20 47.05N 15.22E
Grdelica Yugo. 19 42.54N 22.04E
Great Abaco I. Bahamas 87 26.25N 77.10W
Great Artesian Basin f. Australia 64 26.30S143.02E
Great Australian Bight Australia 63 33.10S129.30E
Great B. U.S.A. 85 39.30N 74.23W
Great Barrier I. New Zealand 60 36.15S175.30E
Great Barrier Reef f. Australia 64 16.30S146.30E
Great Basin f. U.S.A. 80 40.35N116.00W
Great Bear L. Canada 72 66.00N120.00W
Great Bend town U.S.A. 82 38.22N 98.46W
Great Bitter L. see Murrah al Kubrá, Al Buḩayrah al h5ayrah al Egypt 44
Great Blasket I. Rep. of Ire. 13 52.05N 10.32W
Great Coco i. Burma 34 14.06N 93.21E
Great Divide Basin f. U.S.A. 80 42.00N108.10W
Great Dividing Range mts. Australia 67 29.00S152.00E
Great Driffield U.K. 10 54.01N 0.26W
Greater Antillles is. C. America 87 17.00N 70.00W
Greater London d. U.K. 11 51.31N 0.06W
Greater Manchester d. U.K. 10 53.30N 2.18W
Great Exuma i. Bahamas 87 23.00N 76.00W
Great Falls town U.S.A. 80 47.30N111.17W
Great Inagua I. Bahamas 87 21.00N 73.20W
Great Indian Desert see Thar Desert India/Pakistan 40
Great Karroo f. R.S.A. 56 32.40S 22.20E
Great Kei r. R.S.A. 56 32.39S 28.23E
Great L. Australia 65 41.50S146.43E
Great Malvern U.K. 11 52.07N 2.19W
Great Namaland f. Namibia 56 25.30S 17.20E
Great Nicobar i. India 34 7.00N 93.45E
Great North East Channel P.N.G./Australia 64 9.00S144.00E
Great Ouse r. U.K. 10 52.47N 0.23E
Great Ruaha r. Tanzania 55 7.55S 37.52E
Great Salt L. U.S.A. 80 41.10N112.30W
Great Salt Lake Desert U.S.A. 80 40.40N113.30W
Great Sand Hills Canada 75 50.35N109.05W
Great Sandy Desert Australia 62 20.30S123.35E
Great Sandy Desert see An Nafūd des. Saudi Arabia 42
Great Sea Reef Fiji 68 16.25S179.20E
Great Slave L. Canada 74 61.23N115.38W
Great Smoky Mountain Nat. Park U.S.A. 85 35.56N 82.48W
Great Sound b. Bermuda 95 32.18N 64.60W
Great Victoria Desert Australia 63 29.00S127.30E
Great Whernside mtn. U.K. 10 54.09N 1.59W
Great Yarmouth U.K. 11 52.40N 1.45E
Great Zimbabwe ruins Zimbabwe 56 20.30S 30.30E
Gréboun, Mont mtn. Niger 51 20.01N 8.35E
Gredos, Sierra de mts. Spain 16 40.18N 5.20W
Greece Europe 19 39.00N 22.00E
Greeley U.S.A. 80 40.25N104.42W
Green r. U.S.A. 80 38.11N109.53W
Green B. U.S.A. 84 45.00N 87.30W
Green Bay town U.S.A. 82 44.30N 88.01W
Green Bluff f. Australia 67 30.10S153.14E
Greenbush Minn. U.S.A. 82 48.42N 96.11W
Greenbushes Australia 63 33.50S116.00E
Greencastle Ind. U.S.A. 84 39.39N 86.51W
Greene U.S.A. 84 42.20N 75.46W
Greeneville U.S.A. 85 36.10N 82.50W
Greenfield Ill. U.S.A. 82 39.21N 90.21W
Greenfield Iowa U.S.A. 82 41.18N 94.28W
Greenfield Mo. U.S.A. 83 37.25N 93.51W
Greenhills Australia 63 31.58S117.01E
Greening Canada 76 48.08N 74.55W
Greenland N. America 73 68.00N 45.00W
Greenlaw U.K. 12 55.43N 2.28W
Greenly I. Australia 66 34.39S134.50E
Greenock U.K. 12 55.57N 4.45W
Greenore Pt. Rep. of Ire. 13 52.14N 6.19W
Green River town Utah U.S.A. 80 38.59N110.10W
Green River town Wyo. U.S.A. 80 41.32N109.28W
Greensboro N.C. U.S.A. 85 36.04N 79.47W
Greensburg Ind. U.S.A. 84 39.20N 85.29W
Greenville Canada 74 55.03N129.33W
Greenville Liberia 52 5.01N 9.03W
Greenville Ala. U.S.A. 85 31.50N 86.40W
Greenville Mich. U.S.A. 84 43.11N 85.13W
Greenville Miss. U.S.A. 83 33.25N 91.05W
Greenville Mo. U.S.A. 83 37.08N 90.27W
Greenville N.C. U.S.A. 85 35.36N 77.23W
Greenville S.C. U.S.A. 85 34.52N 82.25W
Greenville Tex. U.S.A. 83 33.08N 96.07W
Greenwich Conn. U.S.A. 85 41.05N 73.50W
Greenwood Miss. U.S.A. 83 33.31N 90.11W
Greenwood S.C. U.S.A. 85 34.11N 82.10W
Gregory r. Australia 64 17.53S139.17E
Gregory U.S.A. 82 43.14N 99.26W
Gregory, L. S.A. Australia 66 28.55S139.00E
Gregory, L. W.A. Australia 62 20.10S127.20E
Gregory Range mts. Australia 64 19.00S143.05E
Greifswald E. Germany 20 54.06N 13.24E
Gremikha U.S.S.R. 24 68.03N 39.38E
Grenå Denmark 23 56.25N 10.53E
Grenada C. America 90 12.07N 61.40W
Grenada i. Windward Is. 87 12.15N 61.45W
Grenade France 17 43.47N 1.10E
Grenoble France 17 45.11N 5.43E
Grenville, C. Australia 64 12.00S143.13E
Gresik Indonesia 37 7.12S112.38E
Gretna U.K. 12 55.00N 3.04W
Gretna U.S.A. 83 29.55N 90.03W
Greven W. Germany 14 52.07N 7.38E
Grevenbroich W. Germany 14 51.07N 6.33E
Grevesmühlen E. Germany 20 53.51N 11.10E
Grey r. New Zealand 60 42.28S171.13E
Grey, C. Australia 64 13.00S136.40E
Greybull U.S.A. 80 44.30N108.03W
Grey Is. Canada 77 50.50N 55.37W
Greymouth New Zealand 60 42.28S171.12E
Grey Range mts. Australia 65 27.00S143.35E
Greystones Rep. of Ire. 13 53.09N 6.04W
Greytown R.S.A. 56 29.04S 30.36E
Griffin U.S.A. 79 33.15N 84.17W
Griffith Australia 67 34.18S146.04E
Griggsville U.S.A. 82 39.42N 90.43W
Grignan France 17 44.25N 4.54E
Grigoriopol U.S.S.R. 21 47.08N 29.18E
Grim, C. Australia 65 40.45S144.45E
Grimari C.A.R. 49 5.44N 20.03E
Grimsby Canada 76 43.12N 79.34W
Grimsby U.K. 10 53.35N 0.05W
Grimstad Norway 23 58.20N 8.36E
Grimsvötn mtn. Iceland 22 64.30N 17.10W
Grindavik Iceland 22 63.50N 22.27W
Grindsted Denmark 23 55.45N 8.56E
Grinnell U.S.A. 82 41.45N 92.43W
Griqualand East f. R.S.A. 56 30.40S 29.10E
Griqualand West f. R.S.A. 56 28.50S 23.30E
Griva U.S.S.R. 24 60.35N 50.58E
Grobina U.S.S.R. 23 56.33N 21.10E
Groblershoop R.S.A. 56 28.55S 20.59E
Grodno U.S.S.R. 21 53.40N 23.50E
Grodzisk Poland 20 52.14N 16.22E
Grodzyanka U.S.S.R. 21 53.30N 28.41E
Groenlo Neth. 14 52.02N 6.36E
Groix, Île de i. France 17 47.38N 3.26W
Gronau W. Germany 14 52.14N 7.02E
Grong Norway 22 64.27N 12.19E
Groningen Neth. 14 53.13N 6.35E
Groningen d. Neth. 14 53.15N 6.45E
Groom U.S.A. 83 35.12N101.06W
Groot r. C.P. R.S.A. 56 33.58S 25.03E
Groote Eylandt i. Australia 64 14.00S136.40E
Grootfontein Namibia 56 19.32S 18.07E
Groot Karasberge mts. Namibia 56 27.20S 18.50E
Grootlaagte r. Botswana 56 20.58S 21.42E
Groot Swartberge mts. R.S.A. 56 33.20S 22.00E
Grossenbrode W. Germany 20 54.23N 11.07E
Grossenhain E. Germany 20 51.17N 13.31E
Grosseto Italy 18 42.46N 11.08E
Gross Glockner mtn. Austria 20 47.05N 12.50E
Groswater B. Canada 77 54.20N 57.30W
Grote Nete r. Belgium 14 51.07N 4.20E
Groundhog r. Canada 76 49.40N 82.06W
Grouse Creek town U.S.A. 80 41.22N113.53W
Grover City U.S.A. 81 35.07N120.37W
Groves U.S.A. 83 29.57N 93.55W
Groveton Tex. U.S.A. 83 31.03N 95.08W
Groznyy U.S.S.R. 25 43.21N 45.42E
Grudziądz Poland 21 53.29N 18.45E
Grumeti r. Tanzania 55 2.05S 33.45E
Grünau Namibia 56 27.44S 18.18E
Grundarfjördhur town Iceland 22 64.55N 23.20W
Grundy U.S.A. 85 37.13N 82.08W
Grungedal Norway 23 59.44N 7.43E
Gruzinskaya S.S.R. d. U.S.S.R. 25 42.00N 43.30E
Gryazovets U.S.S.R. 24 58.52N 40.12E
Gryfice Poland 20 53.56N 15.12E
Guachipas Argentina 92 25.31S 65.31W
Guacuí Brazil 94 20.44S 41.40W
Guadalajara Mexico 86 20.30N103.20W
Guadalajara Spain 16 40.37N 3.10W
Guadalcanal i. Solomon Is. 68 9.32S160.12E
Guadalete r. Spain 16 36.37N 6.15W
Guadalmena r. Spain 16 38.00N 3.50W
Guadalquivir r. Spain 16 36.50N 6.20W
Guadalupe Mexico 83 25.41N100.15W
Guadalupe, Isla de i. Mexico 81 29.00N118.16W
Guadalupe, Sierra de mts. Spain 16 39.30N 5.25W
Guadarrama r. Spain 16 39.55N 4.10W
Guadarrama, Sierra de mts. Spain 16 41.00N 3.50W
Guadeloupe C. America 95 16.20N 61.40W
Guadeloupe i. Leeward Is. 87 16.20N 61.40W
Guadiana r. Portugal 16 37.10N 7.36W
Guadix Spain 16 37.19N 3.08W
Guafo, Golfo de g. Chile 93 43.35S 74.15W
Guainía r. Colombia 90 2.01N 67.07W
Guaíra Falls see Sete Quedas, Salto das f. Brazil 92
Guajará Mirim Brazil 90 10.48S 65.22W
Guajira, Península de la pen. Colombia 90 12.00N 72.00W
Gualeguay Argentina 93 33.10S 59.20W
Gualeguay r. Argentina 93 33.18S 59.38W

Gualeguaychu to Harwich

Gualeguaychu Argentina 93 33.00S 58.30W
Guam i. Mariana Is. 37 13.30N144.40E
Guamal Colombia 90 9.10N 74.15W
Guanajuato Mexico 86 21.00N101.16W
Guanajuato d. Mexico 86 21.00N101.00W
Guanare Venezuela 90 9.04N 69.45W
Guanarito Venezuela 90 8.43N 69.12W
Guane Cuba 87 22.13N 84.07W
Guang'an China 33 30.30N106.35E
Guangchang China 33 26.50N116.16E
Guangdong d. China 33 23.00N113.00E
Guanghan China 33 30.59N104.15E
Guanghua China 32 32.26N111.41E
Guangji China 33 29.42N115.39E
Guangming Ding mtn. China 33 30.09N118.11E
Guangnan China 33 24.03N105.03E
Guangrao China 32 37.04N118.22E
Guangxi Zhuangzu d. China 33 23.30N109.00E
Guangyuan China 32 32.29N105.55E
Guangze China 33 27.27N117.23E
Guangzhou China 33 23.08N113.20E
Guanling China 33 25.57N105.38E
Guantánamo Cuba 87 20.09N 75.14W
Guan Xian Shandong China 32 36.29N115.25E
Guan Xian Sichuan China 39 30.59N103.40E
Guanyun China 32 34.17N119.15E
Guaporé r. Bolivia / Brazil 92 12.00S 65.15W
Guaqui Bolivia 92 16.35S 68.51W
Guarabira Brazil 91 6.46S 35.25W
Guarapuava Brazil 94 25.22S 51.28W
Guaratinguetá Brazil 94 22.49S 45.09W
Guarda Portugal 16 40.32N 7.17W
Guardavalle Italy 19 38.30N 16.30E
Guardo Spain 16 42.47N 4.50W
Guareim r. Uruguay see Quarí r. Brazil 93
Guasave Mexico 81 25.34N108.27W
Guasipati Venezuela 90 7.28N 61.54W
Guastalla Italy 15 44.55N 10.39E
Guatemala C. America 87 15.40N 90.00W
Guatemala town Guatemala 86 14.38N 90.22W
Guatemala Basin Pacific Oc. 69 12.00N 95.00W
Guatemala Trench Pacific Oc. 69 15.00N 93.00W
Guatire Venezuela 90 10.28N 66.32W
Guaviare r. Colombia 90 4.00N 67.35W
Guaxupé Brazil 94 21.17S 46.44W
Guayaquil Ecuador 90 2.13S 79.54W
Guayaquil, Golfo de g. Ecuador 90 3.00S 80.35W
Guaymallén Argentina 93 32.54S 68.47W
Guaymas Mexico 81 27.56N110.54W
Guayquiraró r. Argentina 93 30.25S 59.36W
Guba Zaïre 54 10.40S 26.26E
Gubakha U.S.S.R. 24 58.55N 57.30E
Gubeikou China 32 40.41N117.09E
Gubin Poland 20 51.59N 14.42E
Gubio Nigeria 53 12.31N 12.44E
Guchab Namibia 56 19.40S 17.47E
Gucheng China 32 37.20N115.57E
Gúdar, Sierra de mts. Spain 16 40.27N 0.42W
Gudbrandsdalen f. Norway 23 61.30N 10.00E
Gudvangen Norway 23 60.52N 6.50E
Guecho Spain 16 43.21N 3.01W
Guékédou Guinea 52 8.35N 10.11W
Guelma Algeria 51 36.28N 7.26E
Guelph Canada 76 43.34N 80.16W
Guelta Zemmur W. Sahara 50 25.15N 12.20W
Guémené-sur-Scorff France 17 48.04N 3.13W
Guera d. Chad 53 11.22N 18.00E
Guérard, Lac l. Canada 77 56.20N 65.35W
Guéret France 17 46.10N 1.52E
Guernica Spain 16 43.19N 2.40W
Guernsey i. U.K. 11 49.27N 2.35W
Guerra Mozambique 55 13.05S 35.12E
Guerrero d. Mexico 86 18.00N100.00W
Guguan i. Mariana Is. 37 17.20N145.51E
Guiana S. America 91 3.40N 53.00W
Guiana Highlands S. America 90 4.00N 59.00W
Guichón Uruguay 93 32.21S 57.12W
Guidimaka d. Mauritania 50 15.20N 12.00W
Guiding China 33 26.32N107.15E
Guidong China 33 26.12N114.00E
Guiers, Lac de l. Senegal 52 16.12N 15.50W
Gui Jiang r. China 33 23.25N111.20E
Guildford Australia 63 31.55S115.55E
Guildford U.K. 11 51.14N 0.35W
Guilherne Capelo Ihe Angola 54 5.11S 12.10E
Guilin China 33 25.20N110.10E
Guillaume-Delisle, Lac l. Canada 76 56.20N 75.50W
Guimarães Brazil 91 2.08S 44.36W
Guimarães Portugal 16 41.27N 8.18W
Guimeng Ding mtn. China 32 35.34N117.50E
Guinan China 30 35.20N100.50E
Guinea Africa 52 10.30N 11.30W
Guinea, G. of Africa 53 3.00N 3.00E
Guinea Basin f. Atlantic Oc. 95 0.00 5.00W
Guinea Bissau Africa 52 11.30N 15.00W
Güines Cuba 87 22.50N 82.02W
Guingamp France 17 48.34N 3.09W
Guinguinéo Senegal 52 14.20N 15.57W
Guiping China 33 23.20N110.02E
Guir, Hammada du f. Morocco / Algeria 50 31.00N 3.20W
Güiria Venezuela 90 10.37N 62.21W
Guiscard France 15 49.39N 3.03E
Guise France 15 49.54N 3.38E
Guiuan Phil. 37 11.02N125.44E
Guixi China 33 28.12N117.10E
Gui Xian China 33 23.02N109.40E
Guiyang China 33 26.31N106.39E
Guizhou d. China 33 27.00N107.00E
Gujarat d. India 40 22.20N 70.30E
Gūjar Khān Pakistan 40 33.16N 73.19E
Gujrānwāla Pakistan 40 32.26N 74.33E
Gujrāt Pakistan 40 32.34N 74.05E
Gulang Gansu China 32 37.30N102.54E
Gulargambone Australia 67 31.21S148.32E
Gulbarga India 38 17.22N 76.47E
Gulch Ethiopia 48 14.43N 36.45E
Gulfport U.S.A. 83 30.22N 89.06W
Gulgong Australia 67 32.20S149.49E
Gulin China 33 28.07N105.51E
Gulistān Pakistan 40 30.36N 66.35E
Gull Lake town Canada 75 50.08N108.27W
Gulma Nigeria 53 12.41N 4.24E
Gulshad U.S.S.R. 30 46.37N 74.22E
Gulu Uganda 55 2.46N 32.21E
Guluguba Australia 64 26.16S150.03E
Gulwe Tanzania 55 6.27S 36.27E
Gumal r. Pakistan 40 32.08N 69.50E
Gumel Nigeria 53 12.39N 9.23E
Gumla India 41 23.03N 84.33E
Gummersbach W. Germany 14 51.03N 7.32E
Gum Spring town U.S.A. 85 37.47N 77.54W
Gümüşhane Turkey 42 40.26N 39.26E
Guna India 40 24.39N 77.19E
Gunbar Australia 67 34.04S145.25E
Gundagai Australia 67 35.07S148.05E
Gundlupet India 38 11.48N 76.41E
Gungu Zaïre 54 5.43S 19.20E
Gunisao r. Canada 75 53.54N 97.58W
Gunisao L. Canada 75 53.33N 96.15W
Gunnedah Australia 67 30.59S150.15E
Gunnison r. U.S.A. 80 39.03N108.35W
Gunnison Colo. U.S.A. 80 38.33N106.56W
Gunnison Utah U.S.A. 80 39.09N111.49W
Guntersville U.S.A. 85 34.20N 86.18W
Guntersville L. U.S.A. 85 34.45N 86.03W
Guntūr India 39 16.20N 80.27E
Gunungsitoli Indonesia 36 1.17N 97.37E
Gunupur India 41 19.05N 83.49E
Günzburg W. Germany 20 48.27N 10.16E
Guochengyi China 32 36.14N104.52E
Gurais Jammu & Kashmir 40 34.38N 74.50E
Gura Portiţei f. Romania 21 44.40N 29.00E
Gurban Obo China 32 43.05N112.27E
Gurdāspur Jammu & Kashmir 40 32.02N 75.31E
Gurgaon India 40 28.28N 77.02E
Gurgueia r. Brazil 91 6.45S 43.35W
Gūrha India 40 25.14N 71.45E
Gursköy i. Norway 22 62.16N 5.42E
Gurué Mozambique 57 15.30S 36.58E
Gürün Turkey 42 38.44N 37.15E
Gurupá Brazil 91 1.25S 51.39W
Gurupi r. Brazil 91 1.13S 46.06W
Guru Sikhar mtn. India 40 24.39N 72.46E
Guruwe Zimbabwe 56 16.42S 30.40E
Gurvan Sayhan Uul mts. Mongolia 32 43.45N103.30E
Guryev U.S.S.R. 25 47.08N 51.59E
Gusau Nigeria 53 12.12N 6.40E
Gusev U.S.S.R. 21 54.32N 22.12E
Gusong China 33 28.25N105.12E
Guspini Italy 18 39.32N 8.38E
Gustav Holm, Kap c. Greenland 73 67.00N 34.00W
Güstrow E. Germany 20 53.48N 12.11E
Gütersloh W. Germany 20 51.54N 8.22E
Guthrie Ky. U.S.A. 85 36.40N 87.10W
Guthrie Okla. U.S.A. 83 35.53N 97.25W
Guyana S. America 90 4.40N 59.00W
Guyang China 32 41.03N110.03E
Guymon U.S.A. 83 36.41N101.29W
Guyra Australia 67 30.14S151.40E
Guyuan Hebei China 32 41.40N115.41E
Guyuan Ningxia Huizu China 32 36.00N106.25E
Guzhen Anhui China 32 33.19N117.19E
Guzman, Laguna de l. Mexico 81 31.25N107.25W
Gwa Burma 39 17.36N 94.35E
Gwabegar Australia 67 30.34S149.00E
Gwadabawa Nigeria 53 13.23N 5.15E
Gwādar Pakistan 40 25.07N 62.19E
Gwagwada Nigeria 53 10.15N 7.15E
Gwai Zimbabwe 56 19.15S 27.42E
Gwai r. Zimbabwe 56 17.59S 26.55E
Gwalior India 41 26.13N 78.10E
Gwanda Zimbabwe 56 20.59S 29.00E
Gwane Zaïre 49 4.43N 25.50E
Gwasero Nigeria 53 9.30N 8.30E
Gweebarra B. Rep. of Ire. 13 54.52N 8.28W
Gwejam d. Ethiopia 49 11.10N 37.00E
Gwent d. U.K. 11 51.44N 3.00W
Gweru Zimbabwe 56 19.25S 29.50E
Gwydir r. Australia 67 29.35S148.45E
Gwynedd d. U.K. 10 53.00N 4.00W
Gyaca China 41 29.05N 92.55E
Gyangrang China 41 30.47N 85.09E
Gyangzê China 41 28.57N 89.38E
Gyaring Co l. China 41 31.05N 88.00E
Gydanskiy Poluostrov pen. U.S.S.R. 28 70.00N 78.30E
Gyimda China 41 31.03N 97.18E
Gyirong China 41 29.00N 85.15E
Gympie Australia 64 26.11S152.40E
Gyöngyös Hungary 21 47.47N 19.56E
Györ Hungary 21 47.41N 17.40E
Gypsum Pt. Canada 74 61.53N114.35W
Gypsumville Canada 75 51.45N 98.35W

H

Haan W. Germany 14 51.10N 7.02E
Ha'apai Group is. Tonga 69 19.50S174.30W
Haapajärvi Finland 22 63.45N 25.20E
Haapamäki Finland 22 62.15N 24.28E
Haapavesi Finland 22 64.08N 25.22E
Haapsalu U.S.S.R. 23 58.56N 23.33E
Hā Arava r. Israel / Jordan 44 30.30N 35.10E
Haarlem Neth. 14 52.22N 4.38E
Haarlem R.S.A. 56 33.46S 23.28E
Hab r. Pakistan 40 24.53N 66.41E
Habahe China 30 47.53N 86.12E
Ḩabarūt S. Yemen 38 17.18N 52.44E
Habaswein Kenya 55 1.06N 39.26E
Habay-la-Neuve Belgium 14 49.45N 5.38E
Ḩabbān S. Yemen 45 14.21N 47.05E
Hab Chauki Pakistan 40 25.01N 66.53E
Habiganj Bangla. 41 24.23N 91.25E
Habikino Japan 35 34.33N135.37E
Habo Sweden 23 57.55N 14.04E
Hachinohe Japan 31 40.30N141.30E
Hachiōji Japan 35 35.39N139.20E
Hack, Mt. Australia 66 30.44S138.45E
Hadāli Pakistan 40 32.18N 72.12E
Hadano Japan 35 35.22N139.14E
Ḩadāribah, Ra's al c. Sudan 48 22.04N 36.54E
Ḩadbaram Oman 45 17.27N 55.15E
Ḩadd, Ra's al c. Oman 43 22.32N 59.49E
Haddington U.K. 12 55.57N 2.47W
Hadejia Nigeria 53 12.30N 10.03E
Hadejia r. Nigeria 53 12.47N 10.44E
Hadera Israel 44 32.26N 34.55E
Haderslev Denmark 23 55.15N 9.30E
Hadīboh S. Yemen 45 12.39N 54.02E
Hadjer Mornou mtn. Chad 48 17.12N 23.08E
Ha Dong Vietnam 33 20.40N105.58E
Ḩaḑramawt f. S. Yemen 45 16.30N 49.30E
Hadsten Denmark 23 56.20N 10.03E
Hadsund Denmark 23 56.43N 10.07E
Haedo, Cuchilla de mts. Uruguay 93 31.50S 56.10W
Haegeland Norway 23 58.15N 7.50E
Haeju N. Korea 31 38.04N125.40E
Haena Hawaiian Is. 69 22.14N159.34W
Ḩafar al Bāţin Saudi Arabia 43 28.28N 46.00E
Hāfizābād Pakistan 40 32.04N 73.41E
Hafnarfjördhur town Iceland 22 64.04N 21.58W
Haft Gel Iran 43 31.28N 49.35E
Hagen W. Germany 14 51.22N 7.27E
Hagerman U.S.A. 81 33.07N104.20W
Hagerstown U.S.A. 84 39.39N 77.43W
Hagersville Canada 76 42.58N 80.03W
Hagfors Sweden 23 60.02N 13.42E
Ha Giang Vietnam 33 22.50N105.00E
Hags Head Rep. of Ire. 13 52.56N 9.29W
Hague, Cap de la c. France 15 49.44N 1.56W
Haguenau France 17 48.49N 7.47E
Hai'an Shan mts. China 33 23.00N115.30E
Haicheng China 32 40.52N122.48E
Hai Duong Vietnam 34 20.56N106.21E
Haifa see Hefa Israel 44
Haifeng China 33 22.58N115.20E
Haikang China 33 20.55N110.04E
Haikou China 33 20.03N110.27E
Ḩā'il Saudi Arabia 42 27.31N 41.45E
Hailākāndi India 41 24.41N 92.34E
Hailar China 31 49.15N119.41E
Hailong China 32 42.39N125.49E
Hailsham U.K. 11 50.52N 0.17E
Hailun China 31 47.29N126.58E
Hailuoto i. Finland 22 65.02N 24.42E
Haimen China 33 28.41N121.30E
Hainan i. China 33 19.00N109.30E
Hainaut d. Belgium 14 50.30N 3.45E
Haines Alas. U.S.A. 74 59.11N135.23W
Haines Oreg. U.S.A. 80 44.55N117.56W
Haines Junction Canada 74 60.45N137.30W
Haining China 33 30.30N120.35E
Hai Phòng Vietnam 33 20.48N106.40E
Haiti C. America 87 19.00N 73.00W
Haiyang China 32 36.46N121.09E
Haiyuan China 32 36.35N105.40E
Ḩajar Banga Sudan 49 11.30N 23.00E
Hajdúböszörmény Hungary 21 47.41N 21.30E
Hajdúszoboszló Hungary 21 47.27N 21.24E
Hājīpur India 41 25.41N 85.13E
Hakkâri Turkey 43 37.36N 43.45E
Hakodate Japan 31 41.46N140.44E
Hakupu Niue 68 19.07S169.51W
Hala Pakistan 40 25.49N 68.25E
Ḩalab Syria 42 36.14N 37.10E
Ḩalabjah Iraq 43 35.10N 45.59E
Ḩalā'ib Sudan 48 22.13N 36.38E
Ḩalbā Lebanon 44 34.34N 36.05E
Halberstadt E. Germany 20 51.54N 11.04E
Halden Norway 23 59.09N 11.23E
Haldia India 41 22.05N 88.03E
Haldwāni India 41 29.13N 79.31E
Haleyville U.S.A. 85 34.12N 87.38W
Half Assini Ghana 52 5.04N 2.53W
Halfmoon Bay town Canada 74 49.31N123.54W
Haliburton Canada 76 45.03N 78.03W
Haliburton Highlands Canada 76 45.20N 78.00W
Halifax Canada 77 44.39N 63.36W
Halifax U.K. 10 53.43N 1.51W
Halifax U.S.A. 85 36.46N 78.57W
Halifax B. Australia 64 18.50S146.30E
Halīl r. Iran 38 27.35N 58.44E
Halin well Somali Rep. 45 9.08N 48.47E
Halkett, C. U.S.A. 72 71.00N152.00W
Halkirk U.K. 12 58.30N 3.30W
Halladale r. U.K. 12 58.34N 3.54W
Halland d. Sweden 23 56.45N 13.00E
Hall B. Australia 66 34.00S135.03E
Halle Belgium 14 50.45N 4.14E
Halle E. Germany 20 51.28N 11.58E
Halle d. E. Germany 20 51.30N 11.45E
Hällefors Sweden 23 59.47N 14.30E
Hallingdal f. Norway 23 60.30N 9.00E
Hall Is. Pacific Oc. 68 8.37N152.00E
Hall Lake town Canada 73 68.40N 81.30W
Hällnäs Sweden 22 64.19N 19.38E
Hall Pen. Canada 73 63.30N 66.00W
Hallsberg Sweden 23 59.04N 15.07E
Hall's Creek town Australia 62 18.17S127.44E
Hallstavik Sweden 23 60.03N 18.36E
Hallstead U.S.A. 84 41.58N 75.45W
Halmahera i. Indonesia 37 0.45N128.00E
Halmstad Sweden 23 56.39N 12.50E
Halsa Norway 22 63.03N 8.14E
Hälsingborg Sweden 23 56.03N 12.42E
Haltern W. Germany 14 51.45N 7.10E
Haltia Tunturi mtn. Finland 22 69.17N 21.21E
Haltwhistle U.K. 10 54.58N 2.27W
Ham France 15 49.45N 3.04E
Ḩamad, Wādī al r. Saudi Arabia 42 25.49N 36.37E
Hamada f. see Drâa, Hamada du f. W. Sahara 50
Hamadān Iran 43 34.47N 48.33E
Ḩamādat Marzūq f. Libya 51 26.00N 12.30E
Ḩamāh Syria 44 35.09N 36.44E
Hamakita Japan 35 34.48N137.47E
Hamamatsu Japan 35 34.42N137.44E
Hamar Norway 23 60.48N 11.06E
Hamaröy Norway 22 68.05N 15.40E
Ḩamāţah, Jabal mtn. Egypt 42 24.11N 35.01E
Hamborn W. Germany 14 51.29N 6.46E
Hamburg R.S.A. 56 33.17S 27.27E
Hamburg N.J. U.S.A. 85 41.09N 74.35W
Hamburg N.Y. U.S.A. 76 42.43N 78.50W
Hamburg Penn. U.S.A. 85 40.34N 75.59W
Hamburg W. Germany 20 53.33N 10.00E
Häme d. Finland 23 61.20N 24.30E
Hämeenlinna Finland 23 61.00N 24.27E
Hamelin B. Australia 63 34.10S115.00E
Hameln W. Germany 20 52.06N 9.21E
Hamer Koke Ethiopia 49 5.12N 36.45E
Hamersley Range mts. Australia 62 22.00S118.00E
Hamhŭng N. Korea 31 39.54N127.35E
Hami China 30 42.40N 93.30E
Hamilton Australia 66 37.45S142.04E
Hamilton r. Australia 65 27.12S135.28E
Hamilton Bermuda 95 32.18N 64.48W
Hamilton Canada 76 43.15N 79.50W
Hamilton New Zealand 60 37.46S175.18E
Hamilton U.K. 12 55.46N 4.10W
Hamilton Mont. U.S.A. 80 46.15N114.09W
Hamilton Ohio U.S.A. 84 39.23N 84.33W
Hamilton Tex. U.S.A. 83 31.42N 98.07W
Hamley Bridge town Australia 66 34.21S138.41E
Hamlin Tex. U.S.A. 83 32.53N100.08W
Hamm W. Germany 14 51.40N 7.49E
Hammamet, Golfe de g. Tunisia 51 36.05N 10.40E
Hammam Lif Tunisia 51 36.44N 10.20E
Ḩammār, Hawr al l. Iraq 43 30.50N 47.00E
Hammerdal Sweden 22 63.35N 15.20E
Hammerfest Norway 22 70.40N 23.42E
Hammond Australia 66 32.33S138.20E
Hammond La. U.S.A. 83 30.30N 90.28W
Hammond N.Y. U.S.A. 84 44.27N 75.42W
Hammonton U.S.A. 85 39.38N 74.48W
Hamoir Belgium 14 50.25N 5.32E
Hamoyet, Jabal mtn. Sudan 48 17.33N 38.00E
Hampshire d. U.K. 11 51.03N 1.20W
Hampton S.C. U.S.A. 85 32.52N 81.06W
Hampton Va. U.S.A. 85 37.02N 76.23W
Hamra, Saguia el wadi W. Sahara 50 27.15N 13.21W
Ḩamrīn, Jabal mts. Iraq 43 34.40N 44.10E
Hāmūn-e Jaz Mūriān l. Iran 38 27.20N 58.55E
Hana Hawaiian Is. 69 20.45N155.59W
Hanang mtn. Tanzania 55 4.30S 35.21E
Hancheng China 32 35.28N110.29E
Hancock Mich. U.S.A. 84 47.08N 88.34W
Handa Japan 35 34.53N136.56E
Handan China 32 36.37N114.26E
Handeni Tanzania 55 5.25S 38.04E
Hando Somali Rep. 45 10.39N 51.08E
HaNegev des. Israel 44 30.42N 34.55E
Hanford U.S.A. 81 36.20N119.39W
Hanga Roa I. de Pascua 69 27.09S109.26W
Hanggin Houqi China 32 40.50N107.06E
Hanggin Qi China 32 39.56N108.54E
Hangö Finland 23 59.50N 22.57E
Hangu China 32 39.11N117.45E
Hangu Pakistan 40 33.32N 71.04E
Hangzhou China 33 30.14N120.08E
Hangzhou Wan b. China 33 30.25N121.00E
Hanjiang China 33 25.30N119.14E
Hankey R.S.A. 56 33.50S 24.52E
Hankinson U.S.A. 82 46.04N 96.55W
Hanksville U.S.A. 80 38.21N110.44W
Hänle Jammu & Kashmir 41 32.48N 79.00E
Hanmer Springs town New Zealand 60 42.31S172.50E
Hann, Mt. Australia 62 15.55S125.57E
Hanna Canada 75 51.38N111.54W
Hannaford U.S.A. 82 47.19N 98.11W
Hannah B. Canada 76 51.20N 80.00W
Hannibal Mo. U.S.A. 79 39.41N 91.25W
Hannover W. Germany 20 52.23N 9.44E
Hannut Belgium 14 50.40N 5.05E
Hanöbukten b. Sweden 23 55.45N 14.30E
Hà Nôi Vietnam 33 21.01N105.53E
Hanoi see Hà Nôi Vietnam 33
Hanover Canada 76 44.09N 81.02W
Hanover R.S.A. 56 31.04S 24.25E
Hanover Penn. U.S.A. 85 39.48N 76.59W
Hanover, Isla i. Chile 93 50.57S 74.40W
Han Pijesak Yugo. 19 44.04N 18.59E
Hānsdiha India 41 24.36N 87.05E
Hanshou China 33 28.55N111.58E
Han Shui r. China 33 30.32N114.20E
Hānsi Haryana India 40 29.06N 75.58E
Hansi Himachal P. India 41 32.27N 77.50E
Hanson, L. Australia 66 31.02S136.13E
Hantengri Feng mtn. China 30 42.09N 80.12E
Han Ul China 32 45.10N119.48E
Hanyang China 33 30.42N113.50E
Hanyin China 32 32.53N108.37E
Hanzhong China 32 33.08N107.04E
Haouach, Ouadi wadi Chad 51 16.45N 19.35E
Haparanda Sweden 22 65.50N 24.10E
Happy Valley town Canada 77 53.16N 60.14W
Hapsu N. Korea 31 41.12N128.48E
Hāpur India 41 28.43N 77.47E
Ḩaql Saudi Arabia 44 29.14N 34.56E
Ḩaraḑ Saudi Arabia 43 24.12N 49.08E
Harardera Somali Rep. 45 4.32N 47.53E
Harare Zimbabwe 57 17.49S 31.04E
Har-Ayrag Mongolia 32 45.42N109.14E
Haraze Chad 49 9.55N 20.48E
Harbin China 31 45.45N126.41E
Harborcreek U.S.A. 76 42.09N 79.57W
Harbour Deep town Canada 77 50.22N 56.27W
Harbour Grace town Canada 77 47.42N 53.13W
Harburg W. Germany 20 53.27N 9.58E
Harda India 40 22.20N 77.06E
Hardangerfjorden est. Norway 23 60.10N 6.00E
Hardangerjökulen mtn. Norway 23 60.33N 7.26E
Hardanger Vidda f. Norway 23 60.20N 7.30E
Hardeeville U.S.A. 85 32.18N 81.05W
Hardenberg Neth. 14 52.36N 6.40E
Harderwijk Neth. 14 52.21N 5.37E
Harding R.S.A. 56 30.34S 29.52E
Hardman U.S.A. 80 45.10N119.40W
Hardoi India 41 27.25N 80.07E
Hardwār India 41 29.58N 78.10E
Hardwicke B. Australia 66 34.52S137.10E
Hardy U.S.A. 83 36.19N 91.29W
Hare B. Canada 77 51.18N 55.50W
Haren W. Germany 14 52.48N 7.15E
Hārer Ethiopia 49 9.20N 42.10E
Hārergē d. Ethiopia 49 8.00N 41.00E
Harfleur France 15 49.30N 0.12E
Hargeysa Somali Rep. 45 9.31N 44.02E
Har Hu l. China 30 38.20N 97.40E
Hari r. Indonesia 36 1.00S104.15E
Harīpur Pakistan 40 33.59N 72.56E
Harīrūd r. Afghan. 38 35.42N 61.12E
Harlan U.S.A. 82 41.39N 95.19W
Harlech U.K. 10 52.52N 4.08W
Harlem U.S.A. 80 48.32N108.47W
Harlingen Neth. 14 53.10N 5.25E
Harlingen U.S.A. 83 26.11N 97.42W
Harlow U.K. 11 51.47N 0.08E
Harlowton U.S.A. 80 46.26N109.50W
Harnai Pakistan 40 30.06N 67.56E
Harnātānr India 41 27.19N 84.01E
Harney Basin f. U.S.A. 80 43.15N120.40W
Harney L. U.S.A. 80 43.14N119.07W
Härnösand Sweden 22 62.37N 17.55E
Har Nuur l. Mongolia 30 48.00N 93.25E
Haroldswick U.K. 8 60.47N 0.50W
Harper Liberia 52 4.25N 7.43W
Harrai India 41 22.37N 79.13E
Harricana r. Canada 76 51.10N 79.45W
Harrigan, C. Canada 77 55.50N 60.21W
Harrington U.S.A. 85 38.56N 75.35W
Harrington Harbour Canada 77 50.31N 59.30W
Harris Canada 75 51.44N107.35W
Harris i. U.K. 12 57.50N 6.55W
Harris, L. Australia 65 31.08S135.14E
Harris, Sd. of U.K. 12 57.43N 7.05W
Harrisburg Ill. U.S.A. 83 37.44N 88.33W
Harrisburg Oreg. U.S.A. 80 44.16N123.10W
Harrisburg Penn. U.S.A. 84 40.16N 76.52W
Harrismith Australia 63 32.55S117.50E
Harrismith R.S.A. 56 28.15S 29.07E
Harrison Ark. U.S.A. 83 36.14N 93.07W
Harrison Nebr. U.S.A. 82 42.41N103.53W
Harrison, C. Canada 77 54.55N 57.55W
Harrison L. Canada 74 49.33N121.50W
Harrisonville U.S.A. 82 38.39N 94.21W
Harrodsburg U.S.A. 85 37.46N 84.51W
Harrogate U.K. 10 53.59N 1.32W
Harrow U.K. 11 51.35N 0.21W
Harstad Norway 22 68.48N 16.30E
Harsūd India 40 22.06N 76.44E
Hart, L. Australia 66 31.08S136.24E
Hartford U.S.A. 84 41.45N 72.42W
Hartland Canada 77 46.18N 67.32W
Hartland U.K. 11 50.59N 4.29W
Hartland Pt. U.K. 11 51.01N 4.32W
Hartlepool U.K. 10 54.42N 1.11W
Hartley Bay town Canada 74 53.27N129.18W
Hartola Finland 23 61.35N 26.01E
Hartshorne U.S.A. 83 34.51N 95.33W
Hartsville U.S.A. 85 34.23N 80.05W
Hārūnābād Pakistan 40 29.37N 73.08E
Har Us Nuur l. Mongolia 30 48.10N 92.10E
Hārūt r. Afghan. 40 31.35N 61.18E
Harvey Australia 63 33.06S115.50E
Harvey Ill. U.S.A. 82 41.37N 87.39W
Harvey N.Dak. U.S.A. 82 47.47N 99.56W
Harwich U.K. 11 51.56N 1.18E

Haryana d. India 40 29.15N 76.30E
Ḥasā, Wādī al r. Jordan 44 31.01N 35.29E
Hasa Oasis see Aḥsā', Wāḥat al oasis Saudi Arabia 43
Hasdo r. India 41 21.44N 82.44E
Hase r. W. Germany 14 52.42N 7.17E
Haselünne W. Germany 14 52.40N 7.30E
Hasenkamp Argentina 93 31.30S 59.50W
Hashâbah Sudan 48 14.19N 32.19E
Ḥasharūd Iran 43 37.29N 47.05E
Hashimoto Japan 35 34.19N135.37E
Haskell U.S.A. 83 33.10N 99.44W
Haslemere U.K. 11 51.05N 0.41W
Hasselt Belgium 14 50.56N 5.20E
Hassi bel Guebbour Algeria 51 28.30N 6.41E
Hassi er Rmel well Algeria 51 32.57N 3.11E
Hassi Messaoud Algeria 51 31.43N 6.03E
Hassi Tagsist well Algeria 50 25.20N 1.35E
Hässleholm Sweden 23 56.09N 13.46E
Hastings New Zealand 60 39.39S176.52E
Hastings U.K. 11 50.51N 0.36E
Hastings Nebr. U.S.A. 82 40.35N 98.23W
Hastings Range mts. Australia 67 31.14S152.00E
Hatanbulag Mongolia 32 43.08N109.05E
Hatch U.S.A. 81 32.40N107.09W
Hatches Creek town Australia 64 20.56S135.12E
Hatfield Australia 66 33.53S143.47E
Hatfield U.K. 11 51.46N 0.13W
Hāthras India 41 27.36N 78.03E
Hātia I. Bangla. 41 22.40N 90.55E
Ha Tinh Vietnam 34 18.21N105.55E
Hatta India 41 24.07N 79.36E
Hattah Australia 66 34.52S142.23E
Hattem Neth. 14 52.29N 6.06E
Hatteras, C. U.S.A. 85 35.13N 75.32W
Hattiesburg U.S.A. 83 31.19N 89.16W
Hattingen W. Germany 14 51.24N 7.09E
Hatton U.S.A. 80 46.46N118.49W
Hatutu i. Îs. Marquises 69 7.56S140.38W
Hatvan Hungary 21 47.40N 19.41E
Hauge Norway 23 58.18N 6.15E
Haugesund Norway 23 59.25N 5.18E
Haugsdorf Austria 20 48.42N 16.05E
Hauraki G. New Zealand 60 36.30S175.00E
Haut Atlas mts. Morocco 50 31.30N 7.00W
Haut-Bassins d. U. Volta 52 10.45N 3.45W
Haute Kotto d. C.A.R. 49 7.15N 23.30E
Haute Maurice Prov. Park Canada 76 48.38N 74.30W
Haute-Normandie d. France 15 49.30N 1.00E
Hauterive Canada 77 49.11N 68.16W
Haut Mbomou d. C.A.R. 49 6.25N 26.10E
Hautmont France 14 50.16N 3.52E
Hauts Plateau f. Morocco/Algeria 50 34.00N 0.10W
Haut Zaïre d. Zaïre 55 2.00N 27.00E
Havana see La Habana Cuba 87
Havant U.K. 11 50.51N 0.59W
Havel r. E. Germany 20 52.51N 11.57E
Havelange Belgium 14 50.23N 5.14E
Havelberg E. Germany 20 52.50N 12.04E
Havelock New Zealand 60 41.17S173.46E
Haverfordwest U.K. 11 51.48N 4.59W
Haverhill U.K. 11 52.06N 0.27E
Havlíčkuv Brod Czech. 20 49.38N 15.35E
Havre U.S.A. 80 48.33N109.41W
Havre de Grace U.S.A. 85 39.33N 76.06W
Havre St. Pierre Canada 77 50.15N 63.36W
Hawaii d. U.S.A. 78 21.00N156.00W
Hawaii i. Hawaii U.S.A. 78 19.30N155.30W
Hawaiian Is. U.S.A. 78 21.00N157.00W
Hawdon, L. Australia 66 37.09S139.54E
Hawea, L. New Zealand 60 44.30S169.15E
Hawera New Zealand 60 39.35S174.19E
Hawick U.K. 12 55.25N 2.47W
Hawke, C. Australia 67 32.12S152.33E
Hawke B. New Zealand 60 39.18S177.15E
Hawker Australia 66 31.53S138.25E
Hawkers Gate Australia 66 29.46S141.00E
Hawke's Bay d. New Zealand 60 39.40S176.35E
Hawkesbury Canada 77 45.36N 74.37W
Hawkwood Australia 64 25.46S150.48E
Ḥawrān, Wādī r. Iraq 42 33.57N 42.35E
Ḥawsh 'Īsá Egypt 44 30.55N 30.17E
Hawthorne U.S.A. 80 38.32N118.38W
Hay Australia 67 34.31S144.31E
Hay r. Australia 64 25.00S138.00E
Hay r. Canada 74 60.49N115.52W
Haya r. Japan 35 35.30N138.26E
Hayange France 17 49.20N 6.02E
Haybān Sudan 49 11.13N 30.31E
Hayden U.S.A. 81 33.00N110.47W
Hayes r. Canada 75 57.03N 92.09W
Hay-on-Wye U.K. 11 52.04N 3.09W
Hay River town Canada 74 60.51N115.44W
Hays U.S.A. 82 38.53N 99.20W
Hayward U.S.A. 82 46.02N 91.26W
Haywards Heath f. U.K. 11 51.00N 0.05E
Hazārān, Kūh-e mtn. Iran 43 29.30N 57.18E
Hazard U.S.A. 85 37.14N 83.11W
Hazāribāgh India 41 23.59N 85.21E
Hazelton Canada 74 55.20N127.42W
Hazelton U.S.A. 82 46.29N100.17W
Hazen U.S.A. 80 39.34N119.03W
Hazlehurst Ga. U.S.A. 85 31.53N 82.34W
Hazlehurst Miss. U.S.A. 83 31.52N 90.24W
Hazleton U.S.A. 84 40.58N 75.59W
Healdsburg U.S.A. 80 38.37N122.52W
Healesville Australia 67 37.40S145.31E
Healy U.S.A. 72 63.52N148.58W
Heanor U.K. 10 53.01N 1.20W
Hearne L. Canada 74 62.20N113.10W
Hearst Canada 76 49.40N 83.41W
Heathcote Australia 67 36.54S144.42E
Hebei d. China 32 39.00N116.00E
Hebel Australia 67 28.55S147.49E
Heber Springs town U.S.A. 83 35.30N 92.02W
Hebi China 32 35.57N114.05E
Hebrides, Sea of the U.K. 8 57.00N 7.20W
Hebron Canada 73 58.05N 62.30W
Hebron see Al Khalīl Jordan 44
Hebron N.Dak. U.S.A. 82 46.54N102.03W
Hebron Nebr. U.S.A. 82 40.10N 97.35W
Heby Sweden 23 59.56N 16.53E
Hecate Str. Canada 74 53.00N131.00W
Hechi China 33 24.42N108.02E
Hechtel Belgium 14 51.07N 5.22E
Hechuan China 33 30.05N106.14E
Hecla U.S.A. 82 45.53N 98.09W
Hede Sweden 23 62.25N 13.30E
Hedemora Sweden 23 60.17N 15.59E
Hedi Shuiku resr. China 33 21.50N110.19E
Hedley U.S.A. 83 34.52N100.39W
Hedmark d. Norway 23 61.20N 11.30E
Heemstede Neth. 14 52.21N 4.38E
Heerde Neth. 14 52.23N 6.02E
Heerenveen Neth. 14 52.57N 5.55E
Heerlen Neth. 14 50.53N 5.59E
Hefa Israel 44 32.49N 34.59E
Hefei China 33 31.50N117.16E
Hegang China 31 47.36N130.30E
Heide W. Germany 20 54.12N 9.06E
Heidelberg C.P. R.S.A. 56 34.05S 20.58E
Heidelberg W. Germany 20 49.25N 8.42E
Heilbron R.S.A. 56 27.16S 27.57E
Heilbronn W. Germany 20 49.08N 9.14E
Heilongjiang d. China 31 47.00N126.00E
Heiloo Neth. 14 52.37N 4.43E
Heinola Finland 23 61.13N 26.02E
Heinsberg W. Germany 14 51.04N 6.06E
Heishan China 32 41.40N122.03E
Heishui China 32 42.03N119.21E
Heishuisi China 32 36.01N108.56E
Hejaz f. see Al Ḥijāz f. Saudi Arabia 42
Hejian China 32 38.26N116.05E
Hejiang China 33 28.48N105.47E
Hekinan Japan 35 34.51N136.58E
Hekla, Mt. Iceland 22 64.00N 19.45W
Hekou China 39 22.39N103.57E
Helagsfjället mtn. Sweden 22 62.58N 12.25E
Helan China 32 38.35N106.16E
Helan Shan mts. China 32 38.40N106.00E
Helena U.S.A. 80 46.36N112.01W
Helen Reef i. Caroline Is. 37 2.43N131.46E
Helensburgh U.K. 12 56.01N 4.44W
Helensville New Zealand 60 36.40S174.27E
Hellendoorn Neth. 14 52.24N 6.29E
Hellenthal W. Germany 14 50.28N 6.25E
Hellesylt Norway 23 62.05N 6.54E
Hellevoetsluis Neth. 14 51.49N 4.08E
Hellín Spain 16 38.31N 1.43W
Hell-Ville Madagascar 57 13.25S 48.16E
Helmand d. Afghan. 40 31.15N 64.00E
Helmand r. Asia 40 31.12N 61.34E
Helmond Neth. 14 51.28N 5.40E
Helmsdale U.K. 12 58.07N 3.40W
Helmsdale r. U.K. 12 58.05N 3.39W
Helsingfors see Helsinki Finland 23
Helsingör Denmark 23 56.02N 12.37E
Helsinki Finland 23 60.08N 25.00E
Helston U.K. 11 50.07N 5.17W
Helvecia Argentina 93 31.06S 60.05W
Hemaruka Canada 75 51.48N111.10W
Hemel Hempstead U.K. 11 51.46N 0.28W
Hemingford U.S.A. 82 42.19N103.04W
Hempstead N.Y. U.S.A. 85 40.42N 73.37W
Hempstead Tex. U.S.A. 83 30.06N 96.05W
Hemse Sweden 23 57.14N 18.22E
Hemsedal Norway 23 60.52N 8.34E
Henan d. China 32 34.00N114.00E
Henares r. Spain 16 40.26N 3.35W
Henbury Australia 64 24.35S133.15E
Hendaye France 17 43.22N 1.46W
Henderson Ky. U.S.A. 85 37.50N 87.35W
Henderson N.C. U.S.A. 85 36.20N 78.26W
Henderson Nev. U.S.A. 81 36.02N114.59W
Henderson Tex. U.S.A. 83 32.09N 94.48W
Henderson I. Pacific Oc. 69 24.20S128.20W
Hendrik Verwoerd Dam R.S.A. 56 30.37S 25.29E
Hendrina R.S.A. 56 26.09S 29.42E
Hengelo Neth. 14 52.16N 6.46E
Hengshan Hunan China 33 27.14N112.52E
Hengshan Shaanxi China 32 37.57N109.11E
Hengshui China 32 37.40N115.48E
Heng Xian China 33 22.35N109.26E
Hengyang China 33 26.52N112.35E
Hénin-Beaumont France 14 50.25N 2.55E
Henlopen, C. U.S.A. 85 38.48N 75.05W
Hennebont France 17 47.48N 3.16W
Henrietta Maria, C. Canada 76 55.00N 82.15W
Henryetta U.S.A. 83 35.27N 95.59W
Henryville Canada 77 45.08N 73.11W
Hentiesbaai Namibia 56 22.10S 14.19E
Henty Australia 67 35.30S147.03E
Henzada Burma 34 17.36N 95.26E
Heppner U.S.A. 80 45.21N119.33W
Hepu China 33 21.31N109.10E
Heqing China 39 26.34N100.12E
Herāt Afghan. 40 34.20N 62.12E
Herāt d. Afghan. 40 34.10N 62.30E
Herceg-Novi Yugo. 19 42.27N 18.32E
Hereford U.K. 11 52.04N 2.43W
Hereford Md. U.S.A. 85 39.35N 76.40W
Hereford Tex. U.S.A. 83 34.49N102.24W
Hereford and Worcester d. U.K. 11 52.08N 2.30W
Herentals Belgium 14 51.12N 4.42E
Herford W. Germany 20 52.07N 8.40E
Herington U.S.A. 82 38.40N 96.57W
Hermanus R.S.A. 56 34.24S 19.16E
Hermidale Australia 67 31.33S146.44E
Hermiston U.S.A. 80 45.51N119.17W
Hermosillo Mexico 81 29.04N110.58W
Herne W. Germany 14 51.32N 7.12E
Herne Bay town U.K. 11 51.23N 1.10E
Herning Denmark 23 56.08N 8.59E
Heron Bay town Canada 76 48.40N 86.25W
Herowābād Iran 43 37.36N 48.36E
Herrera del Duque Spain 16 39.10N 5.03W
Herstal Belgium 14 50.14N 5.38E
Herten W. Germany 14 51.36N 7.08E
Hertford U.K. 11 51.48N 0.05W
Hertfordshire d. U.K. 11 51.51N 0.05W
Hervey B. Australia 64 25.00S153.00E
Herzliyya Israel 44 32.10N 34.50E
Hesbaye f. Belgium 14 50.32N 5.07E
Hesel W. Germany 14 53.19N 7.35E
Heshui China 32 35.43N108.07E
Heshun China 32 37.19N113.34E
Hessen d. W. Germany 20 50.30N 9.15E
Hesso Australia 66 32.08S137.58E
Hetou China 33 21.05N109.44E
Hettinger U.S.A. 82 46.00N102.39W
Hetzerath W. Germany 14 49.54N 6.50E
Hewett, C. Canada 73 70.20N 68.00W
Hexham U.K. 10 54.58N 2.06W
Hexi China 33 24.51N117.13E
He Xian China 33 24.25N111.31E
Hexigten Qi China 32 43.17N117.24E
Heysham U.K. 10 54.03N 2.53W
Heyuan China 33 23.42N114.48E
Heywood Australia 66 38.08S141.38E
Heywood U.K. 10 53.36N 2.13W
Heze China 32 35.12N115.15E
Hezhang China 33 27.08N104.43E
Hiawatha Kans. U.S.A. 82 39.51N 95.32W
Hiawatha Utah U.S.A. 80 39.29N111.01W
Hibbing U.S.A. 82 47.25N 92.55W
Hickman, Mt. Canada 74 57.11N131.10W
Hickory U.S.A. 85 35.44N 81.23W
Hicks Bay town New Zealand 60 37.35S178.18E
Hickson L. Canada 75 56.17N104.25W
Hicksville U.S.A. 85 40.46N 73.32W
Hidalgo d. Mexico 86 20.50N 98.30W
Hidalgo Nuevo León Mexico 83 25.59N100.27W
Hidalgo Tamaulipas Mexico 86 24.15N 99.26W
Hidalgo del Parral Mexico 81 26.56N105.40W
Hieradhsvotn r. Iceland 22 65.45N 18.50W
Hierro i. Canary Is. 50 27.45N 18.00W
Higashimatsuyama Japan 35 36.02N139.24E
Higashimurayama Japan 35 35.46N139.29E
Higashiōsaka Japan 35 34.39N135.35E
Higgins U.S.A. 83 36.07N100.02W
Higginsville Australia 63 31.46S121.43E
High Hill r. Canada 75 55.52N 94.42W
Highland d. U.K. 12 57.42N 5.00W
Highland town U.S.A. 85 41.43N 73.58W
High Level Canada 74 58.31N117.08W
Highmore U.S.A. 82 44.31N 99.27W
High Peak mtn. U.K. 10 53.22N 1.48W
High Point town U.S.A. 85 35.58N 80.00W
High Prairie Canada 74 55.30N116.30W
Highrock L. Man. Canada 75 55.45N100.30W
Highrock L. Sask. Canada 75 57.04N105.30W
High Willhays mtn. U.K. 11 50.41N 4.00W
High Wycombe U.K. 11 51.38N 0.46W
Hiiumaa i. U.S.S.R. 23 58.52N 22.40E
Híjar Spain 16 41.10N 0.27W
Ḥijāz, Jabal al mts. Saudi Arabia 48 19.45N 41.55E
Hikone Japan 35 35.15N136.15E
Hikurangi New Zealand 60 35.36S174.17E
Hikurangi mtn. New Zealand 60 37.50S178.10E
Hikutavake Niue 68 18.57S169.53W
Hilden W. Germany 14 51.10N 6.56E
Hildesheim W. Germany 20 52.09N 9.58E
Hill City Kans. U.S.A. 82 39.22N 99.51W
Hill City Minn. U.S.A. 82 46.59N 93.44W
Hillegom Neth. 14 52.19N 4.35E
Hill Island L. Canada 75 60.30N109.50W
Hillsboro Oreg. U.S.A. 80 45.31N122.59W
Hillsboro Tex. U.S.A. 83 32.01N 97.08W
Hillsdale U.S.A. 84 41.56N 84.37W
Hillsport Canada 76 49.27N 85.34W
Hillston Australia 67 33.30S145.33E
Hilo Hawaii U.S.A. 78 19.42N155.04W
Hilton U.S.A. 76 43.17N 77.48W
Hilton Head I. U.S.A. 85 32.12N 80.45W
Hiltrup W. Germany 14 51.55N 7.36E
Hilversum Neth. 14 52.14N 5.12E
Himachal Pradesh d. India 40 32.05N 77.15E
Himalaya mts. Asia 41 29.00N 84.30E
Himanka Finland 22 64.04N 23.39E
Himarë Albania 19 40.07N 19.44E
Himatnagar India 40 23.36N 72.57E
Ḥimṣ Syria 44 34.44N 36.43E
Hinchinbrook I. Australia 64 18.23S146.17E
Hinckley U.K. 11 52.33N 1.21W
Hindaun India 40 26.43N 77.01E
Hindmarsh, L. Australia 66 36.03S141.53E
Hindubāgh Pakistan 40 30.49N 67.45E
Hindu Kush mts. Asia 38 36.40N 70.00E
Hindupur India 38 13.49N 77.29E
Hines Creek town Canada 74 56.20N118.40W
Hinganghāt India 41 20.34N 78.50E
Hingol r. Pakistan 40 25.23N 65.28E
Hingoli India 40 19.43N 77.09E
Hinnöy i. Norway 22 68.35N 15.50E
Hinojosa Spain 16 38.30N 5.17W
Hinsdale Mont. U.S.A. 80 48.24N107.05W
Hinton Canada 74 53.25N117.34W
Hipólito Mexico 83 25.41N101.26W
Hippolytushoef Neth. 14 52.57N 4.58E
Hirakata Japan 35 34.48N135.38E
Hīrākud India 41 21.31N 83.57E
Hīrākud resr. India 41 21.31N 83.52E
Hīrāpur India 41 24.22N 79.13E
Hiratsuka Japan 35 35.19N139.21E
Hīrmand r. see Helmand r. Iran 40
Hirok Sāmī Pakistan 40 26.02N 63.25E
Hiroshima Japan 31 34.23N132.27E
Hirson France 14 49.56N 4.05E
Hîrşova Romania 21 44.41N 27.57E
Hirtshals Denmark 23 57.35N 9.58E
Hisai Japan 35 34.40N136.28E
Hisār India 40 29.10N 75.43E
Ḥismá f. Saudi Arabia 44 28.45N 35.56E
Hispaniola i. C. America 87 19.00N 71.00W
Hisua India 41 24.50N 85.25E
Ḥisyah Syria 44 34.24N 36.45E
Hīt Iraq 42 33.38N 42.50E
Hitchin U.K. 11 51.57N 0.16W
Hitra i. Norway 22 63.37N 8.46E
Hiva Oa i. Îs. Marquises 69 9.45S139.00W
Hixon Canada 74 53.27N122.36W
Hjälmaren l. Sweden 23 59.15N 15.45E
Hjalmar L. Canada 75 61.33N109.25W
Hjörring Denmark 23 57.28N 9.59E
Hlotse Lesotho 56 28.52S 28.02E
Ho Ghana 52 6.38N 0.38E
Hòa Bình Vietnam 33 20.40N105.17E
Hoare B. Canada 73 65.20N 62.30W
Hoarusib r. Namibia 56 19.04S 12.33E
Hobart Australia 65 42.54S147.18E
Hobart Ind. U.S.A. 84 41.32N 87.14W
Hobart Okla. U.S.A. 83 35.01N 99.06W
Hobbs U.S.A. 83 32.42N103.08W
Hoboken Belgium 14 51.11N 4.21E
Hoboken U.S.A. 85 40.45N 74.03W
Hobq Shamo des. China 32 40.00N109.00E
Hobro Denmark 23 56.38N 9.48E
Ho Chi Minh City see Thành Pho Ho Chí Minh h Vietnam 34
Hockley U.S.A. 83 30.02N 95.51W
Hodal India 40 27.54N 77.22E
Hodgson Canada 75 51.13N 97.34W
Hod HaSharon Israel 44 32.15N 34.55E
Hodh ech Chargui d. Mauritania 52 19.00N 7.15W
Hodh el Gharbi d. Mauritania 52 16.30N 10.00W
Hódmezövásárhely Hungary 19 46.26N 20.21E
Hodna, Monts du mts. Algeria 51 35.50N 4.50E
Hoek van Holland Neth. 14 51.59N 4.08E
Hof W. Germany 20 50.19N 11.56E
Höfn Iceland 22 64.16N 15.10W
Hofors Sweden 23 60.33N 16.17E
Hofsjökull mtn. Iceland 22 64.50N 19.00W
Hofsos Iceland 22 65.53N 19.26W
Höganäs Sweden 23 56.12N 12.33E
Hogeland U.S.A. 80 48.51N108.39W
Hogem Ranges f. Canada 74 55.40N126.00W
Hohhot China 32 40.42N111.38E
Hoh Tolgoin Sum China 32 44.27N112.41E
Hoi An Vietnam 34 15.54N108.19E
Hoima Uganda 55 1.25N 31.22E
Hojāi India 41 26.00N 92.51E
Hokitika New Zealand 60 42.42S170.59E
Hokkaidō i. Japan 31 43.30N143.20E
Hokksund Norway 23 59.47N 9.59E
Hola Kenya 55 1.29S 40.02E
Holbaek Denmark 23 55.43N 11.43E
Holbrook Australia 67 35.46S147.20E
Holbrook U.S.A. 81 34.54N110.10W
Holdrege U.S.A. 82 40.26N 99.22W
Holguín Cuba 87 20.54N 76.15W
Höljes Sweden 23 60.54N 12.36E
Hollabrunn Austria 20 48.34N 16.05E
Holland Mich. U.S.A. 84 42.46N 86.06W
Holland N.Y. U.S.A. 76 42.38N 78.33W
Holly Kans. U.S.A. 83 38.03N102.07W
Hollywood U.S.A. 85 26.01N 80.09W
Holman Island town Canada 72 70.43N117.43W
Holmavik Iceland 22 65.43N 21.39W
Holmer, Lac l. Canada 77 54.10N 71.44W
Holmestrand Norway 23 59.29N 10.18E
Holmön i. Sweden 22 63.47N 20.53E
Holmsund Sweden 22 63.41N 20.20E
Holon Israel 44 32.01N 34.46E
Holroyd r. Australia 64 14.10S141.36E
Holstebro Denmark 23 56.21N 8.38E
Holstein Canada 76 44.02N 80.42W
Holsteinsborg Greenland 73 66.55N 53.30W
Holsworthy U.K. 11 50.48N 4.21W
Holt U.K. 10 52.55N 1.04E
Holten Neth. 14 52.18N 6.26E
Holwerd Neth. 14 53.22N 5.54E
Holy Cross U.S.A. 72 62.12N159.47W
Holyhead U.K. 10 53.18N 4.38W
Holyhead B. U.K. 10 53.22N 4.40W
Holy I. England U.K. 10 55.41N 1.47W
Holy I. Wales U.K. 10 53.15N 4.38W
Holyoke Colo. U.S.A. 82 40.35N102.18W
Holywood U.K. 13 54.38N 5.50W
Hombori Mali 52 15.20N 1.38W
Home B. Canada 73 69.00N 66.00W
Home Hill town Australia 64 19.40S147.25E
Homer Alas. U.S.A. 72 59.40N151.37W
Homer La. U.S.A. 83 32.48N 93.04W
Homer Tunnel New Zealand 60 44.40S168.15E
Homestead U.S.A. 85 25.29N 80.29W
Homoine Mozambique 57 23.45S 35.09E
Homoljske Planina f. Yugo. 21 44.20N 21.45E
Honda Colombia 90 5.15N 74.50W
Hondeklipbaai R.S.A. 56 30.19S 17.12E
Hondo r. Mexico 87 18.33N 88.22W
Hondo U.S.A. 83 29.21N 99.09W
Honduras C. America 87 14.30N 87.00W
Honduras, G. of Carib. Sea 87 16.20N 87.30W
Honfleur France 15 49.25N 0.14E
Hong'an China 33 31.18N114.33E
Hòn Gay Vietnam 33 21.01N107.02E
Hong Hà r. Vietnam 34 20.15N106.36E
Honghu China 33 29.42N113.26E
Hong Hu l. China 33 29.50N113.15E
Hongjiang China 33 27.08N109.54E
Hongjian Nur l. China 32 39.09N109.56E
Hong Kong Asia 33 22.15N114.15E
Hongor Mongolia 32 45.45N112.56E
Hongshui He r. China 33 23.20N110.04E
Hongtong China 32 36.15N111.37E
Honguedo, Détroit d' str. Canada 77 49.25N 64.00W
Hongze China 32 33.18N118.51E
Hongze Hu l. China 32 33.15N118.40E
Honiton U.K. 11 50.48N 3.13W
Honkajoki Finland 23 62.00N 22.15E
Honokaa Hawaiian Is. 69 20.05N155.28W
Honokahua Hawaiian Is. 69 21.00N156.39W
Honolulu Hawaii U.S.A. 78 21.19N157.50W
Honshū i. Japan 31 36.00N138.00E
Hood Pt. Australia 63 34.23S119.34E
Hood Range mts. Australia 67 28.35S144.30E
Hoogeveen Neth. 14 52.44N 6.29E
Hoogezand Neth. 14 53.10N 6.47E
Hooghly r. India 41 21.55N 88.05E
Hoogstade Belgium 14 50.59N 2.42E
Hooker U.S.A. 83 36.52N101.13W
Hook Head Rep. of Ire. 13 52.07N 6.55W
Hoopa U.S.A. 80 41.03N123.40W
Hoopeston U.S.A. 82 40.28N 87.41W
Hoopstad R.S.A. 56 27.48S 25.52E
Hoorn Neth. 14 52.38N 5.03E
Hoover Dam U.S.A. 81 36.00N114.27W
Hope U.S.A. 83 33.40N 93.36W
Hope, L. Australia 63 32.40S120.10E
Hope, L. Australia 66 28.23S139.19E
Hopedale Canada 77 55.50N 60.10W
Hopefield R.S.A. 56 33.04S 18.19E
Hopetoun Vic. Australia 66 35.43S142.20E
Hopetoun W.A. Australia 63 33.57S120.05E
Hopetown R.S.A. 56 29.37S 24.04E
Hopkins r. Australia 66 38.25S142.00E
Hopkins, L. Australia 62 24.15S128.50E
Hopkinsville U.S.A. 85 36.50N 87.30W
Hopland U.S.A. 80 38.58N123.07W
Hoquiam U.S.A. 80 46.59N123.53W
Hordaland d. Norway 23 60.30N 6.30E
Horde W. Germany 14 51.29N 7.30E
Hörh Uul mts. Mongolia 32 42.20N105.30E
Horinger China 32 40.23N111.53E
Horizonte Mexico 83 25.50N103.48W
Horlick Mts. Antarctica 96 86.00S102.00W
Hormuz, Str. of Asia 43 26.35N 56.20E
Horn Austria 20 48.40N 15.40E
Horn r. Canada 74 61.30N118.01W
Horn, C. see Hornos, Cabo de c. S. America 93
Hornavan l. Sweden 22 66.10N 17.30E
Horncastle U.K. 10 53.13N 0.08W
Horndal Sweden 23 60.18N 16.25E
Hornell U.S.A. 84 42.19N 77.39W
Hornell L. Canada 74 62.20N119.25W
Hornepayne Canada 76 49.14N 84.48W
Hornindal Norway 23 61.58N 6.31E
Horn Mts. Canada 74 62.15N119.15W
Hornos, Cabo de c. S. America 93 55.47S 67.00W
Hornsby Australia 67 33.11S151.06E
Hornsea U.K. 10 53.55N 0.10W
Hořovice Czech. 20 49.50N 13.54E
Horqin Zuoyi Houqi China 32 42.57N122.21E
Horqin Zuoyi Zhongqi China 32 44.08N123.18E
Horru China 41 30.30N 91.32E
Horse Creek town U.S.A. 80 41.25N105.11W
Horsens Denmark 23 55.52N 9.52E
Horsham Australia 66 36.45S142.15E
Horsham U.K. 11 51.04N 0.20W
Horta wadi Chad 48 17.15N 21.52E
Horten Norway 23 59.25N 10.30E
Horton r. Canada 72 70.00N127.00W
Horton L. Canada 72 67.30N122.28W
Hosaina Ethiopia 49 7.38N 37.52E
Hose, Pegunungan mts. Malaysia 36 1.30N114.10E
Hoshāb Pakistan 40 26.01N 63.56E
Hoshangābād India 41 22.45N 77.43E
Hoshiārpur India 40 31.32N 75.54E
Hôsh 'Isa Egypt 44 30.55N 30.17E
Hoskins P.N.G. 61 5.30S150.27E
Hospitalet Spain 16 41.20N 2.06E
Hoste, Isla i. Chile 93 55.10S 69.00W
Hotan China 30 37.07N 79.57E
Hotazel R.S.A. 56 27.16S 22.57E
Hotham r. Australia 63 32.58S116.22E
Hotham, Mt. Australia 67 36.58S147.11E
Hoting Sweden 22 64.07N 16.10E
Hotin Gol China 32 38.58N104.14E
Hot Springs town Ark. U.S.A. 83 34.30N 93.02W
Hot Springs town S.Dak. U.S.A. 82 43.26N103.29W
Hottah L. Canada 72 65.04N118.29W
Houailou N. Cal. 68 21.17S165.38E
Houdan France 15 48.47N 1.36E
Houffalize Belgium 14 50.08N 5.50E
Houghton L. U.S.A. 84 44.16N 84.48W
Houghton-le-Spring U.K. 10 54.51N 1.28W
Houlton U.S.A. 84 46.08N 67.51W
Houma China 32 35.36N111.21E
Houma U.S.A. 83 29.36N 90.43W
Houndé U. Volta 52 11.34N 3.31W
Hourn, Loch U.K. 12 57.06N 5.33W

Houston to Iron Baron

Houston Mo. U.S.A. 83 37.22N 91.58W
Houston Tex. U.S.A. 83 29.46N 95.22W
Hovd Mongolia 30 46.40N 90.45E
Hove U.K. 11 50.50N 0.10W
Hovlya U.S.S.R. 25 49.19N 44.01E
Hövsgöl Mongolia 32 43.36N109.40E
Hövsgöl Nuur l. Mongolia 30 51.00N100.30E
Howa, Ouadi see Howar, Wādī Chad 48
Howar, Wādī Sudan 48 17.30N 27.08E
Howard Australia 64 25.20S152.32E
Howard L. Canada 75 62.15N105.57W
Howe, C. Australia 67 37.30S149.59E
Howell Australia 67 30.00S151.00E
Howick Canada 77 45.11N 73.51W
Howitt, Mt. Australia 67 37.15S146.40E
Howrah India 41 22.35N 88.20E
Howth Head Rep. of Ire. 13 53.22N 6.03W
Hoy i. U.K. 12 58.51N 3.17W
Höyanger Norway 23 61.13N 6.05E
Hoyos Spain 16 40.09N 6.45W
Hradec Králové Czech. 20 50.13N 15.50E
Hron r. Czech. 21 47.49N 18.45E
Hrubieszów Poland 21 50.49N 23.55E
Hrvatska d. Yugo. 21 45.10N 15.30E
Hsenwi Burma 34 23.18N 97.58E
Hsipaw Burma 34 22.42N 97.21E
Hsuphāng Burma 34 20.18N 98.42E
Huab r. Namibia 56 20.55S 13.28E
Huabei Pingyuan f. China 32 35.00N115.30E
Huachi China 32 36.32N108.14E
Huacho Peru 90 11.05S 77.36W
Huachuca City U.S.A. 81 31.34N110.21W
Huade China 32 41.57N114.04E
Hua Hin Thailand 34 12.34N 99.58E
Huahine i. Îs. de la Société 69 16.45S151.00W
Huai'an Hebei China 32 40.40N114.18E
Huai'an Jiangsu China 32 33.29N119.15E
Huaibei China 32 33.58N116.50E
Huaide China 32 43.25N124.50E
Huai He r. China 32 32.58N118.18E
Huaiji China 33 23.58N112.10E
Huailai China 32 40.25N115.27E
Huainan China 32 32.39N117.01E
Huaining China 33 30.21N116.42E
Huairen China 32 39.50N113.07E
Huairou China 32 40.20N116.37E
Huaiyang China 32 33.47N114.59E
Huaiyuan China 32 32.57N117.12E
Huajuápan Mexico 86 17.50N 97.48W
Hualian Taiwan 33 24.00N121.39E
Huallaga r. Peru 90 5.02S 75.30W
Huamanrazo mtn. Peru 90 12.54S 75.04W
Huambo Angola 54 12.47S 15.44E
Huambo d. Angola 54 12.30S 15.45E
Huanan China 31 46.13N130.31E
Huancané Peru 90 15.10S 69.44W
Huancapi Peru 90 13.35S 74.05W
Huancavelica Peru 90 12.45S 75.03W
Huancayo Peru 90 12.05S 75.12W
Huangchuan China 33 32.07N115.02E
Huanggang China 33 30.33N114.59E
Huanggang Shan mtn. China 33 27.50N117.47E
Huang Hai b. N. Korea 32 39.30N123.40E
Huang He r. China 32 38.00N118.40E
Huanghe Kou est. China 32 37.54N118.48E
Huanghua China 32 38.22N117.20E
Huangling China 32 35.36N109.17E
Huangpi China 33 30.52N114.22E
Huangping China 33 26.54N107.53E
Huangshi China 33 30.10N115.04E
Huang Xian China 32 37.38N120.30E
Huangyan China 33 28.42N121.25E
Huan Jiang r. China 32 35.13N108.00E
Huanren China 32 41.16N125.21E
Huanta Peru 90 12.54S 74.13W
Huánuco Peru 90 9.55S 76.11W
Huaráz Peru 90 9.33S 77.31W
Huarmey Peru 90 10.05S 78.05W
Huascaran mtn. Peru 90 9.08S 77.36W
Huasco Chile 92 28.28S 71.14W
Huatabampo Mexico 81 26.50N109.38W
Huatong China 32 40.03N121.56E
Hua Xian Guangdong China 33 23.22N113.12E
Hua Xian Shaanxi China 32 34.31N109.46E
Huayuan China 33 28.37N109.28E
Hubei d. China 33 31.00N112.00E
Hubli India 38 15.20N 75.14E
Hückelhoven W. Germany 14 51.04N 6.10E
Hucknall U.K. 10 53.03N 1.12W
Huddersfield U.K. 10 53.38N 1.49W
Huddinge Sweden 23 59.14N 17.59E
Hudiksvall Sweden 23 61.44N 17.07E
Hudson r. U.S.A. 84 40.42N 74.02W
Hudson N.Y. U.S.A. 84 42.15N 73.47W
Hudson Wyo. U.S.A. 80 42.54N108.35W
Hudson B. Canada 73 58.00N 86.00W
Hudson Bay town Canada 75 52.52N102.25W
Hudson Highlands U.S.A. 85 41.24N 74.15W
Hudson Hope Canada 74 56.03N121.59W
Hudson Mts. Antarctica 96 76.00S 99.00W
Hudson Str. Canada 73 62.00N 70.00W
Hue Vietnam 34 16.28N107.40E
Huedin Romania 21 46.52N 23.02E
Huehuetenango Guatemala 86 15.19N 91.26W
Huelva Spain 16 37.15N 6.56W
Huelva r. Spain 16 37.25N 6.00W
Huércal-Overa Spain 16 37.23N 1.56W
Huesca Spain 16 42.02N 0.25W
Ḥufrat an Naḥās Sudan 49 9.45N 24.19E
Hugh r. Australia 64 25.01S134.01E
Hughenden Australia 64 20.51S144.12E
Hughes U.S.A. 72 66.03N154.16W
Hugo U.S.A. 83 34.01N 95.31W
Hugoton U.S.A. 83 37.11N101.21W
Hugou China 32 33.22N117.07E
Hui'an China 33 25.02N118.48E
Huiarau Range mts. New Zealand 60 38.20S177.15E
Huikou China 33 29.49N116.15E
Huíla d. Angola 54 15.10S 15.30E
Huilai China 33 23.03N116.17E
Huimin China 32 37.30N117.29E
Huining China 32 35.42N105.06E
Huisne r. France 15 47.59N 0.11E
Huixtla Mexico 86 15.09N 92.30W
Huizen Neth. 14 52.18N 5.12E
Huizhou China 33 23.05N114.29E
Hukuntsi Botswana 56 24.02S 21.48E
Ḥulayfā' Saudi Arabia 42 26.00N 40.47E
Hulín Czech. 21 49.19N 17.28E
Hull Canada 77 45.26N 75.45W
Hüls W. Germany 14 51.23N 6.30E
Hulst Neth. 14 51.18N 4.01E
Hultsfred Sweden 23 57.29N 15.50E
Hulun Nur l. China 31 49.00N117.27E
Ḥulwān Egypt 44 29.51N 31.20E
Humaitá Brazil 90 7.31S 63.02W
Humansdorp R.S.A. 56 34.02S 24.45E
Ḥumaydah Sudan 48 14.22N 22.31E
Humber r. U.K. 10 53.40N 0.12W
Humberside d. U.K. 10 53.48N 0.35W
Humble U.S.A. 83 30.00N 95.16W
Humboldt Canada 75 52.12N105.07W
Humboldt U.S.A. 83 35.49N 88.55W
Humboldt r. U.S.A. 80 40.02N118.31W
Hūmedān Iran 43 25.24N 59.39E
Humenné Czech. 21 48.56N 21.55E
Hume Resr. Australia 67 36.06S147.05E
Humphreys Peak mtn. U.S.A. 81 35.20N111.40W
Humpty Doo Australia 62 12.37S131.14E
Hūn Libya 51 29.07N 15.56E
Húnaflói b. Iceland 22 65.45N 20.50W
Hunan d. China 33 27.30N111.30E
Hundred Mile House town Canada 74 51.38N121.18W
Hunedoara Romania 21 45.45N 22.54E
Hungary Europe 21 47.30N 19.00E
Hungerford Australia 66 29.00S144.26E
Hungerford U.K. 11 51.25N 1.30W
Hungfou Hsü i. Taiwan 33 22.03N121.33E
Hŭngnam N. Korea 31 39.49N127.40E
Hung Yen Vietnam 33 20.38N106.05E
Hunsberge mts. Namibia 56 27.40S 17.12E
Hunse r. Neth. 14 53.20N 6.18E
Hunsrück mts. W. Germany 14 49.44N 7.05E
Hunstanton U.K. 10 52.57N 0.30E
Hunte r. W. Germany 20 52.30N 8.19E
Hunter r. Australia 67 32.50S151.42E
Hunter I. Australia 65 40.30S144.46E
Hunter I. Canada 74 51.55N128.00W
Hunter Island Ridge Pacific Oc. 68 21.30S175.00E
Hunter Range mts. Australia 67 32.49S150.20E
Huntingdon U.K. 11 52.20N 0.11W
Huntingdon Penn. U.S.A. 84 40.29N 78.01W
Huntington Ind. U.S.A. 84 40.54N 85.30W
Huntington N.Y. U.S.A. 85 40.51N 73.25W
Huntington Oreg. U.S.A. 80 44.21N117.16W
Huntington Utah U.S.A. 80 39.20N110.58W
Huntington W.Va. U.S.A. 85 38.24N 82.26W
Huntington Beach town U.S.A. 81 33.39N118.01W
Huntly New Zealand 60 37.35S175.10E
Huntly U.K. 12 57.27N 2.47W
Huntsville Canada 76 45.20N 79.13W
Huntsville Ala. U.S.A. 85 34.44N 86.35W
Huntsville Tex. U.S.A. 83 30.43N 95.33W
Hunyani r. Mozambique 57 15.41S 30.38E
Hunyuan China 32 39.45N113.35E
Huon Pen. P.N.G. 37 6.00S147.00E
Huonville Australia 65 43.01S147.01E
Huoshan China 33 31.24N116.20E
Hure Qi China 32 42.44N121.44E
Huretin Sum China 32 40.19N103.02E
Hurlock U.S.A. 85 38.38N 75.52W
Hurmāgai Pakistan 40 28.18N 64.26E
Huron S.Dak. U.S.A. 82 44.22N 98.13W
Huron, L. Canada/U.S.A. 84 44.30N 82.15W
Hurso Ethiopia 49 9.38N 41.38E
Húsavík Iceland 22 66.03N 17.21W
Husevig Faroe Is. 8 61.49N 6.41W
Huşi Romania 21 46.40N 28.04E
Huskvarna Sweden 23 57.48N 14.16E
Husum W. Germany 20 54.29N 9.04E
Hutchinson R.S.A. 56 31.30S 23.10E
Hutchinson U.S.A. 83 38.05N 97.56W
Huttig U.S.A. 83 33.02N 92.11W
Hutuo He r. China 32 39.10N117.12E
Hut Yanchi l. China 32 39.24N105.01E
Huy Belgium 14 50.31N 5.14E
Hvar i. Yugo. 19 43.10N 16.45E
Hvita r. Iceland 22 64.33N 21.45W
Hwange Zimbabwe 56 18.20S 26.29E
Hwange Nat. Park Zimbabwe 56 19.00S 26.30E
Hwang Ho r. see Huang He r. China 32
Hyannis U.S.A. 82 41.59N101.44W
Hyargas Nuur l. Mongolia 30 49.30N 93.35E
Hydaburg U.S.A. 74 55.15N132.50W
Hyde U.K. 10 53.26N 2.06W
Hyden Australia 63 32.27S118.53E
Hyderābād India 39 17.22N 78.26E
Hyderābād Pakistan 40 25.22N 68.22E
Hydesville U.S.A. 80 40.31N124.00W
Hyères France 17 43.07N 6.08E
Hyères, Îles d' is. France 17 43.01N 6.25E
Hyland r. Canada 74 59.50N128.10W
Hyland Post Canada 74 57.40N128.10W
Hyllestad Norway 23 61.10N 5.18E
Hyndland, Mt. Australia 67 30.09S152.25E
Hyndman Peak U.S.A. 80 43.50N114.10W
Hysham U.S.A. 80 46.18N107.14W
Hythe Kent U.K. 11 51.04N 1.05E
Hyvinkää Finland 23 60.38N 24.52E

I

Iakoro Madagascar 57 23.06S 46.40E
Ialomiţa r. Romania 21 44.41N 27.52E
Iar Connacht f. Rep. of Ire. 13 53.21N 9.22W
Iaşi Romania 21 47.09N 27.38E
Iauaretê Brazil 90 0.36N 69.12W
Iaupolo P.N.G. 64 9.34S150.30E
Ibadan Nigeria 53 7.23N 3.56E
Ibagué Colombia 90 4.25N 75.20W
Ibar r. Yugo. 19 43.44N 20.44E
Ibaraki Japan 35 34.49N135.34E
Ibarra Ecuador 90 0.23N 78.05W
Ibb Yemen 45 13.58N 44.11E
Ibba Sudan 49 4.48N 29.06E
Ibba wadi Sudan 49 7.09N 28.41E
Ibbenbüren W. Germany 14 52.17N 7.44E
Iberville Canada 77 45.18N 73.14W
Ibi r. Japan 35 35.03N136.42E
Ibi Nigeria 53 8.11N 9.44E
Ibiapaba, Serra da mts. Brazil 91 5.30S 41.00W
Ibicaraí Brazil 91 14.52S 39.37W
Ibicuy Argentina 93 33.45S 59.13W
Ibina r. Zaïre 55 1.00N 28.40E
Ibitinga Brazil 94 21.43S 48.47W
Ibiza i. Spain 16 39.00N 1.23E
Ibiza town Spain 16 38.55N 1.30E
Ibotirama Brazil 91 12.13S 43.12W
Ibrah, Wadi Sudan 49 10.36N 25.05E
'Ibrī Oman 45 23.14N 56.30E
Ibshawāy Egypt 44 29.21N 30.40E
Içá r. Brazil 90 3.07S 67.58W
Ica Peru 90 14.02S 75.48W
Içana Brazil 90 0.21N 67.19W
Içana r. Brazil 90 0.00 67.10W
Iceland Europe 22 64.45N 18.00W
Ichchāpuram India 41 19.07N 84.42E
Ichihara Japan 35 35.31N140.05E
Ichikawa Japan 35 35.44N139.55E
Ichinomiya Japan 35 35.18N136.48E
Icoraci Brazil 91 1.16S 48.28W
Icy Str. U.S.A. 74 58.20N135.30W
Idabel U.S.A. 83 33.54N 94.50W
Ida Grove U.S.A. 82 42.21N 95.28W
Idah Nigeria 53 7.05N 6.45E
Idaho d. U.S.A. 80 44.58N115.56W
Idaho Falls town U.S.A. 80 43.30N112.02W
Idar India 40 23.50N 73.00E
Idar-Oberstein W. Germany 14 49.43N 7.19E
Iddan Somali Rep. 45 6.03N 49.01E
Ideles Algeria 51 23.49N 5.55E
Idfū Egypt 42 24.58N 32.50E
Ídhi Óros mtn. Greece 19 35.13N 24.45E
Ídhra i. Greece 19 37.20N 23.32E
Idiofa Zaïre 54 4.58S 19.38E
Idmū Egypt 44 28.09N 30.41E
Idre Sweden 23 61.52N 12.43E
Ieper Belgium 14 50.51N 2.53E
Ierápetra Greece 19 35.00N 25.45E
Iesi Italy 18 43.32N 13.15E
Iesolo Italy 15 45.32N 12.38E
Ifakara Tanzania 55 8.09S 36.41E
Ifalik is. Caroline Is. 37 7.15N144.27E
Ifanadiana Madagascar 57 21.19S 47.39E
Ife Oyo Nigeria 53 7.33N 4.34E
Iferouâne Niger 53 19.04N 8.24E
Iga r. Japan 35 34.45N136.01E
Igal Hungary 21 46.31N 17.55E
Igatpuri India 40 19.42N 73.33E
Iggesund Sweden 23 61.38N 17.04E
Iglesias Italy 18 39.18N 8.32E
Igli Algeria 50 30.27N 2.18W
Igloolik Island town Canada 73 69.05N 81.25W
Ignace Canada 76 49.30N 91.40W
Iğneada Burnu c. Turkey 19 41.50N 28.05E
Igoumenítsa Greece 19 39.32N 20.14E
Igra U.S.S.R. 24 57.31N 53.09E
Iguaçu r. Brazil 94 25.33S 54.35W
Iguala Mexico 86 18.21N 99.31W
Igualada Spain 16 41.35N 1.37E
Iguatu Brazil 91 6.22S 39.20W
Iguéla Gabon 54 1.57S 9.22E
Ihiala Nigeria 53 5.51N 6.52E
Ihosy Madagascar 57 22.24S 46.08E
Ihosy r. Madagascar 57 21.58S 43.38E
Ii r. Finland 22 65.19N 25.20E
Iida Japan 35 35.31N137.50E
Iisalmi Finland 22 63.34N 27.11E
Ijebu Ode Nigeria 53 6.47N 3.54E
Ijill, Kediet mtn. Mauritania 50 22.38N 12.33W
IJmuiden Neth. 14 52.28N 4.37E
IJssel r. Zuid Holland Neth. 14 51.54N 4.32E
IJssel r. Overijssel Neth. 14 52.34N 5.50E
IJsselmeer l. Neth. 14 52.45N 5.20E
Ijuí Brazil 94 28.23S 53.55W
Ijzendijke Neth. 14 51.19N 3.37E
Ijzer r. Belgium 14 51.09N 2.44E
Ikaría i. Greece 19 37.35N 26.10E
Ikdū Egypt 44 31.18N 30.18E
Ikela Zaïre 54 1.06S 23.04E
Ikelemba Congo 54 1.15N 16.38E
Ikelemba r. Zaïre 54 0.08N 18.19E
Ikerre Nigeria 53 7.30N 5.14E
Ikopa r. Madagascar 57 16.29S 46.43E
Ila Nigeria 53 8.01N 4.55E
Ilagan Phil. 37 17.07N121.53E
Īlām Iran 43 33.27N 46.27E
Ilām Nepal 41 26.55N 87.56E
Ilan Taiwan 33 24.45N121.44E
Ilangali Tanzania 55 6.50S 35.06E
Ilaro Nigeria 53 6.53N 3.03E
Iława Poland 21 53.37N 19.33E
Ilebo Zaïre 54 4.20S 20.35E
Ilek r. U.S.S.R. 25 51.30N 54.00E
Ileret Kenya 55 4.22N 36.13E
Ilerh, Oued wadi Algeria 51 20.59N 2.14E
Ilesha Oyo Nigeria 53 7.39N 4.45E
Ilford Canada 75 56.04N 95.35W
Ilfracombe Australia 64 23.30S144.30E
Ilfracombe U.K. 11 51.13N 4.08W
Ilhabela Brazil 94 23.47S 45.20W
Ilha Grande, Baía da b. Brazil 94 23.09S 44.30W
Ilhéus Brazil 91 14.50S 39.06W
Ili r. U.S.S.R. 30 45.00N 74.20E
Ilia Romania 21 45.56N 22.39E
Iliamna L. U.S.A. 72 59.30N155.00W
Ilich U.S.S.R. 30 40.50N 68.29E
Iligan Phil. 37 8.12N124.13E
Ilintsy U.S.S.R. 21 49.08N 29.11E
Ilion U.S.A. 84 43.01N 75.02W
Ilkley U.K. 10 53.56N 1.49W
Illapel Chile 92 31.38S 71.10W
Ille-et-Vilaine d. France 15 48.10N 1.30W
Illéla Niger 53 14.30N 5.09E
Iller r. W. Germany 20 48.23N 9.58E
Illeret Kenya 49 4.19N 36.13E
Illiers France 15 48.18N 1.15E
Illinois d. U.S.A. 82 40.30N 89.30W
Illinois r. U.S.A. 82 38.58N 90.27W
Illizi Algeria 51 26.29N 8.28E
Ilmajoki Finland 22 62.44N 22.34E
Ilminster U.K. 11 50.55N 2.56W
Ilo Peru 92 17.38S 71.20W
Iloilo Phil. 37 10.45N122.33E
Ilorin Nigeria 53 8.32N 4.34E
Īlubabor d. Ethiopia 49 7.50N 34.55E
Imala Mozambique 55 14.39S 39.34E
Imandra U.S.S.R. 24 67.53N 33.30E
Imandra, Ozero l. U.S.S.R. 24 67.30N 32.45E
Imbābah Egypt 44 30.05N 31.12E
Imese Zaïre 54 2.07N 18.06E
Īmī Ethiopia 49 6.28N 42.18E
Immingham U.K. 10 53.37N 0.12W
Immokalee U.S.A. 85 26.25N 81.26W
Imo d. Nigeria 53 5.30N 7.20E
Imola Italy 15 44.21N 11.42E
Imperatriz Brazil 91 5.32S 47.28W
Imperia Italy 15 43.53N 8.01E
Imperial Calif. U.S.A. 81 32.51N115.34W
Imperial Nebr. U.S.A. 82 40.31N101.39W
Imperial Dam U.S.A. 81 32.55N114.30W
Imperial Valley f. U.S.A. 81 32.50N115.30W
Impfondo Congo 54 1.36N 17.58E
Imphāl India 39 24.47N 93.55E
Imroz i. see Gökçeada i. Turkey 19
Ina Japan 35 35.50N137.57E
Ina r. Japan 35 34.43N135.28E
In Abbangarit well Niger 53 17.49N 6.15E
Inaccessible I. Tristan da Cunha 95 37.19S 12.44W
I-n-Amguel Algeria 51 23.40N 5.08E
Inangahua Junction New Zealand 60 41.53S171.58E
Inanwatan Indonesia 37 2.08S132.10E
Inarajan Guam 68 13.16N144.45E
Inari l. Finland 22 69.00N 28.00E
Inari town Finland 22 68.54N 27.01E
Inazawa Japan 35 35.15N136.47E
I-n-Belbel Algeria 50 27.54N 1.10E
Inca Spain 16 39.43N 2.54E
Incesu Turkey 42 38.39N 35.12E
Inchiri d. Mauritania 50 20.10N 15.00W
Inch'on S. Korea 31 37.30N126.38E
Indals r. Sweden 22 62.30N 17.20E
Indaw Burma 34 23.40N 94.46E
Independence Calif. U.S.A. 80 36.48N118.12W
Independence Kans. U.S.A. 83 37.13N 95.42W
Independence Mo. U.S.A. 82 39.05N 94.24W
Inderagiri r. Indonesia 36 0.30S103.08E
Inderborskiy U.S.S.R. 25 48.32N 51.44E
India Asia 39 23.00N 78.30E
Indiana d. U.S.A. 84 40.00N 86.15W
Indiana town U.S.A. 84 40.37N 79.09W
Indianapolis U.S.A. 84 39.45N 86.10W
Indian Cabins Canada 74 59.52N117.02W
Indian Harbour Canada 77 54.25N 57.20W
Indian Head Canada 75 50.32N103.40W
Indianola U.S.A. 82 41.22N 93.34W
Indian River B. U.S.A. 85 38.36N 75.05W
Indiga U.S.S.R. 24 67.40N 49.00E
Indigirka r. U.S.S.R. 29 71.00N148.45E
Indija Yugo. 21 45.03N 20.05E
Indio U.S.A. 81 33.43N116.13W
Indonesia Asia 36 6.00S118.00E
Indore India 40 22.43N 75.50E
Indramayu Indonesia 37 6.22S108.20E
Indrāvati r. India 41 18.44N 80.16E
Indre r. France 17 47.16N 0.19W
Indus r. Pakistan 40 24.20N 67.47E
Inebolu Turkey 42 41.57N 33.45E
Inegöl Turkey 42 40.06N 29.31E
I-n-Eker Algeria 51 24.01N 5.05E
I-n-Ezzane well Algeria 51 23.29N 11.15E
Infiesto Spain 16 43.21N 5.21W
I-n-Gall Niger 53 16.47N 6.56E
Ingatestone U.K. 11 51.41N 0.22E
Ingende Zaïre 54 0.17S 18.58E
Ingenika r. Canada 74 56.43N125.07W
Ingersoll Canada 76 43.02N 80.53W
Inggen China 32 41.35N104.47E
Ingham Australia 64 18.35S146.12E
Ingleborough mtn. U.K. 10 54.10N 2.23W
Inglewood Australia 67 28.25S151.02E
Inglewood Canada 76 43.47N 79.56W
Inglewood New Zealand 60 39.09S174.12E
Inglewood U.S.A. 81 33.58N118.21W
Ingolstadt W. Germany 20 48.46N 11.27E
Ingomar Australia 66 29.38S134.48E
Ingulets U.S.S.R. 25 47.43N 33.16E
Ingwiller France 17 48.52N 7.29E
Inhambane Mozambique 57 23.51S 35.29E
Inhambane d. Mozambique 57 22.20S 34.00E
Inhaminga Mozambique 57 18.24S 35.00E
Inharrime Mozambique 57 24.29S 35.01E
Inhassoro Mozambique 57 21.32S 35.10E
Inirida r. Colombia 90 3.59N 67.45W
Inishbofin i. Galway Rep. of Ire. 13 53.38N 10.14W
Inisheer i. Rep. of Ire. 13 53.04N 9.32W
Inishmaan i. Rep. of Ire. 13 53.06N 9.36W
Inishmore i. Rep. of Ire. 13 53.08N 9.43W
Inishowen Pen. Rep. of Ire. 13 55.08N 7.20W
Inishturk i. Rep. of Ire. 13 53.43N 10.08W
Injune Australia 64 25.51S148.34E
Inklin Canada 74 58.56N133.05W
Inklin r. Canada 74 58.50N133.10W
Inn r. Europe 20 48.33N 13.26E
Inner Hebrides is. U.K. 12 56.50N 6.45W
Inner Mongolia d. see Nei Monggol d. China 32
Inner Sd. U.K. 12 57.30N 5.55W
Innisfail Australia 64 17.32S146.02E
Innisfail Canada 74 52.00N113.57W
Innsbruck Austria 20 47.17N 11.25E
Innset Norway 22 68.41N 18.50E
Inongo Zaïre 54 1.55S 18.20E
Inoucdjouac Canada 73 58.25N 78.18W
Inowrocław Poland 21 52.49N 18.12E
I-n-Salah Algeria 51 27.13N 2.28E
Insein Burma 34 16.54N 96.08E
In Tasik well Mali 53 18.03N 2.00E
Interlaken Switz. 20 46.42N 7.52E
International Falls town U.S.A. 82 48.38N 93.26W
Intracoastal Waterway canal U.S.A. 83 28.45N 95.40W
Intute Mozambique 55 14.08S 39.55E
Inuvik Canada 72 68.16N133.40W
Inuyama Japan 35 35.23N136.56E
Inveraray U.K. 12 56.24N 5.05W
Inverbervie U.K. 12 56.51N 2.17W
Invercargill New Zealand 60 46.26S168.21E
Inverell Australia 67 29.46S151.10E
Invergordon U.K. 12 57.42N 4.10W
Inverness U.K. 12 57.27N 4.15W
Inverurie U.K. 12 57.17N 2.23W
Inverway Australia 62 17.49S129.40E
Investigator Group is. Australia 66 33.45S134.30E
Investigator Str. Australia 66 35.25S137.10E
Invinheima r. Brazil 92 22.52S 53.20W
Inya U.S.S.R. 28 50.24N 86.47E
Inyangani mtn. Zimbabwe 57 18.18S 32.50E
Inyonga Tanzania 55 6.43S 32.02E
Inzia r. Zaïre 54 3.47S 17.57E
Ioánnina Greece 19 39.39N 20.49E
Iola U.S.A. 83 37.55N 95.24W
Iona i. U.K. 12 56.20N 6.25W
Iongo Angola 54 9.11S 17.45E
Ionia U.S.A. 84 42.58N 85.06W
Ionian Is. see Iónioi Nísoi is. Greece 19
Ionian Sea Med. Sea 19 38.30N 18.45E
Iónioi Nísoi is. Greece 19 38.45N 20.00E
Íos i. Greece 19 36.42N 25.20E
Iowa d. U.S.A. 82 42.00N 93.30W
Iowa r. U.S.A. 82 41.10N 91.02W
Iowa City U.S.A. 82 41.40N 91.32W
Iowa Falls town U.S.A. 82 42.31N 93.16W
Ipatovo U.S.S.R. 25 45.44N 42.56E
Ipiales Colombia 90 0.52N 77.38W
Ipiaú Brazil 91 14.07S 39.43W
Ipixuna Brazil 90 7.00S 71.30W
Ipoh Malaysia 36 4.36N101.02E
Ippa r. U.S.S.R. 21 52.13N 29.08E
Ippy C.A.R. 49 6.15N 21.12E
Ipswich Australia 67 27.38S152.40E
Ipswich U.K. 11 52.04N 1.09E
Ipu Brazil 91 4.23S 40.44W
Ipuh Indonesia 36 2.58S101.28E
Iquique Chile 92 20.13S 70.10W
Iquitos Peru 90 3.51S 73.13W
Irago-suidō str. Japan 35 34.35N137.00E
Iráklion Greece 19 35.20N 25.08E
Iran Asia 43 32.00N 54.30E
Iran, Pegunungan mts. Indonesia/Malaysia 36 3.20N115.00E
Īrānshahr Iran 43 27.14N 60.42E
Irapuato Mexico 86 20.40N101.40W
Iraq Asia 42 33.00N 44.00E
Irauen, Wādī Libya 51 26.28N 12.00E
Irayel U.S.S.R. 24 64.23N 55.25E
Irazú mtn. Costa Rica 87 9.59N 83.52W
Irbid Jordan 44 32.33N 35.51E
Irbīl Iraq 43 36.12N 44.01E
Irebu Zaïre 54 0.37S 17.45E
Ireland I. Bermuda 95 32.19N 64.51W
Irharrhar, Oued wadi Algeria 51 23.45N 5.55E
Irian Jaya d. Indonesia 37 4.00S138.00E
Iriba Chad 48 15.07N 22.15E
Irié Guinea 52 8.15N 9.10W
Iringa Tanzania 55 7.49S 35.39E
Iringa d. Tanzania 55 8.30S 35.00E
Iriomote jima i. Japan 31 24.30N124.00E
Iriri r. Brazil 91 3.50S 52.40W
Irish Sea U.K./Rep. of Ire. 13 53.30N 5.40W
Irkutsk U.S.S.R. 30 52.18N104.15E
Iron Baron Australia 66 32.59S137.09E

Iron Gate to Joensuu

Iron Gate f. Romania / Yugo. 21 44.40N 22.30E
Iron Knob Australia 66 32.44S137.08E
Iron Mountain town U.S.A. 84 45.51N 88.03W
Iron Mts. Rep. of Ire. 13 54.10N 7.56W
Iron River town U.S.A. 82 46.05N 88.38W
Irons U.S.A. 84 44.08N 85.55W
Ironton U.S.A. 84 38.32N 82.40W
Ironwood U.S.A. 84 46.25N 90.08W
Iroquois Falls town Canada 76 48.40N 80.40W
Irosin Phil. 37 12.45N124.02E
Irō-zaki c. Japan 35 34.36N138.51E
Irpen U.S.S.R. 21 50.31N 30.29E
Irrapatana Australia 66 29.03S136.28E
Irrawaddy d. Burma 34 17.00N 95.00E
Irrawaddy r. Burma 34 15.50N 95.00E
Irrawaddy Delta Burma 34 16.45N 95.00E
Irsha r. U.S.S.R. 21 50.45N 29.30E
Irthing r. U.K. 9 54.55N 2.50W
Irtysh r. U.S.S.R. 28 61.00N 68.40E
Iruma r. Japan 35 35.57N139.30E
Irumu Zaïre 55 1.29N 29.48E
Irún Spain 16 43.20N 1.48W
Irvine U.K. 12 55.37N 4.40W
Irvinestown U.K. 13 54.29N 7.40W
Irving U.S.A. 83 32.49N 96.56W
Irwin, Pt. Australia 63 35.03S116.20E
Is, Jabal mtn. Sudan 48 22.03N 35.28E
Isa Nigeria 53 13.14N 6.24E
Isaac r. Australia 64 22.52S149.20E
Isabella, Cordillera mts. Nicaragua 87 13.30N 85.00W
Ísafjördhur town Iceland 22 66.05N 23.06W
Isaka Tanzania 55 3.52S 32.54E
Isaka Bandundu Zaïre 54 2.35S 18.48E
Isaka Equateur Zaïre 54 1.49S 20.50E
Īsa Khel Pakistan 40 32.41N 71.17E
Isakogorka U.S.S.R. 24 64.23N 40.31E
Isangi Zaïre 54 0.48N 24.03E
Isar r. W. Germany 20 48.48N 12.57E
Isbergues France 14 50.38N 2.24E
Ischia i. Italy 18 40.43N 13.54E
Ise Japan 35 34.29N136.42E
Iseo, Lago d' l. Italy 15 45.43N 10.04E
Isère r. France 17 45.02N 4.54E
Iserlohn W. Germany 14 51.23N 7.42E
Isernia Italy 18 41.36N 14.14E
Ise-wan b. Japan 35 34.45N136.40E
Iseyin Nigeria 53 7.59N 3.36E
Isfahan see Eşfahān Iran 38
Ishim U.S.S.R. 28 56.10N 69.30E
Ishim r. U.S.S.R. 28 57.50N 71.00E
Ishinomaki Japan 31 38.25N141.18E
Ishpeming U.S.A. 84 46.29N 87.40W
Ishurdi Bangla. 41 24.09N 89.03E
Isigny France 15 49.18N 1.06W
Isiolo Kenya 55 0.20N 37.36E
Isipingo Beach town R.S.A. 56 30.00S 30.57E
Isiro Zaïre 55 2.50N 27.40E
Iskenderun Turkey 42 36.37N 36.08E
Iskenderun Körfezi g. Turkey 42 36.40N 35.50E
Iskilip Turkey 42 40.45N 34.28E
Iskûr r. Bulgaria 19 43.42N 24.27E
Isla r. U.K. 12 56.32N 3.22W
Islāmābād Pakistan 40 33.40N 73.10E
Islāmkot Pakistan 40 24.42N 70.11E
Islāmpur Bihār India 41 25.09N 85.12E
Islāmpur W. Bengal India 41 26.16N 88.12E
Island L. Australia 66 31.30S136.40E
Island L. Canada 75 53.47N 94.25W
Island Magee pen. U.K. 13 54.48N 5.44W
Island Pt. Australia 63 30.21S115.01E
Islands, B. of Canada 77 49.10N 58.15W
Islands, B. of New Zealand 60 35.15S174.15E
Islay i. U.K. 12 55.45N 6.20W
Isle r. France 17 45.02N 0.08W
Isle of Portland f. U.K. 11 50.32N 2.25W
Isle of Wight d. U.K. 11 50.40N 1.17W
Isleta U.S.A. 81 34.55N106.42W
Ismael Cortinas Uruguay 93 33.58S 57.06W
Ismay U.S.A. 80 46.30N104.48W
Isnā Egypt 42 25.16N 32.30E
Isoka Zambia 55 10.06S 32.39E
Isola della Scala Italy 15 45.16N 11.00E
Isparta Turkey 42 37.46N 30.32E
Ispica Italy 18 36.46N 14.55E
Ispikān Pakistan 40 26.14N 62.12E
Israel Asia 44 32.00N 34.50E
Israelite B. Australia 63 33.40S123.55E
Issia Ivory Coast 52 6.33N 6.33W
Issoire France 17 45.33N 3.15E
Is-sur-Tille France 17 47.30N 5.10E
Issyk Kul l. U.S.S.R. 30 43.30N 77.20E
Istanbul Turkey 19 41.02N 28.58E
Istanbul Boğazi str. Turkey 19 41.07N 29.04E
Isthmus of Kra Thailand 34 10.20N 99.10E
Istiaía Greece 19 38.57N 23.09E
Istok Yugo. 19 42.47N 20.29E
Istra pen. Yugo. 20 45.12N 13.55E
Itabaiana Brazil 91 7.20S 35.20W
Itabira Brazil 94 19.39S 43.14W
Itabirito Brazil 94 20.21S 43.45W
Itabuna Brazil 91 14.48S 39.18W
Itacajuna r. Brazil 91 5.20S 49.08W
Itacoatiara Brazil 90 3.06S 58.22W
Itagüí Colombia 90 6.10N 75.36W
Itaí Brazil 94 23.23S 49.05W
Itaim r. Brazil 91 6.43S 42.48W
Itaituba Brazil 91 4.17S 55.59W
Itajaí Brazil 94 26.50S 48.39W
Itajubá Brazil 94 22.24S 45.25W
Itaka Tanzania 55 8.51S 32.48E
Italy Europe 18 43.00N 12.00E
Itami Japan 35 34.46N135.25E
Itapecerica Brazil 94 20.28S 45.09W
Itapecuru Mirim Brazil 91 3.24S 44.20W
Itaperuna Brazil 94 21.14S 41.51W
Itapetinga Brazil 91 15.17S 40.16W
Itapetininga Brazil 94 23.36S 48.07W
Itapeva Brazil 94 23.59S 48.59W
Itapicuru r. Brazil 91 11.50S 37.30W
Itapira Brazil 94 22.24S 46.56W
Itaqui Brazil 94 29.07S 56.33W
Itārsi India 41 22.37N 77.45E
Itatiba Brazil 94 22.59S 46.51W
Itatinga Brazil 94 23.06S 48.36W
Itatuba Brazil 90 5.40S 63.20W
Itaúna Brazil 94 20.04S 44.14W
Itbayat i. Phil. 33 20.45N121.50E
Ithaca U.S.A. 84 42.26N 76.30W
Itháki Greece 19 38.23N 20.42E
Itimbiri r. Zaïre 54 2.02N 22.47E
Itmurinkol, Ozero l. U.S.S.R. 25 49.30N 52.17E
Itō Japan 35 34.58N139.05E
Itoko Zaïre 54 1.00S 21.45E
Iton r. France 15 49.09N 1.12E
Iṭsa Egypt 44 29.14N 30.47E
Ittel, Oued wadi Algeria 51 34.18N 6.02E
Itu Brazil 94 23.17S 47.18W
Ituí r. Brazil 90 4.38S 70.19W
Ituiutaba Brazil 94 19.00S 49.25W
Ituri r. Zaïre 55 1.45N 27.06E
Iturup i. U.S.S.R. 31 44.00N147.30E
Ituverava Brazil 94 20.22S 47.48W
Ituxi r. Brazil 90 7.20S 64.50W
Ityāy al Bārūd Egypt 44 30.53N 30.40E
Itzehoe W. Germany 20 53.56N 9.32E
Ivaí r. Brazil 94 23.20S 53.23W
Ivalo Finland 22 68.42N 27.30E
Ivalo r. Finland 22 68.43N 27.36E
Ivanhoe Australia 66 32.56S144.22E
Ivanhoe U.S.A. 82 44.28N 96.12W
Ivano-Frankovsk U.S.S.R. 21 48.55N 24.42E
Ivanovo B.S.S.R. U.S.S.R. 21 52.10N 25.13E
Ivanovo R.S.F.S.R. U.S.S.R. 24 57.00N 41.00E
Ivdel U.S.S.R. 24 60.45N 60.30E
Ivenets U.S.S.R. 21 53.50N 26.40E
Ivigtut Greenland 73 61.10N 48.00W
Ivindo Gabon 54 0.02S 12.13E
Iviza i. see Ibiza i. Spain 16
Ivohibe Madagascar 57 22.29S 45.52E
Ivory Coast Africa 52 8.00N 5.30W
Ivrea Italy 15 45.28N 7.52E
Ivujivik Canada 73 62.24N 77.55W
Ivybridge U.K. 11 50.24N 3.56W
Iwata Japan 35 34.42N137.48E
Iwo Nigeria 53 7.38N 4.11E
Ixiamas Bolivia 92 13.45S 68.09W
Izabal, Lago de l. Guatemala 87 15.30N 89.00W
Izberbash U.S.S.R. 25 42.31N 47.52E
Izhevsk U.S.S.R. 24 56.49N 53.11E
Izhma U.S.S.R. 24 65.03N 53.48E
Izhma r. U.S.S.R. 24 65.16N 53.18E
Izmail U.S.S.R. 21 45.20N 28.50E
Izmir Turkey 19 38.24N 27.09E
Izmir Körfezi g. Turkey 19 38.30N 26.45E
Izmit Turkey 42 40.48N 29.55E
Izozog, Bañados de f. Bolivia 92 18.30S 62.05W
Izozog Marshes f. see Izozog, Bañados de f. Bolivia 92
Izu-hantō pen. Japan 35 34.53N138.55E
Izumi Japan 35 34.29N135.26E
Izumi-ōtsu Japan 35 34.30N135.24E
Izumi-sano Japan 35 34.25N135.19E
Izumo r. Japan 35 34.38N136.33E
Izyaslav U.S.S.R. 21 50.10N 26.46E
Izyum U.S.S.R. 25 49.12N 37.19E

J

Jaba Ethiopia 49 6.17N 35.12E
Jabal, Baḥr al r. Sudan 49 9.30N 30.30E
Jabal al Awliyā' Sudan 48 15.14N 32.30E
Jabal Dūd Sudan 49 13.22N 33.09E
Jabalón r. Spain 16 38.55N 4.07W
Jabalpur India 41 23.10N 79.57E
Jabālyah Egypt 44 31.32N 34.29E
Jabbān, Arḍ al f. Jordan 44 32.08N 36.35E
Jabjabah, Wādī Egypt 48 22.37N 33.17E
Jablah Syria 44 35.22N 35.56E
Jablonec nad Nisou Czech. 20 50.44N 15.10E
Jabori Pakistan 40 34.36N 73.16E
Jaboticabal Brazil 94 21.15S 48.17W
Jabrat Sa'īd wells Sudan 48 16.06N 31.50E
Jaca Spain 16 42.34N 0.33W
Jacareí Brazil 94 23.17S 45.57W
Jackman U.S.A. 84 45.38N 70.16W
Jackson Ky. U.S.A. 85 37.32N 83.24W
Jackson Mich. U.S.A. 84 42.15N 84.24W
Jackson Miss. U.S.A. 83 32.18N 90.12W
Jackson Mo. U.S.A. 83 37.23N 89.40W
Jackson Ohio U.S.A. 84 39.03N 82.40W
Jackson Tenn. U.S.A. 83 35.37N 88.49W
Jackson Wyo. U.S.A. 80 43.29N110.38W
Jackson Bay town Canada 74 50.32N125.57W
Jacksonville Fla. U.S.A. 85 30.20N 81.40W
Jacksonville Ill. U.S.A. 82 39.44N 90.14W
Jacksonville N.C. U.S.A. 85 34.45N 77.26W
Jacksonville Tex. U.S.A. 83 31.58N 95.17W
Jacksonville Beach town U.S.A. 85 30.18N 81.24W
Jacobābād Pakistan 40 28.17N 68.26E
Jacobina Brazil 91 11.13S 40.30W
Jacob Lake town U.S.A. 81 36.41N112.14W
Jacques Cartier, Détroit de str. Canada 77 50.00N 63.30W
Jacques Cartier, Mt. Canada 77 48.59N 65.57W
Jacuí r. Brazil 94 29.56S 51.13W
Jacundá r. Brazil 91 1.57S 50.26W
Jaddi, Rās c. Pakistan 40 25.14N 63.31E
Jade W. Germany 14 53.21N 8.11E
Jadebusen b. W. Germany 14 53.30N 8.12E
Jādū Libya 51 31.57N 12.01E
Jaén Peru 90 5.21S 78.28W
Jaén Spain 16 37.46N 3.48W
Jāfarābād India 40 20.52N 71.22E
Jaffa, C. Australia 66 36.58S139.39E
Jaffna Sri Lanka 39 9.38N 80.02E
Jagādhri India 40 30.10N 77.18E
Jāgan Pakistan 40 28.05N 68.30E
Jagatsingpur India 41 20.16N 86.10E
Jagdalpur India 41 19.04N 82.02E
Jaggang China 41 32.52N 79.45E
Jagtiāl India 41 18.48N 78.56E
Jaguarão Brazil 94 32.30S 53.25W
Jahānābād India 41 25.13N 84.59E
Jahrom Iran 43 28.30N 53.30E
Jailolo Indonesia 37 1.05N127.29E
Jainti India 41 26.42N 89.36E
Jaintiāpur Bangla. 41 25.08N 92.07E
Jaipur India 40 26.53N 75.50E
Jāis India 41 26.15N 81.32E
Jaisalmer India 40 26.55N 70.54E
Jājarkot Nepal 41 28.42N 82.14E
Jajawijaya Mts. Asia 37 4.20S139.10E
Jajjha Pakistan 40 28.45N 70.34E
Jājpur India 41 20.51N 86.20E
Jakarta Indonesia 37 6.08S106.45E
Jakarta d. Indonesia 37 6.10S106.48E
Jakhāu India 40 23.13N 68.43E
Jäkkvik Sweden 22 66.23N 17.00E
Jakobstad see Pietarsaari Finland 22
Jal U.S.A. 83 32.07N103.12W
Jalālābād Afghan. 40 34.26N 70.28E
Jalālah al Baḥrīyah, Jabal mts. Egypt 44 29.20N 32.12E
Jalālat al Qiblīyah, Jabal al mts. Egypt 44 28.42N 32.23E
Jalālpur India 41 26.19N 82.44E
Jalapa Mexico 86 19.45N 96.48W
Jālaun India 41 26.09N 79.21E
Jaldak Afghan. 40 31.58N 66.44E
Jalesar India 41 27.29N 78.19E
Jaleswar India 41 21.49N 87.13E
Jālgaon Mahār. India 40 21.01N 75.34E
Jālgaon Mahār. India 40 21.03N 76.32E
Jalingo Nigeria 53 8.54N 11.21E
Jalisco d. Mexico 86 21.00N103.00W
Jālna India 40 19.50N 75.53E
Jalón r. Spain 16 41.47N 1.02W
Jālor India 40 25.21N 72.37E
Jalpaiguri India 41 26.31N 88.44E
Jālū Libya 51 29.02N 21.33E
Jaluit i. Pacific Oc. 68 6.00N169.35E
Jalūlā Iraq 43 34.16N 45.10E
Jamaari Nigeria 53 11.44N 9.53E
Jamaica C. America 87 18.00N 77.00W
Jamālpur Bangla. 41 24.55N 89.56E
Jamālpur India 41 25.18N 86.30E
Jamame Somali Rep. 55 0.04N 42.46E
Jamanxim r. Brazil 91 4.43S 56.18W
Jamberoo Australia 67 34.40S150.44E
Jambes Belgium 14 50.28N 4.52E
Jambi Indonesia 36 1.36S103.39E
Jambi d. Indonesia 36 2.00S102.30E
Jambusar India 40 22.03N 72.48E
James r. S.Dak. U.S.A. 82 42.55N 97.28W
James r. Va. U.S.A. 85 36.57N 76.26W
James B. Canada 76 53.30N 80.00W
James Bay Prov. Park Canada 76 51.30N 79.00W
Jamestown Australia 66 33.12S138.38E
Jamestown St. Helena 95 15.56S 5.44W
Jamestown N.Dak. U.S.A. 82 46.54N 98.42W
Jamestown N.Y. U.S.A. 84 42.06N 79.14W
Jamestown Tenn. U.S.A. 85 36.24N 84.58W
Jamjodhpur India 40 21.54N 70.01E
Jammerbught b. Denmark 23 57.20N 9.30E
Jammu Jammu & Kashmir 40 32.42N 74.52E
Jammu & Kashmir Asia 40 34.45N 76.00E
Jāmnagar India 40 22.28N 70.04E
Jamnotri India 41 31.01N 78.27E
Jampang Kulon Indonesia 37 7.18S106.33E
Jāmpur Pakistan 40 28.45N 70.36E
Jamsah Egypt 44 27.39N 33.35E
Jämsänkoski Finland 23 61.55N 25.11E
Jamshedpur India 41 22.48N 86.11E
Jämtland d. Sweden 22 63.00N 14.30E
Jamūi India 41 24.55N 86.13E
Jamuna r. Bangla. 41 23.51N 89.45E
Jand Pakistan 40 33.26N 72.01E
Janda, Laguna de la l. Spain 16 36.15N 5.50W
Jandiāla India 40 31.33N 75.02E
Jándula r. Spain 16 38.08N 4.08W
Janesville U.S.A. 82 42.42N 89.02W
Jangamo Mozambique 57 24.06S 35.21E
Jangipur India 41 24.28N 88.04E
Janīn Jordan 44 32.28N 35.18E
Jan Kempdorp R.S.A. 56 27.55S 24.48E
Januária Brazil 94 15.28S 44.23W
Janzé France 15 47.58N 1.30W
Jaora India 40 23.38N 75.08E
Japan Asia 31 36.00N136.00E
Japan, Sea of Asia 31 40.00N135.00E
Japan Trench Pacific Oc. 68 33.00N142.00E
Japla India 41 24.33N 84.01E
Japurá r. Brazil 90 3.00S 64.50W
Jarales U.S.A. 81 34.37N106.46W
Jarama r. Spain 16 40.27N 3.32W
Jarānwāla Pakistan 40 31.20N 73.26E
Jarash Jordan 44 32.17N 35.54E
Jardee Australia 63 34.18S116.04E
Jardines de la Reina is. Cuba 87 20.30N 79.00W
Jardinópolis Brazil 94 20.59S 47.48W
Jargeau France 15 47.52N 2.07E
Jāria Jhānjail Bangla. 41 25.02N 90.39E
Jaridih India 41 23.38N 86.04E
Jarocin Poland 21 51.59N 17.31E
Jarosław Poland 21 50.02N 22.42E
Jarrāḩī r. Iran 43 30.40N 48.23E
Jartai China 32 39.45N105.46E
Jartai Yanchi l. China 32 39.43N105.41E
Jarud Qi China 32 44.30N120.35E
Järvenpää Finland 23 60.28N 25.06E
Jarvis Canada 76 42.53N 80.06W
Jarvis I. Pacific Oc. 68 0.23S160.02W
Jasdan India 40 22.02N 71.12E
Jāsk Iran 43 25.40N 57.45E
Jasło Poland 21 49.45N 21.29E
Jasper Canada 74 52.55N118.05W
Jasper Ala. U.S.A. 85 33.48N 87.18W
Jasper Fla. U.S.A. 85 30.31N 82.58W
Jasper Tex. U.S.A. 83 30.55N 94.01W
Jasper Nat. Park Canada 74 52.50N118.08W
Jasra India 41 25.17N 81.48E
Jastrebarsko Yugo. 20 45.40N 15.39E
Jastrowie Poland 20 53.26N 16.49E
Jászberény Hungary 21 47.30N 19.55E
Jataí Brazil 94 17.58S 51.45W
Jāti Pakistan 40 24.21N 68.16E
Jatibarang Indonesia 37 6.26S108.18E
Jatinegara Indonesia 37 6.12S106.51E
Játiva Spain 16 39.00N 0.32W
Jatni India 41 20.10N 85.42E
Jatobá Brazil 91 4.35S 49.33W
Jaú Brazil 94 22.11S 48.35W
Jauja Peru 90 11.50S 75.15W
Jaunjelgava U.S.S.R. 24 56.34N 25.02E
Jaunpur India 41 25.44N 82.41E
Java i. see Jawa i. Indonesia 37
Javari r. Peru 90 4.30S 71.20W
Java Sea see Jawa, Laut sea Indonesia 36
Java Trench f. Indonesia 36 10.00S110.00E
Jawa i. Indonesia 37 7.25S110.00E
Jawa, Laut sea Indonesia 36 5.00S111.00E
Jawa Barat d. Indonesia 37 7.10S107.00E
Jawa Tengah d. Indonesia 37 7.49S110.35E
Jawa Timur d. Indonesia 37 8.42S113.10E
Jayah, Wādī al see Hā 'Arava Jordan / Israel 44
Jayapura Indonesia 37 2.28S140.38E
Jaynagar India 41 26.32N 86.07E
Jazirah Doberai f. Indonesia 37 1.10S132.30E
Jazzīn Lebanon 44 33.32N 35.34E
Jean U.S.A. 81 35.46N115.20W
Jeanerette U.S.A. 83 29.55N 91.40W
Jean Marie River town Canada 72 61.32N120.40W
Jebāl Bārez, Kūh-e mts. Iran 43 28.40N 58.10E
Jebba Nigeria 53 9.11N 4.49E
Jebri Pakistan 40 27.18N 65.44E
Jedburgh U.K. 12 55.29N 2.33W
Jędrzejów Poland 21 50.39N 20.18E
Jefferson, Mt. Nev. U.S.A. 80 38.46N116.55W
Jefferson, Mt. Oreg. U.S.A. 80 44.40N121.47W
Jefferson City U.S.A. 82 38.34N 92.10W
Jeffersonville U.S.A. 84 38.16N 85.45W
Jega Nigeria 53 12.12N 4.23E
Jēkabpils U.S.S.R. 24 56.28N 25.58E
Jelenia Góra Poland 20 50.55N 15.45E
Jelgava U.S.S.R. 23 56.39N 23.42E
Jelli Sudan 49 5.22N 31.48E
Jember Indonesia 37 8.07S113.45E
Jena E. Germany 20 50.56N 11.35E
Jena U.S.A. 83 31.41N 92.08W
Jenbach Austria 20 47.24N 11.47E
Jenolan Caves town Australia 67 33.53S150.03E
Jepara Indonesia 37 6.32S110.40E
Jeparit Australia 66 36.09S141.59E
Jeppo Finland 22 63.24N 22.37E
Jequié Brazil 91 13.52S 40.06W
Jequitinhonha r. Brazil 94 16.46S 39.45W
Jerada Morocco 50 34.17N 2.13W
Jerantut Malaysia 36 3.56N102.22E
Jérémie Haiti 87 18.40N 74.09W
Jerez Spain 16 38.20N 6.45W
Jerez de la Frontera Spain 16 36.41N 6.08W
Jericho see Arīḩā Jordan 44
Jerilderie Australia 67 35.23S145.41E
Jerome U.S.A. 80 42.43N114.31W
Jersey i. U.K. 11 49.13N 2.08W
Jersey City U.S.A. 85 40.44N 74.04W
Jerseyville U.S.A. 82 39.07N 90.20W
Jerusalem see Yerushalayim Israel / Jordan 44
Jervis B. Australia 67 35.05S150.44E
Jesenice Yugo. 18 46.27N 14.04E
Jessore Bangla. 41 23.10N 89.13E
Jesup U.S.A. 85 31.36N 81.54W
Jesús Carranza Mexico 86 17.26N 95.02W
Jetmore U.S.A. 83 38.03N 99.54W
Jetpur India 40 21.44N 70.37E
Jever W. Germany 14 53.34N 7.54E
Jevnaker Norway 23 60.15N 10.28E
Jewett Tex. U.S.A. 83 31.22N 96.09W
Jeypore India 41 18.51N 82.35E
Jeziorak, Jezioro l. Poland 21 53.40N 19.04E
Jhābua India 40 22.46N 74.36E
Jhajha India 41 24.46N 86.22E
Jhal Pakistan 40 28.17N 67.27E
Jhālakāti Bangla. 41 22.39N 90.12E
Jhālāwār India 40 24.36N 76.09E
Jhal Jhao Pakistan 40 26.18N 65.35E
Jhālod India 40 23.06N 74.09E
Jhang Sadar Pakistan 40 31.16N 72.20E
Jhānsi India 41 25.26N 78.35E
Jharia India 41 23.45N 86.24E
Jhārsuguda India 41 21.51N 84.02E
Jhawāni Nepal 41 27.35N 84.38E
Jhelum Pakistan 40 32.56N 73.44E
Jhelum r. Pakistan 40 31.12N 72.08E
Jhinkpāni India 41 22.25N 85.47E
Jhok Rind Pakistan 40 31.27N 70.26E
Jhūnjhunu India 40 28.08N 75.24E
Jiaganj India 41 24.14N 88.16E
Jialing Jiang r. China 33 29.30N106.35E
Jiamusi China 31 46.50N130.21E
Ji'an China 33 27.03N115.00E
Jianchang China 32 40.50N119.50E
Jiange China 32 32.04N105.26E
Jiangling China 33 30.20N112.14E
Jiangmen China 33 22.31N113.08E
Jiangshan China 33 28.43N118.39E
Jiangsu d. China 32 33.00N119.30E
Jiangxi d. China 33 27.00N115.30E
Jiangyou China 33 31.47N104.45E
Jianhe China 33 26.39N108.35E
Jian'ou China 33 27.04N118.17E
Jianping China 32 41.23N119.40E
Jianshi China 33 30.42N109.20E
Jianyang Fujian China 33 27.19N118.01E
Jianyang Sichuan China 33 30.25N104.32E
Jiaochangba Sichuan China 32 32.05N103.43E
Jiaohe China 31 43.42N127.19E
Jiaolai He r. China 32 43.48N123.00E
Jiaoling China 33 24.40N116.10E
Jiaonan China 32 35.53N119.58E
Jiao Xian China 32 36.16N120.00E
Jiaozou China 32 35.11N113.27E
Jiashan China 32 32.49N118.01E
Jiawang China 32 34.27N117.27E
Jiaxian China 32 38.02N110.29E
Jiaxing China 33 30.52N120.45E
Jiayi Taiwan 33 23.30N120.24E
Jiazi China 33 22.57N116.01E
Jiddah Saudi Arabia 48 21.30N 39.10E
Jiddat al Ḩarāsīs f. Oman 45 19.45N 56.30E
Jiepai China 33 31.11N113.42E
Jiexi China 33 23.26N115.52E
Jiexiu China 32 37.00N111.55E
Jieyang China 33 23.29N116.19E
Jihlava Czech. 20 49.24N 15.35E
Jijel Algeria 51 36.48N 5.46E
Jijiga Ethiopia 45 9.22N 42.47E
Jilib Somali Rep. 55 0.28N 42.50E
Jilin China 31 43.53N126.35E
Jilin d. China 31 43.00N127.30E
Jilong Taiwan 33 25.09N121.45E
Jima Ethiopia 49 7.36N 36.50E
Jimbe Angola 54 10.20S 16.40E
Jiménez Mexico 86 27.08N104.55W
Jimeta Nigeria 53 9.19N 12.25E
Jimo China 32 36.23N120.27E
Jinan China 32 36.40N117.01E
Jind India 40 29.19N 76.19E
Jing'an China 33 28.52N115.22E
Jingbian China 32 37.33N108.36E
Jingchuan China 32 35.15N107.22E
Jingde China 33 30.19N118.31E
Jingdezhen China 33 29.14N117.14E
Jinggu Gansu China 32 35.05N103.41E
Jinggu Yunnan China 39 23.29N100.19E
Jinghai China 33 23.02N116.31E
Jing He r. China 32 34.26N109.00E
Jinghong China 30 21.59N100.49E
Jingmen China 33 31.02N112.06E
Jingning China 32 35.30N105.45E
Jingou China 32 41.37N120.33E
Jingtai China 32 37.10N104.08E
Jingxi China 33 23.03N106.36E
Jing Xian China 33 26.35N109.41E
Jingyuan Gansu China 32 36.40N104.40E
Jingyuan Ningxia Huizu China 32 35.29N106.20E
Jinhua China 33 29.05N119.40E
Jining Nei Monggol China 31 40.56N113.00E
Jining Shantung China 32 35.22N116.45E
Jinja Uganda 55 0.27N 33.10E
Jinotepe Nicaragua 87 11.50N 86.10W
Jinsha Jiang r. China 39 26.30N101.40E
Jinshi China 33 29.35N111.56E
Jintang China 33 30.51N104.27E
Jinxi Fujian China 33 26.12N117.34E
Jinxi Liaoning China 32 40.48N120.46E
Jinxian China 33 28.13N116.34E
Jin Xian Liaoning China 32 39.06N121.49E
Jin Xian Liaoning China 32 41.10N121.20E
Jinxiang China 32 35.08N116.20E
Jinzhou China 32 41.06N121.05E
Jipijapa Ecuador 90 1.23S 80.35W
Jire Somali Rep. 45 5.22N 48.05E
Jirjā Egypt 48 26.20N 31.53E
Jishui China 33 27.13N115.07E
Jitarning Australia 63 32.48S117.57E
Jiu r. Romania 19 43.44N 23.52E
Jiuding Shan mtn. China 33 31.36N103.54E
Jiudongshan China 33 23.44N117.32E
Jiujiang China 33 29.39N116.02E
Jiulian Shan mts. China 33 24.40N115.00E
Jiuling Shan mts. China 33 28.40N114.45E
Jiulong Jiang r. China 33 24.30N117.47E
Jiuzhou Jiang r. China 33 21.25N109.58E
Jixi China 31 45.17N131.00E
Ji Xian Henan China 32 35.25N114.05E
Ji Xian Tianjin China 32 40.03N117.24E
Jīzān Saudi Arabia 48 16.54N 42.32E
Jizl, Wādī al r. Saudi Arabia 42 25.37N 38.20E
João Pessoa Brazil 91 7.06S 34.53W
Jódar Spain 16 37.50N 3.21W
Jodhpur India 40 26.17N 73.02E
Jodiya India 40 22.42N 70.18E
Jodoigne Belgium 14 50.45N 4.52E
Joensuu Finland 24 62.35N 29.46E

Jogdor to **Karakoram Range**

Jogdor China **32** 42.30N115.52E
Johannesburg R.S.A. **56** 26.11S 28.04E
Johi Pakistan **40** 26.41N 67.37E
John Day U.S.A. **80** 44.25N118.57W
John Day *r.* U.S.A. **80** 45.44N120.39W
John O'Groats U.K. **12** 58.39N 3.02W
Johnson U.S.A. **83** 37.34N101.45W
Johnson City Tenn. U.S.A. **85** 36.20N 82.23W
Johnsons Crossing Canada **74** 60.29N133.18W
Johnstone Str. Canada **74** 50.28N126.00W
Johnston I. Pacific Oc. **68** 16.45N169.32W
Johnston Lakes, The Australia **63** 32.25S120.30E
Johnstown Penn. U.S.A. **84** 40.20N 78.55W
Johor Baharu Malaysia **36** 1.29N103.40E
Joigny France **15** 48.00N 3.20E
Joinville Brazil **94** 26.20S 48.49W
Joinville France **17** 48.27N 5.08E
Jokkmokk Sweden **22** 66.37N 19.50E
Jökulsá á Brú *r.* Iceland **22** 65.33N 14.23W
Jökulsá á Fjöllum *r.* Iceland **22** 66.05N 16.32W
Jolfa Iran **43** 32.40N 51.39E
Joliet U.S.A. **82** 41.32N 88.05W
Joliette Canada **77** 46.02N 73.27W
Jolo *i.* Phil. **37** 5.55N121.20E
Jolo *town* Phil. **37** 6.03N121.00E
Jombang Indonesia **37** 7.30S112.21E
Jombo *r.* Angola **54** 10.20S 16.37E
Jomda China **39** 31.30N 98.16E
Jonava U.S.S.R. **23** 55.05N 24.17E
Jonê China **32** 34.35N103.32E
Jonesboro Ark. U.S.A. **83** 35.50N 90.42W
Jonesboro La. U.S.A. **83** 32.15N 92.43W
Jones Sd. Canada **73** 76.00N 85.00W
Jönköping Sweden **23** 57.47N 14.11E
Jönköping *d.* Sweden **23** 57.30N 14.30E
Joplin U.S.A. **83** 37.06N 94.31W
Jora India **41** 26.20N 77.49E
Jordan Asia **42** 31.00N 36.00E
Jordan *r. see* Al Urdunn *r.* Asia **44**
Jordan Mont. U.S.A. **80** 47.19N106.55W
Jordan Valley *town* U.S.A. **80** 42.58N117.03W
Jorhāt India **39** 26.45N 94.13E
Jörn Sweden **22** 65.04N 20.02E
Jos Nigeria **53** 9.54N 8.53E
José de San Martín Argentina **93** 44.04S 70.26W
José Enrique Rodó Uruguay **93** 33.41S 57.34W
Joseph, Lac *l.* Canada **77** 52.45N 65.15W
Joseph Bonaparte G. Australia **62** 14.00S128.30E
Joseph City U.S.A. **81** 34.57N110.20W
Joshīmath India **41** 30.34N 79.34E
Jos Plateau *f.* Nigeria **53** 10.00N 9.00E
Jotunheimen *mts.* Norway **23** 61.38N 8.18E
Joué-lès-Tours France **15** 47.21N 0.40E
Joure Neth. **14** 52.59N 5.49E
Joverega Botswana **56** 19.08S 24.15E
Jowai India **41** 25.27N 92.12E
Juan Aldama Mexico **83** 24.19N103.21W
Juan B. Arruabarrena Argentina **93** 30.25S 58.15W
Juan de Fuca, Str. of Canada / U.S.A. **74** 48.15N124.00W
Juan de Nova *i.* Madagascar **57** 17.03S 42.45E
Juan Fernández, Islas *is.* Pacific Oc. **69** 34.20S 80.00W
Juárez Argentina **93** 37.40S 59.48W
Juárez Chihuahua Mexico **81** 30.20N108.03W
Juárez Coahuila Mexico **83** 27.37N100.44W
Juárez, Sierra de *mts.* Mexico **81** 32.00N115.45W
Juàzeiro Brazil **91** 9.25S 40.30W
Juàzeiro do Norte Brazil **91** 7.10S 39.18W
Juba *r.* Somali Rep. **55** 0.20S 42.40E
Jūbā Sudan **49** 4.51N 31.37E
Jūbāl, Maḑīq *str.* Egypt **44** 27.40N 33.55E
Jubal, Str. of *see* Jūbāl, Maḑīq *str.* Egypt **44**
Jubilee Downs *town* Australia **62** 18.22S125.17E
Juby, Cap *c.* Morocco **50** 27.58N 12.55W
Júcar *r.* Spain **16** 39.10N 0.15W
Juchitán Mexico **86** 16.27N 95.05W
Judenburg Austria **20** 47.10N 14.40E
Judith Basin *f.* U.S.A. **80** 47.10N109.58W
Juist W. Germany **14** 53.41N 7.01E
Juist *i.* W. Germany **14** 53.43N 7.00E
Juiz de Fora Brazil **94** 21.47S 43.23W
Jujuy *d.* Argentina **92** 23.00S 66.00W
Juklegga *mtn.* Norway **23** 61.03N 8.13E
Juliaca Peru **90** 15.29S 70.09W
Julia Creek *town* Australia **64** 20.39S141.45E
Juliana Kanaal *canal* Neth. **14** 51.00N 5.48E
Julianehåb Greenland **73** 60.45N 46.00W
Jülich W. Germany **14** 50.55N 6.21E
Jullundur India **40** 31.20N 75.35E
Jumbo Somali Rep. **55** 0.12S 42.38E
Jumbunna Australia **67** 38.30S145.38E
Jumet Belgium **14** 50.27N 4.27E
Jumilla Spain **16** 38.28N 1.19W
Jumla Nepal **41** 29.17N 82.13E
Jumna *r. see* Yamuna India **41**
Junāgadh India **40** 21.31N 70.28E
Junan China **32** 35.11N118.50E
Junction U.S.A. **83** 30.29N 99.46W
Junction B. Australia **64** 11.50S134.15E
Junction City Kans. U.S.A. **82** 39.02N 96.50W
Junction City Oreg. U.S.A. **80** 44.13N123.12W
Jundah Australia **64** 24.50S143.02E
Jundiaí Brazil **94** 23.10S 46.54W
Juneau U.S.A. **74** 58.26N134.30W
Junee Australia **67** 34.51S147.40E
Jungfrau *mtn.* Switz. **17** 46.30N 8.00E
Junggar Pendi *f.* Asia **30** 44.20N 86.30E
Junglinster Lux. **14** 49.43N 6.13E
Jungshāhi Pakistan **40** 24.51N 67.46E
Junín Argentina **93** 34.35S 60.58W
Junín de los Andes Argentina **93** 39.57S 71.05W
Juniville France **15** 49.24N 4.23E
Jūnīyah Lebanon **44** 33.59N 35.38E
Junlian China **33** 28.08N104.29E
Junnah, Jabal *mts.* Egypt **44** 28.52N 34.15E
Junnar India **40** 19.12N 73.53E
Junsele Sweden **22** 63.40N 16.55E
Juntura U.S.A. **80** 43.46N118.05W
Jun Xian China **32** 32.40N111.18E
Jupiter *r.* Canada **77** 49.29N 63.32W
Jupiter U.S.A. **85** 26.57N 80.08W
Jur *r.* Sudan **49** 7.45N 28.00E
Jura *mts.* Europe **17** 46.55N 6.45E
Jura *i.* U.K. **12** 55.58N 5.55W
Jura, Sd. of U.K. **12** 56.00N 5.45W
Jurado Colombia **90** 7.07N 77.46W
Jura Krakowska *mts.* Poland **21** 50.30N 19.30E
Jurhen Ul Shan *mts.* China **41** 34.00N 91.00E
Jūrmala U.S.S.R. **23** 56.58N 23.42E
Juruá *r.* Brazil **90** 2.33S 65.50W
Juruena Brazil **92** 12.50S 58.58W
Juruena *r.* Brazil **91** 7.20S 57.30W
Juruti Brazil **91** 2.09S 56.04W
Jussey France **17** 47.49N 5.54E
Jutaí *r.* Brazil **90** 2.35S 67.00W
Juticalpa Honduras **87** 14.45N 86.12W
Jutland *pen. see* Jylland *pen.* Denmark **23**
Juye China **32** 35.23N116.06E
Jūyom Iran **43** 28.10N 53.52E
Jwayyā Lebanon **44** 33.14N 35.20E
Jylland *pen.* Denmark **23** 56.00N 9.15E
Jyväskylä Finland **22** 62.14N 25.44E

K

K2 *mtn.* Asia **30** 35.53N 76.32E
Ka *r.* Nigeria **53** 11.35N 4.10E
Kaabong Uganda **55** 3.28N 34.08E
Kaapstad *see* Cape Town R.S.A. **56**
Kaba Guinea **52** 10.08N 11.49W
Kabaena *i.* Indonesia **37** 5.25S122.00E
Kabala Sierra Leone **52** 9.40N 11.36W
Kabale Uganda **55** 1.13S 30.00E
Kabalega Falls *f.* Uganda **55** 2.17N 31.46E
Kabalega Falls Nat. Park Uganda **55** 2.15N 31.45E
Kabalo Zaïre **55** 6.02S 27.00E
Kabambare Zaïre **55** 4.40S 27.41E
Kabanga Zambia **56** 17.36S 26.45E
Kabba Nigeria **53** 7.50N 6.07E
Kabia *i.* Indonesia **37** 6.07S120.28E
Kabinakagami *r.* Canada **84** 50.20N 84.20W
Kabinda Zaïre **54** 6.10S 24.29E
Kabīr Kūh *mts.* Iran **43** 33.00N 47.00E
Kabkābīyah Sudan **49** 13.39N 24.05E
Kabompo Zambia **54** 13.35S 24.10E
Kabompo *r.* Zambia **54** 14.17S 23.15E
Kabongo Zaïre **54** 7.22S 25.34E
Kabonzo Zaïre **55** 6.41S 27.49E
Kaboudia, Ra's *c.* Tunisia **51** 35.14N 11.10E
Kabūd Gonbad Iran **43** 37.02N 59.46E
Kābul Afghan. **40** 34.31N 69.12E
Kābul *d.* Afghan. **40** 34.45N 69.15E
Kabumbu Zaïre **54** 4.07S 26.17E
Kabunda Zaïre **55** 12.27S 29.15E
Kabundi Zaïre **55** 10.07S 27.13E
Kabwe Zambia **55** 14.27S 28.25E
Kāchā Kūh *mts.* Iran **43** 29.30N 61.20E
Kachin *d.* Burma **34** 26.00N 97.30E
Kachiry U.S.S.R. **28** 53.07N 76.08E
Kachisi Ethiopia **49** 9.39N 37.50E
Kadaney *r.* Afghan. **40** 31.20N 65.47E
Kade Ghana **52** 6.08N 0.51W
Kadei *r.* C.A.R. **53** 3.28N 16.05E
Kadi India **40** 23.18N 72.20E
Kadina Australia **66** 33.58S137.14E
Kadioli Mali **52** 10.38N 5.45W
Kadoka U.S.A. **82** 43.50N101.31W
Kadoma Zimbabwe **56** 18.23S 29.52E
Kaduna Nigeria **53** 10.28N 7.25E
Kaduna *d.* Nigeria **53** 11.00N 7.35E
Kaduna *r.* Nigeria **53** 8.45N 5.45E
Kāduqlī Sudan **49** 11.01N 29.43E
Kadusam *mtn.* China **39** 28.30N 96.45E
Kadzherom U.S.S.R. **24** 64.42N 55.59E
Kaédi Mauritania **50** 16.09N 13.30W
Kaélé Cameroon **53** 10.05N 14.28E
Kaesŏng N. Korea **31** 37.59N126.30E
Kafanchan Nigeria **53** 9.38N 8.20E
Kaffrine Senegal **52** 14.08N 15.34W
Kafia Kingi Sudan **49** 9.16N 24.25E
Kafirévs, Ákra *c.* Greece **19** 38.11N 24.30E
Kafo *r.* Uganda **55** 1.40N 32.07E
Kafr ad Dawwār Egypt **44** 31.08N 30.08E
Kafr al Baṭṭīkh Egypt **44** 31.24N 31.44E
Kafr ash Shaykh Egypt **44** 31.07N 30.56E
Kafr az Zayyāt Egypt **44** 30.50N 30.49E
Kafr Salīm Egypt **44** 31.09N 30.07E
Kafta Ethiopia **48** 13.56N 37.13E
Kafue Zambia **55** 15.40S 28.13E
Kafue *r.* Zambia **55** 15.53S 28.55E
Kafue Dam Zambia **55** 15.40S 27.10E
Kafue Nat. Park Zambia **54** 15.30S 25.35E
Kafunzo Uganda **55** 1.05S 30.26E
Kaga Bandoro C.A.R. **53** 7.00N 19.10E
Kāgān Pakistan **40** 34.47N 73.32E
Kagan U.S.S.R. **28** 39.45N 64.32E
Kagarlyk U.S.S.R. **21** 49.50N 30.50E
Kagaznagar India **41** 19.18N 79.50E
Kagera *d.* Tanzania **55** 2.00S 31.20E
Kağizman Turkey **42** 40.08N 43.07E
Kagoshima Japan **31** 31.37N130.32E
Kagul U.S.S.R. **19** 45.54N 28.11E
Kahama Tanzania **55** 3.48S 32.38E
Kahayan *r.* Indonesia **36** 3.20S114.04E
Kahemba Zaïre **54** 7.20S 19.00E
Kahntah *r.* Canada **74** 58.15N120.55W
Kahnūj Iran **43** 27.55N 57.45E
Kahoolawe *i.* Hawaiian Is. **69** 20.33N156.37W
Kahraman Maraş Turkey **42** 37.34N 36.54E
Kai, Kepulauan *is.* Indonesia **37** 5.45S132.55E
Kaiama Nigeria **53** 9.37N 4.03E
Kaiapoi New Zealand **60** 43.23S172.39E
Kaiedin Sudan **49** 9.45N 32.11E
Kaifeng China **32** 34.46N114.22E
Kaikohe New Zealand **60** 35.25S173.49E
Kaikoura New Zealand **60** 42.24S173.41E
Kaikoura Range *mts.* New Zealand **60** 42.00S173.40E
Kailahun Sierra Leone **52** 8.21N 10.21W
Kaili China **33** 26.35N107.55E
Kailu China **32** 43.35N121.12E
Kailua Hawaiian Is. **69** 21.24N157.44W
Kaimana Indonesia **37** 3.39S133.44E
Kaimanawa Mts. New Zealand **60** 39.10S176.15E
Kainantu P.N.G. **37** 6.16S145.50E
Kainji Resr. Nigeria **53** 10.00N 4.35E
Kaintragarh India **41** 20.47N 84.40E
Kaipara Harbour New Zealand **60** 36.30S174.00E
Kaiserslautern W. Germany **14** 49.27N 7.47E
Kaitaia New Zealand **60** 35.08S173.18E
Kaithal India **40** 29.48N 76.23E
Kaitum *r.* Sweden **22** 67.30N 21.05E
Kaiwi Channel Hawaiian Is. **69** 21.15N157.30W
Kaiyuan China **32** 42.45N123.50E
Kaizuka Japan **35** 34.27N135.21E
Kajaani Finland **22** 64.14N 27.41E
Kajabbi Australia **64** 20.02S140.02E
Kajiado Kenya **55** 1.50S 36.48E
Kajo Kaji Sudan **49** 3.53N 31.40E
Kajuru Nigeria **53** 10.19N 7.40E
Kākā Sudan **49** 10.36N 32.11E
Kakamas R.S.A. **56** 28.44S 20.35E
Kakamega Kenya **55** 0.21N 34.47E
Kakamigahara Japan **35** 35.28N136.48E
Kākdwīp India **41** 21.53N 88.11E
Kakegawa Japan **35** 34.46N138.01E
Kakenge Zaïre **54** 4.51S 21.55E
Kakhovskoye Vodokhranilishche *resr.* U.S.S.R. **25** 47.33N 34.40E
Kākī Iran **43** 28.19N 51.34E
Kākināda India **39** 16.59N 82.20E
Kakisa *r.* Canada **74** 61.03N117.10W
Kakisa L. Canada **74** 60.55N117.40W
Kakonko Tanzania **55** 3.19S 30.54E
Kakuma Kenya **55** 3.38N 34.48E
Kakuto Uganda **55** 0.54S 31.26E
Kala *r.* Finland **22** 64.17N 23.55E
Kālābāgh Pakistan **40** 32.58N 71.34E
Kalabahi Indonesia **37** 8.13S124.31E
Kalabáka Greece **19** 39.42N 21.43E
Kalabity Australia **66** 31.53S140.18E
Kalabo Zambia **54** 14.58S 22.33E
Kalach-na-Donu U.S.S.R. **25** 48.43N 43.31E
Kaladan *r.* Burma **34** 20.09N 92.55E
Kalahari Desert Botswana **56** 23.30S 22.00E
Kalahari Gemsbok Nat. Park R.S.A. **56** 25.45S 20.25E
Kalajoki Finland **22** 64.15N 23.57E
Kalakan U.S.S.R. **29** 55.10N116.45E
Kalámai Greece **19** 37.02N 22.05E
Kalamazoo U.S.A. **84** 42.17N 85.36W
Kalamb India **40** 18.56N 73.55E
Kalamera Tanzania **55** 2.07S 33.43E
Kalamurra, L. Australia **66** 28.00S138.00E
Kalannie Australia **63** 30.21S117.04E
Kalanshiyū, Sarīr *des.* Libya **51** 27.00N 21.30E
Kalarash U.S.S.R. **21** 47.18N 28.16E
Kalāt Pakistan **40** 29.02N 66.35E
Kalb, Ra's al *c.* S. Yemen **45** 14.02N 48.41E
Kalchās Pakistan **40** 29.21N 69.42E
Kalecik Turkey **42** 40.06N 33.22E
Kalehe Zaïre **55** 2.05S 28.53E
Kalemie Zaïre **55** 5.57S 29.10E
Kalgan *r.* Australia **63** 34.55S117.58E
Kalgoorlie Australia **63** 30.49S121.29E
Kaliakra, Nos *c.* Bulgaria **19** 43.23N 28.29E
Kalianda Indonesia **36** 5.50S105.45E
Kalima Zaïre **54** 2.35S 26.34E
Kalimantan *d.* Indonesia **36** 1.00S113.00E
Kalimantan *f.* Indonesia **36** 0.05N112.30E
Kalimantan Barat *d.* Indonesia **36** 0.30N110.00E
Kalimantan Selatan *d.* Indonesia **36** 2.30S115.30E
Kalimantan Tengah *d.* Indonesia **36** 2.00S113.30E
Kalimantan Timur *d.* Indonesia **36** 2.20N116.30E
Kálimnos *i.* Greece **19** 37.00N 27.00E
Kālimpong India **41** 27.04N 88.29E
Kalinin U.S.S.R. **24** 56.47N 35.57E
Kaliningrad U.S.S.R. **23** 54.43N 20.30E
Kalinkovichi U.S.S.R. **21** 52.10N 29.13E
Kalinovka U.S.S.R. **21** 49.29N 28.30E
Kalisat Indonesia **37** 8.02S113.50E
Kāli Sindh *r.* India **40** 25.32N 76.17E
Kalispell U.S.A. **80** 48.12N114.19W
Kalisz Poland **21** 51.46N 18.02E
Kaliua Tanzania **55** 5.08S 31.50E
Kalix *r.* Sweden **22** 65.50N 23.11E
Kalkar W. Germany **14** 51.45N 6.17E
Kalkfontein Botswana **56** 22.08S 20.54E
Kalkrand Namibia **56** 24.05S 17.34E
Kallista Australia **65** 42.57S146.10E
Kallsjön *l.* Sweden **22** 63.35N 13.00E
Kalmar Sweden **23** 56.40N 16.22E
Kalmar *d.* Sweden **23** 57.20N 16.00E
Kalmarsund *str.* Sweden **23** 56.40N 16.25E
Kalmthout Belgium **14** 51.23N 4.28E
Kalmykovo U.S.S.R. **25** 49.02N 51.55E
Kālna India **41** 23.13N 88.22E
Kalo P.N.G. **64** 10.05S147.45E
Kalocsa Hungary **21** 46.32N 18.59E
Kaloko Zaïre **54** 6.47S 25.47E
Kālol Gujarat India **40** 22.36N 73.27E
Kālol Gujarat India **40** 23.15N 72.29E
Kalole Zaïre **55** 3.40S 27.22E
Kalomo Zambia **54** 16.55S 26.29E
Kalonje Zambia **55** 12.21S 31.06E
Kālpi India **41** 26.07N 79.44E
Kāl Qal 'eh Afghan. **40** 32.38N 62.32E
Kalsö *i.* Faroe Is. **8** 62.19N 6.42W
Kalsūbai *mtn.* India **40** 19.36N 73.43E
Kaltag U.S.A. **72** 64.20N158.44W
Kaluga U.S.S.R. **24** 54.31N 36.16E
Kālu Khuhar Pakistan **40** 25.08N 67.46E
Kalumburu Australia **62** 14.14S126.38E
Kalundborg Denmark **23** 55.41N 11.06E
Kalush U.S.S.R. **21** 49.02N 24.20E
Kalutara Sri Lanka **39** 6.35N 79.58E
Kalyān India **40** 19.15N 73.09E
Kama *r.* U.S.S.R. **24** 55.30N 52.00E
Kamakura Japan **35** 35.19N139.33E
Kamālia Pakistan **40** 30.44N 72.39E
Kamanashi *r.* Japan **35** 35.33N138.28E
Kamanjab Namibia **56** 19.39S 14.50E
Kamarsuk Canada **77** 56.18N 61.38W
Kamba Nigeria **53** 11.52N 3.42E
Kamba Zaïre **54** 4.00S 22.22E
Kambalda Australia **63** 31.12S121.40E
Kambar Pakistan **40** 27.36N 68.00E
Kambarka U.S.S.R. **24** 56.18N 54.13E
Kambia Sierra Leone **52** 9.09N 12.53W
Kamchatka, Poluostrov *pen.* U.S.S.R. **29** 56.00N160.00E
Kamen *mtn.* U.S.S.R. **29** 68.40N 94.20E
Kamenets Podolskiy U.S.S.R. **21** 48.40N 26.36E
Kamenka R.S.F.S.R. U.S.S.R. **24** 53.10N 44.05E
Kamenka R.S.F.S.R. U.S.S.R. **24** 65.55N 44.02E
Kamenka Bugskaya U.S.S.R. **21** 50.07N 24.30E
Kamen Kashirskiy U.S.S.R. **21** 51.32N 24.59E
Kamen-na-Obi U.S.S.R. **28** 53.46N 81.18E
Kamenskoye U.S.S.R. **29** 62.31N165.15E
Kamensk-Shakhtinskiy U.S.S.R. **25** 48.20N 40.16E
Kamensk-Ural'skiy U.S.S.R. **28** 56.29N 61.49E
Kāmet *mtn.* India / China **41** 30.54N 79.37E
Kameyama Japan **35** 34.51N136.27E
Kamiah U.S.A. **80** 46.14N116.02W
Kamieskroon R.S.A. **56** 30.12S 17.53E
Kamilukuak L. Canada **75** 62.22N101.40W
Kamina Zaïre **54** 8.46S 24.58E
Kaminak L. Canada **75** 62.10N 95.00W
Kamloops Canada **74** 50.40N120.20W
Kamloops Plateau *f.* Canada **74** 50.00N120.20W
Kamo *r.* Japan **35** 35.00N139.52E
Kāmoke Pakistan **40** 31.58N 74.13E
Kamp W. Germany **14** 50.14N 7.37E
Kampa Indonesia **36** 1.46S105.26E
Kampala Uganda **55** 0.19N 32.35E
Kampar *r.* Indonesia **36** 0.20N102.55E
Kampen Neth. **14** 52.33N 5.55E
Kampene Zaïre **54** 3.36S 26.40E
Kamphaeng Phet Thailand **34** 16.28N 99.31E
Kamp-Lintfort W. Germany **14** 51.34N 6.38E
Kâmpóng Cham Kampuchea **34** 11.59N105.26E
Kâmpóng Chhnăng Kampuchea **34** 12.16N104.39E
Kâmpóng Saôm Kampuchea **36** 10.38N103.30E
Kâmpóng Thum Kampuchea **34** 12.42N104.52E
Kâmpôt Kampuchea **34** 10.37N104.11E
Kampti U. Volta **52** 10.07N 3.22W
Kampuchea Asia **34** 12.45N105.00E
Kamsack Canada **75** 51.34N101.54W
Kamskoye Vodokhranilishche *resr.* U.S.S.R. **24** 58.55N 56.20E
Kāmthi India **41** 21.14N 79.12E
Kamyshin U.S.S.R. **25** 50.05N 45.24E
Kana *r.* Zimbabwe **56** 18.30S 26.50E
Kanaaupscow *r.* Canada **76** 53.40N 77.10W
Kanafis Sudan **49** 9.48N 25.40E
Kanagawa *d.* Japan **35** 35.25N139.10E
Kanairiktok *r.* Canada **77** 55.05N 60.20W
Kananga Zaïre **54** 5.53S 22.26E
Kanash U.S.S.R. **24** 55.30N 47.27E
Kanaudi India **41** 23.36N 81.23E
Kanawha *r.* U.S.A. **84** 38.50N 82.08W
Kanazawa Japan **31** 36.35N136.38E
Kanchanaburi Thailand **34** 14.02N 99.28E
Kānchenjunga *mtn.* Nepal / India **41** 27.44N 88.11E
Kānchipuram India **39** 12.50N 79.44E
Kandāhu Pakistan **40** 27.33N 69.24E
Kandalaksha U.S.S.R. **24** 67.09N 32.31E
Kandalakshskaya Guba *g.* U.S.S.R. **24** 66.30N 34.00E
Kandangan Indonesia **36** 2.50S115.15E
Kandavu *i.* Fiji **68** 19.05S178.15E
Kandavu Passage Fiji **68** 18.45S178.00E
Kandhkot Pakistan **40** 28.14N 69.11E
Kandi Benin **53** 11.05N 2.59E
Kāndi India **41** 23.57N 88.02E
Kandiāro Pakistan **40** 27.04N 68.13E
Kandira Turkey **42** 41.05N 30.08E
Kandla India **40** 23.00N 70.10E
Kandos Australia **67** 32.53S149.59E
Kandrāch Pakistan **40** 25.29N 65.29E
Kandreho Madagascar **57** 17.29S 46.06E
Kandy Sri Lanka **39** 7.18N 80.43E
Kane U.S.A. **84** 41.40N 78.49W
Kanem *d.* Chad **53** 15.10N 15.30E
Kanevka U.S.S.R. **24** 67.08N 39.50E
Kang Botswana **56** 23.43S 22.51E
Kangaba Mali **52** 11.56N 8.25W
Kangān Iran **43** 27.50N 52.07E
Kangar Malaysia **36** 6.28N100.10E
Kangaroo I. Australia **66** 35.50S137.06E
Kangding China **30** 30.05N102.04E
Kangean, Kepulauan *is.* Indonesia **37** 7.00S115.30E
Kangerlussuaq *see* Söndreströmfjord Greenland **73**
Kangle China **32** 35.16N103.39E
Kangmar Xizang China **41** 28.30N 89.45E
Kangmar Xizang China **41** 30.45N 85.43E
Kango Gabon **54** 0.15N 10.14E
Kangping China **32** 42.45N123.20E
Kangrinboqê Feng *mtn.* China **41** 31.05N 81.21E
Kangto *mtn.* China **41** 27.54N 92.32E
Kanhar *r.* India **41** 24.28N 83.08E
Kani Ivory Coast **52** 8.34N 6.35W
Kaniama Zaïre **54** 7.32S 24.11E
Kanin, Poluostrov *pen.* U.S.S.R. **24** 68.00N 45.00E
Kaningo Kenya **55** 0.52S 38.31E
Kanin Nos, Mys *c.* U.S.S.R. **24** 68.38N 43.20E
Kaniva Australia **66** 36.33S141.17E
Kanjiža Yugo. **21** 46.04N 20.04E
Kankakee U.S.A. **82** 41.08N 87.52W
Kankan Gabon **54** 0.03S 12.14E
Kankan Guinea **52** 10.22N 9.11W
Kānker India **41** 20.17N 81.29E
Kankossa Mauritania **50** 15.58N 11.31W
Kannack Vietnam **34** 14.07N108.36E
Kannapolis U.S.A. **85** 35.30N 80.36W
Kannauj India **41** 27.04N 79.55E
Kannod India **40** 22.40N 76.44E
Kano *r.* Japan **35** 35.05N138.52E
Kano Nigeria **53** 12.00N 8.31E
Kano *d.* Nigeria **53** 12.00N 9.00E
Kanona Zambia **55** 13.03S 30.37E
Kanowna Australia **63** 30.36S121.36E
Kānpur India **41** 26.28N 80.21E
Kansas *d.* U.S.A. **82** 38.30N 99.00W
Kansas *r.* U.S.A. **82** 39.07N 94.36W
Kansas City Kans. U.S.A. **82** 39.07N 94.39W
Kansas City Mo. U.S.A. **82** 39.05N 94.35W
Kansenia Zaïre **54** 10.19S 26.02E
Kansk U.S.S.R. **29** 56.11N 95.20E
Kansŏng S. Korea **31** 38.20N128.28E
Kantābānji India **41** 20.29N 82.55E
Kantché Niger **53** 13.31N 8.30E
Kantemirovka U.S.S.R. **25** 49.40N 39.52E
Kantō *d.* Japan **35** 35.35N139.30E
Kantōheiya *f.* Japan **35** 36.02N140.10E
Kantō-sanchi *mts.* Japan **35** 36.00N138.35E
Kanye Botswana **56** 24.58S 25.17E
Kanyu Botswana **56** 20.05S 24.39E
Kao *i.* Tonga **69** 19.40S175.01W
Kaoko Veld *f.* Namibia **56** 18.30S 13.30E
Kaolack Senegal **52** 14.09N 16.08W
Kaoma Zambia **54** 14.55S 24.58E
Kapaa Hawaiian Is. **69** 22.05N159.19W
Kapadvanj India **40** 23.01N 73.04E
Kapanga Zaïre **54** 8.22S 22.37E
Kapchagay U.S.S.R. **30** 43.51N 77.14E
Kapenguria Kenya **55** 1.13N 35.07E
Kapfenberg Austria **20** 47.27N 15.18E
Kapiri Mposhi Zambia **55** 13.59S 28.40E
Kapiskau Canada **76** 52.20N 82.01W
Kapiskau *r.* Canada **76** 52.20N 83.40W
Kapit Malaysia **36** 2.01N112.56E
Kapiti I. New Zealand **60** 40.50S174.50E
Kapoeta Sudan **49** 4.47N 33.35E
Kapongolo Zaïre **55** 7.51S 28.12E
Kaposvár Hungary **19** 46.22N 17.47E
Kappar Pakistan **40** 25.19N 62.42E
Kapps Namibia **56** 22.22S 17.52E
Kapsabet Kenya **55** 0.12N 35.05E
Kapsukas U.S.S.R. **23** 54.33N 23.21E
Kaptai Bangla. **41** 22.21N 92.17E
Kapuas *r.* Indonesia **36** 0.13S109.12E
Kapunda Australia **66** 34.21S138.54E
Kapūrthala India **40** 31.23N 75.23E
Kapuskasing Canada **76** 49.25N 82.30W
Kaputar, Mt. Australia **67** 30.20S150.10E
Kapuvár Hungary **21** 47.36N 17.02E
Kara U.S.S.R. **28** 69.12N 65.00E
Kara-Bogaz Gol, Zaliv *b.* U.S.S.R. **43** 41.20N 53.40E
Karabük Turkey **42** 41.12N 32.36E
Karabutak U.S.S.R. **28** 49.55N 60.05E
Karāchi Pakistan **40** 24.52N 67.03E
Karād India **38** 17.17N 74.12E
Karaganda U.S.S.R. **28** 49.53N 73.07E
Karaginskiy, Ostrov *i.* U.S.S.R. **29** 59.00N165.00E
Karakas U.S.S.R. **30** 48.20N 83.30E
Karakelong *i.* Indonesia **37** 4.20N126.50E
Karakoram Pass Asia **39** 35.53N 77.51E
Karakoram Range *mts.* Jammu & Kashmir **38** 35.30N 76.30E

Kidete to Košice

Kidete Morogoro Tanzania 55 6.39S 36.42E
Kidsgrove U.K. 10 53.06N 2.15W
Kiel W. Germany 20 54.20N 10.08E
Kielce Poland 21 50.52N 20.37E
Kieler Bucht b. W. Germany 20 54.30N 10.30E
Kiev see Kiyev U.S.S.R. 21
Kiffa Mauritania 50 16.38N 11.28W
Kigali Rwanda 55 1.59S 30.05E
Kiglapatt, C. Canada 77 57.05N 61.05W
Kigoma Tanzania 55 4.52S 29.36E
Kigoma d. Tanzania 55 4.45S 30.00E
Kigosi r. Tanzania 55 4.37S 31.29E
Kiiminkin r. Finland 22 65.12N 25.18E
Kikinda Yugo. 21 45.51N 20.30E
Kikládhes is. Greece 19 37.00N 25.00E
Kikongo Zaïre 54 4.16S 17.11E
Kikori P.N.G. 37 7.25S144.13E
Kikori r. P.N.G. 37 7.10S144.05E
Kikwit Zaïre 54 5.02S 18.51E
Kil Sweden 23 59.30N 13.19E
Kilafors Sweden 23 61.14N 16.34E
Kila Kila P.N.G. 37 9.31S147.10E
Kilchu N. Korea 31 40.55N129.21E
Kilcoy Australia 65 26.57S152.33E
Kilcullen Rep. of Ire. 13 53.08N 6.46W
Kildare Rep. of Ire. 13 53.10N 6.55W
Kildare d. Rep. of Ire. 13 53.10N 6.50W
Kildonan Zimbabwe 56 17.22S 30.33E
Kilfinan U.K. 12 55.58N 5.18W
Kilgore U.S.A. 83 32.23N 94.53W
Kilifi Kenya 55 3.30S 39.50E
Kilimanjaro d. Tanzania 55 3.45S 37.40E
Kilimanjaro mtn. Tanzania 55 3.02S 37.20E
Kilindoni Tanzania 55 7.55S 39.39E
Kilingi-Nõmme U.S.S.R. 23 58.09N 24.58E
Kilis Turkey 42 36.43N 37.07E
Kiliya U.S.S.R. 21 45.30N 29.16E
Kilkee Rep. of Ire. 13 52.41N 9.40W
Kilkenny Rep. of Ire. 13 52.39N 7.16W
Kilkenny d. Rep. of Ire. 13 52.35N 7.15W
Kilkieran B. Rep. of Ire. 13 53.20N 9.42W
Kilkís Greece 19 40.59N 22.51E
Killala B. Rep. of Ire. 13 54.15N 9.10W
Killard Pt. U.K. 13 54.19N 5.31W
Killarney Australia 67 28.18S152.15E
Killarney Man. Canada 75 49.12N 99.42W
Killarney Rep. of Ire. 13 52.04N 9.32W
Killary Harbour est. Rep. of Ire. 13 53.38N 9.56W
Killdeer U.S.A. 80 47.22N102.45W
Killeen U.S.A. 83 31.08N 97.44W
Killin U.K. 12 56.29N 4.19W
Killíni mtn. Greece 19 37.56N 22.22E
Killorglin Rep. of Ire. 13 52.07N 9.45W
Killybegs Rep. of Ire. 13 54.38N 8.27W
Killyleagh U.K. 13 54.24N 5.39W
Kilmarnock U.K. 12 55.37N 4.30W
Kilmichael Pt. Rep. of Ire. 13 52.44N 6.09W
Kilmore Australia 67 37.18S144.58E
Kilninver U.K. 12 56.21N 5.30W
Kilombero r. Tanzania 55 8.30S 37.28E
Kilosa Tanzania 55 6.49S 37.00E
Kilronan Rep. of Ire. 13 53.08N 9.41W
Kilrush Rep. of Ire. 13 52.39N 9.30W
Kilsyth U.K. 12 55.59N 4.04W
Kilvo Sweden 22 66.50N 21.04E
Kilwa Kivinje Tanzania 55 8.45S 39.21E
Kilwa Masoko Tanzania 55 8.55S 39.31E
Kimaän Indonesia 37 7.54S138.51E
Kimba Australia 66 33.09S136.25E
Kimball U.S.A. 82 41.14N103.40W
Kimberley Canada 74 49.40N115.59W
Kimberley R.S.A. 56 28.44S 24.44E
Kimberley Plateau Australia 62 17.20S127.20E
Kimito i. Finland 23 60.10N 22.30E
Kimparana Mali 52 12.52N 4.59W
Kimry U.S.S.R. 24 56.51N 37.20E
Kimsquit Canada 74 52.45N126.57W
Kinabalu mtn. Malaysia 36 6.10N116.40E
Kincaid Canada 75 49.39N107.00W
Kincardine Canada 76 44.11N 81.38W
Kindersley Canada 75 51.27N109.10W
Kindia Guinea 52 10.03N 12.49W
Kindu Zaïre 54 3.00S 25.56E
Kinel U.S.S.R. 24 53.17N 50.42E
Kineshma U.S.S.R. 24 57.28N 42.08E
Kingaroy Australia 64 26.33S151.50E
King City U.S.A. 81 36.13N121.08W
Kingcome Inlet town Canada 74 50.58N125.15W
King George Is. Canada 76 57.20N 78.25W
King George Sd. Australia 63 35.03S117.57E
King I. Australia 65 39.50S144.00E
King I. Canada 74 52.10N127.40W
Kingisepp U.S.S.R. 23 58.12N 22.30E
King Leopold Ranges mts. Australia 62 17.00S125.30E
Kingman Ariz. U.S.A. 81 35.12N114.04W
Kingman Kans. U.S.A. 83 37.39N 98.07W
Kingman Reef Pacific Oc. 68 6.24N162.22W
Kingoonya Australia 66 30.54S135.18E
Kingri Pakistan 40 30.27N 69.49E
Kings r. U.S.A. 81 36.03N119.49W
Kingsbridge U.K. 11 50.17N 3.46W
Kings Canyon Nat. Park U.S.A. 80 36.48N118.30W
Kingsclere U.K. 11 51.20N 1.14W
Kingscote Australia 66 35.40S137.38E
King Sd. Australia 62 17.00S123.30E
Kingsdown Kent U.K. 11 51.21N 0.17E
Kingsley Dam U.S.A. 78 41.15N101.30W
King's Lynn U.K. 10 52.45N 0.25E
Kingsmill Group is. Kiribati 68 1.00S175.00E
Kings Peaks mts. U.S.A. 80 40.46N110.23W
Kingsport U.S.A. 85 36.33N 82.34W
Kingston Australia 66 36.50S139.50E
Kingston Canada 76 44.14N 76.30W
Kingston Jamaica 87 17.58N 76.48W
Kingston New Zealand 60 45.20S168.43E
Kingston N.Y. U.S.A. 77 41.56N 74.00W
Kingston W.Va. U.S.A. 85 37.58N 81.19W
Kingston upon Hull U.K. 10 53.45N 0.20W
Kingstown St. Vincent 87 13.12N 61.14W
Kingstree U.S.A. 85 33.40N 79.50W
Kingsville U.S.A. 83 27.31N 97.52W
Kingswood Avon U.K. 11 51.27N 2.29W
Kings Worthy U.K. 11 51.06N 1.18W
Kington U.K. 11 52.12N 3.02W
Kingurutik r. Canada 77 56.49N 62.00W
Kingussie U.K. 12 57.05N 4.04W
King William I. Canada 73 69.00N 97.30W
King William's Town R.S.A. 56 32.52S 27.23E
Kinloch Rannoch U.K. 12 56.42N 4.11W
Kinna Sweden 23 57.30N 12.41E
Kinnairds Head U.K. 12 57.42N 2.00W
Kinnegad Rep. of Ire. 13 53.28N 7.08W
Kino r. Japan 35 34.13N135.09E
Kinross U.K. 12 56.13N 3.27W
Kinsale Rep. of Ire. 13 51.42N 8.32W
Kinshasa Zaïre 54 4.18S 15.18E
Kinsley U.S.A. 83 37.55N 99.25W
Kintyre pen. U.K. 12 55.35N 5.35W
Kinuso Canada 74 55.25N115.25W
Kinvara Rep. of Ire. 13 53.08N 8.56W
Kinyeti mtn. Sudan 49 3.57N 32.54E
Kinzia Zaïre 54 3.36S 18.26E
Kiowa Kans. U.S.A. 83 37.01N 98.29W
Kiowa Okla. U.S.A. 83 34.43N 95.54W
Kiparissía Greece 19 37.15N 21.40E
Kipawa, Lac l. Canada 76 47.00N 79.00W
Kipengere Range mts. Tanzania 55 9.15S 34.15E
Kipili Tanzania 55 7.30S 30.39E
Kipini Kenya 55 2.31S 40.32E
Kippure mtn. Rep. of Ire. 13 53.11N 6.20W
Kipushi Zaïre 55 11.46S 27.15E
Kirby U.S.A. 80 43.49N108.10W
Kirbyville U.S.A. 83 30.40N 93.54W
Kircheimbolanden W. Germany 14 49.39N 8.00E
Kirensk U.S.S.R. 29 57.45N108.00E
Kirgiziya Step f. U.S.S.R. 25 50.00N 57.10E
Kirgizskaya S.S.R. d. U.S.S.R. 30 41.30N 75.00E
Kirgiz Steppe see Kirgiziya Step f. U.S.S.R. 25
Kiri Zaïre 54 1.23S 19.00E
Kiribati Pacific Oc. 68 2.00S175.00E
Kirikkale Turkey 42 39.51N 33.32E
Kirillov U.S.S.R. 24 59.53N 38.21E
Kirínia Cyprus 44 35.20N 33.20E
Kiritimati i. Kiribati 69 1.52N157.20W
Kirkby Lonsdale U.K. 10 54.13N 2.36W
Kirkby Stephen U.K. 10 54.27N 2.23W
Kirkcaldy U.K. 12 56.07N 3.10W
Kirkcudbright U.K. 12 54.50N 4.03W
Kirkenes Norway 22 69.40N 30.03E
Kirkland Ariz. U.S.A. 81 34.26N112.43W
Kirkland Wash. U.S.A. 80 47.41N122.12W
Kirkland Lake town Canada 76 48.15N 80.00W
Kirklareli Turkey 19 41.44N 27.12E
Kirkpatrick, Mt. Antarctica 96 85.00S170.00E
Kirksville U.S.A. 82 40.12N 92.35W
Kirkük Iraq 43 35.28N 44.26E
Kirkwall U.K. 12 58.59N 2.58W
Kirkwood R.S.A. 56 33.25S 25.24E
Kirkwood U.S.A. 82 38.35N 90.24W
Kirn W. Germany 14 49.47N 7.28E
Kirov R.S.F.S.R. U.S.S.R. 24 58.38N 49.38E
Kirov R.S.F.S.R. U.S.S.R. 24 53.59N 34.20E
Kirovabad U.S.S.R. 43 40.39N 46.20E
Kirovakan U.S.S.R. 43 40.49N 44.30E
Kirovo-Chepetsk U.S.S.R. 24 58.40N 50.02E
Kirovograd U.S.S.R. 25 48.31N 32.15E
Kirovsk U.S.S.R. 24 67.37N 33.39E
Kirovskiy U.S.S.R. 29 54.25N155.37E
Kirriemuir Canada 75 51.56N110.20W
Kirriemuir U.K. 12 56.41N 3.01W
Kirs U.S.S.R. 24 59.21N 52.10E
Kirsanov U.S.S.R. 25 51.29N 52.30E
Kirşehir Turkey 42 39.09N 34.08E
Kirthar Range mts. Pakistan 40 27.15N 67.00E
Kiruna Sweden 22 67.51N 20.16E
Kisa Sweden 23 57.59N 15.37E
Kisaga Tanzania 55 4.26S 34.26E
Kisangani Zaïre 54 0.33N 25.14E
Kisantu Zaïre 54 5.07S 15.05E
Kisaran Indonesia 36 2.47N 99.29E
Kisarazu Japan 35 35.23N139.55E
Kiselevsk U.S.S.R. 28 54.01N 86.41E
Kishanganj India 41 26.07N 87.56E
Kishangarh Rāj. India 40 27.52N 70.34E
Kishangarh Rāj. India 40 26.34N 74.52E
Kishinev U.S.S.R. 21 47.00N 28.50E
Kishiwada Japan 35 34.28N135.22E
Kishorganj Bangla. 41 24.26N 90.46E
Kishtwār Jammu & Kashmir 40 33.19N 75.46E
Kisii Kenya 55 0.40S 34.44E
Kisiju Tanzania 55 7.23S 39.20E
Kiskitto L. Canada 75 54.16N 98.34W
Kiskörös Hungary 21 46.38N 19.17E
Kiskunfélegyháza Hungary 21 46.43N 19.52E
Kiskunhalas Hungary 21 46.26N 19.30E
Kislovodsk U.S.S.R. 25 43.56N 42.44E
Kismayu Somali Rep. 55 0.25S 42.31E
Kiso Japan 35 35.02N136.45E
Kiso sammyaku mts. Japan 35 35.42N137.50E
Kissamos Greece 19 35.30N 23.38E
Kissidougou Guinea 52 9.48N 10.08W
Kissimmee U.S.A. 85 28.20N 81.24W
Kississing L. Canada 75 55.10N101.20W
Kissū, Jabal mtn. Sudan 48 21.35N 25.09E
Kistna r. see Krishna r. India 38
Kisumu Kenya 55 0.07S 34.47E
Kisvárda Hungary 21 48.13N 22.05E
Kita Mali 52 13.04N 9.29W
Kitab U.S.S.R. 28 39.08N 66.51E
Kitabu Zaïre 54 6.31S 26.40E
Kitakyūshū Japan 31 33.52N130.49E
Kitale Kenya 55 1.01N 35.01E
Kit Carson U.S.A. 82 38.46N102.48W
Kitchener Australia 63 31.01S124.20E
Kitchener Canada 76 43.27N 80.30W
Kitchigama r. Canada 76 51.12N 78.55W
Kitgum Uganda 55 3.17N 32.54E
Kíthira Greece 19 36.09N 23.00E
Kíthira i. Greece 19 36.15N 23.00E
Kíthnos i. Greece 19 37.25N 24.25E
Kitimat Canada 74 54.05N128.38W
Kitinen r. Finland 22 67.20N 27.27E
Kitsman U.S.S.R. 21 48.30N 25.50E
Kittakittaooloo, L. Australia 66 28.09S138.09E
Kittanning U.S.A. 84 40.49N 79.32W
Kittery U.S.A. 84 43.05N 70.45W
Kittilä Finland 22 67.40N 24.54E
Kitui Kenya 55 1.22S 38.01E
Kitunda Tanzania 55 6.48S 33.17E
Kitwe Zambia 55 12.50S 28.04E
Kiumbi Zaïre 54 5.31S 26.34E
Kiunga Kenya 55 1.46S 41.30E
Kivijärvi l. Finland 22 63.10N 25.09E
Kivik Sweden 23 55.41N 14.15E
Kivu d. Zaïre 55 3.00S 27.00E
Kivu, L. Rwanda/Zaïre 55 2.00S 29.10E
Kiyev U.S.S.R. 21 50.28N 30.29E
Kiyevskoye Vodokhranilishche resr. U.S.S.R. 21 51.00N 30.25E
Kizel U.S.S.R. 24 59.01N 57.42E
Kizema U.S.S.R. 24 61.12N 44.52E
Kizil r. Turkey 42 41.45N 35.57E
Kizlyar U.S.S.R. 25 43.51N 46.43E
Kizlyarskiy Zaliv b. U.S.S.R. 25 44.33N 47.00E
Kizu r. Japan 35 34.53N135.42E
Kizyl-Arvat U.S.S.R. 43 39.00N 56.23E
Kizyl Atrek Turkey 43 37.37N 54.49E
Kladno Czech. 20 50.10N 14.05E
Klagenfurt Austria 20 46.38N 14.20E
Klaipeda U.S.S.R. 23 55.43N 21.07E
Klakah Indonesia 37 7.55S113.12E
Klaksvig Faroe Is. 8 62.13N 6.34W
Klamath r. U.S.A. 80 41.33N124.04W
Klamath Falls town U.S.A. 80 42.14N121.47W
Klamath Mts. U.S.A. 80 41.40N123.20W
Klamono Indonesia 37 1.08S131.28E
Klar r. Sweden 23 59.23N 13.32E
Klatovy Czech. 20 49.24N 13.18E
Klawer R.S.A. 56 31.48S 18.34E
Klawock U.S.A. 74 55.33N133.06W
Kleena Kleene Canada 74 51.58N124.50W
Kleinsee R.S.A. 56 29.41S 17.04E
Klerksdorp R.S.A. 56 26.51S 26.38E
Klevan U.S.S.R. 21 50.44N 25.50E
Kleve W. Germany 14 51.47N 6.11E
Klickitat U.S.A. 80 45.49N121.09W
Klimovichi U.S.S.R. 21 53.36N 31.58E
Klimpfjäll Sweden 22 65.04N 14.52E
Klin U.S.S.R. 24 56.20N 36.45E
Klinaklini r. Canada 74 51.21N125.40W
Klintehamn Sweden 23 57.24N 18.12E
Klintsy U.S.S.R. 21 52.45N 32.15E
Klipdale R.S.A. 56 34.18S 19.58E
Klippan Sweden 23 56.08N 13.06E
Klipplaat R.S.A. 56 33.01S 24.19E
Kłobuck Poland 21 50.55N 18.57E
Kłodzko Poland 20 50.27N 16.39E
Klöfta Norway 23 60.04N 11.09E
Klondike Canada 72 64.02N139.24W
Kluane Nat. Park Canada 74 60.32N139.40W
Kluczbork Poland 21 50.59N 18.13E
Klukwan U.S.A. 74 59.25N135.55W
Klungkung Indonesia 37 8.32S115.25E
Knaresborough U.K. 10 54.01N 1.29W
Knight Inlet f. Canada 74 50.45N125.40W
Knighton U.K. 11 52.21N 3.02W
Knin Yugo. 20 44.02N 16.10E
Knockadoon Head Rep. of Ire. 13 51.52N 7.52W
Knockalongy mtn. Rep. of Ire. 13 54.12N 8.45W
Knockmealdown Mts. Rep. of Ire. 13 52.15N 7.55W
Knokke Belgium 14 51.21N 3.17E
Knolls U.S.A. 80 40.44N113.18W
Knossos site Greece 19 35.20N 25.10E
Knox, C. Canada 74 54.11N133.04W
Knox City U.S.A. 83 33.25N 99.49W
Knoxville U.S.A. 85 36.00N 83.57W
Knutsford U.K. 10 53.18N 2.22W
Knyazhevo U.S.S.R. 24 59.40N 43.51E
Knysna R.S.A. 56 34.02S 23.03E
Koartac Canada 73 61.05N 69.36W
Kobar Sink f. Ethiopia 48 14.00N 40.30E
Kōbe Japan 35 34.41N135.10E
København Denmark 23 55.43N 12.34E
Koblenz W. Germany 14 50.21N 7.36E
Kobowen Swamp Sudan 49 5.38N 33.54E
Kobrin U.S.S.R. 21 52.16N 24.22E
Kobroör i. Indonesia 37 6.10S134.30E
Kočani Yugo. 19 41.55N 22.24E
Kočevje Yugo. 18 45.38N 14.52E
Kochkoma U.S.S.R. 24 64.03N 34.14E
Kochmes U.S.S.R. 24 66.12N 60.48E
Kodaira Japan 35 35.44N139.29E
Kodari Nepal 41 27.56N 85.56E
Kodarma India 41 24.28N 85.36E
Kodiak U.S.A. 72 57.49N152.30W
Kodiak I. U.S.A. 72 57.00N153.50W
Kodima U.S.S.R. 24 62.24N 43.57E
Kodinār India 40 20.47N 70.42E
Kodok Sudan 49 9.53N 32.07E
Kodyma U.S.S.R. 21 48.06N 29.04E
Koekelare Belgium 14 51.08N 2.59E
Koekenaap R.S.A. 56 31.30S 18.18E
Koersel Belgium 14 51.04N 5.19E
Koës Namibia 56 25.58S 19.07E
Koffiefontein R.S.A. 56 29.24S 25.00E
Köflach Austria 20 47.04N 15.05E
Koforidua Ghana 52 6.01N 0.12W
Kōfu Japan 35 35.39N138.35E
Koga Tanzania 55 6.10S 32.21E
Kogaluk r. Canada 77 56.12N 61.45W
Køge Denmark 23 55.27N 12.11E
Køge Bugt b. Greenland 73 65.00N 40.30W
Kohak Pakistan 40 25.44N 62.33E
Kohāt Pakistan 40 33.35N 71.26E
Kohima India 39 25.40N 94.08E
Kohler Range mts. Antarctica 96 77.00S110.00W
Kohtla-Järve U.S.S.R. 24 59.28N 27.20E
Koidu Sierra Leone 52 8.41N 10.55W
Koito r. Japan 35 35.21N139.52E
Kojonup Australia 63 33.50S117.05E
Kokand U.S.S.R. 30 40.33N 70.55E
Kokas Indonesia 37 2.45S132.26E
Kokchetav U.S.S.R. 28 53.18N 69.25E
Kokemäki Finland 23 61.15N 22.21E
Kokka Sudan 48 20.00N 30.35E
Kokkola Finland 22 63.50N 23.07E
Koko Sokoto Nigeria 53 11.27N 4.35E
Kokoda P.N.G. 64 8.50S147.45E
Kokomo U.S.A. 84 40.30N 86.09W
Kokonau Indonesia 37 4.42S136.25E
Kokpekty U.S.S.R. 30 48.45N 82.25E
Koksoak r. Canada 73 58.30N 68.15W
Kokstad R.S.A. 56 30.32S 29.25E
Kokuora U.S.S.R. 29 71.33N144.50E
Kolāchi r. Pakistan 40 26.25N 67.50E
Kolahun Liberia 52 8.24N 10.02W
Kolaka Indonesia 37 4.04S121.38E
Kolan Australia 64 24.42S152.10E
Kola Pen. see Kolskiy Poluostrov pen. U.S.S.R. 24
Kolār India 39 13.10N 78.10E
Kolāras India 41 25.14N 77.36E
Kolari Finland 22 67.20N 23.48E
Kolāyat India 40 27.50N 72.57E
Kolbio Kenya 55 1.11S 41.10E
Kolda Senegal 52 12.56N 14.55W
Kolding Denmark 23 55.31N 9.29E
Kole H.Zaïre Zaïre 54 2.07N 25.26E
Kole K.Oriental Zaïre 54 3.28S 22.29E
Kolepom i. see Yos Sudarsa, Pulau i. Indonesia 37
Kolguyev, Ostrov i. U.S.S.R. 24 69.00N 49.00E
Kolhāpur India 38 16.43N 74.15E
Kolia Ivory Coast 52 9.46N 6.28W
Kolín Czech. 20 50.02N 15.10E
Kolka U.S.S.R. 23 57.45N 22.35E
Kolki U.S.S.R. 21 51.09N 25.40E
Köln W. Germany 14 50.56N 6.57E
Kolno Poland 21 53.25N 21.56E
Koło Poland 21 52.12N 18.37E
Kołobrzeg Poland 20 54.10N 15.35E
Kologriv U.S.S.R. 24 58.49N 44.19E
Kolokani Mali 52 13.35N 7.45W
Kololo Ethiopia 49 7.29N 41.58E
Kolomna U.S.S.R. 24 55.05N 38.45E
Kolomyya U.S.S.R. 21 48.31N 25.00E
Kolondiéba Mali 52 11.05N 6.54W
Kolosib India 41 24.14N 92.42E
Kolpashevo U.S.S.R. 28 58.21N 82.59E
Kolpino U.S.S.R. 24 59.44N 30.39E
Kolskiy Poluostrov pen. U.S.S.R. 24 67.00N 38.00E
Kolsva Sweden 23 59.36N 15.50E
Koluszki Poland 21 51.44N 19.49E
Kolvereid Norway 22 64.53N 11.35E
Kolwezi Zaïre 54 10.44S 25.28E
Kolyma r. U.S.S.R. 29 68.50N161.00E
Kolymskiy, Khrebet mts U.S.S.R. 29 63.00N160.00E
Kom r. Cameroon 54 2.20N 10.38E
Kom Kenya 55 1.06N 38.00E
Komadugu Gana r. Nigeria 53 13.06N 12.23E
Komadugu Yobe r. Niger/Nigeria 53 13.43N 13.19E
Komagane Japan 35 35.43N137.55E
Komaga-take mtn. Japan 35 35.47N137.48E
Komaki Japan 35 35.17N136.55E
Komandorskiye Ostrova is. U.S.S.R. 68 55.00N167.00E
Komárno Czech. 21 47.45N 18.09E
Komarom Hungary 21 47.44N 18.08E
Komatipoort R.S.A. 57 25.25S 31.55E
Komba Zaïre 54 2.52N 24.03E
Komló Hungary 21 46.12N 18.16E
Kommunarsk U.S.S.R. 25 48.30N 38.47E
Kommunizma, Pik mtn. U.S.S.R. 30 38.39N 72.01E
Komotiní Greece 19 41.07N 25.26E
Komrat U.S.S.R. 21 46.18N 28.40E
Komsberg mtn. R.S.A. 56 32.40S 20.48E
Komsomolets, Ostrov i. U.S.S.R. 29 80.20N 96.00E
Komsomolets, Zaliv g. U.S.S.R. 25 45.17N 53.30E
Komsomolsk-na-Amure U.S.S.R. 29 50.32N136.59E
Kōnan Japan 35 35.20N136.53E
Konar r. Afghan. 40 34.26N 70.32E
Konārak India 41 19.54N 86.07E
Konar-e Khās Afghan. 40 34.39N 70.54E
Konch India 41 25.59N 79.09E
Kondagaon India 41 19.36N 81.40E
Kondakovo U.S.S.R. 29 69.38N152.00E
Kondinin Australia 63 32.33S118.13E
Kondoa Tanzania 55 4.54S 35.49E
Kondopoga U.S.S.R. 24 62.12N 34.17E
Kondratyevo U.S.S.R. 29 57.22N 98.15E
Kondut Australia 63 30.44S117.06E
Koné N. Cal. 68 21.04S164.52E
Kong Ivory Coast 52 8.54N 4.36W
Kông r. Kampuchea 34 13.32N105.57E
Kong Christian den IX Land f. Greenland 73 68.20N 37.00W
Kong Frederik den VI Kyst f. Greenland 73 63.00N 44.00W
Kong Haakon VII Hav sea Antarctica 96 65.00S 25.00E
Kongolo Zaïre 55 5.20S 27.00E
Kongor Sudan 49 7.10N 31.21E
Kongsberg Norway 23 59.39N 9.39E
Kongsvinger Norway 23 60.12N 12.00E
Kongur Shan mtn. China 30 38.40N 75.30E
Kongwa Tanzania 55 6.13S 36.28E
Konin Poland 21 52.13N 18.16E
Konjic Yugo. 21 43.39N 17.57E
Könkämä r. Sweden/Finland 22 68.29N 22.30E
Konkouré r. Guinea 52 9.55N 13.45W
Konongo Ghana 52 6.38N 1.12W
Konosha U.S.S.R. 24 60.58N 40.08E
Kōnosu Japan 35 36.03N139.31E
Konotop U.S.S.R. 25 51.15N 33.14E
Końskie Poland 21 51.12N 20.26E
Konstanz W. Germany 20 47.40N 9.10E
Kontagora Nigeria 53 10.24N 5.22E
Kontcha Cameroon 53 7.59N 12.15E
Kontiomäki Finland 24 64.21N 28.10E
Kontum Vietnam 34 14.23N108.00E
Kontum, Plateau du f. Vietnam 34 14.00N108.00E
Konya Turkey 42 37.51N 32.30E
Konz W. Germany 14 49.42N 6.34E
Konza Kenya 55 1.45S 37.07E
Kookynie Australia 63 29.20S121.29E
Koolatah Australia 64 15.53S142.27E
Koolkootinnie L. Australia 66 27.58S137.47E
Koolyanobbing Australia 63 30.48S119.29E
Koondrook Australia 66 35.39S144.11E
Koongawa Australia 66 33.11S135.52E
Koonibba Australia 66 31.58S133.29E
Koorawatha Australia 67 34.02S148.33E
Koorda Australia 63 30.50S117.51E
Kootenay L. Canada 74 49.45N117.00W
Kootenay Nat. Park Canada 74 51.00N116.00W
Kootjieskolk R.S.A. 56 31.14S 20.18E
Kopāganj India 41 26.01N 83.34E
Kopargaon India 40 19.53N 74.29E
Kópavogur Iceland 22 64.06N 21.53W
Koper Yugo. 20 45.33N 13.44E
Kopervik Norway 23 59.17N 5.18E
Kopet Dag, Khrebet mts. U.S.S.R. 43 38.00N 58.00E
Köping Sweden 23 59.31N 16.00E
Kopparberg d. Sweden 23 60.50N 15.00E
Koppom Sweden 23 59.43N 12.09E
Koprivnica Yugo. 20 46.10N 16.50E
Kopychintsy U.S.S.R. 21 49.10N 25.58E
Kor r. Iran 43 29.40N 53.17E
Koraput India 41 18.49N 82.43E
Koratla India 41 18.49N 78.43E
Korba India 41 22.21N 82.41E
Korbach W. Germany 20 51.16N 8.53E
Korçë Albania 19 40.37N 20.45E
Korčula i. Yugo. 19 42.56N 16.53E
Kord Kūy Iran 43 36.48N 54.07E
Korea Str. S. Korea/Japan 31 35.00N129.20E
Korem Ethiopia 49 12.30N 39.30E
Korets U.S.S.R. 21 50.39N 27.10E
Korhogo Ivory Coast 52 9.22N 5.31W
Korim Indonesia 37 0.58S136.10E
Korinthiakós Kólpos g. Greece 19 38.15N 22.30E
Kórinthos Greece 19 37.56N 22.55E
Kōriyama Japan 31 37.23N140.22E
Korma U.S.S.R. 21 53.08N 30.47E
Körmend Hungary 20 47.01N 16.37E
Kornat i. Yugo. 18 43.48N 15.20E
Korneshty U.S.S.R. 21 47.21N 28.00E
Kornsjö Norway 23 58.57N 11.39E
Koro i. Fiji 68 17.22S179.25E
Koro Ivory Coast 52 8.36N 7.28W
Koro Mali 52 14.01N 2.58W
Korocha U.S.S.R. 25 50.50N 37.13E
Korogwe Tanzania 55 5.10S 38.35E
Koroit Australia 66 38.17S142.26E
Korong Vale town Australia 66 36.22S143.45E
Koror i. Belau 37 7.30N134.30E
Koro Sea Fiji 68 18.00S179.00E
Korosten U.S.S.R. 21 51.00N 28.30E
Korostyshev U.S.S.R. 21 50.19N 29.03E
Koro Toro Chad 53 16.05N 18.30E
Korrat i. Yugo. 20 43.48N 15.20E
Korsör Denmark 23 55.20N 11.09E
Korsze Poland 21 54.10N 21.09E
Kortrijk Belgium 14 50.49N 3.17E
Koryakskiy Khrebet mts. U.S.S.R. 29 62.20N171.00E
Koryazhma U.S.S.R. 24 61.19N 47.12E
Kos i. Greece 19 36.48N 27.10E
Kosa Ethiopia 49 7.51N 36.51E
Kościan Poland 20 52.06N 16.38E
Kościerzyna Poland 21 54.08N 18.00E
Kosciusko U.S.A. 83 32.58N 89.35W
Kosciusko, Mt. Australia 67 36.28S148.17E
Kosha Sudan 48 20.49N 30.32E
Koshk-e Kohneh Afghan 43 34.52N 62.29E
Košice Czech. 21 48.44N 21.15E

Koski to Lakewood

Koski Finland **23** 60.39N 23.09E
Koslan U.S.S.R. **24** 63.29N 48.59E
Kosovska-Mitrovica Yugo. **19** 42.54N 20.51E
Kossanto Senegal **52** 13.12N 11.56W
Kossovo U.S.S.R. **21** 52.40N 25.18E
Kosta Sweden **23** 56.51N 15.23E
Koster R.S.A. **56** 25.51S 26.52E
Kostopol U.S.S.R. **21** 50.51N 26.22E
Kostroma U.S.S.R. **24** 57.46N 40.59E
Kostrzyn Poland **20** 52.24N 17.11E
Kostyukovichi U.S.S.R. **21** 53.20N 32.01E
Kosyu U.S.S.R. **24** 65.36N 59.00E
Koszalin Poland **20** 54.12N 16.09E
Kota Madhya P. India **41** 22.18N 82.02E
Kota Rāj. India **40** 25.11N 75.50E
Kota Baharu Malaysia **36** 6.07N102.15E
Kota Belud Malaysia **36** 6.00N116.00E
Kotabumi Indonesia **36** 4.52S104.59E
Kot Addu Pakistan **40** 30.28N 70.58E
Kota Kinabalu Malaysia **36** 5.59N116.04E
Kotelnich U.S.S.R. **24** 58.20N 48.10E
Kotelnikovo U.S.S.R. **25** 47.39N 43.08E
Kotel'nyy, Ostrov *i.* U.S.S.R. **29** 75.30N141.00E
Kotka Finland **24** 60.26N 26.55E
Kot Kapūra India **40** 30.35N 74.49E
Kotlas U.S.S.R. **24** 61.15N 46.28E
Kotli Jammu & Kashmir **40** 33.31N 73.55E
Kotlik U.S.A. **72** 63.02N163.33W
Kotor Yugo. **19** 42.28N 18.47E
Kotovsk M.S.S.R. U.S.S.R. **21** 46.50N 28.31E
Kotovsk Ukr.S.S.R. U.S.S.R. **21** 47.42N 29.30E
Kot Pūtli India **40** 27.43N 76.12E
Kotra India **40** 24.22N 73.10E
Kotri Pakistan **40** 25.22N 68.18E
Kotri Allāhrakhio Pakistan **40** 24.24N 67.50E
Kottagūdem India **39** 17.32N 80.39E
Kotto *r.* C.A.R. **49** 4.14N 22.02E
Kotuy *r.* U.S.S.R. **29** 71.40N103.00E
Kotzebue U.S.A. **72** 66.51N162.40W
Kotzebue Sd. U.S.A. **72** 66.20N163.00W
Kouango C.A.R. **49** 4.58N 20.00E
Koudougou U. Volta **52** 12.15N 2.21W
Kouibli Ivory Coast **52** 7.09N 7.16W
Kouki C.A.R. **53** 7.09N 17.13E
Koúklia Cyprus **44** 34.42N 32.34E
Koula Moutou Gabon **54** 1.12S 12.29E
Koulikoro Mali **52** 12.55N 7.31W
Koumac N. Cal. **68** 20.33S164.17E
Koumankou Mali **52** 11.58N 6.06W
Koumbal C.A.R. **49** 9.26N 22.39E
Koumbia Guinea **52** 11.54N 13.40W
Koumbia U. Volta **52** 11.18N 3.38W
Koumbisaleh *site* Mauritania **50** 15.55N 8.05W
Koumongou Togo **52** 10.10N 0.29E
Koumra Chad **53** 8.56N 17.32E
Koupéla U. Volta **52** 12.09N 0.22W
Kouroussa Guinea **52** 10.40N 9.50W
Kousseri Chad **53** 12.05N 14.56E
Koutiala Mali **52** 12.20N 5.23W
Kouto Ivory Coast **52** 9.53N 6.25W
Kouvola Finland **24** 60.54N 26.45E
Kouyou *r.* Congo **54** 0.40S 16.37E
Kovdor U.S.S.R. **24** 67.33N 30.30E
Kovel U.S.S.R. **21** 51.12N 24.48E
Kovpyta U.S.S.R. **21** 51.22N 30.51E
Kovrov U.S.S.R. **24** 56.23N 41.21E
Kovzha *r.* U.S.S.R. **24** 61.05N 36.27E
Kowloon Hong Kong **33** 22.19N114.12E
Kowt-e 'Ashrow Afghan. **40** 34.27N 68.48E
Koyukuk *r.* U.S.A. **72** 64.50N157.30W
Kozan Turkey **42** 37.27N 35.47E
Kozáni Greece **19** 40.18N 21.48E
Kozelets U.S.S.R. **21** 50.54N 31.09E
Kozhim U.S.S.R. **24** 65.45N 59.30E
Kozhposelok U.S.S.R. **24** 63.10N 38.10E
Kpandu Ghana **52** 7.02N 0.17E
Kpessi Togo **53** 8.07N 1.17E
Krabi Thailand **34** 8.08N 98.52E
Krâchéh Kampuchea **34** 12.30N106.00E
Kragan Indonesia **37** 6.40S111.33E
Kragerö Norway **23** 58.52N 9.25E
Kragujevac Yugo. **19** 44.01N 20.55E
Kraków Poland **21** 50.03N 19.55E
Kraljevo Yugo. **19** 43.44N 20.41E
Kramatorsk U.S.S.R. **25** 48.43N 37.33E
Kramer U.S.A. **82** 48.20N100.42W
Kramfors Sweden **22** 62.55N 17.50E
Kranj Yugo. **20** 46.15N 14.21E
Kranskop R.S.A. **56** 28.58S 30.52E
Krapkowice Poland **21** 50.29N 17.56E
Krasavino U.S.S.R. **24** 60.58N 46.25E
Krasilov U.S.S.R. **21** 49.39N 26.59E
Kraskino U.S.S.R. **31** 42.42N130.48E
Krasnaya Gora U.S.S.R. **21** 53.00N 31.36E
Kraśnik Poland **21** 50.56N 22.13E
Krasnodar U.S.S.R. **25** 45.02N 39.00E
Krasnograd U.S.S.R. **25** 49.22N 35.28E
Krasnokamsk U.S.S.R. **24** 58.05N 55.49E
Krasnoperekopsk U.S.S.R. **25** 45.56N 33.47E
Krasnoselkup U.S.S.R. **28** 65.45N 82.31E
Krasnoturinsk U.S.S.R. **24** 59.46N 60.10E
Krasnoufimsk U.S.S.R. **24** 56.40N 57.49E
Krasnouralsk U.S.S.R. **28** 58.25N 60.00E
Krasnovishersk U.S.S.R. **24** 60.25N 57.02E
Krasnovodsk U.S.S.R. **43** 40.01N 53.00E
Krasnovodskiy Poluostrov *pen.* U.S.S.R. **43** 40.30N 53.10E
Krasnovodskiy Zaliv *g.* U.S.S.R. **43** 39.50N 53.15E
Krasnoyarsk U.S.S.R. **29** 56.05N 92.46E
Krasnyy Yar U.S.S.R. **25** 46.32N 48.21E
Kratovo Yugo. **19** 42.05N 22.11E
Krawang Indonesia **37** 6.15S107.15E
Krefeld W. Germany **14** 51.20N 6.32E
Kremenchug U.S.S.R. **25** 49.03N 33.25E
Kremenchugskoye Vodokhranilishche *resr.* U.S.S.R. **25** 49.20N 32.30E
Kremenets U.S.S.R. **21** 50.05N 25.48E
Kremmling U.S.A. **80** 40.03N106.24W
Krems Austria **20** 48.25N 15.36E
Krestovka U.S.S.R. **24** 66.24N 52.31E
Kretinga U.S.S.R. **23** 55.53N 21.13E
Kribi Cameroon **53** 2.56N 9.56E
Krichev U.S.S.R. **21** 53.40N 31.44E
Krishna *r.* India **39** 16.00N 81.00E
Krishnanagar India **41** 23.24N 88.30E
Kristiansand Norway **23** 58.10N 8.00E
Kristianstad Sweden **23** 56.02N 14.08E
Kristianstad *d.* Sweden **23** 56.15N 13.35E
Kristiansund Norway **22** 63.07N 7.45E
Kristiinankaupunki Finland **23** 62.17N 21.23E
Kristinehamn Sweden **23** 59.20N 14.07E
Kristinestad *see* Kristiinankaupunki Finland **23**
Kristinovka U.S.S.R. **21** 48.50N 29.58E
Kríti *i.* Greece **19** 35.15N 25.00E
Kritikón Pélagos *sea* Greece **19** 36.00N 25.00E
Krivaja *r.* Yugo. **21** 44.27N 18.09E
Krivoy Rog U.S.S.R. **25** 47.55N 33.24E
Krk *i.* Yugo. **20** 45.04N 14.36E
Krnov Czech. **21** 50.05N 17.41E
Kroken Norway **22** 65.23N 14.15E
Krokom Sweden **22** 63.20N 14.30E
Krông Kaôh Kông Kampuchea **34** 11.37N102.59E
Kronoberg *d.* Sweden **23** 56.45N 14.15E
Kronprins Olav Kyst *f.* Antarctica **96** 69.00S 42.00E
Kronshtadt U.S.S.R. **24** 60.00N 29.40E
Kroonstad R.S.A. **56** 27.38S 27.12E
Kropotkin U.S.S.R. **25** 45.25N 40.35E
Krosno Poland **21** 49.42N 21.46E
Krotoszyn Poland **21** 51.42N 17.26E
Kroya Indonesia **37** 7.37S109.13E
Kruger Nat. Park R.S.A. **57** 24.10S 31.36E
Krugersdorp R.S.A. **56** 26.06S 27.46E
Krujë Albania **19** 41.30N 19.48E
Krumbach W. Germany **20** 48.14N 10.22E
Krung Thep Thailand **34** 13.44N100.30E
Krupki U.S.S.R. **21** 54.19N 29.05E
Kruševac Yugo. **21** 43.34N 21.20E
Krym *pen.* U.S.S.R. **25** 45.30N 34.00E
Krymsk U.S.S.R. **25** 44.56N 38.00E
Krzyz Poland **20** 52.54N 16.01E
Ksar el Boukhari Algeria **51** 35.53N 2.45E
Ksar-el-Kebir Morocco **50** 35.01N 5.54W
Ksar Rhilane Tunisia **51** 33.00N 9.38E
Ksel, Djebel *mtn.* Algeria **51** 33.44N 1.10E
Kuala Dungun Malaysia **36** 4.47N103.26E
Kualakapuas Indonesia **36** 3.01S114.21E
Kuala Lipis Malaysia **36** 4.11N102.00E
Kuala Lumpur Malaysia **36** 3.08N101.42E
Kuala Trengganu Malaysia **36** 5.10N103.10E
Kuancheng China **32** 40.36N118.27E
Kuandang Indonesia **37** 0.53N122.58E
Kuandian China **32** 40.47N124.43E
Kuantan Malaysia **36** 3.50N103.19E
Kuba U.S.S.R. **43** 41.23N 48.33E
Kuban *r.* U.S.S.R. **25** 45.20N 37.17E
Kubbum Sudan **49** 11.47N 23.47E
Kuchaiburi India **41** 22.16N 86.10E
Kuchāman India **40** 27.09N 74.52E
Kuching Malaysia **36** 1.32N110.20E
Kūchnay Darvīshān Afghan. **40** 30.59N 64.11E
Kūd Jammu & Kashmir **40** 33.05N 75.17E
Kudat Malaysia **36** 6.45N116.47E
Kudus Indonesia **37** 6.46S110.48E
Kufstein Austria **20** 47.36N 12.11E
Kūhpāyeh Iran **43** 32.42N 52.25E
Kūhrān, Kūh-e *mtn.* Iran **43** 26.46N 58.15E
Kuito Angola **54** 12.25S 16.58E
Kuiu I. U.S.A. **74** 56.40N134.00W
Kuivaniemi Finland **22** 65.35N 25.11E
Kuke Botswana **56** 23.19S 24.29E
Kukerin Australia **63** 33.11S118.03E
Kukës Albania **19** 42.05N 20.24E
Kukshi India **40** 22.12N 74.45E
Kūl *r.* Iran **43** 28.00N 55.45E
Kula Turkey **42** 38.33N 28.38E
Kulāchi Pakistan **40** 31.56N 70.27E
Kulakshi U.S.S.R. **25** 47.09N 55.22E
Kulal, Mt. Kenya **55** 2.44N 36.56E
Kulaura Bangla. **41** 24.30N 92.03E
Kuldīga U.S.S.R. **23** 56.58N 21.59E
Kulgera Australia **64** 25.50S133.18E
Kulin Australia **63** 32.40S118.10E
Kulja Australia **63** 30.28S117.17E
Kulkyne *r.* Australia **67** 30.16S144.12E
Kulpara Australia **66** 34.07S137.59E
Kulsary U.S.S.R. **25** 46.59N 54.02E
Kulu India **40** 31.58N 77.07E
Kulu Turkey **25** 39.06N 33.02E
Kulunda U.S.S.R. **28** 52.34N 78.58E
Kulwin Australia **66** 35.02S142.40E
Kulyab U.S.S.R. **30** 37.55N 69.47E
Kuma *r.* U.S.S.R. **25** 44.40N 46.55E
Kumagaya Japan **35** 36.08N139.23E
Kumai Indonesia **36** 2.45S111.44E
Kumamoto Japan **31** 32.50N130.42E
Kumanovo Yugo. **19** 42.08N 21.40E
Kumara New Zealand **60** 42.38S171.11E
Kumarl Australia **63** 32.47S121.33E
Kumasi Ghana **52** 6.45N 1.35W
Kumba Cameroon **53** 4.39N 9.26E
Kumbakonam India **39** 10.59N 79.24E
Kum Dag U.S.S.R. **43** 39.14N 54.33E
Kumdah Saudi Arabia **45** 20.23N 45.05E
Kumertau U.S.S.R. **24** 52.48N 55.46E
Kumi Uganda **55** 1.26N 33.54E
Kumla Sweden **23** 59.08N 15.08E
Kumon Range *mts.* Burma **34** 26.30N 97.15E
Kunashir *i.* U.S.S.R. **31** 44.25N146.00E
Kunchha Nepal **41** 28.08N 84.22E
Kundam India **41** 23.13N 80.21E
Kundelungu Mts. Zaïre **55** 9.30S 27.50E
Kundiān Pakistan **40** 32.27N 71.28E
Kundip Australia **63** 33.44S120.11E
Kundla India **40** 21.20N 71.18E
Kungälv Sweden **23** 57.52N 11.58E
Kungsbacka Sweden **23** 57.29N 12.04E
Kungu Zaïre **54** 2.47N 19.12E
Kungur U.S.S.R. **24** 57.27N 56.50E
Kuningan Indonesia **37** 7.02S108.30E
Kunkuri India **41** 22.45N 83.57E
Kunlong Burma **34** 23.25N 98.39E
Kunlun Shan *mts.* China **30** 36.40N 88.00E
Kunming China **30** 25.04N102.41E
Kunö *i.* Faroe Is. **8** 62.20N 6.39W
Kunsan S. Korea **31** 35.57N126.42E
Kunshan China **33** 31.24N121.08E
Kuntair Gambia **52** 13.36N 16.20W
Kununoppin Australia **63** 31.09S117.53E
Kununurra Australia **61** 15.42S128.50E
Kuolayarvi U.S.S.R. **22** 66.58N 29.12E
Kuopio Finland **24** 62.51N 27.30E
Kupa *r.* Yugo. **20** 45.30N 16.20E
Kupang Indonesia **37** 10.13S123.38E
Kupreanof I. U.S.A. **74** 56.50N133.30W
Kupyansk U.S.S.R. **25** 49.41N 37.37E
Kuqa China **30** 41.43N 82.58E
Kura *r.* U.S.S.R. **43** 39.18N 49.22E
Kuraymah Sudan **48** 18.33N 31.51E
Kurchum U.S.S.R. **30** 48.35N 83.39E
Kurdistan *f.* Asia **43** 37.00N 43.30E
Kurdufān *d.* Sudan **49** 13.00N 29.00E
Kŭrdzhali Bulgaria **19** 41.38N 25.21E
Kurgaldzhino U.S.S.R. **28** 50.35N 70.03E
Kurgan U.S.S.R. **28** 55.20N 65.20E
Kurīgrām Bangla. **41** 25.49N 89.39E
Kurikka Finland **22** 62.37N 22.25E
Kuril Ridge Pacific Oc. **68** 46.10N152.30E
Kurilskiye Ostrova *is.* U.S.S.R. **31** 46.00N150.30E
Kuril Trench Pacific Oc. **68** 46.00N155.00E
Kuring Kuru Namibia **56** 17.36S 18.36E
Kurlovski U.S.S.R. **24** 55.26N 40.40E
Kurmuk Sudan **49** 10.33N 34.17E
Kurnalpi Australia **63** 30.35S121.50E
Kurnool India **39** 15.51N 78.01E
Kurow New Zealand **60** 44.44S170.28E
Kurram Pakistan **40** 30.06N 66.31E
Kurri Kurri Australia **67** 32.49S151.29E
Kurseong India **41** 26.53N 88.17E
Kursk U.S.S.R. **25** 51.45N 36.14E
Kurškiy Zaliv *b.* U.S.S.R. **23** 55.00N 21.00E
Kuršumlija Yugo. **19** 43.09N 21.16E
Kūrtī Sudan **48** 18.07N 31.33E
Kuru Finland **23** 61.52N 23.44E
Kuru Sudan **49** 7.43N 26.31E
Kuruman R.S.A. **56** 27.28S 23.25E
Kuruman *r.* R.S.A. **56** 26.53S 20.38E
Kurur, Jabal *mtn.* Sudan **48** 20.31N 31.32E
Kusatsu Japan **35** 35.02N135.57E
Kusel W. Germany **14** 49.32N 7.21E
Kushālgarh India **40** 23.10N 74.27E
Kushchevskaya U.S.S.R. **25** 46.34N 39.39E
Kushida *r.* Japan **35** 34.36N136.34E
Kushiro Japan **31** 42.58N144.24E
Kushka U.S.S.R. **43** 35.14N 62.15E
Kushtia Bangla. **41** 23.55N 89.07E
Kusiyāra *r.* Bangla. **41** 24.36N 91.44E
Kuskokwim B. U.S.A. **72** 59.45N162.25W
Kuskokwim Mts. U.S.A. **72** 62.50N156.00W
Kusma Nepal **41** 28.13N 83.41E
Kustanay U.S.S.R. **28** 53.15N 63.40E
Küstenkanal W. Germany **14** 53.05N 7.46E
Kūstī Sudan **49** 13.10N 32.40E
Kütahya Turkey **42** 39.25N 29.56E
Kutaisi U.S.S.R. **25** 42.15N 42.44E
Kutch, G. of India **40** 22.40N 69.30E
Kutiyāna India **40** 21.38N 69.59E
Kutná Hora Czech. **20** 49.57N 15.16E
Kutno Poland **21** 52.15N 19.23E
Kutu Zaïre **54** 2.42S 18.09E
Kutubdia I. Bangla. **41** 21.50N 91.52E
Kutum Sudan **48** 14.12N 24.40E
Kutztown U.S.A. **85** 40.31N 75.47W
Kuusamo Finland **24** 65.57N 29.15E
Kuwait Asia **43** 29.20N 47.40E
Kuwait *town see* Al Kuwayt Kuwait **43**
Kuwana Japan **35** 35.04N136.42E
Kuybyshev U.S.S.R. **24** 53.10N 50.15E
Kuybyshevskoye Vodokhranilishche *resr.* U.S.S.R. **24** 55.00N 49.00E
Kuyeda U.S.S.R. **24** 56.25N 55.33E
Kuzey Anadolu Dağlari *mts.* Turkey **42** 40.32N 38.00E
Kuznetsk U.S.S.R. **24** 53.08N 46.36E
Kuzomen U.S.S.R. **24** 66.15N 36.51E
Kuzreka U.S.S.R. **24** 66.35N 34.48E
Kvaenangen *est.* Norway **22** 69.50N 21.30E
Kwale Kenya **55** 4.20S 39.25E
Kwamouth Zaïre **54** 3.11S 16.16E
Kwangju S. Korea **31** 35.07N126.52E
Kwango *r.* Zaïre **54** 3.20S 17.23E
Kwara *d.* Nigeria **53** 8.20N 5.35E
Kwatisore Indonesia **37** 3.18S134.50E
Kwekwe Zimbabwe **56** 18.59S 29.46E
Kwenge *r.* Zaïre **54** 4.53S 18.47E
Kwethluk U.S.A. **72** 60.49N161.27W
Kwidzyn Poland **21** 53.45N 18.56E
Kwigillingok U.S.A. **72** 59.51N163.08W
Kwiguk U.S.A. **72** 62.45N164.28W
Kwilu *r.* Zaïre **54** 3.18S 17.22E
Kwinana Australia **63** 32.15S115.48E
Kwobrup Australia **63** 33.36S117.55E
Kwoka *mtn.* Indonesia **37** 1.30S132.30E
Kyabé Chad **53** 9.28N 18.54E
Kyaiklat Burma **34** 16.25N 95.42E
Kyaikto Burma **34** 17.16N 97.01E
Kyaka Tanzania **55** 1.16S 31.27E
Kyakhta U.S.S.R. **30** 50.22N106.30E
Kyalite Australia **66** 34.57S143.31E
Kyancutta Australia **66** 33.08S135.34E
Kyaukpadaung Burma **34** 20.50N 95.08E
Kyaukpyu Burma **34** 19.20N 93.33E
Kybybolite Australia **66** 36.54S140.58E
Kychema U.S.S.R. **24** 65.32N 42.42E
Kyle of Lochalsh *town* U.K. **12** 57.17N 5.43W
Kyll *r.* W. Germany **14** 49.48N 6.42E
Kyllburg W. Germany **14** 50.03N 6.36E
Kyluchevskaya *mtn.* U.S.S.R. **29** 56.00N160.30E
Kynuna Australia **64** 21.35S141.55E
Kyoga, L. Uganda **55** 1.30N 33.00E
Kyogle Australia **67** 28.36S152.59E
Kyong Burma **34** 20.49N 96.40E
Kyonpyaw Burma **34** 17.18N 95.12E
Kyotera Uganda **55** 0.40S 31.31E
Kyōto Japan **35** 35.00N135.45E
Kyōto *d.* Japan **35** 34.55N135.35E
Kyrön *r.* Finland **22** 63.14N 21.45E
Kyrta U.S.S.R. **24** 64.02N 57.40E
Kyūshū *i.* Japan **31** 32.50N130.50E
Kyushu Palau Ridge Pacific Oc. **68** 15.00N135.00E
Kyustendil Bulgaria **19** 42.18N 22.39E
Kywong Australia **67** 35.01S146.45E
Kyyjärvi Finland **22** 63.02N 24.34E
Kyzyl U.S.S.R. **30** 51.42N 94.28E
Kyzyl Kum, Peski *f.* U.S.S.R. **28** 42.00N 64.30E
Kzyl Orda U.S.S.R. **28** 44.52N 65.28E

L

La Asunción Venezuela **90** 11.06N 63.53W
La Baleine *r.* Canada **73** 58.00N 57.50W
La Banda Argentina **92** 27.44S 64.15W
La Bañeza Spain **16** 42.17N 5.55W
Labao Indonesia **37** 8.12S122.49E
La Barca Mexico **86** 20.20N102.33W
La Barge U.S.A. **80** 42.16N110.12W
La Bassée France **14** 50.32N 2.49E
La Baule France **17** 47.18N 2.23W
Labbezanga Mali **52** 14.57N 0.42E
Labé Guinea **52** 11.17N 12.11W
Labe *r.* Czech. *see* Elbe *r.* W. Germany **20**
La Belle U.S.A. **85** 26.43N 81.27W
Laberge, L. Canada **74** 61.11N135.12W
Labinsk U.S.S.R. **25** 44.39N 40.44E
La Blanquilla *i.* Venezuela **87** 11.53N 64.38W
Labouheyre France **17** 44.13N 0.55W
Laboulaye Argentina **93** 34.05S 63.25W
Labrador *f.* Canada **77** 53.00N 62.00W
Labrador Basin *f.* Atlantic Oc. **95** 55.00N 45.00W
Labrador City Canada **77** 52.57N 66.54W
Labrador Sea Canada / Greenland **73** 57.00N 53.00W
Lábrea Brazil **90** 7.16S 64.47W
Labrit France **17** 44.07N 0.33W
Labuan Indonesia **37** 6.25S105.49E
Labuan *i.* Malaysia **36** 5.20N115.15E
Labuha Indonesia **37** 0.37S127.29E
Labutta Burma **34** 16.09N 94.46E
Labyrinth, L. Australia **66** 30.43S135.07E
Lac *d.* Chad **53** 13.30N 14.35E
La Calera Chile **93** 32.47S 71.12W
La Capelle France **14** 49.59N 3.57E
La Carlota Argentina **93** 33.25S 63.18W
La Carolina Spain **16** 38.16N 3.36W
Lacaune France **17** 43.42N 2.41E
La Ceiba Honduras **87** 15.45N 86.45W
Lacepede B. Australia **66** 36.47S139.45E
Lac Giao Vietnam **34** 12.41N108.02E
Lacha, Ozero *l.* U.S.S.R. **24** 61.25N 39.00E
La Charité France **17** 47.11N 3.01E
La Chartre France **15** 47.44N 0.35E
La Chaux-de-Fonds Switz. **20** 47.07N 6.51E
Lach Dera *r.* Somali Rep. **55** 0.01S 42.45E
Lachhmangarh India **40** 27.49N 75.02E
Lachine Canada **77** 45.26N 73.40W
Lachlan *r.* Australia **66** 34.21S143.58E
Lachute Canada **77** 45.39N 74.20W
Lackan Resr. Rep. of Ire. **13** 53.09N 6.31W
Lackawanna U.S.A. **84** 42.49N 78.49W
Lac la Biche *town* Canada **75** 54.46N111.58W
Lac la Ronge Prov. Park Canada **75** 55.14N104.45W
La Cocha Argentina **92** 27.45S 65.35W
Lacombe Canada **74** 52.30N113.44W
La Concepción Venezuela **90** 10.25N 71.41W
La Concordia Mexico **86** 16.05N 92.38W
La Coruña Spain **16** 43.22N 8.24W
Lac Rémi *town* Canada **77** 46.01N 74.47W
La Crosse Kans. U.S.A. **82** 38.32N 99.18W
La Crosse Wisc. U.S.A. **82** 43.48N 91.15W
La Cruz Mexico **81** 27.50N105.11W
La Cruz Uruguay **93** 33.56S 56.15W
Ladākh Range *mts.* Jammu & Kashmir **41** 34.15N 78.00E
La Demanda, Sierra de *mts.* Spain **16** 42.10N 3.20W
Ladismith R.S.A. **56** 33.29S 21.15E
Ladispoli Italy **18** 41.56N 12.05E
Lādīz Iran **43** 28.57N 61.18E
Lādnun India **40** 27.39N 74.23E
Ladoga *l. see* Ladozhskoye Ozero *l.* U.S.S.R. **24**
La Dorada Colombia **90** 5.27N 74.40W
Ladozhskoye Ozero *l.* U.S.S.R. **24** 61.00N 32.00E
La Dura Mexico **81** 28.22N109.33W
Ladushkin U.S.S.R. **21** 54.30N 20.05E
Ladva Vetka U.S.S.R. **24** 61.16N 34.23E
Ladybrand R.S.A. **56** 29.11S 27.26E
Ladysmith Canada **74** 49.58N123.49W
Ladysmith R.S.A. **56** 28.32S 29.47E
Ladysmith U.S.A. **82** 45.27N 91.07W
Lae P.N.G. **37** 6.45S146.30E
Lae Thailand **34** 19.25N101.00E
Laesö *i.* Denmark **23** 57.16N 11.01E
La Estrada Spain **16** 42.40N 8.30W
La Fayette Ga. U.S.A. **85** 34.42N 85.18W
Lafayette Ind. U.S.A. **84** 40.25N 86.54W
Lafayette La. U.S.A. **83** 30.14N 92.01W
La Fère France **15** 49.40N 3.22E
La Ferté-Bernard France **15** 48.11N 0.40E
La Ferté-Gaucher France **15** 48.47N 3.18E
La Ferté-Macé France **15** 48.36N 0.22W
La Ferté-St. Aubin France **15** 47.43N 1.56E
Lafia Nigeria **53** 8.35N 8.34E
Lafiagi Nigeria **53** 8.50N 5.23E
La Flèche France **15** 47.42N 0.05W
Lafollette U.S.A. **85** 36.23N 84.09W
Laforest Canada **76** 47.04N 81.12W
La Fregeneda Spain **16** 40.58N 6.54W
La Fuente de San Esteban Spain **16** 40.48N 6.15W
Lagan *r.* U.K. **13** 54.37N 5.44W
Lågen *r.* Akershus Norway **23** 60.10N 11.28E
Lågen *r.* Vestfold Norway **23** 59.03N 10.05E
Laghouat Algeria **51** 33.49N 2.55E
Lago Dilolo *town* Angola **54** 11.27S 22.03E
Lagos Mexico **86** 21.21N101.55W
Lagos Nigeria **53** 6.27N 3.28E
Lagos *d.* Nigeria **53** 6.32N 3.30E
Lagos Portugal **16** 37.05N 8.40W
La Goulette Tunisia **51** 36.49N 10.18E
La Grande *r.* Canada **76** 53.50N 79.00W
La Grande U.S.A. **80** 45.20N118.05W
La Grange Australia **62** 18.46S121.49E
La Grange U.S.A. **85** 33.02N 85.02W
La Guaira Venezuela **90** 10.38N 66.55W
La Guerche-de-Bretagne France **15** 47.56N 1.14W
Laguna Brazil **92** 28.29S 48.47W
Laguna Dam U.S.A. **81** 32.55N114.25W
Lagunas Chile **92** 20.59S 69.37W
Lagunas Peru **90** 5.10S 73.35W
Lagunillas Venezuela **90** 10.07N 71.16W
La Habana Cuba **87** 23.07N 82.25W
Lahad Datu Malaysia **36** 5.05N118.20E
La Harpe U.S.A. **82** 40.35N 90.57W
Lahat Indonesia **36** 3.46S103.32E
La Haye-du-Puits France **15** 49.18N 1.33W
Lahij S. Yemen **45** 13.04N 44.53E
Lāhījān Iran **43** 37.12N 50.00E
Lahn *r.* W. Germany **14** 50.18N 7.36E
Lahnstein W. Germany **14** 50.17N 7.38E
Laholm Sweden **23** 56.31N 13.02E
Lahore Pakistan **40** 31.35N 74.18E
Lahri Pakistan **40** 29.11N 68.13E
Lahti Finland **23** 60.58N 25.40E
Laï Chad **53** 9.22N 16.14E
Laiagam P.N.G. **37** 5.31S143.39E
Laibin China **33** 23.42N109.16E
Lai Chau Vietnam **34** 22.04N103.12E
L'Aigle France **15** 48.45N 0.38E
Laignes France **15** 47.50N 4.22E
Laihia Finland **22** 62.58N 22.01E
Laingsburg R.S.A. **56** 33.11S 20.49E
Lainio *r.* Sweden **22** 67.28N 22.50E
Lairg U.K. **12** 58.01N 4.25W
Laisamis Kenya **55** 1.38N 37.47E
Laissac France **17** 44.23N 2.49E
Laitila Finland **23** 60.53N 21.41E
Laiyuan China **32** 39.19N114.41E
Laizhou Wan *b.* China **32** 37.30N119.30E
Lajes Brazil **94** 27.48S 50.20W
La Junta U.S.A. **80** 37.59N103.33W
Lakaband Pakistan **40** 31.00N 69.30E
Lak Bor *r.* Kenya **49** 1.18N 40.40E
Lak Bor *r.* Somali Rep. **55** 0.32N 42.05E
Lake Biddy *town* Australia **63** 33.01S118.51E
Lake Brown *town* Australia **63** 30.57S118.19E
Lake Cargelligo *town* Australia **67** 33.19S146.23E
Lake Charles *town* U.S.A. **83** 30.13N 93.12W
Lake City U.S.A. **85** 30.12N 82.39W
Lake District *f.* U.K. **10** 54.30N 3.10W
Lake George *town* Colo. U.S.A. **80** 38.58N105.23W
Lake Grace *town* Australia **63** 33.06S118.28E
Lake Harbour *town* Canada **73** 62.50N 69.50W
Lake Hart *town* Australia **66** 31.16S136.21E
Lake King *town* Australia **63** 33.05S119.40E
Lakeland *town* U.S.A. **85** 28.02N 81.59W
Lake Mead Nat. Recreation Area U.S.A. **81** 36.00N114.30W
Lake Nash *town* Australia **64** 21.00S137.55E
Lakepa Niue **68** 19.01S169.49W
Lake Placid *town* U.S.A. **84** 44.17N 73.59W
Lake River *town* Canada **76** 54.30N 82.30W
Lakes Entrance *town* Australia **67** 37.53S147.59E
Lakeshore U.S.A. **80** 37.15N119.12W
Lakeside Utah U.S.A. **80** 41.13N112.54W
Lake Stewart *town* Australia **66** 29.22S140.12E
Lake Superior Prov. Park Canada **76** 47.30N 84.50W
Lake Varley *town* Australia **63** 32.46S119.27E
Lakeview U.S.A. **80** 42.11N120.21W
Lake Village U.S.A. **83** 33.20N 91.17W
Lakewood N.J. U.S.A. **85** 40.06N 74.12W
Lakewood N.Mex. U.S.A. **81** 32.39N104.39W

Lakewood to **Liao He**

Lakewood Ohio U.S.A. **84** 41.29N 81.50W
Lākheri India **40** 25.40N 76.10E
Lakhīmpur India **41** 27.57N 80.46E
Lakhnādon India **41** 22.36N 79.36E
Lakhpat India **40** 23.49N 68.47E
Lakonikós Kólpos *g.* Greece **19** 36.35N 22.42E
Lakota Ivory Coast **52** 5.50N 5.30W
Lakota U.S.A. **82** 48.02N 98.21W
Laksefjorden *est.* Norway **22** 70.58N 27.00E
Lakselv Norway **22** 70.03N 24.55E
Lakshadweep Is. Indian Oc. **38** 11.00N 72.00E
Lala India **41** 24.25N 92.40E
Lāla Mūsa Pakistan **40** 32.42N 73.58E
Lalaua Mozambique **55** 14.20S 38.30E
Lālehzār, Kūh-e *mtn.* Iran **43** 29.26N 56.48E
Lālganj India **41** 25.52N 85.11E
Lalībela Ethiopia **49** 12.02N 39.02E
La Libertad El Salvador **87** 13.28N 89.20W
Lalín Spain **16** 42.40N 8.05W
La Línea Spain **16** 36.10N 5.21W
Lalitpur India **41** 24.41N 78.25E
Lalitpur Nepal **41** 27.41N 85.20E
Lālmanir Hāt Bangla. **41** 25.54N 89.27E
La Loche Canada **75** 56.29N109.27W
La Loche, Lac *l.* Canada **75** 56.25N109.30W
La Loupe France **15** 48.28N 1.01E
La Louvière Belgium **14** 50.29N 4.11E
Lālpur India **40** 22.12N 69.58E
Lālsot India **40** 26.34N 76.20E
Lamar U.S.A. **82** 38.05N102.37W
Lambaréné Gabon **54** 0.40S 10.15E
Lambasa Fiji **68** 16.25S179.24E
Lambayeque Peru **90** 6.36S 79.50W
Lambay I. Rep. of Ire. **13** 53.29N 6.01W
Lambert's Bay *town* R.S.A. **56** 32.06S 18.16E
Lamé Chad **53** 9.14N 14.33E
Lame Nigeria **53** 10.27N 9.12E
Lamego Portugal **16** 41.05N 7.49W
Lameroo Australia **66** 35.20S140.33E
La Mesa Calif. U.S.A. **81** 32.46N117.01W
Lamesa Tex. U.S.A. **83** 32.44N101.57W
Lamía Greece **19** 38.53N 22.25E
Lammermuir Hills U.K. **12** 55.51N 2.40W
Lammhult Sweden **23** 57.09N 14.35E
Lamongan Indonesia **37** 7.05S112.26E
Lamont U.S.A. **80** 42.12N107.28W
Lamotrek *i.* Caroline Is. **37** 7.28N146.23E
Lamotte-Beuvron France **15** 47.37N 2.01E
La Moure U.S.A. **82** 46.21N 98.18W
Lampa Peru **90** 15.10S 70.30W
Lampasas U.S.A. **83** 31.04N 98.12W
Lampazos Mexico **83** 27.00N100.30W
Lampedusa *i.* Italy **18** 35.30N 12.35E
Lampeter U.K. **11** 52.06N 4.06W
Lampione *i.* Italy **18** 35.33N 12.18E
Lamu Kenya **55** 2.20S 40.54E
La Mure France **17** 44.54N 5.47E
Lanai *i.* Hawaiian Is. **69** 20.50N156.55W
Lanai City Hawaiian Is. **69** 20.50N156.55W
La Nao, Cabo de Spain **16** 38.42N 0.15E
Lanark U.K. **12** 55.41N 3.47W
Lancang Jiang *r.* China *see* Mekong *r.* Asia **34**
Lancashire *d.* U.K. **10** 53.53N 2.30W
Lancaster U.K. **10** 54.03N 2.48W
Lancaster N.Y. U.S.A. **76** 42.54N 78.40W
Lancaster Canada **77** 45.08N 74.30W
Lancaster Calif. U.S.A. **81** 34.42N118.08W
Lancaster Ohio U.S.A. **84** 39.43N 82.37W
Lancaster Penn. U.S.A. **85** 40.02N 76.19W
Lancaster S.C. U.S.A. **85** 34.43N 80.47W
Lancaster Tex. U.S.A. **83** 32.36N 96.46W
Lancaster Sd. Canada **73** 74.00N 85.00W
Lancelin Australia **63** 31.01S115.19E
Lanchow *see* Lanzhou China **32**
Lancun China **32** 36.24N120.10E
Landau Bayern W. Germany **20** 48.40N 12.43E
Landay Afghan. **40** 30.31N 63.47E
Landeck Austria **20** 47.09N 10.35E
Landen Belgium **14** 50.46N 5.04E
Lander *r.* Australia **64** 20.25S132.00E
Lander U.S.A. **80** 42.50N108.44W
Landerneau France **17** 48.27N 4.16W
Landisville U.S.A. **85** 39.31N 74.55W
Landor Australia **62** 25.06S116.50E
Landrecies France **14** 50.08N 3.40E
Land's End *c.* U.K. **11** 50.03N 5.45W
Landshut W. Germany **20** 48.31N 12.10E
Landskrona Sweden **23** 55.52N 12.50E
Lanett U.S.A. **85** 32.52N 85.12W
Langå Denmark **23** 56.23N 9.55E
La'nga Co *l.* China **41** 30.45N 81.15E
Langadhás Greece **19** 40.45N 23.04E
Langanes *c.* Iceland **22** 66.30N 14.30W
Langao China **32** 32.22N109.04E
Langdon U.S.A. **82** 48.46N 98.22W
Langeais France **15** 47.20N 0.24E
Langeland *i.* Denmark **23** 55.00N 10.50E
Längelmävesi *l.* Finland **23** 61.32N 24.22E
Langeoog *i.* W. Germany **14** 53.46N 7.30E
Langesund Norway **23** 59.00N 9.45E
Langholm U.K. **12** 55.09N 3.00W
Langjökull *ice cap* Iceland **22** 63.43N 20.03W
Langkawi *i.* Malaysia **36** 6.20N 99.30E
Langlade Canada **76** 48.14N 76.00W
Langon France **17** 44.33N 0.14W
Langöy *i.* Norway **22** 68.45N 15.00E
Langres France **17** 47.53N 5.20E
Langsa Indonesia **36** 4.28N 97.59E
Langshan China **32** 41.02N107.27E
Lang Shan *mts.* China **32** 41.30N107.10E
Lang Son Vietnam **33** 21.49N106.45E
Langtry U.S.A. **83** 29.48N101.34W
Languedoc-Roussillon *d.* France **17** 43.50N 3.30E
Langxi China **33** 31.08N119.10E
Lannion France **17** 48.44N 3.27W
Lanoraie Canada **77** 45.58N 73.13W
Lansdale U.S.A. **85** 40.15N 75.17W
Lansdowne India **41** 29.50N 78.41E
L'Anse au Loup Canada **77** 51.34N 56.48W
Lansing U.S.A. **84** 42.44N 84.34W
Lanslebourg France **15** 45.17N 6.52E
Lantewa Nigeria **53** 12.15N 11.45E
Lanxi China **33** 29.17N119.31E
Lanzarote *i.* Canary Is. **50** 29.00N 13.40W
Lanzhou China **32** 36.01N103.46E
Lanzo Torinese Italy **15** 45.16N 7.28E
Laoag Phil. **37** 18.14N120.36E
Lào Cai Vietnam **34** 22.30N104.00E
Laochang China **33** 25.12N104.35E
Laoha He *r.* China **32** 43.30N120.42E
Laois *d.* Rep. of Ire. **13** 53.00N 7.20W
Laojun Shan *mtn.* China **32** 33.45N111.38E
Laon France **15** 49.34N 3.37E
Laona U.S.A. **76** 45.35N 88.40W
La Orotava Canary Is. **95** 28.26N 16.30W
La Oroya Peru **90** 11.36S 75.54W
Laos Asia **34** 18.30N104.00E
Lapage, L. Australia **63** 30.40S121.50E
La Palma *i.* Canary Is. **50** 28.50N 18.00W
La Palma Spain **16** 37.23N 6.33W
La Pampa *d.* Argentina **93** 37.00S 66.00W
La Paragua Venezuela **90** 6.53N 63.22W
La Paz Entre Ríos Argentina **93** 30.45S 59.38W
La Paz Mendoza Argentina **93** 33.28S 67.34W
La Paz Bolivia **92** 16.30S 68.09W
La Paz *d.* Bolivia **92** 16.00S 68.10W
La Paz Mexico **81** 24.10N110.18W
La Paz, Bahía de *b.* Mexico **81** 24.15N110.30W
La Pedrera Colombia **90** 1.18S 69.43W
Lapeer U.S.A. **84** 43.03N 83.09W
La Peña, Sierra de *mts.* Spain **16** 42.30N 0.50W
La Perouse Str. U.S.S.R. **29** 45.50N142.30E
La Pine U.S.A. **80** 43.40N121.30W
Lapinjärvi Finland **23** 60.38N 26.13E
Lapland *f.* Sweden/Finland **22** 68.10N 24.10E
La Plata Argentina **93** 34.55S 57.57W
La Plata Md. U.S.A. **85** 38.32N 76.59W
La Plata Mo. U.S.A. **82** 40.02N 92.29W
La Plata, Río de *est.* Argentina/Uruguay **93** 35.15S 56.45W
Lapointe, Lac *l.* Canada **77** 53.32N 68.56W
Lappajärvi *l.* Finland **22** 63.08N 23.40E
Lappeenranta Finland **24** 61.04N 28.05E
Lappi *d.* Finland **22** 67.20N 26.00E
Laptevykh, More *sea* U.S.S.R. **29** 74.30N125.00E
Lapua Finland **22** 62.57N 23.00E
La Push U.S.A. **80** 47.55N124.38W
La Quiaca Argentina **92** 22.05S 65.36W
L'Aquila Italy **18** 42.22N 13.25E
Lār Iran **43** 27.37N 54.16E
Larache Morocco **50** 35.12N 6.10W
Laramie U.S.A. **80** 41.19N105.35W
Laramie Mts. U.S.A. **80** 42.00N105.40W
Lärbro Sweden **23** 57.47N 18.47E
Larche, Col de France/Italy **15** 44.25N 6.53E
Laredo U.S.A. **83** 27.31N 99.30W
Laredo Sd. Canada **74** 52.30N128.53W
Largeau Chad **53** 17.55N 19.07E
Largs U.K. **12** 55.48N 4.52W
Lariang Indonesia **36** 1.35S119.25E
La Rioja Argentina **92** 29.25S 66.50W
La Rioja *d.* Argentina **92** 29.00S 66.00W
Lárisa Greece **19** 39.36N 22.24E
Lark *r.* U.K. **11** 52.26N 0.20E
Lārkāna Pakistan **40** 27.33N 68.13E
Larkspur U.S.A. **80** 39.13N104.54W
Larnaca *see* Lárnax Cyprus **44**
Lárnax Cyprus **44** 34.54N 33.39E
Larne U.K. **13** 54.51N 5.49W
La Robla Spain **16** 42.50N 5.41W
La Roche Belgium **14** 50.11N 5.35E
La Rochelle France **17** 46.10N 1.10W
La Roche-sur-Yon France **17** 46.40N 1.25W
La Roda Spain **16** 39.13N 2.10W
La Romana Dom. Rep. **87** 18.27N 68.57W
La Ronge Canada **75** 55.06N105.17W
La Ronge, Lac *l.* Canada **75** 55.07N105.15W
Laroquebrou France **17** 44.58N 2.11E
Larrimah Australia **64** 15.35S133.12E
Larvik Norway **23** 59.04N 10.00E
La Sagra *mtn.* Spain **16** 37.58N 2.35W
La Salle U.S.A. **82** 41.20N 89.06W
Las Animas U.S.A. **80** 38.04N103.13W
Las Anod Somali Rep. **45** 8.26N 47.24E
La Sarre Canada **76** 48.45N 79.15W
Las Casitás, Cerro *mtn.* Mexico **81** 23.32N109.59W
Las Cruces U.S.A. **81** 32.23N106.29W
Las Cuevas Mexico **83** 29.38N101.19W
Las Dawa'o Somali Rep. **45** 10.22N 49.03E
Las Dureh Somali Rep. **45** 10.10N 46.01E
La Seine, Baie de France **17** 49.40N 0.30W
La Serena Chile **92** 29.54S 71.16W
La Seyne France **17** 43.06N 5.53E
Las Flores Argentina **93** 36.02S 59.07W
Lāsh-e Joveyn Afghan. **40** 31.43N 61.37E
Las Heras Argentina **93** 32.50S 68.50W
Lashio Burma **34** 22.58N 96.51E
Lashkar Gāh Afghan. **40** 31.30N 64.21E
Las Khoreh Somali Rep. **45** 11.10N 48.16E
Las Lomitas Argentina **92** 24.43S 60.35W
Las Marismas *f.* Spain **16** 37.00N 6.15W
L'Asomption *r.* Canada **77** 45.43N 73.29W
Las Palmas de Gran Canaria Canary Is. **50** 28.08N 15.27W
Las Palomas Mexico **81** 31.44N107.37W
Las Perlas, Archipelago de Panama **87** 8.45N 79.30W
La Spezia Italy **15** 44.07N 9.49E
Las Piedras Uruguay **93** 34.44S 56.13W
Las Plumas Argentina **93** 43.40S 67.15W
Lassay France **15** 48.26N 0.30W
Lassen Peak *mtn.* U.S.A. **80** 40.29N121.31W
L'Assomption Canada **77** 45.50N 73.25W
Last Chance U.S.A. **80** 39.45N103.36W
Last Mountain L. Canada **75** 51.05N105.10W
Lastoursville Gabon **54** 0.50S 12.47E
Lastovo *i.* Yugo. **19** 42.45N 16.52E
Las Tres Vírgenes, Volcán *mtn.* Mexico **81** 27.27N112.37W
Lastrup W. Germany **14** 52.48N 7.55E
La Suze France **15** 47.54N 0.02E
Las Vegas Nev. U.S.A. **81** 36.11N115.08W
Las Vegas N.Mex. U.S.A. **81** 35.36N105.13W
Latacunga Ecuador **90** 0.58S 78.36W
La Tagua Colombia **90** 0.03S 74.40W
Latakia *see* Al Lādhiqīyah Syria **44**
Latambar Pakistan **40** 33.07N 70.52E
Late *i.* Tonga **69** 18.49S174.40W
Lātēhar India **41** 23.45N 84.30E
La Teste-de-Buch France **17** 44.38N 1.09W
Lathen W. Germany **14** 52.54N 7.20E
Lāthi India **40** 21.43N 71.23E
Latina Italy **18** 41.28N 12.52E
Latisana Italy **15** 45.47N 13.00E
La Tortuga *i.* Venezuela **90** 11.00N 65.20W
La Tuque Canada **77** 47.27N 72.47W
Latviyskaya S.S.R. *d.* U.S.S.R. **23** 56.45N 23.00E
Lau Nigeria **53** 9.14N 11.15E
Lauchhammer E. Germany **20** 51.30N 13.48E
Lauenburg W. Germany **20** 53.22N 10.33E
Laughlen, Mt. Australia **64** 23.23S134.23E
Lau Group *is.* Fiji **68** 19.00S178.30W
Launceston Australia **65** 41.25S147.07E
Launceston U.K. **11** 50.38N 4.21W
La Unión Chile **93** 40.15S 73.02W
La Unión Spain **16** 37.38N 0.53W
Laura Australia **66** 33.08S138.19E
La Urbana Venezuela **90** 7.08N 66.56W
Laurel Del. U.S.A. **85** 38.33N 75.34W
Laurel Miss. U.S.A. **83** 31.42N 89.08W
Laurel Mont. U.S.A. **80** 45.40N108.46W
Laurencekirk U.K. **12** 56.50N 2.29W
Laurens U.S.A. **85** 34.29N 82.01W
Laurentides *mts.* Canada **77** 46.25N 73.28W
Laurentides Prov. Park Canada **77** 47.30N 71.30W
Laurinburg U.S.A. **85** 34.46N 79.29W
Lausanne Switz. **20** 46.32N 6.39E
Laut *i.* Indonesia **36** 3.45S116.20E
Lautaro Chile **93** 38.31S 72.27W
Lauterecken W. Germany **14** 49.39N 7.36E
Lautoka Fiji **68** 17.37S177.27E
Lavagh More *mtn.* Rep. of Ire. **13** 54.45N 8.07W
Lava Hot Springs *town* U.S.A. **80** 42.37N112.01W
Laval France **15** 48.04N 0.45W
Laval Canada **77** 45.35N 73.45W
La Vega Dom. Rep. **87** 19.15N 70.33W
La Vela Venezuela **90** 11.27N 69.34W
La Vérendrye Prov. Park Canada **76** 47.32N 77.00W
Laverne U.S.A. **83** 36.43N 99.54W
Laverton Australia **63** 28.49S122.25E
Lavia Finland **23** 61.36N 22.36E
Lavik Norway **23** 61.06N 5.30E
Lavras Brazil **94** 21.15S 44.59W
Lávrion Greece **19** 37.44N 24.04E
Lawgi Australia **64** 24.34S150.39E
Lawra Ghana **52** 10.40N 2.49W
Lawrence New Zealand **60** 45.55S169.42E
Lawrence Kans. U.S.A. **82** 38.58N 95.14W
Lawrence Mass. U.S.A. **84** 42.42N 71.09W
Lawrenceburg U.S.A. **85** 35.16N 87.20W
Lawrenceville Canada **77** 45.25N 72.19W
Lawton Okla. U.S.A. **83** 34.37N 98.25W
Lawz, Jabal al *mtn.* Saudi Arabia **44** 28.40N 35.20E
Laxå Sweden **23** 58.59N 14.37E
Laysan *i.* Hawaiian Is. **68** 25.46N171.44W
Laytonville U.S.A. **80** 39.41N123.29W
Lazio *d.* Italy **18** 42.20N 12.00E
Lead U.S.A. **82** 44.21N103.46W
Leader Canada **75** 50.53N109.31W
Leadhills U.K. **12** 55.25N 3.46W
Leamington U.S.A. **80** 39.31N112.17W
Learmonth Australia **62** 22.13S114.04E
Leavenworth U.S.A. **82** 39.19N 94.55W
Lebak Phil. **37** 6.32N124.03E
Lebango Congo **54** 0.24N 14.44E
Lebanon Asia **44** 34.00N 36.00E
Lebanon Ind. U.S.A. **84** 40.02N 87.28W
Lebanon Kans. U.S.A. **82** 39.49N 98.33W
Lebanon Ky. U.S.A. **85** 37.33N 85.15W
Lebanon Mo. U.S.A. **83** 37.41N 92.40W
Lebanon Oreg. U.S.A. **80** 44.32N122.54W
Lebanon Penn. U.S.A. **84** 40.20N 76.25W
Lebanon Tenn. U.S.A. **85** 36.11N 86.19W
Lebec U.S.A. **81** 34.50N118.52W
Lebesby Norway **22** 70.34N 27.00E
Le Blanc France **17** 46.37N 1.03E
Lebork Poland **21** 54.33N 17.44E
Lebrija Spain **16** 36.55N 6.10W
Lebu Chile **93** 37.37S 73.39W
Le Bugue France **17** 44.55N 0.56E
Le Cateau France **14** 50.07N 3.33E
Le Catelet France **14** 50.00N 3.12E
Lecce Italy **19** 40.21N 18.11E
Lecco Italy **15** 45.51N 9.23E
Lech *r.* W. Germany **20** 48.45N 10.51E
Lechang China **33** 25.08N113.20E
Le Chesne France **14** 49.31N 4.46E
Lechiguanas, Islas de las *is.* Argentina **93** 33.26S 59.42W
Le Creusot France **17** 46.48N 4.27E
Lectoure France **17** 43.56N 0.38E
Ledbury U.K. **11** 52.03N 2.25W
Ledesma Spain **16** 41.05N 6.00W
Le Dorat France **17** 46.14N 1.05E
Leduc Canada **74** 53.20N113.30W
Lee *r.* Rep. of Ire. **13** 51.53N 8.25W
Leech L. U.S.A. **82** 47.09N 94.23W
Leedey U.S.A. **83** 35.52N 99.21W
Leeds U.K. **10** 53.48N 1.34W
Leeds U.S.A. **85** 33.32N 86.31W
Leek U.K. **10** 53.07N 2.02W
Leer W. Germany **14** 53.14N 7.27E
Leesburg Fla. U.S.A. **85** 28.49N 81.54W
Leeton Australia **67** 34.33S146.24E
Leeuwarden Neth. **14** 53.12N 5.48E
Leeuwin, C. Australia **63** 34.22S115.08E
Leeward Is. C. America **87** 18.00N 61.00W
Lefroy, L. Australia **63** 31.15S121.40E
Legazpi Phil. **37** 13.10N123.45E
Legget U.S.A. **80** 39.52N123.34W
Leghorn *see* Livorno Italy **18**
Legion Mine Zimbabwe **56** 21.23S 28.33E
Legionowo Poland **21** 52.25N 20.56E
Legnago Italy **15** 45.11N 11.18E
Legnano Italy **15** 45.36N 8.54E
Legnica Poland **20** 51.12N 16.10E
Le Grand-Lucé France **15** 47.52N 0.28E
Le Grand-Quevilly France **15** 49.25N 1.02E
Leh Jammu & Kashmir **41** 34.10N 77.35E
Le Havre France **15** 49.30N 0.06E
Lehrte W. Germany **20** 52.22N 9.59E
Lehututu Botswana **56** 23.54S 21.52E
Leiah Pakistan **40** 30.58N 70.56E
Leibnitz Austria **20** 46.48N 15.32E
Leicester U.K. **11** 52.39N 1.09W
Leicestershire *d.* U.K. **11** 52.29N 1.10W
Leichardt *r.* Australia **64** 17.35S139.48E
Leiden Neth. **14** 52.10N 4.30E
Leie *r.* Belgium **14** 51.03N 3.44E
Leifeng China **33** 25.35N118.17E
Leigh *r.* Australia **66** 29.49S138.10E
Leigh Creek *town* Australia **66** 30.31S138.25E
Leighton Buzzard U.K. **11** 51.55N 0.39W
Leikanger Norway **23** 61.10N 6.52E
Leipzig E. Germany **20** 51.20N 12.20E
Leipzig *d.* E. Germany **20** 51.15N 12.45E
Leiria Portugal **16** 39.45N 8.48W
Lei Shui *r.* China **33** 26.57N112.33E
Leithbridge Canada **74** 49.40N112.45W
Leitrim *d.* Rep. of Ire. **13** 54.08N 8.00W
Leiyang China **33** 26.30N112.42E
Leizhou Bandao *pen.* China **33** 21.00N110.00E
Lek *r.* Neth. **14** 51.55N 4.29E
Leksvik Norway **22** 63.40N 10.40E
Leland U.S.A. **83** 33.24N 90.54W
Leland Lakes Canada **75** 60.00N110.59W
Lelchitsy U.S.S.R. **21** 51.48N 28.20E
Leleque Argentina **93** 42.24S 71.04W
Leling China **32** 37.45N117.13E
Le Lion-d'Angers France **15** 47.38N 0.43W
Le Lude France **15** 47.39N 0.09E
Lelystad Neth. **14** 52.32N 5.29E
Léman, Lac *l.* Switz. **20** 46.30N 6.30E
Le Mans France **15** 48.01N 0.10E
Le Mars U.S.A. **82** 42.47N 96.10W
Leme Brazil **94** 22.10S 47.23W
Le Merlerault France **15** 48.42N 0.18E
Lemesós Cyprus **44** 34.40N 33.03E
Lemgo W. Germany **20** 52.02N 8.54E
Lemhi Range *mts.* U.S.A. **80** 44.30N113.25W
Lemmer Neth. **14** 52.50N 5.43E
Lemmon U.S.A. **82** 45.56N102.10W
Lemsid W. Sahara **50** 26.32N 13.49W
Lemvig Denmark **23** 56.32N 8.18E
Lena U.S.A. **83** 31.47N 92.48W
Lena *r.* U.S.S.R. **29** 72.00N127.10E
Lenakel Vanuatu **68** 19.32S169.16E
Lendery U.S.S.R. **24** 63.24N 31.04E
Lendinara Italy **15** 45.05N 11.36E
Lengerich W. Germany **14** 52.12N 7.52E
Lengoue *r.* Congo **54** 1.15S 16.42E
Lenina, Kanal *canal* U.S.S.R. **25** 43.46N 45.00E
Lenina, Pik *mtn.* U.S.S.R. **30** 40.14N 69.40E
Leninabad U.S.S.R. **30** 40.14N 69.40E
Leninakan U.S.S.R. **43** 40.47N 43.49E
Leningrad U.S.S.R. **24** 59.55N 30.25E
Leninogorsk U.S.S.R. **28** 50.23N 83.32E
Leninsk U.S.S.R. **25** 48.42N 45.14E
Leninsk Kuznetskiy U.S.S.R. **28** 54.44N 86.13E
Lenkoran U.S.S.R. **43** 38.45N 48.50E
Lenmalu Indonesia **37** 1.58S130.00E
Lenne *r.* W. Germany **14** 51.24N 7.30E
Lennonville Australia **62** 27.58S117.50E
Lenoir U.S.A. **85** 35.56N 81.31W
Lenora U.S.A. **82** 39.38N100.03W
Lenore L. Canada **75** 52.30N105.00W
Lens France **14** 50.26N 2.50E
Lentini Italy **18** 37.17N 15.00E
Lenvik Norway **22** 69.22N 18.10E
Léo U. Volta **52** 11.05N 2.06W
Leoben Austria **20** 47.23N 15.06E
Leominster U.K. **11** 52.15N 2.43W
Leominster U.S.A. **84** 42.32N 71.45W
León Mexico **86** 21.10N101.42W
León *d.* Mexico **83** 25.00N100.20W
León Nicaragua **87** 12.24N 86.52W
León Spain **16** 42.35N 5.34W
León *d.* Spain **16** 41.40N 5.55W
Leon U.S.A. **82** 40.44N 93.45W
Leonardtown U.S.A. **85** 38.17N 76.38W
Leonardville Namibia **56** 23.21S 18.47E
Leonárison Cyprus **44** 35.28N 34.08E
Leongatha Australia **67** 38.29S145.57E
Leonora Australia **63** 28.54S121.20E
Leopoldina Brazil **94** 21.30S 42.38W
Leopoldsburg Belgium **14** 51.08N 5.13E
Leovo U.S.S.R. **21** 46.29N 28.12E
Lepel U.S.S.R. **24** 54.48N 28.40E
Leping China **33** 28.58N117.08E
L'Epiphanie Canada **77** 45.51N 73.30W
Le Puy France **17** 45.03N 3.54E
Le Quesnoy France **14** 50.15N 3.39E
Lerbäck Sweden **23** 58.56N 15.02E
Léré Chad **53** 9.41N 14.17E
Lerici Italy **15** 44.04N 9.55E
Lérida Spain **16** 41.37N 0.38E
Lerma Spain **16** 42.02N 3.46W
Leross Canada **75** 51.17N103.53W
Le Roy Kans. U.S.A. **83** 38.05N 95.38W
Le Roy Mich. U.S.A. **84** 44.03N 85.29W
Le Roy N.Y. U.S.A. **76** 42.59N 77.59W
Lerwick U.K. **12** 60.09N 1.09W
Les Andelys France **15** 49.15N 1.25E
Les Cayes Haiti **87** 18.15N 73.46W
Leschenault, C. Australia **63** 31.50S115.23E
Les Ecrins *mtn.* France **17** 44.50N 6.20E
Leshan China **33** 29.30N103.45E
Leshukonskoye U.S.S.R. **24** 64.55N 45.50E
Lesjaskog Norway **23** 62.15N 8.22E
Leskovac Yugo. **19** 43.00N 21.56E
Leslie Ark. U.S.A. **83** 35.50N 92.34W
Lesotho Africa **56** 29.00S 28.00E
Lesozavodsk U.S.S.R. **31** 45.30N133.29E
Les Pieux France **15** 49.35N 1.50W
Les Riceys France **15** 47.59N 4.22E
Les Sables d'Olonne France **17** 46.30N 1.47W
Lessay France **15** 49.14N 1.30W
Lesser Antilles *is.* C. America **87** 13.00N 65.00W
Lesser Slave L. Canada **74** 55.30N115.25W
Lesser Sunda Is. *see* Nusa Tenggara *is.* Indonesia **36**
Lessines Belgium **14** 50.43N 3.50E
Lesti *r.* Finland **22** 64.04N 23.38E
Le Sueur U.S.A. **82** 44.27N 93.54W
Lésvos *i.* Greece **19** 39.10N 26.16E
Leszno Poland **20** 51.51N 16.35E
Letchworth U.K. **11** 51.58N 0.13W
Lethbridge Canada **72** 49.43N112.48W
Lethem Guyana **90** 3.18N 59.46W
Leti, Kepulauan *is.* Indonesia **37** 8.20S128.00E
Letiahau *r.* Botswana **56** 21.16S 24.00E
Leticia Colombia **90** 4.09S 69.57W
Leting China **32** 39.26N118.56E
Letohatchee U.S.A. **85** 32.08N 86.30W
Le Tréport France **17** 50.04N 1.22E
Lette Australia **66** 34.22S143.15E
Letterkenny Rep. of Ire. **13** 54.56N 7.45W
Leuk Switz. **15** 46.19N 7.38E
Leuser *mtn.* Indonesia **36** 3.50N 97.10E
Leuven Belgium **14** 50.53N 4.45E
Leuze Hainaut Belgium **14** 50.36N 3.37E
Leuze Namur Belgium **14** 50.34N 4.53E
Levanger Norway **22** 63.45N 11.19E
Levanto Italy **15** 44.10N 9.38E
Levelland U.S.A. **83** 33.35N102.23W
Lévêque, C. Australia **62** 16.25S123.00E
Le Verdon France **17** 45.33N 1.04W
Leverkusen W. Germany **14** 51.02N 6.59E
Levice Czech. **21** 48.13N 18.37E
Levin New Zealand **60** 40.37S175.18E
Lévis Canada **77** 46.49N 71.11W
Lévka Cyprus **44** 35.06N 32.51E
Levkás Greece **19** 38.50N 20.41E
Levkás *i.* Greece **19** 38.44N 20.37E
Levkosía Cyprus **44** 35.11N 33.23E
Lewes U.K. **11** 50.53N 0.02E
Lewes U.S.A. **85** 38.47N 75.08W
Lewis *i.* U.K. **12** 58.10N 6.40W
Lewis Pass *f.* New Zealand **60** 42.30S172.15E
Lewisporte Canada **77** 49.15N 55.04W
Lewis Range *mts.* U.S.A. **80** 48.30N113.15W
Lewiston Idaho U.S.A. **80** 46.25N117.01W
Lewiston Maine U.S.A. **84** 44.06N 70.13W
Lewistown Mont. U.S.A. **80** 47.04N109.26W
Lewistown Penn. U.S.A. **84** 40.36N 77.31W
Lexington Ky. U.S.A. **85** 38.03N 84.30W
Lexington Miss. U.S.A. **83** 33.07N 90.03W
Lexington Nebr. U.S.A. **82** 40.47N 99.45W
Lexington Oreg. U.S.A. **80** 45.27N119.41W
Leyburn U.K. **10** 54.19N 1.50W
Leydsdorp R.S.A. **56** 23.59S 30.32E
Leyte *i.* Phil. **37** 10.40N124.50E
Lezignan France **17** 43.12N 2.46E
Lhari China **41** 30.47N 93.24E
Lhasa China **41** 29.39N 91.06E
Lhasa He *r.* China **41** 29.21N 90.45E
Lhazê China **41** 29.10N 87.45E
Lhazhong China **41** 32.02N 86.34E
Lhokseumawe Indonesia **36** 5.09N 97.09E
Lhozhag China **41** 28.23N 90.49E
Lhuntsi Dzong Bhutan **41** 27.39N 91.09E
Lhünzê China **41** 28.26N 92.27E
Lhünzhub China **41** 30.00N 91.12E
Lhut *r.* Somali Rep. **45** 10.25N 51.05E
Li Thailand **34** 17.50N 98.55E
Liancheng China **33** 25.47N116.48E
Liangcheng China **32** 40.31N112.29E
Liangdang China **32** 33.59N106.23E
Lianjiang Fujian China **33** 26.10N119.33E
Lianjiang Guangdong China **33** 21.33N110.19E
Lianshan China **33** 24.37N112.02E
Lianshui China **32** 33.46N119.18E
Lian Xian China **33** 24.52N112.27E
Lianyungang China **32** 34.36N119.10E
Liaocheng China **32** 36.25N115.58E
Liaodong Bandao *pen.* China **32** 40.00N122.20E
Liaodong Wan *b.* China **32** 40.00N121.00E
Liao He *r.* China **32** 40.40N122.20E

Liaoning to Lower California

Liaoning d. China 32 42.00N122.00E
Liaoyang China 32 41.17N123.13E
Liaoyuan China 32 42.50N125.08E
Liard r. Canada 74 61.51N121.18W
Liāri Pakistan 40 25.41N 66.29E
Liart France 15 49.46N 4.20E
Libby U.S.A. 80 48.23N115.33W
Libenge Zaïre 54 3.39N 18.39E
Liberal U.S.A. 83 37.02N100.55W
Liberdade Brazil 94 22.01S 44.22W
Liberec Czech. 20 50.48N 15.05E
Liberia Africa 52 6.30N 9.30W
Liberia Costa Rica 87 10.39N 85.28W
Liberty Tex. U.S.A. 83 30.03N 94.47W
Lībīyah, Aş Şaḩrā' al des. Africa 42 24.00N 25.30E
Libo China 33 25.25N107.53E
Libourne France 17 44.55N 0.14W
Libramont Belgium 14 49.56N 5.22E
Libreville Gabon 54 0.25N 9.30E
Libya Africa 51 26.30N 17.00E
Libyan Desert see Lībīyah, Aş Şaḩrā' al a-' al Africa 42
Libyan Plateau see Aḑ Ḑiffah f. Africa 42
Licantén Chile 93 34.59S 72.00W
Licata Italy 18 37.07N 13.58E
Lichfield U.K. 11 52.40N 1.50W
Lichinga Mozambique 55 13.09S 35.17E
Lichtenburg R.S.A. 56 26.08S 26.09E
Lichtenvoorde Neth. 14 51.59N 6.32E
Lichuan Hubei China 33 30.18N108.51E
Lichuan Jiangxi China 33 27.22N116.59E
Lida U.S.A. 80 37.29N117.29W
Lida U.S.S.R. 21 53.50N 25.19E
Lidköping Sweden 23 58.30N 13.10E
Liechtenstein Europe 20 47.08N 9.35E
Liège Belgium 14 50.38N 5.35E
Liège d. Belgium 14 50.32N 5.35E
Lien-Huong Vietnam 34 11.13N108.48E
Lienz Austria 20 46.50N 12.47E
Liepāja U.S.S.R. 23 56.31N 21.01E
Lier Belgium 14 51.08N 4.35E
Lierneux Belgium 14 50.18N 5.50E
Liești Romania 21 45.38N 27.32E
Liévin France 14 50.27N 2.49E
Lièvre, Rivière du r. Canada 77 45.31N 75.26W
Liffey r. Rep. of Ire. 13 53.21N 6.14W
Liffré France 15 48.13N 1.30W
Lifou, Île i. N. Cal. 68 20.53S167.13E
Liguria d. Italy 15 42.25N 8.40E
Ligurian Sea Med. Sea 18 43.30N 9.00E
Lihou Reef and Cays Australia 64 17.25S151.40E
Lihue Hawaiian Is. 69 21.59N159.23W
Lihula U.S.S.R. 23 58.41N 23.50E
Lijiang China 39 26.50N100.15E
Lijin China 32 37.29N118.16E
Likasi Zaïre 54 10.58S 26.50E
Likati Zaïre 54 3.21N 23.53E
Likona r. Congo 54 0.11N 16.25E
Likouala r. Congo 54 0.51S 17.17E
Liku Niue 68 19.03S169.48W
Lille France 14 50.39N 3.05E
Lille Baelt str. Denmark 23 55.20N 9.45E
Lillebonne France 15 49.31N 0.33E
Lillehammer Norway 23 61.08N 10.30E
Lillers France 14 50.34N 2.29E
Lillesand Norway 23 58.15N 8.24E
Lilleström Norway 23 59.57N 11.05E
Lillhärdal Sweden 23 61.51N 14.04E
Lillooet Canada 74 50.42N121.56W
Lillooet r. Canada 74 49.15N121.57W
Lilongwe Malaŵi 55 13.58S 33.49E
Liloy Phil. 37 8.08N122.40E
Lilydale Australia 66 32.58S139.59E
Lim r. Yugo. 19 43.45N 19.13E
Lima Peru 90 12.06S 77.03W
Lima r. Portugal 16 41.40N 8.50W
Lima Sweden 23 60.56N 13.26E
Lima Mont. U.S.A. 80 44.38N112.36W
Lima Ohio U.S.A. 84 40.43N 84.06W
Limassol see Lemesós Cyprus 44
Limavady U.K. 13 55.03N 6.57W
Limay r. Argentina 93 39.02S 68.07W
Limbang Malaysia 36 4.50N115.00E
Limbdi India 40 22.34N 71.48E
Limbe Cameroon 53 4.01N 9.12E
Limbourg Belgium 14 50.36N 5.57E
Limburg d. Belgium 14 50.36N 5.57E
Limburg d. Neth. 14 51.15N 5.45E
Limeira Brazil 94 22.34S 47.25W
Limerick Rep. of Ire. 13 52.40N 8.37W
Limerick d. Rep. of Ire. 13 52.40N 8.37W
Limfjorden str. Denmark 23 56.55N 9.10E
Liminka Finland 22 64.49N 25.24E
Limmen Bight Australia 64 14.45S135.40E
Límnos i. Greece 19 39.55N 25.14E
Limoges France 17 45.50N 1.15E
Limogne France 17 44.24N 1.46E
Limón Costa Rica 87 10.00N 83.01W
Limon U.S.A. 80 39.16N103.41W
Limone Piemonte Italy 15 44.12N 7.34E
Limousin d. France 17 45.45N 1.30E
Limpopo r. Mozambique 57 25.14S 33.33E
Linah Saudi Arabia 43 28.48N 43.45E
Linakhamari U.S.S.R. 24 69.39N 31.21E
Linares Chile 93 35.51S 71.36W
Linares Mexico 83 24.52N 99.34W
Linares Spain 16 38.05N 3.38W
Lincang China 30 24.00N100.10E
Lincheng China 32 37.26N114.34E
Lincoln Argentina 93 34.55S 61.30W
Lincoln New Zealand 60 43.38S172.29E
Lincoln U.K. 10 53.14N 0.32W
Lincoln Ill. U.S.A. 82 40.10N 89.21W
Lincoln Nebr. U.S.A. 82 40.48N 96.42W
Lincoln N.H. U.S.A. 84 44.03N 71.40W
Lincoln City U.S.A. 80 44.59N124.00W
Lincoln Gap town Australia 66 32.45S137.18E
Lincoln Sea Greenland 96 82.00N 55.00W
Lincolnshire d. U.K. 10 53.14N 0.32W
Lincoln Wolds hills U.K. 10 53.22N 0.08W
Linden Ala. U.S.A. 83 32.18N 87.47W
Lindesnes c. Norway 23 58.00N 7.02E
Líndhos Greece 19 36.05N 28.02E
Lindi Tanzania 55 10.00S 39.41E
Lindi r. Zaïre 54 0.30N 25.06E
Lindsay Canada 76 44.21N 78.44W
Lindsay U.S.A. 81 36.12N119.05W
Line Is. Pacific Oc. 69 3.00S155.00W
Linfen China 32 36.07N111.34E
Lingao China 33 19.54N109.40E
Lingayen Phil. 37 16.02N120.14E
Lingbo Sweden 23 61.03N 16.41E
Lingchuan China 33 25.25N110.20E
Lingen W. Germany 14 52.32N 7.19E
Lingga i. Indonesia 36 0.20S104.30E
Lingling China 33 26.12N111.30E
Lingshan China 33 22.17N109.27E
Lingshui China 33 18.31N110.00E
Linguère Senegal 52 15.22N 15.11W
Linhai China 33 28.49N121.08E
Linhe China 32 40.50N107.30E
Linköping Sweden 23 58.25N 15.37E
Linnhe, Loch U.K. 12 56.35N 5.25W
Linosa i. Italy 18 35.52N 12.50E
Linquan China 32 33.03N115.17E
Linru China 32 34.12N112.45E
Lins Brazil 94 21.40S 49.44W
Linshui China 33 30.18N106.55E
Lintan China 32 34.33N103.40E
Lintao China 32 35.20N104.00E
Linton Ind. U.S.A. 84 39.01N 87.10W
Linton N.Dak. U.S.A. 82 46.16N100.14W
Lintong China 32 34.24N109.13E
Lintorf W. Germany 14 51.19N 6.50E
Linxe France 17 43.56N 1.10W
Linxi China 32 43.31N118.02E
Linxia China 32 35.30N103.10E
Lin Xian China 32 37.57N110.57E
Linyi Shandong China 32 35.08N118.20E
Linyi Shanxi China 32 35.12N110.45E
Linz Austria 20 48.19N 14.18E
Linz W. Germany 14 50.34N 7.19E
Lion, Golfe du g. France 17 43.12N 4.15E
Lions, G. of see Lion, Golfe du g. France 17
Liouesso Congo 54 1.12N 15.47E
Lipéité Congo 54 3.09N 17.22E
Lipetsk U.S.S.R. 24 52.37N 39.36E
Liphook U.K. 11 51.05N 0.49W
Liping China 33 26.16N109.08E
Lipkany U.S.S.R. 21 48.18N 26.48E
Lipova Romania 21 46.05N 21.40E
Lipovets U.S.S.R. 21 49.11N 29.01E
Lippe r. W. Germany 14 51.38N 6.37E
Lippstadt W. Germany 20 51.41N 8.20E
Liptovský Mikuláš Czech. 21 49.06N 19.37E
Lipu China 33 24.28N110.12E
Lira Uganda 55 2.15N 32.55E
Liranga Congo 54 0.43S 17.32E
Liri r. Italy 18 41.12N 13.45E
Liria Spain 16 39.37N 0.35W
Liria Sudan 49 4.38N 32.05E
Lisala Zaïre 54 2.13N 21.37E
Lisboa Portugal 16 38.44N 9.08W
Lisbon see Lisboa Portugal 16
Lisbon N.Dak. U.S.A. 82 46.27N 97.41W
Lisburn U.K. 13 54.30N 6.03W
Lisburne, C. U.S.A. 72 69.00N165.50W
Liscannor B. Rep. of Ire. 13 52.55N 9.24W
Lishi China 32 37.30N111.07E
Lishui China 33 28.28N119.59E
Lisianski i. Hawaiian Is. 68 26.04N173.58W
Lisichansk U.S.S.R. 25 48.53N 38.25E
Lisieux France 15 49.09N 0.14E
Liskeard U.K. 11 50.27N 4.29W
Lismore N.S.W. Australia 67 28.48S153.17E
Lismore Vic. Australia 66 37.58S143.22E
Lismore Rep. of Ire. 13 52.08N 7.57W
Liss U.K. 11 51.03N 0.53W
Lisse Neth. 14 52.18N 4.33E
Listowel Rep. of Ire. 13 52.27N 9.30W
Litang China 33 23.09N109.09E
Litang Qu r. China 39 28.09N101.30E
Litchfield Ill. U.S.A. 82 39.11N 89.40W
Litchfield Minn. U.S.A. 82 45.08N 94.31W
Litchfield Nebr. U.S.A. 82 41.09N 99.09W
Lithgow Australia 67 33.30S150.09E
Lititz U.S.A. 85 40.09N 76.18W
Litovskaya S.S.R. d. U.S.S.R. 21 54.30N 24.00E
Little Andaman i. India 34 10.40N 92.24E
Little Belt Mts. U.S.A. 80 46.45N110.35W
Little Cayman i. Cayman Is. 87 19.40N 80.00W
Little Coco i. Burma 34 13.59N 93.12E
Little Colorado r. U.S.A. 81 36.11N111.48W
Little Current r. Canada 76 50.00N 84.35W
Little Current town Canada 84 45.58N 81.56W
Little Falls town Minn. U.S.A. 82 45.59N 94.21W
Little Falls town N.Y. U.S.A. 84 43.03N 74.52W
Littlefield U.S.A. 83 33.55N102.20W
Littlefork U.S.A. 82 48.24N 93.33W
Little Grand Rapids town Canada 75 52.05N 95.29W
Littlehampton U.K. 11 50.48N 0.32W
Little Inagua i. Bahamas 87 21.30N 73.00W
Little Karroo f. R.S.A. 56 33.40S 21.40E
Little Lake town U.S.A. 81 35.58N117.53W
Little Mecatina r. Canada 77 50.28N 59.35W
Little Missouri r. U.S.A. 82 47.30N102.25W
Little Nicobar i. India 39 7.20N 93.40E
Little Ouse r. U.K. 11 52.34N 0.20E
Little Quill L. Canada 75 51.55N104.05W
Little Rann of Kutch f. India 40 23.25N 71.30E
Little Rock town U.S.A. 83 34.44N 92.15W
Little Smoky r. Canada 74 55.42N117.38W
Littleton Colo. U.S.A. 80 39.37N105.01W
Little Topar Australia 66 31.44S142.14E
Liuba China 32 33.37N106.55E
Liucheng China 33 24.39N109.14E
Liuchong He r. China 33 26.50N106.04E
Liuli Tanzania 55 11.07S 34.34E
Liulin China 32 37.26N110.52E
Liuzhou China 33 24.19N109.12E
Livarot France 15 49.01N 0.09E
Live Oak U.S.A. 85 30.19N 82.59W
Livermore, Mt. U.S.A. 81 30.39N104.11W
Liverpool Australia 67 33.57S150.52E
Liverpool Canada 77 44.02N 64.43W
Liverpool U.K. 10 53.25N 3.00W
Liverpool, C. Canada 73 73.38N 78.06W
Liverpool B. U.K. 10 53.30N 3.10W
Liverpool Plains f. Australia 67 31.20S150.00E
Liverpool Range mts. Australia 67 31.45S150.45E
Livingston U.K. 12 55.54N 3.31W
Livingston Mont. U.S.A. 80 45.40N110.34W
Livingston Tex. U.S.A. 83 30.43N 94.56W
Livingstone see Maramba Zambia 56
Livingstonia Malaŵi 55 10.35S 34.10E
Livo r. Finland 22 65.24N 26.48E
Livorno Italy 18 43.33N 10.18E
Liwale Tanzania 55 9.47S 38.00E
Liwan Sudan 49 4.55N 35.41E
Li Xian Gansu China 32 34.11N105.02E
Li Xian Hunan China 33 29.38N111.45E
Liyujiang China 33 25.59N113.12E
Lizard U.K. 11 49.58N 5.12W
Lizard Pt. U.K. 11 49.57N 5.15W
Ljubljana Yugo. 18 46.04N 14.28E
Ljugarn Sweden 23 57.19N 18.42E
Ljungan r. Sweden 23 62.19N 17.23E
Ljungby Sweden 23 56.50N 13.56E
Ljungdalen Sweden 22 62.54N 12.45E
Ljusdal Sweden 23 61.50N 16.05E
Ljusnan r. Sweden 23 61.12N 17.08E
Ljusne Sweden 23 61.13N 17.08E
Llandeilo U.K. 11 51.54N 4.00W
Llandovery U.K. 11 51.59N 3.49W
Llandrindod Wells U.K. 11 52.15N 3.23W
Llandudno U.K. 10 53.19N 3.49W
Llanelli U.K. 11 51.41N 4.11W
Llanes Spain 16 43.25N 4.45W
Llangadfan U.K. 11 52.41N 3.28W
Llangollen U.K. 10 52.58N 3.10W
Llanidloes U.K. 11 52.28N 3.31W
Llanos f. S. America 90 7.30N 70.00W
Llanwrtyd Wells U.K. 11 52.06N 3.39W
Llerena Spain 16 38.14N 6.00W
Lloret de Mar Spain 16 41.41N 2.53E
Lloydminster Canada 75 53.17N110.00W
Loange r. Zaïre 54 4.18S 20.05E
Lobatse Botswana 56 25.12S 25.39E
Löbau E. Germany 20 51.05N 14.40E
Lobaye r. C.A.R. 53 3.40N 18.35E
Lobería Argentina 93 38.08S 58.48W
Lobito Angola 54 12.20S 13.34E
Lobonäs Sweden 23 61.33N 15.20E
Lobos Argentina 93 35.10S 59.05W
Lobstick L. Canada 77 54.00N 64.50W
Locarno Switz. 20 46.10N 8.48E
Lochboisdale town U.K. 12 57.09N 7.19W
Lochem Neth. 14 52.10N 6.25E
Loches France 17 47.08N 1.00E
Lochgilphead U.K. 12 56.02N 5.26W
Lochinver U.K. 12 58.09N 5.15W
Lochmaddy town U.K. 12 57.36N 7.10W
Lochnagar mtn. U.K. 12 56.57N 3.15W
Lochranza U.K. 12 55.42N 5.18W
Loch Raven Resr. U.S.A. 85 39.27N 76.36W
Lochy, Loch U.K. 12 56.58N 4.55W
Lock Australia 66 33.34S135.46E
Lockeport Canada 77 43.42N 65.07W
Lockerbie U.K. 12 55.07N 3.21W
Lockhart Australia 67 35.16S146.42E
Lockhart U.S.A. 83 29.53N 97.41W
Lockhart, L. Australia 63 33.27S119.00E
Lock Haven U.S.A. 84 41.08N 77.27W
Lockport U.S.A. 84 43.11N 78.39W
Loc Ninh Vietnam 34 11.51N106.35E
Lodalskåpa mtn. Norway 23 61.47N 7.13E
Loddon r. Australia 66 35.40S143.59E
Lodeynoye Pole U.S.S.R. 24 60.43N 33.30E
Lodge Grass U.S.A. 80 45.19N107.22W
Lodhrān Pakistan 40 29.32N 71.38E
Lodi Italy 15 45.19N 9.30E
Lodi Calif. U.S.A. 80 38.08N121.16W
Lodja Zaïre 54 3.29S 23.33E
Lodwar Kenya 55 3.06N 35.38E
Łódź Poland 21 51.49N 19.28E
Loei Thailand 34 17.32N101.34E
Lofoten Vesterålen is. Norway 22 68.15N 13.50E
Log U.S.S.R. 25 49.28N 43.51E
Loga Niger 53 13.40N 3.15E
Logan Australia 67 27.48S153.04E
Logan N.Mex. U.S.A. 81 35.22N103.25W
Logan Utah U.S.A. 80 41.44N111.50W
Logan, Mt. Canada 74 60.34N140.24W
Logansport U.S.A. 84 40.45N 86.25W
Loge r. Angola 54 7.52S 13.08E
Logone r. Cameroon/Chad 53 12.10N 15.00E
Logone Occidental d. Chad 53 8.40N 15.50E
Logone Oriental d. Chad 53 8.10N 16.00E
Logoysk U.S.S.R. 21 54.08N 27.42E
Logroño Spain 16 42.28N 2.26W
Lögstör Denmark 23 56.58N 9.15E
Lohārdaga India 41 23.26N 84.41E
Lohāru India 40 28.27N 75.49E
Lohja Finland 23 60.15N 24.05E
Lohjanjärvi l. Finland 23 60.15N 23.55E
Loikaw Burma 34 19.40N 97.17E
Loimaa Finland 23 60.51N 23.03E
Loir r. France 15 47.29N 0.32W
Loire r. France 15 47.18N 2.00W
Loiret d. France 15 47.55N 2.20E
Loir-et-Cher d. France 15 47.30N 1.30E
Loja Ecuador 90 3.59S 79.16W
Loja Spain 16 37.10N 4.09W
Loka Sudan 49 4.16N 31.01E
Loka Zaïre 54 0.20N 17.57E
Löken Norway 23 59.48N 11.29E
Loken tekojärvi resr. Finland 22 67.55N 27.40E
Lokeren Belgium 14 51.06N 3.59E
Lokichar Kenya 55 2.23N 35.39E
Lokitaung Kenya 55 4.15N 35.45E
Lokka Finland 22 67.49N 27.44E
Lökken Denmark 23 57.22N 9.43E
Lökken Norway 22 63.06N 9.43E
Loknya U.S.S.R. 24 56.49N 30.00E
Lokoja Nigeria 53 7.49N 6.44E
Lokolo r. Zaïre 54 0.45S 19.36E
Lokoro r. Zaïre 54 1.40S 18.29E
Lol r. Sudan 49 9.11N 29.12E
Lolland i. Denmark 23 54.46N 11.30E
Lom Bulgaria 21 43.49N 23.13E
Lom Norway 23 61.50N 8.33E
Loma U.S.A. 80 47.57N110.30W
Lomami r. Zaïre 54 0.45N 24.10E
Lomas de Zamora Argentina 93 34.46S 58.24W
Lombardia d. Italy 15 45.25N 10.00E
Lombok i. Indonesia 36 8.30S116.20E
Lombok, Selat str. Indonesia 37 8.38S115.40E
Lomé Togo 53 6.10N 1.21E
Lomela Zaïre 54 2.15S 23.15E
Lomela r. Zaïre 54 0.14S 20.45E
Lomié Cameroon 53 3.09N 13.35E
Lomme France 14 50.38N 2.59E
Lommel Belgium 14 51.15N 5.18E
Lomond Canada 74 50.21N112.39W
Lomond, Loch U.K. 12 56.07N 4.36W
Lompoc U.S.A. 81 34.38N120.27W
Łomża Poland 21 53.11N 22.04E
Londinières France 15 49.50N 1.24E
London Canada 76 42.58N 81.15W
London Kiribati 69 1.58N157.28W
London U.K. 11 51.32N 0.06W
Londonderry U.K. 13 55.00N 7.21W
Londonderry d. U.K. 13 55.00N 7.00W
Londonderry, C. Australia 62 13.58S126.55E
Londonderry, Isla i. Chile 93 55.03S 70.40W
Londrina Brazil 92 23.30S 51.13W
Lone Pine U.S.A. 81 36.36N118.04W
Longa r. Angola 54 16.15S 19.07E
Longa, Proliv str. U.S.S.R. 29 70.00N178.00E
Long'an China 33 23.11N107.41E
Longarone Italy 15 46.16N 12.18E
Long Beach town Calif. U.S.A. 81 33.46N118.11W
Long Beach town N.Y. U.S.A. 85 40.35N 73.41W
Long Branch U.S.A. 85 40.18N 74.00W
Long Broad Sd. Australia 64 22.20S149.50E
Longchamps Belgium 14 50.05N 5.42E
Longchang China 33 29.18N105.20E
Longchuan China 33 24.12N115.25E
Long Creek town U.S.A. 80 44.43N119.06W
Long Eaton U.K. 10 52.54N 1.16W
Longford Rep. of Ire. 13 53.44N 7.48W
Longford d. Rep. of Ire. 13 53.42N 7.45W
Longhua Hebei China 32 41.17N117.37E
Long I. Bahamas 87 23.00N 75.00W
Long I. Canada 76 54.55N 79.30W
Long I. U.S.A. 84 40.46N 73.00W
Longido Tanzania 55 2.43S 36.41E
Longiram Indonesia 36 0.05S115.45E
Long Jiang r. China 33 24.12N109.30E
Long L. Canada 76 49.30N 86.50W
Longlac town Canada 76 49.45N 86.25W
Longli China 33 26.29N107.59E
Longlin China 33 24.43N105.26E
Longmont U.S.A. 80 40.10N105.06W
Longnan China 33 24.54N114.47E
Longnawan Indonesia 36 1.54N114.53E
Longniddry U.K. 12 55.58N 2.53W
Long Point B. Canada 76 42.40N 80.14W
Long Pt. Canada 76 42.33N 80.04W
Longquan China 33 28.05N119.07E
Long Range Mts. Nfld. Canada 77 48.00N 58.30W
Long Range Mts. Nfld. Canada 77 50.00N 57.00W
Longreach Australia 64 23.26S144.15E
Longsheng China 33 25.59N110.01E
Longs Peak U.S.A. 80 40.15N105.37W
Longtown U.K. 10 55.01N 2.58W
Longué France 15 47.23N 0.06W
Longueuil Canada 77 45.32N 73.30W
Longuyon France 14 49.27N 5.35E
Longview Tex. U.S.A. 83 32.30N 94.44W
Longview Wash. U.S.A. 80 46.08N122.57W
Longwood St. Helena 95 15.57S 5.42W
Longwy France 14 49.32N 5.46E
Longxi China 32 34.59N104.45E
Long Xian China 32 34.52N106.50E
Long Xuyen Vietnam 34 10.23N105.23E
Longyan China 33 25.10N117.02E
Longzhou China 33 22.24N106.50E
Lonigo Italy 15 45.23N 11.23E
Löningen W. Germany 14 52.44N 7.46E
Lönsdal Norway 22 66.46N 15.26E
Lonsdale, L. Australia 66 37.05S142.15E
Lons-le-Saunier France 17 46.40N 5.33E
Looc Phil. 37 12.20N122.05E
Looe U.K. 11 50.51N 4.26W
Lookout, C. U.S.A. 85 34.35N 76.32W
Loolmalassin mtn. Tanzania 55 3.00S 35.45E
Loongana Australia 63 30.57S127.02E
Loop Head Rep. of Ire. 13 52.33N 9.56W
Lopari Zaïre 49 1.15N 19.59E
Lopari r. Zaïre 54 1.20N 20.22E
Lop Buri Thailand 34 14.49N100.37E
Lopez, C. Gabon 54 0.36S 8.40E
Lopi Congo 54 2.57N 16.47E
Lop Nur l. China 30 40.30N 90.30E
Lopphavet est. Norway 22 70.30N 20.00E
Lopydino U.S.S.R. 24 61.10N 52.02E
Lora, Hāmūn-i- l. Pakistan 40 29.20N 64.50E
Lorain U.S.A. 84 41.28N 82.11W
Loralai Pakistan 40 30.22N 68.36E
Lorca Spain 16 37.40N 1.41W
Lord Howe I. Pacific Oc. 68 31.28S159.09E
Lord Howe Rise Pacific Oc. 68 29.00S162.30E
Lordsburg U.S.A. 81 32.21N108.43W
Lorena Brazil 94 22.44S 45.07W
Lorengau P.N.G. 37 2.01S147.15E
Lorenzo Geyres Uruguay 93 32.05S 57.55W
Loreto Brazil 91 7.05S 45.09W
Loreto Italy 18 43.26N 13.36E
Loreto Mexico 81 26.01N111.21W
Lorian Swamp Kenya 55 0.35N 39.40E
Lorient France 17 47.45N 3.21W
Lormes France 15 47.17N 3.49E
Lorne Australia 66 38.34S144.01E
Lorraine d. France 17 49.00N 6.20E
Lorris France 15 47.53N 2.31E
Lorup W. Germany 14 52.58N 7.39E
Los Alamos Mexico 83 28.40N103.30W
Los Alamos U.S.A. 81 35.53N106.19W
Los Andes Chile 93 32.50S 70.37W
Los Angeles Chile 93 37.28S 72.21W
Los Angeles U.S.A. 78 34.00N118.17W
Los Bajíos Mexico 81 28.31N108.25W
Los Banos U.S.A. 80 37.04N120.51W
Los Blancos Argentina 92 23.40S 62.35W
Los Blancos Spain 16 37.37N 0.48W
Los Canarreos, Archipiélago de Cuba 87 21.40N 82.30W
Los Herreras Mexico 83 25.55N 99.24W
Lošinj i. Yugo. 18 44.36N 14.20E
Losinovka U.S.S.R. 21 55.50N 31.57E
Los Llanos de Aridane Canary Is. 95 28.39N 17.54W
Los Lunas U.S.A. 81 34.48N106.44W
Los Mochis Mexico 86 25.45N108.57W
Los Olivos U.S.A. 81 34.40N120.06W
Los Roques is. Venezuela 90 12.00N 67.00W
Lossiemouth U.K. 12 57.43N 3.18W
Lost Cabin U.S.A. 80 43.19N107.36W
Los Teques Venezuela 90 10.25N 67.01W
Los Vilos Chile 92 31.55S 71.31W
Lot r. France 17 44.17N 0.22E
Lota Chile 93 37.05S 73.10W
Lothian d. U.K. 12 55.50N 3.00W
Lotoi r. Zaïre 54 1.30S 18.30E
Lotsani r. Botswana 56 22.42S 28.11E
Lötschberg Tunnel Switz. 17 46.25N 7.53E
Lotuke mtn. Sudan 49 4.07N 33.48E
Louang Namtha Laos 34 20.57N101.25E
Louangphrabang Laos 34 19.53N102.10E
Loudéac France 17 48.11N 2.45W
Loudima Congo 54 4.06S 13.05E
Loué France 15 48.00N 0.09W
Louga Senegal 52 15.37N 16.13W
Loughborough U.K. 10 52.47N 1.11W
Loughrea Rep. of Ire. 13 53.12N 8.35W
Loughros More B. Rep. of Ire. 13 54.48N 8.32W
Louisburgh Rep. of Ire. 13 53.46N 9.49W
Louiseville Canada 77 46.14N 72.56W
Louisiade Archipelago is. P.N.G. 64 11.00S153.00E
Louisiana d. U.S.A. 83 30.60N 92.30W
Louis Trichardt R.S.A. 56 23.03S 29.54E
Louisville Ky. U.S.A. 84 38.13N 85.48W
Louisville Miss. U.S.A. 83 33.07N 89.03W
Louis XIV, Pointe c. Canada 76 54.35N 79.50W
Loukhi U.S.S.R. 24 66.05N 33.04E
Loukouo Congo 54 3.38S 14.39E
Loulé Portugal 16 37.08N 8.02W
Loum Cameroon 53 4.46N 9.45E
Lourches France 14 50.19N 3.20E
Lourdes France 17 43.06N 0.02W
Louth Australia 67 30.34S145.09E
Louth d. Rep. of Ire. 13 53.55N 6.30W
Louth U.K. 10 53.23N 0.00
Louviers France 15 49.13N 1.10E
Louvigné-du-Désert France 15 48.29N 1.08W
Lövånger Sweden 22 64.22N 21.18E
Lovat r. U.S.S.R. 24 58.06N 31.37E
Lovech Bulgaria 19 43.08N 24.44E
Loveland U.S.A. 80 40.24N105.05W
Lovell U.S.A. 80 44.50N108.24W
Lovelock U.S.A. 80 40.11N118.28W
Love Point town U.S.A. 85 39.02N 76.18W
Lovere Italy 15 45.49N 10.04E
Lovington U.S.A. 83 32.57N103.21W
Lovoi r. Zaïre 55 8.14S 26.40E
Lovozero U.S.S.R. 24 68.01N 35.08E
Lovrin Romania 21 45.58N 20.48E
Lovua r. Zaïre 54 6.08S 20.35E
Lowa Zaïre 54 1.24S 25.51E
Lowa r. Kivu Zaïre 54 1.25S 25.55E
Lowell U.S.A. 84 42.39N 71.18W
Lower Arrow L. Canada 74 49.40N118.05W
Lower California pen. see Baja California pen. Mexico 86

Lower Egypt to Makuliro

Lower Egypt see Mişr Baḥrī f. Egypt 44
Lower Hutt New Zealand 60 41.13S174.55E
Lower Lough Erne U.K. 13 54.28N 7.48W
Lower Post Canada 74 59.55N128.30W
Lower Red L. U.S.A. 82 48.00N 94.50W
Lowestoft U.K. 11 52.29N 1.44E
Lowgar d. Afghan. 40 34.10N 69.20E
Łowicz Poland 21 52.06N 19.55E
Lowrah r. Afghan. see Pishīn Lora r. Pakistan 40
Loxton Australia 66 34.38S140.38E
Loyalty Is. see Loyauté, Îles is. N. Cal. 68
Loyauté, Îles is. N. Cal. 68 21.00S167.00E
Loyoro Uganda 55 3.22N 34.16E
Loznica Yugo. 19 44.32N 19.13E
Lua r. Zaïre 54 2.45N 18.28E
Luabo Mozambique 57 18.30S 36.10E
Luachimo Angola 54 7.25S 20.43E
Lualaba r. Zaïre 54 0.18N 25.32E
Luama r. Zaïre 55 4.45S 26.55E
Luampa Zambia 54 15.04S 24.20E
Lu'an China 33 31.47N116.30E
Luancheng Guang. Zhuang. China 33 22.48N108.55E
Luancheng Hebei China 32 37.53N114.39E
Luanda Angola 54 8.50S 13.20E
Luanda d. Angola 54 9.00S 13.30E
Luando Game Res. Angola 54 11.00S 17.45E
Luanginga r. Zambia 54 15.11S 23.05E
Luangwa r. Central Zambia 55 15.32S 30.28E
Luan He r. China 32 39.25N119.10E
Luanping China 32 40.55N117.17E
Luanshya Zambia 55 13.09S 28.24E
Luan Xian China 32 39.45N118.44E
Luao Angola 54 10.41S 22.09E
Luapula r. Zambia 55 9.25S 28.36E
Luarca Spain 16 43.33N 6.31W
Lubalo Angola 54 9.13S 19.21E
Lubango Angola 54 14.52S 13.30E
Lubao Zaïre 54 5.19S 25.43E
Lubbock U.S.A. 83 33.35N101.51W
Lubeck Australia 66 36.47S142.38E
Lübeck W. Germany 20 53.52N 10.40E
Lubefu r. Zaïre 54 4.05S 23.00E
Lubenka U.S.S.R. 25 50.22N 54.13E
Lubersac France 17 45.27N 1.24E
Lubia Angola 54 11.01S 17.06E
Lubika Zaïre 55 7.50S 29.12E
Lubilash r. Zaïre 54 4.59S 23.25E
Lubin Poland 20 51.24N 16.13E
Lublin Poland 21 51.18N 22.31E
Lubliniec Poland 21 50.40N 18.41E
Lubny U.S.S.R. 25 50.01N 33.00E
Lubudi Zaïre 54 9.57S 25.59E
Lubudi r. K.Occidental Zaïre 54 4.00S 21.23E
Lubudi r. Shaba Zaïre 54 9.13S 25.40E
Lubumbashi Zaïre 55 11.44S 27.29E
Lubutu Zaïre 54 0.48S 26.19E
Lucas González Argentina 93 32.25S 59.33W
Lucca Italy 15 43.50N 10.29E
Luce B. U.K. 12 54.45N 4.47W
Lucena Phil. 37 13.56N121.37E
Lucena Spain 16 37.25N 4.29W
Lucena del Cid Spain 16 40.09N 0.17W
Lučenec Czech. 21 48.20N 19.40E
Lucera Italy 18 41.30N 15.20E
Lucerne U.S.A. 80 48.12N120.36W
Lucero Mexico 81 30.49N106.30W
Lucin U.S.A. 80 41.22N113.55W
Lucindale Australia 66 36.59S140.25E
Lucira Angola 54 13.51S 12.31E
Luckeesarai India 41 25.11N 86.05E
Luckenwalde E. Germany 20 52.05N 13.11E
Lucknow India 41 26.51N 80.55E
Lucy Creek town Australia 64 22.25S136.20E
Lüda China 32 38.49N121.48E
Lüdenscheid W. Germany 14 51.13N 7.36E
Lüderitz Namibia 56 26.37S 15.09E
Ludhiāna India 40 30.55N 75.51E
Lüdinghausen W. Germany 14 51.46N 7.27E
Ludington U.S.A. 84 43.58N 86.27W
Ludlow U.K. 11 52.23N 2.42W
Ludogorie mts. Bulgaria 21 43.45N 27.00E
Luduş Romania 21 46.29N 24.05E
Ludvika Sweden 23 60.09N 15.11E
Ludwigsburg W. Germany 20 48.53N 9.11E
Ludwigshafen W. Germany 20 49.29N 8.27E
Luebo Zaïre 54 5.16S 21.27E
Luena Angola 54 11.46S 19.55E
Luena r. Angola 54 12.30S 22.37E
Luena Zaïre 54 9.27S 25.47E
Luena Zambia 55 10.40S 30.21E
Luena r. Western Zambia 54 14.47S 23.05E
Luengue r. Angola 54 16.58S 21.15E
Luenha r. Mozambique 57 16.29S 33.40E
Lüeyang China 32 33.20N106.05E
Lufeng China 33 23.01N115.35E
Lufira r. Zaïre 54 8.15S 26.30E
Lufkin U.S.A. 79 31.21N 94.47W
Luga U.S.S.R. 24 58.42N 29.49E
Lugano Switz. 15 46.01N 8.58E
Lugano, Lago di l. Switz./Italy 15 46.00N 9.00E
Luganville Vanuatu 68 15.32S167.08E
Lugela Mozambique 57 16.25S 36.42E
Lugenda r. Mozambique 55 11.23S 38.30E
Lugh Ganane Somali Rep. 55 3.56N 42.32E
Luginy U.S.S.R. 21 51.05N 28.21E
Lugnaquilla Mtn. Rep. of Ire. 13 52.58N 6.28W
Lugo Italy 15 44.25N 11.54E
Lugo Spain 16 43.00N 7.33W
Lugoj Romania 21 45.42N 21.56E
Luiana Angola 54 17.08S 22.59E
Luiana r. Angola 54 17.28S 23.02E
Luilaka r. Zaïre 54 0.15S 19.00E
Luilu r. Zaïre 54 6.22S 23.53E
Luino Italy 15 46.00N 8.44E
Luiro r. Finland 22 67.18N 27.28E
Luisa Zaïre 54 7.15S 22.27E
Lujiang China 33 31.14N117.17E
Lukala Zaïre 54 5.23S 13.02E
Lukanga Swamp f. Zambia 55 14.15S 27.30E
Lukenie r. Zaïre 54 2.43S 18.12E
Lukka Sudan 48 14.33N 23.42E
Łuków Poland 21 51.56N 22.23E
Lukoyanov U.S.S.R. 24 55.03N 44.29E
Lukuga r. Zaïre 55 5.37S 26.58E
Lukula r. Zaïre 54 4.15S 17.59E
Lukulu Zambia 54 14.35S 23.25E
Lukumbule Tanzania 55 11.34S 37.24E
Lule r. Sweden 22 65.35N 22.03E
Luleå Sweden 22 65.34N 22.10E
Lüleburgaz Turkey 19 41.25N 27.23E
Lüliang Shan mts. China 32 37.00N111.20E
Lulonga r. Zaïre 54 0.42N 18.26E
Lulu r. Zaïre 54 1.18N 23.42E
Lulua r. Zaïre 54 5.03S 21.07E
Lumai Angola 54 13.13S 21.13E
Lumajangdong Co l. China 41 34.02N 81.40E
Lumbala Moxico Angola 54 14.02S 21.35E
Lumbala Moxico Angola 54 12.37S 22.33E
Lumberton Miss. U.S.A. 83 31.00N 89.27W
Lumberton N.Mex. U.S.A. 80 36.55N106.56W
Lumsden New Zealand 60 45.44S168.26E
Lūnāvāda India 40 23.08N 73.37E
Lund Sweden 23 55.42N 13.11E
Lund Nev. U.S.A. 80 38.52N115.00W
Lund Utah U.S.A. 80 38.01N113.28W
Lunda Norte d. Angola 54 8.30S 19.00E
Lunda Sul d. Angola 54 11.00S 20.00E
Lundazi Zambia 55 12.19S 33.11E
Lundi r. Zimbabwe 57 21.20S 32.23E
Lundy i. U.K. 11 51.10N 4.41W
Lune r. U.K. 10 54.03N 2.49W
Lüneburg W. Germany 20 53.15N 10.24E
Lünen W. Germany 14 51.37N 7.31E
Lunéville France 17 48.36N 6.30E
Lunga r. Zambia 54 14.28S 26.27E
Lunge Angola 54 12.13S 16.07E
Lunggar China 41 31.10N 84.01E
Lungwebungu r. Zambia 54 14.20S 23.15E
Lūni India 40 26.00N 73.00E
Lūni r. India 40 24.41N 71.15E
Luninets U.S.S.R. 21 52.18N 26.50E
Luning U.S.A. 80 38.30N118.10W
Lūnkaransar India 40 28.32N 73.50E
Luocheng China 33 24.47N108.54E
Luodian China 33 25.29N106.39E
Luoding China 33 22.44N111.32E
Luofo Zaïre 55 0.12S 29.15E
Luogosanto Italy 18 41.02N 9.12E
Luohe China 32 33.30N114.04E
Luo He r. China 32 34.40N110.15E
Luonan China 32 34.06N110.10E
Luoyang China 32 34.48N112.25E
Lupilichi Mozambique 55 11.45S 35.15E
Luquan China 39 25.35N102.30E
Lūrah r. Afghan. 40 31.20N 65.45E
Lure France 17 47.42N 6.30E
Lurgan U.K. 13 54.28N 6.21W
Lurio Mozambique 55 13.30S 40.30E
Lurio r. Mozambique 55 13.32S 40.31E
Lusaka Zambia 55 15.20S 28.14E
Lusambo Zaïre 54 4.59S 23.26E
Luscar Canada 74 53.05N117.26W
Lu Shan mtn. China 32 36.18N118.03E
Lüshi China 32 34.04N111.02E
Lushnje Albania 19 40.56N 19.42E
Lushoto Tanzania 55 4.48S 38.20E
Lüshun China 32 38.42N121.15E
Lusk U.S.A. 80 42.46N104.27W
Lüta see Lüda China 32
Luton U.K. 11 51.53N 0.25W
Lutsk U.S.S.R. 21 50.42N 25.15E
Lutterworth U.K. 11 52.28N 1.12W
Luverne U.S.A. 82 43.39N 96.13W
Luvua r. Zaïre 55 6.45S 27.00E
Luwegu r. Tanzania 55 8.30S 37.28E
Luwingu Zambia 55 10.13S 30.05E
Luxembourg d. Belgium 14 49.58N 5.30E
Luxembourg Europe 14 49.50N 6.15E
Luxembourg town Lux. 14 49.37N 6.08E
Luxi China 33 28.17N110.10E
Luxor see Al Uqşur Egypt 42
Luza U.S.S.R. 24 60.41N 47.12E
Luza r. U.S.S.R. 24 60.45N 46.25E
Luzarches France 15 49.07N 2.25E
Luzern Switz. 20 47.03N 8.17E
Luzhai China 33 24.29N109.29E
Luzhou China 33 28.48N105.23E
Luziânia Brazil 91 16.18S 47.57W
Luzon i. Phil. 37 17.50N121.00E
Luzon Str. Pacific Oc. 37 20.20N122.00E
Lvov U.S.S.R. 21 49.50N 24.00E
Lyantonde Uganda 55 0.26S 31.08E
Lybster U.K. 12 58.18N 3.18W
Lycksele Sweden 22 64.36N 18.40E
Lydenburg R.S.A. 56 25.06S 30.27E
Lyell I. Canada 74 52.40N131.35W
Lyme B. U.K. 11 50.40N 2.55W
Lyme Regis U.K. 11 50.44N 2.57W
Lymington U.K. 11 50.46N 1.32W
Łyna r. Poland 21 54.37N 21.14E
Lynchburg U.S.A. 85 37.24N 79.10W
Lynd Australia 64 18.56S144.30E
Lynden Canada 76 43.14N 80.09W
Lyndhurst Australia 66 30.19S138.24E
Lyndonville U.S.A. 76 43.19N 78.23W
Lyngdal Norway 23 58.08N 7.05E
Lyngen Norway 22 69.36N 20.10E
Lyngen est. Norway 22 69.35N 20.20E
Lynn U.S.A. 84 42.28N 70.57W
Lynn Canal U.S.A. 74 58.38N135.08W
Lynn Lake town Canada 75 56.51N101.03W
Lynton U.K. 11 51.14N 3.50W
Lynx Canada 76 50.08N 85.55W
Lyon France 17 45.46N 4.50E
Lyons Australia 66 30.34S133.50E
Lyons r. Australia 62 25.02S115.09E
Lysefjorden est. Norway 23 59.00N 6.14E
Lysekil Sweden 23 58.16N 11.26E
Lysva U.S.S.R. 24 58.07N 57.49E
Lysyanka U.S.S.R. 21 49.16N 30.49E
Lysyye Gory U.S.S.R. 25 51.32N 44.48E
Lytham St. Anne's U.K. 10 53.45N 3.01W
Lyubar U.S.S.R. 21 49.58N 27.41E
Lyubech U.S.S.R. 21 51.42N 30.41E
Lyubertsy U.S.S.R. 24 55.38N 37.58E
Lyubeshov U.S.S.R. 21 51.42N 25.32E
Lyushcha U.S.S.R. 21 52.28N 26.41E

M

Ma r. Vietnam 33 19.48N105.55E
Ma, Oued el- wadi Mauritania 50 24.30N 9.10W
Maamakeogh mtn. Rep. of Ire. 13 54.17N 9.29W
Maamturk Mts. Rep. of Ire. 13 53.32N 9.42W
Ma'ān Jordan 44 30.11N 35.43E
Ma'anshan China 33 31.47N118.33E
Maarianhamina Finland 23 60.06N 19.57E
Maas r. Neth. 14 51.44N 4.42E
Maaseik Belgium 14 51.08N 5.48E
Maassluis Neth. 14 51.58N 4.12E
Maastricht Neth. 14 50.51N 5.42E
Maave Mozambique 57 21.06S 34.48E
Maaza Plateau Egypt 44 27.39N 31.45E
Mabalane Mozambique 57 23.49S 32.36E
Mabel Creek town Australia 65 29.01S134.17E
Mablethorpe U.K. 10 53.21N 0.14E
Mabrouk Mali 52 19.29N 1.15W
Macá mtn. Chile 93 45.06S 73.12W
Macaé Brazil 94 22.21S 41.48W
Macalister r. Australia 67 37.55S146.50E
Macapá Brazil 91 0.04N 51.04W
Macaroni Australia 64 16.36S141.30E
Macau Asia 33 22.11N113.33E
Macau Brazil 91 5.05S 36.37W
Macclesfield U.K. 10 53.16N 2.09W
Macdiarmid Canada 76 49.27N 88.08W
Macdoel U.S.A. 80 41.50N122.00W
Macdonald, L. Australia 62 23.30S129.00E
Macdonnell Ranges mts. Australia 64 23.45S133.20E
Macduff U.K. 12 57.40N 2.29W
Macedon mtn. Australia 67 37.27S144.34E
Macedonia see Makedonija d. Yugo. 19
Maceió Brazil 91 9.40S 35.44W
Macenta Guinea 52 8.31N 9.32W
Macerata Italy 18 43.18N 13.30E
MacFarlane r. Canada 75 59.12N107.58W
Macfarlane, L. Australia 66 31.55S136.42E
Macgillycuddy's Reeks mts. Rep. of Ire. 13 52.00N 9.43W
Machado Brazil 94 21.39S 45.33W
Machala Ecuador 90 3.20S 79.57W
Machattie, L. Australia 64 24.50S139.48E
Machece Mozambique 57 19.17S 35.33E
Macheke Zimbabwe 57 18.08S 31.49E
Macheng China 33 31.11N115.02E
Machevna U.S.S.R. 29 60.46N171.40E
Machias Maine U.S.A. 84 44.43N 67.28W
Machichi r. Canada 75 57.03N 92.06W
Machida Japan 35 35.32N139.27E
Machilipatnam India 39 16.13N 81.12E
Machiques Venezuela 90 10.04N 72.37W
Machiya r. Japan 35 35.01N136.42E
Machrihanish U.K. 12 55.25N 5.44W
Machynlleth U.K. 11 52.35N 3.51W
Maciá Argentina 93 32.11S 59.25W
Macia Mozambique 57 25.03S 33.10E
Macintyre r. Australia 67 28.50S150.50E
Mackay Australia 64 21.09S149.11E
MacKay U.S.A. 80 43.55N113.37W
Mackay, L. Australia 62 22.30S149.10E
Mackenzie r. Australia 64 22.48S149.15E
Mackenzie d. Canada 72 65.00N115.00W
Mackenzie r. Canada 72 69.20N134.00W
Mackenzie King I. Canada 72 77.30N112.00W
Mackenzie Mts. Canada 72 64.00N130.00W
Mackinaw City U.S.A. 84 45.47N 84.43W
Mackinnon Road town Kenya 55 3.50S 39.03E
Macklin Canada 75 52.20N109.56W
Macksville Australia 67 30.43S152.55E
Maclean Australia 65 29.27S153.14E
Maclear R.S.A. 56 31.04S 28.21E
Macleay r. Australia 67 30.52S153.01E
Maçobere Mozambique 57 21.14S 32.50E
Macomer Italy 18 40.16N 8.45E
Mâcon France 17 46.18N 4.50E
Macon Ga. U.S.A. 85 32.49N 83.37W
Macon Mo. U.S.A. 82 39.44N 92.28W
Macpherson Range mts. Australia 67 28.15S153.00E
Macquarie r. Australia 67 30.07S147.24E
Macquarie, L. Australia 67 33.05S151.35E
Macquarie-Balleny Ridge Pacific Oc. 68 58.00S160.00E
Macquarie I. Pacific Oc. 68 54.29S158.58E
Macquarie Marshes Australia 67 30.50S147.32E
MacRobertson Land f. Antarctica 96 69.30S 64.00E
Macroom Rep. of Ire. 13 51.54N 8.58W
Macumba r. Australia 65 27.55S137.15E
Ma'dabā Jordan 44 31.44N 35.48E
Madagascar Africa 57 17.00S 46.00E
Madang P.N.G. 37 5.14S145.45E
Madaoua Niger 53 14.05N 6.27E
Mādārīpur Bangla. 41 23.10N 90.12E
Madawaska U.S.A. 84 47.21N 68.20W
Madeira r. Brazil 90 3.20S 59.00W
Madeira i. Madeira Is. 95 32.45N 17.00W
Madeira, Arquipélago da is. Atlantic Oc. 95 32.45N 17.00W
Madeira Is. see Madeira, Arquipélago da is. Atlantic Oc. 95
Madeleine, Îles de la is. Canada 77 47.20N 61.50W
Madera U.S.A. 80 36.57N120.03W
Madera, Sierra de la mts. Mexico 81 30.20N109.00W
Madgaon India 38 15.26N 73.50E
Madhubani India 41 26.22N 86.05E
Madhupur India 41 24.16N 86.39E
Madhya Pradesh d. India 41 23.30N 78.30E
Madibira Tanzania 55 8.13S 34.47E
Madigan G. Australia 66 28.55S137.48E
Madill U.S.A. 83 34.06N 96.46W
Madīnat ash Sha'b S. Yemen 45 12.50N 44.56E
Madison Fla. U.S.A. 79 30.29N 83.39W
Madison Ind. U.S.A. 84 38.46N 85.22W
Madison N.J. U.S.A. 85 40.46N 74.25W
Madison S.Dak. U.S.A. 82 44.00N 97.07W
Madison Tenn. U.S.A. 85 36.16N 86.44W
Madison Wisc. U.S.A. 82 43.05N 89.22W
Madison W.Va. U.S.A. 85 38.03N 81.50W
Madison Junction U.S.A. 80 44.39N110.51W
Madisonville Ky. U.S.A. 85 37.20N 87.30W
Madisonville Tex. U.S.A. 83 30.57N 95.55W
Madiun Indonesia 37 7.37S111.33E
Madoc Canada 76 44.30N 77.28W
Mado Gashi Kenya 55 0.40N 39.11E
Madoi China 30 34.28N 98.56E
Madonna di Campiglio Italy 15 46.14N 10.49E
Madrakah, Ra's al c. Oman 38 19.00N 57.50E
Madras India 39 13.05N 80.18E
Madras U.S.A. 80 44.38N121.08W
Madre, Laguna b. Mexico 83 25.00N 97.40W
Madre, Laguna b. U.S.A. 83 27.00N 97.35W
Madre, Sierra mts. Mexico/Guatemala 86 15.20N 92.20W
Madre de Dios r. Bolivia 90 10.24S 65.30W
Madre del Sur, Sierra mts. Mexico 86 17.00N100.00W
Madre Occidental, Sierra mts. Mexico 81 25.00N105.00W
Madre Oriental, Sierra mts. Mexico 83 28.10N102.10W
Madrid Spain 16 40.25N 3.43W
Madukani Tanzania 55 3.57S 35.49E
Madura i. Indonesia 37 7.02S113.22E
Madurai India 39 9.55N 78.07E
Mae Klong r. Thailand 34 13.21N100.00E
Mae Sot Thailand 34 16.40N 98.35E
Maestra, Sierra mts. Cuba 87 20.10N 76.30W
Maevatanana Madagascar 57 16.56S 46.49E
Maewo i. Vanuatu 68 15.10S168.10E
Mafeking Canada 75 52.43N100.59W
Mafeteng Lesotho 56 29.51S 27.13E
Maffra Australia 67 37.58S146.59E
Mafia I. Tanzania 55 7.50S 39.50E
Mafikeng R.S.A. 56 25.52S 25.36E
Mafra Portugal 16 38.56N 9.20W
Magadan U.S.S.R. 29 59.38N150.50E
Magadi Kenya 55 1.53S 36.18E
Magallanes, Estrecho de str. Chile 93 53.00S 71.00W
Magalluf Spain 16 39.30N 2.31E
Magangué Colombia 90 9.14N 74.46W
Magazine U.S.A. 83 35.10N 93.40W
Magburaka Sierra Leone 52 8.44N 11.57W
Magdalena Argentina 93 35.04S 57.32W
Magdalena Bolivia 92 13.50S 64.08W
Magdalena r. Colombia 90 10.56N 74.58W
Magdalena Mexico 81 30.38N110.59W
Magdalena, Isla i. Chile 93 44.42S 73.10W
Magdalena, Llano de la f. Mexico 81 24.55N111.40W
Magdalene mtn. Malaysia 36 4.25N117.55E
Magdeburg E. Germany 20 52.08N 11.36E
Magdeburg d. E. Germany 20 52.15N 11.30E
Magé Brazil 94 22.37S 43.03W
Magee U.S.A. 83 31.52N 89.44W
Magelang Indonesia 37 7.28S110.11E
Magellan's Str. see Magallanes, Estrecho de str. Chile 93
Magenta Italy 15 45.28N 8.53E
Magenta, L. Australia 63 33.26S119.10E
Mageröya i. Norway 22 71.03N 25.45E
Maggiorasca, Monte mtn. Italy 15 44.33N 9.29E
Maggiore, Lago l. Italy 15 46.00N 8.40E
Maghāghah Egypt 44 28.39N 30.50E
Magherafelt U.K. 13 54.45N 6.38W
Magna U.S.A. 80 40.42N112.06W
Magnitogorsk U.S.S.R. 24 53.28N 59.06E
Magnolia Ark. U.S.A. 83 33.16N 93.14W
Magnolia Miss. U.S.A. 83 31.09N 90.28W
Magnolia Tex. U.S.A. 83 30.13N 95.45W
Magny-en-Vexin France 15 49.09N 1.47E
Magog Canada 77 45.16N 72.09W
Magoye Zambia 55 16.00S 27.38E
Magpie r. Canada 77 50.18N 64.28W
Magrath Canada 74 49.25N112.50W
Magude Mozambique 57 25.01S 32.39E
Magué Mozambique 55 15.46S 31.42E
Maguse River town Canada 75 61.20N 94.25W
Magwe Burma 34 20.08N 95.00E
Magwe d. Burma 34 23.00N 95.00E
Mahābād Iran 43 36.44N 45.44E
Mahābhārat Range mts. Nepal 41 28.00N 84.30E
Mahabo Madagascar 57 20.23S 44.40E
Mahadday Weyne Somali Rep. 55 2.58N 45.32E
Mahādeo Hills India 41 22.15N 78.30E
Mahagi Zaïre 55 2.16N 30.59E
Mahajamba r. Madagascar 57 15.33S 47.08E
Mahājan India 40 28.47N 73.50E
Mahajanga Madagascar 57 15.43S 46.19E
Mahajilo r. Madagascar 57 19.42S 45.22E
Mahalapye Botswana 56 23.04S 26.47E
Maḩallāt Iran 43 33.54N 50.28E
Mahānadi India 41 20.19N 86.45E
Mahānadi r. India 39 20.17N 86.43E
Mahanoro Madagascar 57 19.54S 48.48E
Mahārājpur India 41 25.01N 79.44E
Mahārāshtra d. India 40 19.40N 76.00E
Mahāsamund India 41 21.06N 82.06E
Maha Sarakham Thailand 34 15.50N103.47E
Mahavavy r. Madagascar 57 15.57S 45.54E
Mahbés W. Sahara 50 27.13N 9.44W
Mahd adh Dhahab Saudi Arabia 42 23.30N 40.52E
Mahdia Guyana 90 5.10N 59.12W
Mahendraganj India 41 25.20N 89.45E
Mahenge Tanzania 55 8.46S 36.38E
Mahi r. India 40 22.30N 72.58E
Mahia Pen. New Zealand 60 39.10S177.50E
Mahmūdābād India 41 27.18N 81.07E
Mahmūd-e 'Erāqī Afghan. 40 35.01N 69.20E
Mahnomen U.S.A. 82 47.19N 96.01W
Maho Sri Lanka 39 7.49N 80.17E
Mahoba India 41 25.17N 79.52E
Mahón Spain 16 39.55N 4.18E
Mahone B. Canada 77 44.30N 64.15W
Mahroni India 41 24.35N 78.43E
Mahuva India 40 21.05N 71.48E
Maiāo i. Îs. de la Société 69 17.23S150.37W
Maidenhead U.K. 11 51.32N 0.44W
Maidstone U.K. 11 51.17N 0.32E
Maiduguri Nigeria 53 11.53N 13.16E
Maignelay France 15 49.33N 2.31E
Maihar India 41 24.16N 80.45E
Maikala Range mts. India 41 21.45N 81.00E
Maiko r. Zaïre 54 0.15N 25.35E
Main r. W. Germany 20 50.00N 8.19E
Main Barrier Range mts. Australia 66 31.25S141.25E
Main Camp Kiribati 69 2.01N157.25W
Main Centre Canada 75 50.38N107.20W
Main Channel str. Canada 76 45.22N 81.50W
Mai Ndombe l. Zaïre 54 2.00S 18.20E
Maine d. U.S.A. 84 45.15N 69.15W
Mainland i. Orkney Is. U.K. 12 59.00N 3.10W
Mainoru Australia 64 14.02S134.05E
Mainpuri India 41 27.14N 79.01E
Maintenon France 15 48.35N 1.35E
Maintirano Madagascar 57 18.03S 44.01E
Mainz W. Germany 20 50.00N 8.16E
Maipo mtn. Argentina 93 34.10S 69.50W
Maipú Argentina 93 36.52S 57.54W
Maiquetía Venezuela 90 10.03N 66.57W
Maiskhāl I. Bangla. 41 21.36N 91.56E
Mait Somali Rep. 45 10.57N 47.06E
Maitland N.S.W. Australia 67 32.33S151.33E
Maitland S.A. Australia 66 34.21S137.42E
Maizhokunggar China 41 29.50N 91.44E
Majeigha Sudan 49 11.33N 24.40E
Majene Indonesia 36 3.33S118.59E
Maji Ethiopia 49 6.11N 35.38E
Majiahewan China 32 37.12N105.48E
Majiang China 33 26.30N107.35E
Majorca i. see Mallorca i. Spain 16
Majrūr Sudan 48 14.01N 30.27E
Majuba Hill R.S.A. 56 27.26S 29.48E
Majuro i. Pacific Oc. 68 7.09N171.12E
Makabana Congo 54 3.25S 12.41E
Makale Indonesia 36 3.06S119.53E
Makalu mtn. China/Nepal 41 27.54N 87.06E
Makarikari Salt Pan f. Botswana 56 20.50S 25.45E
Makarikha U.S.S.R. 24 66.17N 58.28E
Makaryev U.S.S.R. 24 57.52N 43.40E
Makasar, Selat str. Indonesia 36 3.00S118.00E
Makassar Str. see Makasar, Selat str. Indonesia 36
Makat U.S.S.R. 25 47.38N 53.16E
Makaw Burma 34 26.27N 96.42E
Makay, Massif du mts. Madagascar 57 21.15S 45.15E
Makaya Zaïre 54 3.22S 18.02E
Makedonija d. Yugo. 19 41.35N 21.30E
Makefu Niue 68 19.01S169.55W
Makeni Sierra Leone 52 8.57N 12.02W
Makere Tanzania 55 4.15S 30.26E
Makeyevka U.S.S.R. 25 48.01N 38.00E
Makhachkala U.S.S.R. 25 42.59N 47.30E
Makham Thailand 34 12.40N102.12E
Makhfar al Quwayrah Jordan 44 29.49N 35.18E
Makhrūq, Wādī al r. Jordan 44 31.30N 37.10E
Makinsk U.S.S.R. 28 52.40N 70.28E
Makkah Saudi Arabia 48 21.26N 39.49E
Makkovik Canada 77 55.00N 59.10W
Makó Hungary 21 46.13N 20.30E
Mako Senegal 52 13.00N 12.26W
Makokou Gabon 54 0.38N 12.47E
Makoua Congo 54 0.01S 15.40E
Makrai India 40 22.04N 77.06E
Makran f. Asia 43 26.30N 61.20E
Makrāna India 40 27.03N 74.43E
Makrān Coast Range mts. Pakistan 40 25.30N 64.30E
Maksamaa Finland 22 63.14N 22.05E
Makuliro Tanzania 55 9.34S 37.26E

Makurdi to Martina Franca

Makurdi Nigeria **53** 7.44N 8.35E
Māl India **41** 26.52N 88.44E
Malabo Equat. Guinea **53** 3.45N 8.48E
Malacca, Str. of Indian Oc. **36** 3.00N100.30E
Malad City U.S.A. **80** 42.12N112.15W
Málaga Spain **16** 36.43N 4.25W
Malaga U.S.A. **81** 32.14N104.04W
Malaimbandy Madagascar **57** 20.20S 45.36E
Malaita Solomon Is. **68** 9.00S161.00E
Malakāl Sudan **49** 9.31N 31.39E
Malakand Pakistan **40** 34.34N 71.56E
Malam Chad **49** 11.27N 20.59E
Malang Indonesia **37** 7.59S112.45E
Malange Angola **54** 9.36S 16.21E
Malange *d.* Angola **54** 9.00S 17.00E
Malangwa Nepal **41** 26.52N 85.34E
Mälaren *l.* Sweden **23** 59.30N 17.12E
Malartic Canada **76** 48.09N 78.09W
Malatya Turkey **42** 38.22N 38.18E
Malaut India **40** 30.11N 74.30E
Malaŵi Africa **55** 12.00S 34.00E
Malaŵi, L. Africa **55** 12.00S 34.30E
Malaya Vishera U.S.S.R. **24** 58.53N 32.08E
Malāyer Iran **43** 34.19N 48.51E
Malaysia Asia **36** 5.00N110.00E
Malazgirt Turkey **42** 39.09N 42.31E
Malbaie *r.* Canada **77** 47.40N 70.05W
Malbaie, Baie de *b.* Canada **77** 48.35N 64.16W
Malbooma Australia **66** 30.41S134.11E
Malbork Poland **21** 54.02N 19.01E
Malcolm Australia **63** 28.56S121.30E
Malcolm, Pt. Australia **63** 33.47S123.44E
Malden Mo. U.S.A. **83** 36.34N 89.57W
Malden I. Kiribati **69** 4.03S154.49W
Maldives Indian Oc. **38** 6.20N 73.00E
Maldon U.K. **11** 51.43N 0.41E
Maldonado Uruguay **94** 34.57S 54.59W
Male Italy **15** 46.21N 10.55E
Maléa, Ákra *c.* Greece **19** 36.27N 23.11E
Malebo Pool *f.* Zaïre **54** 4.15S 15.25E
Mālegaon India **40** 20.33N 74.32E
Malek Sudan **49** 6.04N 31.36E
Malek Dīn Afghan. **40** 32.25N 68.04E
Malekula *i.* Vanuatu **68** 16.15S167.30E
Malema Mozambique **55** 14.55S 37.09E
Malenga U.S.S.R. **24** 63.50N 36.50E
Māler Kotla India **40** 30.32N 75.53E
Malesherbes France **15** 48.18N 2.25E
Malgomaj *l.* Sweden **22** 64.47N 16.12E
Malheur L. U.S.A. **80** 43.20N118.45W
Mali Africa **52** 17.30N 2.30E
Mali *r.* Burma **34** 25.43N 97.29E
Malik, Wādī al Sudan **48** 18.02N 30.58E
Malili Indonesia **37** 2.38S121.06E
Malin U.S.S.R. **21** 50.48N 29.08E
Malinau Indonesia **36** 3.35N116.38E
Malindi Kenya **55** 3.14S 40.08E
Malingping Indonesia **37** 6.45S106.01E
Malin Head Rep. of Ire. **13** 55.23N 7.24W
Malin More Rep. of Ire. **13** 54.42N 8.48W
Malipo China **33** 23.11N104.41E
Malita Phil. **37** 6.19N125.39E
Māliya India **40** 23.05N 70.46E
Malkāpur India **40** 20.53N 76.12E
Mallacoota Australia **67** 37.34S149.43E
Mallacoota Inlet *b.* Australia **67** 37.34S149.43E
Mallaig U.K. **12** 57.00N 5.50W
Mallawi Egypt **44** 27.44N 30.50E
Mallorca *i.* Spain **16** 39.35N 3.00E
Mallow Rep. of Ire. **13** 52.08N 8.39W
Malm Norway **22** 64.04N 11.12E
Malmberget Sweden **22** 67.10N 20.40E
Malmédy Belgium **14** 50.25N 6.02E
Malmesbury R.S.A. **56** 33.28S 18.43E
Malmö Sweden **23** 55.36N 13.00E
Malmöhus *d.* Sweden **23** 55.45N 13.30E
Malmyzh U.S.S.R. **24** 56.34N 50.41E
Maloja Switz. **15** 46.24N 9.41E
Malolos Guam **68** 13.18N144.46E
Malone U.S.A. **84** 44.51N 74.17W
Malonga Zaïre **54** 10.26S 23.10E
Malorita U.S.S.R. **21** 51.50N 24.08E
Målöy Norway **23** 61.56N 5.07E
Malozemelskaya Tundra *f.* U.S.S.R. **24** 67.40N 50.10E
Malpas Australia **66** 34.44S140.43E
Malta Europe **18** 35.55N 14.25E
Malta Mont. U.S.A. **80** 48.21N107.52W
Malta Channel Med. Sea **18** 36.20N 14.45E
Maltby U.K. **10** 53.25N 1.12W
Malton U.K. **10** 54.09N 0.48W
Maluku *d.* Indonesia **37** 4.00S129.00E
Maluku, Laut *sea* Pacific Oc. **37**
Malumfashi Nigeria **53** 11.48N 7.36E
Malundo Angola **54** 14.51S 22.00E
Malung Sweden **23** 60.40N 13.44E
Malūț Sudan **49** 10.26N 32.12E
Mama U.S.S.R. **29** 58.20N112.55E
Mamadysh U.S.S.R. **24** 55.43N 51.20E
Mamaia Romania **21** 44.15N 28.37E
Mambasa Zaïre **55** 1.20N 29.05E
Mamberamo *r.* Indonesia **37** 1.45S137.25E
Mambéré *r.* C.A.R. **53** 3.30N 16.08E
Mambilima Falls *town* Zambia **55** 10.32S 28.45E
Mamers France **15** 48.21N 0.23E
Mamfe Cameroon **53** 5.46N 9.18E
Mamonovo U.S.S.R. **21** 54.30N 19.59E
Mamore *r.* Bolivia **92** 12.00S 65.15W
Mamou Guinea **52** 10.24N 12.05W
Mampika Congo **54** 2.58S 14.38E
Mampikony Madagascar **57** 16.06S 47.38E
Mampong Ghana **52** 7.06N 1.24W
Mamry, Jezioro *l.* Poland **21** 54.08N 21.42E
Mamuju Indonesia **36** 2.41S118.55E
Ma'mūn Sudan **49** 12.15N 22.41E
Man Ivory Coast **52** 7.31N 7.37W
Man Jammu & Kashmir **41** 33.51N 78.32E
Man, Isle of U.K. **10** 54.15N 4.30W
Mana *r.* Ethiopia **49** 6.20N 40.41E
Mana *r.* Guiana **91** 5.35N 53.55W
Mana Hawaiian Is. **69** 22.02N156.46W
Manacapuru Brazil **90** 3.16S 60.37W
Manacor Spain **16** 39.32N 3.12E
Manado Indonesia **37** 1.30N124.58E
Managua Nicaragua **87** 12.06N 86.18W
Managua, Lago de *l.* Nicaragua **87** 12.10N 86.30W
Manahawkin U.S.A. **85** 39.42N 74.16W
Manakara Madagascar **57** 22.08S 48.01E
Manāli India **40** 32.16N 77.10E
Manambao *r.* Madagascar **57** 17.43S 43.57E
Mananara Madagascar **57** 16.10S 49.46E
Mananara *r.* Madagascar **57** 23.21S 47.42E
Mananjary Madagascar **57** 21.13S 48.20E
Manankoro Mali **52** 10.25N 7.26W
Manantenina Madagascar **57** 24.17S 47.19E
Manapouri, L. New Zealand **60** 45.30S167.00E
Manār *r.* India **40** 18.39N 77.44E
Manara Australia **66** 32.28S143.59E
Manāslu *mtn.* Nepal **41** 28.33N 84.35E
Manasquan U.S.A. **85** 40.07N 74.03W
Manau P.N.G. **37** 8.02S148.00E
Manaus Brazil **90** 3.06S 60.00W
Manāwar India **40** 22.14N 75.05E
Mancelona U.S.A. **84** 44.54N 85.03W
Manche *d.* France **15** 49.00N 1.10W
Mancherāl India **41** 18.52N 79.26E
Manchester U.K. **10** 53.30N 2.15W
Manchester Conn. U.S.A. **84** 41.47N 72.31W
Manchester N.H. U.S.A. **84** 42.59N 71.28W
Manchurian Plain *f. see* Dongbei Pingyuan *f.* China **31**
Mand *r.* Iran **43** 28.09N 51.16E
Manda Iringa Tanzania **55** 10.30S 34.37E
Manda Mbeya Tanzania **55** 7.59S 32.27E
Manda, Jabal *mtn.* Sudan **49** 8.39N 24.27E
Mandabe Madagascar **57** 21.03S 44.55E
Mandal Norway **23** 58.02N 7.27E
Mandala Peak Indonesia **37** 4.45S140.15E
Mandalay Burma **34** 21.58N 96.04E
Mandalay *d.* Burma **34** 22.00N 96.00E
Mandalgovi Mongolia **32** 45.40N106.10E
Mandals *r.* Norway **23** 58.02N 7.28E
Mandan U.S.A. **82** 46.50N100.54W
Mandara Mts. Nigeria / Cameroon **53** 10.30N 13.30E
Mandasor India **40** 24.04N 75.04E
Mandeb, Bāb el *str.* Asia **49** 13.00N 43.10E
Mandel Afghan. **40** 33.17N 61.52E
Mandera Kenya **55** 3.55N 41.50E
Mandi India **40** 31.42N 76.55E
Mandiana Guinea **52** 10.37N 8.39W
Mandi Būrewāla Pakistan **40** 30.09N 72.41E
Mandi Dabwāli India **40** 29.58N 74.42E
Mandji Gabon **54** 1.37S 10.53E
Mandla India **41** 22.36N 80.23E
Mandora Australia **62** 19.45S120.50E
Mandoto Madagascar **57** 19.34S 46.17E
Mandra Pakistan **40** 33.22N 73.14E
Mandritsara Madagascar **57** 15.50S 48.49E
Mandu India **40** 22.22N 75.23E
Mandurah Australia **63** 32.31S115.41E
Manduria Italy **19** 40.24N 17.38E
Māndvi India **40** 22.50N 69.22E
Mandya India **38** 12.33N 76.54E
Måne *r.* Norway **23** 59.55N 8.48E
Manendragarh India **41** 23.13N 82.13E
Manerbio Italy **15** 45.21N 10.08E
Manevichi U.S.S.R. **21** 51.19N 25.35E
Manfred Australia **66** 33.21S143.50E
Manfredonia Italy **18** 41.38N 15.54E
Manfredonia, Golfo di *g.* Italy **18** 41.35N 16.05E
Mangaia I. Cook Is. **69** 21.56S157.56W
Mangaldai India **41** 26.26N 92.02E
Mangalia Romania **21** 43.50N 28.35E
Mangalore Australia **64** 26.42S146.08E
Mangalore India **38** 12.54N 74.51E
Mangando Angola **54** 8.02S 17.08E
Mangareva *i.* Pacific Oc. **69** 23.07S134.57W
Mangawān India **41** 24.41N 81.33E
Mangaweka New Zealand **60** 38.49S175.48E
Mangeigne Chad **49** 10.31N 21.19E
Mangnai China **30** 37.52N 91.26E
Mango Togo **52** 10.23N 0.30E
Mangochi Malaŵi **55** 14.29S 35.15E
Mangoky *r.* Madagascar **57** 21.29S 43.41E
Mangombe Zaïre **55** 1.23S 26.50E
Mangonui New Zealand **60** 35.00S173.34E
Mangoro *r.* Madagascar **57** 20.00S 48.45E
Māngrol India **40** 21.07N 70.07E
Mangueira, L. Brazil **94** 33.06S 52.48W
Mangum U.S.A. **83** 34.53N 99.30W
Mangyshlak, Poluostrov *pen.* U.S.S.R. **25** 44.00N 52.30E
Manhattan U.S.A. **82** 39.11N 96.35W
Manhiça Mozambique **57** 25.24S 32.49E
Manhuaçu Brazil **94** 20.16S 42.01W
Manhumirim Brazil **94** 20.22S 41.57W
Mania *r.* Madagascar **57** 19.42S 45.22E
Maniago Italy **15** 46.10N 12.43E
Maniamba Mozambique **55** 12.30S 35.05E
Manica Mozambique **57** 19.00S 33.00E
Manica *d.* Mozambique **57** 20.00S 34.00E
Manicoré Brazil **90** 5.49S 61.17W
Manicouagane *r.* Canada **77** 49.15N 68.20W
Manicouagane, Résr. Canada **77** 51.20N 68.48W
Maniitsoq *see* Sukkertoppen Greenland **73**
Mānikganj Bangla. **41** 23.19N 87.03E
Mānikpur India **41** 25.04N 81.07E
Manila Phil. **37** 14.36N120.59E
Manila U.S.A. **80** 40.59N109.43W
Manildra Australia **67** 33.12S148.41E
Manilla Australia **67** 30.45S150.45E
Maningory *r.* Madagascar **57** 17.13S 49.28E
Maningrida Australia **64** 12.03S134.13E
Manipur *d.* India **39** 25.00N 93.40E
Manisa Turkey **19** 38.37N 27.28E
Manistee U.S.A. **84** 44.14N 86.20W
Manistee *r.* U.S.A. **84** 44.14N 86.20W
Manistique U.S.A. **84** 45.58N 86.17W
Manitoba *d.* Canada **75** 55.00N 96.00W
Manitoba, L. Canada **75** 51.00N 98.45W
Manitoulin I. Canada **76** 45.45N 82.30W
Manitowoc U.S.A. **82** 44.06N 87.40W
Maniwaki Canada **76** 46.23N 75.58W
Manizales Colombia **90** 5.03N 75.32W
Manja Madagascar **57** 21.26S 44.20E
Manjakandriana Madagascar **57** 18.55S 47.47E
Mānjhand Pakistan **40** 25.55N 68.14E
Manjīl Iran **43** 36.44N 49.29E
Manjimup Australia **63** 34.14S116.06E
Mankato U.S.A. **82** 44.10N 94.01W
Mankera Pakistan **40** 31.23N 71.26E
Mankono Ivory Coast **52** 8.01N 6.09W
Manly Australia **67** 33.47S151.17E
Manmād India **40** 20.15N 74.27E
Mann *r.* Australia **64** 12.20S134.07E
Män Na Burma **34** 23.27N 97.14E
Manna Indonesia **36** 4.27S102.55E
Mannahill Australia **66** 32.26S139.59E
Mannar Sri Lanka **39** 8.59N 79.54E
Mannar, G. of India / Sri Lanka **39** 8.20N 79.00E
Mannessier, Lac *l.* Canada **77** 55.28N 70.38W
Mannheim W. Germany **20** 49.30N 8.28E
Mannin B. Rep. of Ire. **13** 53.28N 10.06W
Manning Canada **74** 56.53N117.39W
Manning U.S.A. **85** 33.42N 80.12W
Mannu *r.* Sardegna Italy **18** 39.16N 9.00E
Mannum Australia **66** 34.50S139.20E
Mano Sierra Leone **52** 8.04N 12.02W
Manoharpur India **41** 22.23N 85.12E
Manokwari Indonesia **37** 0.53S134.05E
Manombo Madagascar **57** 22.57S 43.28E
Manono Zaïre **55** 7.18S 27.24E
Manorhamilton Rep. of Ire. **13** 54.18N 8.10W
Manosque France **17** 43.50N 5.47E
Manouane *r.* Canada **77** 49.29N 71.13W
Manouane, Lac *l.* Canada **77** 50.40N 70.45W
Mānpur India **41** 20.22N 80.43E
Manresa Spain **16** 41.43N 1.50E
Mānsa Gujarat India **40** 23.26N 72.40E
Mānsa Punjab India **40** 29.59N 75.23E
Mansa Zambia **55** 11.10S 28.52E
Mānsehra Pakistan **40** 34.20N 73.12E
Mansel I. Canada **73** 62.00N 80.00W
Mansfield U.K. **10** 53.08N 1.12W
Mansfield La. U.S.A. **83** 32.02N 93.43W
Mansfield Mass. U.S.A. **84** 42.02N 71.13W
Mansfield Ohio U.S.A. **84** 40.46N 82.31W
Manso *r.* Brazil **92** 11.59S 50.25W
Mansôa Guinea Bissau **52** 12.08N 15.18W
Manta Ecuador **90** 0.59S 80.44W
Mantaro *r.* Peru **90** 12.00S 74.00W
Manteca U.S.A. **80** 37.48N121.13W
Mantes France **15** 49.00N 1.41E
Mantiqueira, Serra da *mts.* Brazil **94** 22.25S 45.00W
Mantova Italy **15** 45.09N 10.47E
Mänttä Finland **23** 62.02N 24.38E
Manturovo U.S.S.R. **24** 58.20N 44.42E
Mäntyluoto Finland **23** 61.35N 21.29E
Manú Peru **90** 12.14S 70.51W
Manua Is. Samoa **68** 14.13S169.35W
Manuel Benavides Mexico **83** 29.05N103.55W
Manui *i.* Indonesia **37** 3.35S123.08E
Manukau Harbour *est.* New Zealand **60** 37.10S174.00E
Manunda *r.* Australia **66** 32.50S138.58E
Manus *i.* P.N.G. **37** 2.00S147.00E
Manuwalkaninna Australia **66** 29.00S139.08E
Manville U.S.A. **80** 42.47N104.37W
Manyane Botswana **56** 23.23S 21.44E
Manyara, L. Tanzania **55** 3.40S 35.50E
Manych *r.* U.S.S.R. **25** 47.14N 40.20E
Manych Gudilo, Ozero *l.* U.S.S.R. **25** 46.20N 42.45E
Manyinga *r.* Zambia **56** 13.28S 24.25E
Manyoni Tanzania **55** 5.46S 34.50E
Mānzai Pakistan **40** 30.07N 68.52E
Manzanares Spain **16** 39.00N 3.23W
Manzanillo Cuba **87** 20.21N 77.21W
Manzano Mts. U.S.A. **81** 34.48N106.12W
Manzhouli China **31** 49.36N117.28E
Manzil Pakistan **40** 29.15N 63.05E
Manzilah, Buḩayrat al *l.* Egypt **44** 31.20N 32.00E
Manzini Swaziland **56** 26.29S 31.24E
Mao Chad **53** 14.06N 15.11E
Maobitou *c.* Taiwan **33** 22.00N120.45E
Maoke, Pegunungan *mts.* Indonesia **37** 4.00S137.30E
Maokui Shan *mtn.* China **32** 33.55N111.33E
Maoming China **33** 21.50N110.58E
Maoniu Shan *mtn.* China **32** 33.00N103.56E
Mapai Mozambique **57** 22.51S 32.00E
Mapam Yumco *l.* China **41** 30.40N 81.20E
Mapia, Kepulauan *is.* Indonesia **37** 1.00N134.15E
Mapimí, Bolsón de *des.* Mexico **83** 27.30N103.15W
Mapinhane Mozambique **57** 22.19S 35.03E
Mapire Venezuela **90** 7.46N 64.41W
Maple Creek *town* Canada **75** 49.55N109.27W
Mappi Indonesia **37** 7.06S139.23E
Maprik P.N.G. **37** 3.38S143.02E
Mapuera *r.* Brazil **91** 2.00S 55.40W
Maputo Mozambique **57** 25.58S 32.35E
Maputo *d.* Mozambique **57** 26.00S 32.30E
Maqnā Saudi Arabia **44** 28.26N 34.44E
Maqu China **39** 34.05N102.15E
Maquan He *r.* China **41** 29.35N 84.10E
Maquela do Zombo Angola **54** 6.06S 15.12E
Maquinchao Argentina **93** 41.15S 68.44W
Maquoketa U.S.A. **82** 42.04N 90.40W
Mar, Serra do *mts.* Brazil **94** 23.00S 44.40W
Mara Tanzania **55** 1.30S 34.31E
Mara *d.* Tanzania **55** 1.45S 34.30E
Mara *r.* Tanzania **55** 1.30S 33.52E
Maraã Brazil **90** 1.50S 65.22W
Maraa Tahiti **69** 17.46S149.34W
Marabá Brazil **91** 5.23S 49.10W
Marabastad R.S.A. **56** 23.58S 29.21E
Maracaibo Venezuela **90** 10.44N 71.37W
Maracaibo, Lago de *l.* Venezuela **90** 9.50N 71.30W
Maracaju, Serra de *mts.* Brazil **94** 21.38S 55.10W
Maracay Venezuela **90** 10.20N 67.28W
Marādah Libya **51** 29.14N 19.13E
Maradi Niger **53** 13.29N 7.10E
Maradi *d.* Niger **53** 14.00N 8.10E
Marāgheh Iran **43** 37.25N 46.13E
Maragogipe Brazil **91** 12.48S 38.59W
Marahuaca, Cerro *mtn.* Venezuela **90** 3.37N 65.25W
Marajó, Ilha de *i.* Brazil **91** 1.00S 49.40W
Maralal Kenya **55** 1.15N 36.48E
Maralinga Australia **63** 30.13S131.32E
Maramba Zambia **54** 17.40S 25.50E
Maramsilli Resr. India **41** 20.32N 81.41E
Mārān, Koh-i- *mtn.* Pakistan **40** 29.33N 66.53E
Marana U.S.A. **81** 32.27N111.13W
Marand Iran **43** 38.25N 45.50E
Maranhão *d.* Brazil **91** 6.00S 45.30W
Maranoa *r.* Australia **65** 27.55S148.30E
Marañón *r.* Peru **90** 4.40S 73.20W
Marão Mozambique **57** 24.21S 34.07E
Marapi *mtn.* Indonesia **36** 0.20S100.45E
Mărășești Romania **21** 45.52N 27.14E
Marathon Australia **64** 20.49S143.34E
Marathón Greece **19** 38.10N 23.59E
Marathon Tex. U.S.A. **83** 30.12N103.15W
Maratua *i.* Indonesia **36** 2.10N118.35E
Marāveh Tappeh Iran **43** 37.55N 55.57E
Marav L. Pakistan **40** 29.04N 69.18E
Marawī Sudan **48** 18.29N 31.49E
Marbella Spain **16** 36.31N 4.53W
Marble Bar Australia **62** 21.16S119.45E
Marburg W. Germany **20** 50.49N 8.36E
Marcaria Italy **15** 45.07N 10.32E
March U.K. **11** 52.33N 0.05E
Marchant Hill Australia **66** 32.16S138.49E
Marche Belgium **14** 50.13N 5.21E
Marche *d.* Italy **18** 43.35N 13.00E
Marchena Spain **16** 37.20N 5.24W
Mar Chiquita *l.* Argentina **92** 30.42S 62.36W
Marcos Paz Argentina **93** 34.49S 58.51W
Marcounda C.A.R. **53** 7.37N 16.59E
Marcq-en-Baroeul France **14** 50.40N 3.01E
Marcus Hook U.S.A. **85** 39.49N 75.25W
Marcus I. Pacific Oc. **68** 24.18N153.58E
Mardān Pakistan **40** 34.12N 72.02E
Mar del Plata Argentina **93** 38.00S 57.32W
Marden U.K. **11** 51.11N 0.30E
Mardie Australia **62** 21.14S115.57E
Mardin Turkey **42** 37.19N 40.43E
Maré, Île *i.* N. Cal. **68** 21.30S168.00E
Maree, Loch U.K. **12** 57.41N 5.28W
Mareeba Australia **64** 17.00S145.26E
Mareg Somali Rep. **45** 3.47N 47.18E
Marettimo *i.* Italy **18** 37.58N 12.05E
Marfa U.S.A. **83** 30.18N104.01W
Margai Caka *l.* China **39** 35.11N 86.57E
Margaret *r.* Australia **66** 29.26S137.00E
Margaret Bay *town* Canada **74** 51.20N127.20W
Margaret L. Canada **74** 58.56N115.25W
Margaret River *town* W. Aust. Australia **63** 33.57S115.04E
Margaret River *town* W. Aust. Australia **62** 18.38S126.52E
Margarita, Isla de *i.* Venezuela **90** 11.00N 64.00W
Margate R.S.A. **56** 30.51S 30.22E
Margate U.K. **11** 51.23N 1.24E
Mārgow, Dasht-e *des.* Afghan. **40** 30.45N 63.10E
María Elena Chile **92** 22.21S 69.40W
María Grande Argentina **93** 31.40S 59.55W
Maria I. Australia **64** 14.52S135.40E
Mariana Brazil **94** 20.23S 43.23W
Mariana Is. Pacific Oc. **37** 15.00N145.00E
Marianao Cuba **87** 23.03N 82.29W
Mariana Ridge Pacific Oc. **68** 17.00N146.00E
Mariana Trench Pacific Oc. **68** 16.00N148.00E
Marianna Ark. U.S.A. **83** 34.46N 90.46W
Marianna Fla. U.S.A. **85** 30.45N 85.15W
Mariánské Lázně Czech. **20** 49.59N 12.43E
Marias *r.* U.S.A. **80** 47.56N110.30W
Maribo Denmark **23** 54.46N 11.31E
Maribor Yugo. **20** 46.35N 15.40E
Marico *r.* R.S.A. **56** 24.12S 26.57E
Maricopa U.S.A. **81** 35.03N119.24W
Maricourt Canada **73** 61.30N 72.00W
Marīdī Sudan **49** 4.55N 29.28E
Marīdī *r.* Sudan **49** 6.55N 29.00E
Marié *r.* Brazil **90** 0.27S 66.26W
Marieburg Belgium **14** 50.07N 4.30E
Marie-Galante *i.* Guadeloupe **87** 15.54N 61.11W
Mariehamn *see* Maarianhamina Finland **23**
Mariemberg Neth. **14** 52.32N 6.35E
Mariental Namibia **56** 24.38S 17.58E
Mariestad Sweden **23** 58.43N 13.51E
Marietta Ga. U.S.A. **85** 33.57N 84.34W
Marietta Ohio U.S.A. **84** 39.26N 81.27W
Marieville Canada **77** 45.26N 73.10W
Mariga *r.* Nigeria **53** 9.37N 5.55E
Marília Brazil **94** 22.13S 50.20W
Marín Spain **16** 42.23N 8.42W
Marina di Ravenna Italy **15** 44.29N 12.17E
Marineland U.S.A. **85** 29.39N 81.13W
Marinette U.S.A. **82** 45.06N 87.38W
Maringá Brazil **94** 23.36S 52.02W
Maringa Zaïre **49** 1.14N 20.00E
Maringa *r.* Zaïre **54** 1.13N 19.50E
Maringue Mozambique **57** 17.55S 34.24E
Marinha Grande Portugal **16** 39.45N 8.55W
Marion Ill. U.S.A. **83** 37.44N 88.56W
Marion Ind. U.S.A. **84** 40.33N 85.40W
Marion Iowa U.S.A. **82** 42.02N 91.36W
Marion Ohio U.S.A. **84** 40.35N 83.08W
Marion S.C. U.S.A. **85** 34.11N 79.23W
Marion Va. U.S.A. **85** 36.51N 81.30W
Marion, L. U.S.A. **85** 33.30N 80.25W
Marion Reef Australia **64** 19.10S152.17E
Mariposa U.S.A. **80** 37.29N119.58W
Mariscal Estigarribia Paraguay **94** 22.03S 60.35W
Maritsa *r.* Turkey **19** 41.00N 26.15E
Marka Somali Rep. **55** 1.42N 44.47E
Markaryd Sweden **23** 56.26N 13.36E
Marked Tree U.S.A. **83** 35.32N 90.25W
Marken *i.* Neth. **14** 52.28N 5.03E
Markerwaard *f.* Neth. **14** 52.30N 5.15E
Market Drayton U.K. **10** 52.55N 2.30W
Market Harborough U.K. **11** 52.29N 0.55W
Market Rasen U.K. **10** 53.24N 0.20W
Market Weighton U.K. **10** 53.52N 0.04W
Markha *r.* U.S.S.R. **29** 63.37N119.00E
Markham Canada **76** 43.52N 79.16W
Markham, Mt. Antarctica **96** 83.00S164.00E
Marks U.S.S.R. **25** 51.43N 46.45E
Marl W. Germany **14** 51.39N 7.03E
Marlborough Australia **64** 22.51S149.50E
Marlborough *d.* New Zealand **60** 41.40S173.40E
Marlborough U.K. **11** 51.26N 1.44W
Marle France **15** 49.44N 3.46E
Marlette U.S.A. **84** 43.20N 83.04W
Marlin U.S.A. **83** 31.18N 96.53W
Marlo Australia **67** 37.50S148.35E
Marmara *i.* Turkey **19** 40.38N 27.37E
Marmara, Sea of *see* Marmara Denizi *sea* Turkey **19**
Marmara Denizi *sea* Turkey **19** 40.45N 28.15E
Marmaris Turkey **19** 36.50N 28.17E
Marmarth U.S.A. **82** 46.18N103.54W
Marmion L. Canada **76** 48.55N 91.25W
Marmolada *mtn.* Italy **15** 46.26N 11.51E
Marne *d.* France **15** 48.55N 4.10E
Marne *r.* France **15** 48.50N 2.25E
Marnoo Australia **66** 36.40S142.55E
Maroantsetra Madagascar **57** 15.26S 49.44E
Marobi Pakistan **40** 32.36N 69.52E
Marolambo Madagascar **57** 20.02S 48.07E
Maromme France **15** 49.28N 1.02E
Marondera Zimbabwe **57** 18.11S 31.31E
Maroni *r.* Guiana **91** 5.30N 54.00W
Maroua Cameroon **53** 10.35N 14.20E
Marovoay Madagascar **57** 16.06S 46.39E
Marquard R.S.A. **56** 28.39S 27.25E
Marquesas Is. *see* Marquises, Îles *is.* Pacific Oc. **69**
Marquette U.S.A. **84** 46.33N 87.23W
Marquises, Îles *is.* Pacific Oc. **69** 9.00S139.30W
Marra Australia **66** 31.11S144.03E
Marra *r.* Australia **67** 30.05S147.05E
Marracuene Mozambique **57** 25.44S 32.41E
Marradi Italy **15** 44.04N 11.37E
Marradong Australia **63** 32.49S116.27E
Marrah, Jabal *mtn.* Sudan **49** 13.10N 24.22E
Marrakech Morocco **50** 31.49N 8.00W
Marree Australia **66** 29.40S138.04E
Marromeu Mozambique **57** 18.20S 35.56E
Marrupa Mozambique **55** 13.10S 37.30E
Marsá al Burayqah Libya **48** 30.25N 19.35E
Marsabit Kenya **55** 2.20N 37.59E
Marsala Italy **18** 37.48N 12.27E
Marsá Maţrūḩ Egypt **42** 31.21N 27.14E
Marsden Australia **67** 33.46S147.35E
Marseille France **17** 43.18N 5.22E
Marseille-en-Beauvaisis France **15** 49.35N 1.57E
Marsfjället *mtn.* Sweden **22** 65.05N 15.28E
Marshall Liberia **52** 6.10N 10.23W
Marshall Ark. U.S.A. **83** 35.55N 92.38W
Marshall Minn. U.S.A. **82** 44.27N 95.47W
Marshall Mo. U.S.A. **82** 39.07N 93.12W
Marshall Tex. U.S.A. **83** 32.33N 94.23W
Marshall Is. Pacific Oc. **68** 10.00N172.00E
Marshalltown U.S.A. **82** 42.03N 92.55W
Marshyhope Creek *r.* U.S.A. **85** 38.32N 75.45W
Martaban Burma **34** 16.32N 97.35E
Martaban, G. of Burma **34** 15.10N 96.30E
Martapura Indonesia **36** 3.22S114.56E
Marte Nigeria **53** 12.23N 13.46E
Martelange Belgium **14** 49.50N 5.44E
Martés, Sierra *mts.* Spain **16** 39.10N 1.00W
Marthaguy *r.* Australia **67** 30.16S147.35E
Martha's Vineyard *i.* U.S.A. **84** 41.25N 70.40W
Martigny Switz. **20** 46.07N 7.05E
Martin Czech. **21** 49.05N 18.55E
Martin U.S.A. **82** 43.10N101.44W
Martina Franca Italy **19** 40.42N 17.21E

Martinique to Messiniakós, Kólpos

Martinique *i.* Windward Is. **87** 14.40N 61.00W
Martin L. U.S.A. **85** 32.50N 85.55W
Martin Pt. U.S.A. **72** 70.10N143.50W
Martinsburg W.Va. U.S.A. **84** 39.27N 77.58W
Martins Ferry *town* U.S.A. **84** 40.07N 80.45W
Martinsville Ind. U.S.A. **84** 39.25N 86.25W
Martinsville Va. U.S.A. **85** 36.43N 79.53W
Martin Vaz *is.* Atlantic Oc. **95** 20.30S 28.51W
Marton New Zealand **60** 40.04S175.25E
Martos Spain **16** 37.44N 3.58W
Martre, Lac la *l.* Canada **74** 63.15N116.55W
Martti Finland **22** 67.28N 28.28E
Marudi Malaysia **36** 4.15N114.19E
Ma'rūf Afghan. **40** 31.34N 67.03E
Marula Zimbabwe **56** 20.26S 28.06E
Marum Neth. **14** 53.06N 6.16E
Marvejols France **17** 44.33N 3.18E
Marvel Loch *town* Australia **63** 31.31S119.30E
Mārwār India **40** 25.44N 73.36E
Mary U.S.S.R. **28** 37.42N 61.54E
Maryborough Qld. Australia **64** 25.32S152.36E
Maryborough Vic. Australia **66** 37.05S143.47E
Marydale R.S.A. **56** 29.24S 22.06E
Mary Frances L. Canada **75** 63.19N106.13W
Mary Kathleen Australia **64** 20.49S140.00E
Maryland *d.* U.S.A. **84** 39.00N 76.45W
Maryland Beach *town* U.S.A. **85** 38.26N 74.59W
Maryport U.K. **10** 54.43N 3.30W
Mary's Harbour Canada **77** 52.18N 55.51W
Marystown Canada **77** 47.11N 55.10W
Marysvale U.S.A. **80** 38.27N112.11W
Marysville Calif. U.S.A. **80** 39.09N121.35W
Marysville Kans. U.S.A. **82** 39.51N 96.39W
Maryvale Australia **67** 28.04S152.12E
Maryville Mo. U.S.A. **82** 40.21N 94.52W
Maryville Tenn. U.S.A. **85** 35.45N 83.59W
Marzūq Libya **51** 25.55N 13.55E
Marzūq, Ṣaḥrā' *des.* Libya **51** 24.30N 13.00E
Masāhīm, Kūh-e *mtn.* Iran **43** 30.26N 55.08E
Masai Steppe *f.* Tanzania **55** 4.30S 37.00E
Masaka Uganda **55** 0.20S 31.46E
Masan S. Korea **31** 35.10N128.35E
Masasi Tanzania **55** 10.43S 38.48E
Masba Nigeria **53** 10.35N 13.01E
Masbate *i.* Phil. **37** 12.00N123.30E
Mascara Algeria **50** 35.24N 0.08E
Maseru Lesotho **56** 29.18S 27.28E
Mashhad Iran **43** 36.16N 59.34E
Mashkai *r.* Pakistan **40** 26.02N 65.19E
Māshkel *r.* Pakistan **40** 28.02N 63.25E
Māshkel, Hāmūn-i- *l.* Pakistan **40** 28.15N 63.00E
Mashki Chāh Pakistan **40** 29.01N 62.27E
Mashonaland *f.* Zimbabwe **57** 18.20S 32.00E
Mashūray Afghan. **40** 32.12N 68.21E
Masi Norway **22** 69.26N 23.40E
Masīlah, Wādī al *f.* S.Yemen **45** 15.10N 51.08E
Masi-Manimba Zaïre **54** 4.47S 17.54E
Masindi Uganda **55** 1.41N 31.45E
Maṣīrah *i.* Oman **38** 20.30N 58.50E
Maṣīrah, Khalīj *b.* Oman **45** 20.10N 58.10E
Masjed Soleymān Iran **43** 31.59N 49.18E
Mask, Lough Rep. of Ire. **13** 53.38N 9.22W
Maskinongé Canada **77** 46.35N 73.30W
Masoala, Cap, *c.* Madagascar **57** 15.59S 50.13E
Mason Tex. U.S.A. **83** 30.45N 99.14W
Mason City U.S.A. **82** 43.09N 93.12W
Maspalomas Canary Is. **95** 27.42N 15.34W
Masqaṭ Oman **43** 23.36N 58.37E
Massa Italy **15** 44.02N 10.09E
Massachusetts *d.* U.S.A. **84** 42.15N 71.50W
Massakory Chad **53** 13.02N 15.43E
Massa Marittima Italy **18** 43.03N 10.53E
Massangena Mozambique **57** 21.31S 33.03E
Massangulo Mozambique **57** 13.54S 35.24E
Massarosa Italy **15** 43.52N 10.20E
Massena U.S.A. **84** 44.56N 74.54W
Massenya Chad **53** 11.21N 16.09E
Masset Canada **74** 54.00N132.09W
Massif Central *mts.* France **17** 45.00N 3.30E
Massillon U.S.A. **84** 40.48N 81.32W
Massinga Mozambique **57** 23.20S 35.25E
Massingir Mozambique **57** 23.49S 32.04E
Masterton New Zealand **60** 40.57S175.39E
Mastung Pakistan **40** 29.48N 66.51E
Mastūrah Saudi Arabia **42** 23.06N 38.50E
Masvingo Zimbabwe **56** 20.10S 30.49E
Maṣyāf Syria **44** 35.03N 36.21E
Matabeleland *f.* Zimbabwe **56** 19.50S 28.15E
Matachewan Canada **76** 47.56N 80.39W
Matadi Zaïre **54** 5.50S 13.36E
Matagami Canada **76** 49.45N 77.34W
Matagami, L. Canada **76** 49.50N 77.40W
Matagorda B. U.S.A. **83** 28.35N 96.20W
Matakana Australia **67** 32.59S145.53E
Matakana I. New Zealand **60** 37.35S176.15E
Matala Angola **54** 14.45S 15.02E
Matam Senegal **50** 15.40N 13.15W
Matamata New Zealand **60** 37.49S175.46E
Matameye Niger **53** 13.26N 8.28E
Matamoros Coahuila Mexico **83** 25.32N103.15W
Matamoros Tamaulipas Mexico **83** 25.53N 97.30W
Ma'ṭan Bishrah *well* Libya **48** 22.58N 22.39E
Matandu *r.* Tanzania **55** 8.44S 39.22E
Matane Canada **77** 48.51N 67.32W
Matang China **33** 29.30N113.08E
Matankari Niger **53** 13.47N 4.00E
Matanzas Cuba **87** 23.04N 81.35W
Mataram Indonesia **37** 8.36S116.07E
Matarani Peru **92** 16.58S 72.07W
Mataranka Australia **62** 14.56S133.07E
Mataró Spain **16** 41.32N 2.27E
Matatiele R.S.A. **56** 30.19S 28.48E
Matatula, C. Samoa **68** 14.15S170.35W
Mataura *r.* New Zealand **60** 46.34S168.45E
Matautu W. Samoa **68** 13.57S171.56W
Matavera Rarotonga Cook Is. **68** 21.13S159.44W
Matawai New Zealand **60** 38.21S177.32E
Matawin, Résr. Canada **77** 46.45N 73.50W
Maṭāy Egypt **44** 28.25N 30.46E
Matehuala Mexico **86** 23.40N100.40W
Mateke Hills Zimbabwe **56** 21.48S 31.00E
Matera Italy **19** 40.41N 16.36E
Matetsi Zimbabwe **56** 18.17S 25.57E
Matfors Sweden **23** 62.21N 17.02E
Mathews Peak *mtn.* Kenya **55** 1.18N 37.20E
Mathis U.S.A. **83** 28.06N 97.50W
Mathoura Australia **67** 35.49S144.54E
Mathura India **41** 27.30N 77.41E
Mati Phil. **37** 6.55N126.15E
Matias Barbosa Brazil **94** 21.52S 43.21W
Matipó Brazil **94** 20.16S 42.17W
Mātli Pakistan **40** 25.02N 68.39E
Matlock U.K. **10** 53.09N 1.32W
Matochkin Shar U.S.S.R. **28** 73.15N 56.35E
Mato Grosso *d.* Brazil **92** 13.00S 55.00W
Mato Grosso *town* Brazil **92** 15.05S 59.57W
Mato Grosso, Planalto do *f.* Brazil **92** 16.00S 54.00W
Mato Grosso do Sul *d.* Brazil **92** 20.00S 54.30W
Matope Malaŵi **55** 15.20S 34.57E
Matopo Hills Zimbabwe **56** 20.45S 28.30E
Matosinhos Portugal **16** 41.11N 8.42W
Maṭraḥ Oman **43** 23.37N 58.33E
Matsena Nigeria **53** 13.13N 10.04E
Matsiatra *r.* Madagascar **57** 21.25S 45.33E
Matsubara Japan **35** 34.34N135.33E
Matsudo Japan **35** 35.47N139.54E
Matsue Japan **31** 35.29N133.00E
Matsusaka Japan **35** 34.34N136.32E
Matsuyama Japan **31** 33.50N132.47E
Mattagami *r.* Canada **76** 50.43N 81.29W
Mattawa Canada **76** 46.19N 78.42W
Mattawamkeag U.S.A. **84** 45.31N 68.21W
Matterhorn *mtn.* Italy / Switz. **15** 45.58N 7.38E
Matterhorn *mtn.* U.S.A. **80** 41.49N115.23W
Matthews Ridge *town* Guyana **90** 7.30N 60.10W
Matthew Town Bahamas **87** 20.57N 73.40W
Mattice Canada **76** 49.39N 83.20W
Mattmar Sweden **22** 63.19N 13.45E
Mattoon U.S.A. **82** 39.29N 88.21W
Matua Indonesia **36** 2.58S110.52E
Maturín Venezuela **90** 9.45N 63.10W
Maua Mozambique **57** 13.53S 37.10E
Mau Aimma India **41** 25.41N 81.55E
Maubeuge France **14** 50.17N 3.58E
Maudaha India **41** 25.41N 80.07E
Maude Australia **66** 34.27S144.21E
Maués Brazil **91** 3.24S 57.42W
Mauganj India **41** 24.41N 81.53E
Maui *i.* Hawaii U.S.A. **78** 20.45N156.15W
Maulvi Bāzār Bangla. **41** 24.29N 91.42E
Maumee U.S.A. **84** 41.34N 83.41W
Maumee *r.* U.S.A. **84** 41.40N 83.35W
Maumere Indonesia **37** 8.35S122.13E
Maun Botswana **56** 19.52S 23.40E
Maunaloa Hawaiian Is. **69** 21.08N157.13W
Mauna Loa *mtn.* Hawaiian Is. **69** 19.29N155.36W
Maunath Bhanjan India **41** 25.57N 83.33E
Mau Rānīpur India **41** 25.15N 79.08E
Maurice, L. Australia **65** 29.28S130.58E
Maurice Nat. Park Canada **77** 46.42N 73.00W
Mauritania Africa **50** 20.00N 10.00W
Mauston U.S.A. **82** 43.48N 90.05W
Mavinga Angola **54** 15.47S 20.21E
Mavuradonha Mts. Zimbabwe **57** 16.30S 31.20E
Mawjib, Wādī al *r.* Jordan **44** 31.28N 35.34E
Mawlaik Burma **34** 23.50N 94.30E
Maxcanú Mexico **86** 20.35N 89.59W
Maxville Canada **77** 45.17N 74.51W
May, C. U.S.A. **85** 38.58N 74.55W
Maya Spain **16** 43.12N 1.29W
Mayaguana I. Bahamas **87** 22.30N 73.00W
Mayagüez Puerto Rico **87** 18.13N 67.09W
Mayāmey Iran **43** 36.27N 55.40E
Maya Mts. Belize **87** 16.30N 89.00W
Maybole U.K. **12** 55.21N 4.41W
Maych'ew Ethiopia **45** 13.02N 39.34E
Mayen W. Germany **14** 50.19N 7.14E
Mayenne France **15** 48.18N 0.37W
Mayenne *d.* France **15** 48.05N 0.40W
Mayenne *r.* France **15** 47.30N 0.37W
Mayerthorpe Canada **74** 53.57N115.08W
Mayfield U.S.A. **83** 36.44N 88.38W
Maykop U.S.S.R. **25** 44.37N 40.48E
Maymyo Burma **34** 22.05N 96.28E
Maynooth Rep. of Ire. **13** 53.23N 6.37W
Mayo *r.* Mexico **81** 26.45N109.47W
Mayo *d.* Rep. of Ire. **13** 53.47N 9.07W
Mayo, Plains of *f.* Rep. of Ire. **13** 53.46N 9.05W
Mayo Daga Nigeria **53** 6.59N 11.25E
Mayo Landing Canada **72** 63.45N135.45W
Mayor I. New Zealand **60** 37.15S176.15E
Mayotte, Île *i.* Comoros **55** 12.50S 45.10E
May Pen Jamaica **87** 17.58N 77.14W
Mays Landing U.S.A. **85** 39.27N 74.44W
Maysville U.S.A. **84** 38.38N 83.46W
Mayumba Gabon **54** 3.23S 10.38E
Mayville N.Dak. U.S.A. **82** 47.30N 97.19W
Mayville N.Y. U.S.A. **76** 42.15N 79.30W
Mazabuka Zambia **55** 15.50S 27.47E
Mazagão Brazil **91** 0.07S 51.17W
Mazamba Mozambique **57** 18.32S 34.50E
Mazamet France **17** 43.30N 2.24E
Mazán Peru **90** 3.15S 73.00W
Mazarredo Argentina **93** 47.00S 66.45W
Mazarrón Spain **16** 37.38N 1.19W
Mazatenango Guatemala **86** 14.31N 91.30W
Mazatlán Mexico **81** 23.13N106.25W
Mažeikiai U.S.S.R. **23** 56.19N 22.20E
Mazirbe U.S.S.R. **23** 57.41N 22.21E
Mazowe *r.* Mozambique **57** 16.32S 33.25E
Mazowe Zimbabwe **57** 17.30S 30.58E
Mazu Liedao *is.* China **31** 26.12N120.00E
Mazunga Zimbabwe **56** 21.45S 29.52E
Mazurski, Pojezierze *lakes* Poland **21** 53.50N 21.00E
Mbabane Swaziland **56** 26.19S 31.08E
Mbagne Mauritania **50** 16.06N 14.47W
M'Baiki C.A.R. **53** 3.53N 18.01E
Mbala C.A.R. **49** 7.48N 20.51E
Mbala Zambia **55** 8.50S 31.24E
Mbale Uganda **55** 1.04N 34.12E
Mbalmayo Cameroon **53** 3.35N 11.31E
Mbamba Bay *town* Tanzania **55** 11.18S 34.50E
Mbandaka Zaïre **54** 0.03N 18.21E
Mbanza Congo Angola **54** 6.18S 14.16E
Mbarara Uganda **55** 0.36S 30.40E
Mbari *r.* C.A.R. **49** 4.34N 22.43E
Mbeya Tanzania **55** 8.54S 33.29E
Mbeya *d.* Tanzania **55** 8.30S 32.30E
Mbinda Congo **54** 2.11S 12.55E
Mbogo Tanzania **55** 7.26S 33.26E
Mbomou *d.* C.A.R. **49** 5.10N 23.00E
Mbomou *r.* C.A.R. **49** 4.08N 22.26E
Mboro Sudan **49** 6.18N 28.45E
M'Bour Senegal **52** 14.22N 16.54W
Mbout Mauritania **50** 16.02N 12.35W
M'bridge *r.* Angola **54** 7.12S 12.55E
Mbua Fiji **68** 16.48S178.37E
Mbuji Mayi Zaïre **54** 6.08S 23.39E
Mbulamuti Uganda **55** 0.50N 33.05E
Mbura Tanzania **55** 11.14S 35.25E
Mbutha Fiji **68** 16.39S179.50E
Mbuzi Zambia **55** 12.20S 32.17E
McAlester U.S.A. **83** 34.56N 95.46W
McAlister, Mt. Australia **67** 34.27S149.45E
McAllen U.S.A. **83** 26.12N 98.15W
McArthur *r.* Australia **64** 15.54S136.40E
McBride Canada **74** 53.20N120.10W
McCamey U.S.A. **83** 31.08N102.13W
McClintock Canada **75** 57.50N 94.10W
McClintock Channel Canada **73** 71.20N102.00W
McClure Str. Canada **72** 74.30N116.00W
McComb U.S.A. **83** 31.14N 90.27W
McConaughy, L. U.S.A. **82** 41.15N102.00W
McConnel Creek *town* Canada **74** 56.53N126.30W
McCook U.S.A. **82** 40.12N100.38W
McDermitt U.S.A. **80** 41.59N117.36W
McDouall Peak Australia **66** 29.51S134.55E
McGrath U.S.A. **72** 62.58N155.40W
McGregor U.S.A. **82** 46.36N 93.19W
McHenry U.S.A. **82** 42.21N 88.16W
Mchinja Tanzania **55** 9.44S 39.45E
Mchinji Malaŵi **55** 13.48S 32.55E
McIlwraith Range *mts.* Australia **64** 14.00S143.10E
McKeesport U.S.A. **84** 40.21N 79.52W
McKenzie U.S.A. **83** 36.08N 88.31W
McKinley, Mt. U.S.A. **72** 63.00N151.00W
McKinney U.S.A. **83** 33.12N 96.37W
McKittrick U.S.A. **81** 35.18N119.37W
McLaughlin U.S.A. **82** 45.49N100.49W
McLennan Canada **74** 55.42N116.50W
McLeod *r.* Canada **74** 54.08N115.42W
McLeod, L. Australia **62** 24.10S113.35E
McLeod B. Canada **75** 62.53N110.00W
Mcleod Lake *town* Canada **74** 54.58N123.00W
M'Clintock Canada **74** 60.35N134.25W
McMinnville Oreg. U.S.A. **80** 45.13N123.12W
McMinnville Tenn. U.S.A. **85** 35.40N 85.49W
McNary U.S.A. **81** 34.04N109.51W
McPherson U.S.A. **82** 38.22N 97.40W
Mdatsane R.S.A. **56** 32.54S 27.24E
Mead, L. U.S.A. **81** 36.05N114.25W
Meade U.S.A. **83** 37.17N100.20W
Meadow Lake *town* Canada **75** 54.07N108.20W
Meadville U.S.A. **84** 41.38N 80.09W
Mealhada Portugal **16** 40.22N 8.27W
Meander River *town* Canada **74** 59.02N117.42W
Mearim *r.* Brazil **91** 3.20S 44.20W
Meath *d.* Rep. of Ire. **13** 53.32N 6.40W
Meaux France **15** 48.58N 2.54E
Mécatina, Cap *c.* Canada **77** 50.45N 59.01W
Mecca *see* Makkah Saudi Arabia **48**
Mecca U.S.A. **81** 33.35N116.03W
Mechanicsville U.S.A. **85** 38.26N 76.44W
Mechelen Belgium **14** 51.01N 4.28E
Mecheria Algeria **50** 33.33N 0.17W
Mecklenburger Bucht *b.* E. Germany **20** 54.05N 11.00E
Meconta Mozambique **55** 15.00S 39.50E
Mecufi Mozambique **55** 13.20S 40.32E
Meda Portugal **16** 40.58N 7.16W
Medan Indonesia **36** 3.35N 98.39E
Mede Italy **15** 45.06N 8.44E
Médéa Algeria **51** 36.15N 2.48E
Mededsiz *mtn.* Turkey **42** 37.33N 34.38E
Medegue Gabon **54** 0.37N 10.08E
Medellín Colombia **90** 6.15N 75.36W
Medemblik Neth. **14** 52.48N 5.06E
Médenine Tunisia **51** 33.21N 10.30E
Mederdra Mauritania **52** 17.02N 15.41W
Medford Oreg. U.S.A. **80** 42.19N122.52W
Medford Wisc. U.S.A. **82** 45.09N 90.20W
Medgidia Romania **21** 44.15N 28.16E
Medi Sudan **49** 5.04N 30.44E
Media U.S.A. **85** 39.54N 75.23W
Mediaş Romania **21** 46.10N 24.21E
Medicina Italy **15** 44.28N 11.38E
Medicine Bow Mts. U.S.A. **80** 41.10N106.10W
Medicine Bow Peak *mtn.* U.S.A. **80** 41.21N106.19W
Medicine Hat Canada **75** 50.03N110.40W
Medicine Lake *town* U.S.A. **80** 48.30N104.30W
Medicine Lodge U.S.A. **83** 37.17N 98.35W
Medina *see* Al Madīnah Saudi Arabia **42**
Medina N.Dak. U.S.A. **82** 46.54N 99.18W
Medina N.Y. U.S.A. **84** 43.14N 78.23W
Medina del Campo Spain **16** 41.20N 4.55W
Medina de Rioseco Spain **16** 41.53N 5.03W
Mêdog China **30** 29.19N 95.19E
Medstead Canada **75** 53.19N108.02W
Medveditsa *r.* U.S.S.R. **25** 49.35N 42.45E
Medvezhyegorsk U.S.S.R. **24** 62.56N 34.28E
Medvin U.S.S.R. **21** 49.25N 30.48E
Medway *r.* U.K. **11** 51.24N 0.31E
Medzhibozh U.S.S.R. **21** 49.29N 27.28E
Meeberrie Australia **62** 26.58S115.51E
Meekatharra Australia **62** 26.35S118.30E
Meeker U.S.A. **80** 40.02N107.55W
Meer Belgium **14** 51.27N 4.46E
Meerhusener Moor *f.* W. Germany **14** 53.36N 7.33E
Meerut India **41** 28.59N 77.42E
Mega Ethiopia **49** 4.07N 38.16E
Mégara Greece **19** 38.00N 23.21E
Megasini *mtn.* India **41** 21.38N 86.21E
Meghalaya *d.* India **41** 25.30N 91.00E
Meghna *r.* Bangla. **41** 22.50N 90.50E
Mégiscane *r.* Canada **76** 48.36N 76.00W
Mehadia Romania **21** 44.55N 22.22E
Mehar Pakistan **40** 27.11N 67.49E
Mehekar India **40** 20.09N 76.34E
Mehidpur India **40** 23.49N 75.40E
Mehndāwal India **41** 26.59N 83.07E
Mehsāna India **40** 23.36N 72.24E
Mehtar Lām Afghan. **40** 34.39N 70.10E
Meiktila Burma **34** 20.53N 95.50E
Meiningen E. Germany **20** 50.34N 10.25E
Meishan China **33** 30.02N103.50E
Meissen E. Germany **20** 51.10N 13.28E
Mei Xian China **33** 24.20N116.15E
Meiyino Sudan **49** 6.12N 34.40E
Mekatina Canada **76** 46.58N 84.05W
Mekdela Ethiopia **49** 11.28N 39.23E
Mekele Ethiopia **49** 13.33N 39.30E
Mekerrhane, Sebkha *f.* Algeria **50** 26.22N 1.20E
Mekhtar Pakistan **40** 30.28N 69.22E
Meknès Morocco **50** 33.53N 5.37W
Mekong *r.* Asia **34** 10.00N106.40E
Mekong Delta Vietnam **34** 10.00N105.40E
Mekongga *mtn.* Indonesia **37** 3.39S121.15E
Mékôngk *r.* Kampuchea *see* Mekong *r.* Asia **34**
Mékrou *r.* Benin **53** 12.20N 2.47E
Melaka Malaysia **36** 2.11N102.16E
Melanesia *is.* Pacific Oc. **68** 5.00N165.00E
Melbourne Australia **67** 37.45S144.58E
Melbourne U.S.A. **85** 28.04N 80.38W
Mélé C.A.R. **49** 9.46N 21.33E
Melegnano Italy **15** 45.21N 9.19E
Meleuz U.S.S.R. **24** 52.58N 55.56E
Mélèzes, Rivière aux *r.* Canada **77** 57.40N 69.29W
Melfi Chad **53** 11.04N 18.03E
Melfi Italy **18** 40.59N 15.39E
Melfort Canada **75** 52.52N104.36W
Melilla Morocco **50** 35.17N 2.57W
Melilla Spain **16** 35.17N 2.57W
Melipilla Chile **93** 33.42S 71.13W
Melitopol U.S.S.R. **25** 46.51N 35.22E
Melk Austria **20** 48.14N 15.20E
Mellen U.S.A. **82** 46.20N 90.40W
Mellerud Sweden **23** 58.42N 12.28E
Mellit Sudan **48** 14.08N 25.33E
Melmore Pt. Rep. of Ire. **13** 55.15N 7.49W
Melnik Bulgaria **19** 41.30N 23.22E
Mělník Czech. **20** 50.20N 14.29E
Melo Uruguay **94** 32.22S 54.10W
Melrhir, Chott *f.* Algeria **51** 34.20N 6.20E
Melrose U.K. **12** 55.36N 2.43W
Melrose Mont. U.S.A. **80** 45.37N112.41W
Melrose N.Mex U.S.A. **81** 34.26N103.38W
Melstone U.S.A. **80** 46.36N107.52W
Meltaus Finland **22** 66.54N 25.22E
Melton Mowbray U.K. **10** 52.46N 0.53W
Melun France **15** 48.32N 2.40E
Melvich U.K. **12** 58.33N 3.55W
Melville Canada **75** 50.55N102.48W
Melville, C. Australia **64** 14.11S144.30E
Melville, L. Canada **77** 53.45N 59.30W
Melville B. Australia **64** 12.10S136.32E
Melville Hills Canada **72** 69.20N122.00W
Melville I. Australia **64** 11.30S131.00E
Melville I. Canada **72** 75.30N110.00W
Melville Pen. Canada **73** 68.00N 84.00W
Melvin, Lough Rep. of Ire. / U.K. **13** 54.26N 8.12W
Melzo Italy **15** 45.30N 9.25E
Mêmar Co *l.* China **41** 34.10N 82.15E
Memba Mozambique **57** 14.16S 40.30E
Memboro Indonesia **36** 9.22S119.32E
Memmingen W. Germany **20** 47.59N 10.11E
Memphis *ruins* Egypt **44** 29.52N 31.12E
Memphis Tenn. U.S.A. **83** 35.08N 90.03W
Mena U.S.A. **83** 34.35N 94.15W
Mena U.S.S.R. **21** 51.30N 32.15E
Menai Str. U.K. **10** 53.17N 4.20W
Ménaka Mali **51** 15.55N 2.24E
Mènam Khong *r.* Laos *see* Mekong *r.* Asia **34**
Menarandra *r.* Madagascar **57** 25.17S 44.30E
Menard U.S.A. **83** 30.55N 99.47W
Menawashei Sudan **49** 12.40N 24.59E
Mendawai *r.* Indonesia **36** 3.17S113.20E
Mende France **17** 44.32N 3.30E
Mendebo Mts. Ethiopia **49** 7.00N 39.30E
Mendi P.N.G. **37** 6.13S143.39E
Mendip Hills U.K. **11** 51.15N 2.40W
Mendocino, C. U.S.A. **80** 40.25N124.25W
Mendoza Argentina **93** 32.54S 68.50W
Mendoza *d.* Argentina **93** 34.30S 68.00W
Mendung Indonesia **36** 0.31N103.12E
Mene Grande Venezuela **90** 9.51N 70.57W
Menemen Turkey **42** 38.34N 27.03E
Menen Belgium **14** 50.48N 3.07E
Menfi Italy **18** 37.36N 12.59E
Mengcheng China **32** 33.16N116.33E
Mengzi China **39** 23.20N103.21E
Menihek Lakes Canada **77** 54.00N 66.35W
Menindee Australia **66** 32.23S142.30E
Menindee L. Australia **66** 32.21S142.20E
Menominee U.S.A. **82** 45.07N 87.37W
Menomonie U.S.A. **82** 44.53N 91.55W
Menongue Angola **54** 14.40S 17.41E
Menorca *i.* Spain **16** 40.00N 4.00E
Mentawai, Kepulauan *is.* Indonesia **36** 2.50S 99.00E
Mentekab Malaysia **36** 3.29N102.21E
Mentok Indonesia **36** 2.04S105.12E
Menton France **17** 43.47N 7.30E
Menyapa, Gunung *mtn.* Indonesia **36** 1.00N116.20E
Menzel Bourguiba Tunisia **51** 37.10N 9.48E
Menzies Australia **63** 29.41S121.02E
Menzies, Mt. Antarctica **96** 71.50S 61.00E
Meppel Neth. **14** 52.42N 6.12E
Meppen W. Germany **14** 52.42N 7.17E
Mer France **15** 47.42N 1.30E
Merano Italy **18** 46.41N 11.10E
Merauke Indonesia **64** 8.30S140.22E
Merbein Australia **66** 34.11S142.04E
Mercato Saraceno Italy **15** 43.57N 12.12E
Merced U.S.A. **80** 37.18N120.29W
Mercedes Buenos Aires Argentina **93** 34.40S 59.25W
Mercedes Corrientes Argentina **92** 29.15S 58.05W
Mercedes San Luis Argentina **93** 33.40S 65.30W
Mercedes Uruguay **93** 33.16S 58.01W
Mercy, C. Canada **73** 65.00N 63.30W
Mere U.K. **11** 51.05N 2.16W
Meredith Australia **66** 37.50S144.05E
Meredith, L. U.S.A. **83** 35.36N101.42W
Merefa U.S.S.R. **25** 49.49N 36.05E
Mereke C.A.R. **49** 7.34N 23.09E
Mergenevo U.S.S.R. **25** 49.59N 51.19E
Mergui Burma **34** 12.26N 98.38E
Mergui Archipelago *is.* Burma **34** 11.15N 98.00E
Meribah Australia **66** 34.42S140.53E
Meriç *r.* Turkey **19** 40.52N 26.12E
Mérida Mexico **87** 20.59N 89.39W
Mérida Spain **16** 38.55N 6.20W
Mérida Venezuela **90** 8.24N 71.08W
Mérida, Cordillera de *mts.* Venezuela **90** 8.30N 71.00W
Meridian U.S.A. **83** 32.22N 88.42W
Mérignac France **17** 44.50N 0.42W
Merikarvia Finland **23** 61.51N 21.30E
Merino Australia **66** 37.45S141.35E
Merir *i.* Caroline Is. **37** 4.19N132.18E
Merirumã Brazil **91** 1.15N 54.50W
Merizo Guam **68** 13.16N144.40E
Merksem Belgium **14** 51.14N 4.25E
Merlo Argentina **93** 34.40S 58.45W
Merne Merna Australia **66** 31.45S138.21E
Merredin Australia **63** 31.29S118.16E
Merrick *mtn.* U.K. **12** 55.08N 4.29W
Merrill Oreg. U.S.A. **80** 42.01N121.36W
Merrill Wisc. U.S.A. **82** 45.11N 89.41W
Merriman U.S.A. **82** 42.55N101.42W
Merritt Canada **74** 50.10N120.45W
Merriwa Australia **67** 32.08S150.20E
Merrygoen Australia **67** 31.51S149.16E
Mersa Fatma Ethiopia **48** 14.55N 40.20E
Mersch Lux. **14** 49.44N 6.05E
Mersea I. U.K. **11** 51.47N 0.58E
Merseburg E. Germany **20** 51.22N 12.00E
Mersey *r.* U.K. **10** 53.22N 2.37W
Merseyside *d.* U.K. **10** 53.28N 3.00W
Mersin Turkey **42** 36.47N 34.37E
Mersing Malaysia **36** 2.25N103.50E
Merta India **40** 26.39N 74.02E
Merta Road *town* India **40** 26.43N 73.55E
Merthyr Tydfil U.K. **11** 51.45N 3.23W
Mértola Portugal **16** 37.38N 7.40W
Merton U.K. **11** 51.25N 0.12W
Mertzon U.S.A. **83** 31.16N100.49W
Méru France **15** 49.14N 2.08E
Meru *mtn.* Tanzania **55** 3.15S 36.44E
Méry France **15** 48.30N 3.53E
Merzifon Turkey **42** 40.52N 35.28E
Merzig W. Germany **14** 49.26N 6.39E
Mesa U.S.A. **81** 33.25N111.50W
Mesagne Italy **19** 40.33N 17.49E
Mesewa Ethiopia **48** 15.36N 39.29E
Mesewa Channel Ethiopia **48** 15.30N 40.00E
Meslay-du-Maine France **15** 47.57N 0.33W
Mesocco Switz. **15** 46.23N 9.14E
Mesolóngion Greece **19** 38.23N 21.23E
Mesopotamia *f.* Iraq **43** 33.30N 44.30E
Messalo *r.* Mozambique **55** 11.38S 40.27E
Messina Italy **18** 38.13N 15.34E
Messina R.S.A. **56** 22.20S 30.03E
Messina, Stretto di *str.* Italy **18** 38.10N 15.35E
Messíni Greece **19** 37.03N 22.00E
Messiniakós, Kólpos *g.* Greece **19** 36.50N 22.05E

Mesta to **Montigny-le-Roi**

Mesta *r.* Bulgaria *see* Néstos *r.* Greece **19**
Mestre Italy **15** 45.29N 12.15E
Meta *r.* Venezuela **90** 6.10N 67.30W
Metán Argentina **92** 25.30S 65.00W
Metangula Mozambique **55** 12.41S 34.51E
Metković Yugo. **19** 43.03N 17.38E
Metlakatla U.S.A. **74** 55.09N 131.35W
Métsovon Greece **19** 39.46N 21.11E
Metz France **17** 49.07N 6.11E
Meulaboh Indonesia **36** 4.10N 96.09E
Meulan France **15** 49.01N 1.54E
Meuse *r.* Belgium *see* Maas *r.* Neth. **14**
Mexia U.S.A. **83** 31.41N 96.29W
Mexicali Mexico **81** 32.40N 115.29W
Mexico C. America **86** 20.00N 100.00W
México *d.* Mexico **86** 19.45N 99.30W
Mexico Mo. U.S.A. **82** 39.10N 91.53W
Mexico, G. of N. America **86** 25.00N 90.00W
Mexico City *see* Ciudad de México Mexico **86**
Meydān Kalay Afghan. **40** 32.25N 66.44E
Meydān Khvolah Afghan. **40** 33.36N 69.51E
Meymaneh Afghan. **38** 35.54N 64.43E
Mezen U.S.S.R. **24** 65.50N 44.20E
Mezen *r.* U.S.S.R. **24** 65.50N 44.18E
Mézenc, Mont *mtn.* France **17** 44.54N 4.11E
Mezenskaya Guba *g.* U.S.S.R. **24** 66.30N 44.00E
Mezökövesd Hungary **21** 47.50N 20.34E
Mezzolombardo Italy **15** 46.13N 11.05E
Mhow India **40** 22.33N 75.46E
Miahuatlán Mexico **86** 16.20N 96.36W
Miājlar India **40** 26.15N 70.23E
Miami Fla. U.S.A. **85** 25.45N 80.15W
Miami Okla. U.S.A. **83** 36.53N 94.53W
Miami Tex. U.S.A. **83** 35.42N 100.38W
Miami Beach *town* U.S.A. **85** 25.47N 80.07W
Miāndow Āb Iran **43** 36.57N 46.06E
Miandrivazo Madagascar **57** 19.31S 45.28E
Miāneh Iran **43** 37.23N 47.45E
Miang, Phukao *mtn.* Thailand **34** 16.55N 101.00E
Miāni India **40** 21.51N 69.23E
Miāni Hōr *b.* Pakistan **40** 25.34N 66.19E
Miānwāli Pakistan **40** 32.35N 71.33E
Mianyang Hubei China **33** 30.25N 113.30E
Mianyang Sichuan China **33** 31.26N 104.45E
Miao'er Shan *mtn.* China **33** 25.50N 110.22E
Miaoli Taiwan **33** 24.34N 120.48E
Miarinarivo Madagascar **57** 18.57S 46.55E
Miass U.S.S.R. **28** 55.00N 60.00E
Mibu *r.* Japan **35** 35.49N 137.57E
Mica R.S.A. **56** 24.09S 30.49E
Micang Shan *mts.* China **32** 32.40N 107.28E
Michael, L. Canada **77** 54.32N 58.15W
Michalovce Czech. **21** 48.45N 21.55E
Michelson, Mt. U.S.A. **72** 69.19N 144.17W
Michigan *d.* U.S.A. **84** 44.00N 85.00W
Michigan, L. U.S.A. **84** 44.00N 87.00W
Michigan City U.S.A. **84** 41.43N 86.54W
Michikamau L. Canada **77** 54.00N 64.00W
Michipicoten Canada **76** 47.59N 84.55W
Michipicoten I. Canada **76** 47.40N 85.50W
Michoacán *d.* Mexico **86** 19.20N 101.00W
Michurin Bulgaria **19** 42.09N 27.51E
Michurinsk U.S.S.R. **24** 52.54N 40.30E
Micronesia *is.* Pacific Oc. **68** 8.00N 160.00E
Midale Canada **75** 49.22N 103.27W
Mid Atlantic Ridge *f.* Atlantic Oc. **95** 20.00N 45.00W
Middelburg Neth. **14** 51.30N 3.36E
Middelburg C.P. R.S.A. **56** 31.29S 25.00E
Middelburg Trans. R.S.A. **56** 25.45S 29.27E
Middelharnis Neth. **14** 51.46N 4.09E
Middenmeer Neth. **14** 52.51N 4.59E
Middleboro Canada **75** 49.01N 95.21W
Middlebury U.S.A. **84** 44.01N 73.10W
Middle I. Australia **63** 34.07S 123.12E
Middle Loup *r.* U.S.A. **82** 41.17N 98.23W
Middleport N.Y. U.S.A. **76** 43.13N 78.29W
Middlesboro U.S.A. **85** 36.37N 83.43W
Middlesbrough U.K. **10** 54.34N 1.13W
Middleton Canada **77** 44.57N 65.04W
Middleton Reef Pacific Oc. **68** 29.28S 159.06E
Middletown Del. U.S.A. **85** 39.25N 75.47W
Middletown Ind. U.S.A. **84** 39.31N 84.13W
Middletown N.Y. U.S.A. **85** 41.27N 74.25W
Mid Glamorgan *d.* U.K. **11** 51.38N 3.25W
Midi-Pyrénées *d.* France **17** 44.10N 2.00E
Midland Canada **76** 44.45N 79.53W
Midland Mich. U.S.A. **84** 43.38N 84.14W
Midland Tex. U.S.A. **83** 32.00N 102.05W
Midland Junction Australia **63** 31.54S 115.57E
Midleton Rep. of Ire. **13** 51.55N 8.10W
Midnapore India **41** 22.26N 87.20E
Midongy-Sud Madagascar **57** 23.35S 47.01E
Midway Is. Hawaiian Is. **68** 28.15N 177.25W
Midwest U.S.A. **80** 43.25N 106.16W
Midwest City U.S.A. **83** 35.27N 97.24W
Midyan *f.* Saudi Arabia **44** 27.50N 35.30E
Midye Turkey **19** 41.37N 28.07E
Midžor *mtn.* Yugo. **19** 43.23N 22.42E
Mie *d.* Japan **35** 34.42N 136.08E
Miechów Poland **21** 50.23N 20.01E
Miedzychód Poland **20** 52.36N 15.55E
Mielec Poland **21** 50.18N 21.25E
Mienga Angola **54** 17.16S 19.50E
Mieres Spain **16** 43.15N 5.46W
Migang Shan *mtn.* China **32** 35.32N 106.13E
Miguel Hidalgo, Presa *resr.* Mexico **81** 26.41N 108.19W
Migyaunglaung Burma **34** 14.40N 98.09E
Mijares *r.* Spain **16** 39.58N 0.01W
Mikhaylov U.S.S.R. **24** 54.14N 39.00E
Mikhaylovgrad Bulgaria **19** 43.25N 23.11E
Mikhaylovka U.S.S.R. **25** 50.05N 43.15E
Miki Japan **35** 34.48N 134.59E
Mikínai Greece **19** 37.44N 22.45E
Mikindani Tanzania **55** 10.16S 40.05E
Mikkeli Finland **24** 61.44N 27.15E
Mikkwa *r.* Canada **74** 58.25N 114.46W
Míkonos *i.* Greece **19** 37.29N 25.25E
Mikumi Tanzania **55** 7.22S 37.00E
Mikun U.S.S.R. **24** 62.20N 50.01E
Milagro Ecuador **90** 2.11S 79.36W
Milan *see* Milano Italy **15**
Milan Mo. U.S.A. **82** 40.12N 93.07W
Milange Mozambique **55** 16.09S 35.44E
Milano Italy **15** 45.28N 9.10E
Milâs Turkey **19** 37.18N 27.48E
Milbank U.S.A. **82** 45.14N 96.38W
Milbanke Sd. Canada **74** 52.18N 128.33W
Mildenhall U.K. **11** 52.20N 0.30E
Mildura Australia **66** 34.14S 142.13E
Miles Australia **64** 26.40S 150.11E
Miles City U.S.A. **80** 46.25N 105.51W
Milford Del. U.S.A. **85** 38.55N 75.25W
Milford Utah U.S.A. **80** 38.24N 113.01W
Milford Haven *town* U.K. **11** 51.43N 5.02W
Milford Sound *town* New Zealand **60** 44.41S 167.56E
Milgarra Australia **64** 18.10S 140.55E
Miliana Algeria **51** 27.21N 2.28E
Miling Australia **63** 30.27S 116.20E
Milk *r.* U.S.A. **80** 48.05N 106.15W
Millau France **17** 44.06N 3.05E
Millbrook U.S.A. **85** 41.47N 73.42W
Mille Lacs, Lac des *l.* Canada **76** 48.45N 90.35W
Mille Lacs L. U.S.A. **82** 46.10N 93.45W
Miller *r.* Australia **66** 30.05S 136.07E
Millerovo U.S.S.R. **25** 48.55N 40.25E
Millersburg Mich. U.S.A. **84** 45.21N 84.02W
Milleur Pt. U.K. **12** 55.01N 5.07W
Millicent Australia **66** 37.36S 140.22E
Millie Australia **67** 29.49S 149.34E
Millington U.S.A. **85** 39.16N 75.50W
Millinocket U.S.A. **84** 45.39N 68.43W
Millom U.K. **10** 54.13N 3.16W
Mills L. Canada **74** 61.30N 118.10W
Millville U.S.A. **85** 39.24N 75.02W
Milne Inlet *town* Canada **73** 72.30N 80.59W
Milo *r.* Guinea **52** 11.05N 9.05W
Mílos Greece **19** 36.45N 24.27E
Mílos *i.* Greece **19** 36.40N 24.26E
Milparinka Australia **66** 29.45S 141.55E
Milton Australia **67** 35.19S 150.24E
Milton Canada **76** 43.31N 79.53W
Milton Del. U.S.A. **85** 38.47N 75.19W
Milton Keynes U.K. **11** 52.03N 0.42W
Miltou Chad **53** 10.10N 17.30E
Miluo China **33** 28.50N 113.05E
Milwaukee U.S.A. **82** 43.02N 87.55W
Milwaukie U.S.A. **80** 45.27N 122.38W
Milyatino U.S.S.R. **24** 54.30N 34.20E
Mim Ghana **52** 6.55N 2.34W
Miminiska L. Canada **76** 51.32N 88.33W
Mina U.S.A. **80** 38.24N 118.07W
Mīnā 'al Aḥmadī Kuwait **38** 29.04N 48.08E
Mīnāb Iran **43** 27.07N 57.05E
Mīnā Baranīs Egypt **48** 23.55N 35.28E
Minaki Canada **76** 50.00N 94.48W
Minas Uruguay **93** 34.23S 55.14W
Minas Basin *b.* Canada **77** 45.20N 64.00W
Minas Channel *str.* Canada **77** 45.15N 64.45W
Minas de Corrales Uruguay **93** 31.35S 55.28W
Minas de Ríotinto Spain **16** 37.41N 6.37W
Minas Gerais *d.* Brazil **94** 18.00S 45.00W
Minatitlán Mexico **86** 17.59N 94.32W
Minbu Burma **34** 20.09N 94.52E
Mindanao *i.* Phil. **37** 7.30N 125.00E
Mindanao Sea Phil. **37** 9.10N 124.25E
Mindanao Trench Pacific Oc. **68** 9.00N 127.00E
Mindarie Australia **66** 34.51S 140.12E
Minden U.S.A. **83** 32.37N 93.17W
Minden W. Germany **20** 52.18N 8.54E
Minderoo Australia **62** 21.59S 115.04E
Mindif Cameroon **53** 10.25N 14.23E
Mindiptana Indonesia **37** 5.45S 140.22E
Mindona L. Australia **66** 33.09S 142.09E
Mindoro *i.* Phil. **37** 13.00N 121.00E
Mindoro Str. Pacific Oc. **37** 12.30N 120.10E
Mindra *mtn.* Romania **21** 45.20N 23.32E
Minehead U.K. **11** 51.12N 3.29W
Mineola U.S.A. **83** 32.40N 95.29W
Minerva Australia **64** 24.00S 148.05E
Mingan Canada **77** 50.18N 64.02W
Mingary Australia **66** 32.09S 140.46E
Mingela Australia **64** 19.53S 146.40E
Mingenew Australia **63** 29.11S 115.26E
Mingin Burma **34** 22.52N 94.39E
Mingin Range *mts.* Burma **34** 24.00N 95.45E
Minhe China **32** 36.12N 102.59E
Minidoka U.S.A. **80** 42.46N 113.30W
Minigwal, L. Australia **63** 29.35S 123.12E
Min Jiang *r.* China **33** 26.06N 119.15E
Minna Nigeria **53** 9.39N 6.32E
Minneapolis Kans. U.S.A. **82** 39.08N 97.42W
Minneapolis Minn. U.S.A. **82** 44.59N 93.13W
Minnedosa Canada **75** 50.14N 99.51W
Minnesota *d.* U.S.A. **82** 46.00N 94.00W
Minnesota *r.* U.S.A. **82** 44.54N 93.10W
Minnesota Lake *town* U.S.A. **82** 43.51N 93.50W
Minnipa Australia **66** 32.51S 135.09E
Minnitaki L. Canada **76** 50.00N 91.50W
Miño *r.* Spain **16** 41.50N 8.52W
Minobu-sanchi *mts.* Japan **35** 35.05N 138.15E
Mino-kamo Japan **35** 35.26N 137.01E
Mino-mikawa-kōgen *mts.* Japan **35** 35.16N 137.10E
Minorca *i. see* Menorca *i.* Spain **16**
Minot U.S.A. **82** 48.16N 101.19W
Minqin China **32** 38.42N 103.11E
Minsen W. Germany **14** 53.44N 7.59E
Min Shan *mts.* China **32** 32.40N 104.40E
Minsk U.S.S.R. **21** 53.51N 27.30E
Minta Cameroon **53** 4.37N 12.47E
Minto, L. Canada **73** 51.00N 73.37W
Minto, Lac *l.* Canada **76** 57.15N 74.50W
Minturno Italy **18** 41.15N 13.45E
Minūf Egypt **44** 30.28N 30.56E
Min Xian China **32** 34.26N 104.02E
Minyā al Qamḥ Egypt **44** 30.31N 31.21E
Minyar U.S.S.R. **24** 55.06N 57.29E
Miquelon Canada **76** 49.25N 76.32W
Mira Italy **15** 45.26N 12.08E
Mīrābād Afghan. **40** 30.25N 61.50E
Miracema Brazil **94** 21.22S 42.09W
Mīrah, Wādī al *r.* Iraq **42** 32.27N 41.21E
Miraj India **38** 16.51N 74.42E
Miramichi B. Canada **77** 47.08N 65.08W
Mīram Shāh Pakistan **40** 33.01N 70.04E
Mīrān Pakistan **40** 31.24N 70.43E
Miranda de Ebro Spain **16** 42.41N 2.57W
Miranda do Douro Portugal **16** 41.30N 6.16W
Mirande France **17** 43.31N 0.25E
Mirandela Portugal **16** 41.28N 7.10W
Mirando City U.S.A. **83** 27.26N 99.00W
Mirandola Italy **15** 44.53N 11.04E
Mīr Bachcheh Kūt Afghan. **40** 34.45N 69.08E
Mirbāṭ Oman **38** 17.00N 54.45E
Mirecourt France **17** 48.18N 6.08E
Miri Malaysia **36** 4.28N 114.00E
Mirim, L. Brazil **94** 33.10S 53.30W
Mironovka U.S.S.R. **21** 49.40N 30.59E
Miroşi Romania **21** 44.25N 24.58E
Mīrpur Jammu & Kashmir **40** 33.15N 73.55E
Mīrpur Batoro Pakistan **40** 24.44N 68.16E
Mīrpur Khās Pakistan **38** 25.33N 69.05E
Mīrpur Sakro Pakistan **40** 24.33N 67.37E
Miryeny U.S.S.R. **21** 47.00N 29.06E
Mirzāpur India **41** 25.09N 82.35E
Miscou I. Canada **77** 47.57N 64.33W
Mishawaka U.S.A. **84** 41.38N 86.10W
Mishima Japan **35** 35.07N 138.55E
Mishkino U.S.S.R. **24** 55.34N 56.00E
Misima I. P.N.G. **64** 10.40S 152.45E
Misiones *d.* Argentina **92** 27.00S 54.40W
Miskī Sudan **48** 14.51N 24.13E
Miskolc Hungary **21** 48.07N 20.47E
Mismār Sudan **48** 18.13N 35.38E
Misoöl *i.* Indonesia **37** 1.50S 130.10E
Misr al Jadīdah Egypt **44** 30.06N 31.20E
Miṣrātah Libya **51** 32.23N 15.06E
Miṣrātah *d.* Libya **51** 30.30N 17.00E
Mişr Baḥrī *f.* Egypt **44** 30.30N 31.00E
Missinaibi *r.* Canada **76** 50.44N 81.29W
Mission U.S.A. **82** 43.18N 100.40W
Mississauga Canada **76** 43.35N 79.37W
Mississippi *d.* U.S.A. **83** 32.40N 90.00W
Mississippi *r.* U.S.A. **83** 29.00N 89.15W
Mississippi Delta U.S.A. **83** 29.10N 89.15W
Mississippi Sd. U.S.A. **83** 30.15N 88.40W
Missoula U.S.A. **80** 46.52N 114.01W
Missouri *d.* U.S.A. **82** 38.30N 92.00W
Missouri *r.* U.S.A. **82** 38.50N 90.08W
Missouri Valley *town* U.S.A. **82** 41.33N 95.53W
Mistake Creek *town* Australia **62** 17.06S 129.04E
Mistassini Canada **77** 48.54N 72.13W
Mistassini *r.* Canada **77** 48.53N 72.14W
Mistassini, Lac *l.* Canada **77** 51.15N 73.10W
Mistassini Prov. Park Canada **77** 51.30N 73.20W
Mistastin Canada **77** 55.55N 63.30W
Mistinibi, L. Canada **77** 55.55N 64.10W
Mistretta Italy **18** 37.56N 14.22E
Mitchell Australia **64** 26.29S 147.58E
Mitchell *r.* N.S.W. Australia **67** 29.40S 152.18E
Mitchell *r.* Qld. Australia **64** 15.12S 141.35E
Mitchell *r.* Vic. Australia **67** 37.53S 147.41E
Mitchell Oreg. U.S.A. **80** 44.34N 120.09W
Mitchell S.Dak. U.S.A. **82** 43.40N 98.00W
Mitchell, Mt. U.S.A. **85** 35.47N 82.16W
Mitchell River *town* Australia **64** 15.28S 141.44E
Mitchelstown Rep. of Ire. **13** 52.16N 8.17W
Mīt Ghamr Egypt **44** 30.43N 31.16E
Mithapur India **40** 22.25N 69.00E
Mithi Pakistan **40** 24.44N 69.48E
Mitilíni Greece **19** 39.06N 26.34E
Mitla, Mamarr *pass* Egypt **44** 30.00N 32.53E
Mitla Pass *see* Mitla, Mamarr *pass* Egypt **44**
Mitsinjo Madagascar **57** 16.01S 45.52E
Mittagong Australia **67** 34.27S 150.25E
Mittelandkanal W. Germany **14** 52.24N 7.52E
Mitú Colombia **90** 1.08N 70.03W
Mitumba, Monts *mts.* Zaïre **55** 3.00S 28.30E
Mitwaba Zaïre **55** 8.32S 27.20E
Mitzic Gabon **54** 0.48N 11.30E
Miura Japan **35** 35.08N 139.37E
Miya *r.* Japan **35** 34.32N 136.44E
Miyako jima *i.* Japan **31** 24.45N 125.25E
Miyakonojō Japan **31** 31.43N 131.02E
Miyazaki Japan **31** 31.58N 131.50E
Mizdah Libya **51** 31.26N 12.59E
Mizen Head Rep. of Ire. **13** 51.27N 9.50W
Mizil Romania **21** 45.00N 26.26E
Mizoch U.S.S.R. **21** 50.30N 25.50E
Mizoram *d.* India **39** 23.40N 92.40E
Mizpe Ramon Israel **44** 30.36N 34.48E
Mizukaidō Japan **35** 36.01N 139.59E
Mizunami Japan **35** 35.22N 137.15E
Mjölby Sweden **23** 58.19N 15.08E
Mjösa *l.* Norway **23** 60.40N 11.00E
Mkata Tanga Tanzania **55** 5.47S 38.18E
Mkushi Zambia **55** 13.40S 29.26E
Mkuze R.S.A. **57** 27.10S 32.00E
Mkwaja Tanzania **55** 5.46S 38.51E
Mkwiti Tanzania **55** 10.27S 39.18E
Mladá Boleslav Czech. **20** 50.26N 14.55E
Mława Poland **21** 53.06N 20.23E
Mljet *i.* Yugo. **19** 42.45N 17.30E
Mneni Zimbabwe **56** 20.38S 30.03E
Moab U.S.A. **80** 38.35N 109.33W
Moama Australia **67** 36.05S 144.50E
Moamba Mozambique **57** 25.35S 32.13E
Moanda Gabon **54** 1.25S 13.18E
Moapa U.S.A. **81** 36.40N 114.39W
Moatize Mozambique **57** 16.10S 33.40E
Moba Zaïre **55** 7.03S 29.42E
Mobara Japan **35** 35.25N 140.18E
Mobaye C.A.R. **49** 4.19N 21.11E
Moberly U.S.A. **82** 39.25N 92.26W
Mobert Canada **76** 48.41N 85.40W
Mobile U.S.A. **83** 30.42N 88.05W
Mobile B. U.S.A. **83** 30.25N 88.00W
Mobridge U.S.A. **82** 45.32N 100.26W
Moçambique *town* Mozambique **55** 15.00S 40.47E
Mochudi Botswana **56** 24.26S 26.07E
Mocimboa da Praia Mozambique **55** 11.19S 40.19E
Mocimboa do Ruvuma Mozambique **55** 11.05S 39.15E
Moclips U.S.A. **80** 47.14N 124.13W
Mococa Brazil **94** 21.28S 47.00W
Moctezuma Mexico **81** 30.10N 106.28W
Mocuba Mozambique **55** 16.52S 37.02E
Modane France **17** 45.12N 6.40E
Modāsa India **40** 23.28N 73.18E
Modder *r.* R.S.A. **56** 29.03S 23.56E
Modena Italy **15** 44.39N 10.55E
Modena U.S.A. **80** 37.48N 113.57W
Modesto U.S.A. **80** 37.39N 121.00W
Modica Italy **18** 36.51N 14.51E
Modjamboli Zaïre **54** 2.28N 22.06E
Moe Australia **67** 38.10S 146.15E
Moebase Mozambique **57** 17.04S 38.41E
Moelv Norway **23** 60.56N 10.42E
Moffat U.K. **12** 55.20N 3.27W
Moga India **40** 30.48N 75.10E
Mogadisho Somali Rep. **55** 2.02N 45.21E
Mogaung Burma **34** 25.15N 96.54E
Mogi das Cruzes Brazil **94** 23.33S 46.14W
Mogi-Guaçu Brazil **94** 20.55S 48.06W
Mogilev U.S.S.R. **21** 53.54N 30.20E
Mogilev Podolskiy U.S.S.R. **21** 48.29N 27.49E
Mogil-Mogil Australia **67** 29.21S 148.44E
Mogilno Poland **21** 52.40N 17.58E
Mogi-Mirim Brazil **94** 22.29S 46.55W
Mogincual Mozambique **55** 15.33S 40.29E
Mogliano Veneto Italy **15** 45.33N 12.14E
Mogok Burma **34** 23.00N 96.30E
Mogollon Rim *f.* U.S.A. **81** 32.30N 111.00W
Mogumber Australia **63** 31.01S 116.02E
Mohács Hungary **21** 45.59N 18.42E
Mohameru, Gunung *mtn.* Indonesia **37** 8.04S 112.53E
Mohammedia Morocco **50** 33.44N 7.24W
Mohana India **41** 25.54N 77.45E
Mohawk Ariz. U.S.A. **81** 32.41N 113.47W
Mohéli *i.* Comoros **55** 12.22S 43.45E
Mohon France **15** 49.45N 4.44E
Mohoro Tanzania **55** 8.09S 39.07E
Mohoru Kenya **55** 1.01S 34.07E
Moi Norway **23** 58.28N 6.32E
Moincêr China **41** 31.10N 80.52E
Moindi Gabon **54** 3.24S 11.43E
Mointy U.S.S.R. **28** 47.10N 73.18E
Mo-i-Rana Norway **22** 66.19N 14.10E
Mõisaküla U.S.S.R. **23** 58.06N 25.11E
Moisdon France **15** 47.37N 1.22W
Moisie *r.* Canada **77** 50.13N 66.02W
Moissac France **17** 44.07N 1.05E
Moïssala Chad **53** 8.20N 17.40E
Mojave U.S.A. **81** 35.03N 118.10W
Mojave Desert U.S.A. **81** 35.00N 117.00W
Mojokerto Indonesia **37** 7.25S 112.31E
Mokameh India **41** 25.24N 85.55E
Mokau New Zealand **60** 38.41S 174.37E
Mokmer Indonesia **37** 1.13S 136.13E
Mokpo S. Korea **31** 34.50N 126.25E
Mol Belgium **14** 51.11N 5.09E
Molchanovo U.S.S.R. **28** 57.39N 83.45E
Mold U.K. **10** 53.10N 3.08W
Moldavskaya S.S.R. *d.* U.S.S.R. **21** 47.30N 28.30E
Molde Norway **22** 62.44N 7.08E
Molepolole Botswana **56** 24.26S 25.34E
Molfetta Italy **19** 41.12N 16.36E
Molihong Shan *mtn.* China **32** 42.11N 124.43E
Molina de Aragón Spain **16** 40.50N 1.54W
Moline U.S.A. **82** 41.30N 90.30W
Molinella Italy **15** 44.37N 11.40E
Molino Lacy Mexico **81** 30.05N 114.24W
Moliro Zaïre **55** 8.11S 30.29E
Molise *d.* Italy **18** 41.40N 15.00E
Mollendo Peru **92** 17.02S 72.01W
MöIndal Sweden **23** 57.39N 12.01E
Molodechno U.S.S.R. **21** 54.16N 26.50E
Molokai *i.* Hawaii U.S.A. **78** 21.20N 157.00W
Molong Australia **67** 33.08S 148.53E
Molopo *r.* R.S.A. **56** 28.30S 20.22E
Moloundou Cameroon **54** 2.55N 12.01E
Molson L. Canada **75** 54.12N 96.45W
Molt U.S.A. **82** 46.22N 102.20W
Molteno R.S.A. **56** 31.23S 26.21E
Moluccas *is.* Indonesia **37** 4.00S 128.00E
Molucca Sea *see* Maluku, Laut *sea* Pacific Oc. **37**
Moma Mozambique **55** 16.40S 39.10E
Mombasa Kenya **55** 4.04S 39.40E
Momi Zaïre **55** 1.42S 27.03E
Mommark Denmark **20** 54.55N 10.03E
Mompós Colombia **90** 9.15N 74.29W
Mon *d.* Burma **34** 16.45N 97.25E
Mön *i.* Denmark **23** 55.00N 12.20E
Mona *i.* Puerto Rico **87** 18.06N 67.54W
Monaco Europe **17** 43.40N 7.25E
Monadhliath Mts. U.K. **12** 57.09N 4.08W
Monaghan Rep. of Ire. **13** 54.15N 6.58W
Monaghan *d.* Rep. of Ire. **13** 54.10N 7.00W
Monahans U.S.A. **83** 31.36N 102.54W
Monarch Mt. Canada **74** 51.55N 125.57W
Monastir Tunisia **51** 35.35N 10.50E
Mon Cai Vietnam **33** 21.36N 107.55E
Moncalieri Italy **15** 45.00N 7.40E
Monchegorsk U.S.S.R. **24** 67.55N 33.01E
Mönchen-Gladbach W. Germany **14** 51.12N 6.25E
Monchique Portugal **16** 37.19N 8.33W
Monclova Mexico **83** 26.54N 101.25W
Moncton Canada **77** 46.06N 64.47W
Mondo Tanzania **55** 5.00S 35.54E
Mondoubleau France **15** 47.59N 0.54E
Mondovì Italy **15** 44.24N 7.50E
Mondrain I. Australia **63** 34.08S 122.15E
Monessen U.S.A. **84** 40.08N 79.54W
Monet Canada **76** 48.10N 75.40W
Monett U.S.A. **83** 36.55N 93.55W
Monfalcone Italy **18** 45.49N 13.32E
Monforte Spain **16** 42.32N 7.30W
Monga Zaïre **49** 4.12N 22.49E
Mongala *r.* Zaïre **54** 1.58N 19.55E
Mongalla Sudan **49** 5.12N 31.46E
Mong Cai Vietnam **33** 21.36N 107.55E
Monger, L. Australia **63** 29.15S 117.05E
Monghyr India **41** 25.23N 86.28E
Mongo Chad **53** 12.14N 18.45E
Mongolia Asia **30** 46.30N 104.00E
Mongororo Chad **49** 12.01N 22.28E
Mongu Zambia **54** 15.10S 23.09E
Monifieth U.K. **12** 56.29N 2.50W
Monitor Range *mts.* U.S.A. **80** 38.45N 116.30W
Monkoto Zaïre **49** 1.38S 20.39E
Monmouth U.K. **11** 51.48N 2.43W
Monmouth Ill. U.S.A. **82** 40.54N 90.39W
Monmouth Oreg. U.S.A. **80** 44.51N 123.14W
Monocacy *r.* U.S.A. **85** 39.13N 77.27W
Mono L. U.S.A. **80** 38.00N 119.00W
Monopoli Italy **19** 40.56N 17.19E
Monor Hungary **21** 47.21N 19.27E
Monreal del Campo Spain **16** 40.47N 1.20W
Monroe La. U.S.A. **83** 32.33N 92.07W
Monroe Mich. U.S.A. **84** 41.56N 83.21W
Monroe N.C. U.S.A. **85** 35.00N 80.35W
Monroe N.Y. U.S.A. **85** 41.20N 74.11W
Monroe Wisc. U.S.A. **82** 42.36N 89.38W
Monroe City U.S.A. **82** 39.39N 91.44W
Monroeville U.S.A. **85** 31.32N 87.21W
Monrovia Liberia **52** 6.20N 10.46W
Mons Belgium **14** 50.27N 3.57E
Monselice Italy **15** 45.14N 11.45E
Mönsterås Sweden **23** 57.02N 16.26E
Montabaur W. Germany **14** 50.27N 7.51E
Montagnana Italy **15** 45.14N 11.28E
Montague Canada **77** 46.10N 62.39W
Montalbán Spain **16** 40.50N 0.48W
Montalto di Castro Italy **18** 42.21N 11.37E
Montana Switz. **15** 46.18N 7.29E
Montana *d.* U.S.A. **80** 47.14N 109.26W
Montargis France **15** 48.00N 2.44E
Montauban France **17** 44.01N 1.20E
Montbard France **15** 47.37N 4.20E
Montbéliard France **17** 47.31N 6.48E
Montbrison France **17** 45.37N 4.04E
Montceau-les-Mines France **17** 46.40N 4.22E
Mont Cenis, Col du *pass* France **17** 45.15N 6.55E
Montcornet France **15** 49.41N 4.01E
Mont de Marsan *town* France **17** 43.54N 0.30W
Montdidier France **15** 49.39N 2.34E
Monte Alegre *town* Brazil **91** 2.01S 54.04W
Monte Azul *town* Brazil **94** 15.53S 42.53W
Montebello Canada **77** 45.39N 74.56W
Monte Carlo Monaco **17** 43.44N 7.25E
Monte Caseros Argentina **93** 30.15S 57.38W
Montecatini Terme Italy **15** 43.53N 10.46E
Montecollina Australia **66** 29.22S 139.56E
Montecristo *i.* Italy **18** 42.20N 10.19E
Montego Bay *town* Jamaica **87** 18.27N 77.56W
Montélimar France **17** 44.33N 4.45E
Montemor-o-Velho Portugal **16** 40.10N 8.41W
Montenegro *see* Crna Gora *d.* Yugo. **19**
Montepuez Mozambique **57** 13.09S 39.33E
Montereau France **15** 48.22N 2.57E
Monterey Calif. U.S.A. **80** 36.37N 121.55W
Monterey B. U.S.A. **80** 36.45N 121.55W
Montería Colombia **90** 8.45N 75.54W
Montero Bolivia **92** 17.20S 63.15W
Monteros Argentina **92** 27.10S 65.30W
Monterrey Mexico **83** 25.40N 100.19W
Monte Santu, Capo di *c.* Italy **18** 40.05N 9.44E
Montes Claros Brazil **94** 16.45S 43.52W
Montevideo Uruguay **93** 34.53S 56.11W
Montevideo U.S.A. **82** 44.57N 95.43W
Montezuma U.S.A. **83** 37.36N 100.26W
Montfort-sur-Meu France **15** 48.08N 1.57W
Montgomery U.K. **11** 52.34N 3.09W
Montgomery Ala. U.S.A. **85** 32.22N 86.20W
Montguyon France **17** 45.13N 0.11W
Monthey Switz. **15** 46.15N 6.57E
Monthois France **15** 49.19N 4.43E
Monticello Ark. U.S.A. **83** 33.38N 91.47W
Monticello Miss. U.S.A. **83** 31.33N 90.07W
Monticello Utah U.S.A. **80** 37.52N 109.21W
Montichiari Italy **15** 45.25N 10.23E
Montiel, Campo de *f.* Spain **16** 38.46N 2.44W
Montigny-le-Roi France **17** 48.00N 5.30E

Montijo to Mūsa Khel

Montijo Portugal 16 38.42N 8.59W
Montijo Dam Spain 16 38.52N 6.20W
Montilla Spain 16 37.36N 4.40W
Montivilliers France 15 49.33N 0.12E
Mont Joli town Canada 77 48.35N 68.14W
Mont Laurier town Canada 76 46.33N 75.31W
Mont Louis town Canada 77 49.15N 65.46W
Montluçon France 17 46.20N 2.36E
Montmagny Canada 77 46.59N 70.33W
Montmédy France 14 49.31N 5.21E
Montmirail France 15 48.52N 3.32E
Montmorillon France 17 46.26N 0.52E
Montmort France 15 48.55N 3.49E
Monto Australia 64 24.52S151.07E
Montoro Spain 16 38.02N 4.23W
Montpelier Idaho U.S.A. 80 42.20N111.20W
Montpelier Vt. U.S.A. 84 44.16N 72.35W
Montpellier France 17 43.36N 3.53E
Montreal Canada 77 45.30N 73.36W
Montreal r. Canada 76 47.13N 84.40W
Montreal L. Canada 75 54.20N105.40W
Montreal Lake town Canada 75 54.03N105.46W
Montréal-Nord Canada 77 45.36N 73.38W
Montrejeau France 17 43.05N 0.33E
Montreuil France 17 50.28N 1.46E
Montreux Switz. 20 46.27N 6.55E
Montrichard France 15 47.21N 1.11E
Montrose U.K. 12 56.43N 2.29W
Montrose Colo. U.S.A. 80 38.29N107.53W
Montsant, Sierra de mts. Spain 16 41.20N 1.00E
Montserrat i. Leeward Is. 87 16.45N 62.14W
Mont Tremblant Prov. Park Canada 76 46.30N 74.30W
Monument Valley f. U.S.A. 80 36.50N110.20W
Monveda Zaïre 54 2.57N 21.27E
Monywa Burma 34 22.05N 95.15E
Monza Italy 15 45.35N 9.16E
Monze Zambia 55 16.16S 27.28E
Monzón Spain 16 41.52N 0.10E
Moolawatana Australia 66 29.55S139.43E
Mooloogool Australia 62 26.06S119.05E
Moomin r. Australia 67 29.35S148.45E
Moonbi Range mts. Australia 67 31.00S151.10E
Moonie Australia 65 27.40S150.19E
Moonie r. Australia 65 29.30S148.40E
Moonta Australia 66 34.04S137.37E
Moora Australia 63 30.40S116.01E
Mooraberree Australia 64 25.12S140.57E
Moorarie Australia 62 25.56S117.35E
Moorcroft U.S.A. 80 44.16N104.57W
Moore r. Australia 63 31.22S115.29E
Moore, L. Australia 63 29.30S117.30E
Mooréa i. Îs. de la Société 69 17.32S149.50W
Moorfoot Hills U.K. 12 55.43N 3.03W
Moorhead U.S.A. 82 46.53N 96.45W
Moorlands Australia 66 35.20S139.40E
Moornanyah L. Australia 66 33.02S143.58E
Mooroopna Australia 67 36.24S145.22E
Moose Creek town Canada 77 45.15N 74.58W
Moosehead L. U.S.A. 84 45.40N 69.40W
Moose Jaw Canada 75 50.23N105.32W
Moose Lake town U.S.A. 82 46.26N 92.45W
Moosomin Canada 75 50.07N101.40W
Moosonee Canada 76 51.17N 80.39W
Mootwingee Australia 66 31.52S141.14E
Mopanzhang China 32 33.07N117.22E
Mopêia Velha Mozambique 57 17.58S 35.40E
Mopti Mali 52 14.29N 4.10W
Mopti d. Mali 50 15.30N 3.40W
Moqor Afghan. 40 32.55N 67.40E
Moquegua Peru 92 17.20S 70.55W
Mora Cameroon 53 11.02N 14.07E
Mora Spain 16 39.41N 3.46W
Mora Sweden 23 61.00N 14.33E
Mora U.S.A. 82 45.53N 93.18W
Morādābād India 41 28.50N 78.47E
Morafenobe Madagascar 57 17.49S 44.45E
Moralana Australia 66 31.42S138.12E
Moramanga Madagascar 57 18.56S 48.12E
Morar, Loch U.K. 12 56.56N 4.00W
Morava r. Czech. 21 48.10N 16.59E
Morava r. Yugo. 21 44.43N 21.02E
Moravské Budějovice Czech. 20 49.03N 15.49E
Morawhanna Guyana 90 8.17N 59.44W
Moray Firth est. U.K. 12 57.35N 5.15W
Morbach W. Germany 14 49.49N 7.05E
Morbegno Italy 15 46.08N 9.34E
Morcenx France 17 44.02N 0.55W
Morden Australia 66 30.30S142.23E
Morden Canada 75 49.11N 98.05W
Mordialloc Australia 67 38.00S145.05E
Mordovo U.S.S.R. 25 52.06N 40.45E
Moreau r. U.S.A. 82 45.18N100.43W
Morecambe U.K. 10 54.03N 2.52W
Morecambe B. U.K. 10 54.05N 3.00W
Moree Australia 67 29.29S149.53E
Morée France 15 47.55N 1.15E
Morehead U.S.A. 85 38.11N 83.27W
Morehead City U.S.A. 85 34.43N 76.44W
Morelia Mexico 86 19.40N101.11W
Morella Spain 16 40.37N 0.06W
Morelos d. Mexico 86 18.40N 99.00W
Morena India 41 26.30N 78.09E
Morena, Sierra mts. Spain 16 38.10N 5.00W
Morenci U.S.A. 81 33.05N109.22W
Moreno Mexico 81 28.29N110.41W
Möre og Romsdal d. Norway 22 63.00N 9.00E
Moresby I. Canada 74 52.30N131.40W
Moreton I. Australia 65 27.10S153.25E
Morez France 17 46.31N 6.02E
Mórfou Cyprus 44 35.12N 33.00E
Mórfou, Kólpos b. Cyprus 44 35.15N 32.50E
Morgan Australia 66 34.02S139.40E
Morgan U.S.A. 83 32.01N 97.37W
Morgan City U.S.A. 83 29.42N 91.12W
Morganfield U.S.A. 85 37.41N 87.55W
Morgantown U.S.A. 84 39.38N 79.57W
Morghāb r. Afghan. 38 36.50N 63.00E
Moriki Nigeria 53 12.55N 6.30E
Morin Heights Canada 77 45.54N 74.21W
Morioka Japan 31 39.43N141.08E
Morisset Australia 67 33.06S151.29E
Moriyama Japan 35 35.04N135.59E
Morkalla Australia 66 34.22S141.10E
Morlaix France 17 48.35N 3.50W
Mormon Range mts. U.S.A. 80 37.08N114.20W
Mornington Australia 67 38.12S145.05E
Mornington I. Australia 64 16.33S139.24E
Mornington Mission Australia 64 16.40S139.10E
Morobe P.N.G. 37 7.45S147.35E
Morocco Africa 50 32.30N 5.00W
Moro G. Phil. 37 6.30N123.20E
Morogoro Tanzania 55 6.47S 37.40E
Morogoro d. Tanzania 55 8.30S 37.00E
Moroleón Mexico 86 20.08N101.12W
Morombe Madagascar 57 21.45S 43.22E
Morón Argentina 93 34.39S 58.37W
Morón Cuba 87 22.08N 78.39W
Mörön Mongolia 30 49.36N100.08E
Morón Spain 16 37.06N 5.28W
Morondava Madagascar 57 20.17S 44.17E
Moroni Comoros 55 11.40S 43.19E
Morotai i. Indonesia 37 2.10N128.30E
Moroto Uganda 55 2.32N 34.41E
Moroto, Mt. Uganda 55 2.30N 34.46E
Morpeth U.K. 10 55.10N 1.40W
Morrilton U.S.A. 83 35.09N 92.45W
Morrinsville New Zealand 60 37.39S175.32E
Morris Minn. U.S.A. 82 45.35N 95.55W
Morristown Ariz. U.S.A. 81 33.51N112.37W
Morristown N.J. U.S.A. 85 40.48N 74.29W
Morristown S.Dak. U.S.A. 82 45.56N101.43W
Morristown Tenn. U.S.A. 85 36.13N 83.18W
Morrumbene Mozambique 57 23.41S 35.25E
Morsbach W. Germany 14 50.52N 7.44E
Morsi India 41 21.21N 78.00E
Mortagne France 15 48.32N 0.33E
Mortain France 15 48.39N 0.56W
Mortara Italy 15 45.15N 8.44E
Mortes r. Brazil 94 21.09S 45.06W
Mortes r. see Manso r. Brazil 92
Mortlake town Australia 66 38.05S142.48E
Morundah Australia 67 34.56S146.18E
Moruya Australia 67 35.56S150.06E
Morven Australia 64 26.25S147.05E
Morvern f. U.K. 12 56.37N 5.45W
Morvi India 40 22.49N 70.50E
Morwell Australia 67 38.14S146.25E
Morzhovets i. U.S.S.R. 24 66.45N 42.30E
Mosby Norway 23 58.14N 7.54E
Moscow U.S.A. 80 46.44N117.00W
Moscow see Moskva U.S.S.R. 24
Mosel r. W. Germany 14 50.23N 7.37E
Moselle r. see Mosel r. France / Lux. 14
Moses Lake town U.S.A. 80 47.08N119.17W
Mosgiel New Zealand 60 45.53S170.22E
Moshi Tanzania 55 3.20S 37.21E
Mosjöen Norway 22 65.50N 13.10E
Moskenes Norway 22 67.55N 13.00E
Moskenesöy i. Norway 22 67.55N 13.00E
Moskva U.S.S.R. 24 55.45N 37.42E
Moskva r. U.S.S.R. 24 55.08N 38.50E
Mosquera Colombia 90 2.30N 78.29W
Mosquero U.S.A. 81 35.47N103.58W
Mosquitia Plain Honduras 87 15.00N 84.00W
Mosquitos, Costa de f. Nicaragua 87 13.00N 84.00W
Mosquitos, Golfo de los g. Panama 87 9.00N 81.00W
Moss Norway 23 59.26N 10.42E
Mossaka Congo 54 1.20S 16.44E
Mossburn New Zealand 60 45.41S168.15E
Mosselbaai R.S.A. 56 34.11S 22.08E
Mossendjo Congo 54 2.52S 12.46E
Mossgiel Australia 67 33.18S144.05E
Mossman Australia 64 16.28S145.22E
Mossoró Brazil 91 5.10S 37.18W
Mossuril Mozambique 57 14.58S 40.42E
Most Czech. 20 50.31N 13.39E
Mostaganem Algeria 50 35.56N 0.05E
Mostar Yugo. 19 43.20N 17.50E
Mösting, Kap c. Greenland 73 64.00N 41.00W
Mostiska U.S.S.R. 21 49.48N 23.05E
Mosul see Al Mawşil Iraq 42
Motagua r. Guatemala 87 15.56N 87.45W
Motala Sweden 23 58.33N 15.03E
Moth India 41 25.43N 78.57E
Motherwell U.K. 12 55.48N 4.00W
Motīhāri India 41 26.39N 84.55E
Motloutse r. Botswana 56 22.15S 29.00E
Motol U.S.S.R. 21 52.25N 25.05E
Motou China 32 32.17N120.35E
Motril Spain 16 36.44N 3.37W
Mott U.S.A. 80 46.22N102.20W
Motueka New Zealand 60 41.08S173.01E
Motu Iti i. Îs. de la Société 69 16.15S151.50W
Motutapu Niue 68 19.02S169.52W
Mouali Congo 54 0.10N 15.33E
Mouchalagane r. Canada 77 53.32N 69.00W
Moúdhros Greece 19 39.52N 25.16E
Moudjéria Mauritania 50 17.53N 12.20W
Mouila Gabon 54 1.50S 11.02E
Mouka C.A.R. 49 7.16N 21.52E
Moulamein Australia 66 35.03S144.05E
Moulhoulé Djibouti 49 12.36N 43.12E
Moulins France 17 46.34N 3.20E
Moulins-la-Marche France 15 48.39N 0.29E
Moulmein Burma 34 16.55N 97.49E
Moulouya, Oued r. Morocco 50 35.05N 2.25W
Moultrie U.S.A. 85 31.11N 83.47W
Moultrie, L. U.S.A. 85 33.20N 80.05W
Mound City U.S.A. 82 40.07N 95.14W
Moundou Chad 53 8.36N 16.02E
Moundsville U.S.A. 84 39.54N 80.44W
Moundville U.S.A. 83 32.59N 87.38W
Mountain Ash U.K. 11 51.42N 3.22W
Mountain City U.S.A. 80 41.50N115.58W
Mountain Home Ark. U.S.A. 83 36.20N 92.23W
Mountain Home Idaho U.S.A. 80 43.08N115.41W
Mountain Nile r. see Jabal, Baḩr al r. Sudan 49
Mountain Village U.S.A. 72 62.05N163.44W
Mount Airy town Md. U.S.A. 85 39.23N 77.09W
Mount Airy town N.C. U.S.A. 85 36.31N 80.38W
Mount Barker town S.A. Australia 66 35.06S138.52E
Mount Barker town W.A. Australia 63 34.36S117.37E
Mount Bellew town Rep. of Ire. 13 53.28N 8.30W
Mount Brown town Australia 66 29.45S141.52E
Mount Carmel town Ill. U.S.A. 82 38.25N 87.46W
Mount Darwin town Zimbabwe 57 16.46S 31.36E
Mount Douglas town Australia 64 21.31S146.50E
Mount Drysdale town Australia 67 31.11S145.51E
Mount Eba town Australia 66 30.12S135.33E
Mount Fletcher town R.S.A. 56 30.41S 28.30E
Mount Gambier town Australia 66 37.51S140.50E
Mount Goldsworthy town Australia 62 20.20S119.31E
Mount Hagen town P.N.G. 37 5.54S144.13E
Mount Holly town U.S.A. 85 39.59N 74.47W
Mount Hope town N.S.W. Australia 67 32.49S145.48E
Mount Hope town S.A. Australia 66 34.07S135.23E
Mount Isa town Australia 64 20.50S139.29E
Mount Ive town Australia 66 32.24S136.10E
Mount Lofty Range mts. Australia 66 34.40S139.03E
Mount Magnet town Australia 63 28.06S117.50E
Mountmellick Rep. of Ire. 13 53.08N 7.21W
Mount Morgan town Australia 64 23.39S150.23E
Mount Murchison town Australia 66 31.23S143.42E
Mount Newman town Australia 62 23.20S119.40E
Mount Nicholas town Australia 62 22.54S120.27E
Mount Pleasant town Canada 76 43.05N 80.19W
Mount Pleasant town Mich. U.S.A. 84 43.36N 84.46W
Mount Pleasant town S.C. U.S.A. 85 32.48N 79.54W
Mount Pleasant town Tex. U.S.A. 83 33.09N 94.58W
Mount Robson town Canada 74 52.56N119.15W
Mount's B. U.K. 11 50.05N 5.25W
Mount Sterling town U.S.A. 85 38.03N 83.56W
Mount Sturgeon town Australia 64 20.08S144.00E
Mount Swan town Australia 64 22.31S135.00E
Mount Vernon town Australia 62 24.09S118.10E
Mount Vernon town Ill. U.S.A. 82 38.19N 88.52W
Mount Vernon town N.Y. U.S.A. 85 40.54N 73.50W
Mount Vernon town Wash. U.S.A. 80 48.25N122.20W
Mount Willoughby Australia 66 27.58S134.08E
Moura Brazil 90 1.27S 61.38W
Moura Chad 48 13.47N 21.13E
Mourdi, Dépression de f. Chad 48 18.10N 23.00E
Mourdiah Mali 52 14.35N 7.25W
Mourne r. U.K. 9 54.50N 7.29W
Mourne Mts. U.K. 13 54.10N 6.02W
Mouscron Belgium 14 50.46N 3.10E
Moussoro Chad 53 13.41N 16.31E
Moxico Angola 54 11.50S 20.05E
Moxico d. Angola 54 13.00S 21.00E
Moy r. Rep. of Ire. 13 54.10N 9.09W
Moyale Kenya 55 3.31N 39.04E
Moyamba Sierra Leone 52 8.04N 12.03W
Moyen Atlas mts. Morocco 50 33.30N 5.00W
Moyen-Chari d. Chad 53 9.20N 17.35E
Moyeni Lesotho 56 30.24S 27.41E
Moyie Canada 74 49.17N115.50W
Moyobamba Peru 90 6.04S 76.56W
Moyowosi r. Tanzania 55 4.59S 30.58E
Mozambique Africa 57 17.30S 35.45E
Mozambique Channel Indian Oc. 57 16.00S 42.30E
Mozdok U.S.S.R. 25 43.45N 44.43E
Mozyr U.S.S.R. 21 52.02N 29.10E
Mpala Zaïre 55 6.45S 29.31E
M'Pama r. Congo 54 0.59S 15.40E
Mpanda Tanzania 55 6.21S 31.01E
Mpésoba Mali 52 12.31N 5.39W
Mphoengs Zimbabwe 56 21.10S 27.51E
Mpika Zambia 55 11.52S 31.30E
Mponela Malaŵi 55 13.32S 33.43E
Mporokoso Zambia 55 9.22S 30.06E
M'Pouya Congo 54 2.38S 16.08E
Mpunde mtn. Tanzania 55 6.12S 33.48E
Mpwapwa Tanzania 55 6.23S 36.38E
M'qoun, Irhil mtn. Morocco 50 31.31N 6.25W
Mrhila, Djebel mtn. Tunisia 51 35.25N 9.14E
Msaken Tunisia 51 35.42N 10.33E
Mseleni R.S.A. 57 27.21S 32.33E
Msingu Tanzania 55 4.52S 39.08E
Msta r. U.S.S.R. 24 58.28N 31.20E
Mtakuja Tanzania 55 7.21S 30.37E
Mtama Tanzania 55 10.20S 39.19E
Mtito Andei Kenya 55 2.32S 38.10E
Mtsensk U.S.S.R. 24 53.18N 36.35E
Mtwara Tanzania 55 10.17S 40.11E
Mtwara d. Tanzania 55 10.00S 38.30E
Muaná Brazil 91 1.32S 49.13W
Muangangia Angola 54 13.33S 18.04E
Muang Chiang Rai Thailand 34 19.56N 99.51E
Muang Khammouan Laos 34 17.22N104.50E
Muang Khon Kaen Thailand 34 16.25N102.52E
Muang Lampang Thailand 34 18.16N 99.30E
Muang Lamphun Thailand 34 18.36N 99.02E
Muang Nakhon Phanom Thailand 34 17.22N104.45E
Muang Nakhon Sawan Thailand 34 15.42N100.04E
Muang Nan Thailand 34 18.47N100.50E
Muang Ngoy Laos 34 20.43N102.41E
Muang Pak Lay Laos 34 18.12N101.25E
Muang Phaya Thailand 34 19.10N 99.55E
Muang Phetchabun Thailand 34 16.25N101.08E
Muang Phichit Thailand 34 16.29N100.21E
Muang Phitsanulok Thailand 34 16.45N100.18E
Muang Phrae Thailand 34 18.07N100.09E
Muang Sakon Nakhon Thailand 34 17.10N104.08E
Muang Sing Laos 34 21.11N101.09E
Muang Soum Laos 34 18.46N102.36E
Muang Ubon Thailand 34 15.15N104.50E
Muar Malaysia 36 2.01N102.35E
Muara Brunei 36 5.01N115.01E
Muara Indonesia 36 0.32S101.20E
Muarakaman Indonesia 36 0.02S116.45E
Muaratewe Indonesia 36 0.57S114.53E
Muāri, Rās c. Pakistan 40 24.49N 66.40E
Mubende Uganda 55 0.30N 31.24E
Mubi Nigeria 53 10.16N 13.17E
Mucanona Angola 54 8.13S 16.39E
Muchea Australia 63 31.36S115.57E
Muchinga Mts. Zambia 55 12.15S 31.00E
Muck i. U.K. 12 56.50N 6.14W
Mucojo Mozambique 55 12.05S 40.26E
Mudanjiang China 31 44.36N129.42E
Mudgee Australia 67 32.37S149.36E
Mudon Burma 34 16.15N 97.44E
Mudyuga U.S.S.R. 24 63.45N 39.29E
Muèda Mozambique 55 11.40S 39.31E
Muene Quibau Angola 54 11.27S 19.14E
Mufulira Zambia 55 12.30S 28.12E
Mufu Shan mts. China 33 29.30N114.45E
Muganskaya Step f. U.S.S.R. 43 39.40N 48.30E
Mughshin, Wādī Oman 45 19.44N 55.15E
Mugía Spain 16 43.06N 9.14W
Muğla Turkey 19 37.12N 28.22E
Muhamdi India 41 27.57N 80.13E
Muḩammad, Ra's c. Egypt 44 27.42N 34.13E
Mühldorf W. Germany 20 48.15N 12.32E
Mühlhausen E. Germany 20 51.12N 10.27E
Mühlig Hofmann fjella mts. Antarctica 96 72.30S 5.00E
Muhola Finland 22 63.20N 25.05E
Muhos Finland 22 64.48N 25.59E
Muhu i. U.S.S.R. 23 58.32N 23.20E
Muhuru Kenya 49 1.01S 34.07E
Muhu Väin str. U.S.S.R. 23 58.45N 23.30E
Mui Ca Mau c. Vietnam 34 8.30N104.35E
Muine Bheag town Rep. of Ire. 13 52.42N 6.58W
Muir, L. Australia 63 34.30S116.30E
Mukachevo U.S.S.R. 21 48.26N 22.45E
Mukah Malaysia 36 2.56N112.02E
Mukandwara India 40 24.49N 75.59E
Mukawa P.N.G. 64 9.48S150.00E
Mukeriān India 40 31.57N 75.37E
Mukinbudin Australia 63 30.52S118.08E
Muko r. Japan 35 34.41N135.23E
Mukoba Zaïre 54 6.50S 20.50E
Mukongo Zaïre 54 6.32S 23.30E
Muktsar India 40 30.28N 74.31E
Mukwela Zambia 54 17.00S 26.40E
Mūl India 41 20.04N 79.40E
Mula r. India 40 19.35N 74.50E
Mūla r. Pakistan 40 27.57N 67.37E
Mulanje Mts. Malaŵi 55 15.57S 35.33E
Mulchén Chile 93 37.43S 72.14W
Mulde r. E. Germany 20 51.10N 12.48E
Mulgathing Australia 66 30.15S134.00E
Mulgrave Canada 77 45.37N 61.23W
Mulgrave I. Australia 64 10.07S142.08E
Mulhacén mtn. Spain 16 37.04N 3.22W
Mülheim N.-Westfalen W. Germany 14 51.25N 6.50E
Mülheim N.-Westfalen W. Germany 14 50.58N 7.00E
Mulhouse France 17 47.45N 7.21E
Mull i. U.K. 12 56.28N 5.56W
Mull, Sd. of str. U.K. 12 56.32N 5.55W
Mullaghanattin mtn. Rep. of Ire. 13 51.56N 9.51W
Mullaghareirk Mts. Rep. of Ire. 13 52.19N 9.06W
Mullaghmore mtn. U.K. 13 54.51N 6.51W
Mullaley Australia 67 31.06S149.55E
Mullen U.S.A. 82 42.03N101.01W
Mullengudgery Australia 67 31.40S147.23E
Mullens U.S.A. 85 37.35N 81.25W
Mullet Pen. Rep. of Ire. 13 54.12N 10.04W
Mullewa Australia 63 28.33S115.31E
Mullingar Rep. of Ire. 13 53.31N 7.21W
Mullion Creek town Australia 67 33.09S149.09E
Mull of Galloway c. U.K. 12 54.39N 4.52W
Mull of Kintyre c. U.K. 12 55.17N 5.45W
Mullovka U.S.S.R. 24 54.12N 49.26E
Mullumbimby Australia 67 28.32S153.30E
Mulobezi Zambia 56 16.49S 25.09E
Muloorina Australia 66 29.10S137.51E
Muloowurtina Australia 66 30.06S140.04E
Multai India 41 21.46N 78.15E
Multān Pakistan 40 30.11N 71.29E
Multyfarnham Rep. of Ire. 13 53.37N 7.25W
Mulyungarie Australia 66 31.30S140.45E
Mumbwa Zambia 55 14.57S 27.01E
Mun r. Thailand 34 15.15N104.50E
Mun, Jabal mtn. Sudan 48 14.08N 22.42E
Muna i. Indonesia 37 5.00S122.30E
Munābāo India 40 25.45N 70.17E
Munan Pass China / Vietnam 33 22.06N106.46E
Münchberg W. Germany 20 50.11N 11.47E
München W. Germany 20 48.08N 11.35E
Muncho Lake town Canada 74 59.00N125.50W
Muncie U.S.A. 84 40.11N 85.23W
Mundaring Weir Australia 63 31.59S116.13E
Münden W. Germany 20 51.25N 9.39E
Mundiwindi Australia 62 23.50S120.07E
Mundo r. Spain 16 38.20N 1.50W
Mundra India 40 22.51N 69.44E
Mungallala r. Australia 65 28.53S147.05E
Mungari Mozambique 57 17.12S 33.31E
Mungbere Zaïre 55 2.40N 28.25E
Mungeli India 41 22.04N 81.41E
Mungerannie Australia 66 28.00S138.36E
Mungindi Australia 67 28.58S148.56E
Munhango Angola 54 12.10S 18.36E
Munich see München W. Germany 20
Muniz Freire Brazil 94 20.25S 41.23W
Munkfors Sweden 23 59.50N 13.32E
Munning r. Australia 67 31.50S152.30E
Münster N.-Westfalen W. Germany 14 51.58N 7.37E
Muntadgin Australia 63 31.41S118.32E
Muong Hinh Vietnam 33 19.49N105.03E
Muonio Finland 22 67.57N 23.42E
Muonio r. Finland / Sweden 22 67.10N 23.40E
Mupa Angola 56 16.07S 15.45E
Mupa r. Mozambique 57 19.07S 35.50E
Muping China 32 37.23N121.35E
Muqaddam, Wādī Sudan 48 18.04N 31.30E
Mur r. Austria see Mura r. Yugo. 20
Mura r. Yugo. 20 46.18N 16.53E
Murallón mtn. Argentina / Chile 93 49.48S 73.25W
Muranga Kenya 55 0.43S 37.10E
Murashi U.S.S.R. 24 59.20N 48.59E
Murchison r. Australia 62 27.30S114.10E
Murchison New Zealand 60 41.48S172.20E
Murcia Spain 16 37.59N 1.08W
Murcia d. Spain 16 38.30N 1.45W
Murdo U.S.A. 82 43.53N100.43W
Mureş r. Romania 21 46.16N 20.10E
Muret France 17 43.28N 1.19E
Murewa Zimbabwe 57 17.40S 31.47E
Murfreesboro U.S.A. 85 35.50N 86.25W
Murgha Faqīrzai Pakistan 40 31.03N 67.48E
Murgha Kibzai Pakistan 40 30.44N 69.25E
Murgon Australia 64 26.15S151.57E
Murguía Spain 16 42.57N 2.49W
Muri Cook Is. 68 21.14S159.43W
Muriaé Brazil 94 21.08S 42.33W
Müritzsee l. E. Germany 20 52.25N 12.45E
Murjek Sweden 22 66.29N 20.50E
Murliganj India 41 25.54N 86.59E
Murmansk U.S.S.R. 24 68.59N 33.08E
Murnei Sudan 49 12.57N 22.52E
Murom U.S.S.R. 24 55.04N 42.04E
Muroran Japan 31 42.21N140.59E
Murrah al Kubrá, Al Buḩayrah al l. Egypt 44 30.20N 32.20E
Murra Murra Australia 67 28.18S146.48E
Murray r. Australia 66 35.23S139.20E
Murray r. W.A. Australia 63 32.35S115.46E
Murray r. Canada 74 56.11N120.45W
Murray Ky. U.S.A. 83 36.37N 88.19W
Murray Utah U.S.A. 80 40.40N111.53W
Murray, L. P.N.G. 37 7.00S141.30E
Murray, L. U.S.A. 85 34.04N 81.23W
Murray Bridge town Australia 66 35.10S139.17E
Murrayville Australia 66 35.16S141.14E
Murree Pakistan 40 33.54N 73.24E
Murringo Australia 67 34.19S148.36E
Murrumbidgee r. Australia 66 34.38S143.10E
Murrumburrah Australia 67 34.33S148.21E
Murrurundi Australia 67 31.47S150.51E
Murshidābād India 41 24.11N 88.16E
Murtee Australia 66 31.05S143.35E
Murtoa Australia 66 36.40S142.31E
Murud mtn. Malaysia 36 3.45N115.30E
Murwāra India 41 23.51N 80.24E
Murwillumbah Australia 67 28.20S153.24E
Muryo, Gunung mtn. Indonesia 37 6.39S110.51E
Muş Turkey 42 38.45N 41.30E
Mūsá, Jabal mtn. Egypt 44 28.31N 33.59E
Musadi Zaïre 54 2.31S 22.50E
Mūsa Khel Pakistan 40 32.38N 71.44E

Mūsa Khel Bāzār to Nerekhta

Mūsa Khel Bāzār Pakistan 40 30.52N 69.49E
Musala *mtn.* Bulgaria 19 42.11N 23.35E
Mūsā Qal 'eh Afghan. 40 32.05N 64.51E
Mūsā Qal 'eh *r.* Afghan. 40 32.22N 64.46E
Musay'īd Qatar 43 24.47N 51.36E
Mūsāzai Pakistan 40 30.23N 66.32E
Muscat *see* Masqaṭ Oman 43
Muscatine U.S.A. 82 41.25N 91.03W
Musgrave Australia 64 14.47S143.30E
Musgrave Ranges *mts.* Australia 62 26.10S131.50E
Mushie Zaïre 54 2.59S 16.55E
Mushima Zambia 56 14.13S 25.05E
Mushin Nigeria 53 6.33N 3.22E
Musi *r.* Indonesia 36 2.20S104.57E
Muskegon U.S.A. 84 43.13N 86.15W
Muskegon *r.* U.S.A. 84 43.13N 86.16W
Muskegon Heights *town* U.S.A. 84 43.03N 86.16W
Muskogee U.S.A. 83 35.45N 95.22W
Muskoka, L. Canada 76 45.00N 79.25W
Muskwa *r.* Alta. Canada 74 56.16N114.06W
Muskwa *r.* B.C. Canada 74 58.47N122.48W
Musoma Tanzania 55 1.31S 33.48E
Mussari Angola 56 13.07S 17.56E
Musselburgh U.K. 12 55.57N 3.04W
Musselkanaal Neth. 14 52.57N 7.01E
Musselshell *r.* U.S.A. 80 47.21N107.58W
Mussende Angola 54 10.33S 16.02E
Musserra Angola 54 7.31S 13.02E
Mustahil Ethiopia 45 5.12N 44.17E
Mustāng Nepal 41 29.11N 83.57E
Mustjala U.S.S.R. 23 58.28N 22.14E
Muswellbrook Australia 67 32.17S150.55E
Mūṭ Egypt 48 25.29N 28.59E
Mut Turkey 42 36.38N 33.27E
Mutala Mozambique 57 15.54S 37.51E
Mutalau Niue 68 18.58S169.50W
Mutanda Zambia 54 12.23S 26.16E
Mutare Zimbabwe 57 18.59S 32.40E
Mutoko Zimbabwe 57 17.23S 32.13E
Mutooroo Australia 66 32.30S140.58E
Mutoray U.S.S.R. 29 61.20N100.32E
Mutshatsha Zaïre 54 10.39S 24.27E
Mutton Bay *town* Canada 77 50.47N 59.02W
Muwale Tanzania 55 6.22S 33.46E
Muxima Angola 54 9.33S 13.58E
Muya U.S.S.R. 29 56.28N115.50E
Muyinga Burundi 55 2.48S 30.21E
Muynak U.S.S.R. 28 43.46N 59.00E
Muzaffarābād Jammu & Kashmir 40 34.22N 73.28E
Muzaffargarh Pakistan 40 30.04N 71.12E
Muzaffarnagar India 41 29.28N 77.41E
Muzaffarpur India 41 26.07N 85.24E
Muzhi U.S.S.R. 24 65.25N 64.40E
Muzoka Zambia 56 16.43S 27.18E
Muztag *mtn.* China 30 36.25N 87.25E
Mvadhi Gabon 54 1.13N 13.10E
Mvolo Sudan 49 6.03N 29.56E
Mvomero Tanzania 55 6.18S 37.26E
Mvuma Zimbabwe 56 19.16S 30.30E
Mvurwi Range *mts.* Zimbabwe 56 17.10S 30.45E
Mwanza Tanzania 55 2.30S 32.54E
Mwanza *d.* Tanzania 55 3.00S 32.30E
Mwanza Zaïre 54 7.51S 26.43E
Mwaya Mbeya Tanzania 55 9.33S 33.56E
Mweka Zaïre 54 4.51S 21.34E
Mwene Ditu Zaïre 54 7.04S 23.27E
Mwenezi *r.* Mozambique 57 22.42S 31.45E
Mwenezi Zimbabwe 56 21.22S 30.45E
Mweru, L. Zaïre/Zambia 55 9.00S 28.40E
Mwingi Kenya 55 1.00S 38.04E
Mwinilunga Zambia 54 11.44S 24.24E
Mya, Oued *wadi* Algeria 51 31.40N 5.15E
Myanaung Burma 39 18.25N 95.10E
Myaungmya Burma 34 16.33N 94.55E
Myingyan Burma 34 21.22N 95.28E
Myinkyado Burma 34 20.56N 96.42E
Myinmu Burma 34 21.58N 95.43E
Myitkyinā Burma 34 25.24N 97.25E
Mymensingh Bangla. 41 24.45N 90.24E
Myrdal Norway 23 60.44N 7.08E
Myrdalsjökull *ice cap* Iceland 22 63.40N 19.06W
Myrtle Beach *town* U.S.A. 85 33.42N 78.54W
Myrtle Creek *town* U.S.A. 80 43.01N123.17W
Myrtleford Australia 67 36.35S146.44E
Myrtle Point *town* U.S.A. 80 43.04N124.08W
Myślenice Poland 21 49.51N 19.56E
Mysore India 38 12.18N 76.37E
My Tho Vietnam 34 10.27N106.20E
Mytishchi U.S.S.R. 24 55.54N 37.47E
Mziha Tanzania 55 5.53S 37.48E
Mzimba Malaŵi 55 12.00S 33.39E

N

Naab *r.* W. Germany 20 49.01N 12.02E
Naalehu Hawaiian Is. 69 19.04N155.35W
Na'ām *r.* Sudan 49 6.48N 29.57E
Naantali Finland 23 60.27N 22.02E
Naas Rep. of Ire. 13 53.13N 6.41W
Näätämö *r.* Norway 22 69.40N 29.30E
Nababeep R.S.A. 56 29.36S 17.44E
Nabadwīp India 41 23.25N 88.22E
Nabari *r.* Japan 35 34.45N136.01E
Nabeul Tunisia 51 36.28N 10.44E
Nābha India 40 30.22N 76.09E
Nabingora Uganda 55 0.31N 31.11E
Nabī Shu'ayb, Jabal an *mtn.* Yemen 45 15.17N 43.59E
Naboomspruit R.S.A. 56 24.31S 28.24E
Nabq Egypt 44 28.04N 34.26E
Nābulus Jordan 44 32.13N 35.16E
Nacala Mozambique 57 14.34S 40.41E
Nacchio Ethiopia 49 7.30N 40.15E
Nachikapau L. Canada 77 56.44N 68.00W
Nachingwea Tanzania 55 10.21S 38.46E
Nāchna India 40 27.30N 71.43E
Nackara Australia 66 32.51S139.13E
Naco Mexico 81 31.20N109.56W
Nacogdoches U.S.A. 83 31.36N 94.39W
Nadiād India 40 22.42N 72.52E
Nador Morocco 50 35.12N 2.55W
Nadūshan Iran 43 32.03N 53.33E
Nadvoitsy U.S.S.R. 24 63.56N 34.20E
Nadvornaya U.S.S.R. 21 48.37N 24.30E
Nadym U.S.S.R. 28 65.25N 72.40E
Naenwa India 40 25.46N 75.51E
Naeröy Norway 22 64.48N 11.17E
Naestved Denmark 23 55.14N 11.46E
Nafada Nigeria 53 11.08N 11.20E
Nafīshah Egypt 44 30.34N 32.15E
Naft-e Safīd Iran 43 31.38N 49.20E
Nāg Pakistan 40 27.24N 65.08E
Naga Phil. 37 13.36N123.12E
Nāgāland *d.* India 39 26.10N 94.30E
Nagambie Australia 67 36.48S145.12E
Nagano Japan 31 36.39N138.10E
Nagano *d.* Japan 35 35.33N137.50E
Nagaoka Japan 31 37.30N138.50E
Nāgappattinam India 39 10.45N 79.50E
Nagara *r.* Japan 35 35.01N136.43E
Nagar Pārkar Pakistan 40 24.22N 70.45E
Nagarzê China 41 28.58N 90.24E
Nagasaki Japan 31 32.45N129.52E
Nāgaur India 40 27.12N 73.44E
Nāgāvali *r.* India 41 18.13N 83.56E
Nāgda India 40 23.27N 75.25E
Nagele Neth. 14 52.39N 5.43E
Nāgercoil India 38 8.11N 77.30E
Nagichot Sudan 49 4.16N 33.34E
Nagīna India 41 29.27N 78.27E
Nagles Mts. Rep. of Ire. 13 52.06N 8.26W
Nagorskoye U.S.S.R. 24 58.18N 50.50E
Nagoya Japan 35 35.10N136.55E
Nāgpur India 41 21.09N 79.06E
Nagqên China 39 32.15N 96.13E
Nagqu China 41 31.30N 92.00E
Nagykanizsa Hungary 21 46.27N 17.01E
Naha Japan 31 26.10N127.40E
Nāhan India 41 30.33N 77.18E
Nahanni Butte *town* Canada 74 61.02N123.20W
Nahariyya Israel 44 33.01N 35.05E
Nahāvand Iran 43 34.13N 48.23E
Nahe *r.* W. Germany 14 49.58N 7.54E
Nahunta U.S.A. 85 31.12N 82.00W
Nai Ga Burma 34 27.48N 97.30E
Naiman Qi China 32 42.53N120.40E
Nain Canada 77 57.00N 61.40W
Nā'īn Iran 43 32.52N 53.05E
Naini Tāl India 41 29.23N 79.27E
Nainpur India 41 22.26N 80.07E
Nairn U.K. 12 57.35N 3.52W
Nairobi Kenya 55 1.17S 36.50E
Naita, Mt. Ethiopia 49 5.31N 35.18E
Naivasha Kenya 55 0.44S 36.26E
Najd *f.* Saudi Arabia 42 25.00N 45.00E
Naj 'Hammādī Egypt 42 26.04N 32.13E
Najrān *see* Abā as Su'ūd Saudi Arabia 45
Nāka Khārari Pakistan 40 25.15N 66.44E
Nakape Sudan 49 5.47N 28.38E
Nakatsugawa Japan 35 35.29N137.30E
Nakfa Ethiopia 48 16.43N 38.32E
Nakhichevan U.S.S.R. 43 39.12N 45.24E
Nakhodka U.S.S.R. 31 42.53N132.54E
Nakhola India 41 26.07N 92.11E
Nakhon Pathom Thailand 34 13.50N100.01E
Nakhon Ratchasima Thailand 34 14.58N102.06E
Nakhon Si Thammarat Thailand 34 8.24N 99.58E
Nakhtarana India 40 23.20N 69.15E
Nakina Canada 76 50.10N 86.40W
Nakło Poland 21 53.08N 17.35E
Naknek U.S.A. 72 58.45N157.00W
Nakop Namibia 56 28.05S 19.57E
Nakskov Denmark 23 54.50N 11.09E
Näkten *l.* Sweden 22 65.50N 14.35E
Nakuru Kenya 55 0.16S 36.04E
Nāl *r.* Pakistan 40 26.02N 65.19E
Nalbāri India 41 26.26N 91.30E
Nalchik U.S.S.R. 25 43.31N 43.38E
Nalón *r.* Spain 16 43.35N 6.06W
Nālūt Libya 51 31.52N 10.59E
Namacurra Mozambique 55 17.35S 37.00E
Namakī *r.* Iran 43 31.02N 55.20E
Namanga Kenya 55 2.33S 36.48E
Namangan U.S.S.R. 30 40.59N 71.41E
Namanyere Tanzania 55 7.34S 31.00E
Namapa Mozambique 57 13.48S 39.44E
Namaponda Mozambique 57 15.51S 39.52E
Namari Senegal 50 15.05N 13.39W
Namarroi Mozambique 57 15.58S 36.55E
Namatele Tanzania 55 10.01S 38.26E
Namba Angola 54 11.32S 15.33E
Nambala Zambia 56 15.07S 27.02E
Nambour Australia 65 26.40S152.52E
Nambucca Heads *town* Australia 67 30.38S152.59E
Namco China 41 30.53N 91.06E
Nam Co *l.* China 41 30.45N 90.30E
Nam Dinh Vietnam 33 20.21N106.09E
Namecala Mozambique 57 12.50S 39.38E
Nametil Mozambique 57 15.41S 39.30E
Namib Desert Namibia 56 23.00S 15.20E
Namibe Angola 54 15.10S 12.10E
Namibe *d.* Angola 54 15.30S 12.30E
Namibia Africa 56 21.30S 16.45E
Namīn Iran 43 38.25N 48.30E
Namlea Indonesia 37 3.15S127.07E
Namling China 41 29.40N 89.03E
Namoi *r.* Australia 67 30.14S148.28E
Namonuito *i.* Pacific Oc. 68 8.46N150.02E
Namous, Oued *wadi* Algeria 50 30.28N 0.14W
Nampa Canada 74 56.02N117.07W
Nampa U.S.A. 80 43.44N116.34W
Nam Phan *f.* Vietnam 34 10.40N106.00E
Nam Phong Thailand 34 16.45N102.52E
Namp'o N. Korea 31 38.40N125.30E
Nampula Mozambique 57 15.09S 39.14E
Nampula *d.* Mozambique 57 15.00S 39.00E
Namsen *r.* Norway 22 64.27N 12.19E
Namsos Norway 22 64.28N 11.30E
Namtu Burma 34 23.04N 97.26E
Namu Canada 74 51.52N127.41W
Namuchabawashan *mtn.* China 39 29.30N 95.10E
Namungua Mozambique 55 13.11S 40.30E
Namur Belgium 14 50.28N 4.52E
Namur *d.* Belgium 14 50.20N 4.45E
Namur Canada 77 45.54N 74.56W
Namutoni Namibia 56 18.48S 16.58E
Namwala Zambia 54 15.44S 26.25E
Nana Candundo Angola 54 11.28S 23.01E
Nanaimo Canada 74 49.10N124.00W
Nanango Australia 65 26.42S151.58E
Nanchang China 33 28.37N115.57E
Nancheng China 33 27.35N116.33E
Nanchong China 33 30.53N106.05E
Nanchuan China 33 29.12N107.30E
Nancy France 17 48.42N 6.12E
Nanda Devi *mtn.* India 41 30.23N 79.59E
Nandan China 33 24.59N107.32E
Nānded India 40 19.09N 77.20E
Nandewar Range *mts.* Australia 67 30.20S150.45E
Nāndgaon India 40 20.19N 74.39E
Nandi Fiji 68 17.48S177.25E
Nandu Jiang *r.* China 33 20.04N110.20E
Nandurbār India 40 21.22N 74.15E
Nandyāl India 39 15.29N 78.29E
Nanfeng China 33 27.10N116.24E
Nanga Eboko Cameroon 53 4.41N 12.21E
Nānga Parbat *mtn.* Jammu & Kashmir 38 35.10N 74.35E
Nangapinoh Indonesia 36 0.20S111.44E
Nangola Mali 52 12.41N 6.35W
Nangqên China 30 32.15N 96.13E
Nangrūl Pīr India 40 20.19N 77.21E
Nang Xian China 41 29.03N 93.12E
Nanhui China 33 31.03N121.46E
Nanjiang China 32 32.21N106.50E
Nanjing China 33 32.02N118.52E
Nanking *see* Nanjing China 33
Nanling China 33 30.56N118.19E
Nan Ling *mts.* China 33 25.10N110.00E
Nannine Australia 62 26.53S118.20E
Nanning China 33 22.48N108.18E
Nannup Australia 63 33.57S115.42E
Nanortalik Greenland 73 60.09N 45.15W
Nānpāra India 41 27.52N 81.30E
Nanpi China 32 38.02N116.42E
Nanping Fujian China 33 26.38N118.10E
Nanpu Xi *r.* China 33 26.38N118.10E
Nanri *i.* China 33 25.13N119.30E
Nansei shotō *is.* Japan 31 26.30N125.00E
Nansei-Shotō Trench Pacific Oc. 68 25.00N129.00E
Nanshan *is.* S. China Sea 36 10.30N116.00E
Nantes France 15 47.14N 1.35W
Nanteuil-le-Haudouin France 15 49.08N 2.48E
Nanticoke U.S.A. 84 41.12N 76.00W
Nanton Canada 74 50.21N113.46W
Nantong China 32 32.02N120.55E
Nantou Taiwan 33 23.54N120.41E
Nantua France 20 46.09N 5.37E
Nantucket I. U.S.A. 84 41.16N 70.03W
Nantucket Sd. U.S.A. 84 41.30N 70.15W
Nantwich U.K. 10 53.05N 2.31W
Nanumea *i.* Tuvalu 68 5.40S176.10E
Nanwan Shuiku *resr.* China 33 32.05N113.55E
Nanxi China 33 28.52N104.59E
Nan Xian China 33 29.22N112.25E
Nanxiong China 33 25.10N114.16E
Nanyang China 32 33.07N112.30E
Nanzhang China 33 31.47N111.42E
Naococane, Lac *l.* Canada 77 52.50N 70.40W
Naogaon Bangla. 41 24.47N 88.56E
Naokot Pakistan 40 24.51N 69.27E
Napa U.S.A. 80 38.18N122.17W
Napadogan Canada 77 46.24N 67.01W
Napè Laos 34 18.18N105.07E
Napier New Zealand 60 39.29S176.58E
Napierville Canada 77 45.11N 73.25W
Naples *see* Napoli Italy 18
Naples Fla. U.S.A. 85 26.09N 81.48W
Napo China 33 23.23N105.48E
Napo *r.* Peru 90 3.30S 73.10W
Napoleon U.S.A. 84 41.24N 84.09W
Napoli Italy 18 40.50N 14.14E
Napoli, Golfo di *g.* Italy 18 40.42N 14.15E
Naqb Ishtar Jordan 44 30.00N 35.30E
Nara Japan 35 34.41N135.50E
Nara *d.* Japan 35 34.27N135.55E
Nara Mali 50 15.13N 7.20W
Nāra Pakistan 40 24.07N 69.07E
Naracoorte Australia 66 36.58S140.46E
Naradhan Australia 67 33.39S146.20E
Naraini India 41 25.11N 80.29E
Naran Mongolia 32 45.20N113.41E
Narathiwat Thailand 34 6.25N101.48E
Nara Visa U.S.A. 83 35.37N103.06W
Nārāyanganj Bangla. 41 23.37N 90.30E
Narbada *r.* *see* Narmada *r.* India 40
Narbonne France 17 43.11N 3.00E
Nardò Italy 19 40.11N 18.02E
Narembeen Australia 63 32.04S118.23E
Nares Str. Canada 73 78.30N 75.00W
Naretha Australia 63 31.01S124.50E
Nāri *r.* Pakistan 40 29.10N 67.50E
Naria U.S.A. 41 23.18N 90.25E
Narita Japan 35 35.47N140.19E
Narmada *r.* India 40 21.40N 73.00E
Nārnaul India 40 28.03N 76.06E
Nāro, Koh-i- *mtn.* Pakistan 40 29.15N 63.30E
Narodichi U.S.S.R. 21 51.11N 29.01E
Narodnaya *mtn.* U.S.S.R. 24 65.00N 61.00E
Narok Kenya 55 1.04S 35.54E
Narooma Australia 67 36.15S150.06E
Narrabri Australia 67 30.20S149.49E
Narrabri West Australia 67 30.22S149.47E
Narran *r.* Australia 67 29.45S147.20E
Narrandera Australia 67 34.36S146.34E
Narran L. Australia 67 29.40S147.25E
Narrogin Australia 63 32.58S117.10E
Narromine Australia 67 32.17S148.20E
Narsimhapur India 41 22.57N 79.12E
Narsingdi Bangla. 41 23.55N 90.43E
Narsinghgarh India 40 23.42N 77.06E
Narubis Namibia 56 26.56S 18.36E
Narva U.S.S.R. 24 59.22N 28.17E
Narvik Norway 22 68.26N 17.25E
Narwāna India 40 29.37N 76.07E
Naryan Mar U.S.S.R. 24 67.37N 53.02E
Naryilco Australia 66 28.41S141.50E
Naryn U.S.S.R. 28 41.24N 76.00E
Nasa *mtn.* Norway 22 66.29N 15.23E
Nasarawa Nigeria 53 8.35N 7.44E
Naseby New Zealand 60 45.01S170.09E
Nashua Iowa U.S.A. 82 42.57N 92.32W
Nashua Mont. U.S.A. 80 48.08N106.22W
Nashua N.H. U.S.A. 84 42.46N 71.27W
Nashville U.S.A. 85 36.10N 86.50W
Našice Yugo. 21 45.29N 18.06E
Näsijärvi *l.* Finland 23 61.37N 23.42E
Nāsik India 40 19.59N 73.48E
Nāṣir Sudan 49 8.36N 33.04E
Nāṣir, Buḥayrat *l.* Egypt 48 22.40N 32.00E
Nasīrābād India 40 26.18N 74.44E
Nasīrābād Pakistan 40 28.23N 68.24E
Naskaupi *r.* Canada 77 53.45N 60.50W
Naṣr Egypt 44 30.36N 30.23E
Nass *r.* Canada 74 55.00N129.50W
Nassau Bahamas 87 25.05N 77.21W
Nassau I. Cook Is. 68 11.33S165.25W
Nasser, L. *see* Nāṣir, Buḥayrat *l.* Egypt 48
Nassian Ivory Coast 52 8.33N 3.18W
Nässjö Sweden 23 57.39N 14.41E
Nastapoca *r.* Canada 76 56.55N 76.33W
Nastapoka Is. Canada 76 57.00N 77.00W
Nata Botswana 56 20.12S 26.12E
Natal Brazil 91 5.46S 35.15W
Natal Indonesia 36 0.35N 99.07E
Natal *d.* R.S.A. 56 28.30S 30.30E
Natanes Plateau *f.* U.S.A. 81 33.35N110.15W
Naṭanz Iran 43 33.30N 51.57E
Natashquan Canada 77 50.11N 61.49W
Natashquan *r.* Canada 77 50.06N 61.49W
Natchez U.S.A. 83 31.34N 91.23W
Natchitoches U.S.A. 83 31.46N 93.05W
Nāthdwāra India 40 24.56N 73.49E
National City U.S.A. 81 32.40N117.06W
Natitingou Benin 53 10.17N 1.19E
Natoma U.S.A. 82 39.11N 99.01W
Natron, L. Tanzania 55 2.18S 36.05E
Naṭrūn, Wādī an *f.* Egypt 44 30.25N 30.18E
Naturaliste, C. Australia 63 33.32S115.01E
Naturaliste Channel Australia 62 25.25S113.00E
Naubinway U.S.A. 84 46.05N 85.27W
Naumburg E. Germany 20 51.09N 11.48E
Nā'ūr Jordan 44 31.53N 35.50E
Nauroz Kalāt Pakistan 40 28.47N 65.38E
Nauru Pacific Oc. 68 0.32S166.55E
Naushahro Fīroz Pakistan 40 26.50N 68.07E
Naustdal Norway 23 61.31N 5.43E
Nauta Peru 90 4.30S 73.40W
Nautanwa India 41 27.26N 83.25E
Nautla Mexico 86 20.13N 96.47W
Nava Mexico 83 28.25N100.46W
Nava *r.* Zaïre 55 1.45N 27.06E
Navalmoral de la Mata Spain 16 39.54N 5.33W
Navan Rep. of Ire. 13 53.39N 6.42W
Navāpur India 40 21.15N 73.55E
Navarre Australia 66 36.54S143.09E
Navarro Argentina 93 35.00S 59.10W
Navasota U.S.A. 83 30.23N 96.05W
Naver *r.* U.K. 12 58.32N 4.14W
Navlya U.S.S.R. 24 52.51N 34.30E
Navoi U.S.S.R. 28 40.04N 65.20E
Navojoa Mexico 81 27.06N109.26W
Návpaktos Greece 19 38.24N 21.49E
Návplion Greece 19 37.33N 22.47E
Navrongo Ghana 52 10.51N 1.03W
Navsāri India 40 20.57N 72.59E
Nawá Syria 44 32.53N 36.03E
Nawābganj Bangla. 41 24.36N 88.17E
Nawābganj India 41 26.56N 81.13E
Nawābshāh Pakistan 40 26.15N 68.25E
Nawāda India 41 24.53N 85.32E
Nāwah Afghan. 40 32.19N 67.53E
Nawākot Nepal 41 27.55N 85.10E
Nawa Kot Pakistan 40 28.20N 71.22E
Nawalgarh India 40 27.51N 75.16E
Nawāpāra India 41 20.58N 81.51E
Naxi China 33 28.44N105.27E
Náxos Greece 19 37.06N 25.23E
Náxos *i.* Greece 19 37.03N 25.30E
Nayāgarh India 41 20.08N 85.06E
Nayak Afghan. 40 34.44N 66.57E
Nayarit *d.* Mexico 86 21.30N104.00W
Nāy Band Iran 43 27.23N 52.38E
Nāy Band Iran 43 32.20N 57.34E
Nāy Band, Kūh-e *mtn.* Iran 43 32.25N 57.30E
Nazaré Brazil 91 13.00S 39.00W
Nazarovka U.S.S.R. 24 54.19N 41.20E
Nazas *r.* Mexico 86 25.34N103.25W
Nazca Peru 90 14.53S 74.54W
Nazerat Israel 44 32.41N 35.16E
Nazeret Ethiopia 49 8.32N 39.22E
Nazilli Turkey 42 37.55N 28.20E
Nāzir Hāt Bangla. 41 22.38N 91.47E
Nazuo China 33 24.06N105.19E
Nchanga Zambia 55 12.30S 27.55E
Ncheu Malaŵi 55 14.50S 34.45E
Ndalatando Angola 54 9.12S 14.54E
Ndali Benin 53 9.53N 2.45E
Ndasegera *mtn.* Tanzania 55 1.58S 35.41E
Ndélé C.A.R. 49 8.24N 20.39E
Ndélélé Cameroon 53 4.03N 14.55E
N'Dendé Gabon 54 2.20S 11.23E
Ndikiniméki Cameroon 53 4.46N 10.49E
N'Djamena Chad 53 12.10N 14.59E
Ndjolé Gabon 54 0.07S 10.45E
Ndola Zambia 56 12.58S 28.39E
Ndoro Gabon 54 0.24S 12.34E
Ndrhamcha, Sebkha de *f.* Mauritania 50 18.45N 15.48W
Ndungu Tanzania 55 4.25S 38.04E
Nea *r.* Norway 22 63.15N 11.00E
Neagh, Lough U.K. 13 54.36N 6.25W
Néa Páfos Cyprus 44 34.45N 32.25E
Neápolis Greece 19 36.30N 23.04E
Neath U.K. 11 51.39N 3.49W
Nebit-Dag U.S.S.R. 43 39.31N 54.24E
Nebraska *d.* U.S.A. 82 41.50N100.06W
Nebraska City U.S.A. 82 40.41N 95.52W
Nebrodi, Monti *mts.* Italy 18 37.53N 14.32E
Nechako *r.* Canada 74 53.30N122.44W
Neches *r.* U.S.A. 83 29.55N 93.50W
Neckar *r.* W. Germany 20 49.32N 8.26E
Necochea Argentina 93 38.31S 58.46W
Necuto Angola 54 4.55S 12.38E
Nêdong China 41 29.14N 91.48E
Nedroma Algeria 50 35.00N 1.44W
Needles U.S.A. 81 34.51N114.37W
Neepawa Canada 75 50.13N 99.29W
Neerpelt Belgium 14 51.13N 5.28E
Nefta Tunisia 51 33.52N 7.33E
Neftegorsk U.S.S.R. 25 44.21N 39.44E
Nefyn U.K. 10 52.55N 4.31W
Negara Indonesia 37 8.21S114.35E
Negaunee U.S.A. 84 46.31N 87.37W
Negele Ethiopia 49 5.20N 39.36E
Negev *des. see* HaNegev *des.* Israel 44
Negoiu *mtn.* Romania 21 45.36N 24.32E
Negomano Mozambique 55 11.26S 38.30E
Negombo Sri Lanka 39 7.13N 79.50E
Negotin Yugo. 21 44.14N 22.33E
Negrais, C. Burma 34 16.00N 94.12E
Negritos Peru 90 4.42S 81.18W
Negro *r.* Argentina 93 40.50S 63.00W
Negro *r.* Brazil 90 3.00S 59.55W
Negro *r.* Uruguay 93 33.27S 58.20W
Negro B. Somali Rep. 45 7.52N 49.50E
Negros *i.* Phil. 37 10.00N123.00E
Negru-Vodă Romania 21 43.50N 28.12E
Neijiang China 33 29.29N105.03E
Nei Monggol *d.* China 32 41.30N112.00E
Neisse *r.* Poland/E. Germany 20 52.05N 14.42E
Neiva Colombia 90 2.58N 75.15W
Nejanilini L. Canada 75 59.33N 97.48W
Nejo Ethiopia 49 9.30N 35.30E
Nekemte Ethiopia 49 9.02N 36.31E
Neksö Denmark 23 55.04N 15.09E
Nelidovo U.S.S.R. 24 56.13N 32.46E
Neligh U.S.A. 82 42.08N 98.02W
Nelkan U.S.S.R. 29 57.40N136.04E
Nelligen Australia 67 35.39S150.06E
Nellore India 39 14.29N 80.00E
Nelson Australia 66 38.04S141.05E
Nelson Canada 74 49.30N117.20W
Nelson *r.* Canada 75 57.04N 92.30W
Nelson New Zealand 60 41.18S173.17E
Nelson *d.* New Zealand 60 41.40S172.20E
Nelson U.K. 10 53.50N 2.14W
Nelson U.S.A. 81 35.30N113.16W
Nelson, C. Australia 66 38.27S141.35E
Nelson, Estrecho *str.* Chile 93 51.33S 74.40W
Nelson Forks Canada 74 59.30N124.00W
Nelspoort R.S.A. 56 32.07S 23.00E
Nelspruit R.S.A. 56 25.27S 30.58E
Néma Mauritania 50 16.40N 7.15W
Neman *r.* U.S.S.R. 23 55.18N 21.23E
Nembe Nigeria 53 4.32N 6.25E
Nemours France 15 48.16N 2.41E
Nenagh Rep. of Ire. 13 52.52N 8.13W
Nenana U.S.A. 72 64.35N149.20W
Nene *r.* U.K. 10 52.49N 0.12E
Nenjiang China 31 49.10N125.15E
Neodesha U.S.A. 83 37.25N 95.41W
Neosho U.S.A. 83 36.52N 94.22W
Neosho *r.* U.S.A. 82 35.48N 95.18W
Nepal Asia 41 28.00N 84.00E
Nepālganj Nepal 41 28.03N 81.38E
Nepa Nagar India 40 21.28N 76.23E
Nephi U.S.A. 80 39.43N111.50W
Nephin Beg *mtn.* Rep. of Ire. 13 54.02N 9.38W
Nephin Beg Range *mts.* Rep. of Ire. 13 54.00N 9.37W
Nera *r.* Italy 18 42.33N 12.43E
Nérac France 17 44.08N 0.20E
Nerekhta U.S.S.R. 24 57.30N 40.40E

Néret, Lac to **North Frisian Is.**

Néret, Lac *l.* Canada **77** 54.45N 70.50W
Neretva *r.* Yugo. **19** 43.02N 17.28E
Neriquinha Angola **56** 15.50S 21.40E
Nero Deep Pacific Oc. **37** 12.40N145.50E
Néronde France **17** 45.50N 4.14E
Nerriga Australia **67** 35.10S150.03E
Nerva Spain **16** 37.42N 6.30W
Nes Neth. **14** 53.27N 5.46E
Nesbyen Norway **23** 60.34N 9.09E
Nesle France **15** 49.46N 2.51E
Nesna Norway **22** 66.13N 13.04E
Nesöy *i.* Norway **22** 66.35N 12.40E
Ness, Loch U.K. **12** 57.16N 4.30W
Nestaocano *r.* Canada **77** 48.40N 73.25W
Nesterov U.S.S.R. **21** 50.04N 24.00E
Néstos *r.* Greece **19** 40.51N 24.48E
Nesttun Norway **23** 60.19N 5.20E
Nesvizh U.S.S.R. **21** 53.16N 26.40E
Netanya Israel **44** 32.20N 34.51E
Netcong U.S.A. **85** 40.54N 74.42W
Netherlands Europe **14** 52.00N 5.30E
Netherlands Antilles S. America **87** 12.30N 69.00W
Neto *r.* Italy **19** 39.12N 17.08E
Netrakona Bangla. **41** 24.53N 90.43E
Nettilling L. Canada **73** 66.30N 70.40W
Neubrandenburg E. Germany **20** 53.33N 13.16E
Neubrandenburg *d.* E. Germany **20** 53.30N 13.15E
Neuchâtel Switz. **20** 47.00N 6.56E
Neuchâtel, Lac de *l.* Switz. **20** 46.55N 6.55E
Neuenhaus W. Germany **14** 52.30N 6.58E
Neufchâteau Belgium **14** 49.51N 5.26E
Neufchâtel France **15** 49.44N 1.26E
Neuillé-Pont-Pierre France **15** 47.33N 0.33E
Neumarkt W. Germany **20** 49.16N 11.28E
Neumünster W. Germany **20** 54.06N 9.59E
Neuquén Argentina **93** 39.00S 68.05W
Neuquén *d.* Argentina **93** 38.30S 70.00W
Neuquén *r.* Argentina **93** 39.02S 68.07W
Neuruppin E. Germany **20** 52.55N 12.48E
Neuse *r.* U.S.A. **85** 35.06N 76.30W
Neusiedler See *l.* Austria **20** 47.52N 16.45E
Neuss W. Germany **14** 51.12N 6.42E
Neustadt Bayern W. Germany **20** 49.44N 12.11E
Neustrelitz E. Germany **20** 53.22N 13.05E
Neuvic France **17** 45.23N 2.16E
Neuwied W. Germany **14** 50.26N 7.28E
Nevada U.S.A. **83** 37.51N 94.22W
Nevada *d.* U.S.A. **80** 39.50N116.10W
Nevada, Sierra *mts.* Spain **16** 37.04N 3.20W
Nevada, Sierra *mts.* U.S.A. **78** 37.30N119.00W
Nevanka U.S.S.R. **29** 56.31N 98.57E
Nevel U.S.S.R. **24** 56.00N 29.59E
Nevers France **17** 47.00N 3.09E
Nevertire Australia **67** 31.52S147.47E
Nevinnomyssk U.S.S.R. **25** 44.38N 41.59E
Nevşehir Turkey **42** 38.38N 34.43E
Newala Tanzania **55** 10.56S 39.15E
New Albany Ind. U.S.A. **84** 38.17N 85.50W
New Albany Miss. U.S.A. **83** 34.29N 89.00W
New Amsterdam Guyana **91** 6.18N 57.30W
Newark Del. U.S.A. **85** 39.41N 75.45W
Newark N.J. U.S.A. **85** 40.44N 74.11W
Newark N.Y. U.S.A. **84** 43.03N 77.06W
Newark Ohio U.S.A. **84** 40.03N 82.25W
Newark-on-Trent U.K. **10** 53.06N 0.48E
New Athens U.S.A. **82** 38.19N 89.53W
New Bedford U.S.A. **84** 41.38N 70.56W
Newberg U.S.A. **80** 45.18N122.58W
New Bern U.S.A. **85** 35.05N 77.04W
Newberry Mich. U.S.A. **84** 46.22N 85.30W
Newberry S.C. U.S.A. **85** 34.17N 81.39W
Newbiggin-by-the-Sea U.K. **10** 55.11N 1.30W
New Braunfels U.S.A. **83** 29.42N 98.08W
New Britain *i.* P.N.G. **61** 6.00S150.00E
New Brunswick *d.* Canada **77** 46.50N 66.00W
New Brunswick U.S.A. **85** 40.29N 74.27W
Newburgh U.S.A. **85** 41.30N 74.00W
Newbury U.K. **11** 51.24N 1.19W
New Bussa Nigeria **53** 9.53N 4.29E
New Caledonia *is. see* Nouvelle Calédonie *is.* Pacific Oc. **68**
Newcastle Australia **67** 32.55S151.46E
Newcastle N.B. Canada **77** 47.00N 65.34W
Newcastle Ont. Canada **76** 43.55N 78.35W
Newcastle R.S.A. **56** 27.44S 29.55E
Newcastle U.K. **13** 54.13N 5.53W
New Castle Penn. U.S.A. **84** 41.00N 80.22W
Newcastle B. Australia **64** 10.50S142.37E
Newcastle Emlyn U.K. **11** 52.02N 4.29W
Newcastle-under-Lyme U.K. **10** 53.02N 2.15W
Newcastle upon Tyne U.K. **10** 54.58N 1.36W
Newcastle Waters *town* Australia **64** 17.24S133.24E
Newcastle West Rep. of Ire. **13** 52.26N 9.04W
New City U.S.A. **85** 41.09N 73.59W
Newdegate Australia **63** 33.06S119.01E
New Delhi India **40** 28.36N 77.12E
New Denver Canada **74** 50.00N117.25W
New England U.S.A. **82** 46.32N102.52W
New England Range *mts.* Australia **67** 30.30S151.50E
Newenham, C. U.S.A. **72** 58.37N162.12W
Newent U.K. **11** 51.56N 2.24W
Newfane U.S.A. **76** 43.17N 78.43W
New Forest *f.* U.K. **11** 50.50N 1.35W
Newfoundland Australia **67** 30.53S144.38E
Newfoundland *d.* Canada **77** 54.00N 60.10W
Newfoundland *i.* Canada **77** 48.30N 56.00W
New Freedom U.S.A. **85** 39.44N 76.42W
New Galloway U.K. **12** 55.05N 4.09W
Newgate Canada **74** 49.01N115.08W
New Glasgow Canada **77** 45.35N 62.39W
New Guinea *i.* Austa. **37** 5.00S140.00E
New Hampshire *d.* U.S.A. **84** 43.35N 71.40W
New Hanover *i.* Pacific Oc. **61** 2.00S150.00E
Newhaven U.K. **11** 50.47N 0.04E
New Haven U.S.A. **84** 41.18N 72.55W
New Hebrides Basin Pacific Oc. **68** 16.00S162.00E
New Holland U.S.A. **85** 40.06N 76.05W
New Iberia U.S.A. **83** 30.00N 91.49W
New Ireland *i.* P.N.G. **61** 2.30S151.30E
New Jersey *d.* U.S.A. **85** 40.15N 74.30W
New Liskeard Canada **76** 47.31N 79.41W
New London Conn. U.S.A. **84** 41.21N 72.06W
New London Minn. U.S.A. **82** 45.18N 94.56W
Newman U.S.A. **81** 31.55N106.20W
Newmarket Australia **66** 34.43S144.31E
Newmarket Rep. of Ire. **13** 52.13N 9.00W
Newmarket U.K. **11** 52.15N 0.23E
Newmarket on Fergus Rep. of Ire. **13** 52.46N 8.55W
New Martinsville U.S.A. **84** 39.39N 80.52W
New Meadows U.S.A. **80** 44.58N116.32W
New Mexico *d.* U.S.A. **80** 33.30N106.00W
New Milford Conn. U.S.A. **85** 41.35N 73.25W
Newnan U.S.A. **85** 33.23N 84.48W
New Norcia Australia **63** 30.58S116.15E
New Norfolk Australia **65** 42.46S147.02E
New Orleans U.S.A. **83** 29.58N 90.07W
New Philadelphia U.S.A. **84** 40.31N 81.28W
New Plymouth New Zealand **60** 39.03S174.04E
Newport Mayo Rep. of Ire. **13** 53.53N 9.34W
Newport Tipperary Rep. of Ire. **13** 52.42N 8.25W
Newport Dyfed U.K. **11** 52.01N 4.51W
Newport Essex U.K. **11** 51.58N 0.13E
Newport Gwent U.K. **11** 51.34N 2.59W
Newport Hants. U.K. **11** 50.43N 1.18W
Newport Ark. U.S.A. **83** 35.35N 91.16W
Newport Maine U.S.A. **84** 44.50N 69.17W
Newport N.H. U.S.A. **84** 43.21N 72.09W
Newport Oreg. U.S.A. **80** 44.38N124.03W
Newport R.I. U.S.A. **84** 41.13N 71.18W
Newport News U.S.A. **85** 36.59N 76.26W
New Providence I. Bahamas **87** 25.25N 78.35W
Newquay U.K. **11** 50.24N 5.06W
New Quay U.K. **11** 52.13N 4.22W
New Radnor U.K. **11** 52.15N 3.10W
New Rochelle U.S.A. **85** 40.55N 73.47W
New Rockford U.S.A. **82** 47.41N 99.15W
New Romney U.K. **11** 50.59N 0.58E
New Ross Rep. of Ire. **13** 52.24N 6.57W
Newry U.K. **13** 54.11N 6.21W
New Scone U.K. **12** 56.25N 3.25W
New Smyrna Beach *town* U.S.A. **85** 29.01N 80.56W
New South Wales *d.* Australia **67** 32.40S147.40E
Newton Ill. U.S.A. **82** 38.59N 88.10W
Newton Iowa U.S.A. **82** 41.42N 93.03W
Newton Kans. U.S.A. **83** 38.03N 97.21W
Newton Miss. U.S.A. **83** 32.19N 89.10W
Newton N.J. U.S.A. **85** 41.03N 74.45W
Newton Abbot U.K. **11** 50.32N 3.37W
Newton Aycliffe U.K. **10** 54.36N 1.34W
Newtonmore U.K. **12** 57.04N 4.08W
Newton Stewart U.K. **12** 54.57N 4.29W
Newtown U.K. **11** 52.31N 3.19W
Newtownabbey U.K. **13** 54.39N 5.57W
Newtownards U.K. **13** 54.35N 5.41W
Newtown Butler U.K. **13** 54.12N 7.22W
Newtownstewart U.K. **13** 54.43N 7.25W
New Waterford Canada **77** 46.15N 60.05W
New Westminster Canada **74** 49.10N122.52W
New York U.S.A. **85** 40.40N 73.50W
New York *d.* U.S.A. **84** 43.00N 75.00W
New York State Barge Canal U.S.A. **76** 43.05N 78.43W
New Zealand Austa. **60** 41.00S175.00E
New Zealand Plateau Pacific Oc. **68** 50.00S170.00E
Neya U.S.S.R. **24** 58.18N 43.40E
Neyagawa Japan **35** 34.46N135.38E
Neyriz Iran **43** 29.12N 54.17E
Neyshābūr Iran **43** 36.13N 58.49E
Nezhin U.S.S.R. **21** 51.03N 31.54E
Ngala Nigeria **53** 12.21N 14.10E
Ngambwe Rapids *f.* Zambia **54** 17.08S 24.10E
Ngami, L. Botswana **56** 20.32S 22.38E
Ngamiland *f.* Botswana **56** 20.00S 22.30E
Ngamring China **41** 29.14N 87.10E
Ngangla Ringco *l.* China **41** 31.40N 83.00E
Nganglong Kangri *mtn.* China **41** 32.40N 81.00E
Nganglong Kangri *mts.* China **41** 32.15N 82.00E
Ngangzê Co *l.* China **41** 31.00N 87.00E
Nganjuk Indonesia **37** 7.36S111.56E
N'Gao Congo **54** 2.28S 15.40E
Ngaoundéré Cameroon **53** 7.20N 13.35E
Ngara-Binsam Congo **54** 1.36N 13.30E
Ngardiam C.A.R. **49** 9.00N 20.58E
Ngaruawahia New Zealand **60** 37.40S175.09E
Ngaruroro *r.* New Zealand **60** 39.34S176.54E
Ngatangiia Rarotonga Cook Is. **68** 21.14S159.44W
Ngau *i.* Fiji **68** 18.02S179.18E
Ngauruhoe *mtn.* New Zealand **60** 39.10S175.35E
Ngawi Indonesia **37** 7.23S111.22E
Ngaya *mtn.* C.A.R. **49** 9.18N 23.28E
Ng'iro, Mt. Kenya **55** 2.06N 36.44E
Ngiva Angola **56** 17.03S 15.47E
Ngoc Linh *mtn.* Vietnam **34** 15.04N107.59E
Ngoma Zambia **54** 16.04S 26.06E
Ngomba Tanzania **55** 8.16S 32.51E
Ngomeni Kenya **55** 3.00S 40.11E
Ngong Kenya **55** 1.22S 36.40E
Ngonye Falls *f.* Zambia **54** 16.35S 23.39E
Ngorongoro Crater *f.* Tanzania **55** 3.13S 35.32E
Ngouo, Mont *mtn.* C.A.R. **49** 7.55N 24.38E
Ngozi Burundi **55** 2.52S 29.50E
Nguigmi Niger **53** 14.00N 13.11E
Ngunza Angola **54** 11.11S 13.52E
Nguru Nigeria **53** 12.53N 10.30E
Nguruka Tanzania **55** 5.08S 30.58E
Ngwerere Zambia **55** 15.18S 28.20E
Nhaccongo Mozambique **57** 24.18S 35.14E
Nhachengue Mozambique **57** 22.52S 35.10E
Nhandugue *r.* Mozambique **57** 18.47S 34.30E
Nha Trang Vietnam **34** 12.15N109.10E
Nhill Australia **66** 36.20S141.40E
Nhungo Angola **56** 13.17S 20.06E
Niafounké Mali **50** 15.56N 4.00W
Niagara Canada **76** 43.05N 79.20W
Niagara Falls *town* Canada **76** 43.06N 79.04W
Niagara Falls *town* U.S.A. **84** 43.06N 79.02W
Niah Malaysia **36** 3.52N113.44E
Niamey Niger **53** 13.32N 2.05E
Niamey *d.* Niger **53** 14.00N 1.40E
Nianforando Guinea **52** 9.37N 10.36W
Niangara Zaïre **55** 3.47N 27.54E
Nia-Nia Zaïre **55** 1.30N 27.41E
Niapa, Gunung *mtn.* Indonesia **36** 1.45N117.30E
Nias *i.* Indonesia **36** 1.05N 97.30E
Niassa *d.* Mozambique **55** 13.00S 36.30E
Nicaragua C. America **87** 13.00N 85.00W
Nicaragua, Lago de *l.* Nicaragua **87** 11.30N 85.30W
Nicastro Italy **18** 38.58N 16.16E
Nice France **17** 43.42N 7.16E
Nichelino Italy **15** 44.59N 7.38E
Nicholson Australia **62** 18.02S128.54E
Nicholson *r.* Australia **64** 17.31S139.36E
Nicholson L. Canada **75** 62.40N102.35W
Nicobar Is. India **34** 8.00N 93.30E
Nicolet Canada **77** 46.13N 72.37W
Nicolet *r.* Canada **77** 46.14N 72.39W
Nicolls Town Bahamas **87** 25.08N 78.00W
Nicosia *see* Levkosía Cyprus **44**
Nicoya, Golfo de *g.* Costa Rica **87** 9.30N 85.00W
Nicoya, Península de *pen.* Costa Rica **87** 10.30N 85.30W
Nid *r.* Norway **23** 58.24N 8.48E
Nida *r.* Poland **21** 50.18N 20.52E
Nido, Sierra de *mts.* Mexico **81** 29.30N107.00W
Nidzica Poland **21** 53.22N 20.26E
Niederösterreich *d.* Austria **20** 48.20N 15.50E
Niedersachsen *d.* W. Germany **14** 52.55N 7.40E
Niekerkshoop R.S.A. **56** 29.19S 22.48E
Niéllé Ivory Coast **52** 10.05N 5.28W
Nienburg W. Germany **20** 52.38N 9.13E
Niéré Chad **48** 14.30N 21.09E
Niers *r.* Neth. **14** 51.43N 5.56E
Nieuw Nickerie Surinam **91** 5.57N 56.59W
Nieuwpoort Belgium **14** 51.08N 2.45E
Nigde Turkey **42** 37.58N 34.42E
Niger *d.* Nigeria **53** 9.50N 6.00E
Niger *r.* Nigeria **53** 4.15N 6.05E
Niger Delta Nigeria **53** 4.00N 6.10E
Nigeria Africa **53** 9.00N 9.00E
Nightcaps New Zealand **60** 45.58S168.02E
Nightingale I. Tristan da Cunha **95** 37.28S 12.32W
Nihing *r.* Pakistan **40** 26.00N 62.44E
Nihoa *i.* Hawaiian Is. **68** 23.03N161.55W
Niigata Japan **31** 37.58N139.02E
Niihau *i.* Hawaiian Is. **69** 21.55N160.10W
Niiza Japan **35** 35.48N139.34E
Nijmegen Neth. **14** 51.50N 5.52E
Nikel U.S.S.R. **22** 69.20N 30.00E
Nikiniki Indonesia **62** 9.49S124.29E
Nikki Benin **53** 9.55N 3.18E
Nikolayev U.S.S.R. **25** 46.57N 32.00E
Nikolayevskiy U.S.S.R. **25** 50.05N 45.32E
Nikolayevsk-na-Amure U.S.S.R. **29** 53.20N140.44E
Nikolsk U.S.S.R. **24** 59.33N 45.30E
Nikopol U.S.S.R. **25** 47.34N 34.25E
Niksar Turkey **42** 40.35N 36.59E
Nikshahr Iran **43** 26.14N 60.15E
Nikšić Yugo. **19** 42.48N 18.56E
Nikumaroro *i.* Kiribati **68** 4.40S174.32W
Nil, An *r.* Egypt **44** 31.30N 30.25E
Nila *i.* Indonesia **37** 6.45S129.30E
Nile *r. see* Nīl, An *r.* Egypt **44**
Nile Delta Egypt **44** 31.00N 31.00E
Niles Mich. U.S.A. **84** 41.51N 86.15W
Nilgiri India **41** 21.28N 86.46E
Nilgiri Hills India **38** 11.30N 77.30E
Nimach India **40** 24.28N 74.52E
Nimai *r.* Burma **34** 25.44N 97.30E
Nimba, Mt. Guinea **52** 7.35N 8.28W
Nimbin Australia **67** 28.35S153.12E
Nîmes France **17** 43.50N 4.21E
Nim Ka Thāna India **40** 27.44N 75.48E
Nīmrūz *d.* Afghan. **40** 30.40N 62.15E
Nimule Sudan **49** 3.36N 32.03E
Nindigully Australia **67** 28.20S148.47E
Ninety Mile Beach *f.* Australia **67** 38.07S147.30E
Ninety Mile Beach *f.* New Zealand **60** 34.45S173.00E
Nineveh *ruins* Iraq **42** 36.24N 43.08E
Ningbo China **33** 29.56N121.32E
Ningde China **33** 26.41N119.32E
Ningdu China **33** 26.29N115.46E
Ninggang China **33** 26.45N113.58E
Ningguo China **33** 30.38N118.58E
Ningming China **33** 22.04N107.02E
Ningnan China **30** 27.03N102.46E
Ningqiang China **32** 32.49N106.13E
Ningwu China **32** 38.59N112.12E
Ningxia Huizu *d.* China **32** 39.00N105.00E
Ning Xian China **32** 35.27N107.50E
Ningxiang China **33** 28.15N112.33E
Ninh Binh Vietnam **34** 20.14N106.00E
Niningarra Australia **62** 20.35S119.58E
Ninove Belgium **14** 50.50N 4.02E
Niobrara U.S.A. **82** 42.45N 98.02W
Niobrara *r.* U.S.A. **82** 42.45N 98.00W
Nioki Zaïre **54** 2.43S 17.41E
Nioro Mali **50** 15.12N 9.35W
Nioro du Rip Senegal **52** 13.40N 15.50W
Niort France **17** 46.19N 0.27W
Niout *well* Mauritania **50** 16.03N 6.52W
Nipāni India **38** 16.24N 74.23E
Nipigon Canada **76** 49.00N 88.17W
Nipigon, L. Canada **76** 49.50N 88.30W
Nipigon B. Canada **76** 48.55N 88.00W
Nipissing, L. Canada **76** 46.17N 80.00W
Niquelândia Brazil **94** 14.27S 48.27W
Nirasaki Japan **35** 35.42N138.27E
Nirmal India **41** 19.06N 78.21E
Nirmali India **41** 26.19N 86.35E
Nirwāno Pakistan **40** 26.22N 62.43E
Niš Yugo. **19** 43.20N 21.54E
Nisa Portugal **16** 39.31N 7.39W
Nishi China **33** 29.54N110.38E
Nishinomiya Japan **35** 34.43N135.20E
Niskibi *r.* Canada **75** 56.28N 88.10W
Nisko Poland **21** 50.35N 22.07E
Nissedal Norway **23** 59.10N 8.30E
Nisser *l.* Norway **23** 59.10N 8.30E
Nitā' Saudi Arabia **43** 27.13N 48.25E
Nitchequon Canada **77** 53.12N 70.47W
Niterói Brazil **94** 22.54S 43.06W
Nith *r.* U.K. **12** 55.00N 3.35W
Nitra Czech. **21** 48.20N 18.05E
Niue *i.* Cook Is. **68** 19.02S169.52W
Niut, Gunung *mtn.* Indonesia **36** 1.00N110.00E
Nivala Finland **22** 63.55N 24.58E
Nivelles Belgium **14** 50.36N 4.20E
Nixon U.S.A. **83** 29.16N 97.46W
Nizāmābād India **39** 18.40N 78.05E
Nizgān *r.* Afghan. **40** 33.05N 63.20E
Nizhneangarsk U.S.S.R. **29** 55.48N109.35E
Nizhne Kolymsk U.S.S.R. **29** 68.34N160.58E
Nizhneudinsk U.S.S.R. **29** 54.55N 99.00E
Nizhnevartovsk U.S.S.R. **28** 60.57N 76.40E
Nizhniy Tagil U.S.S.R. **24** 58.00N 60.00E
Nizhnyaya Tunguska *r.* U.S.S.R. **29** 65.50N 88.00E
Nizhnyaya Tura U.S.S.R. **24** 58.40N 59.48E
Nizke Tatry *mts.* Czech. **21** 48.54N 19.40E
Nizza Monferrato Italy **15** 44.46N 8.21E
Njombe Tanzania **55** 9.20S 34.47E
Njombe *r.* Tanzania **55** 7.02S 35.55E
Njoro Tanzania **55** 5.16S 36.30E
Nkalagu Nigeria **53** 6.28N 7.46E
Nkawkaw Ghana **52** 6.35N 0.47W
Nkayi Zimbabwe **56** 19.00S 28.54E
Nkhata Bay *town* Malaŵi **55** 11.37S 34.20E
Nkhotakota Malaŵi **55** 12.55S 34.19E
Nkongsamba Cameroon **53** 4.59N 9.53E
Nkungwe Mt. Tanzania **55** 6.15S 29.54E
Noākhāli Bangla. **41** 22.51N 91.06E
Noatak U.S.A. **72** 67.34N162.59W
Noce *r.* Italy **15** 46.09N 11.04E
Nogal *r.* Somali Rep. **45** 7.58N 49.52E
Nogales Mexico **81** 31.20N110.56W
Nogara Italy **15** 45.11N 11.04E
Nogayskiye Step *f.* U.S.S.R. **25** 44.25N 45.30E
Nogent-le-Rotrou France **15** 48.19N 0.50E
Nogent-sur-Seine France **15** 48.29N 3.30E
Nogoyá Argentina **93** 32.22S 59.49W
Noguera Ribagorzana *r.* Spain **16** 41.27N 0.25E
Nohar India **40** 29.11N 74.46E
Nohta India **41** 23.40N 79.34E
Noire *r.* Que. Canada **77** 45.33N 72.58W
Noirmoutier, Île de *i.* France **17** 47.00N 2.15W
Nojima-zaki *c.* Japan **35** 34.56N139.53E
Nokha India **40** 27.35N 73.29E
Nokia Finland **23** 61.28N 23.30E
Nok Kundi Pakistan **40** 28.46N 62.46E
Nokomis Canada **75** 51.30N105.00W
Nokou Chad **53** 14.35N 14.47E
Nola C.A.R. **53** 3.28N 16.08E
Nolinsk U.S.S.R. **24** 57.38N 49.52E
Noman L. Canada **75** 62.15N108.55W
Noma Omuramba *r.* Botswana **56** 19.14S 22.15E
Nombre de Dios Mexico **81** 28.41N106.05W
Nome U.S.A. **72** 64.30N165.30W
Nomgon Mongolia **32** 42.50N105.13E
Nomuka Group *is.* Tonga **69** 20.15S174.46W
Nonancourt France **15** 48.47N 1.11E
Nonburg U.S.S.R. **24** 65.32N 50.37E
Nong Khai Thailand **34** 17.50N102.46E
Nongoma R.S.A. **57** 27.58S 31.35E
Nongpoh India **41** 25.54N 91.53E
Nongstoin India **41** 25.31N 91.16E
Nonning Australia **66** 32.30S136.30E
Nonthaburi Thailand **34** 13.48N100.11E
Noojee Australia **67** 37.57S146.00E
Noonan U.S.A. **82** 48.54N103.01W
Noongaar Australia **63** 31.21S118.55E
Noonkanbah Australia **62** 18.30S124.50E
Noord Beveland *f.* Neth. **14** 51.35N 3.45E
Noord Brabant *d.* Neth. **14** 51.37N 5.00E
Noord Holland *d.* Neth. **14** 52.37N 4.50E
Noordoost-Polder *f.* Neth. **14** 52.45N 5.45E
Noordwijk Neth. **14** 52.16N 4.29E
Noorvik U.S.A. **72** 66.50N161.14W
Nootka I. Canada **74** 49.32N126.42W
Noqui Angola **54** 5.51S 13.25E
Nora Sweden **23** 59.31N 15.02E
Noranda Canada **76** 48.20N 79.00W
Nord *d.* France **14** 50.17N 3.14E
Nordaustlandet *i.* Arctic Oc. **96** 79.55N 23.00E
Norddeich W. Germany **14** 53.35N 7.10E
Nordegg Canada **74** 52.29N116.05W
Norden W. Germany **14** 53.34N 7.13E
Nordenham W. Germany **20** 53.30N 8.29E
Norderney W. Germany **14** 53.43N 7.09E
Norderney *i.* W. Germany **14** 53.45N 7.15E
Nordfjord *est.* Norway **23** 61.54N 5.12E
Nordfjordeid Norway **23** 61.54N 6.00E
Nordfold Norway **22** 67.48N 15.20E
Nordfriesische Inseln *is.* W. Germany **20** 54.30N 8.00E
Nordhausen E. Germany **20** 51.31N 10.48E
Nordhorn W. Germany **14** 52.27N 7.05E
Nordkapp *c.* Norway **22** 71.11N 25.48E
Nordkinnhalvöya *pen.* Norway **22** 70.55N 27.45E
Nordland *d.* Norway **22** 66.50N 14.50E
Nord-Ostsee-Kanal W. Germany **20** 53.54N 9.12E
Nordreisa Norway **22** 69.46N 21.00E
Nordrhein-Westfalen *d.* W. Germany **14** 51.18N 6.32E
Nord Tröndelag *d.* Norway **22** 64.20N 12.00E
Nordvik U.S.S.R. **29** 73.40N110.50E
Nore Norway **23** 60.10N 9.01E
Nore *r.* Rep. of Ire. **13** 52.25N 6.58W
Norfolk *d.* U.K. **11** 52.39N 1.00E
Norfolk Nebr. U.S.A. **82** 42.02N 97.25W
Norfolk Va. U.S.A. **85** 36.54N 76.18W
Norfolk Broads *f.* U.K. **10** 52.43N 1.35E
Norfolk I. Pacific Oc. **68** 29.02S167.57E
Norfolk Island Ridge Pacific Oc. **68** 29.00S167.00E
Norheimsund Norway **23** 60.22N 6.08E
Norilsk U.S.S.R. **29** 69.21N 88.02E
Normal U.S.A. **82** 40.31N 89.00W
Norman *r.* Australia **64** 17.28S140.49E
Norman U.S.A. **83** 35.13N 97.26W
Normanby *r.* Australia **64** 14.25S144.08E
Normanby New Zealand **60** 39.32S174.16E
Normanby I. P.N.G. **64** 10.05S151.05E
Normandie, Collines de *hills* France **15** 48.50N 0.40W
Normanton Australia **64** 17.40S141.05E
Norman Wells Canada **72** 65.19N126.46W
Nornalup Australia **63** 34.58S116.49E
Norquinco Argentina **93** 41.50S 70.55W
Norrahammar Sweden **23** 57.42N 14.06E
Norra Kvarken *str.* Sweden/Finland **22** 63.36N 20.43E
Norra Storfjället *mtn.* Sweden **22** 65.52N 15.18E
Norrbotten *d.* Sweden **22** 67.00N 19.50E
Nörresundby Denmark **23** 57.04N 9.56E
Norris L. U.S.A. **85** 36.18N 83.58W
Norristown U.S.A. **85** 40.07N 75.20W
Norrköping Sweden **23** 58.36N 16.11E
Norrsundet Sweden **23** 60.56N 17.08E
Norrtälje Sweden **23** 59.46N 18.42E
Norseman Australia **63** 32.15S121.47E
Norsk U.S.S.R. **29** 52.22N129.57E
Norte *d.* W. Sahara **50** 26.50N 11.15W
Norte, C. Brazil **91** 1.40N 49.55W
Norte, Cabo *c.* I. de Pascua **69** 27.03S109.24W
Norte, Punta *c.* Argentina **93** 36.17S 56.46W
North, C. Canada **77** 47.01N 60.28W
Northallerton U.K. **10** 54.20N 1.26W
Northam Australia **63** 31.41S116.40E
Northampton Australia **63** 28.21S114.37E
Northampton U.K. **11** 52.14N 0.54W
Northampton Penn. U.S.A. **85** 40.41N 75.30W
Northamptonshire *d.* U.K. **11** 52.18N 0.55W
North Battleford Canada **75** 52.47N108.17W
North Bay *town* Canada **76** 46.19N 79.28W
North Bend Oreg. U.S.A. **80** 43.24N124.14W
North Berwick U.K. **12** 56.04N 2.43W
North Bourke Australia **67** 30.01S145.59E
North C. Antarctica **96** 71.00S166.00E
North C. New Zealand **60** 34.28S173.00E
North Canadian *r.* U.S.A. **83** 35.17N 95.31W
North Caribou L. Canada **76** 52.50N 90.50W
North Carolina *d.* U.S.A. **85** 35.30N 80.00W
North Channel *str.* Canada **76** 46.02N 82.50W
North Channel U.K. **13** 55.15N 5.52W
North Chicago U.S.A. **82** 42.20N 87.51W
North China Plain *f. see* Huabei Pingyuan *f.* China **32**
Northcliffe Australia **63** 34.36S116.04E
North Dakota *d.* U.S.A. **82** 47.00N100.00W
North Dorset Downs *hills* U.K. **11** 50.46N 2.25W
North Downs *hills* U.K. **11** 51.18N 0.40E
North East U.S.A. **76** 42.13N 79.50W
North Eastern *d.* Kenya **55** 1.00N 40.00E
North Eastern Atlantic Basin *f.* Atlantic Oc. **95** 45.00N 17.00W
North East Pt. Kiribati **69** 1.57N157.16W
Northern *d.* Ghana **52** 9.00N 1.30W
Northern Indian L. Canada **75** 57.20N 97.20W
Northern Ireland *d.* U.K. **13** 54.40N 6.45W
Northern Territory *d.* Australia **64** 20.00S133.00E
North Esk *r.* U.K. **12** 56.45N 2.25W
North Fiji Basin Pacific Oc. **68** 17.00S173.00E
North Foreland *c.* U.K. **11** 51.23N 1.26E
North French *r.* Canada **76** 51.04N 80.46W
North Frisian Is. *see* Nordfriesische Inseln *is.* W. Germany **20**

North Head to **Oliva**

North Head *c.* Canada **77** 53.42N 56.24W
North Henik L. Canada **75** 61.45N 97.40W
North Horr Kenya **55** 3.19N 37.00E
North I. Kenya **49** 4.04N 36.03E
North I. New Zealand **60** 39.00S175.00E
Northiam U.K. **11** 50.59N 0.39E
North Knife *r.* Canada **75** 58.53N 94.45W
North Korea Asia **31** 40.00N128.00E
Northland *d.* New Zealand **60** 35.25S174.00E
North Las Vegas U.S.A. **81** 36.12N115.07W
North Little Rock U.S.A. **83** 34.46N 92.14W
North Loup *r.* U.S.A. **82** 41.17N 98.23W
North Mankato U.S.A. **82** 44.15N 94.06W
North Nahanni *r.* Canada **74** 62.15N123.20W
North Ogden U.S.A. **80** 41.18N112.00W
Northome U.S.A. **82** 47.52N 94.17W
North Platte U.S.A. **82** 41.08N100.46W
North Platte *r.* U.S.A. **82** 41.15N100.45W
Northport U.S.A. **85** 33.14N 87.33W
North Powder U.S.A. **80** 45.13N117.55W
North Pt. Canada **77** 47.05N 64.00W
North Rona *i.* U.K. **8** 59.09N 5.43W
North Ronaldsay *i.* U.K. **12** 59.23N 2.26W
North Saskatchewan *r.* Canada **75** 53.15N105.06W
North Sea Europe **20** 54.00N 4.00E
North Seal *r.* Canada **75** 58.50N 98.10W
North Sporades *see* Voríai Sporádhes *is.* Greece **19**
North Sydney Canada **77** 46.13N 60.15W
North Taranaki Bight *b.* New Zealand **60** 38.45S174.15E
North Tawton U.K. **11** 50.48N 3.55W
North Thompson *r.* Canada **74** 50.40N120.20W
North Tonawanda U.S.A. **84** 43.02N 78.54W
North Twin I. Canada **76** 53.20N 80.00W
North Uist *i.* U.K. **12** 57.35N 7.20W
Northumberland *d.* U.K. **10** 55.12N 2.00W
Northumberland, C. Australia **66** 38.04S140.40E
Northumberland Is. Australia **64** 21.40S150.00E
Northumberland Str. Canada **77** 46.00N 63.30W
North Wabasca L. Canada **74** 56.00N113.55W
North Walsham U.K. **10** 52.49N 1.22E
Northway U.S.A. **72** 62.58N142.00W
North West C. Australia **62** 21.48S114.10E
North West Chile Ridge Pacific Oc. **69** 42.00S 90.00W
North West Christmas Island Ridge Pacific Oc. **69** 6.30N159.00W
North Western *d.* Zambia **56** 13.00S 25.00E
North Western Atlantic Basin *f.* Atlantic Oc. **95** 33.00N 55.00W
Northwest Frontier *d.* Pakistan **40** 33.45N 71.00E
North West Highlands U.K. **12** 57.30N 5.15W
North West Pt. Kiribati **69** 2.02N157.29W
North West River *town* Canada **77** 53.32N 60.09W
Northwest Territories *d.* Canada **73** 66.00N 95.00W
Northwich U.K. **10** 53.16N 2.30W
Northwood Iowa U.S.A. **82** 43.27N 93.13W
Northwood N.Dak. U.S.A. **82** 47.44N 97.34W
North York Moors *hills* U.K. **10** 54.21N 0.50W
North Yorkshire *d.* U.K. **10** 54.14N 1.14W
Norton Kans. U.S.A. **82** 39.50N 99.53W
Norton Sound *b.* U.S.A. **72** 63.50N164.00W
Nort-sur-Erdre France **15** 47.26N 1.30W
Norwalk Conn. U.S.A. **85** 41.07N 73.25W
Norwalk Ohio U.S.A. **84** 41.14N 82.37W
Norway Europe **22** 65.00N 13.00E
Norway House *town* Canada **75** 53.59N 97.50W
Norwegian Dependency Antarctica **96** 77.00S 10.00E
Norwegian Sea Europe **96** 65.00N 5.00E
Norwich U.K. **11** 52.38N 1.17E
Norwood Ohio U.S.A. **84** 39.12N 84.21W
Noshul U.S.S.R. **24** 60.04N 49.30E
Nosovka U.S.S.R. **21** 50.55N 31.37E
Noşratābād Iran **43** 29.54N 59.58E
Noss Head U.K. **12** 58.28N 3.03W
Nosy Be *i.* Madagascar **57** 13.20S 48.15E
Nosy Boraha *i.* Madagascar **57** 16.50S 49.55E
Nosy Varika Madagascar **57** 20.35S 48.32E
Noteć *r.* Poland **20** 52.44N 15.26E
Noto Italy **18** 36.53N 15.05E
Notodden Norway **23** 59.34N 9.17E
Notre Dame, Monts *mts.* Canada **77** 48.00N 69.00W
Notre Dame B. Canada **77** 49.45N 55.15W
Notre Dame de la Salette Canada **77** 45.46N 75.35W
Nottawasaga B. Canada **76** 44.40N 80.30W
Nottaway *r.* Canada **76** 51.25N 78.50W
Nottingham U.K. **10** 52.57N 1.10W
Nottinghamshire *d.* U.K. **10** 53.10N 1.00W
Notwani *r.* Botswana **56** 23.46S 26.57E
Nouadhibou Mauritania **50** 20.54N 17.01W
Nouakchott Mauritania **50** 18.09N 15.58W
Nouméa New Caledonia **68** 22.16S166.27E
Nouna U. Volta **52** 12.44N 3.54W
Noupoort R.S.A. **56** 31.11S 24.56E
Nouveau, Lac *l.* Canada **77** 51.59N 68.58W
Nouveau-Comptoir Canada **76** 53.02N 78.55W
Nouvelle Anvers Zaïre **54** 1.38N 19.10E
Nouvelle Calédonie *is.* Pacific Oc. **68** 21.30S165.30E
Nouzonville France **15** 49.49N 4.45E
Nova Caipemba Angola **54** 7.25S 14.36E
Nova Chaves Angola **54** 10.31S 21.20E
Novafeltria Bagnodi Romagna Italy **15** 43.53N 12.17E
Nova Friburgo Brazil **94** 22.16S 42.32W
Nova Gaia Angola **54** 10.09S 17.35E
Nova Iguaçu Brazil **94** 22.45S 43.27W
Nova Lamego Guinea Bissau **52** 12.19N 14.11W
Nova Lima Brazil **94** 19.59S 43.51W
Novara Italy **15** 45.27N 8.37E
Nova Scotia *d.* Canada **77** 45.00N 63.30W
Nova Sofala Mozambique **57** 20.09S 34.24E
Novato U.S.A. **80** 38.06N122.34W
Novaya Ladoga U.S.S.R. **24** 60.09N 32.15E
Novaya Lyalya U.S.S.R. **28** 59.02N 60.38E
Novaya Sibir, Ostrov *i.* U.S.S.R. **29** 75.20N148.00E
Novaya Ushitsa U.S.S.R. **21** 48.50N 27.12E
Novaya Zemlya *i.* U.S.S.R. **28** 74.00N 56.00E
Novelda Spain **16** 38.24N 0.45W
Nové Zámky Czech. **21** 47.59N 18.11E
Novgorod U.S.S.R. **24** 58.30N 31.20E
Novgorod Severskiy U.S.S.R. **24** 52.00N 33.15E
Novi di Modena Italy **15** 44.54N 10.54E
Novigrad Yugo. **20** 45.19N 13.34E
Novi Ligure Italy **15** 44.46N 8.47E
Novi Pazar Yugo. **19** 43.08N 20.28E
Novi Sad Yugo. **21** 45.16N 19.52E
Novoalekseyevka U.S.S.R. **25** 46.14N 34.36E
Novoanninskiy U.S.S.R. **25** 50.32N 42.42E
Novo Arkhangel'sk U.S.S.R. **21** 48.34N 30.50E
Novocherkassk U.S.S.R. **25** 47.25N 40.05E
Novofedorovka U.S.S.R. **25** 47.04N 35.18E
Novograd Volynskiy U.S.S.R. **21** 50.34N 27.32E
Novogrudok U.S.S.R. **21** 53.35N 25.50E
Novo Hamburgo Brazil **94** 29.37S 51.07W
Novokazalinsk U.S.S.R. **28** 45.48N 62.06E
Novokuznetsk U.S.S.R. **28** 53.45N 87.12E
Novomoskovsk R.S.F.S.R. U.S.S.R. **24** 54.06N 38.15E
Novomoskovsk Ukr.S.S.R. U.S.S.R. **25** 48.38N 35.15E
Novorossiysk U.S.S.R. **25** 44.44N 37.46E
Novoshakhtinsk U.S.S.R. **25** 47.46N 39.55E
Novosibirsk U.S.S.R. **28** 55.04N 82.55E
Novosibirskiye Ostrova *is.* U.S.S.R. **29** 76.00N144.00E
Novouzensk U.S.S.R. **25** 50.29N 48.08E
Novo-Vyatsk U.S.S.R. **24** 58.30N 49.40E
Novozybkov U.S.S.R. **21** 52.31N 31.58E
Novska Yugo. **20** 45.21N 16.59E
Nový Jičín Czech. **21** 49.36N 18.00E
Novyy Bykhov U.S.S.R. **21** 53.20N 30.21E
Novyy Port U.S.S.R. **28** 67.38N 72.33E
Nowa Ruda Poland **20** 50.34N 16.30E
Nowa Sól Poland **20** 51.49N 15.41E
Nowendoc Australia **67** 31.35S151.45E
Nowgong Assam India **41** 26.21N 92.40E
Nowgong Madhya P. India **41** 25.04N 79.27E
Nowingi Australia **66** 34.36S142.15E
Nowra Australia **67** 35.54S150.36E
Nowrangapur India **41** 19.14N 82.33E
Nowshera Pakistan **40** 34.01N 71.59E
Nowy Dwór Mazowiecki Poland **21** 52.26N 20.43E
Nowy Korczyn Poland **21** 50.19N 20.48E
Nowy Sącz Poland **21** 49.39N 20.40E
Nowy Targ Poland **21** 49.29N 20.02E
Nowy Tomśyl Poland **20** 52.20N 16.07E
Now Zād Afghan. **40** 32.24N 64.28E
Noxon U.S.A. **80** 48.01N115.47W
Noyant France **15** 47.31N 0.08E
Noyes I. U.S.A. **74** 55.30N133.40W
Noyon France **15** 49.35N 3.00E
Nozay France **15** 47.34N 1.38W
Nsanje Malaŵi **55** 16.55S 35.12E
Nsawam Ghana **52** 5.49N 0.20W
Nsok Equat. Guinea **54** 1.10N 11.19E
Nsombo Zambia **55** 10.50S 29.56E
Nsukka Nigeria **53** 6.51N 7.29E
Nuatja Togo **53** 6.59N 1.11E
Nubian Desert Sudan **48** 20.30N 34.00E
Nueces *r.* U.S.A. **83** 27.50N 97.30W
Nueces Plains *f.* U.S.A. **83** 28.30N 99.15W
Nueltin L. Canada **75** 60.30N 99.30W
Nueva Casas Grandes Mexico **81** 30.25N107.55W
Nueva Gerona Cuba **87** 21.53N 82.49W
Nueva Helvecia Uruguay **93** 34.19S 57.13W
Nueva Palmira Uruguay **93** 33.53S 58.25W
Nueva Rosita Mexico **83** 27.57N101.13W
Nueve de Julio Argentina **93** 35.30S 60.50W
Nuevitas Cuba **87** 21.34N 77.18W
Nuevo *d.* Mexico **83** 26.00N100.00W
Nuevo, Golfo *g.* Argentina **93** 42.42S 64.35W
Nuevo Berlín Uruguay **93** 32.59S 58.03W
Nuevo Laredo Mexico **83** 27.30N 99.31W
Nuevo León *d.* Mexico **86** 26.00N 99.00W
Nuevo Rocafuerte Ecuador **90** 0.56S 75.24W
Nūh, Rās *c.* Pakistan **40** 25.05N 62.24E
Nui *i.* Tuvalu **68** 7.12S177.10E
Nu Jiang *r.* China *see* Salween *r.* Burma **39**
Nukha U.S.S.R. **43** 41.12N 47.10E
Nukhaylah Sudan **48** 19.03N 26.19E
Nuku'alofa Tonga **69** 21.07S175.12W
Nuku Hiva *i.* Îs. Marquises **69** 8.56S140.00W
Nukunonu Pacific Oc. **68** 9.10S171.55W
Nulato U.S.A. **72** 64.43N158.06W
Nullagine Australia **62** 21.56S120.06E
Nullarbor Australia **63** 31.26S130.55E
Nullarbor Plain *f.* Australia **63** 31.30S128.00E
Numalla, L. Australia **66** 28.45S144.21E
Numan Nigeria **53** 9.30N 12.01E
Numazu Japan **35** 35.06N138.52E
Numedal *f.* Norway **23** 60.06N 9.06E
Numurkah Australia **67** 36.05S145.26E
Nundle Australia **67** 31.28S151.08E
Nuneaton U.K. **11** 52.32N 1.29W
Nungo Mozambique **57** 13.25S 37.45E
Nunivak I. U.S.A. **72** 60.00N166.30W
Nunkun *mtn.* Jammu & Kashmir **40** 33.59N 76.01E
Nunthurungie Australia **66** 30.55S142.29E
Nuoro Italy **18** 40.19N 9.20E
Nuqūb S. Yemen **45** 14.59N 45.48E
Nürburg W. Germany **14** 50.20N 6.59E
Nure *r.* Italy **15** 45.03N 9.49E
Nürnberg W. Germany **20** 49.27N 11.05E
Nurri, Mt. Australia **67** 31.44S146.04E
Nusa Tenggara *is.* Indonesia **36** 8.30S118.00E
Nusa Tenggara Barat *d.* Indonesia **36** 8.50S117.30E
Nusa Tenggara Timur *d.* Indonesia **37** 9.30S122.00E
Nusaybin Turkey **42** 37.05N 41.11E
Nushki Pakistan **40** 29.33N 66.01E
Nutak Canada **77** 57.39N 61.50W
Nuuk *see* Godthåb Greenland **73**
Nuwākot Nepal **41** 28.08N 83.53E
Nuwaybi'al Muzayyinah Egypt **44** 28.58N 34.38E
Nuweveldberge *mts.* R.S.A. **56** 32.15S 21.50E
Nuyts, Pt. Australia **63** 35.02S116.32E
Nuyts Archipelago *is.* Australia **65** 32.35S133.17E
Nxaunxau Botswana **56** 18.19S 21.04E
Nyaake Liberia **52** 4.52N 7.37W
Nyabing Australia **63** 33.32S118.09E
Nyahua Tanzania **55** 5.25S 33.16E
Nyahururu Falls *town* Kenya **55** 0.04N 36.22E
Nyainqêntanglha Feng *mtn.* China **41** 30.27N 90.33E
Nyainqêntanglha Shan *mts.* China **41** 30.00N 90.00E
Nyainrong China **41** 32.02N 92.15E
Nyakanazi Tanzania **55** 3.05S 31.16E
Nyaksimvol U.S.S.R. **24** 62.30N 60.52E
Nyala Sudan **49** 12.03N 24.53E
Nyalam China **41** 28.12N 85.58E
Nyamandhlovu Zimbabwe **56** 19.50S 28.15E
Nyamapanda Zimbabwe **57** 16.59S 32.50E
Nyamlell Sudan **49** 9.07N 26.58E
Nyamtukusa Tanzania **55** 3.03S 32.44E
Nyandoma U.S.S.R. **24** 61.33N 40.05E
Nyanga *r.* Gabon **54** 3.00S 10.17E
Nyang Qu *r.* China **41** 29.19N 88.52E
Nyanza *d.* Kenya **55** 0.30S 34.30E
Nyanza Rwanda **55** 2.20S 29.42E
Nyashabozh U.S.S.R. **24** 65.28N 53.42E
Nyaunglebin Burma **34** 17.57N 96.44E
Nyaungu Burma **34** 21.12N 94.55E
Nyborg Denmark **23** 55.19N 10.48E
Nybro Sweden **23** 56.45N 15.54E
Nyda U.S.S.R. **28** 66.35N 72.58E
Nyêmo China **41** 29.25N 90.15E
Nyeri Kenya **55** 0.22S 36.56E
Nyerol Sudan **49** 8.41N 32.02E
Nyhammar Sweden **23** 60.17N 14.58E
Nyika Plateau *f.* Malaŵi **55** 10.25S 33.50E
Nyima China **41** 31.50N 87.48E
Nyimba Zambia **55** 14.33S 30.49E
Nyíregyháza Hungary **21** 47.59N 21.43E
Nyköbing Falster Denmark **23** 54.46N 11.53E
Nyköbing Jylland Denmark **23** 56.48N 8.52E
Nyköbing Sjaelland Denmark **23** 55.55N 11.41E
Nyköping Sweden **23** 58.45N 17.00E
Nylstroom R.S.A. **56** 24.42S 28.24E
Nymagee Australia **67** 32.05S146.20E
Nymboida Australia **67** 29.57S152.32E
Nymboida *r.* Australia **67** 29.39S152.30E
Nymburk Czech. **20** 50.11N 15.03E
Nynäshamn Sweden **23** 58.54N 17.57E
Nyngan Australia **67** 31.34S147.14E
Nyoma Jammu & Kashmir **41** 33.11N 78.38E
Nyong *r.* Cameroon **53** 3.15N 9.55E
Nyons France **17** 44.22N 5.08E
Nysa Poland **21** 50.29N 17.20E
Nysa Kłodzka *r.* Poland **21** 50.49N 17.50E
Nyssa U.S.A. **80** 43.53N117.00W
Nyuksenitsa U.S.S.R. **24** 60.24N 44.08E
Nyunzu Zaïre **55** 5.55S 28.00E
Nyurba U.S.S.R. **29** 63.18N118.28E
Nyuri India **41** 27.42N 92.13E
Nzega Tanzania **55** 4.13S 33.09E
N'zérékoré Guinea **52** 7.49N 8.48W
Nzeto Angola **54** 7.13S 12.56E

O

Oahe Resr. U.S.A. **82** 45.30N100.25W
Oahu *i.* Hawaiian Is. **69** 21.30N158.00W
Oakbank Australia **66** 33.07S140.33E
Oakdale U.S.A. **83** 30.49N 92.40W
Oakesdale U.S.A. **80** 47.08N117.15W
Oakey Australia **65** 27.26S151.43E
Oak Harbour U.S.A. **80** 48.18N122.39W
Oak Hill *town* Fla. U.S.A. **85** 28.52N 80.52W
Oakland Calif. U.S.A. **80** 37.47N122.13W
Oakland Oreg. U.S.A. **80** 43.25N123.18W
Oaklands Australia **67** 35.25S146.15E
Oakley U.S.A. **80** 42.15N113.53W
Oakridge U.S.A. **80** 43.45N122.28W
Oak Ridge *town* U.S.A. **85** 36.02N 84.12W
Oakvale Australia **66** 33.01S140.41E
Oakville Canada **76** 43.27N 79.41W
Oamaru New Zealand **60** 45.07S170.58E
Oates Land *f.* Antarctica **96** 70.00S155.00E
Oaxaca Mexico **86** 17.05N 96.41W
Oaxaca *d.* Mexico **86** 17.30N 97.00W
Ob *r.* U.S.S.R. **24** 66.50N 69.00E
Oba Canada **76** 49.04N 84.07W
Oba *i.* Vanuatu **68** 15.25S167.50E
Oban U.K. **12** 56.26N 5.28W
Obbia Somali Rep. **45** 5.20N 48.30E
Oberá Argentina **92** 27.30S 55.07W
Oberhausen W. Germany **14** 51.28N 6.51E
Oberlin Kans. U.S.A. **82** 39.49N100.32W
Oberösterreich *d.* Austria **20** 48.15N 14.00E
Obi *i.* Indonesia **37** 1.45S127.30E
Obidos Brazil **91** 1.55S 55.31W
Obitsu *r.* Japan **35** 35.24N139.54E
Obo C.A.R. **49** 5.24N 26.30E
Obock Djibouti **49** 11.59N 43.16E
Obodovka U.S.S.R. **21** 48.28N 29.10E
Oboyan U.S.S.R. **25** 51.13N 36.17E
Obozerskiy U.S.S.R. **24** 63.28N 40.29E
Obregón, Presa *resr.* Mexico **81** 28.00N109.50W
Obruk Platosu *f.* Turkey **42** 38.00N 33.30E
Obskaya Guba *g.* U.S.S.R. **28** 68.30N 74.00E
Ōbu Japan **35** 35.00N136.58E
Obuasi Ghana **52** 6.15N 1.36W
Obudu Nigeria **53** 6.42N 9.07E
Ocala U.S.A. **85** 29.11N 82.09W
Ocaña Colombia **90** 8.16N 73.21W
Ocaña Spain **16** 39.57N 3.30W
Occidental, Cordillera *mts.* Colombia **90** 5.00N 76.15W
Occidental, Cordillera *mts.* S. America **92** 17.00S 69.00W
Ocean City Md. U.S.A. **85** 38.20N 75.05W
Ocean City N.J. U.S.A. **85** 39.16N 74.36W
Ocean Falls *town* Canada **74** 52.25N127.40W
Ocean I. *see* Banaba *i.* Kiribati **68**
Oceanside Calif. U.S.A. **81** 33.12N117.23W
Oceanside N.Y. U.S.A. **85** 40.38N 73.38W
Ochamchire U.S.S.R. **25** 42.44N 41.30E
Ochil Hills U.K. **12** 56.16N 3.25W
Ochsenfurt W. Germany **20** 49.40N 10.03E
Ockelbo Sweden **23** 60.53N 16.43E
Ocmulgee *r.* U.S.A. **85** 31.58N 82.32W
Oconee *r.* U.S.A. **85** 31.58N 82.32W
Oconto U.S.A. **82** 44.55N 87.52W
Ocotal Nicaragua **87** 13.37N 86.31W
Ocotlán Mexico **86** 20.21N102.42W
Octeville France **15** 49.37N 1.39W
Ocua Mozambique **57** 13.40S 39.46E
Oda Ghana **52** 5.55N 0.56W
Oda, Jabal *mtn.* Sudan **48** 20.21N 36.39E
Odádhahraun *mts.* Iceland **22** 65.00N 17.30W
Odawara Japan **35** 35.15N139.10E
Odda Norway **23** 60.04N 6.33E
Oddur Somali Rep. **45** 4.10N 43.53E
Ödeborg Sweden **23** 58.33N 12.00E
Odemira Portugal **16** 37.36N 8.38W
Ödemiş Turkey **19** 38.12N 28.00E
Odense Denmark **23** 55.24N 10.23E
Odenwald *mts.* W. Germany **20** 49.40N 9.20E
Oder *r.* E. Germany *see* Odra *r.* Poland **20**
Oderzo Italy **15** 45.47N 12.29E
Odessa Tex. U.S.A. **83** 31.51N102.22W
Odessa U.S.S.R. **21** 46.30N 30.46E
Odienné Ivory Coast **52** 9.36N 7.32W
Odorhei Romania **21** 46.18N 25.18E
Odra *r.* Poland **20** 53.30N 14.36E
Odžak Yugo. **21** 45.03N 18.18E
Odzi *r.* Zimbabwe **57** 19.46S 32.22E
Oegstgeest Neth. **14** 52.12N 4.31E
Oeiras Brazil **91** 7.00S 42.07W
Oelrichs U.S.A. **82** 43.10N103.13W
Oelwein U.S.A. **82** 42.41N 91.55W
Oeno I. Pacific Oc. **69** 23.55S130.45W
Oenpelli Australia **64** 12.20S133.04E
Ofanto *r.* Italy **18** 41.22N 16.12E
Ofaqim Israel **44** 31.19N 34.37E
Offa Nigeria **53** 8.09N 4.44E
Offaly *d.* Rep. of Ire. **13** 53.15N 7.30W
Offenbach W. Germany **20** 50.06N 8.46E
Offenburg W. Germany **20** 48.29N 7.57E
Offerdal Sweden **22** 63.28N 14.03E
Offranville France **15** 49.52N 1.03E
Ofir Portugal **16** 41.31N 8.47W
Ofotfjorden *est.* Norway **22** 68.25N 17.00E
Ofu *i.* Samoa **68** 14.11S169.40W
Ōgaki Japan **35** 35.21N136.37E
Ogallala U.S.A. **82** 41.08N101.43W
Ogbomosho Nigeria **53** 8.05N 4.11E
Ogden Iowa U.S.A. **82** 42.02N 94.02W
Ogden Utah U.S.A. **80** 41.14N111.58W
Ogeechee *r.* U.S.A. **85** 31.51N 81.06W
Ogilvie Mts. Canada **72** 65.00N139.30W
Oginskiy, Kanal *canal* U.S.S.R. **21** 52.25N 25.55E
Oglio *r.* Italy **15** 45.02N 10.39E
Ognon *r.* France **17** 47.20N 5.37E
Ogoja Nigeria **53** 6.40N 8.45E
Ogoki Canada **76** 51.35N 86.00W
Ogoki *r.* Canada **76** 51.35N 86.00W
Ogoki Resr. Canada **76** 51.00N 88.15W
Ogooué *r.* Gabon **54** 1.00S 9.05E
Ogosta *r.* Bulgaria **19** 43.44N 23.51E
Ogr Sudan **49** 12.02N 27.06E
Ogulin Yugo. **20** 45.17N 15.14E
Ogun *d.* Nigeria **53** 6.50N 3.20E
Ohai New Zealand **60** 45.56S167.57E
Ohanet Algeria **51** 28.40N 8.50E
Ohey Belgium **14** 50.26N 5.06E
O'Higgins, Cabo *c.* I. de Pascua **69** 27.05S109.15W
O'Higgins, L. Chile **93** 48.03S 73.10W
Ohio *d.* U.S.A. **84** 40.15N 82.45W
Ohio *r.* U.S.A. **84** 36.59N 89.08W
Ōhito Japan **35** 34.59N138.56E
Ohře *r.* Czech. **20** 50.32N 14.08E
Ohrid Yugo. **19** 41.06N 20.48E
Ohrid, L. Albania / Yugo. **19** 41.00N 20.43E
Ōi *r.* Japan **35** 34.45N138.18E
Oil City U.S.A. **84** 41.26N 79.42W
Oise *d.* France **15** 49.30N 2.30E
Oise *r.* France **15** 49.00N 2.10E
Oisterwijk Neth. **14** 51.34N 5.10E
Ojai U.S.A. **81** 34.27N119.15W
Ojocaliente Mexico **86** 22.35N102.18W
Ojo de Agua Argentina **92** 29.30S 63.44W
Ojos del Salado *mtn.* Argentina / Chile **92** 27.05S 68.05W
Oka Nigeria **53** 7.28N 5.48E
Oka Canada **77** 45.29N 74.06W
Oka *r.* U.S.S.R. **24** 56.09N 43.00E
Okaba Indonesia **37** 8.06S139.46E
Okahandja Namibia **56** 21.58S 16.44E
Okanagan L. Canada **74** 50.00N119.30W
Okanogan U.S.A. **80** 48.39N120.41W
Okanogan *r.* U.S.A. **80** 48.22N119.35W
Okaputa Namibia **56** 20.08S 16.58E
Okāra Pakistan **40** 30.49N 73.27E
Okarito New Zealand **60** 43.14S.170.07
Okaukuejo Namibia **56** 19.12S 15.56E
Okavango *r.* Botswana **56** 18.30S 22.04E
Okavango Basin *f.* Botswana **56** 19.30S 22.30E
Okayama Japan **31** 34.40N133.54E
Okeechobee U.S.A. **85** 27.14N 80.50W
Okeechobee, L. U.S.A. **85** 26.55N 80.45W
Okefenokee Swamp *f.* U.S.A. **85** 30.42N 82.20W
Okehampton U.K. **11** 50.44N 4.01W
Okere *r.* Uganda **55** 1.37N 33.53E
Okha U.S.S.R. **29** 53.35N142.50E
Okhaldhunga Nepal **41** 27.19N 86.31E
Okhansk U.S.S.R. **24** 57.42N 55.20E
Okhotsk U.S.S.R. **29** 59.20N143.15E
Okhotsk, Sea of U.S.S.R. **29** 55.00N150.00E
Okhotskiy Perevoz U.S.S.R. **29** 61.55N135.40E
Okiep R.S.A. **56** 29.36S 17.49E
Oki guntō *is.* Japan **31** 36.30N133.20E
Okinawa jima *i.* Japan **31** 26.30N128.00E
Okino Torishima *i.* Pacific Oc. **37** 20.24N136.02E
Okipoko *r.* Namibia **56** 18.40S 16.03E
Okitipupa Nigeria **53** 6.31N 4.50E
Oklahoma *d.* U.S.A. **83** 35.20N 98.00W
Oklahoma City U.S.A. **83** 35.28N 97.32W
Okmulgee U.S.A. **83** 35.37N 95.58W
Oknitsa U.S.S.R. **21** 48.22N 27.30E
Oko, Wādī Sudan **48** 21.15N 35.56E
Okola Cameroon **53** 4.03N 11.23E
Okolona U.S.A. **83** 34.00N 88.45W
Okondja Gabon **54** 0.03S 13.45E
Okoyo Congo **54** 1.28S 15.00E
Oksskolten *mtn.* Norway **22** 65.59N 14.15E
Oktyabr'sk U.S.S.R. **25** 49.30N 57.22E
Oktyabrskiy B.S.S.R. U.S.S.R. **21** 52.35N 28.45E
Oktyabrskiy R.S.F.S.R. U.S.S.R. **24** 54.30N 53.30E
Oktyabr'skoy Revolyutsii, Ostrov *i.* U.S.S.R. **29** 79.30N 96.00E
Okuru New Zealand **60** 43.56S168.55E
Okuta Nigeria **53** 9.13N 3.12E
Ola U.S.A. **83** 35.02N 93.13W
Ólafsvík Iceland **22** 64.53N 23.44W
Olancha U.S.A. **81** 36.17N118.01W
Öland *i.* Sweden **23** 56.45N 16.38E
Olary Australia **66** 32.18S140.19E
Olascoaga Argentina **93** 35.14S 60.37W
Olavarría Argentina **93** 36.57S 60.20W
Oława Poland **21** 50.57N 17.17E
Olbia Italy **18** 40.55N 9.29E
Old Crow Canada **72** 67.34N139.43W
Oldenburg Nschn. W. Germany **14** 53.08N 8.13E
Oldenburg Sch.-Hol. W. Germany **20** 54.17N 10.52E
Oldenzaal Neth. **14** 52.19N 6.55E
Old Forge Penn. U.S.A. **84** 41.22N 75.44W
Old Fort *r.* Canada **75** 58.30N110.30W
Old Gumbiro Tanzania **55** 10.00S 35.24E
Oldham U.K. **10** 53.33N 2.08W
Old Head of Kinsale *c.* Rep. of Ire. **13** 51.37N 8.33W
Oldman *r.* Canada **75** 49.56N111.42W
Olds Canada **74** 51.50N114.10W
Old Town U.S.A. **84** 44.56N 68.39W
Olean U.S.A. **84** 42.05N 78.26W
Olecko Poland **21** 54.03N 22.30E
Olekma *r.* U.S.S.R. **29** 60.20N120.30E
Olekminsk U.S.S.R. **29** 60.25N120.00E
Olema U.S.S.R. **24** 64.25N 40.15E
Olenëk U.S.S.R. **29** 68.38N112.15E
Olenëk *r.* U.S.S.R. **29** 73.00N120.00E
Olenëkskiy Zaliv *g.* U.S.S.R. **29** 74.00N120.00E
Oléron, Île d' *i.* France **17** 45.55N 1.16W
Oleśnica Poland **21** 51.13N 17.23E
Olevsk U.S.S.R. **21** 51.12N 27.35E
Olga U.S.S.R. **31** 43.46N135.14E
Olga L. Canada **76** 49.44N 77.18W
Ölgiy Mongolia **30** 48.54N 90.00E
Olgopol U.S.S.R. **21** 48.10N 29.30E
Olhão Portugal **16** 37.01N 7.50W
Olifants *r.* Namibia **56** 25.28S 19.23E
Olifants *r.* C.P. R.S.A. **56** 31.42S 18.10E
Olifants *r.* Trans. R.S.A. **56** 24.08S 32.39E
Ólimbos *mtn.* Cyprus **44** 34.55N 32.52E
Ólimbos Greece **19** 35.44N 27.11E
Ólimbos *mtn.* Greece **19** 40.04N 22.20E
Olinda Brazil **91** 8.00S 34.51W
Oliva Argentina **92** 32.05S 63.35W

Oliva to Pakxé

Oliva Spain 16 38.58N 0.15W
Olivares Spain 16 39.45N 2.21W
Oliveira Brazil 94 20.39S 44.47W
Olivenza Spain 16 38.41N 7.09W
Olney U.K. 11 52.09N 0.42W
Olney U.S.A. 82 38.45N 88.05W
Olofström Sweden 23 56.16N 14.30E
Olomouc Czech. 21 49.36N 17.16E
Olonets U.S.S.R. 24 61.00N 32.59E
Oloron France 17 43.12N 0.35W
Olosega i. Samoa 68 14.12S169.38W
Olot Spain 16 42.11N 2.30E
Olovyannaya U.S.S.R. 31 50.58N115.35E
Olpe W. Germany 14 51.02N 7.52E
Olsztyn Poland 21 53.48N 20.29E
Olsztynek Poland 21 53.36N 20.17E
Olt r. Romania 21 43.43N 24.51E
Oltenița Romania 21 44.05N 26.31E
Olteț r. Romania 21 44.13N 24.28E
Olympia U.S.A. 80 47.03N122.53W
Olympic Mts. U.S.A. 80 47.50N123.45W
Olympic Nat. Park U.S.A. 80 47.48N123.30W
Olympus mtn. see Ólimbos mtn. Greece 19
Olympus, Mt. U.S.A. 80 47.48N123.43W
Oma China 41 32.30N 83.14E
Omae-zaki c. Japan 35 34.36N138.14E
Omagh U.K. 13 54.36N 7.20W
Omaha U.S.A. 82 41.16N 95.57W
Oman Asia 38 22.30N 57.30E
Oman, G. of Asia 43 25.00N 58.00E
Omarama New Zealand 60 44.29S169.58E
Omaruru Namibia 56 21.25S 15.57E
Omate Peru 92 16.40S 70.58W
Omboué Gabon 54 1.38S 9.20E
Ombrone r. Italy 18 42.40N 11.00E
Ombu China 41 31.20N 86.34E
Omdurman see Umm Durmân Sudan 48
Omegna Italy 15 45.53N 8.24E
Ometepec Mexico 86 16.41N 98.25W
Om Hajer Ethiopia 48 14.24N 36.46E
Ōmi-hachiman Japan 35 35.08N136.06E
Omineca r. Canada 74 56.05N124.30W
Omitara Namibia 56 22.18S 18.01E
Ōmiya Japan 35 35.54N139.38E
Ommen Neth. 14 52.32N 6.25E
Ömnögovi d. Mongolia 32 43.00N105.00E
Omo r. Ethiopia 49 4.51N 36.55E
Omolon r. U.S.S.R. 29 68.50N158.30E
Omsk U.S.S.R. 28 55.00N 73.22E
Omulew r. Poland 21 53.05N 21.32E
Omuramba Omatako r. Namibia 56 18.19S 19.52E
Omuta Japan 31 33.02N130.26E
Oña Spain 16 42.44N 3.25W
Onaga U.S.A. 82 39.29N 96.10W
Onai Angola 56 16.43S 17.33E
Onancock U.S.A. 85 37.43N 75.46W
Oncocua Angola 56 16.40S 13.25E
Onda Spain 16 39.58N 0.16W
Ondangua Namibia 56 17.59S 16.02E
Ondo d. Nigeria 53 7.10N 5.20E
Onega U.S.S.R. 24 63.57N 38.11E
Onega r. U.S.S.R. 24 63.59N 38.11E
Oneida U.S.A. 84 43.06N 75.39W
O'Neill U.S.A. 82 42.27N 98.39W
Onezhskaya Guba b. U.S.S.R. 24 63.55N 37.30E
Onezhskoye Ozero l. U.S.S.R. 24 62.00N 35.30E
Ongerup Australia 63 33.53S118.29E
Ongiyn Gol r. Mongolia 32 43.40N103.45E
Ongniud Qi China 32 43.00N118.43E
Ongole India 39 15.31N 80.04E
Onilahy r. Madagascar 57 23.34S 43.45E
Onitsha Nigeria 53 6.10N 6.47E
Onslow Australia 62 21.41S115.12E
Onslow B. U.S.A. 85 34.20N 77.20W
Onstwedde Neth. 14 53.04N 7.02E
Ontario d. Canada 76 51.00N 88.00W
Ontario Calif. U.S.A. 81 34.04N117.39W
Ontario Oreg. U.S.A. 80 44.02N116.58W
Ontario, L. Canada/U.S.A. 76 43.40N 78.00W
Ontonagon U.S.A. 84 46.52N 89.18W
Oodnadatta Australia 65 27.30S135.27E
Ooldea Australia 65 30.27S131.50E
Oostelijk-Flevoland f. Neth. 14 52.30N 5.40E
Oostende Belgium 14 51.13N 2.55E
Oosterhout Neth. 14 51.38N 4.50E
Oosterschelde est. Neth. 14 51.35N 3.57E
Oosthuizen Neth. 14 52.33N 5.00E
Oostmalle Belgium 14 51.18N 4.45E
Oost Vlaanderen d. Belgium 14 51.00N 3.45E
Oost Vlieland Neth. 14 53.18N 5.04E
Ootsa L. Canada 74 53.50N126.20W
Opaka Bulgaria 19 43.28N 26.10E
Opal Mexico 83 24.18N102.22W
Opala U.S.S.R. 29 51.58N156.30E
Opala Zaïre 54 0.42S 24.15E
Oparino U.S.S.R. 24 59.53N 48.10E
Opasatika Canada 76 49.30N 82.50W
Opasatika r. Canada 76 50.24N 82.26W
Opasquia Canada 75 53.16N 93.34W
Opava Czech. 21 49.56N 17.54E
Opelousas U.S.A. 83 30.32N 92.05W
Opheim U.S.A. 80 48.51N106.24W
Opinaca r. Canada 76 52.20N 78.00W
Opinnagau r. Canada 76 54.12N 82.21W
Opiscotéo, Lac l. Canada 77 53.10N 68.10W
Opochka U.S.S.R. 24 56.41N 28.42E
Opole Poland 21 50.40N 17.56E
Oporto see Porto Portugal 16
Opotiki New Zealand 60 38.00S177.18E
Opp U.S.A. 85 31.16N 86.18W
Oppdal Norway 22 62.36N 9.41E
Oppland d. Norway 23 61.30N 9.00E
Opportunity U.S.A. 80 47.39N117.15W
Opthalmia Range mts. Australia 62 23.25S120.00E
Opunake New Zealand 60 39.27S173.51E
Ora Italy 15 46.21N 11.18E
Ora Banda Australia 63 30.27S121.04E
Oradea Romania 21 47.03N 21.55E
Öraefajökull mtn. Iceland 22 64.02N 16.39W
Orai India 41 25.59N 79.28E
Oran Algeria 50 35.42N 0.38W
Orán Argentina 92 23.07S 64.16W
Orange Australia 67 33.19S149.10E
Orange France 17 44.08N 4.48E
Orange r. R.S.A. 56 28.38S 16.38E
Orange Tex. U.S.A. 83 30.01N 93.44W
Orange, C. Brazil 91 4.25N 51.32W
Orangeburg U.S.A. 85 33.28N 80.53W
Orange Free State d. R.S.A. 56 28.00S 28.00E
Orangevale U.S.A. 80 38.41N121.13W
Orangeville Canada 76 43.55N 80.06W
Oranienburg E. Germany 20 52.45N 13.14E
Oranjefontein R.S.A. 56 23.27S 27.40E
Oranjemond Namibia 56 28.35S 16.26E
Orarak Sudan 49 6.15N 32.23E
Oras Phil. 37 12.09N125.22E
Orbetello Italy 18 42.27N 11.13E
Orbost Australia 67 37.42S148.30E
Örbyhus Sweden 23 60.14N 17.42E
Orchies France 14 50.28N 3.15E
Orchila i. Venezuela 87 11.52N 66.10W
Orco r. Italy 15 45.10N 7.52E
Ord r. Australia 62 15.30S128.30E
Ordu Turkey 42 41.00N 37.52E
Orduña Spain 16 43.00N 3.00W
Ordzhonikidze U.S.S.R. 25 43.02N 44.43E
Örebro Sweden 23 59.17N 15.13E
Örebro d. Sweden 23 59.30N 15.00E
Oregon d. U.S.A. 80 43.49N120.36W
Oregon City U.S.A. 80 45.21N122.36W
Öregrund Sweden 23 60.20N 18.26E
Orekhovo-Zuyevo U.S.S.R. 24 55.47N 39.00E
Orel U.S.S.R. 24 52.58N 36.04E
Orem U.S.A. 80 40.19N111.42W
Orenburg U.S.S.R. 24 51.50N 55.00E
Orense Spain 16 42.20N 7.52W
Oressa r. U.S.S.R. 21 52.33N 28.45E
Orestiás Greece 19 41.30N 26.33E
Orfanoú, Kólpos g. Greece 19 40.40N 24.00E
Orford U.S.A. 84 43.54N 72.10W
Orford, Mt. Canada 77 45.18N 72.08W
Orfordness c. Australia 64 11.22S142.50E
Orford Ness c. U.K. 11 52.05N 1.36E
Orgeyev U.S.S.R. 21 47.24N 28.50E
Orgūn Afghan. 40 32.55N 69.10E
Orick U.S.A. 80 41.17N124.04W
Orient Australia 66 28.10S142.50E
Oriental, Cordillera mts. Bolivia 92 17.00S 65.00W
Oriental, Cordillera mts. Colombia 90 5.00N 74.30W
Origny France 15 49.54N 3.30E
Orihuela Spain 16 38.05N 0.56W
Orillia Canada 76 44.37N 79.25W
Orimattila Finland 23 60.48N 25.45E
Orinduik Guyana 90 4.42N 60.01W
Orinoco r. Venezuela 90 9.00N 61.30W
Orinoco, Delta del f. Venezuela 90 9.00N 61.00W
Orissa d. India 41 20.20N 84.00E
Oristano Italy 18 39.53N 8.36E
Oristano, Golfo di g. Italy 18 39.50N 8.30E
Orizaba Mexico 86 18.51N 97.08W
Orkanger Norway 22 63.17N 9.52E
Orkney Is. d. U.K. 12 59.00N 3.00W
Orlândia Brazil 94 20.55S 47.54W
Orlando U.S.A. 85 28.33N 81.21W
Orléans France 15 47.54N 1.54E
Orléans Canada 77 45.28N 75.31W
Orléans, Canal d' France 15 47.54N 1.55E
Ormāra Pakistan 40 25.12N 64.38E
Ormāra, Rās c. Pakistan 40 25.09N 64.35E
Ormoc Phil. 37 11.00N124.37E
Ormond New Zealand 60 38.35S177.58E
Ormskirk U.K. 10 53.35N 2.53W
Orne d. France 15 48.40N 0.05E
Orne r. France 15 49.17N 0.10W
Örnsköldsvik Sweden 22 63.17N 18.50E
Orobie, Alpi mts. Italy 15 46.03N 10.00E
Orocué Colombia 90 4.48N 71.20W
Orodara U. Volta 52 11.00N 4.54W
Orogrande U.S.A. 81 32.23N106.28W
Orohena mtn. Tahiti 69 17.37S149.28W
Oromocto Canada 77 45.51N 66.29W
Oron Israel 44 30.55N 35.01E
Oron Nigeria 53 4.49N 8.15E
Orona i. Kiribati 68 4.29S172.10W
Orono Canada 76 43.59N 78.37W
Orono U.S.A. 84 44.53N 68.40W
Orosei Italy 18 40.23N 9.40E
Orosei, Golfo di g. Italy 18 40.15N 9.45E
Orosháza Hungary 21 46.34N 20.40E
Orote Pen. Guam 68 13.26N144.38E
Orotukan U.S.S.R. 29 62.16N151.43E
Oroville Calif. U.S.A. 80 39.31N121.33W
Oroville Wash. U.S.A. 80 48.56N119.26W
Orroroo Australia 66 32.46S138.39E
Orsa Sweden 23 61.07N 14.37E
Orsha U.S.S.R. 24 54.30N 30.23E
Orsières Switz. 15 46.02N 7.09E
Orsk U.S.S.R. 24 51.13N 58.35E
Orșova Romania 21 44.42N 22.22E
Orta Nova Italy 18 41.19N 15.42E
Orthez France 17 43.29N 0.46W
Ortigueira Spain 16 43.41N 7.51W
Ortona Italy 18 42.21N 14.24E
Ortonville U.S.A. 82 45.18N 96.28W
Oruro Bolivia 92 17.59S 67.09W
Oruro d. Bolivia 92 18.00S 72.30W
Orūzgān Afghan. 40 32.56N 66.38E
Orūzgān d. Afghan. 40 33.40N 66.00E
Oryakhovo Bulgaria 19 43.42N 23.58E
Orzinuovi Italy 15 45.24N 9.55E
Os Norway 22 62.31N 11.11E
Osa, Península de pen. Costa Rica 87 8.20N 83.30W
Osage r. U.S.A. 79 38.35N 91.57W
Osage Iowa U.S.A. 82 43.17N 92.49W
Osage Wyo. U.S.A. 80 43.59N104.25W
Ōsaka Japan 35 34.40N135.30E
Ōsaka d. Japan 35 34.24N135.25E
Ōsaka-wan b. Japan 35 34.30N135.18E
Osborne U.S.A. 82 39.26N 98.42W
Osby Sweden 23 56.22N 13.59E
Osceola Iowa U.S.A. 82 41.02N 93.46W
Osceola Mo. U.S.A. 83 38.03N 93.42W
Osen Norway 22 64.18N 10.32E
Osh U.S.S.R. 28 40.37N 72.49E
Oshawa Canada 76 43.53N 78.51W
Ō shima i. Tosan Japan 35 34.43N139.24E
Oshkosh Nebr. U.S.A. 82 41.24N102.21W
Oshmyany U.S.S.R. 21 54.22N 25.52E
Oshnovīyeh Iran 43 37.03N 45.05E
Oshogbo Nigeria 53 7.50N 4.35E
Oshtorān, Kūh mtn. Iran 43 33.18N 49.15E
Oshvor U.S.S.R. 24 66.59N 62.59E
Oshwe Zaïre 54 3.27S 19.32E
Osiān India 40 26.43N 72.55E
Osijek Yugo. 19 45.35N 18.43E
Osipovichi U.S.S.R. 21 53.19N 28.36E
Oskaloosa U.S.A. 82 41.18N 92.39W
Oskarshamn Sweden 23 57.16N 16.26E
Oskol r. U.S.S.R. 25 49.08N 37.10E
Oslo Norway 23 59.56N 10.45E
Oslofjorden est. Norway 23 59.20N 10.35E
Osmancik Turkey 42 40.58N 34.50E
Osmaniye Turkey 42 37.04N 36.15E
Osnabrück W. Germany 14 52.17N 8.03E
Osorno Chile 93 40.35S 73.14W
Osorno Spain 16 42.24N 4.22W
Osöyra Norway 23 60.11N 5.30E
Osprey Reef Australia 64 13.55S146.38E
Oss Neth. 14 51.46N 5.31E
Ossa mtn. Greece 19 39.47N 22.41E
Ossa, Mt. Australia 65 41.52S146.04E
Ossabaw I. U.S.A. 85 31.47N 81.06W
Osse r. Nigeria 53 5.55N 5.15E
Ossining U.S.A. 85 41.10N 73.52W
Ossokmanuan L. Canada 77 53.25N 65.00W
Ostashkov U.S.S.R. 24 57.09N 33.10E
Ost-Berlin d. E. Germany 20 52.30N 13.25E
Ostend see Oostende Belgium 14
Oster U.S.S.R. 21 50.55N 30.53E
Oster r. U.S.S.R. 21 53.47N 31.46E
Österdal r. Sweden 23 61.03N 14.30E
Österdalen f. Norway 23 61.15N 11.10E
Östergötland d. Sweden 23 58.25N 15.35E
Österö i. Faroe Is. 8 62.16N 6.54W
Osteröy i. Norway 23 60.33N 5.35E
Östersund Sweden 22 63.10N 14.40E
Östfold d. Norway 23 59.20N 11.10E
Ostfriesische Inseln is. W. Germany 14 53.45N 7.00E
Östhammar Sweden 23 60.16N 18.22E
Ostrava Czech. 21 49.50N 18.15E
Ostróda Poland 21 53.43N 19.59E
Ostrog U.S.S.R. 21 50.20N 26.29E
Ostrołeka Poland 21 53.06N 21.34E
Ostrov U.S.S.R. 24 57.22N 28.22E
Ostrowiec-Świetokrzyski Poland 21 50.57N 21.23E
Ostrów Mazowiecka Poland 21 52.50N 21.51E
Ostrów Wielkopolski Poland 21 51.39N 17.49E
Ostuni Italy 19 40.44N 17.35E
Osūm r. Bulgaria 19 43.41N 24.51E
Ōsumi shotō is. Japan 31 30.30N131.00E
Osuna Spain 16 37.14N 5.06W
Oswego U.S.A. 84 43.27N 76.31W
Oswestry U.K. 10 52.52N 3.03W
Otago d. New Zealand 60 45.10S169.20E
Otago Pen. New Zealand 60 45.48S170.45E
Otaki New Zealand 60 40.45S175.08E
Otaru Japan 31 43.14N140.59E
Otavalo Ecuador 90 0.14N 78.16W
Otavi Namibia 56 19.37S 17.21E
Otelec Romania 21 45.36N 20.50E
Otematata New Zealand 60 44.37S170.11E
Oti r. Ghana 52 8.43N 0.10E
Otira New Zealand 60 42.51S171.33E
Otish, Monts mts. Canada 77 52.22N 70.30W
Otisville U.S.A. 85 41.28N 74.32W
Otiwarongo Namibia 56 20.30S 16.39E
Otjiwero Namibia 56 17.59S 13.22E
Otju Namibia 56 18.15S 13.18E
Otočac Yugo. 20 44.52N 15.14E
Otog Qi China 32 39.05N107.59E
Otosquen Canada 75 53.17N102.01W
Otra r. Norway 23 58.09N 8.00E
Otradnyy U.S.S.R. 24 53.26N 51.30E
Otranto Italy 19 40.09N 18.30E
Otranto, Str. of Med. Sea 19 40.10N 19.00E
Otrokovice Czech. 21 49.13N 17.31E
Otsego U.S.A. 84 42.26N 85.42W
Otsego Lake town U.S.A. 84 44.55N 84.41W
Ōtsu Japan 35 35.02N135.52E
Ōtsuki Japan 35 35.36N138.57E
Otta Norway 23 61.46N 9.32E
Ottawa Canada 77 45.25N 75.43W
Ottawa r. Canada 76 45.23N 73.55W
Ottawa Ill. U.S.A. 82 41.21N 88.51W
Ottawa Kans. U.S.A. 82 38.37N 95.16W
Ottawa Is. Canada 73 59.50N 80.00W
Otter r. U.K. 11 50.38N 3.19W
Otterbäcken Sweden 23 58.57N 14.02E
Otterburn U.K. 10 55.14N 2.10W
Otter L. Canada 75 55.35N104.39W
Otterndorf W. Germany 20 53.48N 8.53E
Otteröy i. Norway 22 62.45N 6.50E
Ottosdal R.S.A. 56 26.48S 26.00E
Ottumwa U.S.A. 82 41.01N 92.25W
Oturkpo Nigeria 53 7.13N 8.10E
Otway, C. Australia 66 38.51S143.34E
Ou r. Laos 34 20.03N102.19E
Ouachita r. U.S.A. 83 31.38N 91.49W
Ouachita, L. U.S.A. 83 34.40N 93.25W
Ouachita Mts. U.S.A. 83 34.40N 94.25W
Ouada, Djebel mtn. C.A.R. 49 8.56N 23.26E
Ouadane Mauritania 50 20.56N 11.37W
Ouadda C.A.R. 49 8.04N 22.24E
Ouaddaï d. Chad 49 13.00N 21.00E
Ouagadougou U. Volta 52 12.20N 1.40W
Ouahigouya U. Volta 52 13.31N 2.21W
Ouaka d. C.A.R. 49 6.00N 21.00E
Oualâta Mauritania 50 17.18N 7.02W
Ouallam Niger 53 14.23N 2.09E
Ouallene Algeria 50 24.35N 1.17E
Ouanda Djallé C.A.R. 49 8.54N 22.48E
Ouarane f. Mauritania 50 21.00N 9.30W
Ouararda, Passe de pass Mauritania 50 21.01N 13.03W
Ouareau r. Canada 77 45.56N 73.25W
Ouargla Algeria 51 31.57N 5.20E
Ouarra r. C.A.R. 49 5.05N 24.26E
Ouarzazate Morocco 50 30.57N 6.50W
Ouassouas well Mali 50 16.01N 1.26E
Ouddorp Neth. 14 51.49N 3.57E
Oudenaarde Belgium 14 50.50N 3.37E
Oudenbosch Neth. 14 51.35N 4.30E
Oude Rijn r. Neth. 14 52.14N 4.26E
Oudon r. France 15 47.47N 1.02W
Oudtshoorn R.S.A. 56 33.35S 22.11E
Oued-Zem Morocco 50 32.55N 6.30W
Ouellé Ivory Coast 52 7.26N 4.01W
Ouenza Algeria 51 35.57N 8.07E
Ouessant, Île d' i. France 17 48.28N 5.05W
Ouesso Congo 54 1.38N 16.03E
Ouezzane Morocco 50 34.52N 5.35W
Oughter, Lough Rep. of Ire. 13 54.01N 7.28W
Ouham r. Chad 53 9.15N 18.13E
Ouimet Canada 76 48.43N 88.35W
Ouistreham France 15 49.17N 0.15W
Oujda Morocco 50 34.41N 1.45W
Oulu Finland 22 65.01N 25.28E
Oulu d. Finland 22 65.00N 27.00E
Oulu r. Finland 22 65.01N 25.25E
Oulujärvi l. Finland 22 64.20N 27.15E
Oum Chalouba Chad 51 15.48N 20.46E
Oumé Ivory Coast 52 6.25N 5.23W
Oum er Rbia, Oued r. Morocco 50 33.19N 8.21W
Oumm ed Droûs Guebli, Sebkhet f. Mauritania 50 24.03N 11.45W
Oumm ed Droûs Telli, Sebkhet f. Mauritania 50 24.20N 11.30W
Ounas r. Finland 22 66.30N 25.45E
Oundle U.K. 11 52.28N 0.28W
Ounianga Kébir Chad 51 19.04N 20.29E
Our r. Lux. 14 49.53N 6.16E
Ouray U.S.A. 80 40.06N109.40W
Ourcq r. France 15 49.01N 3.01E
Ouri Chad 51 21.34N 19.13E
Ourinhos Brazil 94 23.00S 49.54W
Ouro Fino Brazil 94 22.16S 46.25W
Ouro Prêto Brazil 94 20.54S 43.30W
Ourthe r. Belgium 14 50.38N 5.36E
Ouse r. Humber. U.K. 10 53.41N 0.42W
Outardes, Rivière aux r. Canada 77 49.04N 68.25W
Outer Hebrides is. U.K. 12 57.40N 7.35W
Outjo Namibia 56 20.07S 16.10E
Outlook U.S.A. 80 48.53N104.47W
Ouyen Australia 66 35.06S142.22E
Ouzouer-le-Marché France 15 47.55N 1.32E
Ouzzal, Oued I-n- wadi Algeria 51 20.54N 2.28E
Ovalle Chile 92 30.36S 71.12W
Ovamboland f. Namibia 56 17.45S 16.00E
Ovar Portugal 16 40.52N 8.38W
Ovens r. Australia 67 36.20S146.18E
Overath W. Germany 14 50.56N 7.18E
Overflakkee i. Neth. 14 51.45N 4.08E
Overijssel d. Neth. 14 52.25N 6.30E
Överkalix Sweden 22 66.21N 22.56E
Overland Park town U.S.A. 82 38.59N 94.40W
Overton U.S.A. 81 36.33N114.27W
Övertorneå Sweden 22 66.23N 23.40E
Ovidiopol U.S.S.R. 21 46.18N 30.28E
Oviedo Spain 16 43.21N 5.50W
Ovinishche U.S.S.R. 24 58.20N 37.00E
Övörhangay d. Mongolia 32 45.00N103.00E
Ovruch U.S.S.R. 21 51.20N 28.50E
Owaka New Zealand 60 46.27S169.40E
Owando Congo 54 0.30S 15.48E
Owatonna U.S.A. 82 44.06N 93.10W
Owbeh Afghan. 40 34.22N 63.10E
Owel, Lough Rep. of Ire. 13 53.34N 7.24W
Owen Falls Dam Uganda 55 0.30N 33.07E
Owensboro U.S.A. 85 37.46N 87.07W
Owens L. U.S.A. 81 36.25N117.56W
Owen Sound town Canada 76 44.34N 80.56W
Owen Stanley Range mts. P.N.G. 64 9.30S148.00E
Owerri Nigeria 53 5.29N 7.02E
Owl r. Canada 75 57.51N 92.44W
Owo Nigeria 53 7.10N 5.39E
Owosso U.S.A. 84 43.00N 84.11W
Owyhee r. U.S.A. 80 43.46N117.02W
Oxelösund Sweden 23 58.40N 17.06E
Oxford U.K. 11 51.45N 1.15W
Oxford Md. U.S.A. 85 38.42N 76.10W
Oxford Penn. U.S.A. 85 39.47N 75.59W
Oxfordshire d. U.K. 11 51.46N 1.10W
Oxley Australia 66 34.11S144.10E
Oxnard U.S.A. 81 34.12N119.11W
Oyapock r. Guiana 91 4.10N 51.40W
Oyem Gabon 54 1.34N 11.31E
Oyen Canada 75 51.22N110.28W
Öyer Norway 23 61.12N 10.22E
Öyeren l. Norway 23 59.48N 11.14E
Oykel r. U.K. 12 57.53N 4.21W
Oymyakon U.S.S.R. 29 63.30N142.44E
Oyo Nigeria 53 7.50N 3.55E
Oyo d. Nigeria 53 8.10N 3.40E
Oyonnax France 17 46.15N 5.40E
Ozamiz Phil. 37 8.09N123.59E
Ozarichi U.S.S.R. 21 52.28N 29.12E
Ozark Ala. U.S.A. 85 31.27N 85.40W
Ozark Ark. U.S.A. 83 35.29N 93.50W
Ozark Mo. U.S.A. 83 37.01N 93.12W
Ozark Plateau U.S.A. 83 37.00N 93.00W
Ózd Hungary 21 48.14N 20.18E
Ozernoye U.S.S.R. 24 51.45N 51.29E
Ozersk U.S.S.R. 21 54.26N 22.00E
Ozinki U.S.S.R. 25 51.11N 49.43E
Ozona U.S.A. 83 30.43N101.12W

P

Paamiut see Frederikshåb Greenland 73
Pa-an Burma 34 16.51N 97.37E
Paarl R.S.A. 56 33.44S 18.58E
Pabianice Poland 21 51.40N 19.22E
Pābna Bangla. 41 24.00N 89.15E
Pacaraima, Sierra mts. Venezuela 90 4.00N 62.30W
Pacasmayo Peru 90 7.27S 79.33W
Pachmarhi India 41 22.28N 78.26E
Pāchora India 40 20.40N 75.21E
Pachuca Mexico 86 20.10N 98.44W
Pacific-Antarctic Basin Pacific Oc. 69 58.00S 98.00W
Pacific-Antarctic Ridge Pacific Oc. 69 57.00S145.00W
Pacific Ocean 69
Pacitan Indonesia 37 8.12S111.05E
Packwood U.S.A. 80 46.36N121.40W
Pacy-sur-Eure France 15 49.01N 1.23E
Padam Jammu & Kashmir 40 33.28N 76.53E
Padampur India 41 20.59N 83.04E
Padang Indonesia 36 0.55S100.21E
Padangpanjang Indonesia 36 0.30S100.26E
Padangsidempuan Indonesia 36 1.20N 99.11E
Padany U.S.S.R. 24 63.12N 33.20E
Padauari r. Brazil 90 0.15S 64.05W
Paderborn W. Germany 20 51.43N 8.44E
Padilla Bolivia 92 19.19S 64.20W
Padlei Canada 75 62.10N 97.05W
Padloping Island town Canada 73 67.00N 62.50W
Padova Italy 15 45.27N 11.52E
Pādra India 40 22.14N 73.05E
Padrauna India 41 26.55N 83.59E
Padre I. U.S.A. 83 27.00N 97.15W
Padstow U.K. 11 50.33N 4.57W
Padthaway Australia 66 36.37S140.28E
Padua see Padova Italy 15
Paducah U.S.A. 83 37.05N 88.36W
Paeroa New Zealand 60 37.23S175.41E
Pafúri Mozambique 57 22.27S 31.21E
Pag i. Yugo. 20 44.28N 15.00E
Pagadian Phil. 37 7.50N123.30E
Pagai Selatan i. Indonesia 36 3.00S100.18E
Pagai Utara i. Indonesia 36 2.42S100.05E
Pagan Burma 34 21.07N 94.53E
Pagan i. Mariana Is. 37 18.08N145.46E
Page U.S.A. 80 36.57N111.27W
Pager r. Uganda 55 3.05N 32.28E
Paghmān Afghan. 40 34.36N 68.57E
Pago Pago Samoa 68 14.16S170.42W
Pagosa Springs town U.S.A. 80 37.16N107.01W
Pagri China 41 27.45N 89.10E
Paguchi L. Canada 76 49.38N 91.40W
Pagwa River town Canada 76 50.02N 85.14W
Pahala Hawaii U.S.A. 78 19.12N155.28W
Pahiatua New Zealand 60 40.26S175.49E
Pahlavī Dezh Iran 43 35.51N 46.02E
Paible U.K. 12 57.35N 7.27W
Paide U.S.S.R. 23 58.54N 25.33E
Paihia New Zealand 60 35.16S174.05E
Päijänne l. Finland 23 61.35N 25.30E
Paikü Co l. China 41 28.48N 85.36E
Paimboeuf France 17 47.14N 2.01W
Painan Indonesia 36 1.21S100.34E
Painesville U.S.A. 84 41.43N 81.15W
Pains Brazil 94 20.23S 45.38W
Paintsville U.S.A. 85 37.49N 82.48W
Paisley U.K. 12 55.50N 4.26W
Paiton Indonesia 37 7.42S113.30E
Pajala Sweden 22 67.11N 23.22E
Pajule Uganda 55 2.58N 32.53E
Pakanbaru Indonesia 36 0.33N101.20E
Pakaraima Mts. Guyana 90 5.00N 60.00W
Pakaur India 41 24.38N 87.51E
Paki Nigeria 53 11.33N 8.08E
Pakistan Asia 40 29.00N 67.00E
Pakokku Burma 34 21.20N 95.10E
Pākpattan Pakistan 40 30.21N 73.24E
Paks Hungary 21 46.39N 18.53E
Paktīā d. Afghan. 40 33.25N 69.30E
Pakwach Uganda 55 2.27N 31.18E
Pakxé Laos 34 15.07N105.47E

Peter Pond L. to Portland

Peter Pond L. Canada 75 55.55N108.44W
Petersburg Alas. U.S.A. 74 56.49N132.58W
Petersburg Va. U.S.A. 85 37.14N 77.24W
Petersburg W.Va. U.S.A. 84 39.00N 79.07W
Petersfield U.K. 11 51.00N 0.56W
Petitot *r.* Canada 74 60.14N123.29W
Petit St. Bernard, Col du *pass* France / Italy 15 45.40N 6.53E
Petitsikapau L. Canada 77 54.45N 66.25W
Petlād India 40 22.30N 72.45E
Petoskey U.S.A. 84 45.22N 84.59W
Petra *ruins* Jordan 44 30.19N 35.26E
Petrich Bulgaria 19 41.25N 23.13E
Petrikov U.S.S.R. 21 52.09N 28.30E
Petrodvorets U.S.S.R. 24 59.50N 29.57E
Petrolina Brazil 91 9.22S 40.30W
Petropavlovsk U.S.S.R. 28 54.53N 69.13E
Petropavlovsk Kamchatskiy U.S.S.R. 29 53.03N158.43E
Petrópolis Brazil 94 22.30S 43.06W
Petroşani Romania 21 45.25N 23.22E
Petrovaradin Yugo. 21 45.16N 19.55E
Petrovsk U.S.S.R. 24 52.20N 45.24E
Petrovsk Zabaykal'skiy U.S.S.R. 29 51.20N108.55E
Petrozavodsk U.S.S.R. 24 61.46N 34.19E
Petrus Steyn R.S.A. 56 27.38S 28.08E
Peureulak Indonesia 36 4.48N 97.45E
Pevek U.S.S.R. 29 69.41N170.19E
Pézenas France 17 43.28N 3.25E
Pezinok Czech. 21 48.18N 17.17E
Pezmog U.S.S.R. 24 61.50N 51.45E
Pezu Pakistan 40 32.19N 70.44E
Pfaffenhofen W. Germany 20 48.31N 11.30E
Pfalzel W. Germany 14 49.47N 6.41E
Pforzheim W. Germany 20 48.53N 8.41E
Phagwāra India 40 31.13N 75.47E
Phalodi India 40 27.08N 72.22E
Phangan, Ko *i.* Thailand 36 9.50N100.00E
Phangnga Thailand 34 8.29N 98.31E
Phan Rang Vietnam 34 11.34N109.00E
Phan Thiet Vietnam 34 11.00N108.06E
Pharenda India 41 27.06N 83.17E
Phariāro Pakistan 40 27.12N 68.59E
Phat Diem Vietnam 33 20.06N106.07E
Phatthalung Thailand 34 7.38N100.04E
Phelps L. Canada 75 59.15N103.15W
Phenix City U.S.A. 85 32.28N 85.01W
Phet Buri Thailand 34 13.00N 99.58E
Philadelphia Miss. U.S.A. 83 32.46N 89.07W
Philadelphia Penn. U.S.A. 85 39.57N 75.07W
Philippeville Belgium 14 50.12N 4.32E
Philippines Asia 37 13.00N123.00E
Philippine Sea Pacific Oc. 68 18.00N135.00E
Philippine Trench Pacific Oc. 37 8.45N127.20E
Philipstown R.S.A. 56 30.25S 24.26E
Phillip U.S.A. 82 44.02N101.40W
Phillip I. Australia 67 38.29S145.14E
Phillips *r.* Australia 63 33.55S120.01E
Phillips Maine U.S.A. 84 44.49N 70.21W
Phillips Wisc. U.S.A. 82 45.41N 90.24W
Phillipsburg Kans. U.S.A. 82 39.45N 99.19W
Phillipsburg N.J. U.S.A. 85 40.42N 75.12W
Phillipson, L. Australia 66 29.28S134.28E
Phnom Penh *see* Phnum Pénh Kampuchea 34
Phnum Pénh Kampuchea 34 11.35N104.55E
Phoenix Ariz. U.S.A. 81 33.27N112.05W
Phoenix Is. Kiribati 68 4.00S172.00W
Phoenixville Penn. U.S.A. 85 40.08N 75.31W
Phon Thailand 34 15.50N102.35E
Phôngsali Laos 34 21.40N102.11E
Phou Loi *mtn.* Laos 34 20.16N103.18E
Phu Huu Vietnam 33 19.00N105.35E
Phukao Miang *mtn.* Thailand 39 16.50N101.00E
Phuket Thailand 34 7.55N 98.23E
Phuket, Ko *i.* Thailand 34 8.10N 98.20E
Phu Ly Vietnam 33 20.30N105.58E
Phumi Chuuk Vietnam 34 10.50N104.28E
Phumi Sâmraông Kampuchea 34 14.12N103.31E
Phu Quoc *i.* Kampuchea 34 10.20N104.00E
Phu Tho Vietnam 34 21.23N105.13E
Phu Vinh Vietnam 34 9.57N106.20E
Piacá Brazil 91 7.42S 47.18W
Piacenza Italy 15 45.03N 9.42E
Pian *r.* Australia 67 30.03S148.18E
Piana France 17 42.14N 8.38E
Piangil Australia 66 35.04S143.20E
Pianoro Italy 15 44.22N 11.20E
Pianosa *i.* Italy 18 42.35N 10.05E
Piatra-Neamţ Romania 21 46.56N 26.22E
Piauí *d.* Brazil 91 7.45S 42.30W
Piauí *r.* Brazil 91 6.14S 42.51W
Piave *r.* Italy 15 45.33N 12.45E
Piawaning Australia 63 30.51S116.22E
Pibor *r.* Sudan 49 8.26N 33.13E
Pibor Post Sudan 49 6.48N 33.08E
Pic *r.* Canada 76 48.38N 86.25W
Picardie *d.* France 14 49.47N 3.12E
Pickering U.K. 10 54.15N 0.46W
Pickle Crow Canada 76 51.30N 90.04W
Pickwick L. *resr.* U.S.A. 83 34.55N 88.10W
Picola Australia 67 35.59S145.06E
Picos Brazil 91 7.05S 41.28W
Picquigny France 15 49.57N 2.09E
Picton Australia 67 34.12S150.35E
Picton Canada 76 44.00N 77.08W
Picton New Zealand 60 41.17S174.02E
Picún Leufú Argentina 93 39.30S 69.15W
Pidálion, Akrotírion *c.* Cyprus 44 34.56N 34.05E
Pidarak Pakistan 40 25.51N 63.14E
Piedecuesta Colombia 90 6.59N 73.03W
Piedmont U.S.A. 85 33.55N 85.39W
Piedras *r.* Peru 90 12.30S 69.10W
Piedras, Punta *c.* Argentina 93 35.25S 57.07W
Piedras Negras Mexico 83 28.40N100.32W
Piedra Sola Uruguay 93 32.04S 56.21W
Pielavesi Finland 22 63.14N 26.45E
Pielinen *l.* Finland 24 63.20N 29.50E
Piemonte *d.* Italy 15 44.45N 8.00E
Pierce U.S.A. 80 46.29N115.48W
Pierre U.S.A. 82 44.22N100.21W
Pierreville Canada 77 46.04N 72.49W
Piesseville Australia 63 33.11S117.12E
Piešt'any Czech. 21 48.36N 17.50E
Pietarsaari Finland 22 63.40N 22.42E
Pietermaritzburg R.S.A. 56 29.36S 30.23E
Pietersburg R.S.A. 56 23.54S 29.27E
Pietrasanta Italy 15 43.57N 10.14E
Piet Retief R.S.A. 56 27.00S 30.49E
Pietrosu *mtn.* Romania 21 47.36N 24.38E
Pietrosul *mtn.* Romania 21 47.08N 25.11E
Pieve di Cadore Italy 15 46.26N 12.22E
Pigailoe *i.* Caroline Is. 37 8.08N146.40E
Pigna Italy 15 43.56N 7.40E
Pihtipudas Finland 22 63.23N 25.34E
Pikalevo U.S.S.R. 24 59.35N 34.07E
Pikangikum Canada 75 51.49N 94.00W
Pikes Peak *mtn.* U.S.A. 80 38.51N105.03W
Pikesville U.S.A. 85 39.25N 77.25W
Piketberg R.S.A. 56 32.54S 18.43E
Piketon U.S.A. 84 39.03N 83.01W
Pikeville U.S.A. 85 37.29N 82.33W
Pila Argentina 93 36.00S 58.10W
Piła Poland 20 53.09N 16.44E
Pilar Paraguay 94 26.52S 58.23W
Pilar do Sul Brazil 94 23.48S 47.45W
Pilcomayo *r.* Argentina / Paraguay 92 25.15S 57.43W
Pīlībhīt India 41 28.38N 79.48E
Pilica *r.* Poland 21 51.52N 21.17E
Pilliga Australia 67 30.23S148.55E
Pílos Greece 19 36.55N 21.40E
Pilot Point *town* U.S.A. 83 33.24N 96.58W
Pilsum W. Germany 14 53.29N 7.06E
Pimba Australia 66 31.18S136.47E
Pimenta Bueno Brazil 90 11.40S 61.14W
Pinang, Pulau *i.* Malaysia 36 5.30N100.10E
Pınarbaşi Turkey 42 38.43N 36.23E
Pinar del Río Cuba 87 22.24N 83.42W
Pincher Creek *town* Canada 74 49.30N113.57W
Píndhos Óros *mts.* Albania / Greece 19 39.40N 21.00E
Pindiga Nigeria 53 9.58N 10.53E
Pindi Gheb Pakistan 40 33.14N 72.16E
Pindwāra India 40 24.48N 73.04E
Pine *r.* Canada 74 56.08N120.41W
Pine, C. Canada 77 46.37N 53.30W
Pine Bluff *town* U.S.A. 83 34.13N 92.01W
Pine Bluffs *town* U.S.A. 80 41.11N104.04W
Pine City U.S.A. 82 45.50N 92.59W
Pine Creek *town* Australia 62 13.51S131.50E
Pinega U.S.S.R. 24 64.42N 43.28E
Pinega *r.* U.S.S.R. 24 63.51N 41.48E
Pinehouse L. Canada 75 55.32N106.35W
Pine Is. U.S.A. 85 26.35N 82.06W
Pine Point *town* Canada 74 60.50N114.28W
Pine River *town* Canada 75 51.45N100.40W
Pine River *town* U.S.A. 82 46.43N 94.24W
Pinerolo Italy 15 44.53N 7.21E
Pinetown R.S.A. 56 29.49S 30.52E
Pineville U.S.A. 83 31.19N 92.26W
Piney France 15 48.22N 4.20E
Ping *r.* Thailand 34 15.47N100.05E
Pingaring Australia 63 34.45S118.34E
Pingba China 33 26.25N106.15E
Pingdingshan Henan China 32 33.38N113.30E
Pingdingshan Liaoning China 32 41.28N124.45E
Pingdong Taiwan 33 22.44N120.30E
Pingelap *i.* Pacific Oc. 68 6.15N160.40E
Pingelly Australia 63 32.34S117.04E
Pingle China 33 24.38N110.38E
Pingliang China 32 35.21N107.12E
Pingluo China 32 38.56N106.34E
Pingnan China 33 23.33N110.23E
Pingrup Australia 63 33.33S118.30E
Pingtan *i.* China 33 25.36N119.48E
Pingwu China 32 32.25N104.36E
Pingxiang Guang. Zhuang. China 33 22.07N106.42E
Pingxiang Jiangxi China 33 27.36N113.48E
Pingyang China 33 27.40N120.33E
Pingyao China 32 37.12N112.08E
Pingyi China 32 35.30N117.36E
Pingyuan China 33 24.34N115.54E
Pinhal Brazil 94 22.10S 46.46W
Pinhel Portugal 16 40.46N 7.04W
Pini *i.* Indonesia 36 0.10N 98.30E
Piniós *r.* Greece 19 39.51N 22.37E
Pinjarra Australia 63 32.37S115.53E
Pinnaroo Australia 66 35.18S140.54E
Pinos, Isla de *i.* Cuba 87 21.40N 82.40W
Pinrang Indonesia 36 3.48S119.41E
Pins, Île des *i.* N. Cal. 68 22.37S167.30E
Pinsk U.S.S.R. 21 52.08N 26.01E
Pinto Argentina 92 29.09S 62.38W
Pinto Butte *mtn.* Canada 75 49.22N107.25W
Pinyug U.S.S.R. 24 60.10N 47.43E
Piombino Italy 18 42.56N 10.30E
Piorini, L. Brazil 90 3.34S 63.15W
Piotrków Trybunalski Poland 21 51.25N 19.42E
Piove di Sacco Italy 15 45.18N 12.02E
Pīpār India 40 26.23N 73.32E
Piparia India 41 22.45N 78.21E
Pipestone *r.* Ont. Canada 76 52.48N 89.35W
Pipestone *r.* Sask. Canada 75 58.40N105.45W
Pipestone U.S.A. 82 43.58N 96.10W
Pipinas Argentina 93 35.30S 57.19W
Piplān Pakistan 40 32.17N 71.21E
Pipmouacane, Résr. Canada 77 49.35N 70.30W
Piqua U.S.A. 84 40.08N 84.14W
Piracicaba Brazil 94 22.45S 47.40W
Piracicaba *r.* Brazil 94 22.35S 48.14W
Piracuruca Brazil 91 3.56S 41.42W
Piraeus *see* Piraiévs Greece 19
Piraiévs Greece 19 37.56N 23.38E
Piram I. India 40 21.36N 72.41E
Pirassununga Brazil 94 21.59S 47.25W
Pírgos Greece 19 37.42N 21.27E
Pirna E. Germany 20 50.58N 13.58E
Pirojpur Bangla. 41 22.34N 89.59E
Pirot Yugo. 19 43.10N 22.32E
Pīr Panjāl Range *mts.* Jammu & Kashmir 40 33.50N 74.30E
Piryatin U.S.S.R. 25 50.14N 32.31E
Pisa Italy 18 43.43N 10.24E
Pisciotta Italy 18 40.08N 15.12E
Pisco Peru 90 13.46S 76.12W
Písek Czech. 20 49.19N 14.10E
Pishan China 30 37.30N 78.20E
Pishin Pakistan 40 30.35N 67.00E
Pishin Lora *r.* Pakistan 40 29.09N 64.55E
Pistoia Italy 15 43.55N 10.54E
Pisuerga *r.* Spain 16 41.35N 5.40W
Pisz Poland 21 53.38N 21.49E
Pita Guinea 52 11.05N 12.15W
Pitalito Colombia 90 1.51N 76.01W
Pitarpunga, L. Australia 66 34.23S143.32E
Pitcairn I. Pacific Oc. 69 25.04S130.06W
Pite *r.* Sweden 22 65.14N 21.32E
Piteå Sweden 22 65.20N 21.30E
Piteşti Romania 21 44.52N 24.51E
Pithāpuram India 39 17.07N 82.16E
Pithiviers France 15 48.10N 2.15E
Pithoragarh India 41 29.35N 80.13E
Piti Guam 68 13.28N144.41E
Pitlochry U.K. 12 56.43N 3.45W
Pitt I. Canada 74 53.35N129.45W
Pittsburg Kans. U.S.A. 83 37.25N 94.42W
Pittsburg N.H. U.S.A. 84 45.03N 71.26W
Pittsburg Tex. U.S.A. 83 32.60N 94.58W
Pittsburgh U.S.A. 84 40.26N 80.00W
Pittsfield U.S.A. 84 42.27N 73.15W
Pittston U.S.A. 84 41.19N 75.47W
Pittsville U.S.A. 85 38.24N 75.52W
Pittville U.S.A. 80 41.03N121.20W
Piùí Brazil 94 20.28S 45.58W
Piura Peru 90 5.15S 80.38W
Piuthān Nepal 41 28.06N 82.54E
Placentia Canada 77 47.15N 53.58W
Placentia B. Canada 77 47.15N 54.30W
Plain Dealing U.S.A. 83 32.54N 93.42W
Plainfield N.J. U.S.A. 85 40.37N 74.26W
Plains U.S.A. 80 47.27N114.53W
Plainview U.S.A. 83 34.11N101.43W
Plampang Indonesia 36 8.48S117.48E
Planá Czech. 20 49.52N 12.44E
Plana Cays *is.* Bahamas 87 21.31N 72.14W
Plantagenet Canada 77 45.32N 75.00W
Plasencia Spain 16 40.02N 6.05W
Plassen Norway 23 61.08N 12.31E
Plaster Rock *town* Canada 77 46.54N 67.24W
Platani *r.* Italy 18 37.24N 13.15E
Plate, R. *est. see* La Plata, Río de Argentina / Uruguay 93
Plateau *d.* Nigeria 53 8.50N 9.00E
Platí, Ákra *c.* Greece 19 40.26N 23.59E
Platinum U.S.A. 72 59.00N161.50W
Plato Colombia 90 9.54N 74.46W
Platte *r.* U.S.A. 82 41.04N 95.53W
Platteville U.S.A. 82 42.44N 90.29W
Plattling W. Germany 20 48.47N 12.53E
Plattsburgh U.S.A. 84 44.42N 73.28W
Plauen E. Germany 20 50.29N 12.08E
Plavsk U.S.S.R. 24 53.40N 37.20E
Pleasantville U.S.A. 85 39.23N 74.32W
Pleasonton U.S.A. 83 28.58N 98.29W
Pleiku Vietnam 34 13.57N108.01E
Plenty, B. of New Zealand 60 37.40S176.50E
Plentywood U.S.A. 80 48.47N104.34W
Plesetsk U.S.S.R. 24 62.42N 40.21E
Pleshchenitsy U.S.S.R. 21 54.24N 27.52E
Pleszew Poland 21 51.54N 17.48E
Plétipi, Lac *l.* Canada 77 51.44N 70.06W
Pleven Bulgaria 19 43.25N 24.39E
Pljevlja Yugo. 19 43.22N 19.22E
Płock Poland 21 52.33N 19.43E
Ploieşti Romania 21 44.57N 26.02E
Plomb du Cantal *mtn.* France 17 45.04N 2.45E
Plombières France 17 47.58N 6.28E
Plön W. Germany 20 54.09N 10.25E
Plonge, Lac la *l.* Canada 75 55.05N107.15W
Płońsk Poland 21 52.38N 20.23E
Ploudalmézeau France 17 48.33N 4.39W
Plovdiv Bulgaria 19 42.09N 24.45E
Plumtree Zimbabwe 56 20.30S 27.50E
Plunkett Canada 75 51.56N105.29W
Plymouth U.K. 11 50.23N 4.09W
Plymouth Ind. U.S.A. 84 41.20N 86.19W
Plymouth Wisc. U.S.A. 82 43.44N 87.58W
Plzeň Czech. 20 49.45N 13.22E
Po *r.* Italy 15 44.51N 12.30E
Pô U. Volta 52 11.11N 1.10W
Pobé Benin 53 7.00N 2.56E
Pobeda, Gora *mtn.* U.S.S.R. 29 65.20N145.50E
Pobla de Segur Spain 16 42.15N 0.58E
Pocahontas Canada 74 53.15N118.00W
Pocahontas Ark. U.S.A. 83 36.16N 90.58W
Pocahontas Iowa U.S.A. 82 42.44N 94.40W
Pocatello U.S.A. 80 42.52N112.27W
Pocklington U.K. 10 53.56N 0.48W
Poços de Caldas Brazil 94 21.48S 46.33W
Poděbrady Czech. 20 50.08N 15.07E
Podgaytsy U.S.S.R. 21 49.19N 25.10E
Podkamennaya Tunguska U.S.S.R. 29 61.45N 90.13E
Podkamennaya Tunguska *r.* U.S.S.R. 29 61.40N 90.00E
Podolsk U.S.S.R. 24 55.23N 37.32E
Podor Senegal 52 16.35N 15.02W
Podporozhye U.S.S.R. 24 60.55N 34.02E
Pofadder R.S.A. 56 29.08S 19.22E
Pogrebishche U.S.S.R. 21 49.30N 29.15E
Poh Indonesia 37 1.00S122.50E
P'ohang S. Korea 31 36.00N129.26E
Poinsett, C. Antarctica 96 65.35S113.00E
Point Arena *f.* U.S.A. 80 38.55N123.41W
Pointe-à-Pitre Guadeloupe 87 16.14N 61.32W
Pointe aux Anglais *town* Canada 77 49.34N 67.10W
Pointe-aux-Trembles *town* Canada 77 45.39N 73.29W
Pointe-Claire Canada 77 45.26N 73.50W
Pointe Noire *town* Congo 54 4.46S 11.53E
Point Hope *town* U.S.A. 72 68.21N166.41W
Point Lookout *town* Australia 67 30.33S152.20E
Point Pleasant *town* N.J. U.S.A. 85 40.05N 74.04W
Point Pleasant *town* W.Va. U.S.A. 84 38.53N 82.07W
Poissy France 15 48.56N 2.03E
Poitiers France 17 46.35N 0.20E
Poitou-Charentes *d.* France 17 46.00N 0.00
Poix France 15 49.47N 2.00E
Poix-Terron France 15 49.39N 4.39E
Pokaran India 40 26.55N 71.55E
Pokataroo Australia 67 29.37S148.44E
Pokhara Nepal 41 28.12N 83.59E
Poko Zaïre 54 3.08N 26.51E
Pokoinu Rarotonga Cook Is. 68 21.12S159.50W
Polacca U.S.A. 81 35.50N110.23W
Pola de Lena Spain 16 43.10N 5.49W
Polān Iran 43 25.29N 61.15E
Poland Europe 21 52.30N 19.00E
Polatli Turkey 42 39.34N 32.08E
Polch W. Germany 14 50.18N 7.19E
Polda Australia 66 33.30S135.10E
Pole Zaïre 54 2.51S 23.12E
Polesye *f.* U.S.S.R. 21 52.15N 28.00E
Poli Cameroon 53 8.30N 13.15E
Policastro, Golfo di *g.* Italy 18 40.00N 15.35E
Poligny France 17 46.50N 5.42E
Pólis Cyprus 44 35.02N 32.26E
Políyiros Greece 19 40.23N 23.27E
Pollino *mtn.* Italy 18 39.53N 16.11E
Pollock Reef Australia 63 34.28S123.40E
Polnovat U.S.S.R. 28 63.47N 65.54E
Polonnoye U.S.S.R. 21 50.10N 27.30E
Polotsk U.S.S.R. 24 55.30N 28.43E
Polperro U.K. 11 50.19N 4.31W
Polson U.S.A. 80 47.41N114.09W
Poltava U.S.S.R. 25 49.35N 34.35E
Polunochnoye U.S.S.R. 24 60.52N 60.28E
Polyarnyy U.S.S.R. 24 69.14N 33.30E
Polynesia *is.* Pacific Oc. 68 4.00S165.00W
Pomarkku Finland 23 61.42N 22.00E
Pombal Brazil 91 6.45S 37.45W
Pombal Portugal 16 39.55N 8.38W
Pomene Mozambique 57 22.53S 35.33E
Pomeroy Wash. U.S.A. 80 46.28N117.36W
Pomona Namibia 56 27.09S 15.18E
Pomona U.S.A. 81 34.04N117.45W
Pompano Beach *town* U.S.A. 85 26.14N 80.07W
Pompey's Pillar *town* U.S.A. 80 45.59N107.56W
Ponape *i.* Pacific Oc. 68 6.55N158.15E
Ponca City U.S.A. 83 36.42N 97.05W
Ponce Puerto Rico 87 18.00N 66.40W
Pondicherry India 39 11.59N 79.50E
Pond Inlet *str.* Canada 73 72.30N 75.00W
Ponds, I. of Canada 77 53.24N 55.55W
Ponferrada Spain 16 42.32N 6.31W
Pongani P.N.G. 64 9.05S148.35E
Pongo *r.* Sudan 49 8.52N 27.40E
Pongola *r.* Mozambique 57 26.13S 32.38E
Ponnāni India 38 10.46N 75.54E
Ponnyadaung Range *mts.* Burma 34 22.30N 94.20E
Ponoka Canada 74 52.42N113.40W
Ponorogo Indonesia 37 7.51S111.30E
Ponoy U.S.S.R. 24 67.02N 41.03E
Ponoy *r.* U.S.S.R. 24 67.00N 41.10E
Ponta Grossa Brazil 94 25.00S 50.09W
Pont-à-Mousson France 17 48.55N 6.03E
Ponta Porã Brazil 94 22.27S 55.39W
Pont-Audemer France 15 49.21N 0.31E
Pontax *r.* Canada 76 51.30N 78.48W
Pont Canavese Italy 15 45.25N 7.36E
Pontchartrain, L. U.S.A. 83 30.10N 90.10W
Pont-d'Ain France 17 46.03N 5.20E
Pontedera Italy 18 43.40N 10.38E
Pontefract U.K. 10 53.42N 1.19W
Ponteix Canada 75 49.49N107.30W
Ponte Nova Brazil 94 20.25S 42.54W
Pontevedra Spain 16 42.25N 8.39W
Pontiac Ill. U.S.A. 82 40.54N 88.36W
Pontiac Mich. U.S.A. 84 42.39N 83.18W
Pontianak Indonesia 36 0.05S109.16E
Pontivy France 17 48.05N 3.00W
Pont l'Évêque France 15 49.18N 0.11E
Pontoise France 15 49.03N 2.05E
Pontorson France 15 48.33N 1.31W
Pontremoli Italy 15 44.22N 9.53E
Pontresina Switz. 15 46.28N 9.53E
Pontrilas U.K. 11 51.56N 2.53W
Pont-sur-Yonne France 15 48.17N 3.12E
Pontypool U.K. 11 51.42N 3.01W
Pontypridd U.K. 11 51.36N 3.21W
Ponziane, Isole *is.* Italy 18 40.56N 12.58E
Poochera Australia 66 32.42S134.52E
Poole U.K. 11 50.42N 2.02W
Pooncarie Australia 66 33.23S142.34E
Poopelloe, L. Australia 66 31.39S144.00E
Poopó, Lago de *l.* Bolivia 92 19.00S 67.00W
Popayán Colombia 90 2.27N 76.32W
Poperinge Belgium 14 50.51N 2.44E
Popes Creek *town* U.S.A. 85 38.09N 76.58W
Popilta Australia 66 33.15S141.49E
Popilta L. Australia 66 33.09S141.45E
Poplar *r.* Canada 75 53.00N 97.18W
Poplar U.S.A. 80 48.07N105.12W
Poplar Bluff *town* U.S.A. 83 36.45N 90.24W
Poplarville U.S.A. 83 30.51N 89.32W
Popocatépetl *mtn.* Mexico 86 19.02N 98.38W
Popokabaka Zaïre 54 5.41S 16.40E
Popondetta P.N.G. 64 8.45S148.15E
Poprad Czech. 21 49.03N 20.18E
Popricani Romania 21 47.18N 27.31E
Porāli *r.* Pakistan 40 25.30N 66.25E
Porbandar India 40 21.38N 69.36E
Por Chaman Afghan. 40 33.08N 63.51E
Porcher I. Canada 74 54.00N130.30W
Porcupine *r.* U.S.A. 72 66.25N145.20W
Porcupine Hills Canada 75 52.30N101.45W
Pordenone Italy 15 45.57N 12.39E
Pori Finland 23 61.29N 21.47E
Porirua New Zealand 60 41.08S174.50E
Porjus Sweden 22 66.57N 19.50E
Porkhov U.S.S.R. 24 57.43N 29.31E
Porkkala Finland 23 59.59N 24.26E
Porlamar Venezuela 90 11.01N 63.54W
Pornic France 17 47.07N 2.05W
Porog U.S.S.R. 24 63.50N 38.32E
Poronaysk U.S.S.R. 29 49.13N142.55E
Porosozero U.S.S.R. 24 62.45N 32.48E
Porretta Terme Italy 15 44.09N 10.59E
Porsangen *est.* Norway 22 70.58N 25.30E
Porsangerhalvöya *pen.* Norway 22 70.50N 25.00E
Porsgrunn Norway 23 59.09N 9.40E
Porsuk *r.* Turkey 42 39.41N 31.56E
Portachuela Bolivia 92 17.21S 63.24W
Port Adelaide Australia 66 34.52S138.30E
Portadown U.K. 13 54.25N 6.27W
Portaferry U.K. 13 54.23N 5.33W
Portage Wisc. U.S.A. 82 43.33N 89.28W
Portage la Prairie *town* Canada 75 49.57N 98.25W
Port Alberni Canada 74 49.14N124.48W
Port Albert Australia 67 38.09S146.40E
Portalegre Portugal 16 39.17N 7.25W
Portales U.S.A. 83 34.11N103.20W
Port Alfred R.S.A. 56 33.36S 26.52E
Port Alice Canada 74 50.25N127.25W
Port Angeles U.S.A. 80 48.07N123.27W
Port Antonio Jamaica 87 18.10N 76.27W
Port Arthur Australia 65 43.08S147.50E
Port Arthur U.S.A. 83 29.55N 93.55W
Port Augusta Australia 66 32.30S137.46E
Port au Port Canada 77 48.33N 58.45W
Port-au-Prince Haiti 87 18.33N 72.20W
Port Austin U.S.A. 84 44.04N 82.59W
Port Bergé Madagascar 57 15.33S 47.40E
Port Blair India 34 11.40N 92.40E
Port Bou Spain 16 42.25N 3.09E
Port Bouet Ivory Coast 52 5.14N 3.58W
Port Bradshaw *b.* Australia 64 12.30S136.42E
Port Broughton Australia 66 33.36S137.56E
Port Campbell Australia 66 38.37S143.04E
Port Canning India 41 22.18N 88.40E
Port Cartier Canada 77 50.01N 66.53W
Port Chalmers New Zealand 60 45.49S170.37E
Port Chester U.S.A. 85 41.00N 73.40W
Port Colborne Canada 76 42.53N 79.14W
Port Coquitlam Canada 74 49.20N122.45W
Port Credit Canada 76 43.33N 79.35W
Port Curtis Australia 64 23.50S151.13E
Port Dalhousie Canada 76 43.12N 79.16W
Port-de-Paix Haiti 87 19.57N 72.50W
Port Dover Canada 76 42.47N 80.12W
Port Edward R.S.A. 56 31.03S 30.13E
Portela Brazil 94 21.38S 41.59W
Port Elizabeth R.S.A. 56 33.57S 25.34E
Port Ellen U.K. 12 55.38N 6.12W
Port-en-Bessin France 15 49.21N 0.45W
Port Erin U.K. 10 54.05N 4.45W
Porter Landing Canada 74 58.46N130.05W
Porterville R.S.A. 56 33.01S 19.00E
Porterville U.S.A. 81 36.04N119.01W
Port Fairy Australia 66 38.23S142.17E
Port Gentil Gabon 54 0.40S 8.46E
Port Germein Australia 66 33.01S138.00E
Port Gibson U.S.A. 83 31.58N 90.58W
Portglenone U.K. 13 54.52N 6.30W
Port Harcourt Nigeria 53 4.43N 7.05E
Port Harrison *see* Inoucdjouac Canada 73
Port Hawkesbury Canada 77 45.37N 61.21W
Porthcawl U.K. 11 51.28N 3.42W
Port Hedland Australia 62 20.24S118.36E
Port Henry U.S.A. 84 44.03N 73.28W
Porthill U.S.A. 80 49.00N116.30W
Porthmadog U.K. 10 52.55N 4.08W
Port Hope Canada 76 43.57N 78.18W
Port Huron U.S.A. 84 42.59N 82.28W
Portimão Portugal 16 37.08N 8.32W
Port Isaac B. U.K. 11 50.36N 4.50W
Portiţei, Gura *f.* Romania 19 44.40N 29.00E
Port Jervis U.S.A. 85 41.22N 74.40W
Port Keats Australia 62 14.15S129.35E
Port Kenny Australia 66 33.09S134.42E
Portland N.S.W. Australia 67 33.20S150.00E
Portland Vic. Australia 66 38.21S141.38E
Portland Maine U.S.A. 84 43.39N 70.17W

Portland to **Qom**

Portland Oreg. U.S.A. **80** 45.33N122.36W
Portland Tex. U.S.A. **83** 27.53N 97.20W
Portland Pt. Ascension **95** 7.58S 14.26W
Port-la-Nouvelle France **17** 43.01N 3.03E
Port Laoise Rep. of Ire. **13** 53.03N 7.20W
Port Lavaca U.S.A. **83** 28.37N 96.38W
Port Lincoln Australia **66** 34.43S135.49E
Port Loko Sierra Leone **52** 8.50N 12.50W
Port MacDonnell Australia **66** 38.03S140.46E
Port Macquarie Australia **67** 31.28S152.25E
Port Maitland N.S. Canada **77** 43.59N 66.09W
Port Maitland Ont. Canada **76** 42.52N 79.34W
Portmarnock Rep. of Ire. **13** 53.25N 6.09W
Port Menier Canada **77** 49.49N 64.20W
Port Moresby P.N.G. **64** 9.30S147.07E
Port Musgrave *b.* Australia **64** 11.59S142.00E
Portnaguiran U.K. **12** 58.15N 6.10W
Port Neill Australia **66** 34.07S136.20E
Port Nelson Canada **75** 57.03N 92.36W
Port Nolloth R.S.A. **56** 29.16S 16.54E
Port Norris U.S.A. **85** 39.15N 75.02W
Port-Nouveau Québec Canada **73** 58.35N 65.59W
Porto Portugal **16** 41.09N 8.37W
Pôrto Alegre Brazil **94** 30.03S 51.10W
Porto Alexandre Angola **54** 15.55S 11.51E
Porto Amboim Angola **54** 10.45S 13.43E
Pôrto de Moz Brazil **91** 1.45S 52.13W
Porto Esperança Brazil **94** 19.36S 57.24W
Pôrto Feliz Brazil **94** 23.11S 47.32W
Portoferraio Italy **18** 42.49N 10.19E
Port of Ness U.K. **12** 58.30N 6.13W
Pôrto Franco Brazil **91** 6.21S 47.25W
Port of Spain Trinidad **87** 10.38N 61.31W
Porto Grande Brazil **91** 0.42N 51.24W
Portogruaro Italy **15** 45.47N 12.50E
Pörtom Finland **22** 62.42N 21.37E
Portomaggiore Italy **15** 44.42N 11.48E
Pôrto Mendes Brazil **94** 24.30S 54.20W
Porto Moniz Madeira Is. **95** 32.52N 17.12W
Pôrto Murtinho Brazil **94** 21.42S 57.52W
Porton U.K. **11** 51.08N 1.44W
Pôrto Nacional Brazil **91** 10.42S 48.25W
Porto-Novo Benin **53** 6.30N 2.47E
Porto San Giorgio Italy **18** 43.11N 13.48E
Porto Santo *i.* Madeira Is. **50** 33.04N 16.20W
Porto Tolle Italy **15** 44.56N 12.22E
Porto Torres Italy **18** 40.49N 8.24E
Pôrto Valter Brazil **90** 8.15S 72.45W
Porto Vecchio France **17** 41.35N 9.16E
Pôrto Velho Brazil **90** 8.45S 63.54W
Portoviejo Ecuador **90** 1.07S 80.28W
Portpatrick U.K. **12** 54.51N 5.07W
Port Phillip B. Australia **67** 38.05S144.50E
Port Pirie Australia **66** 33.11S138.01E
Port Radium Canada **72** 66.05N118.02W
Portree U.K. **12** 57.24N 6.12W
Port Renfrew Canada **74** 48.30N124.20W
Portrush U.K. **13** 55.12N 6.40W
Port Said *see* Būr Sa'īd Egypt **44**
Port St. Joe U.S.A. **85** 29.49N 85.19W
Port St. Louis France **17** 43.25N 4.40E
Port Saunders Canada **77** 50.39N 57.18W
Port Shepstone R.S.A. **56** 30.44S 30.27E
Port Simpson Canada **74** 54.32N130.25W
Portsmouth U.K. **11** 50.48N 1.06W
Portsmouth N.H. U.S.A. **84** 43.04N 70.46W
Portsmouth Ohio U.S.A. **84** 38.45N 82.59W
Portsmouth Va. U.S.A. **85** 36.50N 76.20W
Portsoy U.K. **12** 57.41N 2.41W
Port Stanley Canada **84** 42.40N 81.13W
Portstewart U.K. **13** 55.11N 6.43W
Port Sudan *see* Būr Sūdān Sudan **48**
Port Talbot U.K. **11** 51.35N 3.48W
Porttipahdan tekojärvi *resr.* Finland **22** 68.08N 26.40E
Port Townsend U.S.A. **80** 48.07N122.46W
Portugal Europe **16** 39.30N 8.05W
Portumna Rep. of Ire. **9** 53.06N 8.14W
Port Vendres France **17** 42.31N 3.06E
Port Victoria Australia **66** 34.30S137.30E
Port Wakefield Australia **66** 34.12S138.11E
Porvenir Chile **93** 53.18S 70.22W
Porz W. Germany **14** 50.53N 7.05E
Posada Italy **18** 40.38N 9.43E
Posadas Argentina **92** 27.25S 55.48W
Poschiavo Switz. **15** 46.18N 10.04E
Posht *r.* Iran **43** 29.09N 58.09E
Poso Indonesia **37** 1.23S120.45E
Posse Brazil **94** 14.05S 46.22W
Post U.S.A. **83** 33.12N101.23W
Postavy U.S.S.R. **24** 55.07N 26.50E
Poste-de-la-Baleine *town* Canada **76** 55.20N 77.40W
Poste Maurice Cortier Algeria **50** 22.18N 1.05E
Poste Weygand Algeria **50** 24.29N 0.40E
Postmasburg R.S.A. **56** 28.19S 23.03E
Postojna Yugo. **20** 45.47N 14.13E
Postoli U.S.S.R. **21** 52.30N 28.00E
Potchefstroom R.S.A. **56** 26.42S 27.05E
Poteau U.S.A. **83** 35.03N 94.37W
Potenza Italy **18** 40.40N 15.47E
Potgietersrus R.S.A. **56** 24.11S 29.00E
Poti *r.* Brazil **91** 5.01S 42.48W
Poti U.S.S.R. **25** 42.11N 41.41E
Potiskum Nigeria **53** 11.40N 11.03E
Potomac *r.* U.S.A. **85** 38.00N 76.18W
Potosí Bolivia **92** 19.35S 65.45W
Potosí *d.* Bolivia **92** 21.00S 67.00W
Potosi Cerro *mtn.* Mexico **83** 24.50N100.15W
Pototan Phil. **37** 10.54N122.38E
Potsdam E. Germany **20** 52.24N 13.04E
Potsdam *d.* E. Germany **20** 52.30N 12.45E
Potsdam U.S.A. **84** 44.40N 74.59W
Pottstown U.S.A. **85** 40.15N 75.38W
Pouancé France **15** 47.47N 1.11W
Poughkeepsie U.S.A. **85** 41.43N 73.56W
Pouso Alegre Brazil **94** 22.13S 45.49W
Pouté Senegal **50** 15.42N 14.10W
Poŭthisăt Kampuchea **34** 12.27N103.50E
Povenets U.S.S.R. **24** 62.52N 34.05E
Póvoa de Varzim Portugal **16** 41.22N 8.46W
Povorino U.S.S.R. **25** 51.12N 42.15E
Powder *r.* U.S.A. **80** 46.44N105.26W
Powder River *town* U.S.A. **80** 43.03N106.58W
Powell U.S.A. **80** 44.45N108.46W
Powell, L. U.S.A. **80** 37.25N110.45W
Powell Creek *town* Australia **62** 18.05S133.40E
Powell River *town* Canada **74** 49.22N124.31W
Powers U.S.A. **76** 45.42N 87.31W
Powers Lake *town* U.S.A. **82** 48.34N102.39W
Powys *d.* U.K. **11** 52.26N 3.26W
Poyang Hu *l.* China **33** 29.10N116.20E
Požarevac Yugo. **21** 44.38N 21.12E
Poza Rica de Hidalgo Mexico **86** 20.34N 97.26W
Poznań Poland **20** 52.25N 16.53E
Pozoblanco Spain **16** 38.23N 4.51W
Prachin Buri Thailand **34** 14.02N101.23E
Prachuap Khiri Khan Thailand **34** 11.50N 99.49E
Pradera Colombia **90** 3.23N 76.11W
Prades France **17** 42.38N 2.25E
Praestö Denmark **23** 55.07N 12.03E
Prague *see* Praha Czech. **20**
Praha Czech. **20** 50.05N 14.25E
Prainha Amazonas Brazil **90** 7.16S 60.23W
Prainha Para Brazil **91** 1.48S 53.29W
Prairie City U.S.A. **80** 44.28N118.43W
Prairie du Chien *town* U.S.A. **82** 43.03N 91.09W
Prairie Village U.S.A. **82** 39.01N 94.38W
Prang Ghana **52** 8.02N 0.58W
Pratāpgarh India **40** 24.02N 74.47E
Prato Italy **15** 43.52N 11.06E
Pratt U.S.A. **83** 37.39N 98.44W
Pravia Spain **16** 43.30N 6.12W
Predazzo Italy **15** 46.19N 11.36E
Pré-en-Pail France **15** 48.27N 0.12W
Preesall U.K. **10** 53.55N 2.58W
Pregel *r.* U.S.S.R. **21** 54.41N 20.22E
Premer Australia **67** 31.26S149.54E
Premier Canada **74** 56.04N129.56W
Prentice U.S.A. **82** 45.33N 90.17W
Prenzlau E. Germany **20** 53.19N 13.52E
Preparis *i.* Burma **34** 14.51N 93.38E
Přerov Czech. **21** 49.27N 17.27E
Prescott Ariz. U.S.A. **81** 34.33N112.28W
Prescott Ark. U.S.A. **83** 33.48N 93.23W
Presho U.S.A. **82** 43.54N100.04W
Presidencia Roque Sáenz Peña Argentina **92** 26.50S 60.30W
Presidente Epitácio Brazil **94** 21.56S 52.07W
Presidente Hermes Brazil **92** 11.17S 61.55W
Presidente Prudente Brazil **94** 22.09S 51.24W
Presidio U.S.A. **83** 29.33N104.23W
Prešov Czech. **21** 49.00N 21.15E
Prespa, L. Albania/Greece/Yugo. **19** 40.53N 21.02E
Presque Isle *town* Maine U.S.A. **84** 46.41N 68.01W
Prestea Ghana **52** 5.26N 2.07W
Presteigne U.K. **11** 52.17N 3.00W
Preston U.K. **10** 53.46N 2.42W
Preston Idaho U.S.A. **80** 42.06N111.53W
Preston Minn. U.S.A. **82** 43.40N 92.04W
Prestonpans U.K. **12** 55.57N 3.00W
Prestwick U.K. **12** 55.30N 4.36W
Prêto *r.* Brazil **94** 22.00S 43.21W
Pretoria R.S.A. **56** 25.43S 28.11E
Préveza Greece **19** 38.58N 20.43E
Prey Vêng Kampuchea **34** 11.29N105.19E
Priboj Yugo. **19** 43.35N 19.31E
Příbram Czech. **20** 49.42N 14.00E
Price Md. U.S.A. **85** 39.06N 75.58W
Price Utah U.S.A. **80** 39.36N110.48W
Prichard U.S.A. **83** 30.44N 88.07W
Prieska R.S.A. **56** 29.40S 22.43E
Prijedor Yugo. **19** 44.59N 16.43E
Prikaspiyskaya Nizmennost *f.* U.S.S.R. **25** 47.00N 48.00E
Prilep Yugo. **19** 41.20N 21.32E
Priluki R.S.F.S.R. U.S.S.R. **24** 63.05N 42.05E
Priluki Ukr.S.S.R. U.S.S.R. **25** 50.35N 32.24E
Primorsk R.S.F.S.R. U.S.S.R. **24** 60.18N 28.35E
Primrose L. Canada **75** 54.55N109.45W
Primstal W. Germany **14** 49.33N 6.59E
Prince Albert Canada **75** 53.12N105.46W
Prince Albert R.S.A. **56** 33.14S 22.02E
Prince Albert Nat. Park Canada **75** 54.00N106.25W
Prince Albert Sd. Canada **72** 70.25N115.00W
Prince Alfred C. Canada **72** 74.30N125.00W
Prince Charles I. Canada **73** 67.50N 76.00W
Prince Edward Island *d.* Canada **77** 46.45N 63.00W
Prince Frederick U.S.A. **85** 38.33N 76.35W
Prince George Canada **74** 53.50N122.50W
Prince of Wales, C. U.S.A. **72** 66.00N168.30W
Prince of Wales I. Australia **64** 10.40S142.10E
Prince of Wales I. Canada **73** 73.00N 99.00W
Prince of Wales I. U.S.A. **74** 55.00N132.30W
Prince Patrick I. Canada **72** 77.00N120.00W
Prince Regent Inlet *str.* Canada **73** 73.00N 90.30W
Prince Rupert Canada **74** 54.09N130.20W
Princess Charlotte B. Australia **64** 14.25S144.00E
Princess Royal I. Canada **74** 53.00N128.40W
Princeton N.J. U.S.A. **85** 40.21N 74.40W
Princeton Ind. U.S.A. **84** 38.21N 87.33W
Princeton Ky. U.S.A. **85** 37.06N 87.55W
Princeton Mo. U.S.A. **82** 40.24N 93.35W
Príncipe *i.* São Tomé & Príncipe **53** 1.37N 7.27E
Príncipe da Beira Brazil **90** 12.23S 64.28W
Prinzapolca Nicaragua **87** 13.19N 83.35W
Priozersk U.S.S.R. **24** 61.01N 30.08E
Pripet Marshes *see* Polesye *f.* U.S.S.R. **21**
Pripyat *r.* U.S.S.R. **21** 51.08N 30.30E
Priština Yugo. **19** 42.39N 21.10E
Pritzwalk E. Germany **20** 53.09N 12.10E
Privas France **20** 44.44N 4.36E
Privolzhskaya Vozvyshennost *f.* U.S.S.R. **24** 53.15N 45.45E
Prizren Yugo. **19** 42.13N 20.42E
Probolinggo Indonesia **37** 7.45S113.09E
Proddatūr India **39** 14.44N 78.33E
Progreso Mexico **87** 21.20N 89.40W
Prokopyevsk U.S.S.R. **28** 53.55N 86.45E
Prome Burma **34** 18.50N 95.14E
Prophet *r.* Canada **74** 58.48N122.40W
Propriá Brazil **91** 10.15S 36.51W
Proserpine Australia **64** 20.24S148.34E
Prostějov Czech. **21** 49.29N 17.07E
Protection U.S.A. **83** 37.12N 99.29W
Provence-Côte d'Azur *d.* France **17** 43.45N 6.00E
Providence U.S.A. **84** 41.50N 71.25W
Providence Mts. U.S.A. **81** 34.55N115.35W
Providencia, Isla de *i.* Colombia **87** 13.21N 81.22W
Provins France **15** 48.34N 3.18E
Provo U.S.A. **80** 40.14N111.39W
Prozor Yugo. **21** 43.49N 17.37E
Prudhoe Bay *town* U.S.A. **72** 70.20N148.25W
Prüm W. Germany **14** 50.12N 6.25E
Prüm *r.* W. Germany **14** 49.50N 6.29E
Pruszcz Gdański Poland **21** 54.17N 19.40E
Pruszków Poland **21** 52.11N 20.48E
Prut *r.* Romania/U.S.S.R. **21** 45.29N 28.14E
Pruzhany U.S.S.R. **21** 52.23N 24.28E
Prydz B. Antarctica **96** 68.30S 74.00E
Pryor U.S.A. **83** 36.19N 95.19W
Przemyśl Poland **21** 49.48N 22.48E
Przeworsk Poland **21** 50.05N 22.29E
Przhevalsk U.S.S.R. **30** 42.31N 78.22E
Psará *i.* Greece **19** 38.34N 25.35E
Psel *r.* U.S.S.R. **25** 49.00N 33.30E
Pskov U.S.S.R. **24** 57.48N 28.00E
Pskovskoye, Ozero *l.* U.S.S.R. **24** 58.00N 27.55E
Ptich U.S.S.R. **21** 52.15N 28.49E
Ptich *r.* U.S.S.R. **21** 52.09N 28.52E
Ptolemaís Greece **19** 40.31N 21.41E
Puán Argentina **93** 37.30S 62.45W
Pu'an China **33** 25.47N104.57E
Puapua W. Samoa **68** 13.34S172.12W
Pucallpa Peru **90** 8.21S 74.33W
Pucarani Bolivia **92** 16.23S 68.30W
Pucheng China **33** 27.56N118.32E
Pudasjärvi Finland **22** 65.25N 26.50E
Pūdeh Tal *r.* Afghan. **40** 31.00N 61.50E
Pudozh U.S.S.R. **24** 61.50N 36.32E
Pudozhgora U.S.S.R. **24** 62.18N 35.54E
Puebla Mexico **86** 19.03N 98.10W
Puebla *d.* Mexico **86** 18.30N 98.00W
Pueblo U.S.A. **80** 38.16N104.37W
Pueblo Hundido Chile **92** 26.23S 70.03W
Puelches Argentina **93** 38.09S 65.58W
Puelén Argentina **93** 37.32S 67.38W
Puente Alta Chile **93** 33.37S 70.35W
Puente-Genil Spain **16** 37.24N 4.46W
Puerto Aisén Chile **93** 45.27S 72.58W
Puerto Ángel Mexico **86** 15.40N 96.29W
Puerto Armuelles Panama **87** 8.19N 82.15W
Puerto Ayacucho Venezuela **90** 5.39N 67.32W
Puerto Barrios Guatemala **87** 15.41N 88.32W
Puerto Bermúdez Peru **90** 10.20S 75.00W
Puerto Berrío Colombia **90** 6.28N 74.28W
Puerto Cabello Venezuela **90** 10.29N 68.02W
Puerto Cabezas Nicaragua **87** 14.02N 83.24W
Puerto Carreño Colombia **90** 6.08N 67.27W
Puerto Casado Paraguay **92** 22.20S 57.55W
Puerto Coig Argentina **93** 50.54S 69.15W
Puerto Cortés Costa Rica **87** 8.58N 83.32W
Puerto Cortés Honduras **87** 15.50N 87.55W
Puerto de Nutrias Venezuela **90** 8.07N 69.18W
Puerto de Santa Maria Spain **16** 36.36N 6.14W
Puerto Heath Bolivia **90** 12.30S 68.40W
Puerto Juárez Mexico **87** 21.26N 86.51W
Puerto La Cruz Venezuela **90** 10.14N 64.40W
Puerto Leguízamo Colombia **90** 0.12S 74.46W
Puertollano Spain **16** 38.41N 4.07W
Puerto Lobos Argentina **93** 42.01S 65.04W
Puerto Madryn Argentina **93** 42.46S 65.02W
Puerto Maldonado Peru **90** 12.37S 69.11W
Puerto Melendez Peru **90** 4.30S 77.30W
Puerto Montt Chile **93** 41.28S 73.00W
Puerto Natales Chile **93** 51.44S 72.31W
Puerto Páez Venezuela **90** 6.13N 67.28W
Puerto Peñasco Mexico **81** 31.20N113.33W
Puerto Pinasco Paraguay **94** 22.36S 57.53W
Puerto Plata Dom. Rep. **87** 19.48N 70.41W
Puerto Princesa Phil. **36** 9.46N118.45E
Puerto Quepos Costa Rica **87** 9.28N 84.10W
Puerto Rey Colombia **90** 8.48N 76.34W
Puerto Rico C. America **87** 18.20N 66.30W
Puerto Rico Trench Atlantic Oc. **87** 19.50N 66.00W
Puerto Saavedra Chile **93** 38.47S 73.24W
Puerto Santa Cruz Argentina **93** 50.03S 68.35W
Puerto Sastre Paraguay **94** 22.02S 58.00W
Puerto Siles Bolivia **92** 12.48S 65.05W
Puerto Tejado Colombia **90** 3.16N 76.22W
Puerto Vallarta Mexico **86**
Puerto Varas Chile **93** 41.20S 73.00W
Pugachev U.S.S.R. **24** 52.02N 48.49E
Puglia *d.* Italy **19** 41.00N 16.40E
Puisaye, Collines de la *hills* France **15** 47.34N 3.28E
Pujehun Sierra Leone **52** 7.23N 11.44W
Pukaki, L. New Zealand **60** 44.00S170.10E
Pukatawagan Canada **75** 55.45N101.20W
Pukekohe New Zealand **60** 37.12S174.56E
Pukeuri New Zealand **60** 45.02S171.02E
Pukhovichi U.S.S.R. **21** 53.28N 28.18E
Pula Yugo. **20** 44.52N 13.53E
Pulacayo Bolivia **92** 20.25S 66.41W
Pulaski Tenn. U.S.A. **85** 35.11N 87.02W
Pulaski Va. U.S.A. **85** 37.03N 80.47W
Puławy Poland **21** 51.25N 21.57E
Pulgaon India **41** 20.44N 78.20E
Pulkkila Finland **22** 64.16N 25.52E
Pullman U.S.A. **80** 46.44N117.10W
Pulog *mtn.* Phil. **37** 16.50N120.50E
Pulozero U.S.S.R. **24** 68.22N 33.15E
Pulpito, Punta *c.* Mexico **81** 26.31N111.28W
Pułtusk Poland **21** 52.42N 21.02E
Puma Tanzania **55** 5.02S 34.46E
Puma Yumco *l.* China **41** 28.35N 90.20E
Punaauia Tahiti **69** 17.38S149.36W
Punakha Bhutan **41** 27.37N 89.52E
Puncak Jaya *mtn.* Indonesia **37** 4.00S137.15E
Pūnch Jammu & Kashmir **40** 33.46N 74.06E
Pune India **38** 18.34N 73.58E
Punjab *d.* India **40** 30.45N 75.30E
Punjab *d.* Pakistan **40** 30.25N 72.30E
Puno Peru **90** 15.53S 70.03W
Punta Alta *town* Argentina **93** 38.50S 62.00W
Punta Arenas *town* Chile **93** 53.10S 70.56W
Puntabie Australia **66** 32.15S134.13E
Punta Delgada *town* Argentina **93** 42.43S 63.38W
Punta Gorda *town* Belize **87** 16.10N 88.45W
Punta Gorda *town* U.S.A. **85** 26.56N 82.01W
Puntarenas Costa Rica **87** 10.00N 84.50W
Punto Fijo Venezuela **90** 11.50N 70.16W
Puolanka Finland **22** 64.52N 27.40E
Puqi China **33** 29.40N113.52E
Puquio Peru **90** 14.44S 74.07W
Pur *r.* U.S.S.R. **28** 67.30N 75.30E
Pūranpur India **41** 28.31N 80.09E
Purari *r.* P.N.G. **37** 7.49S145.10E
Purcell U.S.A. **83** 35.01N 97.22W
Purgatoire *r.* U.S.A. **80** 38.04N103.10W
Puri India **41** 19.48N 85.51E
Purisima, Sierra de la *mts.* Mexico **83** 26.28N101.45W
Purli India **40** 18.51N 76.32E
Pūrna *r.* India **40** 19.07N 77.02E
Purnea India **41** 25.47N 87.31E
Purros Namibia **56** 18.38S 12.59E
Purūlia India **41** 23.20N 86.22E
Purus *r.* Brazil **90** 3.58S 61.25W
Purwakarta Indonesia **37** 6.30S107.25E
Purwodadi Indonesia **37** 7.05S110.53E
Purwokerto Indonesia **37** 7.28S109.09E
Purworejo Indonesia **37** 7.45S110.04E
Pusad India **41** 19.54N 77.35E
Pusan S. Korea **31** 35.05N129.02E
Pushkar India **40** 26.30N 74.33E
Pushkin U.S.S.R. **24** 59.43N 30.22E
Pushkino U.S.S.R. **25** 51.16N 47.09E
Püspökladány Hungary **21** 47.19N 21.07E
Pustoshka U.S.S.R. **24** 56.20N 29.20E
Putao Burma **34** 27.22N 97.27E
Putaruru New Zealand **60** 38.03S175.47E
Putian China **33** 25.29N119.04E
Puting, Tanjung *c.* Indonesia **36** 3.35S111.52E
Putoran, Gory *mts.* U.S.S.R. **29** 68.30N 96.00E
Putsonderwater R.S.A. **56** 29.14S 21.50E
Puttalam Sri Lanka **39** 8.02N 79.50E
Puttgarden W. Germany **20** 54.30N 11.13E
Putumayo *r.* Brazil **90** 3.05S 68.10W
Puulavesi *l.* Finland **23** 61.50N 26.42E
Puyallup U.S.A. **80** 47.11N122.18W
Puyang China **32** 35.40N115.02E
Puy de Dôme *mtn.* France **17** 45.46N 2.56E
Puysegur Pt. New Zealand **60** 46.10S166.35E
Pūzak, Jehīl-e *l.* Afghan. **40** 31.30N 61.45E
Pwani *d.* Tanzania **55** 7.00S 39.00E
Pweto Zaïre **55** 8.27S 28.52E
Pwllheli U.K. **10** 52.53N 4.25W
Pyaozero, Ozero *l.* U.S.S.R. **24** 66.00N 31.00E
Pyapon Burma **34** 16.15N 95.40E
Pyasina *r.* U.S.S.R. **29** 73.10N 84.55E
Pyatigorsk U.S.S.R. **25** 44.04N 43.06E
Pyhä *r.* Finland **22** 64.28N 24.13E
Pyhäjärvi *l.* Oulu Finland **22** 63.35N 25.57E
Pyhäjärvi *l.* Turku-Pori Finland **23** 61.00N 22.20E
Pyhäjoki Finland **22** 64.28N 24.14E
Pyinmana Burma **34** 19.45N 96.12E
Pyongyang N. Korea **31** 39.00N125.47E
Pyramid U.S.A. **80** 40.05N119.43W
Pyramid Hill *town* Australia **66** 36.03S144.24E
Pyramid Hills Canada **77** 57.35N 65.00W
Pyramid L. U.S.A. **80** 40.00N119.35W
Pyramids Egypt **48** 29.52N 31.00E
Pyrénées *mts.* France/Spain **17** 42.40N 0.30E
Pyrzyce Poland **20** 53.10N 14.55E
Pyttegga *mtn.* Norway **23** 62.13N 7.42E
Pyu Burma **34** 18.29N 96.26E

Q

Qaanaaq *see* Thule Greenland **73**
Qaaqortoq *see* Julianehåb Greenland **73**
Qā'emshahr Iran **43** 36.28N 52.53E
Qagan Nur *l.* China **32** 43.30N114.35E
Qagbasêrag China **41** 30.51N 92.42E
Qagcaka China **41** 32.32N 81.52E
Qahā Egypt **44** 30.17N 31.12E
Qalāt Afghan. **40** 32.07N 66.54E
Qal'at Bīshah Saudi Arabia **48** 19.50N 42.36E
Qal 'eh Kāh Afghan. **40** 32.18N 61.31E
Qal'eh-ye Now Afghan **43** 34.58N 63.04E
Qal'eh-ye Sāber Afghan. **40** 34.02N 69.01E
Qallābāt Sudan **49** 12.58N 36.09E
Qalyūb Egypt **44** 30.11N 31.12E
Qamar, Ghubbat al *b.* S. Yemen **45** 16.00N 52.30E
Qamdo China **30** 31.11N 97.18E
Qamīnis Libya **48** 31.40N 20.01E
Qamr-ud-dīn Kārez Pakistan **40** 31.39N 68.25E
Qanātir Muhammad 'Alī Egypt **44** 30.12N 31.08E
Qandahār Afghan. **40** 31.32N 65.30E
Qandahār *d.* Afghan. **40** 31.00N 65.30E
Qandala Somali Rep. **45** 11.23N 49.53E
Qarā, Jabal al *mts.* Oman **45** 17.15N 54.15E
Qārah Egypt **42** 27.37N 26.30E
Qārat Khazzī *hill* Libya **48** 21.26N 24.30E
Qareh Sū Iran **43** 34.52N 51.25E
Qareh Sū *r.* Iran **43** 35.58N 56.25E
Qarqan He *r.* China **30** 40.56N 86.27E
Qārūn, Birkat *l.* Egypt **44** 29.30N 30.40E
Qaryat al Qaddāhīyah Libya **51** 31.22N 15.14E
Qāsh *r.* Sudan **48** 16.48N 35.51E
Qasigiannguit *see* Christianshåb Greenland **73**
Qaşr al Farāfirah Egypt **42** 27.15N 28.10E
Qaşr al Qarābūllī Libya **51** 32.45N 13.43E
Qaşr-e Qand Iran **43** 26.13N 60.37E
Qa'ţabah Yemen **45** 13.51N 44.42E
Qatanā Syria **44** 33.27N 36.04E
Qatar Asia **43** 25.20N 51.10E
Qaţrānī, Jabal *mts.* Egypt **44** 29.40N 30.36E
Qattara Depression *see* Qaţţārah, Munkhaf. *f.* Egypt **42**
Qaţţārah, Munkhafaḑ al *f.* Egypt **42** 29.40N 27.30E
Qawz Rajab Sudan **48** 16.04N 35.34E
Qāyen Iran **43** 33.44N 59.07E
Qaysān Sudan **49** 10.45N 34.48E
Qāzigund Jammu & Kashmir **40** 33.38N 75.09E
Qazvīn Iran **43** 36.16N 50.00E
Qeqertarsuaq *see* Godhavn Greenland **73**
Qeqertarsuatsiaat *see* Fiskenaesset Greenland **73**
Qeshm Iran **43** 26.58N 57.17E
Qeshm *i.* Iran **43** 26.48N 55.48E
Qezel Owzan *r.* Iran **43** 36.44N 49.27E
Qezi'ot Israel **44** 30.52N 34.28E
Qian'an China **32** 45.00N124.00E
Qianjiang China **33** 29.28N108.43E
Qianxi China **32** 40.10N118.19E
Qianyang China **33** 27.22N110.14E
Qiaotou China **32** 42.56N118.54E
Qidong Hunan China **33** 26.47N112.07E
Qidong Jiangsu China **33** 31.49N121.40E
Qiemo China **30** 38.08N 85.33E
Qijiang China **33** 29.00N106.40E
Qila Abdullāh Pakistan **40** 30.43N 66.38E
Qila Lādgasht Pakistan **40** 27.54N 62.57E
Qila Saifullāh Pakistan **40** 30.43N 68.21E
Qilian Shan *mts.* China **30** 38.30N 99.20E
Qimantag *mts.* China **30** 37.45N 89.40E
Qimen China **33** 29.50N117.38E
Qinā Egypt **42** 26.10N 32.43E
Qinā, Wādī *r.* Egypt **42** 26.07N 32.42E
Qingdao China **32** 36.02N120.25E
Qinghai *d.* China **41** 34.20N 91.00E
Qinghai Hu *l.* China **30** 36.40N100.00E
Qingjian China **32** 37.02N110.06E
Qingjiang China **33** 28.01N115.30E
Qing Jiang Shuiku *resr.* China **33** 30.00N112.12E
Qinglong Guizhou China **33** 25.47N105.12E
Qinglong Hebei China **32** 40.24N118.53E
Qingshui Jiang *r.* China **33** 28.08N110.06E
Qing Xian China **32** 38.35N116.48E
Qingxu China **32** 37.36N112.21E
Qingyang China **32** 36.03N107.52E
Qingyuan Guangdong China **33** 23.42N113.00E
Qingyuan Jilin China **32** 42.05N125.01E
Qingyuan Zhejiang China **33** 27.37N119.03E
Qing Zang Gaoyuan *f.* China **30** 33.40N 86.00E
Qinhuangdao China **32** 39.52N119.42E
Qin Ling *mts.* China **32** 33.30N109.00E
Qin Xian China **32** 36.45N112.41E
Qinyang China **32** 35.06N112.57E
Qinzhou China **33** 21.58N108.34E
Qionghai China **33** 19.12N110.31E
Qiongshan China **33** 19.59N110.30E
Qiongzhou Haixia *str.* China **33** 20.09N110.20E
Qipanshan China **32** 42.05N117.37E
Qiqihar China **31** 47.23N124.00E
Qira China **30** 37.02N 80.53E
Qiryat Gat Israel **44** 31.37N 34.47E
Qiryat Shemona Israel **44** 33.13N 35.35E
Qishn S. Yemen **38** 15.25N 51.40E
Qiuxizhen China **33** 29.54N104.40E
Qi Xian Henan China **32** 34.30N114.50E
Qi Xian Henan China **32** 35.35N114.08E
Qom Iran **43** 34.40N 50.57E

Qonggyai to Riau

Qonggyai China 41 29.03N 91.41E
Qornet'es Sauda mtn. Lebanon 44 34.17N 36.04E
Qoṭūr Iran 43 38.28N 44.25E
Quairading Australia 63 32.00S117.22E
Quakenbrück W. Germany 14 52.41N 7.59E
Quakertown U.S.A. 85 40.26N 75.21W
Qu'ali China 33 29.46N117.15E
Quambatook Australia 66 35.52S143.36E
Quambone Australia 67 30.54S147.55E
Quang Ngai Vietnam 34 15.09N108.50E
Quang Tri Vietnam 34 16.44N107.10E
Quang Yen Vietnam 34 20.56N106.49E
Quan Long Vietnam 34 9.11N105.09E
Quannan China 33 24.45N114.32E
Quantico U.S.A. 85 38.31N 77.17W
Quanzhou Fujian China 33 24.57N118.36E
Quanzhou Guang. Zhuang. China 33 26.00N111.00E
Qu'Appelle r. Canada 75 50.33N101.20W
Quaraí Brazil 93 30.23S 56.27W
Quaraí r. Brazil 93 30.12S 57.36W
Quarryville U.S.A. 85 39.54N 76.10W
Quartu Sant'Elena Italy 18 39.14N 9.11E
Quartzsite U.S.A. 81 33.40N114.13W
Quatsino Sd. Canada 74 50.42N127.58W
Qūchān Iran 43 37.04N 58.29E
Queanbeyan Australia 67 35.24S149.17E
Québec Canada 77 46.50N 71.15W
Québec d. Canada 77 51.20N 68.45W
Quebracho Uruguay 93 31.57S 57.53W
Quedlinburg E. Germany 20 51.48N 11.09E
Queen Anne U.S.A. 85 38.55N 75.57W
Queen Charlotte Canada 74 53.18N132.04W
Queen Charlotte Is. Canada 74 53.00N132.00W
Queen Charlotte Sd. Canada 74 51.30N129.30W
Queen Charlotte Str. Canada 74 51.00N128.00W
Queen Elizabeth Is. Canada 73 78.30N 99.00W
Queen Maud G. Canada 73 68.30N 99.00W
Queen Maud Range mts. Antarctica 96 86.20S165.00W
Queens Channel Australia 62 14.46S129.24E
Queenscliff Australia 67 38.17S144.42E
Queensland d. Australia 64 23.30S144.00E
Queenstown Australia 65 42.07S145.33E
Queenstown New Zealand 60 45.03S168.41E
Queenstown R.S.A. 56 31.52S 26.51E
Queenstown U.S.A. 85 38.59N 76.09W
Queguay Grande r. Uruguay 93 32.09S 58.09W
Queimadas Brazil 91 10.58S 39.38W
Quela Angola 54 9.18S 17.05E
Quelimane Mozambique 55 17.53S 36.57E
Quemado U.S.A. 81 34.20N108.30W
Quemoy i. China 33 24.30N118.20E
Quentico Prov. Park Canada 76 48.20N 91.30W
Quequén Argentina 93 38.34S 58.42W
Querétaro Mexico 86 20.38N100.23W
Querétaro d. Mexico 86 21.03N100.00W
Querobabi Mexico 81 30.03N111.01W
Queshan China 32 32.48N114.01E
Quesnel Canada 74 53.05N122.30W
Quesnel r. Canada 74 52.58N122.29W
Quetta Pakistan 40 30.12N 67.00E
Quettehou France 15 49.36N 1.18W
Quevedo Ecuador 90 0.59S 79.27W
Quezaltenango Guatemala 86 14.50N 91.30W
Quezon City Phil. 37 14.39N121.01E
Quibala Angola 54 10.48S 14.56E
Quibaxi Angola 54 8.34S 14.37E
Quibdó Colombia 90 5.40N 76.38W
Quiberon France 17 47.29N 3.07W
Quibocolo Angola 54 6.20S 15.05E
Quiçama Nat. Park Angola 54 9.40S 13.30E
Quiet L. Canada 74 61.05N133.05W
Quilán, C. Chile 93 43.16S 74.27W
Quilengues Angola 54 14.09S 14.04E
Quillabamba Peru 90 12.50S 72.50W
Quillacollo Bolivia 92 17.26S 66.17W
Quillota Chile 93 32.53S 71.16W
Quilon India 38 8.53N 76.38E
Quilpie Australia 64 26.37S144.15E
Quilpué Chile 93 33.03S 71.27W
Quimbele Angola 54 6.29S 16.25E
Quimilí Argentina 92 27.35S 62.25W
Quimper France 17 48.00N 4.06W
Quimperlé France 17 47.52N 3.33W
Quincy Ill. U.S.A. 82 39.56N 91.23W
Quincy Wash. U.S.A. 80 47.14N119.51W
Qui Nhon Vietnam 34 13.47N109.11E
Quintanar de la Orden Spain 16 39.36N 3.05W
Quintana Roo d. Mexico 87 19.00N 88.00W
Quinter U.S.A. 82 39.04N100.14W
Quinto Spain 16 41.25N 0.30W
Quinzau Angola 54 6.51S 12.46E
Quionga Mozambique 55 10.37S 40.31E
Quirigua ruins Guatemala 87 15.20N 89.25W
Quirimbo Angola 54 10.41S 14.16E
Quiros, C. Vanuatu 68 14.55S167.01E
Quissanga Mozambique 55 12.24S 40.33E
Quissico Mozambique 57 24.42S 34.44E
Quitapa Angola 54 10.10S 18.16E
Quiterajo Mozambique 55 11.46S 40.25E
Quito Ecuador 90 0.14S 78.30W
Qu Jiang r. China 33 30.02N106.20E
Qumigxung China 41 30.53N 86.38E
Quorn Australia 66 32.20S138.02E
Qurayyah, Wādī r. Egypt 44 30.26N 34.01E
Qurdūd Sudan 49 10.17N 29.56E
Qū' Wishām f. Oman 45 18.55N 55.55E
Quxian China 33 30.50N106.54E
Qu Xian China 33 28.59N118.56E
Qūzū China 41 29.21N 90.39E

R

Raahe Finland 22 64.41N 24.29E
Raalte Neth. 14 52.22N 6.17E
Raasay i. U.K. 12 57.25N 6.05W
Rába r. Hungary 21 47.42N 17.38E
Raba Indonesia 36 8.27S118.45E
Rabak Sudan 49 13.09N 32.44E
Rabang China 41 33.03N 80.29E
Rabat Morocco 50 34.02N 6.51W
Rabbitskin r. Canada 74 61.47N120.42W
Rābor Iran 43 29.18N 56.56E
Rabyānah Libya 48 24.14N 21.59E
Rabyānah, Ṣaḥrā' f. Libya 51 24.30N 21.00E
Racconigi Italy 15 44.46N 9.46E
Race, C. Canada 77 46.40N 53.10W
Rach Gia Vietnam 34 10.02N105.05E
Racibórz Poland 21 50.06N 18.13E
Racine U.S.A. 82 42.42N 87.50W
Rădăuţi Romania 21 47.51N 25.55E
Radebeul E. Germany 20 51.06N 13.41E
Radekhov U.S.S.R. 21 50.18N 24.35E
Radford U.S.A. 85 37.07N 80.34W
Rādhanpur India 40 23.50N 71.36E
Radium Hill town Australia 66 32.30S140.32E
Radium Hot Springs town Canada 74 50.48N116.12W
Radom Poland 21 51.26N 21.10E
Radomir Bulgaria 19 42.32N 22.56E
Radomsko Poland 21 51.05N 19.25E
Radomyshl U.S.S.R. 21 50.30N 29.14E
Radöy i. Norway 23 60.38N 5.05E
Radstock U.K. 11 51.17N 2.25W
Radstock, C. Australia 66 33.11S134.21E
Radville Canada 75 49.27N104.17W
Raḍwá, Jabal mtn. Saudi Arabia 42 24.36N 38.18E
Rae Canada 74 62.50N116.03W
Rāe Bareli India 41 26.13N 81.14E
Raeren W. Germany 14 50.41N 6.07E
Raeside, L. Australia 63 29.30S122.00E
Rafaela Argentina 92 31.16S 61.44W
Rafaḥ Egypt 44 31.18N 34.15E
Rafaï C.A.R. 49 4.58N 23.56E
Raffili Mission Sudan 49 6.53N 27.58E
Rafḥā Saudi Arabia 42 29.38N 43.30E
Rafsanjān Iran 43 30.24N 56.00E
Raga Sudan 49 8.28N 25.41E
Ragged, Mt. Australia 63 33.27S123.27E
Ragunda Sweden 22 63.06N 16.23E
Ragusa Italy 18 36.56N 14.44E
Raha Indonesia 37 4.50S122.43E
Raḥá, Ḥarrat ar f. Saudi Arabia 44 28.00N 36.35E
Rahad r. Sudan 48 14.28N 33.31E
Rahad al Bardī Sudan 49 11.18N 23.53E
Rahim Ki Bāzār Pakistan 40 24.19N 69.09E
Rahīmyār Khān Pakistan 40 28.25N 70.18E
Raiatea i. Īs. de la Société 69 16.50S151.25W
Rāichūr India 38 16.15N 77.20E
Raiganj India 41 25.37N 88.07E
Raigarh India 41 21.54N 83.24E
Rainbow Australia 66 35.56S142.01E
Rainelle U.S.A. 85 37.58N 80.47W
Rainier, Mt. U.S.A. 80 46.52N121.46W
Rainy L. Canada/U.S.A. 76 48.42N 93.10W
Rainy River town Canada 76 48.43N 94.29W
Raipur India 41 21.14N 81.38E
Raipur Uplands mts. India 41 20.45N 82.30E
Rairākhol India 41 21.03N 84.23E
Ra'īs Saudi Arabia 42 23.35N 38.36E
Raisen India 41 23.20N 77.48E
Raivavae i. Pacific Oc. 69 23.52S147.40W
Rājahmundry India 39 17.01N 81.52E
Rajāj Sudan 49 10.55N 24.43E
Rajang r. Malaysia 36 2.10N112.45E
Rājanpur Pakistan 40 29.06N 70.19E
Rājapālaiyam India 38 9.26N 77.36E
Rājasthān d. India 40 26.15N 74.00E
Rājasthān Canal India 40 31.10N 75.00E
Rājbāri Bangla. 41 23.46N 89.39E
Rāj Gāngpur India 41 22.11N 84.36E
Rājgarh Madhya P. India 40 23.56N 76.58E
Rājgarh Rāj. India 40 27.14N 76.38E
Rājgarh Rāj. India 40 28.38N 75.23E
Rājkot India 40 22.18N 70.47E
Rāj-Nāndgaon India 41 21.06N 81.02E
Rājpīpla India 40 21.47N 73.34E
Rājpur India 40 21.56N 75.08E
Rājshāhi Bangla. 41 24.22N 88.36E
Rājula India 40 21.01N 71.34E
Rakahanga Atoll Cook Is. 68 10.03S161.06W
Rakaia New Zealand 60 43.45S172.01E
Rakaia r. New Zealand 60 43.52S172.13E
Raka Zangbo r. China 41 29.24N 87.58E
Rakhni Pakistan 40 30.03N 69.55E
Rakhov U.S.S.R. 21 48.02N 24.10E
Rakhshān r. Pakistan 40 27.10N 63.25E
Rakitnoye U.S.S.R. 21 51.18N 27.10E
Rakops Botswana 56 21.00S 24.32E
Rakov U.S.S.R. 21 53.58N 26.59E
Rakulka U.S.S.R. 24 62.19N 46.52E
Råkvåg Norway 22 63.47N 10.10E
Rakvere U.S.S.R. 24 59.22N 26.28E
Raleigh U.S.A. 85 35.46N 78.39W
Raleigh B. U.S.A. 85 35.47N 76.09W
Ralik Chain is. Pacific Oc. 68 8.00N168.00E
Ram r. Canada 74 62.01N123.41W
Rama Nicaragua 87 12.09N 84.15W
Rāmah Saudi Arabia 43 25.33N 47.08E
Rām Allāh Jordan 44 31.55N 35.12E
Ramallo Argentina 93 33.28S 60.02W
Rāmānuj Ganj India 41 23.48N 83.42E
Ramat Gan Israel 44 32.05N 34.48E
Rambau, Lac l. Canada 77 53.40N 70.10W
Rambouillet France 15 48.39N 1.50E
Rām Dās India 40 31.58N 74.55E
Rame Head U.K. 11 50.18N 4.13W
Ramelton Rep. of Ire. 13 55.02N 7.40W
Rāmgarh Bangla. 41 22.59N 91.43E
Rāmgarh Bihār India 41 23.38N 85.31E
Rāmgarh Rāj. India 40 27.15N 75.11E
Rāmgarh Rāj. India 40 27.22N 70.30E
Rāmhormoz Iran 43 31.14N 49.37E
Ramillies Belgium 14 50.39N 4.56E
Ramingstein Austria 20 47.04N 13.50E
Ramis r. Ethiopia 49 7.59N 41.34E
Ramla Israel 44 31.56N 34.52E
Ramlo mtn. Ethiopia 49 13.20N 41.45E
Rāmnagar India 41 25.17N 83.02E
Ramona Calif. U.S.A. 81 33.08N116.52W
Ramona Okla. U.S.A. 83 36.32N 95.55W
Ramore Canada 76 48.30N 80.25W
Ramos Arizpe Mexico 83 25.33N100.58W
Rāmpur Himachal P. India 41 31.27N 77.38E
Rāmpur Uttar P. India 41 28.49N 79.02E
Rampura India 40 24.28N 75.26E
Ramree I. Burma 34 19.06N 93.48E
Rāmsar Iran 43 36.54N 50.41E
Ramsey England U.K. 11 52.27N 0.06W
Ramsey I.o.M. U.K. 10 54.19N 4.23W
Ramsey L. Canada 76 47.10N 82.18W
Ramsgate U.K. 11 51.20N 1.25E
Rāmshīr Iran 43 30.54N 49.24E
Ramsjö Sweden 23 62.11N 15.39E
Rāmtek India 41 21.24N 79.20E
Ramu r. P.N.G. 37 4.00S144.40E
Ramusio, Lac l. Canada 77 55.04N 63.40W
Ranau Malaysia 36 5.58N116.41E
Rancagua Chile 93 34.10S 70.45W
Rancheria r. Canada 74 60.13N129.07W
Rānchī India 41 23.21N 85.20E
Rand Australia 67 35.34S146.35E
Randalstown U.K. 13 54.45N 6.20W
Rānder India 40 21.14N 72.47E
Randers Denmark 23 56.28N 10.03E
Randolph Kans. U.S.A. 82 39.27N 96.44W
Randsburg U.S.A. 81 35.22N117.39W
Randsfjorden l. Norway 23 60.25N 10.24E
Råne r. Sweden 22 65.52N 22.19E
Råneå Sweden 22 65.52N 22.18E
Rāner India 40 28.53N 73.17E
Rangdong China 32 32.51N112.18E
Rangely U.S.A. 80 40.05N108.48W
Rangemore Australia 66 35.19S144.22E
Ranger U.S.A. 85 38.07N 82.10W
Rangia India 41 26.28N 91.38E
Rangiora New Zealand 60 43.18S172.38E
Rangiroa i. Pacific Oc. 69 15.00S147.40W
Rangitaiki r. New Zealand 60 37.55S176.50E
Rangkasbitung Indonesia 37 6.21S106.12E
Rangoon Burma 34 16.47N 96.10E
Rangpur Bangla. 41 25.45N 89.15E
Rānīganj India 41 23.37N 87.08E
Rānīkhet India 41 29.39N 79.25E
Rānīwāra India 40 24.45N 72.13E
Rankin Inlet town Canada 73 62.52N 92.00W
Rankins Springs town Australia 67 33.52S146.18E
Rannoch, Loch U.K. 12 56.41N 4.20W
Rann of Kutch f. India 40 23.50N 69.50E
Ranohira Madagascar 57 22.29S 45.24E
Rano Kao mtn. I. de Pascua 69 27.11S109.27W
Ranong Thailand 34 9.59N 98.40E
Rantauparapat Indonesia 36 2.05N 99.46E
Rantekombola mtn. Indonesia 36 3.30S119.58E
Rao Co mtn. Laos 34 18.10N105.25E
Raoping China 33 23.45N117.05E
Raoul i. Pacific Oc. 68 29.15S177.55W
Rapa i. Pacific Oc. 69 27.35S144.20W
Rapallo Italy 15 44.20N 9.14E
Rāpar India 40 23.34N 70.38E
Rapid Bay town Australia 66 35.33S138.09E
Rapid City U.S.A. 82 44.05N103.14W
Raquette Lake town U.S.A. 84 43.49N 74.41W
Rarotonga i. Cook Is. 68 21.14S159.46W
Ra's al Ḥadd c. Oman 38 22.32N 59.49E
Ra's al Khaymah U.A.E. 43 25.48N 55.56E
Ra's al Unūf Libya 51 30.31N 18.34E
Ra's an Naqb town Egypt 44 29.36N 34.51E
Ra's an Naqb town Jordan 44 30.30N 35.29E
Ras Dashen mtn. Ethiopia 49 13.20N 38.10E
Rās Ghārib Egypt 44 28.22N 33.04E
Rashād Sudan 49 11.51N 31.04E
Rashīd Egypt 44 31.25N 30.25E
Rashīd Qal 'eh Afghan. 40 31.31N 67.31E
Rasht Iran 43 37.18N 49.38E
Raška Yugo. 19 43.17N 20.37E
Rās Koh mtn. Pakistan 40 28.50N 65.12E
Rason, L. Australia 63 28.46S124.20E
Rasra India 41 25.51N 83.51E
Ratak Chain is. Pacific Oc. 68 8.00N172.00E
Ratangarh India 40 28.05N 74.36E
Rat Buri Thailand 34 13.30N 99.50E
Rāth India 41 25.35N 79.34E
Rathcormack Rep. of Ire. 13 52.05N 8.18W
Rathdrum Rep. of Ire. 13 52.56N 6.15W
Rathenow E. Germany 20 52.37N 12.21E
Rathlin I. U.K. 13 55.17N 6.15W
Rath Luirc Rep. of Ire. 13 52.21N 8.41W
Rathmullen Rep. of Ire. 13 55.06N 7.32W
Ratlām India 40 23.19N 75.04E
Ratnāgiri India 38 16.59N 73.18E
Ratno U.S.S.R. 21 51.40N 24.32E
Ratodero Pakistan 40 27.48N 68.18E
Raton U.S.A. 80 36.54N104.24W
Rattlesnake Range mts. U.S.A. 80 42.45N107.10W
Rattray Head U.K. 12 57.37N 1.50W
Rättvik Sweden 23 60.53N 15.06E
Rauch Argentina 93 36.47S 59.05W
Raufoss Norway 23 60.43N 10.37E
Raul Soares Brazil 94 20.04S 42.27W
Rauma Finland 23 61.08N 21.30E
Rauma r. Norway 22 62.32N 7.43E
Raung, Gunung mtn. Indonesia 37 8.07S114.03E
Raurkela India 41 22.13N 84.53E
Rautas Sweden 22 68.00N 19.55E
Ravalgaon India 40 20.38N 74.25E
Rāvar Iran 43 31.14N 56.51E
Rava-Russkaya U.S.S.R. 21 50.15N 23.36E
Ravena U.S.A. 84 42.29N 73.49W
Ravenna Italy 15 44.25N 12.12E
Ravensburg W. Germany 20 47.47N 9.37E
Ravenshoe Australia 64 17.37S145.29E
Ravensthorpe Australia 63 33.35S120.02E
Ravenswood Australia 64 20.05S146.52E
Rāver India 40 21.15N 76.05E
Ravi r. Pakistan 38 30.30N 72.13E
Rawaki i. Kiribati 68 3.43S170.43W
Rāwalpindi Pakistan 40 33.36N 73.04E
Rawāndūz Iraq 43 36.38N 44.32E
Rawdon Canada 77 46.03N 73.44W
Rawene New Zealand 60 35.24S173.30E
Rawicz Poland 20 51.37N 16.52E
Rawlinna Australia 63 31.00S125.21E
Rawlins U.S.A. 80 41.47N107.14W
Rawson Argentina 93 34.40S 60.02W
Raxaul India 41 26.59N 84.51E
Ray U.S.A. 82 48.21N103.10W
Ray, C. Canada 77 47.40N 59.18W
Raya mtn. Indonesia 36 0.45S112.45E
Rāyagada India 41 19.10N 83.25E
Rāyen Iran 43 29.34N 57.26E
Raymond Canada 74 49.30N112.35W
Raymond U.S.A. 80 46.41N123.44W
Raymond Terrace Australia 67 32.47S151.45E
Raymondville U.S.A. 83 26.29N 97.47W
Rayong Thailand 34 12.43N101.20E
Razan Iran 43 35.22N 49.02E
Razdelnaya U.S.S.R. 21 46.50N 30.02E
Razgrad Bulgaria 21 43.32N 26.30E
Ré, Île de i. France 17 46.10N 1.26W
Reading U.K. 11 51.27N 0.57W
Reading U.S.A. 85 40.20N 75.56W
Realicó Argentina 93 35.02S 64.14W
Reay Forest f. U.K. 12 58.17N 4.48W
Rebi Indonesia 37 6.24S134.07E
Rebiana Sand Sea see Rabyānah, Ṣaḥrā' f. Libya 51
Reboly U.S.S.R. 24 63.50N 30.49E
Recalde Argentina 93 36.39S 61.05W
Rechāh Lām Afghan. 40 34.58N 70.51E
Recherche, Archipelago of the is. Australia 63 34.05S122.45E
Rechitsa U.S.S.R. 21 52.21N 30.24E
Recife Brazil 91 8.06S 34.53W
Recklinghausen W. Germany 14 51.36N 7.11E
Reconquista Argentina 92 29.08S 59.38W
Recreo Argentina 92 29.20S 65.04W
Red r. Canada 75 50.20N 96.50W
Red r. U.S.A. 83 31.00N 91.40W
Red r. see Hong Hà r. Vietnam 34
Red Bank U.S.A. 85 40.21N 74.03W
Red Basin f. see Sichuan Pendi f. China 33
Red Bay town Canada 77 51.44N 56.45W
Red Bluff U.S.A. 80 40.11N122.15W
Redcar U.K. 10 54.37N 1.04W
Red Cliffs town Australia 66 34.22S142.13E
Red Cloud U.S.A. 82 40.04N 98.31W
Red Deer Canada 74 52.20N113.50W
Red Deer r. Canada 75 50.56N109.54W
Redding U.S.A. 80 40.35N122.24W
Redditch U.K. 11 52.18N 1.57W
Rede r. U.K. 10 55.08N 2.13W
Redfield U.S.A. 82 44.53N 98.31W
Red Hill town Australia 66 33.34S138.12E
Red Indian L. Canada 77 48.40N 56.50W
Red L. U.S.A. 79 48.00N 95.00W
Red Lake town Canada 75 51.03N 93.49W
Redlands U.S.A. 81 34.03N117.11W
Red Lion U.S.A. 85 39.54N 76.36W
Red Lodge U.S.A. 80 45.11N109.15W
Redmond U.S.A. 80 44.17N121.11W
Red Oak U.S.A. 82 41.01N 95.14W
Redondela Spain 16 42.15N 8.38W
Redondo Portugal 16 38.39N 7.33W
Redondo Beach town U.S.A. 81 33.51N118.23W
Red Rock Canada 74 53.39N122.41W
Redrock U.S.A. 81 32.35N111.19W
Redruth U.K. 11 50.14N 5.14W
Red Sea Africa/Asia 45 20.00N 39.00E
Redstone Canada 74 52.13N123.50W
Red Sucker L. U.S.A. 75 54.09N 93.40W
Red Volta r. Ghana 52 10.32N 0.31W
Redwater Alta. Canada 74 53.55N113.06W
Red Wing U.S.A. 82 44.33N 92.31W
Redwood City U.S.A. 80 37.29N122.13W
Ree, Lough Rep. of Ire. 13 53.31N 7.58W
Reed City U.S.A. 84 43.54N 85.31W
Reeder U.S.A. 82 46.06N102.57W
Reedsport U.S.A. 80 43.42N124.06W
Reefton New Zealand 60 42.07S171.52E
Reese r. U.S.A. 80 40.39N116.54W
Reftele Sweden 23 57.11N 13.35E
Refuge Cove town Canada 74 50.07N124.50W
Refugio U.S.A. 83 28.18N 97.17W
Rega r. Poland 20 54.10N 15.18E
Regensburg W. Germany 20 49.01N 12.07E
Reggane Algeria 50 26.42N 0.10E
Reggio Calabria Italy 18 38.07N 15.38E
Reggio Emilia-Romagna Italy 15 44.40N 10.37E
Reghin Romania 21 46.47N 24.42E
Regina Canada 75 50.25N104.39W
Regiwar Pakistan 40 25.57N 65.44E
Regnéville France 15 49.01N 1.33W
Rehoboth Namibia 56 23.19S 17.10E
Rehoboth B. U.S.A. 85 38.40N 75.06W
Rehoboth Beach town U.S.A. 85 38.43N 75.05W
Rehovot Israel 44 31.54N 34.46E
Reidsville U.S.A. 85 36.21N 79.40W
Reigate U.K. 11 51.14N 0.13W
Reims France 15 49.15N 4.02E
Reindeer L. Canada 75 57.15N102.40W
Reinosa Spain 16 43.01N 4.09W
Reisterstown U.S.A. 85 39.38N 76.50W
Relizane Algeria 51 35.45N 0.33E
Remanso Brazil 91 9.41S 42.04W
Remarkable, Mt. Australia 66 32.48S138.10E
Rembang Indonesia 37 6.45S111.22E
Remeshk Iran 43 26.52N 58.46E
Remich Lux. 14 49.34N 6.23E
Remiremont France 17 48.01N 6.35E
Remo Ethiopia 49 6.50N 41.15E
Remscheid W. Germany 14 51.10N 7.11E
Rena Norway 23 61.08N 11.22E
Rendsburg W. Germany 20 54.19N 9.39E
Renfrew Canada 76 45.28N 76.41W
Rengat Indonesia 36 0.26S102.35E
Rengo Chile 93 34.25S 70.52W
Renheji China 33 31.56N115.07E
Reni India 40 28.41N 75.02E
Reni U.S.S.R. 21 45.28N 28.17E
Renkum Neth. 14 51.59N 5.46E
Renmark Australia 66 34.10S140.45E
Rennell Sd. Canada 74 53.23N132.35W
Renner Springs town Australia 64 18.20S133.48E
Rennes France 15 48.06N 1.40W
Reno r. Italy 15 44.36N 12.17E
Reno U.S.A. 80 39.31N119.48W
Renton U.S.A. 80 47.30N122.11W
Ren Xian China 32 37.07N114.41E
Réo U. Volta 52 12.20N 2.27W
Repki U.S.S.R. 21 51.47N 31.06E
Republic Wash. U.S.A. 80 48.39N118.44W
Republican r. U.S.A. 82 39.03N 96.48W
Republic of Ireland Europe 13 53.00N 8.00W
Republic of South Africa Africa 56 28.30S 24.50E
Repulse B. Australia 64 20.36S148.43E
Repulse Bay town Canada 73 66.35N 86.20W
Requa U.S.A. 80 41.34N124.05W
Requena Peru 90 5.05S 73.52W
Requena Spain 16 39.29N 1.08W
Reserve Canada 75 52.28N102.39W
Resistencia Argentina 92 27.28S 59.00W
Reşiţa Romania 21 45.17N 21.53E
Resolute Canada 73 74.40N 95.00W
Resolution I. Canada 73 61.30N 65.00W
Resolution I. New Zealand 60 45.40S166.30E
Restigouche r. Canada 77 48.04N 66.20W
Rethel France 15 49.31N 4.22E
Réthimnon Greece 19 35.22N 24.29E
Reus Spain 16 41.10N 1.06E
Reusel Neth. 14 51.21N 5.09E
Reutlingen W. Germany 20 48.30N 9.13E
Reutte Austria 20 47.29N 10.43E
Revda U.S.S.R. 24 56.49N 59.58E
Revelstoke Canada 74 51.00N118.00W
Revilla Gigedo, Islas de is. Mexico 86 19.00N111.00W
Revillagigedo I. U.S.A. 74 55.50N131.20W
Revin France 14 49.58N 4.40E
Revue r. Mozambique 57 19.58S 34.40E
Rewa India 41 24.32N 81.18E
Rewāri India 40 28.11N 76.37E
Rexburg U.S.A. 80 43.49N111.47W
Rexford U.S.A. 80 48.53N115.13W
Rey Iran 43 35.35N 51.27E
Reykjavík Iceland 22 64.09N 21.58W
Reynosa Mexico 83 26.07N 98.18W
Rezā'īyeh Iran 43 37.32N 45.02E
Rezé France 17 47.12N 1.34W
Rēzekne U.S.S.R. 24 56.30N 27.22E
Rhayader U.K. 11 52.19N 3.30W
Rheden Neth. 14 52.01N 6.02E
Rhein r. Europe 14 51.53N 6.03E
Rheinbach W. Germany 14 50.39N 6.59E
Rheine W. Germany 14 52.17N 7.26E
Rheinland-Pfalz d. W. Germany 14 50.05N 7.09E
Rhenen Neth. 14 51.58N 5.34E
Rheydt W. Germany 14 51.10N 6.25E
Rhine see Rhein r. Europe 14
Rhinebeck U.S.A. 85 41.56N 73.55W
Rhinelander U.S.A. 82 45.39N 89.23W
Rhino Camp town Uganda 55 2.58N 31.20E
Rhir, Cap c. Morocco 50 30.38N 9.55W
Rho Italy 15 45.32N 9.02E
Rhode Island d. U.S.A. 84 41.40N 71.30W
Rhodes i. see Ródhos i. Greece 19
Rhodopi Planina mts. Bulgaria 19 41.35N 24.35E
Rhondda U.K. 11 51.39N 3.30W
Rhône r. France 17 43.25N 4.45E
Rhône-Alpes d. France 17 45.20N 5.45E
Rhosneigr U.K. 10 53.14N 4.31W
Rhum i. U.K. 12 57.00N 6.20W
Rhyl U.K. 10 53.19N 3.29W
Riachão Brazil 91 7.22S 46.37W
Riāng India 41 27.32N 92.56E
Riāsi Jammu & Kashmir 40 33.05N 74.50E
Riau d. Indonesia 36 0.00 102.35E

Riau, Kepulauan to Rzhev

Riau, Kepulauan *is.* Indonesia **36** 0.50N104.00E
Ribadeo Spain **16** 43.32N 7.04W
Ribarroja, Embalse de *resr.* Spain **16** 41.12N 0.20E
Ribauè Mozambique **55** 14.57S 38.27E
Ribble *r.* U.K. **10** 53.45N 2.44W
Ribe Denmark **23** 55.21N 8.46E
Ribeauvillé France **17** 48.12N 7.19E
Ribécourt France **15** 49.31N 2.55E
Ribeirão Prêto Brazil **94** 21.09S 47.48W
Ribérac France **17** 45.14N 0.22E
Riberalta Bolivia **92** 10.59S 66.06W
Ribnitz-Damgarten E. Germany **20** 54.15N 12.28E
Ribstone Creek *r.* Canada **75** 52.51N110.05W
Riccione Italy **15** 43.59N 12.39E
Rice U.S.A. **81** 34.06N114.50W
Rice Lake *town* U.S.A. **82** 45.30N 91.43W
Richard's Bay *town* R.S.A. **57** 28.47S 32.06E
Richardson *r.* Canada **75** 58.30N111.30W
Richardson U.S.A. **83** 32.57N 96.44W
Richelieu *r.* Canada **77** 46.03N 73.07W
Richfield Idaho U.S.A. **80** 43.03N114.09W
Richfield Utah U.S.A. **80** 38.46N112.05W
Rich Hill *town* U.S.A. **83** 38.06N 94.22W
Richibucto Canada **77** 46.41N 64.52W
Richland U.S.A. **80** 46.17N119.18W
Richmond N.S.W. Australia **67** 33.36S150.46E
Richmond Qld. Australia **64** 20.44S143.08E
Richmond New Zealand **60** 41.20S173.10E
Richmond C.P. R.S.A. **56** 31.24S 23.56E
Richmond U.K. **10** 54.24N 1.43W
Richmond Ind. U.S.A. **84** 39.50N 84.51W
Richmond Ont. Canada **77** 45.11N 75.50W
Richmond Que. Canada **77** 45.40N 72.09W
Richmond Utah U.S.A. **80** 41.55N111.48W
Richmond Va. U.S.A. **85** 37.34N 77.27W
Richmond Hill *town* Canada **76** 43.52N 79.27W
Richmond Range *mts.* Australia **67** 29.00S152.48E
Ricobayo, Embalse de *resr.* Spain **16** 41.40N 5.50W
Ridderkerk Neth. **14** 51.53N 4.39E
Rideau *r.* Canada **77** 45.27N 75.42W
Rideau Lakes Canada **76** 44.40N 76.10W
Ridgway U.S.A. **84** 41.26N 78.44W
Riding Mtn. Canada **75** 50.37N 99.50W
Riding Mtn. Nat. Park Canada **75** 50.55N100.25W
Ried Austria **20** 48.13N 13.30E
Riemst Belgium **14** 50.49N 5.38E
Riesa E. Germany **20** 51.18N 13.18E
Rieti Italy **18** 42.24N 12.53E
Rifle U.S.A. **80** 39.32N107.47W
Rift Valley *d.* Kenya **55** 1.00N 36.00E
Riga U.S.S.R. **23** 56.53N 24.08E
Riga, G. of *see* Rīgas Jūras Līcis *g.* U.S.S.R. **23**
Rīgān Iran **43** 28.40N 58.58E
Rīgas Jūras Līcis *g.* U.S.S.R. **23** 57.30N 23.35E
Rīgestān *f.* Afghan. **40** 30.35N 65.00E
Riggins U.S.A. **80** 45.25N116.19W
Rīg Matī Iran **43** 27.40N 58.11E
Rigo P.N.G. **64** 9.50S147.35E
Rigolet Canada **77** 54.20N 58.35W
Riihimäki Finland **23** 60.45N 24.46E
Riiser-Larsenhalvöya *pen.* Antarctica **96** 68.00S 35.00E
Rijeka Yugo. **18** 45.20N 14.25E
Rijssen Neth. **14** 52.19N 6.31E
Rijswijk Neth. **14** 52.03N 4.22E
Riley U.S.A. **80** 43.31N119.28W
Rimah, Wādī ar *r.* Saudi Arabia **42** 26.10N 44.00E
Rimavská Sobota Czech. **21** 48.23N 20.02E
Rimbo Sweden **23** 59.45N 18.22E
Rimini Italy **15** 44.01N 12.34E
Rîmnicu-Sărat Romania **21** 45.24N 27.06E
Rîmnicu-Vîlcea Romania **21** 45.06N 24.22E
Rimouski Canada **77** 48.27N 68.32W
Rinbung China **41** 29.16N 89.54E
Rinconada Argentina **92** 22.26S 66.10W
Rindal Norway **22** 63.04N 9.13E
Ringebu Norway **23** 61.31N 10.10E
Ringerike Norway **23** 60.10N 10.12E
Ringim Nigeria **53** 12.09N 9.08E
Ringköbing Denmark **23** 56.05N 8.15E
Ringling U.S.A. **80** 46.16N110.49W
Ringsted Denmark **23** 55.27N 11.49E
Ringus India **40** 27.21N 75.34E
Ringvassöy *i.* Norway **22** 69.55N 19.10E
Ringwood Australia **67** 37.51S145.13E
Ringwood U.K. **11** 50.50N 1.48W
Riobamba Ecuador **90** 1.44S 78.40W
Rio Branco Brazil **90** 9.59S 67.49W
Río Bueno Chile **93** 40.20S 72.55W
Rio Casca Brazil **94** 20.13S 42.38W
Rio Claro Brazil **94** 22.19S 47.35W
Río Cuarto Argentina **93** 33.08S 64.20W
Rio de Janeiro Brazil **94** 22.53S 43.17W
Rio de Janeiro *d.* Brazil **94** 22.00S 42.30W
Río Gallegos Argentina **93** 51.37S 69.10W
Río Grande *town* Argentina **93** 53.50S 67.40W
Rio Grande *town* Brazil **94** 32.03S 52.08W
Rio Grande *r.* Mexico/U.S.A. **83** 25.57N 97.09W
Río Grande *r.* Nicaragua **87** 12.48N 83.30W
Rio Grande City U.S.A. **83** 26.23N 98.49W
Rio Grande do Norte *d.* Brazil **91** 6.00S 36.30W
Rio Grande do Sul *d.* Brazil **94** 30.15S 53.30W
Ríohacha Colombia **90** 11.34N 72.58W
Rio Largo Brazil **91** 9.28S 35.50W
Río Negro *d.* Argentina **93** 40.00S 67.00W
Rio Negro Brazil **94** 26.06S 49.48W
Río Negro, Embalse del *resr.* Uruguay **93** 32.45S 56.00W
Rio Novo Brazil **94** 21.15S 43.09W
Rio Piracicaba Brazil **94** 19.54S 43.10W
Rio Pomba Brazil **94** 21.15S 43.12W
Rio Prêto Brazil **94** 22.06S 43.52W
Ríosucio Colombia **90** 7.27N 77.07W
Río Tercero Argentina **92** 32.10S 64.05W
Rio Verde *town* Brazil **92** 17.50S 50.55W
Ripley N.Y. U.S.A. **84** 42.16N 79.43W
Ripon U.K. **10** 54.08N 1.31W
Ripon Canada **77** 45.47N 75.06W
Riparora Brazil **94** 17.20S 45.02W
Risbäck Sweden **22** 64.42N 15.32E
Riscle France **17** 43.40N 0.05W
Rishā, Wādī ar *r.* Saudi Arabia **43** 25.40N 44.08E
Rishikesh India **41** 30.07N 78.42E
Rishon LeZiyyon Israel **44** 31.57N 34.48E
Risle *r.* France **15** 49.26N 0.23E
Rison U.S.A. **83** 33.58N 92.11W
Risör Norway **23** 58.43N 9.14E
Rissani Morocco **50** 31.23N 4.09W
Riti Nigeria **53** 7.57N 9.41E
Ritidian Pt. Guam **68** 13.39N144.51E
Ritzville U.S.A. **80** 47.08N118.23W
Riva Italy **15** 45.53N 10.50E
Rivadavia Argentina **92** 24.11S 62.53W
Rivarolo Canavese Italy **15** 45.25N 7.36E
Rivas Nicaragua **87** 11.26N 85.50W
Rivera Uruguay **93** 30.54S 55.31W
River Cess *town* Liberia **52** 5.28N 9.32W
Rivergaro Italy **15** 44.55N 9.36E
Riverhead U.S.A. **84** 40.55N 72.40W
Riverina *f.* Australia **67** 34.30S145.20E
Rivers Canada **75** 50.02N100.12W
Rivers *d.* Nigeria **53** 4.45N 6.35E
Riversdale R.S.A. **56** 34.05S 21.15E
Riverside U.S.A. **81** 33.59N117.22W
Rivers Inlet *town* Canada **74** 51.40N127.20W
Riverton Australia **66** 34.08S138.24E
Riverton Canada **75** 50.59N 96.59W
Riverton New Zealand **60** 46.21S168.01E
Riverton U.S.A. **80** 43.02N108.23W
Riviera di Levante *f.* Italy **15** 44.00N 9.40E
Riviera di Ponente *f.* Italy **15** 43.40N 8.00E
Rivière-du-Loup *town* Canada **77** 47.50N 69.32W
Rivière Pentecôte *town* Canada **77** 49.47N 67.10W
Rivoli Italy **15** 45.04N 7.31E
Riyadh *see* Ar Riyāḍ Saudi Arabia **43**
Rize Turkey **42** 41.03N 40.31E
Rizhao China **32** 35.26N119.27E
Rizokárpason Cyprus **44** 35.35N 34.24E
Rizzuto, Capo *c.* Italy **19** 38.54N 17.06E
Rjukan Norway **23** 59.52N 8.34E
Roa Norway **23** 60.17N 10.37E
Roag, Loch U.K. **12** 58.14N 6.50W
Roanne France **17** 46.02N 4.05E
Roanoke *r.* U.S.A. **85** 35.56N 76.43W
Roanoke Ala. U.S.A. **85** 33.09N 85.24W
Roanoke Va. U.S.A. **85** 37.15N 79.58W
Roanoke Rapids *town* U.S.A. **85** 36.28N 77.40W
Roaring Springs U.S.A. **83** 33.54N100.52W
Robāţ Iran **43** 30.04N 54.49E
Robe Australia **66** 37.11S139.45E
Robe, Mt. Australia **66** 31.39S141.16E
Roberts, Mt. Australia **67** 28.12S152.21E
Robertsganj India **41** 24.42N 83.04E
Robertson R.S.A. **56** 33.48S 19.52E
Robertsport Liberia **52** 6.45N 11.22W
Robertstown Australia **66** 33.59S139.03E
Roberval Canada **77** 48.31N 72.13W
Robin Hood's Bay *town* U.K. **10** 54.26N 0.31W
Robinson *r.* Australia **64** 16.03S137.16E
Robinson Ranges *mts.* Australia **62** 25.45S119.00E
Robinvale Australia **66** 34.37S142.50E
Robledo Spain **16** 38.46N 2.26W
Roblin Man. Canada **75** 51.17N101.28W
Roboré Bolivia **92** 18.20S 59.45W
Robson, Mt. Canada **74** 53.10N119.10W
Rocas *i.* Atlantic Oc. **95** 3.50S 33.50W
Roccella Italy **19** 38.19N 16.24E
Rocciamelone *mtn.* Italy **15** 45.12N 7.05E
Rocha Uruguay **94** 34.30S 54.22W
Rocha da Gale, Barragem *dam* Portugal **16** 37.42N 7.35W
Rochdale U.K. **10** 53.36N 2.10W
Rochechouart France **17** 45.49N 0.50E
Rochefort Belgium **14** 50.10N 5.13E
Rochefort France **17** 45.57N 0.58W
Rochelle U.S.A. **82** 41.55N 89.05W
Rocher River *town* Canada **74** 61.23N112.44W
Rochester Australia **67** 36.22S144.42E
Rochester Kent U.K. **11** 51.22N 0.30E
Rochester Minn. U.S.A. **82** 44.01N 92.27W
Rochester N.Y. U.S.A. **84** 43.12N 77.37W
Rochfort Bridge Rep. of Ire. **13** 53.25N 7.19W
Rock *r.* Canada **74** 60.07N127.07W
Rock U.S.A. **84** 46.03N 87.10W
Rockall *i.* U.K. **8** 57.39N 13.44W
Rockall Bank *f.* Atlantic Oc. **8** 57.30N 14.00W
Rockdale U.S.A. **85** 39.21N 76.46W
Rockefeller Plateau Antarctica **96** 80.00S140.00W
Rockford U.S.A. **82** 42.17N 89.06W
Rock Hall U.S.A. **85** 39.08N 76.14W
Rockhampton Australia **64** 23.22S150.32E
Rock Hill *town* U.S.A. **85** 34.55N 81.01W
Rockingham Australia **63** 32.16S115.21E
Rockingham U.S.A. **85** 34.56N 79.47W
Rock Island *town* U.S.A. **82** 41.30N 90.34W
Rockland Canada **77** 45.32N 75.19W
Rockland Idaho U.S.A. **80** 42.34N112.53W
Rockland Maine U.S.A. **84** 44.06N 69.06W
Rockland Mich. U.S.A. **84** 46.44N 89.12W
Rocklands Resr. Australia **66** 37.13S141.52E
Rockport U.S.A. **80** 39.45N123.47W
Rock Rapids *town* U.S.A. **82** 43.26N 96.10W
Rock Sound *town* Bahamas **87** 24.54N 76.11W
Rocksprings Tex. U.S.A. **83** 30.01N100.13W
Rock Springs Wyo. U.S.A. **80** 41.35N109.13W
Rockville U.S.A. **85** 39.05N 77.09W
Rockwood Tenn. U.S.A. **85** 35.52N 84.40W
Rocky Ford U.S.A. **78** 38.03N103.44W
Rocky Gully *town* Australia **63** 34.31S117.01E
Rocky Island L. Canada **76** 46.55N 82.55W
Rocky Mount *town* U.S.A. **85** 35.56N 77.48W
Rocky Mountain Foothills *f.* Canada **74** 57.17N123.21W
Rocky Mountain Nat. Park U.S.A. **80** 40.19N105.42W
Rocky Mountain Trench *f.* Canada **74** 56.45N124.47W
Rocky Mts. N. America **80** 43.21N109.50W
Rocky Pt. Australia **63** 33.30S124.01E
Rocky Pt. Namibia **56** 19.00S 12.29E
Rocroi France **14** 49.56N 4.31E
Rod Pakistan **40** 28.06N 63.12E
Rödby Denmark **23** 54.42N 11.24E
Roddickton Canada **77** 50.52N 56.08W
Rodel U.K. **12** 57.44N 6.58W
Rodeo Mexico **83** 25.11N104.34W
Rodez France **17** 44.21N 2.34E
Ródhos *i.* Greece **19** 36.12N 28.00E
Ródhos *town* Greece **19** 36.24N 28.15E
Rodonit, Kep-i- *c.* Albania **19** 41.34N 19.25E
Roe, L. Australia **63** 30.40S122.10E
Roebourne Australia **62** 20.48S117.10E
Roebuck B. Australia **62** 19.04S122.17E
Roermond Neth. **14** 51.12N 6.00E
Roeselare Belgium **14** 50.57N 3.06E
Rogachev U.S.S.R. **21** 53.05N 30.02E
Rogaland *d.* Norway **23** 59.00N 6.15E
Rogers, Mt. U.S.A. **85** 36.35N 81.32W
Rogerson U.S.A. **80** 42.14N114.47W
Roggan *r.* Canada **76** 54.24N 78.05W
Roggan L. Canada **76** 54.10N 77.58W
Roggan River *town* Canada **76** 54.24N 78.05W
Roggeveen, Cabo *c.* I. de Pascua **69** 27.06S109.16W
Rogliano France **17** 42.57N 9.25E
Rogue *r.* U.S.A. **80** 42.26N124.25W
Rohri Pakistan **40** 27.41N 68.54E
Rohtak India **40** 28.54N 76.34E
Rojas Argentina **93** 34.15S 60.44W
Rokan *r.* Indonesia **36** 2.00N101.00E
Rokel *r.* Sierra Leone **52** 8.36N 12.55W
Rola Co *l.* China **39** 35.26N 88.24E
Röldal Norway **23** 59.49N 6.48E
Rolette U.S.A. **82** 48.40N 99.51W
Rolla Mo. U.S.A. **83** 37.57N 91.46W
Rolla N.Dak. U.S.A. **82** 48.52N 99.37W
Rolleston Australia **64** 24.25S148.35E
Rolleville Bahamas **87** 23.41N 76.00W
Rolvsöya *i.* Norway **22** 70.58N 24.00E
Roma Australia **64** 26.35S148.47E
Roma Italy **18** 41.54N 12.29E
Roma Sweden **23** 57.32N 18.28E
Romain, C. U.S.A. **85** 33.00N 79.22W
Romaine *r.* Canada **77** 50.18N 63.47W
Roman Romania **21** 46.55N 26.56E
Romang *i.* Indonesia **37** 7.45S127.20E
Romania Europe **21** 46.30N 24.00E
Romano, C. U.S.A. **85** 25.50N 81.41W
Romans France **17** 45.03N 5.03E
Rome *see* Roma Italy **18**
Rome Ga. U.S.A. **85** 34.01N 85.02W
Rome N.Y. U.S.A. **84** 43.13N 75.27W
Romeo U.S.A. **84** 42.47N 83.01W
Romilly France **15** 48.31N 3.44E
Romney Marsh *f.* U.K. **11** 51.03N 0.55E
Romorantin France **15** 47.22N 1.44E
Rona *i.* U.K. **12** 57.33N 5.58W
Ronan U.S.A. **80** 47.32N114.06W
Ronas Hill U.K. **8** 60.32N 1.26W
Roncesvalles Spain **16** 43.01N 1.19W
Ronda Spain **16** 36.45N 5.10W
Rondane *mtn.* Norway **23** 61.55N 9.45E
Rondônia *d.* Brazil **90** 12.10S 62.30W
Rondonópolis Brazil **91** 16.29S 54.37W
Rongcheng China **32** 37.09N122.23E
Ronge, Lac la *l.* Canada **75** 55.07N104.45W
Rongjiang China **33** 25.56N108.31E
Rongxar China **41** 28.14N 87.44E
Rong Xian China **33** 29.28N104.32E
Roniu *mtn.* Tahiti **69** 17.49S149.12W
Rönne Denmark **23** 55.06N 14.42E
Ronneby Sweden **23** 56.12N 15.18E
Ronse Belgium **14** 50.45N 3.36E
Ronuro *r.* Brazil **91** 11.56S 53.33W
Roof Butte *mtn.* U.S.A. **81** 36.28N109.05W
Roorkee India **41** 29.52N 77.53E
Roosendaal Neth. **14** 51.32N 4.28E
Roosevelt *r.* Brazil **90** 7.35S 60.20W
Roosevelt U.S.A. **80** 40.18N109.59W
Roosevelt I. Antarctica **96** 79.00S161.00W
Root *r.* Canada **74** 62.50N123.40W
Ropcha U.S.S.R. **24** 62.50N 51.55E
Roper *r.* Australia **64** 14.40S135.30E
Roper Valley *town* Australia **64** 14.56S134.00E
Roque Pérez Argentina **93** 35.23S 59.22W
Roraima *d.* Brazil **90** 2.00N 62.00W
Roraima, Mt. Guyana **90** 5.14N 60.44W
Rorketon Canada **75** 51.26N 99.32W
Röros Norway **22** 62.35N 11.23E
Rosa, Monte *mtn.* Italy/Switz. **15** 45.56N 7.51E
Rosamond U.S.A. **81** 34.52N118.10W
Rosario Argentina **93** 32.57S 60.40W
Rosário Brazil **91** 3.00S 44.15W
Rosario Mexico **81** 23.00N105.52W
Rosario Uruguay **93** 34.19S 57.21W
Rosario de la Frontera Argentina **92** 25.50S 64.55W
Rosario del Tala Argentina **93** 32.20S 59.10W
Rosário do Sul Brazil **94** 30.15S 54.55W
Rosarito Mexico **81** 28.38N114.04W
Rosas Spain **16** 42.19N 3.10E
Roscoe S.Dak. U.S.A. **82** 45.27N 99.20W
Roscoff France **17** 48.44N 4.00W
Roscommon Rep. of Ire. **13** 53.38N 8.13W
Roscommon *d.* Rep. of Ire. **13** 53.38N 8.11W
Roscrea Rep. of Ire. **13** 52.57N 7.49W
Roseau *r.* Canada **75** 49.10N 97.20W
Roseau Dominica **87** 15.18N 61.23W
Roseau U.S.A. **82** 48.51N 95.46W
Rose Blanche Canada **77** 47.37N 58.43W
Rosebud Australia **67** 38.21S144.54E
Rosebud *r.* Canada **74** 51.25N112.37W
Roseburg U.S.A. **80** 43.13N123.20W
Rose Harbour Canada **74** 52.15N131.10W
Rosenberg U.S.A. **83** 29.33N 95.48W
Rosenheim W. Germany **20** 47.51N 12.09E
Rosetown Canada **75** 51.33N108.00W
Rosetta R.S.A. **56** 29.18S 29.58E
Roseville Calif. U.S.A. **80** 38.45N121.17W
Roseville Mich. U.S.A. **76** 42.30N 82.56W
Rosières France **15** 49.49N 2.43E
Rosignano Marittimo Italy **18** 43.24N 10.28E
Roşiori-de-Vede Romania **21** 44.07N 25.00E
Rositsa Bulgaria **21** 43.57N 27.57E
Roska *r.* U.S.S.R. **21** 49.27N 29.45E
Roskilde Denmark **23** 55.39N 12.05E
Roslags-Näsby Sweden **23** 59.26N 18.04E
Roslavl U.S.S.R. **24** 53.55N 32.53E
Ross New Zealand **60** 42.54S170.49E
Rossano Italy **19** 39.35N 16.39E
Ross Dependency Antarctica **96** 75.00S170.00W
Rossignol, L. Canada **77** 44.10N 65.10W
Rossing Namibia **56** 22.31S 14.52E
Rossiyskaya S.F.S.R. *d.* U.S.S.R. **28** 62.00N 80.00E
Rosslare Rep. of Ire. **13** 52.17N 6.23W
Rosso Mauritania **50** 16.30N 15.49W
Ross-on-Wye U.K. **11** 51.55N 2.36W
Rossosh U.S.S.R. **25** 50.12N 39.35E
Ross River *town* Canada **74** 62.30N131.30W
Rössvatnet *l.* Norway **22** 65.45N 14.00E
Rosta Norway **22** 68.59N 19.40E
Rosthern Canada **75** 52.40N106.17W
Rostock E. Germany **20** 54.06N 12.09E
Rostock *d.* E. Germany **20** 54.15N 12.30E
Rostov R.S.F.S.R. U.S.S.R. **25** 47.15N 39.45E
Rostov R.S.F.S.R. U.S.S.R. **24** 57.11N 39.23E
Roswell Ga. U.S.A. **85** 34.02N 84.21W
Roswell N.Mex. U.S.A. **81** 33.24N104.32W
Rota *i.* Mariana Is. **37** 14.10N145.15E
Rotem Belgium **14** 51.04N 5.44E
Rothbury U.K. **10** 55.19N 1.54W
Rother *r.* U.K. **9** 50.56N 0.46E
Rotherham U.K. **10** 53.26N 1.21W
Rothes U.K. **12** 57.31N 3.13W
Rothesay Canada **77** 45.23N 66.00W
Rothesay U.K. **12** 55.50N 5.03W
Roti *i.* Indonesia **62** 10.30S123.10E
Roto Australia **67** 33.04S145.27E
Rotondella Italy **19** 40.10N 16.32E
Rotorua New Zealand **60** 38.07S176.17E
Rotorua, L. New Zealand **60** 38.00S176.00E
Rotterdam Neth. **14** 51.55N 4.29E
Rottnest I. Australia **63** 32.01S115.28E
Rottweil W. Germany **20** 48.10N 8.37E
Roubaix France **14** 50.42N 3.10E
Rouen France **15** 49.26N 1.05E
Rougé France **15** 47.47N 1.26W
Rouge *r.* Canada **77** 45.39N 74.41W
Rouku P.N.G. **64** 8.40S141.35E
Round Mt. Australia **67** 30.26S152.15E
Round Pond *l.* Canada **77** 48.10N 56.00W
Roundup U.S.A. **80** 46.27N108.33W
Rousay *i.* U.K. **12** 59.10N 3.02W
Rouyn Canada **76** 48.20N 79.00W
Rovaniemi Finland **22** 66.30N 25.40E
Rovato Italy **15** 45.34N 10.00E
Rovereto Italy **15** 45.53N 11.02E
Rovigo Italy **15** 45.04N 11.47E
Rovinj Yugo. **20** 45.06N 13.39E
Rovno U.S.S.R. **21** 50.39N 26.10E
Rowena Australia **67** 29.49S148.54E
Rowley Shoals *f.* Australia **62** 17.30S119.00E
Roxboro U.S.A. **85** 36.24N 79.00W
Roxburgh New Zealand **60** 45.33S169.19E
Roxen *l.* Sweden **23** 58.30N 15.41E
Roxton Canada **77** 45.29N 72.36W
Roy U.S.A. **81** 35.57N104.12W
Royale, Isle *i.* U.S.A. **84** 48.00N 89.00W
Royal L. Canada **75** 56.00N103.15W
Royal Leamington Spa U.K. **11** 52.18N 1.32W
Royal Tunbridge Wells U.K. **11** 51.07N 0.16E
Royan France **17** 45.37N 1.02W
Roye France **15** 49.42N 2.48E
Royston U.K. **11** 52.03N 0.01W
Rozhishche U.S.S.R. **21** 50.58N 25.15E
Rožňava Czech. **21** 48.40N 20.32E
Rtishchevo U.S.S.R. **24** 52.16N 43.45E
Ruahine Range *mts.* New Zealand **60** 40.00S176.00E
Ruapehu *mtn.* New Zealand **60** 39.20S175.30E
Ruapuke I. New Zealand **60** 46.45S168.30E
Rub 'al Khali *des. see* Ar Rub 'al Khālī *des.* Saudi Arabia **38**
Rubi *r.* Zaïre **54** 2.50N 24.06E
Rubino Ivory Coast **52** 6.04N 4.18W
Rubio Colombia **90** 7.42N 72.23W
Rubryn U.S.S.R. **21** 51.52N 27.30E
Rubtsovsk U.S.S.R. **28** 51.29N 81.10E
Ruby Mts. U.S.A. **80** 40.25N115.35W
Rūdān *r.* Iran **43** 27.02N 56.53E
Rudauli India **41** 26.45N 81.45E
Rūdbār Afghan. **40** 30.09N 62.36E
Rudewa Tanzania **55** 6.40S 37.08E
Rudki U.S.S.R. **21** 49.40N 23.28E
Rudnaya Pristan U.S.S.R. **31** 44.18N135.51E
Rudnichnyy U.S.S.R. **24** 59.10N 52.28E
Rudnik Poland **21** 50.28N 22.15E
Rudnyy U.S.S.R. **28** 53.00N 63.05E
Rudolstadt E. Germany **20** 50.44N 11.20E
Rue France **17** 50.15N 1.40E
Rufā'ah Sudan **48** 14.46N 33.22E
Ruffec France **17** 46.02N 0.12E
Rufiji *r.* Tanzania **55** 8.02S 39.19E
Rufino Argentina **93** 34.16S 62.45W
Rufisque Senegal **52** 14.43N 17.16W
Rufunsa Zambia **55** 15.02S 29.35E
Rugao China **32** 32.25N120.40E
Rugby U.K. **11** 52.23N 1.16W
Rugby U.S.A. **82** 48.22N100.00W
Rügen *i.* E. Germany **20** 54.30N 13.30E
Ruhr *f.* W. Germany **14** 51.22N 7.26E
Ruhr *r.* W. Germany **14** 51.27N 6.41E
Rui'an China **33** 26.50N120.40E
Ruijin China **33** 25.49N116.00E
Ruinen Neth. **14** 52.47N 6.21E
Rukwa *d.* Tanzania **55** 7.05S 31.25E
Rukwa, L. Tanzania **55** 8.00S 32.20E
Ruma Yugo. **21** 44.59N 19.51E
Rumbek Sudan **49** 6.48N 29.41E
Rum Cay *i.* Bahamas **87** 23.41N 74.53W
Rumford U.S.A. **84** 44.33N 70.33W
Rum Jungle Australia **62** 13.01S131.00E
Rummānah Egypt **44** 31.01N 32.40E
Runcorn U.K. **10** 53.20N 2.44W
Rundvik Sweden **22** 63.30N 19.24E
Rungāni Pakistan **40** 26.38N 65.43E
Rungwa *r.* Tanzania **55** 7.38S 31.55E
Rungwa Singida Tanzania **55** 6.57S 33.35E
Rungwe Mt. Tanzania **55** 9.10S 33.40E
Runka Nigeria **53** 12.28N 7.20E
Ruoqiang China **30** 39.00N 88.00E
Ruo Shui *r.* China **30** 42.15N101.03E
Rūpar India **40** 30.58N 76.32E
Rupert *r.* Canada **76** 51.30N 78.45W
Rupununi *r.* Guyana **90** 4.00N 58.30W
Rur *r.* Neth. **14** 51.12N 5.58E
Rurutu *i.* Pacific Oc. **69** 22.25S151.20W
Rusape Zimbabwe **57** 18.30S 32.08E
Ruşayriş, Khazzān ar *resr.* Sudan **49** 11.40N 34.20E
Ruse Bulgaria **19** 43.50N 25.59E
Rusera India **41** 25.45N 86.02E
Rushan China **32** 36.54N121.30E
Rushden U.K. **11** 52.17N 0.37W
Rush Springs *town* U.S.A. **83** 34.47N 97.58W
Rushworth Australia **67** 36.38S145.02E
Russell Canada **77** 45.17N 75.17W
Russellkonda India **41** 19.56N 84.35E
Russell L. Man. Canada **75** 56.15N101.30W
Russell L. N.W.T. Canada **74** 63.05N115.44W
Russell Pt. Canada **72** 73.30N115.00W
Russell Range *mts.* Australia **63** 33.15S123.30E
Russellville U.S.A. **83** 35.17N 93.08W
Russkaya Polyana U.S.S.R. **28** 53.48N 73.54E
Rustavi U.S.S.R. **25** 41.34N 45.03E
Rustenburg R.S.A. **56** 25.39S 27.13E
Ruston U.S.A. **83** 32.32N 92.38W
Rutana Burundi **55** 3.58S 30.00E
Rütenbrock W. Germany **14** 52.51N 7.06E
Ruteng Indonesia **37** 8.35S120.28E
Rutenga Zimbabwe **56** 21.15S 30.46E
Ruth U.S.A. **80** 39.17N114.59W
Ruthin U.K. **10** 53.07N 3.18W
Rutland U.S.A. **84** 43.36N 72.59W
Rutledge *r.* Canada **75** 61.04N112.00W
Rutledge L. Canada **75** 61.33N110.47W
Rutog China **41** 33.27N 79.43E
Rutshuru Zaïre **55** 1.10S 29.26E
Ruvu Coast Tanzania **55** 6.50S 38.42E
Ruvuma *r.* Mozambique/Tanzania **55** 10.30S 40.30E
Ruvuma *d.* Tanzania **55** 10.45S 36.15E
Ruwaybah *wells* Sudan **48** 15.39N 28.45E
Ruwenzori Range *mts.* Uganda/Zaïre **55** 0.30N 30.00E
Ruyigi Burundi **55** 3.26S 30.14E
Ruzayevka U.S.S.R. **24** 54.04N 44.55E
Ruzitgort U.S.S.R. **24** 62.51N 64.52E
Ružomberok Czech. **21** 49.06N 19.18E
Rwanda Africa **55** 2.00S 30.00E
Ryan, Loch U.K. **12** 54.56N 5.02W
Ryasna U.S.S.R. **21** 54.00N 31.14E
Ryazan U.S.S.R. **24** 54.37N 39.43E
Ryazhsk U.S.S.R. **24** 53.40N 40.07E
Rybachiy, Poluostrov *pen.* U.S.S.R. **24** 69.45N 32.30E
Rybachye U.S.S.R. **30** 46.27N 81.30E
Rybinsk U.S.S.R. **24** 58.01N 38.52E
Rybinskoye Vodokhranilishche *resr.* U.S.S.R. **24** 58.30N 38.25E
Rybnik Poland **21** 50.06N 18.32E
Rybnitsa U.S.S.R. **21** 47.42N 29.00E
Ryd Sweden **23** 56.28N 14.41E
Rye U.K. **11** 50.57N 0.46E
Rye *r.* U.K. **10** 54.10N 0.44W
Ryki Poland **21** 51.39N 21.56E
Rylstone Australia **67** 32.48S149.58E
Ryūgasaki Japan **35** 35.54N140.11E
Ryukyu Is. *see* Nansei shotō *is.* Japan **31**
Rzeszów Poland **21** 50.04N 22.00E
Rzhev U.S.S.R. **24** 56.15N 34.18E

Saa to **San Benito**

S

Saa Cameroon **53** 4.24N 11.25E
Saale r. E. Germany **20** 51.58N 11.53E
Saanich Canada **74** 48.28N123.22W
Saar r. W. Germany **14** 49.43N 6.34E
Saarbrücken W. Germany **20** 49.15N 6.58E
Saarburg W. Germany **14** 49.36N 6.33E
Saaremaa i. U.S.S.R. **23** 58.25N 22.30E
Saarijärvi Finland **22** 62.43N 25.16E
Saariselkä mts. Finland **22** 68.15N 28.30E
Saarland d. W. Germany **14** 49.30N 6.50E
Saba i. Leeward Is. **87** 17.42N 63.26W
Šabac Yugo. **21** 44.45N 19.41E
Sabadell Spain **16** 41.33N 2.07E
Sabah d. Malaysia **36** 5.30N117.00E
Sabalān, Kūhhā-ye mts. Iran **43** 38.15N 47.50E
Sabana, Archipiélago de Cuba **87** 23.30N 80.00W
Sabanalarga Colombia **90** 10.38N 75.00W
Sab'atayn, Ramlat as f. Yemen/S. Yemen **45** 15.30N 46.10E
Sabaudia Italy **18** 41.18N 13.01E
Sabbioneta Italy **15** 45.00N 10.39E
Sabhā Libya **51** 27.02N 14.26E
Sabhā d. Libya **51** 27.02N 15.30E
Sabi r. Zimbabwe **57** 21.16S 32.20E
Sabinas Mexico **83** 27.51N101.07W
Sabinas Hidalgo Mexico **83** 26.30N100.10W
Sabine r. U.S.A. **83** 30.00N 93.45W
Sabine L. U.S.A. **83** 29.50N 93.50W
Sabkhat al Bardawīl l. Egypt **44** 31.10N 33.15E
Sablayan Phil. **37** 12.50N120.50E
Sable, C. Canada **77** 43.25N 65.35W
Sable, C. U.S.A. **85** 25.05N 65.50W
Sable I. Canada **73** 43.55N 59.50W
Sablé-sur-Sarthe France **15** 47.50N 0.20W
Sabon Birni Nigeria **53** 13.37N 6.15E
Sabongidda Nigeria **53** 6.54N 5.56E
Sabrina Coast f. Antarctica **96** 67.00S120.00E
Şabyā Saudi Arabia **48** 17.09N 42.37E
Sabzevār Iran **43** 36.13N 57.38E
Sacaca Bolivia **92** 18.05S 66.25W
Sacajawea mtn. U.S.A. **80** 45.15N117.17W
Sacandica Angola **54** 5.58S 15.56E
Sac City U.S.A. **82** 42.25N 95.00W
Sacedón Spain **16** 40.29N 2.44W
Sachigo r. Canada **75** 55.00N 89.00W
Sachigo L. Canada **75** 53.50N 92.00W
Sackville Canada **77** 45.54N 64.22W
Saco U.S.A. **84** 43.29N 70.28W
Sacramento Brazil **94** 19.51S 26.47W
Sacramento U.S.A. **80** 38.35N121.30W
Sacramento r. U.S.A. **80** 38.03N121.56W
Sacramento Mts. U.S.A. **81** 33.10N105.50W
Sacramento Valley f. U.S.A. **80** 39.15N122.00W
Sádaba Spain **16** 42.19N 1.10W
Sadani Tanzania **55** 6.00S 38.40E
Sadda Pakistan **40** 33.42N 70.20E
Sa Dec Vietnam **34** 10.19N105.45E
Sādiqābād Pakistan **40** 28.18N 70.08E
Sadiya India **39** 27.49N 95.38E
Sādri India **40** 25.11N 73.26E
Sadulgarh India **40** 29.35N 74.19E
Şafājah des. Saudi Arabia **42** 26.30N 39.30E
Şafāniyah Egypt **44** 28.49N 30.48E
Şafarābād Iran **43** 38.59N 47.25E
Säffle Sweden **23** 59.08N 12.56E
Saffron Walden U.K. **11** 52.02N 0.15E
Safi Morocco **50** 32.20N 9.17W
Safid r. Iran **43** 37.23N 50.11E
Safonovo R.S.F.S.R. U.S.S.R. **24** 55.08N 33.16E
Safonovo R.S.F.S.R. U.S.S.R. **24** 65.40N 48.10E
Saga China **41** 29.30N 85.09E
Sagaing Burma **34** 22.00N 96.00E
Sagaing d. Burma **34** 24.00N 95.00E
Sagala Mali **52** 14.09N 6.38W
Sagami r. Japan **35** 35.14N139.23E
Sagamihara Japan **35** 35.32N139.23E
Sagami-nada b. Japan **35** 34.55N139.30E
Sāgar India **41** 23.50N 78.43E
Sagara Japan **35** 34.41N138.12E
Sage U.S.A. **80** 41.49N110.59W
Saginaw U.S.A. **84** 43.25N 83.54W
Saginaw B. U.S.A. **84** 43.56N 83.40W
Sagiz U.S.S.R. **25** 47.31N 54.55E
Saglouc Canada **73** 62.10N 75.40W
Sagres Portugal **16** 37.00N 8.56W
Saguache U.S.A. **80** 38.05N106.08W
Sagua la Grande Cuba **87** 22.55N 80.05W
Saguenay r. Canada **77** 48.10N 69.43W
Sagunto Spain **16** 39.40N 0.17W
Sāgwāra India **40** 23.41N 74.01E
Sa'gya China **41** 28.55N 88.03E
Sahaba Sudan **48** 18.55N 30.28E
Sahagún Spain **16** 42.23N 5.02W
Sahand, Kūh-e mtn. Iran **43** 37.37N 46.27E
Sahara des. Africa **51** 22.30N 3.00E
Sahāranpur India **41** 29.58N 77.33E
Saharsa India **41** 25.53N 86.36E
Sahaswān India **41** 28.05N 78.45E
Sahbā, Wādī as r. Saudi Arabia **43** 23.48N 49.50E
Sāhibganj India **41** 25.15N 87.39E
Sāhīwāl Punjab Pakistan **40** 31.58N 72.20E
Sāhīwāl Punjab Pakistan **40** 30.40N 73.06E
Sahtaneh r. Canada **74** 59.02N122.28W
Sahuarita U.S.A. **81** 31.57N110.58W
Saibai i. Australia **64** 9.24S142.40E
Sa'īdābād Iran **43** 29.28N 55.43E
Saidpur Bangla. **41** 25.47N 88.54E
Saidu Pakistan **40** 34.45N 72.21E
Saimaa l. Finland **24** 61.20N 28.00E
Saimbeyli Turkey **42** 38.07N 36.08E
Saindak Pakistan **40** 29.17N 61.34E
St. Abb's Head U.K. **12** 55.54N 2.07W
St. Agapit Canada **77** 46.34N 71.26W
St. Alban's Canada **77** 47.52N 55.51W
St. Albans U.K. **11** 51.46N 0.21W
St. Albans Vt. U.S.A. **84** 44.49N 73.05W
St. Albert Canada **74** 53.37N113.40W
St. Alexis des Monts Canada **77** 46.28N 73.08W
St. Amand France **14** 50.27N 3.26E
St. Amand-Mont-Rond town France **17** 46.43N 2.29E
St. André, Cap c. Madagascar **57** 16.11S 44.27E
St. Andrews U.K. **12** 56.20N 2.48W
St. Andries Belgium **14** 51.12N 3.10E
St. Ann's Bay town Jamaica **87** 18.26N 77.12W
St. Anthony Canada **77** 51.22N 55.35W
St. Anthony U.S.A. **78** 43.59N111.40W
St. Arnaud Australia **66** 36.40S143.20E
St. Augustin r. Canada **77** 51.14N 58.41W
St. Augustine U.S.A. **85** 29.54N 81.19W
St. Augustin Saguenay Canada **77** 51.14N 58.39W
St. Austell U.K. **11** 50.20N 4.48W
St. Barthélemy i. Leeward Is. **87** 17.55N 62.50W
St. Barthélemy Canada **77** 46.12N 73.08W
St. Bees Head U.K. **10** 54.31N 3.39W
St. Boniface Canada **75** 49.55N 97.06W
St. Boswells U.K. **12** 55.35N 2.40W
St. Brides B. U.K. **11** 51.48N 5.03W
St. Brieuc France **17** 48.31N 2.45W
St. Calais France **15** 47.55N 0.45E
St. Casimir Canada **77** 46.40N 72.08W
St. Catharines Canada **76** 43.10N 79.15W
St. Catherine's Pt. U.K. **11** 50.34N 1.18W
St. Céré France **17** 44.52N 1.53E
St. Charles Mo. U.S.A. **82** 38.47N 90.29W
St. Cloud U.S.A. **82** 45.33N 94.10W
St. Croix i. U.S.V.Is. **87** 17.45N 64.35W
St. Cyrille de Wendover Canada **77** 45.56N 72.26W
St. David's U.K. **11** 51.54N 5.16W
St. David's I. Bermuda **95** 32.23N 64.42W
St. Denis France **15** 48.56N 2.21E
St. Dié France **17** 48.17N 6.57E
St. Dizier France **15** 48.38N 4.58E
St. Donat Canada **77** 46.19N 74.13W
Sainte-Agathe-des-Monts Canada **77** 46.03N 74.17W
Sainte Anne de Beaupré Canada **77** 47.02N 70.56W
Sainte Anne de la Pérade Canada **77** 46.35N 72.12W
Sainte-Anne-des-Monts Canada **77** 49.07N 66.29W
Sainte Emelie Canada **77** 46.19N 73.39W
St. Elias, Mt. U.S.A. **74** 60.18N140.55W
St. Elias Mts. Canada **74** 60.30N139.30W
St. Éloi Canada **77** 48.02N 69.13W
Sainte Lucie Canada **77** 46.07N 74.13W
Sainte Marguerite r. Canada **77** 50.10N 66.40W
Sainte Marguerite Canada **77** 46.03N 74.05W
Sainte Marie, Cap c. Madagascar **57** 25.36S 45.08E
Sainte Menehould France **15** 49.05N 4.54E
Sainte Mère-Église France **15** 49.24N 1.19W
Saintes France **17** 45.44N 0.38W
St. Espirit Canada **77** 45.56N 73.40W
Sainte-Thérèse-de-Blainville Canada **77** 45.39N 73.49W
St. Étienne France **17** 45.26N 4.26E
St. Fargeau France **15** 47.38N 3.04E
St. Faustin Canada **77** 46.07N 74.30W
St. Félix Canada **77** 46.10N 73.26W
Saintfield U.K. **13** 54.28N 5.50W
St. Fintan's Canada **77** 48.10N 58.50W
St. Florent France **17** 42.41N 9.18E
St. Florentin France **15** 48.00N 3.44E
St. Flour France **17** 45.02N 3.05E
St. Francis U.S.A. **82** 39.47N101.47W
St. Francisville U.S.A. **83** 30.47N 91.23W
St. Francois r. Canada **77** 46.07N 72.55W
St. Gabriel Canada **77** 46.17N 73.23W
St. Gallen Switz. **20** 47.25N 9.23E
St. Gaudens France **17** 43.07N 0.44E
St. George Australia **65** 28.03S148.30E
St. George Bermuda **95** 32.24N 64.42W
St. George N.B. Canada **77** 45.11N 66.57W
St. George Ont. Canada **76** 43.15N 80.15W
St. George U.S.A. **80** 37.06N113.35W
St. George, C. U.S.A. **85** 29.35N 85.04W
St. George Head Australia **67** 35.11S150.40E
St. Georges Belgium **14** 50.37N 5.20E
St. George's Grenada **87** 12.04N 61.44W
St. Georges Guiana **91** 3.54N 51.48W
St. Georges Canada **77** 46.37N 72.40W
St. George's B. Canada **77** 48.20N 59.00W
St. George's Channel Rep. of Ire./U.K. **13** 51.30N 6.20W
St. George's I. Bermuda **95** 32.24N 64.42W
St. Germain France **15** 48.53N 2.04E
St. Germain de Grantham Canada **77** 45.50N 72.34W
St. Gheorghe's Mouth est. Romania **19** 44.51N 29.37E
St. Gilles-Croix-de-Vie France **17** 46.42N 1.56W
St. Girons France **17** 42.59N 1.08E
St. Gotthard Pass Switz. **17** 46.30N 8.55E
St. Govan's Head U.K. **11** 51.36N 4.55W
St. Grégoire Canada **77** 46.16N 72.30W
St. Guillaume d'Upton Canada **77** 45.53N 72.46W
St. Helena i. Atlantic Oc. **95** 15.58S 5.43W
St. Helena B. R.S.A. **56** 32.35S 18.05E
St. Helens U.K. **10** 53.28N 2.43W
St. Helens U.S.A. **80** 45.52N122.48W
St. Helier U.K. **11** 49.12N 2.07W
St. Hilaire-du-Harcouët France **15** 48.35N 1.06W
St. Hubert Belgium **14** 50.02N 5.22E
St. Hyacinthe Canada **77** 45.38N 72.57W
St. Ignace U.S.A. **84** 45.53N 84.44W
St. Ives U.K. **11** 50.13N 5.29W
St. Jacques Canada **77** 45.57N 73.34W
St. Jean Canada **77** 45.18N 73.20W
St. Jean r. Canada **77** 50.17N 64.20W
St. Jean France **17** 45.17N 6.21E
St. Jean, Lac l. Canada **77** 48.35N 72.00W
St. Jean de Matha Canada **77** 46.10N 73.30W
St. Jean Pied-de-Port France **17** 43.10N 1.14W
St. Jérôme Canada **77** 45.47N 74.00W
St. John Canada **77** 45.16N 66.03W
St. John r. Canada **77** 45.16N 66.04W
St. John U.S.A. **83** 38.00N 98.46W
St. John, C. Canada **77** 50.00N 55.32W
St. John B. Canada **77** 50.40N 57.08W
St. John's Antigua **87** 17.07N 61.51W
St. John's Canada **77** 47.34N 52.43W
St. Johns U.S.A. **81** 34.30N109.22W
St. Johns r. U.S.A. **85** 30.24N 81.24W
St. Johnsbury U.S.A. **84** 44.25N 72.01W
St. John's Pt. U.K. **13** 54.14N 5.39W
St. Joseph La. U.S.A. **83** 31.55N 91.14W
St. Joseph Mich. U.S.A. **84** 42.05N 86.30W
St. Joseph Mo. U.S.A. **82** 39.46N 94.51W
St. Joseph, L. Canada **76** 51.05N 90.35W
St. Jovite Canada **77** 46.07N 74.36W
St. Jude Canada **77** 45.46N 72.59W
St. Junien France **17** 45.53N 0.55E
St. Just-en-Chaussée France **15** 49.30N 2.26E
St. Kilda i. U.K. **8** 57.55N 8.20W
St. Kitts-Nevis Leeward Is. **87** 17.20N 62.45W
St. Lambert Canada **77** 45.30N 73.30W
St. Laurent Man. Canada **75** 50.24N 97.56W
St. Laurent Que. Canada **77** 45.31N 73.41W
St. Laurent du Maroni Guiana **91** 5.30N 54.02W
St. Lawrence r. Canada **77** 48.45N 68.30W
St. Lawrence, G. of Canada **77** 48.00N 62.00W
St. Lawrence I. U.S.A. **72** 63.00N170.00W
St. Léonard d'Aston Canada **77** 46.06N 72.22W
St. Lewis Sd. Canada **77** 52.20N 55.40W
St. Lin Canada **77** 45.51N 73.45W
St. Lô France **15** 49.07N 1.05W
St. Louis Senegal **52** 16.01N 16.30W
St. Louis U.S.A. **82** 38.38N 90.11W
St. Louis Park town U.S.A. **82** 44.56N 93.22W
St. Lucia Windward Is. **87** 14.05N 61.00W
St. Lucia, L. R.S.A. **57** 28.05S 32.26E
St. Magnus B. U.K. **8** 60.25N 1.35W
St. Maixent France **17** 46.25N 0.12W
St. Malo France **15** 48.39N 2.00W
St. Malo, Golfe de g. France **17** 49.20N 2.00W
St.-Marc Haiti **87** 19.08N 72.41W
St. Margaret's Hope U.K. **12** 58.49N 2.57W
St. Maries U.S.A. **80** 47.19N116.35W
St. Martin i. Leeward Is. **87** 18.05N 63.05W
St. Martin U.K. **11** 49.27N 2.34W
St. Martin, L. Canada **75** 51.37N 98.29W
St. Martin's i. U.K. **11** 49.57N 6.16W
St. Mary U.K. **11** 49.14N 2.10W
St. Marys Australia **65** 41.33S148.12E
St. Mary's r. Canada **77** 45.02N 61.54W
St. Mary's i. U.K. **11** 49.55N 6.16W
St. Mary's, C. Canada **77** 46.49N 54.12W
St. Mary's B. Canada **77** 46.50N 53.47W
St. Matthew I. U.S.A. **72** 60.30N172.45W
St. Maur France **15** 48.48N 2.30E
St. Maurice r. Canada **77** 46.22N 72.32W
St. Moritz Switz. **20** 46.30N 9.51E
St. Nazaire France **17** 47.17N 2.12W
St. Neots U.K. **11** 52.14N 0.16W
St. Niklaas Belgium **14** 51.10N 4.09E
St. Omer France **17** 50.45N 2.15E
St. Pacôme Canada **77** 47.24N 69.57W
St. Pascal Canada **77** 47.32N 69.48W
St. Paul r. Canada **77** 51.26N 57.40W
St. Paul Pyr. Or. France **17** 42.49N 2.29E
St. Paul Ark. U.S.A. **83** 35.50N 93.48W
St. Paul Minn. U.S.A. **82** 45.00N 93.10W
St. Paul Nebr. U.S.A. **82** 41.13N 98.27W
St. Paul du Nord Canada **77** 48.27N 69.15W
St. Paulin Canada **77** 46.25N 73.01W
St. Paul Rocks is. Atlantic Oc. **95** 1.00N 29.23W
St. Peter U.S.A. **82** 44.17N 93.57W
St. Peter Port U.K. **11** 49.27N 2.32W
St. Petersburg U.S.A. **85** 27.45N 82.40W
St. Pierre Char. Mar. France **17** 45.57N 1.19W
St. Pierre S. Mar. France **15** 49.48N 0.29E
St. Pierre, Lac l. Canada **77** 46.12N 72.52W
St. Pierre and Miquelon is. N. America **77** 46.55N 56.10W
St. Pierre-Église France **15** 49.40N 1.24W
St. Pölten Austria **20** 48.13N 15.37E
St. Polycarpe Canada **77** 45.18N 74.18W
St. Quentin France **15** 49.51N 3.17E
St. Seine-l'Abbaye France **15** 47.26N 4.47E
St. Siméon Canada **77** 47.55N 69.58W
St. Stephen Canada **77** 45.12N 67.17W
St. Thomas Canada **76** 42.47N 81.12W
St. Thomas i. U.S.V.Is. **87** 18.22N 64.57W
St. Tropez France **17** 43.16N 6.39E
St. Truiden Belgium **14** 50.49N 5.11E
St. Valéry France **15** 49.52N 0.43E
St. Vallier France **17** 45.11N 4.49E
St. Vincent, Cap c. Madagascar **57** 21.57S 43.16E
St. Vincent, G. Australia **66** 35.00S138.05E
St. Vincent and the Grenadines Windward Is. **87** 13.00N 61.15W
St. Vith Belgium **14** 50.15N 6.08E
St. Wendel W. Germany **14** 49.27N 7.10E
St. Yrieix France **17** 45.31N 1.12E
St. Zénon Canada **77** 46.33N 73.49W
Saipan i. Mariana Is. **37** 15.12N145.43E
Saitama d. Japan **35** 35.55N139.00E
Sajama mtn. Bolivia **92** 18.06S 69.00W
Saka Kenya **55** 0.09S 39.18E
Sakai Japan **35** 34.35N135.28E
Sakākah Saudi Arabia **42** 29.59N 40.12E
Sakakawea, L. see Garrison Resr. U.S.A. **82**
Sakami r. Canada **76** 53.40N 76.40W
Sakami, Lac l. Canada **76** 53.10N 77.00W
Sâkâne, Erg i-n f. Mali **50** 21.00N 1.00W
Sakania Zaïre **55** 12.44S 28.34E
Sakarya r. Turkey **42** 41.08N 30.36E
Sakété Benin **53** 6.45N 2.45E
Sakhalin i. U.S.S.R. **31** 50.00N143.00E
Sākhar Afghan. **40** 32.57N 65.32E
Sakhi Sarwar Pakistan **40** 29.59N 70.18E
Sākoli India **41** 21.05N 79.59E
Sakrand Pakistan **40** 26.08N 68.16E
Sakri India **40** 21.02N 74.40E
Sakrivier R.S.A. **56** 30.53S 20.24E
Sakti India **41** 22.02N 82.58E
Sakuma Japan **35** 35.05N137.48E
Sal r. U.S.S.R. **25** 47.33N 40.40E
Sala Ethiopia **48** 16.58N 37.27E
Sala Sweden **23** 59.55N 16.36E
Salaca r. U.S.S.R. **23** 57.45N 24.21E
Salacgriva U.S.S.R. **23** 57.45N 24.21E
Salado r. Buenos Aires Argentina **93** 35.44S 57.22W
Salado r. Santa Fé Argentina **93** 31.40S 60.41W
Salado r. La Pampa Argentina **93** 36.15S 66.55W
Salado r. Mexico **83** 26.50N 99.17W
Salaga Ghana **52** 8.36N 0.32W
Salailua W. Samoa **68** 13.42S172.35W
Salālah Oman **38** 17.00N 54.04E
Salālah Sudan **48** 21.19N 36.13E
Salamanca Spain **16** 40.58N 5.40W
Salamat d. Chad **49** 11.00N 20.40E
Salāmbek Pakistan **40** 28.18N 65.09E
Salamina Colombia **90** 5.24N 75.31W
Salām Khān Afghan. **40** 31.47N 66.45E
Salani W. Samoa **68** 14.02S171.35W
Salatiga Indonesia **37** 7.15S110.34E
Salāya India **40** 22.19N 69.35E
Sala y Gomez i. Pacific Oc. **69** 26.28S105.28W
Salbris France **15** 47.26N 2.03E
Salcombe U.K. **11** 50.14N 3.47W
Saldaña Spain **16** 42.32N 4.48W
Saldanha R.S.A. **56** 33.00S 17.56E
Saldanha B. R.S.A. **56** 33.05S 17.50E
Saldus U.S.S.R. **23** 56.40N 22.30E
Sale Australia **67** 38.06S147.06E
Salé Morocco **50** 34.04N 6.50W
Salekhard U.S.S.R. **24** 66.33N 66.35E
Salelologa W. Samoa **68** 13.43S172.13W
Salem India **39** 11.38N 78.08E
Salem Ind. U.S.A. **84** 38.38N 86.06W
Salem Mo. U.S.A. **83** 37.39N 91.32W
Salem N.J. U.S.A. **85** 39.34N 75.28W
Salem Oreg. U.S.A. **80** 44.57N123.01W
Salem Va. U.S.A. **85** 37.17N 80.04W
Sälen Sweden **23** 61.10N 13.16E
Salerno Italy **18** 40.41N 14.45E
Salerno, Golfo di g. Italy **18** 40.30N 14.45E
Salford U.K. **10** 53.30N 2.17W
Salgótarján Hungary **21** 48.07N 19.48E
Salgueiro Brazil **91** 8.04S 39.05W
Salima Malaŵi **55** 13.45S 34.29E
Salim's Tanzania **55** 10.37S 36.33E
Salina U.S.A. **82** 38.50N 97.37W
Salina Cruz Mexico **86** 16.11N 95.12W
Salinas Ecuador **90** 2.13S 80.58W
Salinas U.S.A. **80** 36.40N121.38W
Salinas r. U.S.A. **78** 36.45N121.48W
Saline r. U.S.A. **82** 38.51N 97.30W
Salinópolis Brazil **91** 0.37S 47.20W
Salins France **17** 46.56N 5.53E
Salisbury U.K. **11** 51.04N 1.48W
Salisbury Md. U.S.A. **85** 38.22N 75.36W
Salisbury N.C. U.S.A. **85** 35.20N 80.30W
Salisbury Plain f. U.K. **11** 51.15N 1.55W
Salisbury Sd. U.S.A. **74** 57.30N135.56W
Şalkhad Syria **44** 32.29N 36.42E
Sallisaw U.S.A. **83** 35.28N 94.47W
Sallyāna Nepal **41** 28.22N 82.12E
Salmās Iran **43** 38.13N 44.50E
Salmi U.S.S.R. **24** 61.19N 31.46E
Salmon r. Canada **74** 54.03N122.40W
Salmon U.S.A. **80** 45.11N113.55W
Salmon r. U.S.A. **80** 45.51N116.46W
Salmon Gums Australia **63** 32.59S121.39E
Salmon River Mts. U.S.A. **80** 44.45N115.30W
Salo Finland **23** 60.23N 23.08E
Salò Italy **15** 45.36N 10.31E
Salobreña Spain **16** 36.45N 3.35W
Salome U.S.A. **81** 33.47N113.37W
Salon France **17** 43.38N 5.06E
Salonga r. Zaïre **54** 0.09S 19.52E
Salonta Romania **21** 46.48N 21.40E
Salsk U.S.S.R. **25** 46.30N 41.33E
Salso r. Italy **18** 37.07N 13.57E
Salsomaggiore Terme Italy **15** 44.49N 9.59E
Salt r. U.S.A. **81** 33.23N112.18W
Salta Argentina **92** 24.47S 65.24W
Salta d. Argentina **92** 25.00S 65.00W
Saltdal Norway **22** 67.06N 15.25E
Saltee Is. Rep. of Ire. **13** 52.08N 6.36W
Saltfjorden est. Norway **22** 67.15N 14.10E
Saltfleet U.K. **10** 53.25N 0.11E
Salt Fork r. U.S.A. **79** 36.41N 97.05W
Saltillo Mexico **83** 25.25N101.00W
Salt Lake City U.S.A. **80** 40.46N111.53W
Salto Argentina **93** 34.17S 60.15W
Salto Brazil **94** 23.10S 47.16W
Salto r. Italy **18** 42.23N 12.54E
Salto Uruguay **93** 31.23S 57.58W
Salto da Divisa Brazil **91** 16.04S 40.00W
Salton Sea l. U.S.A. **81** 33.19N115.50W
Salūmbar India **40** 24.08N 74.03E
Saluzzo Italy **15** 44.39N 7.29E
Salvador Brazil **91** 12.58S 38.29W
Salvador Canada **75** 52.12N109.32W
Salversville U.S.A. **85** 37.43N 83.06W
Salween r. Burma **34** 16.32N 97.35E
Salyany U.S.S.R. **43** 39.36N 48.59E
Salzbrunn Namibia **56** 24.23S 18.00E
Salzburg Austria **20** 47.54N 13.03E
Salzburg d. Austria **20** 47.25N 13.15E
Salzgitter W. Germany **20** 52.02N 10.22E
Salzwedel E. Germany **20** 52.51N 11.09E
Sam India **40** 26.50N 70.31E
Samalambo Angola **54** 14.16S 17.53E
Samālūt Egypt **44** 28.18N 30.43E
Samaná Dom. Rep. **87** 19.14N 69.20W
Samana Cay i. Bahamas **87** 23.05N 73.45W
Samanga Tanzania **55** 8.24S 39.18E
Samannūd Egypt **44** 30.58N 31.14E
Samar i. Phil. **37** 11.45N125.15E
Samara r. U.S.S.R. **24** 53.17N 50.42E
Samarai P.N.G. **64** 10.37S150.40E
Samarinda Indonesia **36** 0.30S117.09E
Samarkand U.S.S.R. **28** 39.40N 66.57E
Sāmarrā Iraq **43** 34.13N 43.52E
Samāstipur India **41** 25.51N 85.47E
Samawāri Pakistan **40** 28.34N 66.46E
Samba Zaïre **54** 0.14N 21.19E
Sambalpur India **41** 21.27N 83.58E
Sambao r. Madagascar **57** 16.40S 44.26E
Sambava Madagascar **57** 14.16S 50.10E
Sambāza Pakistan **40** 31.46N 69.20E
Sambhal India **41** 28.35N 78.33E
Sāmbhar India **40** 26.55N 75.12E
Sāmbhar L. India **40** 26.58N 75.05E
Sambor U.S.S.R. **21** 49.31N 23.10E
Samborombón, Bahía b. Argentina **93** 36.00S 57.00W
Sambre r. Belgium **14** 50.29N 4.52E
Samburu Kenya **55** 3.46S 39.17E
Samch'ŏk S. Korea **31** 37.30N129.10E
Samdari India **40** 25.49N 72.35E
Same Tanzania **55** 4.10S 37.43E
Samnū Libya **51** 27.16N 14.54E
Samoa is. Pacific Oc. **68** 14.20S170.00W
Samoa Is. Pacific Oc. **68** 14.00S171.00W
Samobor Yugo. **20** 45.48N 15.43E
Samorogouan U. Volta **52** 11.21N 4.57W
Sámos i. Greece **19** 37.44N 26.45E
Samothráki i. Greece **19** 40.26N 25.35E
Sampang Indonesia **37** 7.13S113.15E
Sampit Indonesia **36** 2.34S112.59E
Sam Rayburn Resr. U.S.A. **83** 31.27N 94.37W
Samsang China **41** 30.22N 82.57E
Sam Son Vietnam **33** 19.44N105.53E
Samsun Turkey **42** 41.17N 36.22E
Samtredia U.S.S.R. **25** 42.10N 42.22E
Samui, Ko i. Thailand **34** 9.30N100.00E
Samur r. U.S.S.R. **25** 42.00N 48.20E
Samut Prakan Thailand **34** 13.32N100.35E
Samut Sakhon Thailand **34** 13.31N100.13E
San r. Kampuchea **34** 13.32N105.57E
San Mali **52** 13.21N 4.57W
San r. Poland **21** 50.25N 22.20E
Şan'ā' Yemen **45** 15.23N 44.14E
Sana see Şan'ā' Yemen **45**
Sana r. Yugo. **20** 45.03N 16.23E
Sanaba U. Volta **52** 12.25N 3.47W
Sanaga r. Cameroon **53** 3.35N 9.40E
San Ambrosio i. Pacific Oc. **69** 26.28S 79.53W
Sānand India **40** 22.59N 72.23E
Sanandaj Iran **43** 35.18N 47.01E
San Andreas U.S.A. **80** 38.12N120.41W
San Andrés, Isla de i. Colombia **87** 12.33N 81.42W
San Andrés Tuxtla Mexico **86** 18.27N 95.13W
San Angelo U.S.A. **83** 31.28N100.26W
San Antonio Chile **93** 33.35S 71.38W
San Antonio N.Mex. U.S.A. **81** 33.55N106.52W
San Antonio Tex. U.S.A. **83** 29.28N 98.31W
San Antonio, C. Cuba **87** 21.50N 84.57W
San Antonio, Cabo c. Argentina **93** 36.40S 56.42W
San Antonio, Punta c. Mexico **81** 29.45N115.41W
San Antonio, Sierra de mts. Mexico **81** 30.00N110.10W
San Antonio Abad Spain **16** 38.58N 1.18E
San Antonio de Areco Argentina **93** 34.16S 59.30W
San Antonio Oeste Argentina **93** 40.44S 64.57W
San Augustine U.S.A. **83** 31.32N 94.07W
Sanāwad India **40** 22.11N 76.04E
San Benedetto Italy **18** 42.57N 13.53E
San Benedetto Po Italy **15** 45.02N 10.55E
San Benito Guatemala **87** 16.55N 89.54W
San Benito U.S.A. **83** 26.08N 97.38W

San Bernardino to Savant L.

San Bernardino U.S.A. **81** 34.06N117.17W
San Bernardo Chile **93** 33.36S 70.43W
San Blas, C. U.S.A. **85** 29.40N 85.22W
San Bonifacio Italy **15** 45.24N 11.16E
San Carlos Chile **93** 36.25S 71.58W
San Carlos Mexico **83** 29.01N100.51W
San Carlos Nicaragua **87** 11.07N 84.47W
San Carlos Phil. **37** 15.59N120.22E
San Carlos Venezuela **90** 1.55N 67.04W
San Carlos Venezuela **90** 9.39N 68.35W
San Carlos de Bariloche Argentina **93** 41.08S 71.15W
San Carlos del Zulia Venezuela **90** 9.01N 71.55W
Sancerre France **15** 47.20N 2.51E
Sancerrois, Collines du *hills* France **15** 47.25N 2.45E
Sancha He *r.* China **33** 26.50N106.04E
San Clemente U.S.A. **81** 33.26N117.37W
San Clemente *i.* U.S.A. **81** 32.54N118.29W
San Cristóbal Argentina **92** 30.20S 61.41W
San Cristóbal Dom. Rep. **87** 18.27N 70.07W
San Cristóbal Venezuela **90** 7.46N 72.15W
Sancti Spíritus Cuba **87** 21.55N 79.28W
Sand Norway **23** 59.29N 6.15E
Sanda *i.* U.K. **12** 55.17N 5.34W
Sandakan Malaysia **36** 5.52N118.04E
Sandaré Mali **52** 14.40N 10.15W
Sanday *i.* U.K. **12** 59.15N 2.33W
Sandbach U.K. **10** 53.09N 2.23W
Sandefjord Norway **23** 59.08N 10.14E
Sanders U.S.A. **81** 35.13N109.20W
Sanderson U.S.A. **83** 30.09N102.24W
Sandersville U.S.A. **85** 32.59N 82.49W
Sandgate Australia **67** 27.18S153.00E
Sandgirt L. Canada **77** 53.50N 65.10W
Sandhornöy *i.* Norway **22** 67.05N 14.10E
Sāndi India **41** 27.18N 79.57E
Sandia Peru **90** 14.14S 69.25W
San Diego U.S.A. **81** 32.43N117.09W
San Diego, C. Argentina **93** 54.38S 65.05W
Sandīla India **41** 27.05N 80.31E
Sand Lake *town* Canada **76** 47.45N 84.30W
Sandnes Norway **23** 58.51N 5.44E
Sandness U.K. **12** 60.18N 1.38W
Sandö *i.* Faroe Is. **8** 61.50N 6.45W
Sandoa Zaïre **54** 9.41S 22.56E
Sandomierz Poland **21** 50.41N 21.45E
San Donà di Piave Italy **15** 45.38N 12.34E
Sandover *r.* Australia **64** 21.43S136.32E
Sandoway Burma **34** 18.28N 94.20E
Sandown U.K. **11** 50.39N 1.09W
Sandpoint *town* U.S.A. **80** 48.17N116.34W
Sandringham U.K. **10** 52.50N 0.30E
Sandstone Australia **63** 27.59S119.17E
Sandu Shuizu Zizhixian China **33** 25.59N107.52E
Sandusky Ohio U.S.A. **84** 41.27N 82.42W
Sandveld *f.* Namibia **56** 21.25S 20.00E
Sandviken Sweden **23** 60.37N 16.46E
Sandwich B. Canada **77** 53.35N 57.15W
Sandwīp I. Bangla. **41** 22.29N 91.26E
Sandy U.S.A. **80** 40.35N111.53W
Sandy B. St. Helena **95** 16.02S 5.42W
Sandy Bight *b.* Australia **63** 33.53S123.25E
Sandy C. Australia **64** 24.42S153.17E
Sandy Creek *town* U.S.A. **84** 43.39N 76.05W
Sandy Desert Pakistan **40** 28.00N 65.00E
Sandy Hook *f.* U.S.A. **85** 40.27N 74.00W
Sandy L. Nfld. Canada **77** 49.16N 57.00W
Sandy L. Ont. Canada **75** 53.00N 93.00W
Sandy Lake *town* Ont. Canada **75** 53.00N 93.00W
Sandy Lake *town* Sask. Canada **75** 57.00N107.15W
San Enrique Argentina **93** 35.47S 60.22W
San Esteban, Isla *i.* Mexico **81** 28.41N112.35W
San Felipe Chile **93** 32.45S 70.44W
San Felipe Colombia **90** 1.55N 67.06W
San Felipe Mexico **81** 31.00N114.52W
San Felipe Venezuela **90** 10.25N 68.40W
San Felíu de Guixols Spain **16** 41.47N 3.02E
San Félix *i.* Pacific Oc. **69** 26.23S 80.05W
San Fernando Argentina **93** 34.26S 58.34W
San Fernando Chile **93** 34.35S 71.00W
San Fernando *r.* Mexico **83** 24.55N 97.40W
San Fernando Phil. **37** 16.39N120.19E
San Fernando Spain **16** 36.28N 6.12W
San Fernando Trinidad **90** 10.16N 61.28W
San Fernando de Apure Venezuela **90** 7.35N 67.15W
San Fernando de Atabapo Venezuela **90** 4.03N 67.45W
Sanford *r.* Australia **62** 27.22S115.53E
Sanford Fla. U.S.A. **85** 28.49N 81.17W
Sanford N.C. U.S.A. **85** 35.29N 79.10W
San Francisco Argentina **92** 31.29S 62.06W
San Francisco Mexico **81** 30.50N112.40W
San Francisco U.S.A. **80** 37.48N122.24W
San Francisco *r.* U.S.A. **81** 32.59N109.22W
San Francisco, C. Ecuador **90** 0.50N 80.05W
San Francisco del Oro Mexico **81** 26.52N105.51W
San Francisco de Macorís Dom. Rep. **87** 19.19N 70.15W
Sanga Angola **54** 11.09S 15.21E
Sanga-Tolon U.S.S.R. **29** 61.44N149.30E
Sang-e Māsheh Afghan. **40** 33.08N 67.27E
Sanggan He *r.* China **32** 40.23N115.18E
Sangha *r.* Congo **54** 1.10S 16.47E
Sanghar Pakistan **40** 26.02N 68.57E
Sangihe *i.* Indonesia **37** 3.30N125.30E
Sangihe, Kepulauan *is.* Indonesia **37** 2.45N125.20E
San Gil Colombia **90** 6.35N 73.08W
San Giovanni in Persiceto Italy **15** 44.38N 11.11E
Sangkulirang Indonesia **36** 1.00N117.58E
Sāngli India **38** 16.55N 74.37E
Sangmélima Cameroon **53** 2.55N 12.01E
Sangonera *r.* Spain **16** 37.58N 1.04W
San Gottardo, Passo del *pass* Switz. **20** 46.30N 8.55E
Sangre de Cristo Mts. U.S.A. **80** 37.30N105.15W
San Gregorio Uruguay **93** 32.37S 55.40W
Sangri China **41** 29.18N 92.05E
Sangrūr India **40** 30.14N 75.51E
Sangzhi China **33** 29.24N110.09E
Sanhala Ivory Coast **52** 10.01N 6.48W
San Ignacio Bolivia **92** 16.23S 60.59W
San Ignacio Mexico **81** 27.27N112.51W
San Ignacio Paraguay **92** 26.52S 57.03W
San Ignacio, Laguna *l.* Mexico **81** 26.50N113.11W
San Isidro Argentina **93** 34.29S 58.31W
Sanīyah, Hawr as *l.* Iraq **43** 31.52N 46.50E
San Javier Argentina **93** 30.40S 59.55W
San Javier Bolivia **92** 16.22S 62.38W
San Javier Chile **93** 35.35S 71.45W
Sanjāwi Pakistan **40** 30.17N 68.21E
San Joaquin *r.* U.S.A. **80** 38.03N121.50W
San Jorge, Bahía de *b.* Mexico **81** 31.08N113.15W
San Jorge, Golfo *g.* Argentina **93** 46.00S 66.00W
San Jorge, Golfo de *g.* Spain **16** 40.50N 1.10E
San José Costa Rica **87** 9.59N 84.04W
San José Guatemala **86** 13.58N 90.50W
San José Mexico **81** 27.32N110.09W
San Jose U.S.A. **80** 37.20N121.53W
San José, Isla *i.* Mexico **81** 25.00N110.38W
San José de Chiquitos Bolivia **92** 17.53S 60.45W
San José de Feliciano Argentina **93** 30.25S 58.45W
San José de Guanipa Venezuela **90** 8.54N 64.09W
San José del Cabo *town* Mexico **81** 23.03N109.41W
San José del Guaviare Colombia **90** 2.35N 72.38W
San José de Mayo Uruguay **93** 34.20S 56.42W
San José de Ocuné Colombia **90** 4.15N 70.20W
San Juan Argentina **92** 31.30S 68.30W
San Juan *d.* Argentina **92** 31.00S 68.30W
San Juan *r.* Costa Rica **87** 10.50N 83.40W
San Juan Dom. Rep. **87** 18.40N 71.05W
San Juan Peru **92** 15.20S 75.09W
San Juan Phil. **37** 8.25N126.22E
San Juan Puerto Rico **87** 18.29N 66.08W
San Juan *r.* U.S.A. **80** 37.18N110.28W
San Juan, C. Argentina **93** 54.45S 63.50W
San Juan Bautista Spain **16** 39.05N 1.30E
San Juan de Guadalupe Mexico **83** 24.38N102.44W
San Juan del Norte Nicaragua **87** 10.58N 83.40W
San Juan de los Morros Venezuela **90** 9.53N 67.23W
San Juan del Río Durango Mexico **83** 24.47N104.27W
San Juan del Río Querétaro Mexico **86** 20.23N100.00W
San Juan Mts. U.S.A. **80** 37.35N107.10W
San Julián Argentina **93** 49.19S 67.40W
San Justo Argentina **93** 30.47S 60.35W
Sankh *r.* India **41** 22.15N 84.48E
Sankheda India **40** 22.10N 73.35E
Sānkra India **41** 20.18N 82.03E
Sankt Niklaus Switz. **15** 46.11N 7.48E
Sankuru *r.* Zaïre **54** 4.20S 20.27E
San Lázaro, Cabo *c.* Mexico **81** 24.50N112.18W
San Lázaro, Sierra de *mts.* Mexico **81** 23.20N110.00W
San Leonardo Spain **16** 41.49N 3.04W
San Lorenzo Argentina **93** 32.45S 60.44W
San Lorenzo *mtn.* Chile **93** 47.37S 72.19W
San Lorenzo Ecuador **90** 1.17N 78.50W
San Lorenzo *r.* Mexico **81** 24.15N107.25W
San Lorenzo de El Escorial Spain **16** 40.34N 4.08W
Sanlúcar de Barrameda Spain **16** 36.46N 6.21W
Sanlúcar la Mayor Spain **16** 37.26N 6.18W
San Lucas Bolivia **92** 20.06S 65.07W
San Lucas, Cabo *c.* Mexico **81** 22.50N109.55W
San Luis Argentina **93** 33.20S 66.20W
San Luis *d.* Argentina **93** 34.00S 66.00W
San Luis Cuba **87** 20.13N 75.50W
San Luis Obispo U.S.A. **81** 35.17N120.40W
San Luis Potosí Mexico **86** 22.10N101.00W
San Luis Potosí *d.* Mexico **86** 23.00N100.00W
San Luis Rio Colorado Mexico **81** 32.29N114.48W
San Luis Valley *f.* U.S.A. **80** 37.25N106.00W
San Marcos U.S.A. **83** 29.53N 97.57W
San Marino Europe **15** 43.55N 12.27E
San Marino *town* San Marino **15** 43.55N 12.27E
San Martin *r.* Bolivia **92** 12.25S 64.25W
San Mateo U.S.A. **80** 37.35N122.19W
San Matías Bolivia **90** 16.22S 58.24W
San Matías, Golfo *g.* Argentina **93** 41.30S 64.00W
Sanmenxia China **32** 35.45N111.22E
Sanmenxia Shuiku *resr.* China **32** 34.38N111.05E
San Miguel *r.* Bolivia **90** 13.52S 63.56W
San Miguel *r.* Bolivia **92** 12.25S 64.25W
San Miguel El Salvador **87** 13.28N 88.10W
San Miguel del Monte Argentina **93** 35.25S 58.49W
San Miguel de Tucumán Argentina **92** 26.49S 65.13W
San Miguelito Panama **87** 9.02N 79.30W
Sanming China **33** 26.25N117.35E
Sannār Sudan **49** 13.33N 33.38E
Sannicandro Italy **18** 41.50N 15.34E
San Nicolas Argentina **93** 33.20S 60.13W
Sanniquellie Liberia **52** 7.24N 8.45W
Sanok Poland **21** 49.35N 22.10E
San Pablo Phil. **37** 13.58N121.10E
San Pedro Buenos Aires Argentina **93** 33.40S 59.41W
San Pedro Jujuy Argentina **92** 24.14S 64.50W
San Pedro Dom. Rep. **87** 18.30N 69.18W
San Pedro Ivory Coast **52** 4.45N 6.37W
San Pedro Sonora Mexico **81** 27.00N109.53W
San Pedro Paraguay **94** 24.08S 57.08W
San Pedro, Punta *c.* Costa Rica **87** 8.38N 83.45W
San Pedro, Sierra de *mts.* Spain **16** 39.20N 6.20W
San Pedro de las Colonais Mexico **83** 25.45N102.59W
San Pedro Mártir, Sierra *mts.* Mexico **81** 30.45N115.30W
San Pedro Sula Honduras **87** 15.26N 88.01W
San Pellegrino Terme Italy **15** 45.50N 9.40E
San Pietro *i.* Italy **18** 39.09N 8.16E
Sanquhar U.K. **12** 55.22N 3.56W
San Quintín Mexico **81** 30.28N115.58W
San Rafael U.S.A. **80** 37.59N122.31W
San Raphael Argentina **93** 34.40S 68.21W
San Remo Italy **15** 43.48N 7.46E
San Salvador Argentina **93** 31.37S 58.30W
San Salvador *i.* Bahamas **87** 24.00N 74.32W
San Salvador El Salvador **87** 13.40N 89.10W
San Salvador de Jujuy Argentina **92** 24.10S 65.20W
San Sebastián Argentina **93** 53.15S 68.30W
San Sebastián Spain **16** 43.19N 1.59W
San Severo Italy **18** 41.40N 15.24E
Sanshui China **33** 23.09N112.52E
San Simon U.S.A. **81** 32.16N109.14W
Santa *r.* Peru **90** 9.00S 78.35W
Santa Ana Argentina **92** 27.20S 65.35W
Santa Ana Bolivia **92** 13.45S 65.35W
Santa Ana El Salvador **87** 14.00N 89.31W
Santa Ana Mexico **81** 30.33N111.07W
Santa Ana U.S.A. **81** 33.44N117.54W
Santa Bárbara Mexico **81** 26.48N105.49W
Santa Barbara U.S.A. **81** 34.25N119.42W
Santa Catarina *d.* Brazil **94** 27.00S 52.00W
Santa Catarina Mexico **83** 25.41N100.28W
Santa Clara Cuba **87** 22.25N 79.58W
Santa Clara Calif. U.S.A. **80** 37.21N121.57W
Santa Clara Utah U.S.A. **80** 37.08N113.39W
Santa Clotilde Peru **90** 2.25S 73.35W
Santa Comba Dão Portugal **16** 40.24N 8.08W
Santa Cruz *d.* Argentina **93** 48.00S 69.30W
Santa Cruz *r.* Argentina **93** 50.03S 68.35W
Santa Cruz Bolivia **92** 17.45S 63.14W
Santa Cruz *d.* Bolivia **92** 17.45S 62.00W
Santa Cruz Madeira Is. **95** 32.41N 16.48W
Santa Cruz U.S.A. **80** 36.58N122.08W
Santa Cruz *i.* U.S.A. **81** 34.01N119.45W
Santa Cruz de Tenerife Canary Is. **50** 28.28N 16.15W
Santa Cruz Is. Solomon Is. **68** 10.30S166.00E
Santa Domingo Mexico **81** 25.32N112.02W
Santa Elena Argentina **93** 31.00S 59.50W
Santa Elena U.S.A. **83** 26.46N 98.30W
Santa Elena, C. Costa Rica **87** 10.54N 85.56W
Santa Fé Argentina **93** 31.40S 60.40W
Santa Fé *d.* Argentina **92** 30.00S 61.00W
Santa Fe U.S.A. **81** 35.42N106.57W
Santa Filomena Brazil **91** 9.07S 45.56W
Santai China **33** 31.10N105.02E
Santa Inés, Isla *i.* Chile **93** 53.40S 73.00W
Santa Isabel Argentina **93** 36.15S 66.55W
Santa Isabel do Morro Brazil **91** 11.36S 50.37W
Sāntalpur India **40** 23.45N 71.10E
Santa Lucía Uruguay **93** 34.27S 56.24W
Santa Lucía *r.* Uruguay **93** 34.48S 56.22W
Santa Lucia Range *mts.* U.S.A. **81** 36.00N121.20W
Santa Margarita, Isla de *i.* Mexico **81** 24.25N111.50W
Santa Margarita, Sierra de *mts.* Mexico **81** 30.00N110.00W
Santa Margherita Ligure Italy **15** 44.20N 9.12E
Santa María Brazil **94** 29.40S 53.47W
Santa Maria U.S.A. **81** 34.57N120.26W
Santa Maria, Laguna de *l.* Mexico **81** 31.07N107.17W
Santa Maria di Leuca, Capo *c.* Italy **19** 39.47N 18.24E
Santa Maria Madalena Brazil **94** 21.58S 42.02W
Santa Marta Colombia **90** 11.18N 74.10W
Santa Marta, Sierra Nevada de *mts.* Colombia **90** 11.20N 73.00W
Santa Monica U.S.A. **81** 34.01N118.30W
Santana Madeira Is. **95** 32.48N 16.54W
Santana do Livramento Brazil **93** 30.53S 55.31W
Santander Colombia **90** 3.00N 76.25W
Santander Spain **16** 43.28N 3.48W
Santañy Spain **16** 39.20N 3.07E
Santarém Brazil **91** 2.26S 54.41W
Santarém Portugal **16** 39.14N 8.40W
Santa Rosa Argentina **93** 36.00S 64.40W
Santa Rosa Bolivia **90** 10.36S 67.25W
Santa Rosa Brazil **94** 27.52S 54.29W
Santa Rosa Honduras **87** 14.47N 88.46W
Santa Rosa *i.* U.S.A. **81** 33.58N120.06W
Santa Rosa Calif. U.S.A. **80** 38.26N122.34W
Santa Rosa N.Mex. U.S.A. **81** 34.57N104.41W
Santa Rosa, Mt. Guam **68** 13.32N144.55E
Santa Rosa de Cabal Colombia **90** 4.52N 75.37W
Santa Rosalía Mexico **81** 27.19N112.17W
Santa Rosa Range *mts.* U.S.A. **80** 41.00N117.40W
Santa Teresa Mexico **83** 25.19N 97.50W
Santa Vitória do Palmar Brazil **94** 33.31S 53.21W
San Telmo Mexico **81** 31.00N116.06W
Santhià Italy **15** 45.22N 8.10E
Santiago Chile **93** 33.27S 70.40W
Santiago Dom. Rep. **87** 19.30N 70.42W
Santiago Panama **87** 8.08N 80.59W
Santiago *r.* Peru **90** 4.30S 77.48W
Santiago de Compostela Spain **16** 42.52N 8.33W
Santiago de Cuba Cuba **87** 20.00N 75.49W
Santiago del Estero Argentina **92** 27.50S 64.15W
Santiago del Estero *d.* Argentina **92** 27.40S 63.30W
Santiago Vázquez Uruguay **93** 34.48S 56.21W
Sāntipur India **41** 23.15N 88.26E
Santo Amaro Brazil **91** 12.35S 38.41W
Santo André Brazil **94** 23.39S 46.29W
Santo Angelo Brazil **94** 28.18S 54.16W
Santo Antônio do Içá Brazil **90** 3.05S 67.57W
Santo Domingo Dom. Rep. **87** 18.30N 69.57W
Santo Domingo Pueblo U.S.A. **81** 35.31N106.22W
Santoña Spain **16** 43.27N 3.26W
Santos Brazil **94** 23.56S 46.22W
Santos Dumont Brazil **94** 21.30S 43.34W
Santo Tomás Peru **90** 14.34S 72.30W
Santo Tomé Argentina **92** 28.31S 56.03W
Santpoort Neth. **14** 52.27N 4.38E
San Valentin, Cerro *mtn.* Chile **93** 46.40S 73.25W
San Vicente El Salvador **87** 13.38N 88.42W
San Vito al Tagliamento Italy **15** 45.54N 12.52E
Sanyuan China **32** 34.30N108.52E
Sanza Pombo Angola **54** 7.20S 16.12E
São Borja Brazil **94** 28.35S 56.01W
São Caetano do Sul Brazil **94** 23.36S 46.34W
São Carlos Brazil **94** 22.01S 47.54W
São Domingos Guinea Bissau **52** 12.22N 16.08W
São Francisco *r.* Brazil **91** 10.20S 36.20W
São Francisco do Sol Brazil **94** 26.17S 48.39W
São Gabriel Brazil **94** 30.20S 54.19W
São Gonçalo do Sapucaí Brazil **94** 21.54S 45.35W
Sao Hill *town* Tanzania **55** 8.21S 35.10E
São João da Boa Vista Brazil **94** 21.59S 46.45W
São João da Madeira Portugal **16** 40.54N 8.30W
São João del Rei Brazil **94** 21.08S 44.15W
São João do Piauí Brazil **91** 8.21S 42.15W
São Joaquim da Barra Brazil **94** 20.36S 47.51W
São José do Calçado Brazil **94** 21.01S 41.37W
São José do Rio Prêto Brazil **94** 20.50S 49.20W
São José dos Campos Brazil **94** 23.07S 45.52W
São Leopoldo Brazil **94** 29.46S 51.09W
São Lourenço Brazil **94** 22.08S 45.05W
São Luís Brazil **91** 2.34S 44.16W
São Manuel Brazil **94** 22.40S 48.35W
São Manuel *r.* see Teles Pires *r.* Brazil **91**
São Miguel d'Oeste Brazil **94** 26.45S 53.34W
Saona *i.* Dom. Rep. **87** 18.09N 68.42W
Saône *r.* France **20** 45.46N 4.52E
Saoner India **41** 21.23N 78.54E
São Nicolau Angola **54** 14.19S 12.23E
São Paulo Brazil **94** 23.33S 46.39W
São Paulo *d.* Brazil **94** 22.05S 48.00W
São Paulo de Olivença Brazil **90** 3.34S 68.55W
São Roque Brazil **94** 23.31S 47.09W
São Roque, Cabo de *c.* Brazil **95** 5.00S 35.00W
São Sebastião Brazil **94** 23.48S 45.26W
São Sebastião, Ilha de *i.* Brazil **94** 23.53S 45.17W
São Sebastião do Paraíso Brazil **94** 20.54S 46.59W
São Tiago Brazil **94** 20.54S 44.30W
Saoura, Oued *wadi* Algeria **50** 28.48N 0.50W
São Vicente Brazil **94** 23.57S 46.23W
São Vicente, Cabo de *c.* Portugal **16** 37.01N 8.59W
São Vicente de Minas Brazil **94** 21.40S 44.26W
Sapé Brazil **91** 7.06S 35.13W
Sapele Nigeria **53** 5.53N 5.41E
Sapelo I. U.S.A. **85** 31.28N 81.15W
Sapporo Japan **31** 43.05N141.21E
Sapri Italy **18** 40.04N 15.38E
Sapt Kosi *r.* Nepal **41** 26.30N 86.55E
Sapu Angola **54** 12.28S 19.26E
Sapulpa U.S.A. **83** 36.00N 96.06W
Saqin Sum China **32** 42.06N111.03E
Saqqārah Egypt **44** 29.51N 31.13E
Saqqez Iran **43** 36.14N 46.15E
Sarāb Iran **43** 37.56N 47.35E
Sarābiyūm Egypt **44** 30.23N 32.17E
Sara Buri Thailand **34** 14.30N100.59E
Sarāi Naurang Pakistan **40** 32.50N 70.47E
Sarajevo Yugo. **21** 43.52N 18.26E
Saranac Lake *town* U.S.A. **76** 44.20N 74.10W
Sarandí del Yi Uruguay **93** 33.21S 55.38W
Sarandí Grande Uruguay **93** 33.44S 56.20W
Sārangarh India **41** 21.36N 83.05E
Sārangpur India **40** 23.34N 76.28E
Saranpaul U.S.S.R. **24** 64.15N 60.58E
Saransk U.S.S.R. **24** 54.12N 45.10E
Sarapul U.S.S.R. **24** 56.30N 53.49E
Sarar Plain Somali Rep. **45** 9.35N 46.15E
Sarasota U.S.A. **85** 27.20N 82.32W
Sarata U.S.S.R. **21** 46.00N 29.40E
Saratoga U.S.A. **80** 37.16N122.02W
Saratoga Springs U.S.A. **84** 43.05N 73.47W
Saratov U.S.S.R. **25** 51.30N 45.55E
Saravan Laos **34** 15.43N106.24E
Sarawak *d.* Malaysia **36** 2.00N113.00E
Saraychik U.S.S.R. **25** 47.29N 51.42E
Sarbāz Iran **43** 26.39N 61.20E
Sarcelles France **15** 49.00N 2.23E
Sardār Chāh Pakistan **40** 27.58N 64.50E
Sardārpur India **40** 22.39N 74.59E
Sardārshahr India **40** 28.26N 74.29E
Sardegna *d.* Italy **18** 40.05N 9.00E
Sardegna *i.* Italy **18** 40.00N 9.00E
Sardinia *i. see* Sardegna *i.* Italy **18**
Sarek *mtn.* Sweden **22** 67.25N 17.46E
Sareks Nat. Park Sweden **22** 67.15N 17.30E
Sargasso Sea Atlantic Oc. **95** 28.00N 60.00W
Sargodha Pakistan **38** 32.01N 72.40E
Sarh Chad **53** 9.08N 18.22E
Sarhro, Jbel *mts.* Morocco **50** 31.00N 5.55W
Sarī Iran **43** 36.33N 53.06E
Sarigan *i.* Mariana Is. **37** 16.43N145.47E
Sarikamiş Turkey **42** 40.19N 42.35E
Sarikei Malaysia **36** 2.07N111.31E
Sarina Australia **64** 21.26S149.13E
Sarita U.S.A. **83** 37.13N 97.47W
Sark *i.* U.K. **11** 49.26N 2.22W
Sarlat France **17** 44.53N 1.13E
Sărmasu Romania **21** 46.46N 24.11E
Sarmi Indonesia **37** 1.51S138.45E
Sarmiento Argentina **93** 45.35S 69.05W
Särna Sweden **23** 61.41N 13.08E
Sarnia Canada **76** 42.58N 82.23W
Sarny U.S.S.R. **21** 51.21N 26.31E
Saronno Italy **15** 45.38N 9.02E
Saros Körfezi *g.* Turkey **19** 40.32N 26.25E
Sárospatak Hungary **21** 48.19N 21.34E
Sarpsborg Norway **23** 59.17N 11.07E
Sarrebourg France **17** 48.43N 7.03E
Sarreguemines France **17** 49.06N 7.03E
Sarria Spain **16** 42.47N 7.25W
Sarro Mali **52** 13.40N 5.05W
Sartène France **17** 41.36N 8.59E
Sarthe *d.* France **15** 48.00N 0.05E
Sarthe *r.* France **15** 47.29N 0.30W
Sartilly France **15** 48.45N 1.27W
Sartynya U.S.S.R. **28** 63.22N 63.11E
Şarūr Oman **43** 23.25N 58.10E
Sárvár Hungary **20** 47.15N 16.57E
Saryshagan U.S.S.R. **30** 46.08N 73.32E
Sarzana Italy **15** 44.07N 9.58E
Sasabeneh Ethiopia **45** 7.55N 43.39E
Sasarām India **41** 24.57N 84.02E
Sasebo Japan **31** 33.10N129.42E
Saser *mtn.* Jammu & Kashmir **41** 34.50N 77.50E
Saskatchewan *d.* Canada **75** 55.00N106.00W
Saskatchewan *r.* Canada **75** 53.12N 99.16W
Saskatoon Canada **75** 52.07N106.38W
Sasovo U.S.S.R. **24** 54.21N 41.58E
Sassandra Ivory Coast **52** 4.58N 6.08W
Sassandra *r.* Ivory Coast **52** 5.00N 6.04W
Sassari Italy **18** 40.43N 8.33E
Sassnitz E. Germany **20** 54.32N 13.40E
Sasso Marconi Italy **15** 44.24N 11.15E
Sassuolo Italy **15** 44.33N 10.47E
Sastown Liberia **52** 4.44N 8.01W
Sasyk, Ozero *l.* U.S.S.R. **21** 45.38N 29.38E
Satadougou Mali **52** 12.30N 11.30W
Satāna India **40** 20.35N 74.12E
Satanta U.S.A. **83** 37.26N100.59W
Sātāra India **38** 17.43N 74.05E
Satīt *r.* Sudan **48** 14.20N 35.50E
Satkānia Bangla. **41** 22.04N 92.03E
Satna India **41** 24.35N 80.50E
Sátoraljaújhely Hungary **21** 48.24N 21.39E
Sātpura Range *mts.* India **40** 21.30N 76.00E
Satu Mare Romania **21** 47.48N 22.52E
Satun Thailand **34** 6.38N100.05E
Sauce Argentina **93** 30.05S 58.45W
Sauda Norway **23** 59.39N 6.20E
Saudi Arabia Asia **42** 26.00N 44.00E
Sauk Centre U.S.A. **82** 45.44N 94.57W
Saulieu France **15** 47.17N 4.14E
Sault Sainte Marie Canada **76** 46.32N 84.20W
Sault Sainte Marie U.S.A. **84** 46.29N 84.22W
Saumarez Reef Australia **64** 21.50S153.40E
Saumlaki Indonesia **64** 7.59S131.22E
Saumur France **15** 47.16N 0.05W
Saurimo Angola **54** 9.38S 20.20E
Sausar India **41** 21.42N 78.52E
Sava *r.* Yugo. **21** 44.50N 20.26E
Savage U.S.A. **80** 47.27N104.21W
Savai'i *i.* W. Samoa **68** 13.36S172.27W
Savalou Benin **53** 7.55N 1.59E
Savanna U.S.A. **82** 42.06N 90.07W
Savannah *r.* U.S.A. **85** 32.02N 80.53W
Savannah Ga. U.S.A. **85** 32.04N 81.05W
Savannah Tenn. U.S.A. **83** 35.14N 88.14W
Savannakhét Laos **34** 16.34N104.48E
Savant L. Canada **76** 50.48N 90.20W

Savant Lake to Shidao

Savant Lake *town* Canada 76 50.20N 90.40W
Savé Benin 53 8.04N 2.37E
Save *r.* Mozambique 57 20.59S 35.02E
Sâveh Iran 43 35.00N 50.25E
Savelugu Ghana 52 9.39N 0.48W
Saverdun France 17 43.14N 1.35E
Savigliano Italy 15 44.38N 7.40E
Savigny-sur-Braye France 15 47.53N 0.49E
Savona Italy 15 44.18N 8.28E
Savonlinna Finland 24 61.52N 28.51E
Savoonga U.S.A. 72 63.42N170.27W
Savu Sea *see* Sawu, Laut *sea* Pacific Oc. 37
Sawai Mādhopur India 40 25.59N 76.22E
Sawākin Sudan 48 19.07N 37.20E
Sawatch Range *mts.* U.S.A. 82 39.10N106.25W
Sawbridgeworth U.K. 11 51.50N 0.09W
Sawdā', Jabal as *hills* Libya 51 28.40N 15.00E
Sawdā', Qurnat as *mtn.* Lebanon 44 34.17N 36.04E
Sawdirī Sudan 48 14.25N 29.05E
Sawfajjīn, Wādī Libya 51 31.54N 15.07E
Sawhāj Egypt 42 26.33N 31.42E
Şawqirah, Ghubbat *b.* Oman 45 18.35N 57.00E
Sawston U.K. 11 52.07N 0.11E
Sawtooth Mts. U.S.A. 80 44.03N114.35W
Sawu *i.* Indonesia 37 10.30S121.50E
Sawu, Laut *sea* Pacific Oc. 37 9.30S122.30E
Saxmundham U.K. 11 52.13N 1.29E
Saxon Switz. 15 46.09N 7.11E
Say Mali 52 13.08N 2.22E
Say Niger 53 13.08N 2.22E
Sayama Japan 35 35.51N139.24E
Şaydā Lebanon 44 33.32N 35.22E
Sayers Lake *town* Australia 66 32.46S143.20E
Saynshand Mongolia 32 44.58N110.12E
Sayula Mexico 86 19.52N103.36W
Sázava *r.* Czech. 20 49.53N 14.21E
Sbaa Algeria 50 28.13N 0.10W
Scafell Pike *mtn.* U.K. 10 54.27N 3.12W
Scalea Italy 18 39.49N 15.48E
Scalloway U.K. 12 60.08N 1.17W
Scammon Bay *town* U.S.A. 72 61.50N165.35W
Scapa Flow *str.* U.K. 12 58.53N 3.05W
Scarborough Canada 76 43.44N 79.16W
Scarborough Tobago 90 11.11N 60.45W
Scarborough U.K. 10 54.17N 0.24W
Sceale Bay *town* Australia 66 33.00S134.15E
Scenic U.S.A. 80 43.46N102.32W
Schaerbeek Belgium 14 50.54N 4.20E
Schaffhausen Switz. 20 47.42N 8.38E
Schagen Neth. 14 52.47N 4.47E
Schefferville Canada 73 54.50N 67.00W
Schelde *r.* Belgium 14 51.13N 4.25E
Schell Creek Range *mts.* U.S.A. 80 39.10N114.40W
Schenectady U.S.A. 84 42.47N 73.53W
Scheveningen Neth. 14 52.07N 4.16E
Schiedam Neth. 14 51.55N 4.25E
Schiermonnikoog *i.* Neth. 14 53.28N 6.15E
Schio Italy 15 45.43N 11.21E
Schleiden W. Germany 14 50.32N 6.29E
Schleswig W. Germany 20 54.32N 9.34E
Schleswig-Holstein *d.* W. Germany 20 54.00N 10.30E
Schouten, Kepulauan *is.* Indonesia 37 0.45S135.50E
Schouwen *i.* Neth. 14 51.42N 3.45E
Schreiber Canada 76 48.45N 87.20W
Schuler Canada 75 50.22N110.05W
Schuylkill *r.* U.S.A. 85 39.53N 75.12W
Schwandorf W. Germany 20 49.20N 12.08E
Schwaner, Pegunungan *mts.* Indonesia 36 0.45S113.20E
Schwarzrand *mts.* Namibia 56 25.40S 16.53E
Schwarzwald *f.* W. Germany 20 48.00N 7.45E
Schwedt E. Germany 20 53.04N 14.17E
Schweich W. Germany 14 49.50N 6.47E
Schweinfurt W. Germany 20 50.03N 10.16E
Schwelm W. Germany 14 51.17N 7.18E
Schwerin E. Germany 20 53.38N 11.25E
Schwerin *d.* E. Germany 20 53.30N 11.30E
Schwyz Switz. 20 47.02N 8.40E
Sciacca Italy 18 37.31N 13.05E
Scilla Italy 18 38.15N 15.44E
Scilly, Isles of U.K. 11 49.55N 6.20W
Scobey U.S.A. 80 48.47N105.25W
Scone Australia 67 32.01S150.53E
Scotia Calif. U.S.A. 80 40.26N123.31W
Scotia Ridge *f.* Atlantic Oc. 95 60.00S 35.00W
Scotia Sea Atlantic Oc. 95 57.00S 45.00W
Scotland U.K. 12 55.30N 4.00W
Scotsbluff U.S.A. 82 41.52N103.40W
Scott *r.* Australia 66 30.41S137.50E
Scottburgh R.S.A. 56 30.17S 30.45E
Scott City U.S.A. 82 38.29N100.54W
Scott Is. Canada 74 50.48N128.40W
Scott L. Canada 75 59.55N106.18W
Scott Reef Australia 62 14.00S121.50E
Scottsbluff U.S.A. 80 41.52N103.40W
Scottsboro U.S.A. 83 34.40N 86.02W
Scottsdale Australia 65 41.09S147.31E
Scottsdale U.S.A. 81 33.30N111.56W
Scottsville U.S.A. 83 36.45N 86.11W
Scranton U.S.A. 84 41.24N 75.40W
Scugog, L. Canada 76 44.10N 78.51W
Scunthorpe U.K. 10 53.35N 0.38W
Scutari, L. Yugo./Albania 19 42.10N 19.18E
Seabrook, L. Australia 63 30.56S119.40E
Seaford U.S.A. 85 38.39N 75.37W
Seagroves U.S.A. 83 32.57N102.34W
Seahouses U.K. 10 55.35N 1.38W
Sea Isle City U.S.A. 85 39.09N 74.42W
Seal *r.* Canada 75 59.04N 94.48W
Sea Lake *town* Australia 66 35.31S142.54E
Seal Bight Canada 77 52.27N 55.40W
Searchlight U.S.A. 81 35.28N114.55W
Seascale U.K. 10 54.24N 3.29W
Seaside Calif. U.S.A. 80 36.37N121.50W
Seaside Oreg. U.S.A. 80 46.02N123.55W
Seaton U.K. 11 50.43N 3.05W
Seattle U.S.A. 80 47.36N122.20W
Seaview Range *mts.* Australia 64 18.56S146.00E
Sebastian U.S.A. 85 27.50N 80.29W
Sebastián Vizcaíno, Bahía *b.* Mexico 81 28.00N114.30W
Sebba U. Volta 52 13.27N 0.33E
Sebeş Romania 21 45.58N 23.34E
Sebidiro P.N.G. 37 9.00S142.15E
Sebinkarahisar Turkey 42 40.19N 38.25E
Sebou, Oued *r.* Morocco 50 34.15N 6.40W
Sebring U.S.A. 85 27.30N 81.28W
Sechura, Desierto de *des.* Peru 90 6.00S 80.30W
Seclin France 14 50.34N 3.01E
Sêda *r.* Portugal 16 38.55N 7.30W
Sedalia U.S.A. 82 38.42N 93.14W
Sedan Australia 66 34.34S139.19E
Sedan France 15 49.42N 4.57E
Sedan U.S.A. 83 37.08N 96.11W
Seddon New Zealand 60 41.40S174.04E
Sedgewick Canada 75 52.46N111.41W
Sédhiou Senegal 52 12.44N 15.30W
Sedom Israel 44 31.04N 35.23E
Seeheim Namibia 56 26.50S 17.45E
Sées France 15 48.38N 0.10E
Sefrou Morocco 50 33.50N 4.50W
Segbwema Sierra Leone 52 8.00N 11.00W
Seggueur, Oued es *wadi* Algeria 51 31.44N 2.18E
Ségou Mali 52 13.28N 6.18W
Ségou *d.* Mali 52 13.55N 6.20W
Segovia Spain 16 40.57N 4.07W
Segozero, Ozero *l.* U.S.S.R. 24 63.15N 33.40E
Segré France 15 47.41N 0.53W
Segre *r.* Spain 16 41.25N 0.21E
Séguédine Niger 53 20.12N 12.59E
Séguéla Ivory Coast 52 7.58N 6.44W
Seguin U.S.A. 83 29.34N 97.58W
Segura Portugal 16 39.50N 6.59W
Segura *r.* Spain 16 38.07N 0.14W
Segura, Sierra de *mts.* Spain 16 38.00N 2.50W
Sehore India 40 23.12N 77.05E
Sehwān Pakistan 40 26.26N 67.52E
Seiches-sur-le-Loir France 15 47.35N 0.22W
Seiland *i.* Norway 22 70.25N 23.10E
Seinäjoki Finland 22 62.47N 22.50E
Seine *r.* France 15 49.28N 0.25E
Seine, Baie de la *b.* France 15 49.25N 0.15E
Seine-et-Marne *d.* France 15 48.30N 3.00E
Seine-Maritime *d.* France 15 49.45N 1.00E
Sekaju Indonesia 36 2.58S103.58E
Seki Japan 35 35.29N136.55E
Sekoma Botswana 56 24.41S 23.50E
Sekondi-Takoradi Ghana 52 4.57N 1.44W
Sekota Ethiopia 49 12.38N 39.03E
Sekūheh Iran 43 30.45N 61.29E
Selaru *i.* Indonesia 64 8.09S131.00E
Selatan, Tanjung *c.* Indonesia 36 4.20S114.45E
Selbu Norway 22 63.14N 11.03E
Selby U.K. 10 53.47N 1.05W
Selby U.S.A. 82 45.31N100.02W
Selbyville U.S.A. 85 38.28N 75.13W
Seldovia U.S.A. 72 59.27N151.43W
Sele *r.* Italy 18 40.30N 14.50E
Selenga *r.* U.S.S.R. 30 52.20N106.20E
Selenge Mörön *r. see* Selenga Mongolia 30
Sélestat France 20 48.16N 7.28E
Seligman U.S.A. 81 35.20N112.53W
Seljord Norway 23 59.29N 8.37E
Selkirk Man. Canada 75 50.09N 96.52W
Selkirk Ont. Canada 76 42.49N 79.56W
Selkirk U.K. 12 55.33N 2.51W
Selkirk Mts. Canada 74 50.02N116.20W
Selles-sur-Cher France 15 47.16N 1.33E
Sells U.S.A. 81 31.55N111.53W
Selma Ala. U.S.A. 83 32.25N 87.01W
Selma Calif. U.S.A. 81 36.34N119.37W
Selmer U.S.A. 83 35.11N 88.36W
Selseleh ye Safid Kūh *mts.* Afghan 43 34.30N 63.30E
Selsey Bill *c.* U.K. 11 50.44N 0.47W
Selty U.S.S.R. 24 57.19N 52.12E
Sélune *r.* France 15 48.35N 1.15W
Selva Argentina 92 29.50S 62.02W
Selvas *f.* Brazil 90 6.00S 65.00W
Selwyn Australia 64 21.32S140.30E
Selwyn L. Canada 75 60.00N104.30W
Selwyn Mts. Canada 72 63.00N130.00W
Selwyn Range *mts.* Australia 64 21.35S140.35E
Seman *r.* Albania 19 40.53N 19.25E
Semara W. Sahara 50 26.44N 14.41W
Semarang Indonesia 37 6.58S110.29E
Sembabule Uganda 55 0.08S 31.27E
Seminoe Resr. U.S.A. 80 42.00N106.50W
Seminole U.S.A. 83 32.43N102.39W
Semiozernoye U.S.S.R. 28 52.22N 64.06E
Semipalatinsk U.S.S.R. 28 50.26N 80.16E
Semīrom Iran 43 31.31N 52.10E
Semiyarka U.S.S.R. 28 50.52N 78.23E
Semliki *r.* Zaïre 55 1.12N 30.27E
Semmering Pass Austria 20 47.40N 16.00E
Semnān Iran 43 35.31N 53.24E
Semois *r.* France 14 49.53N 4.45E
Semporna Malaysia 36 4.27N118.36E
Semu *r.* Tanzania 55 3.57S 34.20E
Semur-en-Auxois France 15 47.29N 4.20E
Senador Pompeu Brazil 91 5.30S 39.25W
Senaja Malaysia 36 6.49N117.02E
Sena Madureira Brazil 90 9.04S 68.40W
Senanga Zambia 54 15.52S 23.19E
Senatobia U.S.A. 83 34.39N 89.58W
Sendai Tofuku Japan 31 38.16N140.52E
Sendenhorst W. Germany 14 51.52N 7.50E
Sendhwa India 40 21.41N 75.06E
Sendurjana India 41 21.32N 78.17E
Seneca Oreg. U.S.A. 80 44.08N118.58W
Seneca S.C. U.S.A. 85 34.41N 82.59W
Senegal Africa 52 14.30N 14.30W
Sénégal *r.* Senegal/Mauritania 52 16.00N 16.28W
Senekal R.S.A. 56 28.18S 27.37E
Senhor do Bonfim Brazil 91 10.28S 40.11W
Senica Czech. 21 48.41N 17.22E
Senigallia Italy 20 43.42N 13.14E
Senise Italy 18 40.09N 16.18E
Senj Yugo. 20 45.00N 14.58E
Senja *i.* Norway 22 69.15N 17.20E
Senlis France 15 49.12N 2.35E
Senmonoron Vietnam 34 12.27N107.12E
Sennan Japan 35 34.22N135.17E
Sennen U.K. 11 50.04N 5.42W
Senneterre Canada 76 48.25N 77.15W
Sens France 15 48.12N 3.18E
Senta Yugo. 21 45.56N 20.04E
Sentinel U.S.A. 81 32.53N113.12W
Seonāth *r.* India 41 21.44N 82.28E
Seoni India 41 22.05N 79.32E
Seoni Mālwa India 41 22.27N 77.28E
Seorīnārāyan India 41 21.44N 82.35E
Seoul *see* Sŏul S. Korea 31
Sepik *r.* P.N.G. 37 3.54S144.30E
Sepopa Botswana 56 18.45S 22.11E
Sept Îles *town* Canada 77 50.12N 66.23W
Sepúlveda Spain 16 41.18N 3.45W
Seraing Belgium 14 50.37N 5.33E
Seram *i.* Indonesia 37 3.10S129.30E
Seram, Laut *sea* Pacific Oc. 37 2.50S128.00E
Serang Indonesia 37 6.07S106.09E
Serbia *d. see* Srbija *d.* Yugo. 21
Serdo Ethiopia 49 11.59N 41.30E
Seremban Malaysia 36 2.42N101.54E
Serengeti Nat. Park Tanzania 55 2.30S 35.00E
Serengeti Plain *f.* Tanzania 55 3.00S 35.00E
Serenje Zambia 55 13.12S 30.50E
Serenli Somali Rep. 49 2.28N 42.08E
Sergach U.S.S.R. 24 55.32N 45.27E
Sergipe *d.* Brazil 91 11.00S 37.00W
Sergiyevsk U.S.S.R. 24 53.56N 50.01E
Seria Brunei 36 4.39N114.23E
Serian Malaysia 36 1.10N110.35E
Sericho Kenya 49 1.05N 39.05E
Sérifos *i.* Greece 19 37.11N 24.31E
Sérigny *r.* Canada 77 55.59N 68.43W
Serkout, Djebel *mtn.* Algeria 51 23.40N 6.48E
Serle, Mt Australia 66 30.34S138.55E
Sermata *i.* Indonesia 37 8.30S129.00E
Serodino Argentina 93 32.37S 60.57W
Serov U.S.S.R. 24 59.42N 60.32E
Serowe Botswana 56 22.22S 26.42E
Serpa Portugal 16 37.56N 7.36W
Serpentine *r.* Australia 63 32.33S115.46E
Serpent's Mouth *str.* Venezuela 90 9.50N 61.00W
Serpukhov U.S.S.R. 24 54.53N 37.25E
Serra do Navio Brazil 91 0.59N 52.03W
Sérrai Greece 19 41.04N 23.32E
Serra Talhada Brazil 91 8.01S 38.17W
Serravalle Scrivia Italy 15 44.43N 8.51E
Serre *r.* France 14 49.40N 3.22E
Serrinha Brazil 91 11.38S 38.56W
Seru Ethiopia 49 7.50N 40.28E
Serui Indonesia 37 1.53S136.15E
Serule Botswana 56 21.54S 27.17E
Serviceton Australia 66 36.22S141.02E
Şes, Munţii *mts.* Romania 21 47.05N 22.30E
Seseganaga L. Canada 76 50.00N 90.10W
Sese Is. Uganda 55 0.20S 32.30E
Sesepe Indonesia 37 1.30S127.59E
Sesheke Zambia 54 17.14S 24.22E
Sesia *r.* Italy 15 45.05N 8.37E
Sesimbra Portugal 16 38.26N 9.06W
Sestao Spain 16 43.18N 3.00W
Sestri Levante Italy 15 44.16N 9.24E
Sète France 17 43.25N 3.43E
Sete Lagoas Brazil 94 19.29S 44.15W
Sete Quedas, Salto das *f.* Brazil 94 24.00S 54.10W
Sétif Algeria 51 36.10N 5.26E
Seto Japan 35 35.14N137.06E
Settat Morocco 50 33.04N 7.37W
Setté Cama Gabon 54 2.32S 9.46E
Settimo Torinese Italy 15 45.09N 7.46E
Settle U.K. 10 54.05N 2.18W
Settlement of Edinburgh Tristan da Cunha 95 37.03S 12.18W
Setúbal Portugal 16 38.31N 8.54W
Setúbal, Baía de *b.* Portugal 16 38.20N 9.00W
Seul, Lac *l.* Canada 76 50.20N 92.30W
Sevagram India 41 20.45N 78.30E
Sevan, Ozero *l.* U.S.S.R. 43 40.22N 45.20E
Sevastopol' U.S.S.R. 25 44.36N 33.31E
Sevenoaks U.K. 11 51.16N 0.12E
Seven Sisters Peaks *mts.* Canada 74 54.56N128.10W
Sévérac France 17 44.20N 3.05E
Severn *r.* Australia 67 29.08S150.50E
Severn *r.* Canada 75 56.00N 87.38W
Severn *r.* U.K. 11 51.50N 2.21W
Severnaya Zemlya *is.* U.S.S.R. 29 80.00N 96.00E
Severnyy U.S.S.R. 24 69.55N 49.01E
Severnyy Donets *r.* U.S.S.R. 25 49.08N 37.28E
Severnyy Dvina *r.* U.S.S.R. 24 57.03N 24.00E
Severodvinsk U.S.S.R. 24 64.35N 39.50E
Severomorsk U.S.S.R. 24 69.05N 33.30E
Sevier *r.* U.S.A. 80 39.04N113.06W
Sevier L. U.S.A. 80 38.55N113.09W
Sevilla Spain 16 37.24N 5.59W
Sèvre-Nantaise *r.* France 17 47.12N 1.35W
Sèvre Niortaise *r.* France 17 46.35N 1.05W
Sevrey Mongolia 32 43.33N102.13E
Sewa *r.* Sierra Leone 52 7.15N 12.08W
Seward U.S.A. 72 60.05N149.34W
Seward Nebr. U.S.A. 82 40.55N 97.06W
Seward Pen. U.S.A. 72 65.00N164.10W
Seydhisfjördhur *town* Iceland 22 65.16N 14.02W
Seym *r.* U.S.S.R. 25 51.30N 32.30E
Seymour Australia 67 37.01S145.10E
Seymour U.S.A. 83 33.35N 99.16W
Sézanne France 15 48.44N 3.44E
Sfax Tunisia 51 34.45N 10.43E
Sfintu-Gheorghe Romania 21 45.52N 25.50E
'sGravenhage Neth. 14 52.05N 4.16E
Shaanxi *d.* China 32 35.00N108.30E
Shaba *d.* Zaïre 55 8.00S 27.00E
Shabunda Zaïre 55 2.42S 27.20E
Shache China 30 38.27N 77.16E
Shafter U.S.A. 81 35.30N119.16W
Shaftesbury U.K. 11 51.00N 2.12W
Shagamu *r.* Canada 75 55.50N 86.48W
Shāhābād India 41 27.39N 79.57E
Shāhāda India 40 21.28N 74.18E
Shahbā' Syria 44 32.51N 36.37E
Shāhbandar Pakistan 40 24.10N 67.54E
Shāhbāz Kalāt Pakistan 40 26.42N 63.58E
Shahdād Iran 43 30.27N 57.44E
Shāhdādkot Pakistan 40 27.51N 67.54E
Shāhdādpur Pakistan 40 25.56N 68.37E
Shahdol India 41 23.17N 81.21E
Shāhganj India 41 26.03N 82.41E
Shāhgarh India 40 27.07N 69.54E
Shaḩḩāt Libya 48 32.50N 21.52E
Shāh Jahān, Kūh-e *mts.* Iran 43 37.00N 58.00E
Shāhjahānpur India 41 27.53N 79.55E
Shāh Jūy Afghan. 40 32.31N 67.25E
Shāh Kot Pakistan 40 31.34N 73.29E
Shāh Kūh *mtn.* Iran 43 31.38N 59.16E
Shāhpur Pakistan 40 28.43N 68.25E
Shāhpura India 40 25.35N 75.00E
Shāhpur Chākar Pakistan 40 26.09N 68.39E
Shahrak Afghan. 40 34.06N 64.18E
Shahr-e Bābak Iran 43 30.08N 55.04E
Shahrestān Afghan. 40 34.22N 66.47E
Shahrezā Iran 43 32.00N 51.52E
Shahr Kord Iran 43 32.40N 50.52E
Shahsavār Iran 43 36.49N 50.54E
Sha'ib Abā al Qūr *wadi* Saudi Arabia 42 31.02N 42.00E
Shaikhpura India 41 25.09N 85.51E
Shājāpur India 40 23.26N 76.16E
Shakawe Botswana 56 18.22S 21.50E
Shaker Heights *town* U.S.A. 84 41.29N 81.36W
Shakhty U.S.S.R. 25 47.43N 40.16E
Shakhunya U.S.S.R. 24 57.41N 46.46E
Shaki Nigeria 53 8.41N 3.24E
Shakshūk Egypt 44 29.28N 30.42E
Shala, L. Ethiopia 49 7.25N 38.30E
Shalingzi China 32 40.42N114.55E
Shallotte U.S.A. 85 33.58N 78.25W
Shām, Jabal ash *mtn.* Oman 43 23.14N 57.17E
Shāmat al Akbād *des.* Saudi Arabia 42 28.15N 43.05E
Shāmli India 40 29.27N 77.19E
Shamo, L. Ethiopia 49 5.49N 37.35E
Shamokin U.S.A. 84 40.47N 76.34W
Shamrock U.S.A. 83 35.13N100.15W
Shamva Zimbabwe 55 17.20S 31.38E
Shan *d.* Burma 34 22.00N 98.00E
Shandī Sudan 48 16.42N 33.26E
Shandong *d.* China 32 36.00N119.00E
Shandong Bandao *pen.* China 32 37.00N121.30E
Shangcheng China 33 31.48N115.24E
Shangdu China 32 41.33N113.31E
Shanggao China 33 28.15N114.55E
Shanghai China 33 31.18N121.50E
Shanghai *d.* China 33 31.00N121.30E
Shanglin China 33 23.26N108.36E
Shangqiu China 32 34.21N115.40E
Shangrao China 33 28.24N117.58E
Shangshui China 32 33.31N114.39E
Shang Xian China 32 33.49N109.56E
Shangyi China 32 41.06N114.00E
Shangyou Shuiku *resr.* China 33 25.52N114.21E
Shangyu China 33 30.01N120.52E
Shanhaiguan China 32 39.58N119.45E
Shannon *r.* Rep. of Ire. 13 52.39N 8.43W
Shannon, Mouth of the *est.* Rep. of Ire. 13 52.29N 9.57W
Shan Plateau Burma 34 18.50N 98.00E
Shanshan China 30 42.52N 90.10E
Shantarskiy Ostrova *is.* U.S.S.R. 29 55.00N138.00E
Shantou China 33 23.22N116.39E
Shanwa Tanzania 55 3.09S 33.48E
Shanxi *d.* China 32 37.00N112.00E
Shanyin China 32 39.30N112.50E
Shaoguan China 33 24.53N113.31E
Shaoxing China 33 30.01N120.40E
Shaoyang China 33 27.10N111.14E
Shap U.K. 10 54.32N 2.40W
Shapinsay *i.* U.K. 12 59.03N 2.51W
Shapur *ruins* Iran 43 29.42N 51.30E
Shaqrā' Saudi Arabia 43 25.17N 45.14E
Shaqrā' S. Yemen 45 13.21N 45.42E
Sharan Jogīzai Pakistan 40 31.02N 68.33E
Shark B. Australia 62 25.30S113.30E
Sharlyk U.S.S.R. 24 52.58N 54.46E
Sharm ash Shaykh Egypt 44 27.51N 34.16E
Sharon U.S.A. 84 41.16N 80.30W
Sharon Springs *town* U.S.A. 82 38.54N101.45W
Sharqī, Al Jabal ash *mts.* Lebanon 44 34.00N 36.25E
Sharqīyah, Aş Şaḩrā' ash *des.* Egypt 44 27.40N 32.00E
Sharya U.S.S.R. 24 58.22N 45.50E
Shashi *r.* Botswana/Zimbabwe 56 22.10S 29.15E
Shashi China 33 30.18N112.20E
Shasta, Mt. U.S.A. 80 41.20N122.20W
Shatt al Arab *r.* Iraq 43 30.00N 48.30E
Shaunavon Canada 75 49.40N108.25W
Shawangunk Mts. U.S.A. 85 41.35N 74.30W
Shawano U.S.A. 76 44.46N 88.38W
Shawbridge Canada 77 45.52N 74.05W
Shaw I. Australia 64 20.29S149.05E
Shawinigan Canada 77 46.33N 72.45W
Shawinigan Sud Canada 77 46.30N 72.45W
Shawnee Okla. U.S.A. 83 35.20N 96.55W
Sha Xi *r.* China 33 26.38N118.10E
Sha Xian China 33 26.27N117.42E
Shayang China 33 30.42N112.29E
Shaykh, Jabal ash *mtn.* Lebanon 44 33.24N 35.52E
Shaykh 'Uthmān S. Yemen 45 12.52N 44.59E
Shchara *r.* U.S.S.R. 21 53.27N 24.45E
Shchelyayur U.S.S.R. 24 65.16N 53.17E
Shchors U.S.S.R. 21 51.50N 31.59E
Shebele *r.* Ethiopia *see* Shebelle *r.* Somali Rep. 45
Shebelle *r.* Somali Rep. 55 0.30N 43.10E
Sheboygan U.S.A. 82 43.46N 87.36W
Shebshi Mts. Nigeria 53 8.30N 11.45E
Shediac Canada 77 46.13N 64.32W
Sheeffry Hills Rep. of Ire. 13 53.41N 9.42W
Sheelin, Lough Rep. of Ire. 13 53.48N 7.20W
Sheep Range *mts.* U.S.A. 81 36.45N115.05W
Sheet Harbour Canada 77 44.55N 62.32W
Sheffield U.K. 10 53.23N 1.28W
Sheffield Ala. U.S.A. 85 34.46N 87.40W
Sheffield Tex. U.S.A. 83 30.41N101.49W
Shefford U.K. 11 52.02N 0.20W
Shegaon India 40 20.47N 76.41E
Shekatika Bay *town* Canada 77 51.17N 58.20W
Shēkhābād Afghan. 40 34.05N 68.45E
Shek Hasan Ethiopia 49 12.09N 35.54E
Shekhūpura Pakistan 40 31.42N 73.59E
Sheki U.S.S.R. 25 41.12N 47.10E
Sheksna *r.* U.S.S.R. 24 60.00N 37.49E
Shelburne N.S. Canada 77 43.46N 65.19W
Shelburne B. Australia 64 11.49S143.00E
Shelby Mich. U.S.A. 84 43.36N 86.22W
Shelby Mont. U.S.A. 80 48.30N111.51W
Shelbyville Ind. U.S.A. 84 39.31N 85.46W
Shelbyville Tenn. U.S.A. 85 35.29N 86.30W
Sheldon Iowa U.S.A. 82 43.11N 95.51W
Sheldon N.Dak. U.S.A. 82 46.35N 97.30W
Sheldrake Canada 77 50.20N 64.51W
Shelikof Str. U.S.A. 72 58.00N153.45W
Shelley U.S.A. 80 43.23N112.07W
Shellharbour Australia 67 34.35S150.52E
Shell Lake *town* Canada 75 53.18N107.07W
Shelton U.S.A. 80 47.13N123.06W
Shenandoah *r.* U.S.A. 84 39.19N 78.12W
Shenandoah Iowa U.S.A. 82 40.46N 95.22W
Shenandoah Va. U.S.A. 84 38.29N 78.37W
Shenchi China 32 39.08N112.10E
Shëngjin Albania 19 41.49N 19.33E
Shengze China 33 30.53N120.40E
Shenkursk U.S.S.R. 24 62.05N 42.58E
Shenmu China 32 38.54N110.24E
Shennongjia China 33 31.44N110.44E
Shen Xian China 32 36.15N115.40E
Shenyang China 32 41.48N123.27E
Shenzhen China 33 22.32N114.08E
Sheo India 40 26.11N 71.15E
Sheoganj India 40 25.09N 73.04E
Sheopur India 40 25.40N 76.42E
Shepetovka U.S.S.R. 21 50.12N 27.01E
Shepherd Is. Vanuatu 68 16.55S168.36E
Shepparton Australia 67 36.25S145.26E
Sheppey, Isle of U.K. 11 51.24N 0.50E
Sherada Ethiopia 49 7.21N 36.32E
Sherborne U.K. 11 50.56N 2.31W
Sherbro I. Sierra Leone 52 7.30N 12.50W
Sherbrooke Canada 77 45.24N 71.54W
Sherburne U.S.A. 84 42.41N 75.30W
Sheridan U.S.A. 80 44.48N106.58W
Sheringa Australia 66 33.51S135.15E
Sheringham U.K. 10 52.56N 1.11E
Sherkin I. Rep. of Ire. 13 51.28N 9.25W
Sherman N.Y. U.S.A. 76 42.10N 79.36W
Sherman Tex. U.S.A. 83 33.38N 96.36W
Sherman Mills U.S.A. 84 45.52N 68.23W
Sherridon Canada 75 55.07N101.05W
'sHertogenbosch Neth. 14 51.42N 5.19E
Shesh Gāv Afghan. 40 33.45N 68.33E
Shetland Is. *d.* U.K. 12 60.20N 1.15W
Shetpe U.S.S.R. 25 44.09N 52.06E
Shetrunji *r.* India 40 21.20N 72.05E
Shevchenko U.S.S.R. 25 43.37N 51.11E
Shewa *d.* Ethiopia 49 8.40N 38.00E
Shewa Gimira Ethiopia 49 7.00N 35.50E
Sheyang China 32 33.47N120.19E
Sheyenne *r.* U.S.A. 82 47.05N 96.50W
Shibām S. Yemen 45 15.56N 48.38E
Shibīn al Kawm Egypt 44 30.33N 31.00E
Shibīn al Qanāţir Egypt 44 30.19N 31.19E
Shibogama L. Canada 76 53.35N 88.10W
Shidao China 32 36.52N122.26E

Shiel, Loch to Sokółka

Shiel, Loch U.K. 12 56.48N 5.33W
Shiga *d.* Japan 35 34.55N136.00E
Shigaib Sudan 48 15.01N 23.36E
Shihpao Shan *mts.* China 33 30.00N112.00E
Shijiazhuang China 32 38.03N114.26E
Shijiu Hu *l.* China 33 31.20N118.48E
Shikārpur Pakistan 40 27.57N 68.38E
Shikohābād India 41 27.06N 78.36E
Shikoku *i.* Japan 31 33.30N133.30E
Shilabo Ethiopia 45 6.05N 44.48E
Shilka U.S.S.R. 31 51.55N116.01E
Shilka *r.* U.S.S.R. 31 53.20N121.10E
Shillington U.S.A. 85 40.18N 75.58W
Shillong India 41 25.34N 91.53E
Shilong China 33 23.02N113.50E
Shima Japan 35 34.13N136.51E
Shimada Japan 35 34.49N138.11E
Shima-hantō *pen.* Japan 35 34.25N136.45E
Shimizu Japan 35 35.01N138.29E
Shimoda Japan 35 34.40N138.57E
Shimoga India 38 13.56N 75.31E
Shimonoseki Japan 31 33.59N130.58E
Shimpek U.S.S.R. 30 44.50N 74.10E
Shin, Loch U.K. 12 58.06N 4.32W
Shindand Afghan. 40 33.18N 62.08E
Shingleton U.S.A. 84 46.21N 86.28W
Shinkay Afghan. 40 31.57N 67.26E
Shīn Naray Afghan. 40 31.19N 66.43E
Shinshār Syria 44 34.36N 36.45E
Shinshiro Japan 35 34.54N137.30E
Shinyanga Tanzania 55 3.40S 33.20E
Shinyanga *d.* Tanzania 55 3.30S 33.00E
Ship Bottom U.S.A. 85 39.39N 74.11W
Shipka Pass Bulgaria 19 42.45N 25.25E
Shippegan Canada 77 47.45N 64.42W
Shippensburg U.S.A. 84 40.03N 77.31W
Shiprock U.S.A. 80 36.47N108.41W
Shipston on Stour U.K. 11 52.04N 1.38W
Shiqian China 33 27.20N108.10E
Shiqiao China 33 31.19N111.59E
Shiqizhen China 33 22.22N113.21E
Shiquan China 32 33.03N108.17E
Shiquan He *r.* China 41 32.30N 79.40E
Shirakskaya Step *f.* U.S.S.R. 43 41.40N 46.20E
Shirane san *mtn.* Japan 35 35.40N138.15E
Shīrāz Iran 43 29.36N 52.33E
Shirbīn Egypt 44 31.13N 31.31E
Shire *r.* Mozambique 55 17.46S 35.20E
Shīr Kūh *mtn.* Iran 43 31.38N 54.07E
Shirpur India 40 21.21N 74.53E
Shīrvān Iran 43 37.24N 57.55E
Shivpuri India 41 25.26N 77.39E
Shiwan Dashan *mts.* China 33 21.48N107.50E
Shiyan Hubei China 32 32.38N110.47E
Shizuishan China 32 39.14N106.47E
Shizuoka Japan 35 34.58N138.23E
Shizuoka *d.* Japan 35 35.00N138.00E
Shklov U.S.S.R. 21 54.16N 30.16E
Shkodër Albania 19 42.03N 19.30E
Shkumbin *r.* Albania 19 41.01N 19.26E
Shoal C. Australia 63 33.51S121.10E
Sholāpur India 38 17.43N 75.56E
Shonai *r.* Japan 35 35.04N136.50E
Shoshone Calif. U.S.A. 81 35.58N116.17W
Shoshone Idaho U.S.A. 80 42.57N114.25W
Shoshone Mts. U.S.A. 80 39.25N117.15W
Shoshoni U.S.A. 80 43.14N108.07W
Shostka U.S.S.R. 24 51.53N 33.30E
Shou Xian China 32 32.30N116.35E
Shouyang China 32 37.55N113.10E
Show Low U.S.A. 81 34.15N110.02W
Shpola U.S.S.R. 21 49.00N 31.25E
Shreveport U.S.A 83 32.30N 93.45W
Shrewsbury U.K. 11 52.42N 2.45W
Shropshire *d.* U.K. 11 52.35N 2.40W
Shuangliao China 32 43.28N123.27E
Shuangyashan China 31 46.37N131.22E
Shubenacadie Canada 77 45.05N 63.25W
Shubrā al Khaymah Egypt 44 30.06N 31.15E
Shuicheng China 33 26.36N104.51E
Shujāābād Pakistan 40 29.53N 71.18E
Shujālpur India 40 23.24N 76.43E
Shuksan U.S.A. 80 48.55N121.43W
Shule China 30 39.25N 76.06E
Shumagin Is. U.S.A. 72 55.00N160.00W
Shumerlya U.S.S.R. 24 55.30N 46.25E
Shumikha U.S.S.R. 28 55.15N 63.14E
Shumyachi U.S.S.R. 21 53.52N 32.25E
Shunayn, Sabkhat *f.* Libya 48 30.10N 21.00E
Shunchang China 33 26.48N117.47E
Shunde China 33 22.40N113.20E
Shuo Xian China 32 39.19N112.25E
Shūr *r.* Khorāsān Iran 43 34.05N 60.22E
Shūr *r.* Kermān Iran 43 31.14N 55.29E
Shūr *r.* Khorāsān Iran 43 34.11N 60.07E
Shūrāb Iran 43 28.09N 60.18E
Shūrāb *r.* Iran 43 31.30N 55.18E
Shurugwi Zimbabwe 56 19.40S 30.00E
Shūshtar Iran 43 32.04N 48.53E
Shuswap L. Canada 74 50.55N119.03W
Shuttleton Australia 67 32.08S146.08E
Shuwak Sudan 48 14.23N 35.52E
Shuya U.S.S.R. 24 56.49N 41.23E
Shwebo Burma 34 22.35N 95.42E
Shyok Jammu & Kashmir 41 34.11N 78.08E
Siāhān Range *mts.* Pakistan 40 27.30N 64.30E
Siālkot Pakistan 40 32.30N 74.31E
Sian *see* Xi'an China 32
Siargao *i.* Phil. 37 9.55N126.05E
Siari Jammu & Kashmir 40 34.56N 76.44E
Siau *i.* Indonesia 37 2.42N125.24E
Siauliai U.S.S.R. 23 55.56N 23.19E
Sibasa R.S.A. 56 22.56S 30.28E
Šibenik Yugo. 18 43.45N 15.55E
Siberut *i.* Indonesia 36 1.30S 99.00E
Sibi Pakistan 40 29.33N 67.53E
Sibiti Congo 54 3.40S 13.24E
Sibiti *r.* Tanzania 55 3.47S 34.45E
Sibiu Romania 19 45.47N 24.09E
Sibley U.S.A. 82 43.25N 95.43W
Sibolga Indonesia 36 1.42N 98.48E
Sibu Malaysia 36 2.18N111.49E
Sicasica Bolivia 92 17.22S 67.45W
Siccus *r.* Australia 66 31.26S139.30E
Sichuan *d.* China 30 30.30N103.00E
Sichuan Pendi *f.* China 33 31.00N106.00E
Sicilia *d.* Italy 18 37.30N 14.00E
Sicilia *i.* Italy 18 37.30N 14.00E
Sicily *i. see* Sicilia *i.* Italy 18
Sicuani Peru 90 14.21S 71.13W
Sīdamo *d.* Ethiopia 49 4.30N 39.00E
Sidaouet Niger 53 18.34N 8.03E
Sidhi India 41 24.25N 81.53E
Sidhpur India 40 23.55N 72.23E
Sīdī Barrānī Egypt 42 31.38N 25.58E
Sidi bel Abbès Algeria 50 35.12N 0.38W
Sidi Ifni Morocco 50 29.24N 10.12W
Sidi-Kacem Morocco 50 34.15N 5.39W
Sīdī Sālim Egypt 44 31.16N 30.47E
Sidi Smaïl Morocco 50 32.49N 8.30W
Sidlaw Hills U.K. 12 56.31N 3.10W
Sidley, Mt. Antarctica 96 77.30S125.00W
Sidmouth U.K. 11 50.40N 3.13W
Sidney Canada 74 48.39N123.24W
Sidney Mont. U.S.A. 80 47.43N104.09W
Sidney Nebr. U.S.A. 82 41.09N102.59W
Sidney Ohio U.S.A. 84 40.16N 84.10W
Sidon *see* Şaydā Lebanon 44
Sidra, G. of *see* Surt, Khalīj *g.* Libya 51
Siedlce Poland 21 52.10N 22.18E
Sieg *r.* W. Germany 14 50.49N 7.11E
Siegburg W. Germany 14 50.48N 7.13E
Siegen W. Germany 14 50.52N 8.02E
Siemiatycze Poland 21 52.26N 22.53E
Siěmréab Kampuchea 34 13.21N103.50E
Siena Italy 18 43.19N 11.20E
Sieradz Poland 21 51.36N 18.45E
Sierck-les-Bains France 14 49.28N 6.20E
Sierpc Poland 21 52.52N 19.41E
Sierra Blanca *town* U.S.A. 81 31.11N105.12W
Sierra Colorada Argentina 93 40.35S 67.50W
Sierra Leone Africa 52 9.00N 12.00W
Sierra Mojada *town* Mexico 83 27.17N103.42W
Sierra Nevada *mts.* U.S.A. 80 37.45N119.30W
Sierre Switz. 15 46.18N 7.32E
Sifani Ethiopia 49 12.20N 40.24E
Sífnos *i.* Greece 19 36.59N 24.60E
Sig Algeria 50 35.32N 0.11W
Sig U.S.S.R. 24 65.31N 34.16E
Sighetul Marmaţiei Romania 21 47.56N 23.54E
Sighişoara Romania 21 46.13N 24.49E
Sigli Indonesia 36 5.23N 95.57E
Siglufjördhur Iceland 22 66.12N 18.55W
Signy France 15 49.42N 4.25E
Sigüenza Spain 16 41.04N 2.38W
Siguiri Guinea 52 11.28N 9.07W
Sihor India 40 21.42N 71.58E
Sihorā India 41 23.29N 80.07E
Siika *r.* Finland 22 64.50N 24.44E
Siirt Turkey 42 37.56N 41.56E
Sikanni Chief *r.* Canada 74 58.20N121.50W
Sīkar India 40 27.37N 75.09E
Sikasso Mali 52 11.18N 5.38W
Sikasso *d.* Mali 52 11.20N 6.05W
Sikeston U.S.A. 83 36.53N 89.35W
Sikhote Alin *mts.* U.S.S.R. 31 44.00N135.00E
Síkinos *i.* Greece 19 36.39N 25.06E
Sikkim *d.* India 41 27.30N 88.30E
Sil *r.* Spain 16 42.24N 7.15W
Silchar India 39 24.49N 92.47E
Silcox Canada 75 57.12N 94.10W
Silet Algeria 51 22.39N 4.35E
Silgarhi-Doti Nepal 41 29.16N 80.58E
Silghāt India 41 26.37N 92.56E
Silifke Turkey 42 36.22N 33.57E
Silīguri India 41 26.42N 88.26E
Silil Somali Rep. 45 10.59N 43.31E
Siling Co *l.* China 41 31.45N 88.50E
Silistra Bulgaria 19 44.07N 27.17E
Siljan *l.* Sweden 23 60.50N 14.45E
Silkeborg Denmark 23 56.10N 9.34E
Sille-le-Guillaume France 15 48.12N 0.08E
Silloth U.K. 10 54.53N 3.25W
Silogui Indonesia 36 1.10S 98.46E
Silsbee U.S.A 83 30.21N 94.11W
Silvassa India 40 20.17N 73.00E
Silver Bow U.S.A. 80 46.00N112.40W
Silver City U.S.A. 81 32.46N108.17W
Silver Creek *town* U.S.A. 76 42.33N 79.10W
Silver Lake *town* U.S.A. 80 43.08N120.56W
Silver Spring *town* U.S.A. 85 39.02N 77.03W
Silverstone U.K. 11 52.05N 1.03W
Silverthrone Mtn. Canada 74 51.31N126.06W
Silverton Australia 66 31.53S141.13E
Silverton U.S.A. 80 45.01N122.47W
Silvi Italy 18 42.34N 14.06E
Simanggang Malaysia 36 1.10N111.32E
Simàrd, Lac *l.* Canada 76 47.40N 78.40W
Simav *r.* Turkey 19 40.24N 28.31E
Simba Kenya 55 2.10S 37.37E
Simba Zaïre 54 0.36N 22.55E
Simcoe Canada 76 42.50N 80.18W
Simcoe, L. Canada 76 44.25N 79.20W
Simdega India 41 22.37N 84.31E
Simenga U.S.S.R. 29 62.42N108.25E
Simeria Romania 19 45.51N 23.01E
Simeulue *i.* Indonesia 36 2.30N 96.00E
Simferopol' U.S.S.R. 25 44.57N 34.05E
Simikot Nepal 41 29.58N 81.51E
Simitli Bulgaria 19 41.51N 23.09E
Simiyu *r.* Tanzania 55 2.32S 33.25E
Simla India 40 31.06N 77.09E
Simleul Silvaniei Romania 21 47.14N 22.48E
Simmern W. Germany 14 49.59N 7.32E
Simo *r.* Finland 22 65.37N 25.03E
Simojärvo *l.* Finland 22 66.06N 27.03E
Simon, Lac *l.* Canada 77 45.58N 75.05W
Simonstown R.S.A. 56 34.12S 18.26E
Simoom Sound *town* Canada 72 50.45N126.45W
Simplon Pass Switz. 17 46.15N 8.03E
Simplon Tunnel Italy / Switz. 18 46.20N 8.05E
Simpson Desert Australia 64 25.00S136.50E
Simrishamn Sweden 23 55.33N 14.20E
Simuco Mozambique 55 14.00S 40.35E
Sīnā', Shibh Jazīrat *pen.* Egypt 44 29.00N 34.00E
Sinadogo Somali Rep. 45 5.22N 46.22E
Sinai *see* Sīnā', Shibh Jazīrat *pen.* Egypt 44
Sinaloa *d.* Mexico 81 25.00N107.30W
Sinaloa *r.* Mexico 81 25.18N108.30W
Sinan China 33 27.51N108.24E
Sināwin Libya 51 31.02N 10.36E
Sincelejo Colombia 90 9.17N 75.23W
Sinclair U.S.A. 80 41.47N107.07W
Sinclair Mills Canada 74 54.05N121.40W
Sind *r.* India 41 26.26N 79.13E
Sind *d.* Pakistan 40 26.45N 69.00E
Sindara Gabon 54 1.07S 10.41E
Sindari India 40 25.35N 71.55E
Sindhūli Garhi Nepal 41 27.16N 85.58E
Sindri India 41 23.45N 86.42E
Sines Portugal 16 37.58N 8.52W
Sinfra Ivory Coast 52 6.35N 5.56W
Singālila *mtn.* India 41 27.13N 88.01E
Singapore Asia 36 1.20N103.45E
Singapore *town* Singapore 36 1.20N103.45E
Singaraja Indonesia 37 8.06S115.07E
Singatoka Fiji 68 18.08S177.30E
Sing Buri Thailand 34 14.56N100.21E
Singida Tanzania 55 4.45S 34.42E
Singida *d.* Tanzania 55 6.00S 34.30E
Singing India 39 28.53N 94.47E
Singitikós Kólpos *g.* Greece 19 40.12N 24.00E
Singkaling Hkāmti Burma 39 26.00N 95.42E
Singkang Indonesia 37 4.09S120.02E
Singkawang Indonesia 36 0.57N108.57E
Singkep *i.* Indonesia 36 0.30S104.20E
Singleton Australia 67 32.33S151.11E
Singoli India 40 25.00N 75.25E
Singosan N. Korea 31 38.50N127.27E
Sinj Yugo. 19 43.42N 16.38E
Sinjah Sudan 49 13.09N 33.56E
Sinkāt Sudan 48 18.50N 36.50E
Sinnar India 40 19.51N 74.00E
Sînnicolau Mare Romania 19 46.05N 20.38E
Sinnūris Egypt 44 29.25N 30.52E
Sinop Turkey 42 42.02N 35.09E
Sinsheim W. Germany 20 49.15N 8.53E
Sintang Indonesia 36 0.03N111.31E
Sint Eustatius *i.* Leeward Is. 87 17.33N 63.00W
Sint Maarten *i. see* St. Martin *i.* Leeward Is. 87
Sinton U.S.A. 83 29.41N 95.58W
Sinŭiju N. Korea 31 40.04N124.25E
Sinyavka U.S.S.R. 21 52.58N 26.30E
Sinyukha *r.* U.S.S.R. 21 48.03N 30.51E
Siocon Phil. 37 7.42N122.08E
Siófok Hungary 21 46.54N 18.04E
Sion Switz. 15 46.14N 7.21E
Sioux City U.S.A. 82 42.30N 96.23W
Sioux Falls *town* U.S.A. 82 43.32N 96.44W
Sioux Lookout *town* Canada 76 50.06N 91.55W
Siphaqeni R.S.A. 56 31.05S 29.29E
Siping Hubei China 33 31.58N111.10E
Siping Jilin China 32 43.10N124.24E
Sipiwesk L. Canada 75 55.05N 97.35W
Sipura *i.* Indonesia 36 2.10S 99.40E
Sira *r.* Norway 23 58.17N 6.24E
Siracusa Italy 18 37.05N 15.17E
Sirājganj Bangla. 41 24.27N 89.43E
Sirakoro Mali 52 12.41N 9.14W
Sirasso Ivory Coast 52 9.16N 6.06W
Sire Ethiopia 49 9.00N 36.55E
Sir Edward Pellew Group *is.* Australia 64 15.40S136.48E
Siret *r.* Romania 19 45.28N 27.56E
Sirha Nepal 41 26.39N 86.12E
Sirḩān, Wādī as *f.* Saudi Arabia 42 31.00N 37.30E
Sir James MacBrien, Mt. Canada 74 62.07N127.41W
Sirohi India 40 24.53N 72.52E
Sironj India 41 24.06N 77.42E
Síros *i.* Greece 19 37.26N 24.56E
Sirrah, Wādī as *r.* Saudi Arabia 43 23.10N 44.22E
Sirsa India 40 29.32N 75.02E
Sisak Yugo. 18 45.30N 16.21E
Sisaket Thailand 34 15.08N104.18E
Sishen R.S.A. 56 27.46S 22.59E
Sisimiut *see* Holsteinsborg Greenland 73
Sisipuk L. Canada 75 55.45N101.50W
Sisŏphŏn Kampuchea 34 13.37N102.58E
Sisseton U.S.A. 82 45.40N 97.03W
Sissonne France 15 49.34N 3.54E
Sisteron France 17 44.16N 5.56E
Sītāmarhi India 41 26.36N 85.29E
Sītāpur India 41 27.34N 80.41E
Sitka U.S.A. 74 57.05N135.20W
Sittang *r.* Burma 34 17.25N 96.50E
Sittard Neth. 14 51.00N 5.52E
Sittwe Burma 34 20.09N 92.50E
Situbondo Indonesia 37 7.40S114.01E
Siuruan *r.* Finland 22 65.20N 25.55E
Sīvan *r.* Iran 43 29.50N 52.47E
Sivas Turkey 42 39.44N 37.01E
Sivomaskinskiy U.S.S.R. 24 66.45N 62.44E
Sivrihisar Turkey 42 39.29N 31.32E
Sīwah Egypt 42 29.12N 25.31E
Sīwah, Wāḩat *oasis* Egypt 42 29.10N 25.40E
Siwalik Range *mts.* India 41 31.15N 77.45E
Siwān India 41 26.13N 84.22E
Siwa Oasis *see* Sīwah, Wāḩat *oasis* Egypt 42
Sixmilecross U.K. 13 54.34N 7.08W
Siya U.S.S.R. 24 63.38N 41.40E
Sjaelland *i.* Denmark 23 55.30N 11.45E
Sjötorp Sweden 23 58.50N 13.59E
Skagafjördhur *est.* Iceland 22 65.55N 19.35W
Skagen Denmark 23 57.44N 10.36E
Skagerrak *str.* Denmark / Norway 23 57.45N 8.55E
Skagway U.S.A. 74 59.23N135.20W
Skaill U.K. 12 58.56N 2.43W
Skála Oropoú Greece 19 38.20N 23.46E
Skala Podolskaya U.S.S.R. 21 48.51N 26.11E
Skalat U.S.S.R. 21 49.20N 25.59E
Skanderborg Denmark 23 56.02N 9.56E
Skånevik Norway 23 59.44N 5.59E
Skara Sweden 23 58.22N 13.25E
Skaraborg *d.* Sweden 23 58.20N 13.30E
Skarnes Norway 23 60.15N 11.41E
Skarżysko-Kamienna Poland 21 51.08N 20.53E
Skeena *r.* Canada 74 54.09N130.02W
Skeena Mts. Canada 74 57.00N128.30W
Skegness U.K. 10 53.09N 0.20E
Skellefte *r.* Sweden 22 64.42N 21.06E
Skellefteå Sweden 22 64.46N 20.57E
Skelleftehamn Sweden 22 64.41N 21.14E
Skelmersdale U.K. 10 53.34N 2.49W
Skene Sweden 23 57.29N 12.38E
Skerries Rep. of Ire. 13 53.35N 6.07W
Skhíza *i.* Greece 19 36.42N 21.45E
Ski Norway 23 59.43N 10.50E
Skiddaw *mtn.* U.K. 10 54.40N 3.09W
Skidel U.S.S.R. 21 53.37N 24.19E
Skien Norway 23 59.12N 9.36E
Skierniewice Poland 21 51.58N 20.08E
Skikda Algeria 51 36.53N 6.54E
Skipness U.K. 12 56.45N 5.22W
Skipton U.K. 10 53.57N 2.01W
Skíros Greece 19 38.53N 24.33E
Skíros *i.* Greece 19 38.50N 24.33E
Skive Denmark 23 56.34N 9.02E
Skjálfanda Fljót *r.* Iceland 22 65.55N 17.30W
Skjálfandi *est.* Iceland 22 66.08N 17.38W
Skjönsta Norway 22 67.12N 15.45E
Skoghall Sweden 23 59.19N 13.26E
Skole U.S.S.R. 21 49.00N 23.30E
Skopje Yugo. 19 41.58N 21.27E
Skotterud Norway 23 59.59N 12.07E
Skövde Sweden 23 58.24N 13.50E
Skovorodino U.S.S.R. 29 54.00N123.53E
Skreia Norway 23 60.39N 10.56E
Skull Rep. of Ire. 13 51.32N 9.33W
Skuodas U.S.S.R. 23 56.16N 21.32E
Skutskär Sweden 23 60.38N 17.25E
Skvira U.S.S.R. 21 49.42N 29.40E
Skye *i.* U.K. 12 57.20N 6.15W
Slagelse Denmark 23 55.24N 11.22E
Sľalowa Wola Poland 21 50.40N 22.05E
Slamet *mtn.* Indonesia 37 7.14S109.10E
Slaney *r.* Rep. of Ire. 13 52.21N 6.30W
Slantsy U.S.S.R. 24 59.09N 28.09E
Slatina Romania 19 44.26N 24.23E
Slaton U.S.A. 83 33.26N101.39W
Slave *r.* Canada 74 61.18N113.39W
Slavgorod B.S.S.R. U.S.S.R. 21 53.25N 31.00E
Slavgorod R.S.F.S.R. U.S.S.R. 28 53.01N 78.37E
Slavuta U.S.S.R. 21 50.20N 26.58E
Slavyansk U.S.S.R. 25 48.51N 37.36E
Sľawno Poland 20 54.22N 16.40E
Sleaford U.K. 10 53.00N 0.22W
Sleaford B. Australia 66 35.00S136.50E
Sleat, Sd. of *str.* U.K. 12 57.05N 5.48W
Sledge U.S.A. 83 34.26N 90.13W
Sledmere U.K. 10 54.04N 0.35W
Sleeper Is. Canada 76 56.50N 80.30W
Sleetmute U.S.A. 72 61.40N157.11W
Sliedrecht Neth. 14 51.48N 4.46E
Slieve Aughty Mts. Rep. of Ire. 13 53.05N 8.31W
Slieve Bloom Mts. Rep. of Ire. 13 53.03N 7.35W
Slieve Callan *mtn.* Rep. of Ire. 13 52.51N 9.18W
Slieve Donard *mtn.* U.K. 13 54.11N 5.56W
Slieve Gamph *mts.* Rep. of Ire. 13 54.06N 8.52W
Slievekimalta *mtn.* Rep. of Ire. 13 52.45N 8.17W
Slieve Mish *mts.* Rep. of Ire. 13 52.48N 9.48W
Slieve Miskish *mts.* Rep. of Ire. 13 51.41N 9.56W
Slievenamon *mtn.* Rep. of Ire. 13 52.25N 7.34W
Slieve Snaght *mtn.* Donegal Rep. of Ire. 13 55.12N 7.20W
Sligo Rep. of Ire. 13 54.17N 8.28W
Sligo *d.* Rep. of Ire. 13 54.10N 8.35W
Sligo B. Rep. of Ire. 13 54.18N 8.40W
Slite Sweden 23 57.43N 18.48E
Sliven Bulgaria 19 42.41N 26.19E
Sloan U.S.A. 82 42.14N 96.14W
Slobodka U.S.S.R. 21 47.56N 29.18E
Slobodskoy U.S.S.R. 24 58.42N 50.10E
Slonim U.S.S.R. 21 53.05N 25.21E
Slough U.K. 11 51.30N 0.35W
Slovechna *r.* U.S.S.R. 21 51.41N 29.41E
Slovechno U.S.S.R. 21 51.23N 28.20E
Slovenija *d.* Yugo. 18 46.10N 14.45E
Slovenjgradec Yugo. 18 46.31N 15.05E
Sľubice Poland 20 52.20N 14.32E
Sluch *r.* U.S.S.R. 21 52.08N 27.31E
Sluis Neth. 14 51.18N 3.23E
Slunj Yugo. 20 45.07N 15.35E
Sľupsk Poland 21 54.28N 17.01E
Slurry R.S.A. 56 25.48S 25.49E
Slutsk U.S.S.R. 21 53.02N 27.31E
Slyne Head Rep. of Ire. 13 53.25N 10.12W
Slyudyanka U.S.S.R. 30 51.40N103.40E
Smeaton Canada 75 53.30N104.49W
Smederevo Yugo. 19 44.40N 20.56E
Smela U.S.S.R. 25 49.15N 31.54E
Smilde Neth. 14 52.58N 6.28E
Smilovichi U.S.S.R. 21 53.45N 28.00E
Smith Canada 74 55.10N114.00W
Smith Arm *b.* Canada 72 66.15N124.00W
Smithers Canada 74 54.45N127.10W
Smithfield R.S.A. 56 30.11S 26.31E
Smiths Falls *town* Canada 76 44.54N 76.01W
Smithton Australia 65 40.52S145.07E
Smithtown Australia 67 31.03S152.53E
Smoky *r.* Canada 74 56.10N117.21W
Smoky Bay *town* Australia 66 32.22S133.56E
Smoky C. Australia 67 30.55S153.05E
Smoky Hill *r.* U.S.A. 82 39.03N 96.48W
Smöla *i.* Norway 22 63.20N 8.00E
Smolensk U.S.S.R. 24 54.49N 32.04E
Smolevichi U.S.S.R. 21 54.00N 28.01E
Smólikas *mtn.* Greece 19 40.06N 20.55E
Smolyan Bulgaria 19 41.34N 24.45E
Smorgon U.S.S.R. 21 54.28N 26.20E
Smyrna U.S.A. 85 39.18N 75.36W
Snaefell *mtn.* Iceland 22 64.48N 15.34W
Snaefell *mtn.* U.K. 10 54.16N 4.28W
Snake *r.* Idaho U.S.A. 78 43.50N117.05W
Snake *r.* Wash. U.S.A. 80 46.12N119.02W
Snake Range *mts.* U.S.A. 80 39.00N114.15W
Snake River *town* U.S.A. 80 44.10N110.40W
Snake River Plain *f.* U.S.A. 80 43.00N113.00W
Snåsa Norway 22 64.15N 12.23E
Snåsavatn *l.* Norway 22 64.05N 12.00E
Sneek Neth. 14 53.03N 5.40E
Sneem Rep. of Ire. 13 51.50N 9.54W
Sneeuwberg *mtn.* R.S.A. 56 32.30S 19.09E
Śniardwy, Jezioro *l.* Poland 21 53.46N 21.44E
Snina Czech. 21 48.59N 22.07E
Snizort, Loch U.K. 12 57.35N 6.30W
Snöhetta *mtn.* Norway 23 62.20N 9.17E
Snov *r.* U.S.S.R. 21 51.45N 31.45E
Snowbird L. Canada 75 60.45N103.00W
Snowdon *mtn.* U.K. 10 53.05N 4.05W
Snowdrift Canada 75 62.24N110.44W
Snowdrift *r.* Canada 75 62.24N110.44W
Snowflake U.S.A. 81 34.30N110.05W
Snow Hill *town* U.S.A. 85 38.11N 75.23W
Snowtown Australia 66 33.47S138.13E
Snowy *r.* Australia 67 37.49S148.30E
Snowy Mts. Australia 67 36.30S148.20E
Snyatyn U.S.S.R. 21 48.30N 25.50E
Snyder U.S.A. 83 32.44N100.05W
Soacha Colombia 90 4.35N 74.13W
Soalala Madagascar 57 16.06S 45.20E
Soanierana-Ivongo Madagascar 57 16.55S 49.35E
Soasiu Indonesia 37 0.40N127.25E
Soavinandriana Madagascar 57 19.09S 46.45E
Sob *r.* U.S.S.R. 21 48.42N 29.17E
Sobat *r.* Sudan 49 9.30N 31.30E
Sobernheim W. Germany 14 49.47N 7.40E
Soboko C.A.R. 49 6.49N 24.50E
Sobral Brazil 91 3.45S 40.20W
Sochi U.S.S.R. 25 43.35N 39.46E
Société, Îles de la *is.* Pacific Oc. 69 17.00S150.00W
Society Is. *see* Société, Îles de la *is.* Pacific Oc. 69
Socorro Colombia 90 6.30N 73.16W
Socorro U.S.A. 81 34.04N106.54W
Socorro, Isla *i.* Mexico 86 18.45N110.58W
Socotra *i. see* Suquţrá *i.* S. Yemen 45
Socuéllamos Spain 16 39.16N 2.47W
Sodankylä Finland 22 67.29N 26.32E
Söderhamn Sweden 23 61.18N 17.03E
Söderköping Sweden 23 58.29N 16.18E
Södermanland *d.* Sweden 23 59.10N 16.35E
Södertälje Sweden 23 59.12N 17.37E
Sodium R.S.A. 56 30.10S 23.08E
Sodo Ethiopia 49 6.52N 37.47E
Södra Vi Sweden 23 57.45N 15.48E
Soest W. Germany 14 51.34N 8.06E
Sofala Australia 67 33.05S149.42E
Sofala Mozambique 57 19.49S 34.52E
Sofala *d.* Mozambique 57 19.00S 34.39E
Sofia *see* Sofiya Bulgaria 19
Sofia *r.* Madagascar 57 15.27S 47.23E
Sofiya Bulgaria 19 42.41N 23.19E
Sofiysk U.S.S.R. 29 52.19N133.55E
Sofporog U.S.S.R. 24 65.47N 31.30E
Sogamoso Colombia 90 5.43N 72.56W
Sögel W. Germany 14 52.51N 7.31E
Sognefjorden *est.* Norway 23 61.06N 5.10E
Sogn og Fjordane *d.* Norway 23 61.30N 6.50E
Söğüt Turkey 42 40.02N 30.10E
Sog Xian China 41 31.51N 93.40E
Sohāgpur India 41 22.42N 78.12E
Soignies Belgium 14 50.35N 4.04E
Soissons France 15 49.23N 3.20E
Sojat India 40 25.55N 73.40E
Sokal U.S.S.R. 21 50.30N 24.10E
Söke Turkey 19 37.46N 27.26E
Sokodé Togo 53 8.59N 1.11E
Sokol U.S.S.R. 24 59.28N 40.04E
Sokółka Poland 21 53.25N 23.31E

Sokolo to **Streaky Bay**

Sokolo Mali 52 14.53N 6.11W
Sokolov Czech. 20 50.09N 12.40E
Sokoto Nigeria 53 13.02N 5.15E
Sokoto *d.* Nigeria 53 11.50N 5.05E
Sokoto *r.* Nigeria 53 13.05N 5.13E
Solbad Hall Austria 20 47.17N 11.31E
Solec Kujawski Poland 21 53.06N 18.14E
Soledad Venezuela 90 8.10N 63.34W
Solesmes France 14 50.12N 3.32E
Solginskiy U.S.S.R. 24 61.07N 41.30E
Solheim Norway 23 60.53N 5.27E
Soligalich U.S.S.R. 24 59.02N 42.15E
Solihull U.K. 9 52.26N 1.47W
Solikamsk U.S.S.R. 24 59.40N 56.45E
Sol-Iletsk U.S.S.R. 24 51.09N 55.00E
Solingen W. Germany 14 51.10N 7.05E
Sollefteå Sweden 22 63.12N 17.20E
Sollentuna Sweden 23 59.28N 17.54E
Sóller Spain 16 39.47N 2.41E
Sollia Norway 23 61.47N 10.24E
Solola Somali Rep. 49 0.08N 41.30E
Solomon Is. Pacific Oc. 68 8.00S160.00E
Solomons U.S.A. 85 38.21N 76.29W
Solomon Sea Pacific Oc. 61 7.00S150.00E
Solon U.S.A. 84 44.57N 69.52W
Solon Springs U.S.A. 82 46.22N 91.48W
Solothurn Switz. 20 47.13N 7.32E
Solovetskiye, Ostrova *is.* U.S.S.R. 24 65.05N 35.30E
Šolta *i.* Yugo. 18 43.23N 16.17E
Soltānābād Iran 43 36.25N 58.02E
Soltau W. Germany 20 52.59N 9.49E
Sölvesborg Sweden 23 56.03N 14.33E
Solway Firth *est.* U.K. 10 54.50N 3.30W
Solwezi Zambia 54 12.11S 26.23E
Solzach *r.* Austria 20 48.35N 13.30E
Soma Turkey 19 39.11N 27.36E
Somabhula Zimbabwe 56 19.40S 29.38E
Somali Republic Africa 45 5.30N 47.00E
Sombor Yugo. 19 45.48N 19.08E
Sombrerete Mexico 86 23.38N103.39W
Somerset *d.* U.K. 11 51.09N 3.00W
Somerset Ky. U.S.A. 85 37.05N 84.38W
Somerset East R.S.A. 56 32.43S 25.33E
Somerset I. Bermuda 95 32.18N 64.53W
Somerset I. Canada 73 73.00N 93.30W
Somers Point *town* U.S.A. 85 39.20N 74.36W
Somerville N.J. U.S.A. 85 40.34N 74.37W
Somes *r.* Hungary 21 48.40N 22.30E
Somme *r.* France 17 50.01N 1.40E
Sommen *l.* Sweden 23 58.01N 15.15E
Sompeta India 41 18.56N 84.36E
Sompuis France 15 48.41N 4.23E
Son *r.* India 41 25.42N 84.52E
Sonāmarg Jammu & Kashmir 40 34.18N 75.18E
Sonāmura India 41 23.29N 91.17E
Sönderborg Denmark 23 54.55N 9.47E
Sondershausen E. Germany 20 51.22N 10.52E
Söndreströmfjord Greenland 73 66.30N 50.52W
Sondrio Italy 15 46.10N 9.52E
Sonepur India 41 20.50N 83.55E
Songa *r.* Norway 23 59.45N 7.59E
Song-Cau Vietnam 34 13.27N109.13E
Songea Tanzania 55 10.42S 35.39E
Songhua Jiang *r.* China 31 47.46N132.30E
Songjiang China 33 31.01N121.20E
Songkhla Thailand 34 7.12N100.35E
Songololo Zaïre 54 5.40S 14.05E
Songpan China 32 32.36N103.36E
Songtao Miaozu Zizhixian China 33 28.12N109.12E
Song Xian China 32 34.02N111.48E
Sonid Youqi China 32 42.44N112.40E
Sonid Zuoqi China 32 43.58N113.59E
Sonipat India 40 28.59N 77.01E
Son La Vietnam 34 21.20N103.55E
Sonmiāni Pakistan 40 25.26N 66.36E
Sonmiāni B. Pakistan 40 25.15N 66.30E
Sonneberg E. Germany 20 50.22N 11.10E
Sonoita Mexico 81 31.51N112.50W
Sonora *d.* Mexico 81 29.30N110.40W
Sonora *r.* Mexico 81 28.50N111.33W
Sonora U.S.A. 83 30.34N100.39W
Sonsorol *i.* Caroline Is. 37 5.20N132.13E
Son Tay Vietnam 33 21.15N105.17E
Sopi Indonesia 37 2.40N128.28E
Sopo *r.* Sudan 49 8.51N 26.11E
Sopot Poland 21 54.28N 18.34E
Sopotskin U.S.S.R. 21 53.49N 23.42E
Soppero Sweden 22 68.07N 21.40E
Sopron Hungary 20 47.41N 16.36E
Sop's Arm *town* Canada 77 49.46N 56.56W
Sopur Jammu & Kashmir 40 34.18N 74.28E
Sorada India 41 19.45N 84.26E
Sorel Canada 77 46.03N 73.06W
Sörfjorden Norway 22 66.29N 13.20E
Sörfold Norway 22 67.30N 15.30E
Sorgono Italy 18 40.01N 9.06E
Soria Spain 16 41.46N 2.28W
Soriano Uruguay 93 33.24S 58.19W
Sor Kvalöy *i.* Norway 22 69.40N 18.30E
Sörli Norway 22 64.15N 13.50E
Sor Mertvyy Kultuk *f.* U.S.S.R. 25 45.30N 54.00E
Soro India 41 21.17N 86.40E
Sorocaba Brazil 94 23.29S 47.27W
Sorochinsk U.S.S.R. 24 52.29N 53.15E
Soroki U.S.S.R. 21 48.08N 28.12E
Sorol *i.* Caroline Is. 37 8.09N140.25E
Soron India 41 27.53N 78.45E
Sorong Indonesia 37 0.50S131.17E
Soroti Uganda 55 1.40N 33.37E
Söröya *i.* Norway 22 70.35N 22.30E
Sorraia *r.* Portugal 16 39.00N 8.51W
Sorrento Italy 18 40.37N 14.22E
Sör-Rondane *mts.* Antarctica 96 72.30S 22.00E
Sorsele Sweden 22 65.30N 17.30E
Sortavala U.S.S.R. 24 61.40N 30.40E
Sortland Norway 22 68.44N 15.25E
Sör Tröndelag *d.* Norway 22 63.00N 10.20E
Sorūbī Afghan. 40 34.36N 69.43E
Sosnogorsk U.S.S.R. 24 63.32N 53.55E
Sosnovo U.S.S.R. 24 60.33N 30.11E
Sosnovyy U.S.S.R. 24 66.01N 32.40E
Sosnowiec Poland 21 50.18N 19.08E
Sosva U.S.S.R. 24 59.10N 61.50E
Sosyka U.S.S.R. 25 46.11N 38.49E
Sotik Kenya 55 0.40S 35.08E
Sotra *i.* Norway 23 60.15N 5.10E
Sotteville France 15 49.25N 1.06E
Soubré Ivory Coast 52 5.50N 6.35W
Souderton U.S.A. 85 40.19N 75.19W
Soufflay Congo 54 2.00N 14.54E
Souflión Greece 19 41.12N 26.18E
Souk Ahras Algeria 51 36.17N 7.57E
Souk-el-Arba-du-Rharb Morocco 50 34.43N 6.01W
Sŏul S. Korea 31 37.30N127.00E
Sources, Mont-aux- *mtn.* Lesotho 56 28.44S 28.52E
Soure Portugal 16 40.04N 8.38W
Souris *r.* Canada 75 49.39N 99.34W
Souris Man. Canada 75 49.38N100.15W
Souris P.E.I. Canada 77 46.21N 62.15W
Sous, Oued *wadi* Morocco 50 30.27N 9.31W
Sousa Brazil 91 6.41S 38.14W
Sous le Vent, Îles *is.* Îs. de la Société 69 16.30S151.30W
Sousse Tunisia 51 35.48N 10.38E
Soustons France 17 43.45N 1.19W
Southampton Canada 76 44.29N 81.23W
Southampton U.K. 11 50.54N 1.23W
Southampton I. Canada 73 64.30N 84.00W
South Auckland-Bay of Plenty *d.* New Zealand 60 38.00S176.00E
South Aulatsivik I. Canada 77 56.45N 61.30W
South Australia *d.* Australia 66 30.00S137.00E
South Bend Ind. U.S.A. 84 41.40N 86.15W
South Bend Wash. U.S.A. 80 46.40N123.48W
South Boston U.S.A. 85 36.42N 78.58W
South Branch U.S.A. 84 44.29N 83.36W
Southbridge New Zealand 60 43.48S172.15E
South Carolina *d.* U.S.A. 85 34.00N 81.00W
South Cerney U.K. 11 51.40N 1.55W
South China Sea Asia 36 12.30N115.00E
South Dakota *d.* U.S.A. 82 45.00N100.00W
South Dorset Downs *hills* U.K. 11 50.40N 2.25W
South Downs *hills* U.K. 11 50.04N 0.34W
South East C. Australia 65 43.38S146.48E
South Eastern Atlantic Basin *f.* Atlantic Oc. 95 20.00S 0.00
South East Head *c.* Ascension 95 7.58S 14.18W
South East Is. Australia 63 34.23S123.30E
South East Pt. Kiribati 69 1.40N157.10W
Southend-on-Sea U.K. 11 51.32N 0.43E
Southern *d.* Zambia 56 16.30S 26.40E
Southern Alps *mts.* New Zealand 60 43.20S170.45E
Southern Cross Australia 63 31.14S119.16E
Southern Indian L. Canada 75 57.10N 98.40W
Southern Lueti *r.* Zambia 56 16.15S 23.12E
Southern Pines U.S.A. 85 35.12N 79.23W
Southern Uplands *hills* U.K. 12 55.30N 3.30W
Southern Yemen Asia 45 16.00N 49.30E
South Esk *r.* U.K. 12 56.43N 2.32W
Southesk Tablelands *f.* Australia 62 20.50S126.40E
Southey Canada 75 50.56N104.30W
South Fiji Basin Pacific Oc. 68 27.00S176.00E
South Georgia *i.* Atlantic Oc. 95 54.50S 36.00W
South Glamorgan *d.* U.K. 11 51.27N 3.22W
South-haa U.K. 12 60.34N 1.17W
South Hātia I. Bangla. 41 22.19N 91.07E
South Haven U.S.A. 84 42.25N 86.16W
South Henik L. Canada 75 61.30N 97.30W
South Honshu Ridge Pacific Oc. 68 22.00N141.00E
South Horr Kenya 55 2.10N 36.45E
South I. Kenya 55 2.36N 36.38E
South I. New Zealand 60 43.00S171.00E
South Knife *r.* Canada 75 58.55N 94.37W
South Korea Asia 31 36.00N128.00E
South Lake Tahoe *town* U.S.A. 80 38.57N119.57W
Southland *d.* New Zealand 60 45.40S168.00E
South Loup *r.* U.S.A. 82 41.04N 98.40W
South Molton U.K. 11 51.01N 3.50W
South Nahanni *r.* Canada 74 61.03N123.21W
South Orkney Is. Atlantic Oc. 95 60.50S 45.00W
South Platte *r.* U.S.A. 82 41.07N100.42W
Southport Australia 67 27.58S153.20E
Southport U.K. 10 53.38N 3.01W
Southport U.S.A. 85 33.55N 78.00W
South River *town* U.S.A. 85 40.27N 74.23W
South Ronaldsay *i.* U.K. 12 58.47N 2.56W
South Sandwich Is. Atlantic Oc. 95 57.00S 27.00W
South Sandwich Trench *f.* Atlantic Oc. 95 57.00S 25.00W
South Saskatchewan *r.* Canada 75 53.15N105.05W
South Seal *r.* Canada 75 58.48N 98.08W
South Shields U.K. 10 55.00N 1.24W
South Sioux City U.S.A. 82 42.28N 96.24W
South Tasmania Ridge *f.* Pac. Oc./Ind. Oc. 68 46.00S147.00E
South Thompson *r.* Canada 74 50.40N120.20W
South Tucson U.S.A. 81 32.12N110.58W
South Twin I. Canada 76 53.00N 79.50W
South Tyne *r.* U.K. 12 54.59N 2.08W
South Uist *i.* U.K. 12 57.15N 7.20W
South Wabasca L. Canada 74 55.54N113.45W
Southwest C. New Zealand 60 47.15S167.30E
South Western Pacific Basin Pacific Oc. 69 39.00S148.00W
South West Peru Ridge Pacific Oc. 69 20.00S 82.00W
South West Pt. *c.* Kiribati 69 1.52N157.33W
South West Pt. *c.* St. Helena 95 16.00S 5.48W
South Windham U.S.A. 84 43.44N 70.26W
Southwold U.K. 11 52.19N 1.41E
South Yorkshire *d.* U.K. 10 53.28N 1.25W
Soutpansberge *mts.* R.S.A. 56 22.58S 29.50E
Sovetsk Lit.S.S.R. U.S.S.R. 23 55.05N 21.53E
Sovetsk R.S.F.S.R. U.S.S.R. 24 57.39N 48.59E
Sovetskaya Gavan U.S.S.R. 29 48.57N140.16E
Soweto R.S.A. 56 26.16S 27.51E
Soyo Angola 54 6.12S 12.25E
Soyopa Mexico 81 28.47N109.39W
Sozh *r.* U.S.S.R. 21 51.57N 30.48E
Spa Belgium 14 50.29N 5.52E
Spain Europe 16 40.00N 4.00W
Spalding Australia 66 33.29S138.40E
Spalding U.K. 10 52.47N 0.09W
Spalding U.S.A. 82 41.41N 98.22W
Spandau W. Germany 20 52.32N 13.13E
Spanish Fork U.S.A. 80 40.07N111.39W
Sparks U.S.A. 80 39.32N119.45W
Sparrows Point *town* U.S.A. 85 39.13N 76.26W
Sparta N.J. U.S.A. 85 41.02N 74.38W
Sparta Ga. U.S.A. 85 33.17N 82.58W
Sparta Wisc. U.S.A. 82 43.57N 90.47W
Spartanburg U.S.A. 85 34.56N 81.57W
Spárti Greece 19 37.04N 22.28E
Spartivento, Capo *c.* Calabria Italy 18 37.55N 16.04E
Spartivento, Capo *c.* Sardegna Italy 18 38.53N 8.50E
Spátha, Ákra *c.* Greece 19 35.42N 23.43E
Spatsizi Plateau Wilderness Prov. Park Canada 74 57.13N127.53W
Spearman U.S.A. 83 36.12N101.12W
Speculator U.S.A. 84 43.30N 74.17W
Speke G. Tanzania 55 2.20S 33.30E
Spence Bay *town* Canada 73 69.30N 93.20W
Spencer Idaho U.S.A. 80 44.21N112.11W
Spencer Iowa U.S.A. 82 43.09N 95.09W
Spencer S.Dak. U.S.A. 82 43.44N 97.36W
Spencer, C. Australia 66 35.18S136.53E
Spencer G. Australia 66 34.00S137.00E
Spences Bridge *town* Canada 74 50.25N121.20W
Sperrin Mts. U.K. 13 54.49N 7.06W
Spétsai *i.* Greece 19 37.15N 23.10E
Spey *r.* U.K. 12 57.40N 3.06W
Speyer W. Germany 20 49.18N 8.26E
Spiekeroog *i.* W. Germany 14 53.48N 7.45E
Spilimbergo Italy 15 46.07N 12.54E
Spilsby U.K. 10 53.10N 0.06E
Spina *ruins* Italy 15 44.42N 12.08E
Spinazzola Italy 18 40.58N 16.06E
Spin Būldak Afghan. 40 31.01N 66.24E
Spirit River *town* Canada 74 55.45N118.50W
Spišská Nová Ves Czech. 21 48.57N 20.34E
Spithead *str.* U.K. 11 50.45N 1.05W
Spitsbergen *is.* Arctic Oc. 96 78.00N 17.00E
Spittal an der Drau Austria 20 46.48N 13.30E
Split Yugo. 19 43.32N 16.27E
Split L. Canada 75 56.08N 96.15W
Spofford U.S.A. 83 29.11N100.25W
Spokane U.S.A. 80 47.40N117.23W
Spokane *r.* U.S.A. 80 47.44N118.20W
Spooner U.S.A. 82 45.50N 91.53W
Spratly *i.* S. China Sea 36 8.45N111.54E
Spray U.S.A. 80 44.50N119.48W
Spree *r.* E. Germany 20 52.32N 13.15E
Springbok R.S.A. 56 29.40S 17.50E
Springdale Canada 77 49.30N 56.04W
Springer U.S.A. 80 36.22N104.36W
Springerville U.S.A. 81 34.08N109.17W
Springfield Australia 64 25.52S143.06E
Springfield New Zealand 60 43.20S171.56E
Springfield Colo. U.S.A. 83 37.24N102.37W
Springfield Ill. U.S.A. 82 39.49N 89.39W
Springfield Mass. U.S.A. 84 42.07N 72.35W
Springfield Miss. U.S.A. 79 37.11N 93.19W
Springfield Mo. U.S.A. 83 37.14N 93.17W
Springfield Ohio U.S.A. 84 39.55N 83.48W
Springfield Oreg. U.S.A. 80 44.03N123.01W
Springfield Tenn. U.S.A. 85 36.30N 86.54W
Springfield Vt. U.S.A. 84 43.18N 72.29W
Springfontein R.S.A. 56 30.15S 25.41E
Spring Grove U.S.A. 85 39.52N 76.52W
Springhill Canada 77 45.39N 64.03W
Springs *town* R.S.A. 56 26.16S 28.27E
Springsure Australia 64 24.07S148.05E
Spring Valley *town* U.S.A. 82 43.41N 92.23W
Springville Utah U.S.A. 80 40.10N111.37W
Spry U.S.A. 80 37.55N112.28W
Spurn Head U.K. 10 53.35N 0.08E
Spuzzum Canada 74 49.37N121.23W
Squamish Canada 74 49.45N123.10W
Squaw Rapids *town* Canada 75 53.41N103.20W
Squillace Italy 19 38.46N 16.31E
Sragen Indonesia 37 7.24S111.00E
Srbija *d.* Yugo. 19 44.30N 20.30E
Srednekolymsk U.S.S.R. 29 67.27N153.35E
Sredne Russkaya Vozvyshennost *f.* U.S.S.R. 24 53.00N 37.00E
Sredne Sibirskoye Ploskogor'ye *f.* U.S.S.R. 29 66.00N108.00E
Srê Moat Kampuchea 34 13.15N107.10E
Srêpôk *r.* Kampuchea 34 13.33N106.16E
Sretensk U.S.S.R. 31 52.15N117.52E
Sri Dūngargarh India 40 28.05N 74.00E
Sri Gangānagar India 40 29.55N 73.52E
Srīkākulam India 39 18.18N 83.54E
Sri Lanka Asia 39 7.30N 80.50E
Sri Mohangarh India 40 27.17N 71.14E
Srīnagar Jammu & Kashmir 40 34.05N 74.49E
Srīpur Bangla. 41 24.12N 90.29E
Srīrampur India 40 19.30N 74.30E
Srnetica Yugo. 19 44.26N 16.40E
Staaten *r.* Australia 64 16.24S141.17E
Stadskanaal Neth. 14 53.02N 6.55E
Stadtkyll W. Germany 14 50.21N 6.32E
Stadtlohn W. Germany 14 52.00N 6.58E
Staffa *i.* U.K. 12 56.26N 6.21W
Stafford U.K. 10 52.49N 2.09W
Stafford U.S.A. 85 38.09N 76.51W
Staffordshire *d.* U.K. 10 52.40N 1.57W
Staines U.K. 11 51.26N 0.31W
Stainforth U.K. 10 53.37N 1.01W
Stakhanov U.S.S.R. 25 48.34N 38.40E
Stalina Kanal *canal* U.S.S.R. 24 64.33N 34.48E
Stamford U.K. 11 52.39N 0.28W
Stamford Conn. U.S.A. 85 41.03N 73.32W
Stamford N.Y. U.S.A. 84 42.25N 74.37W
Stamford Tex. U.S.A. 83 32.57N 99.48W
Stanberry U.S.A. 82 40.13N 94.35W
Standerton R.S.A. 56 26.57S 29.14E
Stanger R.S.A. 56 29.20S 31.17E
Stanley Canada 72 55.45N104.55W
Stanley Falkland Is. 93 51.42W 57.51W
Stanley U.K. 10 54.53N 1.42W
Stanley Idaho U.S.A. 80 44.13N114.35W
Stanley Wisc. U.S.A. 82 44.58N 90.56W
Stanley Mission Canada 75 55.27N104.33W
Stanovoy Khrebet *mts.* U.S.S.R. 29 56.00N125.40E
Stanthorpe Australia 67 28.37S151.52E
Stanton U.S.A. 83 32.08N101.48W
Stapleton U.S.A. 82 41.29N100.31W
Starachowice Poland 21 51.03N 21.04E
Stara Dorogi U.S.S.R. 21 53.02N 28.18E
Stara Planina *mts.* Bulgaria 19 42.50N 24.30E
Staraya Russa U.S.S.R. 24 58.00N 31.22E
Staraya Sinyava U.S.S.R. 21 49.38N 27.39E
Stara Zagora Bulgaria 19 42.26N 25.37E
Starbuck I. Kiribati 69 5.37S155.55W
Stargard Szczecinski Poland 20 53.21N 15.01E
Staritsa U.S.S.R. 24 56.29N 34.59E
Starke U.S.A. 85 29.55N 82.06W
Starkville U.S.A. 83 33.28N 88.48W
Starnberg W. Germany 20 48.00N 11.20E
Starobin U.S.S.R. 21 52.40N 27.29E
Starogard Gdański Poland 21 53.59N 18.33E
Starokonstantinov U.S.S.R. 21 49.48N 27.10E
Start Pt. U.K. 11 50.13N 3.38W
Staryy Oskol U.S.S.R. 25 51.20N 37.50E
State College U.S.A. 84 40.48N 77.52W
Staten I. *see* Estados, Isla de los *i.* Argentina 93
Statesville U.S.A. 85 35.46N 80.54W
Staunton U.S.A. 85 38.09N 79.04W
Stavanger Norway 23 58.58N 5.45E
Stavelot Belgium 14 50.23N 5.54E
Staveren Neth. 14 52.53N 5.21E
Stavropol' U.S.S.R. 25 45.03N 41.59E
Stavropolskaya Vozvyshennost *mts.* U.S.S.R. 25 45.00N 42.30E
Stawell Australia 66 37.06S142.52E
Stawiski Poland 21 53.23N 22.09E
Stayton U.S.A. 80 44.48N122.48W
Steamboat Springs *town* U.S.A. 80 40.29N106.50W
Steele U.S.A. 82 46.51N 99.55W
Steelpoort R.S.A. 56 24.44S 30.13E
Steelton U.S.A. 84 40.14N 76.49W
Steenbergen Neth. 14 51.36N 4.19E
Steenvoorde France 14 50.49N 2.35E
Steenwijk Neth. 14 52.47N 6.07E
Steep Rock Lake *town* Canada 76 48.50N 91.38W
Steiermark *d.* Austria 20 47.10N 15.10E
Steilloopbrug R.S.A. 56 23.26S 28.37E
Steinbach Canada 75 49.32N 96.41W
Steinkjer Norway 22 64.00N 11.30E
Steinkopf R.S.A. 56 29.16S 17.41E
Stella R.S.A. 56 26.32S 24.51E
Stellarton Canada 77 45.34N 62.40W
Stellenbosch R.S.A. 56 33.56S 18.51E
Stenay France 15 49.29N 5.11E
Stendal E. Germany 20 52.36N 11.52E
Stenträsk Sweden 22 66.20N 19.50E
Stepan U.S.S.R. 21 51.09N 26.18E
Stepanakert U.S.S.R. 43 39.48N 46.45E
Stephens Passage *str.* U.S.A. 74 57.50N133.50W
Stephenville Canada 77 48.33N 58.35W
Stephenville U.S.A. 83 32.13N 98.12W
Stepnyak U.S.S.R. 28 52.52N 70.49E
Steps Pt. *c.* Samoa 68 14.22S170.45W
Sterkstroom R.S.A. 56 31.32S 26.31E
Sterling Colo. U.S.A. 80 40.37N103.13W
Sterling Ill. U.S.A. 82 41.48N 89.43W
Sterling Mich. U.S.A. 84 44.02N 84.02W
Sterlitamak U.S.S.R. 24 53.40N 55.59E
Šternberk Czech. 21 49.44N 17.18E
Stettler Canada 74 52.19N112.40W
Steuben U.S.A. 84 46.12N 86.27W
Steubenville U.S.A. 84 40.22N 80.39W
Stevenage U.K. 11 51.54N 0.11W
Stevenson L. Canada 75 53.56N 96.09W
Stevens Point *town* U.S.A. 82 44.32N 89.33W
Stevenston U.K. 12 55.39N 4.45W
Stewart Canada 74 55.56N130.01W
Stewart I. New Zealand 60 47.00S168.00E
Stewart River *town* Canada 72 63.19N139.26W
Steynsburg R.S.A. 56 31.17S 25.48E
Steyr Austria 20 48.04N 14.25E
Stikine *r.* Canada/U.S.A. 74 56.40N132.30W
Stikine Mts. Canada 72 59.00N129.00W
Stikine Plateau *f.* Canada 74 58.45N130.00W
Stiklestad Norway 22 63.48N 11.22E
Stilbaai R.S.A. 56 34.22S 21.22E
Stillwater U.S.A. 83 36.07N 97.04W
Stillwater Range *mts.* U.S.A. 80 39.50N118.15W
Stilton U.K. 11 52.29N 0.17W
Stimson Canada 76 48.58N 80.36W
Stinchar *r.* U.K. 12 55.06N 5.00W
Stînisoara, Munţii *mts.* Romania 21 47.10N 26.00E
Štip Yugo. 19 41.44N 22.12E
Stirling U.K. 12 56.07N 3.57W
Stirling Range *mts.* Australia 63 34.23S117.50E
Stjernöya *i.* Norway 22 70.17N 22.40E
Stjördalshalsen Norway 22 63.29N 10.51E
Stockaryd Sweden 23 57.18N 14.35E
Stockbridge U.K. 11 51.07N 1.30W
Stockdale U.S.A. 83 29.14N 97.58W
Stockerau Austria 20 48.23N 16.13E
Stockett U.S.A. 80 47.21N111.10W
Stockholm Sweden 23 59.20N 18.03E
Stockholm *d.* Sweden 23 59.40N 18.10E
Stockinbingal Australia 67 34.03S147.53E
Stockport U.K. 10 53.25N 2.11W
Stocksbridge U.K. 10 53.30N 1.36W
Stockton Australia 67 32.55S151.47E
Stockton Calif. U.S.A. 80 37.57N121.17W
Stockton Kans. U.S.A. 82 39.26N 99.16W
Stockton-on-Tees U.K. 10 54.34N 1.20W
Stoeng Tréng Kampuchea 34 13.31N105.59E
Stoffberg R.S.A. 56 25.25S 29.49E
Stoke-on-Trent U.K. 10 53.01N 2.11W
Stokes Bay *town* Canada 76 44.58N 81.18W
Stokhod *r.* U.S.S.R. 21 51.52N 25.38E
Stokksund Norway 22 64.03N 10.05E
Stolac Yugo. 19 43.05N 17.58E
Stolberg W. Germany 14 50.47N 6.12E
Stolbtsy U.S.S.R. 21 53.30N 26.44E
Stolin U.S.S.R. 21 51.52N 26.51E
Stone U.K. 10 52.55N 2.10W
Stone Harbor U.S.A. 85 39.03N 74.45W
Stonehaven U.K. 12 56.58N 2.13W
Stony I. Canada 77 53.00N 55.48W
Stony Rapids *town* Canada 75 59.16N105.50W
Stooping *r.* Canada 76 52.08N 82.00W
Stora Lulevatten *l.* Sweden 22 67.10N 19.16E
Stora Sjöfallets Nat. Park Sweden 22 67.44N 18.16E
Storavan *l.* Sweden 22 65.40N 18.15E
Storby Finland 23 60.13N 19.34E
Stord *i.* Norway 23 59.53N 5.25E
Store Baelt *str.* Denmark 23 55.30N 11.00E
Stor Elvdal Norway 23 61.32N 11.02E
Stören Norway 22 63.03N 10.18E
Storlien Sweden 22 63.20N 12.05E
Storm Lake *town* U.S.A. 82 42.39N 95.10W
Stornoway U.K. 12 58.12N 6.23W
Storozhevsk U.S.S.R. 24 62.00N 52.20E
Storozhinets U.S.S.R. 21 48.11N 25.40E
Storsjön *l.* Sweden 22 63.10N 14.20E
Storuman Sweden 22 65.06N 17.06E
Storuman *l.* Sweden 22 65.10N 16.40E
Stouffville Canada 76 43.59N 79.15W
Stoughton U.S.A. 82 42.55N 89.13W
Stour *r.* Dorset U.K. 11 50.43N 1.47W
Stour *r.* Kent U.K. 11 51.19N 1.22E
Stour *r.* Suffolk U.K. 11 51.56N 1.03E
Stourport-on-Severn U.K. 11 52.21N 2.16W
Stowmarket U.K. 11 52.11N 1.00E
Stow on the Wold U.K. 11 51.55N 1.42W
Strabane U.K. 13 54.50N 7.30W
Stradbally Laois Rep. of Ire. 13 53.01N 7.09W
Stradbroke I. Australia 65 27.38S153.45E
Stradella Italy 15 45.05N 9.18E
Straelen W. Germany 14 51.27N 6.14E
Strahan Australia 65 42.08S145.21E
Strakonice Czech. 20 49.16N 13.55E
Stralsund E. Germany 20 54.18N 13.06E
Strand R.S.A. 56 34.07S 18.50E
Stranda Norway 22 62.19N 6.58E
Strangford Lough U.K. 13 54.28N 5.35W
Strangways Springs *town* Australia 66 29.08S136.35E
Stranraer U.K. 12 54.54N 5.02W
Strasbourg France 17 48.35N 7.45E
Strasburg N.Dak. U.S.A. 82 46.08N100.10W
Stratford Australia 67 37.57S147.05E
Stratford Canada 76 43.22N 80.57W
Stratford New Zealand 60 39.20S174.18E
Stratford Tex. U.S.A. 83 36.20N102.04W
Stratford-upon-Avon U.K. 11 52.12N 1.42W
Strathalbyn Australia 66 35.16S138.54E
Strathclyde *d.* U.K. 12 55.45N 4.45W
Strathcona Prov. Park Canada 74 49.38N125.40W
Strathmore *f.* Tayside U.K. 12 56.44N 2.45W
Strathspey *f.* U.K. 12 57.25N 3.25W
Stratton U.S.A. 82 39.18N102.36W
Straubing W. Germany 20 48.53N 12.35E
Straumnes *c.* Iceland 22 66.30N 23.05W
Strawn U.S.A. 83 32.33N 98.30W
Streaky B. Australia 66 32.36S134.08E
Streaky Bay *town* Australia 66 32.48S134.13E

Streator to Tăndărei

Streator U.S.A. 82 41.07N 88.53W
Street U.K. 11 51.07N 2.43W
Streeter U.S.A. 82 46.39N 99.21W
Streetsville Canada 76 43.35N 79.42W
Stresa Italy 15 45.53N 8.32E
Stretton Australia 63 32.30S117.42E
Strimon r. Greece 19 40.47N 23.51E
Stromboli i. Italy 18 38.48N 15.14E
Stromeferry U.K. 12 57.21N 5.34W
Stromness U.K. 12 58.57N 3.18W
Strömö i. Faroe Is. 8 62.08N 7.00W
Strömsbruk Sweden 23 61.53N 17.19E
Strömstad Sweden 23 58.56N 11.10E
Strömsund Sweden 22 63.51N 15.35E
Strömsvattudal f. Sweden 22 64.15N 15.00E
Strongfield Canada 75 51.20N106.36W
Stronsay i. U.K. 12 59.07N 2.36W
Stroud U.K. 11 51.44N 2.12W
Stroud Road town Australia 67 32.18S151.58E
Struan Australia 66 37.08S140.49E
Struer Denmark 23 56.29N 8.37E
Struga Yugo. 19 41.10N 20.41E
Struma r. Bulgaria see Strimon r. Greece 19
Strumica Yugo. 19 41.26N 22.39E
Strydenburg R.S.A. 56 29.56S 23.39E
Stryker U.S.A. 80 48.40N114.44W
Stryy U.S.S.R. 21 49.16N 23.51E
Strzelecki Creek r. Australia 66 29.37S139.59E
Strzelno Poland 21 52.38N 18.11E
Stuart Fla. U.S.A. 85 27.12N 80.16W
Stuart Nebr. U.S.A. 82 42.36N 99.08W
Stuart Creek town Australia 66 29.43S137.01E
Stuart L. Canada 74 54.30N124.30W
Stuart Range mts. Australia 66 29.10S134.56E
Stuart Town Australia 67 32.51S149.08E
Stupart r. Canada 75 56.00N 93.22W
Sturgeon Bay town U.S.A. 82 44.50N 87.23W
Sturgeon Falls town Canada 76 46.22N 79.55W
Sturgeon L. Ont. Canada 76 50.00N 90.40W
Sturgis U.S.A. 82 44.25N103.31W
Sturminster Newton U.K. 11 50.56N 2.18W
Sturt B. Australia 66 35.24S137.32E
Sturt Creek r. Australia 62 20.08S127.24E
Sturt Desert Australia 66 28.30S141.12E
Sturt Plain f. Australia 64 17.00S132.48E
Stutterheim R.S.A. 56 32.32S 27.25E
Stuttgart W. Germany 20 48.47N 9.12E
Stviga r. U.S.S.R. 21 52.04N 27.54E
Stykkishólmur Iceland 22 65.06N 22.48W
Styr r. U.S.S.R. 21 52.07N 26.35E
Suao Taiwan 33 24.36N121.51E
Subarnarekha r. India 41 21.34N 87.24E
Subay', 'Urūq f. Saudi Arabia 48 22.15N 43.05E
Subei Guangai Zongqu canal China 32 34.06N120.19E
Subotica Yugo. 19 46.04N 19.41E
Suceava Romania 21 47.39N 26.19E
Suck r. Rep. of Ire. 13 53.16N 8.04W
Suckling, Mt. P.N.G. 64 9.45S148.55E
Sucre Bolivia 92 19.02S 65.17W
Sucuriu r. Brazil 94 20.44S 51.40W
Sudan Africa 48 14.30N 29.00E
Sudan U.S.A. 83 34.04N102.32W
Sudbury Canada 76 46.30N 81.00W
Sudbury U.K. 11 52.03N 0.45E
Sudety mts. Czech./Poland 20 50.30N 16.30E
Sudirman, Pegunungan mts. Indonesia 37 3.50S136.30E
Sueca Spain 16 39.12N 0.21W
Suez see As Suways Egypt 44
Suez, G. of see Suways, Khalīj as g. Egypt 44
Suez Canal see Suways, Qanāt as canal Egypt 44
Şufaynah Saudi Arabia 42 23.09N 40.32E
Suffolk d. U.K. 11 52.16N 1.00E
Suffolk U.S.A. 85 36.44N 76.37W
Sugarloaf Pt. Australia 67 32.25S152.30E
Şuḩār Oman 43 24.23N 56.43E
Sühbaatar d. Mongolia 32 45.30N114.00E
Suhl E. Germany 20 50.37N 10.43E
Suhl d. E. Germany 20 50.40N 10.30E
Sūi Pakistan 40 28.37N 69.19E
Suibin China 31 47.19N131.49E
Suichang China 33 28.36N119.16E
Suichuan China 33 26.24N114.31E
Suide China 32 37.35N110.08E
Suihua China 31 46.39N126.59E
Suileng China 31 47.15N127.05E
Suining Jiangsu China 32 33.54N117.56E
Suining Sichuan China 33 30.31N105.32E
Suipacha Argentina 93 34.47S 59.40W
Suippes France 15 49.08N 4.32E
Suir r. Rep. of Ire. 13 52.17N 7.00W
Suita Japan 35 34.45N135.32E
Sui Xian Henan China 32 34.25N115.04E
Sui Xian Hubei China 33 31.45N113.30E
Suiyang Guizhou China 33 27.57N107.11E
Suizhong China 32 40.25N120.25E
Suj China 32 42.02N107.58E
Sūjāngarh India 40 27.42N 74.28E
Sujāwal Pakistan 40 24.36N 68.05E
Sukabumi Indonesia 37 6.55S106.50E
Sukadana Indonesia 36 1.15S110.00E
Sukaraja Indonesia 36 2.23S110.35E
Sukhinichi U.S.S.R. 24 54.07N 35.21E
Sukhona r. U.S.S.R. 24 61.30N 46.28E
Sukhumi U.S.S.R. 25 43.01N 41.01E
Sukkertoppen Greenland 73 65.40N 53.00W
Sukkur Pakistan 40 27.42N 68.52E
Sukoharjo Indonesia 37 7.40S110.50E
Sula i. Norway 23 61.08N 4.55E
Sula, Kepulauan is. Indonesia 37 1.50S125.10E
Sulaimān Range mts. Pakistan 40 30.00N 69.50E
Sulak r. U.S.S.R. 25 43.18N 47.35E
Sulawesi i. Indonesia 37 2.00S120.30E
Sulawesi Selatan d. Indonesia 37 3.45S120.30E
Sulawesi Utara d. Indonesia 37 1.45S120.30E
Sulechów Poland 20 52.06N 15.37E
Sulejów Poland 21 51.22N 19.53E
Sulina Romania 19 45.08N 29.40E
Sulitjelma Norway 22 67.10N 16.05E
Sullana Peru 90 4.52S 80.39W
Sullivan U.S.A. 82 38.13N 91.10W
Sully France 15 47.46N 2.22E
Sulmona Italy 18 42.04N 13.57E
Sulphur U.S.A. 83 34.31N 96.58W
Sultan Canada 76 47.36N 82.47W
Sultan Hamud Kenya 55 2.02S 37.20E
Sultānpur India 41 26.16N 82.04E
Sulu Archipelago Phil. 37 5.30N121.00E
Sulūq Libya 51 31.40N 20.15E
Sulu Sea Pacific Oc. 37 8.00N120.00E
Sumatera i. Indonesia 36 2.00S102.00E
Sumatera Barat d. Indonesia 36 1.00S100.00E
Sumatera Selatan d. Indonesia 36 3.00S104.00E
Sumatera Utara d. Indonesia 36 2.00N 99.00E
Sumatra see Sumatera i. Indonesia 36
Sumatra U.S.A. 80 46.38N107.31W
Sumba i. Indonesia 36 9.30S119.55E
Sumbar r. U.S.S.R. 43 38.00N 55.20E
Sumbawa i. Indonesia 36 8.45S117.50E
Sumbawanga Tanzania 55 7.58S 31.36E
Sumburgh Head U.K. 12 59.51N 1.16W
Sumedang Indonesia 37 6.54S107.55E
Šumen Bulgaria 19 43.15N 26.55E
Sumenep Indonesia 37 7.01S113.51E
Sumgait U.S.S.R. 43 40.35N 49.38E
Summerland Canada 74 49.32N119.41W
Summerside Canada 77 46.24N 63.47W
Summerville Ga. U.S.A. 85 34.29N 85.21W
Summerville S.C. U.S.A. 85 33.02N 80.11W
Šumperk Czech. 20 49.58N 16.58E
Sumprabum Burma 34 26.33N 97.34E
Sumuşta al Waqf Egypt 44 28.55N 30.51E
Sumy U.S.S.R. 25 50.55N 34.49E
Sunām India 40 30.08N 75.48E
Sunāmganj Bangla. 41 25.04N 91.24E
Sunart, Loch U.K. 12 56.43N 5.45W
Sunburst U.S.A. 80 48.53N111.55W
Sunbury Australia 67 37.36S144.45E
Sunda, Selat str. Indonesia 36 6.00S105.50E
Sundance U.S.A. 80 44.24N104.23W
Sundarbans f. India/Bangla. 41 21.45N 89.00E
Sundargarh India 41 22.07N 84.02E
Sundays r. R.S.A. 56 33.43S 25.50E
Sunderland U.K. 10 54.55N 1.22W
Sundsvall Sweden 23 62.23N 17.18E
Sungai Kolok Thailand 34 6.02N101.58E
Sungaipakning Indonesia 36 1.19N102.00E
Sungaipenuh Indonesia 36 2.00S101.28E
Sungguminasa Indonesia 36 5.14S119.27E
Sungurlu Turkey 42 40.10N 34.23E
Sunjikāy Sudan 49 12.20N 29.46E
Sunne Sweden 23 59.50N 13.09E
Sunnyside U.S.A. 80 46.20N120.00W
Suntar U.S.S.R. 29 62.10N117.35E
Suntsar Pakistan 40 25.31N 62.00E
Sun Valley town U.S.A. 78 43.42N114.21W
Sunwu China 31 49.40N127.10E
Sunyani Ghana 52 7.22N 2.18W
Suoyarvi U.S.S.R. 24 62.02N 32.20E
Supaul India 41 26.07N 86.36E
Superior Mont. U.S.A. 80 47.12N114.53W
Superior Wisc. U.S.A. 82 46.42N 92.05W
Superior Wyo. U.S.A. 80 41.46N108.58W
Superior, L. Canada/U.S.A. 84 48.00N 88.00W
Suphan Buri Thailand 34 14.14N100.07E
Suphan Buri r. Thailand 34 13.34N100.15E
Süphan Dagi mtn. Turkey 25 38.55N 42.55E
Süphan Daglari mtn. Turkey 42 38.55N 42.55E
Suqian China 32 33.59N118.25E
Suquţrá i. S. Yemen 45 12.30N 54.00E
Şūr Lebanon 44 33.16N 35.12E
Şūr Oman 43 22.23N 59.32E
Sur d. W. Sahara 50 23.40N 14.15W
Sur, Cabo c. I. de Pascua 69 27.12S109.26W
Sur, Punta c. Argentina 93 36.53S 56.41W
Sura U.S.S.R. 24 53.52N 45.45E
Sūrāb Pakistan 40 28.29N 66.16E
Surabaya Indonesia 37 7.14S112.45E
Surakarta Indonesia 37 7.32S110.50E
Şūrān Syria 44 35.18N 36.44E
Surany Czech. 21 48.06N 18.14E
Surat India 40 21.12N 72.50E
Sūratgarh India 40 29.18N 73.54E
Surat Thani Thailand 34 9.09N 99.23E
Surazh U.S.S.R. 21 53.00N 32.22E
Sûre r. Lux. 14 49.43N 6.31E
Sureau, Lac l. Canada 77 53.10N 70.50W
Surendranagar India 40 22.42N 71.41E
Surfer's Paradise Australia 67 27.58S153.26E
Surgut U.S.S.R. 28 61.13N 73.20E
Sūri India 41 23.55N 87.32E
Surigao Phil. 37 9.47N125.29E
Surin Thailand 34 14.58N103.33E
Surinam S. America 91 4.00N 56.00W
Suriname r. Surinam 91 5.52N 55.14W
Surkole Ethiopia 49 10.25N 34.38E
Surrey d. U.K. 11 51.16N 0.30W
Surt Libya 51 31.13N 16.35E
Surt, Khalīj g. Libya 51 31.45N 17.50E
Surtanāhu Pakistan 40 26.22N 70.00E
Surtsey i. Iceland 22 63.18N 20.30W
Surud Ad mtn. Somali Rep. 45 10.41N 47.18E
Suruga-wan b. Japan 35 34.45N138.30E
Susa Italy 15 45.08N 7.03E
Susanino U.S.S.R. 29 52.46N140.09E
Susanville U.S.A. 80 40.25N120.39W
Susquehanna r. U.S.A. 85 39.33N 76.05W
Sussex N.J. U.S.A. 85 41.13N 74.36W
Sussex Wyo. U.S.A. 80 43.42N106.19W
Sutak Jammu & Kashmir 41 33.12N 77.28E
Sutherland R.S.A. 56 32.23S 20.38E
Sutherlin U.S.A. 80 43.25N123.19W
Sutlej r. Pakistan 40 29.23N 71.02E
Sutton r. Canada 76 55.22N 83.48W
Sutton England U.K. 11 51.22N 0.12W
Sutton Nebr. U.S.A. 82 40.36N 97.52W
Sutton W. Va. U.S.A. 84 38.41N 80.43W
Sutton in Ashfield U.K. 10 53.08N 1.16W
Suva Fiji 68 18.08S178.25E
Suwałki Poland 21 54.07N 22.56E
Suwanee r. U.S.A. 85 29.18N 83.09W
Suways, Khalīj as g. Egypt 44 28.48N 33.00E
Suways, Qanāt as canal Egypt 44 30.40N 32.20E
Suwon S. Korea 31 37.16N126.59E
Suzhou China 33 31.22N120.45E
Suzuka Japan 35 34.51N136.35E
Suzuka r. Japan 35 34.54N136.39E
Suzuka-sammyaku mts. Japan 35 35.00N136.20E
Suzzara Italy 15 45.00N 10.45E
Svalyava U.S.S.R. 21 48.33N 23.00E
Svanvik Norway 22 69.25N 30.00E
Svappavaara Sweden 22 67.39N 21.04E
Svarhofthalvöya Norway 22 70.35N 26.00E
Svartenhuk Halvo c. Greenland 73 71.55N 55.00W
Svartisen mtn. Norway 22 66.40N 13.56E
Svatovo U.S.S.R. 25 49.24N 38.11E
Svay Riĕng Kampuchea 34 11.05N105.48E
Svedala Sweden 23 55.30N 13.14E
Sveg Sweden 23 62.02N 14.21E
Svelgen Norway 23 61.47N 5.15E
Svendborg Denmark 23 55.03N 10.37E
Svenstrup Denmark 23 56.59N 9.52E
Sverdlovsk U.S.S.R. 24 56.52N 60.35E
Svetlograd U.S.S.R. 25 45.25N 42.58E
Svetogorsk U.S.S.R. 24 61.07N 28.50E
Svetozarevo Yugo. 19 43.58N 21.16E
Svinö i. Faroe Is. 8 62.17N 6.18W
Svir r. U.S.S.R. 24 60.09N 32.15E
Svishtov Bulgaria 19 43.36N 25.23E
Svisloch U.S.S.R. 21 53.28N 29.00E
Svitavy Czech. 20 49.45N 16.27E
Svobodnyy U.S.S.R. 31 51.24N128.05E
Svolvaer Norway 22 68.15N 14.40E
Swaffham U.K. 11 52.38N 0.42E
Swain Reefs Australia 64 21.40S152.15E
Swains I. Samoa 68 11.03S171.06W
Swakop r. Namibia 56 22.38S 14.32E
Swakopmund Namibia 56 22.40S 14.34E
Swale r. U.K. 10 54.05N 1.20W
Swan r. Australia 63 32.03S115.45E
Swanage U.K. 11 50.36N 1.59W
Swan Hill town Australia 66 35.23S143.37E
Swan Hills Canada 74 54.42N115.24W
Swan L. Canada 75 52.30N100.45W
Swan River town Canada 75 52.10N101.17W
Swansea Australia 65 42.08S148.00E
Swansea U.K. 11 51.37N 3.57W
Swan Vale town Australia 67 29.43S151.25E
Swastika Canada 76 48.07N 80.06W
Swaziland Africa 56 26.30S 32.00E
Sweden Europe 22 63.00N 16.00E
Swedru Ghana 52 5.31N 0.42W
Sweetwater U.S.A. 83 32.28N100.25W
Swidnica Poland 20 50.51N 16.29E
Swiebodzin Poland 20 52.15N 15.32E
Świetokrzyskie, Góry mts. Poland 21 51.00N 20.30E
Swift Current town Canada 75 50.17N107.50W
Swilly, Lough Rep. of Ire. 13 55.10N 7.32W
Swindon U.K. 11 51.33N 1.47W
Świnoujście Poland 20 53.55N 14.18E
Switzerland Europe 17 47.00N 8.00E
Swords Rep. of Ire. 9 53.27N 6.15W
Syderö i. Faroe Is. 8 61.30N 6.50W
Sydney Australia 67 33.55S151.10E
Sydney Canada 77 46.09N 60.11W
Sydney Mines town Canada 77 46.14N 60.14W
Sydpröven Greenland 73 60.30N 45.35W
Syktyvkar U.S.S.R. 24 61.42N 50.45E
Sylacauga U.S.A. 85 33.10N 86.15W
Sylhet Bangla. 41 24.54N 91.52E
Sylt i. W. Germany 20 54.50N 8.20E
Sylte Norway 22 62.31N 7.07E
Sylvan Lake town Canada 74 52.20N114.10W
Syracuse Kans. U.S.A. 83 37.59N101.45W
Syracuse N.Y. U.S.A. 84 43.03N 76.09W
Syr Darya r. U.S.S.R. 28 46.00N 61.12E
Syria Asia 42 35.00N 38.00E
Syriam Burma 36 16.45N 96.17E
Syrian Desert see Bādiyat ash Shām des. Asia 42
Syzran U.S.S.R. 24 53.10N 48.29E
Szarvas Hungary 21 46.52N 20.34E
Szczecin Poland 20 53.25N 14.32E
Szczecinek Poland 20 53.42N 16.41E
Szczytno Poland 21 53.34N 21.00E
Szécsény Hungary 21 48.06N 19.31E
Szeged Hungary 19 46.16N 20.08E
Székesfehérvár Hungary 21 47.12N 18.25E
Szekszárd Hungary 19 46.22N 18.44E
Szentes Hungary 21 46.39N 20.16E
Szolnok Hungary 21 47.10N 20.12E
Szombathely Hungary 20 47.12N 16.38E
Sztutowo Poland 21 54.20N 19.15E

T

Tabagne Ivory Coast 52 7.59N 3.04W
Ţābah Saudi Arabia 42 27.02N 42.10E
Tabarka Tunisia 51 36.56N 8.43E
Ţabas Khorāsān Iran 43 32.48N 60.14E
Ţabas Khorāsān Iran 43 33.36N 56.55E
Tabasco d. Mexico 86 18.30N 93.00W
Tābask, Kūh-e mtn. Iran 43 29.51N 51.52E
Tabelbala Algeria 50 29.24N 3.15W
Taber Canada 74 49.47N112.08W
Tabili Zaïre 55 0.04N 28.01E
Table B. R.S.A. 56 33.52S 18.26E
Tábor Czech. 20 49.25N 14.41E
Tabora Tanzania 55 5.02S 32.50E
Tabora d. Tanzania 55 5.30S 32.50E
Tabou Ivory Coast 52 4.28N 7.20W
Tabrīz Iran 43 38.05N 46.18E
Tabuaeran i. Kiribati 69 3.52N159.20W
Tabūk Saudi Arabia 44 28.23N 36.36E
Tabulam Australia 67 28.50S152.35E
Ţabūt S. Yemen 45 15.57N 52.09E
Tachia Taiwan 33 24.21N120.37E
Tachikawa Japan 35 35.42N139.25E
Tacloban Phil. 37 11.15N124.59E
Tacna Peru 92 18.01S 70.15W
Tacoma U.S.A. 80 47.15N122.27W
Tacora mtn. Chile 92 17.40S 69.45W
Tacuarembó Uruguay 93 31.44S 55.59W
Tademaït, Plateau du f. Algeria 51 28.30N 2.15E
Tadjetaret, Oued Algeria 51 21.00N 7.30E
Tadjmout Algeria 51 25.30N 3.42E
Tadjoura, Golfe de g. Djibouti 45 11.42N 43.00E
Tadmor New Zealand 60 41.26S172.47E
Tadoule L. Canada 75 58.36N 98.20W
Tadoussac Canada 77 48.09N 69.43W
Tadzhikskaya S.S.R. d. U.S.S.R. 30 39.00N 70.30E
Taegu S. Korea 31 35.52N128.36E
Taejŏn S. Korea 31 36.20N127.26E
Tafalla Spain 16 42.31N 1.40W
Tafassasset, Oued wadi Niger 51 22.00N 9.55E
Tafassasset, Ténéré du des. Niger 53 21.00N 11.00E
Taffanel, Lac l. Canada 77 53.22N 70.56W
Tafí Viejo Argentina 92 26.45S 65.15W
Tafraout Morocco 50 29.40N 8.58W
Taftān, Kūh-e mtn. Iran 43 28.38N 61.08E
Taga W. Samoa 68 13.47S172.30W
Taganrog U.S.S.R. 25 47.14N 38.55E
Taganrogskiy Zaliv g. U.S.S.R. 25 47.00N 38.30E
Tagant d. Mauritania 50 18.30N 10.30W
Tagant f. Mauritania 50 18.20N 11.00W
Tagaytay City Phil. 37 14.07N120.58E
Tagbilaran Phil. 37 9.38N123.53E
Tagish Canada 74 60.19N134.16W
Tagliamento r. Italy 15 45.38N 13.06E
Taglio di Po Italy 15 45.00N 12.12E
Tagounit Morocco 50 29.58N 5.36W
Tagula I. P.N.G. 64 11.30S153.30E
Tagum Phil. 37 7.33N125.53E
Tagus r. Portugal/Spain see Tejo r. Portugal 16
Tahaa i. Îs. de la Société 69 16.38S151.30W
Tahara Japan 35 34.40N137.16E
Tahat mtn. Algeria 51 23.18N 5.32E
Tahe China 31 52.35N124.48E
Tahiti i. Îs. de la Société 69 17.37S149.27W
Tahiti, Archipel de is. Îs. de la Société 69 17.00S149.35W
Tahlequah U.S.A. 83 35.55N 94.58W
Tahoe, L. U.S.A. 80 39.07N120.03W
Tahoua Niger 53 14.57N 5.16E
Tahoua d. Niger 53 15.38N 4.50E
Ţahţā Egypt 42 26.46N 31.30E
Tahuna Indonesia 37 3.37N125.29E
Taï Ivory Coast 52 5.52N 7.28W
Tai'an China 32 36.16N117.13E
Taiarapu, Presqu'île de pen. Tahiti 69 17.47S149.14W
Taibai China 32 36.08N108.41E
Taibai Shan mtn. China 32 33.55N107.45E
Taibus Qi China 32 41.55N115.23E
Taidong Taiwan 33 22.49N121.10E
Taigu China 32 37.23N112.34E
Taihang Shan mts. China 32 36.00N113.35E
Taihape New Zealand 60 39.40S175.48E
Taihe Anhui China 32 33.10N115.36E
Taihe Jiangxi China 33 26.48 114.56E
Tai Hu l. China 33 31.15N120.10E
Tailai China 31 46.23N123.24E
Tain U.K. 12 57.48N 4.04W
Tainan Taiwan 33 23.01N120.12E
Taínaron, Ákra c. Greece 19 36.22N 22.28E
Tai-o-haé Îs. Marquises 69 8.55S140.04W
Taipei Taiwan 33 25.05N121.30E
Taiping Anhui China 33 30.18N118.06E
Taiping Malaysia 36 4.54N100.42E
Taishan China 33 22.10N112.57E
Taitao, Península de pen. Chile 93 46.30S 74.25W
Taitze He r. China 32 41.07N122.43E
Taivalkoski Finland 22 65.34N 28.15E
Taiwan Asia 33 24.00N121.00E
Taiyuan China 32 37.48N112.33E
Taiyue Shan mts. China 32 36.40N112.00E
Taizhong Taiwan 33 24.11N120.40E
Taizhou China 32 32.22N119.58E
Ta'izz Yemen 45 13.35N 44.02E
Tajarḩī Libya 51 24.21N 14.28E
Tajimi Japan 35 35.19N137.08E
Tajitos Mexico 81 30.58N112.18W
Tajo r. Spain see Tejo r. Portugal 16
Tajrīsh Iran 43 35.48N 51.20E
Tajuna r. Spain 16 40.10N 3.35W
Tak Thailand 34 16.51N 99.08E
Takachu Botswana 56 22.37S 21.58E
Takaka New Zealand 60 40.51S172.48E
Takalar Indonesia 36 5.29S119.26E
Takamatsu Japan 31 34.20N134.01E
Takapuna New Zealand 60 36.48S174.47E
Takarazuka Japan 35 34.49N135.21E
Takatsuki Japan 35 34.51N135.37E
Tākestān Iran 43 36.02N 49.40E
Takêv Kampuchea 34 11.00N104.46E
Takhādīd well Iraq 43 29.59N 44.30E
Takla L. Canada 74 55.15N125.45W
Taklimakan Shamo des. China 30 38.10N 82.00E
Taku r. Canada/U.S.A. 74 58.30N133.50W
Talā Egypt 44 30.41N 30.56E
Tala Uruguay 93 34.21S 55.46W
Talagang Pakistan 40 32.55N 72.25E
Talagante Chile 93 33.40S 70.56W
Talāja India 40 21.21N 72.03E
Tālāla India 40 21.02N 70.32E
Talangbetutu Indonesia 36 2.48S104.42E
Talara Peru 90 4.38S 81.18W
Talasskiy Alatau mts. U.S.S.R. 30 42.20N 73.20E
Talata Mafara Nigeria 53 12.37N 6.05E
Talaud, Kepulauan is. Indonesia 37 4.20N126.50E
Talavera de la Reina Spain 16 39.58N 4.50W
Talawdī Sudan 49 10.38N 30.23E
Talbragar r. Australia 67 32.12S148.37E
Talca Chile 93 35.26S 71.40W
Talcahuano Chile 93 36.43S 73.07W
Tālcher India 41 20.57N 85.13E
Taldom U.S.S.R. 24 56.49N 37.30E
Taldy Kurgan U.S.S.R. 30 45.02N 78.23E
Taleh well Somali Rep. 45 9.12N 48.23E
Talia Australia 66 33.16S134.53E
Taliabu i. Indonesia 37 1.50S124.55E
Tali Post Sudan 49 5.54N 30.47E
Talkeetna U.S.A. 72 62.20N150.09W
Ţalkhā Egypt 44 31.04N 31.22E
Tallahassee U.S.A. 85 30.26N 84.19W
Tallangatta Australia 67 36.14S147.19E
Tallard France 17 44.28N 6.03E
Tallinn U.S.S.R. 23 59.22N 24.48E
Tall Kalakh Syria 44 34.40N 36.18E
Tall Kūshik Syria 42 36.48N 42.04E
Tall Salḩab Syria 44 35.15N 36.22E
Tallulah U.S.A. 83 32.25N 91.11W
Talmont France 17 46.28N 1.36W
Talnoye U.S.S.R. 21 48.55N 30.40E
Taloda India 40 21.34N 74.13E
Talofofo Guam 68 13.21N144.45E
Talsi U.S.S.R. 23 57.15N 22.36E
Taltal Chile 92 25.24S 70.29W
Talvik Norway 22 70.05N 22.52E
Talwood Australia 67 28.29S149.25E
Talyawalka r. Australia 66 31.49S143.25E
Tama r. Japan 35 35.32N139.47E
Tamala Australia 62 26.42S113.47E
Tamale Ghana 52 9.26N 0.49W
Tamanar Morocco 50 31.00N 9.35W
Tamanrasset Algeria 51 22.47N 5.31E
Tamanrasset, Oued wadi Algeria 50 21.24N 1.00E
Tamanthi Burma 34 25.19N 95.18E
Tamar r. U.K. 11 50.28N 4.13W
Tamaské Niger 53 14.55N 5.55E
Tamaulipas d. Mexico 83 24.30N 98.50W
Tamazunchale Mexico 86 21.16N 98.47W
Tambacounda Senegal 52 13.45N 13.40W
Tambara Mozambique 55 16.42S 34.17E
Tambellup Australia 63 34.03S117.36E
Tambo Australia 64 24.53S146.15E
Tambo r. Australia 67 37.51S147.48E
Tambohorano Madagascar 57 17.30S 43.58E
Tambor Mexico 81 25.08N105.27W
Tambov U.S.S.R. 24 52.44N 41.28E
Tambre r. Spain 16 42.50N 8.55W
Tambura Sudan 49 5.36N 27.28E
Tamchaket Mauritania 50 17.25N 10.40W
Tâmega r. Portugal 16 41.04N 8.17W
Tamil Nadu d. India 39 11.15N 79.00E
Ţāmiyah Egypt 44 29.29N 30.58E
Tamkuhi India 41 26.41N 84.11E
Tam Ky Vietnam 34 15.34N108.29E
Tammisaari Finland 23 59.58N 23.26E
Tampa U.S.A. 85 27.58N 82.38W
Tampa B. U.S.A. 85 27.45N 82.35W
Tampere Finland 23 61.30N 23.45E
Tampico Mexico 86 22.18N 97.52W
Tamri Morocco 50 30.43N 9.43W
Tamsagbulag Mongolia 31 47.10N117.21E
Tamworth Australia 67 31.07S150.57E
Tamworth U.K. 11 52.38N 1.42W
Tana r. Kenya 55 2.32S 40.32E
Tana Norway 22 70.26N 28.14E
Tana r. Norway 22 69.45N 28.15E
Tana i. Vanuatu 68 19.30S169.20E
Tana, L. Ethiopia 49 12.00N 37.20E
Tanacross U.S.A. 72 63.12N143.30W
Tanafjorden Norway 22 70.54N 28.40E
Tanahgrogot Indonesia 36 1.55S116.12E
Tanahmerah Indonesia 37 6.08S140.18E
Tanakpur India 41 29.05N 80.07E
Tanami Australia 62 19.59S129.43E
Tanana U.S.A. 72 65.11N152.10W
Tanana r. U.S.A. 72 65.09N151.55W
Tanaro r. Italy 15 45.01N 8.46E
Tānda India 41 26.33N 82.39E
Tanda Ivory Coast 52 7.48N 3.10W
Tandaltī Sudan 49 13.01N 31.50E
Tăndărei Romania 21 44.38N 27.40E

Tandil to Three Hills

Tandil Argentina 93 37.18S 59.10W
Tandjilé d. Chad 53 9.45N 16.28E
Tando Ādam Pakistan 40 25.46N 68.40E
Tando Allāhyār Pakistan 40 25.28N 68.43E
Tando Bāgo Pakistan 40 24.47N 68.58E
Tando Muhammad Khan Pakistan 40 25.08N 68.32E
Tandou L. Australia 66 32.38S142.05E
Tandula Tank resr. India 41 20.40N 81.12E
Taneytown U.S.A. 85 39.40N 77.10W
Tanezrouft des. Algeria 50 22.25N 0.30E
Tanga Tanzania 55 5.07S 39.05E
Tanga d. Tanzania 55 5.20S 38.30E
Tangalla Sri Lanka 39 6.02N 80.47E
Tanganyika, L. Africa 55 6.00S 29.30E
Tanger Morocco 50 35.48N 5.45W
Tanggo China 41 31.37N 93.18E
Tanggu China 32 39.01N117.43E
Tanggula Shan mts. China 41 33.00N 90.00E
Tanggula Shankou pass China 41 32.45N 92.24E
Tanggulashanqu China 41 34.10N 92.23E
Tanghe China 32 32.41N112.49E
Tāngi India 41 19.57N 85.30E
Tangi Pakistan 40 34.18N 71.40E
Tangier see Tanger Morocco 50
Tangmarg Jammu & Kashmir 40 34.02N 74.26E
Tangra Yumco l. China 41 31.00N 86.15E
Tangshan China 32 39.32N118.08E
Tangtse Jammu & Kashmir 41 34.02N 78.11E
Tanguiéta Benin 53 10.37N 1.18E
Tanimbar, Kepulauan is. Indonesia 37 7.50S131.30E
Tanishpa mtn. Pakistan 40 31.10N 68.24E
Tanjay Phil. 37 9.31N123.10E
Tanjung Indonesia 36 2.10S115.25E
Tanjungbalai Indonesia 36 2.59N 99.46E
Tanjungkarang Indonesia 36 5.28S105.16E
Tanjungpandan Indonesia 36 2.44S107.36E
Tanjungredeb Indonesia 36 2.09N117.29E
Tānk Pakistan 40 32.13N 70.23E
Tankapirtti Finland 22 68.16N 27.20E
Tännäs Sweden 23 62.27N 12.40E
Tannin Canada 76 49.40N 91.00W
Tannu Ola mts. U.S.S.R. 29 51.00N 93.30E
Tannūrah, Ra's c. Saudi Arabia 45 26.39N 50.10E
Tano r. Ghana 52 5.07N 2.54W
Tanout Niger 53 14.55N 8.49E
Ṭanṭā Egypt 44 30.48N 31.00E
Tanzania Africa 55 5.00S 35.00E
Tao'an China 32 45.20N122.48E
Taole China 32 38.50N106.40E
Taoudenni Mali 52 22.45N 4.00W
Tapachula Mexico 86 14.54N 92.15W
Tapajós r. Brazil 91 2.25S 54.40W
Tapaktuan Indonesia 36 3.30N 97.10E
Tapalquén Argentina 93 36.20S 60.02W
Tapanahoni r. Surinam 91 4.20N 54.25W
Tapanlieh Taiwan 33 21.58N120.47E
Tapanui New Zealand 60 45.57S169.16E
Tapauá r. Brazil 90 5.40S 64.20W
Tapeta Liberia 52 6.25N 8.47W
Tapirapecó, Serra mts. Venezuela/Brazil 90 1.00N 64.30W
Tāplejung Nepal 41 27.21N 87.40E
Tapolca Hungary 21 46.53N 17.27E
Tāpti r. India 40 21.05N 72.40E
Tapurucuara Brazil 90 0.24S 65.02W
Taquari r. Brazil 94 19.00S 57.27W
Taquaritinga Brazil 94 21.23S 48.33W
Tar r. U.S.A. 85 35.33N 77.05W
Tara U.S.S.R. 28 56.55N 74.24E
Tara r. U.S.S.R. 28 56.30N 74.40E
Tara r. Yugo. 19 43.23N 18.47E
Tarabine, Oued Ti-n- wadi Algeria 51 21.16N 7.24E
Tarabuco Bolivia 92 19.10S 64.57W
Ṭarābulus Lebanon 44 34.27N 35.50E
Ṭarābulus d. Libya 51 32.40N 13.15E
Ṭarābulus f. Libya 51 31.00N 13.30E
Ṭarābulus town Libya 51 32.58N 13.12E
Tarago Australia 67 35.05S149.10E
Tarakan Indonesia 36 3.20N117.38E
Taranaki d. New Zealand 60 39.00S174.30E
Tarancón Spain 16 40.01N 3.01W
Taranto Italy 19 40.28N 17.14E
Taranto, Golfo di g. Italy 19 40.00N 17.20E
Tarapacá Colombia 90 2.52S 69.44W
Tarapoto Peru 90 6.31S 76.23W
Tarashcha U.S.S.R. 21 49.35N 30.20E
Tarasovo U.S.S.R. 24 66.14N 46.43E
Tarauacá Brazil 90 8.10S 70.46W
Tarauacá r. Brazil 90 6.42S 69.48W
Taravao, Isthme de Tahiti 69 17.43S149.19W
Tarawa i. Kiribati 68 1.25N173.00E
Tarawera New Zealand 60 39.02S176.36E
Tarbagatay, Khrebet mts. U.S.S.R. 30 47.00N 83.00E
Tarbat Ness c. U.K. 12 57.52N 3.46W
Tarbert Rep. of Ire. 13 52.34N 9.24W
Tarbert Strath. U.K. 12 55.51N 5.25W
Tarbert W. Isles U.K. 12 57.54N 6.49W
Tarbes France 17 43.14N 0.05E
Tarcento Italy 15 46.13N 13.13E
Tarcoola N.S.W. Australia 66 33.31S142.40E
Tarcoola S.A. Australia 66 30.41S134.33E
Tarcoon Australia 67 30.19S146.43E
Tarcutta Australia 67 35.17S147.45E
Taree Australia 67 31.54S152.26E
Tarella Australia 66 30.55S143.06E
Tärendö Sweden 22 67.10N 22.38E
Ṭarfā, Wādī aṭ r. Egypt 44 28.36N 30.50E
Tarfaya Morocco 50 27.58N 12.55W
Tarhjicht Morocco 50 29.05N 9.24W
Tarifa Spain 16 36.01N 5.36W
Tarija Bolivia 92 21.31S 64.45W
Tarija d. Bolivia 92 21.40S 64.20W
Tarīm S. Yemen 45 16.03N 49.00E
Tarim He r. China 30 41.00N 83.30E
Tarīn Kowt Afghan. 40 32.52N 65.38E
Taritatu r. Indonesia 37 2.54S138.27E
Tarka La mtn. Bhutan 41 27.05N 89.40E
Tarkwa Ghana 52 5.16N 1.59W
Tarlac Phil. 37 15.29N120.35E
Tarm Denmark 23 55.55N 8.32E
Tarma Peru 90 11.28S 75.41W
Tarn r. France 17 44.15N 1.15E
Tärnaby Sweden 22 65.43N 15.16E
Tarnak r. Afghan. 40 31.26N 65.31E
Tarnica mtn. Poland 21 49.05N 22.44E
Tarnobrzeg Poland 21 50.35N 21.41E
Tarnów Poland 21 50.01N 20.59E
Taro r. Italy 15 45.00N 10.15E
Taroom Australia 64 25.39S149.49E
Taroudant Morocco 50 30.31N 8.55W
Tarpon Springs town U.S.A. 85 28.08N 82.45W
Tarragona Spain 16 41.07N 1.15E
Tarran Hills Australia 67 32.27S146.27E
Tarrasa Spain 16 41.34N 2.00E
Tarrytown U.S.A. 85 41.05N 73.52W
Tarso Ahon mtn. Chad 53 20.23N 18.18E
Tarso Ouri mtn. Chad 53 21.25N 18.56E
Tarsus Turkey 42 36.52N 34.52E
Tartagal Argentina 92 22.32S 63.50W
Tartu U.S.S.R. 24 58.20N 26.44E
Ṭarṭūs Syria 44 34.55N 35.52E
Tarutino U.S.S.R. 21 46.09N 29.04E
Tarutung Indonesia 36 2.01N 98.54E
Tashan China 32 40.51N120.56E
Tashauz U.S.S.R. 28 41.49N 59.58E
Tashi Gang Dzong Bhutan 41 27.19N 91.34E
Tashkent U.S.S.R. 30 41.16N 69.13E
Tasiilaq see Ammassalik Greenland 73
Tasikmalaya Indonesia 37 7.20S108.16E
Tåsjön Sweden 22 64.15N 15.47E
Tasman B. New Zealand 60 41.00S173.15E
Tasmania d. Australia 65 42.00S147.00E
Tasman Mts. New Zealand 60 41.00S172.40E
Tasman Pen. Australia 65 43.08S147.51E
Tasman Sea Pacific Oc. 68 38.00S162.00E
Tassili-n-Ajjer f. Algeria 51 26.05N 7.00E
Tassili oua-n-Ahaggar f. Algeria 51 20.30N 5.00E
Tataa, Pt. Tahiti 69 17.33S149.36W
Tatabánya Hungary 21 47.34N 18.26E
Tatarsk U.S.S.R. 28 55.14N 76.00E
Tatarskiy Proliv g. U.S.S.R. 29 47.40N141.00E
Tateyama Japan 35 34.59N139.52E
Tathlina L. Canada 74 60.32N117.32W
Tathra Australia 67 36.44S149.58E
Tatinnai L. Canada 75 60.55N 97.40W
Tatnam, C. Canada 75 57.16N 91.00W
Tatong Australia 67 36.46S146.03E
Tatta Pakistan 40 24.45N 67.55E
Tatvan Turkey 42 38.31N 42.15E
Tau i. Samoa 68 14.15S169.30W
Taubaté Brazil 94 23.00S 45.36W
Taulihawa Nepal 41 27.32N 83.05E
Taumarunui New Zealand 60 38.53S175.16E
Taumaturgo Brazil 90 8.57S 72.48W
Taung R.S.A. 56 27.32S 24.46E
Taungdwingyi Burma 34 20.00N 95.30E
Taung-gyi Burma 34 20.49N 97.01E
Taungup Burma 34 18.51N 94.14E
Taunoa Tahiti 69 17.45S149.21W
Taunsa Pakistan 40 30.42N 70.39E
Taunton U.K. 11 51.01N 3.07W
Taunus mts. W. Germany 20 50.07N 7.48E
Taupo New Zealand 60 38.42S176.06E
Taupo, L. New Zealand 60 38.45S175.30E
Taurage U.S.S.R. 23 55.15N 22.17E
Tauranga New Zealand 60 37.42S176.11E
Taurianova Italy 18 38.21N 16.01E
Taurus Mts. see Toros Dağlari mts. Turkey 42
Tautira Tahiti 69 17.45S149.10W
Tavani Canada 75 62.10N 93.30W
Tavda U.S.S.R. 28 58.04N 65.12E
Tavda r. U.S.S.R. 28 57.40N 67.00E
Taveta Kenya 55 3.23S 37.42E
Taveuni i. Fiji 68 16.56S179.58W
Tavira Portugal 16 37.07N 7.39W
Tavistock U.K. 11 50.33N 4.09W
Tavoy Burma 34 14.02N 98.12E
Taw r. U.K. 11 51.05N 4.05W
Tawas City U.S.A. 84 44.16N 83.33W
Tawau Malaysia 36 4.16N117.54E
Tawitawi i. Phil. 37 5.10N120.05E
Ṭawkar Sudan 48 18.26N 37.44E
Tawu Taiwan 33 22.22N120.54E
Tāwurghā', Sabkhat f. Libya 51 31.10N 15.15E
Tay r. U.K. 12 56.21N 3.18W
Tay, L. Australia 63 33.00S120.52E
Tay, Loch U.K. 12 56.32N 4.08W
Tayabamba Peru 90 8.15S 77.15W
Tayan Indonesia 36 0.02S110.05E
Tayegle Somali Rep. 45 4.02N 44.36E
Taylor Tex. U.S.A. 83 30.34N 97.25W
Taylor, Mt. U.S.A. 81 35.14N107.37W
Taylors Island town U.S.A. 85 38.28N 76.18W
Taymā' Saudi Arabia 42 27.37N 38.30E
Taymyr, Ozero l. U.S.S.R. 29 74.20N101.00E
Taymyr, Poluostrov pen. U.S.S.R. 29 75.30N 99.00E
Tay Ninh Vietnam 34 11.21N106.02E
Tayport U.K. 12 56.27N 2.53W
Tayshet U.S.S.R. 29 55.56N 98.01E
Tayside d. U.K. 12 56.35N 3.28W
Taytay Phil. 36 10.47N119.32E
Taz r. U.S.S.R. 28 67.30N 78.50E
Taza Morocco 50 34.16N 4.01W
Tazenakht Morocco 50 30.35N 7.12W
Tazin L. Canada 75 59.40N109.00W
Tāzirbū Libya 48 25.45N 21.00E
Tazovskiy U.S.S.R. 28 67.28N 78.43E
Tbilisi U.S.S.R. 43 41.43N 44.48E
Tchad, Lac see Chad, L. Africa 53
Tchamba Togo 53 9.05N 1.27E
Tchibanga Gabon 54 2.52S 11.07E
Tchien Liberia 52 6.00N 8.10W
Tchigaï, Plateau du f. Niger/Chad 53 21.30N 14.50E
Tcholliré Cameroon 53 8.25N 14.10E
Tczew Poland 21 54.06N 18.47E
Te Anau New Zealand 60 45.25S167.43E
Te Anau, L. New Zealand 60 45.10S167.15E
Teaneck U.S.A. 85 40.53N 74.01W
Teapa Mexico 86 17.33N 92.57W
Te Araroa New Zealand 60 37.38S178.25E
Tea Tree Australia 64 22.11S133.17E
Tébessa Algeria 51 35.22N 8.08E
Tebingtinggi Indonesia 36 3.20N 99.08E
Tebingtinggi Indonesia 36 3.37S103.09E
Tebulos Mta mtn. U.S.S.R. 25 42.34N 45.17E
Techiman Ghana 52 7.36N 1.55W
Tecuci Romania 21 45.49N 27.27E
Tedesa Ethiopia 49 5.07N 37.45E
Tees r. U.K. 10 54.35N 1.11W
Tefé Brazil 90 3.24S 64.45W
Tefé r. Brazil 90 3.35S 64.47W
Tegal Indonesia 37 6.52S109.07E
Tegelen Neth. 14 51.20N 6.08E
Tegina Nigeria 53 10.06N 6.11E
Tego Australia 67 28.48S146.47E
Tegouma well Niger 53 15.33N 9.19E
Tegucigalpa Honduras 87 14.05N 87.14W
Teguidda I-n-Tessoum Niger 53 17.21N 6.32E
Tehamiyam Sudan 48 18.20N 36.32E
Tehata Bangla. 41 23.43N 88.32E
Téhini Ivory Coast 52 9.39N 3.32W
Tehrān Iran 43 35.40N 51.26E
Tehri India 41 30.23N 78.29E
Tehuacán Mexico 86 18.30N 97.26W
Tehuantepec Mexico 86 16.21N 95.13W
Tehuantepec, Golfo de g. Mexico 86 16.00N 95.00W
Tehuantepec, Istmo de f. Mexico 86 17.00N 94.30W
Teifi r. U.K. 11 52.05N 4.41W
Teignmouth U.K. 11 50.33N 3.30W
Teixeiras Brazil 94 20.37S 42.52W
Tejakula Indonesia 37 8.09S115.19E
Tejo r. Portugal 16 39.00N 8.57W
Te Kaha New Zealand 60 37.44S177.52E
Tekamah U.S.A. 82 41.47N 96.13W
Tekapo, L. New Zealand 60 43.35S170.30E
Tekax Mexico 87 20.12N 89.17W
Tekezē r. Ethiopia see Satīt r. Sudan 48
Tekirdağ Turkey 19 40.59N 27.30E
Tekkali India 41 18.37N 84.14E
Tekouiat, Oued wadi Algeria 51 22.20N 2.30E
Tekro well Chad 48 19.30N 20.58E
Te Kuiti New Zealand 60 38.20S175.10E
Tel r. India 41 20.50N 83.54E
Tela Honduras 87 15.56N 87.25W
Telavi U.S.S.R. 43 41.56N 45.30E
Tel Aviv-Yafo Israel 44 32.05N 34.46E
Tele r. Zaïre 54 2.48N 24.00E
Telegraph Creek town Canada 74 57.55N131.10W
Telemark d. Norway 23 59.40N 8.30E
Teleneshty U.S.S.R. 21 47.35N 28.17E
Teles Pires r. Brazil 91 7.20S 57.30W
Telford U.K. 11 52.42N 2.30W
Telfs Austria 20 47.19N 11.04E
Telgte W. Germany 14 51.59N 7.46E
Telichie Australia 66 31.43S139.54E
Télimélé Guinea 52 10.54N 13.02W
Tell Atlas mts. Algeria 51 36.00N 1.00E
Tell City U.S.A. 85 37.56N 86.46W
Teller U.S.A. 72 65.16N166.22N
Telok Anson Malaysia 36 4.00N101.00E
Telpos-Iz mtn. U.S.S.R. 24 63.56N 59.02E
Telsen Argentina 93 42.25S 67.00W
Telšiai U.S.S.R. 23 55.59N 22.15E
Telukbetung Indonesia 36 5.28S105.16E
Tema Ghana 52 5.41N 0.01W
Temagami, L. Canada 76 47.00N 80.05W
Te Manga mtn. Rarotonga Cook Is. 68 21.13S159.45W
Temaverachi, Sierra mts. Mexico 81 29.30N109.30W
Tembo Aluma Angola 54 7.42S 17.15E
Teme r. U.K. 11 52.10N 2.13W
Temir U.S.S.R. 25 49.09N 57.06E
Temirtau U.S.S.R. 28 50.05N 72.55E
Témiscaming Canada 76 46.44N 79.05W
Temora Australia 67 34.27S147.35E
Tempe U.S.A. 81 33.25N111.56W
Tempino Indonesia 36 1.55S103.23E
Tempio Italy 18 40.54N 9.06E
Temple U.S.A. 83 31.06N 97.21W
Temple B. Australia 64 12.10S143.04E
Templemore Rep. of Ire. 13 52.48N 7.51W
Templin E. Germany 20 53.07N 13.30E
Temuco Chile 93 38.44S 72.36W
Tenabo Mexico 86 20.03N 90.14W
Tenaha U.S.A. 83 31.57N 94.15W
Tenasserim Burma 34 12.05N 99.00E
Tenasserim d. Burma 34 13.00N 99.00E
Tenby U.K. 11 51.40N 4.42W
Tendaho Ethiopia 49 11.48N 40.52E
Tende France 17 44.05N 7.36E
Tende, Col de pass France/Italy 15 44.09N 7.34E
Ten Degree Channel Indian Oc. 34 10.00N 93.00E
Tendrara Morocco 50 33.04N 1.59W
Tenenkou Mali 52 14.25N 4.58W
Tenerife i. Canary Is. 50 28.10N 16.30W
Ténès Algeria 51 36.31N 1.18E
Teng r. Burma 34 19.50N 97.40E
Tengchong China 39 25.02N 98.28E
Tengger Shamo des. China 32 39.00N104.10E
Tengiz, Ozero l. U.S.S.R. 28 50.30N 69.00E
Teng Xian China 32 35.08N117.20E
Tenke Zaïre 54 10.34S 26.07E
Tenkodogo U. Volta 52 11.47N 0.19W
Tennant Creek town Australia 64 19.31S134.15E
Tennessee d. U.S.A. 85 35.50N 85.30W
Tennessee r. U.S.A. 85 37.04N 88.33W
Tenosique Mexico 86 17.29N 91.26W
Tenryū Japan 35 34.52N137.49E
Tenryū r. Japan 35 34.39N137.47E
Tensift, Oued r. Morocco 50 32.02N 9.22W
Tenterfield Australia 67 29.01S152.04E
Teófilo Otoni Brazil 94 17.52S 41.31W
Tepa Indonesia 37 7.52S129.31E
Tepa Pt. Niue 68 19.07S169.56W
Tepelenë Albania 19 40.18N 20.01E
Tepic Mexico 86 21.30N104.51W
Teplice Czech. 20 50.40N 13.50E
Ter r. Spain 16 42.02N 3.10E
Téra Niger 52 14.01N 0.45E
Tera r. Portugal 16 38.55N 8.01W
Teramo Italy 18 42.40N 13.43E
Tercan Turkey 42 39.47N 40.23E
Terebovlya U.S.S.R. 21 49.18N 25.44E
Terekhova U.S.S.R. 21 52.13N 31.28E
Teresina Brazil 91 5.09S 42.46W
Teresópolis Brazil 94 22.26S 42.59W
Terevaka mtn. I. de Pascua 69 27.05S109.23W
Tergnier France 15 49.39N 3.18E
Terhazza Mali 52 23.45N 4.59W
Termez U.S.S.R. 28 37.15N 67.15E
Termination I. Australia 63 34.25S121.53E
Termini Italy 18 37.59N 13.42E
Términos, Laguna de b. Mexico 86 18.30N 91.30W
Termoli Italy 18 41.58N 14.59E
Ternate Indonesia 37 0.48N127.23E
Terneuzen Neth. 14 51.20N 3.50E
Terni Italy 18 42.34N 12.44E
Ternopol U.S.S.R. 21 49.35N 25.39E
Terra Bella U.S.A. 81 35.58N119.03W
Terrace Canada 74 54.31N128.35W
Terracina Italy 18 41.17N 13.15E
Terralba Italy 18 39.43N 8.38E
Terre Adélie f. Antarctica 96 80.00S140.00E
Terrebonne Canada 77 45.42N 73.38W
Terre Haute U.S.A. 84 39.27N 87.24W
Terrenceville Canada 77 47.42N 54.43W
Terry U.S.A. 80 46.47N105.19W
Terschelling i. Neth. 14 53.25N 5.25E
Teruel Spain 16 40.21N 1.06W
Tervola Finland 22 66.05N 24.48E
Teryaweynya Australia 66 32.18S143.29E
Tešanj Yugo. 21 44.37N 18.00E
Tesaret, Oued wadi Algeria 51 25.32N 2.52E
Teslin Canada 74 60.10N132.43W
Teslin r. Canada 74 61.34N134.54W
Teslin L. Canada 74 60.15N132.57W
Tessalit Mali 52 20.12N 1.00E
Tessaoua Niger 53 13.46N 7.55E
Tessy-sur-Vire France 15 48.58N 1.04W
Test r. U.K. 11 50.55N 1.29W
Têt r. France 17 42.43N 3.00E
Tetachuck L. Canada 74 53.18N125.55W
Tete Mozambique 57 16.10S 33.30E
Tete d. Mozambique 55 15.30S 33.00E
Teterev r. U.S.S.R. 21 51.03N 30.30E
Teterow E. Germany 20 53.46N 12.34E
Teteven Bulgaria 19 42.55N 24.16E
Tethul r. Canada 74 60.35N112.12W
Tetiaora i. Îs. de la Société 69 17.05S149.32W
Tetiyev U.S.S.R. 21 49.22N 29.40E
Tétouan Morocco 50 35.34N 5.23W
Tetovo Yugo. 19 42.01N 20.58E
Tetuan see Tétouan Morocco 50
Teulada Italy 18 38.58N 8.46E
Teun i. Indonesia 37 6.59S129.08E
Teuva Finland 22 62.29N 21.44E
Tevere r. Italy 18 41.45N 12.16E
Teverya Israel 44 32.48N 35.32E
Teviot r. U.K. 12 55.36N 2.27W
Teviotdale f. U.K. 10 55.26N 2.46W
Teviothead U.K. 12 55.20N 2.56W
Tewkesbury U.K. 11 51.59N 2.09W
Texarkana Ark. U.S.A. 83 33.26N 94.02W
Texarkana Tex. U.S.A. 83 33.26N 94.03W
Texarkana, L. U.S.A. 83 33.16N 94.14W
Texas Australia 67 28.50S151.09E
Texas d. U.S.A. 83 31.30N100.00W
Texas City U.S.A. 83 29.23N 94.54W
Texel i. Neth. 14 53.05N 4.47E
Texoma, L. U.S.A. 83 33.55N 96.37W
Texon U.S.A. 83 31.13N101.43W
Teyvareh Afghan. 40 33.21N 64.25E
Tezpur India 41 26.38N 92.48E
Tha-anne r. Canada 75 60.31N 94.37W
Thabana Ntlenyana mtn. Lesotho 56 29.28S 29.17E
Thabazimbi R.S.A. 56 24.36S 27.23E
Thādiq Saudi Arabia 43 25.18N 45.52E
Thai Binh Vietnam 33 20.30N106.26E
Thailand Asia 34 17.00N101.30E
Thailand, G. of Asia 34 11.00N101.00E
Thai Nguyen Vietnam 33 21.46N105.52E
Thak Pakistan 40 30.32N 70.13E
Thal Pakistan 40 33.22N 70.33E
Thal Desert Pakistan 40 31.30N 71.40E
Thale Luang l. Thailand 34 7.40N100.20E
Thallon Australia 67 28.39S148.49E
Thamarīt Oman 38 17.39N 54.02E
Thames r. Canada 76 42.19N 82.28W
Thames New Zealand 60 37.08S175.35E
Thames r. U.K. 11 51.30N 0.05E
Thāna India 40 19.12N 72.58E
Thāna Pakistan 40 28.55N 63.45E
Thane Australia 67 28.08S151.39E
Thanh Hóa Vietnam 33 19.47N105.49E
Thành Pho Ho Chí Minh Vietnam 34 10.46N106.43E
Thanjāvūr India 39 10.46N 79.09E
Thāno Bula Khān Pakistan 40 25.22N 67.50E
Tharād India 40 24.24N 71.38E
Thar Desert Pakistan/India 40 28.00N 72.00E
Thargomindah Australia 65 27.59S143.45E
Tharrawaddy Burma 34 17.37N 95.48E
Tharthār, Wādī ath r. Iraq 42 34.18N 43.07E
Thásos Greece 19 40.47N 24.42E
Thásos i. Greece 19 40.40N 24.39E
Thatcher U.S.A. 81 32.51N109.56W
Thaton Burma 34 16.50N 97.21E
Thaungdut Burma 34 24.26N 94.45E
Thayer U.S.A. 83 36.31N 91.33W
Thayetmyo Burma 34 19.20N 95.10E
Thazi Burma 34 20.51N 96.05E
Thebes ruins Egypt 42 25.41N 32.40E
The Bight town Bahamas 87 24.19N 75.24W
The Cherokees, L. O' U.S.A. 83 36.45N 94.50W
The Cheviot mtn. U.K. 10 55.29N 2.10W
The Cheviot Hills U.K. 10 55.22N 2.24W
The Coorong g. Australia 66 36.00S139.30E
The Dalles town U.S.A. 80 45.36N121.10W
Thedford U.S.A. 82 41.59N100.35W
The Everglades f. U.S.A. 85 26.00N 80.40W
The Fens f. U.K. 11 55.10N 4.13W
The Granites town Australia 62 20.35S130.21E
The Gulf Asia 43 27.00N 50.00E
The Hague see 'sGravenhage Neth. 14
Thekulthili L. Canada 75 61.03N110.00W
The Little Minch str. U.K. 12 57.40N 6.45W
Thelon r. Canada 75 64.23N 96.15W
The Machers f. U.K. 12 54.45N 4.28W
The Minch str. U.K. 12 58.10N 5.50W
The Needles c. U.K. 11 50.39N 1.35W
Theodore Australia 64 24.57S150.05E
Theodore Roosevelt L. U.S.A. 81 33.30N110.57W
Theog India 40 31.07N 77.21E
The Pas Canada 75 53.50N101.15W
The Pennines hills U.K. 10 55.40N 2.20W
Thérain r. France 15 49.15N 2.27E
Theresa U.S.A. 84 44.13N 75.48W
The Rhinns f. U.K. 12 54.50N 5.02W
Thermaïkós Kólpos g. Greece 19 40.10N 23.00E
Thermopolis U.S.A. 80 43.39N108.13W
Thermopylae, Pass of Greece 19 38.47N 22.34E
The Rock town Australia 67 35.16S147.07E
The Salt L. Australia 66 30.05S142.10E
The Snares is. New Zealand 68 48.00S166.30E
The Solent str. U.K. 11 50.45N 1.20W
The Sound str. Denmark/Sweden 23 55.35N 12.40E
Thessalon Canada 76 46.20N 83.30W
Thessaloníki Greece 19 40.38N 22.56E
Thetford U.K. 11 52.25N 0.44E
Thetford Mines town Canada 77 46.06N 71.18W
The Twins town Australia 66 30.00S135.16E
The Wash b. U.K. 10 52.55N 0.15E
The Weald f. U.K. 11 51.05N 0.20E
Thibodaux U.S.A. 83 29.48N 90.49W
Thicket Portage Canada 75 55.19N 97.42W
Thief River Falls town U.S.A. 82 48.07N 96.10W
Thiene Italy 15 45.42N 11.29E
Thiers France 17 45.51N 3.33E
Thiès Senegal 52 14.50N 16.55W
Thika Kenya 55 1.04S 37.04E
Thimbu Bhutan 41 27.28N 89.39E
Thingvallavatn l. Iceland 22 64.10N 21.10W
Thionville France 17 49.22N 6.11E
Thíra i. Greece 19 36.24N 25.27E
Thirsk U.K. 10 54.15N 1.20W
Thisted Denmark 23 56.57N 8.42E
Thistilfjördhur b. Iceland 22 66.11N 15.20W
Thistle I. Australia 66 35.00S136.09E
Thívai Greece 19 38.21N 23.19E
Thjórsá r. Iceland 22 63.53N 20.38W
Thoa r. Canada 75 60.31N109.47W
Thoen Thailand 34 17.41N 99.14E
Tholen i. Neth. 14 51.34N 4.07E
Thomas U.S.A. 84 39.09N 79.30W
Thomaston U.S.A. 85 32.55N 84.20W
Thomasville Ala. U.S.A. 83 31.55N 87.51W
Thomasville Fla. U.S.A. 85 30.50N 83.59W
Thompson Canada 75 55.45N 97.52W
Thompson Utah U.S.A. 80 38.58N109.43W
Thompson Landing Canada 75 62.56N110.40W
Thompsonville U.S.A. 84 44.32N 85.57W
Thomson r. Australia 64 25.11S142.53E
Thonburi Thailand 34 13.43N100.27E
Thórisvatn l. Iceland 22 64.15N 18.50W
Thorshavn Faroe Is. 8 62.02N 6.47W
Thorshöfn Iceland 22 66.12N 15.17W
Thouars France 17 46.59N 0.13W
Thowa r. Kenya 49 1.33S 40.03E
Thrapston U.K. 11 52.24N 0.32W
Three Forks U.S.A. 80 45.54N111.33W
Three Hills town Canada 74 51.43N113.15W

Three Kings Is. to **Trinkitat**

Three Kings Is. New Zealand **68** 34.09S172.09E
Three Rivers *town* Australia **62** 25.07S119.09E
Three Rivers *town* U.S.A. **83** 28.28N 98.11W
Three Sisters Mt. U.S.A. **80** 44.10N121.46W
Thuin Belgium **14** 50.21N 4.20E
Thul Pakistan **40** 28.14N 68.46E
Thule Greenland **73** 77.30N 69.29W
Thun Switz. **20** 46.46N 7.38E
Thunder Bay *town* Canada **76** 48.25N 89.14W
Thunder Hills Canada **75** 54.30N106.00W
Thung Song Thailand **34** 8.10N 99.41E
Thunkar Bhutan **41** 27.55N 91.00E
Thüringer Wald *mts.* E. Germany **20** 50.40N 10.50E
Thurles Rep. of Ire. **13** 52.41N 7.50W
Thurloo Downs *town* Australia **66** 29.18S143.30E
Thursday I. Australia **68** 10.35S142.13E
Thurso U.K. **12** 58.35N 3.32W
Thurso *r.* U.K. **8** 58.35N 3.32W
Thury-Harcourt France **15** 48.59N 0.29W
Thysville Zaïre **54** 5.15S 14.52E
Tia Australia **67** 31.15S151.40E
Tiandong China **33** 23.36N107.08E
Tian'e China **33** 25.00N107.10E
Tian Head Canada **74** 53.47N133.06W
Tianjin China **32** 39.07N117.08E
Tianjin *d.* China **32** 39.30N117.20E
Tianjun China **30** 37.16N 98.52E
Tianlin China **33** 24.18N106.13E
Tianmen China **33** 30.40N113.25E
Tian Shan *mts.* Asia **30** 42.00N 80.30E
Tianshui China **32** 34.25N105.58E
Tiantai China **33** 29.09N121.02E
Tianyang China **33** 23.45N106.54E
Tiarei Tahiti **69** 17.32S149.20W
Tiaret Algeria **51** 35.28N 1.21E
Tiavea W. Samoa **68** 13.57S171.28W
Tibasti, Sarīr *des.* Libya **51** 24.00N 17.00E
Tibati Cameroon **53** 6.25N 12.33E
Tiber *r. see* Tevere *r.* Italy **18**
Tiberias *see* Teverya Israel **44**
Tiberias, L. *see* Yam Kinneret *l.* Israel **44**
Tibesti *mts.* Chad **53** 21.00N 17.30E
Tibet *d. see* Xizang *d.* China **41**
Tibetan Plateau *see* Qing Zang Gaoyuan *f.* China **30**
Tibooburra Australia **66** 29.28S142.04E
Tiburón, Isla Mexico **81** 29.00N112.20W
Tîchît Mauritania **50** 18.28N 9.30W
Tichla W. Sahara **50** 21.35N 14.58W
Ticino *r.* Italy **15** 45.09N 9.12E
Ticonderoga U.S.A. **84** 43.51N 73.26W
Tidaholm Sweden **23** 58.11N 13.57E
Tidikelt *f.* Algeria **51** 27.00N 1.30E
Tidirhine, Jbel *mtn.* Morocco **50** 34.50N 4.30W
Tidjikdja Mauritania **50** 18.29N 11.31W
Tiel Neth. **14** 51.53N 5.26E
Tieling China **32** 42.13N123.48E
Tielt Belgium **14** 51.00N 3.20E
Tienen Belgium **14** 50.49N 4.56E
Tiénigbé Ivory Coast **52** 8.11N 5.43W
Tientsin *see* Tianjin China **32**
Tierp Sweden **23** 60.20N 17.30E
Tierra Amarilla U.S.A. **80** 36.42N106.33W
Tierra Blanca Mexico **86** 18.28N 96.12W
Tierra del Fuego *d.* Argentina **93** 54.30S 67.00W
Tierra del Fuego *i.* Argentina / Chile **93** 54.00S 69.00W
Tietar *r.* Spain **16** 39.50N 6.00W
Tietê Brazil **94** 23.04S 47.41W
Tifi Ethiopia **49** 6.15N 37.00E
Tifton U.S.A. **85** 31.27N 83.31W
Tiger U.S.A. **80** 48.42N117.24W
Tiger Hills Canada **75** 49.25N 99.30W
Tigil U.S.S.R. **29** 57.49N158.40E
Tiglit Morocco **50** 28.31N 10.15W
Tignère Cameroon **53** 7.23N 12.37E
Tignish Canada **77** 46.57N 64.02W
Tigrē *d.* Ethiopia **48** 14.10N 39.35E
Tigre *r.* Venezuela **90** 9.20N 62.30W
Tigris *r. see* Dijlah *r.* Asia **43**
Tīh, Jabal at *f.* Egypt **44** 28.50N 34.00E
Tihāmah *f.* Saudi Arabia **48** 19.00N 41.00E
Tijuana Mexico **81** 32.32N117.01W
Tīkamgarh India **41** 24.44N 78.50E
Tikaré U. Volta **52** 13.16N 1.44W
Tikhoretsk U.S.S.R. **25** 45.52N 40.07E
Tikhvin U.S.S.R. **24** 59.35N 33.29E
Tikitiki New Zealand **60** 37.47S178.25E
Tiksha U.S.S.R. **24** 64.04N 32.35E
Tiksi U.S.S.R. **29** 71.40N128.45E
Tilburg Neth. **14** 51.34N 5.05E
Tilbury U.K. **11** 51.28N 0.23E
Tilemsi, Vallée du *f.* Mali **52** 16.15N 0.02E
Tilghman U.S.A. **85** 38.42N 76.20W
Tilhar India **41** 27.59N 79.44E
Till *r.* Northum. U.K. **10** 55.41N 2.12W
Tillabéri Niger **53** 14.28N 1.27E
Tillamook U.S.A. **80** 45.27N123.51W
Tílos *i.* Greece **19** 36.25N 27.25E
Tilpa Australia **66** 30.57S144.24E
Timanskiy Kryazh *mts.* U.S.S.R. **24** 66.00N 49.00E
Timaru New Zealand **60** 44.23S171.41E
Timashevsk U.S.S.R. **25** 45.38N 38.56E
Timbákion Greece **19** 35.04N 24.46E
Timbédra Mauritania **50** 16.17N 8.16W
Timboon Australia **66** 38.32S143.02E
Timbuktu *see* Tombouctou Mali **52**
Timimoun Algeria **50** 29.15N 0.15E
Timimoun, Sebkha de *f.* Algeria **50** 29.10N 0.05E
Timiris, Cap *c.* Mauritania **52** 19.23N 16.32W
Timiş *r.* Yugo. / Romania **21** 44.49N 20.28E
Timişoara Romania **21** 45.47N 21.15E
Timişul *r.* Yugo. **19** 44.49N 20.28E
Timmins Canada **76** 48.28N 81.25W
Timok *r.* Yugo. **19** 44.13N 22.40E
Timor *i.* Indonesia **62** 9.30S125.00E
Timor Sea Austa. **62** 11.00S127.00E
Timor Timur *d.* Indonesia **37** 9.00S125.00E
Timpahute Range *mts.* U.S.A. **80** 37.38N115.34W
Tinahely Rep. of Ire. **13** 52.48N 6.19W
Tindouf Algeria **50** 27.42N 8.09W
Tindouf, Sebkha de *f.* Algeria **50** 27.45N 7.30W
Tingha Australia **67** 29.58S151.16E
Tingo María Peru **90** 9.09S 75.56W
Tingping China **33** 26.10N110.17E
Tingréla Ivory Coast **52** 10.26N 6.20W
Tingri China **41** 28.30N 86.34E
Tingsryd Sweden **23** 56.32N 14.59E
Tinguipaya Bolivia **92** 19.11S 65.51W
Tinian *i.* Mariana Is. **37** 14.58N145.38E
Tinkisso *r.* Guinea **52** 11.25N 9.05W
Tinnenburra Australia **67** 28.40S145.30E
Tinnoset Norway **23** 59.43N 9.02E
Tínos *i.* Greece **19** 37.36N 25.08E
Tinsukia India **39** 27.30N 95.22E
Tintinara Australia **66** 35.52S140.04E
Tioman, Pulau *i.* Malaysia **36** 2.45N104.10E
Tionaga Canada **76** 48.05N 82.00W
Tione di Trento Italy **15** 46.02N 10.43E
Tipperary Rep. of Ire. **13** 52.29N 8.10W
Tipperary *d.* Rep. of Ire. **13** 52.37N 7.55W
Tīrān, Jazīrat Saudi Arabia **44** 27.56N 34.34E
Tiranë Albania **19** 41.20N 19.48E
Tirano Italy **15** 46.12N 10.10E
Tiraspol U.S.S.R. **21** 46.50N 29.38E
Tirat Karmel Israel **44** 32.46N 34.58E
Tirebolu Turkey **42** 41.02N 38.49E
Tiree *i.* U.K. **12** 56.30N 6.50W
Tîrgovişte Romania **21** 44.56N 25.27E
Tîrgu-Jiu Romania **21** 45.03N 23.17E
Tîrgu-Lăpuş Romania **21** 47.27N 23.52E
Tîrgu Mureş Romania **21** 46.33N 24.34E
Tîrgu-Neamţ Romania **21** 47.12N 26.22E
Tîrgu-Ocna Romania **21** 46.15N 26.37E
Tîrgu-Secuiesc Romania **21** 46.00N 26.08E
Tiris Zemmour *d.* Mauritania **50** 24.00N 9.00W
Tírnavos Greece **19** 39.45N 22.17E
Tirodi India **41** 21.41N 79.42E
Tirol *d.* Austria **20** 47.15N 11.20E
Tir Pol Afghan. **43** 34.38N 61.19E
Tirso *r.* Italy **18** 39.52N 8.33E
Tiruchchirāppalli India **39** 10.50N 78.43E
Tirunelveli India **38** 8.45N 77.43E
Tirupati India **39** 13.39N 79.25E
Tiruppur India **38** 11.05N 77.20E
Tisa *r.* Yugo. **21** 45.09N 20.16E
Tis'ah Egypt **44** 30.02N 32.35E
Tisdale Canada **75** 52.51N104.04W
Tisza *r.* Hungary *see* Tisa *r.* Yugo. **21**
Tit Algeria **51** 22.58N 5.11E
Titicaca, L. Bolivia / Peru **92** 16.00S 69.00W
Titikaveka Rarotonga Cook Is. **68** 21.16S159.45W
Titiwa Nigeria **53** 12.14N 12.53E
Titlagarh India **41** 20.18N 83.09E
Titograd Yugo. **19** 42.30N 19.16E
Titovo Užice Yugo. **21** 43.52N 19.51E
Titov Veles Yugo. **19** 41.43N 21.49E
Titran Norway **22** 63.42N 8.22E
Titule Zaïre **54** 3.17N 25.32E
Titusville Fla. U.S.A. **85** 28.37N 80.50W
Titusville Penn. U.S.A. **84** 41.38N 79.41W
Tiuni India **41** 30.57N 77.51E
Tivaouane Senegal **52** 14.57N 16.49W
Tiverton U.K. **11** 50.54N 3.30W
Tivoli Italy **18** 41.58N 12.48E
Tiyo Ethiopia **48** 14.40N 40.15E
Tizimín Mexico **87** 21.10N 88.09W
Tizi Ouzou Algeria **51** 36.44N 4.05E
Tiznit Morocco **50** 29.43N 9.44W
Tjeuke Meer *l.* Neth. **14** 52.55N 5.51E
Tjörn *i.* Sweden **23** 58.00N 11.38E
Tlaxcala *d.* Mexico **86** 19.45N 98.20W
Tlemcen Algeria **50** 34.52N 1.19W
Tmassah Libya **51** 26.22N 15.48E
Tni Haïa *well* Algeria **50** 24.15N 2.45W
Toab U.K. **12** 59.53N 1.16W
Toamasina Madagascar **57** 18.10S 49.23E
Toano Italy **15** 44.23N 10.34E
Toanoano Tahiti **69** 17.52S149.12W
Toba Japan **35** 34.29N136.51E
Toba, Danau *l.* Indonesia **36** 2.45S 98.50E
Toba Kākar Range *mts.* Pakistan **40** 31.15N 68.00E
Tobar U.S.A. **80** 40.53N114.54W
Toba Tek Singh Pakistan **40** 30.58N 72.29E
Tobelo Indonesia **37** 1.45N127.59E
Tobermory Canada **76** 45.14N 81.36W
Tobermory U.K. **12** 56.37N 6.04W
Tobl *l.* Caroline Is. **37** 3.01N131.10E
Tobin L. Canada **75** 53.40N103.35W
Toboali Indonesia **36** 3.00S106.30E
Tobol *r.* U.S.S.R. **28** 58.15N 68.12E
Tobolsk U.S.S.R. **28** 58.15N 68.12E
Tobruk *see* Ţubruq Libya **48**
Tobseda U.S.S.R. **24** 68.34N 52.16E
Tocantinópolis Brazil **91** 6.20S 47.25W
Tocantins *r.* Brazil **91** 1.50S 49.15W
Toccoa U.S.A. **85** 34.34N 83.21W
Töcksfors Sweden **23** 59.30N 11.50E
Tocopilla Chile **92** 22.05S 70.12W
Tocorpuri *mtn.* Bolivia / Chile **92** 22.26S 67.53W
Tocumwal Australia **67** 35.51S145.34E
Tocuyo *r.* Venezuela **90** 11.03N 68.23W
Todenyang Kenya **55** 4.34N 35.52E
Todos Santos Mexico **81** 23.27N110.13W
Tofua *i.* Tonga **69** 19.45S175.05W
Togian, Kepulauan *is.* Indonesia **37** 0.20S122.00E
Togo Africa **52** 8.00N 1.00E
Tohen Somali Rep. **45** 11.42N 51.17E
Toi Niue **68** 18.58S169.52W
Toijala Finland **23** 61.10N 23.52E
Tojg Afghan. **40** 32.04N 61.48E
Tokaj Hungary **21** 48.08N 21.27E
Tokala *mtn.* Indonesia **37** 1.36S121.41E
Tokat Turkey **42** 40.20N 36.35E
Tokelau Is. Pacific Oc. **68** 9.00S171.45W
Toki Japan **35** 35.21N137.11E
Toki *r.* Japan **35** 35.12N136.52E
Tokmak U.S.S.R. **30** 42.49N 75.15E
Tokoname Japan **35** 34.53N136.51E
Tokoroa New Zealand **60** 38.13S175.53E
Tokuno shima *i.* Japan **31** 27.40N129.00E
Tōkyō Japan **35** 35.42N139.46E
Tōkyō-wan *b.* Japan **35** 35.25N139.45E
Tolaga Bay *town* New Zealand **60** 38.22S178.18E
Tolbukhin Bulgaria **19** 43.34N 27.52E
Toledo Spain **16** 39.52N 4.02W
Toledo U.S.A. **84** 41.40N 83.35W
Toledo, Montes de *mts.* Spain **16** 39.35N 4.30W
Toledo Bend Resr. U.S.A. **83** 31.46N 93.25W
Toliara Madagascar **57** 23.21S 43.40E
Tolmezzo Italy **15** 46.24N 13.01E
Tolo, Teluk *g.* Indonesia **37** 2.00S122.30E
Tolosa Spain **16** 43.09N 2.04W
Tolstyy-Les U.S.S.R. **21** 51.24N 29.48E
Tolti Jammu & Kashmir **40** 35.02N 76.06E
Toluca Mexico **86** 19.20N 99.40W
Toluca *mtn.* Mexico **86** 19.10N 99.40W
Tol'yatti U.S.S.R. **24** 53.32N 49.24E
Tomah U.S.A. **82** 43.59N 90.30W
Tomar Portugal **16** 39.36N 8.25W
Tomás Gomensoro Uruguay **93** 30.26S 57.26W
Tomaszów Lubelski Poland **21** 50.28N 23.25E
Tomaszów Mazowiecki Poland **21** 51.32N 20.01E
Tombe Sudan **49** 5.49N 31.41E
Tombigbee *r.* U.S.A. **83** 31.04N 87.58W
Tombos Brazil **94** 20.53S 42.03W
Tombouctou Mali **52** 16.49N 2.59W
Tomé Chile **93** 36.37S 72.57W
Tomelilla Sweden **23** 55.33N 13.57E
Tomelloso Spain **16** 39.09N 3.01W
Tomingley Australia **67** 32.06S148.15E
Tomini Indonesia **37** 0.31N120.30E
Tomini, Teluk *g.* Indonesia **37** 0.30S120.45E
Tominian Mali **52** 13.17N 4.35W
Tomintoul U.K. **12** 57.15N 3.24W
Tomkinson Ranges *mts.* Australia **62** 26.11S129.05E
Tom Price Australia **62** 22.49S117.51E
Tomra China **41** 30.52N 87.30E
Tomra Norway **22** 62.34N 6.55E
Tomsk U.S.S.R. **28** 56.30N 85.05E
Toms River *town* U.S.A. **85** 39.57N 74.12W
Tonalá Mexico **86** 16.08N 93.41W
Tonalea U.S.A. **81** 36.20N110.58W
Tonasket U.S.A. **80** 48.42N119.26W
Tonawanda U.S.A. **76** 43.01N 78.53W
Tonbridge U.K. **11** 51.12N 0.16E
Tondano Indonesia **37** 1.19N124.56E
Tönder Denmark **23** 54.56N 8.54E
Tondibi Mali **52** 16.39N 0.14W
Tondoro Namibia **56** 17.45S 18.50E
Tone *r.* Japan **35** 35.44N140.51E
Tonga Pacific Oc. **69** 20.00S175.00W
Tonga Sudan **49** 9.28N 31.03E
Tongaat R.S.A. **56** 29.34S 31.07E
Tong'an China **33** 24.44N118.09E
Tongatapu *i.* Tonga **69** 21.10S175.10W
Tongatapu Group *is.* Tonga **69** 21.10S175.10W
Tonga Trench *f.* Pacific Oc. **68** 20.00S173.00W
Tongchuan China **32** 35.05N109.10E
Tongeren Belgium **14** 50.47N 5.28E
Tongguan Hunan China **33** 28.27N112.48E
Tongguan Shaanxi China **32** 34.32N110.26E
Tonghai China **39** 24.07N102.45E
Tonghua China **31** 41.40N126.52E
Tongking, G. of China / Vietnam **34** 20.00N108.00E
Tongliao China **32** 43.40N122.20E
Tongling China **33** 30.55N117.42E
Tonglu China **33** 29.49N119.40E
Tongo Australia **66** 30.30S143.47E
Tongoa *i.* Vanuatu **68** 16.54S168.34E
Tongobory Madagascar **57** 23.32S 44.20E
Tongoy Chile **92** 30.15S 71.30W
Tongren China **33** 27.41N109.08E
Tongsa Dzong Bhutan **41** 27.31N 90.30E
Tongtianheyan China **41** 33.50N 92.19E
Tongue U.K. **12** 58.28N 4.25W
Tongue *r.* U.S.A. **80** 46.24N105.25W
Tongwei China **32** 35.18N105.10E
Tong Xian China **32** 39.52N116.45E
Tongxin China **32** 36.59N105.50E
Tongyu China **32** 44.48N123.06E
Tongzi China **33** 28.08N106.49E
Tonj Sudan **49** 7.17N 28.45E
Tonk India **40** 26.10N 75.47E
Tônlé Sap *l.* Kampuchea **34** 12.50N104.15E
Tonnerre France **15** 47.51N 3.59E
Tonopah U.S.A. **80** 38.04N117.14W
Tonota Botswana **56** 21.28S 27.24E
Tons *r.* India **41** 25.17N 82.04E
Tönsberg Norway **23** 59.17N 10.25E
Tonstad Norway **23** 58.40N 6.43E
Tonto Basin *town* U.S.A. **81** 33.55N111.18W
Toobeah Australia **67** 28.22S149.50E
Toodyay Australia **63** 31.35S116.26E
Tooele U.S.A. **80** 40.32N112.18W
Tooligie Australia **66** 33.51S135.41E
Toolondo Australia **66** 36.55S142.00E
Toowoomba Australia **65** 27.35S151.54E
Topeka U.S.A. **82** 39.03N 95.41W
Topko *mtn.* U.S.S.R. **29** 57.20N138.10E
Topley Canada **74** 54.32N126.05W
Toplița Romania **21** 46.55N 25.21E
Topock U.S.A. **81** 34.44N114.27W
Topolovgrad Bulgaria **19** 42.05N 26.20E
Topozero, Ozero *l.* U.S.S.R. **24** 65.45N 32.00E
Toppenish U.S.A. **80** 46.23N120.19W
Tora-Khem U.S.S.R. **29** 52.31N 96.13E
Tor B. Australia **63** 35.00S117.40E
Torbat-e Ḩeydarīyeh Iran **43** 35.16N 59.13E
Torbat-e Jām Iran **43** 35.15N 60.37E
Torbay *town* U.K. **11** 50.27N 3.31W
Tördal Norway **23** 59.10N 8.45E
Tordesillas Spain **16** 41.30N 5.00W
Töre Sweden **22** 65.54N 22.39E
Töreboda Sweden **23** 58.43N 14.08E
Torgau E. Germany **20** 51.34N 13.00E
Torhout Belgium **14** 51.04N 3.06E
Tori Ethiopia **49** 7.53N 33.40E
Toride Japan **35** 35.53N140.04E
Torington Australia **67** 29.20S151.40E
Torino Italy **15** 45.04N 7.40E
Torit Sudan **49** 4.24N 32.34E
Tormes *r.* Spain **16** 41.18N 6.29W
Torne *r.* Sweden *see* Tornio *r.* Finland **22**
Torneträsk Sweden **22** 68.15N 19.30E
Torneträsk *l.* Sweden **22** 68.20N 19.10E
Tornio Finland **22** 65.52N 24.10E
Tornio *r.* Finland **22** 65.53N 24.07E
Tornquist Argentina **93** 38.06S 62.14W
Toro Spain **16** 41.31N 5.24W
Toronaíos Kólpos *g.* Greece **19** 40.05N 23.38E
Toronto Canada **76** 43.42N 79.25W
Toropets U.S.S.R. **24** 56.30N 31.40E
Tororo Uganda **55** 0.42N 34.13E
Toros Dağlari *mts.* Turkey **42** 37.15N 34.15E
Torrance U.S.A. **81** 33.50N118.19W
Torreblanca Spain **16** 40.14N 0.12E
Torre de Moncorvo Portugal **16** 41.10N 7.03W
Torrelavega Spain **16** 43.21N 4.00W
Torremolinos Spain **16** 36.38N 4.30W
Torrens *r.* Australia **64** 22.22S145.09E
Torrens, L. Australia **66** 31.00S137.50E
Torrens Creek *town* Australia **64** 20.50S145.00E
Torreón Mexico **83** 25.33N103.26W
Torre Pellice Italy **15** 44.49N 9.13E
Torres Str. Australia **64** 10.30S142.20E
Torres Vedras Portugal **16** 39.05N 9.15W
Torrevieja Spain **16** 37.59N 0.40W
Torrey U.S.A. **80** 38.18N111.25W
Torridge *r.* U.K. **11** 51.01N 4.12W
Torridon U.K. **12** 57.23N 5.31W
Torridon, Loch U.K. **12** 57.35N 5.45W
Torriglia Italy **15** 44.31N 9.10E
Torrington Wyo. U.S.A. **80** 42.04N104.11W
Torsby Sweden **23** 60.08N 13.00E
Tortola *i.* B.V.Is. **87** 18.28N 64.40W
Tortona Italy **15** 44.54N 8.52E
Tortosa Spain **16** 40.49N 0.31E
Tortue, Île de la *i.* Cuba **87** 20.05N 72.57W
Toruń Poland **21** 53.01N 18.35E
Tory I. Rep. of Ire. **13** 55.16N 8.13W
Tory Sd. Rep. of Ire. **13** 55.14N 8.15W
Torzhok U.S.S.R. **24** 57.02N 34.51E
Toscana *d.* Italy **18** 43.35N 11.10E
Tosen Norway **22** 65.16N 12.50E
Tosno U.S.S.R. **24** 59.38N 30.46E
Tostado Argentina **92** 29.15S 61.45W
Totana Spain **16** 37.46N 1.30W
Tôtes France **15** 49.41N 1.03E
Totma U.S.S.R. **24** 59.59N 42.44E
Totora Bolivia **92** 17.42S 65.09W
Tottenham Australia **67** 32.14S147.24E
Tottori Japan **31** 35.32N134.12E
Touba Ivory Coast **52** 8.22N 7.42W
Toubkal *mtn.* Morocco **50** 31.03N 7.57W
Toucy France **15** 47.44N 3.18E
Tougan U. Volta **52** 13.05N 3.04W
Touggourt Algeria **51** 33.06N 6.04E
Tougué Guinea **52** 11.25N 11.50W
Toul France **17** 48.41N 5.54E
Toulnustouc *r.* Canada **77** 49.35N 68.25W
Toulon France **17** 43.07N 5.53E
Toulouse France **17** 43.33N 1.24E
Toummo Niger **51** 22.45N 14.08E
Tounassine, Hamada *des.* Algeria **50** 28.36N 5.00W
Toungoo Burma **34** 18.57N 96.26E
Touques *r.* France **15** 49.22N 0.06E
Tourassine *well* Mauritania **50** 24.40N 11.20W
Tourcoing France **14** 50.44N 3.09E
Tournai Belgium **14** 50.36N 3.23E
Tournon France **17** 45.04N 4.50E
Tournus France **17** 46.33N 4.55E
Tours France **15** 47.23N 0.42E
Toury France **15** 48.11N 1.56E
Touwsrivier *town* R.S.A. **56** 33.20S 20.02E
Towamba Australia **67** 37.09S149.43E
Towcester U.K. **11** 52.07N 0.56W
Tower U.S.A. **82** 47.47N 92.19W
Towerhill *r.* Australia **64** 22.29S144.39E
Towner U.S.A. **82** 48.21N100.25W
Townsend, Mt. Australia **67** 36.24S148.15E
Townshend, C. Australia **64** 22.10S150.30E
Townshend I. Australia **64** 22.15S150.30E
Townsville Australia **64** 19.13S146.48E
Towrzī Afghan. **40** 30.11N 65.59E
Towson U.S.A. **85** 39.24N 76.36W
Towyn U.K. **11** 52.37N 4.08W
Toyah U.S.A. **83** 31.19N103.47W
Toyama Japan **31** 36.42N137.14E
Toyo *r.* Japan **35** 34.47N137.20E
Toyohashi Japan **35** 34.46N137.23E
Toyokawa Japan **35** 34.49N137.24E
Toyota Japan **35** 35.05N137.09E
Tozeur Tunisia **51** 33.55N 8.08E
Traben-Trarbach W. Germany **14** 49.57N 7.07E
Trabzon Turkey **42** 41.00N 39.43E
Tracadie Canada **77** 47.31N 64.54W
Tracy Canada **77** 46.01N 73.09W
Tracy U.S.A. **82** 44.14N 95.37W
Trade Town Liberia **52** 5.43N 9.56W
Trafalgar, Cabo *c.* Spain **16** 36.11N 6.02W
Traiguén Chile **93** 38.15S 72.41W
Trail Canada **74** 49.05N117.40W
Trajanova Vrata *pass* Bulgaria **19** 42.13N 23.58E
Trakt U.S.S.R. **24** 62.40N 51.26E
Tralee Rep. of Ire. **13** 52.16N 9.42W
Tralee B. Rep. of Ire. **13** 52.18N 9.55W
Tranås Sweden **23** 58.03N 14.59E
Trang Thailand **34** 7.35N 99.35E
Trangan *i.* Indonesia **37** 6.30S134.15E
Trangie Australia **67** 32.03S148.01E
Trani Italy **18** 41.17N 16.26E
Tranoroa Madagascar **57** 24.42S 45.04E
Tranqueras Uruguay **93** 31.12S 55.45W
Transkei *f.* R.S.A. **56** 32.12S 28.20E
Transvaal *d.* R.S.A. **56** 24.30S 29.30E
Transylvanian Alps *see* Carpaţii Meridionalimts. *mts.* Romania **19**
Trapani Italy **18** 38.02N 12.30E
Traralgon Australia **67** 38.12S146.32E
Traryd Sweden **23** 56.35N 13.45E
Trarza *d.* Mauritania **50** 18.00N 14.50W
Trarza *f.* Mauritania **50** 18.00N 15.00W
Trasimeno, Lago *l.* Italy **18** 43.09N 12.07E
Trat Thailand **34** 12.14N102.33E
Traunstein W. Germany **20** 47.52N 12.38E
Travellers L. Australia **66** 33.18S142.00E
Travers, Mt. New Zealand **60** 42.05S172.45E
Traverse City U.S.A. **84** 44.46N 85.38W
Travnik Yugo. **19** 44.14N 17.40E
Trayning Australia **63** 31.09S117.46E
Trbovlje Yugo. **20** 46.10N 15.03E
Trebbia *r.* Italy **15** 45.04N 9.41E
Třebíč Czech. **20** 49.13N 15.55E
Trebinje Yugo. **19** 42.43N 18.20E
Trebišov Czech. **21** 48.40N 21.47E
Třeboň Czech. **20** 49.01N 14.50E
Trecate Italy **15** 45.26N 8.44E
Tredegar U.K. **11** 51.47N 3.16W
Tregaron U.K. **11** 52.14N 3.56W
Tregosse Islets and Reefs Australia **64** 17.41S150.43E
Tréguier France **17** 48.47N 3.16W
Treinta-y-Tres Uruguay **94** 33.16S 54.17W
Treis W. Germany **14** 50.10N 7.20E
Trélazé France **15** 47.27N 0.28W
Trelew Argentina **93** 43.15S 65.20W
Trelleborg Sweden **23** 55.22N 13.10E
Trélon France **14** 50.04N 4.05E
Tremadog B. U.K. **10** 52.52N 4.14W
Tremblant, Mont *mtn.* Canada **77** 46.16N 74.35W
Tremp Spain **16** 42.10N 0.52E
Trena Ethiopia **49** 10.45N 40.38E
Trenčín Czech. **21** 48.54N 18.04E
Trenggalek Indonesia **37** 8.01S111.38E
Trenque Lauquen Argentina **93** 35.56S 62.43W
Trent *r.* U.K. **10** 53.41N 0.41W
Trentino-Alto Adige *d.* Italy **15** 46.30N 11.20E
Trento Italy **15** 46.04N 11.08E
Trenton Canada **76** 44.06N 77.35W
Trenton Mo. U.S.A. **82** 40.05N 93.37W
Trenton Nebr. U.S.A. **82** 40.11N101.01W
Trenton N.J. U.S.A. **85** 40.15N 74.43W
Trepassey Canada **73** 46.44N 53.22W
Tres Árboles Uruguay **93** 32.24S 56.43W
Tres Arroyos Argentina **93** 38.26S 60.17W
Três Corações Brazil **94** 21.44S 45.15W
Três Lagoas Brazil **94** 20.46S 51.43W
Três Marias, Reprêsa *resr.* Brazil **94** 18.15S 45.15W
Três Pontas Brazil **94** 21.23S 45.29W
Três Rios Brazil **94** 22.07S 43.12W
Treuchtlingen W. Germany **20** 48.57N 10.55E
Treviglio Italy **15** 45.31N 9.35E
Treviso Italy **15** 45.40N 12.14E
Tribulation, C. Australia **64** 16.03S145.30E
Tribune U.S.A. **82** 38.28N101.45W
Trida Australia **67** 33.00S145.01E
Trier W. Germany **14** 49.45N 6.39E
Trieste Italy **18** 45.40N 13.47E
Triglav *mtn.* Yugo. **18** 46.21N 13.50E
Tríkala Greece **19** 39.34N 21.46E
Tríkomon Cyprus **44** 35.17N 33.53E
Triman Pakistan **40** 29.38N 69.05E
Trincomalee Sri Lanka **39** 8.34N 81.13E
Trinidad Bolivia **92** 14.47S 64.47W
Trinidad Colombia **90** 5.25N 71.40W
Trinidad Cuba **87** 21.48N 80.00W
Trinidad Uruguay **93** 33.32S 56.54W
Trinidad U.S.A. **80** 37.10N104.31W
Trinidad & Tobago S. America **87** 10.30N 61.20W
Trinity *r.* U.S.A. **83** 29.55N 94.45W
Trinity B. Australia **64** 16.56S145.50E
Trinity B. Canada **77** 48.00N 53.40W
Trinity Range *mts.* U.S.A. **80** 40.13N119.12W
Trinkitat Sudan **48** 18.41N 37.43E

Trino to Urdzhar

Trino Italy 15 45.12N 8.18E
Tripoli see Ţarābulus Lebanon 44
Tripoli see Ţarābulus Libya 51
Trípolis Greece 19 37.31N 22.21E
Tripolitania f. see Ţarābulus f. Libya 51
Tripp U.S.A. 82 43.13N 97.58W
Tripura d. India 41 23.50N 92.00E
Tristan da Cunha i. Atlantic Oc. 95 37.50S 12.30W
Trivandrum India 38 8.41N 76.57E
Trnava Czech. 21 48.23N 17.35E
Troarn France 15 49.11N 0.11W
Trobriand Is. P.N.G. 64 8.35S151.05E
Troglav mtn. Yugo. 19 43.57N 16.36E
Troisdorf W. Germany 14 50.50N 7.07E
Trois-Rivières town Canada 77 46.21N 72.34W
Troitsk U.S.S.R. 28 54.08N 61.33E
Troitsko-Pechorsk U.S.S.R. 24 62.40N 56.08E
Troitskoye R.S.F.S.R. U.S.S.R. 24 52.18N 56.26E
Troitskoye UKr.S.S.R. U.S.S.R. 21 47.38N 30.19E
Trölladyngja mtn. Iceland 22 64.54N 17.16W
Trollhättan Sweden 23 58.16N 12.18E
Trollheimen mts. Norway 22 62.50N 9.15E
Troms d. Norway 22 69.20N 19.30E
Tromsö Norway 22 69.42N 19.00E
Trondheim Norway 22 63.36N 10.23E
Trondheimsfjorden est. Norway 22 63.40N 10.30E
Troödos mts. Cyprus 44 34.57N 32.50E
Troon U.K. 12 55.33N 4.40W
Tropic U.S.A. 80 37.37N112.05W
Trosh U.S.S.R. 24 66.24N 56.08E
Trostan mtn. N. Ireland 13 55.03N 6.10W
Trostyanets U.S.S.R. 21 48.35N 29.10E
Trout r. Canada 74 61.19N119.51W
Trout Creek town Canada 76 45.56N 79.24W
Trout L. N.W.T. Canada 74 60.35N121.10W
Trout L. Ont. Canada 76 51.13N 93.20W
Trout River town Canada 77 49.29N 58.08W
Trouville France 15 49.22N 0.55E
Trowbridge U.K. 11 51.18N 2.12W
Troy Ala. U.S.A. 85 31.49N 86.00W
Troy Mo. U.S.A. 82 38.59N 90.59W
Troy Mont. U.S.A. 80 48.28N115.53W
Troy N.Y. U.S.A. 84 42.43N 73.40W
Troy Ohio U.S.A. 84 40.02N 84.12W
Troyes France 15 48.18N 4.05E
Troy Peak mtn. U.S.A. 80 38.19N115.30W
Trpanj Yugo. 19 43.00N 17.17E
Truchas Peak mtn. U.S.A. 81 35.58N105.39W
Truckee U.S.A. 80 39.20N120.11W
Trujillo Honduras 87 15.55N 86.00W
Trujillo Peru 90 8.06S 79.00W
Trujillo Spain 16 39.28N 5.53W
Trujillo Venezuela 90 9.20N 70.37W
Truk Is. Pacific Oc. 68 7.23N151.46E
Trundle Australia 67 32.54S147.35E
Trung-Luong Vietnam 34 13.55N109.15E
Trunmore B. Canada 77 53.48N 57.10W
Truro Australia 66 34.23S139.09E
Truro Canada 77 45.22N 63.16W
Truro U.K. 11 50.17N 5.02W
Truslove Australia 63 33.19S121.40E
Trustrup Denmark 23 56.21N 10.47E
Trust Territory of the Pacific Is. Pacific Oc. 68 10.00N155.00E
Truth or Consequences U.S.A. 81 33.08N107.15W
Trysil Norway 23 61.19N 12.16E
Trysil r. Norway 23 61.03N 12.30E
Trzemeszno Poland 21 52.35N 17.50E
Tsaratanana Madagascar 57 16.47S 47.39E
Tsaratanana, Massif de mts. Madagascar 57 14.00S 49.00E
Tsau Botswana 56 20.10S 22.29E
Tsavo Nat. Park Kenya 55 2.45S 38.45E
Tselinograd U.S.S.R. 28 51.10N 71.28E
Tses Namibia 56 25.58S 18.08E
Tsévié Togo 53 6.28N 1.15E
Tshabong Botswana 56 26.03S 22.25E
Tshane Botswana 56 24.02S 21.54E
Tshela Zaïre 54 4.57S 12.57E
Tshesebe Botswana 56 20.45S 27.31E
Tshikapa Zaïre 54 6.28S 20.48E
Tshofa Zaïre 54 5.13S 25.20E
Tshopo r. Zaïre 54 0.30N 25.07E
Tshuapa r. Zaïre 54 0.14S 20.45E
Tsihombé Madagascar 57 25.18S 45.29E
Tsimlyansk U.S.S.R. 25 47.40N 42.06E
Tsimlyanskoye Vodokhranilishche resr. U.S.S.R. 25 48.00N 43.00E
Tsinan see Jinan China 32
Tsingtao see Qingdao China 32
Tsiribihina Madagascar 57 19.42S 44.31E
Tsiroanomandidy Madagascar 57 18.46S 46.02E
Tsivilsk U.S.S.R. 24 55.50N 47.28E
Tsivory Madagascar 57 24.04S 46.05E
Tskhinvali U.S.S.R. 25 42.14N 43.58E
Tsna r. B.S.S.R. U.S.S.R. 21 52.10N 27.03E
Tsna r. R.S.F.S.R. U.S.S.R. 24 54.45N 41.54E
Tsobis Namibia 56 19.27S 17.30E
Tso Morīri l. Jammu & Kashmir 41 32.54N 78.20E
Tsu Japan 35 34.43N136.31E
Tsuchiura Japan 35 36.05N140.12E
Tsudakhar U.S.S.R. 25 42.20N 47.11E
Tsumeb Namibia 56 19.12S 17.43E
Tsuru Japan 35 35.30N138.56E
Tsushima Japan 35 35.10N136.43E
Tsushima i. Japan 31 34.30N129.20E
Tuam Rep. of Ire. 13 53.32N 8.52W
Tuamotu, Îles is. Pacific Oc. 69 17.00S142.00W
Tuapa Niue 68 18.59S169.54W
Tuapse U.S.S.R. 25 44.06N 39.05E
Tuatapere New Zealand 60 46.08S167.41E
Tubac U.S.A. 81 31.37N111.03W
Tuba City U.S.A. 81 36.08N111.14W
Tuban Indonesia 37 6.55S112.01E
Tubarão Brazil 94 28.30S 49.01W
Ţubayq, Jabal aţ mts. Saudi Arabia 44 29.30N 37.15E
Tubbercurry Rep. of Ire. 13 54.03N 8.45W
Tübingen W. Germany 20 48.32N 9.04E
Ţubjah, Wādī r. Saudi Arabia 42 25.35N 38.22E
Ţubruq Libya 48 32.06N 23.58E
Tubuai i. Pacific Oc. 69 23.23S149.27W
Tubuai Is. Pacific Oc. 69 23.00S150.00W
Tucacas Venezuela 90 10.48N 68.19W
Tuchola Poland 21 53.35N 17.50E
Tuckerton U.S.A. 85 39.36N 74.20W
Tucson U.S.A. 81 32.13N110.58W
Tucumán d. Argentina 92 26.30S 65.20W
Tucumcari U.S.A. 81 35.10N103.44W
Tucupita Venezuela 90 9.02N 62.04W
Tucuruí Brazil 91 3.42S 49.44W
Tudela Spain 16 42.04N 1.37W
Tudmur Syria 42 34.36N 38.15E
Tuen Australia 67 28.33S145.38E
Tufi P.N.G. 64 9.05S149.20E
Tugela R.S.A. 56 29.10S 31.25E
Tuguegarao Phil. 37 17.36N121.44E
Tugur U.S.S.R. 29 53.44N136.45E
Tuineje Canary Is. 95 28.18N 14.03W
Tukangbesi, Kepulauan is. Indonesia 37 5.30S124.00E
Tukayyid well Iraq 43 29.47N 45.36E
Ţūkh Egypt 44 30.21N 31.12E
Tūkrah Libya 51 32.32N 20.34E
Tuktoyaktuk Canada 72 69.27N133.00W
Tukums U.S.S.R. 23 57.00N 23.10E
Tukuyu Tanzania 55 9.20S 33.37E
Tula Mexico 86 23.00N 99.43W
Tula U.S.S.R. 24 54.11N 37.38E
Tūlāk Afghan. 40 33.58N 63.44E
Tulare U.S.A. 81 36.13N119.21W
Tulare L. resr. U.S.A. 81 36.03N119.49W
Tularosa U.S.A. 81 33.04N106.01W
Tulcan Ecuador 90 0.50N 77.48W
Tulcea Romania 19 45.10N 28.50E
Tulchin U.S.S.R. 21 48.40N 28.49E
Tulemalu L. Canada 75 62.58N 99.25W
Tuli Indonesia 37 1.25S122.23E
Tuli Zimbabwe 56 21.50S 29.15E
Tuli r. Zimbabwe 56 21.49S 29.00E
Tulia U.S.A. 83 34.32N101.46W
Ţūlkarm Jordan 44 32.19N 35.02E
Tullahoma U.S.A. 85 35.21N 86.12W
Tullamore Australia 67 32.39S147.39E
Tullamore Rep. of Ire. 13 53.17N 7.31W
Tulle France 17 45.16N 1.46E
Tullins France 17 45.18N 5.29E
Tullow Rep. of Ire. 13 52.49N 6.45W
Tully Australia 64 17.55S145.59E
Tully U.S.A. 84 42.47N 76.06W
Tuloma r. U.S.S.R. 24 68.56N 33.00E
Tulsa U.S.A. 83 36.09N 95.58W
Tulsequah Canada 74 58.39N133.35W
Tuluá Colombia 90 4.05N 76.12W
Tulumbasy U.S.S.R. 24 57.27N 57.40E
Tulun U.S.S.R. 29 54.32N100.35E
Tulungagung Indonesia 37 8.03S111.54E
Tulu Welel mtn. Ethiopia 49 8.53N 34.47E
Tum Indonesia 37 3.28S130.21E
Tumaco Colombia 90 1.51N 78.46W
Tumba Sweden 23 59.12N 17.49E
Tumba, L. Zaïre 54 0.45S 18.00E
Tumbarumba Australia 67 35.49S148.01E
Tumbes Peru 90 3.37S 80.27W
Tumby Bay town Australia 66 34.20S136.05E
Tumd Youqi China 32 40.33N110.30E
Tumd Zuoqi China 32 40.42N111.08E
Tumeremo Venezuela 90 7.18N 61.30W
Tummel, Loch U.K. 12 56.43N 3.55W
Tump Pakistan 40 26.07N 62.22E
Tumsar India 41 21.23N 79.44E
Tumuc Humac Mts. S. America 91 2.20N 54.50W
Tumut Australia 67 35.20S148.14E
Tunari mtn. Bolivia 92 17.18S 66.22W
Tūnat al Jabal Egypt 44 27.46N 30.44E
Tunceli Turkey 42 39.07N 39.34E
Tundubai well Sudan 48 18.31N 28.33E
Tunduma Tanzania 55 9.19S 32.47E
Tunduru Tanzania 55 11.08S 37.21E
Tundzha r. Bulgaria 19 41.40N 26.34E
Tungabhadra r. India 38 16.00N 78.15E
Tungaru Sudan 49 10.14N 30.42E
Tungchiang Taiwan 33 22.28N120.26E
Tungsten Canada 74 62.00N128.15W
Tungsten U.S.A. 80 40.48N118.08W
Tunica U.S.A. 83 34.41N 90.23W
Tunis Tunisia 51 36.47N 10.10E
Tunisia Africa 51 34.00N 9.00E
Tunja Colombia 90 5.33N 73.23W
Tunnsjöen l. Norway 22 64.45N 13.25E
Tunungayualok I. Canada 77 56.05N 61.05W
Tunuyán r. Argentina 93 33.33S 67.30W
Tunxi China 33 29.41N118.22E
Tuoy-Khaya U.S.S.R. 29 62.33N111.25E
Tupã Brazil 94 21.57S 50.28W
Tupelo U.S.A. 83 34.16N 88.43W
Tupinambaranas, Ilha f. Brazil 91 3.00S 58.00W
Tupiza Bolivia 92 21.27S 65.43W
Tuquan China 32 45.22N121.41E
Túquerres Colombia 90 1.06N 77.37W
Tura India 41 25.31N 90.13E
Tura Tanzania 55 5.30S 33.50E
Tura U.S.S.R. 29 64.05N100.00E
Turabah Saudi Arabia 48 21.13N 41.39E
Turangi New Zealand 60 38.59S175.48E
Turbaco Colombia 90 10.20N 75.25W
Turbanovo U.S.S.R. 24 60.05N 50.46E
Turbat Pakistan 40 25.59N 63.04E
Turbo Colombia 90 8.06N 76.44W
Turda Romania 21 46.34N 23.47E
Turek Poland 21 52.02N 18.30E
Turgeon r. Canada 76 50.00N 78.54W
Tŭrgovishte Bulgaria 19 43.14N 26.37E
Turgutlu Turkey 19 38.30N 27.43E
Turhal Turkey 42 40.23N 36.05E
Türi U.S.S.R. 23 58.48N 25.26E
Turia r. Spain 16 39.27N 0.19W
Turiaçu Brazil 91 1.41S 45.21W
Turiaçu r. Brazil 91 1.36S 45.19W
Turin Canada 74 49.59N112.35W
Turin see Torino Italy 15
Turka U.S.S.R. 21 49.10N 23.02E
Turkana, L. Kenya 55 4.00N 36.00E
Turkestan f. Asia 43 40.00N 56.00E
Turkey Asia 42 39.00N 35.00E
Turkey U.S.A. 83 34.23N100.54W
Turkey Creek town Australia 62 17.04S128.15E
Turkmenskaya S.S.R. d. U.S.S.R. 28 40.00N 60.00E
Turks Is. Turks & Caicos Is. 87 21.30N 71.10W
Turku Finland 23 60.27N 22.17E
Turku-Pori d. Finland 23 61.00N 22.35E
Turkwel r. Kenya 55 3.08N 35.39E
Turnagain r. Canada 74 59.06N127.35W
Turnberry Canada 75 53.25N101.45W
Turneffe Is. Belize 87 17.30N 87.45W
Turner U.S.A. 80 48.51N108.24W
Turnhout Belgium 14 51.19N 4.57E
Turnu Măgurele Romania 19 43.43N 24.53E
Turnu Roşu, Pasul pass Romania 19 45.37N 24.17E
Turnu-Severin Romania 19 44.37N 22.39E
Turon r. Australia 67 33.03S149.33E
Turon U.S.A. 83 37.48N 98.26W
Turov U.S.S.R. 21 52.04N 27.40E
Turpan China 30 42.55N 89.06E
Turpan Pendi f. China 30 43.40N 89.00E
Turquino mtn. Cuba 87 20.05N 76.50W
Turret Range mts. Australia 66 29.43S136.42E
Turriff U.K. 12 57.32N 2.28W
Turtkul U.S.S.R. 43 41.30N 61.00E
Turtle Lake town N.Dak. U.S.A. 82 47.31N100.53W
Turtle Lake town Wisc. U.S.A. 82 45.23N 92.09W
Turtle Mtn. Canada/U.S.A. 75 49.05N 99.45W
Turukhansk U.S.S.R. 29 65.21N 88.05E
Turya r. U.S.S.R. 21 51.48N 24.52E
Tuscaloosa U.S.A. 85 33.12N 87.33W
Tuscarora U.S.A. 80 41.19N116.14W
Tuscola Ill. U.S.A. 82 39.48N 88.17W
Tuscola Tex. U.S.A. 83 32.12N 99.48W
Tuticorin India 39 8.48N 78.10E
Tutóia Brazil 91 2.45S 42.16W
Tutrakan Bulgaria 19 44.02N 26.40E
Tuttle U.S.A. 82 47.09N100.00W
Tuttlingen W. Germany 20 47.59N 8.49E
Tutuala Indonesia 37 8.24S127.15E
Tutubu Tanzania 55 5.28S 32.43E
Tutuila i. Samoa 68 14.18S170.42W
Tuţūn Egypt 44 29.09N 30.46E
Tuul Gol r. Mongolia 30 48.53N104.35E
Tuvalu Pacific Oc. 68 8.00S178.00E
Tuwayq, Jabal mts. Saudi Arabia 45 23.30N 46.20E
Tuxpan Mexico 86 21.00N 97.23W
Tuxtla Gutiérrez Mexico 86 16.45N 93.09W
Túy Spain 16 42.03N 8.39W
Tuyen Quang Vietnam 33 21.48N105.21E
Tuz Gölü l. Turkey 42 38.45N 33.24E
Ţūz Khurmātū Iraq 43 34.53N 44.38E
Tuzla Yugo. 19 44.33N 18.41E
Tvaerå Faroe Is. 8 61.34N 6.48W
Tvedestrand Norway 23 58.37N 8.55E
Tveitsund Norway 23 59.01N 8.32E
Tweed r. U.K. 12 55.46N 2.00W
Tweedsmuir Prov. Park Canada 74 52.55N126.20W
Twentynine Palms U.S.A. 81 34.08N116.03W
Twin Bridges town U.S.A. 80 45.33N112.20W
Twin Falls town U.S.A. 80 42.34N114.28W
Twins Creek r. Australia 66 29.10S139.27E
Twin Valley town U.S.A. 82 47.16N 96.16W
Twizel New Zealand 60 44.15S170.06E
Twofold B. Australia 67 37.06S149.55E
Two Harbors town U.S.A. 82 47.02N 91.40W
Twyford U.K. 11 51.01N 1.19W
Tyler Minn. U.S.A. 82 44.17N 96.08W
Tyler Tex. U.S.A. 83 32.21N 95.18W
Tyndinskiy U.S.S.R. 29 55.11N124.34E
Tyne r. U.K. 10 55.00N 1.25W
Tyne and Wear d. U.K. 10 54.57N 1.35W
Tynemouth U.K. 10 55.01N 1.24W
Tynset Norway 23 62.17N 10.47E
Tyre see Şūr Lebanon 44
Tyrifjorden l. Norway 23 60.02N 10.08E
Tyron U.S.A. 85 35.13N 82.14W
Tyrone d. U.K. 13 54.35N 7.15W
Tyrone U.S.A. 84 40.40N 78.14W
Tyrrel Canada 75 54.35N 99.10W
Tyrrell r. Australia 66 35.28S142.55E
Tyrrell, L. Australia 66 35.22S142.50E
Tyrrhenian Sea Med. Sea 18 40.00N 12.00E
Tysnesöy i. Norway 23 60.00N 5.35E
Tyumen U.S.S.R. 28 57.11N 65.29E
Tywi r. U.K. 11 51.46N 4.22W
Tzaneen R.S.A. 56 23.49S 30.10E

U

Ua Huka i. Îs. Marquises 69 8.55S139.32W
Uanda Australia 64 21.34S144.54E
Ua Pu i. Îs. Marquises 69 9.25S140.00W
Uatumã r. Brazil 91 2.30S 57.40W
Uaupés Brazil 90 0.07S 67.05W
Uaupés r. Brazil 90 0.00S 67.10W
Ubá Brazil 94 21.08S 42.59W
Ubangi r. Congo/Zaïre 54 0.25S 17.40E
Ubatuba Brazil 94 23.26S 45.05W
Ubauro Pakistan 40 28.10N 69.44E
Ubayyiḑ, Wādī al r. Iraq 42 32.04N 42.17E
Ubeda Spain 16 38.01N 3.22W
Uberaba Brazil 94 19.47S 47.57W
Uberlândia Brazil 94 18.57S 48.17W
Ubombo R.S.A. 57 27.35S 32.05E
Ubort r. U.S.S.R. 21 52.06N 28.28E
Ubundu Zaïre 54 0.24S 25.28E
Ucayali r. Peru 90 4.40S 73.20W
Uch Pakistan 40 29.14N 71.03E
Udaipur India 40 24.35N 73.41E
Udalguri India 41 26.46N 92.08E
Udaquiola Argentina 93 36.35S 58.30W
Udaypur Nepal 41 26.54N 86.32E
Uddevalla Sweden 23 58.21N 11.55E
Uddjaur l. Sweden 22 65.55N 17.49E
Udhampur Jammu & Kashmir 40 32.56N 75.08E
Udine Italy 15 46.03N 13.15E
Udipi India 38 13.21N 74.45E
Udon Thani Thailand 34 17.25N102.45E
Uele r. Zaïre 49 4.09N 22.26E
Uelzen W. Germany 20 52.58N 10.34E
Ueno Japan 35 34.45N136.08E
Uere r. Zaïre 49 3.42N 25.24E
Ufa U.S.S.R. 24 54.45N 55.58E
Ufa r. U.S.S.R. 24 54.45N 56.00E
Uffculme U.K. 11 50.45N 3.19W
Ugab r. Namibia 56 21.12S 13.37E
Ugalla r. Tanzania 55 5.43S 31.10E
Uganda Africa 55 2.00N 33.00E
Ugep Nigeria 53 5.48N 8.05E
Ughelli Nigeria 53 5.33N 6.00E
Uglegorsk U.S.S.R. 29 49.01N142.04E
Uglovka U.S.S.R. 24 58.13N 33.30E
Ugoma mtn. Zaïre 55 4.00S 28.45E
Ugra r. U.S.S.R. 24 54.30N 36.10E
Uherske Hradiště Czech. 21 49.05N 17.28E
Uig U.K. 12 57.35N 6.22W
Uíge Angola 54 7.40S 15.09E
Uíge d. Angola 54 7.00S 15.30E
Uil U.S.S.R. 25 49.08N 54.43E
Uil r. U.S.S.R. 25 48.33N 52.25E
Uinta Mts. U.S.A. 80 40.45N110.05W
Uitenhage R.S.A. 56 33.46S 25.23E
Uithuizen Neth. 14 53.24N 6.41E
Uivlleq see Nanortalik Greenland 73
Ujhāni India 41 28.01N 79.01E
Uji r. Japan 35 34.53N135.48E
Ujiji Tanzania 55 4.55S 29.39E
Ujjain India 40 23.11N 75.46E
Ujpest Hungary 21 47.33N 19.05E
Ujście Poland 20 53.04N 16.43E
Ujung Pandang Indonesia 36 5.09S119.28E
Uka U.S.S.R. 29 57.50N162.02E
Ukerewe I. Tanzania 55 2.00S 33.00E
Ukhta U.S.S.R. 24 63.33N 53.44E
Ukiah U.S.A. 80 39.09N123.13W
Ukmerge U.S.S.R. 24 55.14N 24.49E
Ukrainskaya S.S.R. d. U.S.S.R. 21 49.45N 27.00E
Ukwi Botswana 56 23.22S 20.30E
Ulaanbaatar Mongolia 30 47.54N106.52E
Ulaangom Mongolia 30 49.59N 92.00E
Ulamba Zaïre 54 9.07S 23.40E
Ulan Bator see Ulaanbaatar Mongolia 30
Ulansuhai Nur l. China 32 40.56N108.49E
Ulan-Ude U.S.S.R. 30 51.55N107.40E
Ulan Ul Hu l. China 39 34.45N 90.25E
Ulcinj Yugo. 19 41.55N 19.11E
Ulenia, L. Australia 66 29.57S142.24E
Ulhāsnagar India 40 19.13N 73.07E
Uliastay Mongolia 30 47.42N 96.52E
Ulindi r. Zaïre 54 1.38S 25.55E
Ulla r. Spain 16 42.38N 8.45W
Ulladulla Australia 67 35.21S150.25E
Ullånger Sweden 22 62.58N 18.16E
Ullapool U.K. 12 57.54N 5.10W
Ullswater l. U.K. 10 54.34N 2.52W
Ulm W. Germany 20 48.24N 10.00E
Ulongwé Mozambique 55 14.34S 34.21E
Ulricehamn Sweden 23 57.47N 13.25E
Ulsan S. Korea 31 35.32N129.21E
Ulsberg Norway 22 62.45N 9.59E
Ultima Australia 66 35.30S143.20E
Ulu Sudan 49 10.43N 33.29E
Ulúa r. Honduras 87 15.50N 87.38W
Uluguru Mts. Tanzania 55 7.05S 37.40E
Ulverston U.K. 10 54.13N 3.07W
Ulverstone Australia 65 41.09S146.10E
Ul'yanovsk U.S.S.R. 24 54.19N 48.22E
Ulysses U.S.A. 83 37.35N101.22W
Umaisha Nigeria 53 8.01N 7.12E
Umala Bolivia 92 17.21S 68.00W
Uman U.S.S.R. 21 48.45N 30.10E
Umaria India 41 23.32N 80.50E
Umarkot Pakistan 40 25.22N 69.44E
Umbria d. Italy 18 42.55N 12.10E
Ume r. Sweden 22 63.47N 20.16E
Ume r. Zimbabwe 56 17.00S 28.22E
Umeå Sweden 22 63.45N 20.20E
Umfors Sweden 22 65.56N 15.00E
Umfuli r. Zimbabwe 56 17.32S 29.23E
Umiat U.S.A. 72 69.25N152.20W
Umm-al-Qaywayn U.A.E. 43 25.32N 55.34E
Umm Badr Sudan 48 14.14N 27.57E
Umm Bel Sudan 49 13.32N 28.04E
Umm Durmān Sudan 48 15.37N 32.59E
Umm el Faḩm Israel 44 32.31N 35.09E
Umm Kuwaykah Sudan 49 12.49N 31.52E
Umm Lajj Saudi Arabia 42 25.03N 37.17E
Umm Qurayn Sudan 49 9.58N 28.55E
Umm Ruwābah Sudan 49 12.54N 31.13E
Umm Shalīl Sudan 49 10.51N 23.42E
Umm Shanqah Sudan 49 13.14N 27.14E
Umniati Zimbabwe 56 18.41S 29.45E
Umniati r. Zimbabwe 56 17.32S 29.23E
Umrer India 41 20.51N 79.20E
Umreth India 40 22.42N 73.07E
Umtata R.S.A. 56 31.35S 28.47E
Umuahia Nigeria 53 5.31N 7.26E
Umzimkulu R.S.A. 56 30.15S 29.56E
Umzimvubu R.S.A. 56 31.37S 29.32E
Una India 40 20.49N 71.02E
Una r. Yugo. 19 45.16N 16.55E
Unalakleet U.S.A. 72 63.53N160.47W
'Unayzah Jordan 44 30.29N 35.48E
'Unayzah Saudi Arabia 43 26.05N 43.57E
'Unayzah, Jabal mtn. Iraq 42 32.15N 39.19E
Uncia Bolivia 92 18.27S 66.37W
Uncompahgre Peak U.S.A. 80 38.04N107.28W
Uncompahgre Plateau f. U.S.A. 80 38.30N108.25W
Underberg R.S.A. 56 29.46S 29.26E
Underbool Australia 66 35.10S141.50E
Undu, C. Fiji 68 16.08S179.57W
Unecha U.S.S.R. 21 52.52N 32.42E
Ungarie Australia 67 33.38S147.00E
Ungava, Péninsule d' pen. Canada 73 60.00N 74.00W
Ungava B. Canada 73 59.00N 67.30W
Unggi N. Korea 31 42.19N130.24E
União Brazil 91 4.35S 42.52W
União da Vitória Brazil 94 26.13S 51.05W
Unimak I. U.S.A. 72 54.50N164.00W
Unini Peru 90 10.41S 73.59W
Union Miss U.S.A. 83 32.34N 89.14W
Union S.C. U.S.A. 85 34.42N 81.37W
Union City Tenn. U.S.A. 83 36.26N 89.03W
Uniondale R.S.A. 56 33.39S 23.07E
Union Gap U.S.A. 80 46.34N120.34W
Union of Soviet Socialist Republics Europe/Asia 21 50.00N 28.00E
Union Springs town U.S.A. 85 32.08N 85.44W
Uniontown U.S.A. 84 39.54N 79.44W
Unionville U.S.A. 82 40.29N 93.01W
United Arab Emirates Asia 43 24.00N 54.00E
United Kingdom Europe 9 55.00N 2.00W
United States of America N. America 78 39.00N100.00W
Unity Canada 75 52.27N109.10W
University Park town U.S.A. 81 32.17N106.45W
Unjha India 40 23.48N 72.24E
Unna W. Germany 14 51.32N 7.41E
Unnão India 41 26.32N 80.30E
Unst i. U.K. 12 60.45N 0.55W
Ünye Turkey 42 41.09N 37.15E
Upata Venezuela 90 8.02N 62.25W
Upemba, L. Zaïre 54 8.35S 26.28E
Upemba Nat. Park Zaïre 54 9.00S 26.30E
Upernavik Greenland 73 72.50N 56.00W
Upington R.S.A. 56 28.26S 21.12E
Upleta India 40 21.44N 70.17E
Upolu i. W. Samoa 68 13.55S171.45W
Upolu Pt. Hawaiian Is. 69 20.16N155.51W
Upper d. Ghana 52 10.30N 1.40W
Upper Arrow L. Canada 74 50.30N117.50W
Upper Egypt see Aş Şa'īd f. Egypt 42
Upper Hutt New Zealand 60 41.07S175.04E
Upper Klamath L. U.S.A. 80 42.23N122.55W
Upper Laberge Canada 74 60.54N135.12W
Upper Lough Erne N. Ireland 13 54.13N 7.32W
Upper Red L. U.S.A. 82 48.05N 94.50W
Upper Tean U.K. 10 52.57N 1.59W
Upper Volta Africa 52 12.30N 2.00W
Upper Yarra Dam Australia 67 37.43S145.56E
Uppsala Sweden 23 59.52N 17.38E
Uppsala d. Sweden 23 60.10N 17.50E
Upshi Jammu & Kashmir 41 33.50N 77.49E
Upton Canada 77 45.39N 72.41W
Upton U.S.A. 80 44.06N104.38W
Uqlat aş Şuqūr Saudi Arabia 42 25.50N 42.12E
Ur ruins Iraq 43 30.55N 46.07E
Uracoa Venezuela 90 9.03N 62.27W
Uraga-suido str. Japan 35 35.10N139.42E
Ural r. U.S.S.R. 25 47.00N 52.00E
Uralla Australia 67 30.40S151.31E
Ural Mts. see Uralskiy Khrebet mts. U.S.S.R. 24
Ural'sk U.S.S.R. 25 51.19N 51.20E
Uralskiy Khrebet mts. U.S.S.R. 24 60.00N 59.00E
Urana Australia 67 35.21S146.19E
Urana, L. Australia 67 35.21S146.19E
Urandangi Australia 64 21.36S138.18E
Uranium City Canada 75 59.28N108.40W
Uraricoera r. Brazil 90 3.10N 60.30W
Urawa Japan 35 35.51N139.39E
Uray U.S.S.R. 28 60.11N 65.00E
Urbana U.S.A. 82 40.07N 88.12W
Urbino Italy 18 43.43N 12.38E
Urcos Peru 90 13.40S 71.38W
Urda U.S.S.R. 25 48.44N 47.30E
Urdzhar U.S.S.R. 28 47.06N 81.33E

Ure to Villa de Santiago

Ure r. U.K. 10 54.05N 1.20W
Urechye U.S.S.R. 21 52.59N 27.50E
Uren U.S.S.R. 24 57.30N 45.50E
Urengoy U.S.S.R. 28 65.59N 78.30E
Ures Mexico 86 29.26N110.24W
Urfa Turkey 42 37.08N 38.45E
Ürgüp Turkey 42 38.39N 34.55E
Uribia Colombia 90 11.43N 72.16W
Urimbin Australia 66 28.15S143.46E
Urisino Australia 66 29.44S143.49E
Urjala Finland 23 61.05N 23.32E
Urk Neth. 14 52.40N 5.36E
Urlingford Rep. of Ire. 13 52.44N 7.35W
Urmia, L. see Daryācheh-ye Rezā'īyeh l. Iran 43
Urnograč Yugo. 20 45.10N 15.57E
Ursus Poland 21 52.12N 20.53E
Uruaçu Brazil 91 14.30S 49.10W
Uruapan Mexico 86 19.26N102.04W
Urubamba Peru 90 13.20S 72.07W
Urubamba r. Peru 90 10.43S 73.55W
Urucará Brazil 91 2.32S 57.45W
Uruçui Brazil 91 7.14S 44.33W
Uruguaiana Brazil 93 29.45S 57.05W
Uruguay r. Argentina / Uruguay 93 34.00S 58.30W
Uruguay S. America 94 33.15S 56.00W
Ürümqi China 30 43.43N 87.38E
Urun P.N.G. 64 8.36S147.15E
Urunga Australia 67 30.30S152.28E
Urup r. U.S.S.R. 25 44.59N 41.12E
Urzhum U.S.S.R. 24 57.08N 50.00E
Urziceni Romania 19 44.43N 26.38E
Usa r. U.S.S.R. 24 65.58N 56.35E
Uşak Turkey 42 38.42N 29.25E
Usakos Namibia 56 22.02S 15.35E
Usambara Mts. Tanzania 55 4.45S 38.25E
Ushant i. see Ouessant, Île d' i. France 17
Ush-Tobe U.S.S.R. 30 45.15N 77.59E
Ushuaia Argentina 93 54.47S 68.20W
Ushumun U.S.S.R. 29 52.48N126.27E
Usisya Malaŵi 55 11.10S 34.12E
Usk r. U.K. 11 51.34N 2.59W
Uskedal Norway 23 59.56N 5.52E
Üsküdar Turkey 19 41.00N 29.03E
Usman U.S.S.R. 25 52.02N 39.43E
Usovo U.S.S.R. 21 51.20N 28.01E
Uspenskiy U.S.S.R. 28 48.41N 72.43E
Ussuriysk U.S.S.R. 31 43.48N131.59E
Ustaoset Norway 23 60.30N 8.04E
Ustica i. Italy 18 38.42N 13.11E
Ust'-Ilga U.S.S.R. 29 54.59N105.00E
Ústí nad Labem Czech. 20 50.41N 14.00E
Ust Ishim U.S.S.R. 28 57.45N 71.05E
Ustka Poland 20 54.35N 16.50E
Ust'kamchatsk U.S.S.R. 29 56.14N162.28E
Ust-Kamenogorsk U.S.S.R. 28 50.00N 82.40E
Ust Kulom U.S.S.R. 24 61.34N 53.40E
Ust Kut U.S.S.R. 29 56.40N105.50E
Ust Lyzha U.S.S.R. 24 65.45N 56.38E
Ust'Maya U.S.S.R. 29 60.25N134.28E
Ust Nem U.S.S.R. 24 61.38N 54.50E
Ust Olenëk U.S.S.R. 29 72.59N120.00E
Ust-Omchug U.S.S.R. 29 61.08N149.38E
Ust Port U.S.S.R. 28 69.44N 84.23E
Ust Tapsuy U.S.S.R. 24 62.25N 61.42E
Ust'Tsilma U.S.S.R. 24 65.28N 53.09E
Ust-Tungir U.S.S.R. 29 55.25N120.15E
Ust Ura U.S.S.R. 24 63.06N 44.41E
Ust Vaga U.S.S.R. 24 62.42N 42.45E
Ust Vym U.S.S.R. 24 62.15N 50.25E
Ustyurt, Plato f. U.S.S.R. 25 43.30N 55.00E
Usu China 30 44.27N 84.37E
Usumacinta r. Mexico 86 18.22N 92.40W
U.S. Virgin Is. C. America 87 18.30N 65.00W
Ut U.S.S.R. 21 52.18N 31.10E
Utah d. U.S.A. 80 39.37N112.28W
Utah L. U.S.A. 80 40.13N111.49W
'Uta Vava'u Tonga 69 18.35S174.00W
'Utaybah, Buḥayrat al l. Syria 44 33.31N 36.37E
Utembo r. Angola 54 17.03S 22.00E
Utengule Tanzania 55 8.55S 35.43E
Utete Tanzania 55 8.00S 38.49E
Uthal Pakistan 40 25.48N 66.37E
Utiariti Brazil 90 13.02S 58.17W
Utica Kans. U.S.A. 82 38.39N100.10W
Utica N.Y. U.S.A. 84 43.05N 75.14W
Utiel Spain 16 39.33N 1.13W
Utikuma L. Canada 74 55.50N115.30W
Utopia Australia 64 22.14S134.33E
Utraula India 41 27.19N 82.25E
Utrecht Neth. 14 52.04N 5.07E
Utrecht d. Neth. 14 52.04N 5.10E
Utrecht R.S.A. 56 27.38S 30.19E
Utrera Spain 16 37.10N 5.47W
Utsjoki Finland 22 69.53N 27.00E
Utsunomiya Japan 31 36.33N139.52E
Utta U.S.S.R. 25 46.24N 46.01E
Uttaradit Thailand 34 17.38N100.05E
Uttarkāshi India 41 30.44N 78.27E
Uttar Pradesh d. India 41 26.30N 81.30E
Uturoa Îs. de la Société 69 16.44S151.25W
Uummannarsuaq see Farvel, Kap c. Greenland 73
Uusikaupunki Finland 23 60.48N 21.25E
Uusimaa d. Finland 23 60.30N 25.00E
Uvalde U.S.A. 83 29.13N 99.47W
Uvarovichi U.S.S.R. 21 52.35N 30.44E
Uvat U.S.S.R. 28 59.10N 68.49E
Uvéa, Île i. N. Cal. 68 20.30S166.35E
Uvinza Tanzania 55 5.08S 30.23E
Uvira Zaïre 55 3.22S 29.06E
Uvs Nuur l. Mongolia 30 50.30N 92.30E
Uwajima Japan 31 33.13N132.32E
Uwayl Sudan 49 8.46N 27.24E
'Uwaynāt, Jabal al mtn. Libya / Sudan 48 21.54N 24.58E
Uxin Qi China 32 38.30N108.53E
Uyo Nigeria 53 5.01N 7.56E
Uyuni Bolivia 92 20.28S 66.50W
Uyuni, Salar de f. Bolivia 92 20.20S 67.42W
Uzbekskaya S.S.R. d. U.S.S.R. 28 42.00N 63.00E
Uzda U.S.S.R. 21 53.28N 27.11E
Uzh r. U.S.S.R. 21 51.15N 30.12E
Uzhgorod U.S.S.R. 21 48.38N 22.15E

V

Vaagö i. Faroe Is. 8 62.03N 7.14W
Vaal r. R.S.A. 56 29.04S 23.37E
Vaala Finland 22 64.26N 26.48E
Vaal Dam R.S.A. 56 26.51S 28.08E
Vaasa Finland 22 63.06N 21.36E
Vaasa d. Finland 22 62.50N 22.50E
Vác Hungary 21 47.49N 19.10E
Vadodara India 38 22.19N 73.14E
Vado Ligure Italy 15 44.17N 8.27E
Vadsö Norway 22 70.05N 29.46E
Vaduz Liech. 20 47.08N 9.32E
Vaeröy i. Norway 22 67.40N 12.40E
Vaga r. U.S.S.R. 24 62.45N 42.48E
Vågåmo Norway 23 61.53N 9.06E
Vaggeryd Sweden 23 57.30N 14.07E
Váh r. Czech. 21 47.40N 17.50E
Vahsel B. Antarctica 96 77.00S 38.00W
Vaiea Niue 68 19.08S169.53W
Vaihu I. de Pascua 69 27.10S109.22W
Vaijāpur India 40 19.55N 74.44E
Vailly-sur-Aisne France 15 49.25N 3.31E
Vairao Tahiti 69 17.48S149.17W
Vaitupu i. Tuvalu 68 7.28S178.41E
Vakaga C.A.R. 49 9.50N 22.30E
Vakarai Sri Lanka 39 8.08N 81.26E
Vålådalen Sweden 22 63.09N 13.00E
Valavsk U.S.S.R. 21 51.40N 28.38E
Valcheta Argentina 93 40.40S 66.10W
Valdagno Italy 15 45.39N 11.18E
Valday U.S.S.R. 24 57.59N 33.10E
Valdayskaya Vozvyshennost mts. U.S.S.R. 24 57.10N 33.00E
Valdemārpils U.S.S.R. 23 57.22N 22.35E
Valdemarsvik Sweden 23 58.12N 16.36E
Valdepeñas Spain 16 38.46N 3.24W
Valdés, Pen. Argentina 93 42.30S 64.00W
Val des Bois Canada 77 45.54N 75.35W
Valdez U.S.A. 72 61.07N146.17W
Val d'Isère France 15 45.27N 6.59E
Valdivia Chile 93 39.46S 73.15W
Val d'Oise d. France 15 49.10N 2.10E
Val d'Or town Canada 76 48.07N 77.47W
Valdosta U.S.A. 85 30.51N 83.51W
Valença Bahia Brazil 91 13.22S 39.06W
Valença R. de Janeiro Brazil 94 22.14S 43.45W
Valença Portugal 16 42.02N 8.38W
Valence France 17 44.56N 4.54E
Valencia Spain 16 39.29N 0.24W
Valencia d. Spain 16 39.30N 0.40W
Valencia Venezuela 90 10.14N 67.59W
Valencia, Golfo de g. Spain 16 39.38N 0.20W
Valencia de Alcántara Spain 16 39.25N 7.14
Valenciennes France 14 50.22N 3.32E
Valentine Nebr. U.S.A. 82 42.52N100.30W
Valentine N.Mex. U.S.A. 81 30.34N104.29W
Vale of Evesham f. U.K. 11 52.05N 1.55W
Vale of Pewsey f. U.K. 11 51.21N 1.45W
Vale of York f. U.K. 10 54.12N 1.25W
Valera Venezuela 90 9.21N 70.38W
Valga U.S.S.R. 24 57.44N 26.00E
Valinco, Golfe de g. France 17 41.40N 8.50E
Valjevo Yugo. 21 44.16N 19.56E
Valkeakoski Finland 23 61.16N 24.02E
Valkenswaard Neth. 14 51.21N 5.27E
Valladolid Mexico 87 20.41N 88.12W
Valladolid Spain 16 41.39N 4.45W
Vall de Uxó town Spain 16 39.49N 0.15W
Valle Norway 23 59.12N 7.32E
Valle d'Aosta d. Italy 15 45.45N 7.25E
Valle de la Pascua Venezuela 90 9.15N 66.00W
Valledupar Colombia 90 10.31N 73.16W
Valle Edén Uruguay 93 31.50S 56.09W
Vallegrande Bolivia 92 18.29S 64.06W
Valle Hermoso Mexico 83 25.39N 97.52W
Vallenar Chile 92 28.35S 70.46W
Valletta Malta 18 35.53N 14.31E
Valley City U.S.A. 82 46.57N 97.58W
Valley Falls town U.S.A. 80 42.29N120.16W
Valleyfield Canada 77 45.15N 74.08W
Valley Stream town U.S.A. 85 40.40N 73.42W
Valleyview Canada 74 55.04N117.17W
Vallgrund i. Finland 22 63.12N 21.14E
Valls Spain 16 41.18N 1.15E
Val Marie Canada 75 49.14N107.44W
Valmiera U.S.S.R. 24 57.32N 25.29E
Valnera mtn. Spain 16 43.10N 3.40W
Valognes France 15 49.31N 1.28W
Valparaíso Chile 93 33.02S 71.38W
Valparaíso Mexico 86 22.46N103.34W
Valparaiso U.S.A. 85 30.30N 86.31W
Vals, Tanjung c. Indonesia 37 8.30S137.30E
Valverde Dom. Rep. 87 19.37N 71.04W
Valverde del Camino Spain 16 37.35N 6.45W
Vammala Finland 23 61.20N 22.54E
Vamsadhāra r. India 41 18.21N 84.08E
Van Turkey 42 38.28N 43.20E
Van Blommestein Meer, W.J. resr. Surinam 91 4.45N 55.05W
Van Buren Ark. U.S.A. 83 35.26N 94.21W
Van Buren Mo. U.S.A. 83 37.00N 91.01W
Vancouver Canada 74 49.20N123.10W
Vancouver U.S.A. 80 45.39N122.40W
Vancouver I. Canada 74 49.45N126.00W
Vandalia Ill. U.S.A. 82 38.58N 89.06W
Vandalia Mo. U.S.A. 82 39.19N 91.29W
Vanderbilt U.S.A. 84 45.09N 84.39W
Vanderlin I. Australia 64 15.44S137.02E
Van Diemen, C. Australia 64 16.31S139.41E
Van Diemen G. Australia 64 11.50S132.00E
Vandry Canada 77 47.50N 73.34W
Vänern l. Sweden 23 59.00N 13.15E
Vänersborg Sweden 23 58.22N 12.19E
Vang Norway 23 61.10N 8.40E
Vanga Kenya 55 4.37S 39.13E
Vangaindrano Madagascar 57 23.21S 47.36E
Van Gölü l. Turkey 42 38.35N 42.52E
Vanier Canada 77 45.26N 75.40W
Vanimo P.N.G. 37 2.40S141.17E
Vankarem U.S.S.R. 29 67.50N175.51E
Vankleek Hill town Canada 77 45.31N 74.39W
Vanna i. Norway 22 70.10N 19.40E
Vännäs Sweden 22 63.58N 19.48E
Vannes France 17 47.40N 2.44W
Vanrhynsdorp R.S.A. 56 31.37S 18.42E
Vansbro Sweden 23 60.31N 14.13E
Vantaa Finland 23 60.13N 25.01E
Van Tassell U.S.A. 80 42.40N104.02W
Vanthali India 40 21.29N 70.20E
Vanua Levu i. Fiji 68 16.33S179.15E
Vanua Mbalavu i. Fiji 68 17.40S178.57W
Vanuatu Pacific Oc. 68 16.00S167.00E
Van Wert U.S.A. 84 40.53N 84.36W
Vanzylsrus R.S.A. 56 26.51S 22.03E
Vapnyarka U.S.S.R. 21 48.31N 28.44E
Var r. France 20 43.39N 7.11E
Varades France 15 47.23N 1.02W
Varallo Italy 15 45.49N 8.15E
Varāmīn Iran 43 35.20N 51.39E
Vārānasi India 41 25.20N 83.00E
Varangerfjorden est. Norway 22 70.00N 30.00E
Varangerhalvöya pen. Norway 22 70.25N 29.30E
Varaždin Yugo. 18 46.18N 16.20E
Varazze Italy 15 44.22N 8.34E
Varberg Sweden 23 57.06N 12.15E
Vardak d. Afghan. 40 34.15N 68.30E
Vardar r. Yugo. see Axiós r. Greece 19
Varde Denmark 23 55.38N 8.29E
Varel W. Germany 14 53.24N 8.08E
Varennes France 17 46.19N 3.24E
Varennes Canada 77 45.41N 73.26W
Varese Italy 15 45.48N 8.48E
Varese Ligure Italy 15 44.22N 9.37E
Varginha Brazil 94 21.33S 45.25W
Varkhān r. Afghan. 40 32.55N 65.30E
Värmland d. Sweden 23 59.55N 13.00E
Varna Bulgaria 21 43.13N 27.57E
Värnamo Sweden 23 57.11N 14.02E
Várpalota Hungary 21 47.12N 18.09E
Vartofta Sweden 23 58.06N 13.40E
Varzo Italy 15 46.12N 8.15E
Varzy France 15 47.21N 3.23E
Vasa see Vaasa Finland 22
Vasai India 40 19.21N 72.48E
Vascongadas y Navarra d. Spain 16 43.00N 2.45W
Vashka r. U.S.S.R. 24 64.55N 45.50E
Vasilkov U.S.S.R. 21 50.12N 30.15E
Vaslui Romania 21 46.38N 27.44E
Västerås Sweden 23 59.37N 16.33E
Västerbotten d. Sweden 22 64.50N 18.10E
Västerdal r. Sweden 23 60.33N 15.08E
Västernorrland d. Sweden 22 63.20N 17.30E
Västervik Sweden 23 57.45N 16.38E
Västmanland d. Sweden 23 59.50N 16.15E
Vasto Italy 18 42.07N 14.42E
Vatan France 17 47.05N 1.48E
Vatiua Mozambique 57 14.15S 37.22E
Vatnajökull mts. Iceland 22 64.20N 17.00W
Vatneyri Iceland 22 65.36N 23.59W
Vatomandry Madagascar 57 19.20S 48.59E
Vatra Dornei Romania 21 47.21N 25.21E
Vättern l. Sweden 23 58.30N 14.30E
Vaughan Canada 76 43.50N 79.32W
Vaughn Mont. U.S.A. 80 47.35N111.34W
Vaughn N.Mex. U.S.A. 81 34.36N105.13W
Vaupés r. Colombia 90 0.20N 69.00W
Vava'u Group is. Tonga 69 18.40S174.00W
Vavuniya Sri Lanka 39 8.45N 80.30E
Växjö Sweden 23 56.52N 14.49E
Vaygach U.S.S.R. 28 70.28N 58.59E
Vaygach, Ostrov i. U.S.S.R. 24 70.00N 59.00E
Vecht r. Neth. 14 52.39N 6.01E
Vecsés Hungary 21 47.26N 19.19E
Veddige Sweden 23 57.16N 12.19E
Veendam Neth. 14 53.08N 6.52E
Veenendaal Neth. 14 52.03N 5.32E
Vega i. Norway 22 65.39N 11.50E
Vega U.S.A. 83 35.15N102.26W
Veghel Neth. 14 51.37N 5.35E
Vegreville Canada 74 53.30N112.05W
Veinticinco de Mayo Argentina 93 35.25S 60.11W
Vejen Denmark 23 55.29N 9.09E
Vejer Spain 16 36.15N 5.59W
Vejle Denmark 23 55.42N 9.32E
Velddrif R.S.A. 56 32.47S 18.09E
Vélez Málaga Spain 16 36.48N 4.05W
Vélez Rubio Spain 16 37.41N 2.05W
Velhas r. Brazil 94 17.20S 44.55W
Velikiye-Luki U.S.S.R. 24 56.19N 30.31E
Velikiy Ustyug U.S.S.R. 24 60.48N 45.15E
Veliko Tŭrnovo Bulgaria 19 43.04N 25.39E
Velizh U.S.S.R. 24 55.36N 31.13E
Velletri Italy 18 41.41N 12.47E
Vellore India 39 12.56N 79.09E
Velsen Neth. 14 52.28N 4.39E
Velsk U.S.S.R. 24 61.05N 42.06E
Veluwe f. Neth. 14 52.17N 5.45E
Vemdalen Sweden 22 62.29N 13.55E
Venado Tuerto Argentina 93 33.45S 61.56W
Venaria Italy 15 45.08N 7.38E
Vence France 15 43.43N 7.07E
Vendas Novas Portugal 16 38.41N 8.27W
Vendeuvre-sur-Barse France 15 48.14N 4.28E
Vendôme France 15 47.48N 1.04E
Veneto d. Italy 15 45.25N 11.50E
Venev U.S.S.R. 24 54.22N 38.15E
Venezia Italy 15 45.26N 12.20E
Venezuela S. America 90 7.00N 65.20W
Venezuela, Golfo de g. Venezuela 90 11.30N 71.00W
Venezuelan Basin f. Carib. Sea. 95 14.30N 68.00W
Vengurla India 38 15.52N 73.38E
Veniaminof Mtn. U.S.A. 72 56.05N159.20W
Venice see Venezia Italy 15
Venice U.S.A. 85 27.05N 82.26W
Venice, G. of Med. Sea 20 45.20N 13.00E
Venlo Neth. 14 51.22N 6.10E
Venraij Neth. 14 51.32N 5.58E
Vent, Îles du is. Îs. de la Société 69 17.30S149.30W
Venta r. U.S.S.R. 23 57.24N 21.33E
Ventersdorp R.S.A. 56 26.19S 26.48E
Ventimiglia Italy 15 43.47N 7.36E
Ventnor U.K. 11 50.35N 1.12W
Ventspils U.S.S.R. 23 57.24N 21.36E
Ventuari r. Venezuela 90 4.00N 67.35W
Venus B. Australia 67 38.40S145.43E
Vera Argentina 94 29.31S 60.30W
Vera Spain 16 37.15N 1.51W
Veracruz Mexico 86 19.11N 96.10W
Veracruz d. Mexico 86 18.00N 95.00W
Verāval India 40 20.54N 70.22E
Verbania Italy 15 45.56N 8.33E
Vercelli Italy 15 45.19N 8.26E
Verde r. Argentina 93 42.10S 65.03W
Verde r. Brazil 92 19.11S 50.44W
Verden W. Germany 20 52.55N 9.13E
Verdon r. France 17 43.42N 5.39E
Verdun Canada 77 45.28N 73.35W
Verdun Meuse France 17 49.10N 5.24E
Vereeniging R.S.A. 56 26.40S 27.55E
Vergelee R.S.A. 56 25.46S 24.09E
Verín Spain 16 41.55N 7.26W
Verkhniy Baskunchak U.S.S.R. 25 48.14N 46.44E
Verkhniy Lyulyukary U.S.S.R. 24 65.45N 64.28E
Verkhniy Shar U.S.S.R. 24 68.21N 50.45E
Verkhniy Ufaley U.S.S.R. 24 56.05N 60.14E
Verkhnyaya Taymyra r. U.S.S.R. 29 74.10N 99.50E
Verkhnyaya Tura U.S.S.R. 24 58.22N 59.50E
Verkhovye U.S.S.R. 24 52.49N 37.14E
Verkhoyansk U.S.S.R. 29 67.25N133.25E
Verkhoyanskiy Khrebet mts. U.S.S.R. 29 66.00N130.00E
Vermenton France 15 47.40N 3.42E
Vermilion Canada 75 53.22N110.51W
Vermilion U.S.A. 84 41.24N 82.21W
Vermilion Bay town Canada 76 49.51N 93.24W
Vermilion Chutes Canada 74 58.22N114.51W
Vermillion U.S.A. 82 42.48N 96.55W
Vermont d. U.S.A. 84 43.50N 72.45W
Vernal U.S.A. 80 40.27N109.32W
Verneuil France 15 48.44N 0.56E
Vernon Canada 74 50.20N119.15W
Vernon France 15 49.05N 1.29E
Vernon U.S.A. 83 34.09N 99.17W
Vero Beach town U.S.A. 85 27.39N 80.24W
Véroia Greece 19 40.31N 22.12E
Verona Italy 15 45.27N 10.59E
Verónica Argentina 93 35.24S 57.22W
Verrès Italy 15 45.40N 7.42E
Versailles France 15 48.48N 2.08E
Versailles U.S.A. 85 38.02N 84.45W
Vert, Cap c. Senegal 52 14.45N 17.25W
Vertou France 17 47.10N 1.28W
Vertus France 15 48.54N 4.00E
Verviers Belgium 14 50.36N 5.52E
Vervins France 15 49.50N 3.54E
Vesanto Finland 22 62.56N 26.25E
Veselí nad Lužnicí Czech. 20 49.11N 14.43E
Vesle r. France 15 49.23N 3.38E
Vesoul France 20 47.38N 6.09E
Vest-Agder d. Norway 23 58.30N 7.10E
Vestfjorden est. Norway 22 68.10N 15.00E
Vestfold d. Norway 23 59.20N 10.10E
Vestmanhavn Faroe Is. 8 62.09N 7.11W
Vestmannaeyjar is. Iceland 22 63.30N 20.20W
Vestvågöy i. Norway 22 68.10N 13.50E
Vesuvio mtn. Italy 18 40.48N 14.25E
Vesyegonsk U.S.S.R. 24 58.38N 37.19E
Veszprém Hungary 21 47.06N 17.55E
Vésztő Hungary 21 46.55N 21.16E
Vetka U.S.S.R. 21 52.35N 31.13E
Vetlanda Sweden 23 57.26N 15.04E
Vetluga U.S.S.R. 24 57.50N 45.42E
Vetluga r. U.S.S.R. 24 56.18N 46.19E
Vettore, Monte mtn. Italy 18 42.50N 13.18E
Veurne Belgium 14 51.04N 2.40E
Vevelstad Norway 22 65.43N 12.30E
Vézelise France 17 48.29N 6.05E
Vézère r. France 17 44.53N 0.55E
Vezhen mtn. Bulgaria 19 42.45N 24.22E
Viacha Bolivia 90 16.40S 68.17W
Viadana Italy 15 44.56N 10.31E
Viana Brazil 91 3.13S 45.00W
Viana Portugal 16 38.20N 8.00W
Viana do Castelo Portugal 16 41.41N 8.50W
Viangchan Laos 34 17.59N102.38E
Viar r. Spain 16 37.45N 5.54W
Viareggio Italy 15 43.52N 10.14E
Viborg Denmark 23 56.26N 9.24E
Vibo Valentia Italy 18 38.40N 16.06E
Vibraye France 15 48.03N 0.44E
Vicente López Argentina 93 34.32S 58.29W
Vicenza Italy 15 45.33N 11.32E
Vich Spain 16 41.56N 2.16E
Vichada r. Colombia 90 4.58N 67.35W
Vichuga U.S.S.R. 24 57.12N 41.50E
Vichy France 17 46.07N 3.25E
Vicksburg U.S.A. 83 32.14N 90.56W
Viçosa Alagoas Brazil 91 9.22S 36.10W
Viçosa Minas Gerais Brazil 94 20.45S 42.53W
Victor Harbour Australia 66 35.36S138.35E
Victoria Argentina 93 32.40S 60.10W
Victoria d. Australia 67 37.20S145.00E
Victoria r. Australia 62 15.12S129.43E
Victoria Canada 74 48.30N123.25W
Victoria Chile 93 38.13S 72.20W
Victoria Guinea 52 10.50N 14.32W
Victoria U.S.A. 83 28.48N 97.00W
Victoria, L. Africa 55 1.00S 33.00E
Victoria, L. Australia 66 34.00S141.15E
Victoria, Mt. Burma 34 21.12N 93.55E
Victoria, Mt. P.N.G. 64 8.55S147.35E
Victoria Beach town Canada 75 50.43N 96.33W
Victoria de las Tunas Cuba 87 20.58N 76.59W
Victoria Downs town Australia 64 20.44S146.21E
Victoria Falls f. Zimbabwe / Zambia 56 17.58S 25.45E
Victoria I. Canada 72 71.00N110.00W
Victoria L. Australia 66 32.29S143.22E
Victoria Nile r. Uganda 55 2.14N 31.20E
Victoria River Downs town Australia 64 16.24S131.00E
Victoriaville Canada 77 46.03N 71.58W
Victoria West R.S.A. 56 31.24S 23.07E
Victorica Argentina 93 36.15S 65.25W
Vidalia U.S.A. 85 32.14N 82.24W
Videle Romania 21 44.16N 25.31E
Viderö i. Faroe Is. 8 62.21N 6.30W
Vidin Bulgaria 21 43.58N 22.51E
Vidisha India 41 23.32N 77.49E
Viedma Argentina 93 40.50S 63.00W
Viedma, L. Argentina 93 49.40S 72.30W
Vienna see Wien Austria 20
Vienna Md. U.S.A. 85 38.29N 75.49W
Vienna S.Dak. U.S.A. 82 44.42N 97.30W
Vienna Va. U.S.A. 85 38.54N 77.16W
Vienne France 17 45.32N 4.54E
Vienne r. France 17 47.13N 0.05W
Vientiane see Viangchan Laos 34
Vieques i. Puerto Rico 87 18.08N 65.30W
Viersen W. Germany 14 51.16N 6.22E
Vierwaldstätter See l. Switz. 20 47.10N 8.50E
Vierzon France 15 47.14N 2.03E
Vietnam Asia 34 15.00N108.30E
Viet Tri Vietnam 33 21.20N105.26E
Vieux-Condé France 14 50.29N 3.31E
Vigan Phil. 37 17.35N120.23E
Vigevano Italy 15 45.19N 8.51E
Vignemale, Pic de mtn. France 17 42.46N 0.08W
Vigo Spain 16 42.15N 8.44W
Vigrestad Norway 23 58.34N 5.42E
Vihāri Pakistan 40 30.02N 72.21E
Vihowa Pakistan 40 31.08N 70.30E
Vijāpur India 40 23.35N 72.45E
Vijayawāda India 39 16.34N 80.40E
Vijosë r. Albania 19 40.39N 19.20E
Vik Norway 22 65.19N 12.10E
Vikajärvi Finland 22 66.37N 26.12E
Vikersund Norway 23 59.59N 10.02E
Vikna i. Norway 22 64.52N 10.57E
Vikulovo U.S.S.R. 28 56.51N 70.30E
Vila Vanuatu 68 17.44S168.19E
Vila da Maganja Mozambique 55 17.25S 37.32E
Vila de Sena Mozambique 55 17.36S 35.00E
Vila Franca Portugal 16 38.57N 8.59W
Vilaine r. France 17 47.30N 2.25W
Vilanculos Mozambique 57 21.59S 35.16E
Vila Nova do Seles Angola 54 11.24S 14.15E
Vila Real Portugal 16 41.17N 7.45W
Vila Real de Santo António Portugal 16 37.12N 7.25W
Vila Vasco da Gama Mozambique 55 14.55S 32.12E
Vila Velha Brazil 94 20.20S 40.17W
Vila Verissimo Sarmento Angola 54 8.08S 20.38E
Vileyka U.S.S.R. 21 54.30N 26.50E
Vilhelmina Sweden 22 64.37N 16.39E
Vilhena Brazil 90 12.40S 60.08W
Viliga Kushka U.S.S.R. 29 61.35N156.55E
Viljandi U.S.S.R. 24 58.22N 25.30E
Vilkavišhkis U.S.S.R. 21 54.39N 23.02E
Vil'kitskogo, Proliv str. U.S.S.R. 29 77.57N102.30E
Vilkovo U.S.S.R. 21 45.28N 29.32E
Villa Angela Argentina 92 27.34S 60.45W
Villa Bella Bolivia 92 10.23S 65.24W
Villablino Spain 16 42.57N 6.19W
Villacañas Spain 16 39.38N 3.20W
Villach Austria 20 46.37N 13.51E
Villa Clara Argentina 93 31.46S 58.50W
Villa Constitución Argentina 93 33.14S 60.21W
Villa de Santiago Mexico 83 25.26N100.09W

Villa Dolores to Waynesboro

Villa Dolores Argentina 92 31.58S 65.12W
Villafranca di Verona Italy 15 45.21N 10.50E
Villagarcía Spain 16 42.35N 8.45W
Villaguay Argentina 93 31.55S 59.00W
Villahermosa Mexico 86 18.00N 92.53W
Villa Hernandarias Argentina 93 31.15S 59.58W
Villa Huidobro Argentina 93 34.50S 64.34W
Villaines-la-Juhel France 15 48.21N 0.17W
Villajoyosa Spain 16 38.31N 0.14W
Villalba Spain 16 43.18N 7.41W
Villa María Argentina 92 32.25S 63.15W
Villa Montes Bolivia 92 21.15S 63.30W
Villanueva de la Serena Spain 16 38.58N 5.48W
Villanueva-y-Geltrú Spain 16 41.13N 1.43E
Villaputzu Italy 18 39.28N 9.35E
Villarrica Chile 93 39.15S 72.15W
Villarrica Paraguay 94 25.45S 56.28W
Villarrobledo Spain 16 39.16N 2.36W
Villa San José Argentina 93 32.12S 58.15W
Villasayas Spain 16 41.24N 2.39W
Villavicencio Colombia 90 4.09N 73.38W
Villaviciosa Spain 16 43.29N 5.26W
Villazón Bolivia 92 22.06S 65.36W
Villedieu France 15 48.50N 1.13W
Villefranche France 17 46.00N 4.43E
Villena Spain 16 38.39N 0.52W
Villenauxe-la-Grande France 15 48.35N 3.33E
Villeneuve France 17 44.25N 0.43E
Villeneuve d'Ascq France 14 50.37N 3.10E
Villeneuve-St. Georges France 15 48.44N 2.27E
Villeneuve-sur-Yonne France 15 48.05N 3.18E
Villers-Bocage France 15 49.05N 0.39W
Villers-Cotterêts France 15 49.15N 3.04E
Villers-sur-Mer France 15 49.21N 0.02W
Villeurbanne France 20 45.46N 4.54E
Vilnius U.S.S.R. 21 54.40N 25.19E
Vilvoorde Belgium 14 50.56N 4.25E
Vilyuy r. U.S.S.R. 29 64.20N 126.55E
Vilyuysk U.S.S.R. 29 63.46N 121.35E
Vimianzo Spain 16 43.07N 9.02W
Vimmerby Sweden 23 57.40N 15.51E
Vimoutiers France 15 48.55N 0.12E
Vina r. Chad 53 7.43N 15.30E
Viña del Mar Chile 93 33.02S 71.34W
Vinaroz Spain 16 40.30N 0.27E
Vincennes France 15 48.51N 2.26E
Vincennes U.S.A. 82 38.41N 87.32W
Vindel r. Sweden 22 63.54N 19.52E
Vindeln Sweden 22 64.12N 19.44E
Vinderup Denmark 23 56.29N 8.47E
Vindhya Range mts. India 40 22.45N 75.30E
Vineland U.S.A. 85 39.29N 75.02W
Vingåker Sweden 23 59.02N 15.52E
Vinh Vietnam 34 18.42N 105.41E
Vinh Long Vietnam 34 10.15N 105.59E
Vinita U.S.A. 83 36.39N 95.09W
Vinju Mare Romania 21 44.26N 22.52E
Vinkovci Yugo. 19 45.17N 18.38E
Vinnitsa U.S.S.R. 21 49.11N 28.30E
Vinson Massif Antarctica 96 78.00S 85.00W
Vintar Phil. 33 18.16N 120.40E
Vinton U.S.A. 82 42.10N 92.01W
Vioolsdrif R.S.A. 56 28.45S 17.33E
Vipava Yugo. 20 45.51N 13.58E
Viqueque Indonesia 37 8.42S 126.30E
Virac Phil. 37 13.35N 124.15E
Viramgām India 40 23.07N 72.02E
Viranşehir Turkey 42 37.13N 39.45E
Virden Canada 75 49.51N 100.55W
Vire France 17 48.50N 0.53W
Vire r. France 15 49.20N 0.53W
Vírgenes, C. Argentina 93 52.00S 68.50W
Virgin Gorda i. B.V.Is. 87 18.30N 64.26W
Virginia U.S.A. 82 47.31N 92.32W
Virginia d. U.S.A. 85 37.30N 78.45W
Virginia Beach town U.S.A. 85 36.51N 75.59W
Virginia City Mont. U.S.A. 80 45.18N 111.56W
Virginia City Nev. U.S.A. 80 39.19N 119.39W
Virovitica Yugo. 21 45.51N 17.23E
Virrat Finland 22 62.14N 23.47E
Virserum Sweden 23 57.19N 15.35E
Virton Belgium 14 49.35N 5.32E
Virtsu U.S.S.R. 23 58.34N 23.31E
Virunga Nat. Park Zaïre 55 0.30S 29.15E
Vis Yugo. 18 43.03N 16.21E
Vis i. Yugo. 18 43.03N 16.10E
Visalia U.S.A. 81 36.20N 119.18W
Visayan Sea Phil. 37 11.35N 123.51E
Visby Sweden 23 57.38N 18.18E
Visconde do Rio Branco Brazil 94 21.00S 42.51W
Viscount Melville Sd. Canada 72 74.30N 104.00W
Visé Belgium 14 50.44N 5.42E
Višegrad Yugo. 19 43.47N 19.20E
Viseu Brazil 91 1.12S 46.07W
Viseu Portugal 16 40.40N 7.55W
Viseu de Sus Romania 21 47.44N 24.22E
Vishākhapatnam India 39 17.42N 83.24E
Visnagar India 40 23.42N 72.33E
Viso, Monte mtn. Italy 15 44.38N 7.05E
Visp Switz. 15 46.18N 7.53E
Vista U.S.A. 81 33.12N 117.15W
Vistula r. see Wisła r. Poland 21
Vitarte Peru 90 12.03S 76.51W
Vitebsk U.S.S.R. 24 55.10N 30.14E
Viterbo Italy 18 42.26N 12.07E
Viti Levu i. Fiji 68 18.00S 178.00E
Vitim U.S.S.R. 29 59.28N 112.35E
Vitim r. U.S.S.R. 29 59.30N 112.36E
Vitória Espírito Santo Brazil 94 20.19S 40.21W
Vitoria Spain 16 42.51N 2.40W
Vitória da Conquista Brazil 91 14.53S 40.52W
Vitré France 15 48.07N 1.12W
Vitry-le-François France 15 48.44N 4.35E
Vitteaux France 15 47.24N 4.30E
Vittoria Italy 18 36.57N 14.21E
Vittorio Veneto Italy 15 45.59N 12.18E
Vivonne Australia 66 35.58S 137.10E
Vivonne B. Australia 66 36.00S 137.00E
Vizcaíno, Desierto de des. Mexico 81 27.40N 114.40W
Vizcaíno, Sierra mts. Mexico 81 27.20N 114.30W
Vizianagaram India 39 18.07N 83.30E
Vizinga U.S.S.R. 24 61.06N 50.05E
Vlaardingen Neth. 14 51.55N 4.20E
Vladimir U.S.S.R. 24 56.08N 40.25E
Vladimirets U.S.S.R. 21 51.28N 26.03E
Vladimir Volynskiy U.S.S.R. 21 50.51N 24.19E
Vladivostok U.S.S.R. 31 43.09N 131.53E
Vlasenica Yugo. 21 44.11N 18.56E
Vlieland i. Neth. 14 53.15N 5.00E
Vlissingen Neth. 14 51.27N 3.35E
Vlorë Albania 19 40.28N 19.27E
Vltava r. Czech. 20 50.22N 14.28E
Voerde W. Germany 14 51.37N 6.39E
Vogelkop f. see Jazirah Doberai f. Indonesia 37
Voghera Italy 15 44.59N 9.01E
Voh N. Cal. 68 20.58S 164.42E
Vohibinany Madagascar 57 18.49S 49.04E
Vohimarina Madagascar 57 13.21S 50.02E
Vohipeno Madagascar 57 22.22S 47.51E
Voi Kenya 55 3.23S 38.35E
Voiron France 17 45.22N 5.35E
Volborg U.S.A. 80 45.50N 105.40W
Volcano Is. Japan 68 25.00N 141.00E
Volda Norway 23 62.09N 6.06E
Volga r. U.S.S.R. 25 45.45N 47.50E
Volgograd U.S.S.R. 25 48.45N 44.30E
Volgogradskoye Vodokhranilishche resr. U.S.S.R. 25 51.00N 46.05E
Volkhov U.S.S.R. 24 59.54N 32.47E
Volkhov r. U.S.S.R. 24 60.15N 32.15E
Völklingen W. Germany 20 49.15N 6.50E
Volkovysk U.S.S.R. 21 53.10N 24.28E
Vollenhove Neth. 14 52.41N 5.59E
Volnovakha U.S.S.R. 25 47.36N 37.32E
Volochanka U.S.S.R. 29 70.59N 94.18E
Volochisk U.S.S.R. 21 49.34N 26.10E
Volodarsk U.S.S.R. 24 56.14N 43.10E
Vologda U.S.S.R. 24 59.10N 39.55E
Volokolamsk U.S.S.R. 24 56.02N 35.56E
Vólos Greece 19 39.22N 22.57E
Volovets U.S.S.R. 21 48.44N 23.14E
Volsk U.S.S.R. 24 52.04N 47.22E
Volta d. Ghana 52 7.30N 0.25E
Volta r. Ghana 52 5.50N 0.41E
Volta, L. Ghana 52 7.00N 0.00
Volta Blanche r. U. Volta see White Volta r. Ghana 52
Volta Noire r. U. Volta see Black Volta r. Ghana 52
Volta-Noire d. U. Volta 52 12.30N 3.25W
Volta Redonda Brazil 94 22.31S 44.05W
Volta Rouge r. U. Volta see Red Volta r. Ghana 52
Volterra Italy 18 43.24N 10.51E
Voltri Italy 15 44.26N 8.45E
Volturno r. Italy 18 41.02N 13.56E
Volzhskiy U.S.S.R. 25 48.48N 44.45E
Vondrozo Madagascar 57 22.49S 47.20E
Voorburg Neth. 14 52.05N 4.22E
Vopnafjördhur est. Iceland 22 65.50N 14.30W
Vopnafjördhur town Iceland 22 65.46N 14.50W
Vorarlberg d. Austria 20 47.15N 9.55E
Vordingborg Denmark 23 55.01N 11.55E
Voríai Sporádhes is. Greece 19 39.00N 24.00E
Vorkuta U.S.S.R. 24 67.27N 64.00E
Vormsi i. U.S.S.R. 23 59.00N 23.20E
Voronezh U.S.S.R. 25 51.40N 39.13E
Voronovo U.S.S.R. 21 54.09N 25.19E
Voroshilovgrad U.S.S.R. 25 48.35N 39.20E
Vosges mts. France 20 48.10N 7.00E
Voss Norway 23 60.39N 6.26E
Vostochno Sibirskoye More sea U.S.S.R. 29 73.00N 160.00E
Vostochnyy Sayan mts. U.S.S.R. 30 51.30N 102.00E
Vostok I. Kiribati 69 10.05S 152.23W
Votkinsk U.S.S.R. 24 57.02N 53.59E
Votkinskoye Vodokhranilishche resr. U.S.S.R. 24 57.00N 55.00E
Votuporanga Brazil 92 20.26S 49.53W
Vouga r. Portugal 16 40.41N 8.38W
Vouillé France 17 46.38N 0.10E
Voulou C.A.R. 49 8.33N 22.36E
Vouziers France 15 49.24N 4.42E
Voves France 15 48.16N 1.37E
Voxna Sweden 23 61.20N 15.30E
Voxna r. Sweden 23 61.17N 16.26E
Voyvozh U.S.S.R. 24 64.19N 55.12E
Vozhega U.S.S.R. 24 60.25N 40.11E
Voznesensk U.S.S.R. 25 47.34N 31.21E
Vrangelya, Ostrov i. U.S.S.R. 29 71.00N 180.00
Vranje Yugo. 19 42.34N 21.52E
Vratsa Bulgaria 19 43.12N 23.33E
Vrbas r. Yugo. 19 45.06N 17.29E
Vrede R.S.A. 56 27.24S 29.09E
Vredendal R.S.A. 56 31.40S 18.28E
Vresse Belgium 14 49.53N 4.57E
Vries Neth. 14 53.06N 6.35E
Vrindāvan India 41 27.35N 77.42E
Vrnograč Yugo. 18 45.10N 15.56E
Vršac Yugo. 21 45.08N 21.18E
Vryburg R.S.A. 56 26.57S 24.42E
Vught Neth. 14 51.39N 5.18E
Vukovar Yugo. 21 45.21N 19.00E
Vung Tau Vietnam 34 10.21N 107.04E
Vyāra India 40 21.07N 73.24E
Vyatka r. U.S.S.R. 28 55.40N 51.40E
Vyatskiye Polyany U.S.S.R. 24 56.14N 51.08E
Vyazma U.S.S.R. 24 55.12N 34.17E
Vyazniki U.S.S.R. 24 56.14N 42.08E
Vyborg U.S.S.R. 24 60.45N 28.41E
Vychegda r. U.S.S.R. 24 61.15N 46.28E
Vychodné Beskydy mts. Europe 21 49.30N 22.00E
Vygozero, Ozero l. U.S.S.R. 24 63.30N 34.30E
Vyrnwy, L. U.K. 10 52.46N 3.30W
Vyshka U.S.S.R. 43 39.19N 54.10E
Vyshniy-Volochek U.S.S.R. 24 57.34N 34.23E
Vytegra U.S.S.R. 24 61.04N 36.27E

W

Wa Ghana 52 10.07N 2.28W
Waal r. Neth. 14 51.45N 4.40E
Waalwijk Neth. 14 51.42N 5.04E
Wabag P.N.G. 37 5.28S 143.40E
Wabasca r. Canada 74 58.22N 115.20W
Wabash U.S.A. 82 40.47N 85.48W
Wabash r. U.S.A. 82 37.46N 88.02W
Wabeno U.S.A. 82 45.27N 88.38W
Wabrzeźno Poland 21 53.17N 18.57E
Wabush City Canada 77 52.53N 66.50W
Waco U.S.A. 83 31.55N 97.08W
Wacouno r. Canada 77 50.50N 65.58W
Wad Pakistan 40 27.21N 66.22E
Wad Bandah Sudan 49 13.06N 27.57E
Waddān Libya 51 29.10N 16.08E
Waddeneilanden is. Neth. 14 53.20N 5.00E
Waddenzee b. Neth. 14 53.15N 5.05E
Wadderin Australia 63 31.57S 118.27E
Waddington, Mt. Canada 74 51.23N 125.15W
Wadena U.S.A. 82 46.26N 95.08W
Wad Ḥāmid Sudan 48 16.30N 32.48E
Wadhurst U.K. 11 51.03N 0.21E
Wādī Ḥalfā' Sudan 42 21.56N 31.20E
Wadikee Australia 66 33.18S 136.12E
Wādī Mūsá town Jordan 44 30.19N 35.29E
Wad Madanī Sudan 48 14.24N 33.32E
Wad Nimr Sudan 48 14.32N 32.08E
Wafrah Kuwait 43 28.39N 47.56E
Wageningen Neth. 14 51.58N 5.39E
Wager B. Canada 73 65.26N 88.40W
Wager Bay town Canada 73 65.55N 90.40W
Wagga Wagga Australia 67 35.07S 147.24E
Wagin Australia 63 33.18S 117.21E
Wagon Mound town U.S.A. 81 36.01N 104.42W
Wāh Pakistan 40 33.48N 72.42E
Wahai Indonesia 37 2.48S 129.30E
Wāḥat Salīmah Sudan 48 21.22N 29.19E
Wahiawa Hawaiian Is. 69 21.30N 158.01W
Wahiba Sands des. Oman 38 21.56N 58.55E
Wahpeton U.S.A. 82 46.16N 96.36W
Waiau New Zealand 60 42.39S 173.03E
Waidhān India 41 24.04N 82.20E
Waidhofen Austria 20 47.58N 14.47E
Waigeo i. Indonesia 37 0.05S 130.30E
Waihi New Zealand 60 37.24S 175.50E
Waikato r. New Zealand 60 37.19S 174.50E
Waikerie Australia 66 34.11S 139.59E
Waikokopu New Zealand 60 39.05S 177.50E
Waikouaiti New Zealand 60 45.36S 170.41E
Wailuku Hawaiian Is. 69 20.53N 156.30W
Waimakariri r. New Zealand 60 43.23S 172.40E
Waimate New Zealand 60 44.45S 171.03E
Waimea Hawaiian Is. 69 20.01N 155.41W
Wainganga r. India 41 18.50N 79.55E
Waingapu Indonesia 37 9.30S 120.10E
Wainwright Canada 75 52.49N 110.52W
Wainwright U.S.A. 72 70.39N 160.00W
Waiouru New Zealand 60 39.39S 175.40E
Waipara New Zealand 60 43.03S 172.45E
Waipawa New Zealand 60 39.56S 176.35E
Waipiro New Zealand 60 38.02S 178.21E
Waipu New Zealand 60 35.59S 174.26E
Waipukurau New Zealand 60 40.00S 176.33E
Wairau r. New Zealand 60 41.32S 174.08E
Wairoa New Zealand 60 39.03S 177.25E
Waitaki r. New Zealand 60 44.45S 171.10E
Waitara New Zealand 60 38.59S 174.13E
Waiuku New Zealand 60 37.15S 174.44E
Wajir Kenya 55 1.46N 40.05E
Waka Ethiopia 49 7.07N 37.26E
Waka Zaïre 54 0.48S 20.10E
Wakatipu, L. New Zealand 60 45.10S 168.30E
Wakayama Japan 35 34.13N 135.11E
Wakefield U.K. 10 53.41N 1.31W
Wakefield Canada 77 45.38N 75.56W
Wake I. Pacific Oc. 68 19.17N 166.36E
Wakema Burma 34 16.36N 95.11E
Wakkanai Japan 31 45.26N 141.43E
Wakre Indonesia 37 0.30S 131.05E
Wakuach, L. Canada 77 55.37N 67.40W
Walamba Zambia 55 13.27S 28.44E
Wałbrzych Poland 20 50.48N 16.19E
Walcha Australia 67 31.00S 151.36E
Walcheren f. Neth. 14 51.32N 3.35E
Wałcz Poland 20 53.17N 16.28E
Waldbröl W. Germany 14 50.52N 7.34E
Waldeck W. Germany 20 51.12N 9.04E
Walden U.S.A. 80 40.34N 106.11W
Waldorf U.S.A. 85 38.37N 76.54W
Waldport U.S.A. 80 44.26N 124.04W
Waldron U.S.A. 83 34.54N 94.05W
Wales d. U.K. 11 52.30N 3.45W
Wales U.S.A. 82 47.13N 91.41W
Walgett Australia 67 30.03S 148.10E
Walikale Zaïre 55 1.29S 28.05E
Walker U.S.A. 82 47.06N 94.35W
Walker L. U.S.A. 80 38.44N 118.43W
Wall U.S.A. 80 43.59N 102.14W
Wallace Idaho U.S.A. 80 47.28N 115.55W
Wallace Nebr. U.S.A. 82 40.50N 101.10W
Wallaceburg Canada 76 42.36N 82.23W
Wallachia f. Romania 21 44.35N 25.00E
Wallambin, L. Australia 63 30.58S 117.30E
Wallangarra Australia 67 28.51S 151.52E
Wallaroo Australia 66 33.57S 137.36E
Walla Walla Australia 67 35.48S 146.52E
Walla Walla U.S.A. 80 46.08N 118.20W
Wallis, Îles is. Pacific Oc. 68 13.16S 176.15W
Wallkill r. U.S.A. 85 41.51N 74.03W
Wallowa U.S.A. 80 45.34N 117.32W
Wallowa Mts. U.S.A. 80 45.10N 117.30W
Wallsend Australia 67 32.55S 151.40E
Walmsley L. Canada 75 63.25N 108.36W
Walpole Australia 63 34.57S 116.44E
Walsall U.K. 11 52.36N 1.59W
Walsenburg U.S.A. 80 37.37N 104.47W
Walterboro U.S.A. 85 32.54N 80.21W
Walton on the Naze U.K. 11 51.52N 1.17E
Walton on the Wolds U.K. 10 52.49N 0.49W
Walvis B. R.S.A. 56 22.55S 14.30E
Walvisbaai R.S.A. 56 22.57S 14.30E
Walvis Bay d. R.S.A. 56 22.56S 14.35E
Walvis Bay town see Walvisbaai R.S.A. 56
Walvis Ridge f. Atlantic Oc. 95 28.00S 4.00E
Wamanfo Ghana 52 7.16N 2.44W
Wamba Kenya 55 0.58N 37.19E
Wamba Nigeria 53 8.57N 8.42E
Wamba Zaïre 55 2.10N 27.59E
Wamba r. Zaïre 54 4.35S 17.15E
Wami r. Tanzania 55 6.10S 38.50E
Wamsasi Indonesia 37 3.27S 126.07E
Wan Indonesia 64 8.23S 137.55E
Wāna Pakistan 40 32.17N 69.35E
Wanaaring Australia 66 29.42S 144.14E
Wanaka New Zealand 60 44.42S 169.08E
Wanaka, L. New Zealand 60 44.30S 169.10E
Wan'an China 33 26.27N 114.46E
Wanapiri Indonesia 37 4.30S 135.50E
Wanapitei r. Canada 76 46.02N 80.51W
Wanapitei L. Canada 76 46.45N 80.45W
Wanbi Australia 66 34.46S 140.19E
Wandana Australia 66 32.04S 133.45E
Wandoan Australia 64 26.09S 149.51E
Wanganella Australia 67 35.13S 144.53E
Wanganui New Zealand 60 39.56S 175.00E
Wangaratta Australia 67 36.22S 146.20E
Wangary Australia 66 34.30S 135.26E
Wangdu China 32 38.43N 115.09E
Wangdu Phodrang Bhutan 41 27.29N 89.54E
Wangerooge i. W. Germany 14 53.50N 7.50E
Wanghai Shan mtn. China 32 41.40N 121.43E
Wangianna Australia 66 29.42S 137.32E
Wangjiang China 33 30.07N 116.41E
Wangpan Yang b. China 33 30.30N 121.30E
Wangyuanqiao China 32 38.24N 106.16E
Wani India 41 20.04N 78.57E
Wānkāner India 40 22.37N 70.56E
Wanle Iten Somali Rep. 45 2.38N 44.55E
Wannian China 33 28.42N 117.03E
Wanning China 33 18.48N 110.22E
Wānow Afghan. 40 32.38N 65.54E
Wantage U.K. 11 51.35N 1.25W
Wanxian China 33 30.52N 108.20E
Wanyang Shan mts. China 33 26.01N 113.48E
Wanyuan China 32 32.04N 108.02E
Wanzai China 33 28.06N 114.27E
Wāpi India 40 20.22N 72.54E
Wapiti r. Canada 74 55.05N 118.18W
Wappingers Falls U.S.A. 85 41.36N 73.55W
Wārāh Pakistan 40 27.27N 67.48E
Warangal India 39 18.00N 79.35E
Waranga Resr. Australia 67 36.32S 145.04E
Wārāseoni India 41 21.45N 80.02E
Waratah B. Australia 67 38.55S 146.04E
Warburton r. Australia 65 27.55S 137.15E
Warburton Range mts. S.A. Australia 66 30.30S 134.32E
Warburton Range mts. W.A. Australia 62 26.09S 126.38E
Ward Rep. of Ire. 13 53.26N 6.20W
Warden R.S.A. 56 27.49S 28.57E
Wardenburg W. Germany 14 53.04N 8.11E
Warder well Ethiopia 45 6.58N 45.21E
Wardha India 41 20.45N 78.37E
Wardha r. India 41 19.38N 79.48E
Ward Hill U.K. 8 58.54N 3.20W
Wardlow Canada 75 50.54N 111.33W
Waren E. Germany 20 53.31N 12.40E
Warendorf W. Germany 14 51.57N 8.00E
Warialda Australia 67 29.33S 150.36E
Wark Forest hills U.K. 10 55.06N 2.24W
Warkopi Indonesia 37 1.12S 134.09E
Warkworth New Zealand 60 36.24S 174.40E
Warley U.K. 11 52.29N 2.02W
Warmbad Namibia 56 28.26S 18.41E
Warminster U.K. 11 51.12N 2.11W
Warm Springs town U.S.A. 80 39.39N 114.49W
Warner Robins U.S.A. 85 32.35N 83.37W
Waroona Australia 63 32.51S 115.50E
Warracknabeal Australia 66 36.15S 142.28E
Warragamba Resr. Australia 67 33.54S 150.36E
Warragul Australia 67 38.11S 145.55E
Warrakalanna, L. Australia 66 28.13S 139.23E
Warrambool r. Australia 67 30.04S 147.38E
Warramutty Australia 66 30.30S 144.04E
Warrego r. Australia 67 30.25S 145.18E
Warrego Range mts. Australia 64 24.55S 146.20E
Warren Australia 67 31.44S 147.53E
Warren Ark. U.S.A. 83 33.37N 92.04W
Warren Mich. U.S.A. 84 42.28N 83.01W
Warren Minn. U.S.A. 82 48.12N 96.46W
Warren Ohio U.S.A. 84 41.15N 80.49W
Warren Penn. U.S.A. 84 41.51N 79.08W
Warrenpoint U.K. 13 54.06N 6.15W
Warrensburg Mo. U.S.A. 82 38.46N 93.44W
Warrenton R.S.A. 56 28.07S 24.49E
Warri Nigeria 53 5.36N 5.46E
Warrina Australia 66 28.10S 135.49E
Warriners Creek r. Australia 66 29.15S 137.03E
Warrington U.K. 10 53.25N 2.38W
Warrington U.S.A. 83 30.23N 87.16W
Warri Warri Australia 66 29.00S 141.56E
Warrnambool Australia 66 38.23S 142.03E
Warroad U.S.A. 82 48.54N 95.19W
Warrumbungle Range mts. Australia 67 31.20S 149.00E
Warsaw see Warszawa Poland 21
Warsaw Ind. U.S.A. 84 41.13N 85.52W
Warshikh Somali Rep. 45 2.19N 45.50E
Warszawa Poland 21 52.15N 21.00E
Warta r. Poland 20 52.45N 15.09E
Warud India 41 21.28N 78.16E
Warwick Australia 67 28.12S 152.00E
Warwick U.K. 11 52.17N 1.36W
Warwick N.Y. U.S.A. 85 41.16N 74.22W
Warwickshire d. U.K. 11 52.13N 1.30W
Wasatch Plateau f. U.S.A. 80 39.20N 111.30W
Wasco Calif. U.S.A. 81 35.36N 119.20W
Wasco Oreg. U.S.A. 80 45.35N 120.42W
Washburn N.Dak. U.S.A. 82 47.17N 101.02W
Washburn Wisc. U.S.A. 82 46.41N 90.52W
Washburn L. Canada 72 70.03N 106.50W
Wāshim India 40 20.06N 77.09E
Washington U.K. 10 54.55N 1.30W
Washington d. U.S.A. 80 47.43N 120.00W
Washington D.C. U.S.A. 85 38.55N 77.00W
Washington Ga. U.S.A. 85 33.43N 82.46W
Washington Ind. U.S.A. 84 38.40N 87.10W
Washington Iowa U.S.A. 82 41.18N 91.42W
Washington N.C. U.S.A. 85 35.33N 77.04W
Washington Utah U.S.A. 80 37.08N 113.30W
Washington Va. U.S.A. 84 38.43N 78.10W
Washington Crossing U.S.A. 85 40.18N 74.52W
Wāshuk Pakistan 40 27.44N 64.48E
Wasian Indonesia 37 1.51S 133.21E
Wasior Indonesia 37 2.38S 134.27E
Waskesiu L. Canada 75 53.56N 106.10W
Wassenaar Neth. 14 52.10N 4.26E
Wassy France 15 48.30N 4.59E
Waswanipi Lac l. Canada 76 49.35N 76.40W
Watampone Indonesia 37 4.33S 120.20E
Watchet U.K. 11 51.10N 3.20W
Waterbury U.S.A. 84 41.33N 73.03W
Waterbury L. Canada 75 58.16N 105.00W
Waterford Rep. of Ire. 13 52.16N 7.08W
Waterford d. Rep. of Ire. 13 52.10N 7.40W
Waterford Harbour est. Rep. of Ire. 13 52.12N 6.56W
Waterloo Belgium 14 50.44N 4.24E
Waterloo Canada 76 43.28N 80.31W
Waterloo Iowa U.S.A. 82 42.30N 92.20W
Waterloo Que. Canada 77 45.21N 72.31W
Waterton Glacier International Peace Park U.S.A./Canada 80 48.47N 113.45W
Watertown N.Y. U.S.A. 84 43.59N 75.55W
Watertown S.Dak. U.S.A. 82 44.54N 97.07W
Watervale Australia 66 33.58S 138.39E
Water Valley town U.S.A. 83 34.09N 89.38W
Waterville Rep. of Ire. 13 51.50N 10.11W
Waterville Maine U.S.A. 84 44.33N 69.38W
Waterville Wash. U.S.A. 80 47.39N 120.04W
Watford U.K. 11 51.40N 0.25W
Watford City U.S.A. 82 47.48N 103.17W
Wa'th Sudan 49 7.24N 28.58E
Wathaman L. Canada 75 56.55N 103.43W
Watonga U.S.A. 83 35.51N 98.25W
Watrous Canada 75 51.40N 105.28W
Watsa Zaïre 55 3.03N 29.29E
Watson Canada 75 52.07N 104.31W
Watson Lake town Canada 74 60.06N 128.49W
Watsonville U.S.A. 80 36.55N 121.45W
Wattiwarriganna r. Australia 66 28.57S 136.10E
Wattle Vale town Australia 66 30.00S 143.30E
Wau P.N.G. 37 7.22S 146.40E
Wauchope Australia 67 31.27S 152.43E
Waukaringa Australia 66 32.18S 139.27E
Waukegan U.S.A. 82 42.22N 87.50W
Waukesha U.S.A. 82 43.01N 88.14W
Waukon U.S.A. 82 43.16N 91.29W
Wauneta U.S.A. 82 40.25N 101.23W
Waurika U.S.A. 83 34.10N 98.00W
Wausau U.S.A. 82 44.58N 89.40W
Wautoma U.S.A. 82 44.05N 89.17W
Wauwatosa U.S.A. 82 43.04N 88.02W
Wave Hill town Australia 62 17.29S 130.57E
Waveney r. U.K. 11 52.29N 1.46E
Waverly Ill. U.S.A. 82 39.36N 89.57W
Waverly Iowa U.S.A. 82 42.44N 92.29W
Wavre Belgium 14 50.43N 4.37E
Wāw Sudan 49 7.42N 28.00E
Wāw al Kabīr Libya 51 25.20N 16.43E
Waxahachie U.S.A. 83 32.24N 96.51W
Waxweiler W. Germany 14 50.08N 6.20E
Waycross U.S.A. 85 31.12N 82.22W
Wayne N.J. U.S.A. 85 40.03N 75.23W
Waynesboro Ga. U.S.A. 85 33.04N 82.01W
Waynesboro Penn. U.S.A. 84 39.45N 77.35W

Waynesboro to Wuda

Waynesboro Va. U.S.A. 85 38.04N 78.53W
Waynesville U.S.A. 85 35.30N 82.58W
Waynoka U.S.A. 83 36.35N 98.53W
Wazay Afghan. 40 33.22N 69.26E
Waziers France 14 50.24N 3.05E
Wazirābād Pakistan 40 32.27N 74.07E
Wear r. U.K. 10 54.55N 1.21W
Weatherford Okla. U.S.A. 83 35.32N 98.42W
Weatherford Tex. U.S.A. 83 32.46N 97.48W
Webera Ethiopia 49 6.25N 40.45E
Webster N.Y. U.S.A. 76 43.13N 77.26W
Webster Wisc. U.S.A. 82 45.53N 92.22W
Webster City U.S.A. 82 42.28N 93.49W
Webster Groves U.S.A. 82 38.35N 90.21W
Weda Indonesia 37 0.30N 127.52E
Wedderburn Australia 66 36.26S 143.39E
Wedgeport Canada 77 43.44N 65.59W
Wedmore U.K. 11 51.14N 2.50W
Wedza Zimbabwe 57 18.37S 31.33E
Weebo Australia 62 28.01S 121.03E
Weeho r. Canada 74 63.20N 115.10W
Weelde Belgium 14 51.25N 5.00E
Weemelah Australia 67 29.02S 149.15E
Weert Neth. 14 51.14N 5.40E
Wee Waa Australia 67 30.34S 149.27E
Wegorzyno Poland 20 53.32N 15.33E
Wegrów Poland 21 52.25N 22.01E
Weichang China 32 41.56N 117.34E
Weiden in der Oberpfalz W. Germany 20 49.40N 12.10E
Weifang China 32 36.40N 119.10E
Weihai China 32 37.28N 122.05E
Wei He r. Shaanxi China 32 34.27N 109.30E
Wei He r. Shandong China 32 36.47N 115.42E
Weilmoringle Australia 67 29.16S 146.55E
Weimar E. Germany 20 50.59N 11.20E
Weinan China 32 34.25N 109.30E
Weipa Australia 64 12.41S 141.52E
Weir r. Australia 67 29.10S 149.06E
Weiser U.S.A. 80 44.37N 116.58W
Weishan Hu l. China 32 34.40N 117.25E
Weishi China 32 34.24N 114.14E
Weissenfels E. Germany 20 51.12N 11.58E
Wei Xian China 32 36.21N 114.56E
Weixin China 33 27.48N 105.05E
Weiya China 30 41.50N 94.24E
Weizhou i. China 33 21.01N 109.03E
Wejherowo Poland 21 54.37N 18.15E
Wekusko Canada 75 54.45N 99.45W
Welbourn Hill town Australia 65 27.21S 134.06E
Weldon U.S.A. 81 35.40N 118.20W
Weldya Ethiopia 49 11.50N 39.36E
Welega d. Ethiopia 49 9.40N 35.50E
Welkom R.S.A. 56 27.59S 26.42E
Welland Canada 76 42.59N 79.14W
Welland r. U.K. 10 52.53N 0.00
Wellesley Is. Australia 64 16.42S 139.30E
Wellin Belgium 14 50.05N 5.07E
Wellingborough U.K. 11 52.18N 0.41W
Wellington N.S.W. Australia 67 32.33S 148.59E
Wellington S.A. Australia 66 35.21S 139.23E
Wellington New Zealand 60 41.17S 174.47E
Wellington d. New Zealand 60 40.00S 175.30E
Wellington Shrops. U.K. 11 52.42N 2.31W
Wellington Somerset U.K. 11 50.58N 3.13W
Wellington Kans. U.S.A. 83 37.16N 97.24W
Wellington Nev. U.S.A. 80 38.45N 119.22W
Wellington, Isla i. Chile 93 49.30S 75.00W
Wells U.K. 11 51.12N 2.39W
Wells Nev. U.S.A. 80 41.07N 114.58W
Wellsboro U.S.A. 84 41.45N 77.18W
Wells Gray Prov. Park Canada 74 52.30N 120.15W
Wells L. Canada 75 57.15N 101.00W
Wells-next-the-Sea U.K. 10 52.57N 0.51E
Wellsville Mo. U.S.A. 82 39.04N 91.34W
Wellton U.S.A. 81 32.40N 114.08W
Welmel r. Ethiopia 49 6.00N 40.20E
Wels Austria 20 48.10N 14.02E
Welshpool U.K. 11 52.40N 3.09W
Welwyn Garden City U.K. 11 51.48N 0.13W
Wem U.K. 10 52.52N 2.45W
Wembere r. Tanzania 55 4.07S 34.15E
Wenatchee U.S.A. 80 47.25N 120.19W
Wenchang China 33 19.37N 110.43E
Wenchi Ghana 52 7.40N 2.06W
Wendel U.S.A. 80 40.20N 120.14W
Wendo Ethiopia 49 6.40N 38.27E
Wendover U.S.A. 80 40.44N 114.02W
Wenebegon L. Canada 76 47.25N 83.05W
Wengfengzhen China 32 34.56N 104.38E
Wenlock r. Australia 64 12.02S 141.55E
Wenquan China 41 33.13N 91.50E
Wenshan China 33 23.20N 104.11E
Wensleydale Australia 66 38.24S 144.01E
Wensleydale f. U.K. 10 54.19N 2.04W
Wentworth Australia 66 34.06S 141.56E
Wen Xian China 32 32.52N 104.40E
Wenzhou China 31 28.02N 120.40E
Weott U.S.A. 80 40.19N 123.54W
Wepener R.S.A. 56 29.43S 27.01E
Werda Botswana 56 25.15S 23.16E
Werdohl W. Germany 14 51.16N 7.47E
Were Ilu Ethiopia 49 10.37N 39.28E
Weri Indonesia 37 3.10S 132.30E
Werne W. Germany 14 51.39N 7.36E
Werra r. W. Germany 20 51.26N 9.39E
Werribee Australia 67 37.54S 144.40E
Werris Creek town Australia 67 31.20S 150.41E
Wesel W. Germany 14 51.39N 6.37E
Weser r. W. Germany 20 53.15N 8.30E
Wesiri Indonesia 37 7.30S 126.30E
Weslaco U.S.A. 83 26.09N 97.59W
Wesleyville Canada 77 49.09N 53.34W
Wesleyville U.S.A. 76 42.08N 80.01W
Wessel, C. Australia 64 10.59S 136.46E
Wessel Is. Australia 64 11.30S 136.25E
Wessington U.S.A. 82 44.27N 98.42W
Wessington Springs town U.S.A. 82 44.05N 98.34W
West U.S.A. 83 31.48N 97.06W
West B. U.S.A. 83 29.15N 94.57W
West Bend U.S.A. 82 43.25N 88.11W
West Bengal d. India 41 23.00N 88.00E
West-Berlin d. W. Germany 20 52.30N 13.20E
West Bromwich U.K. 11 52.32N 2.01W
Westbrook U.S.A. 84 43.41N 70.21W
West Burra i. U.K. 8 60.05N 1.21W
Westby Australia 67 35.29S 147.27E
West Caroline Basin Pacific Oc. 68 5.00N 139.00E
West Chester U.S.A. 85 39.58N 75.36W
West Des Moines U.S.A. 82 41.35N 93.43W
Westende Belgium 14 51.10N 2.46E
Western d. Ghana 52 6.00N 2.40W
Western d. Kenya 55 0.30N 34.30E
Western d. Zambia 56 16.00S 23.45E
Western Australia d. Australia 62 24.20S 122.30E
Western Ghāts mts. India 38 15.30N 74.30E
Western Isles d. U.K. 12 57.40N 7.10W
Western Sahara Africa 50 25.00N 13.30W
Western Samoa Pacific Oc. 68 13.55S 172.00W
Westerschelde est. Neth. 14 51.25N 3.40E
Westerstede W. Germany 14 53.15N 7.56E
Westerwald f. W. Germany 14 50.40N 8.00E
West Falkland i. Falkland Is. 93 51.40W 60.00W
West Felton U.K. 10 52.49N 2.58W
Westfield Mass. U.S.A. 84 42.07N 72.45W
Westfield N.J. U.S.A. 85 40.39N 74.21W
Westfield N.Y. U.S.A. 76 42.19N 79.35W
Westfield Penn. U.S.A. 84 41.55N 77.32W
West Frankfort U.S.A. 83 37.54N 88.55W
West Frisian Is. see Waddeneilanden Neth. 20
West Germany Europe 20 51.00N 8.00E
West Glamorgan d. U.K. 11 51.42N 3.47W
Westhope U.S.A. 82 48.55N 101.01W
West Indies is. C. America 95 21.00N 74.00W
West Lafayette U.S.A. 84 40.26N 86.56W
Westland d. New Zealand 60 43.15S 170.10E
West Linton U.K. 12 55.45N 3.21W
Westlock Canada 74 54.09N 113.55W
Westmeath d. Rep. of Ire. 13 53.30N 7.30W
West Memphis U.S.A. 83 35.08N 90.11W
West Midlands d. U.K. 11 52.28N 1.50W
Westminster U.S.A. 85 39.35N 77.00W
Westmoreland Australia 64 17.18S 138.12E
West Nicholson Zimbabwe 56 21.06S 29.25E
Weston Malaysia 36 5.14N 115.35E
Weston-Super-Mare U.K. 11 51.20N 2.59W
West Palm Beach town U.S.A. 85 26.42N 80.05W
West Plains town U.S.A. 83 36.44N 91.51W
West Point town U.S.A. 83 33.36N 88.39W
Westport New Zealand 60 41.46S 171.38E
Westport Rep. of Ire. 13 53.48N 9.32W
Westport Conn. U.S.A. 85 41.09N 73.22W
Westport Wash. U.S.A. 80 46.53N 124.06W
Westray Canada 75 53.36N 101.24W
Westray i. U.K. 12 59.18N 2.58W
West Road r. Canada 74 53.18N 122.53W
West Siberian Plain f. see Zapadno-Sibirskaya Ravnina f. U.S.S.R. 28
West Sussex d. U.K. 11 50.58N 0.30W
West Terschelling Neth. 14 53.22N 5.13E
West Virginia d. U.S.A. 84 38.45N 80.30W
West Vlaanderen d. Belgium 14 51.00N 3.00E
West Wyalong Australia 67 33.54S 147.12E
West Yellowstone U.S.A. 80 44.30N 111.05W
West York U.S.A. 85 39.57N 76.46W
West Yorkshire d. U.K. 10 53.45N 1.40W
Wetar i. Indonesia 37 7.45S 126.00E
Wetaskiwin Canada 74 52.55N 113.24W
Wetteren Belgium 14 51.00N 3.51E
Wetzlar W. Germany 20 50.33N 8.30E
Wewak P.N.G. 37 3.35S 143.35E
Wewoka U.S.A. 83 35.09N 96.30W
Wexford Rep. of Ire. 13 52.20N 6.28W
Wexford d. Rep. of Ire. 13 52.20N 6.25W
Wexford B. Rep. of Ire. 13 52.27N 6.18W
Weyburn Canada 75 49.41N 103.52W
Weyib r. Ethiopia 49 4.11N 42.09E
Weymouth U.K. 11 50.36N 2.28W
Weymouth, C. Australia 64 12.32S 143.36E
Whakatane New Zealand 60 37.56S 177.00E
Whale Cove town Canada 75 62.11N 92.36W
Whallon r. Australia 67 29.10S 148.42E
Whalsay i. U.K. 12 60.22N 0.59W
Whangarei New Zealand 60 35.43S 174.20E
Wharfe r. U.K. 10 53.50N 1.07W
Wharfedale f. U.K. 10 54.00N 1.55W
Wharton U.S.A. 83 29.19N 96.06W
Whataroa New Zealand 60 43.16S 170.22E
Wheatland U.S.A. 80 42.03N 104.57W
Wheaton Md. U.S.A. 85 39.03N 77.03W
Wheaton Minn. U.S.A. 82 45.48N 96.30W
Wheeler r. Que. Canada 77 58.05N 67.12W
Wheeler r. Sask. Canada 75 57.25N 105.30W
Wheeler Peak mtn. Nev. U.S.A. 80 38.59N 114.19W
Wheeler Peak mtn. N.Mex. U.S.A. 80 36.34N 105.25W
Wheeler Ridge town U.S.A. 81 35.06N 119.01W
Wheeler Springs town U.S.A. 81 34.30N 119.18W
Wheeling U.S.A. 84 40.05N 80.43W
Whernside mtn. U.K. 10 54.14N 2.25W
Whidbey Pt. Australia 66 34.35S 135.07E
Whiskey Gap town Canada 74 49.00N 113.03W
Whitburn U.K. 12 55.52N 3.41W
Whitby Canada 76 43.52N 78.56W
Whitby U.K. 10 54.29N 0.37W
Whitchurch Shrops. U.K. 10 52.58N 2.42W
White r. Ark. U.S.A. 83 33.53N 91.10W
White r. Ind. U.S.A. 84 38.29N 87.45W
White r. S.Dak. U.S.A. 82 43.48N 99.22W
White r. Utah U.S.A. 78 40.04N 109.41W
White, L. Australia 62 21.05S 129.00E
White B. Canada 77 50.00N 56.30W
White Cliffs town Australia 66 30.51S 143.05E
Whitefish U.S.A. 80 48.25N 114.20W
Whitefish B. U.S.A. 84 46.32N 84.45W
Whitefish L. Canada 75 62.41N 106.48W
Whitehall Mont. U.S.A. 80 45.52N 112.06W
Whitehall Wisc. U.S.A. 82 44.22N 91.19W
Whitehaven U.K. 10 54.33N 3.35W
Whitehorse Canada 74 60.43N 135.03W
White L. U.S.A. 83 29.45N 92.30W
Whitemark Australia 65 40.07S 148.00E
White Mountain Peak U.S.A. 80 37.38N 118.15W
White Mts. Calif. U.S.A. 80 37.30N 118.15W
Whitemud r. Canada 74 56.41N 117.15W
White Nile r. see Abyaḍ, Al Baḥr al r. Sudan 48
White Otter L. Canada 76 49.09N 91.50W
White Plains town Liberia 52 6.28N 10.40W
White Plains town U.S.A. 85 41.02N 73.46W
Whitesand r. Canada 75 51.34N 101.55W
White Sea see Beloye More sea U.S.S.R. 24
Whiteshell Prov. Park. Canada 75 50.00N 95.25W
Whitetail U.S.A. 80 48.54N 105.10W
White Volta r. Ghana 52 9.13N 1.15W
Whitewater Baldy mtn. U.S.A. 81 33.20N 108.39W
Whitfield Australia 67 36.49S 146.22E
Whithorn U.K. 12 54.44N 4.25W
Whitianga New Zealand 60 36.50S 175.42E
Whiting U.S.A. 85 39.57N 74.23W
Whitley Bay town U.K. 10 55.03N 1.25W
Whitney Canada 76 45.30N 78.14W
Whitney, Mt. U.S.A. 81 36.35N 118.18W
Whitstable U.K. 11 51.21N 1.02E
Whitsunday I. Australia 64 20.17S 148.59E
Whittier U.S.A. 72 60.46N 148.41W
Whittlesea Australia 67 37.31S 145.08E
Whitton U.K. 10 53.42N 0.39W
Wholdaia L. Canada 75 60.43N 104.20W
Whyalla Australia 66 33.02S 137.35E
Whyjonta Australia 66 29.42S 142.30E
Wichita U.S.A. 83 37.41N 97.20W
Wichita Falls town U.S.A. 83 33.54N 98.30W
Wick U.K. 12 58.26N 3.06W
Wickenburg U.S.A. 81 33.58N 112.44W
Wickepin Australia 63 32.45S 117.31E
Wicklow Rep. of Ire. 13 52.59N 6.03W
Wicklow d. Rep. of Ire. 13 52.59N 6.25W
Wicklow Head Rep. of Ire. 13 52.58N 6.00W
Wicklow Mts. Rep. of Ire. 13 53.06N 6.20W
Widgiemooltha Australia 63 31.30S 121.34E
Widnes U.K. 10 53.22N 2.44W
Wiehl W. Germany 14 50.57N 7.32E
Wieluń Poland 21 51.14N 18.34E
Wien Austria 20 48.13N 16.22E
Wiener Neustadt Austria 20 47.49N 16.15E
Wieprz r. Poland 21 51.34N 21.49E
Wiesbaden W. Germany 20 50.05N 8.15E
Wigan U.K. 10 53.33N 2.38W
Wight, Isle of U.K. 9 50.40N 1.17W
Wigton U.K. 10 54.50N 3.09W
Wigtown U.K. 12 54.47N 4.26W
Wigtown B. U.K. 12 54.47N 4.15W
Wilber U.S.A. 82 40.29N 96.58W
Wilcannia Australia 66 31.33S 143.24E
Wildhorn mtn. Switz. 17 46.22N 7.22E
Wildon Austria 20 46.53N 15.31E
Wildrose U.S.A. 82 48.38N 103.11W
Wildspitze mtn. Austria 20 46.55N 10.55E
Wildwood U.S.A. 85 38.59N 74.49W
Wilgena Australia 66 30.46S 134.44E
Wilhelm, Mt. P.N.G. 37 6.00S 144.55E
Wilhelm II Land Antarctica 96 68.00S 89.00E
Wilhelmshaven W. Germany 14 53.32N 8.07E
Wilkes-Barre U.S.A. 84 41.15N 75.50W
Wilkesboro U.S.A. 85 36.08N 81.09W
Wilkes Land f. Antarctica 96 69.00S 120.00E
Wilkie Canada 75 52.25N 108.43W
Wilkie Canada 72 52.27N 108.42W
Wilkinsburg U.S.A. 84 40.27N 79.53W
Wilkinson Lakes Australia 65 29.40S 132.39E
Willandra Billabong r. Australia 66 33.08S 144.06E
Willara Australia 66 29.14S 144.30E
Willard N.Mex. U.S.A. 81 34.36N 106.02W
Willemstad Neth. Antilles 90 12.12N 68.56W
Willeroo Australia 62 15.17S 131.35E
William, Mt. Australia 66 37.20S 142.41E
William Creek town Australia 66 28.52S 136.18E
Williams Australia 63 33.01S 116.45E
Williams r. Australia 63 32.59S 116.24E
Williamsburg U.S.A. 85 37.17N 76.43W
Williams Lake town Canada 74 52.08N 122.10W
Williamson U.S.A. 85 37.42N 82.16W
Williamsport Penn. U.S.A. 84 41.14N 77.00W
Williamston U.S.A. 85 35.53N 77.05W
Williamstown N.J. U.S.A. 85 39.41N 75.00W
Willie's Range hills Australia 66 28.30S 144.00E
Willis Group is. Australia 64 16.18S 150.00E
Williston R.S.A. 56 31.21S 20.53E
Williston U.S.A. 82 48.09N 103.37W
Williston L. Canada 74 55.40N 123.40W
Willits U.S.A. 80 39.25N 123.21W
Willmar U.S.A. 82 45.07N 95.03W
Willmore Wilderness Park Canada 74 53.45N 119.00W
Willochra Australia 66 32.12S 138.10E
Willochra r. Australia 66 31.57S 137.52E
Willow U.S.A. 72 61.42N 150.08W
Willow Grove U.S.A. 85 40.08N 75.06W
Willow L. Canada 74 62.10N 119.08W
Willowmore R.S.A. 56 33.18S 23.28E
Willow Ranch U.S.A. 80 41.55N 120.21W
Willow River town Canada 74 54.06N 122.28W
Willunga Australia 66 35.18S 138.33E
Wilmette U.S.A. 82 42.04N 87.43W
Wilmington Del. U.S.A. 85 39.44N 75.33W
Wilmington N.C. U.S.A. 85 34.14N 77.55W
Wilmslow U.K. 10 53.19N 2.14W
Wilpena r. Australia 66 31.13S 139.25E
Wilson N.C. U.S.A. 85 35.43N 77.56W
Wilson N.Y. U.S.A. 76 43.19N 78.50W
Wilson's Promontory c. Australia 67 39.06S 146.23E
Wilton r. Australia 64 14.45S 134.33E
Wilton U.K. 11 51.05N 1.52W
Wilton N.Dak. U.S.A. 82 47.10N 100.47W
Wiltshire d. U.K. 11 51.20N 0.34W
Wiltz Lux. 14 49.59N 5.53E
Wiluna Australia 62 26.36S 120.13E
Wimmera r. Australia 66 36.05S 141.56E
Winam b. Kenya 55 0.15S 34.30E
Winbar Australia 67 30.49S 144.50E
Winburg R.S.A. 56 28.30S 27.01E
Wincanton U.K. 11 51.03N 2.24W
Winchester U.K. 11 51.04N 1.19W
Winchester Ky. U.S.A. 85 38.00N 84.10W
Winchester Va. U.S.A. 84 39.11N 78.10W
Winchester Wyo. U.S.A. 80 43.51N 108.10W
Windermere l. U.K. 10 54.20N 2.56W
Windfall Canada 74 54.12N 116.13W
Windhoek Namibia 56 22.34S 17.06E
Windom U.S.A. 82 43.52N 95.07W
Windorah Australia 64 25.26S 142.39E
Wind River Range mts. U.S.A. 80 43.05N 109.25W
Windsor Nfld. Canada 77 48.58N 55.40W
Windsor N.S. Canada 77 44.59N 64.08W
Windsor Ont. Canada 76 42.18N 83.01W
Windsor Que. Canada 77 45.34N 72.00W
Windsor U.K. 11 51.29N 0.38W
Windward Is. C. America 87 13.00N 60.00W
Windward Passage str. Carib. Sea 87 20.00N 74.00W
Winfield Kans. U.S.A. 83 37.15N 96.59W
Wingen Australia 67 31.43S 150.54E
Wingham Australia 67 31.50S 152.20E
Wingham Canada 76 43.53N 81.19W
Winifred U.S.A. 80 47.34N 109.23W
Winisk Canada 76 55.20N 85.15W
Winisk r. Canada 76 55.00N 85.20W
Winisk L. Canada 76 53.00N 88.00W
Winkler Canada 75 49.11N 97.56W
Winneba Ghana 52 5.22N 0.38W
Winnebago, L. U.S.A. 82 44.00N 88.25W
Winnemucca U.S.A. 78 40.58N 117.45W
Winnemucca L. U.S.A. 80 40.09N 119.20W
Winner U.S.A. 82 43.22N 99.51W
Winnfield U.S.A. 83 31.55N 92.38W
Winnininnie Australia 66 32.35S 139.40E
Winnipeg Canada 75 49.53N 97.09W
Winnipeg r. Canada 75 50.38N 96.19W
Winnipeg, L. Canada 75 52.00N 97.00W
Winnipegosis, L. Canada 75 52.30N 100.00W
Winnsboro La. U.S.A. 83 32.10N 91.43W
Winnsboro S.C. U.S.A. 85 34.22N 81.05W
Winona Kans. U.S.A. 82 39.04N 101.15W
Winona Minn. U.S.A. 82 44.03N 91.39W
Winona Miss. U.S.A. 83 33.29N 89.44W
Winooski U.S.A. 84 44.29N 73.11W
Winschoten Neth. 14 53.07N 7.02E
Winsford U.K. 10 53.12N 2.31W
Winslow Ariz. U.S.A. 81 35.01N 110.42W
Winslow Maine U.S.A. 84 44.32N 69.38W
Winston U.S.A. 80 46.28N 111.38W
Winston-Salem U.S.A. 85 36.05N 80.18W
Winsum Neth. 14 53.20N 6.31E
Winter Haven U.S.A. 85 28.02N 81.46W
Winterset U.S.A. 82 41.20N 94.01W
Winterswijk Neth. 14 51.58N 6.44E
Winterthur Switz. 20 47.30N 8.45E
Winthrop Minn. U.S.A. 82 44.32N 94.22W
Winthrop Wash. U.S.A. 80 48.29N 120.11W
Winton Australia 64 22.22S 143.00E
Winton New Zealand 60 46.10S 168.20E
Winton U.S.A. 80 41.45N 109.10W
Wirrabara Australia 66 33.03S 138.18E
Wirraminna Australia 66 31.11S 136.04E
Wirrappa Australia 66 31.28S 137.00E
Wirrega Australia 66 36.11S 140.37E
Wirrida, L. Australia 66 29.45S 134.39E
Wirulla Australia 66 32.24S 134.33E
Wisbech U.K. 11 52.39N 0.10E
Wisconsin d. U.S.A. 82 44.30N 90.00W
Wisconsin r. U.S.A. 82 43.00N 91.15W
Wisconsin Dells U.S.A. 82 43.38N 89.46W
Wisconsin Rapids town U.S.A. 82 44.24N 89.50W
Wisdom U.S.A. 80 45.37N 113.27W
Wisła r. Poland 21 54.23N 18.52E
Wismar E. Germany 20 53.54N 11.28E
Wisner U.S.A. 82 41.59N 96.55W
Wisznice Poland 21 51.48N 23.12E
Witchekan L. Canada 75 53.25N 107.35W
Witham r. U.K. 10 52.56N 0.04E
Withernsea U.K. 10 53.43N 0.02E
Witkowo Poland 21 52.27N 17.47E
Witney U.K. 11 51.47N 1.29W
Witsand R.S.A. 56 34.23S 20.49E
Witten W. Germany 14 51.26N 7.19E
Wittenberg E. Germany 20 51.53N 12.39E
Wittenberge E. Germany 20 52.59N 11.45E
Wittenoom Australia 62 22.19S 118.21E
Wittlich W. Germany 14 49.59N 6.54E
Witu Kenya 55 2.22S 40.20E
Witvlei Namibia 56 22.25S 18.29E
Wiveliscombe U.K. 11 51.02N 3.20W
Wkra r. Poland 21 52.27N 20.44E
Władysławowo Poland 21 54.49N 18.25E
Włocławek Poland 21 52.39N 19.01E
Włodawa Poland 21 51.33N 23.31E
Wodgina Australia 62 21.12S 118.48E
Wodonga Australia 67 36.08S 146.09E
Woerden Neth. 14 52.07N 4.55E
Wohutun China 32 43.40N 123.30E
Wokam i. Indonesia 37 5.45S 134.30E
Woking Canada 74 55.35N 118.50W
Woking U.K. 11 51.20N 0.34W
Woleai i. Pacific Oc. 68 7.21N 143.52E
Wolf r. U.S.A. 82 44.07N 88.43W
Wolf Creek town U.S.A. 80 46.50N 112.20W
Wolfenbüttel W. Germany 20 52.10N 10.33E
Wolf Point town U.S.A. 80 48.05N 105.39W
Wolfsberg Austria 20 46.51N 14.51E
Wolfsburg W. Germany 20 52.27N 10.49E
Wolin Poland 20 53.51N 14.38E
Wollaston L. Canada 75 58.15N 103.20W
Wollaston Pen. Canada 72 70.00N 115.00W
Wollongong Australia 67 34.25S 150.52E
Wolmaransstad R.S.A. 56 27.11S 25.58E
Wołomin Poland 21 52.21N 21.14E
Wolseley Australia 66 36.21S 140.55E
Wolvega Neth. 14 52.53N 6.00E
Wolverhampton U.K. 11 52.35N 2.06W
Womelsdorf U.S.A. 85 40.22N 76.11W
Wondai Australia 64 26.19S 151.52E
Wongan Hills town Australia 63 30.55S 116.41E
Wono Ethiopia 49 8.31N 37.30E
Wonogiri Indonesia 37 7.48S 110.52E
Wonosari Indonesia 37 7.55S 110.39E
Wonosobo Indonesia 37 7.21S 109.56E
Wŏnsan N. Korea 31 39.07N 127.26E
Wonthaggi Australia 67 38.38S 145.37E
Woocalla Australia 66 31.44S 137.10E
Woodbine U.S.A. 85 39.14N 74.49W
Woodbridge U.K. 11 52.06N 1.19E
Woodbridge U.S.A. 85 38.39N 77.15W
Wood Buffalo Nat. Park Canada 74 59.00N 113.41W
Woodburn Australia 67 29.04S 153.21E
Woodbury U.S.A. 85 39.50N 75.10W
Wooded Bluff f. Australia 67 29.22S 153.22E
Woodenbong Australia 67 28.28S 152.35E
Woodland U.S.A. 80 38.41N 121.46W
Woodlark I. P.N.G. 64 9.05S 152.50E
Wood Mts. Canada 75 49.14N 106.20W
Woodroffe, Mt. Australia 64 26.20S 131.45E
Woods, L. Australia 64 17.50S 133.30E
Woods, L. of the Canada/U.S.A. 76 49.15N 94.45W
Woodside Australia 67 38.31S 146.52E
Woods L. Canada 77 54.40N 64.21W
Woodstock Canada 76 43.08N 80.45W
Woodstock U.K. 11 51.51N 1.20W
Woodstown U.S.A. 85 39.39N 75.20W
Woodville New Zealand 60 40.20S 175.52E
Woodward U.S.A. 83 36.26N 99.24W
Wooler U.K. 10 55.33N 2.01W
Woolgangie Australia 63 31.13S 120.30E
Woolgoolga Australia 67 30.07S 153.12E
Woolibar Australia 63 31.03S 121.45E
Wooltana Australia 66 30.28S 139.26E
Woomera Australia 66 31.11S 136.54E
Woonsocket U.S.A. 84 42.00N 71.31W
Wooramel Australia 62 25.42S 114.20E
Wooramel r. Australia 62 25.47S 114.10E
Woorong, L. Australia 66 29.24S 134.06E
Wooroorooka Australia 67 28.59S 145.40E
Worcester R.S.A. 56 33.39S 19.25E
Worcester U.K. 11 52.12N 2.12W
Worcester U.S.A. 84 42.16N 71.48W
Workington U.K. 10 54.39N 3.34W
Worksop U.K. 10 53.19N 1.09W
Workum Neth. 14 53.00N 5.26E
Worland U.S.A. 80 44.01N 107.57W
Worms W. Germany 20 49.38N 8.23E
Worthing U.K. 11 50.49N 0.21W
Worthington Minn. U.S.A. 82 43.37N 95.36W
Worthington Ohio U.S.A. 84 40.03N 83.03W
Worthville U.S.A. 84 38.38N 85.05W
Wosi Indonesia 37 0.15S 128.00E
Wour Chad 53 21.21N 15.57E
Woutchaba Cameroon 53 5.13N 13.05E
Wowoni i. Indonesia 37 4.10S 123.10E
Wragby U.K. 10 53.17N 0.18E
Wrangel I. see Vrangelya, Ostrov i. U.S.S.R. 29
Wrangell U.S.A. 74 56.28N 132.23W
Wrangell Mts. U.S.A. 72 62.00N 143.00W
Wrangle U.K. 10 53.03N 0.09E
Wrath, C. U.K. 12 58.37N 5.01W
Wray U.S.A. 82 40.05N 102.13W
Wrecks, B. of Kiribati 69 1.52N 157.17W
Wrexham U.K. 10 53.05N 3.00W
Wrightville Australia 67 31.36S 145.53E
Wrigley Canada 72 63.16N 123.39W
Wrocław Poland 21 51.05N 17.00E
Wronki Poland 20 52.43N 16.23E
Września Poland 21 52.20N 17.34E
Wubin Australia 63 30.06S 116.38E
Wuchang China 33 30.21N 114.19E
Wucheng China 32 37.12N 116.04E
Wuchuan Guangdong China 33 21.21N 110.40E
Wuchuan Nei Monggol China 32 41.08N 111.24E
Wuda China 32 39.40N 106.40E

Wudham 'Alwā' to Yungas

Wudham 'Alwā' Oman 43 23.48N 57.33E
Wudinna Australia 66 33.03S135.28E
Wudu China 32 33.24N104.50E
Wufeng China 33 30.12N110.36E
Wugang China 33 26.42N110.31E
Wugong Shan mts. China 33 27.15N114.00E
Wuhai China 32 39.50N106.40E
Wuhan China 33 30.37N114.19E
Wuhu China 33 31.25N118.25E
Wūjang China 41 33.38N 79.55E
Wu Jiang r. China 33 29.41N107.24E
Wukari Nigeria 53 7.57N 9.42E
Wulian China 32 35.45N119.12E
Wuliang Shan mts. China 30 24.27N100.43E
Wum Cameroon 53 6.25N 10.03E
Wumbulgal Australia 67 34.25S146.16E
Wuming China 33 23.10N108.16E
Wuning China 33 29.17N115.05E
Wunnummin L. Canada 76 52.50N 89.20W
Wun Rog Sudan 49 9.00N 28.21E
Wuppertal R.S.A. 56 32.16S 19.12E
Wuppertal W. Germany 14 51.15N 7.10E
Wuqi China 32 37.03N108.14E
Wuqiao China 32 37.38N116.22E
Wuqing China 32 39.19N117.05E
Wurno Nigeria 53 13.20N 5.28E
Wurung Australia 64 19.14S140.23E
Würzburg W. Germany 20 49.48N 9.57E
Wusong China 33 31.20N121.30E
Wutongqiao China 33 29.20N103.48E
Wuwei China 32 38.00N102.59E
Wuxi Jiangsu China 33 31.34N120.20E
Wuxi Sichuan China 33 31.28N109.36E
Wuxing China 33 30.59N120.04E
Wuyi Shan mts. China 33 27.00N117.00E
Wuyuan China 32 41.06N108.16E
Wuzhan China 31 50.14N125.18E
Wuzhi Shan mts. China 33 18.50N109.30E
Wuzhou China 33 23.28N111.21E
Wyalkatchem Australia 63 31.21S117.22E
Wyalong Australia 67 33.55S147.17E
Wyandotte U.S.A. 84 42.11N 83.10W
Wyandra Australia 65 27.15S146.00E
Wyangala Resr. Australia 67 33.58S148.55E
Wyara, L. Australia 66 28.42S144.16E
Wye U.K. 11 51.11N 0.56E
Wye r. U.K. 11 51.37N 2.40W
Wymondham U.K. 11 52.34N 1.07E
Wynbring Australia 65 30.33S133.32E
Wyndham Australia 62 15.29S128.05E
Wynne U.S.A. 83 35.14N 90.47W
Wyoming d. U.S.A. 80 43.10N107.36W
Wyong Australia 67 33.17S151.25E
Wyszków Poland 21 52.36N 21.28E
Wytheville U.S.A. 85 36.57N 81.07W

X

Xa Cassau Angola 54 9.02S 20.17E
Xagquka China 41 31.50N 92.46E
Xainza China 41 30.56N 88.40E
Xaitongmoin China 41 29.22N 88.15E
Xai-Xai Mozambique 57 25.05S 33.38E
Xam Nua Laos 34 20.25N104.10E
Xangdoring China 41 32.06N 82.02E
Xangongo Angola 54 16.31S 15.00E
Xanten W. Germany 14 51.40N 6.29E
Xánthi Greece 19 41.07N 24.55E
Xar Hudag China 32 45.07N114.28E
Xar Moron He r. China 32 43.30N120.42E
Xassengue Angola 54 10.26S 18.32E
Xau, L. Botswana 56 21.15S 24.50E
Xebert China 32 44.02N122.00E
Xenia U.S.A. 84 39.41N 83.56W
Xequessa Angola 54 16.47S 19.05E
Xhora R.S.A. 56 31.58S 28.40E
Xiachuan i. China 33 21.40N112.37E
Xiaguan China 30 25.33N100.09E
Xiamen China 33 24.30N118.08E
Xi'an China 32 34.11N108.55E
Xianfeng China 33 29.41N109.02E
Xiangcheng China 32 33.50N113.29E
Xiangfan China 32 32.04N112.05E
Xiangfen China 32 35.52N111.24E
Xiang Jiang r. China 33 28.49N112.30E
Xiangkhoang Laos 34 19.21N103.23E
Xiangquan He r. China 41 31.45N 78.40E
Xiangshan China 33 29.29N121.51E
Xiangtan China 33 27.50N112.49E
Xiangtang China 33 28.26N115.58E
Xiangyin China 33 28.40N112.53E
Xiangyuan China 32 36.32N113.02E
Xiangzhou China 33 23.58N109.41E
Xianju China 33 28.51N120.44E
Xianning China 33 29.53N114.13E
Xian Xian China 32 38.12N116.07E
Xianyang China 32 34.20N108.40E
Xianyou China 33 25.28N118.50E
Xiao Hinggan Ling mts. China 31 48.40N128.30E
Xiaojiang China 33 27.34N120.27E
Xiaojiao China 32 38.24N113.42E
Xiaowutai Shan mtn. China 32 39.57N114.59E
Xiapu China 33 26.58N119.57E
Xiayang China 33 26.45N117.58E
Xichang China 30 27.53N102.18E
Xichou China 33 23.27N104.40E
Xichuan China 32 33.15N111.27E
Xifeng China 33 27.06N106.44E
Xigazê China 30 29.18N 88.50E
Xiheying China 32 39.53N114.42E
Xiji China 32 35.52N105.35E
Xi Jiang r. China 33 22.23N113.20E
Xiliao He r. China 32 43.48N123.00E
Xilin China 33 24.30N105.03E
Ximeng China 39 22.45N 99.29E
Xin'anjiang China 33 29.27N119.14E
Xin'anjiang Shuiku resr. China 33 29.32N119.00E
Xincheng Guang. Zhuang. China 33 24.04N108.40E
Xincheng Ningxia Huizu China 32 38.33N106.10E
Xincheng Shanxi China 32 37.57N112.35E
Xindu China 33 30.50N104.12E
Xinfeng Guangdong China 33 24.04N114.12E
Xinfeng Jiangxi China 33 25.27N114.58E
Xing'an China 33 25.35N110.32E
Xingcheng China 32 40.37N120.43E
Xinghua China 32 32.51N119.50E
Xingkai Hu l. see Khanka, Ozero U.S.S.R./China 31
Xingren China 33 25.26N105.14E
Xingshan China 33 31.10N110.51E
Xingtai China 32 37.04N114.26E
Xingu r. Brazil 91 1.40S 52.15W
Xing Xian China 32 38.31N111.04E
Xingyi China 33 25.00N104.59E
Xinhe Hebei China 32 37.22N115.14E
Xinhe Xin. Uygur China 30 41.34N 82.38E
Xinhua China 33 27.45N111.18E
Xining China 30 36.35N101.55E
Xinji China 32 35.17N115.35E
Xinjiang-Uygur d. China 30 41.15N 87.00E
Xinjie China 32 39.15N109.36E
Xinjin Liaoning China 32 39.27N121.48E
Xinjin Sichuan China 33 30.30N103.47E
Xinle China 32 38.15N114.40E
Xinlitun China 32 42.00N122.09E
Xinmin China 32 42.01N122.48E
Xinning China 33 26.31N110.48E
Xinshao China 33 27.20N111.26E
Xin Xian China 32 38.24N112.47E
Xinxiang China 32 35.12N113.57E
Xinyang China 32 32.08N114.04E
Xinyi Guangdong China 33 22.21N110.57E
Xinyi Jiangsu China 32 34.20N118.30E
Xinyu China 33 27.50N114.55E
Xinzheng China 32 34.25N113.46E
Xinzhu Taiwan 33 24.50N120.58E
Xiping Henan China 32 33.23N114.02E
Xiping Zhejiang China 33 28.27N119.29E
Xique Xique Brazil 91 10.47S 42.44W
Xi Ujimqin Qi China 32 44.32N117.40E
Xiuning China 33 29.48N118.20E
Xiushan China 33 28.27N108.59E
Xiushui China 33 29.01N114.37E
Xixabangma Feng mtn. China 41 28.21N 85.47E
Xixia China 32 33.30N111.30E
Xizang d. China 41 31.45N 87.00E
Xorkol China 30 39.04N 91.05E
Xuancheng China 33 30.59N118.40E
Xuang r. Laos 34 19.59N102.20E
Xuanhan China 33 31.25N107.38E
Xuanhua China 32 40.30N115.00E
Xuanwei China 33 26.16N104.01E
Xuchang China 32 34.02N113.50E
Xuefeng Shan mts. China 33 27.30N111.00E
Xueshuiwen China 31 49.15N129.39E
Xugou China 32 34.40N119.26E
Xunyang China 32 32.48N109.27E
Xupu China 33 27.54N110.35E
Xushui China 32 39.01N115.39E
Xuwen China 33 20.25N110.20E
Xuyong China 33 28.17N105.21E
Xuzhou China 32 34.14N117.20E

Y

Ya Gabon 54 1.17S 14.14E
Ya'an China 39 30.00N102.59E
Yaapeet Australia 66 35.48S142.07E
Yabassi Cameroon 53 4.30N 9.55E
Yabelo Ethiopia 49 4.54N 38.05E
Yablonovyy Khrebet mts. U.S.S.R. 29 53.20N115.00E
Yabrai Shan mts. China 32 39.50N103.30E
Yabrai Yanchang China 32 39.24N102.43E
Yabrūd Syria 44 33.58N 36.40E
Yacheng China 33 18.35N109.13E
Yacuiba Bolivia 92 22.00S 63.25W
Yādgīr India 38 16.46N 77.08E
Yadong China 41 27.29N 88.54E
Yagaba Ghana 52 10.13N 1.14W
Yagoua Cameroon 53 10.23N 15.13E
Yagra China 41 31.32N 82.27E
Yahagi r. Japan 35 34.50N136.59E
Yahisuli Zaïre 54 0.08S 24.04E
Yahuma Zaïre 54 1.06N 23.10E
Yaizu Japan 35 34.52N138.20E
Yajua Nigeria 53 11.27N 12.49E
Yakchāl Afghan. 40 31.47N 64.41E
Yakima U.S.A. 80 46.36N120.31W
Yakmach Pakistan 40 28.45N 63.51E
Yaksha U.S.S.R. 24 61.51N 56.59E
Yakutat U.S.A. 74 59.29N139.49W
Yakutat U.S.A. 72 59.33N139.44W
Yakutat B. U.S.A. 74 59.29N139.49W
Yakutsk U.S.S.R. 29 62.10N129.20E
Yala Thailand 34 6.32N101.19E
Yalgoo Australia 63 28.20S116.41E
Yalinga C.A.R. 49 6.31N 23.15E
Yallourn Australia 67 38.09S146.22E
Yalong Jiang r. China 30 26.35N101.44E
Yalpunga Australia 66 29.04S142.05E
Yalta U.S.S.R. 25 44.30N 34.09E
Yalu Jiang r. China 32 40.10N124.25E
Yalutorovsk U.S.S.R. 28 56.41N 66.12E
Yamal, Poluostrov pen. U.S.S.R. 28 70.20N 70.00E
Yamanashi Japan 35 35.40N138.40E
Yamanashi d. Japan 35 35.30N138.35E
Yamandjo Zaïre 54 1.38N 23.27E
Yaman Tau mtn. U.S.S.R. 24 54.20N 58.10E
Yamaska Canada 77 46.01N 72.55W
Yamaska r. Canada 77 46.06N 72.56W
Yamato Japan 35 35.29N139.29E
Yamato-takada Japan 35 34.31N135.45E
Yamba N.S.W. Australia 67 29.26S153.22E
Yamba S.A. Australia 66 34.15S140.54E
Yambéring Guinea 52 11.49N 12.18W
Yambio Sudan 49 4.34N 28.23E
Yambol Bulgaria 19 42.28N 26.30E
Yamdena i. Indonesia 37 7.30S131.00E
Yamenyingzi China 32 42.23N121.03E
Yamethin Burma 34 20.24N 96.08E
Yam Kinneret l. Israel 44 32.49N 35.36E
Yamma Yamma, L. Australia 64 26.20S141.25E
Yamoussoukro Ivory Coast 52 6.51N 5.18W
Yampol U.S.S.R. 21 48.13N 28.12E
Yamuna r. India 41 25.25N 81.50E
Yamzho Yumco l. China 41 29.00N 90.40E
Yan Nigeria 53 10.05N 12.11E
Yana r. U.S.S.R. 29 71.30N135.00E
Yanac Australia 66 36.09S141.29E
Yan'an China 32 36.45N109.22E
Yanbu'al Baḩr Saudi Arabia 42 24.07N 38.04E
Yancannia Australia 66 30.16S142.50E
Yancheng China 33 33.22N120.05E
Yanchep Australia 63 31.32S115.33E
Yanchi China 32 37.47N107.24E
Yanchuan China 32 36.51N110.05E
Yanco Australia 67 34.36S146.25E
Yanda Australia 67 30.18S145.44E
Yanda r. Australia 67 30.22S145.38E
Yandong China 33 24.02N107.09E
Yandoon Burma 34 17.02N 95.39E
Yanfolila Mali 52 11.11N 8.09W
Yangarey U.S.S.R. 24 68.46N 61.29E
Yangchun China 33 22.03N111.46E
Yangcun China 33 23.26N114.30E
Yangjiang China 33 21.50N111.54E
Yangmingshan Taiwan 33 25.18N121.35E
Yangqu China 32 38.03N112.36E
Yangquan China 32 37.49N113.28E
Yangshan Guangdong China 33 24.29N112.38E
Yangshan Liaoning China 32 41.15N120.18E
Yangshuo China 33 24.47N110.30E
Yangtze r. see Chang Jiang r. China 33
Yang Xian China 32 33.10N107.35E
Yangxin China 33 29.50N115.10E
Yangze China 33 26.59N118.19E
Yangzhou China 32 32.22N119.26E
Yanhuqu China 41 32.32N 82.44E
Yanji China 31 42.45N129.25E
Yanko r. Australia 67 35.25S145.27E
Yanko Glen town Australia 66 31.43S141.39E
Yankton U.S.A. 82 42.53N 97.23W
Yanqi China 30 42.00N 86.30E
Yanshan China 39 23.36N104.20E
Yanshiping China 41 33.35N 92.04E
Yanskiy Zaliv g. U.S.S.R. 29 72.00N136.10E
Yantabulla Australia 67 29.13S145.01E
Yantai China 32 37.27N121.26E
Yanxi China 33 28.11N110.58E
Yanzhou China 32 35.35N116.52E
Yao Chad 53 12.52N 17.34E
Yao Japan 35 34.37N135.36E
Yaopu China 33 26.05N105.42E
Yaoundé Cameroon 53 3.51N 11.31E
Yao Xian China 32 34.52N109.01E
Yap i. Caroline Is. 37 9.30N138.09E
Yapehe Zaïre 54 0.10S 24.20E
Yapen i. Indonesia 37 1.45S136.10E
Yaqui r. Mexico 81 27.37N110.39W
Yar U.S.S.R. 24 58.13N 52.08E
Yaraka Australia 64 24.53S144.04E
Yaransk U.S.S.R. 24 57.22N 47.49E
Yardea Australia 66 32.23S135.32E
Yare r. U.K. 11 52.34N 1.45E
Yaremcha U.S.S.R. 21 48.26N 24.29E
Yarensk U.S.S.R. 24 62.10N 49.07E
Yaretsk U.S.S.R. 21 46.25N 28.20E
Yaritagua Venezuela 90 10.05N 69.07W
Yarkant He r. China 30 40.30N 80.55E
Yarlung Zangbo Jiang r. China see Brahmaputra r. Asia 41
Yarmouth Canada 77 43.50N 66.07W
Yaroslavl U.S.S.R. 24 57.34N 39.52E
Yarra r. Australia 67 37.51S144.54E
Yarram Australia 67 38.30S146.41E
Yarran Range mts. Australia 64 18.08S136.40E
Yarrawonga Australia 67 36.02S145.59E
Yarrow r. U.K. 12 55.32N 2.51W
Yar Sale U.S.S.R. 28 66.50N 70.48E
Yartsevo R.S.F.S.R. U.S.S.R. 24 55.06N 32.43E
Yartsevo R.S.F.S.R. U.S.S.R. 29 60.17N 90.02E
Yarumal Colombia 90 6.59N 75.25W
Yasanyama Zaïre 49 4.18N 21.11E
Yaselda r. U.S.S.R. 21 52.07N 26.28E
Yasen U.S.S.R. 21 53.10N 28.55E
Yashi Nigeria 53 12.23N 7.54E
Yashkul U.S.S.R. 25 46.10N 45.20E
Yasinya U.S.S.R. 21 48.12N 24.20E
Yasothon Thailand 34 15.46N104.12E
Yass Australia 67 34.51S148.55E
Yatakala Niger 52 14.52N 0.22E
Yaté N. Cal. 68 22.09S166.57E
Yates Center U.S.A. 83 37.53N 95.44W
Yathkyed L. Canada 75 62.40N 98.00W
Yāval India 40 21.10N 75.42E
Yavatmāl India 41 20.24N 78.08E
Yaví, Cerro mtn. Venezuela 90 5.32N 65.59W
Yavorov U.S.S.R. 21 49.59N 23.20E
Yawng-hwe Burma 34 20.35N 96.58E
Yaxi China 33 27.35N106.40E
Ya Xian China 33 18.19N109.32E
Yazd Iran 43 31.54N 54.22E
Yazmān Pakistan 40 29.08N 71.45E
Yazoo r. U.S.A. 83 32.22N 91.00W
Yazoo City U.S.A. 83 32.51N 90.28W
Ybbs Austria 20 48.11N 15.05E
Ye Burma 34 15.15N 97.50E
Yea Australia 67 37.12S145.25E
Yecla Spain 16 38.35N 1.05W
Yedintsy U.S.S.R. 25 48.09N 27.18E
Yeeda River town Australia 62 17.36S123.39E
Yefremov U.S.S.R. 24 53.08N 38.08E
Yegorlyk r. U.S.S.R. 25 46.30N 41.52E
Yegoryevsk U.S.S.R. 24 55.21N 39.01E
Yegros Paraguay 94 26.24S 56.25W
Yei Sudan 49 4.05N 30.40E
Yei r. Sudan 49 7.20N 30.39E
Yeji China 33 31.51N115.01E
Yelets U.S.S.R. 24 52.36N 38.30E
Yeletskiy U.S.S.R. 24 67.04N 64.00E
Yélimané Mali 52 15.08N 10.34W
Yell i. U.K. 12 60.35N 1.05W
Yellowdine Australia 63 31.19S119.36E
Yellowhead Pass Canada 74 52.53N118.25W
Yellowknife Canada 74 62.27N114.21W
Yellowknife r. Canada 74 62.27N114.19W
Yellow Mt. Australia 67 32.19S146.50E
Yellow Sea Asia 31 35.00N123.00E
Yellowstone r. U.S.A. 82 47.58N103.59W
Yellowstone r. U.S.A. 78 47.55N103.45W
Yellowstone L. U.S.A. 80 44.25N110.38W
Yellowstone Nat. Park U.S.A. 80 44.30N110.35W
Yell Sd. U.K. 12 60.30N 1.11W
Yelma Australia 62 26.30S121.40E
Yelsk U.S.S.R. 21 51.50N 29.10E
Yelwa Nigeria 53 10.48N 4.42E
Yemen Asia 45 15.15N 44.30E
Yemilchino U.S.S.R. 21 50.58N 27.40E
Yenagoa Nigeria 53 4.59N 6.15E
Yenangyaung Burma 34 20.28N 94.54E
Yen Bai Vietnam 34 21.43N104.44E
Yendi Ghana 52 9.29N 0.01W
Yengan Burma 34 21.06N 96.30E
Yenisey r. U.S.S.R. 29 69.00N 86.00E
Yeniseysk U.S.S.R. 29 58.27N 92.13E
Yeniseyskiy Zaliv g. U.S.S.R. 28 73.00N 79.00E
Yenshui Taiwan 33 23.20N120.16E
Yenyuka U.S.S.R. 29 57.57N121.15E
Yeo, L. Australia 63 28.04S124.23E
Yeola India 40 20.02N 74.29E
Yeovil U.K. 11 50.57N 2.38W
Yeppoon Australia 64 23.08S150.45E
Yerbent U.S.S.R. 43 39.23N 58.35E
Yercha U.S.S.R. 29 69.34N147.30E
Yerepol U.S.S.R. 29 65.15N168.43E
Yerevan U.S.S.R. 43 40.10N 44.31E
Yerington U.S.A. 80 38.59N119.10W
Yermak U.S.S.R. 28 52.03N 76.55E
Yermitsa U.S.S.R. 24 66.56N 52.20E
Yermo Mexico 83 26.23N104.01W
Yermo U.S.A. 81 34.54N116.50W
Yershov U.S.S.R. 25 51.22N 48.16E
Yertom U.S.S.R. 24 63.31N 47.51E
Yerushalayim Israel/Jordan 44 31.47N 35.13E
Yeşil r. Turkey 42 41.22N 36.37E
Yeso U.S.A. 81 34.26N104.37W
Yessey U.S.S.R. 29 68.29N102.15E
Yetman Australia 67 28.55S150.49E
Yeu Burma 34 22.49N 95.26E
Yeu, Île d' i. France 17 46.43N 2.20W
Yevpatoriya U.S.S.R. 25 45.12N 33.20E
Yevstratovskiy U.S.S.R. 25 50.07N 39.45E
Ye Xian China 32 37.10N119.56E
Yeysk U.S.S.R. 25 46.43N 38.17E
Yí r. Uruguay 93 33.17S 58.08W
Yiannitsá Greece 19 40.48N 22.25E
Yibin China 33 28.42N104.34E
Yibug Caka l. China 41 33.50N 87.00E
Yichang China 33 30.21N111.21E
Yichuan China 32 34.25N112.26E
Yidu China 32 36.45N118.24E
Yifag Ethiopia 49 12.02N 37.44E
Yijun China 32 35.23N109.07E
Yilan China 31 46.22N129.31E
Yilehuli Shan mts. China 31 51.20N124.20E
Yilliminning Australia 63 32.54S117.22E
Yilong China 33 31.34N106.24E
Yimen China 32 34.21N107.07E
Yinan China 32 35.33N118.27E
Yinchuan China 32 38.27N106.18E
Yindarlgooda, L. Australia 63 30.45S121.55E
Yingcheng China 33 30.57N113.33E
Yingde China 33 24.07N113.20E
Yinggehai China 33 18.31N108.40E
Yingkou China 32 40.39N122.18E
Yingshan China 33 31.06N106.35E
Yingshang China 32 32.42N116.20E
Yingtan China 33 28.11N116.55E
Yinkanie Australia 66 34.21S140.20E
Yinning China 30 43.57N 81.23E
Yin Shan mts. China 32 41.30N109.00E
Yirga Alem Ethiopia 49 6.52N 38.22E
Yirol Sudan 49 6.33N 30.30E
Yirwa Sudan 49 7.47N 27.15E
Yishan China 33 24.37N108.32E
Yíthion Greece 19 36.46N 22.34E
Yiwu China 33 29.18N120.04E
Yi Xian China 32 41.30N121.14E
Yiyang Henan China 32 34.30N112.10E
Yiyang Hunan China 33 28.20N112.30E
Yiyuan China 32 36.12N118.08E
Yizhang China 33 25.24N112.57E
Ylitornio Finland 22 66.19N 23.40E
Ylivieska Finland 22 64.05N 24.33E
Yoakum U.S.A. 83 29.17N 97.09W
Yodo r. Japan 35 34.41N135.25E
Yogyakarta Indonesia 37 7.48S110.24E
Yogyakarta d. Indonesia 37 7.48S110.22E
Yokadouma Cameroon 53 3.26N 15.06E
Yokkaichi Japan 35 34.58N136.37E
Yoko Cameroon 53 5.29N 12.19E
Yokohama Japan 35 35.27N139.39E
Yokosuka Japan 35 35.18N139.40E
Yola Nigeria 53 9.14N 12.32E
Yom r. Thailand 34 15.47N100.05E
Yona Guam 68 13.25N144.47E
Yongcheng China 32 33.56N116.22E
Yongchuan China 33 29.19N105.55E
Yongchun China 33 25.19N118.17E
Yongdeng China 32 36.44N103.24E
Yonghe China 32 36.44N110.39E
Yongnian China 32 36.47N114.30E
Yongring China 33 22.45N108.29E
Yongshou China 32 34.40N108.04E
Yongxiu China 33 28.58N115.43E
Yonkers U.S.A. 85 40.56N 73.54W
Yonne d. France 15 47.55N 3.45E
Yonne r. France 15 48.22N 2.57E
York Australia 63 31.55S116.45E
York Canada 76 43.41N 79.29W
York U.K. 10 53.58N 1.07W
York r. U.S.A. 85 37.15N 76.23W
York Nebr. U.S.A. 82 40.52N 97.36W
York Penn. U.S.A. 85 39.58N 76.44W
York, C. Australia 64 10.42S142.31E
Yorke Pen. Australia 66 35.00S137.30E
Yorketown Australia 66 35.02S137.35E
York Factory town Canada 75 57.00N 92.18W
Yorkshire Wolds hills U.K. 10 54.00N 0.39W
Yorkton Canada 75 51.13N102.28W
Yoro Honduras 87 15.09N 87.07W
Yōrō Japan 35 35.32N140.04E
Yosemite Nat. Park U.S.A. 80 37.45N119.35W
Yoshino r. Japan 35 34.22N135.40E
Yoshkar Ola U.S.S.R. 24 56.38N 47.52E
Yos Sudarsa, Pulau i. Indonesia 37 8.00S138.30E
Yŏsu S. Korea 31 34.46N127.45E
Youghal Rep. of Ire. 13 51.58N 7.51W
You Jiang r. Guang. Zhuang. China 33 23.28N111.18E
Youkou Ivory Coast 52 5.16N 7.16W
Youkounkoun Guinea 52 12.35N 13.11W
Young Australia 67 34.19S148.20E
Young r. Australia 63 33.45S121.12E
Young Uruguay 93 32.41S 57.38W
Young U.S.A. 81 34.06N110.57W
Younghusband, L. Australia 66 30.51S136.05E
Younghusband Pen. Australia 66 36.00S139.15E
Youngstown Canada 75 51.32N111.13W
Youngstown U.S.A. 84 41.05N 80.40W
You Xian China 33 26.59N113.12E
Youyang China 33 28.52N108.45E
Youyu China 32 39.59N112.27E
Yoxford U.K. 11 52.16N 1.30E
Yozgat Turkey 42 39.50N 34.48E
Yreka U.S.A. 80 41.44N122.38W
Ystad Sweden 23 55.25N 13.49E
Ythan r. U.K. 12 57.21N 2.01W
Ytterhogdal Sweden 23 62.12N 14.51E
Yu'alliq, Jabal mtn. Egypt 44 30.21N 33.31E
Yuanbaoshan China 32 42.15N119.14E
Yuan Jiang r. Hunan China 33 29.00N111.55E
Yuan Jiang r. Yunnan China see Hong Hà r. Vietnam 30
Yuanling China 33 28.28N110.15E
Yuanping China 32 38.42N112.46E
Yuba City U.S.A. 80 39.08N121.27W
Yubdo Ethiopia 49 9.00N 35.22E
Yucatán d. Mexico 87 19.30N 89.00W
Yucatan Channel Carib. Sea 87 21.30N 86.00W
Yucatan Pen. Mexico 86 19.00N 90.00W
Yucca U.S.A. 81 34.52N114.09W
Yuci China 32 37.37N112.47E
Yudino U.S.S.R. 28 55.49N 48.54E
Yudu China 33 25.57N115.16E
Yueqing China 33 28.08N120.57E
Yuexi China 30 28.36N102.35E
Yueyang China 33 29.22N113.10E
Yugan China 33 28.41N116.41E
Yugorskiy Poluostrov pen. U.S.S.R. 24 69.00N 62.30E
Yugoslavia Europe 19 44.00N 20.00E
Yuhang China 33 30.25N120.18E
Yuhebu China 32 37.59N109.51E
Yukon r. U.S.A. 72 62.35N164.20W
Yukon Territory d. Canada 72 65.00N135.00W
Yuleba Australia 64 26.37S149.20E
Yulin Guang. Zhuang. China 33 22.38N110.10E
Yulin Shaanxi China 32 38.11N109.33E
Yuma Ariz. U.S.A. 81 32.43N114.37W
Yuma Colo. U.S.A. 80 40.08N102.43W
Yumen China 30 40.19N 97.12E
Yunan China 33 23.14N111.35E
Yuncheng China 32 35.02N111.00E
Yungas f. Bolivia 92 16.20S 65.00W

OCEANIA
MAPS 58 – 69

NORTH AMERICA
MAPS 70 – 87

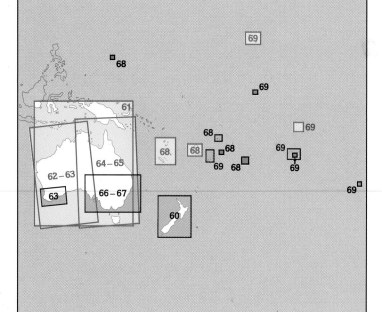

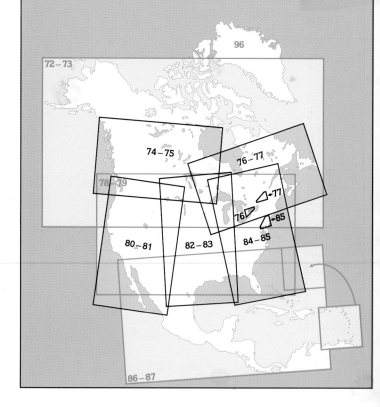

Continuation from Front Endpaper